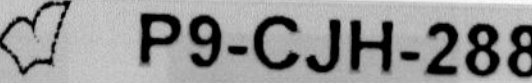

Reims

NORTHEAST FRANCE

Strasbourg

Troyes

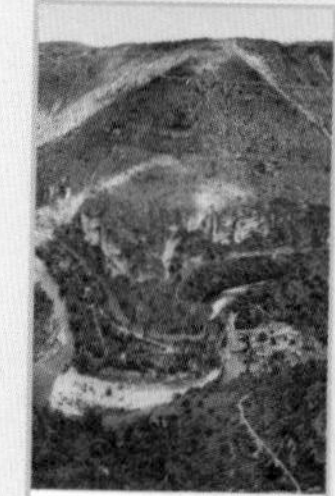

Dijon

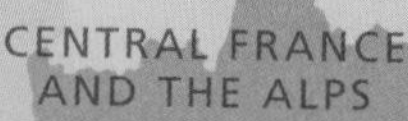

Lyon

Grenoble

THE SOUTH OF FRANCE

EYEWITNESS TRAVEL

FRANCE

EYEWITNESS TRAVEL
FRANCE
DK

LONDON, NEW YORK,
MELBOURNE, MUNICH AND DELHI
www.dk.com

Project Editor Rosemary Bailey
Art Editor Janis Utton
Editors Tanya Colbourne, Fiona Morgan, Anna Streiffert, Celia Woolfrey
Designers Joy FitzSimmons, Erika Lang, Clare Sullivan

Map Co-ordinators
Simon Farbrother, David Pugh

Researcher
Philippa Richmond

Main Contributors
John Ardagh, Rosemary Bailey, Judith Fayard, Lisa Gerard-Sharp, Colin Jones, Alister Kershaw, Alec Lobrano, Anthony Roberts, Alan Tillier, Nigel Tisdall

Photographers
Max Alexander, Neil Lukas, John Parker, Kim Sayer

Illustrators
Stephen Conlin, John Lawrence, Maltings Partnership, John Woodcock

Printed and bound by South China Printing Co. Ltd., China

First American edition, 1995

14 15 16 17 10 9 8 7 6 5 4 3 2

Published in the United States by
DK Publishing, 345 Hudson Street,
New York, New York 10014

Reprinted with revisions 1995, 1996, 1997, 1999, 2000, 2001, 2002, 2003, 2004, 2006, 2008, 2010, 2012, 2014

Published in Great Britain by Dorling Kindersley Limited.
A catalog record for this book is available from the Library of Congress.

ISSN 1542–1554
ISBN 978-1-4654-1151-8

Floors are referred to throughout in accordance with French usage; i.e., the "first floor" is the floor above ground level.

MIX
Paper from responsible sources
FSC™ C018179

The information in this DK Eyewitness Travel Guide is checked regularly.
Every effort has been made to ensure that this book is as up-to-date as possible at the time of going to press. Some details, however, such as telephone numbers, opening hours, prices, gallery hanging arrangements, and travel information are liable to change. The publishers cannot accept responsibility for any consequences arising from the use of this book, nor for any material on third-party websites, and cannot guarantee that any website address in this book will be a suitable source of travel information. We value the views and suggestions of our readers very highly. Please write to: Publisher, DK Eyewitness Travel Guides, Dorling Kindersley, 80 Strand, London WC2R 0RL, Great Britain, or email: travelguides@dk.com.

Front cover main image: Lavender fields, Plateau de Vaucluse, Provence

◀ The stunning cliffs at Etretat, famous for their naturally formed archways and pointed "needle"

Contents

Bust of Charlemagne

The fishing village of St-Jean-de-Luz in the Pyrenees

Northeast France

Grape harvest in Alsace

Western France

Central France and the Alps

Southwest France

The South of France

Travelers' Needs

Survival Guide

Palais des Papes, Avignon

HOW TO USE THIS GUIDE

This guide helps you to get the most from your visit to France. It provides both expert recommendations and detailed practical information. *Introducing France* maps the country and sets it in its historical and cultural context. The 15 regional chapters, plus *Paris and Ile de France*, describe important sights, with maps, pictures, and illustrations. Throughout, features cover topics from food and wine to culture and beaches. Restaurant and hotel recommendations can be found in *Travelers' Needs*. The *Survival Guide* has tips on everything from the French telephone system to transport.

Paris and Ile de France

The center of Paris has been divided into five sightseeing areas. Each has its own chapter, which opens with a list of the sights described. Another section covers Ile de France. All sights are numbered and plotted on an area map. The detailed information for each sight follows the map's numerical order, making sights easy to locate within the chapter.

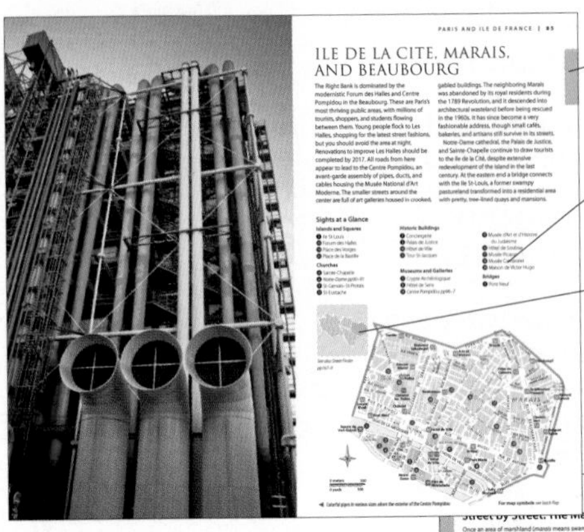

All pages relating to Paris and Ile de France have green thumb tabs.

Sights at a Glance lists the chapter's sights by category: Churches, Museums and Galleries; Historic Buildings, Squares, and Gardens.

A locator map shows where you are in relation to other areas of the city center.

1 Area Map For easy reference, the sights are numbered and located on a map. Sights in the city center are also shown on the Paris Street Finder on pages 160–73.

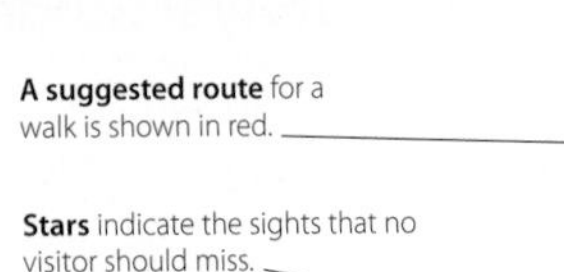

A suggested route for a walk is shown in red.

Stars indicate the sights that no visitor should miss.

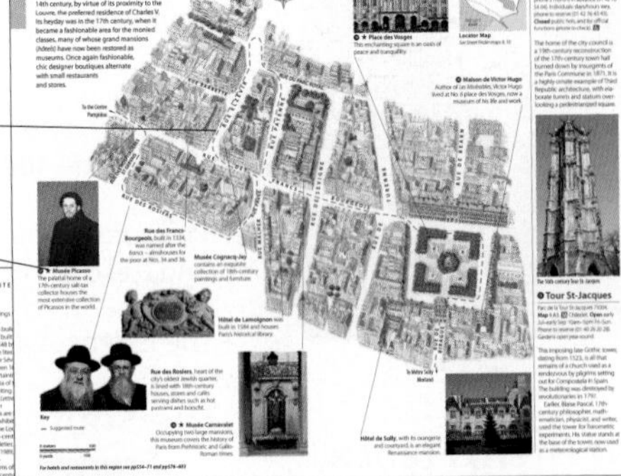

2 Street by Street Map This gives a bird's eye view of the key areas in each chapter.

3 Detailed information The sights in Paris and Ile de France are described individually. Addresses, telephone numbers, opening hours, and information on admission charges and wheelchair access are also provided for each entry.

France Area by Area

Apart from Paris and Ile de France, France has been divided into 15 regions, each of which has a separate chapter. The most interesting towns and places to visit have been numbered on a *Regional Map*.

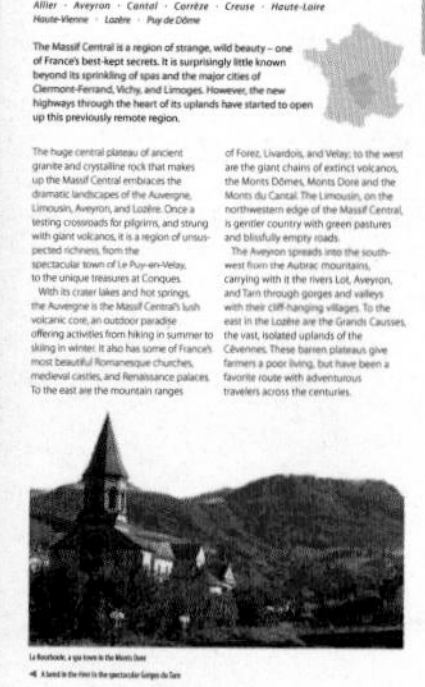

1 **Introduction** The landscape, history, and character of each region is described here, showing how the area has developed over the centuries and what it offers to the visitor today.

Each area of France can be quickly identified by its color coding, shown on the inside front cover.

2 **Regional Map** This shows the road network and gives an illustrated overview of the whole region. All interesting places to visit are numbered and there are also useful tips on getting around the region by car and train.

3 **Detailed information** All the important towns and other places to visit are described individually. They are listed in order, following the numbering on the Regional Map. Within each town or city, there is detailed information on important buildings and other sights.

For all the top sights, a Visitor's Checklist provides the practical information you will need to plan your visit.

Story boxes highlight noteworthy features of the top sights.

4 **France's top sights** These are given two or more full pages. Historic buildings are dissected to reveal their interiors. The most interesting towns or city centers are shown in a bird's eye view, with sights picked out and described.

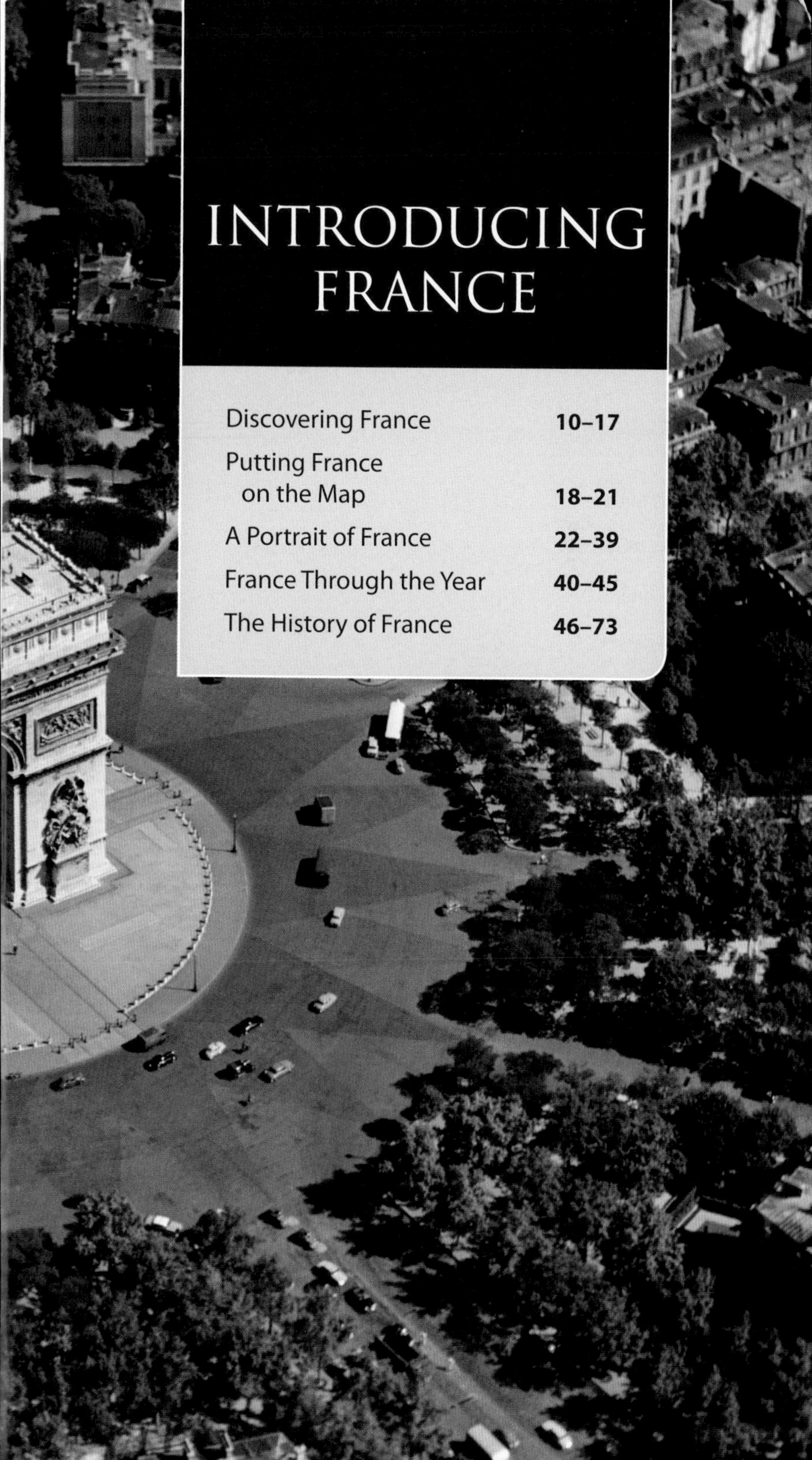

INTRODUCING FRANCE

DISCOVERING FRANCE

The following tours have been designed to take in as many of the country's highlights as possible, while keeping long-distance travel to a minimum. First comes a two-day visit to France's unmissable heart, Paris. Next is a one-week tour of the greatest architectural monuments around the capital – Versailles, Loire châteaus, great Gothic cathedrals. Two more seven-day tours cover Northern France and the Rhône Valley, and the Southwest. These can be combined to make a superb two-week tour. Finally, two seven-day routes focus on regions legendary for fine wines and food – Burgundy, Périgord, and Bordeaux – and the beauties of the Mediterranean coast. Suggestions are provided for those who want to extend their stay, so pick and combine your favorite tours, or simply be inspired.

A Week in Northern France

- Admire the vibrant colors of Monet's garden at **Giverny**.
- Linger over dinner beside the old harbor of **Honfleur**.
- Take in the fascinating details of the **Bayeux Tapestry**.
- Go to the **Normandy beaches** where the 1944 D-Day landings took place.
- Wonder at the majesty of **Mont-St-Michel**, rising up out of the sea.
- Follow the Loire Valley from Gothic **Tours** to Renaissance **Chambord**.
- Visit the historic center of **Dijon**, once home to the grand Burgundian court.

A Wine and Food Tour of Burgundy, Périgord, and Bordeaux

- Wander through beautiful vineyards along the Côte d'Or around **Beaune**.
- Eat creamy mountain cheeses like **St-Nectaire** and **Cantal** in the Auvergne.
- Go truffle-tasting in pretty villages along the **Dordogne** valley.
- Explore the town of **St-Émilion**, dedicated to wine for over ten centuries.
- Relax over a glass of fine wine in **Bordeaux**.
- Sample world-famous brandy in the historic cellars of **Cognac**.

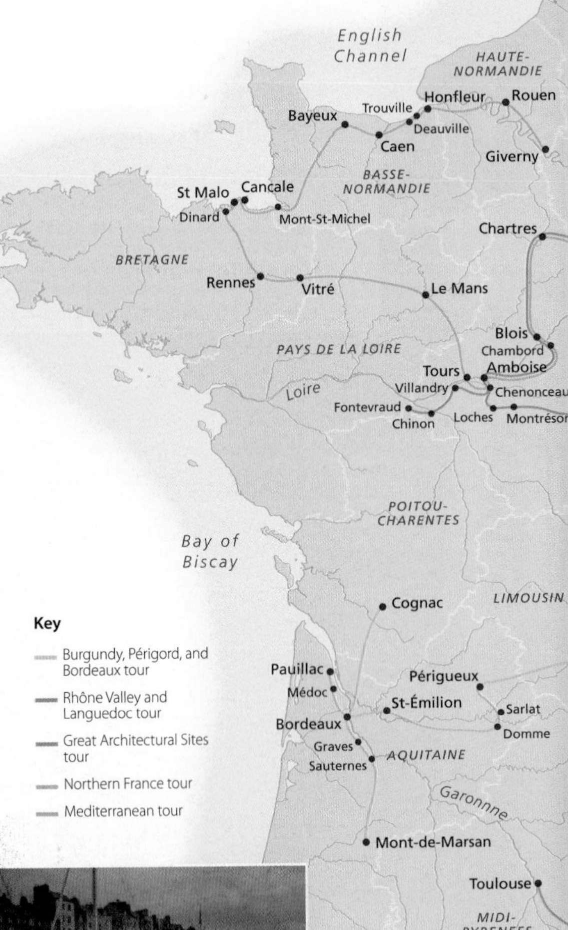

Honfleur
Views of Honfleur's harbor and Vieux Bassin (Old Dock) have appealed to artists from the 19th century to the present.

Versailles
In 1668, Louis XIV began work on enlargements to his father's old hunting lodge just outside Paris. Over the course of the next century, the Château was transformed into one of the finest palaces in the world.

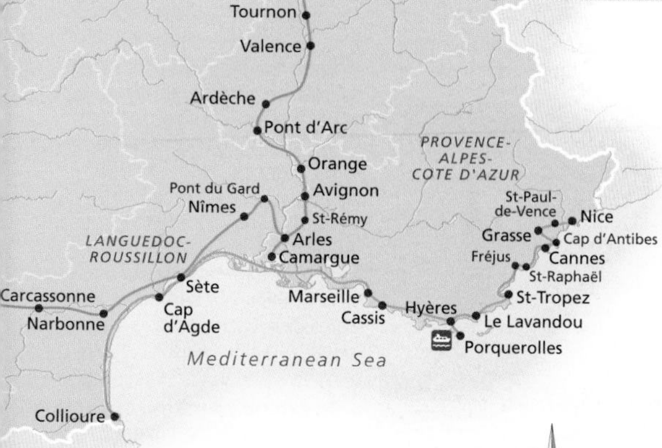

A One-Week Tour of Great Architectural Sites

- Take in the extravagance of **Versailles** and explore Le Nôtre's magnificent gardens.
- Trace the stories told by the stunning stained-glass windows at **Chartres** cathedral.
- View the famous chateaus of **Chenonceau** and **Villandry**.
- Marvel at the skills of medieval stonemasons at **Troyes, Reims**, **Laon**, and **Amiens**.

A Week in the Rhône Valley and Languedoc

- Enjoy a hearty meal in a traditional restaurant in **Lyon**, one of France's culinary capitals.
- Taste the renowned wines of the **Côtes du Rhône**.
- Explore wild mountain landscapes around the magnificent gorges of the **Ardèche**.
- Visit a former papal palace in historic **Avignon**.
- Enter a medieval fantasy in the walled city of **Carcassonne**.

A Week in the Mediterranean

- Delight in work by a great 20th-century artist at the **Musée Matisse** in **Nice**.
- Take in breathtaking views of the coast from the clifftop village of **Èze**.
- Join the rich and famous in the harbor at **St-Tropez**.
- Discover perfect pine-ringed beaches on the **Iles d'Hyères**.
- Taste the local seafood in the lively harbor restaurants of **Sète**.

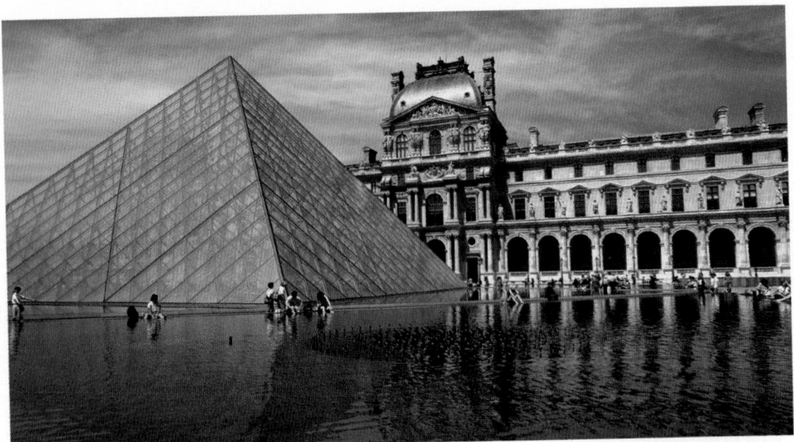

The great glass pyramid entrance to the Musée du Louvre, viewed from across the fountain pool

Two Days in Paris

With its great art, glorious architecture, chic shopping, gourmet food, and unique street life, the French capital offers an array of attractions.

- **Arriving** Charles-de-Gaulle international airport is about 18 miles (30 km) from the city. RER Line B trains run frequently to central Paris (40 mins). International trains arrive at seven Paris stations, all with connections to the city Métro network.

Day 1

Morning There is so much to see and do in Paris that a two-day visit can only be a taster, but for a first dose of Parisian atmosphere begin with a café breakfast on the riverside quays of **Ile St-Louis** *(p89)*, for a fabulous view of the Seine and the buttresses of **Notre-Dame cathedral** *(pp90–1)*. Then stroll across to **Ile de la Cité** to visit the cathedral itself and see the Gothic jewel of **Sainte-Chapelle** *(p88)*. Cross to the Left Bank on the historic **Pont Neuf** *(p87)* and walk along the quays to the **Musée d'Orsay** *(pp124–5)*. Allow about two hours, and don't miss the Impressionist masterpieces and stunning paintings by Van Gogh and Toulouse Lautrec. Then cross back to the Right Bank for a rest and lunch in one of the **Louvre**'s courtyard restaurants.

Afternoon Give at least two hours to the **Louvre** *(pp104–7)*. The display of historic art is vast and awe-inspiring. Be sure to see the *Mona Lisa* and the Greek and Roman sculptures. Then take a break in the **Jardin des Tuileries** *(p102–3)* and wander up to **Place de la Concorde** *(p102)* for majestic vistas. From there, take a taxi or bus along the **Champs-Elysées** *(pp110–12)* to the **Arc de Triomphe** *(p103)*, and go to the top to watch the crazy traffic below. Return to the center for dinner, stopping to browse chic boutiques on **Rue St-Honoré** *(p147)* and glittering food shops in **Place de la Madeleine** *(p101)*.

Day 2

Morning Explore the bohemian Left Bank, beginning at the **Panthéon** and the **Sorbonne** in the old **Latin Quarter** *(pp128–9)*.

The iconic Eiffel Tower, from across the River Seine

Wander through the district toward the river, perhaps with a stop at **Musée de Cluny** for Roman baths and medieval art, then head west to **St-Germain-des-Prés**, past lively **rue de Buci** with its street market. Stop for coffee in one of the classic intellectual cafés, **Café de Flore** or the **Deux Magots**. Then cross the Seine through Ile de la Cité and head right to enter the **Marais** *(pp92–3)* district for lunch in the **Place des Vosges**, Paris's most charming square.

Afternoon Stroll around the 17th-century streets of the Marais, with their trendy shops, cafés, and historic Jewish Quarter. Return to modern Paris at the **Centre Pompidou** *(pp96–7)* (2 hours), to see works by Picasso, Matisse, and other 20th-century masters, and the views from the tubelike escalators. Then take the Métro or a taxi – or walk part of the way along the river – to the **Eiffel Tower** *(pp116–17)*, and get to the top in time for the views at sunset. Dine in one of the Tower restaurants, or for less view but more Parisian color head to Boulevard du Montparnasse to eat in one of its classic 1920s brasseries.

To extend your trip...
Spend a day in the **Luxembourg Quarter** *(pp130–31)* and window-shop on **Rue du Faubourg-St-Honoré**.

A One-Week Tour of Great Architectural Sites

Within a short distance of Paris, discover an extraordinary range of famous buildings – Gothic, Renaissance, and Baroque.

- **Airports** Arrive and depart from Paris.
- **Transport** A rental car is essential for the full route, but many places can be visited by train on day trips from Paris.
- **Booking ahead** Advisable at Versailles in July–August.

Day 1: Versailles, Vaux-le-Vicomte, Fontainebleau

Louis XIV's palace of **Versailles** *(pp178–9)* is the epitome of regal grandeur. Take time to walk through the equally magnificent gardens to the **Trianon** palaces and Marie Antoinette's village. Rest for lunch, then drive south to more discreet **Vaux-le-Vicomte** *(pp182–3)*, model of French 17th-century mansion style, and Napoleon's favorite palace at **Fontainebleau** *(p184)*. Relax after châteaus-visiting in the lovely surrounding forest.

Day 2: Chartres to the Loire Valley

Head west to **Chartres** *(pp310–13)* to the most intact of all medieval **cathedrals**. The stories and images in its stunning stained glass are fascinating to trace. Move on to Renaissance architecture at **Blois** *(pp308–9)*, one of the first royal châteaus. Explore the old town before a short hop east to François I's vast palace at **Chambord** *(p306)*, surrounded by a delightful wooded park.

Day 3 : The Loire: Amboise to Chinon

Looming over the tiny town, the royal château of **Amboise** *(p305)* has a dramatic history, and a few streets away is the **Clos-Lucé mansion**, where Leonardo da Vinci lived just before his death. Nearby, **Chenonceau** *(pp302–3)* and its gardens typify the grand life of the Loire Valley châteaus. For one of the loveliest French gardens, stop at **Château de Villandry** *(p300)*. A very different château is **Chinon** *(pp298–9)*, a 12th-century fortress built for Henry II of England, in a medieval town known for fine wines.

Day 4: Fontevraud to Bourges Morning

The Benedictine **Abbaye Royale de Fontevraud** *(p298)* reflects the deep spirituality of the Middle Ages. To the east, the rugged ruined keep at **Loches** *(p304)* is one of the oldest Loire castles, set in an exquisite walled town. Nearby is idyllic **Montrésor** *(p305)* with its 15th-century castle. In the afternoon head to **Bourges** *(p317)*, a little-known gem with a giant cathedral and a Gothic merchant mansion, the **Palais Jacques Coeur**.

Stained-glass window at Chartres Cathedral in the Loire Valley

Day 5: Into Champagne

Northeast from Bourges, stop in **Auxerre** *(p332)* in Burgundy for the cathedral and its fine stained glass. Champagne and Picardy contain several of the greatest Gothic monuments. Ancient **Troyes** *(pp220)* has a wonderful old center of Gothic churches and courtyards. Carry on north through green hills and vineyards to **Epernay** *(p215)*, home of champagne, and visit at least one cellar for a tasting.

Day 6: Reims to Amiens

Explore **Reims** and its magnificent **cathedral** *(pp216–17)*, site of the coronations of French kings. To the northeast in Picardy are a number of astonishing Gothic cathedrals: **Laon** *(p209)* with its curious carvings, harmonious **Noyon** *(p205)* and glorious **Amiens** *(p204)*, with a facade that has been called "the Bible in stone."

Day 7: Royal Compiègne and Chantilly

The château and forest at **Compiègne** *(p205)* were a royal hunting estate for centuries. Napoleon III's own Neo-Gothic castle is nearby at **Pierrefonds**. To the south, visit the **Musée Conde** inside the rambling **Château de Chantilly** *(pp208–9)*. Don't miss the *Très Riches Heures du Duc de Berry*, one of the world's finest medieval manuscripts.

Champagne vineyards at Ville-Dommange, near Reims

A Week in Northern France

- **Airports** Arrive and depart from Paris.
- **Transport** A rental car is essential for the full route, but many places can be visited by train on separate trips from Paris.
- **Booking ahead** Advisable at champagne cellars on weekends.

Day 1: Giverny, Rouen, and Honfleur
Travel to **Giverny** *(p270)* in time for the 10am opening of Claude Monet's house (Apr–Oct only), and enjoy the stunning colors of the artist's garden with the fewest crowds. In the afternoon, continue down the Seine Valley to lively **Rouen** *(pp268–9)*, and its three great Gothic jewels: the churches of **St-Ouen** and **St-Maclou**, and the magnificent **cathedral**, painted many times by Monet. Finish the day with dinner beside the quaint harbor at **Honfleur** *(p266)*.

Day 2: Heart of Normandy
Living up to its name, the "Flowery Coast" west of Honfleur contains attractive beach resorts like bohemian **Trouville** and elegant **Deauville** *(p259)*. Just inland is Normandy's most exuberantly lush green countryside, in the cider farms of the **Pays d'Auge** *(p259)*. Linger there, or go on to **Caen** *(p257–8)* to visit the two great Abbeys built by William the Conqueror and his Queen. From there it's a short drive to **Bayeux** *(pp256–7)*, where the unmissable **tapestry** portrays the vivid details of William's invasion of England. Bayeux is also an ideal base for visiting the coast nearby at **Arromanches** and **Omaha Beach** *(p255)*, which witnessed the dramatic events of the June 1944 Allied invasion.

Day 3: Mont-St-Michel and St-Malo
Soaring up out of the sea, **Mont-St-Michel** *(pp260–61)* is one of France's greatest sights, a magical monument to medieval ambition. It dominates the view as you continue west around the giant bay, past charming **Cancale** *(p287)*, toward **St-Malo** *(p286)* and its fascinating walled city. Relax on the city's beaches or across the river at **Dinard** *(p285)*, a classic Breton seaside resort.

Day 4: Rennes to Tours
Turn inland to visit Brittany's capital, **Rennes** *(p289)*, with its half-timbered houses, and on the way west don't miss **Vitré** *(p289)*, a picture-book medieval walled town. Stop for lunch in **Le Mans** *(p295)*, famed for sports car racing but also for its fascinating ancient city and Roman walls. Join the Loire Valley at **Tours** *(pp300–1)* and visit the soaring Gothic cathedral and atmospheric riverside old quarter.

Normandy's Mont-St-Michel, one of the most enchanting sights in France

Day 5: Loire Valley Highlights
The Loire is famously studded with magnificent mansions. Be sure to see luxurious **Chenonceau**, regal **Amboise**, and majestic **Chambord** *(pp306–7)*. Then cross the river north to **Chartres** *(pp311–15)*, and stay in the town to enjoy the spectacular light show around the **cathedral** (mid-Apr–mid-Sep only).

The imposing facade of the cathedral at Reims

Day 6: Reims and Champagne Country
Start early and drive east around Paris on the outer-ring highways to **Reims** and its sumptuous **cathedral** *(pp216–17)*. Relax after the drive by visiting some of the famous champagne houses in Reims and in the soft green countryside towards **Epernay** *(p215)*. Continue on to **Troyes**, with another fine Gothic cathedral and a delightfully preserved old city.

Day 7: Into Burgundy
Burgundy's capital **Dijon** *(pp344–5)* has a particular grandeur inherited from the days when the region's dukes were a great power in the medieval world. To the south, some of the world's most celebrated vine-yards, many open to visitors, extend along the **Côte d'Or** down to the delightful old wine town of **Beaune** *(p348)*, with its superb **Hôtel-Dieu** *(pp350–1)*.

To extend your trip...
Continue through the southern Côte d'Or to **Lyon** *(pp382–5)* or head east to the south of **Besançon** *(p354)*.

For practical information on traveling around France, see pp618–41

The famous medieval fortified town of Carcassonne

A Week in the Rhône Valley and Languedoc

- **Airports** Arrive at Lyon and depart from Toulouse airport, or arrive and depart from Paris and take trains to Lyon (2 hours) and back from Toulouse (5½ hours).
- **Transport** A rental car is essential to tour the route after Lyon.

Day 1: Lyon
France's sophisticated second city, **Lyon** *(pp382–5)* has an array of attractions, from Roman amphitheaters and a lovely old quarter to trendy shops and a variety of museums. It's also one of France's culinary capitals, so be sure to sample *cuisine lyonnais* in a *bouchon* or traditional restaurant.

Day 2: Vienne and the Côtes du Rhône
Rent a car and make the short journey south to **Vienne** *(p386)*, a charming town with an extraordinary concentration of Roman relics as well as a Gothic cathedral. In the afternoon continue down the Rhône Valley to **Valence** *(p388)*, with detours east near **Tournon** to taste subtle red Côtes du Rhône wines in the village of **Tain l'Hermitage**.

Day 3: The Ardèche
The rugged rocky hills west of the Rhône contain dramatic scenery around the spectacular gorges of the fast-flowing **Ardèche** *(pp388–9)* river. Make a detour to wander among captivating hill villages and enjoy stunning views, ending up at the fabulous natural bridge **Pont d'Arc**, near **Vallon-Pont d'Arc**.

Day 4: Orange and Avignon
Return to the Rhône and head for **Orange** *(p506)*, with its Roman Theater (Théâtre Antique) and Arc de Triomphe. Nearby, the vineyards of **Châteauneuf-du-Pape** *(pp506–7)* are famed for their powerful red wines. **Avignon** *(p507)* is perhaps the archetypal southern French city, with its golden stone walls, relaxing squares, and warm sunlight, plus the 14th-century **Palais des Papes** *(pp508–9)*, 12th-century bridge, and vibrant summer arts festival.

Day 5: Arles to the Camargue
Little **St-Rémy-de-Provence** *(p511)* is where Vincent Van Gogh produced many of his famous paintings. He is also associated with **Arles** *(pp512–13)*, where many places he painted are easy to recognize. Don't miss the Roman Amphitheater.

Diners in Lyon enjoying traditional cuisine at a small café known as a *bouchon*

The misty flat landscape of the **Camargue** *(pp514–15)* also begins just outside town. Head back north to the astonishing Roman aqueduct **Pont du Gard** *(pp498–9)* before arriving in Nîmes for the night.

Day 6: Nîmes to Narbonne
Ancient **Nîmes** *(pp500–1)* has France's most complete Roman monuments in the Maison Carrée, the giant Arènes amphitheater and more. Spend much of the day there, or head southwest along the coast for lunch in the great Mediterranean port of **Sète** *(p496)*. Take a walk along the beach and then continue to **Narbonne** *(pp490–91)*. See the Gothic cathedral and cloisters, before ending the day in Carcassonne.

Day 7: Carcassonne and Toulouse
Carcassonne *(pp492–3)*, a carefully restored medieval city of stone walls and winding alleys, stuns everyone who sees it. Visitors who stay overnight can explore before the crowds arrive towards midday. From there it's a short distance to **Toulouse** *(pp450–51)*, with at its heart a charming old town and historic buildings such as the **Jacobins** church and **Musée des Augustins**, housed around an exquisite Gothic cloister.

To extend your trip...
Relax and catch some waves on the Atlantic surf beaches around **Biarritz** *(p456)*.

View of the Dordogne river from the village of Tremolat, near Sarlat

A Wine and Food Tour of Burgundy, Périgord, and Bordeaux

This tour takes you to some of France's classic regions for fine wines and food, focusing on local specialties along the way.

- **Airports** Arrive at Paris, and depart from there or Bordeaux. Rent a car in Paris or take trains to Auxerre (2 hours) and back from Bordeaux (3¼ hours).
- **Transport** A rental car is essential.
- **Booking ahead** Required at larger Burgundy vineyards and the châteaus wine estates near Bordeaux.

Day 1: Chablis to the Côte d'Or

Burgundy's northernmost wine district is found just east of **Auxerre** *(pp334–5)* around the pleasant village of **Chablis** *(p335)*, famed for delicious whites.
Make a brief stop in Dijon before reaching one of the most famous and beautiful wine regions in the world along the **Côte d'Or** *(p348)*. The roads here are lined with village names magnetic to any wine lover – **Nuits-St-Georges**, **Gevrey-Chambertin** *(p348)* – and there are plenty of great opportunities for tasting.
End the day in lovely **Beaune** *(p348)*, which has a wine museum in a Gothic palace as well as the famous Hôtel-Dieu hospital.

Day 2: Beaune to Beaujolais

Continue down the southern half of the **Côte d'Or**, and for a change from wines stop to visit the impressive ruins of **Cluny Abbey** *(p349)*. In the afternoon, leave the main routes south of Mâcon to explore the charming villages and vineyards of the **Beaujolais** *(p381)* district.
Stay the night in **Lyon** *(pp382–5)*, and enjoy some of the city's famous cuisine.

Day 3: The Auvergne

To the west, beyond Clermont-Ferrand and the extinct volcanos, the **Monts Dore**, the mountains of the Auvergne are known for fine soft cheeses such as **Cantal** *(p367)* and **St-Nectaire** *(p364)*. Driving westwards through rugged landscapes, be sure to explore the enticing displays of local produce in village shops and markets, reaching the borders of Périgord in the evening.

Vineyards and fields in the wine district around Chablis

Day 4: Périgord and Dordogne

The Périgord region and Dordogne valley are equally famed for beautiful scenery and delicious foods. Window-shop and learn about truffles in the capital **Périgueux** *(p435)*, and be sure to catch the spectacular market in **Sarlat** *(pp436–7)*.
Try the Périgord's famed specialties – truffles, duck, *foie gras* – in the restaurants of the many gorgeous villages along the Dordogne, like **Domme** *(p439)*.

Day 5: St-Emilion to Bordeaux

St-Emilion *(p426)* has been producing wine since Roman times, and its winding streets are full of historic buildings and early medieval churches. Visit famous estates in the village of **Figeac** *(p427)*, and in nearby **Libourne** and **Pomerol** *(pp402–3)*. Then head into Bordeaux to end the day with a relaxing drink in the city's Maison du Vin wine center.

Day 6: Bordeaux and Graves

The center of **Bordeaux** *(pp424–5)* retains its 18th-century grandeur. Admire the huge Neo-Classical **Grand Théâtre**, and stroll along the quays beside the River Garonne. Later, explore the southern areas of Bordeaux's wine region around **Graves** and **Sauternes**, known for sweet dessert wines or, if you have time, head south to **Mont-de-Marsan** *(p429)*, home of Armagnac.

Day 7: Médoc and Cognac

The grandest Bordeaux wines – Château Mouton-Rothschild, Château Latour – all come from the **Médoc** district north of the city around **Pauillac** *(p427)*, from estates presided over by grand châteaus that provide a luxurious setting for tasting. If there's time, return to Bordeaux and head north to **Cognac** *(pp422–3)* for a sample of its famous brandy.

To extend your trip…
Relax on the beaches and sample seafood at **La Rochelle** *(p420)* and **Ile d'Oléron** *(pp421)*.

A Week in Mediterranean France

This tour visits some of the finest beaches and beauty spots of France's celebrated south coast.

- **Airports** Arrive and depart from Nice, Toulouse, or Paris. Return to Nice (6½ hours) or Paris (5–6 hours) by train from Perpignan.
- **Transport** Several parts of the trip can be made by train but for others a car is essential.
- **Booking ahead** Prebook boat trips from Cassis to the Calanques in July–August.

Bright sun and Mediterranean colors seen from the perched village of Eze

Day 1: Nice
Capital of the Côte d'Azur, **Nice** *(pp530–31)* has superb restaurants and an elegant seafront. Don't miss the Musée Matisse, with stunning works by the painter who celebrated Mediterranean colors more than any other artist. In the afternoon, rent a car to visit the exquisite coastline east of the city, at **Cap Ferrat** *(p532)* and especially the clifftop village of **Eze** *(p533)*, for unforgettable views over the Riviera.

Day 2: St-Paul-de-Vence to Cannes
Take a car and drive inland to **St-Paul-de-Vence** *(pp528–9)*, an artists' mecca full of echoes of Picasso and Chagall, and the perfume capital of **Grasse** *(p521)*, ringed by fields of lavender and jasmine. Drop down to the sea again for a look at opulent **Cap d'Antibes** *(p525)* before ending the day in ever-fashionable **Cannes** *(p524)*.

Day 3: West to St-Tropez
All along the winding coast road west from Cannes there are magnificent views and seascapes. The road runs into **St-Raphaël** and **Fréjus** *(p521)*, two pleasant, relaxed resorts with long beaches. Farther west again, **St-Tropez** *(p520)* has been the chicest spot on the Riviera since Brigitte Bardot arrived in the 1950s. Watch the fashion parade around the harbor, and count the luxury yachts.

Day 4: Island Beaches
The coast road west through **Le Lavandou** to the charming harbor of **Hyères** *(p518)* is one of the loveliest on the Côte d'Azur, but there is also a faster inland road. From Hyères take a boat to **Porquerolles**, largest of the **Iles d'Hyères** *(p519)*, with turquoise seas and perfect beaches that are easily explored by rented bicycle. Return to Hyères to stay for the night.

To extend your trip...
Stay overnight to enjoy **Porquerolles'** beaches to the full, or spend a day exploring **Marseille** *(p516)*.

Day 5: Cassis and the Calanques
Cassis *(p517)* is one of the most vibrant small towns of the Provençal coast, with a lively café-lined fishing harbor. The surrounding coast is magnificently wild and rocky, and boats run regularly to the **Calanques** *(p517)*, jagged inlets accessible only by sea that are fabulous for swimming and contain an abundance of birds and wild flowers.

Day 6: Sète and Cap d'Agde
Leave your car in Marseille and take an early train to **Sète** *(p496)* (2 hours) to transfer to a very different Mediterranean coast, in Languedoc. Sète is an atmospheric old port town, with superb, no-frills seafood restaurants along its canalside quays. Walk or take a train or bus beside the endless sandy beaches south towards **Cap d'Agde** *(p491)*, and watch the colorful sails running in the wind at one of Europe's foremost windsurfing and kitesurfing locations.

Day 7: Collioure
Take another train down the coast to **Collioure** *(p487)*, a classic small Mediterranean harbor loved by artists such as Matisse and Derain. Explore the old port and medieval Catalan castle, then lie back on the beaches with a superb view of the town's imposing stone church.

To extend your trip...
Catch a boat or plane to **Corsica** *(pp537–47)* for some of France's purest Mediterranean beaches.

Rocky coastline and the narrow inlet of Calanque d'En-Vau near Bouches du Rhone

Putting France on the Map

France, one of the largest countries in Europe, has airline connections with most cities in the world. Paris is the major transport hub with two international airports; others include Bordeaux, Lille, Lyon, Nice, and Toulouse. There are good, high-speed rail links with the rest of Europe, and a network of efficient highways. A number of ferry routes cross the Mediterranean to Corsica and beyond. Cross-Channel ferries serve several ports, with the Channel Tunnel providing an alternative link by rail.

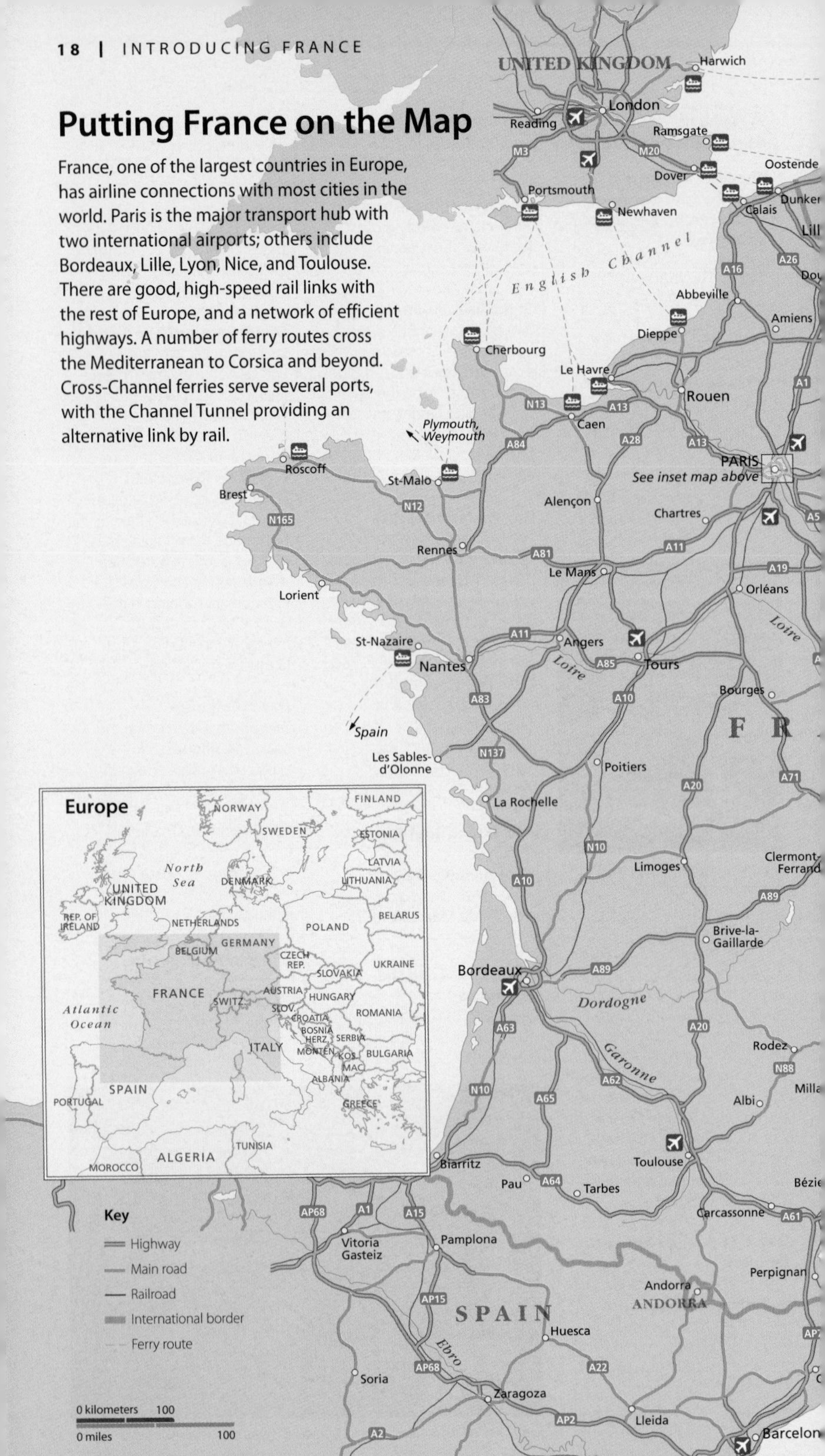

Key

- Highway
- Main road
- Railroad
- International border
- Ferry route

0 kilometers 100

0 miles 100

For additional map symbols *see back flap*

Greater Paris
St Denis
Bezons
Asniéres-sur-Seine
Bobigny
BLVD PÉRIPHÉRIQUE
Nanterre
PARIS
St-Cloud
Boulogne
Vincennes
Versailles
Montrouge
Créteil
Sceaux
0 kilometers 5
0 miles 5
Den Haag
Rotterdam
NETHERLANDS
Dortmund
Essen
Antwerpen
Düsseldorf
Bruxelles
Köln
BELGIUM
Bonn
Liège
LUXEMBOURG
Charleville-Méziers
Luxembourg
Saarbrücken
Reims
Metz
Nancy
Strasbourg
Troyes
Donau
München
GERMANY
Mulhouse
Bodensee
Basel
Zürich
Innsbruck
AUSTRIA
Dijon
Besançon
Bern
SWITZERLAND
Bolzano
Lac Léman
Mâcon
Genève
Udine
Lyon
Aosta
Trento
Chambéry
Bergamo
Milano
Venezia
Grenoble
Torino
Piacenza
Po
Valence
Parma
Rhône
Gap
Ravenna
Cuneo
Genova
Bologna
ITALY
Savona
La Spezia
Avignon
Nîmes
Firenze
Nice
Monaco
Pisa
Aix-en-Provence
Livorno
Cannes
Marseille
Siena
Toulon
Perugia
Piombino
Ile Rousse
Bastia
Orbetello
Corsica
Mediterranean Sea
Roma
Ajaccio
Porto-Vecchio
Sardinia

Regional France

France has a population of around 61 million, and receives over 75 million visitors a year. It covers an area of 210,025 miles (543,965 sq km). Paris is the largest city, followed by Lyon, Marseille and the conurbation of Lille-Lens-Valenciennes. The Loire, Seine, Garonne, and Rhône are the longest of France's many rivers. This book divides the country into 15 regions, plus a separate section for Paris and Ile de France, although officially France comprises 22 *régions*.

Key
Highway
Major road
Minor road

0 kilometers 100
0 miles 100

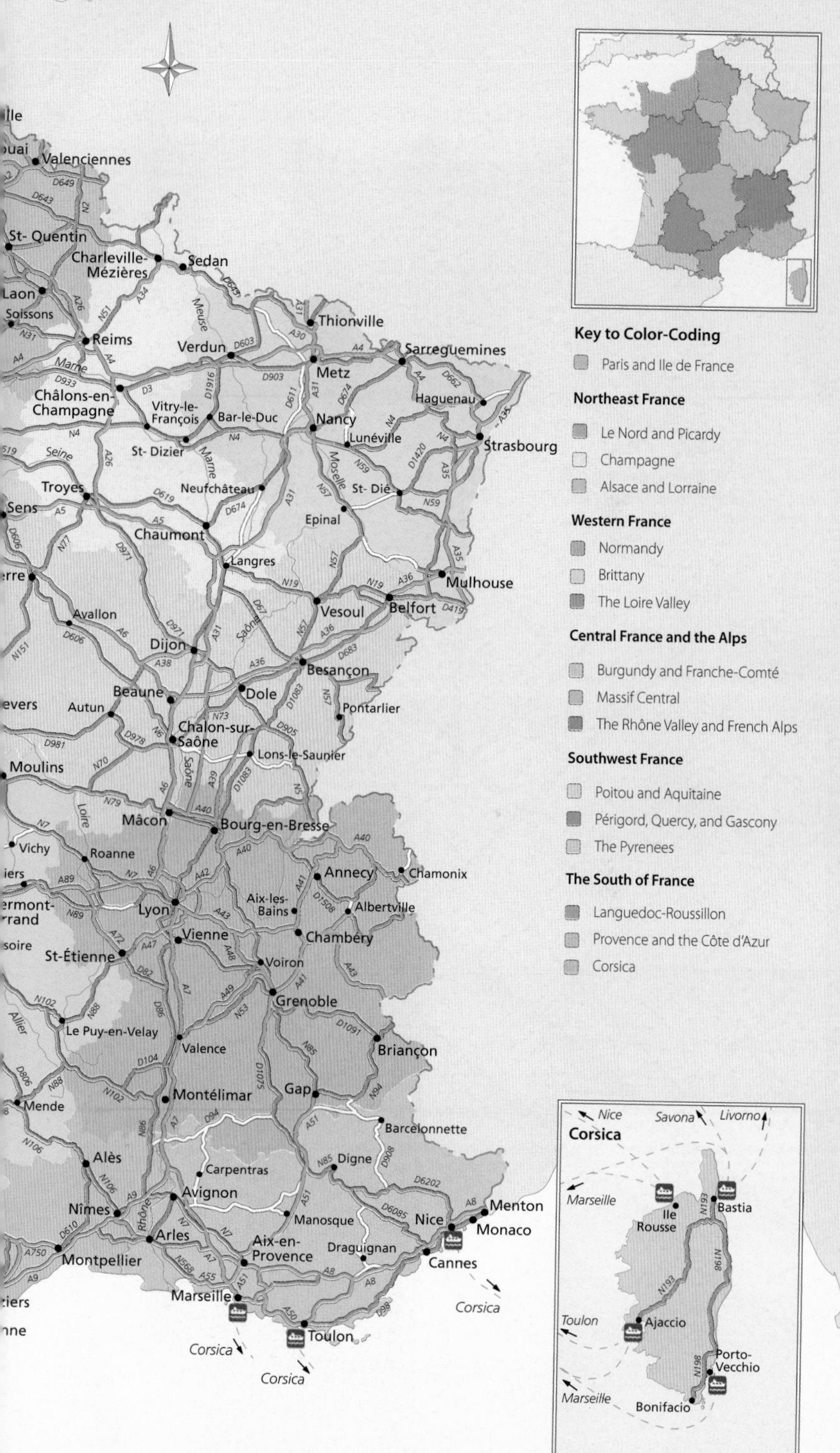
Key to Color-Coding
Paris and Ile de France
Northeast France
Le Nord and Picardy
Champagne
Alsace and Lorraine
Western France
Normandy
Brittany
The Loire Valley
Central France and the Alps
Burgundy and Franche-Comté
Massif Central
The Rhône Valley and French Alps
Southwest France
Poitou and Aquitaine
Périgord, Quercy, and Gascony
The Pyrenees
The South of France
Languedoc-Roussillon
Provence and the Côte d'Azur
Corsica
Valenciennes
St- Quentin
Charleville-Mézières
Sedan
Laon
Soissons
Reims
Verdun
Thionville
Sarreguemines
Metz
Haguenau
Châlons-en-Champagne
Vitry-le-François
Bar-le-Duc
Nancy
Lunéville
Strasbourg
St- Dizier
Troyes
Neufchâteau
St- Dié
Sens
Epinal
Chaumont
Langres
Mulhouse
Belfort
Vesoul
Avallon
Dijon
Besançon
Beaune
Dole
Autun
Pontarlier
Chalon-sur-Saône
Lons-le-Saunier
Moulins
Mâcon
Bourg-en-Bresse
Vichy
Roanne
Annecy
Chamonix
Lyon
Aix-les-Bains
Albertville
Vienne
Chambéry
St-Étienne
Voiron
Grenoble
Le Puy-en-Velay
Valence
Briançon
Mende
Montélimar
Gap
Barcelonnette
Alès
Carpentras
Digne
Avignon
Nîmes
Manosque
Nice
Menton
Monaco
Arles
Aix-en-Provence
Draguignan
Cannes
Montpellier
Marseille
Toulon
Corsica
Corsica
Nice
Savona
Livorno
Marseille
Ile Rousse
Bastia
Toulon
Ajaccio
Porto-Vecchio
Marseille
Bonifacio

A PORTRAIT OF FRANCE

The French are convinced that their way of life is best, and that their country is the most civilized on earth. Many millions of visitors agree with them. The food and wine are justly celebrated. French culture, literature, art, cinema, and architecture can be both profound and provocative. Whether cerebral, sensual, or sportive, France is a country where anyone might feel at home.

France's landscape ranges from mountain plateaus to lush farmland, traditional villages to chic boulevards. Its regional identities are equally diverse. The country belongs to both northern and southern Europe, and encompasses Brittany with its Celtic maritime heritage, the Mediterranean sunbelt, Germanic Alsace-Lorraine, and the hardy mountain regions of the Auvergne and the Pyrenees. Paris remains the linchpin, with its famously brusque citizens and intense tempo. Other cities range from the industrial conglomeration of Lille in the north, to Marseille, the biggest port on the Mediterranean. The differences between north and south, country and city are well-entrenched, indeed cherished. Advances such as the TGV (high-speed train), Internet and mobile phone technology have helped reduce distance (both physical and emotional) yet have simultaneously provoked an opposite reaction: as life in France becomes more city-based and industrialized, so the desire grows to safeguard the old, traditional ways and to value rural life.

The idea of life in the country – *douceur de vivre* (the Good Life), tables set in the sun for the wine and anecdotes to flow – is as seductive as ever for residents and visitors alike. Nevertheless, the rural way of life has been changing. Whereas in 1945 one person in three worked in farming, today it is only one in 25.

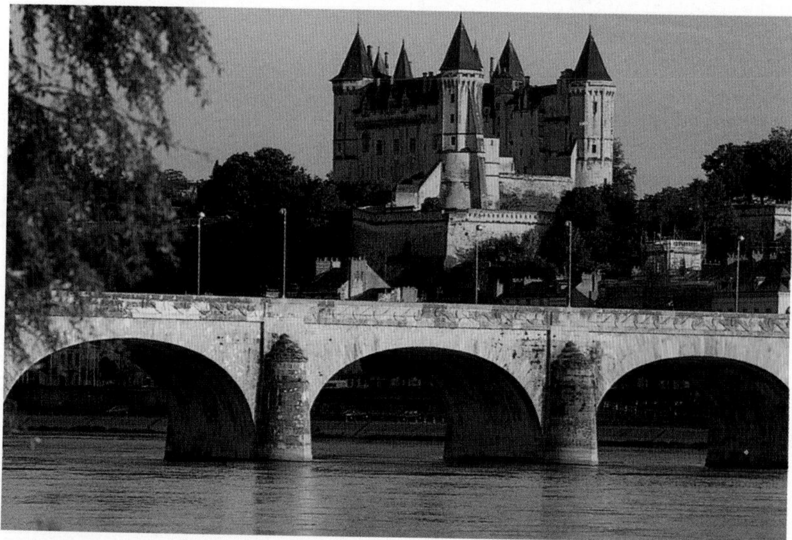

Château de Saumur, one of the Loire's most romantic and complete castles

◀ Glass pyramid entrance to the Musée du Louvre, Paris

France's main exports used to be luxury goods such as perfumes and Cognac; these have been overtaken by cars, aircraft, nuclear power stations, and telecommunications equipment, although exports of alcoholic beverages, and especially Cognac, have made a resurgence in recent years.

The popular scooter

People remain firmly committed to their roots, and often retain a place in the country for holidays or retirement. On average, more French people have second homes than any other nationality; and in many areas, such as Provence, dying villages have found new life as chic summer residences for Parisians. Many artists and artisans now live and work in the country, and entrepreneurs have set up factory workshops there, more feasible in the age of the Internet.

Chanel chic

The decline in the influence of the Catholic Church has resulted in social changes. Today only 9 percent of people attend mass regularly. Many couples live together before marriage, and are allowed the same tax status as married couples. Abortion is now legal, and since 2013, same-sex couples can legally marry.

Feminism in France has quite a different look than in Anglo-Saxon countries. French feminists are unwilling to condemn frivolous sex-appeal. As EU citizens, women in France have legal equality with men, but French attitudes remain traditional. It may have seemed like a milestone in 1991, when Edith Cresson became France's first woman prime minister, but her unpopularity and the 1999 corruption case against her arguably held back women's equality in French politics. Ségolène Royal re-established a prominent political role for women when she won 47 percent of the vote in the 2007 presidential elections, as did Martine Aubry in 2008, when she became head of the French Socialist party.

Social Customs and Politics

French social life, except between close friends, has always been marked by formality – handshaking, the use of titles, the preference for the formal *vous* rather than the intimate *tu*. However, this is changing among the younger generation,

The May 1968 disturbances, a catalyst for profound change in France

Farming in Alsace-Lorraine

who now call you by your first name. Standards of dress have become much more informal too, though the French still dress well.

Formality lingers on, however, and France remains very legalistic – whether you are buying a house or exporting an antique. But the French are insouciant about their famous red tape. Rules and laws are there to be ingeniously evaded, twisted, or made more human. This sport of avoiding cumbersome bureaucracy has a name of its own, *le système D*, to be accompanied with a shrug and a smile.

Charles de Gaulle

Since the end of the Cold War, the sharp Left/Right divisions in French society have been replaced by pragmatic centrism. For 14 years, President François Mitterrand – elected in 1981 as head of a Socialist Communist coalition – steadily moved towards a more central-focused political agenda. In 1995, he was replaced by Jacques Chirac who promised right-wing policies; he too moved to the center. By 2002, immigration and security fears, broken electoral promises, and political corruption had caused widespread disenchantment and a swing to the Front National. The result was elimination of Socialist Lionel Jospin in the first round of the presidential elections and the election of Chirac by default in the second round. Further electoral discontent was revealed by the rejection of the European Constitution in 2005.

In 2007, Chirac's Deputy Prime Minister, Nicolas Sarkozy, won the presidency by addressing public fears and promising an end to corruption. He forged a closer relationship with the US, re-engaged France in the European Union, and opened up his government to ministers from the Left. But his popularity waned in 2010, after his plans to raise the retirement age provoked strikes, and deportation of gypsies drew criticism from other European states.

On 6 May 2012, François Hollande was elected France's second Socialist president. Early reforms included increasing the income tax rate on high earnings, and supporting same-sex marriage. He also sent French troops to curtail Islamic extremists in Mali.

Culture and the Arts

Culture is taken seriously in France, and writers, intellectuals, artists, and fashion designers are held in high social esteem.

Designer John Galliano at a 2010 haute couture show in Paris

As a result, the state finances a large network of provincial arts centers and has traditionally given subsidies that allow experimentation in art and design. The French remain justly proud of their own cinematic tradition and are determined to defend it against pressures from Hollywood. Other activities – from the music industry to the French language itself – are subject to the same protectionist attitudes.

Traditional Breton costumes, worn for festivals and *pardons*

Avant-garde art and literature and modern architecture all enjoy strong patronage in France. Some of the more exciting architectural projects range from the striking modern buildings in Paris – the Louvre pyramid and La Grande Arche at La Défense – to the Post-Modern housing developments of Nîmes, Montpellier, and Marseille in the south.

Modern Life

While one half of the French were heralding the new millennium in true Gallic style, the other half were plunged into darkness caused by some of the worst storms ever to hit Europe. This is an extreme illustration of French ambivalence towards modernism. France's agro-business is one of the most advanced in the world, but the peasant farmer is deeply revered. France hankers after a leading role in the world, yet the country effectively closes down for the whole of August, when the French take to the roads and coastal resorts of France! However, two factors have forced a change of pace: the Internet, which France has embraced keenly, and the Euro, which, in one fell swoop, has swept away Europe's oldest decimalized currency, the Franc.

La Grande Arche, part of the huge business complex on the edge of Paris

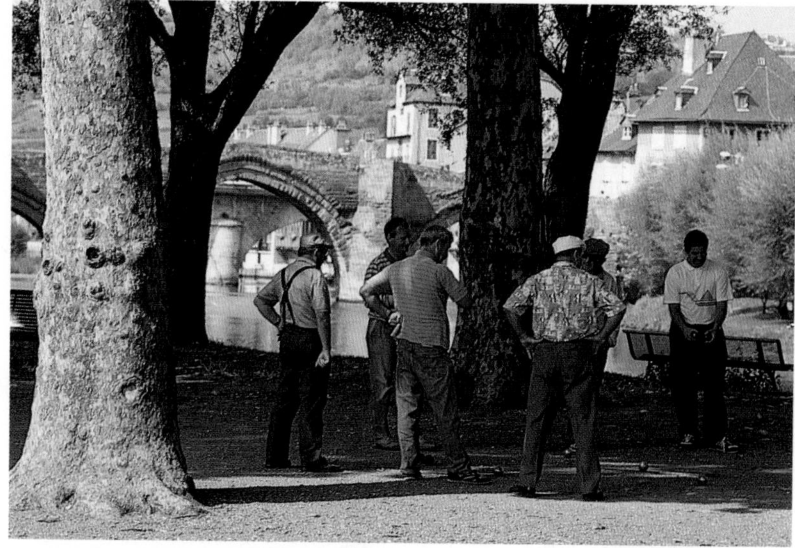

The traditional game of *boules* or *pétanque,* still extremely popular – especially in the south

The French are enthusiastic, discerning consumers. Even small towns have stylish clothes shops and street markets with the best of local produce. France also has Europe's largest hypermarkets, which have been steadily ousting the local grocery or corner store. These are remarkably French in what they sell: a long delicatessen counter may display 100 or so French cheeses and charcuterie, while the range of fresh vegetables and fruit is a tribute to their role in French cuisine.

Southern produce: melons, peaches, and apricots

However, modern pressures have been changing eating habits in a curious way. The French used to eat well daily as a matter of course. Today many are in a hurry, and for most weekly meals will eat simply – either a quick steak or pasta dish at home, or a snack in town (hence the wave of fast-food places that have sprung up, in defiance of French tradition).

But meals still remain an important part of French culture – not just for the food and wines, but also for the pleasure of lengthy meals and good conversation around a table of family or friends. They will reserve their gastronomy for the once-or-twice-a-week special occasion, or the big family Sunday lunch, an important French ritual. It is at these times that the French zest for life really comes into its own.

Remote farm – a nostalgic reminder of rural life

The Classic French Menu

The traditional French meal consists of at least three courses. *Les entrées* or *hors d'oeuvre* (starters or appetizers) include soups, egg dishes, salads, or *charcuterie*, such as sliced sausage or hams. There may be a separate fish course before the main course. Otherwise, *les plats* (main courses) will be a choice of meat and fish dishes, often served with a sauce and accompanied by potatoes, rice, or pasta and vegetables. The cheese course comes before the dessert. Desserts may include sorbets, fruit tarts, and creamy or chocolate concoctions. A fixed-price menu is the cheapest option. For more information on French restaurants, see pp572–5.

Escargots à la Bourguignonne In Bourgogne, snails are served in their shells with parsley and garlic butter.

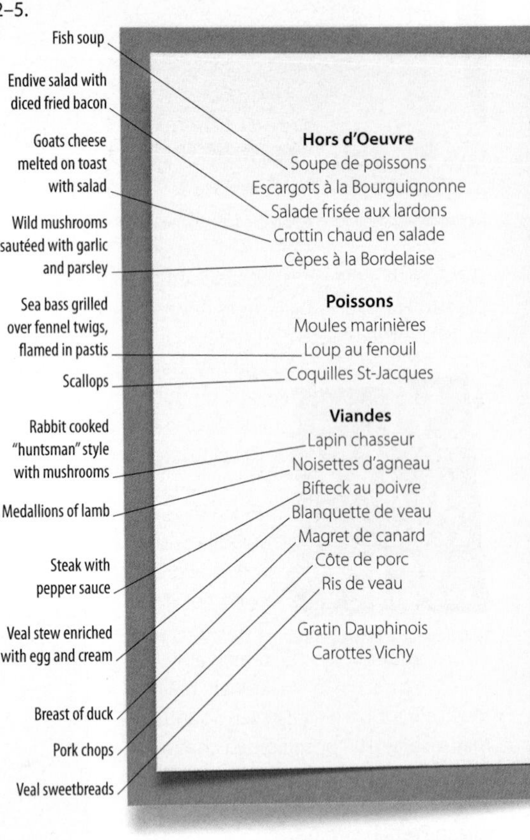

Moules marinières In this classic dish, mussels are cooked in dry white wine with shallots and parsley.

Gratin Dauphinois Layers of potato are covered in cream, topped with Gruyère cheese, and slowly baked.

Carottes Vichy Cooked in Vichy water with sugar, carrots take on a delicious, sweet glaze. They are served garnished with parsley.

Breakfast

The French rarely eat cereal, eggs, or meat for breakfast; assorted breads, spread with butter and jams, are their morning choice. These include *croissants* (flaky, buttery crescent-shaped pastries); a piece of *baguette* (the classic long thin loaf); *pain au chocolat* (an oblong of croissant dough rolled around a tablet of chocolate, then baked); and *brioche* (an airy, egg-enriched yeast bread or roll). They are accompanied by coffee or tea, or hot chocolate for children. Hotels will usually offer fresh fruit juice, too. The most common form of coffee at breakfast is *café au lait*, espresso served with warm milk.

Typical French breakfast selection

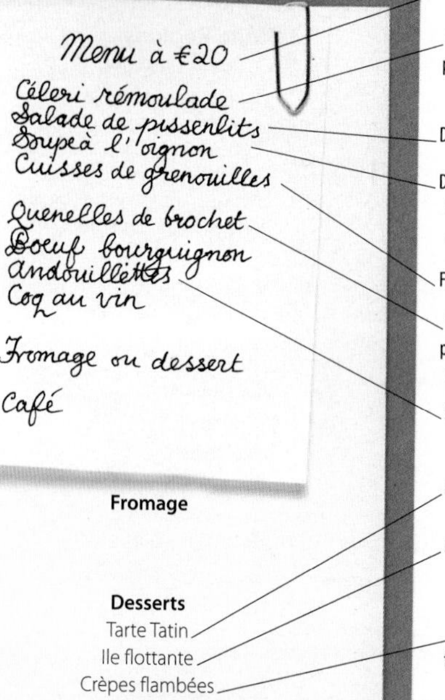

Menu à €20
Céleri rémoulade
Salade de pissenlits
Soupe à l'oignon
Cuisses de grenouilles
Quenelles de brochet
Boeuf bourguignon
Andouillettes
Coq au vin
Fromage ou dessert
Café
Fromage
Desserts
Tarte Tatin
Ile flottante
Crèpes flambées
Clafoutis
Crème caramel
Crème brulée

Fixed-price menu of the day

Grated celeriac in a piquant mayonnaise

Dandelion-leaf salad

Dark, rich onion soup topped with bread and grilled cheese

Frogs' legs

Light, fluffy poached pike dumplings

Small tripe sausages, usually grilled

Upside-down baked apple tart

Meringues floating in a creamy sauce

Sugared crêpes flamed in liqueur

Baked fruit and batter dessert, often made with cherries

Egg custard with a caramel sauce

Boeuf Bourguignon Beef is cooked in red Burgundy wine with bacon, baby onions, and button mushrooms.

Coq au vin A male chicken is flamed in brandy, then stewed in wine with button mushrooms and onions.

Fromage Any good French restaurant will take pride in offering a good range of perfectly matured regional cheeses, including, as available, cows', ewes', and goats' milk, blue, soft, and hard varieties.

Crème Brulée This rich, creamy custard is covered with brown sugar, grilled to form a crisp topping.

The Wine of France

Winemaking in France dates back to pre-Roman times, although it was the Romans who disseminated the culture of the vine and the practice of winemaking throughout the country. The range, quality, and reputation of the fine wines of Bordeaux, Burgundy, the Rhône, and Champagne in particular have made them role models the world over. France's everyday wines can be highly enjoyable too, with plenty of good value wines now emerging from the southern regions.

Traditional vineyard cultivation

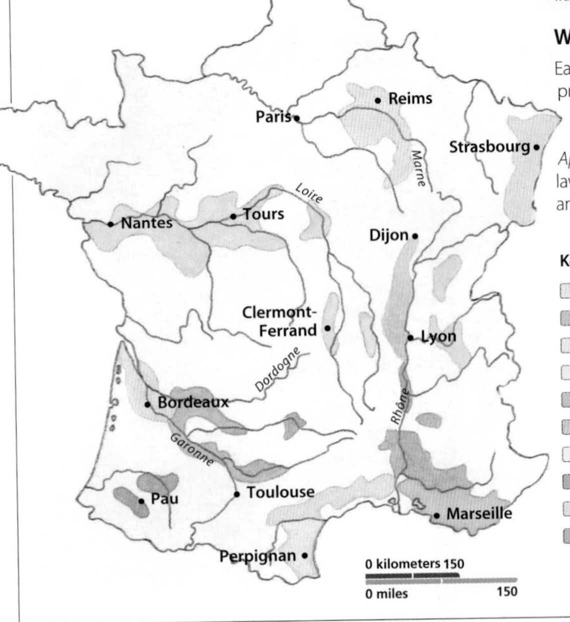

Wine Regions

Each of the 10 principal wine-producing regions has its own identity, based on grape varieties, climate, and *terroir* (soil). *Appellation d'Origine Protégée* laws guarantee a wine's origins and production methods.

Key

- Bordeaux
- Burgundy
- Champagne
- Alsace
- Loire
- Provence
- Jura and Savoie
- The Southwest
- Languedoc-Roussillon
- Rhône

How to read a wine label

Even the simplest label will identify the wine and provide a key to its quality. It will bear the name of the wine and its producer, its vintage, if there is one, and whether it comes from a strictly defined area (*Appellation d'Origine Protégée*), or is a more general *IGP* (*Indication Géographique Protégée*) wine or *vin de France*. It may also have a regional grading, as with the *crus classés* in Bordeaux. The shape and color of the bottle is also a guide to the kind of wine it contains. Green glass is often used since this helps to protect the wine from light.

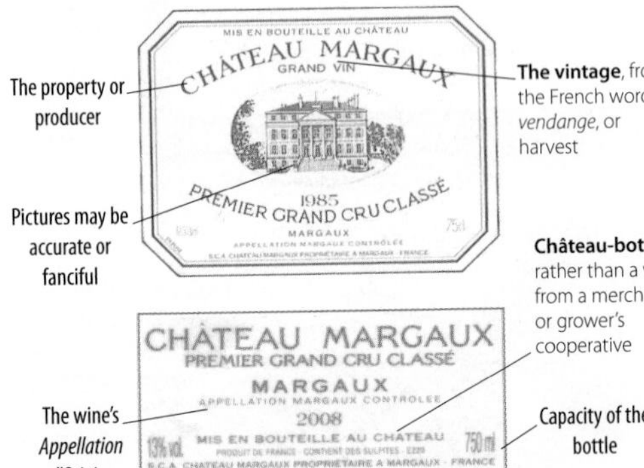

How Wine is Made

Wine is the product of the juice of freshly picked grapes, after natural or cultured yeasts have converted the grape sugars into alcohol during the fermentation process. The yeasts, or lees, are normally filtered out before bottling.

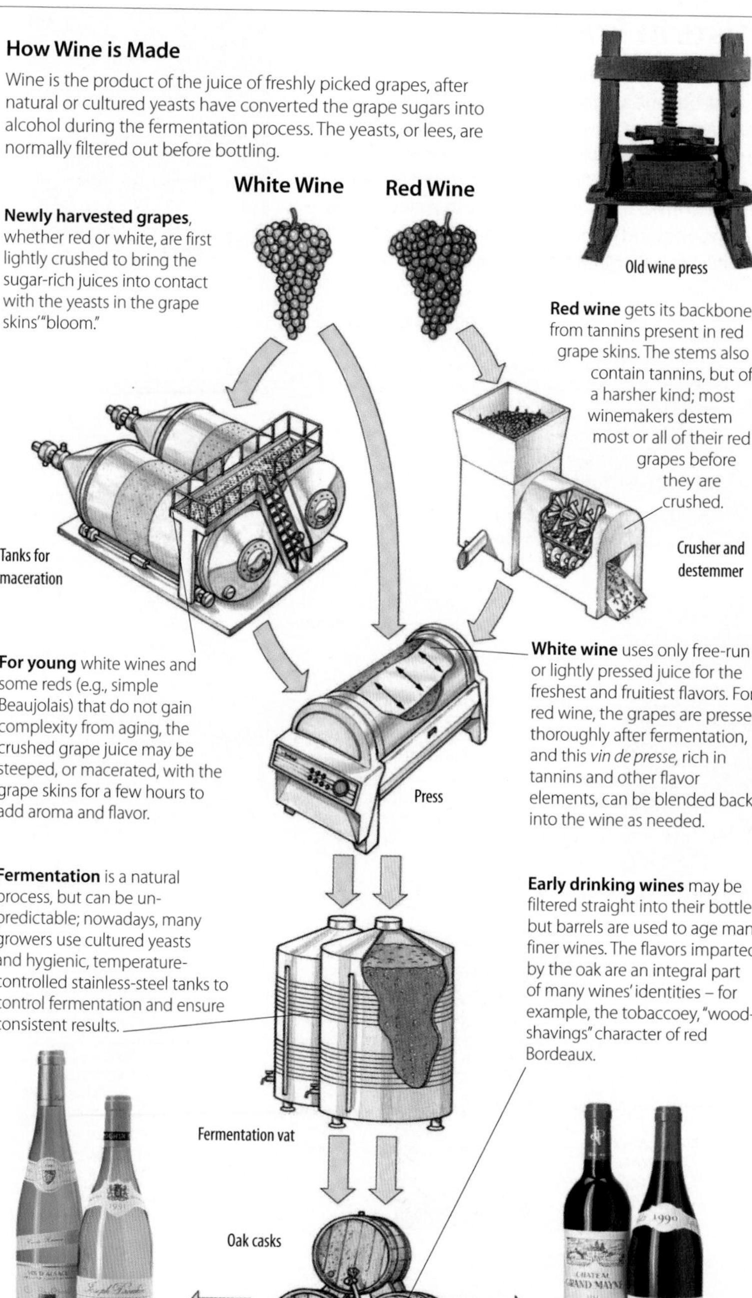

Newly harvested grapes, whether red or white, are first lightly crushed to bring the sugar-rich juices into contact with the yeasts in the grape skins' "bloom."

Old wine press

Red wine gets its backbone from tannins present in red grape skins. The stems also contain tannins, but of a harsher kind; most winemakers destem most or all of their red grapes before they are crushed.

For young white wines and some reds (e.g., simple Beaujolais) that do not gain complexity from aging, the crushed grape juice may be steeped, or macerated, with the grape skins for a few hours to add aroma and flavor.

White wine uses only free-run or lightly pressed juice for the freshest and fruitiest flavors. For red wine, the grapes are pressed thoroughly after fermentation, and this *vin de presse*, rich in tannins and other flavor elements, can be blended back into the wine as needed.

Fermentation is a natural process, but can be unpredictable; nowadays, many growers use cultured yeasts and hygienic, temperature-controlled stainless-steel tanks to control fermentation and ensure consistent results.

Early drinking wines may be filtered straight into their bottles, but barrels are used to age many finer wines. The flavors imparted by the oak are an integral part of many wines' identities – for example, the tobaccoey, "wood-shavings" character of red Bordeaux.

Different shades of glass identify the wine regions

Bottle shapes typical of red Bordeaux (left) and Burgundy

Artists in France

Artists have always been inspired by France, especially since landscape became a legitimate subject for art in the 19th century. Art and tourism have been closely linked for over a century, when the establishment of artists' colonies in the forest of Fontainebleau, Brittany, and the south of France did much to make these areas attractive to visitors. Today, one of the pleasures of touring the countryside is the recognition of landscapes made famous in paintings.

A few months before his tragic death in July 1890, Vincent Van Gogh painted the *Church at Auvers*. He noted that the building "appears to have a violet-hued blue color; pure cobalt."

Gustave Courbet, socialist and leader of the Realist School of painting, captured this famous coastal town in *The Cliffs at Etretat after a Storm* (1869).

Emile Bernard was fascinated by the wild, almost primitive character of the Breton landscape and the individuality of its inhabitants. He was one of the community of artists based in Pont Aven. His *La Ronde Bretonne* (1892) portrays local Celtic customs.

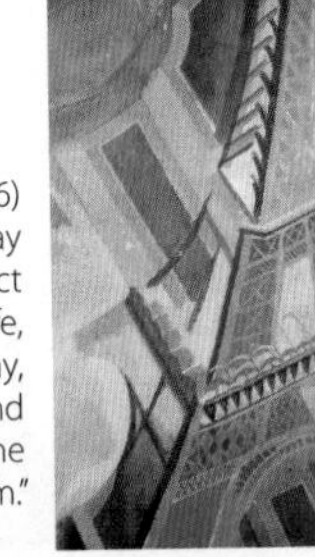

In his Eiffel Tower (1926) Robert Delaunay investigated the abstract qualities of color. His wife, artist Sonia Delaunay, said, "The Eiffel Tower and the Universe were one and the same to him."

Neo-Impressionist artist and exponent of Pointillism, Paul Signac indulged his love of maritime subjects on the coasts of France. *Entrance to the Port at La Rochelle* (1921) shows his use of myriad dots of color to represent nature.

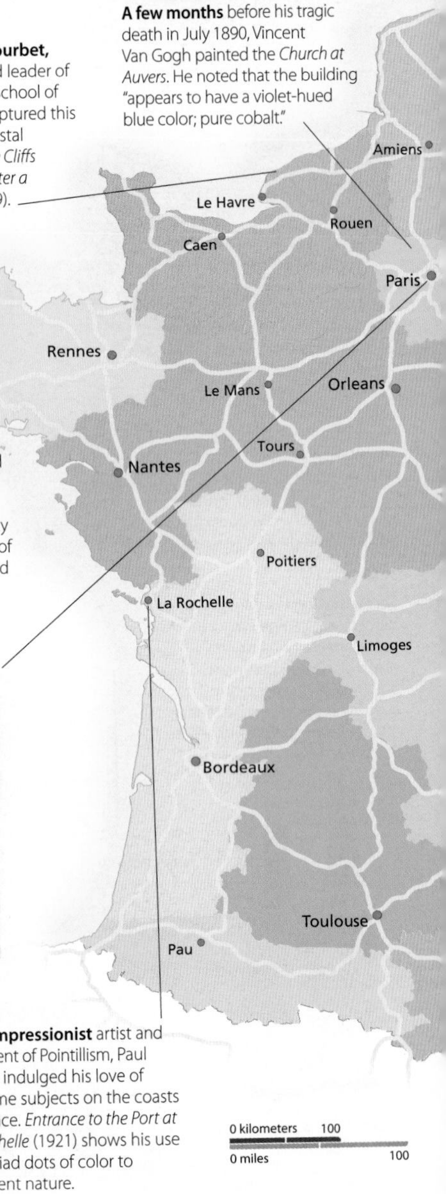

Amiens
Le Havre
Rouen
Caen
Paris
Rennes
Le Mans
Orleans
Tours
Nantes
Poitiers
La Rochelle
Limoges
Bordeaux
Toulouse
Pau

0 kilometers 100
0 miles 100

Follower of the French Classical tradition of landscape painting, Jean-Baptiste-Camille Corot recorded *The Belfry of Douai* (1871).

Scenes from everyday life were realistically rendered by Gustave Courbet, as here in *Young Ladies of the Village Giving Alms to a Cow Girl in a Valley near Ornans* (1851–2).

Maurice Utrillo painted this village scene, *The Church of Saint Bernard in Summer* (1924), while staying at his mother's home. The somber tone and emptiness reflect his unhappy life.

Théodore Rousseau, the leading light of the Barbizon School *(see p185)* of landscape painters, visited the Auvergne in 1830. It was here that he began to paint "en plein air" (in the open air). The results are seen in this sensitively observed scene, *Sunset, Auvergne* (c.1830).

The French Riviera attracted many artists *(see pp476–7)*. Raoul Dufy particularly appreciated its pleasures, seen in this typical scene of blue skies and palm trees, *La Jetée Promenade à Nice* (1928).

Landscape at Collioure (1905) depicts the vivid colors of this little Catalan fishing village. It was here that Henri Matisse founded the art movement of the Fauves, or "Wild Beasts," who used exceptionally bright, expressive colors.

Writers in France

Writers and intellectuals traditionally enjoy high prestige in France. One of the most august of French institutions is the Academie Française, whose 40 members, most of them writers, have pronounced on national events and, on occasion, held public office.

The work of many French novelists is deeply rooted in their native area, ranging from the Normandy of Gustave Flaubert to Jean Giono's Provence. In addition to their literary merit, these novels provide a unique guide to France's regional identities.

The Novel

The farmland of the Beauce, where Zola based his novel, *La Terre*

The first great French writer was Rabelais, in the 16th century, a boisterous, life-affirming satirist *(see p299)*. Many writers in the Age of Enlightenment which followed emphasized the tradition of reason, clarity, and objectivity in their work. The 19th century was the golden age of the French humanist novel, producing Balzac, with his vast fresco of contemporary society; Stendhal, a critic of the frailties of ambition in *Scarlet and Black*; and Victor Hugo, known for epics such as *Les Misérables*. George Sand broke ground with her novels such as *The Devil's Pool* which depicted peasant life, albeit in an idealized way. In the same century, Flaubert produced his masterwork *Madame Bovary*, a study of provincialism and misplaced romanticism. In contrast, Zola wrote *Germinal*, *La Terre*, and other studies of lower-class life.

Marcel Proust, author of *Remembrance of Things Past*

Marcel Proust combined a poetic evocation of his boyhood with a portrait of high society in his long novel, *Remembrance of Things Past*. Others have also written poetically about their child-

Colette's house in Burgundy

hood, such as Alain-Fournier in *Le Grand Meaulnes* and Colette in *My Mother's House*.

A new kind of novel emerged after World War I. Jean Giono's *Joy of Man's Desiring*, and François Mauriac's masterly *Thérèse Desqueyroux*, explored the impact of landscape upon human character. Mauriac, and also George Bernanos in his *Diary of a Country Priest*, used lone spiritual struggle as a theme. The free-thinker André Gide was another leading writer of the inter-war years with his *Strait is the Gate* and the autobiographical *If it Die*.

In the 1960s Alain Robbe-Grillet and others experimented with the Nouveau Roman, which subordinated character and plot to detailed physical description. Critics held it in part responsible for the recent decline of the novel. Despite this, the 2008 Nobel Prize for literature was awarded to Franco-Mauritian Jean-Marie Gustave Le Clézio.

Hugo's novel *Les Misérables*, made into a musical in the 1980s

Theater

The three classic playwrights of French literature, Racine, Molière, and Corneille, lived in the 17th century. Molière's comedies satirized the vanities and foibles of human nature. Corneille and Racine wrote noble verse tragedies. They were followed in the 18th century by Marivaux, writer of romantic comedies, and Beaumarchais whose *Barber of Seville* and *Marriage of Figaro* later became operas. Victor Hugo's dramas were the most vigorous product of the 19th century. The exceptional dramatists of the 20th century range from Jean Anouilh, author of urbane philosophical comedies, to Jean Genet, ex-convict critic of the establishment. In the 1960s, Eugene Ionesco from Romania and Samuel Beckett from Ireland were among the pioneers of a new genre, the "theater of the absurd." Since then, no major playwrights have emerged but experimental work flourishes in state-subsidized theater companies.

Molière, the 17th-century dramatist

Poetry

The greatest of early French poets was Ronsard, who wrote sonnets about nature and love in the 16th century. Lamartine, a major poet of the early 19th century, also took nature as one of his themes (his poem *Le Lac* laments a lost love). Later the same century, Baudelaire *(Les Fleurs du mal)* and Rimbaud *(Le Bateau Ivre)* were judged to be provocative in their day. Nobel prizewinner in 1904, Frédéric Mistral wrote in his native Provençal tongue. The greatest poet of the 20th century is considered to be Paul Valéry, whose work is profoundly philosophical.

Philosophy

France has produced a large number of major philosophers in the European humanist tradition. One of the first was Montaigne, in the 16th century, an inspired moralist. Then came Descartes, the master of logic, and Pascal. The 18th century produced Voltaire, the supreme liberal, and Rousseau, who preached the harmonizing influence of living close to nature.

In the 20th century, Sartre, de Beauvoir, and Camus used the novel as a philosophical vehicle. Sartre led the existentialist movement in Paris in the early 1940s with his novel *Nausea* and his treatise *Being and Nothingness*. Camus' novel, *The Outsider*, was equally influential.

The 1970s and 1980s brought the structuralists, such as Foucault and Barthes, with their radical ideas. Post-structuralism took this rationalist approach into the 1990s, with Derrida, Kristeva, Deleuze, and Lyotard. At the start of the 21st century, Badiou, known for his political ideas, is one of France's key philosophers.

Sartre and de Beauvoir in La Coupole restaurant in Paris, 1969

Novels by Albert Camus, who won the Nobel Prize in 1957

Foreign Writers

Many foreign writers have visited and been inspired by France, from Petrarch in 14th-century Avignon to Goethe in Alsace in 1770–71. In the 20th century the Riviera attracted novelists Somerset Maugham, Katherine Mansfield, Ernest Hemingway, and Graham Greene. In 1919 the American Sylvia Beach opened the first Shakespeare and Company bookshop in Paris, which became a cultural center for expatriate writers. In 1922 she was the first to publish James Joyce's masterwork, *Ulysses*.

Hemingway with Sylvia Beach and friends, Paris 1923

Romanesque and Gothic Architecture in France

France is rich in medieval architecture, ranging from small Romanesque churches to great Gothic cathedrals. As the country emerged from the Dark Ages in the 11th century, there was a surge in Romanesque building, based on the Roman model of thick walls, round arches, and heavy vaults. French architects improved this basic structure, leading to the flowering of Gothic in the 13th century. Pointed arches and flying buttresses were the key inventions that allowed for much taller buildings with larger windows.

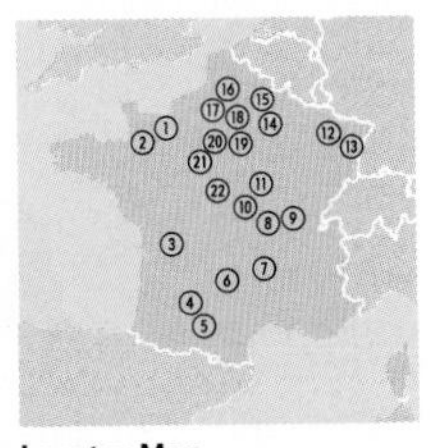

Locator Map

① *Romanesque abbeys & churches*

⑬ *Gothic cathedrals*

Romanesque Features

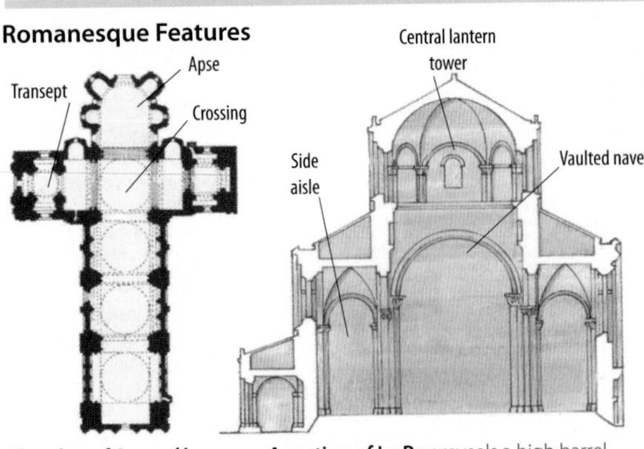

The plan of Angoulême shows the cross-shape and the rounded eastern apse typical of Romanesque architecture.

A section of Le Puy reveals a high barrel-vaulted nave with round arches and low side aisles. Light could enter through windows in the side aisles and the central lantern tower.

The massive walls of the nave bays of St-Etienne support a three-story structure of arcades, a gallery, and clerestory.

Gothic Features

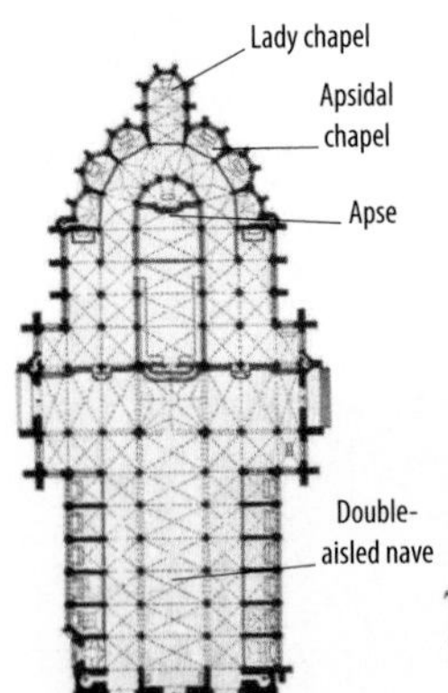

The plan of Amiens shows the nave and apse flanked by a continuous row of chapels.

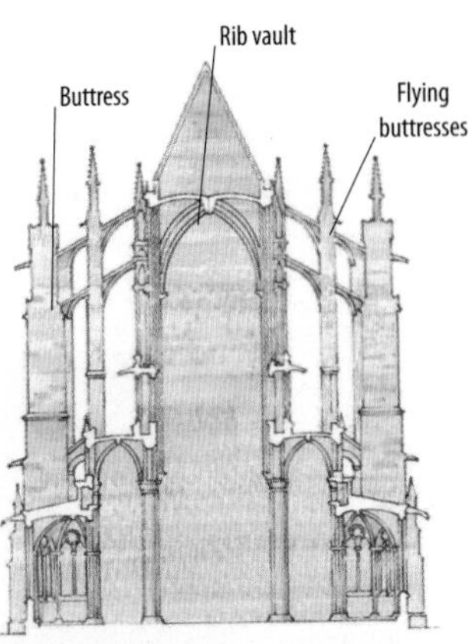

A section of Beauvais shows how the nave could be raised to staggering heights thanks to exterior support from flying buttresses.

Pointed arches withstood greater stress, permitting larger windows as in the nave at Reims.

Where to find Romanesque Architecture

① St-Etienne, Caen *p258*
② Mont-St-Michel, Normandy *pp260–63*
③ St-Pierre, Angoulême *p423*
④ Notre-Dame, Le Puy *p369*
⑤ St-Pierre, Moissac *pp446–7*
⑥ St-Sernin, Toulouse *p451*
⑦ Ste-Foy, Conques *pp372–3*
⑧ Sacré-Coeur, Paray-le-Monial *p349*
⑨ St-Philibert, Tournus *p348–9*
⑩ St-Etienne, Nevers *p342*
⑪ Ste-Madeleine, Vézelay *pp340–1*
⑫ Marmoutier, Saverne *p237*

Where to find Gothic Architecture

⑬ Notre-Dame, Strasbourg *p234*
⑭ Notre-Dame, Reims *pp216–7*
⑮ Notre-Dame, Laon *p209*
⑯ Notre-Dame, Amiens *pp206–7*
⑰ St-Pierre, Beauvais *p204*
⑱ St-Denis, Ile-de-France *pp176–7*
⑲ Sainte-Chapelle, Paris *pp88–9*
⑳ Notre-Dame, Paris *pp90–91*
㉑ Notre-Dame, Chartres *pp312–15*
㉒ St-Etienne, Bourges *p317*

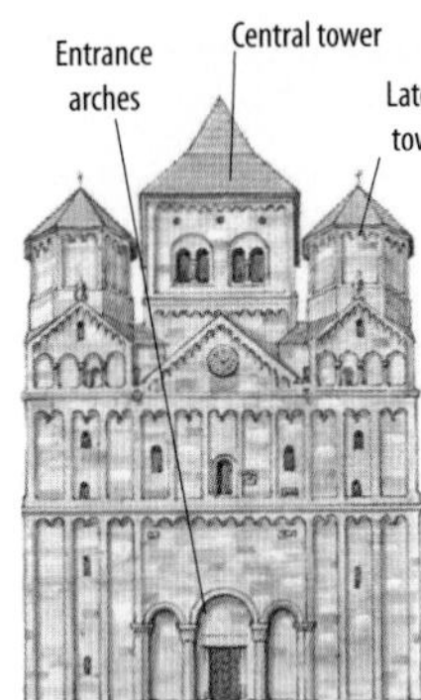

The west facade of Marmoutier Abbey with its towers, narrow windows, and small portal give it a fortified appearance.

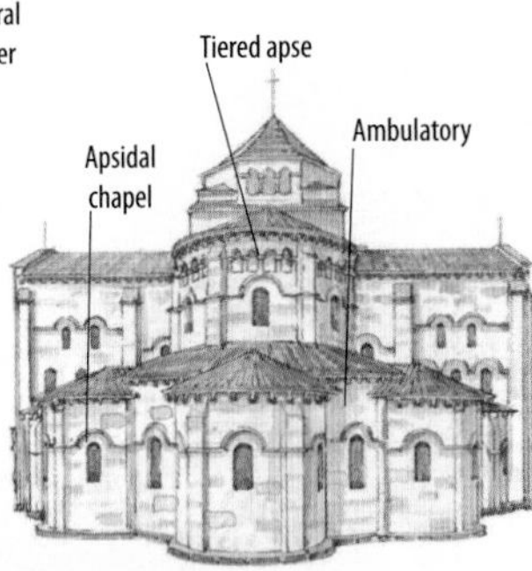

The east end of Nevers has a rounded apse surrounded by a semi-circular ambulatory and radiating chapels. The chapels were added to provide space for altars.

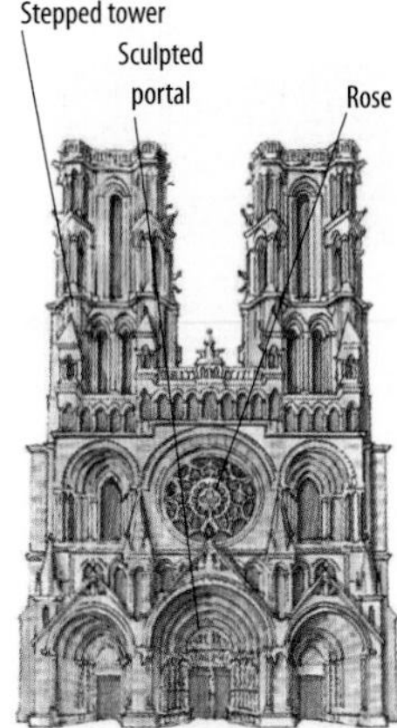

The west facade of Laon has decorative, sculpted portals and a rose window characteristic of Gothic style.

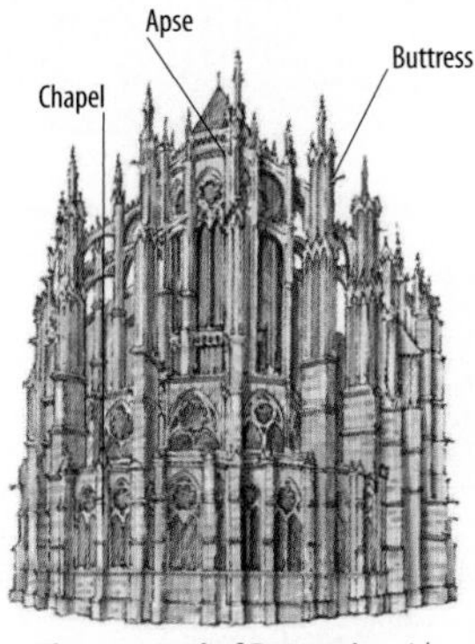

The east end of Beauvais, with its delicate buttresses topped by pinnacles, is the culmination of High Gothic.

Terms used in this Guide

Basilica: Early church with two aisles and nave lit from above by clerestory windows.

Clerestory: A row of windows illuminating the nave from above the aisle roof.

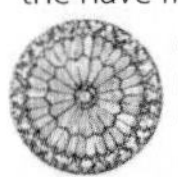

Rose: Circular window, often stained glass.

Buttress: Mass of masonry built to support a wall.

Flying buttress: An arched support transmitting thrust of the weight downwards.

Portal: Monumental entrance to a building, often decorated.

Tympanum: Decorated space, often carved, over a door or window lintel.

Vault: Arched stone ceiling.

Transept: Two wings of a cruciform church at right angles to the nave.

Crossing: Center of cruciform where transept crosses nave.

Lantern: Turret with windows to illuminate interior, often with cupola (domed ceiling).

Triforium: Middle story between arcades and clerestory.

Apse: Termination of the church, often rounded.

Ambulatory: Aisle running around east end, passing behind the sanctuary.

Arcade: Set of arches and supporting columns.

Rib vault: Vault supported by projecting ribs of stone.

Gargoyle: Carved grotesque figure, often a water spout.

Tracery: Ornamental carved stone pattern within Gothic window.

Flamboyant Gothic: Carved stone tracery resembling flames.

Capital: Top of a column, usually carved.

Rural Architecture

French farmhouses are entirely products of the soil, built of stone, clay or wood, depending on what materials are found locally. As the topography changes so does the architecture, from the steeply-sloped roofs covered in flat tiles in the north to the broad canal-tiled roofs of the south.

Despite this rich regional diversity, French farm-houses fall into three basic categories: the *maison bloc,* where house and outbuildings share the same roof; the high house, with living quarters upstairs and livestock or wine cellar below; and courtyard farmsteads, their buildings set around a central court.

Shuttered window in Alsace

The chalet is typical of the Jura, Alps, and Vosges mountains. The *maison bloc* housed both family and livestock throughout the winter. Gaps between the gable planks allowed air to circulate around crops stored in the loft, and an earth ramp behind gave wagons access. Many lofts also had a threshing floor.

Half-timbered houses are typical of Normandy, Alsace, Champagne, Picardy, the Landes, and Basque country. The filling between the timbers was wattle and daub or in some cases brick, but it is the arrangement of the smaller posts, different in each region, that best expresses the local style.

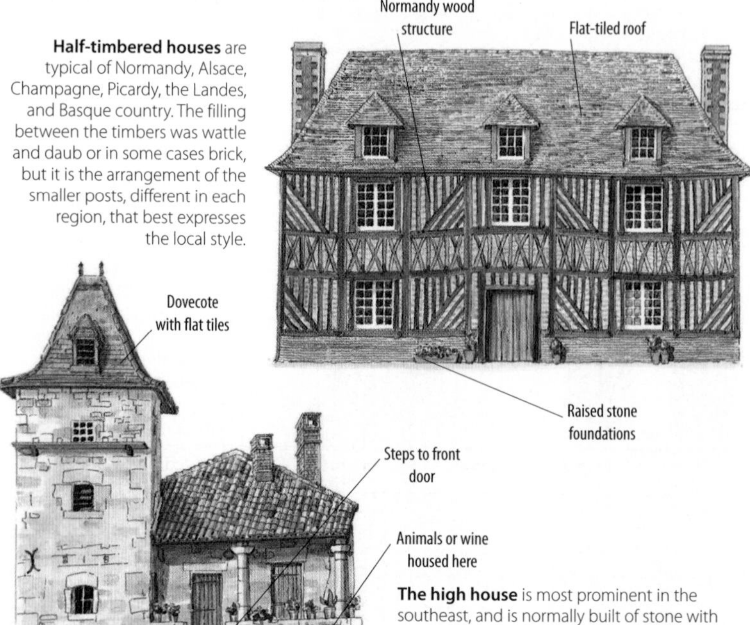

The high house is most prominent in the southeast, and is normally built of stone with an exterior stone staircase and upstairs porch. Wine growers' barrels could be stored on the ground floor without hoisting, or livestock stabled there. High houses in the Lot Valley often boast a dovecote.

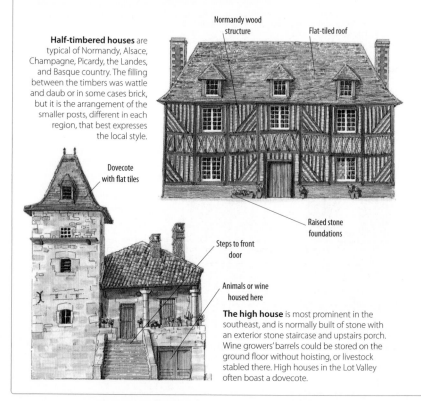

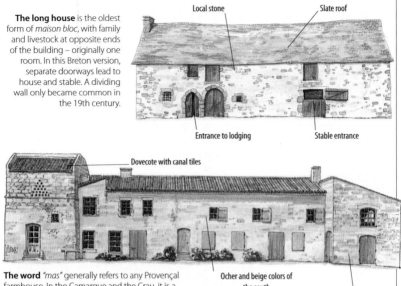

The long house is the oldest form of *maison bloc*, with family and livestock at opposite ends of the building – originally one room. In this Breton version, separate doorways lead to house and stable. A dividing wall only became common in the 19th century.

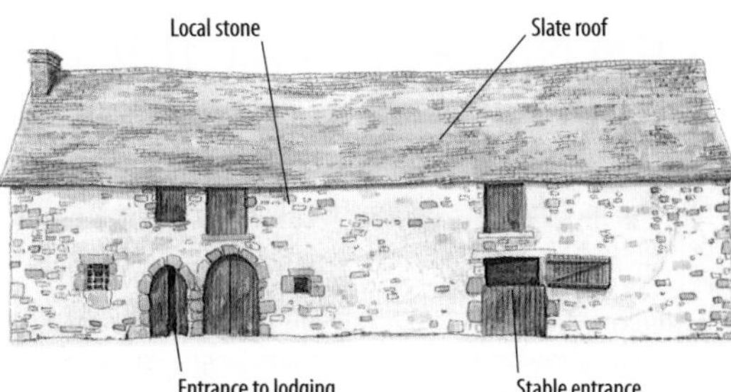

The word *"mas"* generally refers to any Provençal farmhouse. In the Camargue and the Crau, it is a farmstead for large-scale sheep farming built in an "agglomerated" style: the outbuildings, although attached to one another, are of different heights. Often, a dovecote is included.

Pebble and brick wall

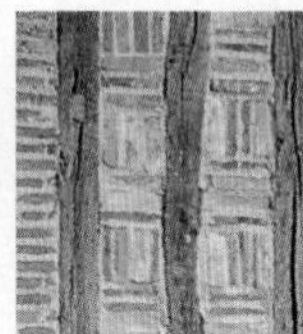
Half-timber and brick

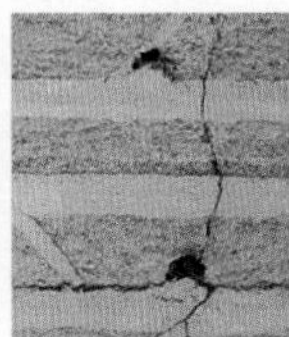
Compressed cob: *pisé*

Sun-dried adobe bricks

Pebbles in lime mortar

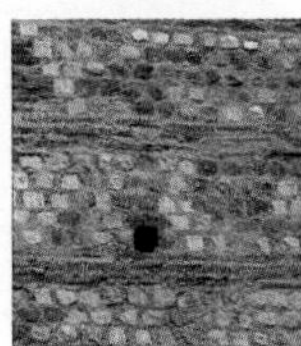
Brick, flint, and chalk

Walls

Limestone, granite, sandstone, and pebbles were all used for building walls. But if no stone was available, clay was dug for infilling half-timbered houses, as wattle and daub. The alternative was to use a cob mixture *(pisé)*, pressed into blocks in a process called *banchange*. Adobe (sun-dried brick) was also used but fired brick was fairly rare as it was expensive to bake. However, brick was sometimes used as trim or combined with chalk or pebbles in a "composite" walling. Walls were generally rendered with mortar.

Flat terracotta tiles in colors of local sand

Pantiles, used in Flanders and Picardy

Canal clay tiles typical of the south

Roofing

Two roof styles distinguish the north and south. Northern roofs are steeply pitched, so that any rainwater runs off easily. In the south, roofs are covered with canal clay tiles, and more gently sloped to prevent the tiles sliding off.

FRANCE THROUGH THE YEAR

The French, with their farming roots, are deeply aware of the changing seasons, and the mild climate means they can celebrate outdoors most of the year. History and tradition are honored with *fêtes*, such as Bastille Day (July 14). For culture lovers, thousands of arts festivals are held throughout France, ranging from the huge Avignon Theater Festival down to small village events. Large national sports events, such as the Tour de France cycle race, are a key feature in the calendar. Throughout the year, festivals take place celebrating every kind of food and wine. In high summer, the cities empty and French and foreign visitors flock to the beaches and countryside.

Spring

France's outdoor life resumes in spring, terrace-cafés filling up in the sunshine. Easter is a time of Catholic processions, and concerts of sacred music. The Cannes Film Festival in May is the best known of the season's many conventions and trade fairs.

March

International Half Marathon, Paris. Beginning and ending at Château de Vincennes *(see p142)*.

Six Nations Rugby Tournament, Stade de France, Paris.

Tinta' Mars *(two weeks)*, Langres. Cabaret and musical evenings at various venues.

Babel Med Music, Marseille (*mid-Mar*). Three-day international music festival.

Europa Jazz Festival *(mid-Mar–mid-May)*, Le Mans.

La Bravade procession honoring Saint Torpès in St-Tropez

Formula One racing at the Monaco Grand Prix

April

Festival de Pâques *(Easter week)*, Deauville. Chamber music festival.

Feria Pascale *(Easter week)*, Arles. Start of the bullfighting season *(see pp512–13)*.

Lourdes Pilgrimage *(Palm Sun to Oct, see pp462–3)*.

Banlieues Blues Jazz Festival *(early Apr)*, Saint-Denis. Jazz music.

Les Détours de Babel *(two weeks early Apr)*, Grenoble. Contemporary world music festival.

Floréal Musical d'Epinal *(early Apr–mid-May)*, Epinal. Multigenre music festival.

Bourges Spring Festival *(end Apr/early May, see p317)*. Modern music.

Joan of Arc Festival *(end Apr–early May)* Orléans. Pageant and cathedral service *(see p316)*.

Paris International Marathon, from Place de la Concorde to Avenue Foch.

May

Asparagus harvest, notably in the Loire.

International Grand Prix de Monaco *(Ascension weekend, see p534)*.

La Bravade *(May 16–18)*, St-Tropez *(see p520)*.
Cannes Film Festival *(second and third week, see p524)*.
Gypsy Pilgrimage *(late May)*, Stes-Maries-de-la-Mer *(see p514)*.
Fête de la Transhumance *(end May)*. Herds are taken up to summer pastures.
International Garden Festival *(May–mid-Oct)*, Chaumont sur Loire.
Nîmes Feria *(Pentecost)*. Bullfights and street music *(see pp500–501)*.
Grandes Eaux Musicales *(Apr–Oct: Sat–Sun; mid-May–Jun: Tue)*, Versailles. Fountain jets set to classical music in the grounds of the château.

Traditional transhumance of animals to summer pastures

Puy du Fou Pageant *(May–Sep)*. Actors, audio-guides, and horse stunts make a "living pageant" which evokes local life through the ages *(see p294)*.
Football Cup Final *(second week)*, Stade de France, Paris.
Le Printemps des Arts *(mid-May–Jun)*, Nantes area. Baroque dance and music.

Summer

The French holiday season begins in mid-July, with the return to work and school *(la rentrée)* in early September. Beaches, marinas, and camp sites are all full to bursting. Each village has its *fête* and there are festivals, sporting events, and flea markets.

June

French Tennis Open *(last week May–first week Jun)*, Stade Roland Garros, Paris.
International Sailing Week *(early Jun)*, La Rochelle.
Le Mans 24-Hour Automobile Race *(second or third weekend, see p295)*. The world's oldest endurance sports car race.
Fête de la Musique *(Jun 21)*. Music events all over France.
Fête de St-Jean *(Jun 24)*. Music, bonfires, and fireworks all over France.
Gay Pride March *(Jun 23)*. The march engulfs Paris.
Des Rives et Des Notes *(1 week late Jun)*, Oloron-Ste-Marie (near Pau). Jazz festival.
Tarasque Festival *(last weekend)*, Tarascon *(see p511)*.

July

Festival d'Art Lyrique *(Jun–Jul)*, Aix-en-Provence. International classical music festival.
Avignon Theater Festival *(all month, see p507)*.
Troménie *(Sun Jul)*, Locronan. Procession of penitents *(see p277)*.

Cyclists in the final stage of the Tour de France cycle race

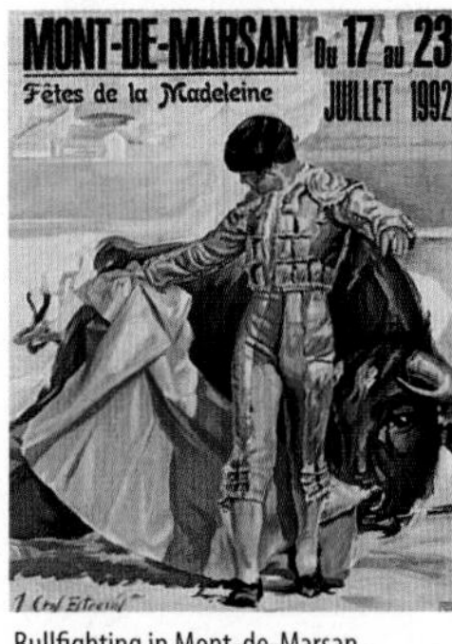

Bullfighting in Mont-de-Marsan

Tombées de la Nuit *(first week)*, Rennes. Arts festival.
Jazz Vienne *(first 2 weeks)*, Vienne *(see p386)*.
Tour de France cycle race *(first 3 weeks)*. The grand finale takes place on the Champs-Elysées, Paris.
Paris-Plage *(mid-Jul–mid-Aug)*. Paris and other cities get an annual temporary beach.
Mont-de-Marsan Feria *(third weekend)*. Bullfights and music *(see p429)*.
International Jazz Festival *(second half)*, Antibes and Juan-les-Pins *(see p525)*.
Nice Jazz Festival *(late-Jul)*.
Comminges Music Festival *(Jul–end Aug, see p466)*.
Pablo Casals Festival *(end Jul–mid-Aug)*, Prades *(see p484)*.
Francofolies *(mid-Jul)*. Music festival at La Rochelle.

Holiday-makers on a crowded beach in Cannes on the Côte d'Azur

August

Mimos *(first week)*, Périgueux. World famous international mime festival.

Fête du Jasmin *(first weekend)*, Grasse. Floats, music, dancing in town.

Foire aux Sorciers *(first Sun)*, Bué (nr Bourges). Costumed witch and wizard festival and folk groups.

Parade of Lavender Floats *(first or second weekends)*, Digne *(see p521)*.

Fête de la Véraison *(first or second weekend)*, Châteauneuf-du-Pape *(see p506)*. Medieval celebration of thanksgiving for the fruit harvest.

Interceltic Festival *(second week)*, Lorient. Celtic arts and music.

Feria – Bullfight *(mid-Aug)*, Dax *(see p429)*.

St-Jean-Pied-de-Port-Basque Fête *(mid-Aug, see p458)*. Celebration of Basque culture with music and dancing.

Fête de St-Louis *(around Aug 25)*, Sète *(see p496)*.

Les Rendezvous de l'Erdre *(last weekend)*, Nantes. Jazz and river boats.

Autumn

In wine regions, the grape harvest is the occasion for much jollity, and every wine village has its wine festival. When the new wine is ready in November there are more festivities. The hunting season begins – everywhere there is game shooting. In the southwest, migrating birds are trapped.

September

Deauville American Film Festival *(first two weeks)*.

Le Puy "Roi de l'Oiseau," *(second week)*. Renaissance-style festival *(see p369)*.

Grape harvest, wine regions throughout France.

Journées du Patrimoine, *(third weekend)*. Over 14,000 historical buildings can be visited, many not normally open.

Biennale de Lyon *(mid-Sep–Dec)*. Dance festival and art festival alternate years.

Musica *(late Sep–early Oct)*, Strasbourg. International music festival.

Ceremony for the Induction of new Chevaliers at the Hospice de Beaune

October

Dinard British Film Festival *(first week,)*.

Prix de l'Arc de Triomphe *(first Sun)*. Horse racing at Longchamp, Paris.

Jazz Pulsations *(mid-Oct)*, Nancy. International jazz fest.

Espelette Pepper Festival *(last weekend, see p457)*.

Festival de Lanvellec and Trégor *(mid-Oct)*. Baroque music festival.

Les Castagnades *(Oct–Nov)*. Chestnut festival throughout the Ardéche.

November

Dijon International Food and Wine Festival *(first 2 weeks)*. Traditional gastronomic fair.

Wine Auctions and Les Trois Glorieuses *(third weekend)*, Beaune *(see p350)*.

Truffle season *(until Mar)*, Périgord, Quercy, and Provence.

Winter

At Christmas, traditional nativity plays are held in churches, and there are fairs and markets throughout France. In the Alps and the Pyrenees, and even the Vosges and Massif Central, the ski-slopes are crowded. In Flanders and Nice, carnivals take place before Lent.

December
Critérium International de la Première Neige *(early Dec)*, Val d'Isère. First competition of the season.

January
Monte-Carlo Rally *(usually mid-Jan, see p534)*.
Limoux Carnival *(until Mar)*. Street festival held since the Middle Ages.
Fashion shows, Paris. Summer collections.

Downhill skier on the slopes in the French Alps

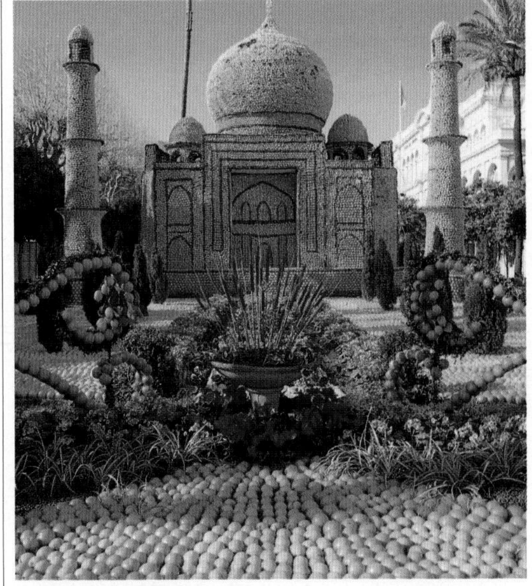
The Taj Mahal re-created at the Lemon Festival in Menton

Festival du Cirque *(end)*, Monaco. International event.
Festival de la Bande Dessinée *(last weekend)*. International strip cartoon festival, Angoulême.

February
Lemon Festival *(mid-Feb–Mar)*, Menton *(see p533)*.
Nice Carnival and the Battle of Flowers *(late Feb–early Mar, see p530)*.
Paris Carnaval, *(date varies, check)*, Quartier St-Fargeau.
Fête de Mimosa, *(third Sun)*, Bormes-les-Mimosas.

Celebrating the Nice Carnival and the Battle of Flowers

Bastille Day parade past the Arc de Triomphe

Public Holidays

New Year's Day (Jan 1)
Easter Sunday and Monday
Ascension Day (sixth Thursday after Easter)
Whit Monday (second Monday after Ascension)
Labor Day (May 1)
VE Day (May 8)
Bastille Day (Jul 14)
Assumption Day (Aug 15)
All Saints' Day (Nov 1)
Remembrance Day (Nov 11)
Christmas Day (Dec 25)

The Climate of France

Set on Europe's western edge, France has a varied, temperate climate. An Atlantic influence prevails in the northwest, with westerly sea winds bringing humidity and warm winters. The east experiences Continental temperature extremes with frosty, clear winters and often stormy summers. The south enjoys a Mediterranean climate with hot, dry summers and mild winters, punctuated by violent winds.

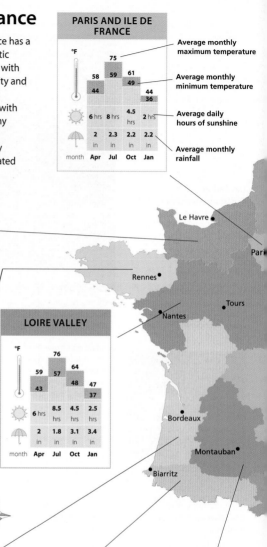

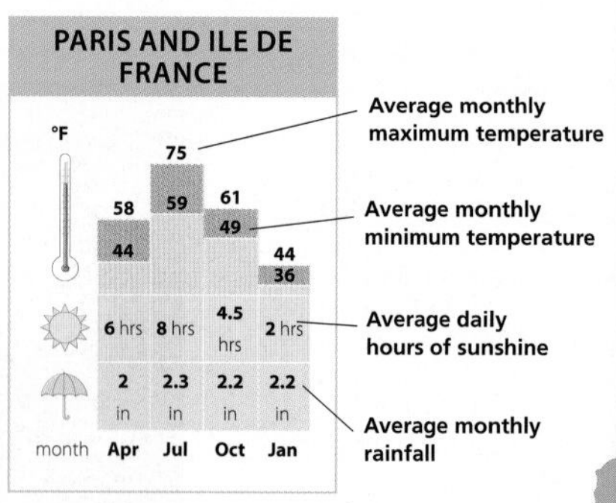

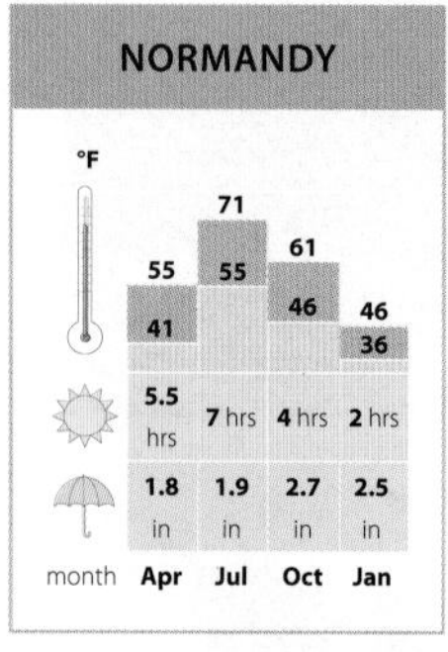

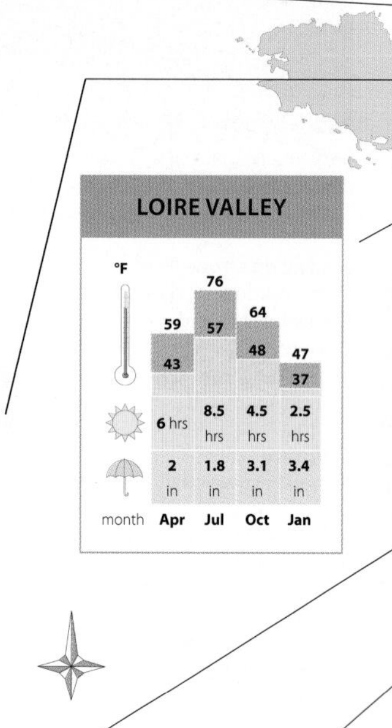

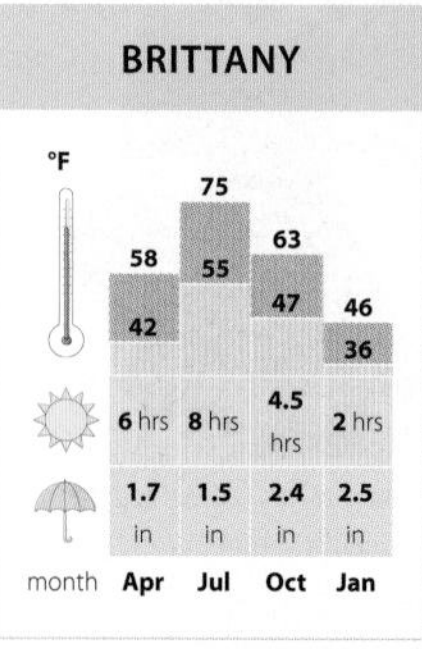

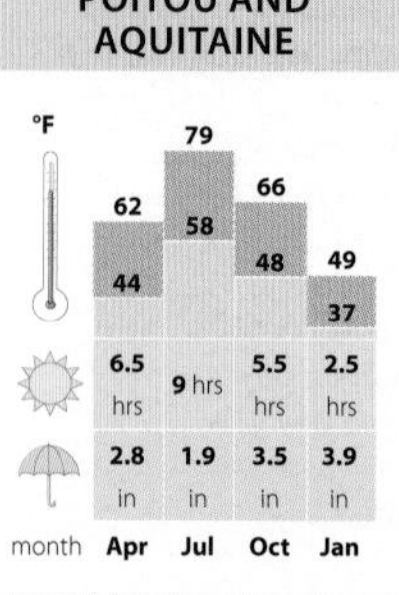

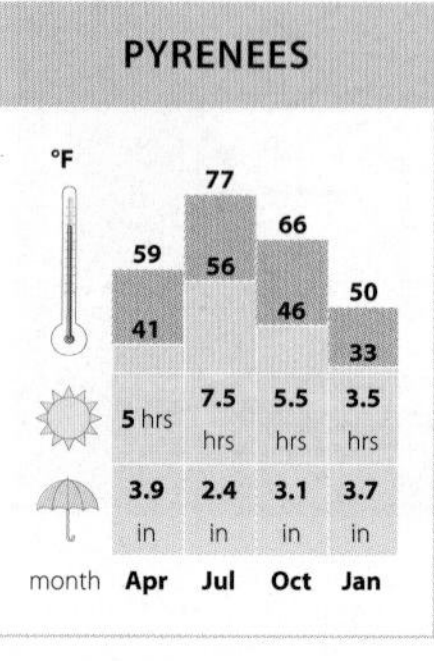

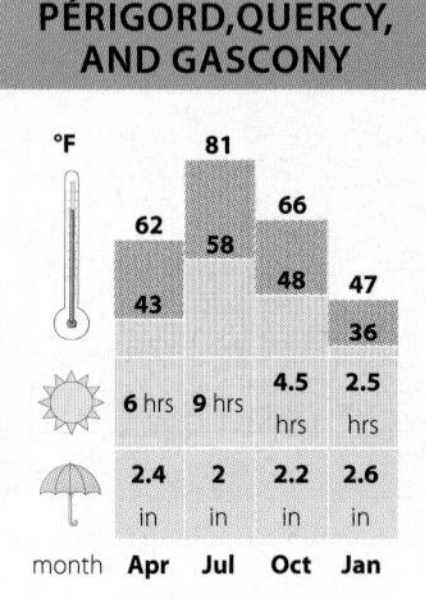

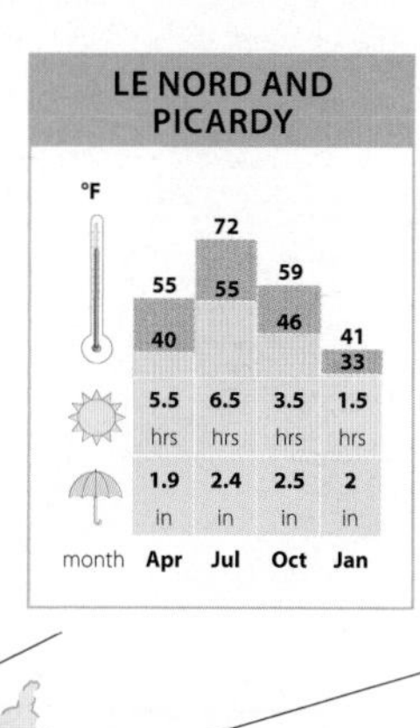

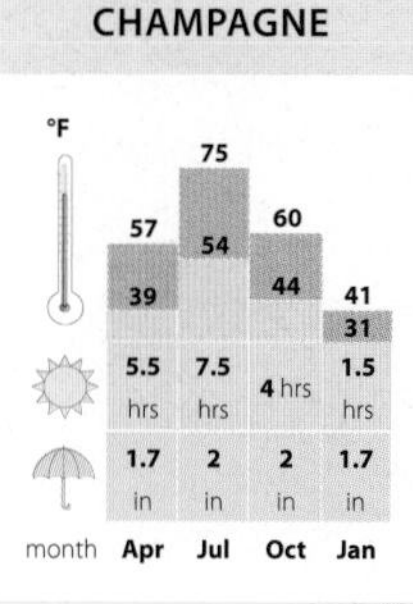

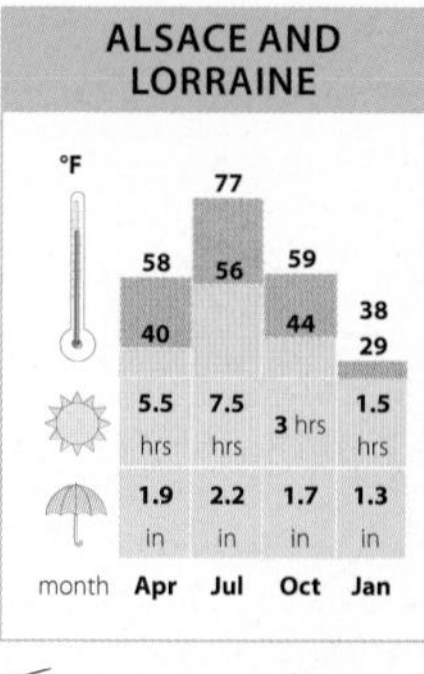

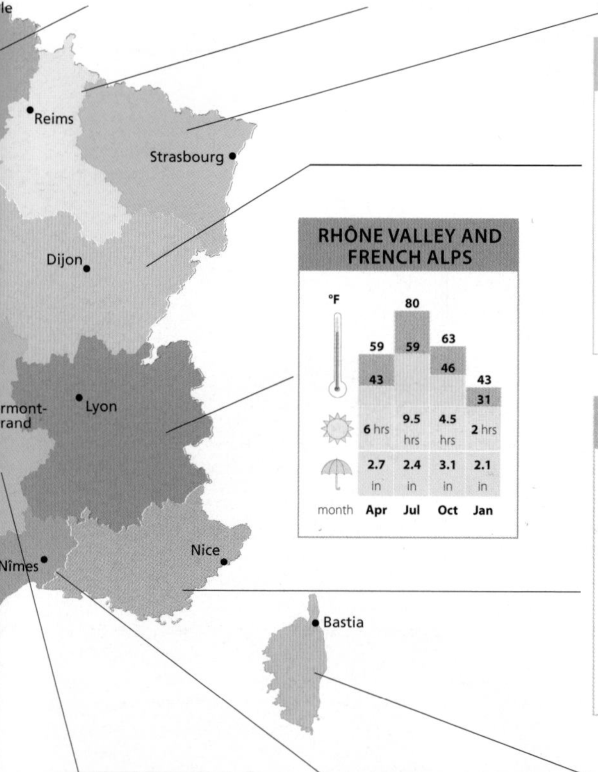

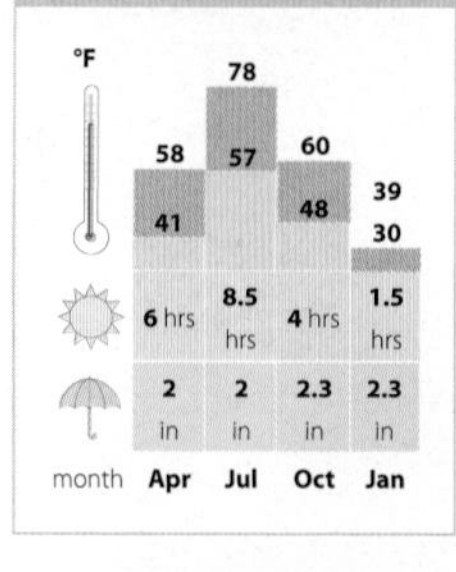

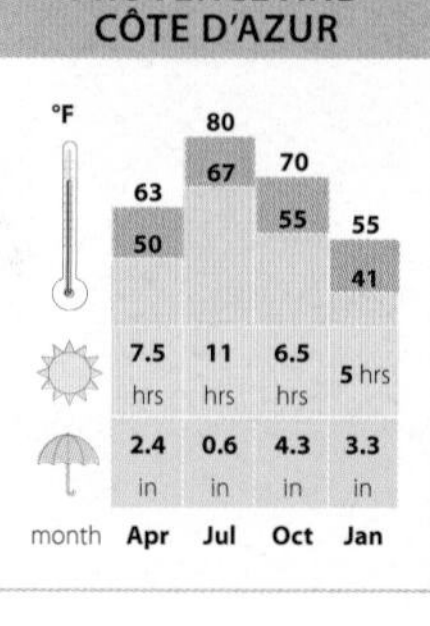

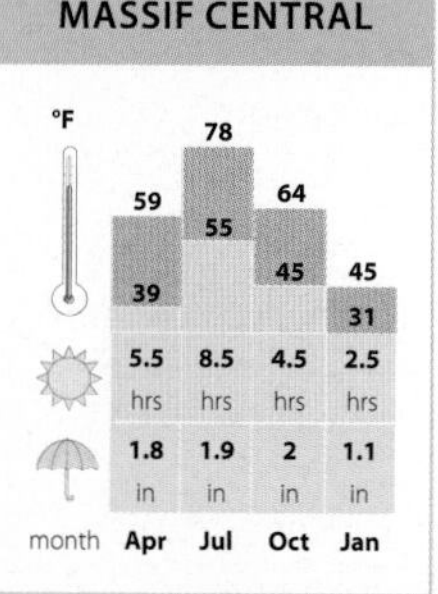

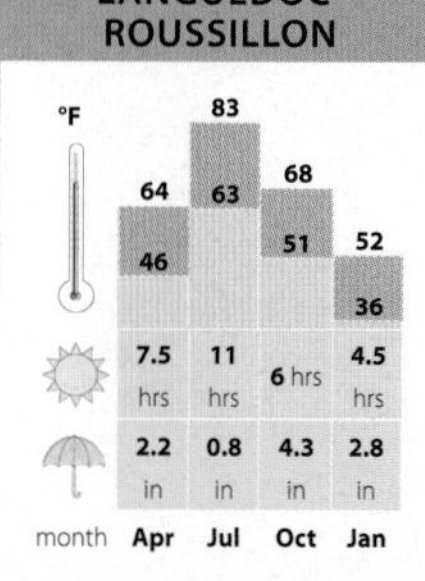

CORSICA

month	Apr	Jul	Oct	Jan
°F	64 / 47	83 / 64	71 / 55	56 / 41
sun	7 hrs	11 hrs	6.5 hrs	4.5 hrs
rain	2.6 in	0.6 in	4.2 in	2.4 in

THE HISTORY OF FRANCE

The only European country facing both the North Sea and the Mediterranean, France has been subject to a particularly rich variety of cultural influences. Though famous for the rootedness of its peasant population, it has also been a European melting pot, even before the arrival of the Celtic Gauls in the centuries before Christ, through to the Mediterranean immigrations of the 20th century. Roman conquest by Julius Caesar had an enduring impact, but from the 4th and 5th centuries AD, waves of Barbarian invaders destroyed much of the Roman legacy. The Germanic Franks provided political leadership in the following centuries, but when their line died out in the late 10th century, France was socially and politically fragmented.

The Formation of France

The Capetian dynasty gradually pieced France together over the Middle Ages, a period of great economic prosperity and cultural vitality. The Black Death and the Hundred Years' War brought setbacks, and the dynasty's power was seriously threatened by the rival Burgundian dukes. France recovered and despite the wars of religion flourished during the Renaissance, followed by the grandeur of Louis XIV's reign. During the Enlightenment, in the 18th century, French culture was the envy of Europe.

The Revolution of 1789 ended the absolute monarchy and introduced major social and institutional reforms, many of which were endorsed and consolidated by Napoleon. Yet the Revolution also inaugurated the instability that remained a hallmark of French politics until de Gaulle and the Fifth Republic: since 1789, France has known five republics, two empires, and three brands of royal power, plus the Vichy government in World War II.

Modernization in the 19th and 20th centuries proved a slow process. Railways, the military service, and radical educational reforms were crucial in forming a sense of French identity among the citizens.

Rivalry with Germany dominated French politics for most of the late 19th and early 20th century. The population losses in World War I were traumatic for France, while during 1940–44 the country was occupied by Germany. Yet since 1945, the two countries have proved the backbone of the developing European Union.

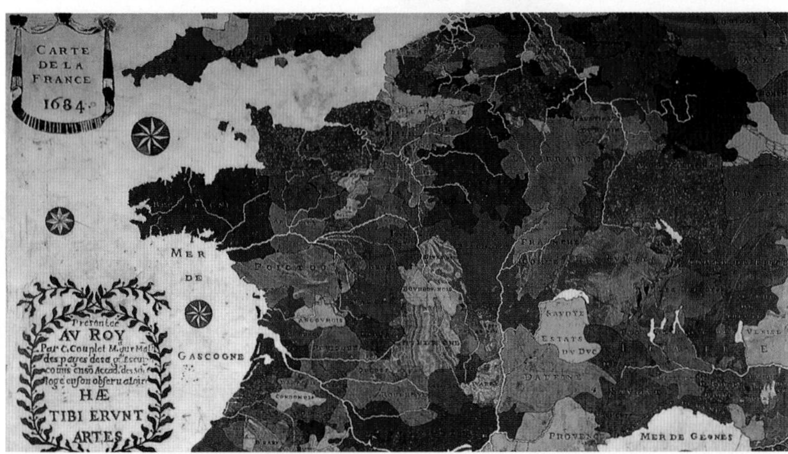

Inlaid marble table top showing the map of France in 1684

◀ *La République*, painted by Charles Landelle in 1848

Prehistoric France

The earliest traces of human life in France date back to around 2 million BC. From around 40,000 BC, *Homo sapiens* lived an itinerant existence as hunters and gatherers. Around 6000 BC, following the end of the Ice Age, a major shift in lifestyle occurred, as people settled down to herd animals and cultivate crops. The advent of metal-working allowed more effective tools and weapons to be developed. The Iron Age is associated particularly with the Celts, who arrived from the east during the first millennium BC. A more complex social hierarchy developed, consisting of warriors, farmers, artisans, and druids (Celtic priests).

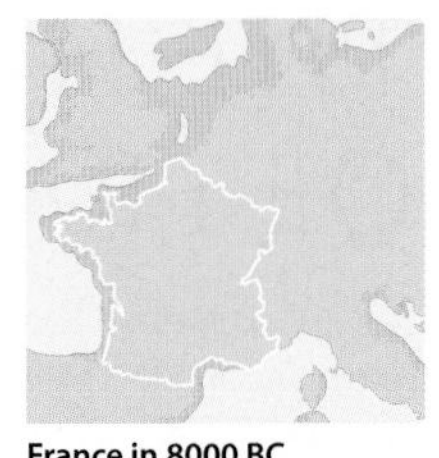

France in 8000 BC

Former coastline

Present-day land mass

Carnac Stone Alignments (4500–4000 BC)
The purpose of the extensive networks of megaliths around Carnac *(see p282–3)* remains obscure. They possibly served in pagan rituals or as an astronomical calendar.

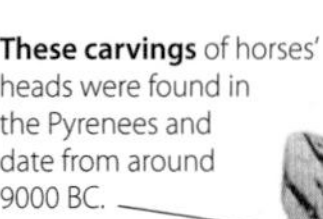

These carvings of horses' heads were found in the Pyrenees and date from around 9000 BC.

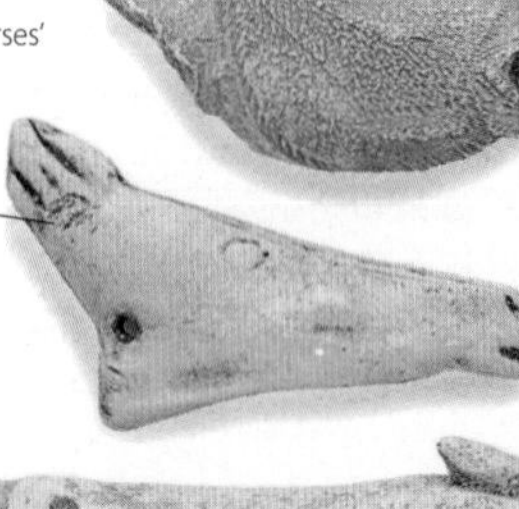

The mammoth, here carved from animal bone, was a thick-coated giant who died out after the end of the Ice Age.

Cro-Magnon Man
This skull, dating to c.25,000 BC, was discovered at Cro-Magnon in the Dordogne in 1868. In comparison with most of his predecessors, Cro-Magnon Man was tall, robust, and had a large head. He differed only marginally from us.

Prehistoric Art

The rich deposits of cave art in France have only been recognized as authentic for just over a century. They include wall paintings and daubings but also various engraved objects. Venus figurines, carved with flint tools, probably had ritual and religious rather than erotic purposes.

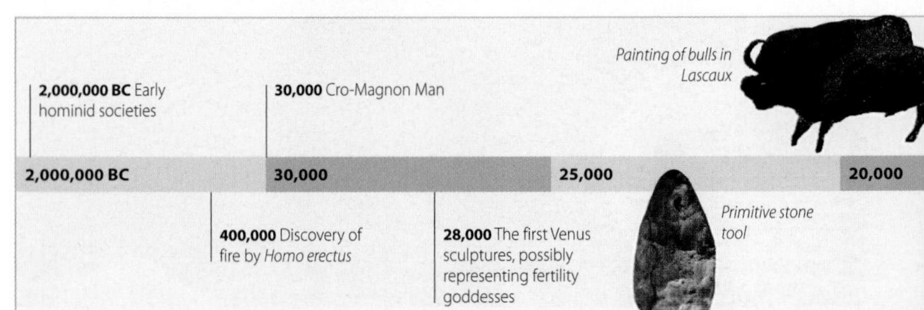

2,000,000 BC Early hominid societies

400,000 Discovery of fire by *Homo erectus*

30,000 Cro-Magnon Man

28,000 The first Venus sculptures, possibly representing fertility goddesses

Painting of bulls in Lascaux

Primitive stone tool

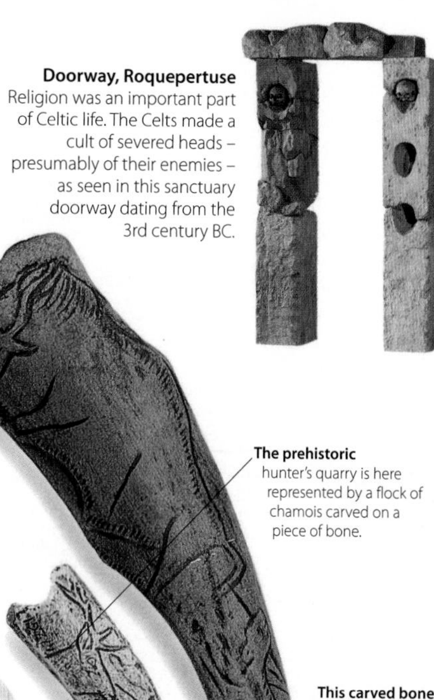

Doorway, Roquepertuse
Religion was an important part of Celtic life. The Celts made a cult of severed heads – presumably of their enemies – as seen in this sanctuary doorway dating from the 3rd century BC.

Where to see Prehistoric France

The Lascaux cave paintings in Périgord *(see p438)* are among the best in the world. More cave decoration is found around Les Eyzies *(pp438–9)*, at the Vallée des Merveilles near Tendes in the Alpes-Maritimes *(p533)*, and in the Grotte du Pech Merle in the Lot Valley *(p442)*. The intriguing menhirs at Filitosa in Corsica *(pp546–7)* are about 4,000 years old.

The Lascaux cave paintings, dating from 16,000 –14,000 BC, include images of bulls and mammoths.

The prehistoric hunter's quarry is here represented by a flock of chamois carved on a piece of bone.

This carved bone, found in Laugerie Basse in the Dordogne, shows a bison chased by a man with a spear.

Copper Axe (c.2000 BC)
Copper tools preceded the arrival of the stronger and more malleable bronze alloy. Iron was to prove the toughest and most useful metal of all.

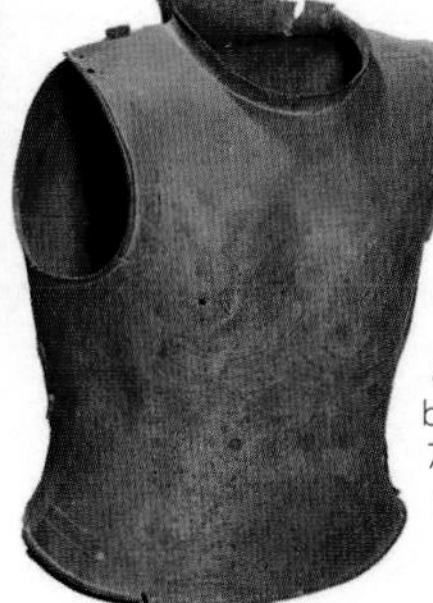

Bronze Armor
Bronze and Iron Age people were highly warlike. The Celtic Gauls were feared even by Romans. Their protective armor, such as this breastplate dating from 750–475 BC, was light but reasonably effective.

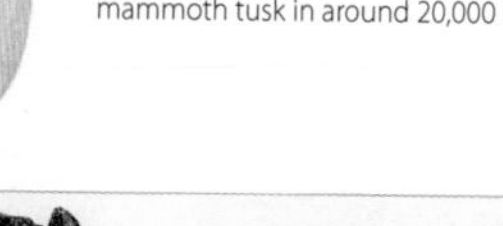

This highly stylized female figure, a Venus figurine found in southwest France, was carved from mammoth tusk in around 20,000 BC.

15,000 Hunters live on wandering herds of mammoth, rhinoceros, and reindeer. Art includes the Lascaux caves and Val Camonica/Mont Bego engravings

15,000

10,000 End of Ice Age. More regions become inhabitable

10,000–6000 Mammoth herds disappear and hunters must rely on animals of the forest, including wild boar and aurochs

10,000

7000–4500 Neolithic revolution: farming, megaliths, and menhir stone sculptures

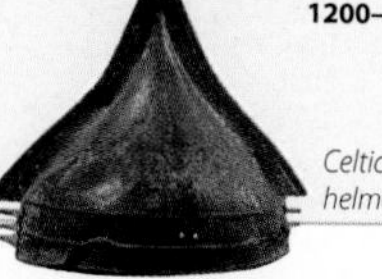

Celtic helmet

5,000

1200–700 Arrival of the Celts during the Bronze and Iron Ages

600 Greek colony at Marseille. Mediterranean luxury goods exchanged for tin, copper, iron, and slaves. Early urban development

500 Celtic nobles bury their dead with riches such as the Vix treasure *(see p338)*

Roman Gaul

The Romans had annexed the southern fringe of France by 125–121 BC. Julius Caesar brought the rest of Gaul under Roman control in the Gallic Wars (58–51 BC). The province of Gaul prospered: it developed good communications, a network of cities crammed with public buildings and leisure facilities such as baths and amphitheaters, while in the countryside large villas were established. By the 3rd century AD, however, barbarian raids from Germany were causing increasing havoc. From the 5th century barbarians began to settle throughout Gaul.

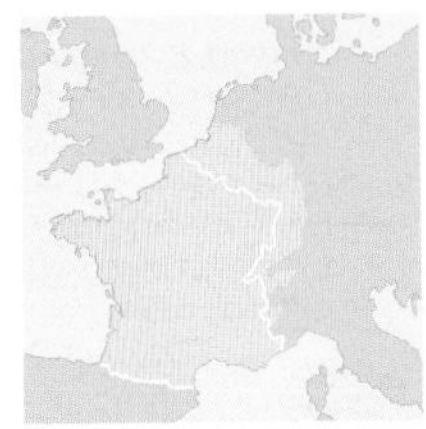

France in 58 BC

Roman Gaul

Emperor Augustus, who was considered a living God, was worshiped at this altar.

Roman Dolce Vita
The Romans brought material comfort and luxury, and wine-growing became widespread. This 19th-century painting by Couture conveys a contemporary view of Roman decadence.

Vercingetorix
The Celtic chieftain Vercingetorix was Julius Caesar's greatest military opponent. This bronze statue is at Alise-Sainte-Reine *(see p338)*, the Gauls' final stand in 51 BC.

La Turbie

This impressive monument near Monaco was erected in 6 BC by the Roman Senate. It celebrates Augustus's victory over the Alpine tribes in 14–13 BC. Badly pillaged for its stone, restoration only began in the 1920s.

Augustus

125–121 BC Roman colonization of Southern Gaul

31 BC Frontiers of the Three Gauls *(Gallia Celtica, Gallia Aquitania,* and *Gallia Belgica)* established by Augustus

200 BC | 100 | 0 | AD 100

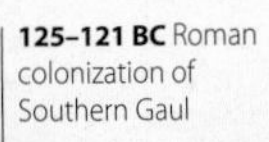

Julius Caesar

58–51 BC Julius Caesar's Gallic Wars result in establishment of Roman Gaul

52–51 BC Vercingetorix revolt

16 BC Maison Carrée built in Nîmes *(see pp500–501)*

AD 43 Lugdunum (Lyon) established as capital of the Three Gauls

Dancing Girl
Celtic art continued uninfluenced by Roman naturalistic ideals. This bronze statuette of a young woman dates from the 1st–2nd century AD.

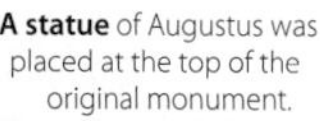

A statue of Augustus was placed at the top of the original monument.

Enameled Brooch
This decorative Gallo-Roman brooch dates from the second half of the 1st century BC.

Where to see Gallo-Roman France

Gallo-Roman remains are to be found all over France, many of them in Provence. In addition to La Turbie *(see p533)*, there is the Roman amphitheater in Arles *(p512–13)*, and the theater and triumphal arch in Orange *(p506)*. Elsewhere, there are ruins at Autun in Burgundy *(p343)*, the Temple d'Auguste et Livie in Vienne *(p386)*, Les Arènes in Nîmes *(pp500–501)*, and fragments of Vesunna in Périgueux *(p435)*.

Les Arènes in Nîmes, built at the end of the 1st century AD, is still in use today.

The Claudian Tables
In AD 48, Emperor Claudius persuaded the Senate to allow Gauls full Roman citizenship. The grateful Gauls recorded the event on stone tables found at Lyon.

The 44 tribes subjugated by Augustus are listed on an inscription, with a dedication to the emperor.

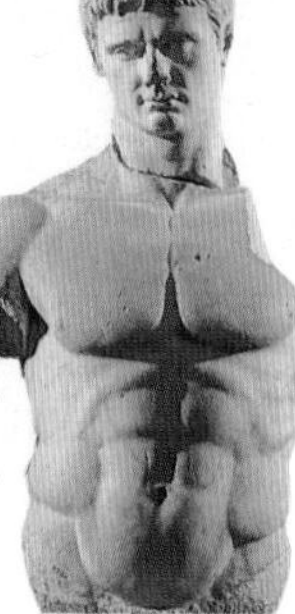

Emperor Augustus
Augustus, the first Roman Emperor (27 BC–AD 14), upheld the Pax Romana, an enforced peace which allowed the Gauls to concentrate on culture rather than war.

AD 177 First execution of Christian martyrs, Lyon. Sainte Blandine is thrown to the lions, who refuse to harm her

Sainte Blandine

360 Julian, prefect of Gaul, proclaimed Roman Emperor. Lutetia changes name to Paris

200 | 300 | 400

275 First Barbarian raids

313 Christianity officially recognized as religion under the rule of Constantine, the first Christian emperor

406 Barbarian invasion from the east. Settlement of the Franks and Germanic tribes

476 Overthrow of the last Roman emperor leads to end of the western Roman Empire

The Monastic Realm

The collapse of the Roman Empire led to a period of instability and invasions. Both the Frankish Merovingian dynasty (486–751) and the Carolingians (751–987) were unable to bring more than spasmodic periods of political calm. Throughout this turbulent period, the Church provided an element of continuity. As centers for Christian scholars and artists, the monasteries helped to restore the values of the ancient world. They also developed farming and viticulture and some became extremely powerful, dominating the country economically as well as spiritually.

France in 751

Carolingian Empire

Stable with lay brethren's quarters above

Charlemagne (742–814)
The greatest of Carolingian rulers, Charlemagne created an empire based on strictly autocratic rule. Powerful and charismatic, he could neither read nor write.

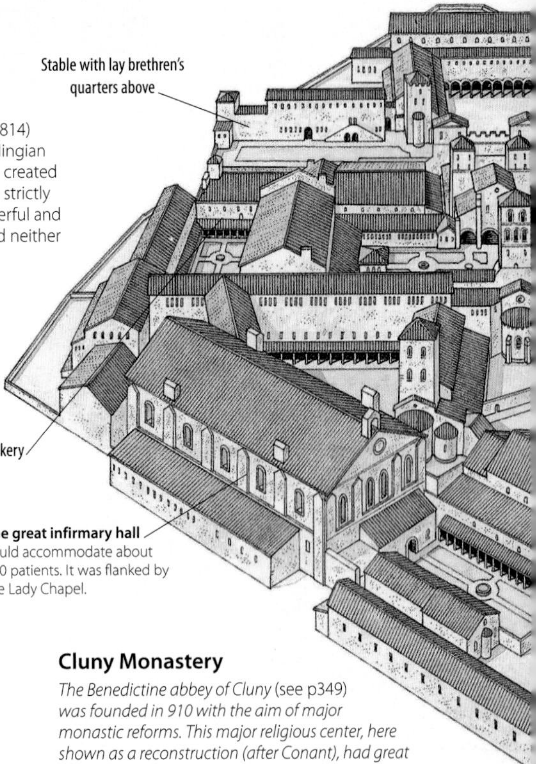

Bakery

The great infirmary hall could accommodate about 100 patients. It was flanked by the Lady Chapel.

Saint Benedict
Saint Benedict established the Benedictine rule: monks were to divide their time between work and prayer.

Cluny Monastery

The Benedictine abbey of Cluny (see p349) *was founded in 910 with the aim of major monastic reforms. This major religious center, here shown as a reconstruction (after Conant), had great influence over hundreds of monasteries throughout Europe.*

481 Clovis the Frank becomes first Merovingian king

496 Conversion of Clovis, king of the Franks, to Christianity

500

508 Paris made capital of the Frankish kingdom

c.590 Saint Colombanus introduces Irish monasticism to France

600

629–37 Dagobert I, the last effective ruler of the Merovingian dynasty, brings temporary unity to the Frankish kingdom

Dagobert I

700

732 Battle of Poitiers: Charles Martel repulses Arab invasion

751 Pepin becomes first king of the Carolingian dynasty

Baptism of Clovis
The Frankish chieftain Clovis was the first barbarian ruler to convert to Christianity. He was baptized in Reims in 496.

Where to see Monastic France

Cluny capitals

The monastic realm has survived in austere Cistercian abbeys in Burgundy, such as Fontenay *(see pp336–7)*. Little remains of Cluny, but some of the superb capitals can still be admired *(p349)*. The best way to experience monastic France might be to retrace the steps of medieval pilgrims and visit the monastic centers on the route to Santiago de Compostela *(pp404–5)*, such as Vézelay *(pp340–41)*, Le Puy *(pp368–9)*, Conques *(pp372–3)*, Moissac *(pp446–7)*, and St-Sernin in Toulouse *(pp450–51)*.

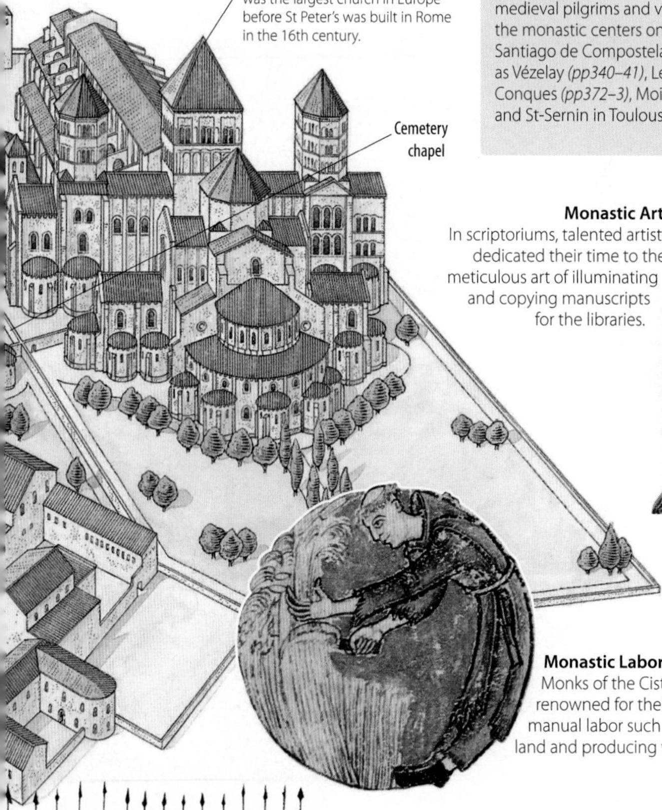

The abbey church, begun in 1088, was the largest church in Europe before St Peter's was built in Rome in the 16th century.

Cemetery chapel

Monastic Arts
In scriptoriums, talented artists dedicated their time to the meticulous art of illuminating and copying manuscripts for the libraries.

Monastic Labor
Monks of the Cistercian rule were renowned for their commitment to manual labor such as cultivating the land and producing wine and liqueurs.

Carolingian soldiers

987 Hugh Capet, first Capetian ruler

1066 Conquest of England by the Normans

1096 First Crusade

800 | 900 | 1000

800 Coronation of Charlemagne as Holy Roman Emperor

843 Treaty of Verdun: division of the Carolingian Empire into three parts including West Francia

910 Foundation of the Benedictine monastery of Cluny

1077 Bayeux tapestry

William the Conqueror steering his ship on the Bayeux tapestry

Gothic France

The Gothic style, epitomized by soaring cathedrals *(see pp36–7)*, emerged in the 12th century at a time of growing prosperity and scholarship, crusades, and an increasingly dominant monarchy. The rival French and Burgundian courts *(see p347)* became models of fashion and etiquette for all of Europe. *Chansons de gestes* (epic poems) performed by troubadours celebrated the code of chivalry.

France in 1270

Royal territory

Other fiefs

Ciborium of Alpais
Alpais, a renowned 12th-century goldsmith in Limoges, made this superb ciborium used to hold wafers for the Holy Communion.

Courtly Love
According to the code of chivalry, knights dedicated their service to an ideal but unapproachable lady. Courtesy and romance were introduced in art and music.

Winch to lift up stone sections

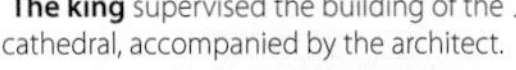

The king supervised the building of the cathedral, accompanied by the architect.

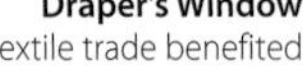

Draper's Window
The textile trade benefited from the era of urban prosperity. This stained-glass window in a church in Semur-en-Auxois *(see p339)* shows wool washers at work.

c.1100 First edition of the epic poem *Chanson de Roland*

1115 Saint Bernard founds the Cistercian abbey at Clairvaux

1117 Secret marriage of the scholar Abelard and his student Héloise. Her uncle, canon Filibert, does not approve and forces him to become a monk while she retires as a nun

1120 Rebuilding of the abbey of St-Denis; birth of the Gothic style

1154 Angevin Empire created by Anglo-Norman dynasty starting with Henry Plantagenet, count of Anjou and king of England (as Henry II)

1180–1223 Reign of Philip Augustus

1100 | 1125 | 1150 | 1175

King Philip Augustus, who adopted the fleur-de-lis emblem

The Crusades
In an attempt to win back the Holy Land from the Turks, Philip Augustus set out on the Third Crusade (1189) alongside England's Richard the Lion-Heart and Holy Roman Emperor Frederick Barbarossa.

Eleanor of Aquitaine

Strong-willed and vivacious Eleanor, duchess of independent Aquitaine, contributed to the conflict between France and England. In 1137 she married the pious Louis VII of France. Returning from a Crusade, Louis found that their marriage had broken down. After the annulment in 1152, Eleanor married Henry of Anjou, taking her duchy with her. Two years later Henry successfully claimed the throne of England. Aquitaine came under English rule and thus the Angevin Empire began.

Eleanor of Aquitaine and Henry II are buried in Fontevraud *(p298)*.

Lacelike sculpture adorned the facades of the Gothic cathedrals.

Stone masons cut stones on site.

St Bernard (1090–1153) Key figure of the Cistercian rule and counsellor to the pope, St Bernard preached rigorous simplicity of life.

Holy Relic
Throughout the Middle Ages most churches could boast at least one saint's relic. The cult of relics brought pilgrims and more riches.

The Building of a Cathedral

In affluent, mercantile towns, skilled masons constructed towering Gothic cathedrals of revolutionary design, such as Chartres (see pp312–15) *and Amiens* (pp206–7). *With their improbable height and lightness they were a testimony to both faith and prosperity.*

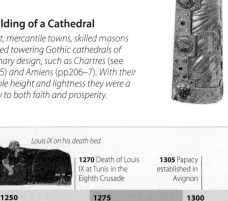

Louis IX on his death bed

1200 | **1225** | **1250** | **1275** | **1300**

1214 Battle of Bouvines. Philip Augustus begins to drive the English out of France

1226 Louis IX crowned king

1259 Normandy, Maine, Anjou, and Poitou acquired from England

1270 Death of Louis IX at Tunis in the Eighth Crusade

1285 Philip the Fair crowned

1297 Louis IX is canonized, becoming Saint Louis

1305 Papacy established in Avignon

The Hundred Years' War

The Hundred Years' War (1337–1453), pitting England against France for control of French land, had devastating effects. The damage of warfare was amplified by frequent famines and the ravages of bubonic plague in the wake of the Black Death in 1348. France came close to being permanently partitioned by the king of England and the duke of Burgundy. In 1429–30 the young Joan of Arc helped rally France's fortunes and within a generation the English had been driven out of France.

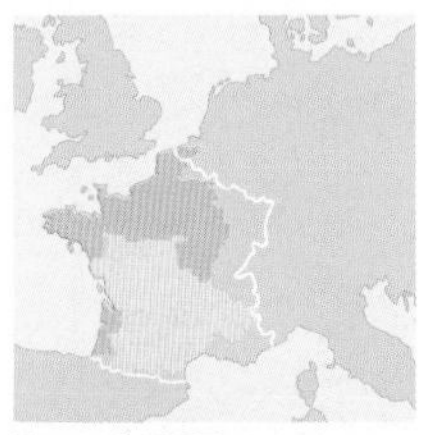

France in 1429

France

Anglo-Burgundy

Men of War
One of the reasons men enlisted as soldiers was hope for plunder. Both the French and English armies lived off the land, at the expense of the peasantry.

Angels with trumpets announce the Last Judgment.

The elect, springing resurrected from their graves, are ushered into heaven.

The Black Death
The plague of 1348–52 caused 4–5 million deaths, about 25 percent of the French population. For want of medicines people had to put their faith in prayers and holy processions.

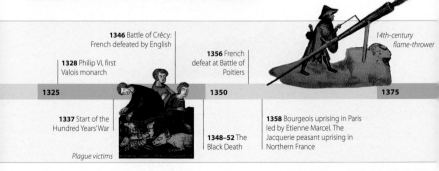

1328 Philip VI, first Valois monarch

1337 Start of the Hundred Years' War

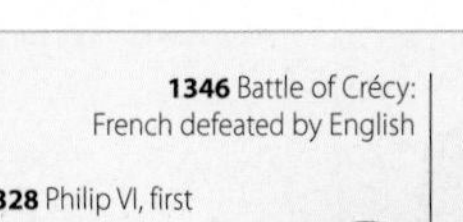

Plague victims

1346 Battle of Crécy: French defeated by English

1348–52 The Black Death

1356 French defeat at Battle of Poitiers

1358 Bourgeois uprising in Paris led by Etienne Marcel. The Jacquerie peasant uprising in Northern France

14th-century flame-thrower

1325 | 1350 | 1375

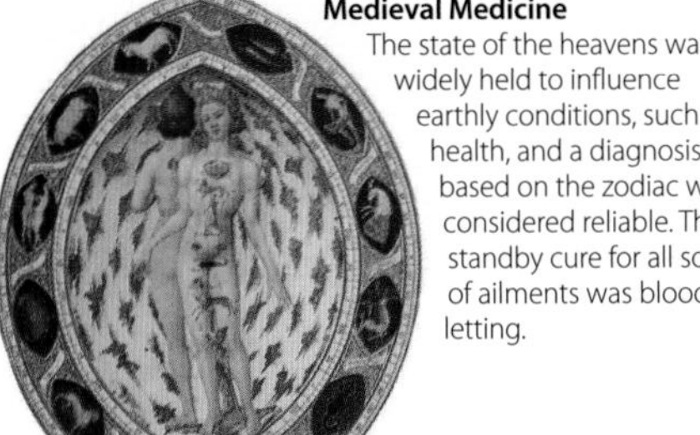

Medieval Medicine
The state of the heavens was widely held to influence earthly conditions, such as health, and a diagnosis based on the zodiac was considered reliable. The standby cure for all sorts of ailments was blood letting.

English Longbow
The king's troops fought against England, but the individual French duchies supported whichever side seemed more favorable. In the confused battles, English bowmen excelled. Their longbows caused chaos among the hordes of mounted French cavalry.

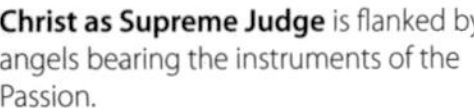

Christ as Supreme Judge is flanked by angels bearing the instruments of the Passion.

Archangel Michael, resplendent with peacock wings, holds the judgment scales. The weight of sinners outbalances the elect.

John the Baptist is accompanied by the 12 apostles and the Virgin Mary, dressed in blue.

The damned, with hideously twisted faces, fall into Hell.

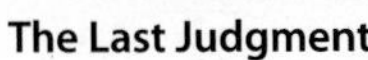

The Last Judgment

With war, plague, and famine as constant visitors, many people feared that the end of the world was nigh. Religious paintings, such as the great 15th-century altar screen by Rogier van der Weyden in the Hôtel-Dieu in Beaune (see pp350–51), *reflected the moral fervor of the time.*

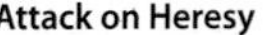

Attack on Heresy
The general anxiety spilled over into anti-Semitic pogroms and attacks on alleged heretics, who were burned at the stake.

1400 | 1425 | 1450

1411 *Les Très Riches Heures du Duc du Berry* prayer book, by Paul and Jean de Limbourg *(see p208)*

1415 Battle of Agincourt. French defeat by Henry V of England

1419 Charles VI of France makes Henry V of England his heir

1429 Intervention of Joan of Arc: Charles VII crowned king

1431 Joan of Arc burned at stake as witch by the English

1453 End of the Hundred Years' War. Only Calais remains in English hands

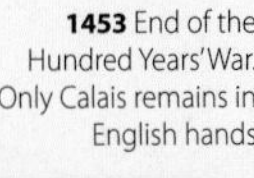

Joan of Arc

Renaissance France

As a result of the French invasion of Italy in 1494, the ideals and aesthetic of the Italian Renaissance spread to France, reaching their height during the reign of François I. Known as a true Renaissance prince, he was skilled in letters and art as well as sports and war. He invited Italian artists, such as Leonardo and Cellini, to his court and enjoyed Rabelais' bawdy stories. Another highly influential Italian was Catherine de' Medici (1519–89). Widow of Henri II, she virtually ruled France through her sons, François II, Charles IX, and Henri III. She was also one of the major players in the Wars of Religion (1562–93) between Catholics and Protestants, which divided the nobility and tore the country to pieces.

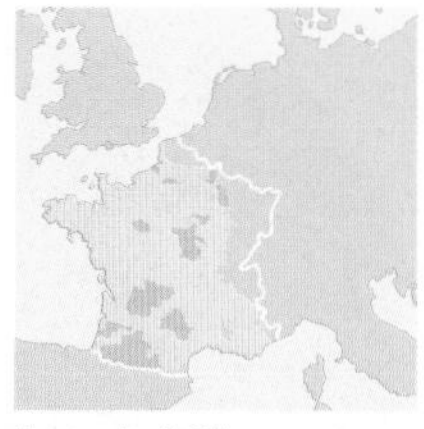

France in 1527

Royal territory

Other fiefs

Galerie François I, Fontainebleau
The artists of the School of Fontainebleau blended late Italian Renaissance style with French elements.

Power Behind the Throne
Catherine de' Medici dominated French politics from 1559–89.

The corner towers are a Gothic feature transformed by Italian lightness of touch into pure decoration.

Azay-le-Rideau

One of the loveliest of the Loire châteaux, Azay was begun in 1518 (see p300). *Italian influences are visible and it is clear that this is a dwelling meant for pleasure rather than defence.*

1470 First printing presses established in France

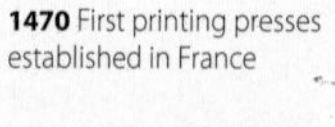

Prototype tank by Leonardo da Vinci

1519 Leonardo da Vinci dies in the arms of François I at the French court in Amboise

1536 Calvin's *Institutes of the Christian Religion* leads to a new form of Protestantism

1470	1480	1490	1500	1510	1520	1530

1477 Final defeat of the dukes of Burgundy, who sought to establish a middle kingdom between France and Germany

1494–1559 France and Austria fight over Italian territories in the Italian Wars

1515 Reign of François I begins

Golden coin showing the fleur-de-lis an the salamand of François I

Gold Pomander
Pomanders containing sweet-smelling herbs such as amber and cinnamon were carried in time of plague to ward off the bad air held responsible for contagion.

Ballroom with Flemish tapestries
The staircase was in the new Italian fashion with double flights of steps rather than a spiral.
The Red Room

Where to see Renaissance France

In Paris, many churches and the impressive place des Vosges *(see p95)* date from the Renaissance. There are countless 16th-century châteaus in the Loire and Burgundy. Among the finest are Chenonceau *(pp302–3)* and Tanlay *(p335)*.
Salers *(p367)* is a virtually intact Renaissance town. The historic center of Toulouse *(pp450–51)* has many elegant Renaissance palaces.

This fireplace stands in François I's room at Château de Chenonceau.

François I and the Italian Influence
François I, here receiving Raphael's painting *The Holy Family* in 1518, collected Italian art at Fontainebleau. Among the favored painters were Michelangelo, Leonardo, and Titian.

New France
French expansion and quest for colonies started with Cartier's expedition to Canada in 1534 *(see p286)*.

1559 Treaty of Cateau–Cambrésis ends the Italian Wars

1572 Massacre of Protestants on St Bartholomew's Eve in Paris

1589 Henry III murdered. The Huguenot Henry IV becomes first Bourbon king of France

1598 Edict of Nantes: tolerance for Protestantism

1608 Foundation of Quebec

1540 | 1550 | 1560 | 1570 | 1580 | 1590 | 1600

539 Edict of Villers Cotterets nakes French the official anguage of state

1562 Wars of Religion between Catholics and Protestants start

St Bartholomew's Day Massacre

1593 Henry IV converts to Catholicism and ends the Wars of Religion

The Grand Siècle

The end of the Religious Wars heralded a period of exceptional French influence and power. The cardinal ministers Richelieu and Mazarin paved the way for Louis XIV's absolute monarchy. Political development was matched by artistic styles of unprecedented brilliance: enormous Baroque edifices, the drama of Molière and Racine, and the music of Lully. Versailles *(see pp178–81)*, built under the supervision of Louis' capable finance minister Colbert, was the glory of Europe, but its cost and Louis XIV's endless wars proved expensive for the French state and led to widespread misery by the end of his reign.

France in 1661

Royal territory

Avignon (papal enclave)

Molière (1622–73)
Actor-playwright Molière performed many plays for Louis XIV and his court, though some of his satires were banned. After his death, his company became the basis of the French state theater, the Comédie Française.

The Sun King and his Family

Claiming to be monarch by divine right, Louis XIV commanded court painter Jean Nocret to devise this allegorical scene in 1665. Surrounded by his family, the king appears as the sun god Apollo.

Madame de Maintenon
In 1684, following the death of his first wife Marie-Thérèse, Louis secretly married his mistress Mme de Maintenon, then aged 49.

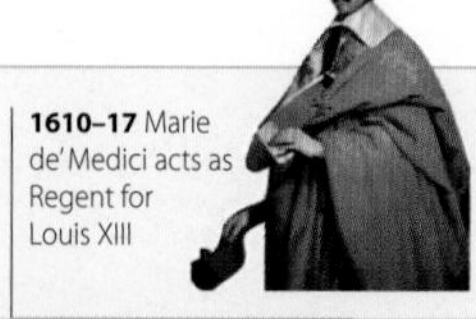

Cardinal Richelieu

- **1610–17** Marie de' Medici acts as Regent for Louis XIII
- **1617** Louis XIII accedes at the age of 17
- **1624** Cardinal Richelieu becomes principal minister
- **1631** Foundation of *La Gazette*, France's first newspaper
- **1634** Foundation of the literary society Académie Française
- **1635** Richelieu actively involves France in the Thirty Years' War
- **1637** Descartes' *Discourse on Method*
- **1642–3** Death of Louis XIII and Cardinal Richelieu. Accession of Louis XIV with Mazarin as principal minister
- **1648–52** The Fronde: French civil wars

1610 | 1620 | 1630 | 1640 | 1650

Louis XIV's Book of Hours
After a lively and libertine youth, Louis became increasingly religious. His *Book of Hours* (1688–93) is in Musée Condé *(see p209)*.

Royal Wedding
Louis XIII and Anne of Austria were married in 1615. After his death, Anne became regent for the young Louis XIV with Cardinal Mazarin as minister.

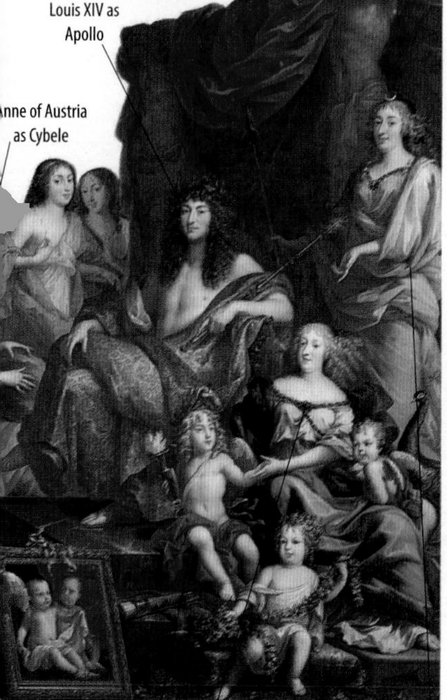

Baroque Figurine
The royal glory was reflected in the arts. This *objet d'art* features a Christ in jasper on a pedestal decorated with gilded cherubs and rich enameling.

Where to see architecture of the Grand Siècle

Paris boasts many imposing Grand Siècle buildings, such as the Hôtel des Invalides *(see p118)*, the Dôme church *(p119)*, and the Palais du Luxembourg *(pp130–31)*, but the Château de Versailles *(pp178–81)* is the ultimate example of the flamboyance of the period. Reminders of this glory include the sumptuous Palais Lascaris in Nice *(p530)* and the Corderie Royale in Rochefort *(p421)*. At the same time, military architect Vauban constructed mighty citadels, such as Neuf-Brisach *(see pp230–31)*.

Versailles' interior is a typical example of the gilded Baroque style.

Playwright Jean Racine (1639–99)

1661 Death of Mazarin: Louis XIV becomes his own principal minister

1662 Colbert, finance minister, reforms finances and the economy

1680 Creation of the theatre Comédie Française

1682 Royal court moves to Versailles

1685 Revocation of the Edict of Nantes of 1598: Protestantism banned

1686 Opening of the Café Procope (first coffee house in Paris)

1689 Major wars of Louis XIV begin

1709 Last great famine in French history

1660 | 1670 | 1680 | 1690 | 1700

17th-century cannon

Enlightenment and Revolution

In the 18th century, Enlightenment philosophers such as Voltaire and Rousseau redefined man's place within a framework of natural principles, thus challenging the old aristocratic order. Their essays were read across Europe and even in the American colonies. But although France exported worldly items as well as ideas, the state's increasing debts brought social turmoil, triggering the 1789 Revolution. Under the motto "Liberty, Equality, Fraternity," the new Republic and its reforms had a far-reaching impact on the rest of Europe.

France in 1789

Royal France

Avignon (papal enclave)

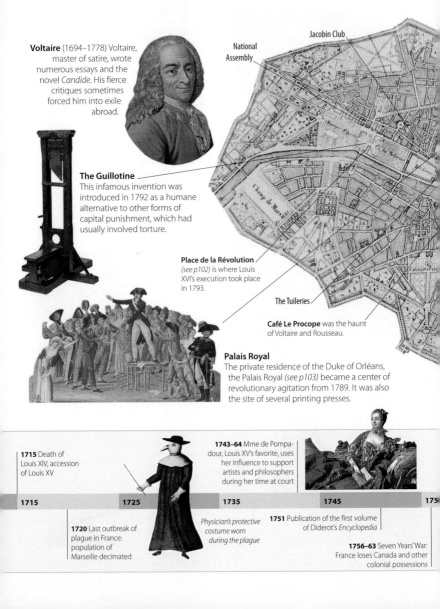

Voltaire (1694–1778) Voltaire, master of satire, wrote numerous essays and the novel *Candide*. His fierce critiques sometimes forced him into exile abroad.

Jacobin Club

National Assembly

The Guillotine
This infamous invention was introduced in 1792 as a humane alternative to other forms of capital punishment, which had usually involved torture.

Place de la Révolution *(see p102)* is where Louis XVI's execution took place in 1793.

The Tuileries

Café Le Procope was the haunt of Voltaire and Rousseau.

Palais Royal
The private residence of the Duke of Orléans, the Palais Royal *(see p103)* became a center of revolutionary agitation from 1789. It was also the site of several printing presses.

1715 Death of Louis XIV, accession of Louis XV

1720 Last outbreak of plague in France: population of Marseille decimated

Physician's protective costume worn during the plague

1743–64 Mme de Pompadour, Louis XV's favorite, uses her influence to support artists and philosophers during her time at court

1751 Publication of the first volume of Diderot's *Encyclopedia*

1756–63 Seven Years' War: France loses Canada and other colonial possessions

1715 | 1725 | 1735 | 1745 | 175

Revolutionary Symbols
The motifs of the Revolution such as the blue, white, and red of the tricolor even appeared on wallpaper in the 1790s.

Queen Marie-Antoinette
Marie-Antoinette's frivolous behavior helped discredit the monarchy. She was held in the Conciergerie and brought to the guillotine in 1793.

The Marais, earlier an aristocratic area, fell into decay as a result of the Revolution.

Bastille

Revolutionary Paris

From 1789, Paris housed numerous political clubs, such as the left-wing Jacobins, and many revolutionary newspapers. The war tune La Marseillaise, *introduced by volunteers from the south, was soon heard everywhere.*

Where to see 18th-Century France

The Palais de l'Elysée, built in 1718 *(see p112)*, is an outstanding example of 18th-century Parisian architecture. Examples across France include the curious Saline Royale in Arc-et-Senans *(p354)*, the Grand Théâtre in Bordeaux *(p426)*, the elegant mansions in Condom *(p444)*, and the merchants' houses in Ciboure *(p457)*. The Château de Laàs in Sauveterre de Béarn is a feast of 18th-century art and furniture *(p458)*.

The Grand Théâtre in Bordeaux is an excellent example of elegant 18th-century architecture.

Revolutionary Calendar
A new calendar was introduced, the months named after seasonal events. This engraving shows Messidor, the month of harvest.

1765 | 1775 | 1785 | 1795

1762 Rousseau's *Emile* and the *Social Contract*

1768 Annexation of Corsica

1774 Accession of Louis XVI

1778–83 France aids the 13 colonies in the War of American Independence

1783 First balloon ascent, by the Montgolfier brothers

1789 Storming of the Bastille, and establishment of constitutional monarchy: abolition of feudal laws

Model of the Bastille

Electors' card for the Convention of 1792

1792 Overthrow of Louis XVI: establishment of First Republic

1794 Overthrow of Robespierre and end of the Terror

Napoleonic France

Two generations of Napoleons dominated France from 1800 to 1870. Napoleon Bonaparte took the title of Emperor Napoleon I. He extended his empire throughout most of western Europe, placing his brothers and sisters on the thrones of conquered countries. Defeated in 1814 and replaced by the restored Bourbon dynasty, followed by the 1830 Revolution and the so-called July Monarchy, the Napoleonic clan made a comeback after 1848. Napoleon I's nephew, Louis Napoleon, became President of the Second Republic, then made himself emperor as Napoleon III. During his reign Paris was modernized and the industrial transformation of France began.

Europe in 1812
- Napoleonic rule
- Dependent states

Musée du Louvre
The museum had opened in 1792, but it flourished during Napoleon's reign. He took a personal interest in both acquisitions and organization.

The Laurel, crown of the Roman emperors

Napoleon, as First Consul, is crowned by Chronos, the God of Time.

The revolutionary tricolor flag was kept throughout the empire.

Légion d'Honneur medal

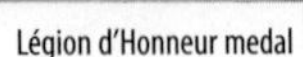

Imperial Insignia
Napoleon I created a new titled aristocracy, who were allowed coats of arms. Only his, however, was permitted a crown. The eagle symbol was adopted in 1800, an evocation of Imperial Rome.

1800 Establishment of the Bank of France

1802 Treaty of Amiens brings temporary peace to Europe

1802 Establishment of the Légion d'Honneur

1803 Resumption of wars to create the Napoleonic Empire

1804 Napoleon crowned as Emperor. Napoleonic Civil Code established

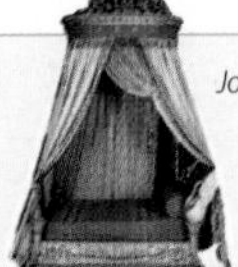

Josephine's bed at Malmaison

1806 Arc de Triomphe commissioned

1809 Josephine and Napoleon divorce. She retains Château Malmaison *(see p177)*

1814 Defeat of Napoleon by the Allies (England, Russia, Austria, and Prussia). Napoleon exiled to Elba

1815 The "Hundred Days": Napoleon returns from Elba, is defeated at Waterloo, and exiled to St Helena

1800 | 1810 | 1820

July Revolution
Three days of street-fighting in July 1830 ended unpopular Bourbon rule.

The Napoleons
This imaginary group portrait depicts Napoleon I (seated), his son "Napoleon II" *(right)* – who never ruled – Napoleon's nephew Louis Napoleon (Napoleon III), and the latter's infant son.

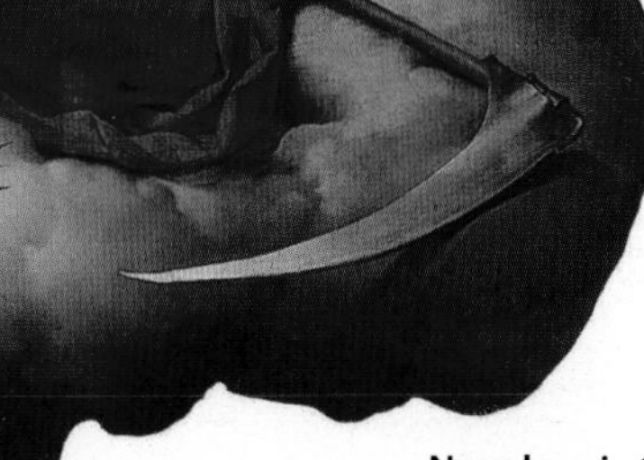

The Civil Code, created by Napoleon, is here shown as a tablet.

Napoleonic Glory

Though professing himself a true revolutionary, Napoleon developed a taste for imperial pomp. However, he also achieved some long-lasting reforms such as the Civil Code, the new school system, and the Bank of France.

Napoleon on Campaign
A dashing general in the late 1790s, Napoleon remained a remarkable military commander throughout his reign.

Empire Fashion

Greek and Roman ideals were evident in architecture, furniture, design, and fashion. Women wore light, Classical tunics, the most daring with one shoulder or more bare. David and Gérard were the fashionable portraitists, while Delacroix and Géricault created many Romantic masterpieces.

Madame Récamier held a popular salon and was renowned for her beauty and wit. David painted her in 1800.

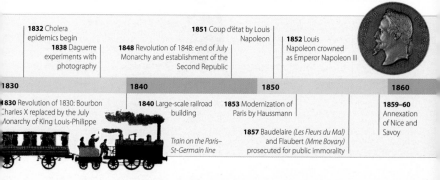

1832 Cholera epidemics begin

1838 Daguerre experiments with photography

1848 Revolution of 1848: end of July Monarchy and establishment of the Second Republic

1851 Coup d'état by Louis Napoleon

1852 Louis Napoleon crowned as Emperor Napoleon III

1830 | **1840** | **1850** | **1860**

1830 Revolution of 1830: Bourbon Charles X replaced by the July Monarchy of King Louis-Philippe

1840 Large-scale railroad building

Train on the Paris–St-Germain line

1853 Modernization of Paris by Haussmann

1857 Baudelaire *(Les Fleurs du Mal)* and Flaubert *(Mme Bovary)* prosecuted for public immorality

1859–60 Annexation of Nice and Savoy

The Belle Epoque

The decades before World War I became the *Belle Epoque* for the French, remembered as a golden era forever past. Nevertheless this was a politically turbulent time, with working-class militancy, organized socialist movements, and the Dreyfus Affair polarizing the country between Left and anti-semitic Right. New inventions such as electricity and vaccination against disease made life easier at all social levels. The cultural scene thrived and took new forms with Impressionism and Art Nouveau, the realist novels of Gustave Flaubert and Emile Zola, cabaret and cancan and, in 1895, the birth of the cinema.

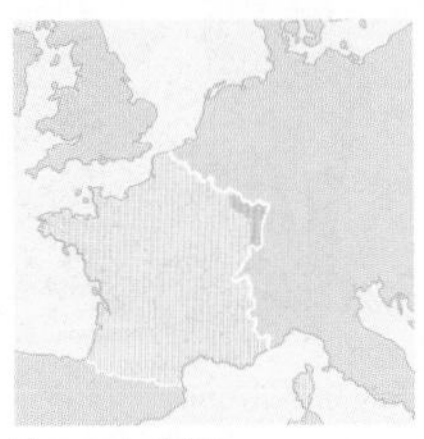

France in 1871

Under Third Republic

Alsace and Lorraine

Universal Exhibition
The 1889 Paris exhibition was attended by 3.2 million people. Engineer Eiffel's breathtaking iron structure dominated the exhibition and caused great controversy at the time.

Statue of Apollo by Aimé Millet

Copper-green roofed cupola

Stage

Backstage area

The auditorium in gold and purple seated over 2,000 guests.

Peugeot Car (1899) The car and bicycle brought new freedom, becoming a part of people's leisure time. Peugeot, Renault, and Citroën were all founded before World War I.

Woman on the barricades in 1871

1865

1869 Opening of the Suez Canal, built by Ferdinand de Lesseps

1870–71 Franco-Prussian War: defeat and overthrow of Napoleon III; France cedes Alsace and Lorraine to Germany

1870

1871 The Paris Commune leads to the Third Republic

1874 Impressionist movement begins

1875

1880s Scramble for colonies in Africa and Asia begins

1881–6 Reforms in education by Jules Ferry

1880

1885 Pasteur produces vaccine for rabies, the first tested on a human

1885

1889 Universal Exhibition in Paris; Eiffel Tower built

1890 Peugeot constructs one of the earliest automobiles

Poster Art
The poster was revolutionized by Art Nouveau, with designs by Alphonse Mucha particularly popular. This one from 1897 is for beer, the beverage of the lost Alsace and Lorraine, which became a "patriotic" drink.

Where to see the Belle Epoque

Belle Epoque buildings include the Negresco Hotel, Nice *(see p530)*, the Grand Casino in Monte-Carlo *(p534)*, and the Palais Hotel in Biarritz *(p456)*. The Musée d'Orsay in Paris *(pp124–5)* exhibits Art Nouveau objects and furniture.

Guimard's Métro entrance is a typical example of the elegant, swirling lines of Art Nouveau.

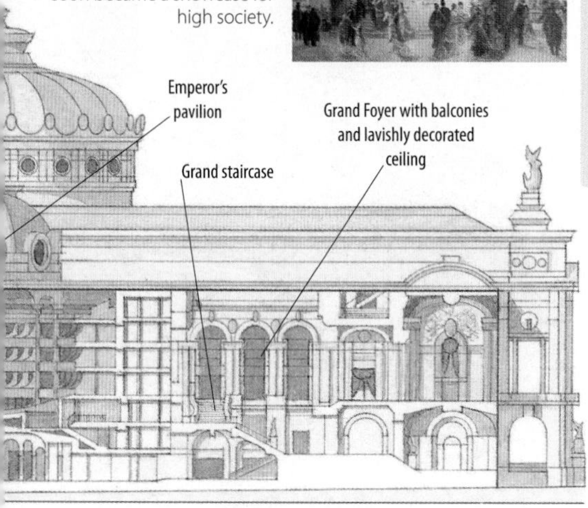

Staircase at the Opera
The grand staircase had colored marble columns and a frescoed ceiling. As this painting by Beroud from 1887 shows, it soon became a showcase for high society.

Emperor's pavilion

Grand staircase

Grand Foyer with balconies and lavishly decorated ceiling

Opera National Garnier

Founded by Napoleon III in 1862, the new opera was opened to great public acclaim in 1875 and became a focus of Belle Epoque social life. Designed by Charles Garnier, its extravagant exterior was matched by its sumptuous interior decor.

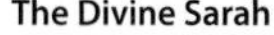

The Divine Sarah
Actress Sarah Bernhardt (1844–1923) worked in all theatrical genres, dominating the Paris stage.

Caricature of Zola

1894–1906 The alleged treason of Dreyfus sparks the Dreyfus Affair, involving the author Zola among others

1895 First public cinema by the Lumière brothers

1898 Marie and Pierre Curie discover radium

1905 Official separation of church and state

1909 Blériot flies the Channel

1913 Publication of Proust's first volume of *Remembrance of Things Past*

1914 World War I breaks out

1916 Battle of Verdun

1917 Mutinies in the army suppressed by Pétain

1918 Germany asks for armistice to end war

French recruit, 1916

1919 Treaty of Versailles

1895 | 1900 | 1905 | 1910 | 1915

Avant-Garde France

Despite the devastation wrought by two world wars, France retained its international renown as a center for the avant garde. Paris in particular was a magnet for experimental writers, artists, and musicians. The cafés were full of American authors and jazz musicians, French surrealists and film makers. The French Riviera also attracted colonies of artists and writers, from Matisse and Picasso to Hemingway and F. Scott Fitzgerald, along with the wealthy industrialists and aristocrats arriving in automobiles or the famous Train Bleu. And from 1936 paid holidays meant that the working classes could also enjoy the new fashion for sunbathing.

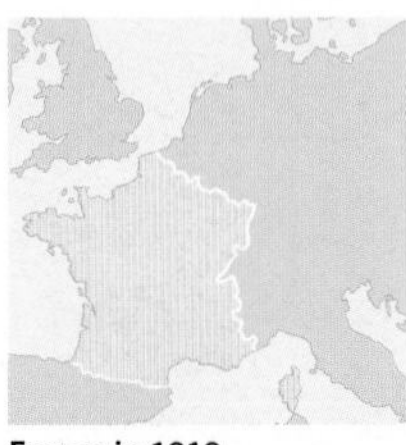

France in 1919

French territory

Art Deco 1925 The International Exhibition in Paris in 1925 launched the Art Deco style: geometrical shapes and utilitarian designs, adapted for mass-production.

African Gods of Creation

Dancers in heavy cardboard costumes

The costumes and scenery by the Cubist Léger were striking and made to look partly mechanical.

The Jazz Age Paris welcomed American jazz musicians, such as Sidney Bechet in 1925 and Dizzy Gillespie (left), co-founder of Bebop in the 1940s.

Citroën Goddess (1956) This elegant model became an icon of the new French consumerism evident in the 1950s and '60s.

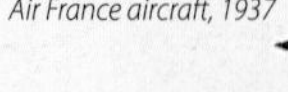

Air France aircraft, 1937

1920 French Communist Party founded. Publication of Tristan Tzara's Dadaist Manifesto

1928 Premiere of *Un Chien Andalou* by Luis Buñuel and Salvador Dalí

1933 Air France begins operation

1937 Premiere of *La Grande Illusion* by Jean Renoir

1920

1930

1924 Olympic Games in Paris. André Breton publishes the *Surrealist Manifesto*

Detail of poster for the 1924 Olympics

1929–39 The Depression

1936–38 The "Popular Front": radical social program introduced, including paid holidays

1938 Munich Conference height of appeasement

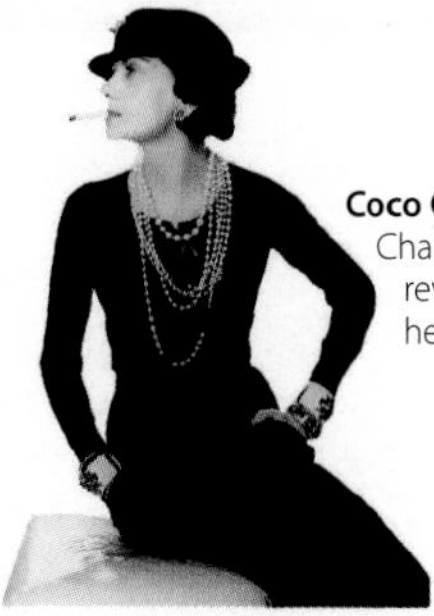

Coco Chanel (1883–1971)
Chanel, here photographed by Man Ray, revolutionized fashion in the 1920s with her elegant but comfortable clothes.

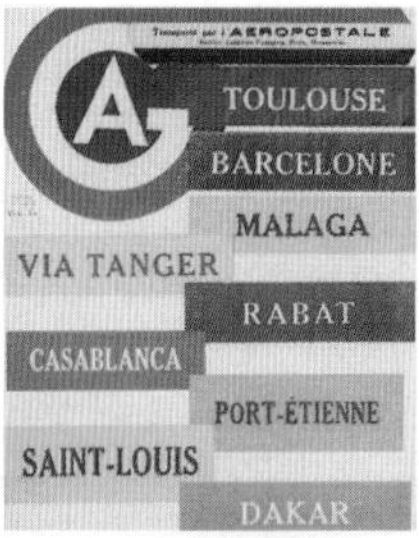

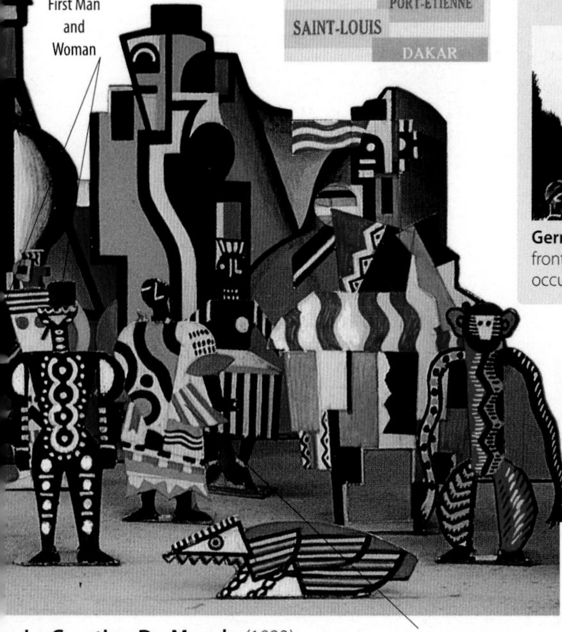

World War II

Following the collapse of the Third Republic in 1940, Paris and the north and west parts of France were occupied by the Germans until the Liberation in 1944. South-east France formed the collaborationist Vichy state, led by Marshal Pétain and Pierre Laval. Meanwhile, the Free French movement was led by Charles de Gaulle, with Jean Moulin coordinating the operations of the many different Resistance factions.

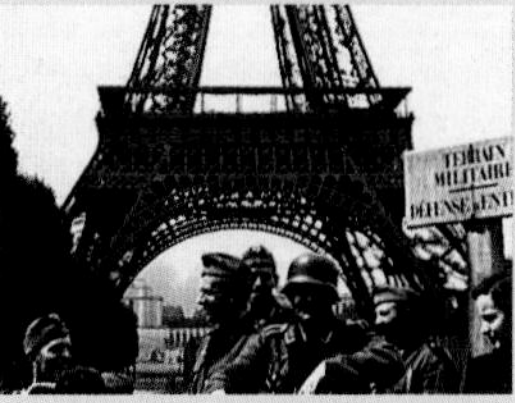

German soldiers liked to pose in front of the Eiffel Tower during the occupation of Paris.

AEROPOSTALE
TOULOUSE
BARCELONE
MALAGA
VIA TANGER
RABAT
CASABLANCA
PORT-ÉTIENNE
SAINT-LOUIS
DAKAR

Par Avion
France pioneered the use of airmail, starting in 1927.

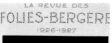

First Man and Woman
The African theme was based on text by Blaise Cendrars.

La Creation Du Monde *(1923)*

Artistic experimentation thrived in the early 20th century. La Création du Monde *by Les Ballets Suédois had costumes by Léger and music by Milhaud. Diaghilev's Ballets Russes also competed for avant-garde artists like Picabia, Cocteau, Satie, and Sonia Delaunay.*

LA REVUE DES
FOLIES-BERGERE
1926-1927

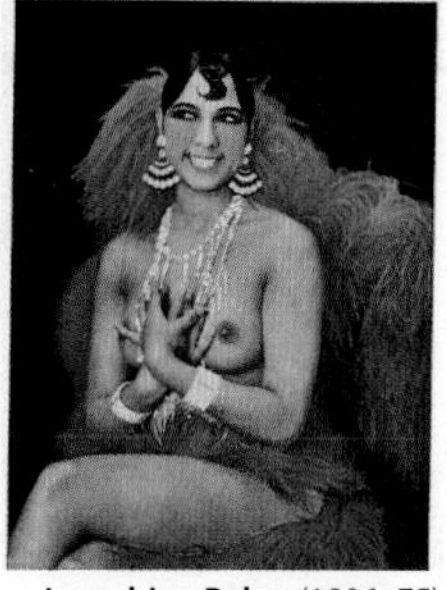

Josephine Baker (1906–75)
The music hall flourished in the 1920s with Mistinguett and Josephine Baker as its undisputed queens.

1940 The Fall of France. Vichy government led by Pétain. De Gaulle fights on from London

1942 The whole of France controlled by Germany

1949 Establishment of NATO. Founding of the Council of Europe

1958 Fifth Republic begins under President de Gaulle

1956 Late in her career, Edith Piaf crowns her success at Carnegie Hall, New York

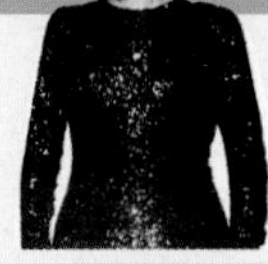

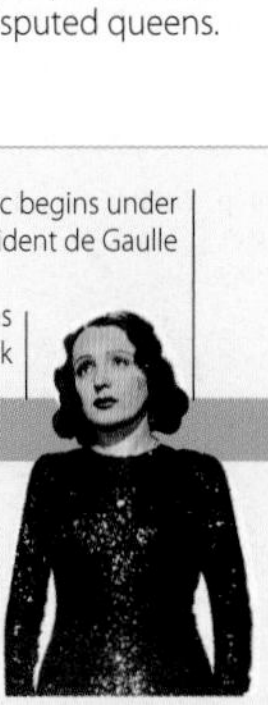

1940

1950

1944 D-Day: Allied landings in Normandy (June). Liberation of Paris (August)

1946 Sartre establishes *Les Temps Modernes*. First Cannes Film Festival

1954 France withdraws from Indo-China after Battle of Dien Bien Phu. Start of Algerian insurrection

39 Declaration Vorld War II

1945 End of the war. Fourth Republic begins. Votes for women

Modern France

After the 1950s, the traditional foundations of French society changed: the number of peasant farmers plummeted, old industries decayed, jobs in the service sector and high-technology industries grew dramatically, and the French came to enjoy the benefits of mass culture and widespread consumerism. High prestige projects, such as Concorde, TGV, La Défense, and the Centre Pompidou, brought international acclaim. Efforts for European integration and the inauguration of the Channel Tunnel aim towards closer relations with France's neighbors.

France Today
France
European Union

Centre Pompidou (1977)
The Centre Pompidou's controversial building changed the aspect of the historic quarter of Beaubourg. A major arts center, it has revitalized the formerly rundown area *(see pp96–7)*.

New Wave Film
Directors like Godard and Truffaut launched a refreshing, personal style of films, such as *Jules et Jim* (1961).

La Grande Arche was opened in 1989 to commemorate the bicentennial of the Revolution.

Shopping center

La Défense

The huge modernist business center at La Défense (see p134), *on the edge of Paris, was developed in the 1960s and has become a prime site for the headquarters of major multinational companies.*

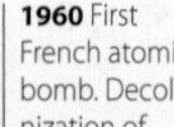

1960 First French atomic bomb. Decolonization of black Africa

1962 Evian agreements lead to Algerian independence

1963 First French nuclear power station

1967 Common Agricultural Policy, subsidizing Europe's farmers

1968 May demonstrations

1969 Pompidou replaces de Gaulle as president

1973 Extension of the Common Market (EU) from six to nine states

1974 Giscard d'Estaing elected president

1976 Concorde's first commercial flight

1977 Jacques Chirac is first mayor of Paris since 1871. Opening of Centre Pompidou

1980 Giverny, Monet's garden, opens to the public *(see p270)*

1981 Socialist Mitterrand becomes president for 14 years

1987 Mitterrand and Thatcher sign agreement for Channel Tunnel. Trial in Lyon of ex-SS Officer Klaus Barbie

1989 Bicente celebr of the Fr Revol

1960 — 1970 — 1980

François Mit

EU Flag
France has been one of the leading forces in the European Union ever since the move toward closer European collaboration began in the 1950s.

TGV
The TGV (Train à Grande Vitesse) is one of the world's fastest trains *(see pp632–3)*. It typifies the French government's commitment to high technology and improved communications.

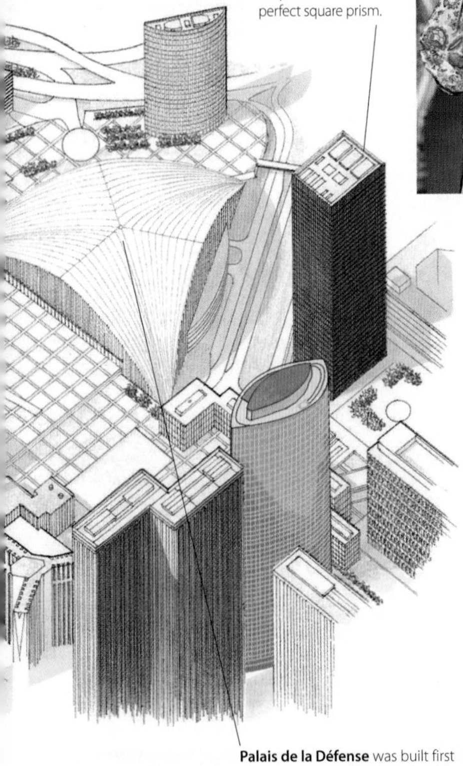

Fashion by Lacroix
Despite less demand for *haute couture*, Paris is still a major fashion center. The designs shown on the catwalk, here by Christian Lacroix, remain proof of the world-renowned skills of French designers.

The Areva (Fiat) Tower is 584 ft (178 m) tall. Its shape is that of a perfect square prism.

Palais de la Défense was built first and houses the center for industry.

May 1968

The events of May 1968 began as a political revolt by left-wing students against the Establishment and had a profound influence on French society. Around 9 million workers, and leading intellectuals like Jean-Paul Sartre, joined the rebellion, demanding better pay, better study conditions, and the overhaul of traditional values and institutions.

Student riots starting in Nanterre, just outside Paris, sparked widespread rioting and industrial unrest in France.

1994 Channel Tunnel opens

2002 National Front defeat Socialists in 1st round of presidential campaign. France re-elects Jacques Chirac

Prince Albert II

2010 The head of France's King Henry IV is found after it was lost in 1793

2013 Legalization of same-sex marriage

)

2000

2010

2020

991 Edith Cresson is irst woman prime ninister

2002 Euro replaces franc as legal tender

1996 Mitterrand dies after a long illness

2005 Prince Rainier III of Monaco dies and is succeeded by his only son, Prince Albert II

2008 Jean-Marie Gustave Le Clézio wins the Nobel Prize for literature

2007 Center-right Nicolas Sarkozy is elected president

2012 Socialist candidate Francois Hollande is elected as president

Kings and Emperors of France

Following the break-up of the Roman Empire, the Frankish king Clovis consolidated the Merovingian dynasty. It was followed by the Carolingians, and from the 10th century by Capetian rulers. The Capetians established royal power, which passed to the Valois branch in the 14th century, and then to the Bourbons in the late 16th century, following the Wars of Religion. The Revolution of 1789 seemed to end the Bourbon dynasty, but it made a brief come-back in 1814–30. The 19th century was dominated by the Bonapartes, Napoleon I and Napoleon III. Since the overthrow of Napoleon III in 1870, France has been a republic.

768–814 Charlemagne

447–458 Merovich

458–482 Childéric I

482–511 Clovis I

511–558 Childebert I

558–562 Clothaire I

562–566 Caribert

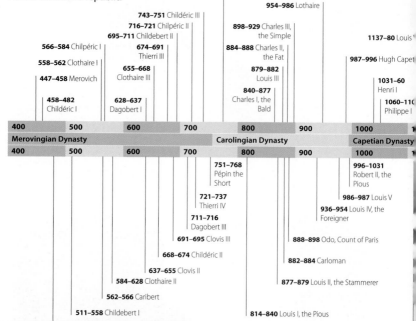

566–584 Chilpéric I

584–628 Clothaire II

628–637 Dagobert I

637–655 Clovis II

655–668 Clothaire III

668–674 Childéric II

674–691 Thierri III

691–695 Clovis III

695–711 Childebert II

711–716 Dagobert III

716–721 Chilpéric II

721–737 Thierri IV

743–751 Childéric III

751–768 Pépin the Short

814–840 Louis I, the Pious

840–877 Charles I, the Bald

877–879 Louis II, the Stammerer

879–882 Louis III

882–884 Carloman

884–888 Charles II, the Fat

888–898 Odo, Count of Paris

898–929 Charles III, the Simple

936–954 Louis IV, the Foreigner

954–986 Lothaire

986–987 Louis V

987–996 Hugh Capet

996–1031 Robert II, the Pious

1031–60 Henri I

1060–11… Philippe I

1108–37 Louis VI, the Fat

1137–80 Louis…

400	500	600	700	800	900	1000
Merovingian Dynasty				Carolingian Dynasty		Capetian Dynasty

482–511 Clovis I

1108–37 Louis VI, the Fat

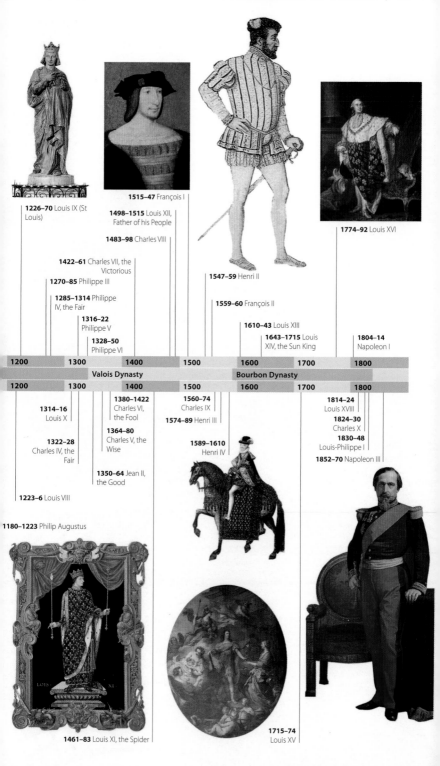

1226–70 Louis IX (St Louis)

1515–47 François I

1498–1515 Louis XII, Father of his People

1483–98 Charles VIII

1774–92 Louis XVI

1422–61 Charles VII, the Victorious

1270–85 Philippe III

1547–59 Henri II

1285–1314 Philippe IV, the Fair

1559–60 François II

1316–22 Philippe V

1610–43 Louis XIII

1328–50 Philippe VI

1643–1715 Louis XIV, the Sun King

1804–14 Napoleon I

1200	1300	1400	1500	1600	1700	1800
	Valois Dynasty			Bourbon Dynasty		
1200	1300	1400	1500	1600	1700	1800

1380–1422 Charles VI, the Fool

1560–74 Charles IX

1814–24 Louis XVIII

1314–16 Louis X

1574–89 Henri III

1824–30 Charles X

1364–80 Charles V, the Wise

1830–48 Louis-Philippe I

1322–28 Charles IV, the Fair

1589–1610 Henri IV

1852–70 Napoleon III

1350–64 Jean II, the Good

1223–6 Louis VIII

1180–1223 Philip Augustus

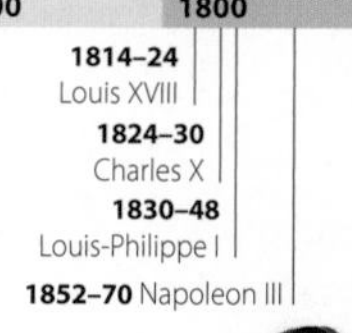

1715–74 Louis XV

1461–83 Louis XI, the Spider

PARIS AND ILE DE FRANCE

Introducing Paris and Ile de France

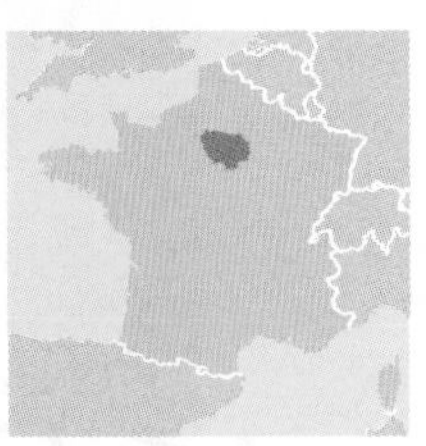

The French capital is rich in museums, art galleries, and monuments. The Louvre, Eiffel Tower, and Centre Pompidou are among the most popular sights.

Surrounding Paris, the Ile de France takes in 4,600 sq miles (12,000 sq km) of busy suburbs and commuter towns punctuated by châteaus, the most celebrated being Versailles. Farther out, suburbia gives way to farmland, forests, and the magnificent palace of Fontainebleau.

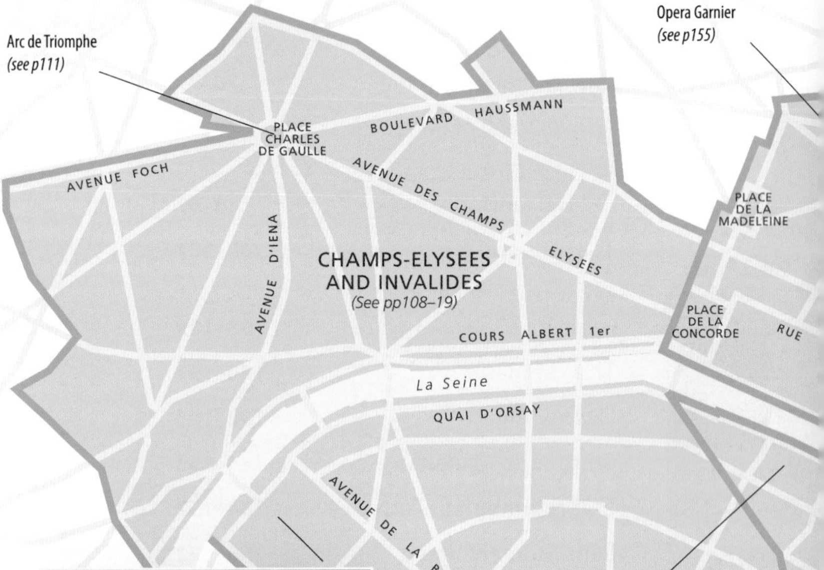

Arc de Triomphe *(see p111)*

Opera Garnier *(see p155)*

PLACE CHARLES DE GAULLE

BOULEVARD HAUSSMANN

AVENUE FOCH

AVENUE DES CHAMPS ELYSEES

AVENUE D'IENA

PLACE DE LA MADELEINE

CHAMPS-ELYSEES AND INVALIDES
(See pp108–19)

PLACE DE LA CONCORDE

RUE

COURS ALBERT 1er

La Seine

QUAI D'ORSAY

AVENUE DE LA BOURDONNAIS

RUE DE BABYLONE

The Eiffel Tower, designed for the Universal Exhibition of 1889, scandalized contemporary critics but is now the capital's most famous landmark *(see p117)*.

The Musée d'Orsay, opened in 1986, was created from a late 19th-century railroad terminal *(see pp124–5)*. Its magnificent collection of 19th- and early 20th-century art (notably Impressionist art) includes Jean-Baptiste Carpeaux's *Four Quarters of the World* (1872).

◀ View of the iconic Eiffel Tower from below

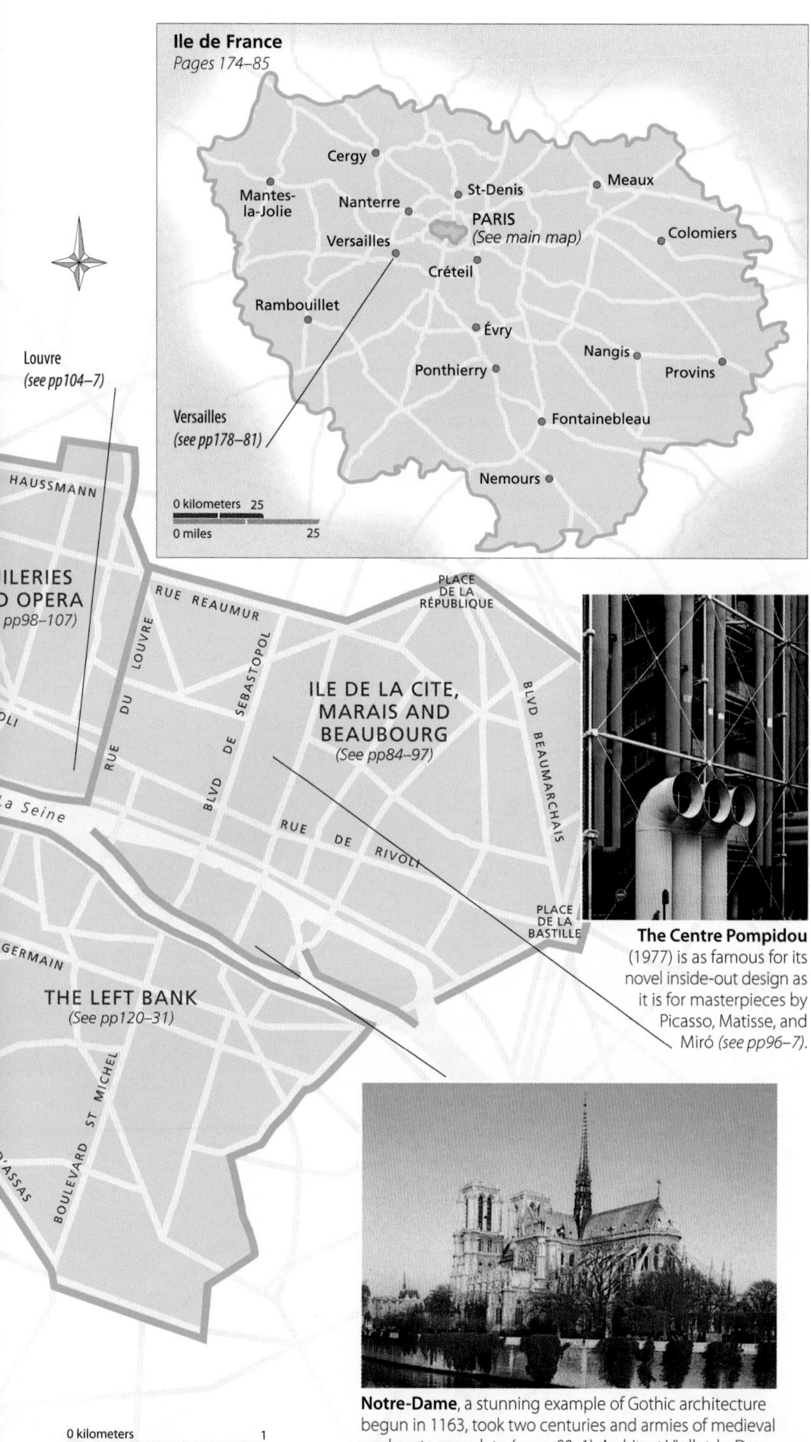

The Centre Pompidou (1977) is as famous for its novel inside-out design as it is for masterpieces by Picasso, Matisse, and Miró *(see pp96–7)*.

Notre-Dame, a stunning example of Gothic architecture begun in 1163, took two centuries and armies of medieval workers to complete *(see pp90–1)*. Architect Viollet-le-Duc designed the spire in the 19th century.

A RIVER VIEW OF PARIS

The remarkable French music hall star Mistinguett described the Seine as a "pretty blonde with laughing eyes." The river most certainly has a beguiling quality, but the relationship that exists between it and the city of Paris is far more than one of flirtation.

No other European city defines itself by its river in the same way as Paris. The Seine is the essential point of reference to the city: distances are measured from it, street numbers determined by it, and it divides the capital into two distinct areas, the Right Bank on the north side of the river and the Left Bank on the south side. These are as well-defined as any of the official boundaries. The city is also divided historically: the east is linked to the city's ancient roots and the west to the 19th–20th centuries. Practically every building of note in Paris is either along the river bank or within a stone's throw of it. The quays are lined by fine bourgeois apartments, magnificent townhouses, world-renowned museums, and striking monuments.

Above all, the river is very much alive. For centuries fleets of small boats used it, but motorized land traffic stifled this once-bustling scene. Today, the river is busy with commercial barges and massive *bâteaux mouches* (pleasure boats) carrying sightseers up and down the river.

The Latin Quarter Quayside is on the left bank of the Seine. Associated with institutes of learning since the Middle Ages, it acquired its name from the early Latin-speaking students.

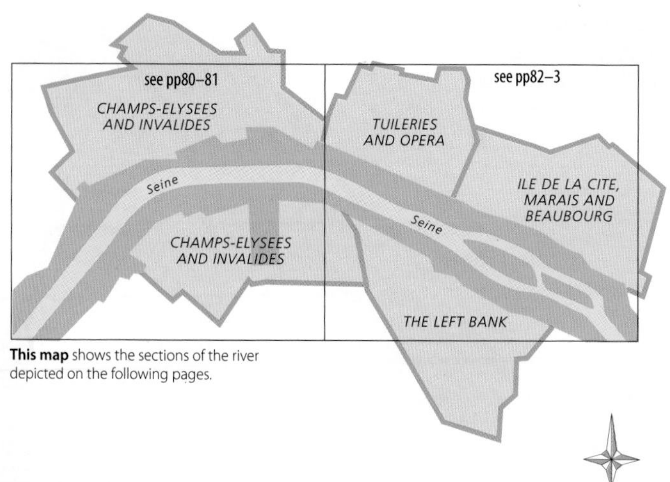

This map shows the sections of the river depicted on the following pages.

Les Bouquinistes, the bookstalls on the river banks, are treasure troves of second-hand books and prints, and perfect for an afternoon's browsing.

◀ River view of Paris from the height of the Eiffel Tower

From Pont de Grenelle to Pont de la Concorde

The grand monuments along this stretch of the river are remnants of the Napoleonic era and the Industrial Revolution. The elegance of the Eiffel Tower, the Petit Palais, and the Grand Palais is matched by more recent buildings, such as the Palais de Chaillot and the Musée du Quai Branly.

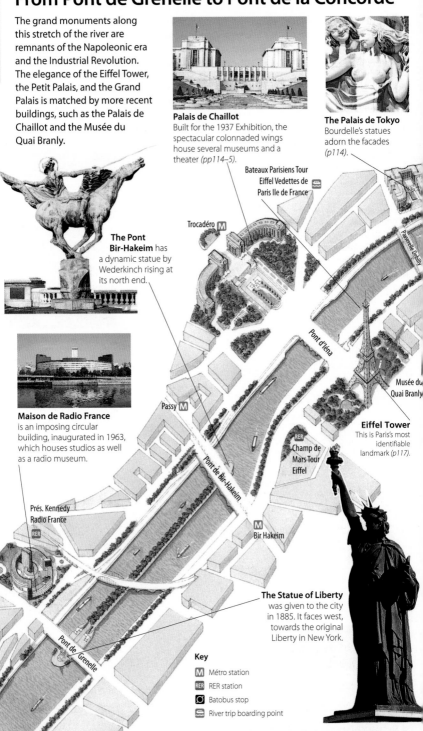

Palais de Chaillot
Built for the 1937 Exhibition, the spectacular colonnaded wings house several museums and a theater *(pp114–5)*.

The Palais de Tokyo
Bourdelle's statues adorn the facades *(p114)*.

The Pont Bir-Hakeim has a dynamic statue by Wederkinch rising at its north end.

Maison de Radio France
is an imposing circular building, inaugurated in 1963, which houses studios as well as a radio museum.

Eiffel Tower
This is Paris's most identifiable landmark *(p117)*.

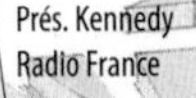

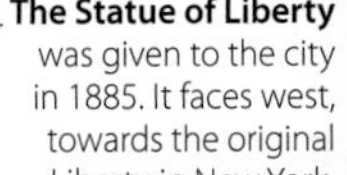

The Statue of Liberty
was given to the city in 1885. It faces west, towards the original Liberty in New York.

Key

Métro station

RER station

Batobus stop

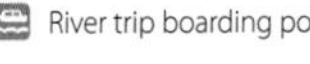
River trip boarding point

Grand Palais
Major exhibitions and a science museum are based here *(p113)*.

Petit Palais
Now the Paris museum of fine arts, this was first designed as a companion to the Grand Palais *(p112)*.

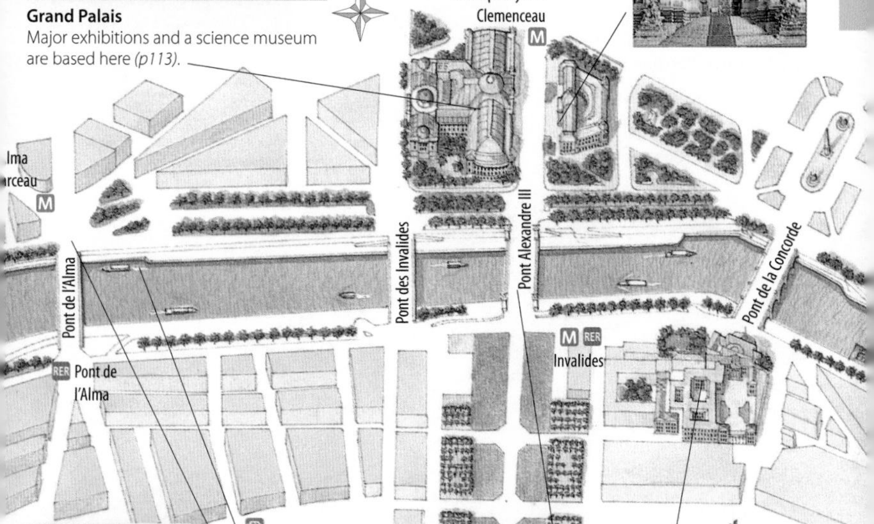

The Zouave, a statue on the Pont de l'Alma, is a useful gauge for checking flood levels.

The Liberty Flame is a memorial to the fighters of the French Resistance during World War II.

The Assemblée Nationale Palais-Bourbon was originally built for Louis XIV's daughter. It has accommodated the lower house of the French Parliament since 1830.

Dôme des Invalides
The majestic dome *(p119)*, now used as a burial site for many of France's war heroes, is here seen from Pont Alexandre III. Napoleon's tomb is in the crypt.

Pont Alexandre III
Flamboyant statuary decorates Paris's most ornate bridge *(p113)*.

From Pont de la Concorde to Pont de Sully

The historic heart of Paris lies on the banks and islands of the east river. At its center is the Ile de la Cité, a natural stepping stone across the Seine and the cultural core of medieval Paris. Today it is still vital to Parisian life.

Jardin des Tuileries
These are laid out in the formal style *(pp102–3)*.

Musée du Louvre
Before becoming the world's greatest museum and home to the *Mona Lisa*, this was Europe's largest royal palace *(pp104–7)*.

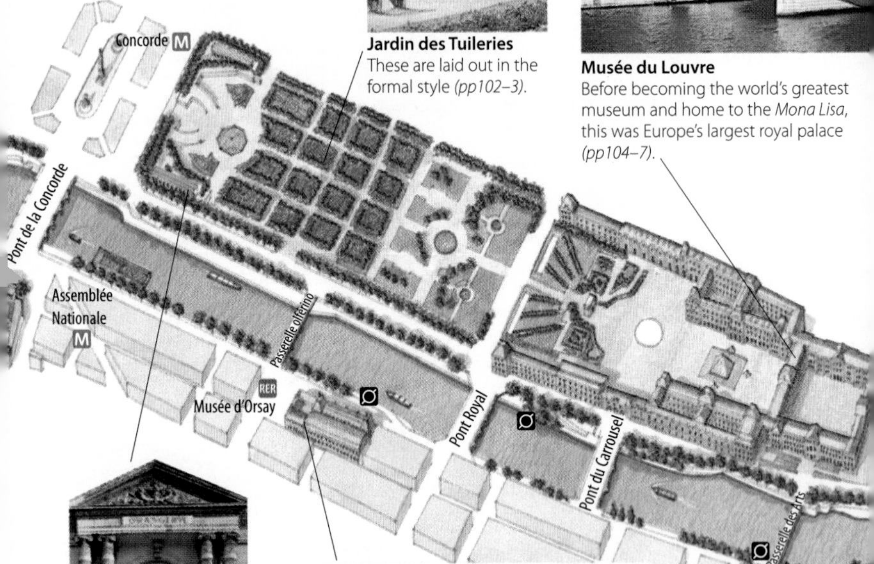

Concorde
Pont de la Concorde
Assemblée Nationale
Passerelle Solférino
RER Musée d'Orsay
Pont Royal
Pont du Carrousel
Passerelle des Arts

Musée de l'Orangerie
An important collection of 19th-century paintings is on display here *(p102)*.

Musée d'Orsay
This converted railway station houses Paris's outstanding collection of Impressionist art *(pp124–5)*.

Bateaux Vedettes du Pont Neuf

Batobus cruises

The boarding points are: **Eiffel Tower. Map** 6 D3. Ⓜ Bir Hakeim. **Champs-Elysées. Map** 7 A1. Ⓜ Champs-Elysées-Clemenceau or Concorde. **Musée d'Orsay. Map** 8 D2. Ⓜ Assemblée Nationale. **Louvre. Map** 8 D2. Ⓜ Palais Royal-Musée du Louvre. **Hôtel de Ville. Map** 9 B4. Ⓜ Hôtel de Ville. **Notre-Dame. Map** 9 B4. Ⓜ St-Michel or Maubert-Mutualité. **St-Germain-des-Prés. Map** 8 E3. Ⓜ St-Germain des Prés. **Jardin des Plantes. Map** 13 C1. Ⓜ Jussieu or Cardinal-Lemoines. ***Departures*** *early Sep–early Apr: 10am–7pm (every 25 mins); early Apr–early Sep: 10am–9:30pm (every 20 mins).* Ⓦ **batobus.com**

Passerelle des Arts
This steel reconstruction of Paris's first cast-iron bridge (1804) was inaugurated in 1984.

Monnaie de Paris,
the Mint, was built in 1778, and has an extensive coin and medallion collection in its old milling halls.

For hotels and restaurants in this region see pp554–71 and pp576–603

How to Take a Seine Cruise

Bateaux Vedettes du Pont-Neuf
Boarding point: **Square du Vert-Galant** (Pont Neuf). **Map** 8 F3. **Tel** 01 46 33 98 38. Ⓜ Pont Neuf. RER Châtelet/St-Michel. 🚌 27, 58, 67, 70, 72, 74, 75. **Departures** Mar 15–Oct 31: 10:30 am, 11:15am, noon, 1:30–10:30pm (every 30 mins) daily; Nov–Mar 14: 10:30am, 11:15am, noon, 2–6:30pm (every 45 mins), 8pm, 10pm Mon–Thu & 10:30am, 11:15am, noon, 2–6:30pm (every 30 mins), 8pm, 9pm, 10pm Fri–Sun. **Duration** 1 hr. Snacks available.
W vedettesdupontneuf.fr

Bateaux Mouches
Boarding point: **Pont de l'Alma. Map** 6 F1. **Tel** 01 42 25 96 10. Ⓜ Alma-Marceau. RER Pont de l'Alma. 🚌 28, 42, 63, 72, 80, 81, 92. **Departures** Apr–Sep: 10:15am–10:30pm daily (every 20–45 mins); Oct–Mar: 11am–9pm Mon–Fri, 10:15am–9pm Sat–Sun (every 30–60 min). **Duration** 1hr 10 mins. **Lunch cruise** 1pm Sat, Sun, bank hols (boards 12:15pm). **Dinner cruise** 8:30pm daily (boards 7:30–8:15pm). **Duration** 2 hr 15 mins. Jacket and tie.
W bateaux-mouches.fr

Vedettes de Paris Ile de France
Boarding point: **Port du Suffren. Map** 6 D3. **Tel** 01 44 18 19 50. Ⓜ Trocadéro, Bir Hakeim. RER Champ-de-Mars–Tour Eiffel. 🚌 22, 30, 32, 42, 44, 63, 69, 72, 82, 87. **Departures** Apr–Sep: 10:30am–11pm daily; Nov–mid-Feb: 11:15am–9pm Mon–Fri, 10:30am–10pm Sat–Sun; mid-Feb–Mar: 10:30am–9pm daily (every 20–45 mins). **Duration** 1hr. **Champagne cruise** 6pm Thu–Sat (May–Aug 6:30pm daily). **Duration** 1hr. **Dinner cruise** 9:15pm daily. **Duration** 2 hrs 30 mins.
W vedettesdeparis.com

Bateaux Parisiens Tour Eiffel
Boarding point: **Port de la Bordonnais** (foot of Eiffel Tower) **& Quai de Montbello** (Apr–Nov). **Map** 6 D2. **Tel** 08 25 01 01 01. Ⓜ Trocadéro, Bir Hakeim. RER Champ-de-Mars–Tour Eiffel. 🚌 42, 82. **Departures** Apr–Sep: 10am–10:30pm (Jun–Aug to 11pm); Oct–Mar: 10:30am–10pm (every 30 mins). **Duration** 1 hr. **Lunch cruise** 12:30pm daily (duration 2 hrs). **Dinner cruises** 6pm (boards 5–6pm, duration 1.5 hrs) & 8:30pm (boards 7:15–8:15pm, duration 2.5 hrs) daily. Jacket and tie.
W bateauxparisiens.com

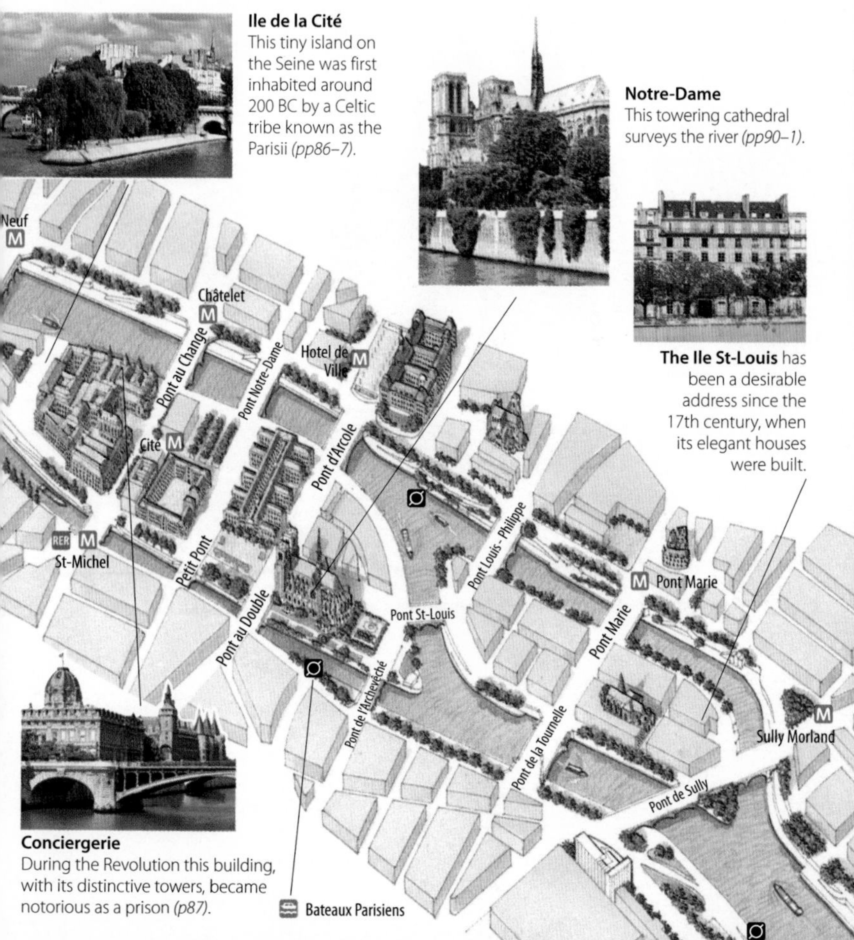

Ile de la Cité
This tiny island on the Seine was first inhabited around 200 BC by a Celtic tribe known as the Parisii *(pp86–7)*.

Notre-Dame
This towering cathedral surveys the river *(pp90–1)*.

The Ile St-Louis has been a desirable address since the 17th century, when its elegant houses were built.

Conciergerie
During the Revolution this building, with its distinctive towers, became notorious as a prison *(p87)*.

ILE DE LA CITE, MARAIS, AND BEAUBOURG

The Right Bank is dominated by the modernistic Forum des Halles and Centre Pompidou in the Beaubourg. These are Paris's most thriving public areas, with millions of tourists, shoppers, and students flowing between them. Young people flock to Les Halles, shopping for the latest street fashions, but you should avoid the area at night. Renovations to improve Les Halles should be completed by 2017. All roads from here appear to lead to the Centre Pompidou, an avant-garde assembly of pipes, ducts, and cables housing the Musée National d'Art Moderne. The smaller streets around the center are full of art galleries housed in crooked, gabled buildings. The neighboring Marais was abandoned by its royal residents during the 1789 Revolution, and it descended into architectural wasteland before being rescued in the 1960s. It has since become a very fashionable address, though small cafés, bakeries, and artisans still survive in its streets.

Notre-Dame cathedral, the Palais de Justice, and Sainte-Chapelle continue to draw tourists to the Ile de la Cité, despite extensive redevelopment of the island in the last century. At the eastern end a bridge connects with the Ile St-Louis, a former swampy pastureland transformed into a residential area with pretty, tree-lined quays and mansions.

Sights at a Glance

Islands and Squares

7 Ile St-Louis
13 Forum des Halles
19 Place des Vosges
21 Place de la Bastille

Churches

4 Sainte-Chapelle
6 *Notre-Dame pp90–91*
9 St-Gervais–St-Protais
12 St-Eustache

Historic Buildings

2 Conciergerie
3 Palais de Justice
10 Hôtel de Ville
11 Tour St-Jacques

Museums and Galleries

5 Crypte Archéologique
8 Hôtel de Sens
14 *Centre Pompidou pp96–7*
15 Musée d'Art et d'Histoire du Judaisme
16 Hôtel de Soubise
17 Musée Picasso
18 Musée Carnavalet
20 Maison de Victor Hugo

Bridges

1 Pont Neuf

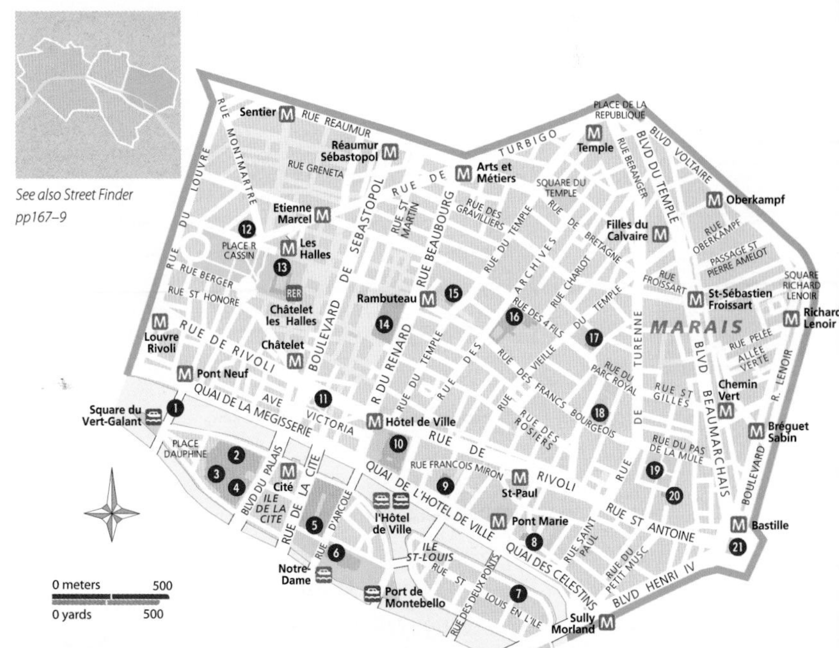

See also Street Finder pp167–9

◀ Colorful pipes in various sizes adorn the exterior of the Centre Pompidou

For map symbols *see back flap*

Street by Street: Ile de la Cité

The origins of Paris are on the Ile de la Cité, the boat-shaped island on the Seine first inhabited by Celtic tribes in the 3rd century BC. One tribe, the Parisii, eventually gave its name to the city. The island offered a convenient river crossing on the route between northern and southern Gaul and was easily defended. In later centuries the settlement was expanded by the Romans, the Franks, and the Capetian kings to form the nucleus of today's city.

Remains of the first buildings can still be seen today in the archeoological crypt of the great medieval cathedral of Notre-Dame. At the other end of the island is Sainte-Chapelle, another Gothic masterpiece.

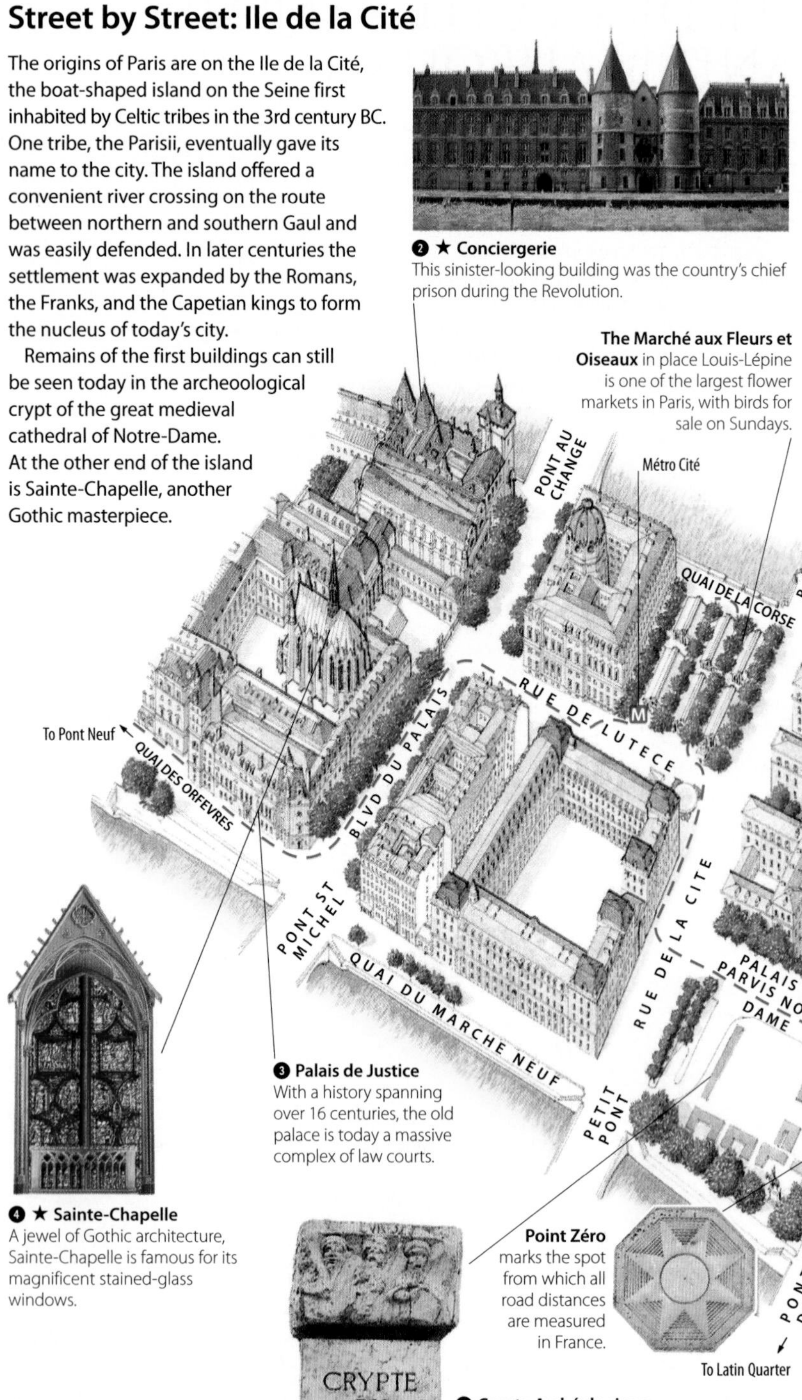

❷ ★ **Conciergerie**
This sinister-looking building was the country's chief prison during the Revolution.

The Marché aux Fleurs et Oiseaux in place Louis-Lépine is one of the largest flower markets in Paris, with birds for sale on Sundays.

❸ **Palais de Justice**
With a history spanning over 16 centuries, the old palace is today a massive complex of law courts.

❹ ★ **Sainte-Chapelle**
A jewel of Gothic architecture, Sainte-Chapelle is famous for its magnificent stained-glass windows.

Point Zéro marks the spot from which all road distances are measured in France.

❺ **Crypte Archéologique**
Deep under the square lie remnants of houses dating back 2,000 years.

Key

— Suggested route

Hôtel Dieu, the oldest hospital in Paris, was founded in AD 651 by St Landry, Bishop of Paris.

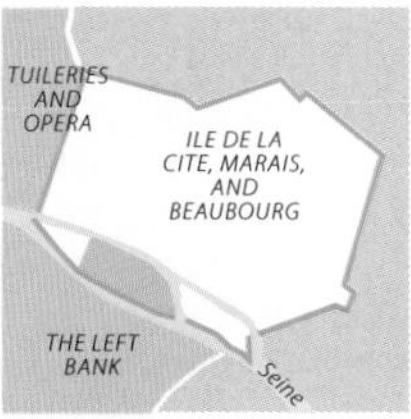

TUILERIES AND OPERA
ILE DE LA CITE, MARAIS, AND BEAUBOURG
THE LEFT BANK
Seine

Locator Map
See Street Finder maps 9, 10

6 ★ Notre-Dame
This cathedral, with its magnificent south-facing rose window and impressive array of gargoyles, is one of the finest examples of French Gothic architecture.

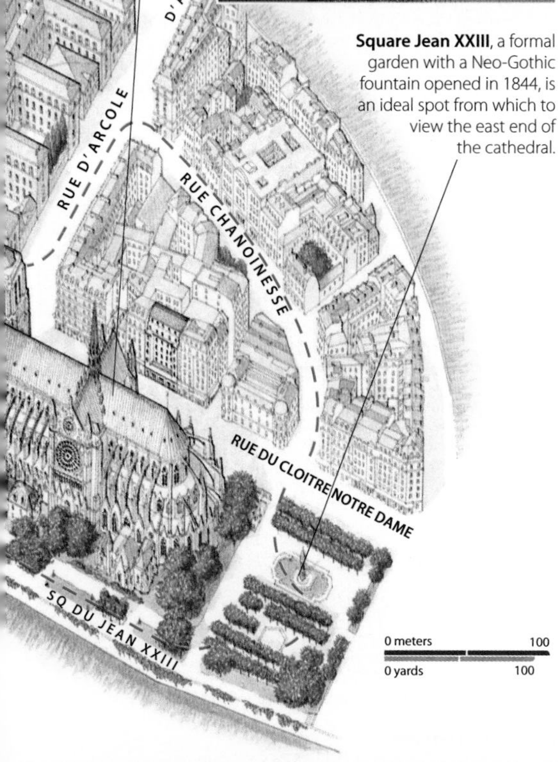

PONT D'ARCOLE
RUE D'ARCOLE
RUE CHANOINESSE
RUE DU CLOITRE NOTRE DAME
SQ DU JEAN XXIII

Square Jean XXIII, a formal garden with a Neo-Gothic fountain opened in 1844, is an ideal spot from which to view the east end of the cathedral.

0 meters 100
0 yards 100

Pont Neuf, the city's oldest bridge

1 Pont Neuf

75001. **Map** 8 F3. M Pont Neuf, Cité.

Despite its name (New Bridge), this bridge is the oldest in Paris and has been immortalized by major literary and artistic figures. The first stone was laid by Henri III in 1578, but it was Henri IV (whose statue stands at the center) who inaugurated it and gave it its name in 1607.

2 Conciergerie

2 bd du Palais 75001. **Map** 9 A3. **Tel** 01 53 40 60 80. M Cité. **Open** 9:30am–6pm daily (9am–5pm Nov–Feb; last adm 30 mins before closing). **Closed** Jan 1, May 1, Dec 25. Combined ticket with Sainte-Chapelle *(see p88)* available. phone to check. W **conciergerie.monuments-nationaux.fr**

Forming part of the huge Palais de Justice, the historic Conciergerie served as a prison from 1391–1914. Henri IV's assassin, François Ravaillac, was imprisoned and tortured here in 1610.

During the Revolution the building was packed with over 4,000 prisoners. Its most celebrated inmate was Marie-Antoinette, who was held in a tiny cell until her execution in 1793. Others included Charlotte Corday, who stabbed Revolutionary leader Marat.

The Conciergerie has a superb four-aisled Gothic hall, where guards of the royal household once lived. Renovated during the 19th century, the building retains its 11th-century torture chamber and 14th-century clock tower.

A sculptured relief on the Palais de Justice

❸ Palais de Justice

4 bd du Palais (entrance at 8 bd du Palais) 75001. **Map** 9 A3. **Tel** 01 44 32 52 52. Ⓜ Cité. **Open** 9am–6pm Mon–Fri. **Closed** public hols & Aug recess.

This huge block of buildings making up the law courts of Paris stretches the entire width of the Ile de la Cité. It is a splendid sight with its Gothic towers lining the quays. The site has been occupied since Roman times when it was the governors' residence. It was the seat of royal power until Charles V moved the court to the Marais following a bloody revolt in 1358. In April 1793 the notorious Revolutionary Tribunal began dispensing justice from the Première Chambre Civile, or first civil chamber. Today the site embodies Napoleon's great legacy – the French judicial system.

❺ Crypte Archéologique

Parvis Notre-Dame–7 pl Jean-Paul II 75004. **Map** 9 A4. **Tel** 01 55 42 50 10. Ⓜ Cité. **Open** 10am–6pm Tue–Sun (last adm 30 mins before closing). **Closed** Jan 1, May 1 & 8, Nov 1 & 11, Dec 25. Ⓦ **crypte-paris.fr**

Situated beneath the *parvis* (main square) of Notre-Dame and stretching 393 ft (120 m) underground, the crypt was opened in 1980.

There are Gallo-Roman streets and houses with an underground heating system, sections of Lutetia's 3rd-century BC wall, and remains of the cathedral. Models explain the development of Paris from a settlement of the Parisii, the Celtic tribe who inhabited the island 2,000 years ago.

❻ Notre-Dame

See pp90–91.

❹ Sainte-Chapelle

6 bd du Palais 75001. **Map** 9 A3. **Tel** 01 53 40 60 80. Ⓜ Cité. **Open** Mar–Oct: 9:30am–6pm daily; Nov–Feb: 9am–5pm daily. **Closed** Jan 1, May 1, Dec 25. Combined ticket with Conciergerie *(see p87)* available. No sharp objects permitted. Ⓦ **sainte-chapelle.monuments-nationaux.fr**

Ethereal and magical, Sainte-Chapelle has been hailed as one of the greatest architectural masterpieces of the Western world. In the Middle Ages the devout likened this church to "a gateway to heaven." Today no visitor can fail to be transported by the blaze of light created by the 15 magnificent stained-glass windows, separated by pencil-like columns soaring 50 ft (15 m) to the star-studded roof. The windows portray more than 1,000 biblical scenes in a kaleidoscope of red, gold, green, and blue. Starting from the left near the entrance and proceeding clockwise, you can trace the scriptures from Genesis through to the Crucifixion and the Apocalypse.

The chapel was completed in 1248 by Louis IX to house what was believed to be Christ's Crown of Thorns and fragments of the True Cross (now in the treasury at Notre-Dame). The king, who was canonized for his good works, purchased the relics from the Emperor of Constantinople, paying three times more for them than for the entire construction of Sainte-Chapelle.

The building actually consists of two separate chapels. The somber lower chapel was used by servants and lower court officials, while the exquisite upper chapel, reached via a narrow spiral staircase, was reserved for the royal family and its courtiers. A discreetly placed window enabled the king to take part in the celebrations unobserved.

During the Revolution the building was badly damaged and became a warehouse. It was renovated a century later by Felix Duban and Jean-Baptiste Lassus.

Today, evening concerts of classical music are held regularly in the chapel, taking advantage of its superb acoustics.

The magnificent interior of Sainte-Chapelle

7 Ile St-Louis

75004. **Map** 9 B-C4-5. Ⓜ Pont Marie, Sully Morland. **St-Louis-en-l'Ile** 19 rue Saint-Louis en l'Ile. **Tel** 01 46 34 11 60. **Open** 9:30am–1pm, 2–7:30pm daily (7pm Sun, public hols). ✝ 6:45pm Mon–Fri, 6:30pm Sat, 11am Sun. Concerts **W saintlouisenlile.catholique.fr**

Across Pont St-Louis from Ile de la Cité, Ile St-Louis is a little haven of quiet streets and riverside quays. The luxurious restaurants and shops include the famous ice-cream maker Berthillon. Almost everything on the Ile was built in Classical style in the 17th century. The church of **St-Louis-en-l'Ile**, with its marble and gilt Baroque interior, was completed in 1726 from plans by royal architect Louis de Vau. Note the 1741 iron clock at the church entrance, the pierced iron spire, and a plaque given in 1926 by St Louis, Missouri. The church is twinned with Carthage cathedral in Tunisia, where St-Louis is buried.

The interior of St-Louis-en-l'Ile

8 Hôtel de Sens

1 rue du Figuier 75004. **Map** 9 C4. **Tel** 01 42 78 14 60. Ⓜ Pont-Marie. **Open** 10am–7:30pm Wed, Thu (from 1pm Tue, Fri, Sat). **Closed** public hols. **W bibliotheques.paris.fr**

One of only a handful of medieval buildings still standing in Paris, the Hôtel de Sens is home to the Forney arts library. During the period of the Catholic League in the 16th century, it was turned into a fortified mansion and occupied by the Bourbons, the Guises, and Cardinal de Pellevé.

9 St-Gervais–St-Protais

Pl St-Gervais 75004. **Map** 9 B3. **Tel** 01 48 87 32 02. Ⓜ Hôtel de Ville. **Open** 5:30am–9pm daily. Organ concerts.

Named after Gervase and Protase, two Roman soldiers martyred by the Emperor Nero, the origins of this magnificent church go back to the 6th century. It boasts the earliest Classical facade in Paris, dating from 1621, with a triple-tiered arrangement of Doric, Ionic, and Corinthian columns.

Behind the facade lies a late Gothic church renowned for its association with religious music. François Couperin (1668–1733) composed his two masses for this church's organ.

Upper Chapel Windows

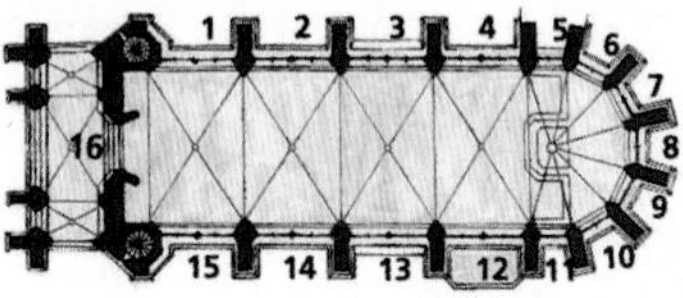

1 2 3 4 5 6 7 8 9 10 11 12 13 14 15 16

- **1** Genesis
- **2** Exodus
- **3** Numbers
- **4** Deuteronomy: Joshua
- **5** Judges
- **6** *left* Isaiah *right* Rod of Jesse
- **7** *left* St John the Evangelist *right* Childhood of Christ
- **8** Christ's Passion
- **9** *left* St John the Baptist *right* Story of Daniel
- **10** Ezekiel
- **11** *left* Jeremiah *right* Tobias
- **12** Judith and Job
- **13** Esther
- **14** Book of Kings
- **15** Story of the Relics
- **16** Rose Window: The Apocalypse

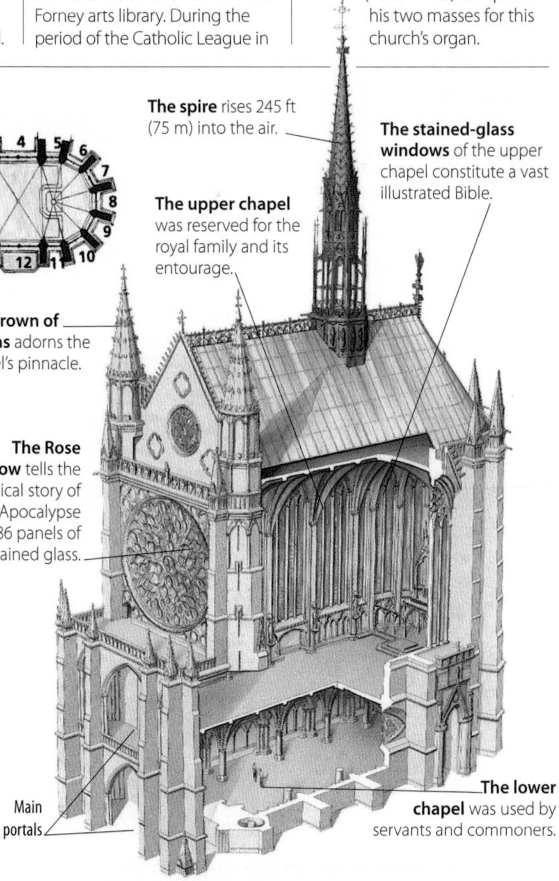

The spire rises 245 ft (75 m) into the air.

The stained-glass windows of the upper chapel constitute a vast illustrated Bible.

The upper chapel was reserved for the royal family and its entourage.

The Crown of Thorns adorns the chapel's pinnacle.

The Rose Window tells the biblical story of the Apocalypse in 86 panels of stained glass.

Main portals

The lower chapel was used by servants and commoners.

❻ Notre-Dame

No other building epitomizes the history of Paris more than Notre-Dame. Built on the site of a Roman temple, the cathedral was commissioned by Bishop de Sully in 1159. The first stone was laid in 1163, marking the start of two centuries of toil by armies of Gothic architects and medieval craftsmen. It has been witness to great events of French history ever since, including the coronations of Henry VI in 1422 and Napoleon Bonaparte in 1804. During the Revolution the building was desecrated and rechristened the Temple of Reason. Extensive renovations (including the addition of the spire and gargoyles) were carried out in the 19th century by architect Viollet-le-Duc.

★ West Facade
The beautifully proportioned west facade is a masterpiece of French Gothic architecture.

★ Galerie des Chimères
The cathedral's legendary gargoyles *(chimères)* gaze menacingly from the cathedral's ledge.

KEY

① **The Kings' Gallery** features 28 stone images of the kings of Judah.

② **West Rose Window** depicts the Virgin in a medallion of rich reds and blues.

③ **387 steps** lead to the top of the south tower, where the famous Emmanuel bell is housed.

④ **The spire** designed by Viollet-le-Duc, soars to a height of 315 ft (96 m).

⑤ **The treasury** houses the cathedral's religious treasures, including ancient manuscripts and reliquaries.

⑥ **The transept** was built at the start of Philippe-Auguste's reign, in the 13th century.

Portal of the Virgin
The Virgin surrounded by saints and kings is a fine composition of 13th-century statues.

For hotels and restaurants in this region see pp554–71 and pp576–603

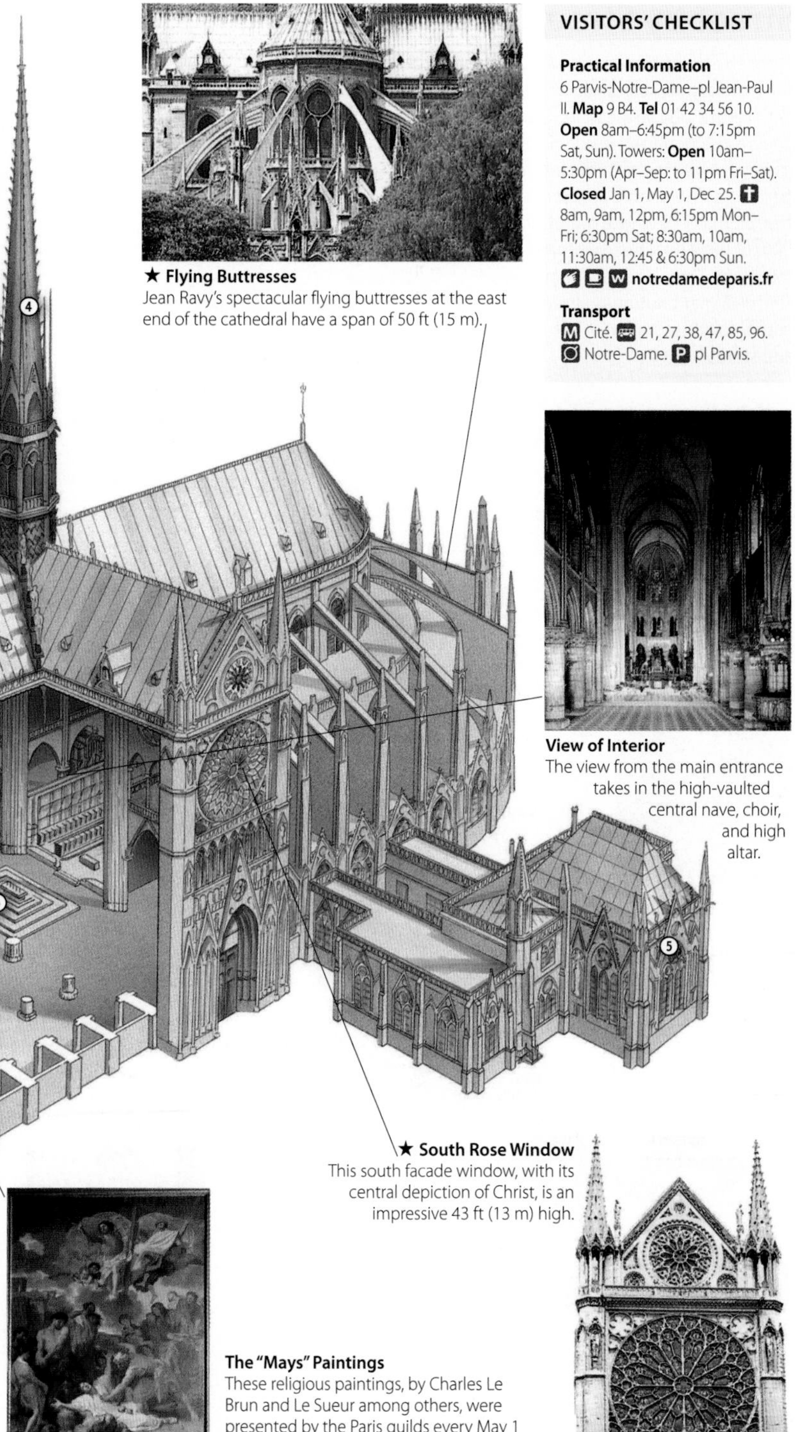

★ Flying Buttresses
Jean Ravy's spectacular flying buttresses at the east end of the cathedral have a span of 50 ft (15 m).

VISITORS' CHECKLIST

Practical Information
6 Parvis-Notre-Dame–pl Jean-Paul II. **Map** 9 B4. **Tel** 01 42 34 56 10.
Open 8am–6:45pm (to 7:15pm Sat, Sun). Towers: **Open** 10am–5:30pm (Apr–Sep: to 11pm Fri–Sat).
Closed Jan 1, May 1, Dec 25. 8am, 9am, 12pm, 6:15pm Mon–Fri; 6:30pm Sat; 8:30am, 10am, 11:30am, 12:45 & 6:30pm Sun.
notredamedeparis.fr

Transport
M Cité. 21, 27, 38, 47, 85, 96. Notre-Dame. P pl Parvis.

View of Interior
The view from the main entrance takes in the high-vaulted central nave, choir, and high altar.

★ South Rose Window
This south facade window, with its central depiction of Christ, is an impressive 43 ft (13 m) high.

The "Mays" Paintings
These religious paintings, by Charles Le Brun and Le Sueur among others, were presented by the Paris guilds every May 1 from 1630 to 1707.

Street by Street: The Marais

Once an area of marshland (*marais* means swamp), the Marais grew steadily in importance from the 14th century, by virtue of its proximity to the Louvre, the preferred residence of Charles V. Its heyday was in the 17th century, when it became a fashionable area for the monied classes, many of whose grand mansions (*hôtels*) have now been restored as museums. Once again fashionable, chic designer boutiques alternate with small restaurants and stores.

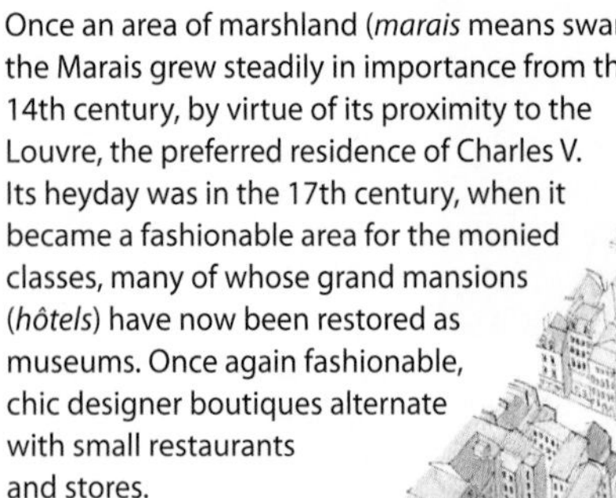

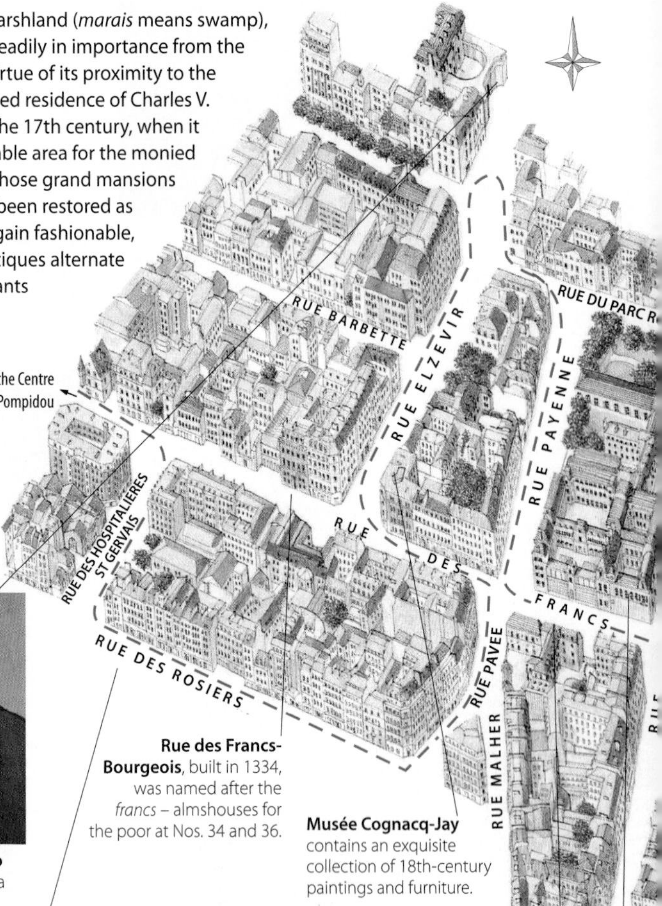

⓱ ★ Musée Picasso
The palatial home of a 17th-century salt-tax collector houses the most extensive collection of Picassos in the world.

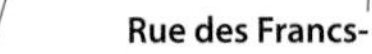

Rue des Francs-Bourgeois, built in 1334, was named after the *francs* – almshouses for the poor at Nos. 34 and 36.

Musée Cognacq-Jay contains an exquisite collection of 18th-century paintings and furniture.

Hôtel de Lamoignon was built in 1584 and houses Paris's historical library.

Rue des Rosiers, heart of the city's oldest Jewish quarter, is lined with 18th-century houses, stores and cafés serving dishes such as hot pastrami and borscht.

⓲ ★ Musée Carnavalet
Occupying two large mansions, this museum covers the history of Paris from Prehistoric and Gallo-Roman times.

Key

— Suggested route

0 meters 100
0 yards 100

For hotels and restaurants in this region see pp554–71 and pp576–603

⑲ ★ Place des Vosges
This enchanting square is an oasis of peace and tranquillity.

Locator Map
See Street Finder maps 9, 10

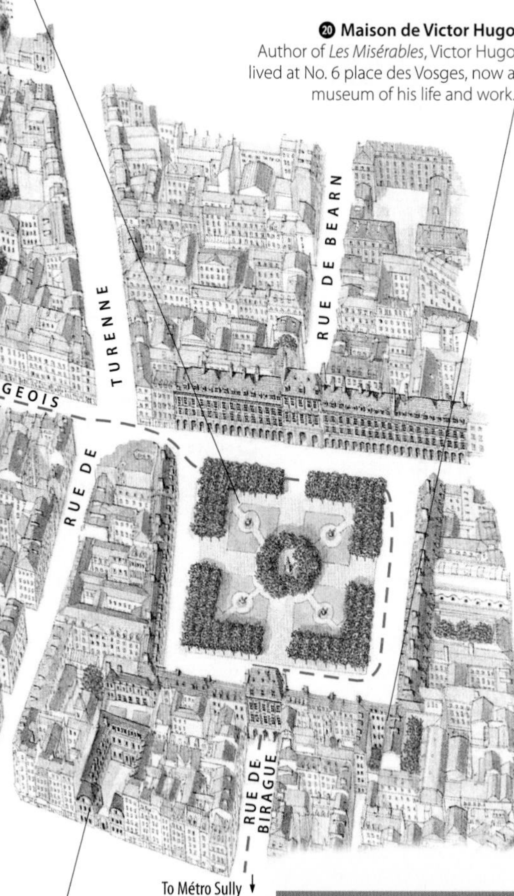

⑳ Maison de Victor Hugo
Author of *Les Misérables*, Victor Hugo lived at No. 6 place des Vosges, now a museum of his life and work.

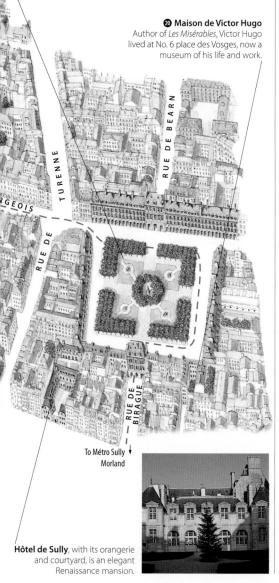

To Métro Sully Morland

Hôtel de Sully, with its orangerie and courtyard, is an elegant Renaissance mansion.

⑩ Hôtel de Ville

Pl de l'Hôtel de Ville, 29 rue de Rivoli 75004. **Map** 9 B3. **Tel** 01 42 76 40 40. Ⓜ Hôtel-de-Ville. **Open** Groups: phone 2 months in advance (01 42 76 54 04). Individuals: days/hours vary, phone to reserve (01 42 76 43 43). **Closed** public hols, and for official functions *(phone to check)*.

The home of the city council is a 19th-century reconstruction of the 17th-century town hall burned down by insurgents of the Paris Commune in 1871. It is a highly ornate example of Third Republic architecture, with elaborate turrets and statues overlooking a pedestrianized square.

The 16th-century Tour St-Jacques

⑪ Tour St-Jacques

Parc de la Tour St-Jacques 75004. **Map** 9 A3. Ⓜ Châtelet. **Open** early Jul–early Sep: 10am–5pm Fri–Sun. Phone to reserve (01 40 26 20 28). Gardens open year-round.

This imposing late Gothic tower, dating from 1523, is all that remains of a church used as a rendezvous by pilgrims setting out for Compostela in Spain. The building was destroyed by revolutionaries in 1797.

Earlier, Blaise Pascal, 17th-century philosopher, mathematician, physicist, and writer, used the tower for barometric experiments. His statue stands at the base of the tower, now used as a meteorological station.

⓬ St-Eustache

2 impasse St-Eustache 75001. **Map** 9 A1. **Tel** 01 42 36 31 05. Ⓜ Les Halles. RER Châtelet-Les-Halles. **Open** 9:30am–7pm Mon–Fri, 10am–7pm Sat–Sun. ✝ 12:30pm Mon–Fri, 6pm Sat, 11am, 6pm Sun. Concerts.
W saint-eustache.org

With its Gothic plan and Renaissance decoration, St-Eustache is one of Paris's most beautiful churches. Its massive interior is modeled on Notre-Dame, with five naves and side and radial chapels. The 105 years (1532–1637) it took to complete the church saw the flowering of the Renaissance style, which is evident in the magnificent arches, pillars, and columns.

St-Eustache has hosted many ceremonial events, including the baptisms of Cardinal Richelieu and Madame de Pompadour, and the funerals of fabulist La Fontaine, Colbert (prime minister to Louis XIV), 17th-century dramatist Molière, and the revolutionary orator Mirabeau. It was here that Berlioz first performed his *Te Deum* in 1855. Today talented choir groups perform regularly, and organ recitals are often held here.

⓭ Forum des Halles

101 Porte Bergere, 75001. **Map** 13 A2. **Tel** 01 44 76 95 56. Ⓜ Les Halles. RER Châtelet-Les-Halles. **Open** 10am–8pm Mon–Sat (cinemas/restaurants 9:30am–11pm). Le Forum des Images: 2 rue du Cinéma. **Tel** 01 44 76 62 00. **Open** 12:30–10pm Tue–Fri, 2–10pm Sat, Sun. **W forumdeshalles.com**
W forumdesimages.fr

Known simply as Les Halles and built amid controversy on the site of a famous fruit and vegetable market, the 750,000 sq ft (7 ha) complex, partly above and partly below ground, has a reputation for being unsafe, particularly at night. Underground levels 2 and 3 are occupied by a varied array of stores, as well as two multi-screen cinemas and a cinema resource center, Le **Forum des Images**. Above ground are gardens, pergolas, and mini-pavilions. Extensive renovations are due to finish at the end of 2016.

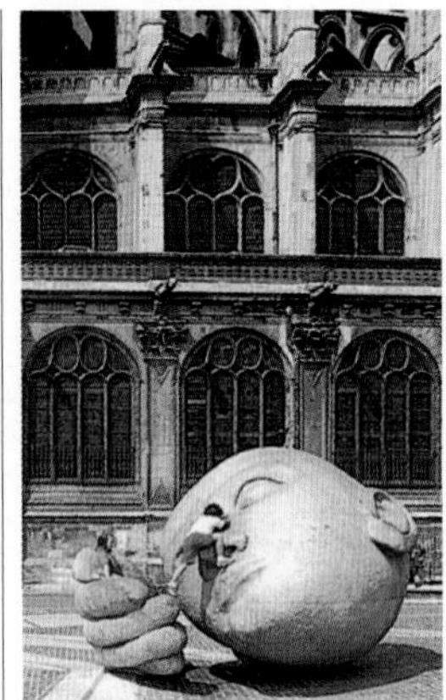

St-Eustache and sculptured head, *l'Ecoute*, by Henri de Miller

⓮ Centre Pompidou

See pp96–7.

⓯ Musée d'Art et d'Histoire du Judaïsme

Hôtel de St-Aignan, 71 rue du Temple 75003. **Map** 13 B2. **Tel** 01 53 01 86 60. Ⓜ Rambuteau. **Open** 11am–6pm Mon–Fri, 10am–6pm Sun. **Closed** Jewish hols. **W mahj.org**

This museum in a Marais mansion, the elegant Hôtel de St-Aignan, brings together collections formerly scattered around the city, and commemorates the culture of French Jewry from medieval times to the present. Visitors learn that there has been a sizable Jewish community in France since Roman times, and some of the world's greatest Jewish scholars – Rashi, Rabenu Tam, the Tosafists – were French. Much exquisite craftsmanship is displayed, with elaborate silverware, Torah covers, fabrics, and items of fine Judaica and religious objects for use both in the synagogue and in the home. There are also photographs, paintings, and cartoons and historical documents, including some on the antisemitic Dreyfus Affair more than a century ago.

⓰ Hôtel de Soubise

60 rue des Francs-Bourgeois 75003. **Map** 9 C2. **Tel** 01 40 27 60 96 (guided tours: 01 40 27 62 18). Ⓜ Rambuteau. **Open** 10am–5:30pm Mon, Wed–Fri; 2–5:30pm Sat & Sun. **Closed** public hols.

This imposing mansion, built from 1705 to 1709 for the Princesse de Rohan, houses the Musée des Archives Historique and the Musée de l'Histoire de France. It boasts a majestic courtyard and 18th-century interior decoration by some of the best-known artists of the time.

Notable items held here include Natoire's *rocaille* work in the Princess's bedchamber and Napoleon's will. Some of the rooms are accessible only to historical researchers, by appointment.

⓱ Musée Picasso

Hôtel Salé, 5 rue de Thorigny, 75003. **Map** 10 D2. **Tel** 01 42 71 25 21. Ⓜ St-Sébastien Froissart. **Closed** until late 2013; telephone for opening hours. groups by appointment only.
W musee-picasso.fr

On the death of the Spanish-born artist Pablo Picasso (1881–1973), who lived most of his life in France, the French State inherited one quarter of his works in lieu of death duties. In 1986, it used them to create the Musée Picasso in the beautifully restored

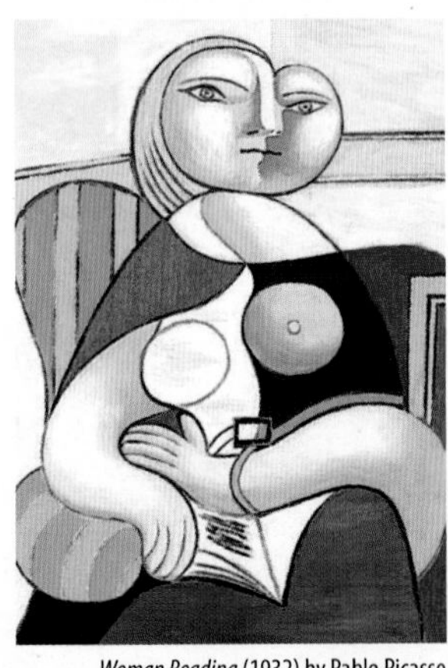

Woman Reading (1932) by Pablo Picasso

Hôtel Salé, one of the loveliest buildings in the Marais. It was built in 1656 for Aubert de Fontenay, collector of the dreaded salt tax (*salé* means "salty").

Comprising over 200 paintings, 158 sculptures, 88 ceramic works, and some 3,000 sketches and engravings, this unique collection shows the enormous range and variety of Picasso's work, including examples from his Blue, Pink, and Cubist periods.

Highlights to look out for are his Blue period *Self-portrait*, painted at age 20; *Still Life with Caned Chair*, which introduced collage to Cubism; the Neo-Classical *Pipes of Pan;* and *The Crucifixion.*

The museum frequently loans canvases for special exhibitions elsewhere, so some works will be on show in other galleries.

A magnificent 17th-century ceiling painting by Charles Le Brun

⓲ Musée Carnavalet

23 rue de Sevigné 75003. **Map** 10 D3. **Tel** 01 44 59 58 58. M St-Paul. **Open** 10am–6pm Tue–Sun (rooms open in rotas: phone to check). **Closed** public hols. telephone for times. **W carnavalet.paris.fr**

Devoted to the history of Paris since Prehistoric times, this vast museum is in two adjoining mansions. They include entire decorated rooms with gilded paneling, furniture, and *objets d'art*; many works of art, such as paintings and sculptures of prominent personalities; and engravings showing Paris being built.

The main building is the Hôtel Carnavalet, built as a town house in 1548 by Nicolas Dupuis. The literary hostess Madame de Sévigné lived here between 1677 and 1696, entertaining the intelligentsia of the day and writing her celebrated *Lettres*. Many of her possessions are in the first-floor exhibit covering the Louis XIV era.

The 17th-century Hôtel le Peletier, opened in 1989, features reconstructions of early 20th-century interiors and artifacts from the Revolution and Napoleonic era. The Orangery houses a department devoted to Prehistory and Gallo-Roman Paris. The collection includes pirogues discovered in 1992, during an archeological dig in the Parc de Bercy, which unearthed a Neolithic village.

⓳ Place des Vosges

75003, 75004. **Map** 10 D3. M Bastille, St-Paul.

This perfectly symmetrical square, laid out in 1605 by Henri IV, is considered among the most beautiful in the world. Thirty-six houses, nine on each side, are built over arcades which today accommodate antiques shops and fashionable cafés. The square has been the scene of many historical events over the centuries, including a three-day tournament in celebration of the marriage of Louis XIII to Anne of Austria in 1615.

⓴ Maison de Victor Hugo

6 pl des Vosges 75004. **Map** 10 D4. **Tel** 01 42 72 10 16. M Bastille. **Open** 10am–6pm Tue–Sun. **Closed** public hols. **Library** **W musee-hugo.paris.fr**

The French poet, dramatist and novelist lived on the second floor of the former Hôtel de Rohan-Guéménée, the largest house on the square, from 1832 to 1848. It was here that he wrote most of *Les Misérables*. On display are reconstructions of some of the rooms in which he lived, complete with his desk, furniture he made, his drawings and mementos from key periods of his life, from his childhood to his exile between 1852 and 1870. There are also regular temporary exhibitions.

Marble bust of Victor Hugo by Auguste Rodin

㉑ Place de la Bastille

75004. **Map** 10 E4. M Bastille.

Nothing remains of the infamous prison stormed by the revolutionary mob on July 14, 1789, the event that sparked the French Revolution.

The 164-ft (50-m) Colonne de Juillet stands in the middle of the traffic-clogged square to honor the victims of the July Revolution of 1830. On the south side of the square (at 120 rue de Lyon) is the 2,700-seat **Opéra National Bastille**, completed in 1989, the bicentennial of the French Revolution.

The "genius of liberty" statue on top of the Colonne de Juillet

⓮ Centre Pompidou

The Pompidou is like a building turned inside out: escalators, lifts, air and water ducts, and even the massive steel struts that make up the building's skeleton are all on the outside. This allowed the architects, Richard Rogers, Renzo Piano, and Gianfranco Franchini, to create a flexible exhibition space. Among the artists featured in the museum are Matisse, Picasso, Miró, and Pollock, representing such schools as Fauvism, Cubism, and Surrealism. The Pompidou also keeps abreast of the Paris art scene with frequently changing temporary exhibitions. Outside in the Piazza, crowds gather to watch street performers.

Key

- Exhibition space
- Nonexhibition space

This riotous jumble of glass and steel, known as Beaubourg, is Paris's top tourist attraction, built in 1977 and drawing over 7 million visitors a year.

Mobile on Two Planes (1955) 20th-century American artist Alexander Calder introduced the mobile as an art form.

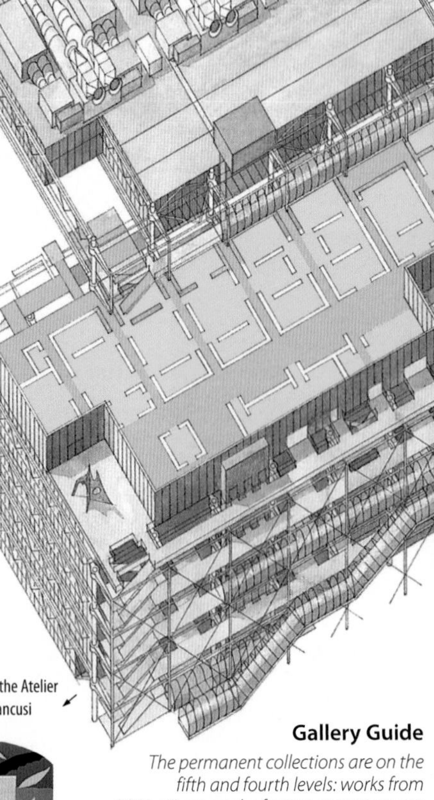

Gallery Guide

The permanent collections are on the fifth and fourth levels: works from 1905–60 are on the former, contemporary art on the latter. The first and sixth levels are for temporary exhibitions; the second and third house a library. The lower levels make up "The Forum," the focal public area, with a performance center, a cinema, shops, and a children's workshop.

Sorrow of the King (1952) This collage was created by Matisse using gouache-painted paper cut-outs.

Basin and Sculpture Terrace

Portrait of the Journalist Sylvia von Harden (1926)
The surgical precision of Otto Dix's style makes this a harsh caricature.

VISITORS' CHECKLIST

Practical Information
Centre d'Art et de Culture Georges Pompidou, pl G Pompidou, 75004.
Map 9 B2. **Tel** 01 44 78 12 33.
Open 11am–10pm Wed–Mon (ticket office closes 8pm); MNAM & temp exhibs: 11am–9pm Wed–Mon; Atelier Brancusi: 2– 6pm Wed–Mon; Library: noon–10pm Mon, Wed–Fri, 11am–10pm w/e.

centrepompidou.fr

Transport
Rambuteau, Châtelet, Hôtel de Ville. 21, 29, 38, 47, 58, 69, 70, 72, 74, 75, 76, 81, 85, 96. RER Châtelet-Les-Halles. P Centre G Pompidou.

Le Duo (1937) Georges Braque, like Picasso, developed the Cubist technique of representing different views of a subject in a single picture.

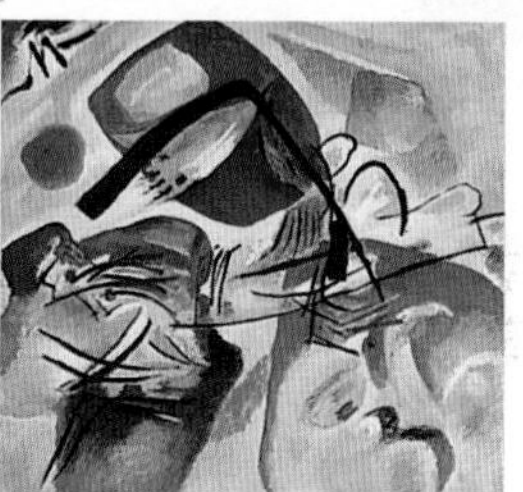

With the Black Arc (1912) The transition to Abstraction, one of the major art forms of the 20th century, can be seen in the works of Wassily Kandinsky.

Stravinsky Fountain
This fountain, which was inaugurated in 1983, is in the place Igor Stravinsky near the Centre Pompidou. It was designed by sculptors Jean Tinguely and Niki de Saint Phalle, both of whom are represented in the Centre Pompidou.

Brancusi Workshop

The Atelier Brancusi, on the rue Rambuteau side of the piazza, is a reconstruction of the workshop of the Romanian-born artist Constantin Brancusi (1876–1957), who lived and worked in Paris. He bequeathed his entire collection of works to the French state on condition that his workshop be rebuilt as it was. The collection includes over 200 sculptures and plinths, 1600 photographs, exhibited in rotation, and tools Brancusi used to create his works. Also featured are some of his more personal items such as documents, pieces of furniture, and his book collection.

Interior of the Brancusi workshop, designed by Renzo Piano

TUILERIES AND OPERA

The 19th-century grandeur of Baron Haussmann's *grands boulevards* offsets the bustle of bankers, theater-goers, sightseers, and shoppers who frequent the area around the Opéra. A profusion of shops and department stores, ranging from the exclusively expensive to the popular, draws the crowds. Much of the area's older character is found in the early 19th-century shopping arcades, with elaborate steel and glass roofs. They are known as *galeries* or *passages*, and were restored to their former glory in the 1970s. Galerie Vivienne, which is the smartest, has an elaborate, patterned mosaic floor. The passage des Panoramas, passage Verdeau, and tiny passage des Princes are more old-style Parisian. These streets abound with curious stores of all kinds, from mouthwatering food stores, to antique book shops, and stamp collectors.

The Tuileries area lies between the Opéra and the river, bounded by the vast place de la Concorde in the west and the Louvre to the east. The Louvre palace combines one of the world's greatest art collections with I. M. Pei's avant-garde glass pyramid. Elegant squares and formal gardens give the area its special character. Monuments to monarchy and the arts coexist with modern luxury at its most ostentatious. Place Vendôme, home to exquisite jewelry shops and the luxurious Ritz Hotel, is a heady mix of the wealthy and the chic. Parallel to the Jardin des Tuileries are two of Paris's foremost shopping streets, the rue de Rivoli and rue St-Honoré, full of expensive boutiques, bookstores, and deluxe hotels.

Sights at a Glance

Museums and Galleries

3 Grévin
6 Galerie Nationale du Jeu de Paume
8 Musée de l'Orangerie
11 Musée des Arts Décoratifs
14 *Musée du Louvre pp104–7*

Squares, Parks, and Gardens

9 Jardin des Tuileries
5 Place Vendôme
7 Place de la Concorde

Monuments

12 Arc de Triomphe du Carrousel

Historic Buildings

2 Opéra National de Paris Garnier
13 Palais Royal

Churches

1 La Madeleine
10 St-Roch

Shops

4 Les Passages

See also Street Finder pp162–3 and pp166–8

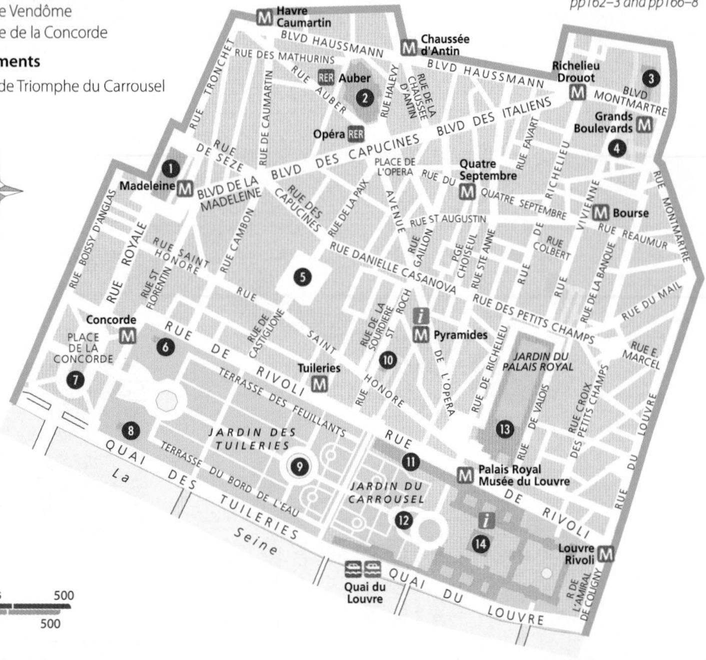

◀ Ceiling in the Grand Foyer at the Opéra National de Paris Garnier

For map symbols *see back flap*

Street by Street: Opéra Quarter

It has been said that the whole world will pass you by if you sit for long enough at the Café de la Paix (opposite the Opéra National Garnier). During the day, the area is a center of commerce, tourism, and shopping, with mammoth department stores lining the *grands boulevards*. In the evening, the clubs and theaters attract a totally different crowd, and the cafés along boulevard des Capucines throb with life.

2 ★ Opéra National de Paris Garnier
Dating from 1875, the grandiose opera house has come to symbolize the opulence of the Second Empire.

Statue by Gumery on the Opéra

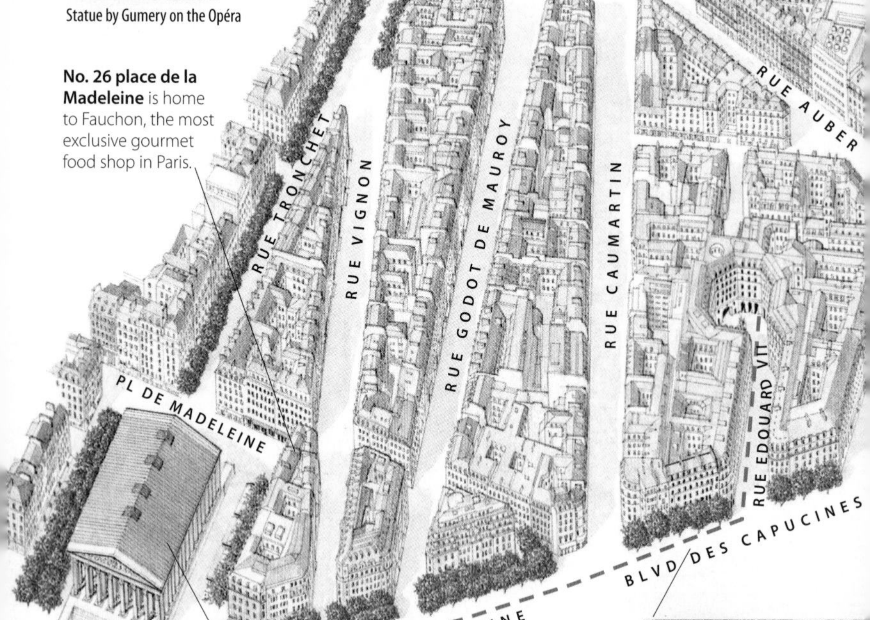

No. 26 place de la Madeleine is home to Fauchon, the most exclusive gourmet food shop in Paris.

RUE TRONCHET
RUE VIGNON
RUE GODOT DE MAUROY
RUE CAUMARTIN
RUE AUBER
RUE EDOUARD VII
PL DE MADELEINE
BLVD DES CAPUCINES
BLVD DE LA MADELEINE
M

Métro Madeleine

1 ★ La Madeleine
The original model of the Madeleine can be seen at the Musée Carnavalet *(see p95)*.

Boulevard des Capucines
(No. 14) is where the Lumière brothers staged the first public screening of a movie on December 28, 1895.

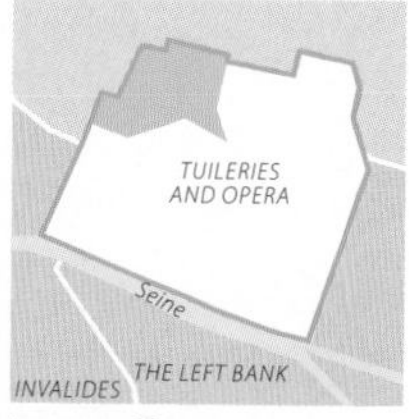

Locator Map
See Street Finder maps 4, 7, 8

Bibliothèque and Musée de l'Opéra contains the scores of every ballet and opera performed at the Opéra, and memorabilia from Nijinsky's dancing shoes to Pavlova's tiara.

Place de l'Opéra was designed by Baron Haussmann and is one of Paris's busiest intersections.

Key

▬ Suggested route

0 meters 100

0 yards 100

Marochetti's *Mary Magdalene Ascending to Heaven* in La Madeleine

❶ La Madeleine

Pl de la Madeleine 75008. **Map** 3 C5. **Tel** 01 44 51 69 00. Ⓜ Madeleine. **Open** 9:30am–7pm daily. ✝ 12:30pm Mon–Sat, 6:30pm Tue–Fri, 6pm Sat, 9:30am, 11am, 7pm Sun. Concerts. **W eglise-lamadeleine.com**

Modeled after a Greek temple, La Madeleine was begun in 1764 but not consecrated until 1845. Before that, there were proposals to turn it into a stock exchange, a bank, or a theater.

Corinthian columns encircle the building, supporting a sculptured frieze. Three ceiling domes crown the inside, which is richly decorated with sculptures, rose marble, and gilt.

❷ Opéra National de Paris Garnier

Pl de l'Opéra 75009. **Map** 4 DF. **Tel** 0892 89 90 90. Ⓜ Opéra. **Open** 10am–4:30pm daily (until 5:30pm mid-Jul–Aug and 1pm on matinée days). **Closed** public hols. **W operadeparis.fr**

Sometimes compared to a giant wedding cake, this lavish building was designed by Charles Garnier for Napoleon III in 1862. The Prussian War and the 1871 uprising delayed the opening until 1875.

The interior is famous for its Grand Staircase made of white Carrara marble, topped by a huge chandelier, as well as for its auditorium bedecked in red velvet and gold, with a false ceiling painted by Chagall in 1964. Restored to its full glory, it is primarily used for dance, but shares operatic productions with the Opéra Bastille *(see p157)*.

❸ Grévin

10 bd Montmartre 75009. **Map** 4 F4. **Tel** 01 47 70 85 05. Ⓜ Grands Boulevards. **Open** 10am–6:30pm Mon–Fri (7pm Sat, Sun & school hols). **W grevin.com**

Sign outside the Grévin

Founded in 1882, this is a Paris landmark, on a par with Madame Tussauds. The historical scenes include Louis XIV at Versailles and the arrest of Louis XVI. Notable figures from the worlds of art, politics, film, and sport are also on display.

On the first floor is a holography museum devoted to optical tricks. The museum also houses a 320-seat theater.

❹ Les Passages

75002. **Map** 4 F5. Ⓜ Bourse.

The early 19th-century glass-roofed shopping arcades (known as *galeries* or *passages*) are concentrated between boulevard Montmartre and rue St-Marc. They house an eclectic mixture of small stores selling anything from designer jewelry to rare books and art supplies. One of the most charming is the Galerie Vivienne (off the rue Vivienne or the rue des Petits Champs) with its mosaic floor and excellent tearoom.

❺ Place Vendôme

75001. **Map** 8 D1. Ⓜ Tuileries.

Perhaps the best example of 18th-century elegance in the city, the architect Jules Hardouin-Mansart's royal square was begun in 1698. The original plan was to house academies and embassies behind its arcaded facades, but instead bankers moved in and created sumptuous mansions for themselves. The square's most famous residents include Frédéric Chopin, who died here in 1849 at No. 12, and César Ritz, who established his famous hotel at No. 15 in 1898.

Monet's *Waterlilies (Nymphéas)* on display in the Musée de l'Orangerie

❻ Galerie Nationale du Jeu de Paume

Jardin des Tuileries, 1 place de la Concorde 75008. **Map** 7 C1. **Tel** 01 47 03 12 50. Ⓜ Concorde. **Open** 11am–9pm Tue, 11am–7pm Wed–Sun. **Closed** Jan 1, May 1, Dec 25. **jeudepaume.org**

The Jeu de Paume – literally "game of the palm" – was built as two royal tennis courts by Napoleon III in 1851 on the north side of the Tuileries gardens. The courts were later converted into an art gallery and exhibition space. The Jeu de Paume has rotating exhibitions of contemporary art and houses the Centre National de la Photographie. Its sister site is the Hôtel de Sully *(see p93)*.

❼ Place de la Concorde

75008. **Map** 7 C1. Ⓜ Concorde.

One of Europe's most magnificent and historic squares, covering over 20 acres (8 ha), the place de la Concorde was a swamp until the mid-18th century. It became the *place* in 1775 when royal architect Jacques-Ange Gabriel was asked by the Louis XV to design a suitable setting for an equestrian statue of himself.

The monument, which lasted here less than 20 years, was replaced by the guillotine (the Black Widow, as it came to be known), and the square was renamed place de la Révolution. On January 21, 1793 Louis XVI was beheaded, followed by over 1,300 other victims including Marie Antoinette, Madame du Barry, Charlotte Corday (Marat's assassin), and revolutionary leaders Danton and Robespierre.

The blood-soaked square was optimistically renamed place de la Concorde after the Reign of Terror finally came to an end in 1794. A few decades later the 3,200-year-old Luxor obelisk was presented to King Louis-Philippe as a gift from the viceroy of Egypt (who also donated Cleopatra's Needle in London).

Flanking the rue Royale on the north side of the square are two of Gabriel's Neo-Classical mansions, the Hôtel de la Marine and the exclusive Hôtel Crillon.

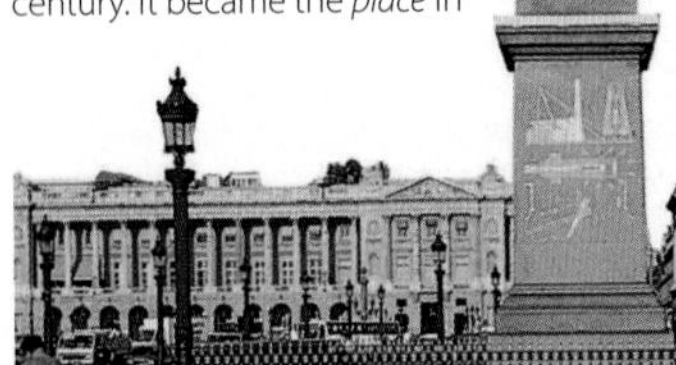

The 3,200-year-old obelisk from Luxor

❽ Musée de l'Orangerie

Jardin des Tuileries, place de la Concorde 75001. **Map** 7 C1. **Tel** 01 44 77 80 07. Ⓜ Concorde. **Open** 9am–6pm Wed–Mon. **Closed** May 1, Dec 25. by appt. **musee-orangerie.fr**

Paintings from Claude Monet's crowning work, representing part of his waterlily series, fill the two oval upper floor rooms. Known as the *Nymphéas*, most of the canvases were painted between 1899 and 1921.

This superb work is complemented by the Walter-Guillaume collection, including 27 Renoirs, notably *Young Girls at the Piano*, works by Soutine, and 14 Cézannes, including *The Red Rock*. Picasso is represented by works including *The Female Bathers*, and Rousseau by 9 paintings, notably *The Wedding*. Other works are by Matisse, Derain, Utrillo, and Modigliani.

❾ Jardin des Tuileries

75001. **Map** 8 D1. Ⓜ Tuileries, Concorde. **Open** Apr–May: 7am–9pm; Jun–Aug: 7am–11pm; Sep: 7am–9pm; Oct–Mar: 7:30am–7:30pm.

These Neo-Classical gardens once belonged to the Palais des Tuileries, which the Communards razed to the ground in 1871. They were laid out in the 17th century by André Le Nôtre, who created the broad central avenue and geometric topiary. Ongoing restoration has created a new garden with lime and chestnut trees, and modern sculptures.

⑩ St-Roch

296 rue St-Honoré 75001. **Map** 8 E1. **Tel** 01 42 44 13 20. Ⓜ Tuileries, Pyramides. **Open** 8:30am–7pm daily. **Closed** non- religious public hols. ✝ 12:30pm, 6:30pm Mon, Wed–Fri; 6:30pm Sat; 11am, 12:15pm, 6:30pm Sun. Concerts.

This huge church was designed by Jacques Lemercier, architect of the Louvre, and its foundation stone was laid by Louis XIV in 1653. It is a treasure house of religious art, much of it from now-vanished churches and monasteries, and contains the tombs of the playwright Pierre Corneille, the royal gardener André Le Nôtre, and the philosopher Denis Diderot.

Vien's *St Denis Preaching to the Gauls* (1767) in St-Roch

⑪ Musée des Arts Décoratifs

Palais du Louvre, 107–111 rue de Rivoli 75001. **Map** 8 E2. **Tel** 01 44 55 57 50. Ⓜ Palais Royal, Tuileries. **Open** 11am–6pm Tue–Sun (until 9pm Thu). Library: **Tel** 01 44 55 59 36. **Open** 1–7pm Mon, 10am–7pm Tue, 10am–6pm Wed–Fri. **Closed** public hols.
W **lesartsdecoratifs.fr**

Occupying the northwest wing of the Palais du Louvre (along with the Musée de la Publicité and the Musée de la Mode et du Textile), this museum offers an eclectic mix of decorative art and domestic design from the Middle Ages to the present day. The Art Nouveau and Art Deco rooms include a reconstruction of the home of couturier Jeanne Lanvin. Other floors show Louis XIV, XV, and XVI styles of decoration and furniture. Contemporary designers are also represented. The restaurant has breathtaking views over the Tuileries gardens.

The Buren Columns in the main courtyard of the Palais Royal

⑫ Arc de Triomphe du Carrousel

Pl du Carrousel 75001. **Map** 8 E2. Ⓜ Palais Royal.

This rose-marble arch was built by Napoleon to celebrate various military triumphs, notably the Battle of Austerlitz in 1805. The crowning statues, added in 1828, are copies of the famous Horses of St Mark's, which Napoleon had stolen from Venice and was subsequently forced to return after his defeat at Waterloo in 1815.

⑬ Palais Royal

Pl du Palais Royal 75001. Gardens: 6 rue de Montpensier. **Map** 8 E1. **Tel** 01 47 03 92 16. Ⓜ Palais Royal. Gardens and court: **Open** Apr–May: 7am–10:15pm; Jun–Aug: 7am–11pm; Sep: 7am–9:30pm; Oct–Mar: 7am–8:30pm. **W** **palais-royal.monuments-nationaux.fr**

This former royal palace, built by Cardinal Richelieu in the early 17th century, passed to the Crown on his death and became the childhood home of Louis XIV. Under the 18th-century royal dukes of Orléans, it became the epicenter of brilliant gatherings, interspersed with periods of gambling and debauchery. It was from here that the clarion call to revolution roused the mobs to storm the Bastille on July, 14 1789.

Today the south section of the building houses the Councils of State and the Ministry of Culture. Just to the west is the Comédie Française, established by Louis XIV in 1680. At the back of the palace are luxury shops where artists such as Colette and Cocteau once lived.

The Arc de Triomphe du Carrousel crowned by Victory riding a chariot

⑭ Musée du Louvre

The Musée du Louvre, containing one of the most important art collections in the world, has a history dating back to medieval times. First built as a fortress in 1190 by King Philippe-Auguste to protect Paris against Viking raids, it lost its keep in the reign of François I, who replaced it with a Renaissance-style building. Thereafter, four centuries of kings and emperors improved and enlarged it. Visitors should request a schedule of room closures from the information point as not all rooms are open on any given day.

The Louvre's east facade, facing St-Germain l'Auxerrois

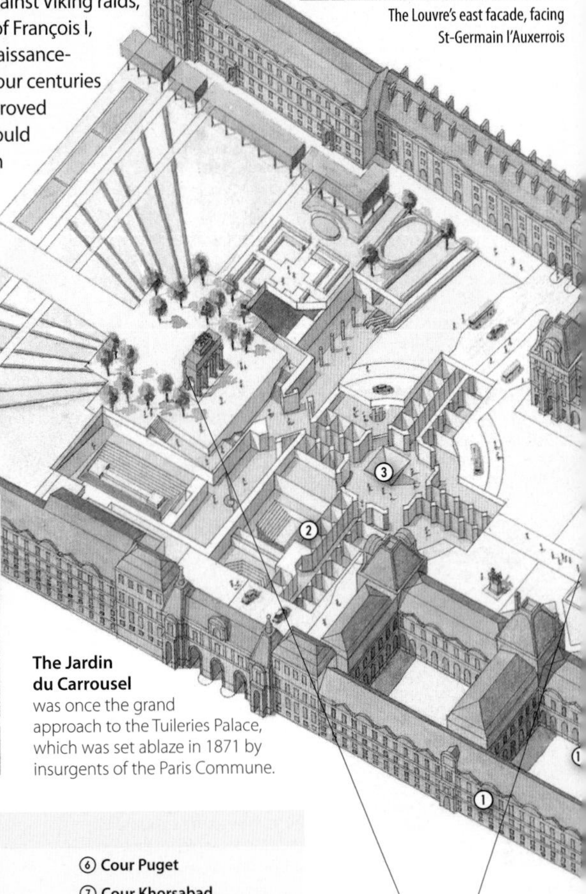

The Jardin du Carrousel was once the grand approach to the Tuileries Palace, which was set ablaze in 1871 by insurgents of the Paris Commune.

Pyramid entrance

★ Arc de Triomphe du Carrousel
This triumphal arch was built to celebrate Napoleon's military victories in 1805.

KEY

① **Denon Wing**

② **The Carrousel du Louvre,** an underground visitors' complex (1993), with galleries, gift shops, restrooms, parking and an information desk, lies beneath the Arc de Triomphe du Carrousel.

③ **The inverted glass pyramid** brings light to the subterranean complex, echoing the museum's main entrance in the Cour Napoléon.

④ **Cour Marly** is the glass-roofed courtyard that now houses the Marly Horses *(see p107)*.

⑤ **Richelieu Wing**

⑥ **Cour Puget**

⑦ **Cour Khorsabad**

⑧ **Cour Carrée**

⑨ **The Salle des Caryatides** is named after the four monumental statues created by Jean Goujon in 1550 to support the upper gallery. Built for Henri II, it is the oldest room in the palace.

⑩ **Sully Wing**

⑪ **Cour Napoléon**

⑫ **Hall Napoléon** is situated under the pyramid.

⑬ **Cour Visconti** houses Islamic art: over 3,000 objects from the 7th to the 19th centuries.

The Glass Pyramid

Plans for the modernization and expansion of the Louvre were first conceived in 1981. They included the transfer of the Ministry of Finance from the Richelieu wing of the Louvre to new offices elsewhere, as well as a new main entrance designed by architect I. M. Pei in 1989. Made of metal and glass, the pyramid enables the visitor to see the buildings around the palace, while allowing light down into the underground visitors' reception area.

VISITORS' CHECKLIST

Practical Information

Map 12 E2. P Carrousel du Louvre (entrance via av du Général Lemonnier); pl du Louvre, rue St-Honoré.

Open 9am–5:45pm Mon, Thu, Sat & Sun, 9am–9:45pm Wed & Fri. **Closed** Jan 1, May 1, Dec 25. (free 1st Sun of each month and for under 18s). Main switchboard 01 40 20 50 50, reception 01 40 20 53 17. **louvre.fr**

Advance bookings:
ticketweb.com
fnac.com

Transport

M Palais Royal, Musée du Louvre. 21, 24, 27, 39, 48, 68, 69, 72, 81, 95. RER Châtelet-Les-Halles. Louvre.

The Louvre of Charles V
In about 1360, Charles V transformed Philippe-Auguste's old fortress, with its distinctive tower and keep, into a royal residence.

★ Perrault's Colonnade
The east facade, with its majestic rows of columns, was built by Claude Perrault, who worked on the Louvre with Louis Le Vau in the mid-17th century.

Building the Louvre

Over many centuries the Louvre was enlarged by a succession of French rulers, shown below with their dates.

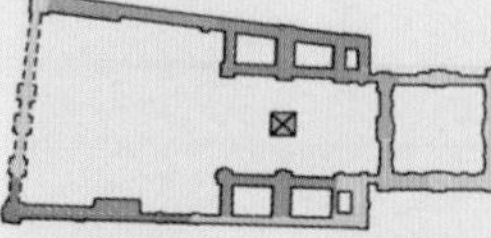

Major Alterations

- Reign of François I (1515–47)
- Catherine de' Medici (about 1560)
- Reign of Henri IV (1589–1610)
- Reign of Louis XIII (1610–43)
- Reign of Louis XIV (1643–1715)
- Reign of Napoleon I (1804–15)
- Reign of Napoleon III (1852–70)
- I. M. Pei (1989) (architect)

★ Medieval Moats
The base of the twin towers and the drawbridge support of Philippe-Auguste's fortress can be seen in the excavated area.

Exploring the Louvre's Collection

Owing to the vast size of the Louvre's collection, it is useful to set a few viewing priorities before starting. The collection of European paintings (1400–1848) is comprehensive, with over half the works by French artists. The extensively renovated departments of Oriental, Egyptian, Greek, Etruscan, and Roman antiquities feature numerous new acquisitions and rare treasures. The varied display of *objets d'art* includes furniture and jewelry.

The Raft of the Medusa (1819) by Théodore Géricault

European Painting: 1200 to 1848

Painting from northern Europe (Flemish, Dutch, German, and English) is well covered. One of the earliest Flemish works is Jan van Eyck's *Madonna of the Chancellor Rolin* (about 1435), showing the Chancellor of Burgundy kneeling in prayer before the Virgin and Child. Hieronymus Bosch's *Ship of Fools* (1500) is a satirical account of the futility of human existence. In the fine Dutch collection, Rembrandt's *Self-portrait*, his *Disciples at Emmaus* (1648), and *Bathsheba* (1654) are examples of the artist's genius.

Mona Lisa (about 1504) by Leonardo da Vinci

The three major German painters of the 15th and 16th centuries are represented by important works. There is a youthful *Self-portrait* (1493) by Albrecht Dürer, a *Venus* (1529) by Lucas Cranach, and a portrait of the great humanist scholar Erasmus by Hans Holbein.

The impressive collection of Italian paintings is arranged in chronological order from 1200 to 1800. The father figures of the early Renaissance, Cimabue and Giotto, are here, as is Fra Angelico, with his *Coronation of the Virgin* (1430–32), and Raphaël, with his stately portrait of Count Baldassare Castiglione (1514–15). Several paintings by Leonardo da Vinci are on display, for instance the *Virgin with the Infant Jesus and St Anne*, which is as enchanting as his *Mona Lisa*.

The Louvre's fine collection of French painting ranges from the 14th century to 1848. Paintings after this date are housed in the Musée d'Orsay *(see pp124–5)*. Outstanding is Jean Fouquet's portrait of Charles VII (1450–55). The great 18th-century painter of melancholy, J. A. Watteau, is represented, as is J. H. Fragonard, master of the Rococo, whose delightfully frivolous subjects are evident in *The Bathers* from 1770.

European Sculpture: 1100 to 1848

Early Flemish and German sculpture in the collection has many masterpieces such as Tilman Riemenschneider's *Virgin of the Annunciation* from the end of the 15th century, and a life-size nude figure of the penitent Mary Magdalen by Gregor Erhart (early 16th century). An important work of Flemish sculpture is Adrian de Vries's long-limbed *Mercury and Psyche* from 1593, which was originally made for the court of Rudolph II in Prague.

The French section opens with early Romanesque works, such as the figure of Christ by a 12th-century Burgundian sculptor, and a head of St. Peter. With its eight black-hooded mourners, the late 15th-century tomb of Philippe Pot (a high-ranking official in Burgundy) is one of the more unusual pieces. Diane de Poitiers, Henri II's mistress, had a large figure of her namesake Diana, goddess of the hunt, installed in the courtyard of her castle west of Paris. It is now in the Louvre. The works of

The tomb of Philippe Pot (late 15th century) by Antoine le Moiturier

The celebrated *Marly Horses* (1745) by Guillaume Coustou

French sculptor Pierre Puget (1620–94) have been assembled in the Cour Puget. They include a figure of Milo of Crotona, the Greek athlete who got his hands caught in the cleft of a tree stump and was eaten by a lion. The wild horses of Marly now stand in the Cour Marly, surrounded by other masterpieces of French sculpture, including Jean-Antoine Houdon's early 19th-century busts of famous men such as Diderot and Voltaire.

The collection of Italian sculpture includes such splendid exhibits as Michelangelo's *Slaves* and Benvenuto Cellini's Fontainebleau *Nymph*.

Oriental, Egyptian, Greek, Etruscan, and Roman Antiquities

A substantial overhaul of the Louvre has boosted its collection of antiquities, which range from the Neolithic period to the fall of the Roman Empire. Among the exhibits are Greek and Roman glassware dating from the 6th century BC. Important works of Mesopotamian art include one of the world's oldest legal documents, a basalt block bearing the code of the Babylonian King Hammurabi, dating from about 1700 BC.

The warlike Assyrians are represented by delicate carvings and a spectacular reconstruction of part of Sargon II's (722–705 BC) palace with its winged bulls. A fine example of Persian art is the enameled brickwork depicting the king of Persia's personal guard of archers (5th century BC). Most Egyptian art was made for the dead, who were provided with the things they would need for the afterlife. Examples include the lifelike funeral portraits, such as the *Squatting Scribe* and several sculptures of married couples.

The departments of Greek, Roman, and Etruscan antiquities contain a vast array of fragments, among them some exceptional pieces. There is a geometric head from the Cyclades (2700 BC) and an elegant swan-necked bowl hammered out of a gold sheet (2500 BC). The two most famous Greek marble statues, the *Winged Victory of Samothrace* and the *Venus de Milo*, both belong to the Hellenistic period (late 3rd to 2nd century BC), when more natural-looking human forms were produced.

Venus de Milo (Greece, late 3rd–early 2nd century BC)

The undisputed star of the Etruscan collection is the terracotta sarcophagus of a married couple who look as though they are attending an eternal banquet, while the highlight of the Roman section is a 2nd-century bronze head of the Emperor Hadrian.

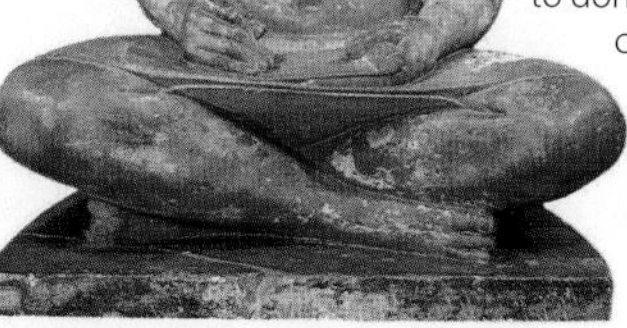

Squatting Scribe (about 2500 BC), a life-like Egyptian funeral sculpture

Objets d'Art

The catch-all term *objets d'art* (art objects) covers a vast range of items: jewelry, furniture, clocks, watches, sundials, tapestries, miniatures, silver and glassware, cutlery, Byzantine and Parisian carved ivory, Limoges enamels, porcelain, French and Italian stoneware, rugs, snuffboxes, scientific instruments, and armor. The Louvre has well over 8,000 pieces, from many ages and regions.

Many of these precious objects came from the Abbey of St-Denis, where the kings of France were crowned. The treasures include a serpentine stone plate from the 1st century AD with a 9th-century border of gold and precious stones, a porphyry vase which Suger, Abbot of St-Denis, had mounted in gold in the shape of an eagle, and the golden sceptre made for King Charles V in about 1380.

The French crown jewels include the coronation crowns of Louis XV and Napoleon, scepters, swords, and other accessories of the coronation ceremonies. On view also is the Regent, one of the purest diamonds in the world, which Louis XV wore at his coronation in 1722.

One whole room is taken up with a series of tapestries called the *Hunts of Maximilian,* originally executed for Emperor Charles V in 1530. The large collection of French furniture ranges from the 16th to the 19th centuries and is assembled by period, or in rooms devoted to donations by distinguished collectors. On display are pieces by exceptionally prominent furniture-makers such as André-Charles Boulle, cabinet-maker to Louis XIV, who worked at the Louvre in the late 17th to mid-18th centuries.

CHAMPS-ELYSEES AND INVALIDES

The River Seine bisects this area, much of which is built on a monumental scale from the imposing 18th-century buildings of Les Invalides to the Art Nouveau avenues surrounding the Eiffel Tower. Two of Paris's grandest avenues dominate the neighborhood to the north of the Seine: the Champs-Elysées has many smart hotels and shops but today is more downmarket; while the more chic rue du Faubourg St-Honoré has the heavily guarded Palais de l'Elysée. The village of Chaillot was absorbed into the city in the 19th century, and many of its opulent Second Empire mansions are now embassies or company headquarters. Streets around the place du Trocadéro and Palais de Chaillot are packed full of museums and elegant cafés.

Sights at a Glance

Historic Buildings and Streets

2 Avenue des Champs-Elysées
3 Palais de l'Elysée
14 Les Egouts
17 No. 29 Avenue Rapp
18 Champ-de-Mars
19 Ecole Militaire
21 Hôtel des Invalides
10 Cité de l'Architecture et du Patrimoine
11 Musée Dapper
13 Palais de Chaillot

Museums and Galleries

4 Petit Palais
5 Grand Palais
7 Musée d'Art Moderne de la Ville de Paris
8 Musée Galliera
9 Musée National des Arts Asiatiques Guimet
15 Musée du Quai Branly
22 Musée de l'Armée
25 Musée Rodin
27 Musée Maillol

Churches

23 St-Louis-des-Invalides
24 Dôme Church
26 Sainte-Clotilde

Monuments and Fountains

1 Arc de Triomphe
16 *Eiffel Tower p117*

Modern Architecture

20 UNESCO

Gardens

12 Jardins du Trocadéro

Bridges

6 Pont Alexandre III

See also Street Finder pp158–73

◀ View of Champs-Elysées from the Arc de Triomphe

For map symbols *see back flap*

Street by Street: Champs-Elysées

The formal gardens that line the Champs-Elysées from the place de la Concorde to the Rond-Point have changed little since they were laid out by the architect Jacques Hittorff in 1838. The gardens were used as the setting for the World Fair of 1855, which included the Palais de l'Industrie, Paris's response to London's Crystal Palace. The Palais was later replaced by the Grand Palais and the Petit Palais, which was created as a showpiece of the Third Republic for the Universal Exhibition of 1900. They sit on either side of an impressive vista that stretches from the place Clémenceau across the elegant curve of the Pont Alexandre III, with its four strong anchoring columns, to the Invalides.

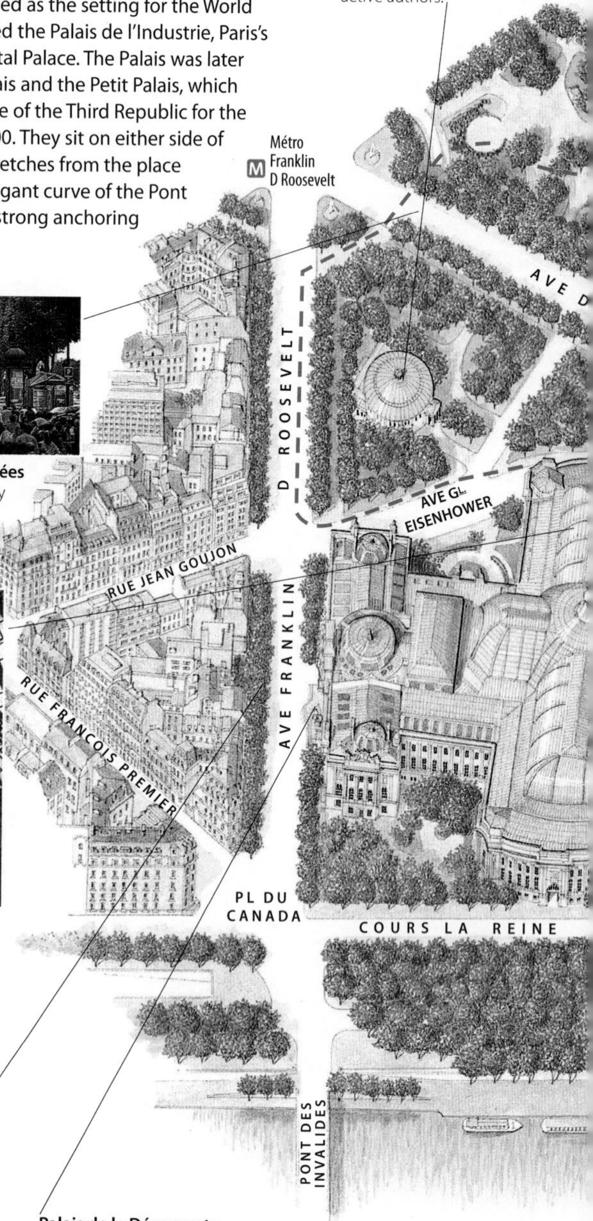

Théâtre du Rond Point, an original Champs-Elysées building, presents the work of active authors.

Métro Franklin D Roosevelt

❷ ★ Avenue des Champs-Elysées
This was the setting for the victory parades following the two World Wars.

❺ ★ Grand Palais
Designed by Charles Girault, and built between 1897 and 1900, this elaborate exhibition hall with its splendid glass dome is frequently used for major exhibitions.

The Lasserre restaurant is decorated in the style of a luxury ocean liner dating from the 1930s.

Palais de la Découverte, a museum of scientific discovery, was originally opened in the Grand Palais for the World Fair of 1937.

0 meters 100
0 yards 100

Key
— Suggested route

The Jardins des Champs-Elysées, with their fountains, flowerbeds, and pleasure pavilions, have been a popular spot since the 19th century.

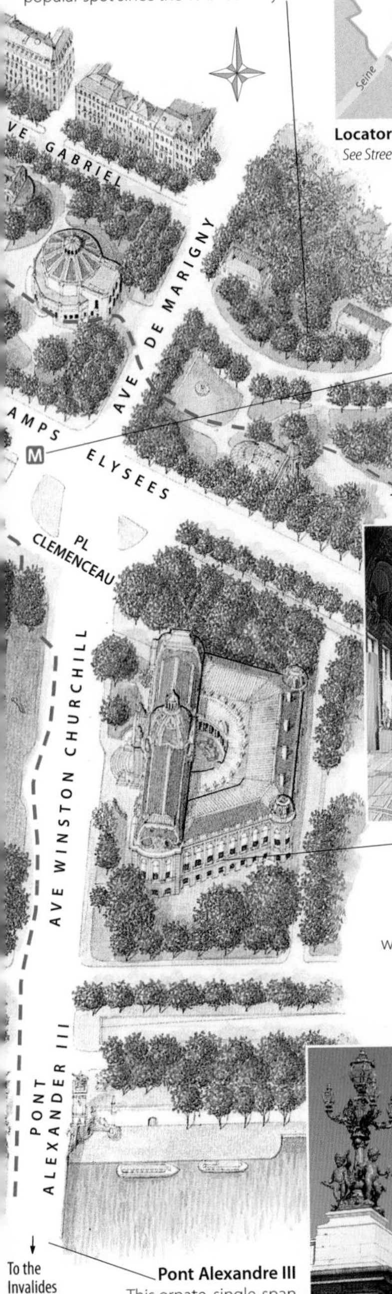

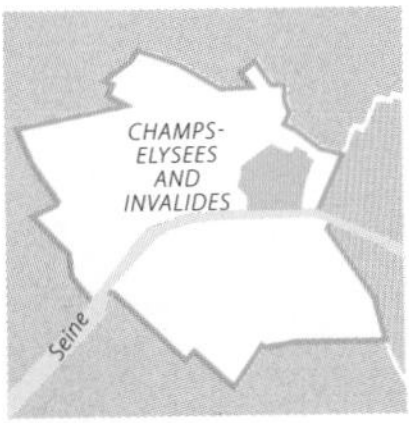

Locator Map
See Street Finder maps 2, 3, 6, 7

Métro Champs-Elysées-Clémenceau

To place de la Concorde

4 ★ Petit Palais
The art collections of the city of Paris are housed here. They contain 19th-century works from objets d'art to paintings by the Barbizon School.

To the Invalides

Pont Alexandre III
This ornate, single-span structure symbolizes the optimism of the Belle Epoque at the turn of the 20th century.

The east facade of the Arc de Triomphe

1 Arc de Triomphe

Place Charles de Gaulle, 75008. **Map** 2 D4. Ⓜ Charles de Gaulle-Etoile. **Tel** 01 55 37 73 77. Museum: **Open** Apr–Sep: 10am–11pm daily; Oct–Mar: 10am–10.30pm daily (last adm 30 mins earlier); May 8, Jul 14, Nov 11: am only (last adm 45 mins before closing). **Closed** Jan 1, May 1, Dec 25.
W arc-de-triomphe.monuments-nationaux.fr

After his greatest victory, the Battle of Austerlitz in 1805, Napoleon promised his men they would "go home beneath triumphal arches." The first stone of the world's most famous triumphal arch was laid in 1806, but disruptions to architect Jean Chalgrin's plans and the demise of Napoleonic power delayed completion. Standing 164 ft (50 m) high, the Arc is encrusted with reliefs, shields, and sculptures, and offers splendid views.

On November 11, 1920, the body of the Unknown Soldier was placed beneath the arch to commemorate the dead of World War I. The tomb's eternal flame is lit every evening.

High relief by J. P. Corot, celebrating the Triumph of Napoleon

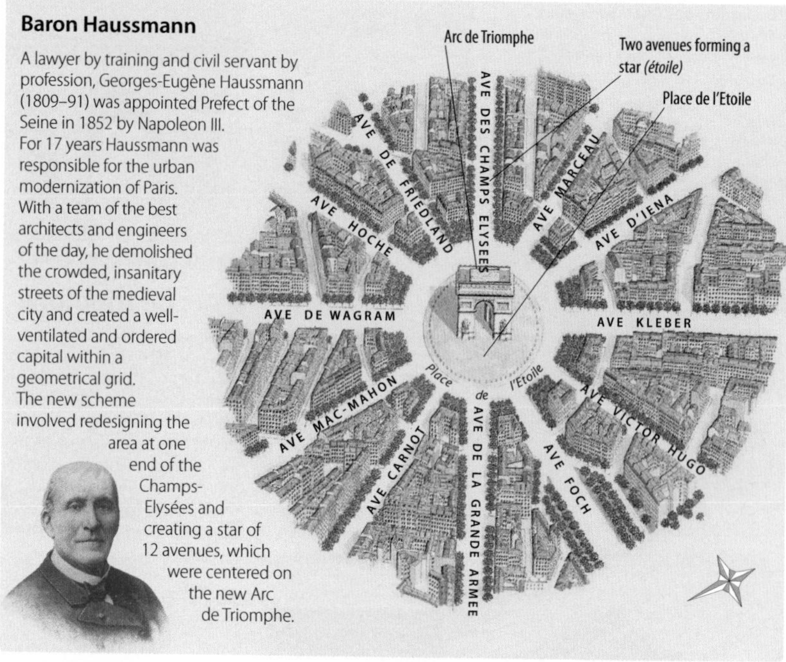

Baron Haussmann

A lawyer by training and civil servant by profession, Georges-Eugène Haussmann (1809–91) was appointed Prefect of the Seine in 1852 by Napoleon III. For 17 years Haussmann was responsible for the urban modernization of Paris. With a team of the best architects and engineers of the day, he demolished the crowded, insanitary streets of the medieval city and created a well-ventilated and ordered capital within a geometrical grid. The new scheme involved redesigning the area at one end of the Champs-Elysées and creating a star of 12 avenues, which were centered on the new Arc de Triomphe.

❷ Avenue des Champs-Elysées

75008. **Map** 3 A5. Ⓜ Charles de Gaulle-Etoile, George V, Franklin D Roosevelt, Champs-Elysées-Clemenceau, Concorde.

The majestic avenue "of the Elysian Fields" (the name refers to a mythical Greek heaven for heroes), first laid out in the 1660s by the landscape designer André Le Nôtre, forms a 2 mile (3 km) straight line from the huge place de la Concorde to the Arc de Triomphe. The 19th century saw it transformed from horseride into elegant boulevard. Today it's a crowded tourist trap with notorious traffic, but the Champs-Elysées keeps its style, its memories, and a special place in the French heart. National parades are held here, the finish of the annual Tour de France cycle race is always in the Champs-Elysées, and, above all, it is where Parisians instinctively go at times of great national celebration.

❸ Palais de l'Elysée

55 rue du Faubourg-St-Honoré 75008. **Map** 3 B5. Ⓜ St-Philippe-du-Roule. **Closed** to the public.

Amid splendid gardens, the Elysée Palace was built in 1718 and has been the official residence of the President of the Republic since 1848. Several occupants left their mark. Louis XV's mistress, Madame de Pompadour, had the whole site enlarged. After the Revolution, it became a dance hall. In the 19th century, it was home to Napoleon's sister Caroline Murat, and his wife Empress Josephine. The President's Apartments are today on the first floor.

❹ Petit Palais

Av Winston Churchill 75008. **Map** 7 B1. **Tel** 01 53 43 40 00. Ⓜ Champs-Elysées-Clemenceau. **Open** 10am–6pm Tue–Sun. **Closed** public hols. for exhibitions. **W petitpalais.paris.fr**

Built for the Universal Exhibition in 1900 to stage a major display of French art, this jewel of a building was renovated in 2005 and houses the **Musée des Beaux-Arts de la Ville de Paris**. The architect, Charles Girault, arranged the palace around a

Grand Palais

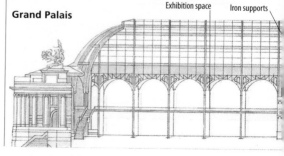

Exhibition space

Iron supports

Pont Alexandre III, built 1896–1900 for the Universal Exhibition

semi-circular courtyard and garden. Permanent exhibits, housed on the Champs-Elysées side, include the Dutuit Collection of medieval and Renaissance *objets d'art*, paintings, and drawings; the Tuck Collection of 18th-century furniture and *objets d'art*; and the City of Paris collection, with work by Ingres, Delacroix, and Courbet, and the landscape painters of the Barbizon School. Temporary exhibitions are housed in the Cours de la Reine wing.

Entrance to the Petit Palais

❺ Grand Palais

Porte A, av Général Eisenhower 75008. **Map** 7 A1. **Tel** 01 44 13 17 17. Ⓜ Champs-Elysées-Clemenceau. **Open** for temporary exhibitions only; 10am–8pm Wed–Mon. **Closed** May 1, Dec 25.  **W grandpalais.fr**

Palais de la Decouverte: av Franklin D. Roosevelt 75008. **Tel** 01 44 43 20 20. Ⓜ Franklin D. Roosevelt. **Open** 9:30am–6pm Tue–Sat, 10am–7pm Sun. **Closed** Jan 1, May 1, Jul 14, Dec 25. **W palais-decouverte.fr**

Built at the same time as the Petit Palais opposite, this huge, glass-roofed palace has a fine Classical facade adorned with statuary and Art Nouveau ironwork. Bronze flying horses and chariots stand at the four corners. The Great Hall and the glass cupola can be admired during the palace's superb exhibitions. The **Palais de la Découverte**, on the west side of the building, is an imaginative child-oriented science museum.

❻ Pont Alexandre III

75008. **Map** 7 A1. Ⓜ Champs-Elysées-Clemenceau.

This is Paris's prettiest bridge, with exuberant Art Nouveau decoration of gilt and bronze lamps, cupids and cherubs, nymphs, and winged horses at either end. It was built between 1896 and 1900 to commemorate the 1892 French-Russian alliance, and in time for the Universal Exhibition in 1900. Pont Alexandre III was named after Tsar Alexander III (father of Nicholas II), who laid the foundation stone in October 1896.

The style of the bridge reflects that of the Grand Palais, to which it leads on the Right Bank. The construction of the bridge is a marvel of 19th-century engineering. It consists of a 18-ft- (6-m-) high single-span steel arch across the Seine. The design was subject to strict controls that prevented the bridge from obscuring the view of the Champs-Elysées or the Invalides, so today you can still enjoy the magnificent views from here.

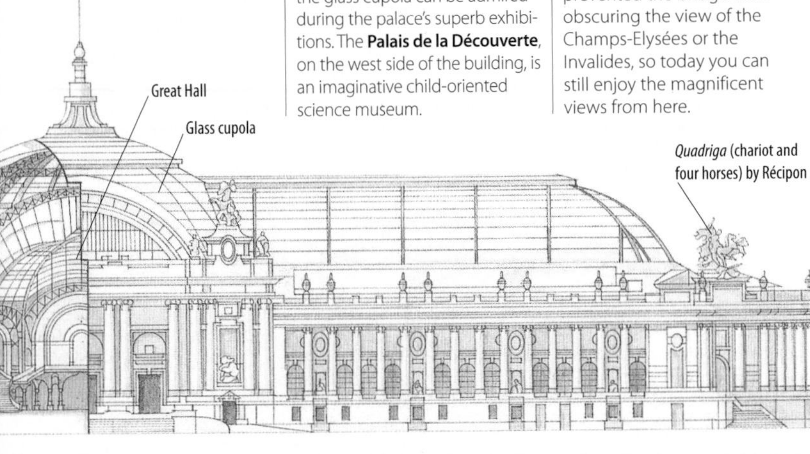

❼ Musée d'Art Moderne de la Ville de Paris

Palais du Tokyo, 11 av du Président-Wilson 75016. **Map** 6 E1. **Tel** 01 53 67 40 00. Ⓜ Iéna, Alma-Marceau. **Open** 10am–6pm Tue–Sun (until 10pm Thu for temporary exhibitions). **Closed** public hols. for temporary exhibitions. **W mam.paris.fr**

This museum covers trends in 20th-century art and is located in the east wing of the Palais de Tokyo. The Fauves and Cubists are well represented here. Highlights include Raoul Dufy's gigantic mural, *The Spirit of Electricity* (created for the 1937 World Fair), and Matisse's *The Dance* (1932). There is also a collection of Art Deco furniture.

❽ Musée Galliera

10 ave Pierre 1er de Serbie 75116. **Map** 6 D1. **Tel** 01 56 52 86 00. Ⓜ Iéna, Alma–Marceau. **Open** 10am–6pm Tue–Sun. **Closed** some public holidays (check website). Children's Room. **W galliera.paris.fr**

Devoted to the evolution of fashion, this museum, also known as the Musée de la Mode et du Costume, is housed in the Renaissance-style palace built for the Duchesse Maria de Ferrari Galliera in 1892. The collection includes more than 100,000 outfits and fashion accessories, from the 18th century to the present day. Donations have been made by such fashionable women as Baronne Hélène de Rothschild and Princess Grace of Monaco. Eminent couturiers such as Balmain and Balenciaga have donated their designs to the museum.

Often extremely fragile, the fashion exhibits are displayed in rotation, usually in two major exhibitions each year. These shows can highlight a particular couturier's career or explore a single theme.

Trocadéro fountains in front of the Palais de Chaillot

⓫ Musée Dapper

35bis rue Paul-Valéry, 75016. **Map** 2 D5. **Tel** 01 45 00 91 75. Ⓜ Victor-Hugo. **Open** 11am–7pm Wed, Fri–Mon. **W dapper.com.fr**

A world-class ethnographic research center, this is one of France's premier showcases of African art and culture. Located in an attractive building with an "African" garden, it is a treasure house of color and powerful, evocative work from the black nations. The focus is on pre-colonial folk arts, with sculpture, carvings, and tribal work, but there is later art, too. The highlight is tribal masks, with a dazzling, extraordinary array of richly carved religious, ritual, and funerary masks, as well as theatrical ones used for comic, magical, or symbolic performances.

⓬ Jardins du Trocadéro

75016. **Map** 6 D2. Ⓜ Trocadéro. Cinéaqua: **Tel** 01 40 69 23 23. **Open** 7am–11pm daily. **Closed** Jul 14.

These beautiful gardens cover 25 acres (10 ha). Their centerpiece is a long rectangular ornamental pool, bordered by stone and bronze-gilt statues, which looks spectacular at night when the fountains are illuminated. The statues include *Woman* by Georges Braque and *Horse* by Georges Lucien Guyot. On either side of the pool, the slopes of the Chaillot hill lead gently down to the Seine and the Pont d'Iéna. Cinéaqua, the hi-tech aquarium here, has over 25 sharks and a petting pool for children.

⓭ Palais de Chaillot

Pl du Trocadéro 75016. **Map** 5 C2. Ⓜ Trocadéro. Théâtre National de Chaillot: **Tel** 01 53 65 30 00. **W theatre-chaillot.fr** Musée de l'Homme: **Tel** 01 44 05 72 72. **Closed** for renovation until 2015. **W museedelhomme.fr** Musée National de la Marine: **Tel** 01 53 65 69 69. **Open** 11am–6pm Wed–Mon (to 7pm Sat–Sun). **Closed** Jan 1, May 1, Dec 25. **W musee-marine.fr**

The Palais, with its huge, curved, colonnaded wings each culminating in a vast pavilion, has three museums and a theater. Designed in Neo-Classical style for the 1937 Paris Exhibition by Azéma, Louis-Auguste Boileau, and Jacques Carlu, it is adorned with sculptures and bas-reliefs; inside, the gold inscriptions on the walls were written by the poet and essayist Paul Valéry.

For hotels and restaurants in this region see pp554–71 and pp576–603

Buddha head from Musée Guimet

9 Musée National des Arts Asiatiques Guimet

6 pl d'Iéna 75016. **Map** 6 D1. **Tel** 01 56 52 53 00. M Iéna. **Open** 10am–6pm Wed–Mon. Panthéon Bouddhique, 19 av d'Iéna. **Tel** 01 40 73 88 00. **Open** 10am– 5:45pm (phone ahead), garden 10am–5pm. **Closed** Jan 1, May 1, Dec 25. W **guimet.fr**

One of the world's leading museums of Asian art, the Guimet has a fine collection of Cambodian (Khmer) art. It was set up in Lyon in 1889 by Emile Guimet, and later moved to Paris. It includes a comprehensive Asian research center.

10 Cité de l'Architecture et du Patrimoine

Palais de Chaillot, pl du Trocadéro 75016. **Map** 5 C2. **Tel** 01 58 51 52 00. M Trocadéro. **Open** 11am–7pm Wed–Mon (until 9pm Thu). **Closed** Jan 1, May 1, Dec 25. W **citechaillot.fr**

This museum charts French architecture through the ages and includes models of great French cathedrals, such as Chartres *(see pp311–15)*. There is also a reconstruction of an apartment designed by Le Corbusier.

Palais de Chaillot

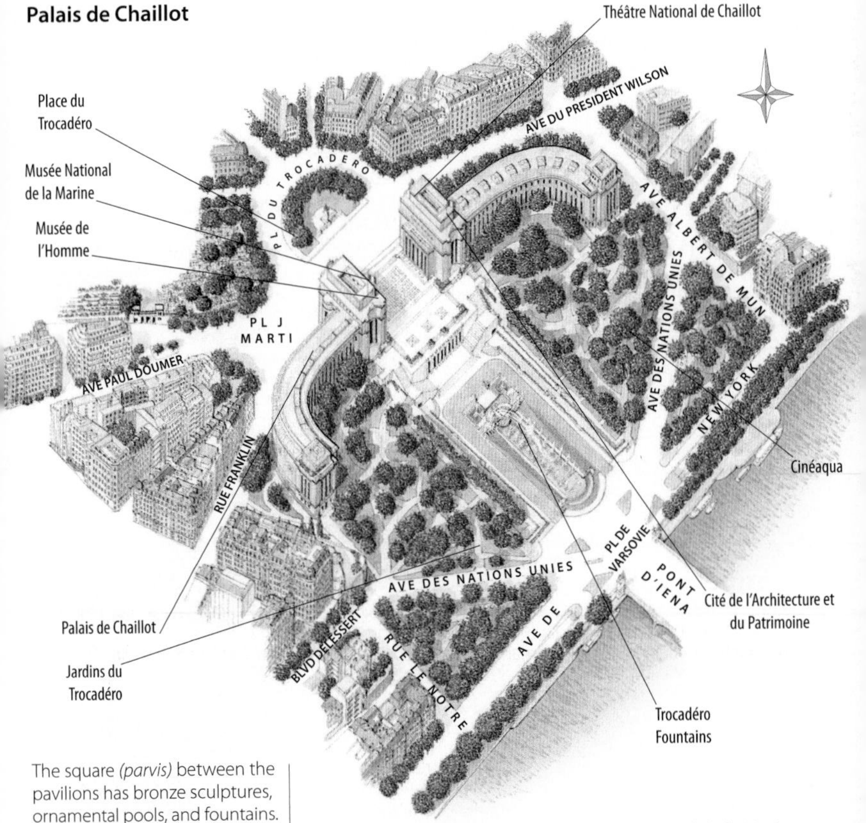

Théâtre National de Chaillot

Place du Trocadéro

Musée National de la Marine

Musée de l'Homme

Cinéaqua

Cité de l'Architecture et du Patrimoine

Palais de Chaillot

Jardins du Trocadéro

Trocadéro Fountains

AVE DU PRESIDENT WILSON

PL DU TROCADERO

AVE ALBERT DE MUN

AVE DES NATIONS UNIES

NEW YORK

PL J MARTI

AVE PAUL DOUMER

RUE FRANKLIN

PL DE VARSOVIE

PONT D'IENA

AVE DE

BLVD DELESSERT

RUE LE NOTRE

The square *(parvis)* between the pavilions has bronze sculptures, ornamental pools, and fountains. Steps lead down from the terrace to the **Théatre National de Chaillot**, offering an experimental approach to all genres.

The **Musée de l'Homme**, in the west wing, stages temporary exhibitions tracing human evolution through a series of anthropological exhibits. The museum is undergoing extensive renovation and is closed until 2015. Next door is the **Musée National de la Marine**, devoted to French naval history and aspects of the modern-day navy. The east wing contains the **Cité de l'Architecture et du Patrimoine** *(see above)*.

⓮ Les Egouts

Pont d'Álma, opposite 93 quai d'Orsay 75007. **Map** 6 F2. **Tel** 01 53 68 27 81 (in English). M Alma-Marceau. RER Pont-de-l'Alma. **Open** 11am–4pm (5pm in summer) Sat–Wed. **Closed** last 3 wks Jan.

One of Baron Haussmann's finest achievements, the majority of Paris's sewers (*égouts*) date from the Second Empire. If laid end to end, the 1,490 miles (2,400 km) of sewers would stretch from Paris to Istanbul. Tours of this popular attraction have been limited to an area around the quai d'Orsay entrance and are on foot (visiting the sewers without a guide can be dangerous, and is against the law). Visitors can discover the mysteries of underground Paris in the sewer museum and learn how the machinery used has changed over the years.

⓯ Musée du Quai Branly

37 quai Branly 75007, or 206/218 rue de l'Université. **Map** 6 E2. **Tel** 01 56 61 70 00. M Alma-Marceau. RER Pont-de-l'Alma. **Open** 11am–7pm Tue, Wed, Sun, 11am–9pm Thu–Sat. **Closed** May 1, Dec 25. free 1st Sun of month & for 18–25s after 6pm Sat. Exhibitions, theater, film, library.
W quaibranly.fr

Built to give the arts of Africa, Asia, Oceania, and the Americas a platform as shining as that for Western art in the city, this museum has a massive collection of more than 300,000 objects. It is particularly strong on Africa, with stone, wooden, and ivory masks, as well as ceremonial tools. The Jean Nouvel-designed building, which is raised on stilts, is a worthwhile sight in itself, while the ingenious use of glass in its construction allows the surrounding greenery to act as a natural backdrop.

Aztec mask, Musée du Quai Branly

⓰ Eiffel Tower

See p117.

Original Art Nouveau doorway at No. 29 avenue Rapp

⓱ No. 29 Avenue Rapp

75005. **Map** 6 E2. M Alma-Marceau. RER Pont-de-l'Alma.

A prime example of Art Nouveau architecture, No. 29 avenue Rapp won its designer, Jules Lavirotte, first prize at the Concours des Façades de la Ville de Paris in 1901. Its ceramics and brickwork are decorated with animal and flower motifs intermingling with female figures. These are superimposed on a multicolored sandstone base to produce a facade that is deliberately erotic, and was certainly subversive in its day. Also worth visiting nearby is Lavirotte's earlier apartment building, complete with watchtower, which can be found in the square Rapp.

⓲ Champ-de-Mars

75007. **Map** 6 E3. M Ecole-Militaire. RER Champ-de-Mars–Tour-Eiffel.

The vast gardens stretching from the Eiffel Tower to the Ecole Militaire (Military School) were originally a parade ground for young officer cadets. The area has since been used for horse-racing, balloon ascents, and mass ceremonies to celebrate the anniversary of the Revolution on July 14th. The first ceremony was held in 1790, in the presence of a glum, captive, Louis XVI.

Mammoth exhibitions were held here in the late 19th century, among them the 1889 World Fair for which the Eiffel Tower was erected.

⓳ Ecole Militaire

1/21 pl Joffre 75007. **Map** 6 F4. **Tel** 01 80 50 14 00. M Ecole-Militaire. Visits: by special permission only – contact the Commandant by writing to École de Guerre, Case 46, 75700 Paris SP 07.

The Royal Military Academy of Louis XV was founded in 1751 to educate 500 sons of impoverished officers. Louis XV and Madame de Pompadour commissioned architect Jacques-Ange Gabriel to design a building that would rival Louis XIV's Hôtel des Invalides. Financing the building became a problem so a lottery was authorized and a tax was raised on playing-cards. One of the main features is the central pavilion – a magnificent example of the French Classical style, with ten Corinthian columns and a quadrangular dome. Four figures adorn the entablature frieze, symbolizing France, Victory, Force, and Peace.

An early cadet at the academy was Napoleon, whose passing-out report stated that "he could go far if the circumstances are right."

A 1751 engraving showing the planning of the Ecole Militaire

16 Eiffel Tower

Built for the Universal Exhibition of 1889, and to commemorate the centennial of the Revolution, the 1,063 ft (324 m) Eiffel Tower (Tour Eiffel) was meant to be a temporary addition to Paris's skyline. Designed by Gustave Eiffel, and fiercely decried by 19th-century aesthetes, it was the world's tallest building until 1931, when New York's Empire State Building was completed. Most of the tower is open while the first floor is being renovated for the first time in 30 years.

VISITORS' CHECKLIST

Practical Information
Quai Branly and Champ-de-Mars, 75007. **Map** 6 D3. **Tel** 08 92 70 12 39. **Open** mid-Jun–Aug: 9am–12:45am; Sep–mid-Jun: 9:30am–11:45pm daily. (Access to top restricted for inclement weather.) **tour-eiffel.fr**

Transport
M Bir Hakeim. 42, 69, 72, 82, 87 to Champ-de-Mars. RER Champ-de-Mars. Tour Eiffel.

Daring Feats

The tower has always inspired crazy stunts. In 1912, Reichelt, a Parisian tailor, attempted to fly from the parapet with only a cape for wings. He plunged to his death in front of a large crowd.

Stuntman Reichelt

The third level, 905 ft (276 m) above the ground, can hold 400 people at a time.

★ Viewing Gallery
On a clear day it is possible to see for 45 miles (72 km), including a distant view of Chartres Cathedral.

The double-decker elevators have a limited capacity, and during the tourist season there can be long waits. Lining-up for the elevators requires patience and a good head for heights.

The second level is at 380 ft (116 m), separated from the first level by 359 steps or a few minutes in the elevator.

Cineiffel
This small audio-visual museum is closed for renovation until August 2014.

Jules Verne restaurant is rated highly in Paris, offering not only superb food, but a breathtaking panoramic view.

★ Eiffel Bust
The achievement of Eiffel (1832–1923) was honored by Antoine Bourdelle, who placed this bust under the tower in 1929.

The first level, 187 ft (57 m) high, can be reached by evevator or by 345 steps. The renovation will add a new and more accessible visitor center.

Les Invalides

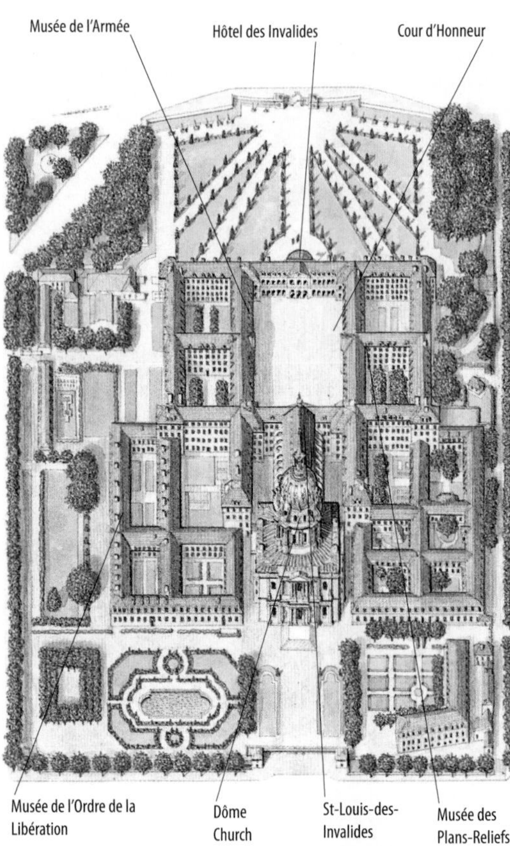

⓱ UNESCO

7 pl de Fontenoy 75007. **Map** 6 F5. **Tel** 01 45 68 10 00. Ⓜ Ségur, Cambronne. **Open** for guided tours only (reservations essential): 3pm Mon (French), 3pm Wed (English). **Closed** public hols. **unesco.org**

This is the headquarters of the United Nations Educational, Scientific, and Cultural Organization (UNESCO). Its aim is to contribute to international peace through education, science, and culture.

UNESCO is a treasure-trove of modern art, including an enormous mural by Picasso, ceramics by Joan Miró, and sculptures by Henry Moore, and the calm Japanese garden by Nogushi. Exhibitions and films are also held here.

㉑ Hôtel des Invalides

Esplanade des Invalides 75007. **Map** 7 A3. **Tel** 08 10 11 33 99. Ⓜ Latour-Maubourg, Invalides, Varenne. **Open** 7:30am–7pm daily (Apr–Sep: to 9pm Tue). **Closed** Jan 1, May 1, Dec 25. good for admission to all attractions. book ahead online. **musee-armee.fr**

This imposing building, from which the area takes its name, was commissioned by Louis XIV in 1670 for his wounded and homeless veterans. Designed by Libéral Bruand, it was completed in 1676 by Jules Hardouin-Mansart. He later incorporated the Dôme Church, with its golden roof, which was built as Louis XIV's private chapel. Nearly 6,000 soldiers once lived here. Today there are fewer than 100.

The harmonious Classical facade is one of the most impressive sights in Paris. The building houses the Musée de l'Armée and the Musée de l'Ordre de la Libération, set up to honor feats of heroism during World War II under the leadership of Charles de Gaulle. The story is told using film, photographs, and mementos. The Musée des Plans-Reliefs also houses a large collection of military models of French forts.

㉒ Musée de l'Armée

129 rue Grenelle 75007 (also esplanade des Invalides or pl Vaubon). **Map** 7 A3. **Tel** 08 10 11 33 99. Ⓜ Varenne, Latour-Maubourg, Invalides. RER Invalides. **Open** 10am–6pm daily (to 5pm Nov–Mar; to 5:30pm school hols). **Closed** 1st Mon of month Oct–Jun, Jan1, May 1, Dec 25. for admission to all attractions. **musee-armee.fr**

One of the most comprehensive museums of military history in the world is housed in two galleries on either side of the magnificent courtyard of the Hôtel des Invalides. The newly opened "Priests' Wing" holds the World War II galleries.

A major exhibit of France's victories and defeats, dedicated mainly to the Napoleonic era, includes the emperor's death mask and stuffed horse, Vizier. Also on display are François I's ivory hunting horns and a model of the 1944 Normandy landing.

The facade of the Musée de l'Armée

For hotels and restaurants in this region see pp554–71 and pp576–603

Altar of St-Louis-des-Invalides with banners seized in battle

㉓ Cathedral of St-Louis-des-Invalides

Esplanade des Invalides, Hôtel des Invalides 75007. **Map** 7 A3. M Invalides, Latour-Maubourg, Varenne. **Tel** 08 10 11 33 99. **Open** 10am–6pm daily (Jul–Aug: to 7pm; Apr–Sep: to 9pm Tue). W **musee-armee.fr**

Also known as the "soldiers' church," this is the chapel of the Hôtel des Invalides. It was built from 1679 to 1708 by Jules Hardouin-Mansart, to Bruand's design. The stark, Classical interior is well proportioned, designed in the shape of a Greek cross.

There is a fine 17th-century organ on which the first performance of Berlioz's *Requiem* was given on December 5, 1837, with more than 200 musicians and choristers participating.

㉔ Dôme Church

Esplanade des Invalides, Hôtel des Invalides, 129 rue de Grenelle, 75007. **Map** 7 A3. **Tel** 08 10 11 33 99. M Latour-Maubourg, Varenne, Invalides. 82, 92 to Les Invalides. RER Invalides. Tour Eiffel. **Open** 10am–6pm daily (Apr–Sep: to 9pm Tue; Jul–Aug: to 7pm). **Closed** Jan 1, May 1, Dec 25. restr. W **musee-armee.fr**

Jules Hardouin-Mansart was asked in 1676 by the Sun King, Louis XIV, to build the Dôme Church to complement the existing buildings of the Invalides military refuge, designed by Libéral Bruand. The Dôme was to be reserved for the exclusive use of the Sun King and as the location of royal tombs.

The resulting masterpiece is one of the greatest examples of 17th-century French architecture, the period known as the *grand siècle*. After Louis XIV's death, plans to bury the royal family in the church were abandoned.

The main attraction is the tomb of Napoleon; 20 years after his death on the island of St Helena, his body was returned to France and installed in this magnificent crypt, encased in six coffins in a vast red porphyry sarcophagus.

Dôme Church with cupola, first gilded in 1715

㉕ Musée Rodin

79 rue de Varenne 75007. **Map** 7 B3. **Tel** 01 44 18 61 10. M Varenne. **Open** 10am–5:45pm Tue–Sun. **Closed** Jan 1, May 1, Dec 25. free 1st Sun of month & for 18–25s after 6pm Sat. restricted. W **musee-rodin.fr**

Auguste Rodin (1840–1917), regarded as one of the greatest French sculptors, lived and worked in the Hôtel Biron, an elegant 18th-century mansion, from 1908 until his death. In return for a state-owned flat and studio, Rodin left his work to the nation, and it is now exhibited here. Some of his most celebrated sculptures are on display in the garden: *The Burghers of Calais, The Thinker, The Gates of Hell* *(see p124)*, and *Balzac*.

The indoor exhibits are arranged in chronological order, spanning the whole of Rodin's career. Highlights include *The Kiss* and *Eve*.

Rodin's *The Thinker* in museum garden

㉖ Sainte-Clotilde

23 bis rue Las Cases 75007. **Map** 7 B3. **Tel** 01 44 18 62 60. M Solférino, Varenne, Invalides. **Open** 9am–7:30pm Mon–Fri, 10am–8pm Sat & Sun. **Closed** non-religious public hols. Concerts.

Designed by the German-born architect Franz Christian Gau and built in 1846–56, this Neo-Gothic church was inspired by the 19th-century enthusiasm for the Middle Ages, popularized by such writers as Victor Hugo.

Inside are wall paintings by James Pradier and stained-glass windows with scenes relating to the patron saint of the church. The composer César Franck was organist here from 1858 to 1890.

㉗ Musée Maillol

61 rue de Grenelle 75007. **Map** 7 C4. **Tel** 01 42 22 59 58. M Rue du Bac, Sèvres-Babylone. **Open** 10:30am–7pm (9:30pm Fri). **Closed** pub hols. W **museemaillol.com**

This museum was created by Dina Vierny, muse to Aristide Maillol. His work is exhibited here in all its diverse forms: drawings, engravings, paintings, sculpture, and decorative objects. The museum also plays host to two major temporary exhibitions a year. Allegorical figures of the city of Paris and the four seasons adorn Bouchardon's fountain outside.

THE LEFT BANK

The Left Bank has long been associated with poets, philosophers, artists, and radical thinkers of all kinds. It still has its share of bohemian street life and sidewalk cafés, but the smart set has moved in, patronizing Yves St-Laurent and the exclusive interior design shops in rue Jacob.

The Latin Quarter is the ancient area lying between the Seine and Luxembourg Gardens, and is today filled with bookshops, art galleries, and cafés. The boulevard St-Michel, bordering the Latin quarter, and St-Germain-des-Prés, has slowly given way to commerce, and is full of fast-food outlets and cheap stores. The surrounding maze of narrow, cobbled streets has retained its character, with ethnic shops and avant-garde theaters dominated by the facade of the Sorbonne, France's first university, built in 1253. Many Parisians dream of living near the Luxembourg Gardens, a quiet area with charming old streets, gateways, and elaborate gardens full of paths, lawns, and tree-lined avenues. Students come here to chat, and on warm days, Parisian men still meet underneath the chestnut trees to play chess or the traditional French game of *boules*.

Sights at a Glance

Churches

- 5 St-Germain-des-Prés
- 9 St-Séverin
- 10 St-Julien-le-Pauvre
- 12 St-Etienne-du-Mont
- 13 Panthéon
- 15 St-Sulpice
- 17 Val-de-Grâce

Museums and Galleries

- 1 *Musée d'Orsay pp124–5*
- 6 Musée Eugène Delacroix
- 8 Musée de Cluny
- 16 Fontaine de l'Observatoire

Historic Buildings and Streets

- 2 Boulevard St-Germain
- 3 Quai Voltaire
- 4 Ecole Nationale Supérieure des Beaux Arts
- 7 Rue de l'Odéon
- 11 La Sorbonne
- 14 Palais du Luxembourg

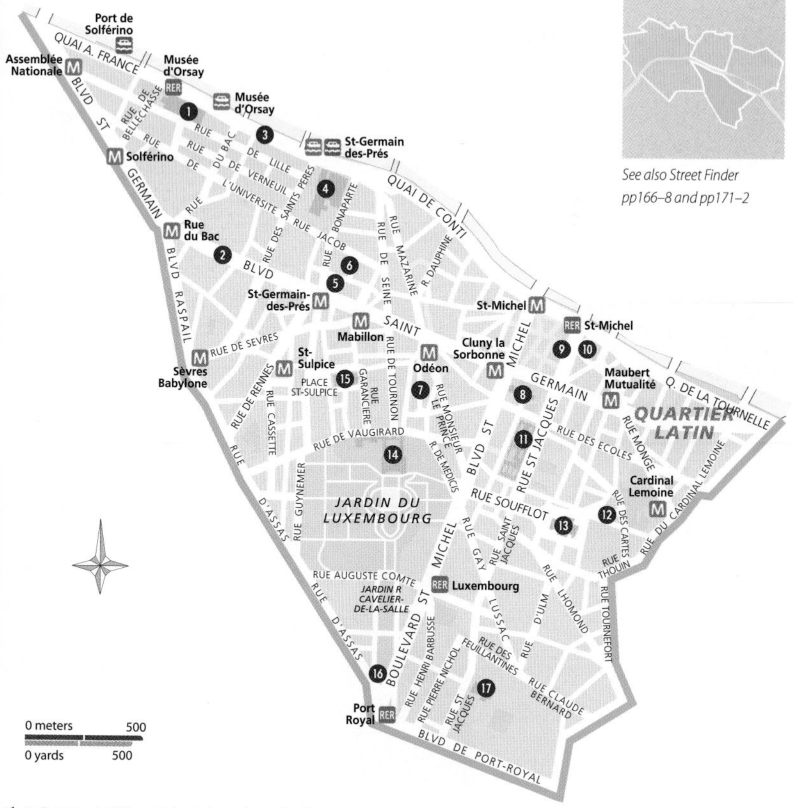

See also Street Finder pp166–8 and pp171–2

◀ La Fontaine de l'Observatoire, in Luxembourg Gardens

For map symbols *see back flap*

Street-by-Street: St-Germain-des-Prés

After World War II, St-Germain des-Prés became synonymous with intellectual life centered on bars and cafés. Philosophers, writers, actors, and musicians mingled in the cellar nightspots and brasseries, where existentialist philosophy co-existed with American jazz. The area is now smarter than in the heyday of Jean-Paul Sartre and Simone de Beauvoir, the enigmatic singer Juliette Greco and the New Wave film-makers. However, the writers are still around, enjoying the pleasures of sitting in Les Deux Magots, Café de Flore, and other haunts. The 17th-century buildings have survived, but signs of change are evident in boutiques for the affluent dealing in antiques, books, and fashion.

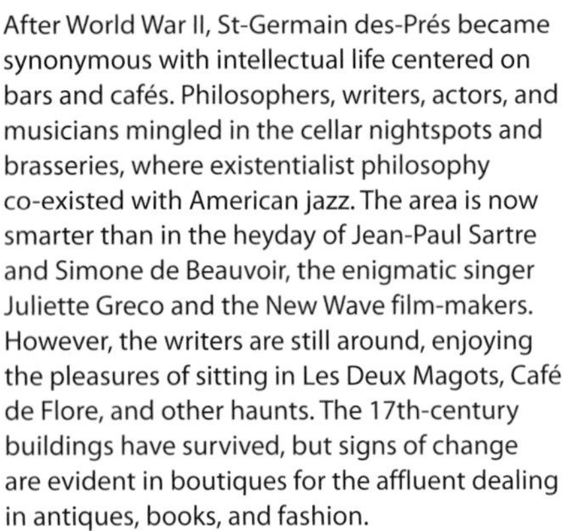

Les Deux Magots became a focus of bohemian and literary activity in the 1920s.

Café de Flore, the former favorite haunt of Jean-Paul Sartre, Simone de Beauvoir, and other French intellectuals, still has a classic Art Deco interior.

Brasserie Lipp, decorated with colorful ceramics, is a renowned brasserie frequented by politicians.

Métro St-Germain-des-Prés

5 ★ St-Germain-des-Prés
The philosopher René Descartes is among the notables buried here in Paris's oldest church.

2 ★ Boulevard St-Germain
Café terraces, boutiques, cinemas, restaurants, and bookshops characterize the central section of the Left Bank's main street.

For hotels and restaurants in this region see pp554–71 and pp576–603

Key

▬ Suggested route

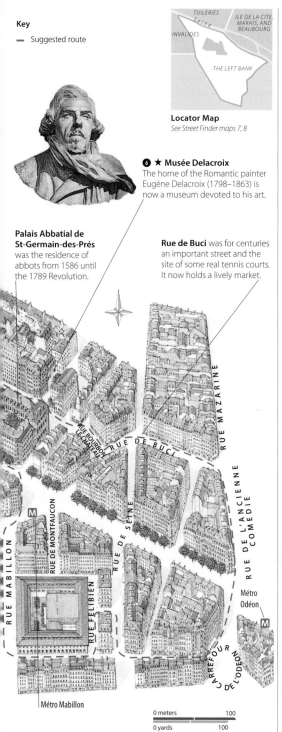

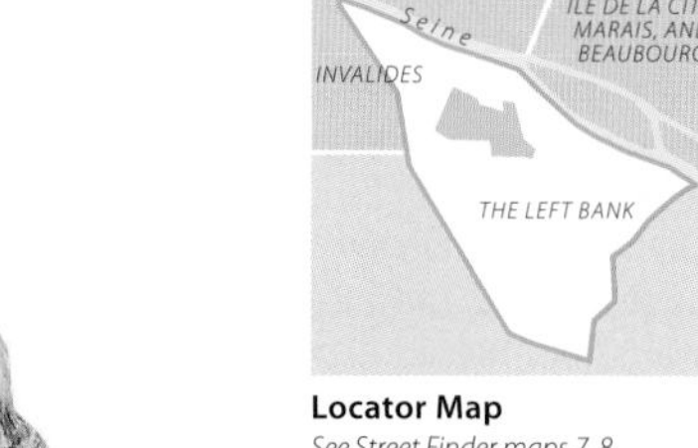

Locator Map
See Street Finder maps 7, 8

6 ★ Musée Delacroix
The home of the Romantic painter Eugène Delacroix (1798–1863) is now a museum devoted to his art.

Palais Abbatial de St-Germain-des-Prés was the residence of abbots from 1586 until the 1789 Revolution.

Rue de Buci was for centuries an important street and the site of some real tennis courts. It now holds a lively market.

Métro Mabillon

Métro Odéon

❶ Musée d'Orsay

See pp124–5.

❷ Boulevard St-Germain

75006, 75007. **Map** 8 D4. Ⓜ Solférino, Rue du Bac, St-Germain-des-Prés, Mabillon, Odéon, Cluny-La Sorbonne, Maubert-Mutualité.

The Left Bank's most celebrated thoroughfare curves across three districts from the Ile St-Louis to the Pont de la Concorde. The architecture is homogeneous because the boulevard was another of Baron Haussmann's bold strokes of urban planning, but it encompasses a wide range of different lifestyles from bohemian to bourgeois.

Starting from the east, it passes Musée de Cluny and the Sorbonne. It is most lively from boulevard St-Michel to St-Germain-des-Prés, with its café culture.

❸ Quai Voltaire

75006, 75007. **Map** 8 D3. Ⓜ Rue du Bac. RER Museé d'Orsay.

The quai Voltaire is now home to some of the most important antique dealers in Paris. Many famous people have lived in the attractive 18th-century houses, among others Voltaire at No. 27 and Richard Wagner, Jean Sibelius, and Oscar Wilde at No. 19.

Plaque marking the house in quai Voltaire where Voltaire died in 1778

❶ Musée d'Orsay

In 1986, 47 years after it had closed as a mainline railroad station, Victor Laloux's turn-of-the-century building reopened as the Musée d'Orsay. Built as the Orléans railway terminus in the heart of Paris, it narrowly avoided demolition in the 1970s. In the conversion to a museum, much of the original architecture was retained. The museum presents the rich diversity of visual arts from 1848 to 1914 and explains the social and technological context in which they were created. Exhibits include paintings, sculptures, furniture, and decorative objects. The museum also has a program of classical music concerts. Exhibits and access are subject to change due to major ongoing renovations.

The Gates of Hell (1880–1917)
Rodin included figures that he had already created, such as *The Thinker* and *The Kiss*, in this famous gateway.

Dancing at the Moulin de la Galette (1876)
Renoir painted this picture outside to capture the light as it filtered through the trees.

The Dance (1867–8)
Carpeaux's dynamic sculpture caused a scandal when it was first unveiled in 1869.

Key to Floorplan

- Architecture & Decorative Arts
- Sculpture
- Painting before 1870
- Impressionism
- Neo-Impressionism
- Naturalism and Symbolism
- Art Nouveau
- Temporary exhibitions
- Nonexhibition space

For hotels and restaurants in this region see pp554–71 and pp576–603

Doctor Paul Gachet (1890)
This portrait by Van Gogh is one of three and was painted the same year the artist died.

Gallery Guide

The ground floor has works from the mid- to late 19th century. The middle level features Art Nouveau, decorative art, and late-19th- to early 20th-century paintings and sculptures. The upper level is currently not open to the public.

Upper level

Middle level

Entrance

Ground floor

Shop entrance

VISITORS' CHECKLIST

Practical Information
Quai Anatole France 75007. **Map** 8 D2. **Tel** 01 40 49 48 14. P Carrousel du Louvre/Bac Montalembert. **Open** 9:30am–6pm Tue–Sun (to 9:45pm Thu; last entry 1 hr before closing). **Closed** Jan 1, May 1, Dec 25. Events: call 01 53 63 04 63. W **musee-orsay.fr**

Transport
M Solférino. 24, 68, 69, 84 to quai A. France; 73 to rue de la Légion d'Honneur; 63, 83, 84, 94 to bd St-Germain. RER Musée d'Orsay.

Exploring the Musée d'Orsay

Many of the paintings in the Musée d'Orsay came from the Louvre and the Impressionist collection once in the Jeu de Paume. Paintings from before 1870 are on the ground floor, presided over by Thomas Couture's massive *Romans of the Decadence*. Neo-Classical masterpieces, like Ingres's *La Source*, hang near Romantic works like Delacroix's turbulent *Tiger Hunt*. These exotic visions contrast with Realist works by artists like Courbet and early canvases by Degas and Manet, including the latter's famous *Olympia*.

The museum's central aisle overflows with sculpture, from Daumier's satirical busts of members of parliament to Carpeaux's exuberant *The Dance* and Rodin's *The Gates of Hell*. Decorative arts and architecture are on the middle level, where there is also a display of Art Nouveau – sinuous lines characterize Lalique's jewelry and glassware and the designs of Hector Guimard, who produced the characteristic curvy entrances of the Paris Métro.

Blue Waterlilies (1919) by Claude

Among the many highlights of the Impressionist rooms are Monet's *Rouen Cathedral* series *(see p271)* and Renoir's joyful *Moulin de la Galette*. The Post-Impressionist collection on the middle level includes the *Eglise d'Auvers* by Van Gogh, Seurat's pointillist compositions such as *Le Cirque*, Gauguin's highly colored Symbolist works, and Toulouse-Lautrec's depictions of Parisian nightlife. Among the highlights of the post-1900 display is Matisse's *Luxe, Calme et Volupté*. Some exhibits may be moved due to ongoing renovation work.

Le Déjeuner sur l'Herbe (1863) by Edouard Manet

The facade of the Ecole Nationale Supérieure des Beaux Arts

❹ Ecole Nationale Supérieure des Beaux Arts

14 rue Bonaparte 75006. **Map** 8 E3. **Tel** 01 47 03 50 00. Ⓜ St-Germain-des-Prés. **Open** for guided visits only (01 42 46 92 02 to book). Library. **W ensba.fr**

The main French school of fine arts has an enviable position at the corner of the rue Bonaparte and the riverside quai Malaquais. It is housed in several buildings, the most imposing being the 19th-century Palais des Etudes. A host of budding French and foreign painters and architects have crossed the courtyard, which contains a 17th-century chapel, to learn in the ateliers of the school. Many American architects have studied here over the past century.

❺ Paroisse St-Germain-des-Prés

3 pl St-Germain-des-Prés 75006. **Map** 8 E4. **Tel** 01 55 42 81 10. Ⓜ St-Germain-des-Prés. **Open** 8am–7pm daily. Concerts: 8pm (days vary but generally Thu–Fri). **W eglise-sgp.org**

This the oldest church in Paris, originating in 542 as a basilica to house holy relics. It became an immensely powerful Benedictine abbey, rebuilt in the 11th century, but most of it was destroyed by fire in 1794. Major restoration took place in the 19th century. One of the three original towers survives, housing one of the oldest belfries in France. The interior is an interesting mix of styles, with 6th-century marble columns, Gothic vaulting, and Romanesque arches. Famous tombs include that of 17th-century philosopher René Descartes.

❻ Musée Eugène Delacroix

6 rue de Fürstenberg 75006. **Map** 8 E4. **Tel** 01 44 41 86 50. Ⓜ St-Germain-des-Prés. **Open** 9:30am–5pm Wed–Mon. **Closed** Jan 1, May 1, Dec 25. free 1st Sun of month & for 18–25s (EU residents). **W musee-delacroix.fr**

The leading Romantic painter Eugène Delacroix lived and worked here from 1857 until his death in 1863. Here he painted *The Entombment of Christ* and *The Way to Calvary* (which hang in the museum). He also created murals for the Chapel of the Holy Angels in the nearby St-Sulpice church.

The apartment and studio has a portrait of George Sand and Delacroix self-portraits.

Jacob Wrestling with the Angel by Delacroix, in St-Sulpice *(see p131)*

❼ Rue de l'Odéon

75006. **Map** 8 F5. Ⓜ Odéon.

Opened in 1779 to improve access to the Odéon theater, this was the first street in Paris to have sidewalks with gutters and it still has many 18th-century houses.

Sylvia Beach's bookstore, the original Shakespeare & Company, stood at No. 12 from 1921 to 1940. It was a magnet for writers like James Joyce, Ezra Pound, and Hemingway.

❽ Musée de Cluny

6 pl Paul-Painlevé. **Map** 9 A5. **Tel** 01 53 73 78 16. Ⓜ St-Michel, Odéon, Cluny. RER St-Michel. **Open** 9:15am–5:45pm Wed–Mon. **Closed** Jan 1, May 1, Dec 25. Concerts: **W musee-moyenage.fr**

The museum (officially the Musée National du Moyen Age) is a unique combination of Gallo-Roman ruins, incorporated

Stone heads of the Kings of Judah carved around 1220

❾ St-Séverin

1 rue-des-Prêtres-St-Séverin 75005. **Map** 9 A4. **Tel** 01 42 34 93 50. Ⓜ St-Michel. **Open** 11am–7:30pm Mon–Sat, 9am–8:30pm Sun.

St-Séverin, one of the most beautiful churches in Paris, is named after a 6th-century hermit who lived in the area. It is a perfect example of the Flamboyant Gothic style. Finished in the early 16th century, it includes a remarkable double aisle encircling the chancel. In the garden stands the church's medieval gable-roofed charnel house.

Gargoyles adorning the gables of the Flamboyant Gothic St-Séverin

The School woodcarving (English, early 16th century)

into a medieval mansion (in newly created medieval gardens), and one of the world's finest collections of medieval art and crafts. Its name comes from Pierre de Chalus, Abbot of Cluny, who bought the ruins in 1330. The present building dates from 1485–98. Among the star exhibits are the tapestries, remarkable for their quality, age, and state of preservation. The highlight of the sculpture section is the Gallery of the Kings, while one of Cluny's most precious items, the Golden Rose of Basel from 1330, is found in the collection of jewelry and metalwork. Other treasures include stained glass, woodcarvings, and books of hours.

Lady with the Unicorn Tapestries

These six outstanding tapestries are fine examples of the millefleur style. Developed in the 15th and early 16th centuries, the style is noted for its graceful depiction of animals and people, and its fresh and harmonious colors.

The poetic elegance of a unicorn on the sixth tapestry

⑩ St-Julien-le-Pauvre

79 rue Galande 75005. **Map** 9 A4. **Tel** 01 43 54 52 16. Ⓜ St-Michel. **Open** 9:30am–1pm, 3–6:30pm daily. ✝ 12:15pm Tue & Thurs; 10am, 11am & 6pm Sun. Concerts. Ⓦ **sjlpmelkites.fr**

The church is one of the oldest in Paris, dating from between 1165 and 1220. The university held its official meetings in the church until 1524, when a student protest created so much damage that they were barred from the church by parliament. It has belonged to the Melchite sect of the Greek Orthodox Church since 1889 and is now the setting for classical and religious concerts.

⑪ La Sorbonne

1 rue Victor Cousin 75005. **Map** 9 A5. **Tel** 01 40 46 22 11. Ⓜ Cluny-La Sorbonne, Maubert-Mutualité. only by appt. Write to Service des Visites or visites.sorbonnes@ac-paris.fr. Ⓦ **paris-sorbonne.fr**

The Sorbonne, one of the oldest universities in the world, was established in 1253 by Robert de Sorbon, confessor to Louis IX, for 16 poor scholars to study theology. It went on to become the center of scholastic theology. In 1469, three printing machines were brought from Mainz, and the first printing house in France was founded. The college's opposition to liberal 18th-century philosophical ideas led to its suppression during the Revolution. It was re-established by Napoleon in 1806, and the 17th-century buildings replaced. In 1969, the Sorbonne split into 13 separate universities, but the building still holds some lectures.

⑫ St-Etienne-du-Mont

Pl Ste-Geneviève 75005. **Map** 13 A1. **Tel** 01 43 54 11 79. Ⓜ Cardinal Lemoine. **Open** 8:45am–7:45pm daily (summer: from 10am Tue–Sat). **Closed** midday. ✝ 6:45pm daily & 11am Sat & Sun. Ⓦ **saintetiennedumont.fr**

This remarkable church houses the shrine of the patron saint of Paris, Saint Geneviève, and the remains of the great literary figures Racine and Pascal. The building is part Gothic and part eye-catching Renaissance design.

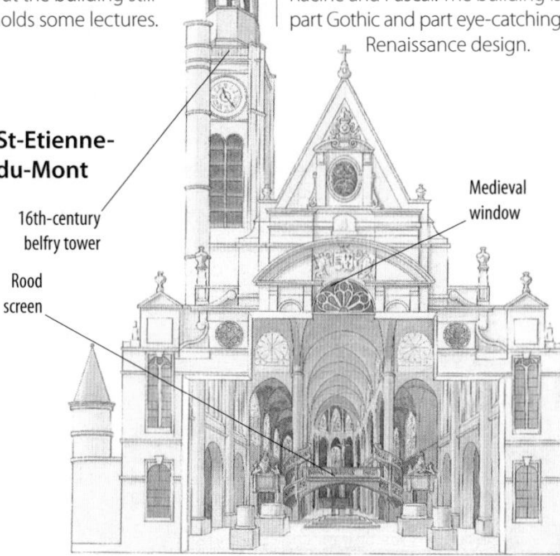

Street by Street: Latin Quarter

Since the Middle Ages this riverside quarter has been dominated by the Sorbonne, and acquired its name from the early Latin-speaking students. It dates back to the Roman town across from the Ile de la Cité; at that time the rue St-Jacques was one of the main roads out of Paris. The area is generally associated with artists, intellectuals, and a bohemian way of life; it also has a history of political unrest. In 1871, the place St-Michel became the center of the Paris Commune, and in May 1968 it was a site of student uprisings. Today the eastern half has become sufficiently chic, however, to house members of the Establishment.

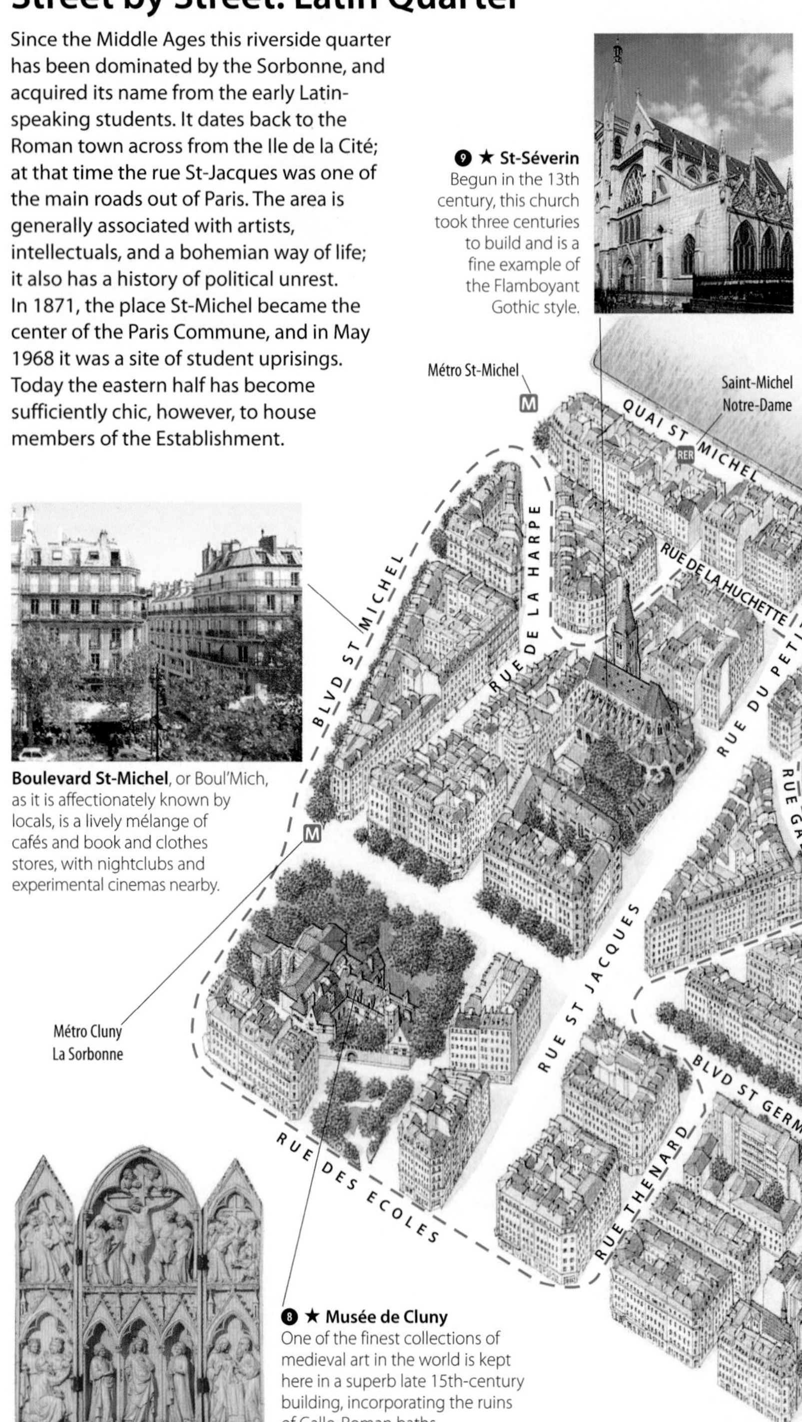

9 ★ St-Séverin
Begun in the 13th century, this church took three centuries to build and is a fine example of the Flamboyant Gothic style.

Boulevard St-Michel, or Boul'Mich, as it is affectionately known by locals, is a lively mélange of cafés and book and clothes stores, with nightclubs and experimental cinemas nearby.

8 ★ Musée de Cluny
One of the finest collections of medieval art in the world is kept here in a superb late 15th-century building, incorporating the ruins of Gallo-Roman baths.

For hotels and restaurants in this region see pp554–71 and pp576–603

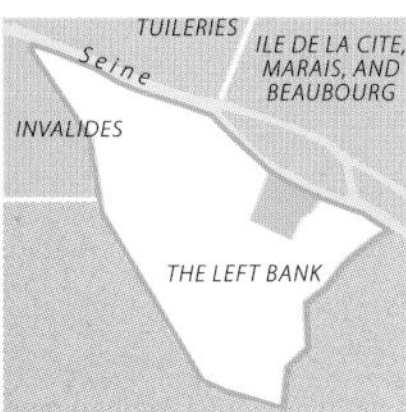

Locator Map
See Street Finder maps 8, 9, 12, 13

⑩ ★ St-Julien-le-Pauvre
Rebuilt in the 17th century, this church was used to store animal feed in the Revolution.

Métro Maubert Mutualité

0 meters 100
0 yards 100

Key

— Suggested route

⑬ Panthéon

Pl du Panthéon 75005. **Map** 13 A1. **Tel** 01 44 32 18 00. Ⓜ Maubert-Mutualité, Cardinal-Lemoine. RER Luxembourg. **Open** Apr–Sep: 10am–6:30pm daily; Oct–Mar: 10am–6pm daily (last adm 45 mins before closing). **Closed** Jan 1, May 1, Dec 25. **pantheon.monuments-nationaux.fr**

When Louis XV recovered from illness in 1744, he was so grateful that he conceived a magnificent church to honor Saint Geneviève, the patron saint of Paris. The French architect Jacques-Germain Soufflot planned the church in Neo-Classical style. Work began in 1764 and was completed in 1790 under the control of Guillaume Rondelet. But with the Revolution underway, the church was soon turned into a pantheon – a monument housing the tombs of France's great heroes. Napoleon returned it to the Church in 1806, but it was secularized and then desecularized once more before finally being made a civic building in 1885.

The facade, inspired by the Rome Pantheon, has a pediment relief depicting the mother country granting laurels to her great men. Those resting here include Voltaire, Rousseau, and Zola, and the ashes of Pierre and Marie Curie, and André Malraux.

The Panthéon Interior
The interior has four aisles arranged in the shape of a Greek cross, from the center of which the great dome rises.

Iron-Framed Dome
The fresco in the dome's stone cupola represents the *Glorification of Sainte Geneviève*, commissioned by Napoleon in 1811.

The dome lantern

The dome galleries

Entrance

Crypt
Under the building, the vast crypt divides into galleries flanked by Doric columns. Many French notables rest here, including Voltaire and Emile Zola.

Street by Street: Luxembourg Quarter

Situated only a few steps from the bustle of St-Germain-des-Prés, this graceful and historic area offers a peaceful haven in the heart of a modern city. The Jardin du Luxembourg and Palais du Luxembourg dominate the surroundings. The gardens became fully open to the public in the 19th century under the ownership of the Comte de Provence (later to become Louis XVIII), when for a small fee visitors could come in and feast on fruit from the orchard. Today the gardens, palace, and old houses on the streets to the north remain unspoilt and attract many visitors.

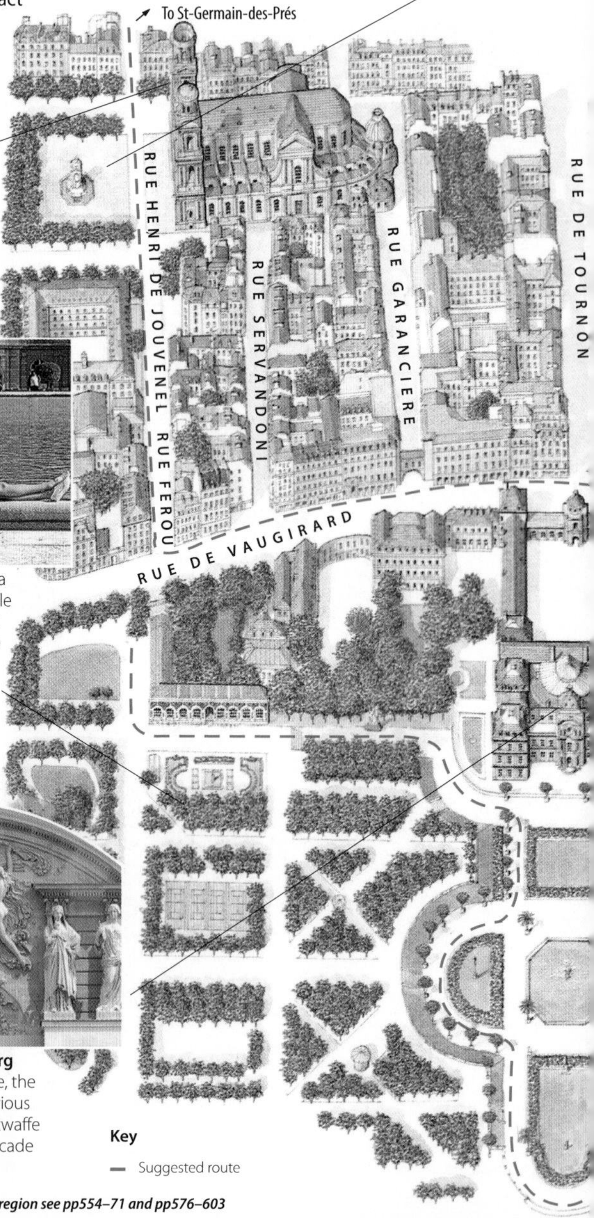

Place St-Sulpice ringed by floweri chestnut trees, w begun in 1754.

To St-Germain-des-Prés

RUE HENRI DE JOUVENEL

RUE FEROU

RUE SERVANDONI

RUE GARANCIERE

RUE DE TOURNON

RUE DE VAUGIRARD

15 ★ St-Sulpice
This huge Classical church, by six different architects, took more than a century to build.

Jardins du Luxembourg is a popular garden where people come to relax, sunbathe, sail boats in the pond, or admire the many beautiful statues erected in the 19th century.

0 meters 100
0 yards 100

14 ★ Palais du Luxembourg
First built as a royal residence, the palace has been used for various purposes from prison to Luftwaffe headquarters. This garden facade was added in 1841.

Key

— Suggested route

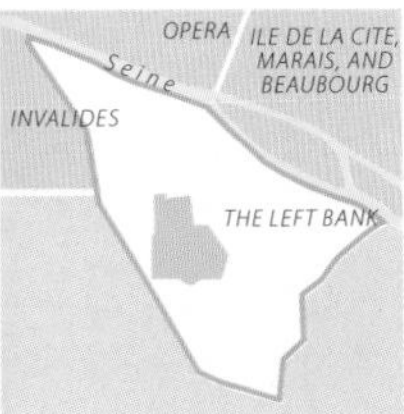

Locator Map
See Street Finder maps 8, 12, 13

Fontaine de Médicis is a 17th-century fountain in the style of an Italian grotto. It is thought to have been designed by Salomon de Brosse.

Saint Geneviève, patron saint of Paris, whose prayers saved Paris from the Huns in AD 451, is honored by this statue by Michel-Louis Victor in 1845.

⓮ Palais du Luxembourg

15 rue de Vaugirard 75006. **Map** 8 E5. **Tel** 01 44 54 19 49. M Odéon. RER Luxembourg. groups: Mon, Fri, Sat (apply 3 months in advance: 01 42 34 20 60); indiv: one Sat per month (01 44 54 19 30). W **senat.fr/visite** Museum: **Open** 10am–7:30pm daily during exhibitions. **Closed** May 1. W **museeduluxembourg.fr**

Now home to the French Senate, this palace was built to remind Marie de' Médici, widow of Henri IV, of her native Florence. It was designed by Salomon de Brosse in the style of Florence's Pitti Palace. By the time it was finished (1631), Marie had been banished from Paris, but it remained a royal palace until the Revolution. In World War II it became the Luftwaffe headquarters. The first public museum in France, the Musée du Luxembourg in the east gallery hosts world-class art exhibitions.

⓯ St-Sulpice

2 rue Palatine, pl St-Sulpice 75006. **Map** 8 E5. **Tel** 01 42 34 59 98. M St-Sulpice. **Open** 7:30am–7:30pm daily. call 01 43 25 03 10. Concerts. W **paroisse-saint-sulpice-paris.org**

This huge and imposing church, started in 1646, took more than a century to finish. The result is a simple facade with two tiers of elegant columns and two mismatched towers at the ends. Large arched windows fill the vast interior with light. The side chapel to the right has murals by Eugène Delacroix, including *Jacob Wrestling with the Angel (see p126)* and *Heliodorus Driven from the Temple.*

The Classical two-storey west front of St-Sulpice with its two towers

Carpeaux's fountain sculpture

⓰ Fontaine de l'Observatoire

Pl Ernest Denis, av de l'Observatoire 7500. **Map** 12 E2. RER Port Royal.

Situated at the southern tip of the Jardin du Luxembourg, this is one of the finest fountains in Paris. The central sculpture, by Jean-Baptiste Carpeaux, was erected in 1873. Made of bronze, it has four women holding aloft a globe representing four continents – the fifth, Oceania, was left out for reasons of symmetry. There are some subsidiary figures, including dolphins, horses, and a turtle.

⓱ Val-de-Grâce

1 pl Alphonse-Laveran 75005. **Map** 12 F2. **Tel** 01 40 51 51 92. M Gobelins. RER Port Royal. **Open** 2–6pm Mon–Sat, 9am–noon & 2–6pm Sun. **Closed** Aug. 11am Sun. except for nave. W **valdegrace.org**

This is one of the most beautiful churches in France, and forms part of a military hospital complex. Built for Anne of Austria (wife of Louis XIII) in gratitude for the birth of her son, young Louis XIV himself laid the first stone in 1645.

The church is noted for its dome. In the cupola is Pierre Mignard's enormous fresco, with over 200 triple-life-size figures. The six huge marble columns framing the altar are similar to St Peter's in Rome.

FARTHER AFIELD

Many of Paris's famous sights are slightly out of the city center. Montmartre, long a mecca for artists and writers, still retains much of its bohemian atmosphere, and Montparnasse is full of bustling cafés and theater crowds. The famous Cimetière du Père Lachaise numbers Chopin, Oscar Wilde, and Jim Morrison among its dead and, along with the parks and gardens, provides a tranquil escape from sightseeing. Modern architecture can be seen at Fondation Le Corbusier and La Défense, and there is a huge selection of museums to visit. To the northeast, the science museum at La Villette provides an educational family day out.

Sights at a Glance

Museums and Galleries

5 Musée Marmottan Claude Monet
6 Musée du Cristal de Baccarat
9 Musée Gustave Moreau
15 *Cité des Sciences et de l'Industrie pp140–41*
20 Cité Nationale de l'Histoire de l'Immigration
24 Musée National d'Histoire Naturelle

Churches and Mosques

7 St-Alexandre-Nevsky
11 Sacré-Coeur
27 Mosquée de Paris

Parks and Gardens

2 Bois de Boulogne
8 Parc Monceau
17 Parc des Buttes-Chaumont
23 Parc Montsouris
25 Jardin des Plantes
28 Parc André Citroën

Cemeteries

13 Cimetière de Montmartre
18 Cimetière du Père Lachaise
30 Cimetière du Montparnasse

Historic Districts

10 *Montmartre pp136–7*
16 Canal St-Martin
29 Montparnasse

Historic Buildings and Streets

4 Rue La Fontaine
12 Moulin Rouge
21 Château de Vincennes
31 Catacombes

Modern Architecture

1 La Défense
3 Fondation Le Corbusier
19 Bercy
22 Bibliothèque Nationale de France
26 Institut du Monde Arabe

Markets

14 Marché aux Puces de St-Ouen

Key

Main sightseeing area
Highway
Main road
Other road
Railroad

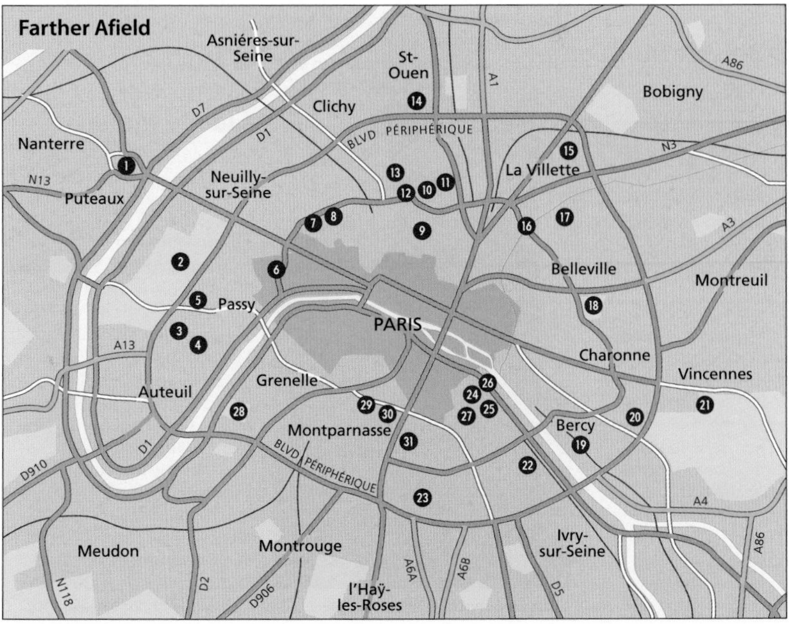

0 kilometers 4
0 miles 2

◀ La Grande Arche at La Défense

West of the City

❶ La Défense

La Grande Arche. **Tel** 01 49 07 27 55. RER La Défense. **Open** 10am–7pm daily (to 8pm Apr–Aug). Rooftop: **Closed** for renovation; phone for information. *See The History of France pp70–71.* **W grandearche.com**

This skyscraper business city on the western edge of Paris is the largest office development in Europe. La Grande Arche is an enormous hollow cube large enough to contain Notre-Dame cathedral. Designed by Danish architect Otto von Spreckelsen in the late 1980s, the arch houses a gallery, conference center, computer museum, and video game museum, and has superb views.

La Grande Arche in La Défense

❷ Bois de Boulogne

75016. M Porte Maillot, Porte Dauphine, Porte d'Auteuil, Sablons. **Open** 24 hrs daily. to specialist gardens and museum.

Located between the western edges of Paris and the River Seine, this 3.3 sq miles (8.6 sq km) park offers a vast belt of greenery for strolling, cycling, riding, boating, picnicking, or spending a day at the races. The Bois de Boulogne was once part of the immense Forêt du Rouvre. In the mid-19th century Napoleon III had the Bois designed and landscaped by Baron Haussmann, along the lines of Hyde Park in London. Several self-contained parks within the forest include the Jardin d'Acclimatation, a fun park for children, and the Bagatelle gardens, with architectural follies and an 18th-century villa famous for its rose garden. The villa was built in just 64 days after a bet between the Comte d'Artois and Marie-Antoinette.

By day the Bois is busy with families, joggers, and walkers, but after dark it is notoriously seedy – and best avoided.

A landscaped island in the Bois de Boulogne

❸ Fondation Le Corbusier

8–10 square du Docteur-Blanche 75016. Villa La Roche: **Tel** 01 42 88 75 72. M Jasmin. **Open** 1:30–6pm Mon, 10am–6pm Tue–Sat. **Closed** public hols. in English 2pm Tue (and Fri during summer). Films, videos. **W fondationlecorbusier.fr**

In a quiet corner of Auteuil stand the villas La Roche and Jeanneret, the first two Parisian houses built by the influential 20th-century architect Charles-Edouard Jeanneret, better known as Le Corbusier. Built at the start of the 1920s, they demonstrate his revolutionary use of white concrete in Cubist forms. Rooms flow into each other allowing maximum light and volume, and the houses stand on stilts with windows along their entire length.

Villa La Roche was owned by the art patron Raoul La Roche. Today, the villas hold lectures on Le Corbusier and his work.

An Art Nouveau window in the rue la Fontaine

❹ Rue la Fontaine

75016. **Map** 5 A4. M Michel-Ange-Auteuil, Jasmin. RER Radio-France.

The rue la Fontaine and surrounding streets act as a showcase for some of the most exciting early 20th-century, low-cost architecture, featuring sinuous decorative detail. At No. 14 stands the Castel Béranger, which firmly established the reputation of architect Hector Guimard. He went on to design the city's Art Nouveau Métro entrances.

❺ Musée Marmottan-Claude Monet

2 rue Louis Boilly 75016. **Tel** 01 44 96 50 33. M Muette. **Open** 10am–6pm Tue–Sun (to 8pm Thu). **Closed** 1 Jan, 1 May, 25 Dec. **W marmottan.com**

The museum was created in the 19th-century mansion of the famous art historian, Paul Marmottan, in 1932. He bequeathed his house, plus his Renaissance, Consular, and First Empire paintings and furniture, to the Institut de France.

In 1966 the museum acquired a fabulous collection of work by Impressionist painter Claude Monet, the bequest of his son, Michel. Some of Monet's most famous paintings are here, including *Impression – Sunrise*

For hotels and restaurants in this region see pp554–71 and pp576–603

(hence the term "Impressionist"), a painting of Rouen Cathedral *(see p271)*, and the *Waterlilies* series *(see p102)*. Also here is the work painted at Giverny during the last years of Monet's life. This includes *The Japanese Bridge* and *The Weeping Willow*. The iridescent colors and daring brush-strokes make these some of the museum's most powerful works.

Part of Monet's personal art collection was passed on to the museum, including work by fellow Impressionists Camille Pissarro, Pierre-Auguste Renoir, and Alfred Sisley. The museum also displays medieval illuminated manuscripts and 16th-century Burgundian tapestries. Piano and chamber music concerts are held here on occasion.

❻ Musée du Cristal de Baccarat

11 pl des Etats Unis 75016. **Tel** 01 40 22 11 00. M Boissière. **Open** 10am–6:30pm Mon, Wed–Sat (last adm 5pm). **Closed** public hols. by appt. W **baccarat.fr**

The Musée du Cristal, also known as the Galerie-Musée Baccarat, displays over 400 items made by the Baccarat company, which was founded in 1764 in Lorraine in eastern France. These include dinner services created for the royal and imperial courts of Europe and many of the best contemporary pieces produced in the workshops, such as fine vases, candelabras, decanters, and perfume bottles, as well as watches and jewelry.

In the glassworks itself you can see some of the technical skills used to shape and decorate the crystal ware, such as fine cutting, wheel-engraving, gilding and enameling.

Le Vase d'Abyssinie, made of Baccarat crystal and bronze

Colonnade beside the *naumachia* basin in Parc Monceau

North of the City

St-Alexandre-Nevsky Cathedral

❼ St-Alexandre-Nevsky

12 rue Daru 75008. **Map** 2 F3. **Tel** 01 42 27 37 34. M Courcelles, Ternes. **Open** 3–5pm Tue, Fri, Sun. by appt, call 03 86 91 97 88. 6pm Sat, 10:30am Sun.

This imposing Russian Orthodox cathedral with its five golden-copper domes signals the presence of a large Russian community in Paris. Designed by members of the St Petersburg Fine Arts Academy and financed jointly by Tsar Alexander II and the local Russian community, it was completed in 1861.

Inside, a wall of icons divides the church in two. The Greek-cross plan and the rich mosaics and frescoes decorating the interior are Neo-Byzantine, while the exterior and gilt domes are traditional Russian Orthodox.

❽ Parc Monceau

Bd de Courcelles 75017. **Map** 3 A3. **Tel** 01 42 27 08 64. M Monceau. **Open** 7am–8pm daily (10pm summer). by appt.

This green haven dates back to 1778 when the Duc de Chartres commissioned the painter-writer and amateur landscape designer Louis Carmontelle to create a magnificent garden. The result was an exotic landscape full of architectural follies in the English and German style.

In 1852 the garden became a chic public park. A few original features remain, among them the *naumachia* basin – an ornamental version of a Roman pool used for simulating naval battles.

❾ Musée Gustave Moreau

14 rue de la Rochefoucauld 75009. **Map** 4 E3. **Tel** 01 48 74 38 50. M Trinité. **Closed** ground floor closed for renovation until late 2014. Call for information. W **musee-moreau.fr**

The Symbolist painter Gustave Moreau (1826–98), known for his symbolic works depicting biblical and mythological fantasies, lived and worked in this handsome town house. *Jupiter and Semele*, one of the artist's outstanding works, is displayed here, along with other major paintings, and some of the collection's 7,000 drawings and 1,000 oils and watercolors.

⑩ Montmartre

The steep *butte* (hill) of Montmartre has been associated with artists for 200 years. Théodore Géricault and Camille Corot came here at the start of the 19th century, and in the 20th century Maurice Utrillo immortalized the streets in his works. Today, street artists thrive predominantly on the tourist trade, but much of the area still preserves its rather louche, villagey pre-war atmosphere.
The name of the area is ascribed to martyrs who were tortured and killed in the area around AD 250, hence *mons martyrium*.

Clos Montmartre
This is the last Parisian vineyard. The harvest is celebrated on the first Saturday in October.

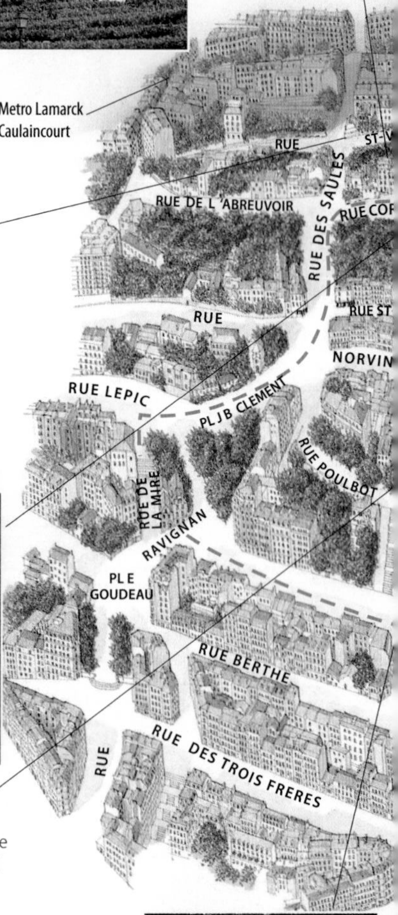

Metro Lamarck Caulaincourt

RUE ST-V
RUE DE L'ABREUVOIR
RUE DES SAULES
RUE COR
RUE
RUE ST
NORVIN
RUE LEPIC
PL J B CLEMENT
RUE POULBOT
RUE DE LA MIRE
RAVIGNAN
PL E GOUDEAU
RUE BERTHE
RUE
RUE DES TROIS FRERES

Au Lapin Agile
"The Agile Rabbit," once a literary haunt and cabaret, is now a nightclub.

Musée de Montmartre
Changing, Montmartre-related exhibitions usually include works by artists who lived here, such as this *Portrait of a Woman* (1918) by Amedeo Modigliani.

Espace Montmartre Salvador Dalí
Some 330 works by the Surrealist painter and sculptor are on display here.

Place du Tertre
The tourist center of Montmartre is full of portraitists. Artists first exhibited in the square in the 19th century.

Key

— Suggested route

0 meters 100
0 yards 100

A la Mère Catherine
This was a favorite restaurant of Russian cossacks. They would shout "Bistro!" (meaning "quick") – which gave the bistro its name.

Locator Map
See Street Finder maps 3, 4

⓫ Sacré-Coeur
This Neo-Romanesque church, started in the 1870s and completed in 1914, contains many treasures, such as this figure of the *Virgin Mary and Child* (1896) by P. Brunet.

St-Pierre de Montmartre
This is an early Parisian church with origins dating back to the 6th century.

To metro Anvers

The funiculaire, or cable railroad, at the end of the rue Foyatier takes you to the foot of the basilica of the Sacré-Coeur. Metro tickets are valid for it.

Square Willette lies below the forecourt of the Sacré-Coeur. It is laid out on the side of the hill in a series of descending terraces with lawns, shrubs, trees, and flowerbeds.

Musée de la Halle Saint Pierre
Exhibitions here showcase Outsider Art and Art Brut, such as this piece by S. Feleggakis.

⓫ Sacré-Coeur

33–35 rue du Chevalier-de-la-Barre, Parvis de Notre Dame 75018. **Map** 4 F1. **Tel** 01 53 41 89 00. Ⓜ Abbesses (then funiculaire to steps of Sacré-Coeur), Anvers, Jules Joffrin, Pigalle. 30, 31, 80, 85. Basilica: **Open** 6am–11pm daily. **Closed** Tue–Wed Oct–Apr. Dome & crypt: **Open** 9am–6pm daily. 3–4 times a day (call for hours). Vespers 4pm Sun.
W sacre-coeur-montmartre.com

The Sacré-Coeur basilica, dedicated to the Sacred Heart of Christ and consecrated in 1919, was built as a result of a private religious vow made at the outbreak of the Franco-Prussian war. Two Catholic businessmen, Alexandre Legentil and Hubert Rohault de Fleury, promised to finance the basilica should France be spared from assault. Despite the war and the Siege of Paris, invasion was averted and work began in 1875 to Paul Abadie's designs. Never considered very graceful, the basilica is vast and impressive, and one of France's most important Roman Catholic buildings.

The stained glass gallery affords a view of the whole interior.
The ovoid dome is the second-highest point in Paris, after the Eiffel Tower.
The Great Mosaic of Christ (1912–22), by Luc Olivier Merson, dominates the chancel vault.
Bronze doors in the portico show the Last Supper and other biblical scenes.
The crypt vaults house a chapel containing Alexandre Legentil's heart in a stone urn.

⓬ Moulin Rouge

82 bd de Clichy 75018. **Map** 4 E1. **Tel** 01 53 09 82 82. Ⓜ Blanche. Dinner: 7pm. Shows: 9pm & 11pm daily.
W moulinrouge.com

Built in 1885, the Moulin Rouge was turned into a dance hall as early as 1900. Henri de Toulouse-Lautrec immortalized the wild and colorful cancan shows here in his posters and drawings of famous dancers such as Jane Avril. The high-kicking routines continue today in glitzy, Las Vegas-style revues.

⓭ Cimetière de Montmartre

20 av Rachel 75018. **Map** 4 D1. **Tel** 01 53 42 36 30. Ⓜ Place de Clichy. **Open** 8am–6pm Mon–Fri (from 8:30am Sat, from 9am Sun).

This has been the resting place for many luminaries of the creative arts since the beginning of the 19th century. The composers Hector Berlioz and Jacques Offenbach (who wrote the famous cancan tune), Russian dancer Vaslav Nijinsky, and film director François Truffaut are just a few of the famous people who have been buried here over the years.

There is also a Montmartre cemetery near square Roland-Dorgelès, known as the St-Vincent cemetery. This is where the French painter Maurice Utrillo is buried.

African stall in the Marché aux Puces de St-Ouen

⓮ Marché aux Puces de St-Ouen

Rue des Rosiers, St-Ouen 93406. Ⓜ Porte-de-Clignancourt, Garibaldi. **Open** 9am–6pm Sat, 10am–6pm Sun, 11am–5pm Mon (reduced hours in summer). *See Shops and Markets p144.*
W marcheauxpuces-saintouen.com

This is the oldest and largest of the Paris flea markets, covering 15 acres (6 ha) near the Porte de Clignancourt. In the 19th century, rag merchants and tramps would gather outside the fortifications that marked the city limits and offer their wares for sale. Today the area is divided into separate markets, and is well-known for its heavy Second Empire furniture and ornaments. Although there are few bargains to be had, this does not deter the huge weekend crowds.

⓯ Cité des Sciences et de l'Industrie

See pp140–41.

⑯ Canal St-Martin

Ⓜ Jaurès, J Bonsergent, Goncourt.

A walk along the quays on either side of the Canal St-Martin gives a glimpse of how this thriving, industrial, working-class area of the city looked at the end of the 19th century. The 3-mile (5-km) canal, opened in 1825, provided a shortcut for river traffic between loops of the Seine. A smattering of brick-and-iron factories and warehouses survive from this time along the quai de Jemmapes. Here, too, is the legendary Hôtel du Nord, from Marcel Carné's 1930s film of the same name. The canal itself is quietly busy with barges and anglers; around it are tree-lined quays with quirky shops and cafés, iron footbridges, and public gardens. At Jaurès, it meets the Canal de l'Ourcq, which offers a pleasant stroll to Parc de la Villette *(see p140)*.

⑰ Parc des Buttes-Chaumont

Place Armand Carrel 75019. No phone. Ⓜ Botzaris, Buttes-Chaumont. **Open** May–Sep: 7am–10pm daily; Oct–Apr: 7am–8pm daily.

For many this is the most pleasant park in Paris. Urban planner Baron Haussmann converted the hilly site from a garbage dump and quarry with gallows at the foot, to English-style gardens in the 1860s. His colleague was landscape architect Adolphe Alphand, who was responsible for a vast 1860s program to provide Haussmann's new pavement-lined Parisian avenues with benches, streetlights, kiosks, and urinals *(see p112)*.

Others involved in the creation of this highly praised park were the engineer Darcel and the landscape gardener Barillet-Deschamps. They created a lake, made an island with real and artificial rocks, gave it a Roman-style temple, and added a waterfall, streams, and footbridges leading to the island. Today, in summer, visitors will also find boating facilities, donkey rides, and puppet (*guignol*) shows for the kids, and beautiful lawns.

Boats moored at Port de l'Arsenal

East of the City

⑱ Cimetière du Père Lachaise

16 rue du Repos 75020. **Tel** 01 55 25 82 10. Ⓜ Père Lachaise, A Dumas. 60, 69, 102 to Pl Gambetta. Ⓟ Pl Gambetta. **Open** 8am–5:30pm daily (to 6pm Apr–Nov; from 9am Sun & hols).

Paris's most prestigious cemetery is set on a wooded hill overlooking the city. The land was once owned by Père de la Chaise, Louis XIV's confessor, but it was bought by order of Napoleon in 1803. The cemetery became so popular that the boundaries were extended six times in the 19th century. Here are buried celebrities such as writer Honoré de Balzac and composer Frédéric Chopin, singer Jim Morrison, and actors Yves Montand and Simone Signoret.

⑲ Bercy

75012. Ⓜ Bercy, Cour St-Emilion. 24, 64, 87. Cinémathèque Française: 51 rue de Bercy. **Tel** 01 71 19 33 33. **Open** noon–7pm Mon–Sat, 10am–8pm Sun.

This former wine-trading quarter just east of the city center, with its once-grim riverside warehouses and pavilions and slum housing, has been transformed into an ultra-modern district beside the Seine. An automatic Métro line (Line 14) links it to the heart of the city.

The centerpiece of this district is the Palais d'Omnisports de Paris-Bercy (POPB), which is the city center's principal concert venue, as well as its premier sports stadium. The vast pyramidal structure, its sides clad with real lawns, has become a landmark for the eastern part of central Paris.

Other architecturally adventurous buildings dominate the skyline, notably Chemetov's Ministry of Finance building, and Frank Gehry's American Center, which houses the **Cinémathèque Française**, a cinema museum with film screenings, a library, and retrospectives on directors.

At the foot of these structures, the 173-acre (70-ha) Parc de Bercy provides a welcome green space. Former wine stores and cellars along Cours St-Emilion have been restored as restaurants, bars, and shops. Some of the warehouses have been restructured as the Pavillons de Bercy, one of which contains the Musée des Arts Forains (Fairground Museum).

Bercy's striking American Center, designed by Frank Gehry

⑮ Cité des Sciences et de l'Industrie

This hugely popular science and technology museum occupies the largest of the old Villette slaughterhouses, which now form part of a massive urban park. Architect Adrien Fainsilber has created an imaginative interplay of light, vegetation, and water in the high-tech, five-story building, which soars 133 ft (40 m) high, stretching over 7 acres (3 ha). At the museum's heart is the Explora exhibit, a fascinating guide to the worlds of science and technology. Visitors can take part in computerized games on space, the earth and ocean, computers, and sound. On other levels there are a children's science city, cinemas, a science newsroom, a library, and shops.

Planetarium
In this 260-seat auditorium you can watch eclipses and fly over Martian landscapes, thanks to their 3-D video system.

Le Nautile
This full-scale model of the Nautile, France's technologically advanced exploration submarine, represents one of the most sophisticated machines in the world.

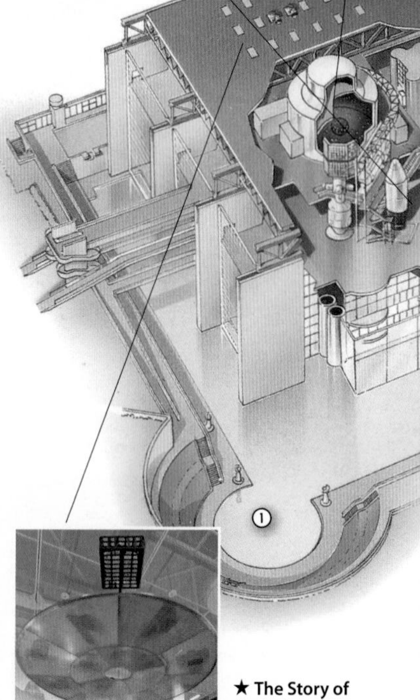

KEY

① **The moat** was designed by Fainsilber so that natural light could penetrate into the lower levels of the building.

② **The main hall** is vast, with a soaring network of shafts, bridges, escalators, and balconies, and has a cathedral-like atmosphere.

③ **The greenhouse** is a square hothouse, 105 ft (32 m) high and wide, linking the park to the building.

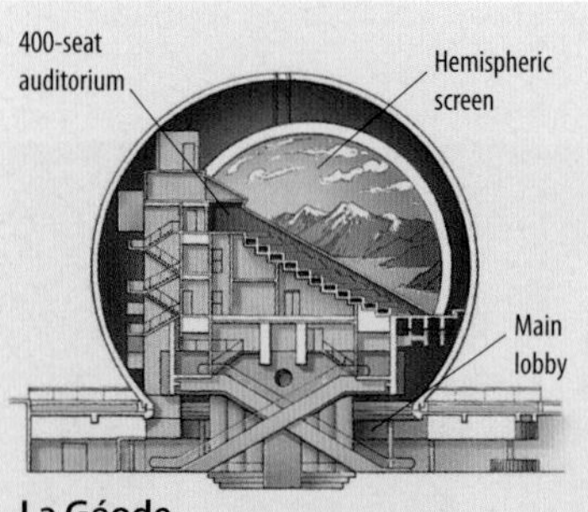

La Géode

This giant entertainment sphere houses a huge hemispherical cinema screen, 11,000 sq ft (1,000 sq m), showing IMAX films on nature, travel, history, and space.

★ The Story of the Universe
An exploration of the birth of the universe, this exhibit takes you back 13.7 billion years to the creation of the first atom.

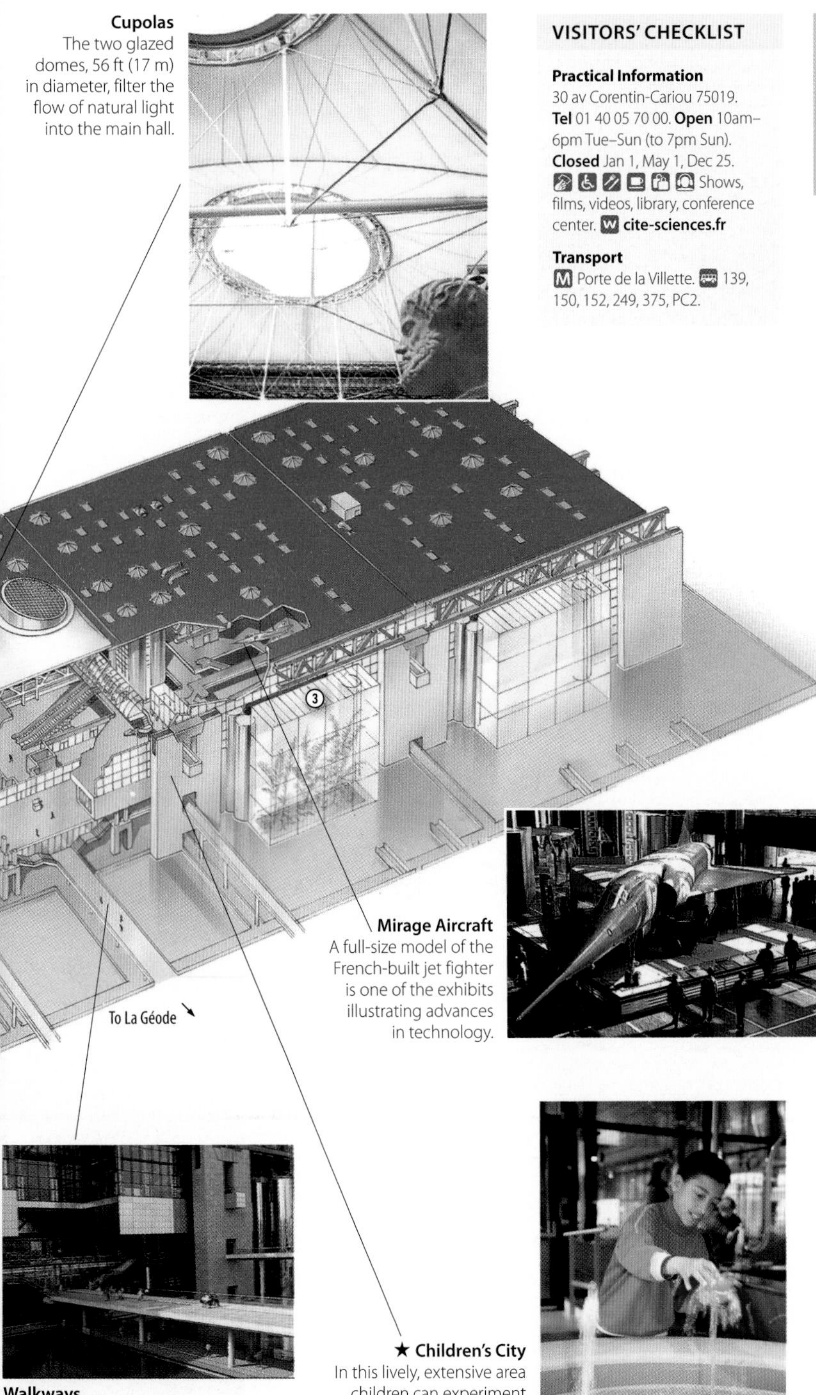

Cupolas
The two glazed domes, 56 ft (17 m) in diameter, filter the flow of natural light into the main hall.

VISITORS' CHECKLIST

Practical Information
30 av Corentin-Cariou 75019.
Tel 01 40 05 70 00. **Open** 10am–6pm Tue–Sun (to 7pm Sun).
Closed Jan 1, May 1, Dec 25.
Shows, films, videos, library, conference center. **cite-sciences.fr**

Transport
Porte de la Villette. 139, 150, 152, 249, 375, PC2.

Mirage Aircraft
A full-size model of the French-built jet fighter is one of the exhibits illustrating advances in technology.

Walkways
The walkways cross the encircling moat to link the various floors of the museum to the Géode and the park.

★ Children's City
In this lively, extensive area children can experiment and play with machines that show how scientific principles work.

Bibliothèque Nationale de France

⑳ Cité Nationale de l'Histoire de l'Immigration

293 av Daumesnil 75012. **Tel** 01 53 59 58 60. Porte Dorée. **Open** 10am–5:30pm Tue–Fri (7pm Sat & Sun). **Closed** Jan 1, May 1, Jul 14, Dec 25. restricted. **histoire-immigration.fr**

Housed in the Palais de la Porte Dorée, this museum is devoted to immigration in France. The palace is an Art Deco building designed by Albert Laprade and Léon Jaussely for the city's grand colonial exhibition in 1931.

The cellar also contains tropical fish collections, along with tortoises and crocodiles.

㉑ Château de Vincennes

Av de Paris 94300 Vincennes. **Tel** 01 48 08 31 20. Château de Vincennes. Vincennes. **Open** 10am–5pm daily (6pm mid-May–Sep). **Closed** Jan 1, May 1, Nov 1 & 11, Dec 25. Chapel & donjon: **chateau-vincennes.fr**

The Château de Vincennes was the permanent royal residence until the 17th century, before the court moved to Versailles. The donjon, the tallest fortified medieval building in Europe, the Gothic chapel, 17th-century pavilions, and moat are all worth seeing.

Beyond lies the Bois de Vincennes. Once a royal hunting ground, it is now a landscaped forest with ornamental lakes and a racecourse.

㉒ Bibliothèque Nationale de France

Quai François-Mauriac 75013. **Tel** 01 53 79 59 59. Bibliothèque François-Mitterrand. **Open** 10am–8pm Tue–Sat, 1–7pm Sun. **Closed** public hols, 2 wks Sep. **bnf.fr**

These four great book-shaped towers house 10 million volumes. The libraries offer over 400,000 titles. Other resources include digitized illustrations and sound archives. There are also frequent temporary exhibitions.

South of the City

㉓ Parc Montsouris

2 rue Gazan, bd Jourdan 75014. **Tel** 01 40 71 75 60. Pte d'Orléans. Cité Universitaire, Glacière. **Open** 9am–9:30pm (5:30pm winter) daily.

This English-style park, the second largest in Paris, was laid out by Adolphe Alphand from 1865–1878. Its restaurant, lawns, and lake – home to a variety of birds – are popular with students and children.

Skull of the reptile dimetrodon

㉔ Musée National d'Histoire Naturelle

36 rue Geoffroy Saint-Hilaire 75006. **Map** 14 D1. **Tel** 01 40 79 54 79. Jussieu, Austerlitz. **Open** 10am–6pm Wed–Mon. **Closed** May 1. Library. **mnhn.fr**

The highlight of the museum is the Grande Galerie de l'Evolution. There are also four other departments: paleontology, featuring skeletons, casts of various animals, and an exhibition showing the evolution of the vertebrate skeleton; paleobotany, devoted to plant fossils; mineralogy, including gemstones; and entomology, with some of the oldest fossilized insects on earth. The bookstore is in the house that was occupied by the naturalist Buffon, from 1772 until his death in 1788.

㉕ Jardin des Plantes

57 rue Cuvier 75005. **Map** 13 C1. Tel 01 40 79 56 01. Jussieu, Austerlitz. **Open** 8am–8pm daily (5:30pm winter). **jardindesplantes.net**

The botanical gardens were established in 1626 when Jean Hérouard and Guy de la Brosse, Louis XIII's physicians, obtained permission to found a royal medicinal herb garden. A school of botany, natural history, and pharmacy followed and the garden opened to the public in 1640. One of the city's great parks, it contains a natural history museum, botanical school, and zoo.

As well as vistas and walkways flanked by ancient statues, the park has an alpine garden with plants from Corsica, Morocco, the Alps, and the Himalayas, and an unrivaled display of herbaceous and wild plants. The Cedar of Lebanon here, originally from Britain's Kew Gardens, was the first to be planted in France.

Rue Mouffetard, one of several markets near Jardin des Plantes

㉖ Institut du Monde Arabe

1 rue des Fossés St-Bernard, Pl Mohammed V 75005. **Map** 9 C5. **Tel** 01 40 51 38 38. Ⓜ Jussieu, Cardinal-Lemoine. Museum & temp exhibs: **Open** Jul–Aug: 1–6pm Tue–Sat; Sep–Jun: 10am–6pm Tue–Sun. **Closed** May 1. **W imarabe.org**

This magnificent modern building was designed by French architect Jean Nouvel, and cleverly combines high-tech details with the spirit of traditional Arab architecture. From the fourth to seventh floors there is a comprehensive display of Islamic art from the 9th to 19th centuries, including glassware, ceramics, and sculpture. The museum's highlight is its collection of astrolabes, the much-prized tool used by ancient Arab astronomers.

Institut du Monde Arabe, covered with photosensitive lightscreens

㉗ Mosquée de Paris

2 pl du Puits de l'Ermite 75005. **Tel** 01 45 35 97 33. Ⓜ Place Monge. **Open** 9am–noon, 2–6pm Sat–Thu. **Closed** Muslim hols. Library. **W mosquee-de-paris.org**

Built in the 1920s in the Hispano-Moorish style, these buildings are the center for Paris's Muslim community. Once used solely by scholars, the mosque has expanded over the years and now houses some salubrious but fun Turkish baths, a fine restaurant, and a beautiful *salon de thé*.

㉘ Parc André Citroën

2 rue Cauchy, Quai André Citroën 75015. **Tel** 01 40 71 75 60. Ⓜ Balard. **Open** May–Sep: 8am–8:30 pm daily; Oct–Apr: 9am–7pm daily.

Designed by both landscapers and architects, this park is a fascinating blend of styles, ranging from wildflower meadow in the north to sophisticated monochrome mineral and sculpture gardens in the southern section. Modern water sculptures dot the park.

Tour Montparnasse

㉙ Montparnasse

75014 & 75015. **Map** 11 & 12. Ⓜ Montparnasse, Vavin, Raspail, Edgar Quinet. Tour Montparnasse: 33 av du Maine. **Open** Apr–Sep: 9:30am–11:30pm; Oct–Mar: 9:30am–10:30pm. **W tourmontparnasse56.com**

The name Montparnasse was first used ironically, when 17th-century arts students performed on a "mount" of rubble left over from quarrying. In ancient Greece, Mount Parnassus was dedicated to poetry, music, and beauty. By the 19th century, crowds were drawn to the local cabarets and bars by duty-free prices. The mixture of art and high living was particularly potent in the 1920s and 1930s when Hemingway, Picasso, Cocteau, Giacometti, Matisse, and Modigliani were "Montparnos," as the residents were called. The modern *quartier* is dominated by the much-hated **Tour Montparnasse**, although the view from the top (the 56th floor) is spectacular.

㉚ Cimetière du Montparnasse

3 bd Edgar Quinet 75014. **Map** 12 D3. **Tel** 01 44 10 86 50. Ⓜ Edgar Quinet. **Open** mid-Mar–Nov: 8am–6pm Mon–Fri, 8:30am–6pm Sat, 9am–6pm Sun; Dec–mid-Mar: closes 5:30pm. 01 40 33 85 85

Montparnasse cemetery opened in 1824. Among those buried here are Serge Gainsbourg, Charles Baudelaire, Jean-Paul Sartre and Simone de Beauvoir, and Guy de Maupassant.

㉛ Catacombes

1 av du Colonel Henri Rol-Tanguy 75014. **Map** 12 E3. **Tel** 01 43 22 47 63. Ⓜ Denfert-Rochereau. **Open** 10am–5pm Tue–Sun. **Closed** public hols. **W catacombes.paris.fr**

A long series of quarry tunnels built in the 13th century, the catacombs are now lined with ancient bones and skulls. Thousands of rotting corpses were transported here in the 1780s to absorb the excess from the insanitary Les Halles cemetery.

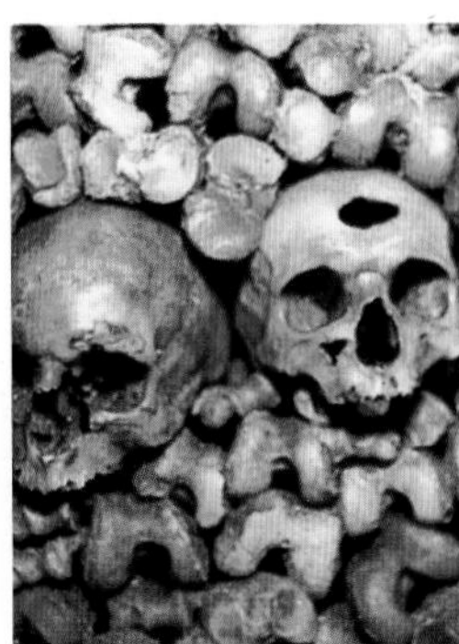

Skulls and bones stored in the catacombs

SHOPS AND MARKETS

For many people, Paris epitomizes luxury and good living. Exquisitely dressed men and women sip wine by the banks of the Seine against the backdrop of splendid French architecture, or browse at small specialist shops. The least expensive way of joining the chic set is to create French style with accessories or costume jewelry. Alternatively, try shopping in the January or July sales. If your budget allows, take the opportunity to buy world-famous Paris fashions, or feast on the wonderful gourmet delicacies displayed with consummate artistry. Parisian shopping streets and markets are the ideal place to indulge in the French custom of strolling for the express purpose of seeing and being seen. For up-to-the-minute high fashion, the rue du Faubourg-St-Honoré is hard to beat, with its exquisite couture window displays. Browsing around the bookstalls along the Seine is another favorite French pastime. A survey of some of the best and most famous places to shop follows.

Shopping in avenue Montaigne

Opening Hours

Shops are usually open from 10am–7pm, Monday to Saturday, but hours can vary. Many department stores stay open late on Thursday, while boutiques may shut for an hour or two at midday. Markets and local neighborhood shops usually close on Mondays. Some places shut for the summer, usually in August, but they may leave a note on the door suggesting an equivalent shop nearby that is open.

Payment and VAT

Cash is readily available from the ATMs in most banks, which accept both credit and bank debit cards. Visa and MasterCard are the most widely accepted credit cards.

A sales tax (TVA) from 5.5–19.6 per cent is imposed on most goods and services in EU countries. Non-EU residents shopping in France are entitled to a refund of this if they spend a minimum of €175 in one store in one day. You must have been resident in France for less than six months and either carry the goods with you out of the country within three months of purchase, or get the store to forward them to you. Larger stores will generally supply a form *(bordereau de détaxe* or *bordereau de vente)* and help you to fill it in. When you leave France or the EU you present the form to Customs, who either permit you to be reimbursed straightaway, or forward your claim to the place where you bought the merchandise; the store eventually sends you a refund.

The Chanel logo, recognized worldwide

Sales

The best sales *(soldes)* are held in January and July, although more and more you can find good deals throughout the year. If you see goods labeled *Stock*, it means that they are stock items, reduced for clearance. *Dégriffé* means designer labels, (with the label cut out) marked down, frequently from the previous year's collections. *Fripes* indicates that the clothes are secondhand.

The Center of Paris Couture

The couture houses are concentrated on the Right Bank, around rue du Faubourg-St-Honoré and avenue Montaigne.

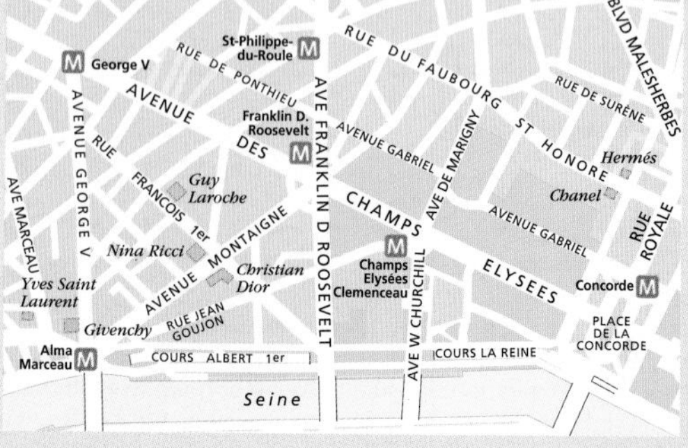

Department Stores

Much of the pleasure of shopping in Paris is derived from going to the small specialist shops. But if time is short, try the *grands magasins* (department stores). Some still operate a ticket system for selling goods. The shop assistant writes up a ticket for goods from their own boutique. You take the ticket to one of the cashiers, and then return with the validated ticket to pick up your purchase. This can be time-consuming, so go early in the morning and don't shop on Saturdays, unless you enjoy a crush. The French do not pay much attention to lines so be assertive! One peculiarity of a visit is that the security guards may ask to inspect your bags as you leave. These are random checks and should not be taken as an implication of theft.

All department stores have places to eat, although the stores themselves tend to have different emphases. **Au Printemps** is noted for its exciting and innovative household goods section, vast cosmetic range, and large menswear store. The clothes departments for women and children are well stocked. Fashion shows are held at 10am on Tuesdays (and each Friday from April to October: by invitation only). The lovely domed restaurant in the cupola often hosts chic after-hours parties, which are private, but a visit to the restaurant during shopping hours is worthwhile.

Kenzo designerwear in the place des Victoires

The 1865 facade of Au Printemps department store

Cartier, one of the world's most exclusive stores

BHV (Le Bazar de l'Hôtel de Ville) is a DIY enthusiast's paradise, and sells a host of other items, such as fashion decor. The Left Bank's **Le Bon Marché** was Paris's first department store and today is its chicest. The designer clothing sections are well-sourced, the high-end accessories are excellent, and the own-brand linen has a good quality to price ratio. The prepared food and gourmet grocery sections serve restaurant-quality fare to take away.

Galeries Lafayette is perhaps the best-known department store and has a wide range of clothes available at all price levels. Its first-floor trends section plays host to lots of innovative designers. Galeries Lafayette Gourmet, the food court, sells a range of French and international delicacies. Across the road is the store's homeware building, which stocks a good range of kitchenware.

FNAC specializes in records, books (foreign editions can be found at Les Halles), and electronic equipment, while **FNAC Odéon** sells a wide range of the latest technological equipment. **Gibert Joseph** has an impressive selection of books, records, and DVDs.

Addresses

Au Printemps

64 bd Haussmann 75009. **Map** 4 D4. **Tel** 01 42 82 50 00. **W printemps.com**

BHV

55 rue de la Rivoli 75004. **Map** 9 B3. **Tel** 09 77 40 14 00. **W bhv.fr**

Le Bon Marché

24 rue de Sèvres 75007. **Map** 7 C5. **Tel** 01 44 39 80 00. **W lebonmarche.com**

FNAC

Forum des Halles, 1/7 rue Pierre Lescot 75001. **Map** 9 A2. **Tel** 0825 020 020. **W fnac.com**

FNAC Odéon

77–81 bd St-Germain 75006. **Map** 9 A5. **Tel** 0825 020 020.

Galeries Lafayette

40 bd Haussmann 75009. **Map** 4 E4. **Tel** 01 42 82 34 56. **W galerieslafayette.com**

Gibert Joseph

5 rue Pierre Sarrazin 75006. **Map** 8 F5. **Tel** 01 44 41 88 88. **W gibertjoseph.com**

Clothes and Accessories

For many people Paris is synonymous with fashion, and Parisian style is the ultimate in chic. More than anywhere else in the world, women in Paris seem to be in tune with current trends and when a new season arrives appear, as one, to don the look. Though less trend-conscious generally, Parisian men are aware of style, and mix and match patterns and colors with *élan*. Finding the right clothes at the right price means knowing where to shop. For every luxury boutique on the avenue Montaigne, there are ten young designers' shops waiting to become the next Jean-Paul Gaultier – and hundreds more selling imitations.

Haute Couture

Paris is the home of *haute couture*. The original *couture* garments, as opposed to the imitations and adaptations, are one-off creations, designed by one of the nine *haute couture* houses listed with the Fédération Française de la Couture. The rules for being classified are fairly strict, and many of the top designers are not included. Astronomical prices put *haute couture* beyond the reach of all but a few immensely deep pockets, but it is still the lifeblood of the fashion industry providing inspiration for the mass market.

Women's Clothes

Most *couture* houses are found on or near the rue du Faubourg-St-Honoré and avenue Montaigne: **Christian Dior**, **Pierre Cardin**, **Chanel**, **Christian Lacroix**, **Versace**, **Givenchy**, **Nina Ricci**, **Georgio Armani** and **Yves Saint Laurent**.

Hermès has classic country chic. **MaxMara**'s Italian elegance is popular in France, and no one can resist a **Giorgio Armani** suit. The legendary **Prada** store has stuck to the Right Bank, but many fashion houses prefer the Left Bank.

Many designers have a Left Bank branch in addition to their Right Bank bastions, and they all have ready-to-wear shops here. For sheer quality there's **Georges Rech**, and **Jil Sander** for exquisite tailoring. Try **Sonia Rykiel** for knitwear, and **Barbara Bui** for soft, feminine clothes. **Comptoir des Cotonniers** has branches throughout Paris and stocks excellent basics, and **Vanessa Bruno** is extremely popular for feminine flair.

For ready-to-wear, head to place des Victoires. **Kenzo** is here (although its flagship store is located near the Pont Neuf), along with fellow Japanese designers **Comme des Garçons**, with quirky fashion for both sexes. In nearby rue du Jour, find the timeless elegance of **Agnès B**.

The Marais is a haven for up-and-coming designers. One of the best streets is the rue des Rosiers, which includes the wonderful **L'Eclaireur**. **Anne Fontaine** is on the neighboring rue des Francs-Bourgeois, and daring designer **Azzedine Alaïa** is just around the corner.

The Bastille area has trendy boutiques, as well as established names, including **Jean-Paul Gaultier** and high-street stores like **Petit Bateau**. **Isabel Marant's** boutique is renowned for its originality.

Young designers' clothes are found at **Colette**, **Stella Cadente**, and **Zadig & Voltaire**.

Children's Clothes

Lots of options for children exist in various styles and many price ranges. Many top designers of adult clothes also have boutiques for children. These include **Kenzo**, **Baby Dior**, and **Agnès B**. Ready-to-wear shops such as **Jacadi** and **Du Pareil au Même** are serviceable and wide-ranging, and **Tartine et Chocolat**'s best-selling garments are overalls. **Bonpoint** stocks adorably chic clothing for mini-Parisians. **Petit Bateau** is coveted as much by grown-ups as it is by children. The inevitable has finally happened – children now have their own concept store in **Bonton**.

For little feet, **Froment-Leroyer** probably offers the best all-round classics.

Men's Clothes

Men don't have the luxury of *haute couture* dressing and their choice is limited to ready-to-wear. On the Right Bank, there's **Giorgio Armani**, **Pierre Cardin**, **Lanvin** (also good for accessories), and **Yves Saint Laurent**. On the Left Bank, **Michel Axel** and **Jean-Charles de Castelbajac** are known for their ties, and **Francesco Smalto**'s elegant creations are worn by some of the world's leading movie stars. Yohji Yamamoto's clothes in **Y3** are for those who are intent on making a serious fashion statement, while **Gianni Versace** is classic, suave, and Italian in style.

The ultimate in Parisian elegance for men, however, is a suit, custom-made shirt, or silk tie from **Charvet**.

Vintage and Secondhand Stores

The vintage craze hit Paris some time back and there are some wonderful shops to plunder for a retro look. The best of the bunch is **Didier Ludot**, where an Aladdin's Cave of chic *haute couture* is elegantly displayed. The **Depôt-Vente de Buci-Bourbon** is another good place to bargain hunt. A cheaper option is to head for one of the secondhand consignment stores. Chic Parisians discard their outfits with the seasons so it is very easy to pick up some quality items, often in top condition, from places such as **Réciproque** in Passy or **Alternatives** in the Marais.

A cheaper option for sample pieces and sale stock can be found at **Le Mouton à Cinq Pattes**.

Jewelry

The *couture* houses probably stock some of the best jewelry and scarves. **Chanel**'s jewels are classics and **Christian Lacroix**'s are fun. **Boutique YSL** is a great place for accessories.

Among the main expensive Paris jewelry outlets are **Boucheron**, **Mauboussin**, and **Poiray**. They are for the serious jewelry buyer. Other top retailers include **Harry Winston** and **Cartier**. **Dinh Van** has some quirky pieces, whilst **Mikimoto** is a must for pearls, and **H. Stern** has some innovative designs using semi-precious and precious stones. For a range of more unusual jewelry and accessories, try the **Swarovski Boutique**, which is owned by the Swarovksi crystal family.

Shoes and Bags

For both classic and wild footwear designs, you can't beat **Miu Miu**. **Rodolphe Ménudier** and **Christian Louboutin** are mainstays for sexy stilettos. **Carel** stocks smart basics, and **Jonak** is a must for good imitations of designer footwear.

For ladies' handbags, nothing beats **Chanel** or **Dior** at the top end of the scale, although **Goyard** comes close. Mid-range bags from **Furla** are a great compromise. Fabric bags from **Jamin Puech** or **Vanessa Bruno** are a feature in every chic Parisian closet. For those with tighter purse strings, cheap, cheerful, and stylish bags can be found at **Lollipops**.

Lingerie

For modern lingerie go to **Fifi Chachnil**, whose shop is filled with colorful underwear. **La Boîte à Bas** sells fine French stockings, whereas **Princesse Tam Tam** offers quality items at reasonable prices, while divine designer underwear can be found at cult store **Sabbia Rosa**. The ultimate in Parisian lingerie can be bought off the peg or made to order at **Cadolle**, the store which invented the bra.

DIRECTORY

Women's Clothes

Agnès B.
2–3–6–19 rue du Jour 75001. **Map** 9 A1. **Tel** 01 45 08 56 56. **W** agnesb.com
One of several branches.

Anne Fontaine
17 rue Francois 1er 75008. **Map** 6 F1. **Tel** 01 44 59 81 59. One of several branches.

Azzedine Alaïa
7 rue de Moussy 75004. **Map** 9 C3. **Tel** 01 42 72 19 19.

Barbara Bui
23 rue Etienne-Marcel 75001. **Map** 9 A1. **Tel** 01 40 26 43 65. **W** barbarabui.com
One of several branches.

Chanel
51 av Montaigne 75008. **Map** 3 A5. **Tel** 01 44 50 73 00. **W** chanel.com
One of several branches.

Christian Dior
30 av Montaigne 75008. **Map** 6 F1. **Tel** 01 40 73 73 73. **W** dior.com

Christian Lacroix
2 rue Saint-Sulpice 75006. **Map** 8 E4. **Tel** 01 46 33 48 95. **W** christian-lacroix.fr

Colette
213 rue St-Honoré 75001. **Map** 8 D1. **Tel** 01 55 35 33 90. **W** colette.fr

Comme des Garçons
54 rue du Faubourg St-Honoré 75008. **Map** 2 E3. **Tel** 01 53 30 27 27.

Comptoir des Cotonniers
12 pl St-Sulpice 75006. **Map** 8 E4. **Tel** 01 56 81 00 20.

L'Eclaireur
40 rue de Sévigné 75003. **Map** 10 D4. **Tel** 01 48 87 10 22. **W** leclaireur.com

Georges Rech
181 blvd St-Germain 75006. **Map** 8 D4. **Tel** 01 45 48 31 77 51. **W** georges-rech.fr
One of several branches.

Giorgio Armani
18 av Montaigne 75008. **Map** 2 E3. **Tel** 01 42 61 55 09. **W** armani.com

Givenchy
3 av Georges V 75008. **Map** 2 E5. **Tel** 01 44 31 51 25. **W** givenchy.com

Hermès
24 rue du Faubourg-St-Honoré 75008. **Map** 3 C5. **Tel** 01 40 17 46 00. **W** hermes.com
One of several branches.

Isabel Marant
16 rue de Charonne 75011. **Map** 10 F4. **Tel** 01 49 29 71 55. **W** isabelmarant.com

Jean-Paul Gaultier
6 rue Vivienne 75002. **Map** 8 F1. **Tel** 01 42 86 05 05. **W** jeanpaulgaultier.com
One of two branches.

Jil Sander
56 av Montaigne 75008. **Map** 6 F1. **Tel** 01 44 95 06 70. **W** jilsander.com

Kenzo
3 pl des Victoires 75001. **Map** 8 F1. **Tel** 01 40 39 72 03. **W** kenzo.com
One of several branches.

MaxMara
31 av Montaigne 75008. **Map** 6 F1. **Tel** 01 47 20 61 13. **W** maxmara.com
One of several branches.

Nina Ricci
39 av Montaigne 75008. **Map** 6 F1. **Tel** 01 40 88 64 61. **W** ninaricci.fr

Pierre Cardin
59 Faubourg St-Honoré 75008. **Map** 3 B5. **Tel** 01 42 66 68 98. **W** pierrecardin.com

Prada
10 av Montaigne 75008. **Map** 6 F1. **Tel** 01 53 23 99 42. **W** prada.com

Sonia Rykiel
175 bd St-Germain 75006. **Map** 8 D4. **Tel** 01 49 54 60 60. **W** soniarykiel.com
One of several branches.

Stella Cadente
102 blvd Beaumarchais 75011. **Map** 10 E2. **Tel** 09 50 90 25 55. **W** stella-cadente.com

Vanessa Bruno
25 rue St-Sulpice 75006. **Map** 8 E5. **Tel** 01 43 54 41 04. **W** vanessabruno.com

Versace
45 ave Montaigne 75008. **Map** 3 A5. **Tel** 01 47 42 88 02. **W** versace.com

Yves Saint Laurent
38 rue du Faubourg-St-Honoré 75008. **Map** 3 C5. **Tel** 01 42 65 74 59. **W** ysl.com
One of several branches.

Zadig & Voltaire
9 rue du 29 Juillet 75001. **Map** 8 D1. **Tel** 01 42 92 00 61. **W** zadig-et-voltaire.com One of several branches.

DIRECTORY

Children's Clothes

Bonpoint
320 rue St-Honoré 75001. **Map** 9 A2. **Tel** 01 49 27 94 82. **w bonpoint.com**

Bonton
82 rue de Grenelle 75007. **Map** 6 F3. **Tel** 01 44 39 09 20. **w bonton.fr**

Du Pareil au Même
1 rue St-Denis 75001. **Map** 9 B3. **Tel** 01 42 36 07 57. **w dpam.com**

Froment-Leroyer
7 rue Vavin 75006. **Map** 12 E1. **Tel** 01 43 54 33 15. **w froment-leroyer.fr**

Jacadi
17 rue Tronchet 75008. **Map** 3 C5. **Tel** 01 42 65 84 98. **w jacadi.com**

Petit Bateau
116 av des Champs Elysées 75008. **Map** 2 E4. **Tel** 01 40 74 02 03. **w petit-bateau.com**

Tartine et Chocolat
84 rue du Faubourg-St-Honoré 75008. **Map** 3 B5. **Tel** 01 45 62 44 04. **w tartine-et-chocolat.fr**

Men's Clothes

Charvet
28 pl Vendôme 75001. **Map** 4 D5. **Tel** 01 42 60 30 70. **w charvet.com**

Francesco Smalto
44 rue François 1er 75008. **Map** 2 F5. **Tel** 01 47 20 96 04. **w smalto.com**

Gianni Versace
45 av Montaigne 75008. **Map** 2 F5. **Tel** 01 47 42 88 02. **w versace.com**

Giorgio Armani
(see p147).

Jean-Charles de Castelbajac
61 rue des Saints Pères 75006. **Map** 8 D4. **Tel** 09 64 48 48 54. **w jc-de-castelbajac.com**

Kenzo
(see p147).

Lanvin
15 rue du Faubourg St-Honoré 75008. **Map** 10 F4. **Tel** 01 44 71 31 25. **w lanvin.com**

Michel Axel
44 rue du Dragon 75006. **Map** 8 E4. **Tel** 01 42 84 13 86. **w michelaxel.com**

Pierre Cardin
(see p147).

Y3
47 rue Etienne Marcel 75001. **Map** 9 A1. **Tel** 01 45 08 82 45. **w y-3.com**

Yves Saint Laurent
6 pl St-Sulpice 75006. **Map** 8 D4. **Tel** 01 43 29 43 00. **w ysl.com**

Vintage and Secondhand Stores

Alternatives
18 rue du Roi-de-Sicile 75004. **Map** 9 C3. **Tel** 01 42 78 31 50.

Depôt-Vente de Buci Bourbon
4/6 rue de Bourbon-le-Château 75006. **Map** 8 E4. **Tel** 01 44 51 51 82.

Didier Ludot
24 Galerie Montpensier 75001. **Map** 8 E1. **Tel** 01 42 96 06 56. **w didierludot.fr**

Le Mouton à Cinq Pattes
8/18 rue St-Placide 75006. **Map** 8 D5. **Tel** 01 45 48 86 26. **w moutonacinq pattesparis.com**

Réciproque
89–101 rue de la Pompe 75016. **Map** 5 A1. **Tel** 01 47 04 30 28. **w reciproque.fr**

Jewelry

Boucheron
26 pl Vendôme 75001. **Map** 4 D5. **Tel** 01 42 61 58 16. **w boucheron.com**

Cartier
13 rue de la Paix 75002. **Map** 4 D5. **Tel** 01 58 18 23 00. **w cartier.fr**

Dinh Van
16 rue de la Paix 75002. **Map** 4 D5. **Tel** 01 42 61 74 49. **w dinhvan.com**

H. Stern
3 rue Castiglione 75001. **Map** 8 D1. **Tel** 01 42 60 22 27. **w hstern.net**

Harry Winston
29 av Montaigne 75008. **Map** 6 F1. **Tel** 01 47 20 03 09. **w harrywinston.com**

Mauboussin
20 pl Vendôme 75001. **Map** 4 D5. **Tel** 01 44 55 10 00. **w mauboussin.fr**

Mikimoto
8 pl Vendôme 75001. **Map** 4 D5. **Tel** 01 42 60 33 55. **w mikimoto.fr**

Poiray
1 rue de la Paix 75002. **Map** 4 D5. **Tel** 01 42 61 70 58. **w poiray.com**

Swarovski Boutique
146 av des Champs Elysées 75008. **Map** 2 E4. **Tel** 01 45 61 13 80. **w swarovski.com**

Shoes and Bags

Carel
2 rue Tronchet 75008. **Map** 4 D4. **Tel** 01 42 66 21 58. **w carel.fr**

Christian Louboutin
38-40 rue de Grenelle 75007. **Map** 6 F3. **Tel** 01 42 22 33 07. **w christian louboutin.com**

Furla
74 av des Champs-Elysées 75008. **Map** 2 F5. **Tel** 01 40 75 02 40. **w furla.com**

Goyard
233 rue St-Honoré 75001. **Map** 3 C5. **Tel** 01 42 60 57 04. **w goyard.com**

Jamin Puech
26 rue Cambon 75001. **Map** 4 D5. **Tel** 01 40 20 40 28. **w jamin-puech.com**

Jonak
70 rue de Rennes 75006. **Map** 12 D1. **Tel** 01 45 48 27 11. **w jonak.fr**

Lollipops
60 rue Tiquetonne 75002. **Map** 9 A1. **Tel** 01 42 33 15 72. **w lollipopsparis.fr**

Miu Miu
219 rue St-Honoré 75001. **Map** 8 D1. **Tel** 01 58 62 53 20. **w miumiu.com**

Rodolphe Ménudier
14 rue de Castiglione 75001. **Map** 8 D1. **Tel** 06 07 02 81 91. **w rodolphmenudier. com**

Vanessa Bruno
25 rue St-Sulpice 75006. **Map** 8 E5. **Tel** 01 43 54 41 04. **w vanessabruno.com**

Lingerie

La Boîte à Bas
27 rue Boissy-d'Anglas 75008. **Map** 3 C5. **Tel** 01 42 66 26 85.

Cadolle
4 rue Cambon 75001. **Map** 4 D5. **Tel** 01 42 60 94 22. **w cadolle.com**

Fifi Chachnil
231 rue St-Honoré 75001. **Map** 8 D1. **Tel** 01 42 61 21 83. **w fifichachnil.com**

Princesse Tam Tam
52 bd St-Michel 75006. **Map** 8 F5. **Tel** 01 40 51 72 99. **w princessetamtam. com**

Sabbia Rosa
73 rue des Sts-Pères 75006. **Map** 8 D4. **Tel** 01 45 48 88 37.

Gifts and Souvenirs

Paris has a wealth of stylish gift options, from designer accessories to Eiffel Tower paperweights. Shops on the rue de Rivoli and around major tourist attractions offer a range of cheap holiday paraphernalia, or go to one of the souvenir stores such as **Les Drapeaux de France.**

Perfume

Many shops advertise discounted perfume. They include **Eiffel Shopping** near the Eiffel Tower. The **Sephora** chain has a big selection, or try the department stores for a range of beauty brands which are hard to find elsewhere.

Parfums Caron has many scents created at the turn of the 19th century, which are unavailable elsewhere. Beautifully packaged perfumes made from natural essences are available from **Annick Goutal**. **Guerlain** has the ultimate in beauty care, while the elegant shops of **L'Artisan Parfumeur** specialize in exquisitely packaged scents evoking specific memories.

Household Goods

It is difficult to ignore some of the world's most elegant tableware. Luxury homeware stores line the rue Royale. **Lalique**'s Art Nouveau and Art Deco glass sculptures are collected all over the world. Impeccable silverware comes from **Christofle**.

For significant savings on porcelain and crystal, try **Editions Paradis**, which stocks Baccarat, Daum, and Limoges crystal, or why not go to **Baccarat** itself.

La Chaise Longue has a selection of fun gift ideas to suit most tastes, and **BoConcept** has a wide range of contemporary goods to add a new lease of life to any home.

Books

Some department stores have a books section, and there are several English-language bookshops such as **W. H. Smith** and **Brentano's**. The cozy **Shakespeare & Company** and **Galignani** (the first English bookstores in Europe) are good for convivial browsing among expats. French-language bookstores include **La Hune**, specializing in art, cinema, fashion, and photography, and **Gibert Joseph** for educational books.

Specialist Shops

A La Civette is perhaps Paris's most beautiful tobacconist's, stocking a vast range of cigars behind specially humidified store windows. **La Boîte à Joujoux** is one of the largest dollhouse boutiques in Paris, while the name **Cassegrain** is synonymous with high-quality stationery and paper products.

DIRECTORY

Souvenir Shops

Les Drapeaux de France
1 pl Colette 75001.
Map 8 E1. **Tel** 01 40 20 00 11. **W drapeaux-de-france.net**

Perfume

Annick Goutal
16 rue de Bellechasse 75007. **Map** 7 C3.
Tel 01 45 51 36 13.
W annickgoutal.com

L'Artisan Parfumeur
24 bd Raspail 75007. **Map** 12 D1. **Tel** 01 42 22 23 32.
W artisanparfumeur.com One of several branches.

Eiffel Shopping
9 av de Suffren 75007. **Map** 6 D3.
Tel 01 45 66 55 30.

Guerlain
68 av des Champs-Elysées 75008. **Map** 2 F5.
Tel 01 45 62 52 57.
W guerlain.com

Parfums Caron
34 av Montaigne 75008.
Map 6 F1.
Tel 01 47 23 40 82.
W parfumscaron.com

Sephora
70–72 av des Champs-Elysées 75008. **Map** 7 B1.
Tel 01 53 93 22 50.
W sephora.fr

Household Goods

Baccarat
11 pl de la Madeleine 75008. **Map** 3 C5. **Tel** 01 42 65 36 26. **W baccarat.fr**

BoConcept
8 bd Sebastopol 75004.
Map 9 A3. **Tel** 01 42 78 66 66. **W boconcept.fr**

La Chaise Longue
30 rue Croix-des-Petits-Champs 75001. **Map** 8 F1.
Tel 01 42 96 32 14.
W lachaiselongue.fr

Christofle
24 rue de la Paix 75002.
Map 4 D5. **Tel** 01 42 65 62 43. **W christofle.com**

Lalique
11 rue Royale 75008.
Map 3 C5.
Tel 01 53 05 12 81.
W lalique.com

Editions Paradis
29 rue de Paradis 75010.
Tel 01 42 46 60 29.
W editionsparadis.com

Books

Brentano's
37 av de l'Opéra 75002.
Map 4 E5. **Tel** 01 42 60 87 37. **W librairie-brentanos-paris.com**

Gibert Joseph
26–34 bd St-Michel 75006. **Map** 8 F5.
Tel 01 44 41 88 88.
W gibertjoseph.com

La Hune
18 rue de l'Abbaye 75006. **Map** 8 D4.
Tel 01 45 48 35 85.

Librairie Galignani
224 rue de Rivoli 75001.
Tel 01 42 60 76 07.
W galignani.com

Shakespeare & Company
37 rue de la Bûcherie 75005.
Map 9 A4.
Tel 01 43 25 40 93.
W shakespeareandcompany.com

W. H. Smith
248 rue de Rivoli 75001.
Map 7 C1.
Tel 01 44 77 88 99.
W whsmith.fr

Specialist Shops

A La Civette
157 rue St-Honoré 75001. **Map** 8 F2.
Tel 01 42 96 04 99.
W alacivette.fr

La Boîte à Joujoux
41–43 passage Jouffroy 75009.
Tel 01 48 24 58 37.
W joujoux.com

Cassegrain
422 rue St-Honoré 75008.
Map 3 C5.
Tel 01 42 60 20 08.
W cassegrain.fr.

Food and Drink

Paris is as famous for food as it is for fashion. Gastronomic treats include *foie gras*, cold meats from the *charcuterie*, cheese, and wine. Certain streets are so overflowing with food shops that you can put together a picnic for 20 in no time: try the rue Montorgueil *(see Map 9 A1)*. The rue Rambuteau, running on either side of the Centre Pompidou, has a marvellous row of fishmongers and delicatessens.

Bread and Cakes

There is a vast range of breads and pastries in France's capital. The *baguette* is often translated as "French bread," a *bâtard* is similar but thicker, while a *ficelle* is thinner. A *fougasse* is a crusty, flat loaf often filled with onions, cheese, herbs, or spices.

Croissants can be bought *ordinaire* or *au beurre* – the latter is flakier and more buttery. *Pain au chocolat* is a chocolate-filled pastry eaten for breakfast, and *chausson aux pommes* is filled with apples. There are also pear, plum, and rhubarb variations. A *pain aux raisins* is a bread-like wheel filled with custard and raisins.

Poilâne sells perhaps the only bread in Paris known by the name of its baker (the late Lionel, brother of Max) and his hearty whole-wheat loaves are tremendously popular.

Many think **Ganachaud** bakes the best bread in Paris. Thirty different kinds, with ingredients such as walnuts and fruit, are made in the old-fashioned ovens.

Maison Kayser, a high-end chain bakery, produces a variety of artisan breads including *pain au cèrèale* (multi-grain bread) and *pain d'amande* (almond bread), the owner's favorite.

The Jewish delicatessens have the best ryes and the only pumpernickels in town. One of the best is **Sacha Finkelsztajn**.

Le Moulin de la Vierge uses a wood fire to bake organic breads and rich pound cakes. **Boulanger et Pâtisserie Secco** is known for light, airy madeleines and "Paris–Brest" (*choux* pastry filled with hazelnut praline butter-cream, in honor of the famous bicycle race).

Pierre Hermé is to cakes what Chanel is to fashion, while **Ladurée**'s macaroons are legendary.

Chocolate

Like all food in France, chocolate is to be savored. **Christian Constant**'s low-sugar creations are made with pure cocoa and are known to connoisseurs. **Dalloyau** makes all types of chocolate and is not too expensive (it is also known for its pâtisserie and cold meats). **Fauchon** is world famous for its luxury food products. Its chocolates are excellent, as is the pâtisserie. Robert Linxe at **La Maison du Chocolat** is constantly inventing fresh, rich chocolates with mouthwatering exotic ingredients. **Richart** boasts beautifully presented and hugely expensive chocolates, which are usually liqueur-filled or coated with dark chocolate.

Charcuterie and Foie Gras

Charcuteries often sell cheese, snails, truffles, smoked salmon, caviar, and wine as well as cold meats. **Fauchon** has a good grocery, as does the department store **Le Bon Marché**. **Hédiard** is a luxury shop similar to Fauchon, and **Maison de la Truffe** sells *foie gras* and sausages as well as truffles. For Beluga caviar, Georgian tea, and Russian vodka, go to **Petrossian**.

Award-winning charcutier **Gilles Verot**'s delicacies are internationally renowned. His shops are a feast for the eyes as well as the stomach. **Maison Pou** is a sparklingly clean and popular store selling *pâté en croute* (pâté baked in pastry), *boudins* (black and white puddings), Lyonnais sausages, ham, and *foie gras*. Just off the Champs-Elysées, **Vignon** has superb *foie gras* and Lyonnais sausages as well as popular prepared food.

Together with truffles and caviar, *foie gras* is the ultimate in gourmet food. Though most specialist food shops sell *foie gras*, you can be sure of quality at **Comtesse du Barry**, which has six outlets in Paris. **Divay** is relatively inexpensive and will ship overseas. **Lafitte** has a wide range of *foie gras* and wines including gift boxes suitable for giving as presents.

Cheese

Although camembert is undoubtedly a favorite, there is an overwhelming range of cheeses available and a friendly *fromager* will always help you choose. **Marie-Anne Cantin** is one of the leading figures in the fight to protect traditional production methods, and her fine cheeses are available from the store that she inherited from her father. Some say that **Alléosse** is the best cheese delicatessen in Paris – all the cheeses are made according to traditional methods. **Fromagerie Quatrehomme** sells farm-made cheeses, many of which are in danger of becoming extinct. These include a rare and delicious truffle Brie (when in season). **Le Jardin Fromager** is one of the best shops in Paris for all types of cheese – the *chèvre* (goat's cheese) is particularly good, as are the *camemberts au lait cru* (cheese made with unpasteurized milk), which ooze over the plate. **Laurent Dubois**, medaled cheese maker in the boulevard Saint-Germain, is known for his marinated goat's cheese.

Androuët is a Parisian institution with several branches across the city. Try a pungent Munster or a really ripe Brie. A charming cheese shop, **La Fermette** offers a dazzling array of dairy products, which the staff will encase in plastic for the journey home, imperative when bringing cheese through customs.

Well-heeled locals line up down the street to buy oozing *livarot* and sharp *chèvre* from **La Fromagerie d'Auteuil**.

Wine

The chain store which has practically cornered the everyday tippling market is **Nicolas** – there is a branch in every neighborhood that can provide a range of wines to suit all pockets. As a rule, the salespeople at Nicolas are knowledgeable and helpful. Try the charming **Legrand Filles et Fils** for a carefully chosen selection of high-end champagnes. **Caves Taillevent** on the rue du Faubourg-St-Honoré is well worth a sightseeing tour. It is an enormous, overwhelming cellar with some of the most expensive wine available.

Cave Péret on the rue Daguerre has a vast selection of wines, and staff can offer personal advice to help you with your purchase. The beautiful **Ryst-Dupeyron**, in the St-Germain quarter, displays whiskies, wines, ports, and Monsieur Ryst's own Armagnac. On request, he will even personalize a bottle for that special occasion.

Other great wine stores in Paris include **Lavinia**, which is the largest in Europe. The staff in **Les Caves Augé** are also very knowledgeable and friendly.

DIRECTORY

Bread and Cakes

Boulangerie et Pâtisserie Secco
18 rue Jean Nicot 75007.

Boulangerie Flute Gana by Ganachaud
226 rue des Pyrénées 75020. **Tel** 01 43 58 42 62. **W gana.fr**

Ladurée
75 av des Champs-Elysées 75008. **Map** 2 F5. **Tel** 01 40 75 08 75. **W laduree.fr**

Le Moulin de la Vierge
105 rue Vercingétorix 75014. **Map** 11 A4. **Tel** 01 45 43 09 84. **W lavierge.com**

Maison Kayser
8 rue Monge 75005. **Map** 9 B5. **Tel** 01 44 07 01 42. **W maison-kayser.com**

Pierre Hermé
72 rue Bonaparte 75006. **Map** 8 E4. **Tel** 01 43 54 47 77. **W pierreherme.com**

Poilâne
8 rue du Cherche-Midi 75006. **Map** 8 D4. **Tel** 01 45 48 42 59. **W poilane.com**

Sacha Finkelsztajn
27 rue des Rosiers 75004. **Map** 9 C3. **Tel** 01 42 72 78 91. **W finkelsztajn.com**

Chocolate

Christian Constant
37 rue d'Assas 75006. **Map** 12 E1. **Tel** 01 53 63 15 15. **W christianconstant.fr**

Dalloyau
101 rue du Faubourg-St-Honoré 75008. **Map** 3 B5. **Tel** 01 42 99 90 00. **W dalloyau.fr**

Fauchon
24–26, 30 pl de la Madeleine 75008. **Map** 3 C5. **Tel** 01 70 39 38 00. **W fauchon.fr**

La Maison du Chocolat
225 rue du Faubourg-St-Honoré 75008. **Map** 2 E3. **Tel** 01 42 27 39 44. **W lamaisonduchocolat.com**

Richart
258 bd St-Germain 75007. **Map** 7 C2. **Tel** 01 45 55 66 00. **W richart-chocolates.com**

Charcuterie and Foie Gras

Comtesse du Barry
1 rue de Sèvres 75006. **Map** 8 D4. **Tel** 01 45 48 32 04. **W comtessedubarry.com**

Divay
4 rue Bayen 75017. **Map** 2 D2. **Tel** 01 43 80 16 97. **W fois-gras-divay.com**

Gilles Verot
7 rue Lecourbe 75015. **Map** 11 A. **Tel** 01 47 34 01 03. **W verot-charcuterie.fr**

Hédiard
21 pl de la Madeleine 75008. **Map** C5. **Tel** 01 43 12 88 88. **W hediard.com**

Lafitte
Ile Saint-Louis, 8 rue Jean du Bellay 75004. **Map** 9 B4. **Tel** 01 43 26 08 63. **W lafitte.fr**

Le Bon Marché
24 rue de Sèvres 75007. **Map** 7 C5. **Tel** 01 44 39 80 00. **W lebonmarche.com**

Maison de la Truffe
19 pl de la Madeleine 75008. **Map** 3 C5. **Tel** 01 42 65 53 22. **W maison-de-la-truffe.com**

Maison Pou
16 av des Ternes 75017. **Map** 2 D3. **Tel** 01 43 80 19 24. **W maisonpou.com**

Petrossian
18 bd Latour-Maubourg 75007. **Map** 7 A2. **Tel** 01 44 11 32 25. **W petrossian.fr**

Vignon
13 rue Clément-Marot 75008. **Map** 2 E5. **Tel** 01 47 20 10 01.

Cheese

Alléosse
13 rue Poncelet 75017. **Map** 2 E3. **Tel** 01 46 22 50 45. **W fromage-alleosse.com**

Androuët
134 rue Mouffetard 75005. **Map** 13 B1. **Tel** 01 45 87 85 05. **W androuet.com**

Fromagerie Quatrehomme
62 rue de Sèvres 75007. **Map** 7 C5. **Tel** 01 47 34 33 45. **W quatrehomme.fr**

La Fermette
86 rue Montorgeuil 75002. **Map** 9 A1. **Tel** 01 42 36 70 96.

La Fromagerie d'Auteuil
58 rue d'Auteuil 75016. **Map** 5 A5. **Tel** 01 45 25 07 10. **W lafromageriedauteuil.fr**

Laurent Dubois
47 ter bd St-Germain 75007. **Map** 9 A5. **Tel** 01 43 54 50 93. **W fromageslaurentdubois.fr**

Le Jardin Fromager
53 rue Oberkampf 75011. **Map** 10 E1. **Tel** 01 48 05 19 96.

Marie-Anne Cantin
12 rue du Champ-de-Mars 75007. **Map** 6 F3. **Tel** 01 45 50 43 94. **W cantin.fr**

Wine

Cave Péret
6 rue Daguerre 75014. **Map** 12 D4. **Tel** 01 43 22 57 05.

Les Caves Augé
116 bd Haussman 75008. **Map** 3 C4. **Tel** 01 45 22 16 97. **W cavesauge.com**

Caves Taillevent
199 rue du Faubourg-St-Honoré 75008. **Map** 2 F3. **Tel** 01 45 61 14 09. **W taillevent.com**

Lavinia
3–5 bd de la Madeleine 75008. **Map** 4 D5. **Tel** 01 42 97 20 20. **W lavinia.fr**

Legrand Filles et Fils
1 rue de la Banque 75002. **Map** 8 F1. **Tel** 01 42 60 07 12. **W caves-legrand.com**

Nicolas
35 bd Malesherbes 75008. **Map** 3 C5. **Tel** 01 42 65 00 85. **W nicolas.com**

Ryst-Dupeyron
79 rue du Bac 75007. **Map** 8 D3. **Tel** 09 54 39 72 78. **W vintageandco.com**

Art and Antiques

In Paris you can buy art and antiques either from shops and galleries with established reputations, or from flea markets and avant-garde galleries. Many of the prestigious antique shops and galleries are located around the rue du Faubourg-St-Honoré and are worth a visit even if you can't afford to buy. On the Left Bank is Le Carré Rive Gauche, an organization of 30 antiques dealers.

Exporting

Objets d'art over 50 years old, worth more than a given amount, will require a *Certificat pour un bien culturel* to be exported (provided by the vendor), plus a *licence d'exportation* for non-EU countries. Seek professional advice from the large antique shops. The **Centre des Renseignements des Douanes** has a booklet, *Bulletin Officiel des Douanes*, with all the details.

Antiques

If you wish to buy antiques, you might like to stroll around the areas that boast the most galleries – in Le Carré Rive Gauche around quai Malaquais, try **L'Arc en Seine** and **Anne-Sophie Duval** for Art Nouveau and Art Deco. Rue Jacob is still one of the best places to seek beautiful objects, antique or modern. Close to the Louvre, the **Louvre des Antiquaires** comprises 250 shops selling mainly expensive, quality furniture. Many of the prestigious antique stores are near rue du Faubourg-St-Honoré, including **Didier Aaron**, expert on furniture from the 17th and 18th centuries. **Village St-Paul** is the most charming group of antique shops and is also open on Sundays. In the south of the city, **Le Village Suisse** also groups many art and antique dealers.

Art Galleries

Established art galleries are located on or around avenue Montaigne. The **Louise Leiris** gallery was founded by D. H. Kahnweiler, the dealer who "discovered" both Georges Braque and Pablo Picasso. The gallery still shows Cubist masterpieces.

On the Left Bank **Galerie Maeght** has a tremendous stock of paintings at prices to suit most budgets; he also publishes fine art books.

Rue Louise-Weiss, known as Scène Est, has become the area for cutting-edge creativity and innovation. The **Air de Paris** gallery is popular.

In the Marais try **Yvon Lambert** and **Galerie du Jour Agnès B.**; in the Bastille, try **Lavignes-Bastille** and **L et M Durand-Dessert**, also a fashionable place to buy catalogs on new artists, if not their works.

Auction Houses

The great Paris auction center, in operation since 1858, is **Drouot-Richelieu**. Bidding can be intimidating since most of it is done by dealers. Beware of the auctioneer's high-speed patter. *La Gazette de L'Hôtel Drouot* tells you what auctions are coming up when. Drouot-Richelieu also has its own auction catalog. The house only accepts cash and French checks, but there is an exchange desk inhouse. A 10–15 percent commission to the house is charged, so remember to add it on to any price you hear. You may view from 11am–6pm on the day before the sale, and from 11am to noon on the morning of the sale.

DIRECTORY

Exporting

Centre des Renseignements des Douanes
Tel 08 11 20 44 44 or 01 72 40 78 40.
W douane.gouv.fr

Antiques

Anne-Sophie Duval
5 quai Malaquais 75006. **Map** 8 E3. **Tel** 01 43 54 51 16. **W annesophieduval.com**

L'Arc en Seine
31 rue de Seine 75006. **Map** 8 E3. **Tel** 01 43 29 11 02. **W arcenseine.com**

Didier Aaron
118 rue du Faubourg-St-Honoré 75008. **Map** 3 C5. **Tel** 01 47 42 47 34. **W didieraaron.com**

Louvre des Antiquaires
2 pl du Palais Royal 75001. **Map** 8 E2. **Tel** 01 42 97 27 27. **W louvre-antiquaires.com**

Village St-Paul
Between the rues St-Paul, Ava Maria, Charlemagne and Jardins St-Paul 75004. **Map** 9 C4. **W levillagesaintpaul.com**

Le Village Suisse
78 av de Suffren 75015. **Map** 6 E4. **Tel** 01 73 79 15 41. **W villagesuisse.com**

Art Galleries

Air de Paris
32 rue Louise-Weiss 75013. **Map** 14 E4. **Tel** 01 44 23 02 77. **W airdeparis.com**

Galerie du Jour Agnès B.
44 rue Quincampoix 75004. **Map** 9 B2. **Tel** 01 44 54 55 90. **W galeriedujour.com**

Galerie Maeght
42 rue du Bac 75007. **Map** 8 D3. **Tel** 01 45 48 45 15. **W maeght.com/galeries**

L et M Durand-Dessert
28 rue de Lappe 75011. **Map** 10 F4. **Tel** 01 48 06 92 23.

Lavignes-Bastille
27 rue de Charonne 75011. **Map** 10 F4. **Tel** 01 47 00 88 18. **W lavignesbastille.com**

Louise Leiris
47 rue de Monceau 75008. **Map** 3 A3. **Tel** 01 45 63 28 85.

Yvon Lambert
108 rue Vieille-du-Temple 75003. **Map** 10 D2. **Tel** 01 42 71 09 33. **W yvon-lambert.com**

Auction Houses

Drouot-Richelieu
9 rue Drouot 75009. **Map** 4 F4. **Tel** 01 48 00 20 20. **W drouot.fr**

Markets

For eye-catching displays of wonderful food, or a lively shopping atmosphere, there is no better place than a Paris market. There are large covered food markets, markets where stalls change regularly, and permanent street markets. Some of the more famous markets, with approximate opening times, follow. While you are enjoying browsing round the stalls, remember to keep an eye on your money and be prepared to bargain.

Food Markets

The French still shop daily, hence food markets are always packed. Most fruit and vegetable markets are open from around 8am–1pm and from 4–7pm Tuesday to Saturday, and from 9am–1pm Sunday. Watch out for rotten goods – buy produce loose, not in boxes. A little language is useful for specifying *pas trop mûr* (not too ripe), or *pour manger ce soir* (to be eaten tonight).

Flea Markets

It is often said that you can no longer find bargains at the Paris flea markets. Though this may be true, it is still worth going to one for the sheer fun of browsing. Whether you pick up any real bargains has as much to do with luck as with judgment. Often the sellers themselves have little or no idea of the true value of their goods – which can work either for or against you. The biggest and most famous market, incorporating several smaller ones, is the Marché aux Puces de St-Ouen. Keep an eye on your wallet, as pickpockets frequent these markets.

Marché d'Aligre

Pl d'Aligre 75012. **Map** *10 F5.* M *Ledru-Rollin.* **Open** *7am–1pm, 4–8pm Tue–Sat, 7am–2pm Sun.*
W **marchedaligre.free.fr**

Reminiscent of a Moroccan bazaar, this must be the cheapest and liveliest market in the city. Traders hawk ingredients such as North African olives, peanuts and hot peppers, and there are even a few halal butchers. Stalls on the square sell mostly second-hand clothes and bric-à-brac. This is a less affluent area of town with few tourists and many Parisians.

Marché des Enfant Rouges

39 rue de Bretagne 75003. **Map** *10 D2.* M *Temple, Filles-du-Calvaire.* **Open** *8:30am–1pm, 4–7:30pm Tue–Sat (8pm Fri & Sat), 8:30am–2pm Sun.*
This part-covered fruit and vegetable market is the oldest covered market in Paris and dates from 1620. Famous for the freshness of its produce, on Sunday mornings street singers and accordionists enliven the proceedings. There are also plenty of cheap eateries.

Marché Raspail

Between blvd Raspail, rue Cherche-Midi and rue de Rennes, 75006. **Map** *8 D4.* M *Rennes.* **Open** *7am–2:30pm Tue & Fri, 9am– 3pm Sun.*
Conveniently sited between Montparnasse and St-Germain, this market sells fresh produce during the week and organic-only produce on Sundays.

Marché St-Germain

4–86 rue Lobineau 75006. **Map** *8 E4.* M *Mabillon.* **Open** *8:30am–1pm, 4–8pm Mon–Sat; 8am–1:30pm Sun.*
St-Germain is one of the few covered markets left in Paris. Here you can buy Italian, Mexican, Greek, Asian, and organic produce.

Rue Montorgueil

75001 & 75002. **Map** *9 A1.* M *Les Halles.* **Open** *10am–6pm Mon–Sat; Sun am only (subject to change).*
The paved rue Montorgueil is what remains of the old Les Halles market. Here you can buy exotic fruit and vegetables like green bananas and yams, or sample offerings from the delicatessens. Expect high prices.

Rue Mouffetard

75005. **Map** *13 B2.* M *Pl Monge.* **Open** *8am–1pm Tue–Sun.*
This is one of the oldest market streets in Paris, and although it has become touristy it is still a charming winding street full of quality food. There is also a lively African market down the nearby side street of rue Daubenton.

Rue Poncelet

75017. **Map** *2 E3.* M *Ternes.* **Open** *8am–1pm, 4–7:30pm Tue–Sat, 8am–1pm Sun.*

Situated away from the main tourist areas, this market street is worth visiting for its authentic French atmosphere. Choose from many bakeries, pâtisseries, and *charcuteries*.

Marché aux Puces de la Porte de Vanves

Av Georges-Lafenestre & av Marc-Sangnier 75014. M *Porte-de-Vanves.* **Open** *7am–2 or 5pm Sat & Sun.*
W **pucesdevanves.typepad.com**
Porte de Vanves is a small market selling good-quality bric-à-brac and junk, as well as some secondhand furniture. It's best to get to the market early on Saturday morning for the best choice of wares. Artists exhibit nearby.

Marché aux Puces de Montreuil

Porte de Montreuil, 93 Montreuil 75020. M *Porte-de-Montreuil.* **Open** *7am–7:30pm Sat–Mon.*
Go early to the Porte de Montreuil flea market for a better chance of picking up a bargain. The substantial secondhand clothes section attracts many young people. Stalls sell everything from used bicycles to bric-à-brac and exotic spices.

Marché aux Puces de St-Ouen

(See p138).

This is the most well-known, the most crowded, and the most expensive of all the flea markets. Here you'll find a range of markets, locals dealing from their car boots, and large buildings packed with stalls. Some of them are very upmarket; others sell junk. *A Guide des Puces* (guide to the flea markets) can be obtained from the information kiosk in the Marché Biron on the rue des Rosiers.

Rue de Seine and Rue de Buci

75006. **Map** *8 E4.* M *Odéon.* **Open** *8am–1pm, 4–7pm Tue–Sat, 9am–1pm Sun.*
The stalls here are expensive and crowded but sell quality fruit and vegetables. There is also a large florist's and two excellent pâtisseries.

ENTERTAINMENT IN PARIS

Whether your preference is for classical drama, avant-garde theater, ballet, opera, or jazz, cinema or dancing the night away, Paris has it all. There is plenty of free entertainment too, from the street performers outside the Centre Pompidou to musicians busking all over town and in the Métro.

Parisians themselves like nothing better than strolling along the boulevards or sitting at a sidewalk café nursing a drink as they watch the world go by. If, however, you're looking for the ultimate "Oh la-la!" experience, you can take in any of the celebrated nightclubs.

For fans of spectator sports there is tennis, the Tour de France, or horse racing. Recreation centers and gyms cater to the more active. And for those disposed to more leisurely pursuits, there is always a quiet game of *boules* to be played in the park.

The glass facade of the Bastille Opéra

Booking Tickets

Depending on the event, tickets can be bought at the door, but for popular events it is wiser to check online for availability and purchase tickets in advance at one of the **FNAC** stores or by **Virgin Mega Online**. Theater box offices open daily from about 11am–7pm. Credit cards are accepted for bookings online or by telephone.

Theater

From the grandeur of the **Comédie Française** to slapstick farce and avant-garde drama, theater is flourishing, both in Paris and in its suburbs. Founded in 1680 by royal decree, the Comédie Française is the bastion of French theater, aiming to keep classical drama in the public eye and to perform works by the best modern playwrights. Formerly the second theater of the Comédie Française, the **Odéon Théâtre de l'Europe** now specializes in plays from other countries, performed in their original language. In an underground auditorium in the Art Deco Palais de Chaillot, the **Théâtre National de Chaillot** is famed for staging some very lively productions of European classics. The **Théâtre National de la Colline** specializes in contemporary drama.

Among the most important of the serious independents is the **Comédie des Champs-Elysées**, while for over 100 years the **Palais Royal** has been known as the temple of risqué farce. The café theaters such as **Théâtre d'Edgar** and **Le Point Virgule** are always good venues for seeing the best of the emerging new talent. In the summer, street theater thrives in tourist areas such as the Centre Pompidou, Les Halles, and St-Germain-des-Prés. Open-air performances of Shakespeare and classic French plays are given at the Shakespeare Garden in the Bois de Boulogne.

Classical Music

Paris has many first-class venues with an excellent range of opera, classical, and contemporary music productions. Opened in 1989, the stylish, 2,700-seat **Opéra National de Paris Bastille** stages classic and modern operas. The beautifully renovated **Opéra National Garnier** puts on mostly ballets.

The **Salle Pleyel** is Paris's principal concert hall, housing the Orchestre de Paris and Radio France's Philharmonic Orchestra. Both the **Théâtre des Champs-Elysées** and the **Théâtre du Châtelet** are recommended for their varied high-quality programs. Venues for chamber music include the **Salle Gaveau** and the **Théâtre de la Ville**. The **Cité de la Musique** in the Parc

Listings Magazines

Pariscope and *L'Officiel des Spectacles* are the best listings magazines in Paris. Published every Wednesday, you can pick them up at any newsstand. *Le Figaro* also has a good listings section on Wednesdays. *Time Out Paris* online or *Premier* online are also handy websites for up-to-date events listings.

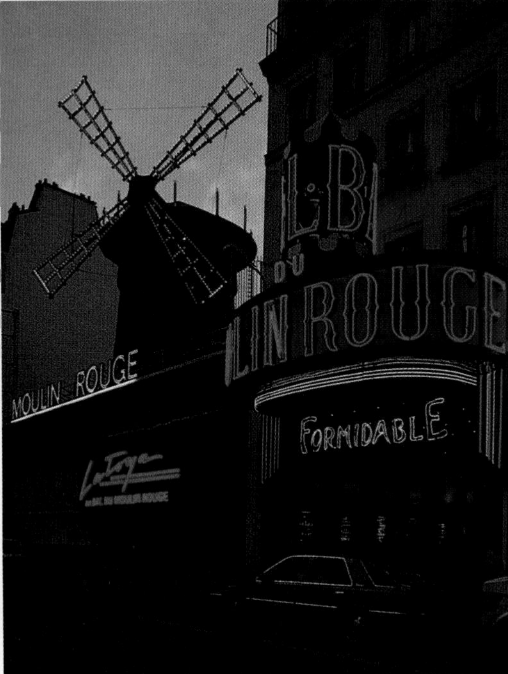

The famous silhouette of the Moulin Rouge nightclub

de la Villette is one of Paris's most vibrant concert halls. The venue is renowned for its eclectic music programs and workshops, while the museum charts the history of music and exhibits over 4,000 instruments.

Dance

The French are very vocal in their appreciation or dislike of dance, and those who fail to please are subjected to boos, hisses and mass walk-outs mid-performance.

The opulent **Opéra National Garnier** has space for 450 artists and is home to the Ballet de l'Opéra de Paris, which has earned a reputation as one of the best classical ballet companies in the world. Government support has helped the **Théâtre de la Ville** to become Paris's most important venue for modern dance, with subsidies keeping ticket costs relatively low.

The **Maison des Arts de Créteil** stages famous over-seas companies, as well as its own much praised productions.

Clubs and Cabaret

Music in Paris clubs tends to follow the trends set in the US and Britain. Only a few clubs such as **Balajo**, once frequented by Edith Piaf, and the ultra-hip **Showcase**, under the Alexandre III bridge, are genuinely up-to-the-minute with their music.

Le Baron is a trendy night-spot, attracting people from the fashion world and from show business. For comedy in English, try **La Java**. The stage of this club, where Edith Piaf once performed, now showcases British and American comedians.

When it comes to picking a cabaret, the rule of thumb is simple: the better known places are best. The **Folies-Bergère** is the oldest music hall in Paris and probably the most famous in the world. It is closely rivaled by the **Lido** and the **Moulin Rouge**, birthplace of the cancan. **Paradis Latin** is the most "French" cabaret in the city. It shows variety acts whose sketches are enlivened by remarkable special effects and scenery.

Rock, Jazz, and World Music

The top international acts are usually to be found at the enormous arenas such as **Palais Omnisports Paris-Bercy** or the **Zénith**. For a more intimate atmosphere, the legendary **Olympia** has assigned seating and good acoustics. To hear indigenous rock groups like Les Negresses Vertes and Mano Negra go to **La Cigale** or **Elysée-Montmartre** in the Pigalle area.

Jazz-crazy Paris has innumerable packed clubs where the best talent in the world can be heard on any evening. All the great jazz musicians have performed at **New Morning**, which also hosts African, Brazilian, and other sounds. For Dixieland go to **Le Petit Journal St-Michel**.

World music and jazz lovers alike can see top acts and dance until dawn at the excellent **Chapelle des Lombards**.

The spectacular facade of the Opéra National Garnier

Cinema

Paris is the world's capital of film appreciation. It was the cradle of the cinematograph nearly 100 years ago. Then in the late 1950s and early 1960s the city nurtured that very Parisian vanguard movement, the New Wave, when film directors such as François Truffaut and Jean-Luc Godard revolutionized the way films were made and perceived.

There are now more than 370 screens within the city limits, distributed among over 100 cinemas. Most are concentrated in cinema belts, which enjoy the added appeal of nearby restaurants and shops. The Champs-Elysées has the densest cinema strip in town, where you can see the latest Hollywood smash or French *auteur* triumph, as well as some classic reissues.

In the vicinity of the Opéra de Paris Garnier, the cinemas in the Grands Boulevards include two notable landmarks: the 2,800-seat **Le Grand Rex**, with its Baroque decor, and the **Max Linder Panorama**, which was completely refurbished in the 1980s. The place de Clichy is the last Parisian stronghold of Pathé, while the hub of Right Bank cinema is in the Forum des Halles mall. France's largest screen is at **La Géode**.

On the Left Bank, Odéon-St-Germain-des-Prés has taken over from the Latin Quarter as the city's heartland for art and repertory cinemas. The new, and huge, **MK2 Bibliothèque** points to the future with its collection of 14 screens, a bar, shops, and exhibition space.

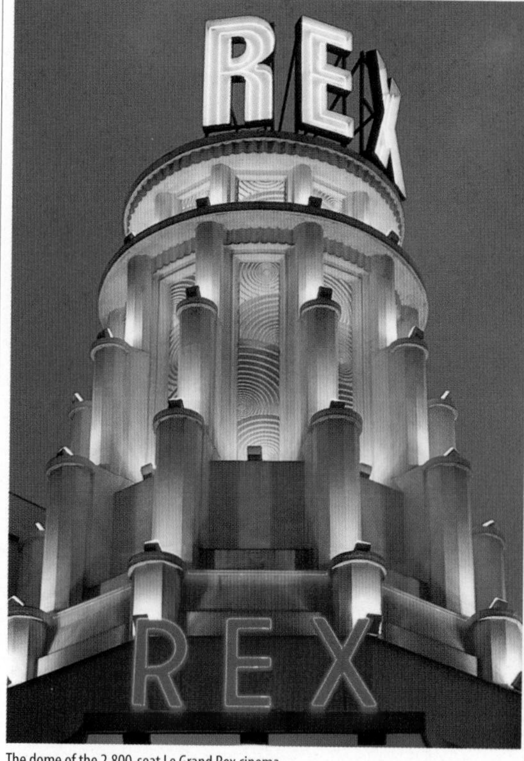

The dome of the 2,800-seat Le Grand Rex cinema

Sport

Paris is host to some of the foremost sporting events in the world. City-wide frenzy sweeps Paris when the Tour de France bicycle race finishes there in July. From late May to mid-June Parisians live and breathe tennis during the **Roland Garros** national tennis championship. The Prix de l'Arc de Triomphe, held at the **Hippodrome de Longchamp** on the first Sunday in October, provides the opportunity to see the rich in all their finery as well as first-class flat racing.

The **Palais Omnisports Paris-Bercy** is the venue for a vast range of events, including the Paris tennis open and rock concerts, as is the new **Stade de France** at St-Denis. **Parc des Princes** is home to Paris's top soccer team, Paris St-Germain.

The Celebrated Cafés of Paris

One of the most enduring images of Paris is the Left Bank café scene where great artists, writers, and eminent intellectuals consorted. Before World War I, hordes of Russian revolutionaries, including Lenin and Trotsky, whiled away their days in the Rotonde and the Dôme in Montparnasse. In the 1920s, Surrealists dominated café life. Later came the American writers led by Ernest Hemingway and F. Scott Fitzgerald, whose haunts included La Coupole. After World War II, Jean-Paul Sartre and other Existentialists shifted the cultural scene northwards to St-Germain.

Newspaper reading remains a typical café pastime

DIRECTORY

Booking Tickets

FNAC
26–30 av des Ternes 75017. **Map** 2 D3. **Tel** 0825 020 020.
Forum Les Halles, 1 rue Pierre Lescot 75001. **Map** 9 A2. **Tel** 0825 020 020. **W fnac.com**

Virgin Mega
Tel 01 49 97 51 91. **W virginmega.fr**

Theater

Comédie des Champs-Elysées
15 av Montaigne 75008. **Map** 6 F1. **Tel** 01 53 23 99 19. **W comedie deschampselysees**

Comédie Française
1 pl Colette 75001. **Map** 8 E1. **Tel** 0825 10 16 80. **W comedie-francaise.fr**

Odéon Théâtre de l'Europe
Place de l'Odéon 75006. **Map** 12 F5. **Tel** 01 44 85 40 40. **W theatre-odeon.eu**

Le Point Virgule
7 rue Ste-Croix de la Bretonnerie 75004. **Map** 9 C3. **Tel** 01 42 78 67 03. **W lepointvirgule.com**

Théâtre d'Edgar
58 bd Edgar-Quinet 75014. **Map** 12 D2. **Tel** 01 42 79 97 97.

Théâtre National de Chaillot
Pl du Trocadéro 75016. **Map** 5 C2. **Tel** 01 53 65 30 00. **W theatre-chaillot.fr**

Théâtre National de la Colline
15 rue Malte-Brun 75020. **Tel** 01 44 62 52 52. **W colline.fr**

Théâtre du Palais Royal
38 rue Montpensier 75001. **Map** 8 E1. **Tel** 01 42 97 40 00. **W theatrepalais royal.com**

Classical Music

Cité de la Musique
221 av Jean-Jaurès 75019. **Tel** 01 44 84 44 84. **W citedelamusique.fr**

Opéra National de Paris Bastille
Pl de la Bastille, 120 rue de Lyon 75012. **Map** 10 E4. **Tel** 08 92 89 90 90. **W operadeparis.fr**

Opéra National de Paris Garnier
Pl de l'Opera 75009. **Map** 4 E5. **Tel** 08 92 89 90 90.

Salle Gaveau
45–47 rue la Boétie 75008. **Map** 3 B4. **Tel** 01 49 53 05 07. **W sallegaveau.com**

Salle Pleyel
252 rue du Faubourg St-Honoré 75008. **Map** 2 E3. **Tel** 01 42 56 13 13. **W sallepleyel.fr**

Théâtre des Champs-Elysées
15 av Montaigne 75008. **Map** 6 F1. **Tel** 01 49 52 50 00. **W theatrechamps elysees.fr**

Théâtre du Châtelet
Pl du Châtelet 75001. **Map** 9 A3. **Tel** 01 40 28 28 40. **W chatelet-theatre.com**

Théâtre de la Ville
2 pl du Châtelet 75004. **Map** 9 A3. **Tel** 01 42 74 22 77. **W theatredelaville-paris.com**

Dance

Maison des Arts de Créteil
Pl Salvador Allende 94000 Créteil. **Tel** 01 45 13 19 19. **W maccreteil.com**

Opéra Garnier
(See Classical Music.)

Théâtre de la Ville
(See Classical Music.)

Clubs and Cabaret

Balajo
9 rue de Lappe 75011. **Map** 10 E4. **Tel** 09 54 94 54 09. **W balajo.fr**

Le Baron
6 av Marceau 75008. **Map** 6 E1. **Tel** 01 47 20 04 01.

Folies-Bergère
32 rue Richer 75009. **Tel** 08 92 68 16 50. **W foliesbergere.com**

La Java
105 rue du Faubourg-du-Temple 75010. **Tel** 01 42 02 20 52. **W la-java.fr**

Lido
116 bis av des Champs-Elysées 75008. **Map** 2 E4. **Tel** 01 40 76 56 10. **W lido.fr**

La Machine du Moulin Rouge
90 bd de Clichy 75018. **Map** 4 D1. **Tel** 01 53 41 88 99. **W lamachinedu moulinrouge.fr**

Moulin Rouge
82 bd de Clichy 75018. **Map** 4 E1. **Tel** 01 53 09 82 82. **W moulinrouge.fr**

Paradis Latin
28 rue du Cardinal-Lemoine 75008. **Map** 9 B5. **Tel** 01 43 25 28 28. **W paradislatin.com**

Showcase
Under Pont Alexandre III. Porte des Champs-Elysées 75008. **Map** 7 A1. **Tel** 01 45 61 25 43. **W showcase.fr**

Rock, Jazz, and World Music

Chapelle des Lombards
19 rue de Lappe 75011. **Map** 10 F4. **Tel** 01 43 57 24 24. **W la-chapelle-des-lombards.com**

La Cigale
120 bd Rochechouart 75018. **Map** 4 F2. **Tel** 01 49 25 89 99. **W lacigale.fr**

Elysée-Montmartre
72 bd Rochechouart 75018. **Map** 4 F2. **Tel** 01 55 07 06 03.

New Morning
7–9 rue des Petites-Ecuries 75010. **Tel** 01 45 23 51 41. **W newmorning.com**

Olympia
28 bd des Capucines 75009. **Map** 4 D5. **Tel** 08 92 68 33 68. **W olympiahall.com**

Palais Omnisports Paris-Bercy
8 bd de Bercy 75012. **Map** 14 F2. **Tel** 08 92 39 04 90. **W bercy.fr**

Le Petit Journal St-Michel
71 bd St-Michel 75005. **Map** 12 F1. **Tel** 01 43 26 28 59. **W lepetitjournal saintmichel.com**

Zénith
211 av de Jean-Jaurès 75019. **Tel** 08 90 71 02 07. **W zenith-paris.com**

Cinema

La Géode
26 av Corentin-Cariou 75019. **Tel** 08 92 68 45 40. **W lageode.fr**

Le Grand Rex
1 bd Poissonnière 75002. **Tel** 08 92 68 05 96. **W legrandrex.com**

Max Linder Panorama
24 bd Poissonnière 75009. **Tel** 01 48 00 90 24. **W maxlinder.cine. allucine**

MK2 Bibliothèque
128–162 av de France 75013. **Tel** 08 92 69 84 84. **W mk2.com**

Sport

Hippodrome de Longchamp
Route des Tribunes 75016. **Tel** 01 44 30 75 00.

Palais Omnisports Paris-Bercy
(See Rock section.)

Parc des Princes
24 rue du Commandant-Guilbaud 75016. **Tel** 3275. **W leparcdesprinces.fr**

Stade de France
Rue Henri Delaunay, La Plaine St-Denis 93210. **Tel** 08 92 70 09 00. **W stadedefrance.fr**

Stade Roland Garros
2 av Gordon-Bennett 75016. **Tel** 01 47 43 48 00. **W fft.fr/rolandgarros**

PARIS STREET FINDER

The map references given with sights, shops, and entertainment venues described in the Paris section of the guide refer to the maps on the following pages. Map references are also given for Paris hotels *(see pp554–71)* and restaurants *(pp576–603)*, and for useful addresses in the *Travelers' Needs* and *Survival Guide* sections at the back of the book. The maps include not only the main sightseeing areas but also the most important districts for hotels, restaurants, shopping, and entertainment venues. The key map below shows the area of Paris covered by the *Street Finder*, with the *arrondissement* numbers for the various districts. The symbols used for sights and other features on the *Street Finder* maps are listed opposite.

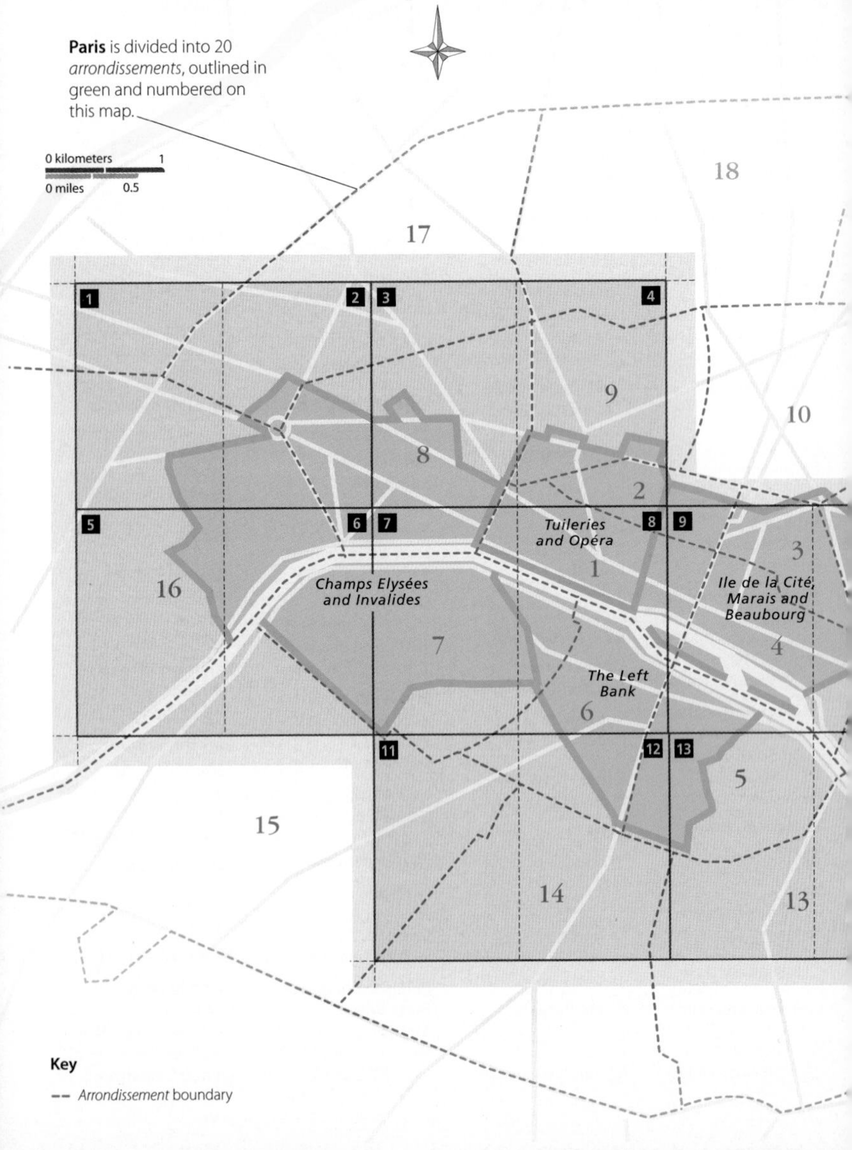

Paris is divided into 20 *arrondissements*, outlined in green and numbered on this map.

Key

-- *Arrondissement* boundary

How the Map References Work

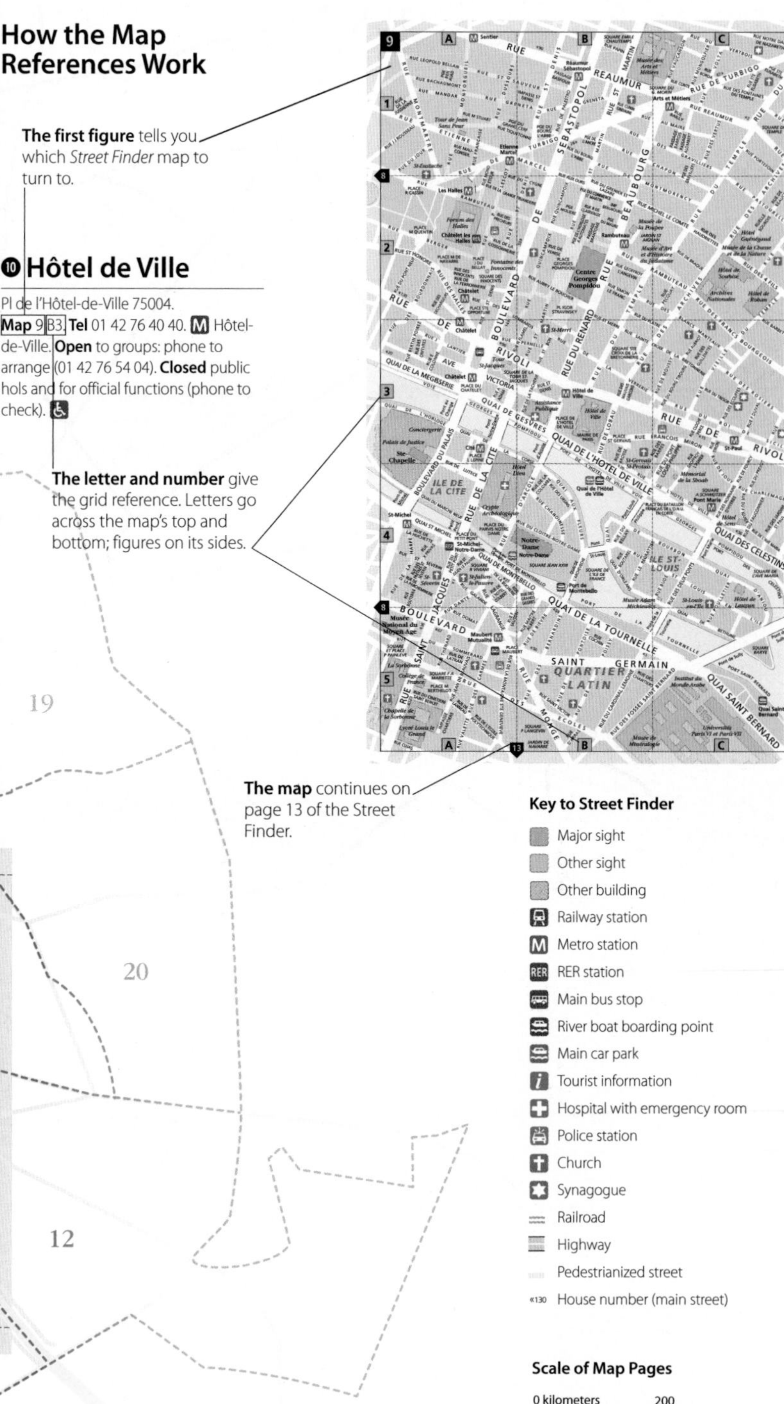

The first figure tells you which *Street Finder* map to turn to.

⑩ Hôtel de Ville

Pl de l'Hôtel-de-Ville 75004. **Map** 9 B3. **Tel** 01 42 76 40 40. Ⓜ Hôtel-de-Ville. **Open** to groups: phone to arrange (01 42 76 54 04). **Closed** public hols and for official functions (phone to check). ♿

The letter and number give the grid reference. Letters go across the map's top and bottom; figures on its sides.

The map continues on page 13 of the Street Finder.

Key to Street Finder

- Major sight
- Other sight
- Other building
- Railway station
- Metro station
- RER station
- Main bus stop
- River boat boarding point
- Main car park
- Tourist information
- Hospital with emergency room
- Police station
- Church
- Synagogue
- Railroad
- Highway
- Pedestrianized street
- «130 House number (main street)

Scale of Map Pages

0 kilometers 200

0 miles 200

1:12,000

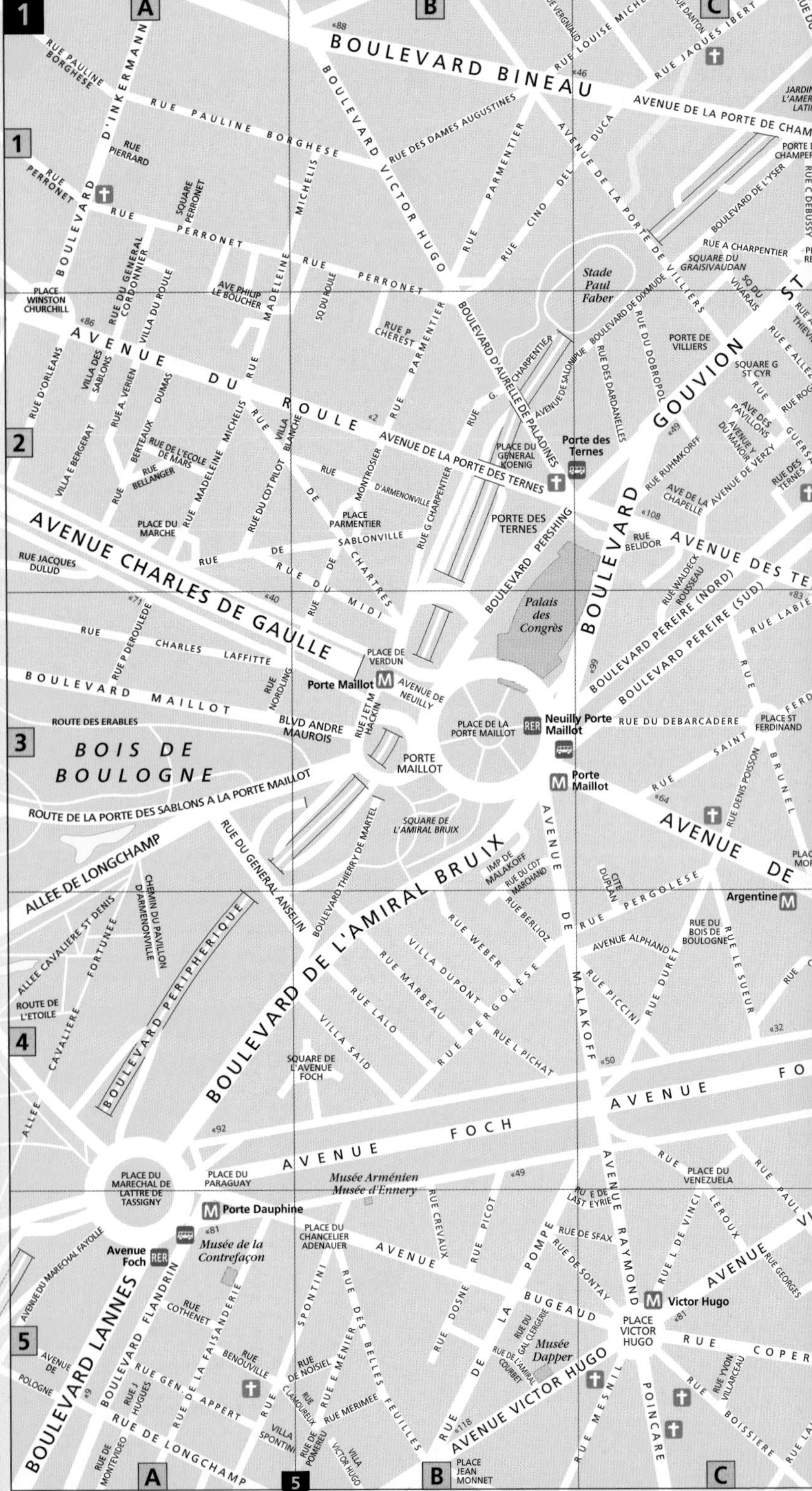
1
A
B
C
BOULEVARD BINEAU
AVENUE DE LA PORTE DE CHAMPERRET
RUE LOUISE MICHEL
RUE DANTON
RUE JACQUES IBERT
RUE VERGNIAUD
RUE PAULINE BORGHESE
BOULEVARD D'INKERMANN
RUE PIERRARD
RUE PERRONET
SQUARE PERRONET
BOULEVARD VICTOR HUGO
RUE DES DAMES AUGUSTINES
RUE PARMENTIER
RUE CINO DEL DUCA
AVENUE DE LA PORTE DE VILLIERS
BOULEVARD DE L'YSER
RUE A CHARPENTIER
SQUARE DU GRAISIVAUDAN
SQ DU VIVARAIS
Stade Paul Faber
PLACE WINSTON CHURCHILL
RUE DU GENERAL CORDONNIER
VILLA DU ROULE
AVE PHILIP LE BOUCHER
RUE MADELEINE MICHELIS
SQ DU ROULE
RUE P CHEREST
AVENUE DU ROULE
RUE D'ORLEANS
VILLA DES SABLONS
RUE A VERIEN
DUMAS
BOULEVARD D'AURELLE DE PALADINES
BOULEVARD DE DIXMUDE
AVENUE DE SALONIQUE
RUE DU DOBROPOL
RUE DES DARDANELLES
PORTE DE VILLIERS
BOULEVARD GOUVION ST CYR
SQUARE G ST CYR
AVENUE DES PAVILLONS
AVENUE Y DU MANOIR
AVENUE DE VERZY
RUE RUHMKORFF
AVE DE LA CHAPELLE
RUE DES TERNES
2
VILLA DE BERGERAT
BERTEAUX
RUE DE L'ECOLE DE MARS
RUE BELLANGER
VILLA BLANCHE
RUE DU CDT PILOT
RUE D'ARMENONVILLE
RUE MONTROSIER
AVENUE DE LA PORTE DES TERNES
PLACE DU GENERAL KOENIG
Porte des Ternes
PORTE DES TERNES
BOULEVARD PERSHING
PLACE PARMENTIER
RUE G CHARPENTIER
PLACE DU MARCHE
RUE DE SABLONVILLE
RUE DE CHARTRES
RUE DU MIDI
RUE JACQUES DULUD
AVENUE CHARLES DE GAULLE
AVENUE DES TERNES
RUE BELIDOR
RUE WALDECK ROUSSEAU
BOULEVARD PEREIRE (NORD)
BOULEVARD PEREIRE (SUD)
Palais des Congrès
RUE CHARLES LAFFITTE
RUE P DEROULEDE
PLACE DE VERDUN
Porte Maillot
AVENUE DE NEUILLY
RUE NORDLING
BOULEVARD MAILLOT
ROUTE DES ERABLES
BLVD ANDRE MAUROIS
RUE J ET M HACKIN
PLACE DE LA PORTE MAILLOT
Neuilly Porte Maillot
RUE DU DEBARCADERE
PLACE ST FERDINAND
RUE SAINT FERDINAND
RUE BRUNEL
3
BOIS DE BOULOGNE
PORTE MAILLOT
Porte Maillot
RUE DENIS POISSON
ROUTE DE LA PORTE DES SABLONS A LA PORTE MAILLOT
ALLEE DE LONGCHAMP
RUE DU GENERAL ANSELIN
BOULEVARD THIERRY DE MARTEL
SQUARE DE L'AMIRAL BRUIX
AVENUE DE MALAKOFF
IMP DE MALAKOFF
RUE DU CDT MARCHAND
CITE DUPLAN
AVENUE DE LA GRANDE ARMEE
Argentine
CHEMIN DU PAVILLON D'ARMENONVILLE
ALLEE CAVALIERE ST DENIS
FORTUNEE
BOULEVARD PERIPHERIQUE
BOULEVARD DE L'AMIRAL BRUIX
RUE BERLIOZ
RUE PERGOLESE
RUE WEBER
AVENUE ALPHAND
RUE DU BOIS DE BOULOGNE
RUE LE SUEUR
VILLA DUPONT
RUE MARBEAU
RUE PICCINI
RUE DURET
ROUTE DE L'ETOILE
ALLEE CAVALIERE
RUE LALO
VILLA SAID
RUE L PICHAT
4
SQUARE DE L'AVENUE FOCH
AVENUE FOCH
PLACE DU MARECHAL DE LATTRE DE TASSIGNY
PLACE DU PARAGUAY
Musée Arménien
Musée d'Ennery
PLACE DU VENEZUELA
RUE PAUL VALERY
RUE LEROUX
RUE DE LASTEYRIE
RUE CREVAUX
RUE PICOT
Porte Dauphine
PLACE DU CHANCELIER ADENAUER
Musée de la Contrefaçon
Avenue Foch
AVENUE DU MARECHAL FAYOLLE
RUE DE SFAX
RUE DE SONTAY
AVENUE BUGEAUD
RUE DE LA POMPE
AVENUE RAYMOND POINCARE
RUE L DE VINCI
AVENUE VICTOR HUGO
RUE GEORGES BIZET
Victor Hugo
PLACE VICTOR HUGO
RUE COPERNIC
BOULEVARD LANNES
BOULEVARD FLANDRIN
RUE COTHENET
RUE DE LA FAISANDERIE
RUE BENOUVILLE
RUE SPONTINI
RUE DES BELLES FEUILLES
RUE DOSNE
RUE DU GAL CLERGERIE
Musée Dapper
RUE DE L'AMIRAL COURBET
5
AVENUE DE POLOGNE
RUE GEN. APPERT
RUE J HUGUES
RUE DE NOISIEL
RUE E MENIER
RUE CLAMOUREUX
RUE MERIMEE
VILLA SPONTINI
RUE DE POMEREU
VILLA VICTOR HUGO
RUE DE LONGCHAMP
RUE DE MONTEVIDEO
PLACE JEAN MONNET
RUE MESNIL
RUE YVON VILLARCEAU
RUE BOISSIERE
RER
5

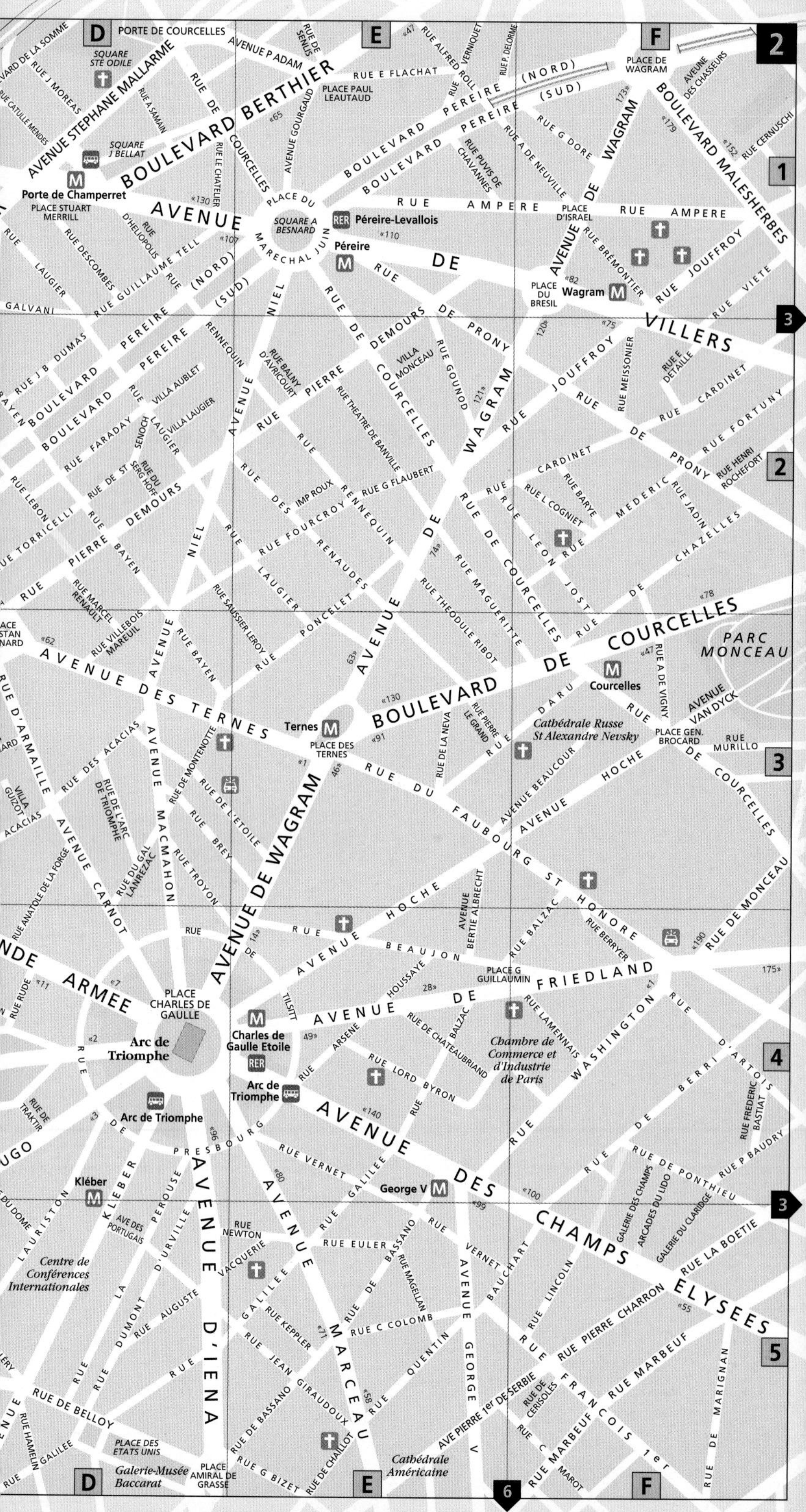

D
E
F
2
PORTE DE COURCELLES
SQUARE STE ODILE
AVENUE STEPHANE MALLARME
BOULEVARD BERTHIER
AVENUE P ADAM
RUE DE SENLIS
RUE E FLACHAT
PLACE PAUL LEAUTAUD
RUE ALFRED ROLL
RUE VERNIQUET
RUE P. DELORME
BOULEVARD PEREIRE (NORD)
BOULEVARD PEREIRE (SUD)
PLACE DE WAGRAM
AVENUE DES CHASSEURS
BOULEVARD MALESHERBES
RUE CERNUSCHI
RUE J MOREAS
RUE CATULLE MENDES
RUE A SAMAIN
SQUARE J BELLAT
Porte de Champerret
PLACE STUART MERRILL
RUE LE CHATELIER
RUE DE COURCELLES
AVENUE GOURGAUD
RUE PUVIS DE CHAVANNES
RUE A DE NEUVILLE
RUE G DORE
AVENUE DE WAGRAM
1
AVENUE DE VILLIERS
RUE AMPERE
PLACE DU MARECHAL JUIN
SQUARE A BESNARD
Péreire-Levallois
Péreire
PLACE D'ISRAEL
RUE BREMONTIER
RUE JOUFFROY
RUE VIETE
PLACE DU BRESIL
Wagram
RUE D'HELIOPOLIS
RUE DESCOMBES
RUE LAUGIER
RUE GUILLAUME TELL
GALVANI
3
RUE DE PRONY
RUE DEMOURS
AVENUE NIEL
RUE RENNEQUIN
RUE BALNY D'AVRICOURT
RUE PIERRE DEMOURS
VILLA MONCEAU
RUE GOUNOD
RUE MEISSONIER
RUE E DETAILLE
RUE CARDINET
RUE FORTUNY
RUE J B DUMAS
BOULEVARD PEREIRE
VILLA AUBLET
VILLA LAUGIER
RUE THEATRE DE BANVILLE
RUE FARADAY
RUE SENOCH
RUE DE ST SENOCH
RUE DU SERG HOFF
RUE G FLAUBERT
IMP ROUX
RUE HENRI ROCHEFORT
RUE L COGNIET
RUE BARYE
RUE MEDERIC
RUE JADIN
RUE DE CHAZELLES
RUE LEON JOST
RUE LEBON
RUE TORRICELLI
RUE BAYEN
RUE DES RENAUDES
RUE FOURCROY
RUE THEODULE RIBOT
RUE MAGUERITTE
RUE MARCEL RENAULT
RUE SAUSSIER LEROY
RUE PONCELET
BOULEVARD DE COURCELLES
PARC MONCEAU
RUE A DE VIGNY
Courcelles
RUE VILLEBOIS MAREUIL
AVENUE DES TERNES
RUE D'ARMAILLE
RUE DES ACACIAS
VILLA GUIZOT
RUE DE L'ARC DE TRIOMPHE
AVENUE MACMAHON
RUE DE MONTENOTTE
RUE DE L'ETOILE
RUE BREY
Ternes
PLACE DES TERNES
RUE DU FAUBOURG ST HONORE
RUE DE LA NEVA
RUE PIERRE LE GRAND
RUE DARU
Cathédrale Russe St Alexandre Nevsky
AVENUE VAN DYCK
PLACE GEN. BROCARD
RUE MURILLO
AVENUE HOCHE
AVENUE BEAUCOUR
AVENUE CARNOT
RUE DU GAL LANREZAC
RUE TROYON
RUE ANATOLE DE LA FORGE
AVENUE BERTIE ALBRECHT
RUE BALZAC
RUE BERRYER
RUE DE MONCEAU
AVENUE DE LA GRANDE ARMEE
RUE DE TILSITT
RUE BEAUJON
PLACE G GUILLAUMIN
AVENUE DE FRIEDLAND
RUE RUDE
PLACE CHARLES DE GAULLE
Arc de Triomphe
Charles de Gaulle Etoile
RUE ARSENE HOUSSAYE
RUE DE CHATEAUBRIAND
RUE LAMENNAIS
Chambre de Commerce et d'Industrie de Paris
RUE WASHINGTON
RUE D'ARTOIS
4
RUE LORD BYRON
RUE DE BERRI
RUE FREDERIC BASTIAT
RUE DE TRAKTIR
AVENUE VICTOR HUGO
RUE DE PRESBOURG
AVENUE DES CHAMPS ELYSEES
RUE VERNET
George V
RUE DE PONTHIEU
RUE P BAUDRY
Kléber
AVENUE KLEBER
RUE LAURISTON
RUE DU DOME
AVE DES PORTUGAIS
RUE LA PEROUSE
RUE D'URVILLE
AVENUE D'IENA
RUE NEWTON
RUE VACQUERIE
RUE GALILEE
AVENUE MARCEAU
RUE EULER
RUE DE BASSANO
RUE MAGELLAN
AVENUE GEORGE V
RUE BAUCHART
GALERIE DES CHAMPS
ARCADES DU LIDO
GALERIE DU CLARIDGE
RUE LA BOETIE
Centre de Conférences Internationales
RUE DUMONT D'URVILLE
RUE AUGUSTE VACQUERIE
RUE KEPPLER
RUE C COLOMB
RUE QUENTIN BAUCHART
RUE LINCOLN
RUE PIERRE CHARRON
5
RUE JEAN GIRAUDOUX
RUE DE BELLOY
RUE HAMELIN
AVE PIERRE 1er DE SERBIE
RUE DE CERISOLES
RUE FRANCOIS 1er
RUE MARBEUF
RUE DE MARIGNAN
RUE C MAROT
PLACE DES ETATS UNIS
Galerie-Musée Baccarat
PLACE AMIRAL DE GRASSE
RUE G BIZET
RUE DE CHAILLOT
Cathédrale Américaine
6

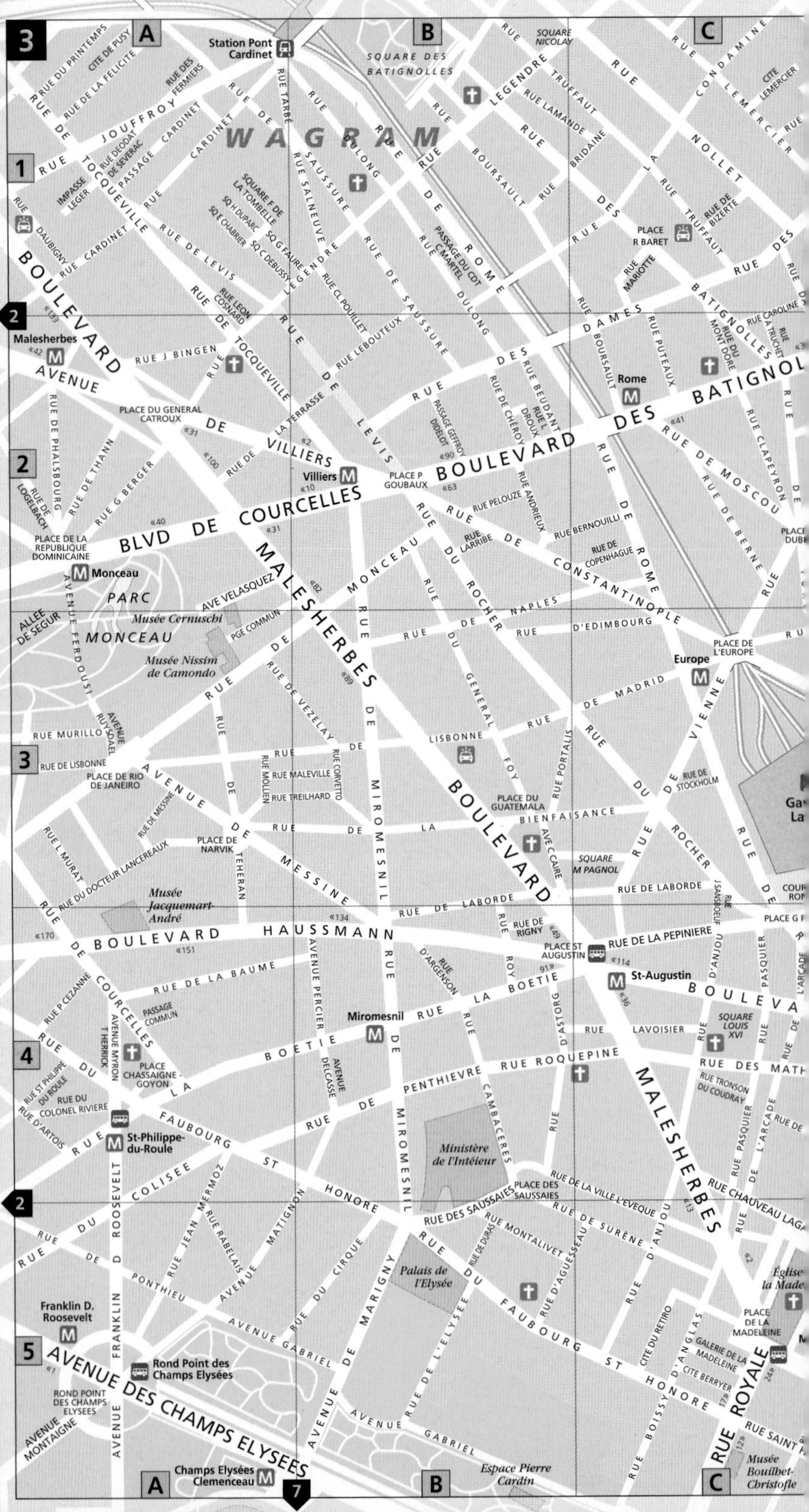
3
A
B
C
1
2
3
4
5
7
Station Pont Cardinet
SQUARE DES BATIGNOLLES
SQUARE NICOLAY
WAGRAM
RUE DU PRINTEMPS
CITE DE PUSY
RUE DE LA FELICITE
RUE DES FERMIERS
RUE JOUFFROY
RUE DE TOCQUEVILLE
RUE DEODAT DE SEVERAC
PASSAGE CARDINET
IMPASSE LEGER
RUE DAUBIGNY
RUE CARDINET
RUE DE LEVIS
RUE TARDE
RUE DE SAUSSURE
RUE SALNEUVE
RUE DULONG
RUE LEGENDRE
SQUARE F DE LA TOMBELLE
SQ H DUPARC
SQ CHABRIER
SQ G FAURE
SQ C DEBUSSY
RUE LEON COSNARD
RUE CL POUILLET
PASSAGE DU CDT C MARTEL
RUE DE ROME
RUE BOURSAULT
RUE LAMANDE
RUE TRUFFAUT
RUE BRIDAINE
RUE DES DAMES
RUE NOLLET
RUE CONDAMINE
CITE LEMERCIER
RUE LEMERCIER
PLACE R BARET
RUE DE BIZERTE
RUE MARIOTTE
RUE DES BATIGNOLLES
RUE CAROLINE
RUE LA TRUCHET
RUE DU MONT DORE
RUE PUTEAUX
Rome
BOULEVARD DES BATIGNOLLES
Malesherbes
BOULEVARD MALESHERBES
AVENUE DE VILLIERS
RUE J BINGEN
RUE LEBOUTEUX
RUE DE LA TERRASSE
PLACE DU GENERAL CATROUX
RUE DE PHALSBOURG
RUE DE THANN
RUE DE LOGELBACH
RUE G BERGER
Villiers
PLACE P GOUBAUX
PASSAGE GEFFROY DIDELOT
RUE DE CHEROY
RUE BEUDANT
RUE L DROUX
RUE DE MOSCOU
RUE CLAPEYRON
RUE PELOUZE
RUE ANDRIEUX
RUE BERNOUILLI
RUE LARRIBE
RUE DE CONSTANTINOPLE
RUE DE COPENHAGUE
RUE DE BERNE
PLACE DE LA REPUBLIQUE DOMINICAINE
BLVD DE COURCELLES
Monceau
PARC MONCEAU
Musée Cernuschi
Musée Nissim de Camondo
ALLEE DE SEGUR
AVENUE FERDOUSI
AVE VELASQUEZ
PGE COMMUN
RUE DE MONCEAU
RUE DU ROCHER
RUE DE NAPLES
RUE D'EDIMBOURG
PLACE DE L'EUROPE
Europe
RUE DE MADRID
RUE DE VIENNE
RUE DE VEZELAY
RUE DU GENERAL FOY
RUE MURILLO
AVENUE RUYSDAEL
RUE DE LISBONNE
LISBONNE
RUE PORTALIS
RUE DE STOCKHOLM
PLACE DE RIO DE JANEIRO
RUE MOLLIEN
RUE MALEVILLE
RUE CORVETTO
RUE TREILHARD
RUE DE MIROMESNIL
BOULEVARD MALESHERBES
PLACE DU GUATEMALA
RUE DE LA BIENFAISANCE
AVE C AIRE
SQUARE M PAGNOL
AVENUE DE MESSINE
RUE DE MESSINE
RUE DE TEHERAN
PLACE DE NARVIK
RUE L MURAT
RUE DU DOCTEUR LANCEREAUX
Musée Jacquemart-André
RUE DE LABORDE
RUE J SANSBOEUF
BOULEVARD HAUSSMANN
RUE DE RIGNY
PLACE ST AUGUSTIN
RUE DE LA PEPINIERE
St-Augustin
PLACE G P
RUE DE COURCELLES
RUE DE LA BAUME
AVENUE PERCIER
RUE D'ARGENSON
RUE ROY
RUE LA BOETIE
RUE P CEZANNE
PASSAGE COMMUN
Miromesnil
RUE LAVOISIER
SQUARE LOUIS XVI
RUE D'ANJOU
RUE PASQUIER
RUE DE L'ARCADE
AVENUE MYRON T HERRICK
PLACE CHASSAIGNE-GOYON
AVENUE DELCASSE
RUE DE PENTHIEVRE
RUE ROQUEPINE
RUE D'ASTORG
RUE DES MATH
RUE TRONSON DU COUDRAY
RUE ST PHILIPPE DU ROULE
RUE DU COLONEL RIVIERE
RUE D'ARTOIS
RUE DU FAUBOURG ST HONORE
St-Philippe-du-Roule
RUE CAMBACERES
Ministère de l'Intéieur
RUE DE LA VILLE L'EVEQUE
PLACE DES SAUSSAIES
RUE DES SAUSSAIES
RUE CHAUVEAU LAGA
RUE DU COLISEE
RUE JEAN MERMOZ
RUE RABELAIS
AVENUE MATIGNON
RUE DE SURENE
RUE MONTALIVET
RUE DE DURAS
RUE D'AGUESSEAU
AVENUE FRANKLIN D ROOSEVELT
RUE DE PONTHIEU
RUE DU CIRQUE
Palais de l'Elysée
RUE DE L'ELYSEE
Eglise la Made
Franklin D. Roosevelt
AVENUE GABRIEL
AVENUE DE MARIGNY
CITE DU RETIRO
RUE BOISSY D'ANGLAS
GALERIE DE LA MADELEINE
PLACE DE LA MADELEINE
CITE BERRYER
RUE ROYALE
Rond Point des Champs Elysées
ROND POINT DES CHAMPS ELYSEES
AVENUE MONTAIGNE
AVENUE DES CHAMPS ELYSEES
Champs Elysées Clemenceau
Espace Pierre Cardin
RUE SAINT F
Musée Bouilbet-Christofle

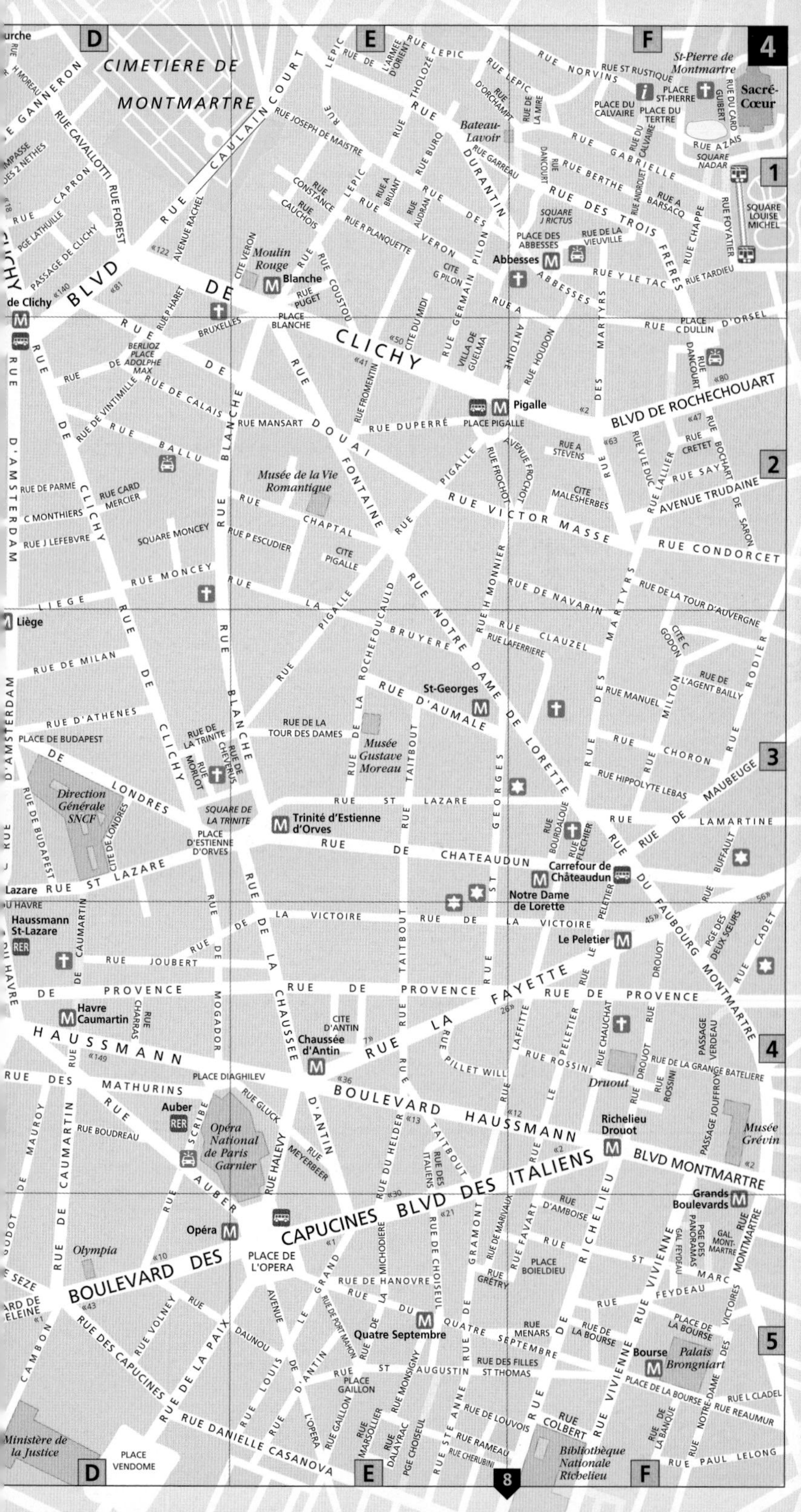

4
D
E
F
1
2
3
4
5
8
CIMETIERE DE MONTMARTRE
St-Pierre de Montmartre
Sacré-Cœur
RUE LEPIC
RUE NORVINS
RUE ST RUSTIQUE
PLACE ST-PIERRE
PLACE DU CALVAIRE
PLACE DU TERTRE
RUE DU CARD GUIBERT
RUE AZAIS
SQUARE NADAR
SQUARE LOUISE MICHEL
RUE FOYATIER
RUE CHAPPE
RUE TARDIEU
RUE GABRIELLE
RUE BERTHE
RUE DES TROIS FRERES
RUE A BARSACQ
RUE ANDROUET
RUE DU CALVAIRE
RUE DE LA MIRE
RUE D'ORCHAMPT
RUE DE L'ARMEE D'ORIENT
RUE THOLOZÉ
Bateau-Lavoir
RUE GARREAU
RUE DANCOURT
SQUARE J RICTUS
PLACE DES ABBESSES
RUE DE LA VIEUVILLE
Abbesses
RUE DES ABBESSES
RUE Y LE TAC
RUE CAULAINCOURT
RUE JOSEPH DE MAISTRE
RUE DURANTIN
RUE BURQ
RUE A BRUANT
RUE AUDRAN
RUE VERON
RUE R PLANQUETTE
CITE G PILON
RUE GERMAIN PILON
RUE CONSTANCE
RUE CAUCHOIS
RUE LEPIC
RUE GANNERON
RUE CAVALLOTTI
RUE H MOREAU
IMPASSE DES 2 NETHES
RUE CAPRON
RUE FOREST
PGE LATHUILLE
PASSAGE DE CLICHY
AVENUE RACHEL
CITE VERON
Moulin Rouge
Blanche
RUE PUGET
RUE COUSTOU
de Clichy
BLVD DE CLICHY
RUE P HARET
PLACE BLANCHE
BRUXELLES
CITE DU MIDI
VILLA DE GUELMA
RUE ANTOINE
RUE HOUDON
RUE DES MARTYRS
PLACE C DULLIN
RUE D'ORSEL
RUE DANCOURT
BLVD DE ROCHECHOUART
RUE FROMENTIN
Pigalle
PLACE PIGALLE
RUE DUPERRÉ
RUE DE DOUAI
RUE MANSART
BERLIOZ
PLACE DE ADOLPHE MAX
RUE DE CALAIS
RUE DE VINTIMILLE
RUE BALLU
RUE BLANCHE
RUE CARD MERCIER
RUE DE PARME
C MONTHIERS
RUE J LEFEBVRE
SQUARE MONCEY
RUE MONCEY
RUE DE CLICHY
RUE D'AMSTERDAM
Musée de la Vie Romantique
RUE CHAPTAL
RUE P ESCUDIER
CITE PIGALLE
RUE FONTAINE
RUE PIGALLE
AVENUE FROCHOT
RUE FROCHOT
RUE A STEVENS
CITE MALESHERBES
RUE VICTOR MASSE
RUE V LE DUC
RUE LALLIER
RUE CRETET
RUE BOCHART DE SARON
RUE SAY
AVENUE TRUDAINE
RUE CONDORCET
RUE H MONNIER
RUE DE NAVARIN
RUE DE LA TOUR D'AUVERGNE
RUE CLAUZEL
RUE LAFERRIERE
CITE C GODON
RUE RODIER
LIEGE
Liège
RUE DE LA BRUYERE
RUE LA ROCHEFOUCAULD
RUE NOTRE DAME DE LORETTE
RUE DE MILAN
St-Georges
RUE D'AUMALE
RUE MANUEL
RUE MILTON
RUE DE L'AGENT BAILLY
RUE D'ATHENES
PLACE DE BUDAPEST
RUE DE LA TRINITE
RUE DE CHEVREUS
RUE MORLOT
RUE DE LA TOUR DES DAMES
Musée Gustave Moreau
RUE TAITBOUT
RUE ST GEORGES
RUE CHORON
RUE HIPPOLYTE LEBAS
RUE DE MAUBEUGE
RUE DE LONDRES
Direction Générale SNCF
RUE DE BUDAPEST
CITE DE LONDRES
SQUARE DE LA TRINITE
PLACE D'ESTIENNE D'ORVES
Trinité d'Estienne d'Orves
RUE ST LAZARE
RUE DE CHATEAUDUN
RUE BOURDALOUE
RUE FLECHIER
RUE LAMARTINE
RUE BUFFAULT
Carrefour de Châteaudun
Notre Dame de Lorette
Lazare
RUE DU HAVRE
Haussmann St-Lazare
RER
RUE DE CAUMARTIN
RUE JOUBERT
RUE DE LA VICTOIRE
RUE DE MOGADOR
RUE DE LA CHAUSSEE D'ANTIN
Le Peletier
RUE LE PELETIER
RUE DU FAUBOURG MONTMARTRE
PGE DES DEUX SŒURS
RUE CADET
RUE DROUOT
RUE DE PROVENCE
RUE LA FAYETTE
Havre Caumartin
RUE CHARRAS
CITE D'ANTIN
Chaussée d'Antin
RUE LAFFITTE
RUE CHAUCHAT
PASSAGE VERDEAU
RUE PILLET WILL
RUE ROSSINI
RUE DE LA GRANGE BATELIERE
Drouot
PASSAGE JOUFFROY
Musée Grévin
HAUSSMANN
BOULEVARD HAUSSMANN
RUE DES MATHURINS
PLACE DIAGHILEV
Auber
RUE SCRIBE
RUE GLUCK
Opéra National de Paris Garnier
RUE HALEVY
RUE MEYERBEER
RUE DU HELDER
RUE TAITBOUT
RUE DES ITALIENS
Richelieu Drouot
BLVD MONTMARTRE
RUE BOUDREAU
RUE DE CAUMARTIN
RUE AUBER
Opéra
PLACE DE L'OPERA
BOULEVARD DES CAPUCINES
BLVD DES ITALIENS
RUE DE MARIVAUX
RUE FAVART
RUE D'AMBOISE
RUE DE RICHELIEU
Grands Boulevards
Olympia
RUE DE LA MICHODIERE
RUE DE CHOISEUL
RUE DE GRAMONT
PLACE BOIELDIEU
RUE GRETRY
RUE ST MARC
RUE VIVIENNE
GAL FEYDEAU
PGE DES PANORAMAS
GAL MONTMARTRE
RUE MONTMARTRE
RUE FEYDEAU
RUE DE HANOVRE
RUE DU QUATRE SEPTEMBRE
Quatre Septembre
RUE DE PORT MAHON
RUE MENARS
RUE DE LA BOURSE
PLACE DE LA BOURSE
RUE DES VICTOIRES
Bourse
Palais Brongniart
RUE VOLNEY
RUE DAUNOU
RUE DE LA PAIX
RUE DES CAPUCINES
RUE CAMBON
RUE SEZE
RUE LOUIS LE GRAND
AVENUE DE L'OPERA
RUE D'ANTIN
RUE ST AUGUSTIN
PLACE GAILLON
RUE GAILLON
RUE MONSIGNY
RUE DES FILLES ST THOMAS
RUE NOTRE-DAME
RUE L CLADEL
RUE REAUMUR
RUE DE LA BANQUE
RUE DE LOUVOIS
RUE COLBERT
RUE STE ANNE
RUE RAMEAU
RUE CHERUBINI
RUE MARSOLLIER
RUE DALAYRAC
PGE CHOISEUL
RUE DANIELLE CASANOVA
Ministère de la Justice
PLACE VENDOME
Bibliothèque Nationale Richelieu
RUE PAUL LELONG

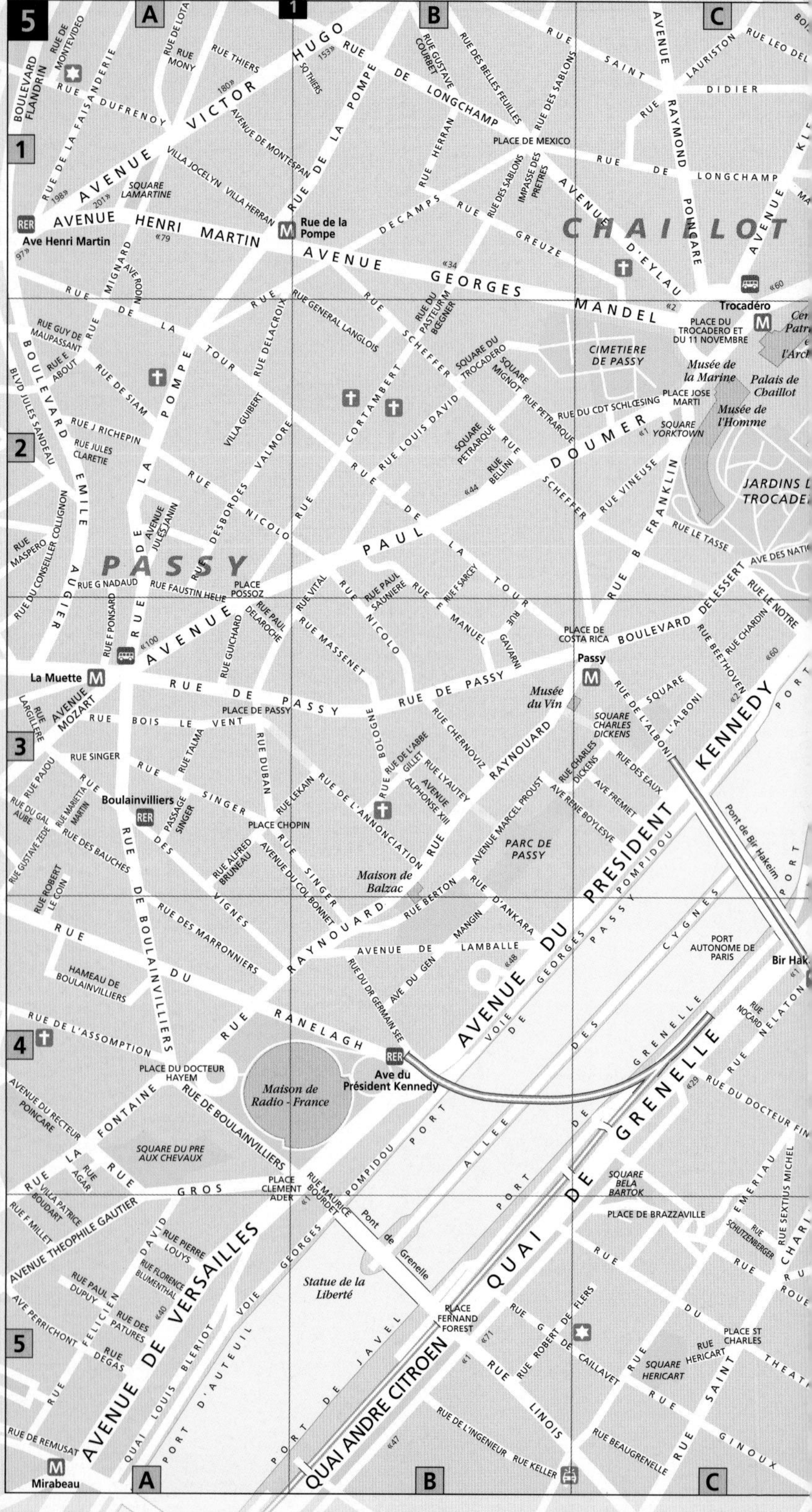

5
A
B
C
1
2
3
4
5
CHAILLOT
PASSY
BOULEVARD FLANDRIN
RUE DE MONTEVIDEO
RUE DE LA FAISANDERIE
RUE DUFRENOY
RUE DE LOTA
RUE MONY
RUE THIERS
AVENUE VICTOR HUGO
SQ THIERS
RUE DE LONGCHAMP
RUE GUSTAVE COURBET
RUE DES BELLES FEUILLES
RUE DES SABLONS
PLACE DE MEXICO
RUE SAINT DIDIER
AVENUE RAYMOND POINCARE
RUE LAURISTON
RUE LEO DELIBES
AVENUE DE MONTESPAN
VILLA JOCELYN
VILLA HERRAN
SQUARE LAMARTINE
RUE DE LA POMPE
RUE HERRAN
RUE DES SABLONS
IMPASSE DES PRETRES
AVENUE D'EYLAU
RUE DECAMPS
RUE GREUZE
AVENUE HENRI MARTIN
Ave Henri Martin
Rue de la Pompe
AVENUE GEORGES MANDEL
Trocadéro
PLACE DU TROCADERO ET DU 11 NOVEMBRE
RUE MIGNARD
AVE RODIN
RUE DE LA TOUR
RUE GUY DE MAUPASSANT
RUE E ABOUT
BOULEVARD EMILE AUGIER
BLVD JULES SANDEAU
RUE DE SIAM
RUE J RICHEPIN
RUE JULES CLARETIE
RUE DELACROIX
RUE GENERAL LANGLOIS
RUE SCHEFFER
RUE DU PASTEUR M BOEGNER
SQUARE DU TROCADERO
SQUARE MIGNOT
CIMETIERE DE PASSY
Musée de la Marine
Palais de Chaillot
Musée de l'Homme
PLACE JOSE MARTI
RUE DU CDT SCHLŒSING
RUE PETRARQUE
SQUARE YORKTOWN
JARDINS DU TROCADERO
VILLA GUIBERT
RUE VALMORE
RUE CORTAMBERT
RUE LOUIS DAVID
SQUARE PETRARQUE
RUE BELLINI
AVENUE PAUL DOUMER
RUE VINEUSE
RUE FRANKLIN
RUE LE TASSE
AVE DES NATIONS
RUE DESBORDES VALMORE
RUE NICOLO
AVENUE JULES JANIN
RUE DU CONSEILLER COLLIGNON
RUE MASPERO
RUE G NADAUD
RUE FAUSTIN HELIE
PLACE POSSOZ
RUE VITAL
RUE PAUL SAUNIERE
RUE E MANUEL
RUE F SARCEY
RUE GAVARNI
RUE B FRANKLIN
BOULEVARD DELESSERT
RUE LE NOTRE
PLACE DE COSTA RICA
RUE CHARDIN
RUE BEETHOVEN
RUE F PONSARD
AVENUE PAUL DOUMER
RUE GUICHARD
RUE PAUL DELAROCHE
RUE MASSENET
La Muette
RUE DE PASSY
Passy
Musée du Vin
SQUARE L'ALBONI
RUE DE L'ALBONI
SQUARE CHARLES DICKENS
AVENUE DU PRESIDENT KENNEDY
AVENUE MOZART
RUE LARGILLIERE
PLACE DE PASSY
RUE BOIS LE VENT
RUE CHERNOVIZ
RUE BOLOGNE
RUE DE L'ABBE GILLET
RUE LYAUTEY
AVENUE ALPHONSE XIII
RUE RAYNOUARD
RUE CHARLES DICKENS
RUE DES EAUX
AVE FREMIET
AVE RENE BOYLESVE
RUE SINGER
RUE TALMA
RUE DUBAN
RUE PAJOU
RUE MARIETTA MARTIN
Boulainvilliers
PASSAGE SINGER
RUE LEKAIN
RUE DE L'ANNONCIATION
PLACE CHOPIN
AVENUE MARCEL PROUST
PARC DE PASSY
Pont de Bir Hakeim
PORT DE PASSY
RUE DU GAL AUBE
RUE DES BAUCHES
RUE GUSTAVE ZEDE
RUE ROBERT LE COIN
RUE DES VIGNES
RUE ALFRED BRUNEAU
AVENUE DU COLONEL BONNET
Maison de Balzac
RUE BERTON
RUE D'ANKARA
AVENUE DE LAMBALLE
RUE MANGIN
VOIE GEORGES POMPIDOU
ALLEE DES CYGNES
PORT AUTONOME DE PARIS
Bir Hakeim
RUE DES MARRONNIERS
RUE DU RANELAGH
HAMEAU DE BOULAINVILLIERS
RUE DE BOULAINVILLIERS
RUE DE L'ASSOMPTION
AVE DU GEN MANGIN
RUE DU DR GERMAIN SEE
RUE NOCARD
RUE NELATON
PLACE DU DOCTEUR HAYEM
Maison de Radio - France
Ave du Président Kennedy
PORT DE GRENELLE
RUE DU DOCTEUR FINLAY
AVENUE DU RECTEUR POINCARE
RUE LA FONTAINE
SQUARE DU PRE AUX CHEVAUX
RUE AGAR
RUE GROS
PLACE CLEMENT ADER
RUE MAURICE BOURDET
QUAI DE GRENELLE
SQUARE BELA BARTOK
PLACE DE BRAZZAVILLE
RUE EMERIAU
RUE SCHUTZENBERGER
RUE SEXTIUS MICHEL
RUE CHARLES MICHELS
RUE VILLA PATRICE BOUDART
RUE F MILLET
AVENUE THEOPHILE GAUTIER
RUE DAVID
RUE PIERRE LOUYS
RUE FLORENCE BLUMENTHAL
RUE PAUL DUPUY
RUE FELICIEN DAVID
RUE DES PATURES
AVENUE DE VERSAILLES
Pont de Grenelle
Statue de la Liberté
PLACE FERNAND FOREST
RUE DU THEATRE
RUE ROBERT DE FLERS
RUE G DE CAILLAVET
SQUARE HERICART
RUE HERICART
PLACE ST CHARLES
RUE SAINT CHARLES
RUE DE LA ROUEN
AVE PERRICHONT
RUE DEGAS
VOIE D'AUTEUIL
RUE LOUIS BLERIOT
QUAI LOUIS BLERIOT
PORT D'AUTEUIL
PORT DE JAVEL
QUAI ANDRE CITROEN
RUE LINOIS
RUE DE L'INGENIEUR
RUE KELLER
RUE BEAUGRENELLE
RUE GINOUX
RUE DE REMUSAT
Mirabeau

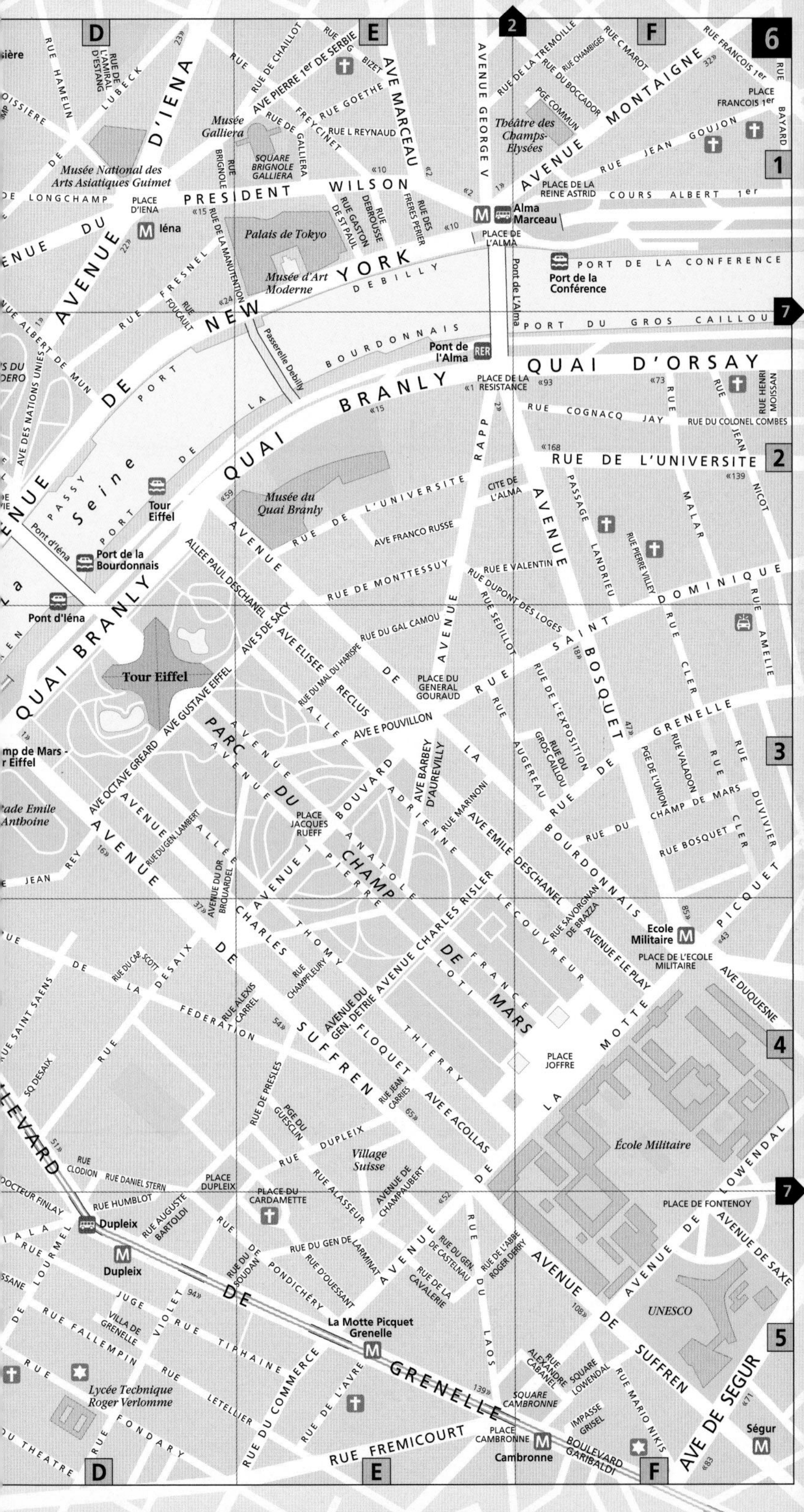

6
D
E
F
2
7
1
2
3
4
5
Musée National des Arts Asiatiques Guimet
Musée Galliera
Square Brignole Galliera
Théâtre des Champs-Elysées
Palais de Tokyo
Musée d'Art Moderne
Iéna
Alma Marceau
Place de l'Alma
Port de la Conférence
Pont de l'Alma
Place de la Résistance
Tour Eiffel
Port de la Bourdonnais
Pont d'Iéna
Musée du Quai Branly
Seine
Parc du Champ de Mars
Place Jacques Rueff
Place du Général Gouraud
Ecole Militaire
Place de l'Ecole Militaire
Place Joffre
École Militaire
Place de Fontenoy
UNESCO
Village Suisse
Place Dupleix
Place du Cardamette
Dupleix
La Motte Picquet Grenelle
Square Cambronne
Place Cambronne
Cambronne
Ségur
Lycée Technique Roger Verlomme
Avenue du Président Wilson
Avenue de New York
Quai Branly
Quai d'Orsay
Avenue d'Iéna
Avenue Marceau
Avenue George V
Avenue Montaigne
Cours Albert 1er
Rue de l'Université
Rue Saint Dominique
Avenue Bosquet
Avenue Rapp
Rue de Grenelle
Avenue de la Bourdonnais
Avenue de Suffren
Avenue de la Motte Picquet
Boulevard de Grenelle
Avenue de Ségur
Avenue de Saxe
Avenue de Lowendal
Rue Cler
Avenue Duquesne
Rue de la Fédération
Rue du Commerce
Rue Fremicourt
Boulevard Garibaldi

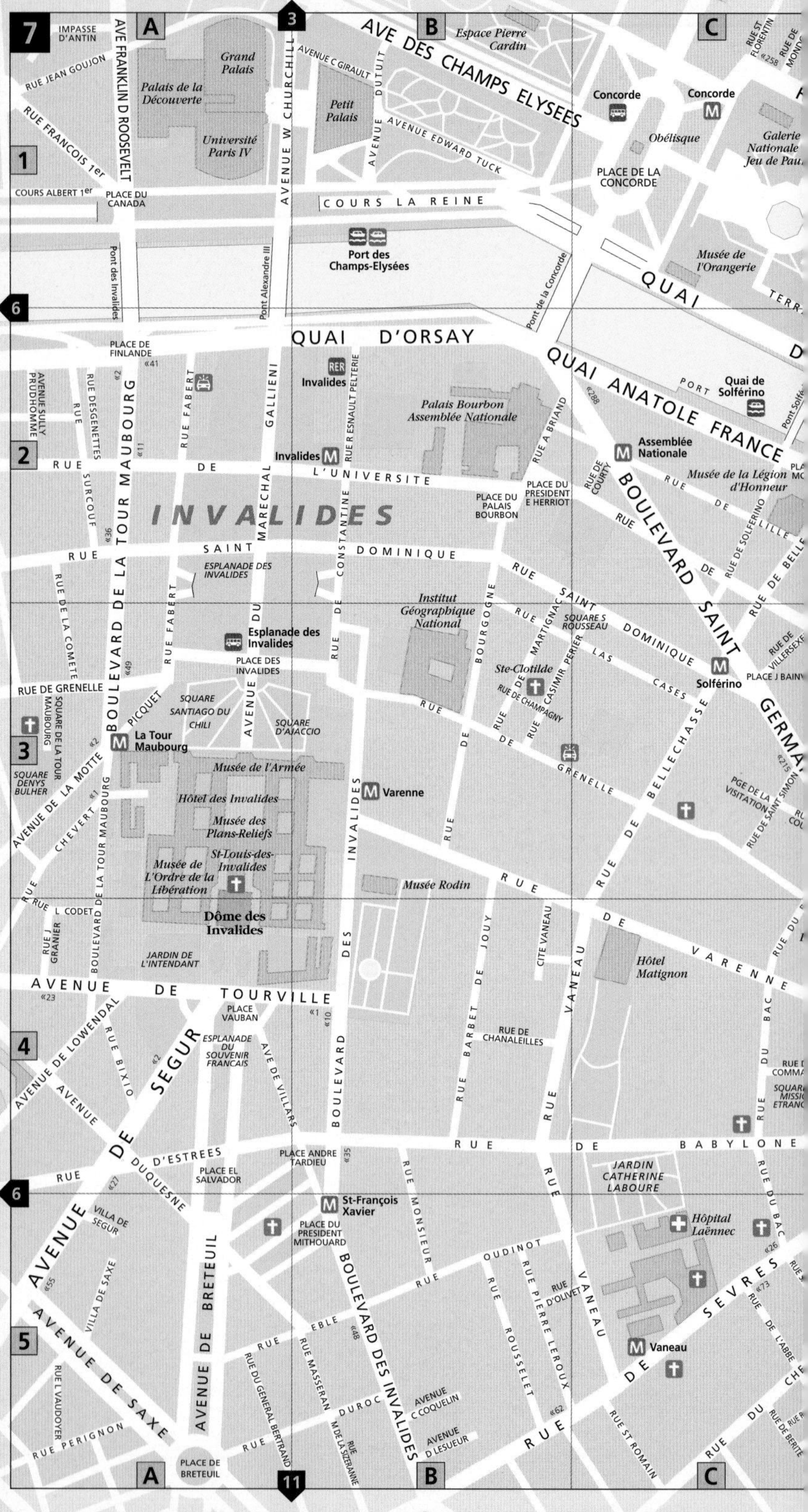
7
A
B
C
1
2
3
4
5
6
3
11
IMPASSE D'ANTIN
AVE FRANKLIN D ROOSEVELT
RUE JEAN GOUJON
RUE FRANCOIS 1er
COURS ALBERT 1er
PLACE DU CANADA
Grand Palais
Palais de la Découverte
Université Paris IV
AVENUE W CHURCHILL
AVENUE C GIRAULT
Petit Palais
AVENUE DUTUIT
AVE DES CHAMPS ELYSEES
Espace Pierre Cardin
AVENUE EDWARD TUCK
COURS LA REINE
Port des Champs-Elysées
Concorde
Obélisque
PLACE DE LA CONCORDE
Galerie Nationale Jeu de Pau
Musée de l'Orangerie
QUAI
RUE ST FLORENTIN
Pont des Invalides
Pont Alexandre III
Pont de la Concorde
QUAI D'ORSAY
PLACE DE FINLANDE
Invalides
QUAI ANATOLE FRANCE
PORT
Quai de Solférino
Palais Bourbon Assemblée Nationale
AVENUE SULLY PRUDHOMME
RUE DESGENETTES
RUE FABERT
GALLIENI
RUE R ESNAULT PELTERIE
RUE A BRIAND
Assemblée Nationale
RUE DE COURTY
BOULEVARD SAINT GERMAIN
Musée de la Légion d'Honneur
RUE DE LILLE
RUE DE L'UNIVERSITE
RUE SURCOUF
BOULEVARD DE LA TOUR MAUBOURG
PLACE DU PALAIS BOURBON
PLACE DU PRESIDENT E HERRIOT
INVALIDES
RUE SAINT DOMINIQUE
RUE DE SOLFERINO
RUE DE BELLECHASSE
ESPLANADE DES INVALIDES
AVENUE DU MARECHAL
RUE DE CONSTANTINE
Institut Géographique National
RUE DE BOURGOGNE
RUE DE MARTIGNAC
SQUARE S ROUSSEAU
RUE LAS CASES
RUE CASIMIR PERIER
RUE DE LA COMETE
Esplanade des Invalides
PLACE DES INVALIDES
Ste-Clotilde
RUE DE CHAMPAGNY
Solférino
RUE DE VILLERSEXEL
PLACE J BAINVILLE
RUE DE GRENELLE
SQUARE DE LA TOUR MAUBOURG
RUE PICQUET
SQUARE SANTIAGO DU CHILI
SQUARE D'AJACCIO
La Tour Maubourg
SQUARE DENYS BULHER
AVENUE DE LA MOTTE
Musée de l'Armée
Hôtel des Invalides
Musée des Plans-Reliefs
St-Louis-des-Invalides
Musée de L'Ordre de la Libération
Dôme des Invalides
Varenne
PGE DE LA VISITATION
RUE DE SAINT SIMON
RUE CHEVERT
BOULEVARD DE LA TOUR MAUBOURG
Musée Rodin
RUE DE VARENNE
RUE L CODET
RUE J GRANIER
JARDIN DE L'INTENDANT
RUE DE JOUY
CITE VANEAU
RUE VANEAU
Hôtel Matignon
RUE DU BAC
AVENUE DE TOURVILLE
PLACE VAUBAN
BOULEVARD DES INVALIDES
RUE BARBET DE JOUY
RUE DE CHANALEILLES
AVENUE DE LOWENDAL
RUE BIXIO
AVENUE DE SEGUR
ESPLANADE DU SOUVENIR FRANCAIS
AVE DE VILLARS
RUE DE BABYLONE
PLACE ANDRE TARDIEU
RUE D'ESTREES
RUE DUQUESNE
PLACE EL SALVADOR
JARDIN CATHERINE LABOURE
St-François Xavier
RUE MONSIEUR
VILLA DE SEGUR
PLACE DU PRESIDENT MITHOUARD
Hôpital Laënnec
RUE OUDINOT
AVENUE DE BRETEUIL
VILLA DE SAXE
RUE D'OLIVET
RUE PIERRE LEROUX
RUE ROUSSELET
RUE DE SEVRES
RUE DE L'ABBE
RUE EBLE
RUE MASSERAN
Vaneau
AVENUE DE SAXE
RUE L VAUDOYER
RUE DU GENERAL BERTRAND
RUE DUROC
AVENUE C COQUELIN
AVENUE D LESUEUR
RUE M DE LA SIZERANNE
RUE ST ROMAIN
RUE DU CHE
RUE DE BERITE
RUE PERIGNON
PLACE DE BRETEUIL

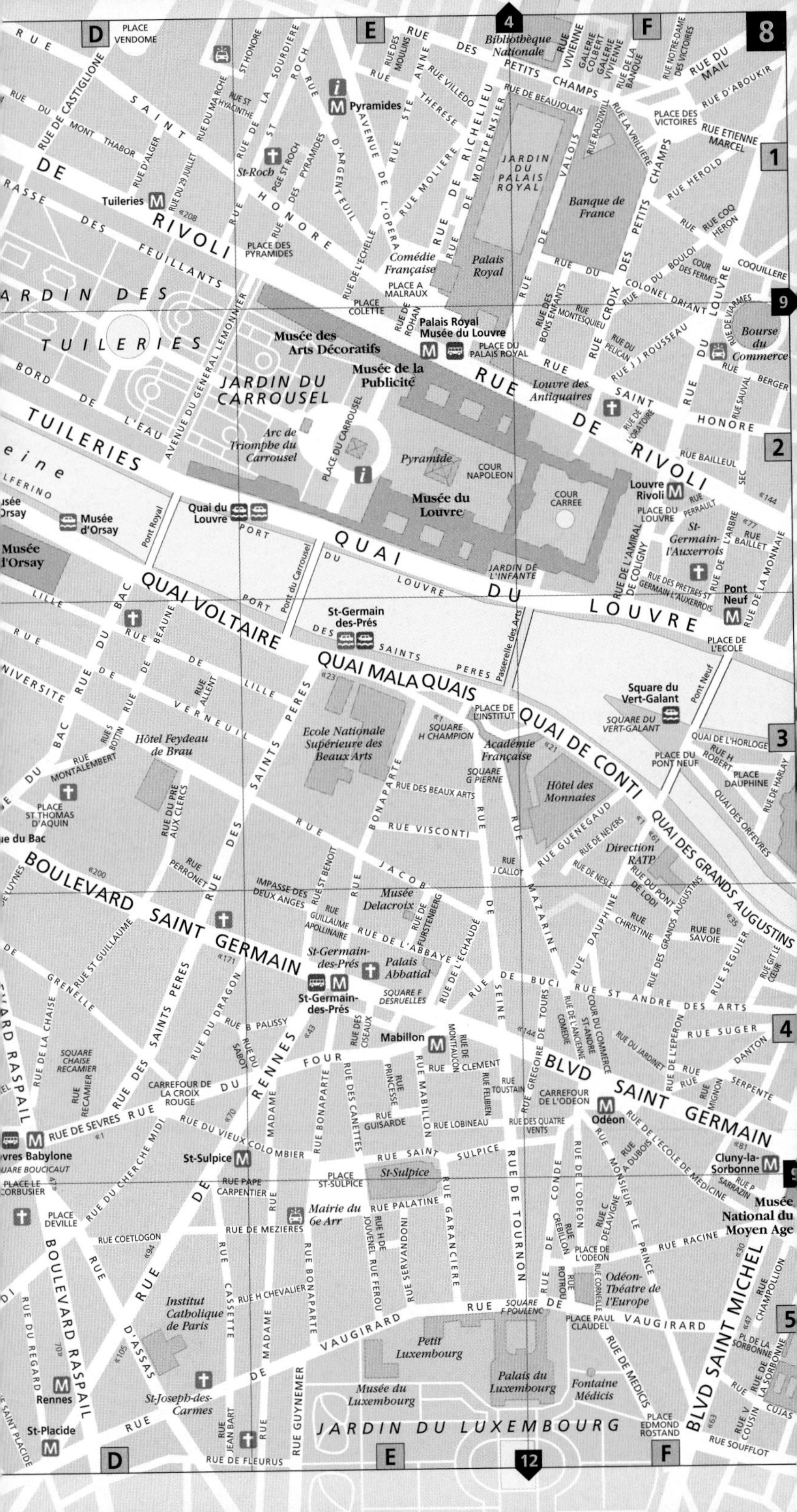

8
D
E
F
4
1
2
3
4
5
9
12
PLACE VENDOME
RUE DE CASTIGLIONE
RUE DU MONT THABOR
RUE SAINT HONORE
RUE DE RIVOLI
RUE D'ALGER
RUE DU 29 JUILLET
Tuileries
RUE DU MARCHE ST HONORE
RUE ST HYACINTHE
RUE DE LA SOURDIERE
RUE ST ROCH
St-Roch
PGE ST ROCH
RUE DES PYRAMIDES
PLACE DES PYRAMIDES
Pyramides
AVENUE DE L'OPERA
RUE D'ARGENTEUIL
RUE DE L'ECHELLE
RUE DES MOULINS
RUE STE ANNE
RUE THERESE
RUE VILLEDO
RUE MOLIERE
RUE DE RICHELIEU
RUE DE MONTPENSIER
RUE DES PETITS CHAMPS
Bibliothèque Nationale
RUE VIVIENNE
GALERIE COLBERT
GALERIE VIVIENNE
RUE DE LA BANQUE
RUE NOTRE-DAME DES VICTOIRES
RUE DU MAIL
RUE D'ABOUKIR
PLACE DES VICTOIRES
RUE ETIENNE MARCEL
RUE DE BEAUJOLAIS
RUE RADZIWILL
RUE LA VRILLIERE
JARDIN DU PALAIS ROYAL
Banque de France
RUE DE VALOIS
RUE HEROLD
RUE COQ HERON
Comédie Française
Palais Royal
PLACE A MALRAUX
PLACE COLETTE
RUE DE ROHAN
Palais Royal Musée du Louvre
PLACE DU PALAIS ROYAL
RUE DES BONS ENFANTS
RUE MONTESQUIEU
RUE CROIX DES PETITS CHAMPS
RUE DU COLONEL DRIANT
RUE DU BOULOI
COUR DES FERMES
RUE COQUILLERE
RUE DU LOUVRE
RUE DE VIARMES
Bourse du Commerce
RUE DU PELICAN
RUE J J ROUSSEAU
RUE BERGER
RUE SAUVAL
Louvre des Antiquaires
RUE DE L'ORATOIRE
RUE BAILLEUL
RUE DE L'ARBRE SEC
TERRASSE DES FEUILLANTS
JARDIN DES TUILERIES
Musée des Arts Décoratifs
Musée de la Publicité
JARDIN DU CARROUSEL
AVENUE DU GENERAL LEMONNIER
BORD DE L'EAU
TUILERIES
Seine
Arc de Triomphe du Carrousel
PLACE DU CARROUSEL
Pyramide
COUR NAPOLEON
COUR CARREE
Musée du Louvre
Louvre Rivoli
RUE PERRAULT
PLACE DU LOUVRE
St-Germain-l'Auxerrois
RUE BAILLET
RUE DE LA MONNAIE
RUE DE L'AMIRAL DE COLIGNY
RUE DES PRETRES ST GERMAIN L'AUXERROIS
Pont Neuf
JARDIN DE L'INFANTE
QUAI DU LOUVRE
PORT DU LOUVRE
Quai du Louvre
Musée d'Orsay
Pont Royal
Pont du Carrousel
RUE DE LILLE
QUAI VOLTAIRE
PORT DES SAINTS PERES
St-Germain des-Prés
Passerelle des Arts
PLACE DE L'ECOLE
QUAI MALAQUAIS
Square du Vert-Galant
SQUARE DU VERT-GALANT
Pont Neuf
QUAI DE L'HORLOGE
RUE H ROBERT
PLACE DU PONT NEUF
PLACE DAUPHINE
RUE DE HARLAY
QUAI DES ORFEVRES
RUE DU BAC
RUE DE BEAUNE
RUE DE L'UNIVERSITE
RUE ALLENT
RUE DE VERNEUIL
RUE DES SAINTS PERES
Hôtel Feydeau de Brau
RUE S BOTTIN
RUE MONTALEMBERT
PLACE ST THOMAS D'AQUIN
RUE DU PRE AUX CLERCS
Ecole Nationale Supérieure des Beaux Arts
PLACE DE L'INSTITUT
SQUARE H CHAMPION
Académie Française
QUAI DE CONTI
Hôtel des Monnaies
SQUARE G PIERNE
RUE DES BEAUX ARTS
RUE BONAPARTE
RUE VISCONTI
RUE DE SEINE
RUE MAZARINE
RUE J CALLOT
RUE GUENEGAUD
RUE DE NEVERS
RUE DE NESLE
Direction RATP
QUAI DES GRANDS AUGUSTINS
RUE DU PONT DE LODI
RUE DAUPHINE
RUE CHRISTINE
RUE DES GRANDS AUGUSTINS
RUE DE SAVOIE
RUE SEGUIER
RUE GIT LE COEUR
Rue du Bac
BOULEVARD SAINT GERMAIN
RUE PERRONET
RUE DE L'UNIVERSITE
IMPASSE DES DEUX ANGES
RUE ST BENOIT
RUE JACOB
Musée Delacroix
RUE DE FURSTENBERG
RUE GUILLAUME APOLLINAIRE
RUE DE L'ABBAYE
RUE DE L'ECHAUDE
RUE ST GUILLAUME
RUE DE GRENELLE
St-Germain-des-Prés
Palais Abbatial
SQUARE F DESRUELLES
RUE DE BUCI
RUE ST ANDRE DES ARTS
RUE DE L'ANCIENNE COMEDIE
COUR DU COMMERCE ST-ANDRE
RUE GREGOIRE DE TOURS
RUE DU JARDINET
RUE DE L'EPERON
RUE SUGER
RUE DANTON
RUE SERPENTE
RUE MIGNON
RUE DE LA CHAISE
SQUARE CHAISE RECAMIER
RUE RECAMIER
RUE DES SAINTS PERES
RUE DU DRAGON
RUE B PALISSY
RUE DU SABOT
RUE DE RENNES
RUE DES CISEAUX
Mabillon
RUE DE MONTFAUCON
RUE DU FOUR
RUE CLEMENT
RUE FELIBIEN
RUE TOUSTAIN
CARREFOUR DE L'ODEON
BLVD SAINT GERMAIN
Odéon
RUE DE L'ECOLE DE MEDICINE
CARREFOUR DE LA CROIX ROUGE
RUE DE SEVRES
RUE DU CHERCHE MIDI
RUE DU VIEUX COLOMBIER
RUE MADAME
RUE DES CANETTES
RUE PRINCESSE
RUE MABILLON
RUE GUISARDE
RUE LOBINEAU
RUE DES QUATRE VENTS
RUE A DUBOIS
Cluny-la-Sorbonne
Sèvres Babylone
SQUARE BOUCICAUT
St-Sulpice
RUE SAINT SULPICE
PLACE ST-SULPICE
St-Sulpice
RUE PAPE CARPENTIER
PLACE LE CORBUSIER
PLACE DEVILLE
RUE DE MEZIERES
Mairie du 6e Arr
RUE PALATINE
RUE H DE JOUVENEL
RUE FEROU
RUE SERVANDONI
RUE GARANCIERE
RUE DE TOURNON
RUE DE CONDE
RUE DE L'ODEON
RUE CREBILLON
RUE C DELAVIGNE
RUE MONSIEUR LE PRINCE
RUE P SARRAZIN
Musée National du Moyen Age
RUE RACINE
RUE COETLOGON
BOULEVARD RASPAIL
RUE D'ASSAS
RUE CASSETTE
RUE H CHEVALIER
PLACE DE L'ODEON
RUE ROTROU
RUE CORNEILLE
Odéon-Théatre de l'Europe
Institut Catholique de Paris
RUE DE VAUGIRARD
SQUARE F POULENC
PLACE PAUL CLAUDEL
BLVD SAINT MICHEL
RUE CHAMPOLLION
PL DE LA SORBONNE
RUE DE LA SORBONNE
Petit Luxembourg
Palais du Luxembourg
Fontaine Médicis
RUE DE MEDICIS
Musée du Luxembourg
RUE GUYNEMER
RUE DU REGARD
Rennes
St-Joseph-des-Carmes
RUE JEAN BART
RUE DE FLEURUS
JARDIN DU LUXEMBOURG
PLACE EDMOND ROSTAND
RUE V COUSIN
RUE CUJAS
RUE SOUFFLOT
St-Placide
RUE ST PLACIDE

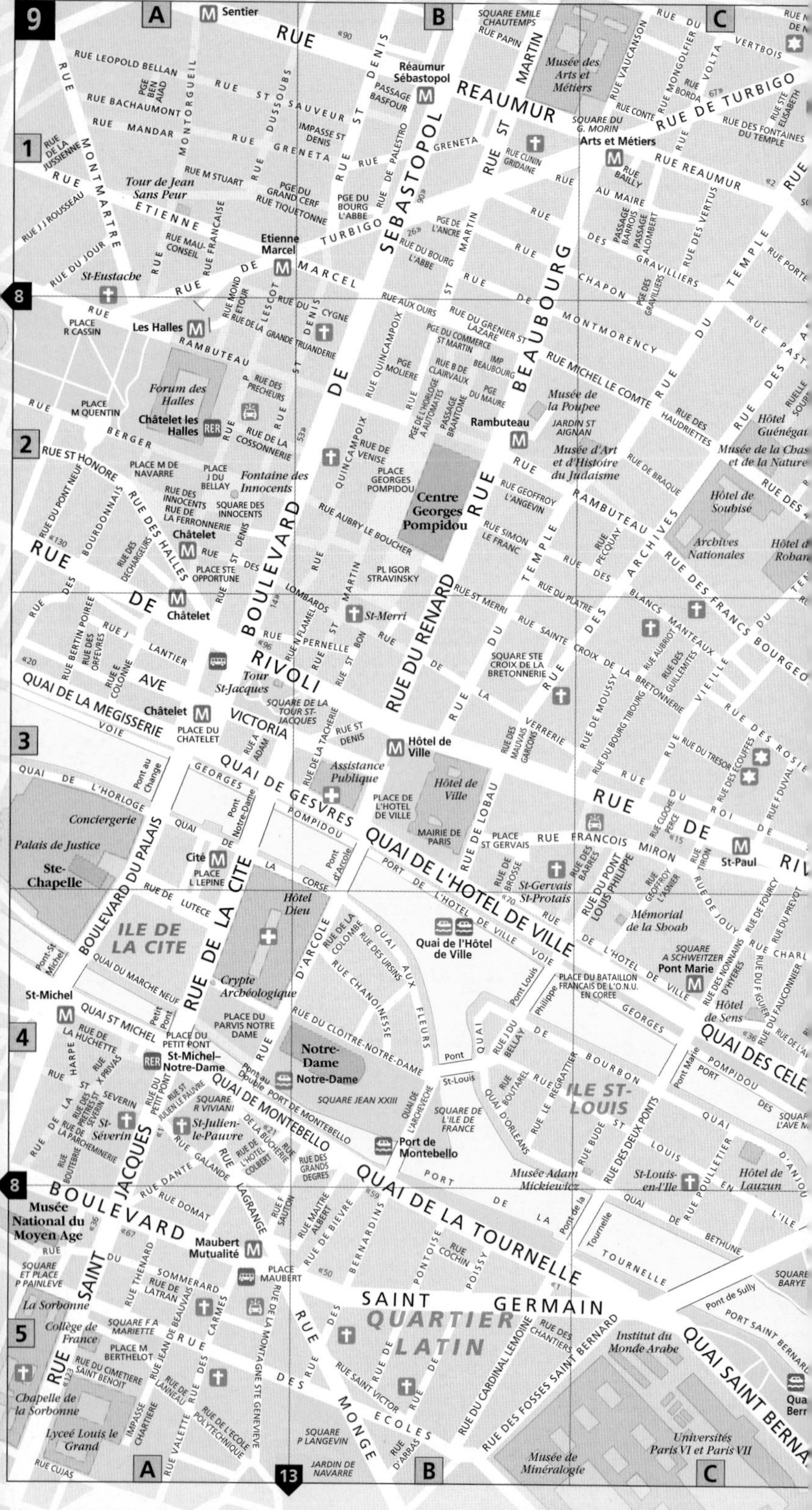
9
A
B
C
1
2
3
4
5
8
13
Sentier
Réaumur Sébastopol
Arts et Métiers
Etienne Marcel
Les Halles
Châtelet les Halles
Rambuteau
Châtelet
Hôtel de Ville
Cité
St-Michel
St-Michel–Notre-Dame
Maubert Mutualité
Pont Marie
St-Paul
RUE REAUMUR
RUE DE TURBIGO
RUE ETIENNE MARCEL
RUE MONTMARTRE
RUE MONTORGUEIL
RUE ST DENIS
BOULEVARD DE SEBASTOPOL
RUE ST MARTIN
RUE BEAUBOURG
RUE DU TEMPLE
RUE RAMBUTEAU
RUE DE RIVOLI
RUE DU RENARD
RUE DES ARCHIVES
RUE DES FRANCS BOURGEOIS
RUE DU ROI DE SICILE
RUE VIEILLE DU TEMPLE
RUE DE LA VERRERIE
RUE ST HONORE
RUE BERGER
RUE DE LA FERRONNERIE
RUE DES LOMBARDS
AVE VICTORIA
RUE FRANCOIS MIRON
RUE DE LOBAU
RUE DE LA CITE
BOULEVARD DU PALAIS
QUAI DE LA MEGISSERIE
QUAI DE GESVRES
QUAI DE L'HOTEL DE VILLE
QUAI DES CELESTINS
QUAI DE L'HORLOGE
QUAI DE LA CORSE
QUAI AUX FLEURS
QUAI DU MARCHE NEUF
QUAI ST MICHEL
QUAI DE MONTEBELLO
QUAI DE LA TOURNELLE
QUAI DE BOURBON
QUAI D'ORLEANS
QUAI D'ANJOU
QUAI DE BETHUNE
QUAI SAINT BERNARD
RUE ST LOUIS EN L'ILE
RUE DU CLOITRE-NOTRE-DAME
RUE D'ARCOLE
BOULEVARD ST GERMAIN
BOULEVARD SAINT MICHEL
RUE SAINT JACQUES
RUE DES ECOLES
RUE MONGE
RUE DE LA HUCHETTE
RUE GALANDE
RUE LAGRANGE
RUE DES CARMES
RUE DE LA MONTAGNE STE GENEVIEVE
RUE DU CARDINAL LEMOINE
RUE DES FOSSES SAINT BERNARD
RUE DES BERNARDINS
RUE DE POISSY
RUE DE PONTOISE
Tour de Jean Sans Peur
St-Eustache
Forum des Halles
Fontaine des Innocents
Centre Georges Pompidou
Musée des Arts et Métiers
Musée de la Poupee
Musée d'Art et d'Histoire du Judaïsme
Hôtel de Soubise
Archives Nationales
Hôtel de Rohan
Hôtel Guénégaud
Musée de la Chasse et de la Nature
St-Merri
Tour St-Jacques
Assistance Publique
Hôtel de Ville
Mairie de Paris
Conciergerie
Palais de Justice
Ste-Chapelle
ILE DE LA CITE
Hôtel Dieu
Crypte Archéologique
Notre-Dame
St-Gervais St-Protais
Mémorial de la Shoah
Hôtel de Sens
ILE ST-LOUIS
Musée Adam Mickiewicz
St-Louis-en-l'Ile
Hôtel de Lauzun
St-Julien-le-Pauvre
St-Séverin
Musée National du Moyen Age
La Sorbonne
Collège de France
Chapelle de la Sorbonne
Lycée Louis le Grand
QUARTIER LATIN
Institut du Monde Arabe
Universités Paris VI et Paris VII
Musée de Minéralogie
Quai de l'Hôtel de Ville
Notre-Dame
Port de Montebello
Pont au Change
Pont Notre-Dame
Pont d'Arcole
Pont Louis Philippe
Pont St-Louis
Pont Marie
Pont de la Tournelle
Pont de Sully
Pont au Double
Petit Pont
Pont St-Michel
PLACE DU CHATELET
PLACE GEORGES POMPIDOU
PLACE DE L'HOTEL DE VILLE
PLACE DU PARVIS NOTRE DAME
PLACE MAUBERT
PL IGOR STRAVINSKY
SQUARE JEAN XXIII
SQUARE DE L'ILE DE FRANCE
SQUARE RENE VIVIANI
SQUARE DE LA TOUR ST-JACQUES
SQUARE DU TEMPLE

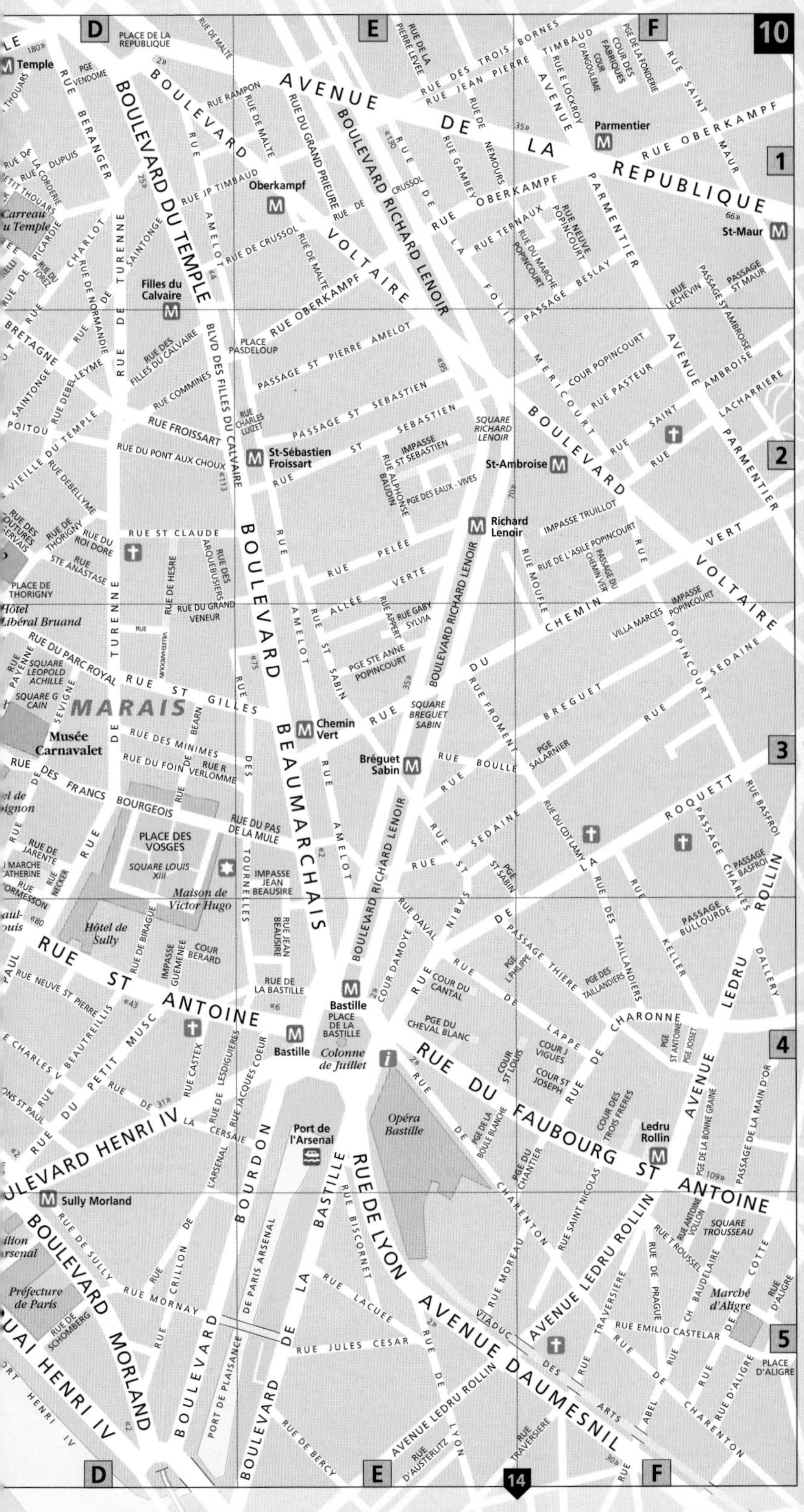

10
D
E
F
1
2
3
4
5
14
PLACE DE LA REPUBLIQUE
RUE DE MALTE
Temple
PGE VENDOME
RUE BERANGER
BOULEVARD DU TEMPLE
BOULEVARD VOLTAIRE
AVENUE DE LA REPUBLIQUE
RUE DE LA PIERRE LEVEE
RUE DES TROIS BORNES
RUE JEAN PIERRE TIMBAUD
RUE E LOCKROY
COUR D'ANGOULEME
COUR DES FABRIQUES
PGE DE LA FONDERIE
RUE SAINT MAUR
RUE OBERKAMPF
Parmentier
AVENUE PARMENTIER
RUE RAMPON
RUE AMELOT
RUE DU GRAND PRIEURE
BOULEVARD RICHARD LENOIR
RUE DE CRUSSOL
RUE GAMBEY
RUE DE NEMOURS
RUE DE LA FOLIE MERICOURT
RUE DUPUIS
RUE DE LA CORDERIE
RUE JP TIMBAUD
Oberkampf
RUE TERNAUX
RUE NEUVE POPINCOURT
RUE DU MARCHE POPINCOURT
St-Maur
Carreau du Temple
RUE DE PICARDIE
RUE CHARLOT
RUE DE TURENNE
RUE DE SAINTONGE
RUE DE NORMANDIE
RUE DU FOREZ
Filles du Calvaire
PASSAGE BESLAY
RUE LECHEVIN
PASSAGE ST AMBROISE
PASSAGE ST MAUR
RUE DE BRETAGNE
RUE DES FILLES DU CALVAIRE
BLVD DES FILLES DU CALVAIRE
PLACE PASDELOUP
PASSAGE ST PIERRE AMELOT
RUE COMMINES
RUE DEBELLEYME
PASSAGE ST SEBASTIEN
COUR POPINCOURT
RUE PASTEUR
AVENUE ST AMBROISE
RUE LACHARRIERE
RUE CHARLES LUIZET
RUE FROISSART
RUE DU PONT AUX CHOUX
RUE VIEILLE DU TEMPLE
RUE DE POITOU
St-Sébastien Froissart
RUE ST SEBASTIEN
IMPASSE ST SEBASTIEN
RUE ALPHONSE BAUDIN
PGE DES EAUX - VIVES
SQUARE RICHARD LENOIR
St-Ambroise
RUE SAINT AMBROISE
Richard Lenoir
IMPASSE TRUILLOT
RUE DE L'ASILE POPINCOURT
PASSAGE DU CHEMIN VERT
RUE DES COUTURES ST GERVAIS
RUE DE THORIGNY
RUE DU ROI DORE
RUE ST CLAUDE
RUE DE HESRE
RUE DES ARQUEBUSIERS
RUE PELEE
RUE MOUFLE
RUE STE ANASTASE
PLACE DE THORIGNY
Hôtel Libéral Bruand
RUE DU GRAND VENEUR
ALLEE VERTE
RUE APPERT
RUE GABY SYLVIA
RUE DU CHEMIN VERT
VILLA MARCES
IMPASSE POPINCOURT
RUE POPINCOURT
RUE DU PARC ROYAL
RUE PAYENNE
SQUARE LEOPOLD ACHILLE
RUE ST GILLES
PGE STE ANNE POPINCOURT
RUE SEDAINE
SQUARE G CAIN
MARAIS
RUE DE BEARN
RUE DE SEVIGNE
RUE FROMENT
RUE BREGUET
Musée Carnavalet
RUE DES MINIMES
Chemin Vert
SQUARE BREGUET SABIN
RUE DU FOIN
RUE R VERLOMME
Bréguet Sabin
RUE BOULLE
PGE SALARNIER
RUE DES FRANCS BOURGEOIS
RUE DE LA ROQUETTE
RUE BASFROI
PASSAGE CHARLES DALLERY
PASSAGE BASFROI
RUE DU PAS DE LA MULE
RUE DU CDT LAMY
PLACE DES VOSGES
SQUARE LOUIS XIII
BOULEVARD BEAUMARCHAIS
RUE DES TOURNELLES
IMPASSE JEAN BEAUSIRE
RUE ST SABIN
PGE ST SABIN
RUE DE JARENTE
MARCHE CATHERINE
RUE NECKER
RUE D'ORMESSON
Maison de Victor Hugo
RUE DAVAL
RUE DES TAILLANDIERS
RUE KELLER
AVENUE LEDRU ROLLIN
RUE DE LAPPE
PASSAGE BULLOURDE
Hôtel de Sully
RUE DE BIRAGUE
IMPASSE GUEMENEE
COUR BERARD
RUE JEAN BEAUSIRE
COUR DAMOYE
COUR DU CANTAL
PASSAGE THIERE
PGE L PHILIPPE
PGE DES TAILLANDIERS
RUE DE CHARONNE
RUE NEUVE ST PIERRE
RUE ST ANTOINE
RUE DE LA BASTILLE
Bastille
PLACE DE LA BASTILLE
PGE DU CHEVAL BLANC
PGE ST ANTOINE
PGE JOSSET
RUE BEAUTREILLIS
RUE CHARLES V
RUE DU PETIT MUSC
RUE CASTEX
RUE DE LESDIGUIERES
RUE JACQUES COEUR
Colonne de Juillet
RUE DU FAUBOURG ST ANTOINE
COUR J VIGUES
COUR ST LOUIS
COUR ST JOSEPH
COUR DES TROIS FRERES
RUE DES JARDINS ST PAUL
BOULEVARD HENRI IV
RUE DE LA CERISAIE
BOULEVARD BOURDON
Port de l'Arsenal
RUE DE L'ARSENAL
Opéra Bastille
RUE DE CHARENTON
PGE DE LA BOULE BLANCHE
PGE DU CHANTIER
Ledru Rollin
PGE DE LA BONNE GRAINE
PASSAGE DE LA MAIN D'OR
Sully Morland
RUE DE SULLY
RUE DE CRILLON
BOULEVARD DE LA BASTILLE
RUE BISCORNET
RUE DE LYON
RUE SAINT NICOLAS
RUE ANTOINE VOLLON
SQUARE TROUSSEAU
RUE T ROUSSEL
Pavillon de l'Arsenal
BOULEVARD MORLAND
PORT DE PARIS ARSENAL
RUE LACUEE
RUE MOREAU
RUE TRAVERSIERE
RUE DE PRAGUE
RUE CH BAUDELAIRE
RUE DE COTTE
RUE D'ALIGRE
Marché d'Aligre
Préfecture de Paris
RUE DE SCHOMBERG
RUE MORNAY
VIADUC DES ARTS
RUE EMILIO CASTELAR
PLACE D'ALIGRE
QUAI HENRI IV
RUE JULES CESAR
AVENUE DAUMESNIL
RUE ABEL
PORT DE PLAISANCE
RUE DE BERCY
AVENUE LEDRU ROLLIN
RUE D'AUSTERLITZ

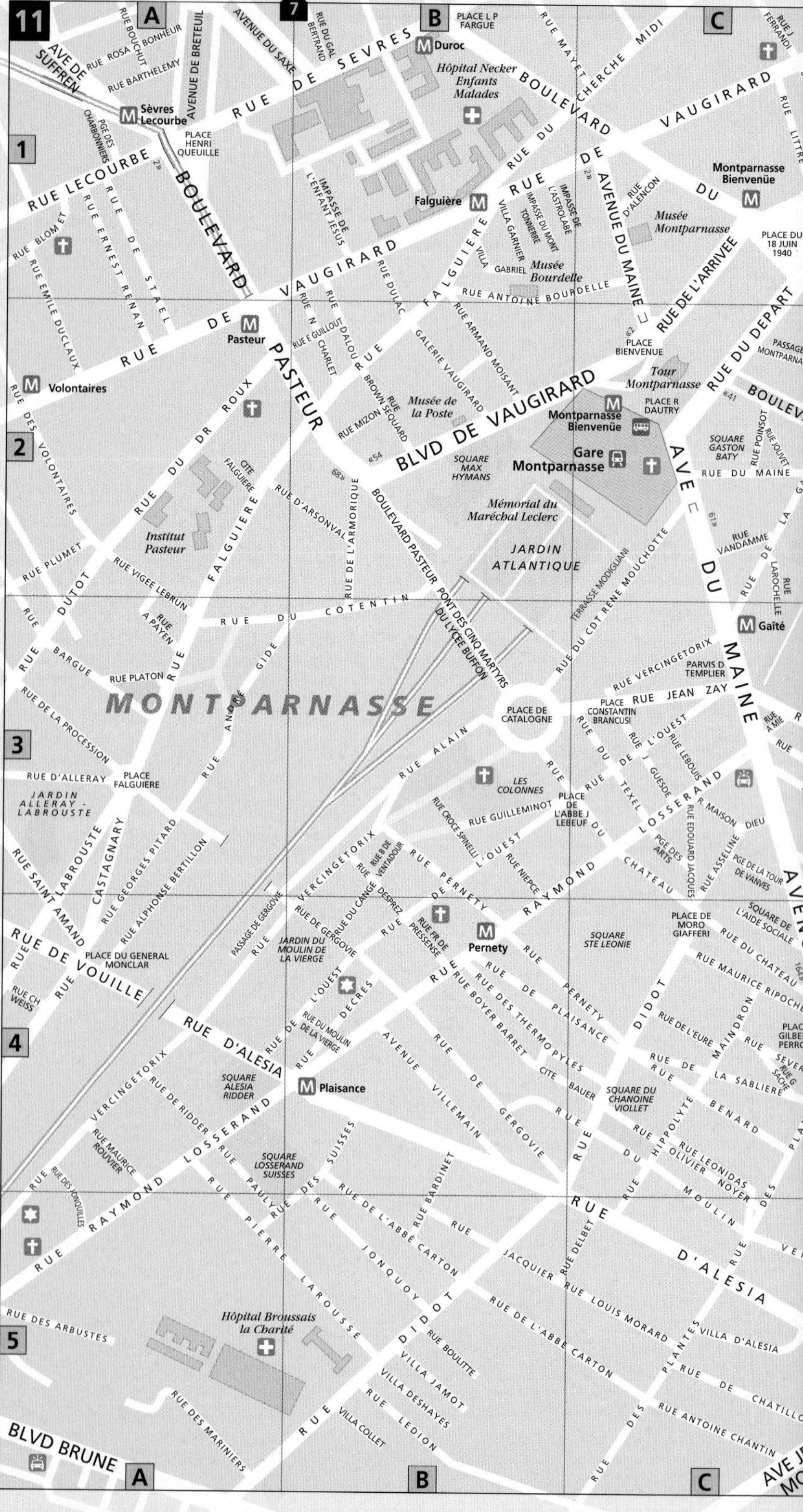
MONTPARNASSE
Rue de Sèvres
Duroc
Hôpital Necker Enfants Malades
Sèvres Lecourbe
Boulevard Pasteur
Rue de Vaugirard
Boulevard de Vaugirard
Pasteur
Volontaires
Falguière
Montparnasse Bienvenüe
Musée Montparnasse
Musée Bourdelle
Musée de la Poste
Tour Montparnasse
Gare Montparnasse
Institut Pasteur
Mémorial du Maréchal Leclerc
Jardin Atlantique
Place de Catalogne
Gaîté
Les Colonnes
Pernety
Jardin du Moulin de la Vierge
Rue d'Alesia
Plaisance
Square Alesia Ridder
Square Losserand Suisses
Hôpital Broussais la Charité
Blvd Brune
Rue Raymond Losserand
Avenue du Maine
Rue Vercingetorix
Rue de Vouille
Jardin Alleray - Labrouste
Place Falguiere
Place du General Monclar
Square Ste Leonie
Square du Chanoine Viollet
Rue Didot
Rue des Plantes
Rue de l'Abbé Carton
Rue Jacquier
Rue Louis Morard
Villa d'Alesia
Rue Antoine Chantin
Rue des Arbustes
Rue des Mariniers
Rue Ledion
Villa Collet
Villa Deshayes
Villa Jamot
Rue Boulitte
Rue Larousse
Rue Pierre
Rue Jonquoy
Rue Bardinet
Avenue Villemain
Rue de Gergovie
Rue Boyer Barret
Rue des Thermopyles
Rue de Plaisance
Rue Pernety
Rue du Château
Rue Maurice Ripoche
Rue Bénard
Rue Hippolyte
Rue du Moulin Vert
Rue Olivier Noyer
Rue Leonidas
Rue de la Sablière
Rue Maindron
Rue de l'Eure
Rue Guilleminot
Place de l'Abbé J Lebeuf
Rue de l'Ouest
Rue Jean Zay
Place Constantin Brancusi
Rue du Texel
Rue du Cdt René Mouchotte
Rue du Cotentin
Rue de l'Armorique
Rue d'Arsonval
Rue Falguiere
Rue du Dr Roux
Rue Dutot
Rue Plumet
Rue Vigée Lebrun
Rue Platon
Rue Bargue
Rue de la Procession
Rue d'Alleray
Rue Labrouste
Rue Castagnary
Rue Georges Pitard
Rue Alphonse Bertillon
Rue Saint Amand
Rue Lecourbe
Rue Blomet
Rue Emile Duclaux
Rue Ernest Renan
Rue de Staël
Rue des Volontaires
Rue Dalou
Rue Dulac
Rue Armand Moisant
Galerie Vaugirard
Rue Antoine Bourdelle
Rue de l'Arrivée
Rue du Départ
Place du 18 Juin 1940
Rue du Cherche Midi
Boulevard du Montparnasse
Avenue de Breteuil
Avenue de Suffren
Avenue du Saxe
Place Henri Queuille
Square Max Hymans
Place Bienvenue
Place R Dautry
Square Gaston Baty
Rue Vandamme
Rue de la Gaîté
Rue Brown Sequard
Rue Mizon
Pont des Cinq Martyrs du Lycée Buffon
Terrasse Modigliani

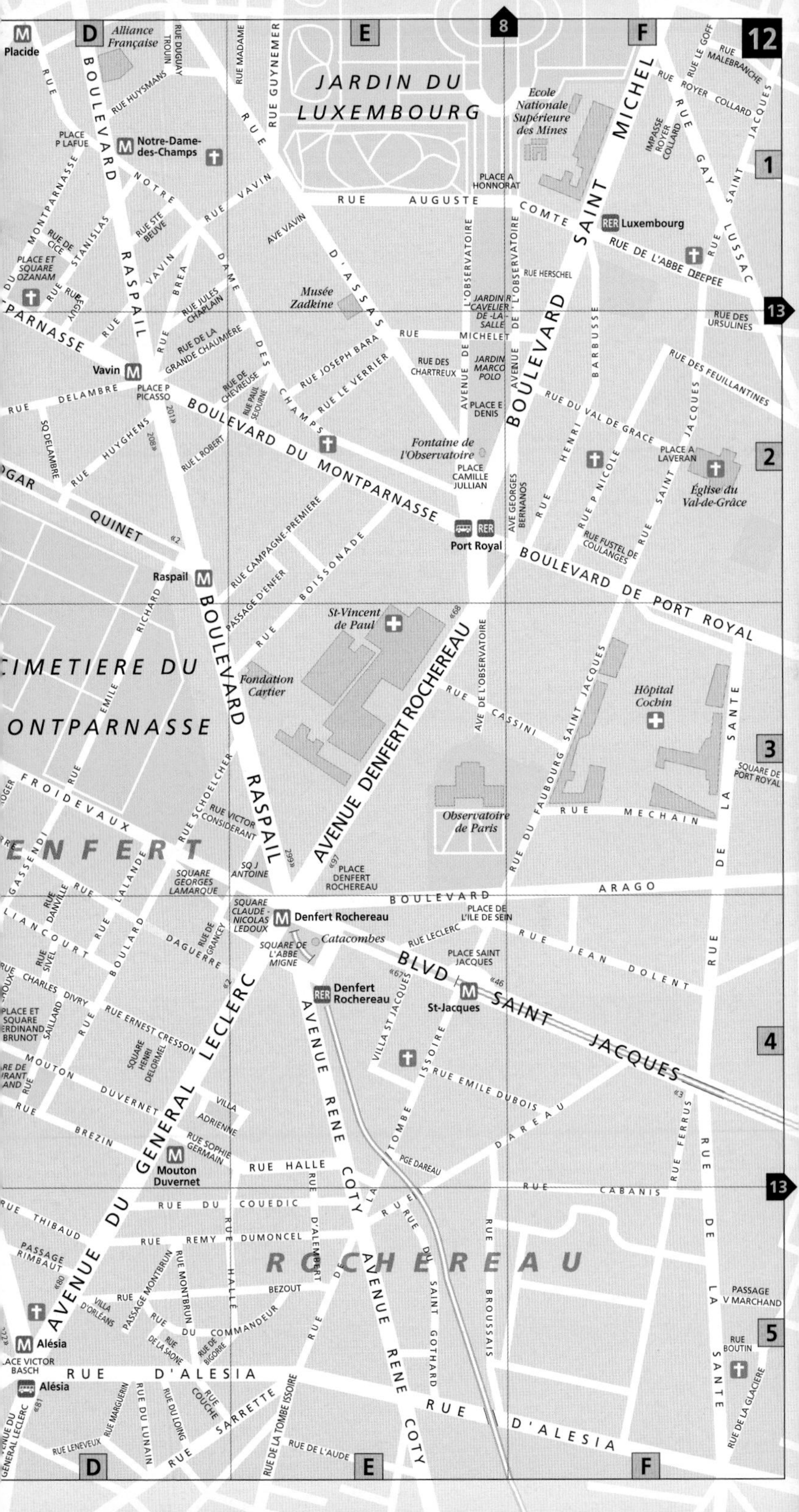

12
D
E
F
8
13
1
2
3
4
5
Placide
Alliance Française
RUE DUGUAY TROUIN
RUE MADAME
RUE GUYNEMER
JARDIN DU LUXEMBOURG
Ecole Nationale Supérieure des Mines
BOULEVARD SAINT MICHEL
RUE MALEBRANCHE
RUE LE GOFF
RUE ROYER COLLARD
IMPASSE ROYER COLLARD
RUE GAY LUSSAC
RUE SAINT JACQUES
RUE HUYSMANS
PLACE P LAFUE
Notre-Dame-des-Champs
BOULEVARD RASPAIL
RUE NOTRE DAME DES CHAMPS
RUE VAVIN
PLACE A HONNORAT
RUE AUGUSTE COMTE
Luxembourg
RUE DE L'ABBE DE L'EPEE
RUE MONTPARNASSE
RUE STANISLAS
RUE DE CICE
RUE STE BEUVE
AVE VAVIN
PLACE ET SQUARE OZANAM
RUE BREA
RUE D'ASSAS
AVENUE DE L'OBSERVATOIRE
RUE HERSCHEL
Musée Zadkine
RUE JULES CHAPLAIN
JARDIN R CAVELIER-DE-LA-SALLE
RUE DES URSULINES
RUE MICHELET
RUE DE LA GRANDE CHAUMIÈRE
RUE JOSEPH BARA
RUE DES CHARTREUX
JARDIN MARCO POLO
RUE HENRI BARBUSSE
RUE DES FEUILLANTINES
Vavin
RUE LE VERRIER
PLACE P PICASSO
RUE DE CHEVREUSE
RUE PAUL SEJOURNE
RUE DELAMBRE
PLACE E DENIS
RUE DU VAL DE GRACE
SQ DELAMBRE
RUE HUYGHENS
BOULEVARD DU MONTPARNASSE
Fontaine de l'Observatoire
PLACE CAMILLE JULLIAN
PLACE A LAVERAN
RUE P NICOLE
Église du Val-de-Grâce
RUE L ROBERT
EDGAR QUINET
AVE GEORGES BERNANOS
RUE CAMPAGNE-PREMIERE
Port Royal
RUE FUSTEL DE COULANGES
BOULEVARD DE PORT ROYAL
RUE BOISSONADE
Raspail
PASSAGE D'ENFER
St-Vincent de Paul
RUE RICHARD
AVENUE DENFERT ROCHEREAU
AVE DE L'OBSERVATOIRE
CIMETIERE DU MONTPARNASSE
Fondation Cartier
RUE CASSINI
Hôpital Cochin
RUE EMILE
RUE DU FAUBOURG SAINT JACQUES
SQUARE DE PORT ROYAL
RUE FROIDEVAUX
RUE SCHOELCHER
RUE VICTOR CONSIDERANT
Observatoire de Paris
RUE MECHAIN
RUE DE LA SANTE
DENFERT
RUE GASSENDI
SQ J ANTOINE
PLACE DENFERT ROCHEREAU
BOULEVARD ARAGO
SQUARE GEORGES LAMARQUE
RUE LALANDE
RUE DANVILLE
SQUARE CLAUDE-NICOLAS LEDOUX
Denfert Rochereau
PLACE DE L'ILE DE SEIN
RUE JEAN DOLENT
RUE LIANCOURT
RUE DE GRANCEY
RUE DAGUERRE
SQUARE DE L'ABBE MIGNE
Catacombes
RUE LECLERC
PLACE SAINT JACQUES
RUE BOULARD
RUE SIVEL
RUE CHARLES DIVRY
BLVD SAINT JACQUES
St-Jacques
VILLA ST JACQUES
PLACE ET SQUARE FERDINAND BRUNOT
RUE SAILLARD
RUE ERNEST CRESSON
SQUARE HENRI DELORMEL
AVENUE DU GENERAL LECLERC
AVENUE RENE COTY
RUE DE LA TOMBE ISSOIRE
RUE EMILE DUBOIS
RUE MOUTON DUVERNET
VILLA ADRIENNE
RUE DAREAU
RUE FERRUS
RUE BREZIN
RUE SOPHIE GERMAIN
Mouton Duvernet
RUE HALLE
PGE DAREAU
RUE CABANIS
RUE THIBAUD
RUE DU COUEDIC
RUE D'ALEMBERT
RUE DE LA TOMBE ISSOIRE
RUE BROUSSAIS
PASSAGE RIMBAUT
RUE REMY DUMONCEL
RUE MONTBRUN
ROCHEREAU
RUE DU SAINT GOTHARD
PASSAGE V MARCHAND
VILLA D'ORLÉANS
PASSAGE MONTBRUN
BEZOUT
RUE DU COMMANDEUR
RUE DE LA SAONE
RUE DE BIGORRE
Alésia
RUE BOUTIN
PLACE VICTOR BASCH
RUE D'ALESIA
RUE DE LA GLACIERE
RUE MARGUERIN
RUE DU LUNAIN
RUE DU LOING
RUE COUCHE
RUE SARRETTE
RUE LENEVEUX
RUE DE L'AUDE

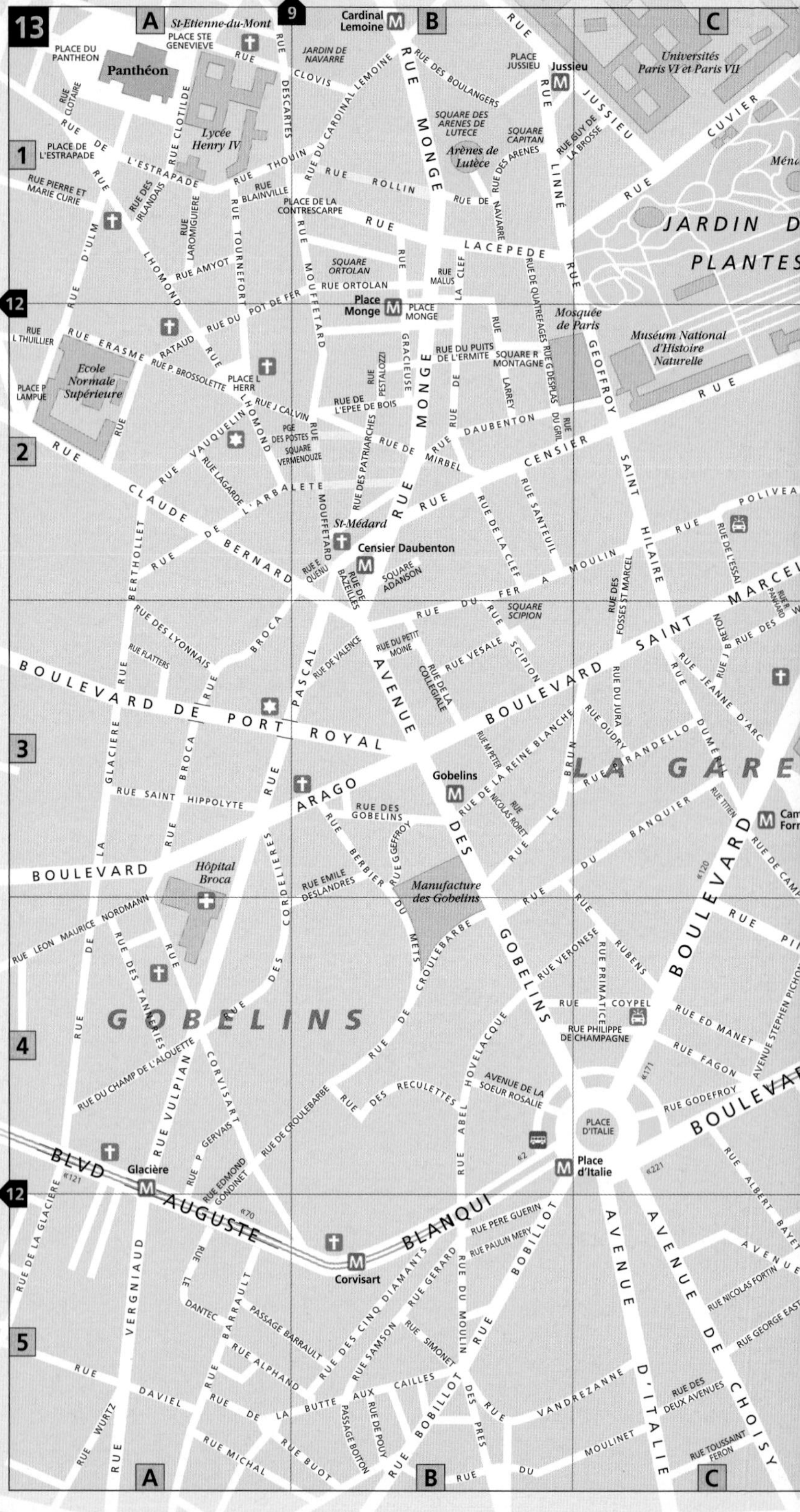
13
A
B
C
1
2
3
4
5
9
12
St-Etienne-du-Mont
Cardinal Lemoine
Place du Panthéon
Panthéon
Place Ste Geneviève
Lycée Henry IV
Jardin de Navarre
Place Jussieu
Jussieu
Universités Paris VI et Paris VII
Square des Arènes de Lutèce
Arènes de Lutèce
Square Capitan
Place de l'Estrapade
Place de la Contrescarpe
Jardin des Plantes
Square Ortolan
Place Monge
Mosquée de Paris
Muséum National d'Histoire Naturelle
Square R Montagne
Ecole Normale Supérieure
Place P Lampué
Place L Herr
PGE des Postes
Square Vermenouze
St-Médard
Censier Daubenton
Square Adanson
Square Scipion
Boulevard de Port Royal
Boulevard Saint Marcel
Boulevard Arago
Avenue des Gobelins
Gobelins
La Gare
Hôpital Broca
Manufacture des Gobelins
Gobelins
Place d'Italie
Boulevard Auguste Blanqui
Glacière
Corvisart
Avenue d'Italie
Avenue de Choisy
Rue Monge
Rue Mouffetard
Rue Lacépède
Rue Claude Bernard
Rue Geoffroy Saint Hilaire
Rue de la Glacière
Rue Vergniaud
Rue Bobillot
Rue de la Butte aux Cailles
Rue de Tolbiac

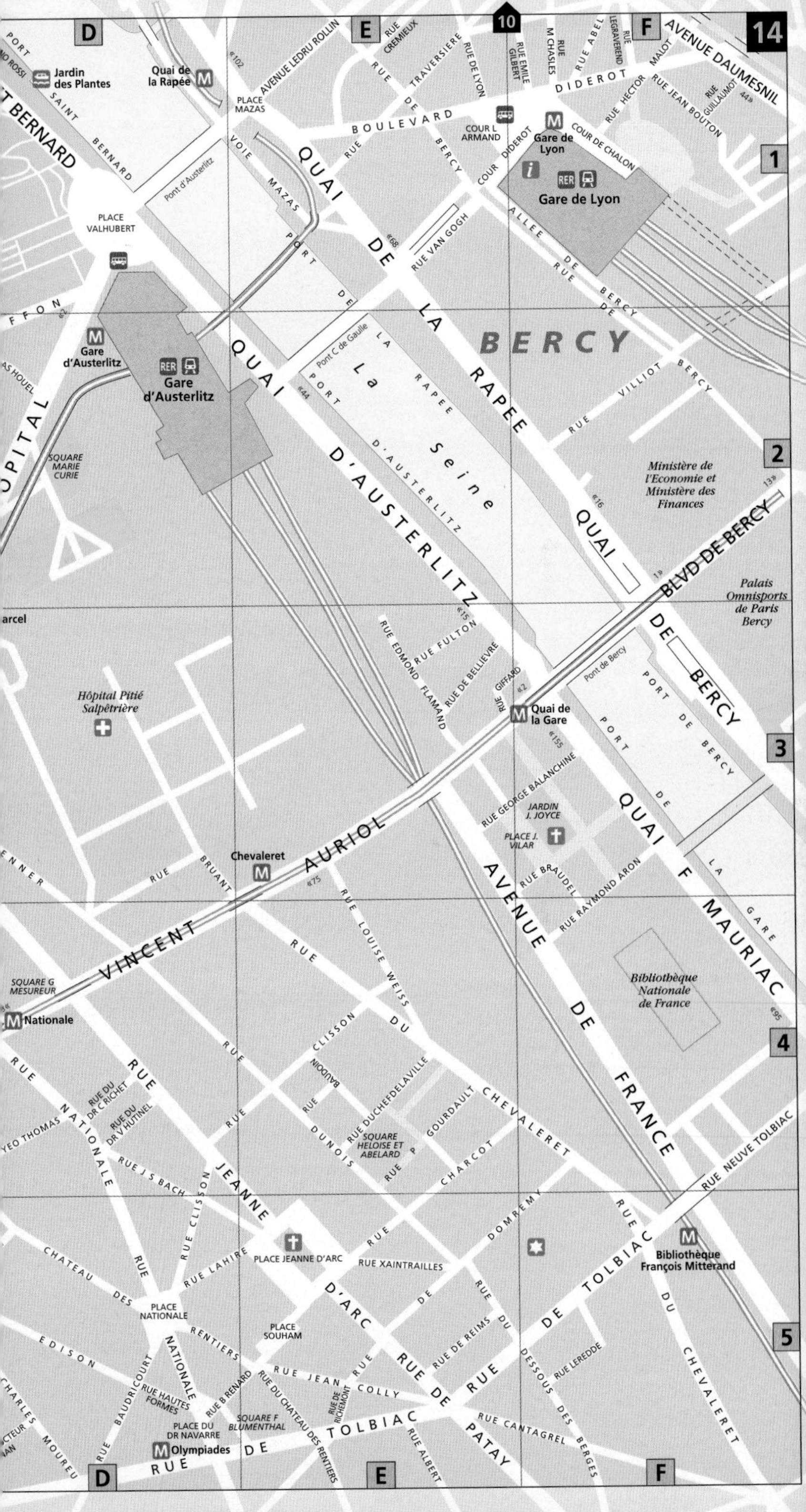
D
E
F
10
1
2
3
4
5
Jardin des Plantes
Quai de la Rapée
Gare de Lyon
Gare d'Austerlitz
BERCY
La Seine
Ministère de l'Economie et Ministère des Finances
Palais Omnisports de Paris Bercy
Hôpital Pitié Salpêtrière
Quai de la Gare
Chevaleret
Bibliothèque Nationale de France
Nationale
Bibliothèque François Mitterand
Olympiades
QUAI DE LA RAPEE
QUAI D'AUSTERLITZ
QUAI DE BERCY
QUAI F MAURIAC
BLVD DE BERCY
VINCENT AURIOL
AVENUE DE FRANCE
BOULEVARD DIDEROT
AVENUE DAUMESNIL
AVENUE LEDRU ROLLIN
RUE JEANNE D'ARC
RUE DE TOLBIAC
RUE NATIONALE
RUE DU CHEVALERET
PLACE VALHUBERT
PLACE MAZAS
PLACE JEANNE D'ARC
PLACE NATIONALE
PLACE SOUHAM
SQUARE MARIE CURIE
SQUARE G MESUREUR
JARDIN J. JOYCE
PLACE J. VILAR
SQUARE HELOISE ET ABELARD
SQUARE F BLUMENTHAL
PLACE DU DR NAVARRE
Pont d'Austerlitz
Pont C de Gaulle
Pont de Bercy

ILE DE FRANCE

Set at the heart of France, with Paris as its hub, Ile de France extends well beyond the densely populated suburbs of the city. Its rich countryside incorporates a historic royal region of monumental splendor central to *"la gloire de la France."*

The region became a favorite with French royalty after François I transformed Fontainebleau into a Renaissance palace in 1528. Louis XIV kept the Ile de France as the political axis of the country when he started building Versailles in 1661. This Classical château created by the combined genius of Le Nôtre, Le Vau, Le Brun, and Jules Hardouin-Mansart is France's most visited sight. It stands as a monument to the power of the Sun King and is still used for state occasions. Rambouillet, closely linked with Louis XVI, is now the summer residence of the French president, while Malmaison was the favorite home of Empress Josephine. To the north, the Château d'Ecouen offers a showcase of Renaissance life and to the south Vaux-le-Vicomte boasts some of the loveliest formal gardens in France.

Nourished by the Seine and Marne rivers, the Ile de France is a patchwork of chalky plains, wheatfields, and forests. The serene, poplar-lined avenues, and rustic charm of the region have been an inspiration to painters such as Corot, Rousseau, Pissarro, and Cézanne.

Sights at a Glance

Châteaux and Museums

2 Musée National de la Renaissance
5 Château de Malmaison
6 Château de Versailles
7 Château de Sceaux
8 Château de Dampierre
9 Château de Rambouillet
11 Château de Vaux-le-Vicomte
13 Château de Fontainebleau

Towns

4 St-Germain-en-Laye
12 Provins

Abbeys and Churches

1 Abbaye de Royaumont
3 Basilique St-Denis

Theme Parks

10 Disneyland® Resort Paris

Key

Greater Paris
Central Paris
Highway
Major road
Minor road

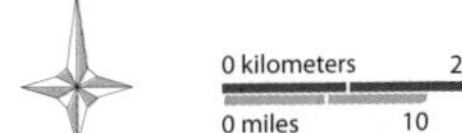

Ile de France

◀ Stunning formal gardens at the Château de Fontainbleau

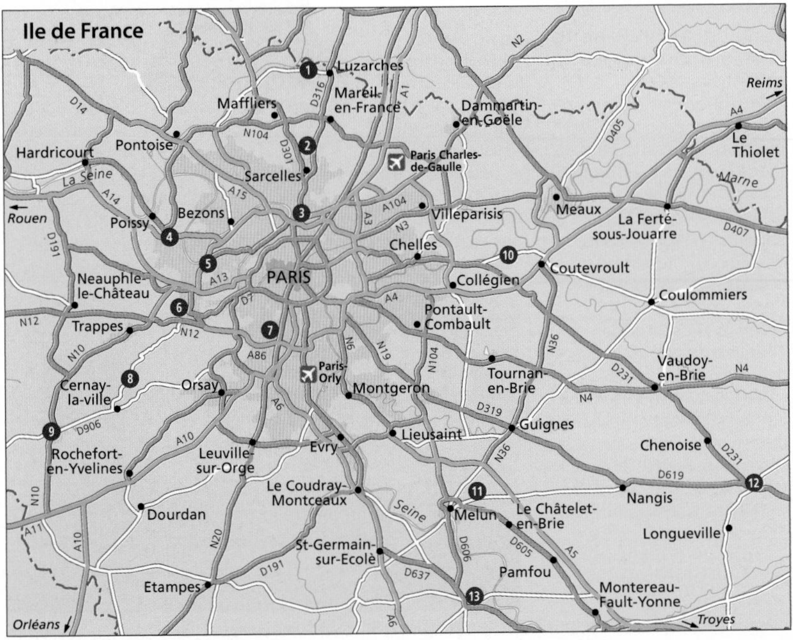

For additional map symbols *see back flap*

The vaulted Gothic refectory of Abbaye de Royaumont

1 Abbaye de Royaumont

Fondation Royaumont, Asnières-sur-Oise, Val-d'Oise. **Tel** 01 30 35 59 70. **Open** daily. Concerts. **royaumont.com**

Set among woods "near water and far from mankind," 22 miles (35 km) north of Paris, Royaumont is the finest Cistercian abbey in the Ile de France. Chosen for its remoteness, the abbey's stark stonework and simplicity of line reflect the austere teachings of St-Bernard. However, unlike his Burgundian abbeys, Royaumont was founded in 1228 by Louis IX and his mother, Blanche de Castille. "St-Louis" showered the abbey with riches and chose it as a royal burial site.

The abbey retained its royal links until the Revolution, when much of it was destroyed. It was then a textiles mill and orphanage until its revival as a cultural center. The original pillars still remain, along with a gravity-defying corner tower and the largest Cistercian cloisters in France, which enclose a charming Classical garden. The monastic quarters border one side of the cloisters.

The Château de Royaumont, erected as the abbot's palace on the eve of the Revolution, is set apart and resembles an Italianate villa. In the grounds are monks' workshops, woods, ponds, and Cistercian canals.

In summer, concerts are held in the abbey on weekends *(01 34 68 05 50 for details; www.3emeacte.com for tickets).*

2 Musée National de la Renaissance

Rue Jean Bulant, Château d'Ecouen, Val-d'Oise. **Tel** 01 34 38 38 50. **Open** 9:30am–12:30pm, 2–5:15pm Wed–Mon. **Closed** Jan 1, May 1, Dec 25. Park: no animals. museum only.

This imposing moated château is curiously adrift, halfway between St-Denis and Royaumont. Now a Renaissance museum, Ecouen's magnificent quadrilateral exterior provides an authentic setting for an impressive collection of paintings, tapestries, coffers, carved doors, and staircases salvaged from other 16th-century châteaus.

Ecouen was built in 1538 for Anne de Montmorency, adviser to François I and Commander-in-Chief of his armies. As the second most powerful person in the kingdom, he employed Ecole de Fontainebleau artists and craftsmen to adorn his palace. Their influence is apparent in the ravishing painted fireplaces, depicting biblical and Classical themes in mysterious landscapes. The most striking room is the chapel, containing a gallery and vaulted ceilings painted with the Montmorency coat of arms.

Upstairs is one of the finest series of 16th-century tapestries in France. Equally compelling are the princely apartments, the library of illuminated manuscripts, vivid ceramics from Lyon, Nevers, Venice and Faenza, and Iznik, and a display of early mathematical instruments. Recent acquisitions include 16th- and 17th-century engravings from France, Italy, and Germany.

3 Basilique St-Denis

1 rue de la Légion d'Honneur, St-Denis, Seine-St-Denis. **Tel** 01 48 09 83 54. Line 13 Basilique de St-Denis. **Open** Apr–Sep: 10am–6:15pm Mon–Sat, noon–6:15pm Sun. **Closed** Jan 1, May 1, Dec 25. 8:30am & 10am Sun.

According to legend, the decapitated St-Denis struggled here clutching his head, and an abbey was erected to commemorate the martyred bishop. Following the burial of Dagobert I in the basilica in 638, a royal link with St-Denis began, which was to span 12 centuries. Most French kings were entombed in St-Denis, and all the queens of France were crowned here. The elegant, early Gothic basilica rests on Carolingian and Romanesque crypts. Of the medieval effigies, the most impressive are of Charles V (1364) and a 12th-century likeness in enameled copper of Blanche de France with

Statue of Louis XVI at St-Denis

The west wing of Musée National de la Renaissance

The Renaissance tomb of Louis XII and Anne de Bretagne in St-Denis

her dog. The masklike serenity of these effigies is in sharp contrast with the graphically realistic Renaissance portrayal of agony present in the grotesque mausoleum of Louis XII and Anne de Bretagne. Both are represented as naked figures, their faces eerily captured at the moment of death. Above the mausoleum, effigies of the finely dressed royal couple contemplate their own nakedness. As a reflection of humanity in the face of death, the tombs have few rivals.

❹ St-Germain-en-Laye

Yvelines. 42,200. Maison Claude Debussy, 38 rue au Pain. **Tel** 01 30 87 20 63. **Open** Oct–Apr: Tue–Sat; May–Sep: daily. Tue–Wed, Fri–Sun.

Dominating the Place Général de Gaulle in this chic suburb is the legendary Château de St-Germain, birthplace of Louis XIV. Louis VI built the original stronghold in 1122 but only the keep and St-Louis chapel remain. Under François I and Henri II, the medieval upper tiers were demolished, leaving a moated pentagon. Henri IV built the pavilion and terraces that run down to the Seine, and Louis XIV had Le Nôtre landscape the gardens before leaving for Versailles in 1682.

Today the château houses the **Musée d'Archéologie Nationale**, which exhibits archeological finds from prehistory to the Middle Ages. Created by Napoleon III, the collection includes a 22,000-year-old carved female, a megalithic tomb, a bronze helmet from the 3rd century BC, and Celtic jewelry. The finest treasure is the Gallo-Roman mosaic pavement.

Musée d'Archéologie Nationale
Château de St-Germain-en-Laye. **Tel** 01 39 10 13 00. **Open** 10am–5pm Wed–Mon. **W** **musee-archeologienationale.fr**

❺ Château de Malmaison

Rueil-Malmaison, Hauts-de-Seine. **Tel** 01 41 29 05 55. **Open** 10am–12:30pm, 1:30–5:15pm daily (to 5:45pm Apr–Sep and weekends year-round). **Closed** Jan 1, Dec 25. **W** **chateau-malmaison.fr**

Situated 9 miles (15 km) west of Paris, this 17th-century estate is best known for its Napoleonic associations. Bought by Josephine as a retreat from the formality of the Emperor's residences at the Tuileries and Fontainebleau, it has charming rural grounds. While Josephine loved this country manor, Napoleon scorned its entrance as fit only for servants, and so he had a curious drawbridge built at the back of the château.

The finest rooms are the frescoed and vaulted library, the canopied campaign room, and the sunny Salon de Musique. Napoleon's restrained, yellow canopied bedroom contrasts with the bedchamber Josephine died in, a magnificent indulgence bedecked in red. Many of the rooms overlook the romantic "English" gardens and the famous rose garden Josephine cultivated after her divorce.

Memorabilia abound, from imperial eagles to David's moody portrait of Napoleon, or Gérard's painting of the languid Josephine reclining on a chaise-longue.

Château Bois Préau, set in the wooded grounds, houses a museum dedicated to Napoleon's exile and death.

Empress Josephine's bed at Château de Malmaison

6 Château de Versailles

The present palace, started by Louis XIV in 1668, grew around Louis XIII's original hunting lodge. Architect Louis Le Vau built the first section, which expanded into an enlarged courtyard. From 1678, Jules Hardouin-Mansart added north and south wings, and the Hall of Mirrors. He also designed the chapel, completed in 1710. The Opera House (L'Opéra) was added by Louis XV in 1770. André Le Nôtre enlarged the gardens and broke the monotony of the symmetrical layout with expanses of water and creative use of uneven ground. Opposite the château is the Academie du Spectacle Equestre, where you can watch dressage shows.

★ Formal Gardens
Geometric paths and shrubberies are features of the gardens.

★ Château
Under Louis XIV, Versailles became the center of political power in France.

Fountain of Latona
Four marble basins rise to Balthazar Marsy's statue of the goddess Latona.

KEY

① **Fountain of Neptune** sculptures spray spectacular jets of water in Le Nôtre's 17th-century garden.

② **Ornamental Pools (Parterre d'Eau)**

③ **The Orangery** was built beneath the Parterre du Midi to house exotic plants in winter.

④ **The king's garden** features a mirror pool in the 19th-century garden created by Louis XVIII.

⑤ **Colonnade** is a series of marble arches designed by Mansart in 1685.

Dragon Fountain
The fountain's centerpiece is a winged monster.

For hotels and restaurants in this region see pp554–71 and pp576–603

The Grand Canal was the setting for Louis XIV's boating parties.

VISITORS' CHECKLIST

Practical Information
Pl d'Ármes, Versailles, Yvelines. **Tel** 01 30 83 78 00. Château: **Open** 9am–6:30pm (5:30pm Nov–Mar) Tue–Sun. **Closed** some public hols; phone to check. Grand Trianon, Petit Trianon: **Open** noon–6:30pm (5:30pm Nov–Mar) Tue–Sun. Gardens: **Open** 8am–8:30pm daily. Park: **Open** 7am–8:30pm daily (7pm for cars; 6pm Nov–Mar). **Closed** Jan 1, May 1, Dec 25. Les Fêtes de Nuit (Aug–Sep); Les Grandes Eaux Nocturnes (Apr–Sep: Sat). **chateauversailles.fr**

Transport
171 from Paris. RER Versailles Rive Gauche. Versailles Chantiers, Versailles Rive Droite.

Petit Trianon
Built in 1762 as a retreat for Louis XV, this small château became a favorite with Marie-Antoinette.

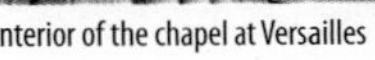

Interior of the chapel at Versailles

★ Grand Trianon
Louis XIV built this small palace of stone and pink marble in 1687 to escape the rigors of court life, and to enjoy the company of Madame de Maintenon.

Inside the Château de Versailles

The sumptuous main apartments are on the first floor of this vast château complex. Around the Marble Courtyard are the private apartments of the king and queen. The apartments of the dauphin (the heir) and the mesdames (the daughters of Louis XV), on the ground floor, are also open to visitors. On the garden side are the state apartments where official court life took place. These were richly decorated by Charles Le Brun with marble, stone, and wood carvings, murals, velvet, silver, and gilded furniture. Beginning with the Salon d'Hercule, each state room is dedicated to an Olympian deity. The climax is the Hall of Mirrors, where 17 vast mirrors face tall arched windows. Not all rooms are open at the same time so check on arrival.

★ Queen's Bedroom
In this room the queens of France gave birth to the royal children in public view.

The Salon du Sacre is adorned with huge paintings of Napoleon by Jacques-Louis David.

The Marble Courtyard is overlooked by a gilded balcony.

Stairs to ground floor reception area

★ Chapelle Royale
The chapel's first floor was reserved for the royal family and the ground floor for the court. The beautiful interior is decorated with Corinthian columns and white marble, gilding, and Baroque murals.

Key to Floorplan

- South wing
- Coronation room
- Madame de Maintenon's apartments
- Queen's apartments and private suite
- State apartments
- King's apartments and private suite
- North wing
- Nonexhibition space

For hotels and restaurants in this region see pp554–71 and pp576–603

★ Hall of Mirrors
Great state occasions were held in this room stretching 233 ft (70 m) along the west façade. Here in 1919 the Treaty of Versailles was ratified, ending World War I.

Oeil-de-Boeuf

The King's Bedroom is where Louis XIV died in 1715.

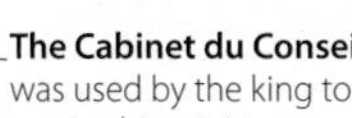

The Cabinet du Conseil was used by the king to receive his ministers and family.

Salon de la Guerre
The room's theme of war is reinforced by Antoine Coysevox's stuccoed relief of Louis XIV riding to victory.

Louis XVI's library features Neo-Classical paneling and the king's terrestrial globe.

★ Salon de Vénus
A statue of Louis XIV stands amid the rich marble decor of this room.

Salon d'Apollon
Designed by Le Brun and dedicated to the god Apollo, this was Louis XIV's throne room. A copy of Hyacinthe Rigaud's famous portrait of the king (1701) hangs here.

Salon d'Hercule

Louis XV

1650 1700 1750 1800 1850 1900

1661 Louis XIV enlarges château

1667 Grand Canal begun

1668 Construction of new château by Le Vau

1671 Interior decoration by Le Brun begun

1682 Louis XIV and Marie-Thérèse move to Versailles

1715 Death of Louis XIV. Versailles abandoned by court

1722 12-year-old Louis XV occupies Versailles

1774 Louis XVI and Marie-Antoinette live at Versailles

1789 King and Queen forced to leave Versailles for Paris

1793 Louis XVI and Marie-Antoinette executed

1833 Louis-Philippe turns the château into a museum

1919 Treaty of Versailles signed on June 28

❼ Château de Sceaux

Domaine de Sceaux, Hauts-de-Seine. **Tel** 01 41 87 29 50. **Open** Apr–Oct: 10am–1pm Mon–Fri (to 6:30pm Sat–Sun); Nov–Mar: 10am–5pm Wed–Mon. **Closed** public hols & lunchtimes. **domaine-de-sceaux.fr**

The Parc de Sceaux, bounded by elegant villas, is an appealing mixture of formal gardens, woods, and water. The gardens, designed by Le Nôtre, use water to great effect, with tiered waterfalls and fountains presenting a moving staircase that cascades into an octagonal basin. This feeds into the Grand Canal and offers a poplar-lined view to the Pavillon de Hanovre. This elegant pavilion is one of several that adorn the park, which also contains Mansart's Classical Orangerie. Today it is the setting for exhibitions and music concerts.

Built for Colbert in 1670, the original château was demolished and rebuilt in Louis XIII style in 1856. The stylish fake contains the Musée de l'Ile de France, which celebrates the landscapes and châteaux of the region with paintings, furniture, and sculpture.

❽ Château de Dampierre

Dampierre-en-Yvelines, Yvelines. **Tel** 01 30 52 53 24. **Open** Apr–Sep: 11am–6:30pm daily. **Closed** Sun lunch. restricted. **chateau-de-dampierre.fr**

After Versailles and Rambouillet, Dampierre is the most celebrated château southwest of Paris. Built in 1675 for the Duc de Chevreuse, the exterior of the château is a harmonious composition of rose-colored brick and cool stone, designed by Hardouin-Mansart.

By contrast, the interior sumptuously evokes Versailles, particularly in the royal apartments and the Louis XIV dining room. The grandest room is the frescoed Salle des Fêtes, remodeled in the 19th century in triumphal Roman style. The rooms overlook gardens landscaped by Le Nôtre.

Château de Rambouillet

❾ Château de Rambouillet

Rambouillet, Yvelines. **Tel** 01 34 83 00 25. **Open** Wed–Mon. **Closed** Jan 1, May 1, Nov 1 & 11, Dec 25, when president in residence & lunchtimes. **chateau-rambouillet.monuments-nationaux.fr**

The château borders the deep Forêt de Rambouillet, once the favorite royal hunting ground. This ivy-covered red-brick château, flanked by five stone towers, is curious rather than beautiful. Adopted as a feudal castle, country estate, royal palace, and Imperial residence, it reflects a composite of French royal history. Since 1897, it has been the president's official summer residence.

Inside, oak-paneled rooms are adorned with Empire-style furnishings and Aubusson tapestries. The main facade overlooks Classical parterres. Nearby is the Queen's Dairy, given by Louis XVI to Marie-Antoinette so that she could play milkmaid.

Environs

About 17 miles (28 km) north on the D11, the **Château de Thoiry** has a safari park and an innovative play area for children.

❿ Disneyland® Resort Paris

Marne-la-Vallée, Seine-et-Marne. **Tel** 08 25 30 02 22. **Open** daily. RER Marne-la-Vallée-Chessy. TGV from Lille or Lyon. from both airports. **disneylandparis.com**

Disneyland® Resort Paris covers 500 acres (200 ha), with 2 theme parks, seven hotels, facilities for shopping and dining, and convention centers. Most interesting are the Parks – the first with its five themed Lands, offering magic dominated by Sleeping Beauty Castle and Walt Disney Studios®.

Minnie Mouse

⓫ Château de Vaux-le-Vicomte

Maincy, Seine-et-Marne. **Tel** 01 64 14 41 90. shuttle from Melun railway station. **Open** mid-Mar–early Nov. **Closed** Wed (except Jul & Aug). **vaux-le-vicomte.com**

Set north of Melun, not far from Fontainebleau, the château enjoys a peaceful rural location. Nicolas Fouquet, a powerful

Sèvres Porcelain

In 1756 Madame de Pompadour and Louis XV opened a porcelain factory near Versailles at Sèvres to supply the royal residences with tableware and *objets d'art*. Thus began the production of exquisite dinner services, statuettes, Etruscan-style vases, romantic cameos and porcelain paintings, depicting grand châteaus or mythological scenes. Sèvres porcelain is typified by its translucence, durability and narrow palette of colours.

Le Pugilat (1832), one of a pair of vases from Sèvres

Andre Le Nôtre

As the greatest French landscape gardener, Le Nôtre (1613–1700) created masterpieces in château gardens all over France. His Classical vision shaped many in the Ile de France, such as those at Dampierre, Sceaux, and Vaux-le-Vicomte. At Vaux he perfected the concept of the jardin à la française: avenues framed by statues and box hedges; water gardens with fountains and ornate pools; graceful terraces and geometrical parterres "embroidered" with motifs. His genius lay in architectural orchestration and a sense of symmetry, typified by the sweeping vistas of Versailles, his greatest triumph.

court financier to Louis XIV, challenged the architect Le Vau and the decorator Le Brun to create the most sumptuous palace of the day. The result is one of the greatest 17th-century French châteaus. However, it also led to his downfall. Louis and his ministers were so enraged – because its luxury cast the royal palaces into the shade – that they arrested Fouquet.

The interior is a gilded banquet of frescoes, stucco, caryatids, and giant busts. The Salon des Muses boasts Le Brun's magnificent frescoed ceiling of dancing nymphs and poetic sphinxes. La Grande Chambre Carrée is decorated in Louis XIII style with paneled walls and an impressive triumphal frieze, evoking Rome. However, its many rooms feel intimate and the scale is not overwhelming.

Yet Vaux-le-Vicomte's continuing fame is due to André Le Nôtre's stunning gardens. The landscape designer's early training as a painter is evident in the magnificent succession of terraces, ornamental lakes, and fountains, which descend to a formal canal. On Saturday evenings from May to October, the castle is lit with over 2,000 candles and classical music is played in the gardens.

⓬ Provins

Seine-et-Marne. 12,000. Chemin de Villecran 77482 (01 64 60 26 26). Sat. **provins.net**

As a Roman outpost, Provins commanded the border of Ile de France and Champagne. Today, it offers a coherent vision of the medieval world. Ville Haute, the upper town, is clustered within high 12th-century ramparts, complete with crenellations and defensive ditches. The ramparts to the west are the best preserved. Here, between the fortified gateways of Porte de Jouy and Porte St-Jean, the fortifications are dotted with square, round, and rectangular towers.

The town is dominated by Tour César, a keep with four corner turrets and a pyramid shaped roof. The moat and fortifications were added by the English during the Hundred Years' War. A guard-room leads to a gallery and views over the place du Chatel, a busy square of medieval gabled houses, and over the wheatfields beyond.

Provins is proud of its crimson roses. Every June, a floral celebration is held in the riverside rose garden, marked by a medieval festival with falconry and jousting.

Château de Vaux-le-Vicomte seen across the gardens designed by Le Nôtre

⓭ Château de Fontainebleau

Fontainebleau is not the product of a single vision but is a bewildering cluster of styles from different periods. Louis VII built an abbey here which was consecrated by Thomas Becket in 1169. A medieval tower survives but the present château harks back to François I. Originally drawn by the local hunting, the Renaissance king created a decorative château modeled on Florentine and Roman styles.

Fontainebleau's abiding charm comes from its relative informality and spectacular forest setting. While impossible to cover in a day, the *grands appartements* provide a sumptuous introduction to this royal palace.

Jardin de Diane
Now more romantic than Classical, the garden features a bronze fountain of Diana as huntress.

★ Escalier du Fer-à-Cheval
This imposing horseshoe-shaped staircase by Jean Androuet du Cerceau, built in 1634, lies at the end of Cour du Cheval Blanc. Its ingenious design allowed carriages to pass beneath the two arches.

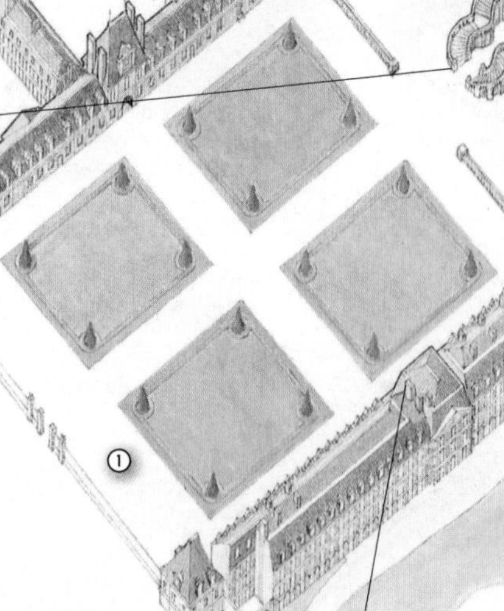

KEY

① **Cour du Cheval Blanc**, was once a simple enclosed courtyard. It was transformed by Napoleon I into the main approach to the château.

② **Chapelle de la Sainte Trinité**, was designed by Henri II in 1550. The chapel acquired its vaulted and frescoed ceiling under Henri IV and was completed by Louis XIII.

③ **Cour Oval**

④ **Cour de la Fontaine**

⑤ **The Appartements de Napoléon I**, house his grandiose throne in the Emperor's Salle du Trône, formerly the Chambre du Roi.

⑥ **The Jardin Anglais**, is a romantic "English" garden, planted with cypress and plantain trees. It was redesigned in the 19th century by Maximilien-Joseph Hurtault.

Key to Floorplan

- Petits Appartements
- Galerie des Cerfs
- Musée Chinois
- Musée Napoléon
- Grands Appartements
- Salle Renaissance
- Appartements de Madame de Maintenon
- Grands Appartements des Souverains
- Escalier de la Reine/ Appartements des Chasses
- Chapelle de la Trinité
- Appartement Intérieur de l'Empereur

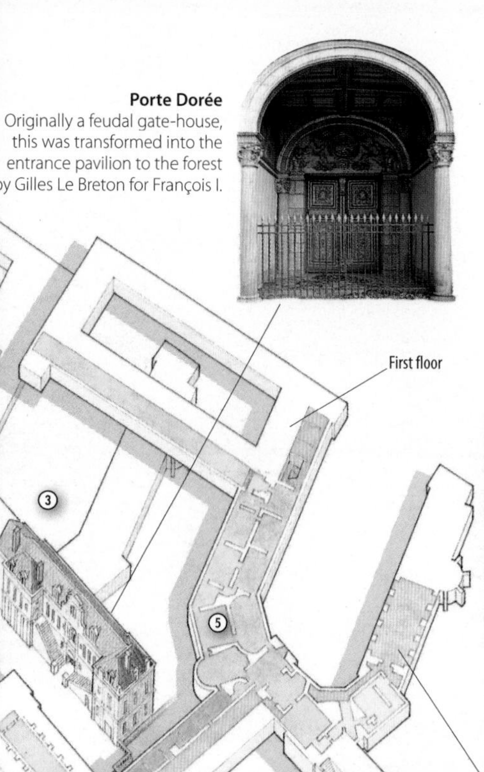

Porte Dorée
Originally a feudal gate-house, this was transformed into the entrance pavilion to the forest by Gilles Le Breton for François I.

VISITORS' CHECKLIST

Practical Information
Seine-et-Marne. **Tel** 01 60 71 50 70. **Open** 9:30am–5pm Wed–Mon (6pm Apr–Sep). Gardens: **Open** 9am–5pm daily (6pm Mar–Apr & Oct, 7pm May–Sep). **Closed** Jan 1, May 1, Dec 25. **W musee-chateau-fontainebleau.fr**

★ Salle de Bal
The Renaissance ballroom, designed by Primaticcio (1552), was finished under Henri II. His emblems adorn the walnut coffered ceiling, forming a pattern reflected in the parquet floor.

★ Galerie François I
This gilded gallery is a tribute to the Italian artists in the *Ecole de Fontainebleau*. Rosso Fiorentino's allegorical frescoes pay homage to the king's wish to create "a second Rome."

The Barbizon School

Artists have been drawn to the glades of Fontainebleau since the 1840s, when a group of landscape painters, determined to paint only from nature, formed around Théodore Rousseau and Millet. They settled in the nearby hamlet of Barbizon where the Auberge Ganne, a museum dedicated to the *Ecole de Barbizon*, is located.

Spring at Barbizon, painted by Jean-François Millet (1814–75)

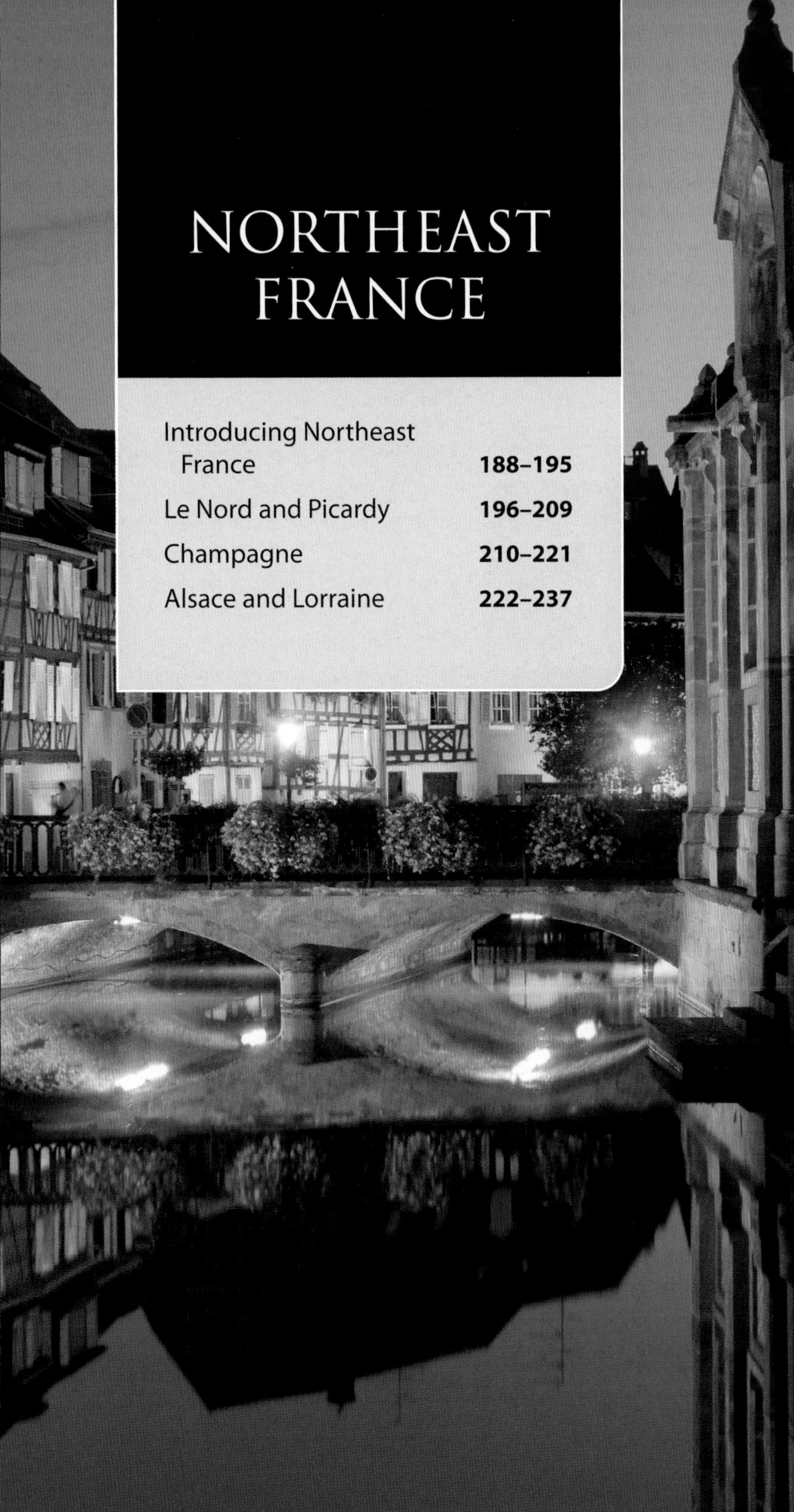

NORTHEAST FRANCE

Introducing Northeast France

The rolling plains of Northern France run from the English Channel to the wooded Ardennes hills and the Vosges mountains of Alsace. Apart from somber battle memorials, the area has France's finest Gothic cathedrals – and a long tradition of brewing good quality beers. There is fine wine, too, in Champagne and Alsace. The old heavy industry has gone, while Lille's growth as a transport hub has brought new prosperity. This map shows some of the most interesting sights.

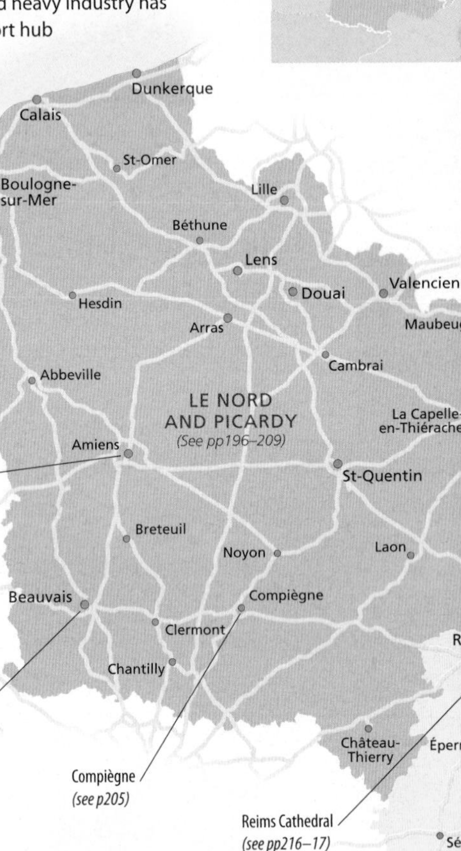

Amiens cathedral is renowned for its fine wood carvings and its nave, the highest in France *(see pp206–7)*.

Compiègne *(see p205)*

Reims Cathedral *(see pp216–17)*

The pride of Beauvais is its Gothic cathedral and astronomical clock *(see p204)*, which escaped heavy bombing during World War II.

Half-timbered houses ar Renaissance mansions lin the streets and alleys of Troyes' Old Town *(see p22C* rebuilt after the great fire i 1524. Its cathedral has remarkable stained-glass windows.

◀ River Lauch by night, Colmar

The legacy of World War I is strong in this area of former battlefields. The Douaumont Memorial outside Verdun *(see pp194–5)*, with its 15,000 graves, is only one of many memorials and cemeteries here.

Haut-Koenigsbourg, a castle painstakingly rebuilt by Kaiser Wilhelm II when Alsace-Lorraine was under German rule, is one of Alsace's most popular attractions *(see p232)*.

Strasbourg, seat of the Council of Europe, has a fine Gothic cathedral *(see pp234–5)* surrounded by delightful historic buildings.

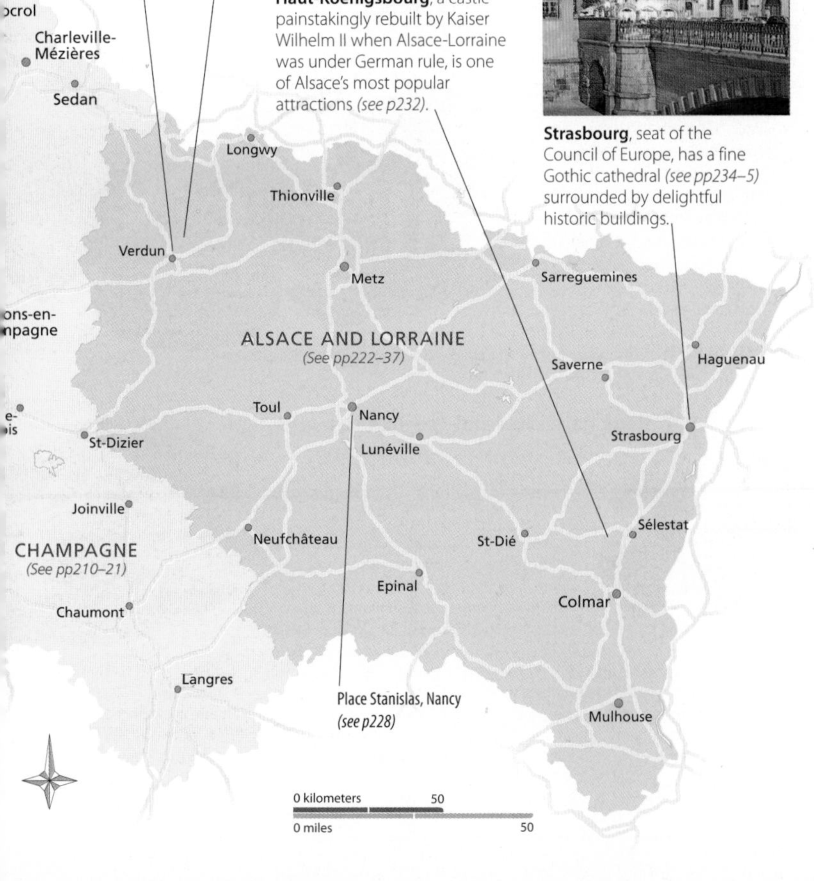

Porte Chaussée, Verdun
(see p226)

Place Stanislas, Nancy
(see p228)

ALSACE AND LORRAINE
(See pp222–37)

CHAMPAGNE
(See pp210–21)

Charleville-Mézières
Sedan
Longwy
Thionville
Verdun
Metz
Sarreguemines
Haguenau
Saverne
Toul
Nancy
St-Dizier
Lunéville
Strasbourg
Joinville
Neufchâteau
St-Dié
Sélestat
Epinal
Colmar
Chaumont
Langres
Mulhouse

0 kilometers 50
0 miles 50

The Flavors of Northeast France

The cuisine of northeast France is robust and warming, with rich beef stews, suckling pig, sausages and hams, dumplings, and sauerkraut dishes, many of them closely related to German or Flemish staples. There is good fish from the Atlantic and from freshwater lakes and rivers. Vegetables and fruit are produced in abundance, and often served in a variety of savory and sweet tarts, of which *quiche lorraine*, with bacon, eggs, and cream, is the best known. Rich cakes are popular, especially *Kougelhopf*, a ring-shaped cake of raisins and almonds soaked in *kirsch*, and madeleine sponge cakes.

Leeks from a local market

Golden mirabelle plums alongside the more usual variety

Le Nord and Picardy

The northern coast offers a wide variety of fish dishes, the most popular being steamed mussels served with fries. Herrings are pickled, soused, grilled, or smoked and North Sea shrimps fried and eaten whole. Chicken may be cooked in beer, duck is made into pies and terrines, and eel is served smoked as an appetizer. The market gardens *(hortillons)* of Picardy are famous for their vegetables, often made into delicious soups. Leeks or endive, braised or in gratins, accompany many dishes. Strong, washed-rind cheeses, such as Maroilles, are typical of the region.

Beer is often drunk with meals in the northeast, where traditional methods and small breweries thrive.

Champagne

Champagne encompasses arable plains and wooded uplands as well as vineyards, and produces game, *charcuterie* and delicious freshwater fish. Nothing, however, can compete with its main claim to fame champagne itself, which is often used as a luxury cooking ingredient as well as, of course, being enjoyed in its own right.

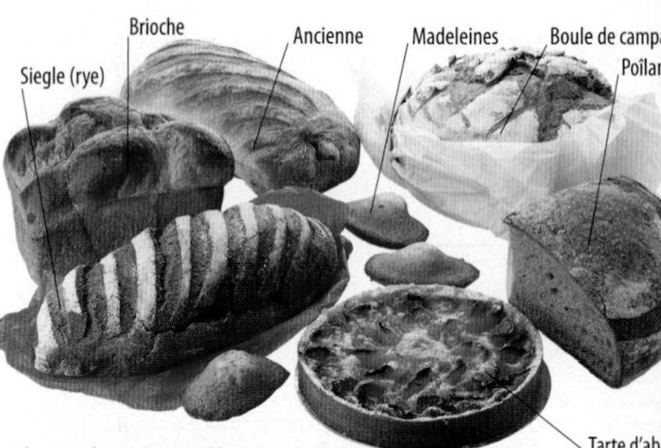

Selection of typical regional breads and pâtisserie

Regional Dishes and Specialties

Beets

The classic dish of the region is *choucroute garni*, a platter of pickled cabbage, flavored with juniper berries, and cooked with white wine, ham hock, and smoked pork belly. Smoked Montbeliard and Strasbourg sausages are added towards the end of cooking. Sausages come in many variations, from *saucisses de Strasbourg* to *bratwurst*, made from veal and pork, *lewerzurscht* (liver sausage), *andouillettes* (spicy chitterling sausages), *boudin noir* (pork and pig's blood sausage), and *boudin blanc* (white meat without blood). There are also smoked hams, cooked hams, and many different terrines, such as *presskopf* (headcheese) and the jellied white meat terrine, *potjevleesch. Langue lucullus* is smoked ox tongue studded with *foie gras*, a speciality of Valenciennes.

Ficelle picardie Pancakes are filled with mushrooms and ham in crème fraîche sauce, and baked with grated cheese.

Display of traditional northern French charcuterie

Wild boar, deer, rabbit, hare, quail, partridge, and woodcock are all found in the Ardennes, made into game pâtés and terrines as well as roasts and stews. The Ardennes is also noted for its fine quality smoked ham, while *jambon de Reims* is cooked ham with mustard, champagne, and Reims vinegar. Troyes is famous for its *andouillettes*, usually served with onions or baked in a creamy mustard sauce. Fish come from the small lakes east of Troyes and trout are abundant in the clear streams of the Ardennes. The two best cheeses of Champagne are Chaource and

Alsace and Lorraine

Rolling pastures, orchards, pine forests, and rivers produce the ingredients of Alsatian cooking. Meat is important, particularly pork, roasted or made into hams and sausages. In winter, game stews abound. There is a strong tradition of raising geese; after all, *foie gras* production originated in Strasbourg. The rivers are a

Shopping at the fish market in the port of Boulogne

good source of pike, trout, crayfish, and carp, often cooked in beer and served on festive occasions. Locally grown vegetables include cabbage, potatoes, and turnips, and fruit includes blueberries, quince, red currants, and the golden mirabelle plums of Lorraine, the latter prized for both jam and *eau de vie* (fruit brandy). The best-known cheese is Munster, a soft cow's milk cheese.

The white wines of Alsace range from steely, bone-dry Riesling (the region's finest variety) to aromatic Muscat and Gerwurztraminer. For more on the wines of Alsace, *see pp236–7.*

ON THE MENU

Anguille au vert Eel baked with green herbs and potatoes.

Cassolette de petits gris Snails in champagne sauce.

Flamiche aux poireaux Leek tart.

Flammekueche Pizza-style tart topped with bacon, crème fraîche, and onions.

Marcassin à l'Ardennaise Wild boar with celeriac.

Potée champenoise Pork, ham, sausage, beans, and vegetable stew.

Potée Lorraine Casserole of salt pork with vegetables.

Zewelwai A rich onion tart.

Truite à l'Ardennaise Trout is stuffed with breadcrumbs and finely chopped Ardennes ham, then baked.

Carbonnade de boeuf Steak and caramelized onions are covered with beer and cooked for three hours.

Babas au rhum These are dry yeast cakes of raisins, eggs, and butter, doused in rum and served with cream.

France's Wine Regions: Champagne

Since its fabled "invention" by the monk Dom Pérignon in the 17th century, no other wine has rivaled champagne as the symbol of luxury and celebration. Only wines made in this region by the *Méthode Champenoise* can be called champagne *(see p214)*. Most champagne is nonvintage: the skill of the blenders, using reserves of older wines, creates consistency and excellence year on year. The "big names" *(grandes marques)*, command the prestige and prices, but many small growers and cooperatives also produce excellent-value wines well worth seeking out.

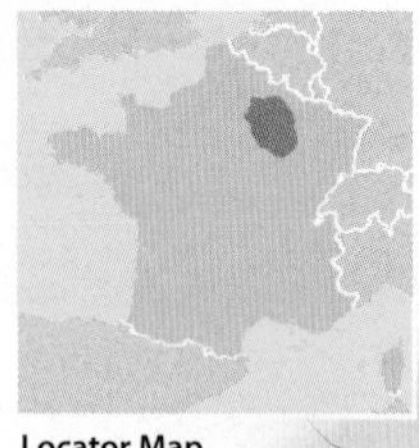

Locator Map

Champagne wine region

Soissons

Neuilly-Saint-Front

Château-Thierry

La Ferté-sous-Jouarre

A4

Grapes going for pressing, Montagne de Reims

Wine Regions

Champagne is a compact wine region, largely in the French département *of the Marne. Certain areas within it are particularly identified with certain styles of wine. The Aube produces 25 percent of all champagne as well as the exclusive Rosé des Riceys.*

Key Facts about Champagne

Location and Climate
The cool, marginal climate creates the finesse that other sparkling wines strive for, but seldom achieve. Chalky soils and east- and north-facing aspects help produce the relatively high acidity champagne needs.

Grape Varieties

Three varieties are grown, red ***Pinot Noir*** and ***Pinot Meunier***, and white ***Chardonnay***. Most champagne is a blend of all three, though Blanc de Blancs is 100 percent Chardonnay and Blanc de Noirs, although white, is made only from red grapes.

Good Producers
Grandes Marques: Bollinger, Gosset, Krug, Möet et Chandon, Joseph Perrier, Louis Roederer, Pol Roger, Billecart-Salmon, Veuve Clicquot, Taittinger, Ruinart, Laurent Perrier, Salon.
Négociants, cooperatives & growers: Boizel, M. Arnould, Cattier, Bricout, Drappier, Ployez-Jacquemart, H. Blin, Gimmonet, Andre Jacquart, Chartogne-Taillet, Vilmart, Alfred Gratien, Emile Hamm, B. Paillard, P. Gerbais.

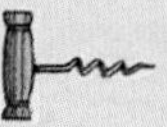

Good Vintages
2005, 2003, 2000, 1998, 1996, 1990.

From a name famous even to nonwine lovers, this is in the classic *brut* (dry) style; only *brut non dosage* or *brut sauvage* is drier.

KEY

- Vallée de la Marne district
- Montagne de Reims district
- Côte de Sézanne district
- Côte des Blancs district
- Aube district

0 kilometers 15

0 miles 15

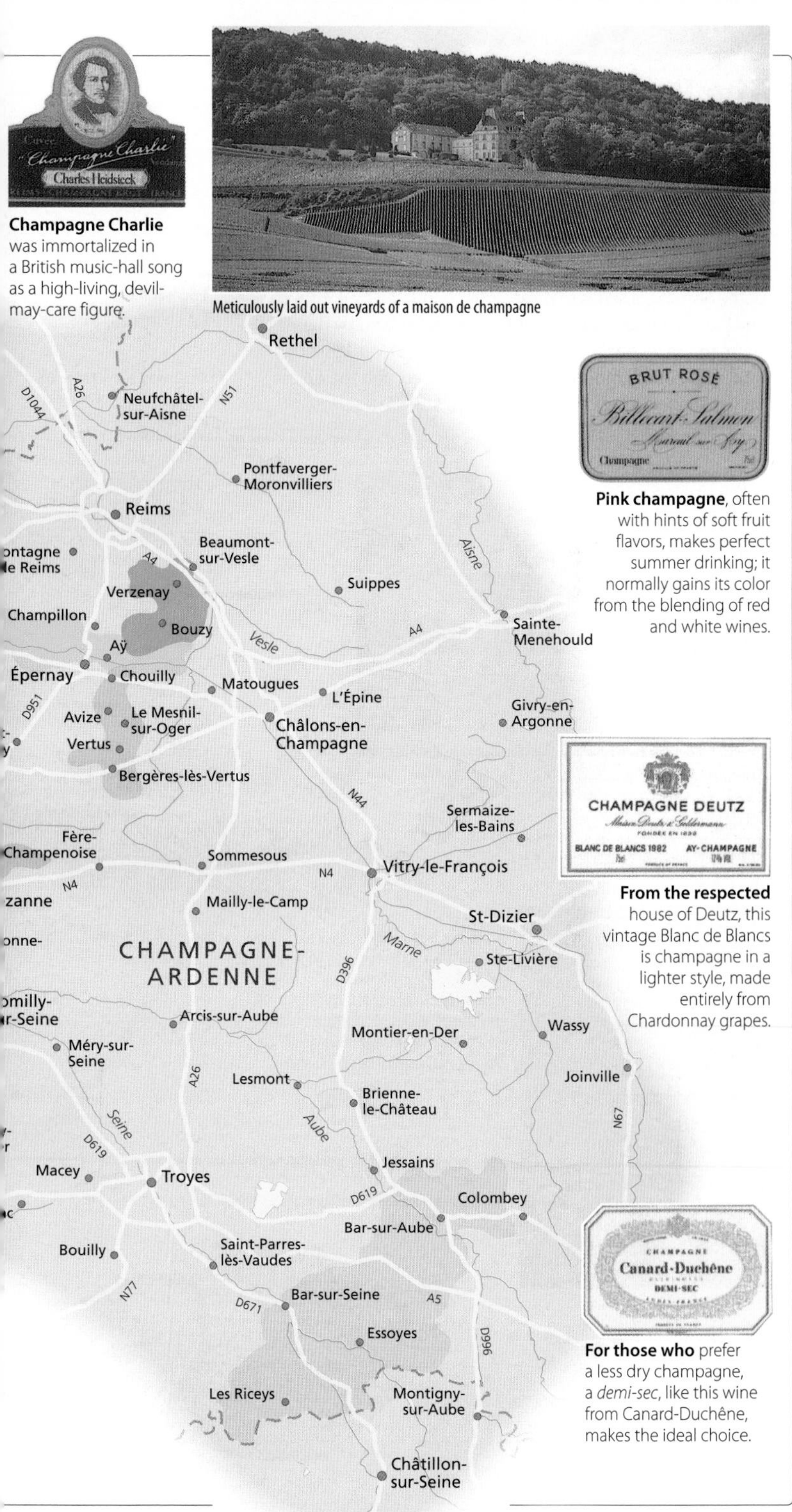

Champagne Charlie was immortalized in a British music-hall song as a high-living, devil-may-care figure.

Meticulously laid out vineyards of a maison de champagne

Pink champagne, often with hints of soft fruit flavors, makes perfect summer drinking; it normally gains its color from the blending of red and white wines.

From the respected house of Deutz, this vintage Blanc de Blancs is champagne in a lighter style, made entirely from Chardonnay grapes.

For those who prefer a less dry champagne, a *demi-sec*, like this wine from Canard-Duchêne, makes the ideal choice.

The Battle of the Somme

The many cemeteries that cover the Somme region serve as a poignant reminder of the mass slaughter that took place on the Western Front in World War I (which ended with the Armistice on November 11, 1918). Between July 1 and November 21, 1916, the Allied forces lost more than 600,000 men and the Germans at least 465,000. The Battle of the Somme, a series of campaigns conducted by British and French armies against fortified positions held by the Germans, relieved the hard-pressed French at Verdun; but hopes of a breakthrough never materialized, and the Allies only managed to advance 10 miles (16 km).

Locator Map

Somme battlefield

Beaumont Hamel Memorial Park, a tribute to the Royal Newfoundland Regiment, has a huge bronze caribou.

Thiepval Memorial was designed by Sir Edwin Lutyens. It dominates the landscape of Thiepval, one of the most hard-fought areas of the battle, appropriately chosen as a memorial to the 73,367 British soldiers with no known grave.

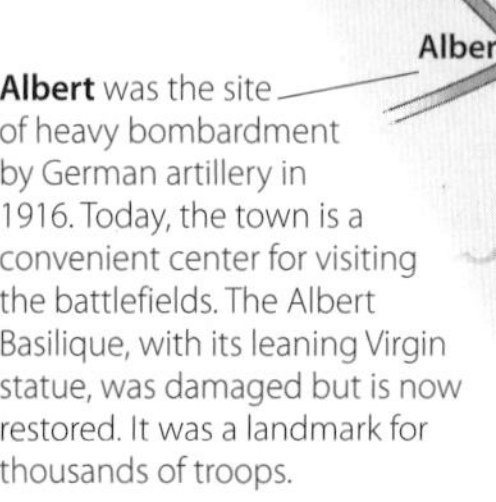

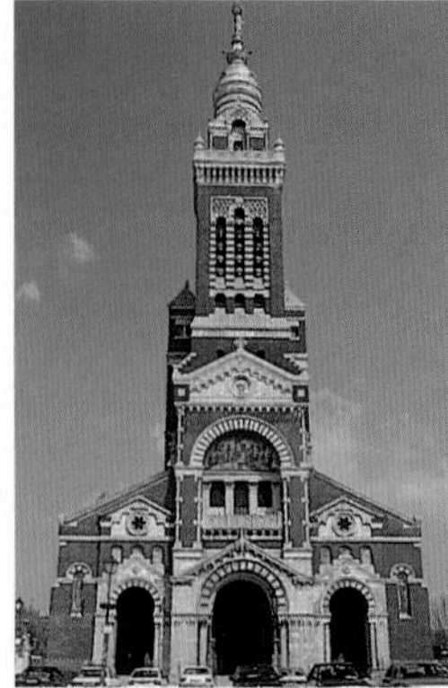

Albert was the site of heavy bombardment by German artillery in 1916. Today, the town is a convenient center for visiting the battlefields. The Albert Basilique, with its leaning Virgin statue, was damaged but is now restored. It was a landmark for thousands of troops.

Lochnager Mine Crater, formed by the largest of the British mines exploded on July 1, 1916, lies on the ridge by La Boiselle.

The British Tank Memorial, on the main road from Albert to Bapaume, commemorates the first use of tanks in warfare on September 15, 1916. The attack was a limited success; the tanks of World War I were too few before 1918 to transform warfare dominated by artillery, machine guns, and barbed wire.

For hotels and restaurants in this region see pp554–71 and pp576–603

Propaganda in World War I was employed by both sides to maintain support at home. This French postcard has a popular image for civilian consumption. It shows a dying soldier kissing the flag, under the tender gaze of a ministering nurse, affirming his faith in the cause with his last breath.

Delville Wood South African Memorial and Museum show the importance of Commonwealth forces in the Somme.

VISITORS' CHECKLIST

Practical Information

D929, D938 from Albert. 30 pl de la République, 80800 Corbie. **Tel** 03 22 96 95 76. somme-tourisme.com Albert Basilique, Beaumont Hamel Memorial Park, Delville Wood, La Boiselle, Thiepval, & Pozières memorials: **Open** daily. Ulster Tower: **Tel** 03 22 74 81 11. **Open** Feb–Mar: Tue–Sun; Apr–Nov: daily. South African Memorial, Delville Wood, Longueval. **Tel** 03 22 85 02 17. **Open** Feb–Nov: Tue–Sun. **Closed** hols. Historial de Péronne: **Tel** 03 22 83 14 18. **Open** May–Sep: daily; Oct– Apr: Tue–Sun. **Closed** mid-Dec–mid-Jan. **historial.org**

paume
N17
D1017
A1
A2
Flers
Morval
nchy
Canal du Nord
Maurepas
court
D917
la Somme
Péronne
D1
0 kilometers 5
0 miles 5

Poppies were one of the few plants to grow on the battlefield. Ghengis Khan brought the first white poppy from China and, according to legend, it turned red after battle. Today poppies are a symbol of remembrance.

Key

- Allied forces
- German forces
- Front Line before July 1, 1916
- Front Line progress July–September 1916
- Front Line progress September–November 1916

The Front Line trenches stretched from the North Sea to the Swiss frontier; only by keeping underground could men survive the terrible conditions. Trenches remain in a few areas, including the Beaumont Hamel Park.

LE NORD AND PICARDY

Pas de Calais · Nord · Somme · Oise · Aisne

Beneath the modern skin of France's northernmost region, the sights and monuments bear witness to the triumphs and turbulence of its past: soaring Gothic cathedrals, stately châteaus along the river Oise, and the battlefields and memorials of World War I.

The Channel ports of Dunkerque, Calais, and Boulogne, and the refined resort of Le Touquet, are the focal points along a busy coastline that stretches from the Somme estuary to the Belgian frontier. Boulogne has a genuine maritime flavor, and the white cliffs running from here to Calais provide the most dramatic scenery along the Côte d'Opale.

Flemish culture holds sway along the border with Belgium: an unfamiliar France of windmills and canals where the local taste is for beer, hotpots, and festivals with gallivanting giants. Lille is the dominant city here, a sprawling modern metropolis with a lively historic heart and an excellent art museum. To the southwest, the grace of Flemish architecture is handsomely displayed in the central squares of Arras, the capital of Artois. From here to the Somme valley the legacy of World War I, with its memorial cemeteries and poppy-strewn battlefields, makes compelling viewing. Cathedrals are the main appeal of Picardy. In Amiens, its capital, Cathédrale Notre-Dame is a pinnacle of the Gothic style – its magnificence echoed by the dizzying achievements at Beauvais farther south. Splendid cathedrals at Noyon, Senlis, and the delightful hilltop town of Laon chart the evolution of the Gothic. Closer to Paris, two châteaus command attention. Chantilly, the epicenter of French equestrianism, boasts gardens by Le Nôtre and a 19th-century château housing copious art treasures. Compiègne, bordered by a large and inviting forest, plays host to a lavish royal palace favored by French rulers from Louis XV to Napoleon III.

Memorial cemetery in Vallée de la Somme, an area still haunted by the memory of World War I

◀ Château de Pierrefonds, overlooking the Forêt de Compiègne

Exploring Le Nord and Picardy

As the gateway to England and Belgium, this northern corner of France is buzzing with business and industries, with the large, Euro-oriented city of Lille offering great culture as well as a new high-tech district. Yet peace and quiet is never far away. The coast between the historic port of Boulogne-sur-Mer and the Vallée de la Somme has a rich birdlife and is perfect for a relaxing seaside visit. Inland, the many Gothic cathedrals such as Amiens and Beauvais make an impressive tour, and the World War I battlefields and memorials provide an important insight into 20th-century history. Further south, the grand châteaux at Compiègne and Chantilly – which has the fascinating Musée Condé – are easily visited en route to or from Paris.

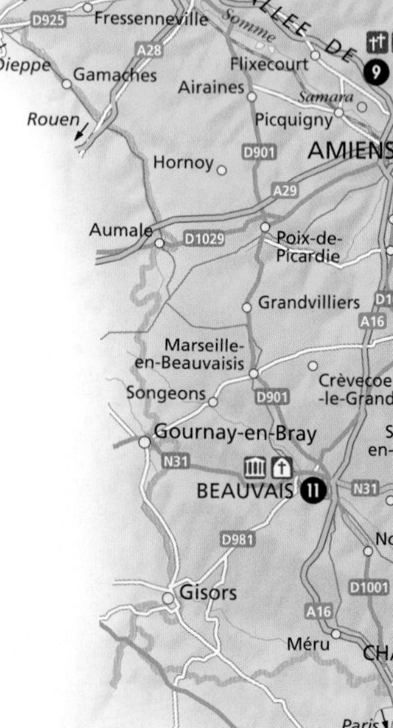

Key

- Highway
- Major road
- Secondary road
- Minor road
- Scenic route
- Main railroad
- Minor railroad
- International border
- Regional border

Lively outdoor café in the historic Grand'place in the heart of Arras

For additional map symbols *see back flap*

Sights at a Glance

1. Le Touquet
2. Boulogne-sur-Mer
3. Calais
4. Dunkerque
5. St-Omer
6. Flandre Maritime
7. Lille
8. Arras
9. Vallée de la Somme
10. Amiens
11. Beauvais
12. Noyon
13. Compiègne
14. Château de Pierrefonds
15. Senlis
16. Chantilly
17. Parc Astérix
18. Laon

The meandering waters in the Vallée de la Somme

Getting Around

The main entry point into the region is Calais (and the Channel Tunnel terminal 2 miles/3 km south). From here, highways A16 and A26/A1, several major N and D roads, and mainline rail services run directly to Paris. In addition, TGVs serve Calais-Frethun, Lille, and Paris. There is a dense road network throughout the region. With their many local bus and train connections, Lille and Amiens make good bases. The A26 (or *Autoroute des Anglais*) crosses the whole region from Calais to Troyes, via Arras and Laon, giving easy access to eastern Picardy. It's also a useful route if you're heading south and want to avoid Paris.

Poppies, the symbol of World War I battlefields, in the Vallée de la Somme

Le Touquet beach at low tide

❶ Le Touquet

Pas de Calais. 5,500. Palais du Congrès, pl de l'Hermitage (03 21 06 72 00). Thu & Sat (Jun–mid-Sep: also Mon). **letouquet.com**

Properly known as Le Touquet Paris-Plage, this resort was created in the 19th century and became fashionable with the rich and famous between the two World Wars. A vast pine forest, planted in 1855, spreads around the town sheltering stately villas. To the west, a grid of smart hotels, holiday residences, and sophisticated shops and restaurants borders a long, sandy beach. A racecourse and casino are complemented by seaside amusements and sports facilities, including two excellent golf courses, horseback riding and land yachting.

Further inland, the hilltop town of **Montreuil** has lime-washed 17th-century houses, abundant restaurants, and a tree-shaded rampart walk.

❷ Boulogne-sur-Mer

Pas de Calais. 45,000. Parvis de Nausicaa (03 21 10 88 10). Wed & Sat *(pl Dalton)*, Sun *(pl Vignon)*. **tourisme-boulognesurmer.com**

An important fishing port and busy marina, Boulogne rewards its visitors well. Its attractions come neatly boxed in a walled Haute Ville, with the Porte des Dunes opening on to a 17th–19th-century ensemble of Palais de Justice, Bibliothèque, and Hôtel de Ville in **place de la Résistance**.

The 19th-century **Basilique Notre-Dame** is capped by a dome visible for miles. Inside, a bejeweled wooden statue represents Boulogne's patroness, Notre-Dame de Boulogne. She is wearing a *soleil*, a headdress also worn by women during the *Grande Procession* held annually in her honor. Nearby, the powerful moated 13th-century **Château**, built for the Counts of Boulogne, is now a well-organized historical museum.

In the center of town, shops, hotels, and fish restaurants line the quai Gambetta on the east bank of the river Liane. To the north lie Boulogne's beach and **Nausicaa**, a vast, spectacular, and innovative aquarium and Sea Center.

North of the town, the **Colonne de la Grande Armée** was erected in 1841 as a monument to Napoleon I's planned invasion of England in 1803–5. From the top there is a panoramic view along the coast towards Calais. This is the most scenic stretch of the Côte d'Opale (Opal Coast), with the windblown headlands of **Cap Gris-Nez** and **Cap Blanc-Nez** offering breathtakingly extensive views across the Channel.

Château
Rue de Bernet. **Tel** 03 21 10 02 20. **Open** Tue–Sun. **Closed** Jan 1, May 1, Dec 24–Jan 2.

Aquarium Nausicaa
Bd Sainte-Beuve. **Tel** 03 21 30 99 99. **Open** daily. **Closed** 3 wks Jan, Dec 25. **nausicaa.fr**

❸ Calais

Pas de Calais. 76,000. 12 bd Clémenceau (03 21 96 62 40). Wed, Thu & Sat. **calais-cotedopale.com**

Calais is a busy cross-Channel port with a sandy beach to the west. Clumsily rebuilt after World War II, it seems to have little to offer at first sight. Many visitors never get closer than the huge Cité Europe shopping mall by the Eurotunnel exit.

The **Musée des Beaux Arts**, however, has works by the Dutch and Flemish Schools. Also on show are studies for Auguste Rodin's famous statue *The Burghers of Calais* (1895). The statue stands outside the Hôtel de Ville, and celebrates

The windswept Cap Blanc-Nez on the Côte d'Opale

For hotels and restaurants in this region see pp554–71 and pp576–603

The Burghers of Calais by Auguste Rodin (1895)

an event during Edward III's siege of Calais in 1347, when six burghers offered their lives to save the rest of the town.

The **Cité de la Dentelle et de la Mode** recalls the town's lace-making industry. **Musée Mémoire 1939–1945**, housed in a battle-scarred German blockhouse, offers a detailed account of local events during World War II.

Musée des Beaux Arts
25 rue Richelieu. **Tel** 03 21 46 48 40. **Open** Tue–Sat, Sun pm.

Cité de la Dentelle
Quai du Commerce. **Tel** 03 21 00 42 30. **Open** Wed–Mon. **Closed** first 2 wks Jan, May 1, Dec 25.

Musée Mémoire 1939–1945
Parc Saint Pierre. **Tel** 03 21 34 21 57. **Open** call for hours.

❹ Dunkerque

Nord. 376,000. Rue Amiral Ronarc'h (03 28 66 79 21). Wed, Sat. **ot-dunkerque.fr**

Though a major industrial port, Dunkerque has much Flemish character. Start a tour from place du Minck, with its fresh fish stalls. Nearby **Musée Portuaire** celebrates the town's maritime history. In the old center, a statue commemorates local hero Jean Bart, a 17th-century corsair, who lies in **Eglise St-Eloi**. Its belfry (1440) offers fine views.

Le Mémorial du Souvenir has an exhibition of the dramatic evacuation of 350,000 British and French troops in 1940. The **Lieu d'Art et d'Action Contemporaine (LAAC)** features ceramics and glassware.

Musée Portuaire
9 quai de la Citadelle. **Tel** 03 28 63 33 39. **Open** Wed–Mon. **Closed** Jan 1, May 1, Dec 25.

The port at Dunkerque

Le Memorial du Souvenir
Rue des Chantiers de France. **Tel** 03 28 66 79 21. **Open** Apr–Sep: daily; Oct–Mar: call for hours. **Closed** Jan 1, Nov 1, Dec 25. gr. fl. only.

Lieu d'Art et d'Action Contemporaine
Jardin des Sculptures. **Tel** 03 28 29 56 00. **Open** Tue–Sun. **Closed** public hols.

❺ St-Omer

Pas de Calais. 15,000. 4 rue Lion d'Or (03 21 98 08 51). Wed, Thu, Sat. **tourisme-saintomer.com**

St-Omer appears untouched. Pilasters adorn the 17th- and 18th-century houses lining the cobbled streets, one of which, **Hôtel Sandelin**, is now a fine and decorative arts museum. The cathedral boasts 13th-century tiles and a huge organ. The **Bibliothèque d'Agglomération** contains rare manuscripts from the Abbaye St-Bertin, a ruined 15th-century abbey east of town. Three miles (5 km) from St-Omer, **La Coupole** is an informative WWII museum inside a converted bunker.

Hôtel Sandelin
14 rue Carnot. **Tel** 03 21 38 00 94. **Open** Wed–Sun. gr. fl.

Bibliothèque d'Agglomération
40 rue Gambetta. **Tel** 03 21 38 35 08. **Open** Tue–Sat. **Closed** public hols.

La Coupole
Tel 03 21 12 27 27. **Open** daily. **Closed** last week Dec–first week Jan.

Channel Crossings

Calais is only 22 miles (36 km) southeast of the English coast, and crossing the waters of the Channel – which the French know as La Manche (the Sleeve) – has inspired many intrepid exploits. The first crossing by balloon was in 1785 by Jean Pierre Blanchard; Captain M. Webb made the first swim in 1875; and Louis Blériot's pioneering flight followed in 1909. Plans for an undersea tunnel, first laid as early as 1751, were finally achieved in 1994 with the opening of a railroad link between Fréthun and Folkestone.

Children watching Louis Blériot taking off, 1909

6 Flandre Maritime

Nord. 5,000. Lille. Bergues. Dunkerque. Bergues, Le Beffroi, pl Henri Billiaert (03 28 68 71 06).

South of Dunkerque lies a flat, agricultural plain with narrow waterways and expansive skies – an archetypal Flemish landscape with canals, cyclists, and ancient windmills. The large **Noordmeulen**, built of graying wood and just north of Hondschoote in 1127, is thought to be the oldest windmill in Europe.

From Hondschoote the D3 follows the Canal de la Basse Colme west to Bergues, a fortified wool town with fine 16th–17th-century Flemish works in its **Musée Municipal**. Farther south, the hilltop town of **Cassel** has a cobbled Grande place with 16th–18th-century buildings, and views across Flanders and Belgium from its Jardin Public.

Musée Municipal
1 rue du Mont de Piété, Bergues. **Tel** 03 28 68 13 30. **Open** Thu–Mon. **Closed** Oct–Apr.

Place du General de Gaulle in Lille's historic center

7 Lille

Nord. 232,000. Palais Rihour (08 91 56 20 04). Tue–Sun. **lilletourism.com**

Lille has excellent shops and markets and a powerful sense of its historic Flemish identity – the Flemish name, Rijssel, is still used and some of the area's one million residents speak a Franco-Flemish patois. With heavy industry declining, the city has turned to high tech. A modern commercial quarter, including the ultra-modern Euralille shopping mall, adjoins Lille Europe station, the TGV/Eurostar/Thalys rail interchange. The city's Métro VAL, is a driverless automatic train.

The city's charm lies in its historic center, Vieux Lille – a mass of cobbled squares and narrow streets that are packed with stylish shops, cafés, and restaurants. Place du Général de Gaulle forms its hub, with facades including the 17th-century **Vieille Bourse** (Old Exchange), which boasts an arcaded courtyard. Adjacent stand the **Nouvelle Bourse** and the **Opéra**, both built in the early 20th century. The moated five-point brick Citadel by Vauban is also worth a look.

Flower stalls in the arcades of the Vieille Bourse in Lille

Musée de l'Hospice Comtesse
32 rue de la Monnaie. **Tel** 03 28 36 84 00. **Open** Wed–Sun, Mon pm.

A hospital was founded here in 1237. Now its 15th- and 17th-century buildings house exhibitions. The Sick Room has a barrel-vaulted ceiling, the Community Wing a Delft kitchen. There is a collection of ancient instruments.

Palais des Beaux-Arts
Pl de la République. **Tel** 03 20 06 78 00. **Open** Wed–Sun, Mon pm. **Closed** Jan 1, May 1, Jul 14, 1st w/e Sep, Nov 1, Dec 25.

One of the best art collections outside Paris, the museum is strong on Flemish works, including Rubens and Van Dyck. Other highlights are *Paradise and Hell* by Dirk Bouts, Van Goyen's *The Skaters*, Goya's *The Letter*, Delacroix's *Médée*, as well as works by Courbet and Impressionist paintings.

For hotels and restaurants in this region see pp554–71 and pp576–603

❽ Arras

Pas de Calais. 45,000.
Hôtel de Ville, pl des Héros (03 21 51 26 95). Wed, Thu, Sat, Sun.
ot-arras.fr

The center of Arras, capital of the Artois region, is graced by two picturesque cobbled squares enclosed by 155 houses with 17th-century Flemish-style facades. A triumph of postwar reconstruction, each residence in the **Grand' place** and the smaller place des Héros has a slightly varying design, with some original shop signs still visible.

A monumental **Hôtel de Ville** rebuilt in the Flamboyant Gothic style stands at the west end of place des Héros – in the foyer are two giants, Colas Dédé and Jacqueline, who swagger around the town during local festivals. From the basement you can take an elevator up to the belfry for superb views, or take a guided tour into the labyrinth of underground passages below Arras. These were cut in the limestone in the 10th century. They have often served as shelter; during World War I as a subterranean army camp.

The huge Abbaye St-Vaast includes an 18th–19th-century Neo-Classical cathedral and the **Musée des Beaux-Arts**. The museum contains some fine examples of medieval sculpture including a pair of beautiful 13th-century angels. Among other exhibits are a local *arras* (hanging tapestry) and 19th-century works by the School of Arras, a group of realist landscape painters.

Hôtel de Ville
Pl des Héros. **Tel** 03 21 51 26 95. **Open** Jul–Aug: daily. oblig for tunnels.

Musée des Beaux-Arts
22 rue Paul Doumer. **Tel** 03 21 71 26 43. **Open** Wed–Mon. **Closed** pub hols.

❾ Vallée de la Somme

Somme. Amiens. 16 pl André Audinot, Péronne (03 22 84 42 38). **somme-tourisme.com**

The name of the Somme is synonymous with the slaughter and horror of trench warfare during World War I *(see pp190-91)*. Yet the Somme valley also means pretty countryside, a vast estuary wetland, and abundant wildlife. Lakes and woods alongside provide enjoyable camping, walking, and fishing. Battlefields lie along the river and its tributaries north and northeast of Amiens, and extend north to Arras. Neat World War I Commonwealth cemeteries cover the area. The **Historial de la Grande Guerre** at Péronne gives a thoughtful introduction. Parc Mémorial Beaumont-Hamel, near Albert, is a real battlefield being allowed to disappear in its own time. Travel to Vimy Ridge Canadian Memorial, near Arras, to see a bloodbath battle site preserved as it was, and to Notre-Dame de Lorette, the landmark French National Cemetery.

Roadside shrine, Somme Valley

Boating on the river Somme

West of Amiens, **Samara** – Amiens' Gallo-Roman name – is France's largest archeological park, with reconstructions of prehistoric dwellings, and exhibitions explaining early crafts like flint-cutting and corn-grinding. Farther downstream, Eglise St-Vulfran at Abbeville is noted for its Flamboyant Gothic west front with beautifully carved 16th-century door panels.

St-Valéry-sur-Somme is a charming harbor resort with a historic upper town and a tree-lined promenade looking across the estuary. William departed for England from here in 1066. Bird-watchers should visit the Maison de l'Oiseau on the D3 nearby, or the Parc Ornithologique de Marquenterre on the far shore near delightful Le Crotoy. In summer, a little train links the two sides, passing through dunes and marshes.

Historial de la Grande Guerre
Château de Péronne. **Tel** 03 22 83 14 18. **Open** Apr–Sep: daily; Oct–Mar: Tue–Sun. **Closed** mid-Dec–mid-Jan.
historial.org

Samara
La Chaussée-Tirancourt. **Tel** 03 22 51 82 83. **Open** mid-Mar–mid-Nov: daily.
 **samara.fr**

16th-century carvings on Eglise St-Vulfran in Abbeville, Somme Valley

⑩ Amiens

Somme. 130,000. 6 bis rue Dusevel (03 22 71 60 50). Wed & Sat. **amiens-tourisme.com**

There is more to Amiens, the capital of Picardy, than its **Cathédrale Notre-Dame** *(see pp206–7)*. The picturesque quarter of St-Leu is a pedestrianized area of low houses and flower-lined canals with waterside restaurants, bars, and artisans' shops. Farther east are **Les Hortillonnages**, a colorful patchwork of marshland market gardens, once tended by farmers using punts which now ferry visitors around the protected natural site.

The **Musée de Picardie** has many fine medieval and 19th-century sculptures and 16th–20th-century paintings, including a remarkable set of 16th-century group portraits, commissioned as offerings to the cathedral. To the south is the Cirque d'Hiver which Jules Verne (1828–1905) inaugurated in 1889. **Maison de Jules Verne**, his renovated home, has over 700 objects spread over four floors relating to the famous author, who lived here from 1882 until 1900.

Musée de Picardie
48 rue de la République. **Tel** 03 22 97 14 00. **Open** Tue–Sun. **Closed** Jan 1, May 1, Nov 1, Nov 11, Dec 25.

Maison de Jules Verne
2 rue Charles Dubois. **Tel** 03 22 45 45 75. **Open** Easter–mid-Oct: daily; mid-Oct–Easter: Wed–Mon.

The clock depicts Christ surrounded by the 12 apostles.
Mechanical figures perform scenes from the Last Judgment.
Solstice indicator
Clock showing age of the world

Astronomical clock in Beauvais cathedral

⑪ Beauvais

Oise. 61,000. 1 rue Beauregard (03 44 15 30 30). Mon, Wed, Thu, Sat. **beauvaistourisme.fr**

Heavily bombed in World War II, Beauvais is now a modern town with one outstanding jewel. Though never completed, **Cathédrale St-Pierre** is a poignant, neck-cricking finale to the vaulting ambition that created the great Gothic cathedrals. In 1227 work began on a building designed to soar above all predecessors, but the roof of the chancel caved in twice from lack of support before its completion in the early 14th century. Delayed by wars and inadequate funds, the transept was not completed until 1550. In 1573 its crossing collapsed after a tower and spire were added. What remains today is nevertheless a masterpiece, rising 157 ft (48 m) high. In the transept much of the original 16th-century stained glass survives, while near the north door is a 90,000-part astronomical clock assembled in the 1860s. What would have been the nave is still occupied by the remnants of a 10th-century church known as the Basse-Oeuvre.

The former Bishop's Palace is now home to the **Musée Départemental de l'Oise**. The collection includes archeological finds, medieval sculpture, tapestries, and local ceramics. Beauvais has a long tradition of tapestry manufacture, and examples from the

Viollet-Le-Duc

The renowned architectural theorist Viollet-le-Duc (1814–79) was the first to fully appreciate Gothic architecture. His 1854 dictionary of architecture celebrated medieval building techniques, showing that the arches and tracery of Gothic cathedrals were solutions to architectural problems, not mere decoration. His restoration work included Château de Pierrefonds, Notre-Dame in Paris *(see pp90–91)*, and Carcassonne *(see pp492–3)*.

Medieval architects, as drawn by Viollet-le-Duc

French national collection are shown in the **Galerie Nationale de la Tapisserie.**

Musée Départemental de l'Oise
Ancien Palais Episcopal, 1 rue du Musée. **Tel** 03 44 10 40 50. **Open** Wed–Mon. **Closed** Jan 1, Easter, May 1, Jun 9, Nov 1, Dec 25.

Galerie Nationale de la Tapisserie
22 rue St-Pierre. **Tel** 03 44 15 39 10. **Open** Tue–Sun. **Closed** Jan 1, May 1, Dec 25.

The rib-vaulted nave of Cathédrale de Notre-Dame, Noyon

⓬ Noyon

Oise. 15,200. pl de l'Hôtel de Ville (03 44 44 21 88). Wed & Sat, first Tue of each month.
noyon-tourisme.com

Noyon has long been a religious center. The **Cathédrale de Notre-Dame**, dating from 1150, is the fifth to be built on this site and was completed by 1290. It provides a harmonious example of the transition from Romanesque to Gothic style.

A local history museum, the **Musée du Noyonnais**, occupies part of the former Bishop's Palace, and at the cathedral's east end is a rare half-timbered chapter library built in 1506.

Jean Calvin, the Protestant theologian and one of the leaders of the Reformation, was born here in 1509 and is commemorated in the small **Musée Jean Calvin.**

Musée du Noyonnais
Ancien Palais Episcopal, 7 rue de l'Evêché. **Tel** 03 44 09 43 41. **Open** Tue–Sun. **Closed** Jan 1, Nov 11, Dec 25.

⓭ Compiègne

Oise. 70,000. pl de l'Hôtel de Ville (03 44 40 01 00). Tue–Sat.
compiegne-tourisme.fr

Compiegne is where Joan of Arc was captured by the Burgundians in 1430. A 16th-century Hôtel de Ville with a towering belfry rules over the center, but the town is most famous for its royal **Château**.

Designed as a summer residence for Louis XV, the château was completed by Louis XVI, restored by Napoleon, and later became a residence of Napoleon III and Empress Eugénie. Tours of the Imperial Apartments take in private chambers, such as the sumptuous bedrooms of Napoleon I and Marie-Louise.

Within the château, the Musée du Second Empire and Musée de l'Impératrice display furniture, memorabilia, and portraits, while the Musée de la Voiture is an entertaining assembly of historic carriages, bicycles, and early motor cars.

South and east of the town, the old hunting grounds of **Forêt de Compiègne** spread as far as Pierrefonds, with ample space for walks and picnics beneath its oaks and beeches. East of the D130, Les Beaux Monts provide majestic views back to the château.

The Clairière de l'Armistice, north of the N31, marks the spot where the armistice of World War I was signed on November 11, 1918. The small **Musée Wagon de l'Armistice** has a replica of the train carriage where the ceremony took place, which was used again in World War II by Hitler as a humiliating venue for the signing of the French surrender on June 22, 1940.

Château de Compiègne
Pl du Général de Gaulle. **Tel** 03 44 38 47 00. **Open** Wed–Mon. **Closed** Jan 1, May 1, Dec 25. **musee-chateau-compiegne.fr**

Musée Wagon de l'Armistice
Clairière de l'Armistice (direc. Soissons). **Tel** 03 44 85 14 18. **Open** Wed–Mon. **Closed** Jan 1, Jan & Feb am, Dec 25.

⓮ Château de Pierrefonds

Oise. **Tel** 03 44 42 72 72. **Open** daily. **Closed** Mon (Sep 5–Apr), Jan 1, May 1, Nov 1 & 11, Dec 25. Concerts.

The immense Château de Pierrefonds dominates the small village below. A mighty castle was constructed here by Louis d'Orléans in the 14th century, but by 1813 it had become a picturesque ruin which Napoleon I purchased for less than 3,000 francs.

In 1857, Napoleon III commissioned the architect Viollet-le-Duc to restore it, and in 1884 Pierrefonds was reborn as a museum of fortification. The exterior, with its moat, drawbridge, towers, and double sentry walks, is a diligent reconstruction of medieval military architecture. The interior, by contrast, is enlivened by the romantic fancies of Viollet-le-Duc and his patron. There are guided tours and a historical exhibition.

Path through Forêt de Compiègne

Amiens Cathedral

Work on France's largest cathedral started around 1220. It was built to house the head of St John the Baptist, brought back from the Crusades in 1206, which is still displayed here. Within 50 years, Notre-Dame was complete, a masterpiece of engineering – Gothic architecture carried to a bold extreme. Restored in the 1850s by Viollet-le-Duc *(see p204)*, and having miraculously survived two World Wars, the cathedral is famous for its statues and reliefs, which inspired John Ruskin's *The Bible of Amiens* in 1884. The annual *La Cathédrale en Couleurs* sound-and-light show recreates the original colors of the statuary around the west door.

★ West Front
The King's Gallery, a row of 22 colossal statues representing the kings of France, spans the west front. The statues are also thought to symbolize the Kings of Judah.

Weeping Angel
Sculpted by Nicolas Blasset in 1628, this sentimental statue in the ambulatory became a popular image during World War I.

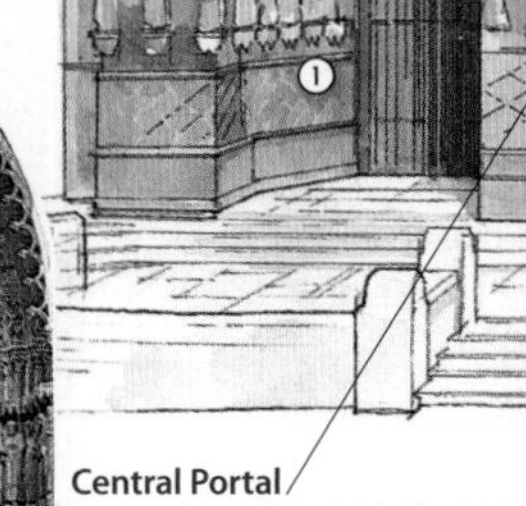

KEY

① **The Calendar** shows signs from the Zodiac, with the corresponding monthly labors below. It depicts everyday life in the 13th century.

② **St Firmin Portal** is decorated with figures and scenes from the life of St Firmin, the martyr who brought Christianity to Picardy and became the first bishop of Amiens.

③ **The Flamboyant tracery** of the rose window was created in the 16th century.

④ **A double row** comprising 22 elegant flying buttresses supports the construction.

⑤ **The flooring** was laid down in 1288 and reassembled in the late 19th century. The faithful followed its labyrinthine shape on their knees.

Central Portal
Scenes from the Last Judgment adorn the tympanum, with the *Beau Dieu*, a statue of Christ, between the doors.

Towers
Two towers of unequal height frame the west front. The south tower was completed in 1366; the north in 1402. The spire was replaced twice, in 1627 and 1887.

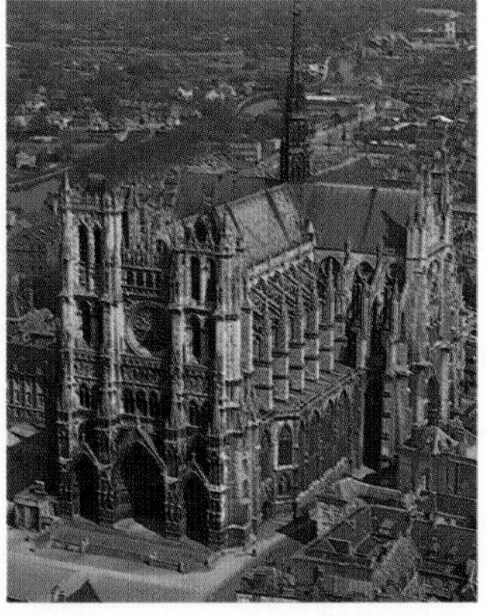

VISITORS' CHECKLIST

Practical Information
Cathédrale Notre-Dame, pl Notre-Dame. **Tel** 03 22 71 60 50.
Open Apr–Sep: 8:30am–6:15pm; Oct–Mar: 8:30am–5:15pm. Jun–Dec (nightly): La Cathédrale en Couleurs light show. **Closed** Jan 1, last Sun Sep. 9am daily (noon Wed); 9am, 10:15am, 11:30am, 6pm Sun. **amiens-cathedrale.fr**

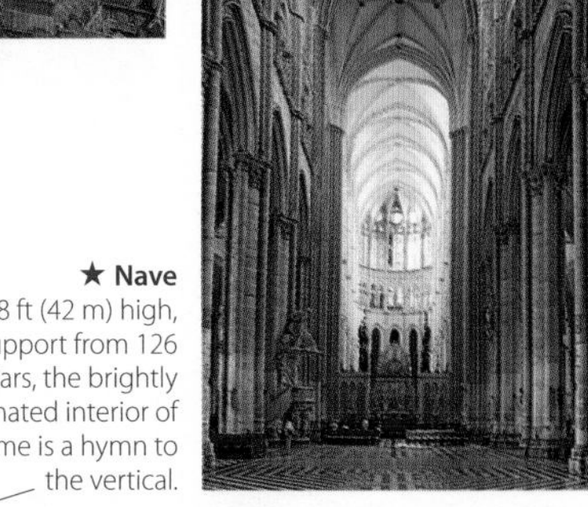

★ Nave
Soaring 138 ft (42 m) high, with support from 126 slender pillars, the brightly illuminated interior of Notre-Dame is a hymn to the vertical.

★ Choir Stalls
The 110 oak choir stalls (1508–19) are delicately carved with over 4,000 biblical, mythical, and real life figures.

★ Choir Screens
Vivid scenes from the lives of St. Firmin and St. John, carved in the 15th–16th centuries, adorn the ambulatory.

⓯ Senlis

Oise. 17,000. pl du Parvis Notre-Dame (03 44 53 06 40). Tue & Fri. **senlis-tourisme.fr**

Senlis, 6 miles (10 km) east of Chantilly, is worth visiting for its Gothic cathedral and the well-preserved historic streets that surround it. **Cathédrale Notre-Dame** was constructed during the 12th century, and the sculpted central doorway of its west front, depicting the Assumption of the Virgin, influenced later cathedrals such as Amiens *(see pp206–7)*. The south tower's spire dates from the 13th century, while the Flamboyant south transept, built in the mid-16th century, makes an ornate contrast with the austerity of earlier years. Opposite the west front, a gateway leads to the ruins of the Château Royal and its gardens. Here the **Musée de la Vénerie**, housed in a former priory, celebrates hunting through paintings, old weapons, and trophies.

The **Musée d'Art** recalls the town's Gallo-Roman past, and also has an excellent collection of early Gothic sculpture.

Musée de la Vénerie
Château Royal, pl du Parvis Notre-Dame. **Tel** 03 44 29 49 93. **Open** Tue pm, Wed–Sun all day. **Closed** Jan 1, May 1, Dec 25. oblig.

Musée d'Art et d'Archéologie
Ancien Evêché, 2 pl Notre-Dame. **Tel** 03 44 24 86 72. **Open** Wed pm, Thu–Mon all day.

Les Très Riches Heures du Duc de Berry, on show in Chantilly

⓰ Chantilly

Oise. 11,200. 60 av du Maréchal Joffre (03 44 67 37 37). Wed & Sat. **chantilly-tourisme.com**

The horse-racing capital of France, Chantilly offers a classy combination of château, park, and forest that has long made it a popular excursion. With origins in Gallo-Roman times, the château of today started to take shape in 1528, when the famous Anne de Montmorency, Constable of France, had the old fortress replaced and added the Petit Château. During the time of the Great Prince of Condé (1621–86), renovation work continued and Le Nôtre created a park and fountains which made even Louis XIV jealous. Destroyed in the Revolution, the

Chantilly Horse Racing

Prix Equipage de Hermès, one of many prestigious races at Chantilly

Chantilly is the capital of thoroughbred racing in France, a shrine to the long-standing love affair between the French upper classes and the world of horses. It was the firm belief of Prince Louis-Henri de Bourbon, creator of Chantilly's monumental Grandes Ecuries, that he would one day be reincarnated as a horse. Horse racing was introduced from England around 1830 and soon became very popular. The first official race meeting was held here in 1834 and today around 3,000 horses are trained in the surrounding forests and countryside. Every June, Chantilly becomes the focus of the social and flat racing season when top riders and their thoroughbreds compete for its two historic trophies, the Prix du Jockey-Club and Prix de Diane-Hermès.

Grand Château was again rebuilt and its receptions and hunting parties became crowded by the fashionable high society of the 1820s–30s. It was finally replaced by a Renaissance-style château in the late 19th century.

Today the Grand Château and the Petit Château form the **Musée Condé**, displaying art treasures collected by its last private owner, the Duke of Aumale. These include work by Raphael, Botticelli, Poussin, and Ingres, and an entertaining gallery of 16th-century portraits by the Clouet brothers. Among the most precious items is the famous 15th-century illuminated manuscript *Les Très Riches Heures du Duc de Berry*, reproductions of which are on view. You can also tour the stately apartments, with decorative conceits ranging from frolicking monkeys to triumphant battles.

Asterix with friends, Parc Astérix

Both châteaus are somewhat upstaged by the magnificent stables (Grandes Ecuries), an equestrian palace designed by Jean Aubert in 1719 which could accommodate 240 horses and 500 dogs. It is occupied by the **Musée Vivant du Cheval**, presenting various breeds of horses and ponies, and riding displays.

Musée Condé
Château de Chantilly. **Tel** 03 44 62 62 62. **Open** Wed–Mon.

Musée Vivant du Cheval
Grandes Ecuries du Prince de Condé, Chantilly. **Tel** 03 44 27 31 80. **Open** phone for information.

17 Parc Astérix

Plailly. **Tel** 08 26 46 26 26. **Open** Jun–Aug daily & French schools hols (check). **parcasterix.fr**

Near Charles de Gaulle Airport a small fortified Gaulish village has its own customs controls, currency and radio station (Menhir FM). One of the most popular theme parks in France, it is dedicated to Asterix the Gaul and all the other characters in Goscinny and Uderzo's famous cartoon strip: Getafix, Obelix, Cacofonix *et al.* The Romans are driven crazy as they try to subdue these larger than life Gauls, who dodge patrolling Roman centurions. Hilarious battles take place.

The Parc is as much about French history as about the cartoons. Via Antiqua and the Roman City are lighthearted but genuinely educational. Rue de Paris shows Paris through the centuries, including the construction of Notre-Dame cathedral. There are nonhistorical attractions too, like a dolphinarium and Zeus' Thunder high-speed rollercoaster. Check out the latest rides – there's usually something new every year.

18 Laon

Aisne. 27,000. Hôtel-Dieu, pl du Parvis Gauthier de Montagne (03 23 20 28 62). Tue–Sat. **tourisme-paysdelaon.com**

The capital of the Aisne *département*, Laon occupies a dramatic site on top of a long, narrow ridge surrounded by

The pedestrianized rue Châtelaine, a main shopping street in Laon

Rose window in the 13th-century Cathédrale de Notre-Dame, Laon

wide plains. The old town, on top of the mount, is best approached by Poma, an automated cable car that swings up from the train station to the place du Général Leclerc.

The pedestrianized rue Châtelaine leads to Laon's splendid **Cathédrale de Notre-Dame**. Completed in 1235, the cathedral lost two of its original seven towers in the Revolution but remains an impressive monument to the early Gothic style.

Details include the deep porches of the west facade, the four-story nave, and the carved Renaissance screens enclosing its side chapels. The immense 13th-century rose window in the apse represents the Glorification of the Church. Protruding from the cathedral's western towers are statues paying tribute to the oxen used to haul up stone for its construction.

The rest of medieval Laon rewards casual strolling: a promenade rings the 16th-century **Citadelle** farther east, while to the south you can follow the ramparts past the Porte d'Ardon and Porte des Chenizelles to **Eglise St-Martin**, with views of the cathedral from rue Thibesard.

South of Laon is Chemin des Dames, named after Louis XV's daughters who used to take this route, but more often remembered as a World War I battlefield and lined with cemeteries and memorials.

CHAMPAGNE

Marne · Ardennes · Aube · Haute-Marne

Champagne is a name of great resonance, conjuring up images of celebration and the world-famous cathedral at Reims. Yet beyond the glamor lies an unspoiled rural idyll of two strikingly contrasting landscapes: the rolling plains of Champagne, giving way to lakes and water meadows to the south, and the dense forests and hills of the Ardennes in the north.

The so-called "sacred triangle of Champagne," linking Épernay, Reims, and Châlons-en-Champagne, is like a magnet for wine lovers. Here, the experience of drinking fine champagne is enhanced by gourmet meals of stuffed trout, Ardennes ham, and the famous tripe sausages called *andouillettes*.

The sign-posted *route touristique du champagne* wends its way through vineyards toward endless cereal plains stretching southward to the "lake district," an area of oak forests, water meadows, and streams.

On the border between France and Belgium lies the Ardennes, named after the Celtic word for deep forest. This wild border land of dramatic valleys, deciduous forests, and hills is cut by the meanderings of the river Meuse. Border fortifications include the vast citadel of Sedan and the star-shaped town and fortress of Rocroi, as well as the Maginot Line outposts built before World War II. The Ardennes may offer appealing countryside but Champagne is culturally superior, with impressive towns that have painstakingly restored historic centers. It has some striking churches, from the Gothic majesty of Reims cathedral to the rustic charm of its typical half-timbered *champenoises* churches. These feature vivid stained-glass windows by the famous School of Troyes, whose subtle craftsmanship seems to typify the appeal of this quiet region.

Timber-framed *champenoise* church at Lac du Der-Chantecoq

◀ Interior of Cathédrale Notre-Dame, Reims

Exploring Champagne

Champagne's fizz draws wine lovers to the sacred triangle between Reims, Épernay, and Châlons-en-Champagne, but the region also attracts culture lovers to its great churches, notably Reims Cathedral. Reims abounds in gastronomic restaurants but Troyes, the former capital of Champagne, makes the most delightful base. Much of Champagne is flat or gently undulating, and the wild and wooded Ardennes to the north attracts walkers and nature-lovers. North of Reims, the Ardennes canal can be explored by barge or pleasure boat from Rethel; to the south, watersports are popular on the lakes to the east of Troyes.

Fishing by a canal in Montier-en-Der near Lac du Der-Chantecoq

Getting Around

The region's main *autoroute* is the A26, which reaches Reims in under 3 hours from Calais, and also provides easy access to most of the region all the way down to Troyes and Langres (via the A5). The A4 highway also links Reims to Paris and Alsace. Paris–Reims by the TGV high-speed train takes 45 minutes. Rail transport within the region is reasonably good, and so are the roads. To explore the wine-growing region, follow the signposted roads marked "Route de Champagne."

Windmill at Verzenay, Parc Naturel de la Montagne de Reims

For additional map symbols *see back flap*

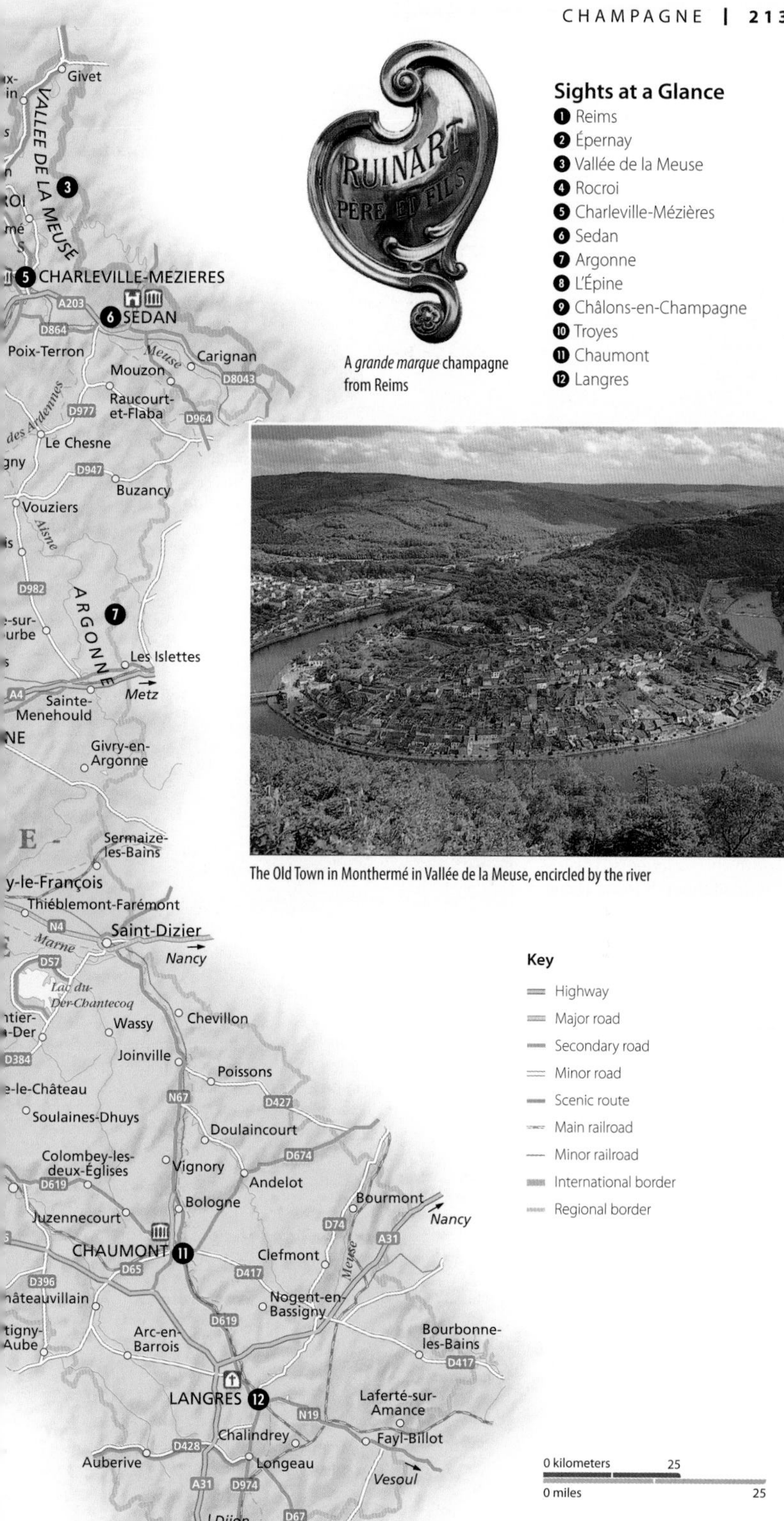

A *grande marque* champagne from Reims

Sights at a Glance

1. Reims
2. Épernay
3. Vallée de la Meuse
4. Rocroi
5. Charleville-Mézières
6. Sedan
7. Argonne
8. L'Épine
9. Châlons-en-Champagne
10. Troyes
11. Chaumont
12. Langres

The Old Town in Monthermé in Vallée de la Meuse, encircled by the river

Key

- Highway
- Major road
- Secondary road
- Minor road
- Scenic route
- Main railroad
- Minor railroad
- International border
- Regional border

0 kilometers 25

0 miles 25

Interior of Basilique St-Remi, Reims

❶ Reims

Marne. 185,000.
12 boulevard de General Leclerc (03 26 77 45 18). daily. **reims-tourisme.com**

Pronounced like the French word "prince" without the "p", Reims is home to some of the best known *grandes marques* in Champagne, and several are grouped around the Basilique St-Remi. But the city has another, much earlier, claim to fame: since the 11th century, all the kings of France have come to this "city of coronations" to be crowned in its remarkable Gothic **Cathédrale Notre-Dame** *(see pp216–17)*.

Although World War II bombing destroyed much of Reims' architectural coherence, there are some remarkable monuments here. The **Cryptoportique**, part of the forum, and Porte Mars, a triumphal Augustan arch, recall the Roman past. In 1945, the German surrender was taken in the **Musée de la Reddition** in Eisenhower's French HQ during World War II. **Musée des Beaux-Arts** houses a fine collection of 15th- and 16th-century canvases depicting biblical scenes, portraits by the Cranachs, *The Death of Marat* by David, and more than 20 landscapes by Corot. Also here are the Barbizons, Impressionists, and modern masters.

In 1996 Reims celebrated the 1,500-year anniversary of the baptism of Clovis, first King of the Franks, in its cathedral.

Ancien Collège des Jésuites & Planetarium

1 pl Museux. **Tel** 03 26 35 34 70. **Collège** (Planetarium).

Founded in 1606, this college was a hospice until 1976. Nowadays its 18th-century vines, Romanesque wine cellars, and Baroque interior play their part as atmospheric movie sets, notably for the film of Zola's *Germinal* (1992) and *Queen Margot* (1993). Highlights include the refectory's ceiling and the kitchen, the only room where fireplaces were permitted in an austere Jesuit establishment. A double spiral staircase leads to a Baroque library with yet another magnificent ceiling. Housed in the same building since 1979 is the **Planetarium**, with views of the sky from everywhere in the world.

Basilique St-Remi

Pl St-Rémi. **Open** daily.

This Benedictine abbey church, the oldest church in Reims, began as a Carolingian basilica dedicated to Saint Rémi (440–533). Inside, an Early Gothic choir and radiating chapels can be seen, as well as sculpted Romanesque capitals in the north transept.

Porte Mars, a reminder of Reims in Roman times

Methode Champenoise

To produce its characteristic bubbles, champagne has to undergo a process of double fermentation. **First fermentation:** The base wine, made from rather acidic grapes, is fermented at 68–72°F in either stainless steel tanks or, occasionally, in oak barrels. It is then siphoned off from the sediment and kept at colder temperatures to clear completely, before being drawn off and blended with wines from other areas and years (except in the case of vintage champagne). The wine is bottled and the *liqueur de tirage* (sugar, wine, and yeast) is added. **Second fermentation:** The bottles are stored for a year or more in cool, chalky cellars. The yeast converts the sugar to alcohol and carbon dioxide, which produces the sparkle, and the yeast cells die leaving a deposit. To remove this, the inverted bottles are turned and tapped daily *(remuage)* to shift the deposits into the neck of the bottle. Finally, the deposits are expelled by the process known as *dégorgement*, and a bit of sugar syrup *(liqueur d'expédition)* is added to adjust the sweetness before the final cork is inserted.

Champagne Mumm of Reims

Musée St-Remi

53 rue Simon. **Tel** 03 26 35 36 90. **Open** daily pm only. **Closed** Jan 1, May 1, Jul 14, Nov 1 & 11, Dec 25.

Set in the former abbey, the adjoining museum encloses the original Gothic chapter-house within its cloistered 17th-century shell. On display are archeological artifacts, 15th-century tapestries depicting the life of Saint Remi, and a collection of weapons dating from the 16th–19th centuries.

Fort de la Pompelle

5 miles (8 km) southeast of Reims. **Tel** 03 26 49 11 85. **Open** Wed–Mon.

Built to protect Reims after the Franco-Prussian War, this fort houses a museum of German imperial military headgear.

2 Épernay

Marne. 25,000. 7 av de Champagne (03 26 53 33 00). daily. **ot-epernay.fr**

The sole reason for visiting Épernay is to burrow into the chalky *caves* and taste the champagne. This rather undistinguished town lives off the fruits of its profitable champagne industry. As proof, the

Statue of Dom Perignon at Moët

avenue de Champagne quarter abounds in mock-Renaissance mansions. **Moët & Chandon**, dating back to 1743, is the largest and slickest *maison*, the star of the Moët-Hennessy stable. Its cellars stretch some 18 miles (28 km) underground.

The group also owns other champagne houses, such as Mercier, Krug, Pommery, Veuve Clicquot, and Canard Duchêne. There is little to choose between a visit to the cellars of Moët & Chandon or **Mercier** – both are in Avenue de Champagne. Mercier has the distinction of displaying a giant tun (cask) created for the 1889 Paris Exhibition, and takes you through the *caves* in an electric train.

De Castellane offers a more personalized tour, accompanied by a heady *dégustation*.

Moët & Chandon

20 av de Champagne. **Tel** 03 26 51 20 20. **Open** end Mar–mid-Nov: daily; mid-Nov–Dec, Feb–end Mar: Mon–Fri. only. **moet.com**

Mercier

70 av de Champagne. **Tel** 03 26 51 22 22. **Open** mid-Mar–Nov: daily; Dec–mid-Mar: Thu–Mon. oblig. **champagnemercier.com**

De Castellane

57 rue de Verdun. **Tel** 03 26 51 19 19. **Open** daily (Jan–Mar: Sat & Sun only). restr. oblig. **castellane.com**

Dégorgement is the final removal of the yeast deposits from the bottle. The neck of the bottle is plunged in freezing brine and the frozen block of sediment is then removed.

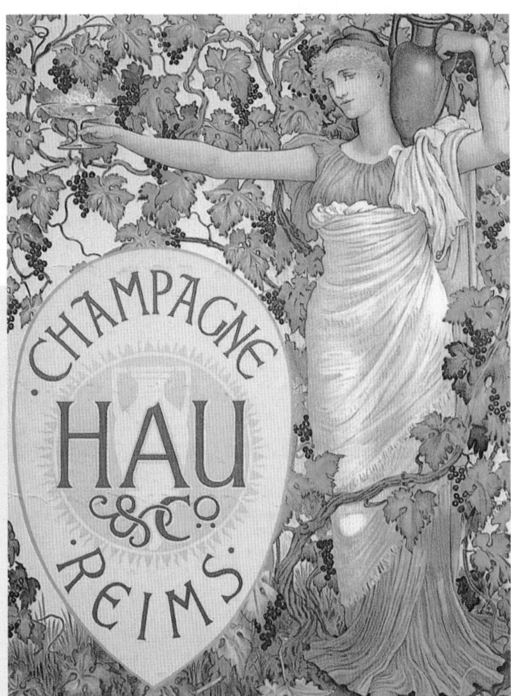

Seductive marketing of champagne since the 19th century has ensured its continuing success.

The bubbles in champagne are produced during the second fermentation. Champagnes, especially vintage ones, improve with aging.

Reims Cathedral

The magnificent Gothic Cathédrale Notre-Dame at Reims is noted for its monumentality. A cathedral has stood on this site since 401, but the present building was begun in 1211. Reims has been the backdrop for coronations from medieval times till 1825, when Charles X was crowned. The coronation of Charles VII here in 1429 was attended by Joan of Arc.

During the Revolution, the rood screen and windows were destroyed but the stonework survived. World War I damage was fully restored in 1996, to coincide with the 1,500th anniversary of the baptism of Clovis, King of the Franks, at Reims, which was considered the first coronation of a French king.

The Nave
Compared with the nave at Chartres *(see pp312–13)*, Reims is taller. Its elegant capitals are decorated with naturalistic floral motifs such as ivy and berries.

★ Great Rose Window
Best seen at sunset, the 13th-century window shows the Virgin surrounded by the apostles and angel musicians. It is set within a larger window, a feature common in 13th-century architecture.

WEST FACADE

SOUTH FACADE

KEY

① **South transept**

② **The clerestory windows** pioneered Gothic tracery by dividing the lights with slender bars of stone, creating a decorative, intersecting pattern.

③ **The radiating chapels** of the apse are supported by flying buttresses and adorned with octagonal pinnacles.

④ **Pinnacles** on the flying buttresses shelter guardian angels, symbolic protectors of the cathedral.

★ Smiling Angel
Rich in statuary, Reims is often called "the cathedral of angels." Situated above the left (north) portal, this enigmatic angel with unfurled wings is the most celebrated of the many that grace the building.

★ Gallery of the Kings
The harmonious west facade, decorated with over 2,300 statues is the most notable feature at Reims. Fifty-six stone effigies of French kings form the Gallery of the Kings.

Palais du Tau

The archbishop's palace adjoining the cathedral is named after its T-shaped design, based on early episcopal crosses. (Tau is Greek for T.) The palace, built in 1690 by Mansart and Robert de Cotte, encloses a Gothic Chapel and the 15th-century Salle du Tau, rooms associated with French coronations. On the eve of a coronation, the future king would spend the night in the palace. After being crowned in the cathedral, he held a magnificent banquet in the palace. The Salle du Tau, or banqueting hall, is the finest room in the palace, with a magnificent barrel-vaulted ceiling and walls hung with 15th-century Arras tapestries. The palace now houses a museum of statuary and tapestries from the cathedral, including a 15th-century tapestry of the baptism of Clovis, the first Christian king.

Salle du Tau – the banqueting hall

VISITORS' CHECKLIST

Practical Information
Cathédrale Notre-Dame,pl du Cardinal Luçon. **Tel** 03 26 47 55 34. **Open** 7:30am–7:30pm daily. 8am & 7pm Mon, Wed, Fri, 8am Tue, Thu, Sat, 9:30am & 11am Sun. by appt only.
cathedrale-reims.com
Palais du Tau: **Tel** 03 26 47 81 79. **Open** Tue–Sun. **Closed** Jan 1, May 1, Nov 1 & 11, Dec 25.

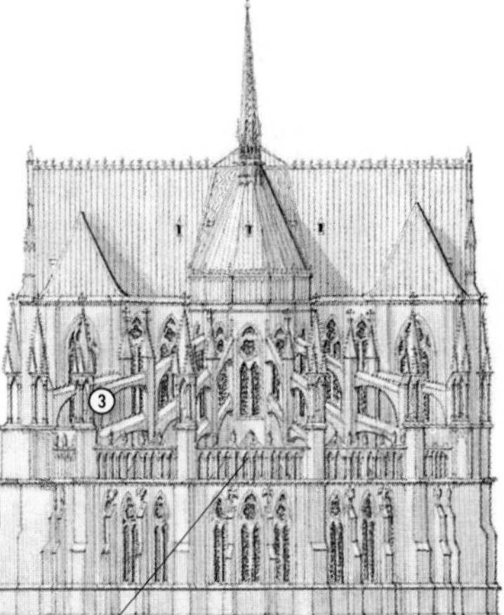

APSE

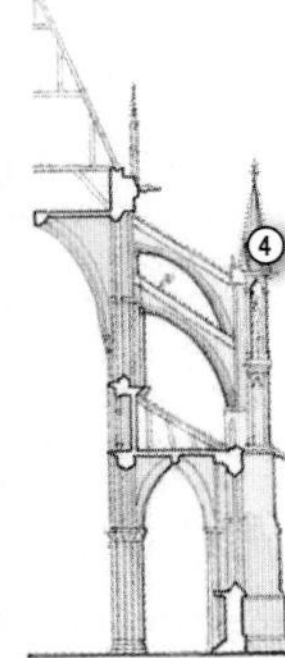

SIDE SECTION

Apse Gallery
The restored *claire-voie* (open work) gallery on the apse is crowned by statues of mythological beasts.

Chagall Window
The windows in the axial chapel were designed by the 20th-century artist Marc Chagall and made by local craftsmen. This one depicts the Crucifixion and the Sacrifice of Isaac.

The *sentier touristique*, a walk along the ramparts of Rocroi

❸ Vallée de la Meuse

Ardennes. 8,900. Revin. 65 quai Edgar Quinet, Revin (03 24 40 19 59). **tourisme-meuse.com**

The Meuse meanders through the Ardennes among spectacular scenery of wild gorges, woods, and warped rock formations of granite or schist.

Dramatically situated on a double meander of the Meuse, **Revin** is an unremarkable town in an exceptional site, with the Vieille Ville enfolded in the north bend. From the quay, you can see wooded **Mont Malgré Tout** and a route dotted with observation points and steep trails. Just south is **Dames de la Meuse**, a rocky outcrop over the river gorge.

Monthermé lies on two banks, with the Vieille Ville clustered on the charming left bank. The rocky gorges around **Roche à Sept Heures** on the far bank entice climbers and ramblers. The jagged crest of **Rocher des Quatre Fils d'Aymon** suggests the silhouette of four legendary local horsemen.

❹ Rocroi

Ardennes. 2,430. Revin. 14 pl d'Armes (03 24 54 20 06). Tue & first Mon of month. **otrocroi.com**

Set on the Ardennes plateau, the star-shaped citadel of Rocroi was originally built under Henri II in 1555, and later made impregnable by Vauban in 1675 *(see p226)*. The main attraction is the walk along the ramparts from the southern gateway. The nature reserve at Rièzes is home to orchids and carnivorous plants.

❺ Charleville-Mézières

Ardennes. 58,000. 4 pl Ducale (03 24 55 69 90). Tue, Thu & Sat. **charleville-tourisme.com**

This riverside ford was originally two towns. The somber medieval citadel of Mézières only merged with the neat Classical town of Charleville in 1966. Mézières has irregular slate-covered houses curving around a bend in the Meuse. Battered fortifications and gateways are visible from avenue de St-Julien. Tucked into the ramparts is the much remodeled Gothic **Notre-Dame de l'Espérance**.

The centerpiece of Charleville is **place Ducale**, a model of Louis XIII urban planning, echoing place des Vosges in Paris *(see p91)*. The poet Arthur Rimbaud was born nearby in 1854. His modest birthplace at No. 12 rue Bérégovoy is still there, along with his childhoo home on the Meuse at 7 quai Arthur Rimbaud.

Just along the quayside is th Vieux Moulin, the town house whose view inspired *Le Bateau Ivre*, Rimbaud's greatest poem. Inside is the small **Musée Rimbaud**, with manuscripts an photographs by the poet.

Musée Rimbaud
Quai Arthur Rimbaud. **Tel** 03 24 32 44 65. **Open** Tue–Sun. **Closed** Jan 1, May Dec 25. (free first Sun of month).

❻ Sedan

Ardennes. 20,000. 32 rue du Menil (03 24 27 73 73). We & Sat. **tourisme-sedan.fr**

Just to the east of Charleville is the **Château de Sedan**, the largest fortified castle in Europe There has been a bastion on these slopes since the 11th century, but each Ardennes conflict has spelt a new tier of defences for Sedan.

In 1870, during the Franco-Prussian War, with 700 Prussian cannons turned on Sedan, Napoleon III surrendered and 83,000 French prisoners were deported to Prussia. In May 1940 after capturing Sedan, German forces reached the French coast a week later.

The seven-storied bastion contains sections dating from medieval times to the 16th

The 19th-century poet Rimbaud, whose birthplace was Charleville

century. Highlights of any visit are the ramparts, the 16th-century fortifications and the magnificent 15th-century eaves in one tower. The **Musée du Château**, in the south wing, is rather jumbled, with a section on military campaigns.

The bastion is surrounded by 17th-century slate-roofed houses which hug the banks of the Meuse. These reflect the city's earlier prosperity as a Huguenot stronghold.

Musée du Château
1 pl du Château. **Tel** 03 24 27 73 73. **Open** Jul & Aug: daily; Sep–mid-Mar: Tue–Sun. Tue–Fri pms.

Environs
Farther south is **Fort de Villy-la-Ferté**, one of the few forts on the Maginot line to have been captured in devastating combat with the enemy in 1940.

Courtyard inside the heavily fortified Château de Sedan

Gargoyle on Basilique de Notre-Dame de l'Epine

7 Argonne

Ardennes & Meuse. Châlons. Ste-Menehould. 5 pl du Général Leclerc, Ste-Menehould (03 26 60 85 83). **argonne.fr**

East of Reims, the Argonne is a compact region of picturesque valleys and forests, dotted with priories, trenches, and war cemeteries.

As a wooded border between the rival bishoprics of Champagne and Lorraine, the Argonne was home to abbeys and priories. Now ruined, the Benedictine abbey of **Beaulieu-en-Argonne** boasts a 13th-century wine press and has forest views. Just north is **Les Islettes**, known for its faïence pottery and tiles. The hilly terrain here was a battleground during the Franco-Prussian War and World War I. The disputed territory of **Butte de Vauquois**, north of Les Islettes, bears a war memorial.

8 L'Épine

Marne. 670. Châlons. 33 av du Luxembourg, Mairie (03 26 66 96 99).

L'Épine is worth visiting if only for a glimpse of the **Basilique de Notre-Dame de l'Épine** surrounded by wheatfields. Designed on the scale of a cathedral, this 15th-century Flamboyant Gothic church has been a pilgrimage site since medieval times. Even French kings have come here to venerate a "miraculous" statue of the Virgin.

On the facade, three gabled portals are offset by floating tracery, a gauzy effect reminiscent of Reims cathedral. All around are gruesome gargoyles, symbolizing evil spirits and deadly sins, chased out by the holy presence within. Unfortunately, the most risqué sculptures were destroyed, judged obscene by 19th- century puritans. The subdued Gothic interior contains a 15th-century rood-screen and the venerated statue of the Virgin.

Champagne Timber Churches

Skirting Lac du Der-Chantecoq lies a region of woodland and water meadows, containing twelve Romanesque and Renaissance half-timbered churches with curious pointed gables and *caquetoirs*, rickety wooden porches. They have intimate and often beautifully carved interiors with stained-glass windows designed in the vivid colors of the School of Troyes. Rural roads link churches at Bailly-le-Franc, Chatillon-sur-Broué, Lentilles, Vignory, Outines, Chavanges, and Montier-en-Der.

16th-century timber church in Lentilles

9 Châlons-en-Champagne

Marne. 48,000. 3 quai des Arts (03 26 65 17 89). Wed, Fri am, Sat, Sun am. **chalons-tourisme.com**

Encircled by the river Marne and minor canals, Châlons' sleepy bourgeois charm is made up of half-timbered houses and gardens mirrored in canals. Nearby are vineyards producing Blanc de Blancs.

From quai de Notre-Dame there are views of old bridges and the Romanesque towers of **Notre-Dame-en-Vaux**, a masterpiece of Romanesque-Gothic. Behind the church is a well-restored medieval quarter and the **Musée du Cloître**, containing the original Romanesque cloisters.

Cathédrale St-Etienne, by the canal, is a cool Gothic affair with a Baroque portal, Romanesque crypt, and vivid medieval windows. Beyond is **Le Petit Jard**, riverside gardens overlooking the Château du Marché, and a turreted toll gate built by Henri IV. Excellent river tours of the city are available from the tourist office.

Musée du Cloître de Notre-Dame-en-Vaux

Rue Nicolas Durand. **Tel** 03 26 69 38 53. **Open** Wed–Mon. **Closed** Jan 1, May 1, Nov 1 & 11, Dec 25.

10 Troyes

Aube. 63,000. 16 bd Carnot (08 92 22 46 09). daily. **tourisme-troyes.com**

Troyes is a delight, a city of magnificent Gothic churches and charming 16th-century courtyards, in a historical center shaped like a champagne cork. The city is famous for its heritage of stained glass and sausages *(andouillettes)*, its knitwear industry and factory shops.

The battered Flamboyant Gothic west front of the **Cathédrale St-Pierre-et-St-Paul** opens on to a splendid vaulted interior. The nave is bathed in mauvish-red rays from the 16th-century rose window, complemented by the discreet turquoise of the Tree of Jesse window, and the intense blue of the medieval windows of the apse.

Statuary in Troyes' Cathédrale St-Pierre-et-St-Paul

Nearby, **Eglise St-Nizier** glitters in the faded quarter behind the cathedral with its shimmering tiled Burgundian roof. Inside, it is lit by windows in a range of warm mauves and soothing blues.

The Gothic **Basilique St-Urbain** boasts grand flying buttresses and particularly fine 13th-century windows. **Eglise Ste-Madeleine** is noted for its elaborate 16th-century rood screen resembling lacey foliage, grapes, and figs. Beyond is a wall of windows in browns, reds, and blues. The ruelle des Chats, which is a quaint covered passageway, connects rue Charbonnet and rue Champeaux.

Rue Larivey, a typical street with half-timbered houses, in Troyes

Set in one of the best-preserved quarters, **Eglise St-Pantaléon** faces a Renaissance mansion. A Gothic and Renaissance interior houses an imposing collection of 16th-century statuary and severe *grisaille* windows.

Musée d'Art Moderne

14 pl St-Pierre. **Tel** 03 25 76 26 80. **Open** Tue–Sun. **Closed** public hols.

Beside the cathedral, the former episcopal palace is now a museum of modern art, with a sculpture by Rodin and an especially fine collection of Fauvist paintings, as well as other modern art.

Hôtel du Petit Louvre

Rue de la Montée St-Pierre. Courtyard only **Open** daily.

Set off quai Dampierre, this well restored *hôtel particulier* boasts a fish-scale roof, medieval tower, Renaissance courtyard, staircase, and well. The highlight is a facade adorned with quizzical multicolored faces.

For hotels and restaurants in this region see pp554–71 and pp576–603

Environs
The city's green playground, **Lac et Forêt d'Orient**, is 15 miles (25 km) east of Troyes. The forest is dotted with marshes, nature reserves and smaller lakes. Lac d'Orient, the largest artificial lake in Europe, is popular for sailing, with water-skiing on Lac Amance, and fishing at Lac du Temple.

⓫ Chaumont

Haute-Marne. 26,000.
37 rue de Verdun (03 25 03 80 80). Wed & Sat. **tourisme-chaumont-champagne.com**

As the former residence of the Counts of Champagne, this feudal town enjoyed great prestige in the 13th century. On the far side of a ravine, the old town is on a rocky spur, with the Palais de Justice and the medieval castle keep dominating.

The keep is a reminder that this quiet administrative center had a formidable past. This impression is confirmed by the Renaissance town houses which are bulging with *tourelles d'escaliers*, turreted staircases.

Basilique St-Jean-Baptiste, a gray-stone Champenois church, is the most remarkable monument in Chaumont. The interior is enlivened by a spider's web of vaulting, a striking turreted staircase, and Renaissance galleries. Near the entrance is a tiny chapel containing an unsettling *Mise au Tombeau* (1471), an intense multicolored stone group of 10 mourners gathered around Christ laid out on a shroud in his tomb. In the left transept is a bizarre but beguiling *Tree of Jesse*. On this ill-lit Renaissance stone relief, a family tree sprouts from the sleeping Jesus.

Environs
Fourteen miles (23 km) northwest of Chaumont, **Colombey-les-Deux-Eglises** will forever be associated with General Charles de Gaulle (1890–1970). The de Gaulles bought their home, **La Boisserie**, in 1933, but had to abandon it during the war,

Cathédrale St-Mammès in Langres

when it was badly damaged. After its restoration, de Gaulle would return to La Boisserie from Paris at weekends to write his memoirs. He died here on November 9, 1970. The house is now a museum.

In the village churchyard, the General lies in a simple tomb, but a giant granite cross of Lorraine, erected in 1972, dominates the skyline. At its foot is the **Mémorial**, a museum dedicated to de Gaulle's life.

La Boisserie
Colombey-les-Deux-Eglises. **Tel** 03 25 01 52 52. **Open** mid-Apr–mid-Oct: daily; mid-Oct–mid-Apr: Wed–Mon.

Mémorial Charles de Gaulle
Tel 03 25 30 90 80. **Open** May–Sep: daily; Oct–Apr: Wed–Mon.
memorial-charlesdegaulle.fr

⓬ Langres

Haute-Marne. 9,000. square Olivier Lahalle (03 25 87 67 67). Fri. **tourisme-langres.com**

Set on a rocky spur, Langres lies beyond Chaumont, in the backwaters of southern Champagne. This ancient bishopric was one of the gateways to Burgundy and the birthplace of the encyclopedist, Denis Diderot (1713–84). Langres promotes itself as a land of springs, claiming that its proximity to the sources of the Seine and Marne grant it mystical powers.

Virtually the whole town is enclosed by medieval ramparts, Langres' undoubted attraction. A succession of towers and parapets provide glimpses of romantic town gates and sculpted Renaissance mansions, with panoramic views of the Marne valley, the Langres plateau, the Vosges, and, on a clear day, even Mont Blanc.

Near Porte Henri IV is the much-remodeled **Cathédrale St-Mammès**. The gloomy vaulted interior, in Burgundian Romanesque style, is redeemed by the sculpted capitals in the apse, reputedly taken from a temple of Jupiter. The town's Musée d'Art et d'Histoire has some interesting collections.

Langres' lively summer season includes historical re-enactments, theater, and fireworks.

Memorial to General de Gaulle at Colombey-les-Deux-Eglises

ALSACE AND LORRAINE

Meurthe-et-Moselle · Meuse · Moselle · Bas-Rhin · Haut-Rhin · Vosges

As border regions, Alsace and Lorraine have been fought over for centuries by France, Austria, and Germany, their beleaguered past recalled by many a military stronghold and cemetery. Today, the region presents only a peaceful aspect with pastel-painted villages, fortified towns, and sleepy vineyards.

At the northeast frontier of France, bordered by the Rhine, Alsace forms a fertile watershed between the mountains of the Vosges and the Black Forest in Germany. Lorraine, with its rolling landscape on the other side of the mountains, is the poorer cousin but is more overtly French in character.

Embattled Territory

Caught in the wars between France and Germany, Alsace and part of Lorraine have changed nationality four times since 1871. Centuries of strife have made border citadels of Metz, Toul, and Verdun in Lorraine, while Alsace abounds with castles, from the faithfully reconstructed Haut-Koenigsbourg to Saverne's ruined fortress, built to guard a strategic pass in the Vosges. However, the area has a strong identity of its own, taking pride in local costumes, traditions, and dialects. In Alsace, Route des Vins vineyards nudge pretty villages in the Vosges foothills. Strasbourg, the capital, is a cosmopolitan city with a 16th-century center, while Nancy, Lorraine's historical capital, represents elegant 18th-century architecture.

Much of the attraction of this region lies in its cuisine. Lorraine offers beer and quiche lorraine. In Alsace, cozy *winstubs*, or wine cellars, serve sauerkraut and flowery white wines, such as Riesling and Gewürztraminer. There are also fine restaurants here.

Villagers enjoying the view from their window in Hunspach, north of Strasbourg in the northern Vosges

◀ Half-timbered houses lining the canals of Petite Venise, Colmar

Exploring Alsace and Lorraine

Visitors seeking art and architecture will be amply rewarded by the charming medieval towns and excellent city museums of the region. Undiscovered Lorraine is the place to clamber over military citadels, walk in unspoiled countryside, and unwind at relaxing spas. By contrast, Alsace offers magnificent forests and rugged mountain drives in the Vosges, quaint villages, and rich wines. The Route des Vins *(see pp236–7)* is one of the region's many scenic routes. It is particularly popular during the wine harvest festivities but is worth visiting in any season.

Sights at a Glance

1. Verdun
2. Toul
3. Metz
4. Nancy
5. Gérardmer
6. Mulhouse
7. Guebwiller
8. Neuf-Brisach
9. Eguisheim
10. Colmar
11. Riquewihr
12. Ribeauvillé
13. Château du Haut-Koenigsbourg
14. Sélestat
15. Obernai
16. Strasbourg
17. Saverne
18. Betschdorf

Field of sunflowers just outside the village of Turckheim

For additional map symbols *see back flap*

The picturesque village of Riquewihr on the Route du Vin

Getting Around

There are good roads and rail links between Strasbourg, Colmar, Metz, and Nancy, and on to Switzerland and Germany. The main roads to and through the regions are the N4, A31, A35, A4 to Paris, and N59, and the tunnel under the Vosges. The spectacular journey over the Vosges and along the Route des Vins is best made by car or on organized trips from Colmar or Strasbourg. The TGV link to the region from Paris takes 2 hours 20 minutes.

Key

- Highway
- Major road
- Secondary road
- Minor road
- Scenic route
- Main railroad
- Minor railroad
- International border
- Regional border
- △ Summit

The Ossuaire de Douaumont, a sentinel for the regiments of crosses on the battlefields of Verdun

❶ Verdun

Meuse. 21,000. pl de la Nation (03 29 86 14 18). Fri.
verdun-tourisme.com

Verdun will be forever remembered for the horrors of the 1916–1917 Battle of Verdun, when about a million men died in almost a whole year of continuous bloodshed that is considered the worst single battle of the Great War. The Germans intended to strike a blow at French morale by destroying the forts of Douaumont and Vaux (which had been built to prevent a repeat of the humiliating French defeat of the Franco-Prussian War of 1870) and capture Verdun, France's northeastern stronghold. The French fought simply to prevent the town being taken. The stalemate and the killing continued here right up to the end of the war, and not until 1918 did the Germans draw back from their positions just 3 miles (5 km) from the town.

Several poignant museums, memorials, battle sites, and cemeteries can be visited in the hills just outside Verdun on the north side. In this devastated region, nine villages were obliterated without trace. The **Musée-Memorial de Fleury** tells their story. Nearby, the **Ossuaire de Douaumont** contains the unidentified bones of over 130,000 French and German dead. One of the most striking monuments to the Battle of Verdun is Rodin's memorial in Verdun itself. It depicts the winged figure of Victory unable to soar triumphant because she has become caught in the remains of a dead soldier.

The town of Verdun was heavily fortified over the centuries. The crenellated **Porte Chaussée**, a medieval river gateway, still guards the eastern entrance to the town and is the most impressive of the remaining fortifications.

Although battered by war damage, the **Citadelle de Verdun** retains its 12th-century tower, the only relic from the original abbey that Vauban incorporated into his new military design. Now a war museum, the **Citadelle Souterraine**, it recreates Verdun's role in WWI. The citadel casemates come to life as grim trenches, and the presentation ends by showing how the "Unknown Soldier" was chosen for the symbolic tomb under the Arc de Triomphe in Paris *(see p111)*.

The town center is dominated by the cathedral, where Romanesque elements were rediscovered after the 1916 bombardments.

The 16th-century cloisters of Eglise St-Gengoult in Toul

Citadelle Souterraine
Ave du 5ième R.A.P. **Tel** 03 29 84 84 42
Open daily. **Closed** Jan & Dec 25.

❷ Toul

Meurthe-et-Moselle. 16,500. 1 pl Charles de Gaulle (03 83 64 90 60). Wed, Fri & Sat.
lepredenancy.fr

Lying within dark forests west of Nancy, the octagonal fortress city of Toul is encircled by the Moselle and the Canal de la Marne. Along with Verdun and Metz, Toul was one of the 4th-century bishoprics. In the early 18th century, Vauban built the citadel, from which the ring of defensive waterways, the octagonal city ramparts, and the **Porte de Metz** remain.

The **Cathédrale St-Etienne**, begun in the 13th century, took over 300 years to build. It suffered damage in World War II but the purity of the Champenois style has survived, notably in the arched, high-galleried interior. The imposing Flamboyant Gothic facade is flanked by octagonal towers. Rue du Général-Gengoult, behind the Gothic **Eglise St-Gengoult**, contains a clutch of sculpted Renaissance houses. North of the city the local "gray" Côtes de Toul wines are produced.

Environs
South of Toul, near the town of Neufchâteau, is the birthplace of Joan of Arc at Domrémy-La-Pucelle. Next door to the house where she was born

s an exhibition about her emarkable life.

The vast **Parc Régional de orraine** takes in red-tiled ottages, vineyards, forests, ropland, *chaumes* (high pasture-and), marshes, and lakes. Inns in he area are especially noted for heir quiche lorraine nd *potée lorraine*, a acon casserole.

upiter Slaying a Monster on the Column of 1erten in La Cour d'Or

3 Metz

Aoselle. 125,000. pl d'Armes (03 87 55 53 76). Tue, Thu & Sat. **tourisme.metz.fr**

An austere yet appealing city, Metz sits at the confluence of the Moselle and the Seille. Twenty bridges crisscross the rivers and canals, and there are pleasant walks along the banks. This Gallo-Roman city, now the capital of Lorraine, has always been a pawn n the game of border chess – annexed by Germany in 1871, regained by France in 1918.

Set on a hill above the Moselle, the **Cathédrale St-Etienne** overlooks the historic center. nside, there are stained-glass windows, including some by Chagall.

To the northwest of the cathedral, a narrow wooden bridge leads across to the island of Petit Saulcy, site of the oldest French theater still in use. Located on the other side of the cathedral, the **Porte des Allemands**, spanning a river, more resembles a medieval castle because of its bridge, defensive towers and 13th-century gate with pepper-pot towers.

In the Vieille Ville, place St-Louis is a delightful square bordered by arcaded 14th-century mansions. **Eglise St-Pierre-aux-Nonnains** claims to be one of France's oldest churches. The external walls and facade date from Roman times, while much of the rest belongs to the 7th century. Nearby is the 13th-century **Chapelle des Templiers**, built by the Knights Templar.

Centre Pompidou Metz

1 parvis des Droits de l'Homme. **Tel** 03 87 15 39 39. **Open** Wed–Mon. **Closed** May 1.

This museum is an annex to the Centre Pompidou in Paris *(see pp96–7)*. Modern European art is displayed inside an unusual hexagonal building.

Musée de la Cour d'Or

2 rue du Haut-Poirier. **Tel** 03 87 20 13 20. **Open** Wed–Mon. **Closed** public hols.

Also known as the Musée d'Art et d'Histoire, this is set in the Petits-Carmes, a deconsecrated 17th-century monastery incorporating Gallo-Roman baths and a medieval barn. On display are Merovingian stone carvings; Gothic painted ceilings, and a variety of German, Flemish, and French paintings.

White Storks

The white stork, traditionally a symbol of good fortune in Alsace, used to be a frequent sight in northeast France. White storks spend the winter in Africa but migrate north to breed. However, the gradual draining of marshy ground, pesticides, and electric cables have threatened their survival here. A program to reintroduce them to the area has set up breeding centers, as at Molsheim and Turckheim, which means these striking birds can once again be seen in Alsace-Lorraine.

The 13th-century Chapelle des Templiers, with restored frescoes, in Metz

Place Stanislas in Nancy, with statue of Stanislas Leczinski, Duke of Lorraine and father-in-law of Louis XV

4 Nancy

Meurthe-et-Moselle. 108,000. 14 pl Stanislas (03 83 35 22 41). Tue–Sat. **ot-nancy.fr**

Lorraine's historic capital backs on to the Canal du Marne and the river Meurthe. In the 18th century, Stanislas Leczinski, Duke of Lorraine *(see p306)*, transformed the city, making it a model of 18th-century town planning.

Nancy's second golden age was the turn of this century, when glassmaker Emile Gallé founded the Ecole de Nancy, a forerunner of the Art Nouveau movement in France.

Nancy's principal and most renowned landmark is **place Stanislas**. Laid out in the 1750s, this elegantly proportioned square is enclosed by highly ornate gilded wrought-iron gates and railings, which have been beautifully restored. Lining the square are fine *hôtels particuliers* (town houses) and chic restaurants.

An Arc de Triomphe leads to Place de la Carrière, a gracious, tree-lined square. At the far end, flanked by semicircular arcades, is the Gothic **Palais du Gouvernement**. Next door in the Parc de la Pépinière is Rodin's statue of Claude Lorrain, the landscape painter, born near Nancy.

The Grande Rue provides a glimpse of medieval Nancy. Of the original fortifications only the Porte de la Craffe remains, which was used as a prison after the Revolution.

Eglise et Couvent des Cordeliers et Musée Régional des Arts et Traditions Populaires

64 & 66 grande rue. **Tel** 03 83 32 18 74. **Open** Tue–Sun. **Closed** Jan 1, Easter Sun, May 1, Jul 14, Nov 1, Dec 25.

The Dukes of Lorraine are buried in the crypt, and the adjoining converted monastery contains the Musée Régional des Arts et Traditions Populaires, covering folklore, furniture, costumes, and crafts.

Musée des Beaux-Arts

3 pl Stanislas. **Tel** 03 83 85 30 72. **Open** Wed–Mon. **Closed** some public hols.

A renovation and modern extension have enabled 40 percent more of the museum's remarkable collection of 14th- to 20th-century European art to be seen, including works by Delacroix, Manet, Monet, Utrillo, and Modigliani. The Daum glassware is stunning.

Musée Historique Lorraine

Palais Ducal, 64 grande rue. **Tel** 03 83 32 18 74. **Open** Tue–Sun. **Closed** Jan 1, May 1, Jul 14, Nov 1, Dec 25.

The Museum of the History of Lorraine has a rich collection of archeological finds, sculptures, and paintings, including two by Georges de la Tour.

Musée de l'Ecole de Nancy

36–38 rue de Sergent Blandan. **Tel** 03 83 40 14 86. **Open** Wed–Sun. **Closed** Jan 1, May 1, July 14, Nov 1, Dec 25.

Exhibits in reconstructed Art Nouveau settings include furniture, fabrics, and jewelry, as well as the fanciful glassware of Emile Gallé, founder of the Ecole de Nancy.

Arc de Triomphe in place Stanislas, leading to place de la Carrière

Vosges landscape seen from the Route des Crêtes

The Route des Crêtes

This strategic mountain road, 83 km (50 miles) long, connects the Vosges valleys from Col du Bonhomme to Cernay, east of Thann, often through woodland. Hugging the western side of the Vosges, the Route des Crêtes was created during World War I to prevent the Germans from observing French troop movements. When not shrouded in mist, there are breathtaking views over Lorraine from its many "ridges" *(crêtes)*.

5 Gérardmer

Vosges. 10,000. 4 pl des Déportés (03 29 27 27 27). Thu & Sat. **gerardmer.net**

Nestling on the Lorraine side of the Vosges, on the shore of a magnificent lake stretching out before it, Gérardmer is a setting rather than a city. In November 1944, just before its liberation, Gérardmer was razed by the Nazi scorched-earth policy, but has since been reconstructed. Saw mills and wood-carving remain local trades, though tourism is fast replacing the textile industry.

Gérardmer is now a popular holiday resort. In winter, the steep slopes of the Vosges Cristallines around the town turn it into a ski resort, while the lake is used for watersports in summer. The town's attractions also include lake-side walks and boat trips, as well as Géromée cheese, similar to the more famous Munster, from just over the Alsatian border. Gérardmer also boasts the oldest tourist information office in the country, dating from 1875.

The scenic drives and mountain hikes in the Vosges attract adventurous visitors. Most leave the lakeside bowl to head for the Alsatian border and the magnificent **Route des Crêtes**, which can be joined at the mountain pass of Col de la Schlucht.

The lake at Gérardmer, offering sporting and leisure activities

Recreating village crafts in Ecomusée d'Alsace in Ungersheim

6 Mulhouse

Haut Rhin. 115,000. 1 av Robert Schuman (03 89 35 48 48). Tue, Thu & Sat. **tourisme-mulhouse.com**

Close to the Swiss border, Mulhouse is an industrial city, which was badly damaged in World War II. However, there are technical museums and shopping galleries, as well as Alsatian taverns and Swiss wine bars. Most visitors use the city as a base for exploring the rolling hills of the Sundgau on the Swiss border.

Of the museums, **Musée de l'Impression sur Etoffes**, at 14 rue Jean-Jaques Henner, is devoted to textiles and fabric painting, while **Musée Français du Chemin de Fer**, at 2 rue Alfred Glehn, has a collection of steam and electric locomotives. A revamped **Musée National de l'Automobile**, at 192 avenue de Colmar, boasts over 100 Bugattis, a clutch of Mercedes and Ferraris, and Charlie Chaplin's Rolls Royce. In Place de la République is the **Musée Historique**, in the Renaissance former town hall.

Alsatian black pig in Ecomusée d'Alsace in Ungersheim

Environs

At Ungersheim, north of Mulhouse, the **Ecomusée d'Alsace** displays and preserves the region's rural heritage. The 12th-century fortified house from Mulhouse is a dramatic building, complete with Gothic garden. Farms are run along traditional lines, with livestock such as the Alsatian black pig. Rural crafts can be seen in their original settings.

Ecomusée d'Alsace
Chemin du Grosswald. **Tel** 03 89 74 44 74. **Open** Apr–Oct & Dec: daily.

7 Guebwiller

Haut Rhin. 12,000. 71 rue de la République (03 89 76 10 63). Tue & Fri. **tourisme-guebwiller.fr**

Surrounded by vineyards and flower-filled valleys, Guebwiller is known as "the gate-way to the valley of flowers." However, as an industrial town producing textiles and machine tools, it feels cut off from this rural setting. The *caves* and churches make it worth a visit.

Set on a pretty square, **Eglise Notre-Dame** combines Baroque theatricality with Neo-Classical elegance, while **Eglise des Dominicains** boasts Gothic frescoes and a fine rood screen. **Eglise St-Léger**, the richly decorated Romanesque church, is the most rewarding, especially the facade, triple porch, and portal.

Eglise St-Léger in Guebwiller

Environs

The scenic Lauch valley, north-west of Guebwiller, is known as "Le Florival" because of its floral aspect. **Lautenbach** is used as a starting point for hikes through this recognized *zone de tranquillité*. The village has a pink Romanesque church, whose portal depicts human passion and the battle between Good and Evil. The square leads to the river, a small weir, *lavoir* (public washing place), and houses overhanging the water.

8 Neuf-Brisach

Haut Rhin. 2,100. Palais du Gouverneur, 6 pl d'Armes (03 89 72 17 65). Sat. **tourisme-paysdebrisach.com**

Situated near the German border, this octagonal citadel is the military strategist Vauban's masterpiece. Built between 1698 and 1707, the citadel forms a typical starshaped pattern, with symmetrical towers enclosing 48 equal squares. In the center, from where straight streets radiate for ease of defense, is the

The Citadel of Neuf-Brisach

The outer ring of defenses was built around two moats.
Porte de Bâle
Place d'Armes, once the parade ground, provided the innermost refuge.
Porte de Strasbourg was originally protected by a draw-bridge.
Bastion
The fortress is divided into 48 ilôts or squares.
The fortress walls are 30 ft (9 m) high and 14.5 ft (4.5 m) wide at their base.
The Porte de Belfort houses the Musée Vauban. A walk links Porte de Belfort with Porte de Colmar.
Porte de Colmar

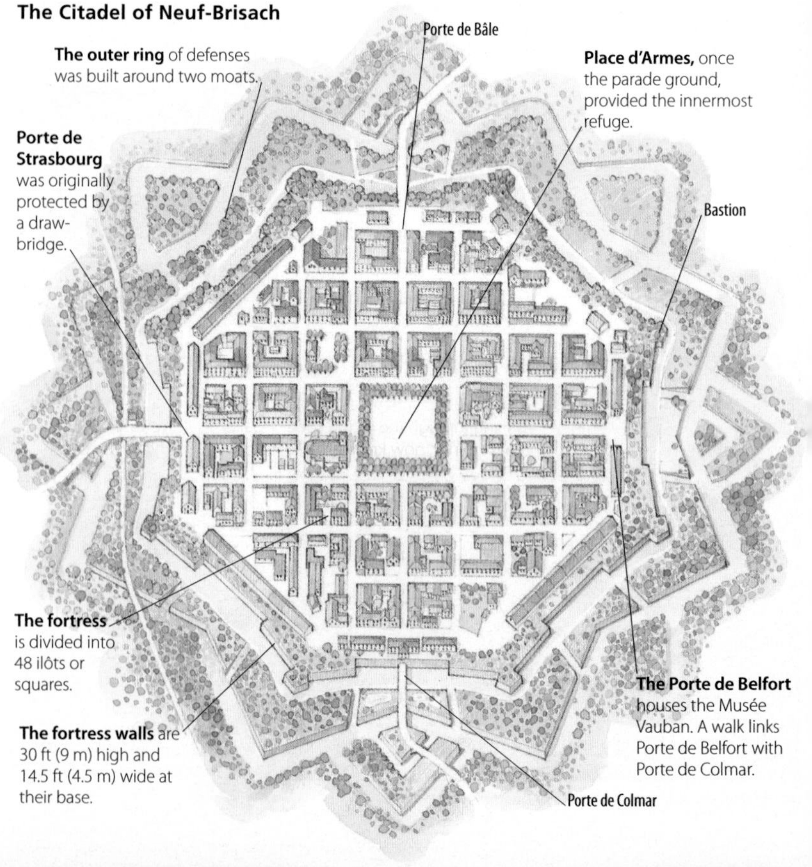

The celebrated Issenheim altarpiece by Matthias Grünewald in Colmar

place d'Armes and the Eglise St-Louis, which was added in 1731–6. This was the usual homage to Louis XV, implying that the church was dedicated to the King, rather than the saint.

The Porte de Belfort houses the **Musée Vauban**, which includes a model of the town, showing the outlying defenses, now concealed by woodland. They represent Vauban's barrier to the fortress and it is to his credit that the citadel was never taken.

Musée Vauban
Pl Porte de Belfort. **Tel** 03 89 72 03 93. **Open** May–Oct: Wed–Mon; Nov–Apr: groups only, by appt.

9 Eguisheim

Haut Rhin. 1,600.
22a grand'rue (03 89 23 40 33).
ot-eguisheim.fr

Eguisheim is a most exquisite small town, laid out within three concentric rings of 13th-century ramparts. The ensemble of austere fortifications and domestic elegance within makes for a surprisingly harmonious whole.

In the center of town is the octagonal feudal **castle** of the Counts of Eguisheim. A Renaissance fountain in front has the statue of Bruno Eguisheim, born here in 1002. He became Pope Léon IX and was later canonized.

The Grand'Rue is lined with half-timbered houses, many showing their construction date. Close to the castle is the **Marbacherhof**, a monastic tithe barn and cornhall. On a neighboring square, the modern parish church retains the original Romanesque sculpted tympanum.

The rest of the town has its share of Hansel-and-Gretel atmosphere, while inviting courtyards offer tastings of *grands crus*. From rue de Hautvilliers, outside the ramparts, a marked path leads through scenic vineyards.

10 Colmar

Haut Rhin. 68,000.
32 cours Sainte-Anne (03 89 20 68 92). Mon, Wed, Thu & Sat.
ot-colmar.fr

Colmar is the best preserved city in Alsace. As a trading post and river port, Colmar had its heyday in the 16th century, when wine merchants shipped their wine along the waterways running through the picturesque canal quarter, now known as **Petite Venise**. "Little Venice" is best seen on a leisurely boat trip that takes you from the tanners' quarter to the Rue des Tanneurs. The adjoining Place de l'Alsacienne Douane is dominated by the **Koifhüs**, a galleried customs house with a Burgundian tiled roof, overlooking half-timbered pastel houses which sport sculpted pillars.

Nearby, the place de la Cathédrale quarter is full of 16th-century houses. **Eglise St-Martin**, essentially Gothic, has a noted south portal. To the west, the place des Dominicains, with cafés, is dwarfed by the Gothic **Eglise Dominicaine**. Inside is *La Vierge au Buisson de Roses* (1473), the red and gold "Virgin of the Rosebush" by Martin Schongauer, a renowned painter and native son of Colmar.

Place d'Unterlinden, the adjoining square, has the **Musée d'Unterlinden**. Set in a Dominican monastery, it displays early Rhenish paintings. The highlight is the Issenheim altarpiece. A masterpiece of emotional intensity, it is part of an early 16th-century Alsatian panel painting by Matthias Grünewald.

In the historic center, the quaint rue des Têtes has the former wine exchange, a Renaissance town house known as the Maison des Têtes because of the grimacing heads on the gabled facade. And in rue Mercière, **Maison Pfister**, with its slender stair turret and galleried flower-decked facade, has come to typify the city.

Along the Quai de la Poissonerie in the Petite Venise area of Colmar

For hotels and restaurants in this region see pp554–71 and pp576–603

⓫ Riquewihr

Haut Rhin. 1,300. 2 rue de 1ère Armée (03 89 73 23 23). Fri.
ribeauville-riquewihr.com

Vineyards run right up to the ramparts of Riquewihr, the prettiest village on the Route des Vins *(see pp236–7)*. Deeply pragmatic, Riquewihr winemakers plant roses at the end of each row of vines – both for their pretty effect and as early detectors of parasites. The village belonged to the Counts of Wurtemberg until the Revolution and has grown rich on wine, from Tokay and Pinot Gris to Gewürztraminer and Riesling. Virtually an open-air museum, Riquewihr abounds in cobbled alleys, geranium-clad balconies, galleried courtyards, romantic double ramparts, and watchtowers.

From the Hôtel de Ville, the **rue du Général de Gaulle** climbs gently past medieval and Renaissance houses, half-timbered, stone-clad or corbelled. Oriel windows vie with sculpted portals and medieval sign boards. On the right lies the idyllic **place des Trois Eglises**. A passageway leads through the ramparts to the vineyards on the hill. Farther up lies the **Dolder**, a 13th-century belfry, followed by the **Tour des Voleurs** (both are museums, the latter with a medieval torture chamber), marking the second tier of ramparts. Beyond the gateway is the **Cour des Bergers**, gardens laid out around the 16th-century ramparts. Visitors outnumber the locals in summer or during the superb Christmas market.

The pretty – and popular – village of Riquewihr, set among vineyards

⓬ Ribeauvillé

Haut Rhin. 5,000. 1 grand'rue (03 89 73 23 23). Fri & Sat. **ribeauville-riquewihr.com**

Overlooked by three ruined castles, Ribeauvillé is stiflingly prettified, as may be expected from a favored town on the Route du Vin. This status is partly due to healthy sales of the celebrated *grands crus* of Alsace, especially Riesling. There are ample opportunities for tastings, particularly near the park, in the lower part of town *(see p236)*.

On the grand'rue (No. 14) is the **Pfifferhüs**, the minstrels' house. As locals declare, Ribeauvillé is the capital of the *kougelhopf*, the almond-flavored Alsatian cake.

Tortuous alleys wind past steep-roofed artisans' and *vignerons'* houses in the upper part of the town. Beyond are Renaissance fountains, painted facades, and **St-Grégoire-le-Grand**, the Gothic parish church. A marked path, which begins in this part of town, leads into the vineyards.

⓭ Château du Haut-Koenigsbourg

Orschwiller. **Tel** 03 69 33 25 00.
Open daily. **Closed** Jan 1, May 1, Dec 25.
haut-koenigsbourg.fr

Looming above the pretty village of St-Hippolyte, this castle is the most popular attraction in Alsace. In 1114, the Swabian Emperor, Frederick of Hohenstaufen, built the first Teutonic castle here, which was destroyed in 1462. Rebuilt and added to under the Habsburgs, it burned down in 1633. At the end of the 19th century, Kaiser Wilhelm II commissioned Berlin architect Bodo Ebhardt to restore the castle. The result of his painstaking work was a precise reconstruction of the original building.

With a drawbridge, fierce keep, and rings of fortifications, this warm sandstone hybrid is a sophisticated feudal château. The Cour d'Honneur is a breathtaking recreation, with a pointed corner turret and creaky arcaded galleries. Inside are gloomy "Gothic" chambers and "Renaissance" rooms. La Grande Salle is the most far-fetched, with a Neo-Gothic gallery and ornate paneling. From the battlements, almost 2,500 ft (750 m) above the Alsace plain, stretches a Rhineland panorama, bordered by the Black Forest and the Alps. On the other side are views from the high Vosges to villages and vineyards below.

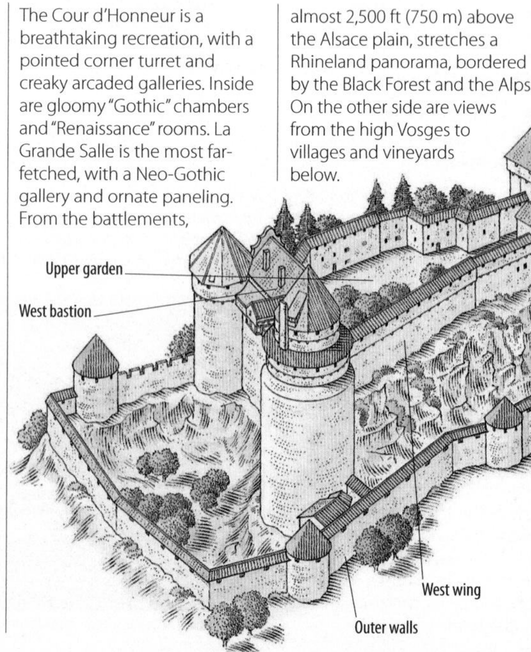

hapelle St-Sébastien outside Dambach-la-Ville, along the Route du Vin

Sélestat

as Rhin. 17,000.
Commanderie Saint Jean, bd du
én-éral Leclerc (03 88 58 87 20).
Tue, Sat. **selestat-tourisme.com**

)uring the Renaissance, Sélestat vas the intellectual center of \lsace, with a tradition of ıumanism fostered by Beatus :henanus, a friend of Erasmus. 'he **Bibliothèque Humaniste** ıas a collection of editions of ome of the earliest printed)ooks, including the first book o name America, in 1507. \learby are the Cour des Prélats, turreted ivy-covered mansion, and the Tour de l'Horloge, a clocktower. **Eglise Ste-Foy** is 12th-century, with an octagonal belltower. Opposite is **Eglise St-Georges**, glittering with green and red "Burgundian tiles."

Bibliothèque Humaniste
1 rue de la Bibliothèque. **Tel** 03 88 58 07 20. **Open** Mon, Wed–Sat am; (Jul–Aug: Wed–Mon exc. Sun am). **Closed** public hols.
bibliotheque-humaniste.eu

Environs

Medieval **Dambach-la-Ville**, another pretty town, is linked to Andlau and red-tiled Itterswiller by a delightful rural road through vineyards.

Ebersmunster, a picturesque hamlet, has an onion-domed abbey church, whose Baroque interior is a sumptuous display of gilded stucco.

15 Obernai

Bas Rhin. 11,000. pl du Beffroi (03 88 95 64 13). Thu.
obernai.fr

Young *Alsaciens* in traditional costume

At the north end of the Route du Vin, Obernai retains a flavor of authentic Alsace: residents speak Alsatian, at festivities women wear traditional costume, and church services are well-attended in the cavernous Neo-Gothic **Eglise St-Pierre-et-St-Paul**.

The place du Marché is well-preserved and features the gabled **Halle aux Blés**, a 16th-century corn hall (now a restaurant) above a former butcher's shop, with a facade adorned with cows' and dragons' heads. Place de la Chapelle, the adjoining square, has a Renaissance fountain and the 16th-century **Hôtel de Ville** and the **Kapellturm**, the galleried Gothic belfry. Side streets have Renaissance and medieval timber-framed houses. A stroll past the cafés on rue du Marché ends in a pleasant park by the ramparts.

Environs

Odile, Alsace's seventh-century patron saint, was born in Obernai but she is venerated on **Mont Sainte-Odile**, to the west.

Molsheim, a former bishopric and fortified market town 6 miles (10 km) north, is noted for its Metzig, a Renaissance-style butchers' guildhall.

Le Mémorial de l'Alsace-Moselle at Schirmeck commemorates the 10,000 who died at the Struthof concentration camp across the valley.

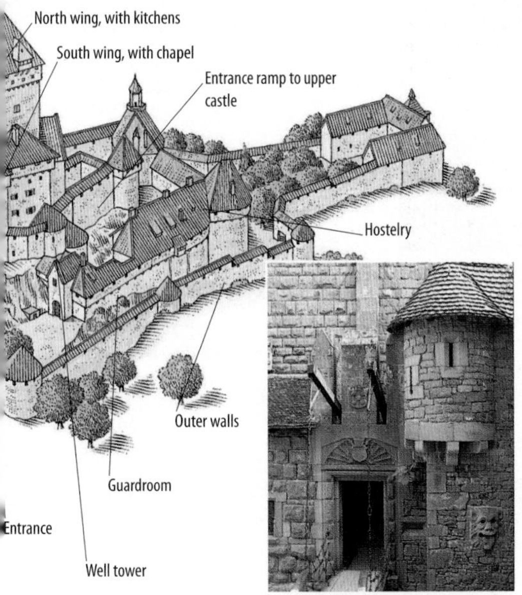

Drawbridge within the walls of Château du Haut-Koenigsbourg

⓰ Strasbourg

Halfway between Paris and Prague, Strasbourg is not surprisingly often known as "the crossroads of Europe." The city wears its European cosmopolitanism with ease – after all, its famous cathedral has catered to both Catholic and Protestant congregations – and as one of the capitals of the European Union has sensibly located the futuristic European Parliament building some way from the historic center. One of the ways to see this, along with the more traditional city sights, is to take a boat trip along the waterways encircling the Old Town. On the way you will take in the Ponts-Couverts, covered bridges linked by medieval watchtowers that provide an observation point for the four Ill canals, and the scenic Petite France, once the tanners' district, dotted with mills and crisscrossed by bridges.

Barge on the canal

The central portal of the west facade of the cathedral

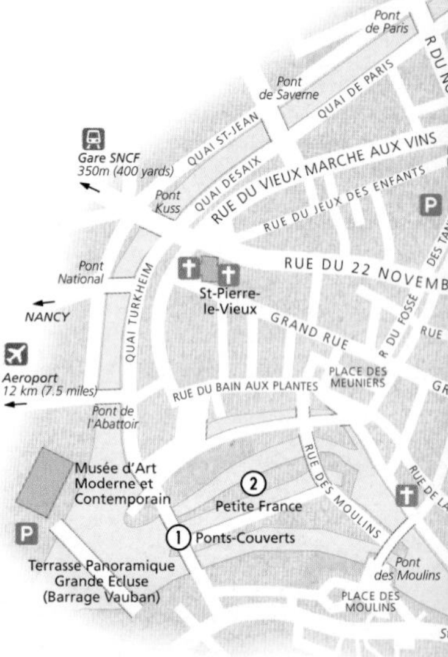

Cathédrale Notre-Dame

A masterpiece of stone lacework, the sandstone cathedral "rises like a most sublime, wide-arching tree of God," as Goethe marveled. Though construction began in the late 11th century (the choir is Romanesque, the nave is Gothic), it ended only in 1439, with the completion of the west facade, begun in 1277. The three portals are ornamented with statues. But the crowning glory is the rose window. The south portal leads to the Gothic Pillar of Angels (c.1230), set beside the Astronomical Clock: mechanical figures appear accompanied by chimes at 12:31pm. There are wonderful views over the city from the viewing platform, and on some summer evenings there are organ concerts.

In place de la Cathédrale, Maison Kammerzell, now a popular restaurant, was once a rich merchant's mansion, its highly elaborate, carved facade dating from the mid-15th to late-16th centuries.

Palais Rohan

2 pl du Château. **Tel** 03 88 80 50 50. **Open** Wed–Mon. **Closed** Jan 1, Good Fri, May 1, Nov 1 & 11, Dec 25. **musee-strasbourg.org**

Designed by the king's architect Robert de Cotte, in 1730, this grand Classical palace was intended for the Prince-Bishops of Strasbourg. It houses three museums: the Musée des Beaux Arts; the Musée Archéologique; and the Musée des Arts Décoratifs, which contains the sumptuous State Apartments and one of the finest collections of ceramics in France.

e Musée d'Art Moderne et Contemporain on Strasbourg's waterfront

VISITORS' CHECKLIST

Practical Information
Bas Rhin. 500,000. 17 pl de la Cathédrale (03 88 52 28 28). Wed, Fri & Sat. International Music Festival (Jun–Jul). **ot-strasbourg.fr**

Transport
7.5 miles (12 km) SW Strasbourg. pl de la Gare (08 92 35 35 35). pl des Halles (03 88 23 43 23).

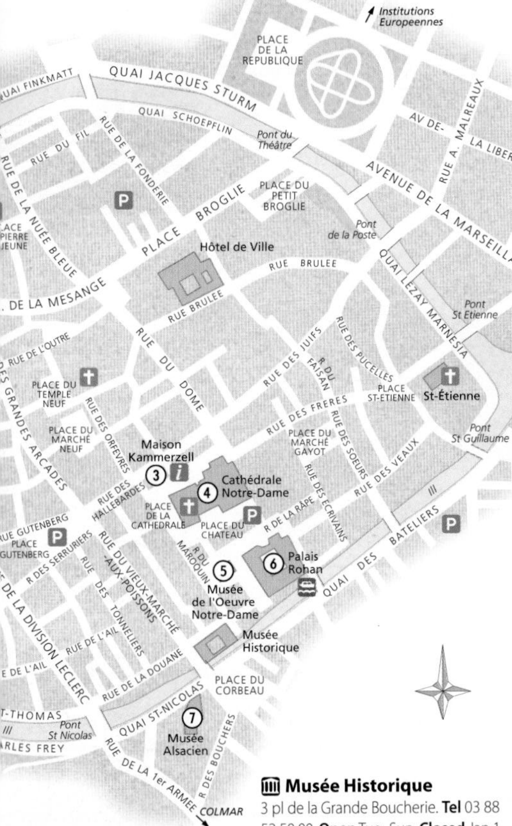

Strasbourg City Center

1. Ponts-Couverts
2. Petite France
3. Maison Kammerzell
4. Cathédrale Notre-Dame
5. Musée de l'Oeuvre Notre-Dame
6. Palais Rohan
7. Musée Alsacien

meters 250
yards 250

Key to Symbols *see back flap*

Musée Historique

3 pl de la Grande Boucherie. **Tel** 03 88 52 50 00. **Open** Tue–Sun. **Closed** Jan 1, Good Fri, May 1, Nov 1 & 11, Dec 25.

The museum occupies the 16th-century city abattoir and focuses on Strasbourg's political and military history.

Musée Alsacien

23 quai St-Nicolas. **Tel** 03 88 52 50 00. **Open** Wed–Mon. **Closed** Jan 1, Good Fri, May 1, Nov 1, Dec 25.

Housed in a series of interconnecting Renaissance buildings, the museum has fascinating exhibits on local traditions, and popular arts and crafts.

Musée de l'Oeuvre Notre-Dame

3 pl du Château. **Tel** 03 88 52 50 00. **Open** Tue–Sun. **Closed** Jan 1, Good Fri, May 1, Nov 1, Dec 25. ground fl.

The cathedral's impressive museum contains much of its original sculpture, as well as magnificent 11th-century stained glass. This somber gabled house also displays a collection of Medieval and Renaissance Alsatian art.

Musée d'Art Moderne et Contemporain

1 pl Hans-Jean Arp. **Tel** 03 88 23 31 31. **Open** Tue–Sun. **Closed** Jan 1, Good Fri, May 1, Nov 1 & 11, Dec 25. Concerts, cinema.

Adrien Fainsilber's cultural flagship for the 21st century is a marvel of glass and light (particularly at night when it appears to float on the river). Its superb collections run from 1860–1950 and from 1950 onwards. The Art Café is welcome respite for art-weary feet.

Ponts-Couverts with medieval watchtowers over the canals

The Alsace Route des Vins

Meandering over 110 miles (180 km) from Marlenheim to Thann, the picturesque wine route takes in historic towns with cobbled streets, medieval timber-framed houses, and Renaissance fountains. Romantically appointed *winstubs*, or cellars, offer traditional *choucroute garnie* and flowery white Alsatian wines. Dedicated wine lovers could spend two or three days covering the route at leisure, or may want to make shorter trips in either direction to or from Colmar. For a refreshing contrast from the unremitting charm of the towns and villages, escape occasionally into *sentiers viticoles* – lovely paths through the vineyards themselves.

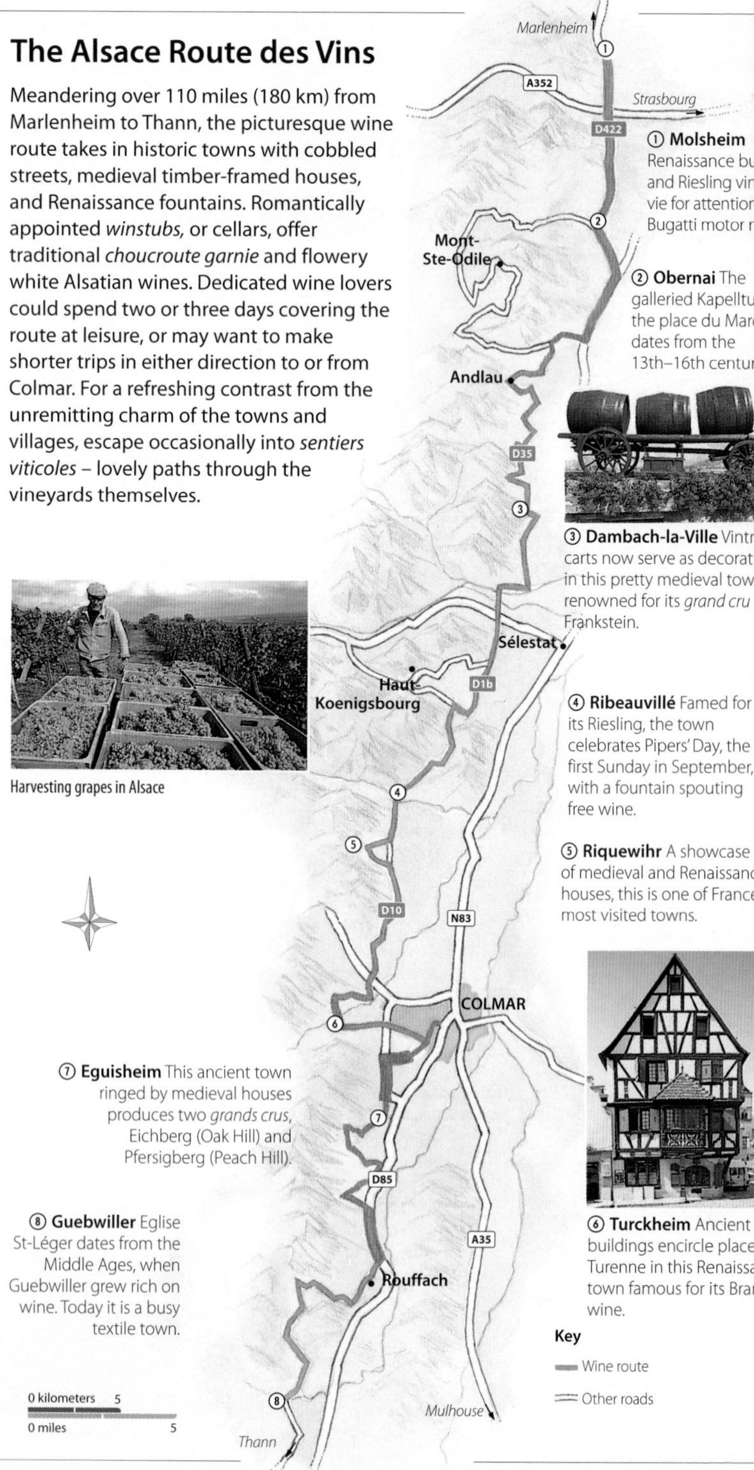

Marlenheim
A352
Strasbourg
D422
① Molsheim
Renaissance bu
and Riesling vin
vie for attention
Bugatti motor m
Mont-Ste-Odile
② Obernai The
galleried Kapelltu
the place du Marc
dates from the
13th–16th centur
Andlau
D35
③ Dambach-la-Ville Vintn
carts now serve as decorati
in this pretty medieval tow
renowned for its grand cru
Frankstein.
Sélestat
Haut-Koenigsbourg
D1b
④ Ribeauvillé Famed for
its Riesling, the town
celebrates Pipers' Day, the
first Sunday in September,
with a fountain spouting
free wine.
⑤ Riquewihr A showcase
of medieval and Renaissanc
houses, this is one of France
most visited towns.
D10
N83
COLMAR
⑦ Eguisheim This ancient town
ringed by medieval houses
produces two grands crus,
Eichberg (Oak Hill) and
Pfersigberg (Peach Hill).
D85
⑧ Guebwiller Eglise
St-Léger dates from the
Middle Ages, when
Guebwiller grew rich on
wine. Today it is a busy
textile town.
A35
Rouffach
⑥ Turckheim Ancient
buildings encircle place
Turenne in this Renaissa
town famous for its Brar
wine.
Key
Wine route
Other roads
0 kilometers 5
0 miles 5
Mulhouse
Thann

Harvesting grapes in Alsace

e Wine

wines are usually aromatic, d full-bodied. All are white Pinot Noir, used for light reds.

arvested Alsatian classic

Facts

Location and climate
Protected by the Vosges, Alsace has a climate and France's lowest al rainfall.

Grape varieties
Alsace wines are known simply by their grape variety. *irztraminer,* with its exotic petal character, is most typi- Alsatian, although the ***Ries-*** s arguably the finest. ***Muscat*** other aromatic variety. Spicy ss assertive than Gewür- iner, ***Pinot Gris*** and the er, dry ***Pinot Blanc*** go well food. ***Pinot Noir*** is the only ariety. sciously rich, sweet, late- sted wines are an Alsace ality.

producers
Albert Boxler, Marcel Deiss, Rolly Gassmann, Beyer, Meyer-Fonne, Kuentz-Bas, Domaine Weinbach, Dopff & Irion, Olivier Humbrecht, Charles ret, Domaines Schlumberger, aine Ostertag, Domaine bach, Hugel & Fils, Cave de heim.

Good vintages
2008, 2004, 2001, 1998, 1996, 1995.

The 12th-century chapel of the Château du Haut-Barr, near Saverne

⑰ Saverne

Bas Rhin. 12,300. 37 grand rue (03 88 91 80 47). Tue & Thu. **ot-saverne.fr**

Framed by hills, and situated on the river Zorn and the Marne-Rhine canal, Saverne is a pretty sight. The town was a fief of the prince-bishops of Strasbourg and its sandstone Château des Rohan was a favorite summer residence. Today, it houses the **Musée du Château de Rohan-Pontivy**, whose collection traces Saverne's past. On the far side of the château, the grand'rue is studded with restaurants and timber-framed Renaissance houses.

Musée du Château de Rohan-Pontivy
Château des Rohan. **Tel** 03 88 91 06 28. **Open** Jan–mid-Jun & mid-Sep–Dec: Mon–Fri pm, 10am–6pm Sat & Sun; mid-Jun–mid-Sep: 10am–6pm daily. **Closed** Tue. restricted.

Environs
To the southwest, perched on a rocky spur, the ruined **Château du Haut-Barr** – the "Eye of Alsace" – once commanded the pass of Col de Saverne. In **Marmoutier**, 3.5 miles (6 km) south, is an abbey church with a Romanesque-Lombard facade and octagonal towers.

⑱ Betschdorf

Bas Rhin. 4,000. 1 rue des Francs, La Mairie (03 88 54 48 00). **betschdorf.com**

The vibrant village of Betschdorf borders the Forêt de Haguenau, 27 miles (45 km) north of Strasbourg. Many residents occupy timber-framed houses dating from the 18th century, when pottery made the village prosperous. Generations of potters have passed down the knowledge of the characteristic blue-gray glaze to their sons, while the women have been entrusted with decorating it in cobalt blue. A pottery museum, with a workshop attached, displays rural ceramics. Betschdorf is a good place to try *tartes flambées* – hot, crispy bases topped with cheese or fruit.

Betschdorf pottery

Environs
Another pottery village, **Soufflenheim**, lies 6 miles (10 km) southeast. Its earth-colored pottery is usually painted with bold flowers. To the north, close to the German border, the picturesque town of **Wissembourg** has many half-timbered houses and the second-largest church in Alsace after Strasbourg Cathedral, Eglise St-Pierre et St-Paul.

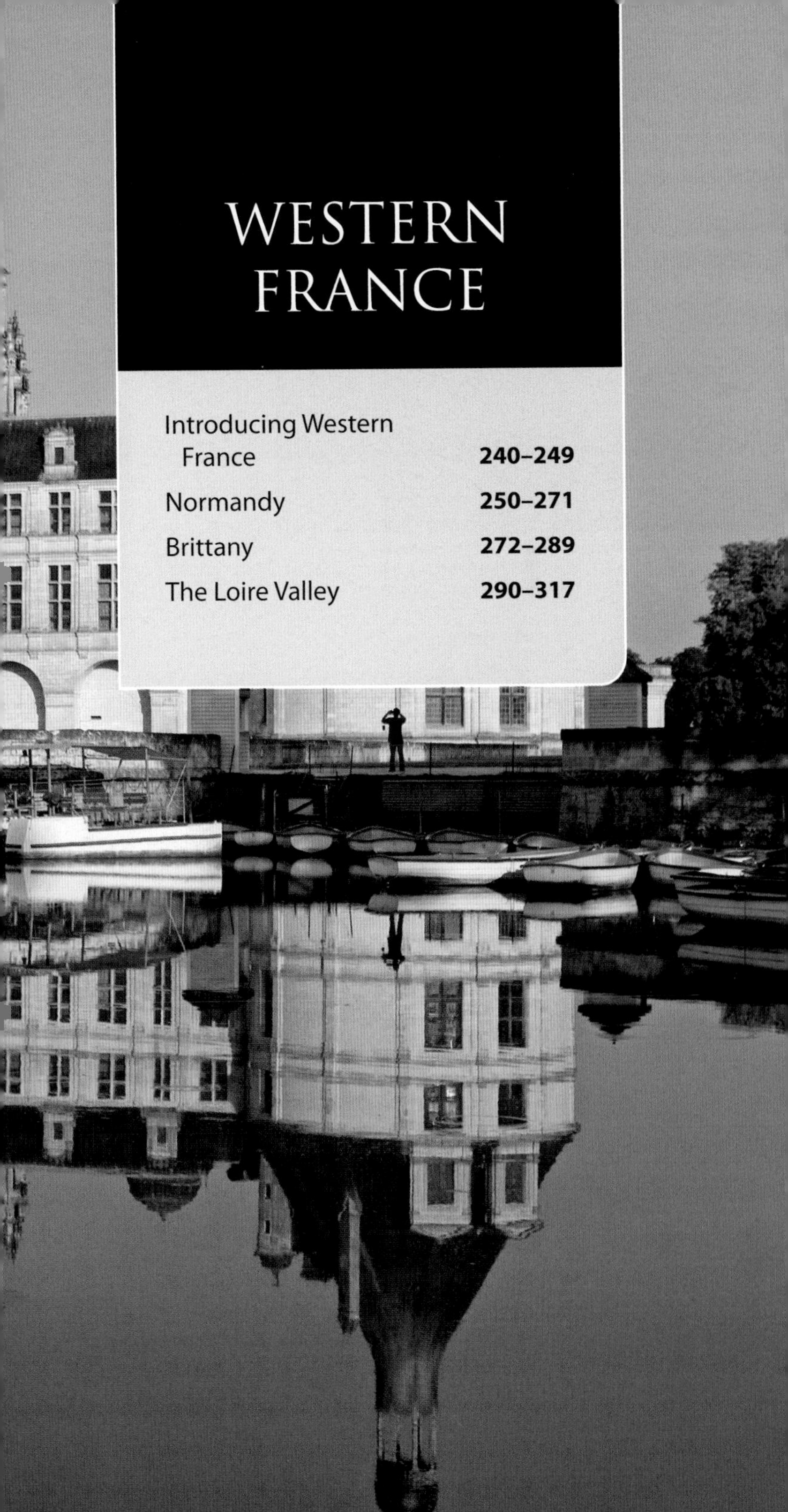

WESTERN FRANCE

Introducing Western France

The western regions of France have played very different historical roles, from the royal heartland of the Loire Valley to separatist Celtic Brittany. These are mainly rich farming regions, with fishing important along the coasts. Heavy industry and oil refineries are concentrated around Rouen and Le Havre. Visitors come for the wonderful beaches, quiet rural byways, and the sumptuous Loire châteaux. This map shows some of the region's most celebrated sights.

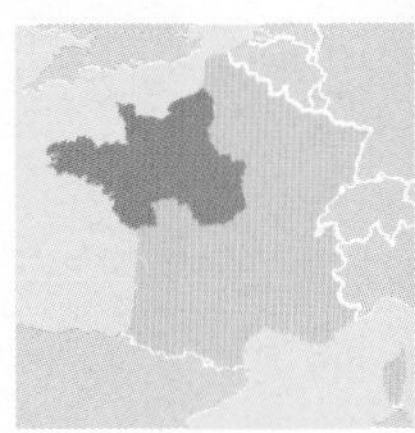

The evocative silhouette of Mont-St-Michel has welcomed pilgrims since the 11th century. Today nearly one million visitors a year walk across the footbridge to the island abbey *(see pp260–65).*

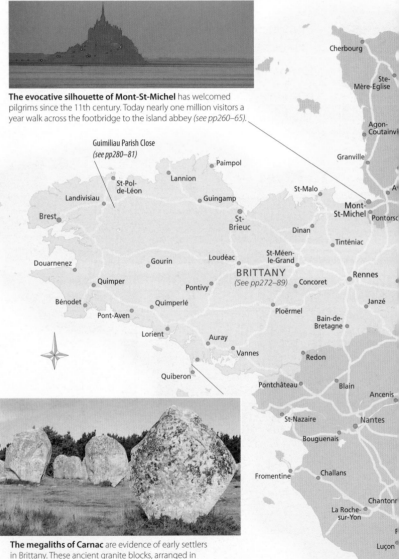

Guimiliau Parish Close *(see pp280–81)*

BRITTANY *(See pp272–89)*

The megaliths of Carnac are evidence of early settlers in Brittany. These ancient granite blocks, arranged in intriguing patterns, date back to 4000 BC and are thought to have had a religious or astronomical purpose *(see p283).*

◀ Château de Chambord, reflected in the river Cossan

The Bayeux Tapestry *(see pp256–7)* shows William the Conqueror's invasion of England from the French point of view. Among its 58 scenes, key events such as the Battle of Hastings in 1066 are depicted with great vigor and finesse. Here, two of William's messengers are shown hurrying to meet him.

Château de Chambord is the largest and most extravagant of the Loire châteaux (*see pp306–7*). François I transformed the original hunting lodge to a luxurious moated castle in 1519. Its splendor was completed by Louis XIV in 1685. Inside the 440 rooms are François' salamander emblem and 365 fireplaces, one for every day of the year.

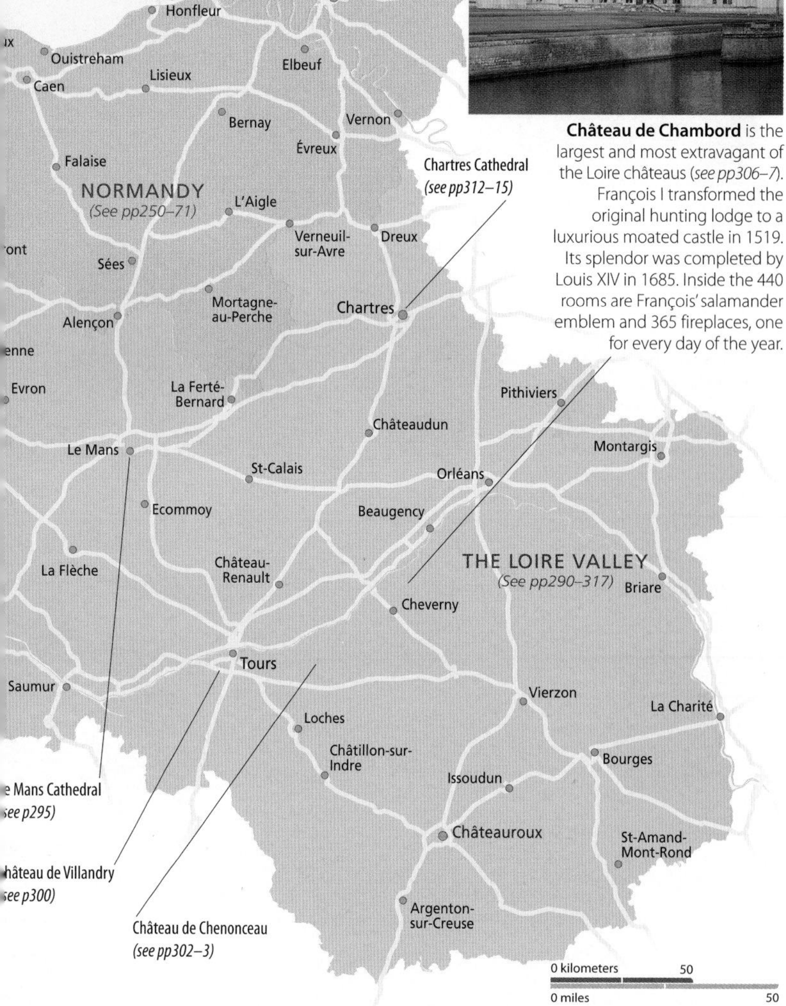

Rouen Cathedral
(see pp268–9)

Chartres Cathedral
(see pp312–15)

NORMANDY
(See pp250–71)

THE LOIRE VALLEY
(See pp290–317)

e Mans Cathedral
see p295)

hâteau de Villandry
see p300)

Château de Chenonceau
(see pp302–3)

Le Tréport
Dieppe
St-Valery-en-Caux
Tôtes
Etretat
Yvetot
Harfleur
Rouen
Honfleur
Ouistreham
Elbeuf
Caen
Lisieux
Bernay
Vernon
Évreux
Falaise
L'Aigle
Verneuil-sur-Avre
Dreux
Sées
Mortagne-au-Perche
Chartres
Alençon
Evron
La Ferté-Bernard
Pithiviers
Châteaudun
Le Mans
Montargis
St-Calais
Orléans
Ecommoy
Beaugency
La Flèche
Château-Renault
Briare
Cheverny
Tours
Saumur
Vierzon
La Charité
Loches
Châtillon-sur-Indre
Bourges
Issoudun
Châteauroux
St-Amand-Mont-Rond
Argenton-sur-Creuse

0 kilometers 50
0 miles 50

The Flavors of Western France

The Atlantic coast, the rich agricultural hinterland of dairy farms, orchards and vegetable fields, and the rivers of the Loire Valley combine to produce some of France's best loved food. Vegetables are grown in abundance in Brittany and the alluvial soils of the Loire, and the orchards of Normandy are bountiful. Fish from the windswept coast of Brittany or the channel ports of Normandy play a key role in the cuisine. Hearty meat dishes range from the celebrated duck of Rouen to the rabbit and game of the Sologne in the Loire. Fine cheeses are made here, and butter is the favored cooking medium.

Normandy apples

Norman cheese-producer displaying his wares

Normandy

Normandy's lush green pastures, dotted with brown and white cows, and orchards heavy with apples, make it a great source of veal, milk, cheese, cream, butter, apples, and pears. Duck is a speciality, as is *pre-salé* lamb from the salt-rich marshes around Mont-St-Michel. Many vegetables are grown and wild mushrooms thrive in the damp meadows and woodlands in autumn. Fish is important, with catches of sole, plaice and mackerel, skate and herrings, and 80 percent of France's scallops, plus a great variety of shellfish.

Camembert is Normandy's most famous cheese; others include Pont l'Evêque, the pungent-smelling Livarot, rich Brillat-Savarin and Petit-Suisse, a small, fresh white cheese eaten with sugar. Apples symbolize Normandy above all, and cider is traditionally drunk with food while Calvados, the powerful apple brandy, is served with meals as *le trou normand*.

Brittany

Thousands of miles of coastline yield an abundance of fish and seafood. Oysters are highly prized, as are mussels, harvested both wild and cultivated.

Some of the favorite vegetables of western France

Regional Dishes and Specialties

Fish dominates the menus here, most spectacularly in the *plateau de fruits de mer*, featuring oysters, crabs, langoustines, shrimps, cockles, and clams, piled on a bed of ice. Oysters are served simply with lemon or shallot vinegar, but can also come stuffed, gratinéed, or wrapped in pastry. Fresh fish may be grilled, baked in sea salt (*sel de Guérande* is the best), braised in cider or served with *beurre blanc* ("white butter" sauce with shallots, wine vinegar and cream). Lobster is often served *à l'armoricaine*. *Cotriade*, the Breton fish stew, combines a selection of the catch of the day with onions and potatoes. *Moules marinières* (mussels steamed in white wine with shallots and butter) is the popular classic. As a change from fish, look for *gigot de sept heures* – lamb slowly pot-roasted for seven hours.

Pears

Homard à l'armoricaine
Lobster, served in a herby tomato and onion sauce, enriched with brandy.

Superb Breton oysters for sale at a regional fish market

Other fish caught include monkfish, tuna, sardines, scallops, and lobster. Pig-rearing is important, so expect roast pork, smoked sausages, hams, and *boudin noir* (blood sausage), delicious served with apples. A great delicacy is the *pre-salé* lamb from Ile de Ouessant, served with haricot beans. Artichokes are the symbol of Brittany, an indication of the importance of vegetables, especially winter produce like cauliflower, onions, and potatoes.

Crêpes (pancakes), both sweet and savory, are a key element of the Breton diet. They come as buckwheat *galettes* with savory fillings such as ham, cheese, spinach, or mushrooms, or as lacy light dessert versions with sweet fillings and known as *crêpes dentelles* (*dentelle* meaning "lace").

The Loire Valley

This huge region takes pride in a truly diverse range of specialties. Grass-fed cattle are raised in Anjou, and sheep in the Berry region. Excellent free-range chickens, *poulet fermier Loué*, are raised in Touraine and the Orléanais. The forests and lakes of the Sologne yield deer, wild boar, pheasant, partridge, hare, and duck. Charcuterie includes *rillettes*, (shredded and potted pork), and ham from the Vendée. The Atlantic coast produces a variety of fish and the Loire itself is a source of pike, shad, tench, salmon, eels, and lampreys. Mushrooms are cultivated in the limestone caves around Saumur, but of the many vegetables grown, best of all is Sologne asparagus. Superb goats' cheeses include St Maure de Touraine, ash-coated Valençay, and the little Crottins de Chavignol.

Cheese and charcuterie at Loches market in the Loire Valley

ON THE MENU

Alose à l'oseille Shad in a sorrel sauce.

Côte de veau vallée d'Auge Veal in mushrooms, cream, and cider or Calvados.

Far aux pruneaux Egg batter pudding baked with prunes.

Kig ha farz Meat and vegetable hotpot with buckwheat dumpling.

Marmite Dieppoise Assorted fish stewed in cider or white wine with cream.

Tergeule Creamy baked rice pudding with cinnamon.

Tripes à la Mode de Caen Tripe with calves' feet, onions or leeks, herbs, and cider.

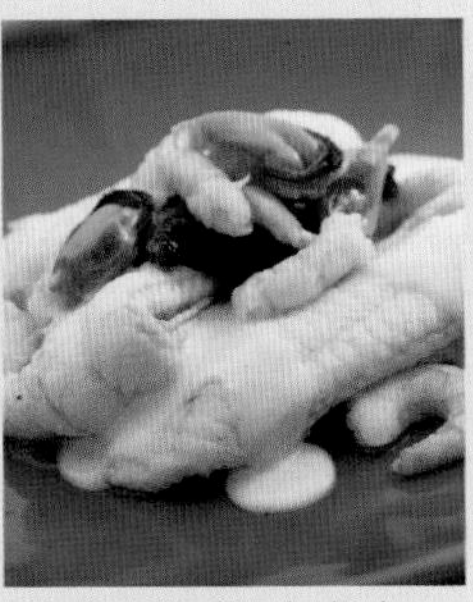

Sole Normande Baked sole in sauce of egg and cream, garnished with mussels, oysters, mushrooms, and shrimps.

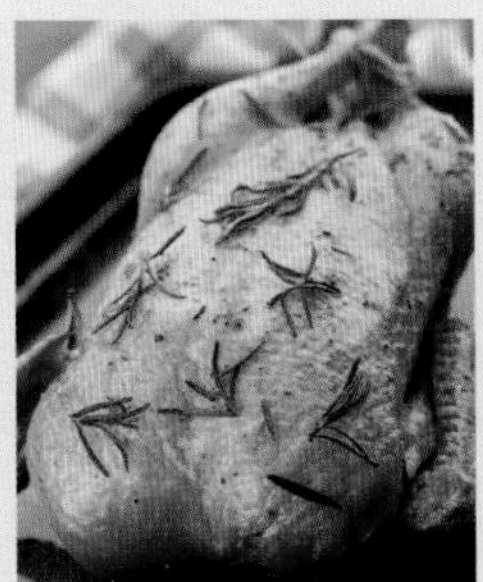

Canard Rouennais Duclair duck, part-roasted then finished in a rich sauce of duck liver and shallots.

Tarte tatin Caramelized upside-down apple tart, originally made at the Hotel Tatin in the Loire Valley.

France's Wine Regions: the Loire

With a few exceptions, the Loire is a region of good rather than great wines. The fertile agricultural soils of the meandering flatlands of the "Garden of France" are fine for fruit and vegetables, less so for the production of great wines. The cool, northern, Atlantic-influenced climate nonetheless produces refreshing reds and summer rosés, both dry and lusciously sweet white wines, and attractively bracing sparkling wines. Dry white wines are very much in the majority here, and are usually intended for early consumption, so vintages in the Loire tend to matter less than in the classic red wine regions.

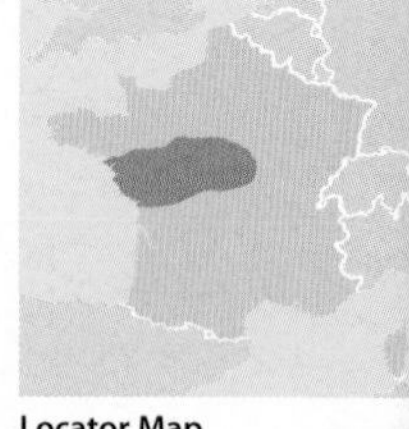

Locator Map

Loire wine region

The sweet wine of Quarts de Chaume, within the Coteaux du Layon appellation, is little-known outside France.

Muscadet with the words *sur lie* on the label has been aged on its "lees" *(see p31)*, giving the wine more flavor and interest.

Wine Regions

The Loire, flowing for some 620 miles (1,000 km), links the major wine areas of the Loire Valley. From its source in the Ardèche, it flows north through the center of France to the Sancerre and Pouilly Fumé vineyards, then west through Touraine and Anjou, finally reaching the coastal flats of the Pays Nantais, home of Muscadet.

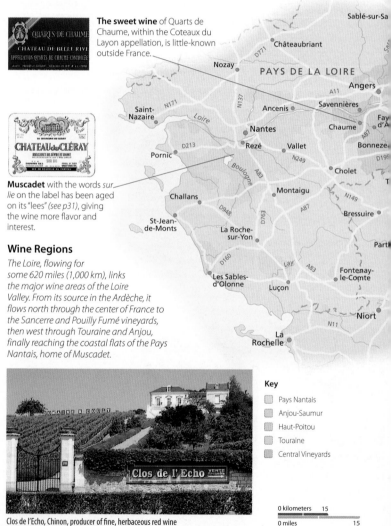

Clos de l'Echo, Chinon, producer of fine, herbaceous red wine

Key

- Pays Nantais
- Anjou-Saumur
- Haut-Poitou
- Touraine
- Central Vineyards

0 kilometers 15

0 miles 15

'his red wine has been ıade using grapes from *'ieilles vignes* – the oldest ınd the best vines on the ırower's property.

Red wine vineyards at Bourgueil

Vouvray makes still and sparkling white wine, the latter often aged in chalk caves very like those in Champagne.

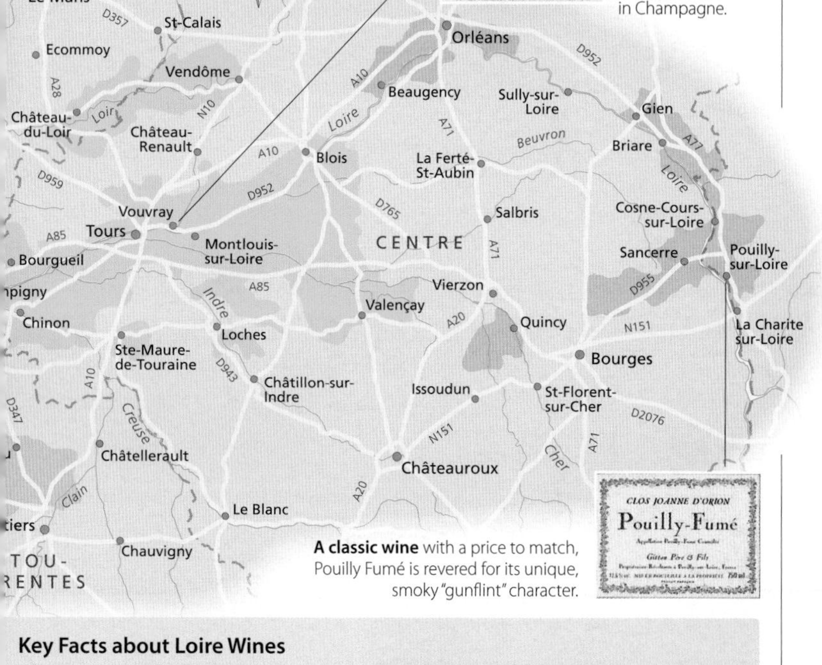

A classic wine with a price to match, Pouilly Fumé is revered for its unique, smoky "gunflint" character.

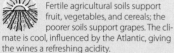

Key Facts about Loire Wines

Location and Climate

Fertile agricultural soils support fruit, vegetables, and cereals; the poorer soils support grapes. The climate is cool, influenced by the Atlantic, giving the wines a refreshing acidity.

Grape Varieties

The ***Melon de Bourgogne*** makes simple, dry white wines. The ***Sauvignon*** makes gooseberryish, flinty dry whites, finest in Sancerre and Pouilly Fumé but also good in Touraine. The ***Chenin Blanc*** makes dry and medium Anjou, Savennières, Vouvray, Montlouis, and Saumur, sparkling Vouvray and Saumur, and the famous sweet whites, Bonnezeaux,

Vouvray, and Quarts de Chaume. Summery reds are made from the ***Gamay*** and the fruity, herbaceous ***Cabernet Franc***.

Good Producers

Muscadet: Sauvion, Guy Bossard, Michel Bregeon. *Anjou, Savennières, Vouvray*: Richou, Ogereau, Nicolas Joly, Huet, Domaine des Aubuissières, Bourillon-Dorléans, Jacky Blot, Domaine Gessey. *Touraine* (white): Pibaleau. *Saumur-Champigny* (red): Filliatreau, Chateâu du Hureau. *Chinon, Bourgueil*: Couly-Dutheil, Yves Loiseau. *Sancerre, Pouilly Fumé, Ménétou-Salon*: Francis Cotat, Vacheron, Mellot, Vincent Pinard.

From Defense to Decoration

The great châteaus of the Loire Valley gradually evolved from purely defensive structures to decorative palaces. With the introduction of firearms, castles lost their defensive function, and comfort and taste predominated. Defensive elements like towers, battlements, moats, and gatehouses were retained largely as symbols of rank and ancestry. Renaissance additions, like galleries and dormer windows, added elegance.

Salamander emblem of François 1

Angers *(see p295)*, a fortress built from 1230–40 by Louis IX, stands on a rocky hill in the town center. In 1585, Henri III removed the pepper-pot shaped towers from 17 fortifications which were formerly 98 ft (30 m) high.

Circular tower, formerly defensive

Corbeled walkways, once useful in battle

Chaumont *(see p310)* was rebuilt in 1445–1510 in Renaissance style by the Amboise family. Although it has a defensive appearance, with circular towers, corbeled walkways and a gatehouse, these features are mainly decorative. It was restored after 1833.

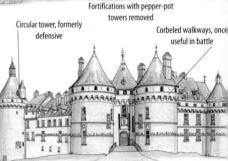

Decorated turret

Azay-le-Rideau *(see p300)*, regarded as one of the most elegant and well-designed Renaissance châteaus, was built by finance minister Gilles Berthelot (1518–1527) and his wife Philippa Lesbahy. It is a mixture of traditional turrets with Renaissance pilasters and pinnacles. Most dramatic is the interior staircase with its three storys of twin bays and an intricately decorated pediment.

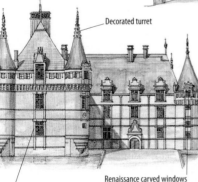

Renaissance carved windows

Pilasters (columns)

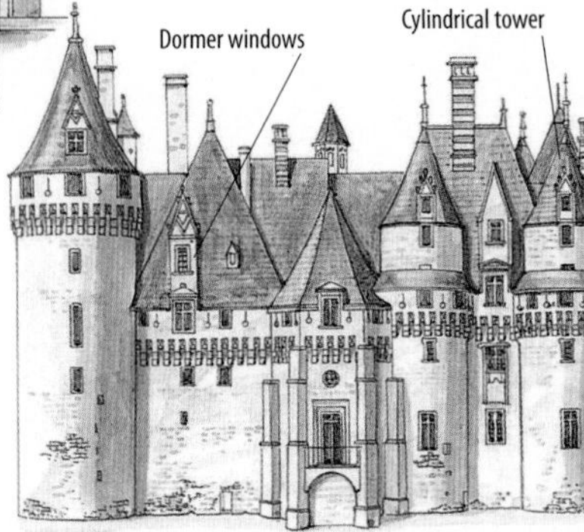

Ussé *(see p299)* was built in 1462 by Jean de Bueil as a fortress with parapets containing openings for missiles, battlements, and gunloops. The Espinay family, chamberlains to both Louis XI and Charles VIII, bought the château and changed the walls overlooking the main courtyard to Renaissance style with dormer windows and pilasters. In the 17th century the north wing was demolished to create palatial terraces.

Breton Traditions

Brittany was christened Breiz Izel (Little Britain) by the Welsh and Cornish migrants who fled here in the 5th and 6th centuries AD and imposed their customs, language, and religion on the local Gauls. Brittany resisted Charlemagne, the Vikings, the Normans, English alliances, and even French rule until 1532. Today, Breton is taught in some schools, and a busy calendar keeps Brittany in touch with its past and with other Celtic regions.

Bigouden lace headdresses

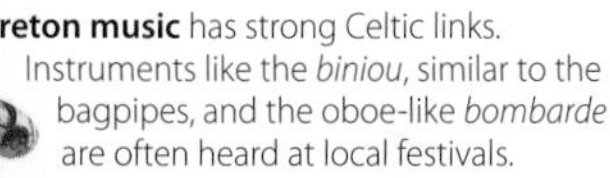

Breton music has strong Celtic links. Instruments like the *biniou*, similar to the bagpipes, and the oboe-like *bombarde* are often heard at local festivals.

A pardon is an annual religious festival honoring a local saint. The name derives from the granting of indulgences to pardon the sins of the past year. Some *pardons*, like those at Ste-Anne d'Auray and Ste-Anne-la-Palud, still attract thousands of pilgrims who carry banners and holy relics through the streets. Most *pardons* take place between April and September.

Breton costumes, still seen at *pardons* and weddings, varied as each area had distinctive headdresses or *coiffes*. Artists like Gauguin often painted the costumes. There are good museum collections in Quimper *(see p278)* and Pont l'Abbé in Pays Bigouden *(see p277)*.

Brittany's Coastal Wildlife

With its granite cliffs, sweeping bays, rias, and deep estuaries, the Brittany coastline contains a wealth of varied wildlife habitats. Parts of the coast have a tidal range of more than 150 ft (50 m), the highest in France, and this great variation in sea level divides marine life into several distinct zones. Most of the region's famous shellfish, including mussels, clams, and oysters, live on the lower shore, either on rocks or in muddy sand where they are submerged for most of the day. Higher zones are the preserve of limpets and barnacles, and several kinds of seaweed which can survive out of the water for long periods. Above the sea, towering cliffs offer a nursery for seabirds and a foothold for many kinds of wild flowers.

Cliffs at the Pointe du Raz, Brittany

The Ile de Bréhat at low tide

Features of the Coast

This scene shows some of the wildlife habitats found on the Brittany coastline. When exploring the shore, make a note of the tide times, particularly if you plan to walk along the foot of the cliffs.

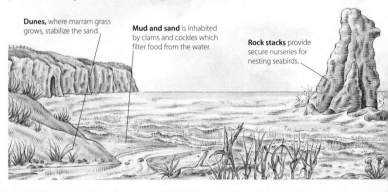

Salt-marsh flowers are their best in late summ

Dunes, where marram grass grows, stabilize the sand.

Mud and sand is inhabited by clams and cockles which filter food from the water.

Rock stacks provide secure nurseries for nesting seabirds.

Oyster Beds

Like most marine molluscs, oysters begin their lives as tiny floating larvae. The first step in *ostréiculture*, or oyster cultivation, consists of providing the larvae with somewhere to settle, which is usually a stack of submerged tiles. The developing oysters are later transferred to beds and left to mature before being collected for the market.

Oyster beds at Cancale

Clifftop turf often contains a narrow band of wild flowers sandwiched between fields and the sea.

Rockpools are flooded twice daily by the tide. They are inhabited by fish, molluscs, sea anemones, and sponges.

Coastal Wildlife

The structure of this shore determines the wildlife that lives on it. In a world beset by wind and waves, rocks provide solid anchorage for plants and a secure habitat for many small animals. Muddy sand is rich in nutrients, and has a greater abundance of life – although most of this is concealed beneath the surface.

Cliffs

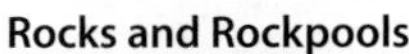

The rock dove is a cliff-dwelling ancestor of the well-known city pigeon.

Thrift is a common spring flower, found on exposed ledges near the sea.

Rocks and Rockpools

Seaweed of many different varieties is exposed each day by the falling tide.

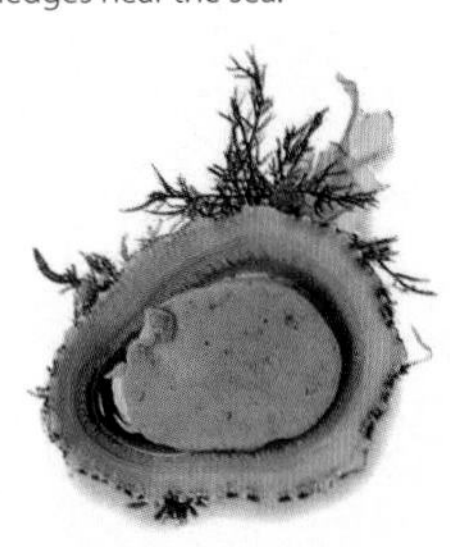

The limpet, a slow-moving creature, scrapes tiny plants from the rock surface.

The goby, with its sharp eyesight, dashes for cover at the first sign of movement above.

Crabs live at many different water depths. Some species are extremely good swimmers.

Mud and Sand

Cockles live in large numbers just beneath the surface of muddy sand.

The curlew has a forceps-like curved beak for extracting shell-fish from mud and sand.

atamarans.com
LE CLIPPER

NORMANDY

Eure · Seine-Maritime · Manche · Calvados · Orne

The quintessential image of Normandy is of a lush, pastoral region of apple orchards and contented cows, cider and pungent cheeses – but the region also spans the windswept beaches of the Cotentin and the wooded banks of the Seine valley. Highlights include the great abbey churches of Caen, the mighty island of Mont-St-Michel, and Monet's garden at Giverny.

Normandy gets its name from the Viking Norsemen who sailed up the river Seine in the 9th century. Pillagers turned settlers, they made their capital at Rouen – today a cultured cathedral city that commands the east of the region. Here the Seine meanders seaward past the ancient abbeys at Jumièges and St-Wandrille to a coast that became an open-air studio for Impressionist painters during the mid- and late 19th century.

North of Rouen are the chalky cliffs of the Côte d'Albâtre. The mood softens at the port of Honfleur and the elegant resorts of the Côte Fleurie to the west. Inland lies the Pays d'Auge, with its half-timbered manor houses and patch-eyed cows. The western half of Normandy is predominantly rural, a *bocage* countryside of small, high-hedged fields with windbreaks composed of beech trees.

The modern city of Caen is worth visiting for its two great 11th-century abbey churches built by William the Conqueror and his queen, Matilda. Close by in Bayeux, the story of William's invasion of England is told in detail by the town's famous tapestry. Memories of another invasion, the D-Day Landings of 1944, still linger along the Côte de Nacre and the Cotentin Peninsula. Thousands of Allied troops poured ashore on to these magnificent beaches in the closing stages of World War II. The Cotentin Peninsula is capped by the port of Cherbourg, still a strategic naval base. At its western foot stands one of France's greatest attractions: the monastery island of Mont-St-Michel.

Half-timbered manor house in the village of Beuvron-en-Auge, near Lisieux

◀ The harbor at Honfleur, Calvados

Exploring Normandy

Normandy's rich historical sights and diverse landscape make it ideal for touring by car or bicycle. Rewarding coastal drives and good beaches can be found along the windswept Côte d'Albâtre and the Cotentin Peninsula. Further south is one of France's most celebrated sights, Mont-St-Michel. Inland, follow the meanders of the Seine valley, passing cider orchards and half-timbered houses along the way, to visit historic Rouen and Monet's garden at Giverny.

Apple trees in blossom in the Pays d'Auge

The Côte d'Albâtre coastline

Key

- Highway
- Major road
- Secondary road
- Minor road
- Scenic route
- Main railroad
- Minor railroad
- Regional border

Sights at a Glance

1. Cotentin
2. Cherbourg
3. Coutances
4. Granville
5. Avranches
6. Mont-St-Michel
7. Côte de Nacre
8. Bayeux
9. Caen
10. Suisse Normande
11. Parc Naturel Régional de Normandie-Maine
12. Côte Fleurie
13. Pays d'Auge
14. Honfleur
15. Le Havre
16. Côte d'Albâtre
17. Dieppe
18. Basse-Seine
19. Rouen
20. Haute-Seine
21. Giverny
22. Évreux

For additional map symbols *see back flap*

;etting Around

.ccess to and through the region from Calais is quick and direct n the A16, which links up with the A28–A29 and A13 highways ɔ Paris, and runs west to Caen, and beyond on the A84. There re also main road and rail links to the cross-Channel ports of ieppe, Le Havre, Caen (Ouistreham), and Cherbourg. Travel y public transport beyond these arteries is limited. he region is threaded with minor roads, particularly lelightful in the Pays d'Auge and Cotentin eninsula. The main airports are at Rouen, e Havre, and Caen.

The town of Les Andelys shrouded in mist

Rugged cliffs on the Cotentin Peninsula

❶ Cotentin

Manche. Cherbourg.
2 quai Alexandre III, Cherbourg (02 33 93 52 02).
manchetourisme.com

Thrusting into the English Channel, the Cotentin Peninsula has a landscape similar to Brittany's. Its long sandy beaches have wild and windblown headlands around Cap de la Hague and Nez de Jobourg. The latter is popular among bird-watchers – gannets and shearwaters fly by in large numbers. Along the east coast stretches Utah Beach, where American troops landed as part of the Allied invasion on June 6, 1944. Inland, Ste-Mère-Eglise commemorates these events with its **Musée Airborne** (Airborne Troops Museum). Just outside Ste-Mère-Eglise, the **Ferme Musée du Cotentin** has farm animals and activities, which give an insight into rural life in the early 1900s, while farther north, in the market town of Valognes, the **Musée Régional du Cidre et du Calvados** celebrates the thriving local talent for making cider and Calvados.

Two fishing ports command the Peninsula's northeast corner: Barfleur and St-Vaast-la-Hougue, the latter famous for oysters and a base for boat trips to the Ile de Tatihou. The Val de Saire is ideal for a scenic drive, with a view point at La Pernelle the best place to survey the coast. On the west side of the Peninsula, warmed by the Gulf Stream, the resort of Barneville-Carteret offers sandy beaches and summer boat trips to the Channel Islands. The low-lying, marshy landscape east of Carentan forms the heart of the Parc Régional des Marais du Potentin et du Bessin.

Musée Airborne
14 rue Eisenhower, Ste-Mère-Eglise. **Tel** 02 33 41 41 35. **Open** Feb–Nov: daily; Christmas hols. Open during renovation. **Closed** Jan, Dec 24, 25 & 31. **musee-airborne.com**

Ferme Musée du Cotentin
Rte de Beauvais, Ste-Mère-Eglise. **Tel** 02 33 95 40 20. **Open** Jul–Aug: daily; Apr–Jun, Easter & Nov school hols: daily pms only. **Closed** May 1.

Musée Régional du Cidre et du Calvados
Rue du Petit-Versailles, Valognes. **Tel** 02 33 40 22 73. **Open** Apr–Sep: Wed–Mon pms only (mid-Jun–mid-Sep: daily). **Closed** Sun am.

❷ Cherbourg

Manche. 44,100.
2 quai Alexandre III (02 33 93 52 02). Tue, Thu & Sat.
cherbourgtourisme.com

Cherbourg has been a strategic port and naval base since the mid-19th century. The French Navy still uses its harbors, as do transatlantic ships and cross-Channel ferries from England and Ireland. For a good view of the port, drive to the hilltop **Fort du Roule**, which houses the **Musée de la Libération**, recalling the D-Day invasion and the subsequent liberation of Cherbourg. Most activity is centered on the flower-filled market square, place Général de Gaulle, and along shopping streets such as rue Tour-Carrée and rue de la Paix. The fine art in the **Musée Thomas Henry** includes 17th-century Flemish works, and portraits by Jean François Millet, born in Gréville-Hague. **Parc Emmanuel Liais** has small botanical gardens and a densely packed **Musée d'Histoire Naturelle**.

The **Cité de la Mer**, a completely bilingual center, has a cylindrical deep-sea aquarium, the world's largest visitable submarine, and other wonders.

Cherbourg town center

Musée de la Libération
Fort du Roule. **Tel** 02 33 20 14 12. **Open** May–Sep: Tue–Sat & Sun pm; Oct–Apr: Tue–Sun pms. **Closed** public hols. free Sun.

Musée Thomas-Henry
Rue Vastel. **Tel** 02 33 23 39 30. **Closed** for renovation until 2015.

La Cité de la Mer
Gare Maritime Transatlantique. **Open** Feb–Oct: daily; Nov–Dec: Tue–Sun. **Closed** Jan, Dec 25. **Tel** 02 33 20 26 69.
citedelamer.com

❸ Coutances

Manche. 11,500. pl Georges Leclerc (02 33 19 08 10). Thu. **tourisme-coutances.fr**

From Roman times until the Revolution, the hill-top town of Coutances was the capital of the Cotentin. The slender **Cathédrale Notre-Dame**, a fine example of Norman Gothic architecture, has a soaring 217 ft (66 m) lantern tower. Founded in the 1040s by Bishop Geoffroi de Montbray, it was financed by the local de Hauteville family using moneys gained in Sicily where they had founded a kingdom a few years earlier.

The town was badly damaged during World

War II but the cathedral, the churches of St. Nicholas and St. Peter, and the beautiful public gardens with their rare plants, all survived.

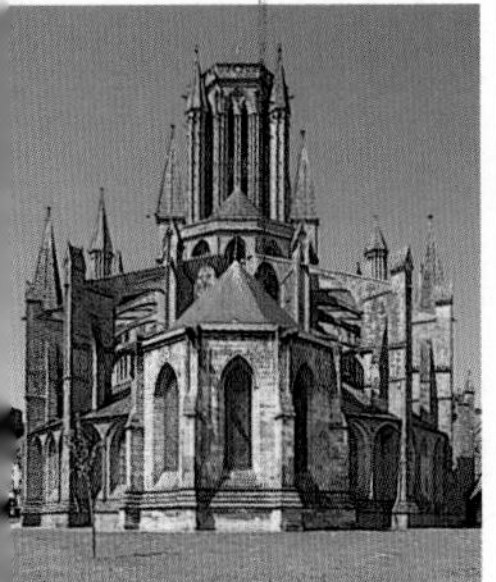

The back of Coutances cathedral with its squat lantern tower

❹ Granville

Manche. 13,500. 4 cours Jonville (02 33 91 30 03). Sat. **ville-granville.fr**

Ramparts enclose the upper town of Granville, which sits on a spur overlooking the Baie du Mont-St-Michel. The walled town was developed from fortifications built by the English in 1439.

The **Musée de Vieux Granville**, in the town gatehouse, recounts Granville's long seafaring tradition. The chapel walls of the **Eglise de Notre-Dame** are lined with tributes from local fishermen to their patroness, Notre-Dame du Cap Lihou. The lower town is an old-fashioned seaside resort with a casino, promenades, and public gardens. From the port there are boat trips to the Iles Chausey, a scattering of low-lying granite islands.

Le Musée Christian Dior is housed in Les Rhumbs, the fashion designer's childhood home, surrounded by a beautiful cliff garden.

Musée de Vieux Granville
2 rue Le Carpentier. **Tel** 02 33 50 44 10. **Open** Apr–Sep: Wed–Mon; Oct–Mar: Wed, Sat & Sun pms. **Closed** Nov 1, Dec 22–Jan.

Musée Christian Dior
Villa les Rhumbs. **Tel** 02 33 61 48 21. **Open** mid-May–Sep: daily; Oct–mid-May: Sat–Sun pms. Gardens: open all year.

D-Day Landings

In the early hours of June 6, 1944, Allied forces began landing on the shores of Normandy, the first step in a long-planned invasion of German-occupied France, known as Operation Overlord. Parachutists were dropped near Ste-Mère-Eglise and Pegasus Bridge, and sea-borne assaults were made along a string of code-named beaches. US troops landed on Utah and Omaha in the west, while British and Canadian troops, which included a contingent of Free French commandos, landed at Gold, Juno, and Sword. The beaches are still referred to by their code names. Pegasus Bridge, where the first French house was liberated, is a natural starting point for a tour around the sights and memorials. Farther west, evocative ruins of the artificial harbor towed across from England survive at Arromanches-les-Bains. There are British, German, and American war cemeteries at La Cambe, Ranville, and St-Laurent-sur-Mer. War museums at Bayeux, Caen, St-Mère-Eglise, and Cherbourg provide background on D-Day and the ensuing Battle for Normandy.

American troops coming ashore during the Allied invasion of France

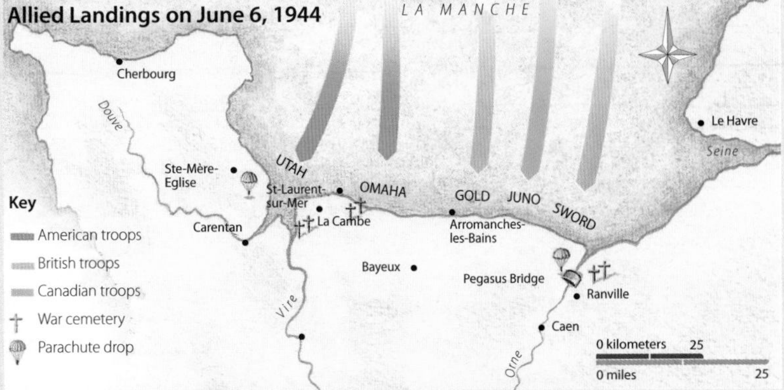

By the end of D-Day, over 135,000 men had been brought ashore, with losses totaling around 10,000.

❺ Avranches

Manche. 9,500. 2 rue Général-de-Gaulle (02 33 58 00 22). Sat. **ot-avranches.com**

Avranches has been a religious center since the 6th century and is the final staging-post for visitors to the abbey on Mont-St-Michel. The origins of the famous abbey lie in a vision experienced by Aubert, the Bishop of Avranches. One night in 708 the Archangel Michael instructed him to build a church on the nearby island. Aubert's skull, with the finger-hole made in it by the angel, can be seen in the treasury of **St-Gervais** in Avranches. The best views of Mont-St-Michel are from the **Jardin des Plantes**. After the Revolution, 203 illuminated manuscripts were rescued from Mont-St-Michel's abbey. These and many others are held in the **Musée des Manuscrits du Mont-St-Michel**. Multimedia displays show how monks copied and illuminated the texts. The **Musée d'Art et d'Histoire** details life in the Cotentin over the centuries, with a collection devoted to representations of Mont-St-Michel.

Musée des Manuscrits du Mont-St-Michel
Pl d'Estouteville. **Tel** 02 33 79 57 00. **Open** Tue–Sun (Jul–Aug: daily). **Closed** Jan, May 1, Nov 1, Dec 25.

Musée d'Art et d'Histoire
Place Jean de Saint-Avit. **Open** Jun–Sep: daily.

Remains of Mulberry Harbor from World War II off the Côte de Nacre

❻ Mont-St-Michel

See pp260–63.

❼ Côte de Nacre

Calvados. Caen. Caen, Bayeux. Caen-Ouistreham. pl St-Pierre, Caen (02 31 27 14 14). Fri, Sun. **caen-tourisme.fr**

The stretch of coast between the mouths of the rivers Orne and Vire was dubbed the Côte de Nacre (Mother of Pearl Coast) in the 19th century. More recently it has become known as the site of the D-Day Landings when Allied troops poured ashore at the start of Operation Overlord *(see p255)*. The associated cemeteries, memorials, and museums, and the remnants of the Mulberry Harbor at Arromanches-les-Bains, provide focal points for a visit. However, the coastline is equally popular as a summer holiday destination, offering long, sandy beaches backed by seaside resorts such as Courseulles-sur-Mer and Luc-sur-Mer, which are more relaxed than the resorts of the Côte Fleurie farther east.

❽ Bayeux

Calvados. 15,500. Pont St-Jean (02 31 51 28 28). Sat, Wed. **bessin-normandie.com**

Bayeux was the first town to be liberated by the Allies in 1944 and fortunate to escape war damage. Today, an attractive nucleus of 15th–19th-century buildings remains around its central high streets, rue St-Martin and rue St-Jean. The latter is lined with shops and cafés.

Bayeux Tapestry

A lively comic strip justifying William the Conqueror's invasion of England, this 230-ft (70-m) long embroidered hanging was commissioned by Bishop Odo of Bayeux. Offering insights into 11th-century life, and an action-packed account of the defeat of Harold, the King of England, at the Battle of Hastings, the tapestry is valued as a work of art, a historical document, an early example of spin, and an entertaining read.

Harold's retinue sets off for France to inform William that he will succeed to the English throne.

Trees with interlacing branches are sometimes used to divide the tapestry's 58 scenes.

Above the town rise the spires and domed lantern tower of the Gothic **Cathédrale Notre-Dame**. Beneath its interior is an 11th-century crypt decorated with restored 15th-century frescoes of angels playing musical instruments. The original Romanesque church that stood here was consecrated in 1077, and it is likely that Bayeux's famous tapestry was commissioned for this occasion by one of its key characters, Bishop Odo.

The tapestry is displayed in a renovated seminary, **Centre Guillaume-le-Conquérant-Tapisserie de Bayeux**, which gives a detailed audio-visual explanation of events leading up to the Norman conquest. On the southwest side of the town, the restored **Musée Mémorial de la Bataille de Normandie** traces the events of the Battle of Normandy in World War II, with an excellent film compilation made from contemporary newsreels.

Centre Guillaume-le-Conquérant-Tapisserie
Rue de Nesmond. **Tel** 02 31 51 25 50. **Open** daily. **Closed** 3 wks early Jan, Dec 25–26. **bayeuxmuseum.com**

Musée Mémorial de la Bataille de Normandie
Bd Fabian-Ware. **Tel** 02 31 51 46 90. **Open** mid-Feb–Dec: daily. **Closed** Jan 1, Dec 25.

The Abbaye aux Hommes in Caen

9 Caen

Calvados. 117,200. pl St-Pierre (02 31 27 14 14). Fri & Sun. **caen-tourisme.fr**

In the mid-11th century Caen became the favored residence of William the Conqueror and Queen Matilda, and despite the destruction of three-quarters of the city during World War II, much remains of their creation. The monarchs built two great abbeys and a castle on the north bank of the river Orne, bequeathing Caen a core of historic interest that justifies penetrating its industrial areas and postwar housing. Much-loved by the citizens of Caen, the **Eglise St-Pierre** was built on the south side of the castle in the 13th–14th centuries, with an impressively ornate Renaissance east end added in the early 16th century. The frequently copied 14th-century belltower was destroyed in 1944 but has now been restored. To the east, rue du Vaugeux is the central street in Caen's small Vieux Quartier (Old Quarter). Now pedestrianized, the street still has some lovely half-timbered buildings. A walk west, along rue St-Pierre or boulevard du Maréchal Leclerc, leads to the city's main shopping district.

The English have a last meal on land before boarding with hunting dogs and falcons.

Wide moustaches distinguish the English characters from the clean-shaven Normans.

The colored wool used to embroider the linen has faded little since the 11th century.

Latin inscriptions caption each main scene in the work and embody the heroic ideals shared by all the participants.

Borders provide wry comment through fables and asides.

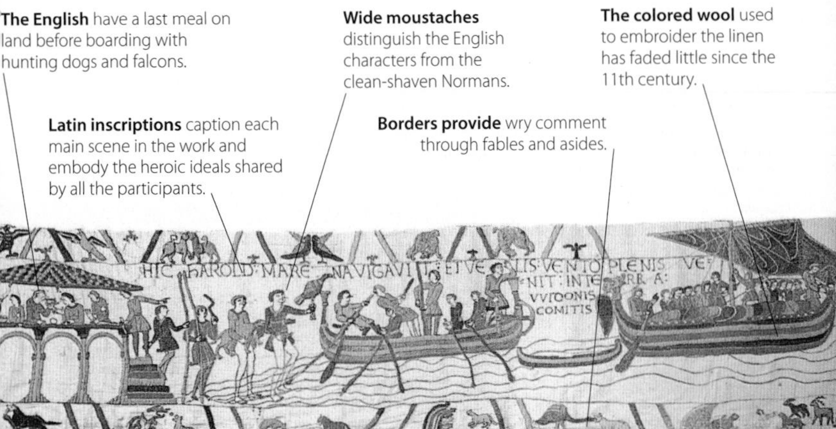

Caen City Center

① Abbaye aux Hommes
② Eglise St-Etienne
③ Château Ducal
④ Eglise St-Pierre
⑤ La Trinité
⑥ Abbaye aux Dames

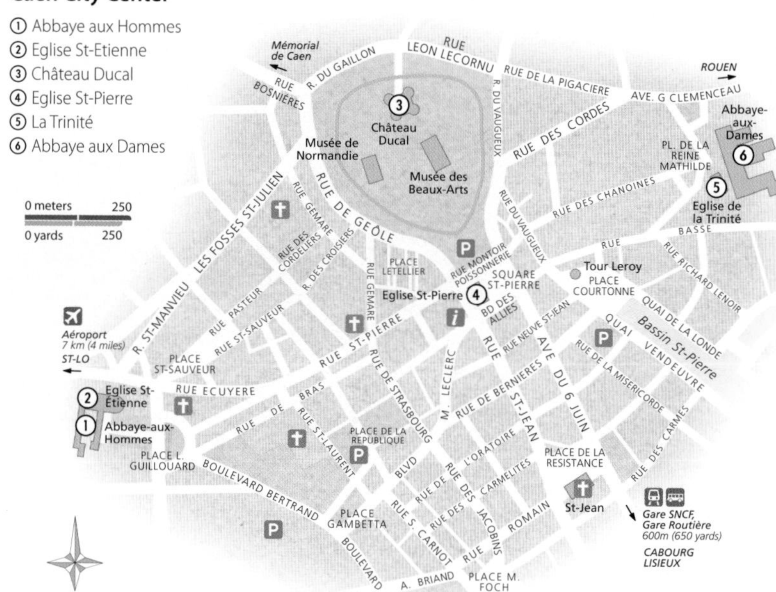

Key to Symbols *see back flap*

Abbaye-aux-Hommes

Esplanade Jean-Marie Louvel. **Tel** 02 31 30 42 81. **Open** daily. **Closed** Jan 1, May 1, Dec 25. restr. oblig.

Work began on William's Abbey for Men in 1063 and was almost complete by his death 20 years later. The abbey church, **Eglise St-Etienne**, is a masterpiece of Norman Romanesque, with a severe, unadorned west front crowned with 13th-century spires. The sparingly decorated nave was roofed in the early 12th century with stone vaulting that anticipates the Gothic style.

Abbaye-aux-Dames

Pl de la Reine Mathilde. **Tel** 02 31 06 98 98. **Open** daily pms only. **Closed** Jan 1, May 1, Dec 25. oblig.

Like William's Abbaye-aux-Hommes, Matilda's Abbey for Women also has a Norman Romanesque church, **La Trinité**, flanked by 18th-century buildings. Begun in 1060, it was consecrated 6 years later. Queen Matilda lies buried in the choir under a slab of black marble, and her beautifully restored abbey, with its creamy Caen stone, makes a serene, dignified mausoleum.

Château Ducal

Esplanade du Château. Musée des Beaux Arts: **Tel** 02 31 30 47 70. **Open** Wed–Mon. Musée de Normandie: **Tel** 02 31 30 47 60. **Open** Jun–Oct: daily: Nov–May: Wed–Mon. **Closed** Jan 1, Easter, May 1, Ascension, Nov 1, Dec 25 (both museums).

The ruins of Caen's castle, one of the largest fortified enclosures in Europe, offer spacious lawns, museums and rampart views. A fine art collection, strong on 17th-century French and Italian painting, is exhibited in the **Musée des Beaux Arts**. The **Musée de Normandie** recalls traditional life in the region with utensils and displays on farming and lace.

Mémorial de Caen

Esplanade Dwight-Eisenhower. **Tel** 02 31 06 06 45. **Open** mid-Feb–Oct: daily; Nov–mid-Feb: Tue–Sun. **Closed** 3 weeks in Jan, Dec 25. **memorial-caen.fr**

Northwest of Caen, close to the N13 ring-road (exit 7), this museum is dedicated to peace, placing D-Day into the context of World War II using a host of interactive and audio-visual techniques, including stunning compilations of archive and fictional film.

A modern extension gives a wider perspective on cultural, religious, border, and ecological conflicts in the second half of the 20th century.

Lush Orne valley in the Suisse Normande

Suisse Normande

alvados & Orne. Caen. aen, Argentan. 2 pl St-Sauveur, ury-Harcourt (02 31 79 70 45). **ot-suisse-normande.com**

hough hardly like the iountains of Switzerland, the iffs and valleys carved out y the river Orne as it winds orth to Caen have become opular for walking, climbing, amping, and river sports. ne area is also ideal for a ıral drive. Its highest and iost impressive point is the)ëtre Rock, off the D329, /here you can look down over ıe dramatic gorges created y the river Rouvre.

❶ Parc Naturel Régional de Normandie-Maine

)rne & Manche. Alençon. rgentan. Carrouges (02 33 81 13 3). **parc-naturel-normandie-naine.fr**

he southern fringes of central Normandy have been ncorporated into France's ırgest regional park. Among ne farmland and forests of oak nd beech are several small owns. **Domfront** rests on a spur verlooking the river Varenne. he spa town **Bagnoles-de-'Orne** offers a casino and sports acilities, while **Sées** has a Gothic cathedral. The **Maison du Parc** at Carrouges has nformation on walks, cycling, nd canoeing.

Poster of Deauville, about 1930

Maison du Parc
Carrouges. **Tel** 02 33 81 13 33.
Open May–Sep: Tue–Sun, Oct–Apr: Tue–Fri. **Closed** public hols.

Environs
Just north of the park is the **Chateau d'O**, a Renaissance château with fine 17th-century frescoes. The **Haras du Pin** is France's national stud, called "a horses' Versailles" for its 17th-century architecture. Horse shows, dressage events, and various tours take place throughout the year.

⓬ Côte Fleurie

Calvados. Deauville. 112 rue Victor Hugo, Deauville (02 31 14 40 00). **deauville.org**

The Côte Fleurie (Flowery Coast) between Villerville and Cabourg has been planted with chic resorts which burst into bloom every summer. **Trouville** was once a humble fishing village, but in the mid-19th century caught the attention of writers Gustave Flaubert and Alexandre Dumas. By the 1870s Trouville had acquired grand hotels, a train station, and pseudo-Swiss villas along the beachfront. It has, however, long been outclassed by its neighbor, **Deauville**, created by the Duc de Morny in the 1860s. This resort boasts a casino, racecourses, marinas, and the famous beachside catwalk, Les Planches.

For something quieter, head west to smaller resorts such as Villers-sur-Mer or Houlgate. **Cabourg** farther west is dominated by the turn-of-the-century Grand Hôtel where novelist Marcel Proust spent many summers. Proust used the resort as a model for the fictional Balbec in his novel *Remembrance of Things Past*.

⓭ Pays d'Auge

Calvados. Deauville. Lisieux. 11 rue d'Alençon, Lisieux (02 31 48 18 10). **lisieux-tourisme.com**

Inland from the Côte Fleurie, the Pays d'Auge is classic Normandy countryside, lushly woven with fields, wooded valleys, cider orchards, dairy farms, and manor houses. Its capital is **Lisieux**, a cathedral town devoted to St. Thérèse of Lisieux, canonized in 1925, who attracts hundreds of thousands of pilgrims each year. Lisieux is an obvious base for exploring the region, but nearby market towns, such as St-Pierre-sur-Dives and Orbec, are smaller and more attractive.

The best way to enjoy the Pays d'Auge is to potter around its minor roads. There is a tourist route devoted to cider, and picturesque manor houses, farmhouses, and châteaus testify to the wealth of this fertile land. **St-Germain-de-Livet** can be visited, as can **Crèvecoeur-en-Auge**, and the half-timbered village of **Beuvron-en-Auge** is charming.

Apples and Cider

Apple orchards are a familiar feature of the Normandy countryside, and their fruit a fundamental ingredient in the region's gastronomic repertoire. No selfrespecting pâtisserie would be without its *tarte normande* (apple tart), and every country lane seems to sport an *Ici Vente Cidre* (cider sold here) sign. Much of the harvest forms the raw material for cider and Calvados, an apple brandy aged in oak barrels for at least two years. A local brew is also made from pears, and known as *poiré* (perry).

A crop ranging from sour cider apples to sweet eating varieties

❻ Mont-St-Michel

Shrouded by mist, encircled by sea, soaring proudly above glistening sands – the silhouette of Mont-St-Michel is one of the most enchanting sights in France. Now linked to the mainland by a causeway, the island of Mont-Tombe (Tomb on the Hill) stands at the mouth of the river Couesnon, crowned by a fortified abbey that almost doubles its height. Lying strategically on the frontier between Normandy and Brittany, Mont-St-Michel grew from a humble 8th-century oratory to become a Benedictine monastery that had its greatest influence in the 12th and 13th centuries. Pilgrims known as *miquelots* journeyed from afar to honor the cult of St. Michael, and the monastery was a renowned center of medieval learning. Major engineering works to reverse the silting up of the sea around the island will be in place until 2015.

St. Aubert's Chapel
A small 15th-century chapel built on an outcrop of rock is dedicated to Aubert, the founder of Mont-St-Michel.

★ Gabriel Tower
Three floors of cannons point in all directions from this imposing 16th-century tower.

700

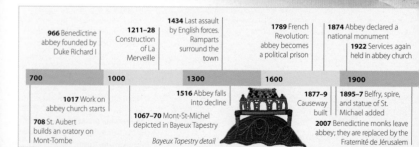

708 St. Aubert builds an oratory on Mont-Tombe

966 Benedictine abbey founded by Duke Richard I

1000

1017 Work on abbey church starts

1067–70 Mont-St-Michel depicted in Bayeux Tapestry

1211–28 Construction of La Merveille

1300

1434 Last assault by English forces. Ramparts surround the town

1516 Abbey falls into decline

Bayeux Tapestry detail

1600

1789 French Revolution: abbey becomes a political prison

1874 Abbey declared a national monument

1877–9 Causeway built

1895–7 Belfry, spire, and statue of St. Michael added

1900

1922 Services again held in abbey church

2007 Benedictine monks leave abbey; they are replaced by the Fraternité de Jérusalem

Tides of Mont-St-Michel
Extremely strong tides in the Baie du Mont-St-Michel act as a natural defence. They rise and fall with the lunar calendar and can reach speeds of 6 mph (10 km/h).

VISITORS' CHECKLIST

Practical Information
bd de l'Avancée (02 33 60 14 30). **ot-montsaint michel.com** Abbey: **Tel** 02 33 89 80 00. **Open** May–Aug: 9am–7pm; Sep–Apr: 9:30am–6pm. Nocturnal visits in summer (recommended). **Closed** Jan 1, May 1, Dec 25. 12:15pm Tue–Sat, 11:30am Sun. **mont-saint-michel.monuments-nationaux.fr**

Transport
to Pontorson, then bus.

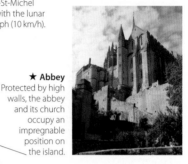

★ Abbey
Protected by high walls, the abbey and its church occupy an impregnable position on the island.

2
3
4
5

KEY

① **Gautier's Leap**, the terrace at the top of the Inner Staircase, is named after a prisoner who leapt to his death.

② **Eglise St-Pierre**

③ **Liberty Tower**

④ **The Arcade Tower** provided lodgings for the abbot's soldiers.

⑤ **King's Tower**

★ Grande Rue
Now crowded with restaurants, the pilgrims' route, followed since the 12th century, climbs up past Eglise St-Pierre to the abbey gates.

The Abbey of Mont-St-Michel

The present buildings bear witness to the time when the abbey served both as a Benedictine monastery and, for 73 years after the Revolution, as a political prison. In 1017 work began on a Romanesque church at the island's highest point, building over its 10th-century predecessor, now the Chapel of Our Lady Underground. A monastery built on three levels, La Merveille (The Miracle) was added to the church's north side in the early 13th century.

★ Church
Four bays of the Romanesque nave survive. Three were pulled down in 1776, creating the West Terrace.

★ La Merveille
The Miracle is a Gothic masterpiece – a three-story monastic complex built in only 16 years.

Refectory
The monks took their meals in this long, narrow room, which is flooded with light through tall windows.

Knights' Room
The rib vaults and finely decorated capitals are typically Gothic.

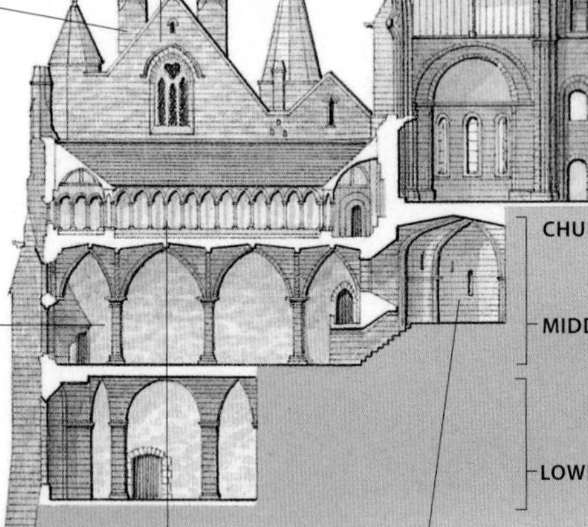

Crypt of the Thirty Candles is one of two 11th-century crypts bui to support the transept the main church.

★ Cloisters
The cloisters with their elegant columns in staggered rows are a beautiful example of early 13th-century Anglo-Norman style.

For hotels and restaurants in this region see pp554–71 and pp576–603

isiting the Abbey

he three levels of the abbey reflect the monastic ierarchy. The monks lived at the highest level, in n enclosed world of church, cloister, and refec- ory. The abbot entertained his noble guests on the niddle level. Soldiers and pilgrims farther down on he social scale were received at the lowest level. uided tours begin at the West Terrace at the hurch level and end in the almonry, where alms vere dispensed to the poor. The almonry is now a ookstore and souvenir hall.

CHURCH LEVEL

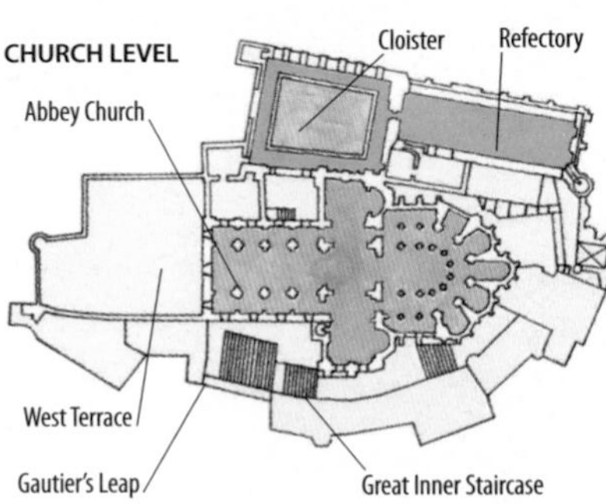

Church Interior
A Flamboyant Gothic choir was built in 1446–1521, held up by crypts with massive supporting pillars.

MIDDLE LEVEL

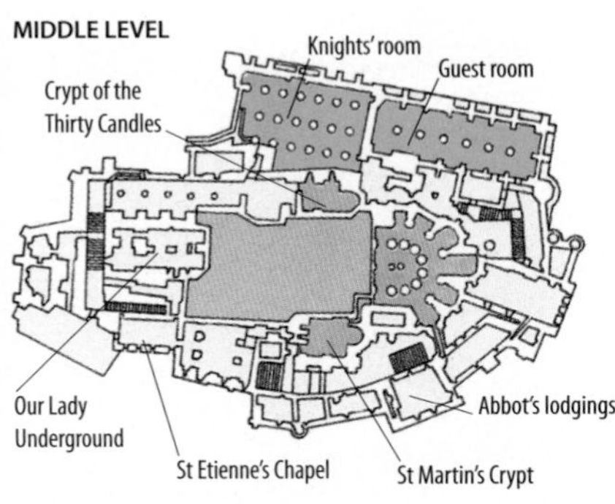

LOWER LEVEL

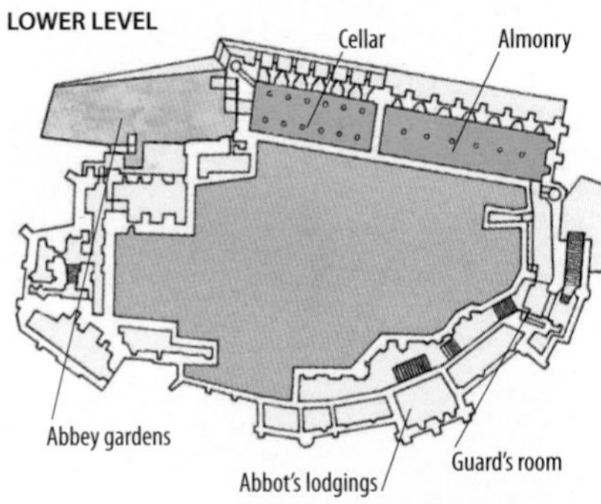

St Martin's Crypt is an 11th-century barrel-vaulted chapel that preserves the austere forms of the original Romanesque abbey.

The abbot's lodgings were close to the abbey entrance, and he received prestigious visitors in the guest room. Poorer pilgrims were received in the almonry.

West Terrace
Guided tours start here, at the West Terrace. The Fraternité de Jérusalem, a small monastic community, lives in the abbey and welcomes visitors.

Mont-St-Michel by night ▶

⓮ Honfleur

Calvados. 8,500. Deauville. quai Lepaulmier (02 31 89 23 30). Wed, Sat; Thu, Sun: fish market at harbor. **ot-honfleur.fr**

A major defensive port in the 15th century, Honfleur has become one of Normandy's most appealing harbors. At its heart is the 17th-century **Vieux Bassin** (Old Dock), with its pretty tall houses (6–7 storys).

Honfleur became a center of artistic activity in the 19th century. Eugène Boudin, the painter, was born here in 1824, as was the composer Erik Satie in 1866. Courbet, Sisley, Renoir, Pissarro, and Cézanne all visited Honfleur, often meeting at the Ferme St-Siméon, now a luxury hotel. Painters still work from Honfleur's quayside, and exhibit in the **Greniers à Sel**, two salt warehouses built in 1670. These lie to the east of the Vieux Bassin in an area known as l'Enclos, which made up the fortified heart of the town in the 13th century.

The **Musée d'Ethnographie et d'Art Populaire Normand** displays mementos of Honfleur's nautical past, with a warren of Norman interiors next door in the former prison. Place Ste-Catherine has an unusual 15th-century church built by ship's carpenters. The **Musée Eugène-Boudin** documents the artistic appeal of Honfleur and the Seine estuary, with works from Boudin to Raoul Dufy. **Les Maisons Satie** use extracts from Satie's music to guide you round reconstructions of the rooms.

Greniers à Sel
Rue de la Ville. 02 31 89 23 30. **Open** for guided tours & exhibitions. obligatory, except during summer exhibs.

Musée d'Ethnographie et d'Art Populaire Normand
Quai St Etienne. **Tel** 02 31 89 14 12. **Open** mid-Feb–Mar, Oct–mid-Nov: Tue–Fri *(pms only)*, Sat, Sun; Apr–Sep: daily. **Closed** May 1.

Musée Eugène-Boudin
Pl Erik Satie, rue de l'Homme de Bois. **Tel** 02 31 89 54 00. **Open** mid-Feb–mid-Mar & Oct–Dec: Wed–Mon pms, Sat, Sun; mid-Mar–Sep: Wed–Mon. **Closed** May 1, Jul 14, Dec 25.

Les Maisons Satie
67 bd Charles V. **Tel** 02 31 89 11 11. **Open** mid-Feb–Dec: Wed–Mon. **Closed** public hols.

Quai St-Etienne in Honfleur

⓯ Le Havre

Seine-Maritime. 194,000. 186 bd Clemenceau (02 32 74 04 04). daily. **lehavretourisme.com**

Strategically positioned on the Seine estuary, Le Havre (The Harbor) was created in 1517 by François I after the nearby port of Harfleur silted up. During World War II it was virtually obliterated by Allied bombing, but despite a vast industrial zone which stands beside the port, it still has appeal. It is an important yachting center, and its beach has two blue flags (very clean!).

Much of the city center was rebuilt in the 1950s–1960s by August Perret, whose towering **Eglise St-Joseph** (a UNESCO World Heritage site) pierces the skyline. On the seafront, the **Musée Malraux** has works by, amongst others, local artist Raoul Dufy. France's biggest skateboard park is also on the seafront.

Musée Malraux
2 bd Clemenceau. **Tel** 02 35 19 62 62. **Open** Wed–Mon. **Closed** public hol **muma-lehavre.fr**

⓰ Côte d'Albâtre

Seine-Maritime. Pont Jehan Ango, Dieppe (02 32 14 40 60 **dieppetourisme.com**

The Alabaster Coast gets its name from the chalky cliffs and milky waters that characterize the Normandy coastline between Le Havre and Le Tréport. It is best known for the **Falaise d'Aval** west of Etretat, eroded into an arch. The author Guy de Maupassant, born near Dieppe in 1850, compared these cliffs to an elephant dipping its trunk into the sea. From Etretat, a chain of coastal roads runs east across a switchback of breezy headlands and wooded valleys to Dieppe.

Fécamp is the only major town along this route. Its Benedictine abbey was once an important pilgrimage center after a tree trunk said to contain drops of Christ's Blood was washed ashore here in the 7th century. This is enshrined in a reliquary at the entrance to the Lady Chapel of the abbey church, La Trinité.

The vast **Palais Bénédictine** a Neo-Gothic-and-Renaissance homage to the ego of Alexander Le Grand, a local wine and spirits merchant who rediscovered the monks' recipe for Bénédictine, the famous herbal liqueur. Built in 1882, it

Woman with Parasol (1880) by Boudin in the Musée Eugène-Boudin

For hotels and restaurants in this region see pp554–71 and pp576–603

The cliffs at Falaise d'Aval, famously likened to an elephant dipping its trunk into the sea

incorporates a distillery and an eccentric museum packed with curios. The adjacent halls provide an aromatic account and tastings of the 27 herbs and spices which make up the elixir.

Palais Bénédictine
110 rue Alexandre Le Grand, Fécamp. **Tel** 02 35 10 26 10. **Open** daily. **Closed** Jan–mid-Feb, May 1, Dec 25.

View of Dieppe from the château and museum above the town

⓱ Dieppe

Seine-Maritime. 36,000.
Pont Jean Ango (02 32 14 40 60).
Tue, Thu & esp. Sat.
dieppetourisme.com

Dieppe exploits a break in the chalky cliffs bordering the Pays de Caux, and has won historical prestige as a Channel fort, port, and resort. Prosperity came during the 16th and 17th centuries, when local privateer Jehan Ango raided the Portuguese and English fleets, and a trading post called Petit Dieppe was founded on the West African coast. At that time, Dieppe's population was already 30,000, and included a 300-strong community of craftsmen carving imported ivory. This maritime past is celebrated in **Le Château-Musée**, the 15th-century castle crowning the headland to the west of the seafront. Here you can see historical maps and model ships, a collection of Dieppe ivories, and paintings that evoke the town's development as a fashionable seaside resort during the 19th century. Dieppe had the nearest beach to Paris and quickly responded to the developing passion for promenading, seawater cures, and bathing.

Today Dieppe's broad seafront is given over to lawns, seaside amusements, and car parks, and its liveliest streets surround the battle-scarred **Eglise St-Jacques** to the south. If the weather is poor, visit **L'Estran-La Cité de la Mer**, an exhibition center with models on maritime themes, and an aquarium.

Le Château-Musée
Tel 02 35 06 61 99. **Open** Jun & Sep: Mon pm, Tue–Sun; Jul–Aug: daily. **Closed** Jan 1, May 1, Nov 1, Dec 25. **dieppe.fr**

L'Estran-La Cité de la Mer
37 rue de l'Asile Thomas. **Tel** 02 35 06 93 20. **Open** daily. **Closed** Jan 1, Dec 25.

⓲ Basse-Seine

Seine-Maritime & Eure. Le Havre, Rouen. Yvetot. Le Havre.
Yvetot (02 35 95 08 40).

Meandering seaward from Rouen to Le Havre, the river Seine is crossed by three spectacular road bridges: the Pont de Brotonne, the Pont de Tancarville, and the Pont de Normandie (linking Le Havre and Honfleur). The grace and daring of these modern bridges echo the soaring aspirations of the abbeys founded on the river's banks in the 7th and 8th centuries. The abbeys now provide good stepping stones for a tour of the Lower Seine valley.

West of Rouen is the harmonious Eglise de St-Georges at **St-Martin-de-Boscherville** which until the Revolution was the church of a small walled abbey. Its 12th-century chapter house has remarkable biblical statues and carved capitals. From here the D67 runs south to the riverside village of La Bouille.

As you head northwest, an hourly car ferry at Mesnil-sous-Jumièges takes you over to the colossal ruins of the **Abbaye de Jumièges**. The abbey was founded in 654 and once housed 900 monks and 1,500 servants. The main abbey church dates from the 11th century; its consecration in 1067 was a major event, with William the Conqueror in attendance.

The D913 strikes through oak and beech woods in the Parc Régional de Brotonne to the 7th-century **Abbaye de St-Wandrille** (closed for renovation until 2015). The Musée de la Marine de Seine at **Caudebec-en-Caux** gives an engrossing account of many aspects of life on this great river since the late 19th century.

Monk from Abbaye de St-Wandrille

⓳ Rouen

Rouen, a thriving port on the river Seine

Founded at the lowest point where the Seine could be bridged, Rouen has prospered through maritime trade and industrialization to become a rich and cultured city. Despite the severe damage of World War II, the city boasts a wealth of historic sights on its right bank, all within walking distance of the central Cathédrale Notre-Dame, frequently painted by Monet. In turn a Celtic trading post, Roman garrison, and Viking colony, Rouen became the capital of the Norman Duchy in 911. It was captured by Henry V in 1419 after a siege during the Hundred Years' War. In 1431 Joan of Arc was burned at the stake here in place du Vieux-Marché.

Exploring Rouen

From the cathedral, the rue du Gros Horloge runs west under the city's Great Clock, to the place du Vieux Marché and its post-war Eglise Ste-Jeanne-d'Arc. Rue aux Juifs leads past the 15th-century Gothic **Palais de Justice**, once Normandy's parliament, to the smart shops and cafés around rue des Carmes. Farther east, between the St-Maclou and St-Ouen churches, are half-timbered houses in the rue Damiette and rue Eau de Robec. North, in place Général de Gaulle, is the 18th-century **Hôtel de Ville**.

Cathédrale Notre-Dame

This Gothic masterpiece is dominated by the famous west facade *(see p271)*, painted by Monet, which is framed by two unequal towers – the northern Tour St-Romain, and the later Tour du Beurre, supposedly paid for by a tax on butter consumption in Lent. Above the central lantern tower rises a Neo-Gothic spire, made from cast iron and erected in 1876. Recently restored, both the 14th-century northern Portail des Libraires and the 14th-century southern Portail de la Calende are worth seeing for their precise sculpting and delicate tracery. Many of the cathedral's riches are accessible by guided tour only, including the tomb of Richard the Lionheart, whose heart was buried here, and the rare 11th-century semicircular hall crypt, rediscovered in 1934. The choir/chancel was badly hit by the 1999 storm.

Cathédrale Notre-Dame, Rouen

Eglise St-Maclou

This Flamboyant Gothic church has an intensively decorated west facade with a five-bay porch and carved wooden

Sights at a Glance

1. Place du Vieux-Marché
2. Gros-Horloge
3. Palais de Justice
4. Musée de la Céramique
5. Musée des Beaux Arts
6. Musée le Secq des Tournelles
7. Cathédrale Notre-Dame
8. Eglise St-Maclou
9. Aître St-Maclou
10. Eglise St-Ouen
11. Hôtel de Ville
12. Musée d'Histoire Naturelle

doors depicting biblical scenes. Behind the church, its *aître*, or ossuary, is a rare surviving example of a medieval cemetery for the burial of plague victims. The timbers of its buildings, set around the quadrangle, are carved with a macabre array of grinning skulls, crossed bones, coffins, and grave-diggers' implements.

Musée d'Histoire Naturelle

198 rue Beauvoisine. **Tel** 02 35 71 41 50. **Open** Tue–Sun pms. **Closed** public hols.

The second largest museum of its kind in France, this museum holds more than 800,000 objects.

Eglise St-Ouen

Once part of a formidable Benedictine abbey, St-Ouen is a solid Gothic church with a lofty, unadorned interior made all the more beautiful by its restored 14th-century stained glass. Behind the church there is a pleasant park which is ideal for picnics.

Musée des Beaux Arts

Square Verdrel. **Tel** 02 35 71 28 40. **Open** Wed–Mon. **Closed** public hols except Easter & Whitsun.

The city's collection includes major art works: masterpieces by Caravaggio and Velázquez, and paintings by Normandy-born artists Théodore Géricault, Eugène Boudin, and Raoul Dufy. Also on display is Monet's *Rouen Cathedral, The Portal, Gray Weather.*

Musée de la Céramique

Hôtel d'Hocqueville,1 rue Faucon. **Tel** 02 35 07 31 74. **Open** Wed–Mon pms. **Closed** public hols.

Jug from Musée de la Céramique

Exhibits of 1,000 pieces of Rouen faïence – colorful glazed earthenware – together with other pieces of French and foreign china are displayed in a 17th-century town house. The works trace the history of Rouen faïence to its zenith in the 18th century.

VISITORS' CHECKLIST

Practical Information

Seine Maritime. 108,800. 25 pl de la Cathédrale (02 32 08 32 40). Tue–Sun. Feast of Joan of Arc (late May). **rouentourisme.com**

Transport

7 miles (11 km) SE Rouen. gare rive droite, pl Bernard Tissot (08 92 35 35 35). 25 rue des Charrettes. **Tel** 02 35 52 52 52.

Musée Le Secq des Tournelles

Rue Jacques-Villon. **Tel** 02 35 88 42 92. **Open** Wed–Mon pms. **Closed** public hols. ground floor only.

Located in a 15th-century church, this wrought ironwork museum exhibits antique iron-mongery ranging from keys to corkscrews and Gallo-Roman spoons to mighty tavern signs.

Musée Flaubert

51 rue de Lecat. **Tel** 02 35 15 59 95. **Open** Tue–Sat. **Closed** public hols.

Flaubert's father was a surgeon at Rouen Hospital, and his family home combines memorabilia with an awesome – and occasionally gruesome – display of 17th–19th-century medical equipment.

Gustave Flaubert

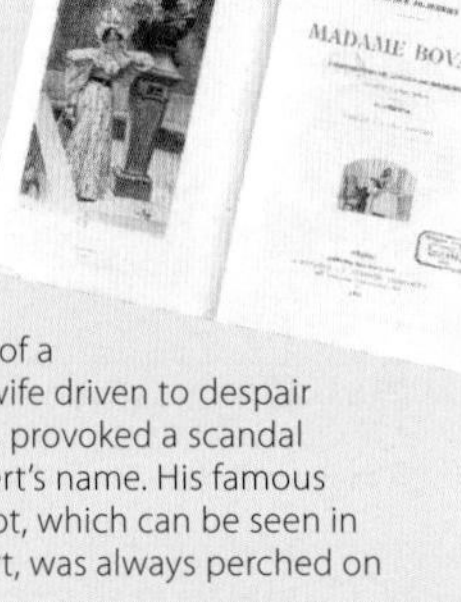

The novelist Gustave Flaubert (1821–80) was born and raised in Rouen, and the city provides the backdrop for some memorable scenes in his masterpiece, *Madame Bovary*. Published in 1857, this realistic study of a country doctor's wife driven to despair by her love affairs provoked a scandal that made Flaubert's name. His famous stuffed green parrot, which can be seen in the Musée Flaubert, was always perched on his writing desk.

Flaubert's stuffed parrot

Château Gaillard and the village of Les Andelys, in a loop of the river Seine

⑳ Haute-Seine

Eure. Rouen. Vernon, Val de Reuil. Gisors, Les Andelys. Les Andelys (02 32 54 41 93). **lesandelys-tourisme.fr**

Southeast of Rouen, the river Seine follows a convoluted course, with most points of interest on its north bank. At the center of the Forêt de Lyons, once the hunting ground for the Dukes of Normandy, is the country town of **Lyons-la-Forêt**, with half-timbered houses and an 18th-century covered market.

To the south the D313 follows the gracefully curving Seine to the town of **Les Andelys**. Above it tower the ruins of Château Gaillard which Richard the Lionheart, as King of England and Duke of Normandy, built in 1197 to defend Rouen from the French. They eventually took the castle in 1204.

㉑ Giverny

Eure. 600. 80 rue Claude Monet, Giverny 27620 (02 32 64 45 01). **cape-tourisme.fr**

In 1883 the Impressionist painter Claude Monet rented a house in the small village of Giverny, and worked here until his death. The house, known as the **Fondation Claude Monet**, and its garden are open to the public. The house is decorated in the color schemes that Monet admired; the gardens are famous as the subject of some of the artist's studies. Only copies are on show, but there are outstanding original 19th- and 20th-century art works in the **Musée des Impressionnismes** nearby.

Fondation Claude Monet
Giverny, Gasny. **Tel** 02 32 51 28 21. **Open** Apr–Oct: daily.
fondation-monet.fr

Musée des Impressionnismes
99 rue Claude Monet, Giverny. **Tel** 02 32 51 94 65. **Open** Apr–Oct.

㉒ Évreux

1 Eure. 55,000. 1ter pl du Général de Gaulle (02 32 24 04 43). Wed & Sat. **grandevreuxtourisme.fr**

Though considerably damaged in the war, Évreux is a pleasant cathedral town set in wide, agricultural plains. At its heart, the **Cathédrale Notre-Dame** is renowned for its 14th–15th century stained glass. The building is predominantly Gothic, though Romanesque arches survive in the nave and Renaissance screens adorn its chapels. Next door, the former Bishop's Palace houses the **Musée de l'Ancien Evêché**, with Roman bronze statues of Jupiter and Apollo, and fine 18th-century furniture and decorative art.

Monet's garden at Giverny, restored to its original profuse glory

For hotels and restaurants in this region see pp554–71 and pp576–603

Monet's Cathedral Series

In the 1890s Claude Monet made almost 30 paintings of Rouen's cathedral, several of which are now in the Musée d'Orsay in Paris *(see pp124–5)*. He studied the effects of changing light on its facades, and described both the surface detail and huge bulk, putting color before contour. The archetypal Impressionist, Monet said he conceived this series when he watched the effects of light on a country church, "as the sun's rays slowly dissolved the mists … that wrapped the golden stone in an ideally vaporous envelope."

Harmony in Blue and Gold (1894)
Monet selected a close vantage point for the series and was keen on this southwest view. The sun would cast afternoon shadows across the carved west front, accentuating the cavernous portals and the large rose window.

Monet's sketch, one of many of Rouen, parallels the shimmering effect of the paintings.

Harmony in Brown (1894) is the only finished version of a frontal view of the west facade. Analysis has shown that it was begun as a south-west view like the others.

Harmony in Blue (1894), compared with Harmony in Blue and Gold, shows the stone of the west facade further softened by the diffuse light of a misty morning.

The Portal, Gray Weather (1894) was one of several canvases in the gray color group which showed the cathedral facade in the soft light of an overcast day.

BRITTANY

Finistère · Côtes d'Armor · Morbihan · Ille-et-Vilaine

Jutting defiantly into the Atlantic, France's northwest corner has long been culturally and geographically distinct from the main bulk of the country. Known to the Celts as Armorica, the land of the sea, Brittany's past swirls with the legends of drowned cities and Arthurian forests. Prehistoric megaliths arise mysteriously from land and sea, and the medieval is never far from the modern.

A long, jagged coastline is the region's great attraction. Magnificent beaches line its northern shore, swept clean by huge tides and interspersed with well-established seaside resorts, seasoned fishing ports, and abundant oysterbeds. The south coast is gentler, with wooded river valleys and a milder climate, while the west, being exposed to the Atlantic winds, has a drama that justifies the name Finistère – the End of the Earth.

Inland lies the Argoat – once the Land of the Forest, now a patchwork of undulating fields, woods, and rolling moorland. Parc Régional d'Armorique occupies much of central Finistère, and it is in western Brittany that Breton culture remains most evident. In Quimper, and in the Pays Bigouden, crêpes and cider, traditional costumes, and Celtic music are still a genuine part of the Breton lifestyle. Eastern Brittany has a more conventional appeal. Vannes, Dinan, and Rennes, the Breton capital, have well-preserved medieval quarters where half-timbered buildings shelter inviting markets, shops, crêperies, and restaurants. The walled port of St-Malo on the Côte d'Emeraude recalls the region's maritime prowess, while the remarkably intact castles at Fougères and Vitré are reminders of the mighty border-fortresses that protected Brittany's eastern frontier before its final union with France in 1532.

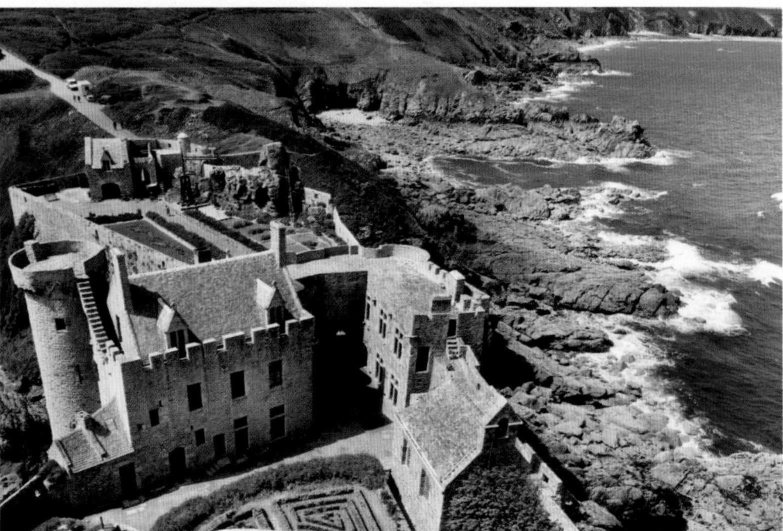

Fort la Latte, a medieval castle, offers spectacular views of the Côte d'Emeraude

◄ The sun sets over the dramatic coastline at the Pointe du Raz

Exploring Brittany

Ideal for a seaside holiday, Brittany offers enjoyable drives along the headlands and beaches of the northern Côte d'Emeraude and Côte de Granit Rose, while the south coast boasts wooded valleys and the prehistoric sites of Carnac and the Golfe du Morbihan. The parish closes *(see pp280–81)* provide an intriguing insight into Breton culture, as does the cathedral town of Quimper. Be sure to visit the regional capital, Rennes, and the great castle at Fougères, and in summer take a boat trip to one of Brittany's islands.

Sights at a Glance

1. Ile d'Ouessant
2. Brest
3. Parc Régional d'Armorique
4. Douarnenez
5. Locronan
6. Pointe du Raz
7. Pays Bigouden
8. Quimper
9. Concarneau
10. Pont-Aven
11. Le Pouldu
12. Roscoff
13. St-Thégonnec
14. Guimiliau
15. Lampaul-Guimiliau
16. Côte de Granit Rose
17. Tréguier
18. Ile de Bréhat
19. Carnac
20. Presqu'île de Quiberon
21. Belle-Ile-en-Mer
22. Vannes
23. Golfe du Morbihan
24. Josselin
25. Forêt de Paimpont
26. Côte d'Emeraude
27. St-Malo
28. Cancale
29. Dinan
30. Combourg
31. Rennes
32. Fougères
33. Vitré

Key

- Highway
- Major road
- Secondary road
- Minor road
- Scenic route
- Main railroad
- Minor railroad
- Regional border

For additional map symbols *see back flap*

Lighthouse on the Ile de Bréhat, Côte de Granit Rose

Getting Around

Expressways N12/N165 encircle Brittany, giving easy access to coastal areas, while the N12 and N24 give direct access to Rennes, Brittany's capital. Brittany can be reached by air to Brest, Nantes, and Rennes airports, by Channel ferries to St-Malo and Roscoff, by highways from Normandy, the Loire, and A11 from Paris, or by TGV direct from Paris and Lille.

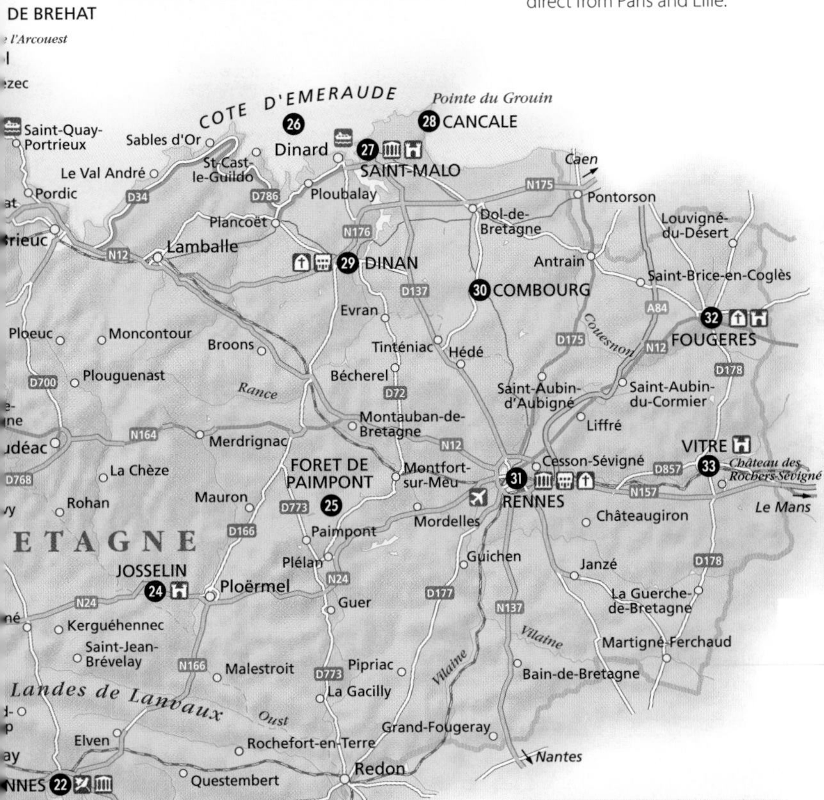

0 kilometers 25

0 miles 25

Half-timbered houses in the medieval part of Rennes

❶ Ile d'Ouessant

Finistère. 930. Ouessant (via Brest). Brest, then boat. Le Conquet, then boat. pl de l'Eglise, Lampaul (02 98 48 85 83).
ot-ouessant.fr

A well-known Breton proverb declares "He who sees Ouessant sees his own blood." Also known as Ushant, the island is notorious among sailors for its fierce storms and strong currents. However, this westerly point of France has a pleasant climate in summer and, though often bleak and stormy, can be surprisingly mild in winter. Part of the Parc Naturel Régional d'Armorique, the windswept island supports migrating birds and a small seal population, which may be observed from the Pern and Pen-ar-Roc'h headlands.

Two museums shed light on the island's defiant history, dogged by shipwreck and tragedy. At Niou Uhella, the **Ecomusée d'Ouessant** has furniture made from driftwood and wrecks, often painted blue and white in honor of the Virgin Mary. Nearby at Phare du Créac'h, the **Musée des Phares et Balises** explains the history of Brittany's many lighthouses and their keepers.

Ecomusée d'Ouessant
Maison du Niou. **Tel** 02 98 48 86 37. **Open** Apr–Sep: daily; Oct–Mar: Tue–Sun pms.

Musée des Phares et Balises
Pointe de Créac'h. **Tel** 02 98 48 80 70. **Open** Apr–Sep: daily; Oct–Mar: Tue–Sun pms.

❷ Brest

Finistère. 153,000. to islands only. 8 av Georges Clemenceau (02 98 44 24 96). daily.
brest-metropole-tourisme.fr

A natural harbor protected by the Presqu'île de Crozon, Brest is France's premier Atlantic naval port with a rich maritime history. Heavily bombed during World War II, it is now a modern commercial city where cargo vessels, yachts, and fishing boats ply the waters. The Cours Dajot promenade has good views of the Rade de Brest. The

Windswept moorlands near Ménez-Meur, Parc Régional d'Armorique

Château houses a naval museum with historic maps, maritime paintings, model ships, carved wooden, figureheads, and nautical instruments.

Across the Penfeld river – reached by Europe's largest lifting bridge, the Pont de Recouvrance – is the 14th-century **Tour de la Motte Tanguy**. By the Port de Plaisance, **Océanopolis** "sea center" has three vast pavilions simulating temperate, tropical, and polar ecosystems.

Château de Brest
Tel 02 98 22 12 39. **Open** Feb–Mar & Oct–Dec: daily pms only; Apr–Sep: daily. **Closed** May 1, Dec 25.

Tour de la Motte Tanguy
Sq Pierre Peron. **Tel** 02 98 00 88 60. **Open** Jun–Sep: daily; Oct–May: Wed–Thu, Sat–Sun pms. **Closed** Jan 1, May 1, Dec 25.

Océanopolis
Port de Plaisance du Moulin Blanc. **Tel** 02 98 34 40 40. **Open** mid-Apr–Sep: daily; Oct–mid-Apr: Tue–Sun. **Closed** 2 wks Jan, Dec 25.
oceanopolis.com

Traditional boatbuilding at Le Port Musée, Douarnenez

❸ Parc Naturel Régional d'Armorique

Finistère. Brest. Chateaulin, Landernau. Le Faou, Huelgoat, Carhaix. Le Faou (02 98 81 90 08).
pnr-armorique.fr

The Armorican Regional Nature Park stretches west from the moorlands of the Monts d'Arrée to the Presqu'île de Crozon and Ile d'Ouessant. Within this protected area lies a mixture of farmland, heaths, remains of ancient oak forest, and wild, open spaces. The park and its scenic coastline is ideal for walking, riding, and touring by bicycle or car.

Huelgoat is a good starting point for inland walks, while **Ménez-Hom** (1,082 ft/330 m) at the start of the Crozon Peninsula, has excellent views. The main park information center is at **Le Faou**. Nearby at **Ménez-Meur** is a wooded estate with wild and farm animals, and a Breton horse museum. Scattered around the park are 16 small specialist museums, some paying tribute to country traditions like hunting, fishing, and tanning. The **Musée de l'Ecole Rurale** (closed for renovation until mid-2014; call 02 98 26 04 72) at Trégarvan recreates an early 20th-century rural school. Other museums cover subjects such as medieval monastic life, rag-and-bone men, and the lifestyle of a Breton country priest. The **Maison des Artisans** in Brasparts displays contemporary crafts and art.

Douarnenez

nistère. 16,700. 2 rue
ı Docteur Mével (02 98 92 13 35).
Mon–Sat. **douarnenez-**
urisme.com

t the start of this century ouarnenez used to be France's ading sardine port; today it is ill devoted to fishing, but is so a tourist resort with eaches on both sides of the ouldavid estuary.

Nearby lies the tiny **Ile Tristan**, nked with the tragic love story of istan and Iseult. In the 16th entury it was the stronghold of a otorious brigand, La Fontenelle.

The picturesque **Port du osmeur** offers cafés, fish estaurants, and boat trips ound the bay, with a lively arly morning *criée* (fish uction) held in the nearby ouveau Port. The Port-Rhu has een turned into a floating useum, **Le Port Musée**, with ver 100 boats and several ipyards. Some of the larger essels can be visited.

Le Port Musée
de l'Enfer. **Tel** 02 98 92 65 20. **Open** ıl–Aug: daily; Feb–Jun & Sep–Oct: ue–Sun. **port-musee.org**

ocronan's 15th-century Eglise St-Ronan, een from the churchyard

Locronan

nistère. 1,000. pl de la Mairie 2 98 91 70 14).
locronan-tourisme.com

uring the 15th–17th centuries ocronan grew wealthy from the anufacture of sail-cloth. After ouis XIV ended the Breton onopoly on this trade, the own declined – leaving an elegant ensemble of Renaissance buildings that attract many visitors. In the town's central cobbled square stands a late 15th-century church dedicated to the Irish missionary St. Ronan. Down Rue Moal is the delightful **Chapelle Notre-Dame-de-Bonne-Nouvelle** with a calvary and a fountain. Every July Locronan is the scene of a *Troménie*, a hilltop pilgrimage held in honour of St. Ronan. The more elaborate *Grande Troménie* takes place every 6 years.

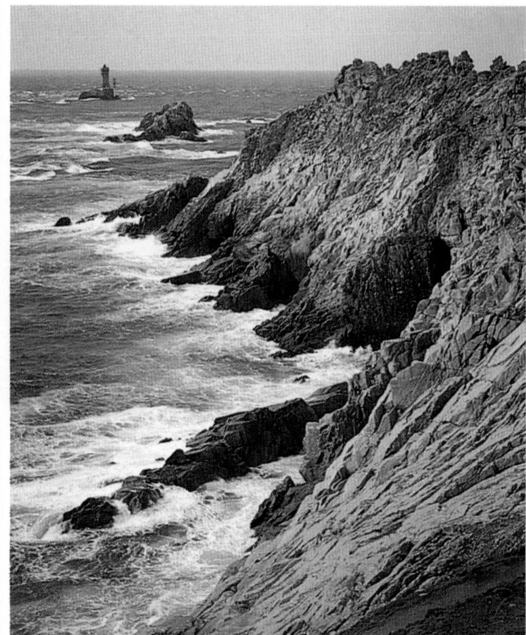

The awe-inspiring cliffs of Pointe du Raz

6 Pointe du Raz

Finistère. Quimper. Quimper, then bus. Audierne (02 98 70 12 20); Maison du Site (02 98 70 67 18).
pointeduraz.com

The dramatic Pointe du Raz, almost 262 ft (80 m) high, is a headland jutting into the Atlantic at the tip of Cap Sizun. The views of jagged rocks and pounding seas are breathtaking. Farther west is the flat Ile de Sein and beyond that the lighthouse of Ar Men. Despite being only 5 ft (1.5 m) above sea level, Ile de Sein is nevertheless home to 260 inhabitants, and can be reached by boat from Audierne in an hour.

7 Pays Bigouden

Finistère. Pont l'Abbé.
Pont l'Abbé (02 98 82 37 99).
ot-pontlabbe29.fr

Brittany's southwest tip is known as the Pays Bigouden, a windy peninsula with proud and ancient traditions. The region is famous for the women's tall *coiffes* still worn at festivals and *pardons* *(see p247)*, which can also be seen at the **Musée Bigouden**.

Along the Baie d'Audierne is a brooding landscape of hamlets and isolated chapels – the 15th-century calvary at **Notre-Dame-de-Tronoën** is the oldest in Brittany. There are invigorating sea views from **Pointe de la Torche** (a good surfing spot) and from the **Eckmühl lighthouse**.

Musée Bigouden
Le Château, Pont l'Abbé. **Tel** 02 98 66 09 03. **Open** Jun–Sep: daily; Feb–May & Oct–mid-Nov: Sat–Sun pms (sch hols: Tue–Sun pms);. **Closed** May 1.

8 Quimper

Finistère. 67,250. pl de la Résistance (02 98 53 04 05). Wed, Sat. **quimper-tourisme.com**

The ancient capital of Cornouaille, Quimper has a distinctly Breton character. Here you can find Breton language books and music on sale, buy a traditional costume, and tuck into some of the best crêpes and cider in Brittany. Quimper gets its name from *kemper*, a Breton word meaning the confluence of two rivers, and the Steir and Odet still flow through this relaxed cathedral city.

West of the cathedral lies a pedestrianized area known as **Vieux Quimper**, full of shops, crêperies, and half-timbered houses. Rue Kéréon is the main thoroughfare, with the place au Beurre and the picturesque *hôtels particuliers* (mansions) of rue des Gentilshommes to the north.

Quimper has been producing faïence, elegant hand-painted pottery, since 1690. The design often features decorative flowers and animals framed by blue and yellow borders. Now mainly decorative, faïence is today exported to collectors all over the world. In the southwest of the city lies the oldest factory, **Faïenceries HB-Henriot**, which is open to visitors all year round.

Cathédrale St-Corentin

Quimper's cathedral is dedicated to the city's founder-bishop St. Corentin. Begun in 1240 – its colorfully painted interior now restored – it is the earliest Gothic building in Lower Brittany, and was bizarrely constructed with its choir at a slight angle to the nave, perhaps to fit in with some since-disappeared buildings. The two spires of the west facade were added in 1856. Between them rides a statue of King Gradlon, the mythical founder of the

The Martyrdom of St Triphine (1910) by Sérusier, Pont-Aven School

drowned city of Ys. After this deluge he chose Quimper as his new capital and St. Corentin as his spiritual guide.

Typical faïence plate from Quimper

Musée des Beaux-Arts

40 pl St-Corentin. **Tel** 02 98 95 45 20. **Open** Jul–Aug: daily; Sep–Jun: Wed–Mon. **Closed** most public hols; Nov–Mar: Sun am. **mbaq.fr**

Quimper's art museum is one of the best in the region. The collection is strong on late 19th- and early 20th-century artists, and their work – such as Jean-Eugène Buland's *Visite à Ste-Marie de Bénodet* – offers a valuable insight into the way visiting painters perpetuated a romantic view of Brittany. Also on show are works by members of the Pont-Aven School and local artists like J-J Lemordant and Max Jacob.

Musée Départemental Breton

1 rue de Roi-Gradlon. **Tel** 02 98 95 21 60. **Open** Jun–Sep: daily; Oct–May: Tue– Sat; Sun pm.

The 16th-century Bishop's Palace has collections of Breton costumes, furniture, and faïence, including Cornouaille *coiffes*, ornately carved box-beds and wardrobes, and turn-of-the-century tourist posters for Brittany.

9 Concarneau

Finistère. 20,000. only for islands. quai d'Aiguillon (02 98 97 01 44). Mon & Fri. **tourismeconcarneau.fr**

An important fishing port, Concarneau's principal attraction is its 14th-century **Ville Close** (walled town), built on an island in the harbor and encircled by massive lichen-covered granite ramparts. Access is by bridge from place Jean Jaurès. Parts of the ramparts can be toured, and the narrow streets are full of shops and restaurants. The **Musée de la Pêche**, housed in the port's ancient barracks, explains the local techniques and history of sea-fishing.

Musée de la Pêche

3 rue Vauban. **Tel** 02 98 97 10 20. **Open** Feb–Nov: daily. **Closed** public hols.

Fishing boats in Concarneau's busy harbor

For hotels and restaurants in this region see pp554–71 and pp576–603

Pont-Aven

ıistère. 3,000. 5 pl de ôtel de Ville (02 98 06 04 70). Tue, Sat. **pontaven.com**

nce a market town of "14 mills ıd 15 houses," Pont-Aven's cturesque location in the ooded Aven estuary made it tractive to many late 9th-century artists.

In 1888 Paul Gauguin, along ith like-minded painters Emile ernard and Paul Sérusier, eveloped a crude, colorful yle of painting known as ynthetism. Drawing inspiration om the Breton landscape and people, the Ecole de Pont-ven (Pont-Aven School) orked here and in nearby Pouldu until 1896.

The town is devoted to art ıd has 50 private galleries, ong with the informative **usée de Pont-Aven** which ocuments the achievements the Pont-Aven School. The ırrounding woods proved ıspirational to many artists, ıd offer pleasant walks – ne leads through the Bois Amour to the **Chapelle de rémalo**, where the wooden hrist in Gauguin's *Le Christ une* still hangs.

Musée de Pont-Aven
de l'Hôtel de Ville. **Tel** 02 98 06 14 3. **Closed** for renovation until 2015.

Notre-Dame-de-Kroaz-Baz, Roscoff

⓫ Le Pouldu

Finistère. 4,000. Pouldu Plage, rue C. Filiger (02 98 39 93 42).

A quiet port at the mouth of the river Laïta, Le Pouldu has a small beach and good walks. Its main attraction is **Maison Musée du Pouldu**, a reconstruction of the inn where Paul Gauguin and other artists stayed between 1889 and 1893. They covered every inch of the dining room, including the windowpanes, with self-portraits, caricatures, and still-lifes. These were discovered in 1924 beneath layers of wallpaper.

Maison Musée du Pouldu
10 rue des Grands Sables. **Tel** 02 98 39 98 51. **Open** May–mid-June & mid-Sep–Oct Sat–Sun pm; mid-Jun–mid-Sep: Tue–Sun. **museedu pouldu.clohars-carnoet.fr**

⓬ Roscoff

Finistère. 3,690. Quai d'Auxerre (02 98 61 12 13). Wed. **roscoff-tourisme.com**

Once a Corsairs' haunt, Roscoff is a thriving Channel port and seaside resort. Signs of its wealthy seafaring past can be found in the old port, along rue Amiral Réveillère and in place Lacaze-Duthiers. The granite facades of the 16th- and 17th-century shipowners' mansions, and the weather-beaten caravels and cannons decorating the 16th-century **Eglise Notre-Dame-de-Kroaz-Baz**, testify to the days when the privateers of Roscoff were as notorious as those of St-Malo *(see p286)*.

The famous French onion sellers (Johnnies) first crossed the Channel in 1828, selling braided onions door to door. The **Maison des Johnnies** tells their colorful history.

The **Centre de Découverte des Algues** is an informative seaweed exhibition center. From the harbor you can take a boat trip to the peaceful **Ile de Batz**. Near Pointe de Bloscon are tropical gardens.

Maison des Johnnies
48 rue Brizeux. **Tel** 02 98 61 25 48. **Open** mid-Jun–mid-Sep: Mon–Fri; mid-Sep–mid-Jun: Mon, Tue, Thu & Fri pm. **Closed** Jan.

Centre de Découverte des Algues
Quai Auxerre. **Open** Mon–Sat. **Closed** Sep–mid-Jul: Sun & Mon am. **algopole.fr**

Paul Gauguin in Brittany

Carving, Chapelle de Trémalo

Paul Gauguin's (1848–1903) story reads like a romantic novel. At the age of 35 he left his career as a stockbroker to become a full-time painter. From 1886 to 1894 he lived and worked in Brittany, at Pont-Aven and Le Pouldu, where he painted the landscape and its people. He chose to concentrate on the intense, almost "primitive" quality of the Breton Catholic faith, attempting to convey it in his work. This is evident in *Le Christ Jaune* (Yellow Christ), inspired by a woodcarving in the Trémalo chapel. In Gauguin's painting, the Crucifixion is a reality in the midst of the contemporary Breton landscape, rather than a remote or symbolic event. This theme recurs in many of his paintings from the period, including *Jacob Wrestling with the Angel* (1888).

Le Christ Jaune (1889) by Paul Gauguin

⓭ St-Thégonnec

Finistère. **Open** daily.

This is one of the most complete parish closes in Brittany. Passing through its triumphal archway, the ossuary is to the left. The calvary, directly ahead, was built in 1610 and perfectly illustrates the extraordinary skills Breton sculptors developed as they worked with the local granite. Among the many animated figures surrounding the central cross, a small niche contains a statue of St. Thégonnec with a cart pulled by wolves.

⓮ Guimiliau

Finistére. **Open** daily.

Almost 200 figures adorn Guimiliau's intensely decorated calvary (1581–88), many wearing 16th-century dress. Among them you can contemplate the legendary torment of Katell Gollet, a servant girl tortured by demons for stealing a consecrated wafer to please her lover. The church is dedicated to St. Miliau and has a richly decorated south porch. The baptistry's elaborate carved oak canopy dates from 1675.

Font canopy from 1675, Guimiliau

⓯ Lampaul-Guimiliau

Finistère. **Open** daily.

Entering through the monumental gate, the chapel and ossuary lie to the left, while the calvary is to the right. Here, however, it is the church that demands most attention. The interior is zealously painted and carved, including some naive scenes from the Passion depicted along the 16th-century rood-beam dividing the nave and choir.

Parish Closes

Reflecting the religious fervor of the Bretons, the Enclos Paroissiaux (parish closes) were built during the 15th–18th centuries. At that time Brittany had few urban centers but many wealthy rural settlements that profited from maritime trading and the manufacture of cloth. Gran religious monuments, some taking over 200 years to complete, were built by small villages inspired by spiritual zeal and the more earthly desire to rival their neighbors. Some of the finest parish closes lie in the Elorn valley, linked by a well-signposted Circuit des Enclos Paroissiaux.

The enclosure, surrounded by a stone wall, is the hallowed area. By following the wall, visitors are drawn towards the triumphal arch, shown here in Pleyben.

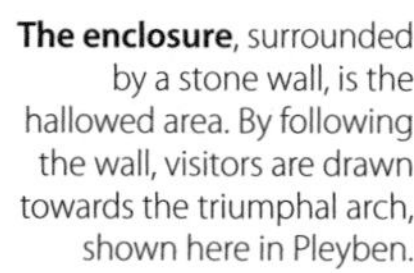

The small cemetery reflects the size of the community that built these great churches.

Guimiliau Parish Close

The three essential features of a parish close are a triumphal gateway marking the entry into the hallowed enclosure, a calvary depicting scenes from the Passion and Crucifixion, and an ossuary beside the church porch.

The calvary is unique to Brittany, and may have been inspired by the crosses set on top of menhirs *(see p283)* by the early Christians. They provide a walk-around Bible lesson, often with the characters in 17th-century costumes as in this example from St-Thégonnec.

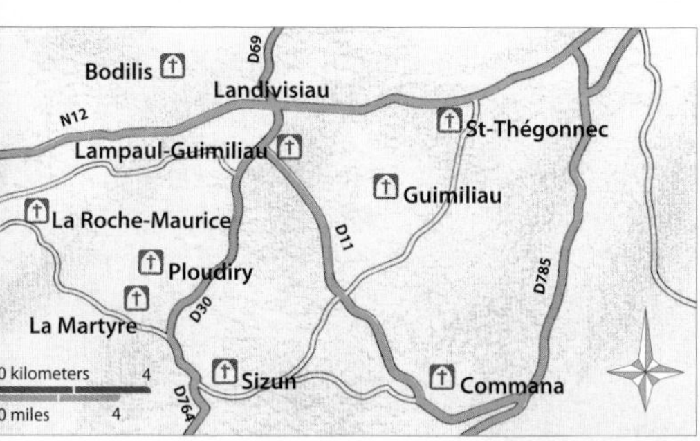

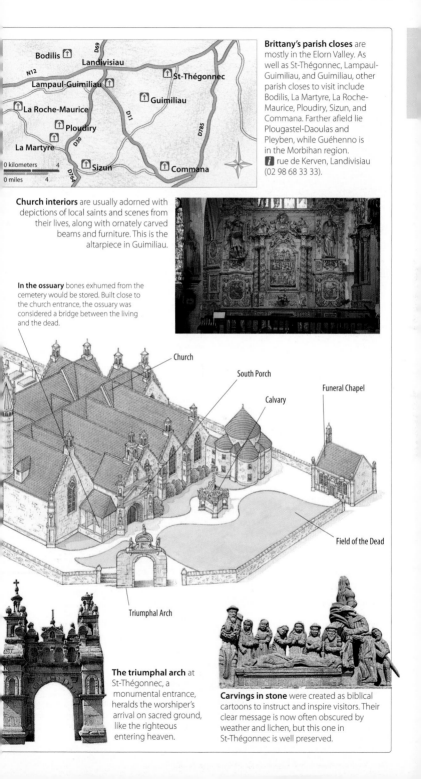

Brittany's parish closes are mostly in the Elorn Valley. As well as St-Thégonnec, Lampaul-Guimiliau, and Guimiliau, other parish closes to visit include Bodilis, La Martyre, La Roche-Maurice, Ploudiry, Sizun, and Commana. Farther afield lie Plougastel-Daoulas and Pleyben, while Guéhenno is in the Morbihan region.
i rue de Kerven, Landivisiau (02 98 68 33 33).

Church interiors are usually adorned with depictions of local saints and scenes from their lives, along with ornately carved beams and furniture. This is the altarpiece in Guimiliau.

In the ossuary bones exhumed from the cemetery would be stored. Built close to the church entrance, the ossuary was considered a bridge between the living and the dead.

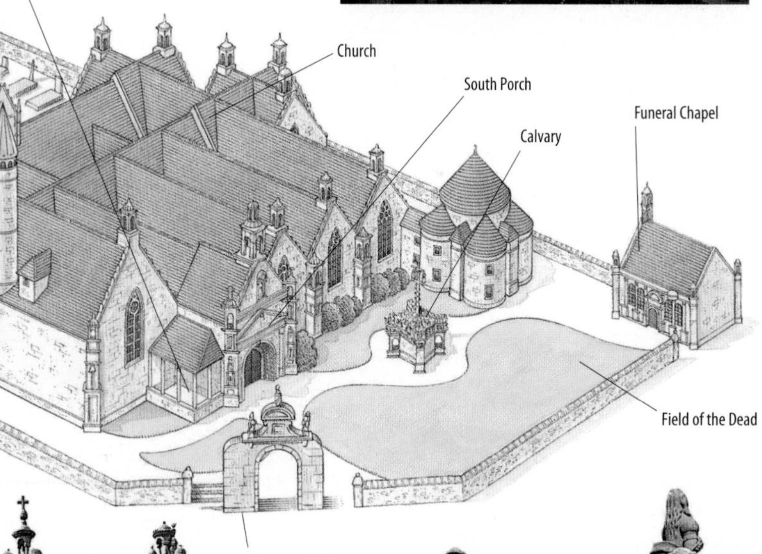

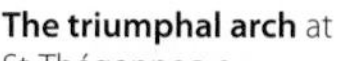

The triumphal arch at St-Thégonnec, a monumental entrance, heralds the worshiper's arrival on sacred ground, like the righteous entering heaven.

Carvings in stone were created as biblical cartoons to instruct and inspire visitors. Their clear message is now often obscured by weather and lichen, but this one in St-Thégonnec is well preserved.

The chapel of Notre-Dame, perched on the cliffs above the beach of Port-Blanc, Côte de Granit Rose

⑯ Côte de Granit Rose

Côtes d'Armor. ✈ 🚉 🚌 Lannion. ℹ Lannion (02 96 05 60 70). Thu. **bretagne-cotedegranitrose.com**

The coast between Paimpol and Trébeurden is known as the Côte de Granit Rose due to its pink cliffs. These are best between Trégastel and Trébeurden; their granite is also used in neighboring towns. The coast between Trébeurden and Perros-Guirec is one of Brittany's most popular family holiday areas.

Farther east there are quieter beaches and coves, as at **Trévou-Tréguignec** and **Port-Blanc**. Beyond Tréguier, **Paimpol** is a working fishing port that once sent huge cod and whaling fleets to fish off Iceland and Newfoundland.

⑰ Tréguier

Côtes d'Armor. 2,950. ℹ 13 pl de l'Eglise, Penvenan (02 96 92 81 09). Wed.

Overlooking the estuary of the Jaundy and Guindy rivers, Tréguier stands apart from the resorts of the Côte de Granit Rose. It is a typically Breton market town, with one main attraction, the 14th–15th century **Cathédrale St-Tugdual**. It has three towers: one Gothic, one Romanesque, and one 18th-century. The last, financed by Louis XVI with winnings from the Paris Lottery, has holes in the shapes of playing-card suits.

Environs

Chapelle St-Gonery in Plougrescant has a leaning lead spire and a 15th-century painted wooden ceiling.

⑱ Ile de Bréhat

Côtes d'Armor. 420. 🚉 🚌 Paimpol, then bus to Pointe de l'Arcouest (Mon–Sat winter; daily summer), then boat. ℹ Paimpol (02 96 20 83 16). **paimpol-goelo.com**

A 15-minute crossing from the Pointe de l'Arcouest, the Ile de Bréhat is actually 2 islands, joined by a bridge, which together are only 2.2 miles (3.5 km) long. With motorized traffic banned, and a climate mild enough for mimosa and a variety of fruit trees to flourish, it has a relaxing atmosphere. Bicycle hire and boat tours are available in the main town, **Port-Clos**, and you can walk to the island's highest point, the **Chapelle St-Michel**.

Chapelle St-Michel, a landmark on Ile de Bréhat

⑲ Carnac

Morbihan. 4,600. 🚌 ℹ 74 avenue des Druides (02 97 52 13 52). **ot-carnac.fr**

Carnac, a popular seaside resort, is also one of the world's great prehistoric sites, with almost 3,000 menhirs in parallel rows, and an excellent **Musée de Préhistoire**.

The 17th-century **Eglise St-Cornély** is dedicated to St Cornelius, patron saint of horned animals. His life is depicted on its ceiling.

Maison des Megaliths
Tel 02 97 52 29 81. **Open** daily. **Closed** Jan 1, May 1, Dec 25. Apr–Oct. oblig. Apr–Oct.

Musée de Préhistoire
10 pl de la Chapelle. **Tel** 02 97 52 22 04. **Open** Feb–Jun & Sep–Dec: Wed–Mon; Jul–Aug: daily. **Closed** Jan, May 1, Dec 25.

⑳ Presqu'île de Quiberon

Morbihan. 5,200. ✈ Quiberon (via Lorient). 🚉 Jul–Aug. 🚌 ⛴ Quiberon. ℹ Quiberon (02 97 50 07 84). Sat, Wed (summer). **quiberon.com**

Once an Island, the slender Quiberon peninsula has a bleak west coast with sea-punished cliffs, known as the Côte Sauvage. The east is more benign. At the peninsula's southern tip is the fishing port and resort of **Quiberon**, with a car ferry to Belle-Ile. In 1795 10,000 Royalist troops were massacred here in an ill-fated attempt to reverse the French Revolution.

Brittany's Prehistoric Monuments

At Carnac, thousands of ancient granite rocks were arranged in mysterious lines and patterns by Megalithic tribes as early as 4000 BC. Their original purpose remains obscure: the significance was probably religious, but the precise patterns also suggest an early astronomical calendar. Celts, Romans, and Christians have since adapted them to their own beliefs.

The Gavrinis Tumulus, Golfe du Morbihan

Megaliths

There are many different formations of megaliths, all with a particular purpose. Words from the Breton language, such as men *(stone),* dole *(table) and* hir *(long), are still used to describe them.*

Menhirs, the most common megaliths, are upright stones, standing alone or arranged in lines. Those in circles are known as cromlechs.

Dolmen, two upright stones roofed by a third, were used as a burial chamber, such as the Merchant's Table at Locmariaquer.

Allée couverte, upright stones placed in a row and roofed to form a covered alley, can be seen at Carnac.

A tumulus is a dolmen covered with stones and soil to form a burial mound.

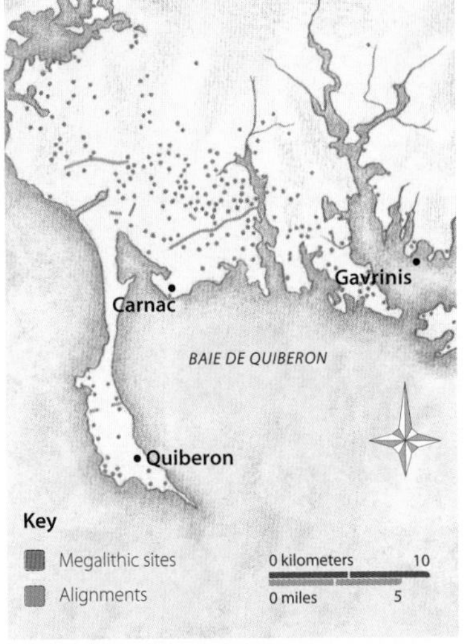

Brittany's major megalithic sites

Alignment at Carnac

Menhirs of all shapes in a field near Carnac

㉑ Belle-Ile-en-Mer

Morbihan. 5,200. Quiberon (via Lorient). from Quiberon. quai Bonnelle, Le Palais (02 97 31 81 93). daily. **belle-ile.com**

Brittany's largest island lies 9 miles (14 km) south of Quiberon and can be reached in 45 minutes by car ferry from Quiberon. The coast has cliffs and good beaches; inland lie exposed highlands intersected by sheltered valleys. In the main town, Le Palais, stands the **Citadelle Vauban**, a 16th-century star-shaped fortress, and there are fine walks and views along the southern Côte Sauvage.

Breton seafarer, off Belle-Ile's coast

Cloisters of St-Pierre in Vannes

㉒ Vannes

Morbihan. 58,000. 1 quai Tabarly (02 97 47 24 34). Wed & Sat. **tourisme-vannes.com**

Standing at the head of the Golfe du Morbihan, Vannes was the capital of the Veneti, a seafaring Armorican tribe defeated by Caesar in 56 BC. In the 9th century Nominoë, the first Duke of Brittany, made it his power base. The city remained influential up until the signing of the union with France in 1532, when Rennes became the Breton capital. Today it is a busy commercial city with a well-preserved medieval quarter, and a good base for exploring the Golfe du Morbihan.

The impressive eastern walls of old Vannes can be viewed from the promenade de la Garenne. Two of the city's old gates survive at either end: Porte-Prison in the north, and the southern Porte-Poterne with a row of 17th-century wash houses close by.

Walking up from Porte St-Vincent, you find the city's old market squares, still in use today. The **place des Lices** was once the scene of medieval tournaments and the streets around the rue de la Monnaie are full of well-preserved 16th-century houses.

Begun in the 13th century, **Cathédrale St-Pierre** has since been drastically remodeled and restored. The Chapel of the Holy Sacrament houses the revered tomb of Vincent Ferrier, a Spanish saint who died in Vannes in 1419.

Opposite the west front of the cathedral, the old covered market **La Cohue** (meaning throng or hubbub) was once the city's central meeting place. Parts of the building date from the 13th century, and a small museum inside displays art and artifacts relevant to the history of the area.

Housed in the 15th-century Château Gaillard, the **Musée d'Histoire** is a rich assembly of finds from Morbihan's many prehistoric sites, including jewelry, pottery, and weapons. There is also a gallery of mediev and Renaissance *objets d'art.*

Musée d'Histoire
Château Gaillard, 2 rue Noé. **Tel** 02 9 01 63 00. **Open** Jun–Sep: daily. **Closed** public hols.

Environs
To the south of the city the **Par du Golfe** is a beautiful leisure park with many amusements, a butterfly conservatory, a conservatory set in a tropical forest and an aquarium that boasts over 400 species of fish. Northeast of Vannes, off the N166, lie the romantic ruins of the 15th-century **Tours d'Elver**

㉓ Golfe du Morbihan

Morbihan. Lorient. Vannes. Vannes (02 97 47 24 34). **tourisme-vannes.com**

Morbihan means "little sea" in Breton, an apt description for this landlocked expanse of tida water. Only connected to the Atlantic by a small channel between the Locmariaquer anc Rhuys peninsulas, the gulf is dotted with islands. Around 40 are inhabited, with the **Ile d'Arz** and the **Ile aux Moines** the largest. These are served by regular ferries from Conleau an Port-Blanc respectively.

Around the gulf several small harbors earn a living from fishing, oyster cultivation, and tourism. There is a wealth of

The picturesque fishing port of Le Bono in Golfe du Morbihan

e seaside resort of Dinard, on the Côte d'Emeraude

ıegalithic sites, notably the and of **Gavrinis** where stone ırvings have been excavated *ee p283)*. There are boat trips) Gavrinis from Larmor-Baden ıd around the gulf from ɔcmariaquer, Auray, Vannes, ıd Port-Navalo.

e medieval Château de Josselin on the ınks of the river Oust

Josselin

orbihan. 2,500. 26 rue de ente (02 97 22 36 43). Sat. josselin-communaute.fr

verlooking the river Oust, ɔsselin is dominated by a ıedieval **château** owned by ıe de Rohan family since the ıd of the 15th century. ınly four of its nine towers ırvive. The elaborate inner ranite facade incorporates the tter "A" – a tribute to the uch-loved Duchess Anne of rittany (1477–1514), who esided over Brittany's "Golden ge." Tours are given of the 9th-century interior, and in e former stables there is a usée des Poupées with 600 ɔlls. In the town, **Basilique Notre-Dame-du-Roncier** contains the mausoleum of the castle's most famous owner and constable of France, Olivier de Clisson (1336–1407). West of Josselin at Kerguéhennec, the grounds of an 18th-century château have become a modern sculpture park.

Château de Josselin
Tel 02 97 22 36 45. **Open** Apr–Aug: daily (Apr–mid-Jul & Sep: pms only); Oct: Sat & Sun pms.

25 Forêt de Paimpont

Ille-et-Vilaine. Rennes. Monfort-sur-Meu. Rennes. Montauban de Bretagne (02 99 06 86 07). **broceliande-tourisme.info**

Also known as the Forêt de Brocéliande, this is a remnant of the dense primeval woods that once covered much of Armorica. It has long been associated with the legends of King Arthur, and visitors still search for the magical spring where the sorcerer Merlin first met the Lady of the Lake. The small village of **Paimpont** is a good base for exploring both the forest and its myths.

Legendary sorcerer Merlin and Viviane, the Lady of the Lake

26 Côte d'Emeraude

Ille et Vilaine & Côtes d'Armor. Dinard–St-Malo. Dinard (02 99 46 94 12). **ot-dinard.com**

Between Le Val-André and the Pointe du Grouin, near Cancale, sandy beaches, rocky headlands, and classic seaside resorts stretch along Brittany's northern shore. Known as the Emerald Coast, its self-proclaimed Queen is the aristocratic resort of **Dinard**, "discovered" in the 1850s and still playing host to the international rich.

To its west are resorts like St-Jacut-de-la-Mer, St-Cast-le-Guildo, Sables d'Or-les-Pins, and Erquy, all with tempting beaches. In the Baie de la Frênaye, the medieval **Fort La Latte** provides good views from high in its ancient watchtower, while the lighthouse that dominates **Cap Fréhel** nearby offers even more extensive panoramas.

East of Dinard, the D186 runs across the **Barrage de la Rance** to St-Malo. Built in 1966 it was the world's first dam to generate electricity by using tidal power. Beyond St-Malo, coves and beaches surround La Guimorais, while around the Pointe du Grouin the seas are often truly emerald.

Seafarers of St-Malo

St-Malo owes its wealth and reputation to the exploits of its mariners. In 1534 Jacques Cartier, born in nearby Rothéneuf, discovered the mouth of the St Lawrence river in Canada and claimed the territory for France. It was Breton sailors who voyaged to South America in 1698 to colonize the Iles Malouines, known today as Las Malvinas or the Falklands. By the 17th century St-Malo was the largest port in France and famous for its corsairs – privateers licensed by the king to prey on foreign ships. The most illustrious were the swashbuckling René Duguay-Trouin (1673–1736), who captured Rio de Janeiro from the Portuguese in 1711, and the intrepid Robert Surcouf (1773–1827), whose ships hounded vessels of the British East India Company. The riches won by trade and piracy enabled St-Malo's ship-owners to build great mansions known as *malouinières*.

Explorer Jacques Cartier (1491–1557)

㉗ St-Malo

Ille-et-Vilaine. 53,000. esplanade St-Vincent (08 25 13 52 00). Tue & Fri. **saint-malo-tourisme.fr**

Once a fortified island, St-Malo stands in a commanding position at the mouth of the river Rance.

The city is named after Maclou, a Welsh monk who came here in the 6th century to spread the Christian message. During the 16th–19th centuries the port won prosperity and power through the exploits of its seafarers. St-Malo was heavily bombed in 1944 but has since been scrupulously restored and is now a major port and ferry terminal as well as a resort.

The old city is encircled by ramparts that provide fine views of St-Malo and its islands. Take the steps up by the **Porte St-Vincent** and walk clockwise, passing the 15th-century **Grande Porte**.

Within the city is a web of cobbled streets with tall 18th-century buildings housing stores, fish restaurants, and crêperies. Rue Porcon-de-la-Barbinais leads to **Cathédrale St-Vincent**, with its somber 12th-century nave contrasting with the stained glass of the chancel. On cour La Houssaye, the 15th-century Maison de la Duchesse Anne has been carefully restored.

St-Malo seen at low tide through the gate of Fort National

Château de St-Malo

Pl Châteaubriand, near the Marina. **Tel** 02 99 40 71 57. **Open** Apr–Sep: daily; Oct–Mar: Tue–Sun. **Closed** Jan 1, May 1, Nov 1 & 11, Dec 25.

St-Malo's castle dates from the 14th–15th centuries. The great keep contains a museum of the city's history, including the adventures of its state-sponsored corsairs. From its watch towers there is an impressive view. Nearby, in the place Vauban, a tropical aquarium has been built into the ramparts, while on the edge of town, the Grand Aquarium has a shark tank and simulated submarine rides.

Fort National

Open Jun–Sep: daily at low tide.

Constructed in 1689 by Louis XIV's famous military architect, Vauban, this fort can be reached on foot at low tide and offers good views of St-Malo and its ramparts. At low tide you can also walk out to **Petit Bé Fort** (open Easter–mid-Nov) and **Grand Bé**, where St-Malo-born writer François-René de Chateaubriand lies buried. From the top there are great views along the whole of Côte d'Emeraude *(see p285)*.

Tour Solidor

St-Servan. **Tel** 02 99 40 71 58. **Open** Apr–Oct: daily; Nov–Mar: Tue–Sun. **Closed** Jan 1, May 1, Nov 1 & 1[illegible], Dec 25.

To the west of St-Malo in St-Servan, the three-towered Tour Solidor was built in 1382. Formerly a toll house, it was al[illegible] a prison under the Revolution, and now houses an intriguing museum devoted to the ships and sailors that rounded Cape Horn, with ship models, logs, ar[illegible] various nautical instruments.

Environs

When the tide is out, good beaches are revealed around St-Malo and in the nearby suburbs of St-Servan and Param[illegible]. A passenger ferry runs to Dinar[illegible] in summer *(see p285)* and the Channel Islands, and there are boat trips up the Rance to Dina[illegible] and out to the Iles Chausey, Ile de Cézembre, and Cap Fréhel.

At Rothéneuf you can visit the **Manoir Limoëlou**, home [illegible] the navigator Jacques Cartier. Nearby, on the coast, Les Roch[illegible] Sculptés is a beguiling array o[illegible]

ncale oysters, prized for their taste since oman times

ranite faces and figures carved nto the cliffs by a local priest, bbé Fouré, at the end of the 9th century.

Manoir Limoëlou
ue D Macdonald-Stuart, Limoëlou-othéneuf. **Tel** 02 99 40 97 73. **Open** ul–Aug: daily; Sep–Jun: Mon–Sat. **losed** public hols. oblig.

Cancale

le-et-Vilaine. 5,350. 44 rue u Port (02 99 89 63 72). Sun. **cancale-tourisme.fr**

A small port with views across he Baie du Mont-St-Michel, ancale is entirely devoted o the cultivation and onsumption of oysters. Prized y the Romans, the acclaimed lavor of Cancale's oysters is said o derive from the strong tides hat wash over them daily. You an survey the beds from a *sentier des douaniers* coastguards' footpath, the GR34) running along the cliffs.

There are plenty of opportu-nities for sampling the local speciality provided by a multitude of bars and restaurants along the busy docks of the Port de la Houle, where the fishing boats arrive at high tide. Devotees should pay a visit to the **Musée de l'Huître, du Coquillage et de la Mer.**

Musée de l'Huître, du Coquillage et de la Mer – La Ferme Marine
Aurore. **Tel** 02 99 89 69 99. **Open** mid-Feb–Jun & mid-Sep–Oct: Mon–Fri pms; Jul–mid-Sep: daily.

29 Dinan

Côtes d'Armor. 10,000. 9 rue du Château (02 96 87 69 76). Thu. **dinan-tourisme.com**

Set on a hill overlooking the wooded Rance valley, Dinan is a modern market town with a medieval heart. Surrounded by ramparts, the well-kept, half-timbered houses and cobbled streets of its Vieille Ville have an impressive, unforced unity best appreciated by climbing to the top of its 15th-century **Tour d'Horloge**, in rue de l'Horloge. Nearby, **Basilique St-Sauveur** contains the heart of Dinan's most famous son, the 14th-century warrior Bertrand du Guesclin.

Behind the church, Les Jardins Anglais offer good views of the river Rance and the viaduct spanning it. A couple of streets farther north, the steep, geranium-decorated rue du Jerzual winds down through the 14th-century town gate to the port. Once a busy harbor from which cloth was shipped, it is now a quiet backwater where you can take a pleasure cruise, or walk along a towpath to the restored 17th-century **Abbaye St-Magloire** at Léhon.

The **Musée du Château** houses a small museum of local history. Next to it is the 15th-century **Tour de Coëtquen**. From here are walks beside the ramparts along the promenade des Petits Fossés and the promenade des Grands Fossés.

Musée du Château
Château de la Duchesse Anne, rue du Château. **Tel** 02 96 39 45 20. **Open** daily (Oct–May: pms only). **Closed** mid-Nov–Easter, public hols.

Author and diplomat François-René de Chateaubriand (1768–1848)

30 Combourg

Ille-et-Vilaine. 5,000. 23 pl Albert Parent (02 99 73 13 93). Mon. **combourg.org**

A small, sleepy town beside a lake, Combourg is completely overshadowed by the great, haunting **Château de Combourg**. The buildings seen today date from the 14th and 15th centuries. In 1761 the château was bought by the Comte de Chateaubriand, and the melancholic childhood spent there by his son, the author and diplomat François-René de Chateaubriand (1768–1848), is candidly described in his entertaining chronicle, *Mémoires d'Outre-Tombe*.

Empty after the Revolution, the château was restored in the 19th century and is open for tours. One room has the belongings of François-René de Chateaubriand.

Château de Combourg
23 rue des Princes. **Tel** 02 99 73 22 95. **Open** Apr–Jun & Sep–Oct: Mon–Fri & Sun pm; Jul–Aug: daily. **combourg.net**

View over Dinan and the Gothic bridge crossing the river Rance

Rennes City Center

① Portes Mordelaises
② Cathédrale St-Pierre
③ Eglise St-Sauveur
④ Hôtel de Ville
⑤ Théâtre de Rennes
⑥ Palais du Parlement de Bretagne
⑦ Parc du Thabor
⑧ Eglise St-Germain
⑨ Musée des Beaux Arts

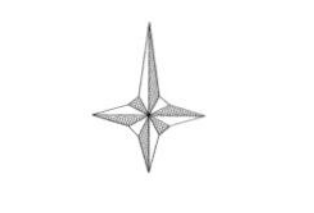

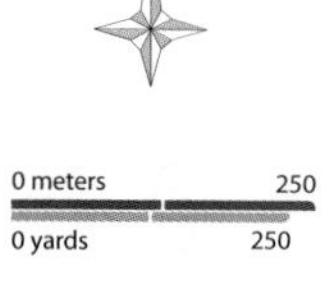

㉛ Rennes

Ille-et-Vilaine. 214,800. 11 rue St-Yves (02 99 67 11 11). Tue–Sat. **tourisme-rennes.com**

Founded by the Gauls and colonized by the Romans, Rennes is strategically located where the Vilaine and Ille rivers meet. After Brittany's union with France in 1532, the town became regional capital.
In 1720 a fire lasting for six days devastated the city. Today a small part of the medieval city survives, together with the neat grid of 18th-century buildings that arose from the ashes.

The imposing Neo-Classical facade of Cathédrale St-Pierre

Around this historic core are the tower blocks and hi-tech factories of modern Rennes – a confident provincial capital with two universities and a thriving cultural life.

Wandering through the streets that radiate from the place des Lices and the place Ste-Anne, it is easy to imagine what Rennes was like before the Great Fire. Now mostly pedestrianized, this area has become the city's youthful heart with plenty of bars, crêperies, and designer shops. At the western end of rue de la Monnaie stands the 15th-century **Portes Mordelaises**, once part of the city's ramparts.

Close by, **Cathédrale St-Pierre** was completed in 1844, the third on this site. Note the carved 16th-century Flemish altar piece. Nearby is the 18th-century **Eglise St-Sauveur**. Just south of the attractive rue St-George, **Eglise St-Germain** has a typically Breton belfry and wooden vaulting. In the place de la Mairie stands the early 18th-century **Hôtel de Ville** and the Neo-Classical **Théâtre de Rennes**. The **Parc du Thabor**, once part of a Benedictine monastery, is ideal for walks and picnics.

Half-timbered houses lining the narrow streets of old Rennes

Palais du Parlement de Bretagne

Pl du Parlement. **Open** Tourist Office for guided tours (02 99 67 11 66). **tourisme-rennes.com**

Rennes' Law Courts, built in 1618–55, were the seat of the region's governing body until the Revolution. Severely damaged by fire during riots over fish prices in 1994, the major restoration work is all but complete, including the unique coffered ceiling and gilded woodwork of the Grande Chambre. Today, the Salle des Pas Perdus, with its vaulted ceilings, can again be admired by the public.

For hotels and restaurants in this region see pp554–71 and pp576–603

Musée des Beaux Arts
0 quai Zola. **Tel** 02 23 62 17 45. **Open** Tue–Sun. **Closed** public hols. **mbar.org**. Musée Bretagne 10 cours des Alliés. **Tel** 02 23 40 66 70. **Open** Tue–Sun pm only. **Closed** public hols. **musee-bretagne.fr**

The **Musée des Beaux Arts** has a wide-ranging collection of art from the 14th century to the present, including a room of art on Breton themes. There are paintings by Gauguin, Bernard, and other members of the Pont-Aven School *(see p279)*, and three works by Picasso, including the lively *Baigneuse* painted at Dinard in 1928.

Housed in the Rennes cultural center along with the Science Museum and Planetarium, the **Musée de Bretagne** includes examples of traditional Breton furniture and costume, and displays on Brittany's prehistoric megaliths, the growth of Rennes, rural crafts, and the fishing industry.

Environs

Just south of Rennes, the **Ecomusée du Pays de Rennes** traces the history of a local farm since the 17th century.

Some 10 miles (16 km) to the southeast of Rennes is **Châteaugiron**, a charming medieval village, with an imposing castle and houses preserving their wooden eaves.

Ecomusée du Pays de Rennes
Ferme de la Bintinais, rte de Châtillon-sur-Seiche. **Tel** 02 99 51 38 15. **Open** Tue–Fri (Sat, Sun pm only). **Closed** public hols. **ecomusee-rennes-metropole.fr**

Château de Châteaugiron
Open mid-Jun–mid-Sep: daily; call 02 99 37 89 02.

32 Fougères

Ille-et-Vilaine. 23,000. 2 rue Nationale (02 99 94 12 20). Sat. **ot-fougeres.fr**

A fortress town close to the Breton border, Fougères rests on a hill overlooking the Nançon river. In the valley below, and still linked to the Haute Ville by a curtain of ancient ramparts, stands the mighty 11th–15th century **Château de Fougères**.

The mighty fortifications of Château de Fougères

To get a good overview of the château, go to the gardens of place aux Arbres behind the 16th-century **Eglise St-Léonard**. From here you can descend to the river and the medieval houses around place du Marchix. The Flamboyant Gothic **Eglise St-Sulpice**, with its 18th-century wood-paneled interior and granite retables, is well worth visiting.

A walk around the castle's massive outer fortifications reveals the ambitious scale of its construction, with 13 towers and walls over 10 ft (3 m) thick. You can still climb the castle's ramparts to get a feel of what it was like to live within its staggered defences. Much of the action in Balzac's novel *Les Chouans* (1829) takes place in and around Fougères and its castle.

Château de Fougères
Pl Pierre-Simon. **Tel** 02 99 99 79 59. **Open** Jul–Aug: daily; Sep–Jun: Tue–Sun. **Closed** Jan, Dec 25. **chateau-fougeres.com**

Overhanging timber-frame houses on rue Beaudrairie, Vitré

33 Vitré

Ille-et-Vilaine. 16,000. pl Général de Gaulle (02 99 75 04 46). Mon & Sat. **ot-vitre.fr**

The fortified town of Vitré is set high on a hill overlooking the Vilaine valley. Its medieval **Château** is complete with pencil-point turrets and picturesque 15th–16th century buildings in attendance. The castle was rebuilt in the 14th–15th centuries and follows a triangular plan, with some of its ramparts walkable. There is a museum in the Tour St-Laurent.

To the east, rue Beaudrairie and rue d'Embas have overhanging timber-frame houses with remarkable patterning.

The 15th–16th century **Cathédrale Notre-Dame**, built in Flamboyant Gothic style, has a south facade with an exterior stone pulpit. Further along rue Notre-Dame, the promenade du Val skirts around the town's ramparts.

To the southeast of Vitré on the D88, the **Château des Rochers-Sévigné** was once the home of Mme de Sévigné (1626–96), famous letter-writer and chronicler of life at the court of Louis XIV. The park, chapel, and some of her rooms are open to the public.

Château de Vitré
Tel 02 99 75 04 54. **Open** Apr–Sep: daily; Oct–Mar: Wed–Mon (closed Sun am). **Closed** Jan 1, Easter, Nov 1, Dec 25.

Château des Rochers-Sévigné
Tel 02 99 96 76 51. **Open** Apr–Sep: daily; Oct–Mar: Fri–Sun pms. restricted.

THE LOIRE VALLEY

Indre · Indre-et-Loire · Loir-et-Cher · Loiret · Eure-et-Loir
Cher · Vendée · Maine-et-Loire · Loire-Atlantique · Sarthe

Renowned for its sumptuous châteaux, the glorious valley of the Loire, now classified a UNESCO World Heritage Site, is rich both in history and architecture. Like the river Loire, this vast region runs through the heart of French life. Its sophisticated cities, luxuriant landscape, and magnificent food and wine add up to a bourgeois paradise.

The lush Loire Valley is supremely regal. Orléans was France's intellectual capital in the 13th century, attracting artists, poets, and troubadours to the royal court. But the medieval court never stayed in one place for long, which led to the building of magnificent châteaux all along the Loire. Chambord and Chenonceau, the two greatest Renaissance châteaux, remain prestigious symbols of royal rule, resplendent amid vast hunting forests and waterways.

Due to its central location, culture, and fine cuisine, Tours is the natural visitors' capital. Angers is a close second but more authentic are the historic towns of Saumur, Amboise, Blois, and Beaugency, strung out like jewels along the river. This is the classic Loire Valley, a château trail which embraces the Renaissance gardens of Villandry and the fairytale turrets of Ussé. Venture northwards and the cathedral cities of Le Mans and Chartres reign supreme, their medieval centers bordered by Gallo-Roman walls. Nantes in the west is a breezy, forward-looking port and gateway to the Atlantic.

Southwards, the windswept Vendée is edged by a wild, sandy coastline that is perfect for windsurfers and nature lovers alike. Inland, the Loire's more peaceful tributaries and the watery Sologne beg to be explored. Also ripe for discovery are troglodyte caves, sleepy hamlets, and small Romanesque churches decorated with frescoes. Inviting inns offer game, fish, and abundant fresh vegetables to be lingered over with a light white Vouvray wine or a fruity Bourgeuil. Overindulgence is no sin in this rich region.

The river Loire at Montsoreau, southeast of Saumur

◀ Formal gardens at the Château de Villandry

Exploring the Loire Valley

The lush valley landscape, studded with France's greatest châteaux, is the main attraction. Numerous river cruises are available, while the sandy Atlantic coast offers beach holidays. Peaceful country holidays can be had in the Vendée, and in the Loir and Indre valleys. Wine tours focus on Bourgueil, Chinon, Muscadet, Saumur, and Vouvray vintages. The most charming bases are Amboise, Blois, Beaugency, and Saumur, but culture-lovers are well-provided for throughout the region.

Countryside around Vouvray

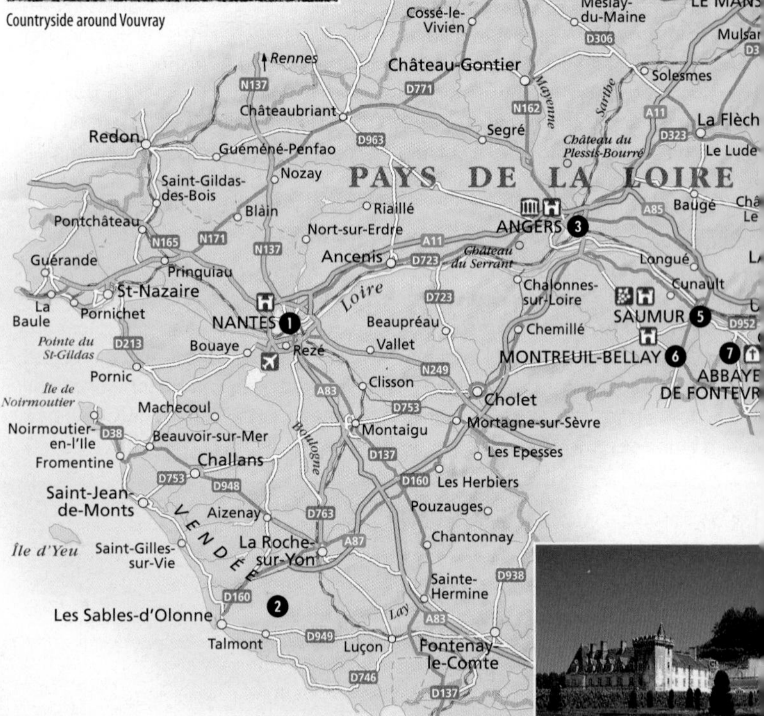

Getting Around

The region is well served by transport links. Nantes and Tours airports have international flights; Tours airport also serves Marseille and Figari (Corsica). Chartres, Le Mans, Angers, and Nantes are reached from Paris by the A11, and the A10 links Orléans, Blois, and Tours. The TGV train travels from Paris to Le Mans (1 hr); Tours (1 hr); Angers (90 mins); and Nantes (2 hrs). There is also TGV access from Lille (Eurostar interchange). The smaller châteaus can be difficult to reach by public transport, but there are tours from major tourist centers.

The 16th-century Château de Villandry and its famous gardens

For additional map symbols *see back flap*

Sights at a Glance

1. Nantes
2. The Vendée
3. Angers
4. Le Mans
5. Saumur
6. Montreuil-Bellay
7. Abbaye Royale de Fontevraud
8. Chinon
9. Ussé
10. Langeais
11. Azay-le-Rideau
12. Villandry
13. Tours
14. Vouvray
15. Loches
16. Montrésor
17. Chenonceau
18. Amboise
19. Chambord
20. Blois
21. Beaugency
22. Vendôme
23. The Loir
24. Chartres
25. Orléans
26. St-Benoît-sur-Loire
27. Bourges

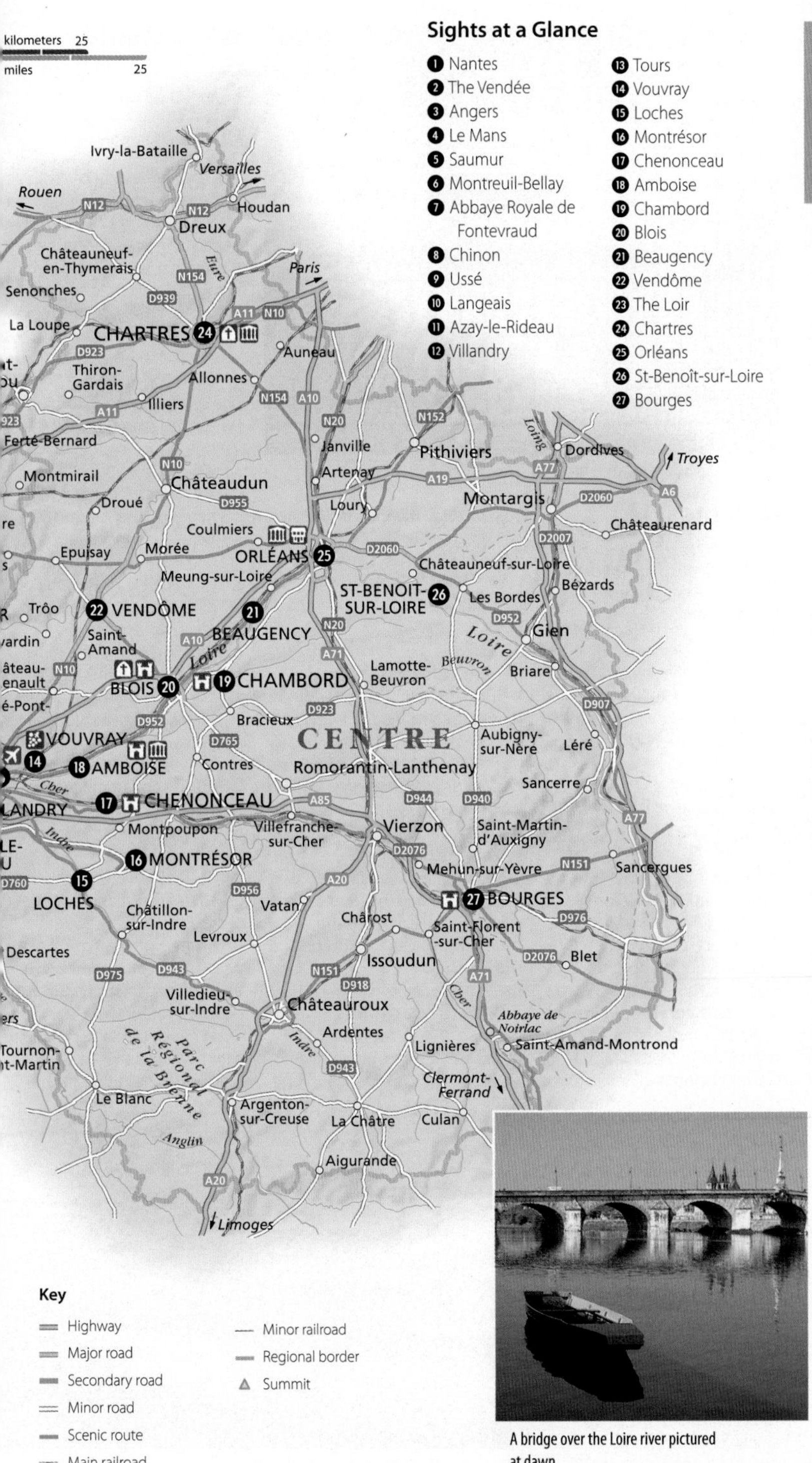

Key

- Highway
- Major road
- Secondary road
- Minor road
- Scenic route
- Main railroad
- Minor railroad
- Regional border
- Summit

A bridge over the Loire river pictured at dawn

Tomb of François II and his wife, Marguerite de Foix, in Cathédrale St-Pierre

❶ Nantes

Loire-Atlantique. 270,000. 9 rue des Etats (08 92 46 40 44). Tue–Sun. **nantes-tourisme.com**

For centuries, Nantes disputed with Rennes the title of capital of Brittany. Yet links with the Plantagenets and Henri IV also bound it to the "royal" river Loire. Since the 1790s it has officially ceased to be part of Brittany, and, though still Breton at heart, it is today capital of the Pays de la Loire.

Visually, Nantes is a city of variety, with high-tech towers overlooking the port, canals, and Art Nouveau squares. Chic bars and restaurants cram the medieval nucleus, bounded by place St-Croix and the château.

The **Cathédrale St-Pierre et St-Paul**, completed in 1893, is notable both for its sculpted Gothic portals and Renaissance tomb of François II, the last duke of Brittany.

More impressive is the **Château des Ducs de Bretagne**, where Anne of Brittany was born in 1477 and where the Edict of Nantes was signed by Henri IV in 1598, granting Protestants religious freedom. Following major restoration work the château now houses the lively, interactive **Musée d'Histoire**. It charts the history of Nantes through 32 rooms of exhibits, including Turner's painting of the Loire embankments in Nantes and a virtual visit of the city in 1757.

Château des Ducs de Bretagne
Pl Marc Elder. **Tel** 08 11 46 46 44. **Open** Jul–Aug: daily; Sep–Jun: Tue–Sun. **Closed** Jan 1, May 1, Nov 1, Dec 25.

Environs

From Nantes, boats cruise the Erdre and Sèvre Nantaise rivers, passing châteaux and vineyards. Some 20 miles (30 km) southeast of Nantes is **Clisson**, a town razed to the ground during the Vendée Uprising of 1793, and later rebuilt by sculptor François-Frédéric Lemot along Italian lines, with Neo-Classical villas and red-tiled roofs. On a spur overlooking the Sèvre Nantaise river is the ruined 13th-century **Château de Clisson**.

Château de Clisson
Tel 02 40 54 02 22. **Open** Wed–Mon (Oct–Apr: Wed–Mon pms only). **Closed** May 1, Christmas hols.

❷ The Vendée

Vendée and Maine-et-Loire. Nantes. La Roche-sur-Yon. La Roche-sur-Yon (02 51 36 00 85). **vendee-tourisme.com**

The counter-revolutionary movement which swept western France between 1793 and 1799 began as a series of uprisings in the Vendée, still an evocative name to the French. As a bastion of the *Ancien Régime*, the region rebelled against urban Republican values. But a violent massacre in 1793 left 80,000 royalists dead in one day as they tried to cross the Loire at St-Florent-le-Vieil. The Vendée farmers were staunch royalists, and, although they ultimately lost, the region remains colored by conservatism and religious fervor to this day.

This local history is dramatically retraced at **Le Puy du Fou** in Les Epesses, south of Cholet, with its spectacular summer evening live show, *Cinéscenie*. More sober accounts are given at Logis de La Chabotterie near St-Sulpice-de-Verdon (closed for renovation until mid-2014), and the Musée du Textile in Cholet, whose flax and hemp textiles provided the royalist heroes with their kerchiefs: originally white, then blood-red.

The tranquil Vendée offers green tourism inland, in the *bocage vendéen*, a wooded backwater with paths and nature trails. The Atlantic coast between the Loire and La Rochelle has beaches, yet the only sizable resort here is **Les Sables d'Olonne** with boat trips to the salt-marshes, out to sea or to the

The harbor at Ile de Noirmoutier in the Vendée

nearby **Ile d'Yeu**. To the north, the marshy **Ile de Noirmoutier** is connected to the mainland at low tide via the Gois causeway.

Inland lies the remote **Marais Poitevin** *(see p412)*, its marshes home to bird sanctuaries and fine churches (Maillezais, Vix, Maillé) in hamlets bordered by canals. It is France's largest complex of man-made waterways, largely reclaimed for farming in the west, while farther east is a nature lover's paradise. Coulon is the main center for hiring punts.

The Apocalypse Tapestry in Angers

3 Angers

Maine-et-Loire. 156,300. 7 pl Kennedy (02 41 23 50 00). Tue–Sun. **angersloiretourisme.com**

Angers is the historic capital of Anjou, home of the Plantagenets and gateway to the Loire Valley. The town has a formidable 13th-century **Château** *(see p246)*. Inside is the longest (338 ft/103 m) and one of the finest medieval tapestries in the world. It tells the story of the Apocalypse, with battles between hydras and angels.

A short walk from the castle is the **Cathédrale St-Maurice**, noted for its facade and 13th-century stained-glass windows. Close by is Maison d'Adam, with carvings showing the tree of life. The nearby **Galerie David d'Angers**, housed in the glass-covered ruins of a 13th-century church, celebrates the sculptor born in Angers. Across the river Maine, the Hôpital St-Jean, a hospital for the poor from 1174 to 1854, houses the **Musée Jean Lurçat**. Its prize exhibit is the exquisite *Chant du Monde* tapestry, which was created by Lurçat in 1957. In the same building is **Le Musée de la Tapisserie Contemporaine**, with displays of ceramics and paintings.

Château d'Angers
Tel 02 41 86 48 77. **Open** daily. **Closed** Jan 1, May 1, Nov 1 & 11, Dec 25.

Galerie David d'Angers
33 bis rue Toussaint. **Tel** 02 41 05 38 00. **Open** mid-May–mid-Sep: daily; mid-Sep–mid-May: Tue–Sun. **Closed** most public hols.

Musée Jean Lurçat / Le Musée de la Tapisserie Contemporaine
4 bd Arago. **Tel** 02 41 24 18 45. **Open** Jun–Sep: daily; Oct–May: Tue–Sun. **Closed** most public hols.

Environs

Within a 13-mile (20-km) radius of Angers lie the Classical **Château de Serrant** and the moated **Château du Plessis-Bourré**, a decorative pleasure dome encased in a feudal shell. Follow the Loire east along the sandbanks and dykes, enjoying the fish restaurants en route.

Château de Serrant
St-Georges-sur-Loire. **Tel** 02 41 39 13 01. **Open** call or check website for opening schedules. oblig. **chateau-serrant.net**

Château du Plessis-Bourré
Ecuillé. **Tel** 02 41 32 06 72. **Open** Apr–Jun & Sep: Thu pm–Tue; Feb, Mar, Oct, Nov: Thu–Tue pms only; Jul– Aug: daily. oblig. **plessis-bourre.com**

4 Le Mans

Sarthe. 150,000. rue de l'Etoile (02 43 28 17 22). Tue–Sun. **lemanstourisme.com**

Ever since Monsieur Bollée became the first designer to place an engine under a car bonnet, Le Mans has been synonymous with the motor trade. Bollée's son created an embryonic Grand Prix, since when the event *(see p41)* and associated **Musée Automobile de la Sarthe** have remained star attractions. Cité Plantagenêt, the ancient fortified center, is surrounded by the greatest Roman walls in France, best seen from the quai Louis Blanc. Once abandoned, the area has been restored, and is now used for filming epics such as *Cyrano de Bergerac*, set amongst Renaissance mansions, half-timbered houses, arcaded alleys, and tiny courtyards.

The crown is the Gothic **Cathédrale St-Julien**, borne aloft by flying buttresses, with its Romanesque portal rivaling that of Chartres. Inside, the Angevin nave opens into a Gothic choir, complemented by sculpted capitals and a 12th-century Ascension window.

Stained-glass Ascension window in the Cathédrale St-Julien, Le Mans

Musée Automobile de la Sarthe
9 pl Luigi Chinetti. **Tel** 02 43 72 72 24. **Open** Apr–Sep: daily; Oct–Mar: Wed–Mon (Jan: Sat–Sun only).

Le Mans racetrack: a 1933 print from the French magazine *Illustration*

❺ Saumur

Maine-et-Loire. 32,000. pl de la Bilange (02 41 40 20 60). Thu, Sat. **saumur-tourisme.com**

The Château de Saumur and spire of St-Pierre seen from the Loire

Saumur is celebrated for its fairytale château, cavalry school, mushrooms, and sparkling wines. Its stone mansions recall the city's 17th-century heyday, when it was a bastion of Protestantism and vied with Angers as the intellectual capital of Anjou.

High above both town and river is the turreted **Château de Saumur**. The present structure was started in the 14th-century by Louis I of Anjou and remodeled later by his grandson, King René. Collections include medieval sculpture and equestrian exhibits.

King René's coat of arms

The Military Cavalry School, established in Saumur in 1814, led to the creation of the **Musée des Blindés**, which exhibits 150 different armored vehicles, and of the prestigious Cadre Noir horseback-riding formation.

Morning training sessions and stable visits, along with occasional evening performances, can be seen at the **Ecole Nationale d'Equitation**. The nearby subterranean **Parc Pierre et Lumière** (sculptures in the tufa cave walls of prominent local tourist sites), is well worth a visit; as is Europe's largest dolmen, with its collection of prehistoric implements, in Bagneux.

Before you leave the area, be sure to sample the local *méthode champenoise* sparkling wine – the best in France outside Champagne – in one of the many wine cellars or at the Maison des Vins in town.

Château de Saumur
Tel 02 41 40 24 40. **Open** Apr–Oct: Tue–Sun (mid-Jun–mid-Sep: daily).

Ecole Nationale d'Equitation
St-Hilaire-St-Florent. **Tel** 02 41 53 50 6(**Open** mid-Feb–early Nov: call for performance times. **Closed** public hol oblig. **cadrenoir.fr**

Environs

The lovely **Eglise Notre-Dame** at Cunault, an 11th-century Romanesque priory church, has a fine west door and carved capitals, while an amazing subterranean fort and myriad caves and tunnels can be seen at **Château de Brézé**.

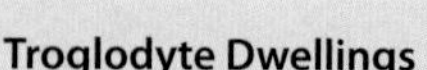

Troglodyte Dwellings

Some of the best troglodyte settlements in France have been carved out of the soft limestone (tufa) of the Loire Valley, especially around Saumur, Vouvray, and along the river Loir. The caves, cut out of cliff-faces or dug underground, have been a source of cheap, secure accommodation for centuries. Today they are popular as *résidences secondaires*, or used for wine storage and mushroom growing. Some are now restaurants or hotels, and old quarries at Doué-la-Fontaine accommodate a zoo and a 15th-century amphitheater. At Rochemenier, near Saumur, is a well-preserved troglodyte village museum. A central pit is surrounded by a warren of caves, barns, wine cellars, dwellings, and even a simple underground chapel.

Heralded by chimney pots, the underground hamlet of La Fosse was inhabited until the late 20th century by three families, and is now a museum of family life underground.

A typical troglodyte dwelling

❻ Montreuil-Bellay

Maine-et-Loire. 4,500. pl du Concorde (02 41 52 32 39). Tue (& Sun, mid-Jun–mid-Sep). **ville-montreuil-bellay.fr**

Set on the river Thouet 11 miles (17 km) south of Saumur, Montreuil-Bellay is one of the region's most gracious small towns and is an ideal base for touring Anjou. The towering roofline of the Gothic collegiate church overlooks walled mansions and surrounding vineyards (wine-tasting recommended). The **Chapelle St-Jean** was an ancient hospice and pilgrimage center.

The imposing **Château de Montreuil-Bellay**, established in 1025, is a veritable fortress with its 13 interlocking towers, barbican, and ramparts.

A 15th-century house lies beyond the fortified gateway, complete with vaulted medieval kitchen and an oratory decorated with 15th-century frescoes.

Château de Montreuil-Bellay
Tel 02 41 52 33 06. **Open** Apr–mid-Nov: Wed–Mon (Jul–Aug: daily).

Court Life in the Renaissance

François I's reign, from 1515 to 1547, witnessed the apogee of the French Renaissance, characterized by an intense period of château-building and an interest in humanism and the arts. The itinerant court traveled between the pleasure palaces of Amboise, Blois, and Chambord in the Loire. Days were devoted to hunting, falconry, *fêtes champêtres* (country festivals), or *jeu de paume*, a forerunner of tennis. Nights were given over to feasting, balls, poetry, and romantic assignations.

Lute and mandolin music were much in vogue, as were Italian recitals and masquerades. Musicians played at the twice-weekly balls, where the pavane and galliard were danced.

The antics of François I's fools, Triboulet and Caillette, amused the court. Yet they were often mistreated: courtiers regularly nailed Caillette's ears to a post for fun, daring him to remain silent.

Renaissance Feasts

Dinner usually took place before 7pm to the accompaniment of Italian music. Humanist texts were read aloud and the king's fools amused the courtiers.

Courtiers used their own knives at dinner. Forks were still rare, although their use was spreading from Italy.

A typical royal dinner comprised smoked eel, salted ham, veal pâté, egg and saffron soups, roast game, and boiled meats, as well as fish dishes in lemon or gooseberry sauce.

The cost of lavish damask, satin, and silk costumes often sent courtiers into debt.

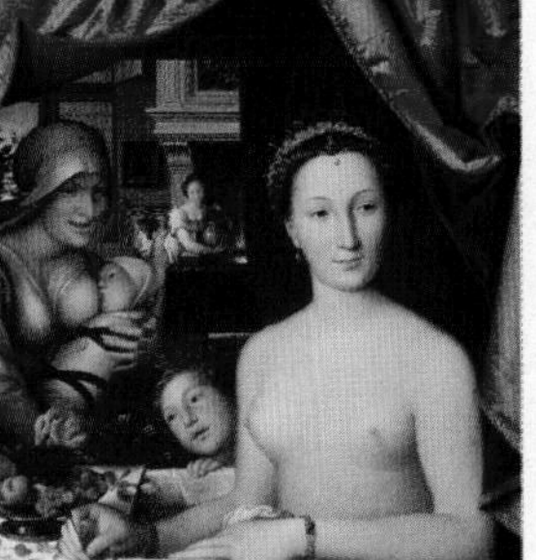

Diane de Poitiers (1499–1566) became the mistress of the future Henri II when he was 12 years old. Two years later he married Catherine de' Medici, but Diane remained his favorite until his death.

Artists symbolized love in different ways during the Renaissance. Winged hearts charmingly perform the function here.

The Grand Moûtier cloisters

❼ Abbaye Royale de Fontevraud

Maine-et-Loire. from Saumur. **Tel** 02 41 51 73 52. **Open** Apr–mid-Nov: daily; mid-Nov–Mar: Tue–Sun. **Closed** Jan, 25 Dec. **abbayedefontevraud.com**

The Abbaye Royale de Fontevraud is the largest and most remarkably intact medieval abbey in Europe. It was founded in the early 12th century by Robert d'Arbrissel, a visionary itinerant preacher who set up a Benedictine community of monks, nuns, nobles, lepers, and vagabonds. The radical founder entrusted the running of the abbey to an abbess, usually from a noble family, and the abbey became a favorite sanctuary for the female aristocracy, including Eleanor of Aquitaine.

From 1804 to 1963 the abbey was used as a prison, since when the buildings have been undergoing painstaking restoration by the French State. Wandering around the abbey buildings and gardens gives a fascinating insight into monastic life.

Tour Evraud

Pepperpot chimneys top the towers of the kitchen, restored in the 20th century.

Fireplace alcoves that look like side chapels housed the ovens.

The focal point was the Romanesque abbey church, consecrated in 1119. It boasts beautifully carved capitals and an immense nave with four domes, one of the finest examples of a cupola nave in France. Inside are the painted effigies of the Plantagenets, dating from the early 13th century: Henry II of England, his redoubtable wife Queen Eleanor of Aquitaine, their crusading son Richard the Lion-Heart, and Isabelle d'Angoulême, widow of his infamous brother, King John of England.

The abbey's nuns lived around the Renaissance **Grand Moûtier cloisters**, forming one of the largest nunneries in France. The leper colony was once housed in the **St-Lazare priory**, now a hotel *(due to reopen in 2014 following renovation)*. The monastic quarters of **St-Jean de l'Habit** no longer exist. Most impressive is the octagonal kitchen with its fireplaces and chimneys in the **Tour Evraud**, a rare example of secular Romanesque architecture.

The abbey, now an important arts center, regularly hosts concerts and exhibitions.

The Plantagenets

The legendary counts of Anjou were named after the *genêt*, the sprig of broom Geoffrey Plantagenet wore in his cap. He married Matilda, daughter of England's Henry I. In 1154, when their son Henry – who married Eleanor of Aquitaine *(see p55)* – acceded to the English throne, the Plantagenet dynasty of English kings was founded, fusing French and English destinies for 300 years.

Effigies of Henry II, Plantagenet king of England, and Eleanor of Aquitaine

❽ Chinon

Indre-et-Loire. 9,000. pl Hofheim (02 47 93 17 85). Thu. **chinon-valdeloire.com**

The Château de Chinon is an important shrine in Joan of Arc country and, as such, wheedles money from all passing pilgrims. It was here in 1429 that the saint first recognized the disguised dauphin (later Charles VII), and persuaded him to give her an army to drive the English out of France. Before that, Chinon was the Plantagenet kings' favorite castle. Although the **château** is now mostly in ruins, the ramparts are an impressive sight from the opposite bank of the Vienne river. The town's bijou center is like a medieval film set. **Rue Voltaire**, lined with 15th- and 16th-century houses and once enclosed by the castle walls, represents a cross-section of Chinonais history. At No. 12 is the **Musée Animé du Vin**, where animated figures tell the story of wine-making. Nearby, at 44 rue Haute St-Maurice, is the Musée d'Art et d'Histoire, a stone

Stallholder at Chinon's market

Vineyard in the Chinon wine region

mansion where, in 1199, Richard the Lion-Heart is said to have died. The grandest mansion is the **Palais du Gouverneur,** with its double staircase and loggia. More charming is the **Maison Rouge** in the Grand Carroi, studded with a red-brick herringbone pattern.

The neighboring 15th-century **Château de Marçay**, built on an earlier 11th-century fortress *(see p561)* now offers luxurious rooms for a stay in the Loire Valley.

The 1900s market, with stall-holders in period costume, folk dancing, and music is a must (third Saturday of August).

Musée Animé du Vin
12 rue Voltaire. **Tel** 02 47 93 25 63.
Open Easter–Sep: daily.

Environs

Three miles (5 km) southwest of Chinon is **La Devinière,** birth-place of François Rabelais, the 16th-century writer, priest, doctor, and humanist scholar.

La Devinière
Seuilly. **Tel** 02 47 95 91 18. **Open** Apr–Sep: daily; Oct–Mar: Wed–Mon.
Closed 1 Jan, 25 Dec.

9 Château d'Ussé

Indre-et-Loire. Chinon, then taxi.
Tel 02 47 95 54 05. **Open** mid-Feb–mid-Nov: daily.
chateaudusse.fr

The fairytale Château d'Ussé enjoys a bucolic setting by the river Indre. Its romantic turrets, pointed towers, and chimneys inspired Charles Perrault's *Sleeping Beauty*.

Constructed in the 15th century, the castle was gradually transformed into an aristocratic château, which is still privately owned *(see p246)*. However, the sunless and musty interior is rather disappointing and the *Sleeping Beauty* tableaux are clumsily presented.

The château's delightful Renaissance chapel, framed by the oak forest of Chinon, has lost its Aubusson tapestries, but retains a lovely della Robbia terracotta *Virgin*.

10 Château de Langeais

Indre-et-Loire. Langeais. **Tel** 02 47 96 72 60. **Open** daily. **Closed** Jan 1, Dec 25. **chateau-de-langeais.com**

Compared with neighboring towns, Langeais is distinctly untouristy and has a welcoming, unpretentious feel. Its château is fiercely feudal, built strictly for defence with a drawbridge, portcullis, and no concessions to the Renaissance. It was constructed by Louis XI in just four years, from 1465–9, with hardly an alteration since then. The ruins of an impressive keep, built by Foulques Nerra in AD 994, stand in the small château courtyard.

A *son et lumière* in the Salle de la Chapelle represents the marriage of Charles VIII and Anne of Brittany in 1491. Many of the rooms have intricate designs on the tiled floors, and all are hung with fine 15th- and 16th-century Flemish and Aubusson tapestries.

François Rabelais

Rabelais, born in 1494, was a priest, doctor, diplomat, and humanist scholar noted for his wisdom and tolerance. He is best remembered for his many ribald satires (written as "medicine" for his patients), such as *Pantagruel* and *Gargantua*, set around his native Chinon.

Infant Pantagruel, depicted by Doré in 1854, was fed on the milk of 17,913 cows

⓫ Château d'Azay-le-Rideau

Indre-et-Loire. Azay-le-Rideau. **Tel** 02 47 45 42 04. **Open** daily. **Closed** Jan 1, May 1, Dec 25. Son et Lumière: Jul–Aug.

Balzac called Azay-le-Rideau "a multi-faceted diamond set in the Indre." It is the most beguiling and feminine of Loire châteaus, created in the early 16th century by Philippa Lesbahy, wife of François I's corrupt finance minister. Although Azay is superficially Gothic *(see pp58–59, 246)*, it clearly shows the transition to the Renaissance: the turrets are purely decorative and the moats are picturesque pools. Azay was a pleasure palace, lived in during fine weather and deserted in winter.

The interior is equally delightful, an airy, creaking mansion smelling faintly of cedarwood and full of lovingly re-created domestic detail. The first floor is furnished in the Renaissance style, with a fine example of a portable Spanish cabinet and exquisite tapestries. The ground floor has 19th-century furniture, dating from the period of the château's restoration. The four-story grand staircase is unusual for its time, being straight as opposed to spiral.

Wine-tasting opportunities in the village are a welcome reminder that vineyards are all around. Unlike most Loire villages, Azay is lively at night, thanks to the château's poetic *son et lumière*.

Château d'Azay-le-Rideau reflected in the river Indre

The Château de Villandry's *jardin d'ornement*

⓬ Château de Villandry

Indre-et-Loire. Tours, then taxi. **Tel** 02 47 50 02 09. **Open** Château: mid-Feb–mid-Nov & mid-Dec–early Jan: daily. Gardens: daily. Mar–Oct. **chateauvillandry.fr**

Villandry was the last great Renaissance château built in the Loire Valley, a perfect example of 16th-century architecture. Its gardens were restored to their original splendor early in the last century by Dr Joachim Carvallo, whose grandson continues his work.

The result is a patchwork of sculpted shrubs and flowers on three levels: the kitchen garden *(jardin potager)*, the ornamental garden *(jardin d'ornement)*, and, on the highest level, the water garden *(jardin d'eau)*. There are signs to explain the history and meaning behind each plant: the marrow squash, for instance, symbolized fertility; the cabbage, sexual and spiritual corruption. Plants were also prized for their medicinal properties: cabbage was thought to help cure hangovers, while pimento aided digestion.

The delicate roots of the 32 miles (52 km) of box hedge that outline and highlight each section mean that the whole 10 acres (4 ha) of gardens must be hand-weeded.

A *chocolatier* in Tours

⓭ Tours

Indre-et-Loire. 140,000. 78 rue Bernard Palissy (02 47 70 37 37). Tue–Sun. **tours-tourisme.fr**

Tours is the most appealing of the major Loire cities, thanks to bourgeois prosperity, an intelligent restoration program and its university population. It is built on the site of a Roman town, and was a center of Christianity in the 4th century under St Martin, bishop of Tours. In 1461 Louis XI made the city the French capital. However, during Henri IV's reign the city lost favor with the monarchy and the capital left Tours for Paris.

Bombarded by the Prussians in 1870, and bombed in World War II, Tours suffered extensive damage. By 1960, the middle classes had abandoned the historic center and it became a slum, full of crumbling medieval masonry.

generation of the city has cceeded due to the popular licies of Jean Royer, mayor of urs from 1958 to 1996.

The pedestrianized **place umereau** is Tours' most mospheric quarter, set in the edieval heart of the city and l of cafés, boutiques, and lleries. Streets such as rue çonnet reveal half-timbered cades, hidden courtyards, and oked towers. A gateway ads to place St-Pierre-le-ellier, a square with sunken llo-Roman remains and a manesque church converted to a café. A few streets away in ace de Châteauneuf lies the manesque **Tour Charlemagne**, that remains of St Martin's st church. West of here is the ghly yuppified artisans' arter, centered on the rue du tit St-Martin.

The **Cathédrale St-Gatien**, in e eastern sector of the city, was gun in the early 13th century d completed in the 16th. Flamboyant Gothic facade is ackened and crumbling but ll truly impressive, as are the edieval stained-glass windows.

The **Musée des Beaux Arts**, set the former archbishop's palace earby, overlooks Classical gardens and a giant cedar of Lebanon. Its star exhibits are *Christ in the Garden of Olives* and *The Resurrection* by Mantegna, and a room devoted to the modern artist Olivier Debré.

Cathédrale St-Gatien in Tours

Further west, is the **Eglise St-Julien**, whose Gothic monastic cells and chapter-house contain a small wine museum. Next door, the **Musée du Compagnonnage** displays hundreds of finely created works by master craftsmen of the guilds. Across the rue Nationale lies the town's finest Renaissance building, the **Hôtel Goüin**, which houses regular art exhibitions.

Musée des Beaux Arts
18 pl François Sicard. **Tel** 02 47 05 68 73. **Open** Wed–Mon. **Closed** Jan 1, May 1, Jul 14, Nov 1 & 11, Dec 25.

Musée du Compagnonnage
8 rue Nationale. **Tel** 02 47 21 62 20. **Open** mid-Jun–mid-Sep: daily; mid-Sep–mid-Jun: Wed–Mon. **Closed** Jan 1, May 1, Jul 14, Nov 1 & 11, Dec 25.

Environs

Just outside Céré la Ronde, on the D764 from Montrichard to Loches, lies the 15th-century **Château de Montpoupon** and its excellent Musée du Veneur, which looks at the important role of horses in hunting.

Backgammon players in Tours' place Plumereau

ours Town Center

1. Tour Charlemagne
2. Hôtel Goüin
3. Eglise St-Julien
4. Château Royal
5. Cathédrale St-Gatien
6. Musée des Beaux Arts

0 meters 100
0 yards 100

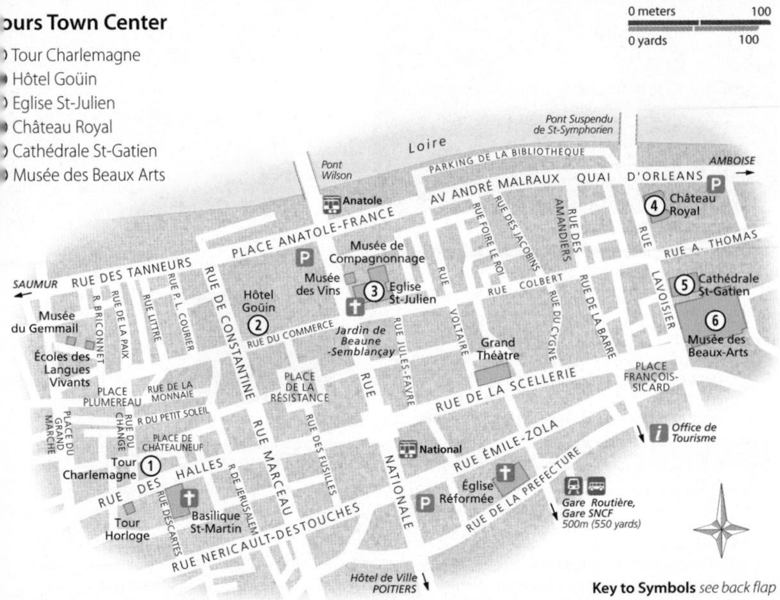

Key to Symbols *see back flap*

⑰ Château de Chenonceau

A romantic pleasure palace, Chenonceau was created from the Renaissance onwards by a series of aristocratic women. A magnificent avenue bordered by plane trees leads to symmetrical gardens and the serene vision that Flaubert praised as "floating on air and water." The château stretches across the river Cher with a 197-ft (60-m) gallery built over a series of arches, its elegant beauty reflected in the languid waters. The grandeur continues inside with splendidly furnished rooms, airy bedchambers, and fine paintings and tapestries.

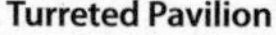

Turreted Pavilion
This was built between 1513 and 1521 by Catherine Briçonnet and her husband, Thomas Bohier, over the foundations of an old water mill.

Chapelle
The chapel has a vaulted ceiling and pilasters sculpted with acanthus leaves and cockleshells. The stained glass, destroyed by a bomb in 1944, was replaced in 1953.

Catherine de' Medici's Garden
Lavish court receptions and transvestite balls were held under Catherine's auspices.

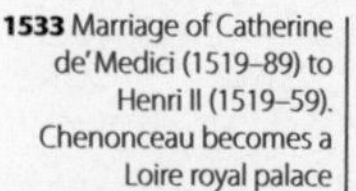

1533 Marriage of Catherine de' Medici (1519–89) to Henri II (1519–59). Chenonceau becomes a Loire royal palace

1559 On Henri's death, Catherine forces the disgraced Diane to accept the Château de Chaumont in exchange for Chenonceau

Catherine de' Medici

1789 Chenonc
is spared in the
French Revoluti
thanks to
Madame Dupin

1500	1600	1700	1800

1513 Thomas Bohier acquires medieval Chenonceau. His wife, Catherine Briçonnet, rebuilds it in Renaissance style

1575 Louise de Lorraine (1554–1601) marries Henri III, Catherine's third and favorite son

1547 Henri II offers Chenonceau to Diane de Poitiers, his lifelong mistress

1863 Madame Pelouze rest
château to its origir

1730–99 Madame Dupin, a "farmer-general's" wife, makes Chenonceau a salon for writers and philosophers

VISITORS' CHECKLIST

Practical Information
Tel 02 47 23 90 07. **Open** daily. gr. fl. only. Promenades Nocturnes: Jul–Aug (walks in the illuminated grounds to the sound of classical music). chenonceau.com

Transport
Chenonceaux. from Tours.

Grande Galerie
The elegant gallery crowning the bridge is Florentine in style, created by Catherine de' Medici from 1570 –76.

1913 The château is bought by the Menier family, the chocolatiers who still own it today

1900

1941 Chenonceau chapel is damaged in a bombing raid

Diane de Poitiers

The Creation of Chenonceau

The women responsible for Chenonceau each left their mark. Catherine Briçonnet, wife of the first owner, built the turreted pavilion and one of the first straight staircases in France; Henri II's mistress, Diane de Poitiers, added the formal gardens and arched bridge over the river; Catherine de' Medici transformed the bridge into an Italian-style gallery (having evicted Diane following her husband's death in 1559); Louise de Lorraine, bereaved wife of Henri III, inherited the château in 1590 and painted the ceiling of her bedchamber black and white (the color of royal mourning); Madame Dupin, a cultured 18th-century châtelaine, saved the château from destruction in the Revolution; and Madame Pelouze undertook a complete restoration in 1863.

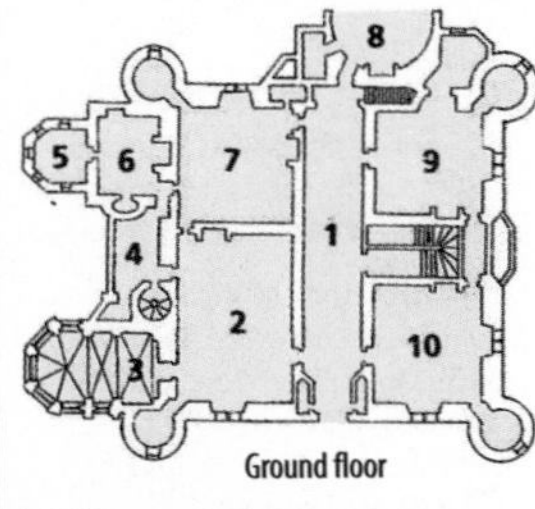

Ground floor

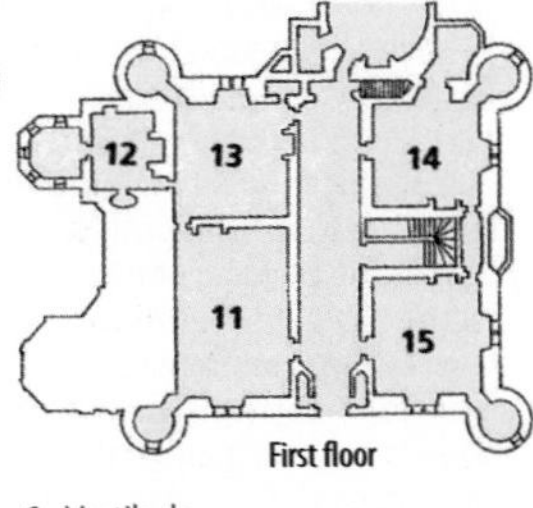

First floor

Château Guide

The main living area was in the square-shaped turreted pavilion in the middle of the river Cher. Four principal rooms open off the Vestibule on the ground floor: the Salle des Gardes and the Chambre de Diane de Poitiers, both hung with 16th-century Flemish tapestries; the Chambre de François I, with a Van Loo painting; and the Salon Louis XIV. On the first floor, reached via the Italianate staircase, are other sumptuous apartments including the Chambre de Catherine de' Médicis and the Chambre de Vendôme.

1 Vestibule
2 Salle des Gardes
3 Chapelle
4 Terrasse
5 Librairie de Catherine de' Médicis
6 Cabinet Vert
7 Chambre de Diane de Poitiers
8 Grande Galerie
9 Chambre de François
10 Salon Louis XIV
11 Chambre des Cinq Reines
12 Cabinet des Estampes
13 Chambre de Catherine de' Médicis
14 Chambre de Vendôme
15 Chambre de Gabrielle d'Estrées

Chambre de Catherine de' Médicis

⓮ Vouvray

Indre-et-Loire. 3,500. 12 rue Rabelais (02 47 52 68 73). Tue & Fri. **tourismevouvray-valdeloire.com**

Just east of Tours is the village of Vouvray, home of the delicious white wine that Renaissance author Rabelais likened to taffeta.

The quality of Vouvray's wines has not changed. The star vineyard is **Huet**, where, since 1990, grapes have been grown according to biodynamic methods: manual weeding and natural fertilizers. In the preface to his novel *Quentin Durward,* Sir Walter Scott sang the praises of its dry white wines, which are still matured in chestnut barrels. Gaston Huet also hit the headlines in 1990 with his protests against the building of tracks for the TGV train over Vouvray vineyards. A compromise was eventually reached and tunnels were built under the hilly vineyards.

The **Chateau de Montcontour**, where monks first planted vines in the 4th century, has its own wine-making museum in the impressive 10th-century cellars hewn out of the tufa rock.

The medieval town of Loches

Huet
11–13 rue de la Croix-Buisée. **Tel** 02 47 52 78 87. **Open** Mon–Sat; wine tastings and cellar visits by reservation only. **Closed** public hols. for groups.

Château de Moncontour
Route de Rochecorbon. **Tel** 02 47 52 60 77. **Open** Easter–Sep: daily; Oct–before Easter: Mon–Fri. Visits can be followed by wine tastings.
moncontour.com

⓯ Loches

Indre-et-Loire. 7,000. pl de la Marne (02 47 91 82 82). Wed & Sat. **loches- tourainecotesud.com**

This unspoilt medieval town is removed from the château trail i the Indre valley. It is a backwater of late Gothic gateways and sculpted facades. Its keep boasts the deepest dungeons in the Loire. The Logis Royal is associate with Charles VII and his mistress Agnès Sorel. It is also where Joar of Arc pleaded with Charles to g to Reims and be crowned. Anne of Brittany's chapel is decorated with ermines, and contains an effigy of Agnès Sorel.

Logis Royal de Loches
Tel 02 47 59 01 32. **Open** daily. **Closed** Jan 1, Dec 25.

The Heroine of France

Joan of Arc is the quintessential French national heroine, a virginal warrior, a woman martyr, a French figurehead. Her divinely led campaign to "drive the English out of France" during the Hundred Years' War has inspired plays, poetry, and films from Voltaire to Cecil B de Mille. Responding to heavenly voices, she appeared on the scene as champion of the dauphin, the uncrowned Charles VII. He faced an Anglo-Burgundian alliance which held most of northern France, and had escaped to the royal châteaus on the Loire. Joan convinced him of her mission, mustered the French troops, and in May 1429 led them to victory over the English at Orléans. She then urged the dithering Charles to go to Reims to be crowned. However, in 1430 she was captured and handed over to the English. Accused of witchcraft, she was burnt at the stake in Rouen in 1431 at the age of 19. Her legendary bravery and tragic martyrdom led to her canonization in 1920.

Earliest known drawing of Joan of Arc (1429)

Portrait of Joan of Arc in the Archives Nationales in Paris. She saved the city from the English on May 8, 1429, a date the Orléannais still celebrate annually *(see p316)*.

Montrésor

dre-et-Loire. 400. 43 grande
e (02 47 92 70 71). **tourisme-**
ldindrois-montresor.com

lassed as one of "the most eautiful villages in France," ontrésor does not disappoint. et on the river Indrois, it ecame a Polish enclave in e 1840s. In 1849 a Polish obleman, Count Branicki, ought the 15th-century **hâteau**, built on the site of ne of Foulques Nerra's 1th-century fortifications.

rm building and poppy fields near the lage of Montrésor

It has remained in the family ever since, its interior unchanged.

Château de Montrésor
Tel 02 47 92 60 04. **Open** daily.

17 Château de Chenonceau

See pp302–3.

18 Amboise

Indre-et-Loire. 12,000.
quai du Général de Gaulle (02 47 57 09 28). Fri & Sun am.
amboise-valdeloire.com

Few buildings are more historically important than the **Château d'Amboise**. Louis XI lived here; Charles VIII was born and died here; François I was brought up here, as were Catherine de' Medici's 10 children. The château was also the setting for the 1560 Amboise Conspiracy, an ill-fated Huguenot plot against François II. Visitors are shown the metal lacework balcony which served as a gibbet for 12 of the 1,200 conspirators who were put to death. The **Tour des Minimes**, the château's original entrance, is famous for its huge spiral ramp up which horsemen could ride to deliver provisions.

Amboise seen from the Loire

On the ramparts is the beautifully restored Gothic **Chapelle St-Hubert,** Leonardo da Vinci's burial place. Under the patronage of François I, the artist lived in the nearby manor house of **Clos-Lucé,** whose gardens exhibit models of Leonardo's inventions constructed from his sketches.

Château d'Amboise
Tel 02 47 57 00 98. **Open** daily.
Closed Jan 1, Dec 25.
chateau-amboise.com

Clos-Lucé
2 rue de Clos-Lucé. **Tel** 02 47 57 00 73.
Open daily. **Closed** Jan 1, Dec 25.
restricted. **vinci-closluce.com**

A romantic heroine, Joan of Arc was a popular subject for artists. This painting of her is by François Léon Benouville (1821–59).

Burned at the stake – a scene from *St. Joan*, Otto Preminger's 1957 epic film, which starred Jean Seberg.

⓳ Château de Chambord

Henry James once said, "Chambord is truly royal – royal in its great scale, its grand air, and its indifference to common considerations." The Loire's largest residence, brainchild of the extravagant François I, began as a hunting lodge in the Forêt de Boulogne. In 1519 this was razed and the creation of present-day Chambord began, to a design probably initiated by Leonardo da Vinci. By 1537 the towers, keep, and terraces had been completed by 1,800 men and three master masons. At one point, François suggested diverting the Loire to flow in front of his château, but he settled for redirecting the nearby Cosson instead. His son Henry II continued his work, and Louis XIV completed the 440-roomed edifice in 1685.

The Château de Chambord with the river Cosson, a tributary of the Loire, in the foreground

★ Roof Terraces
This skyline of delicate cupolas has been likened to a miniature Oriental town. The roof terraces include a forest of elongated chimney pots, miniature spires, shell-shaped domes, and richly sculpted gables.

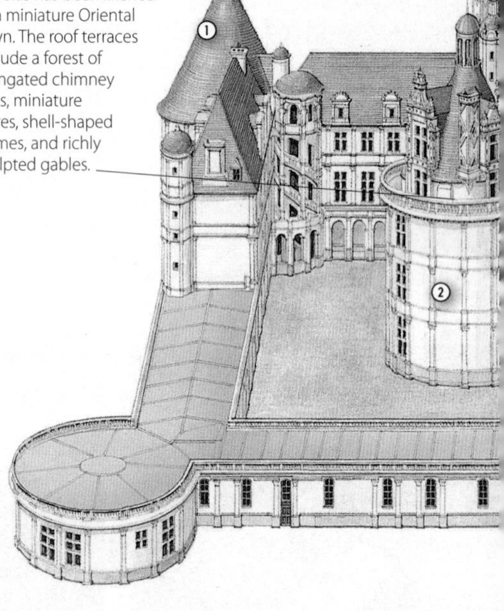

KEY

① **The chapel** was begun by François I shortly before his death in 1547. Henri II added the second story and Louis XIV the roof.

② **The central keep** (donjon), with its four circular towers, forms the nucleus of the château.

③ **The lantern tower** is 105 ft (32 m) high. Surmounting the terrace, it is supported by arched buttresses and crowned by a fleur-de-lis.

④ **François I's Bedchamber** is where the king, hurt by a failed romance, scratched a message on a pane of glass: "Souvent femme varie, bien fol est qui s'y fie." (Every woman is fickle, he who trusts one is a fool.)

1500 — **1600** — **1700** — **1800** — **1900**

1519–47 The Count of Blois' hunting lodge demolished by François I and the château created

1547 Death of François I

1547–59 Henri II adds the west wing and second storey of the chapel

1669–85 Louis XIV completes the building, then abandons it

1670 Molière's *Le Bourgeois Gentilhomme* staged at Chambord

1725–33 Inhabited by Stanislas Leczinski, exiled king of Poland who was made duke of Lorraine

1748 The Maréchal de Saxe acquires Chambord. On his death two years later, the château yet again falls into decline

1840 Chambord declared a *Monument Historique*

1970s Chambord is restored and refurnished and the moats re-dug.

Molière

Vaulted Guardrooms
ranged in the form of a eek cross around the and Staircase, the ulted guardrooms ere once the setting royal balls and ays. Their ceilings are corated with François I's tials and salamander motif.

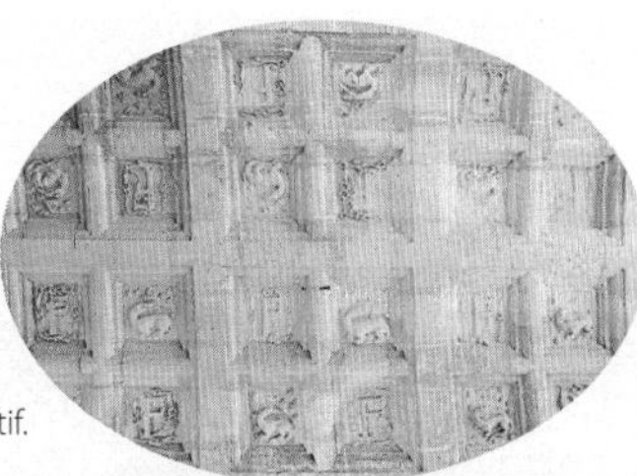

VISITORS' CHECKLIST

Practical Information
Open Jan–Mar: 10am–5pm daily; Apr–Sep: 9am–6pm daily; Oct–Dec: 10am–5pm daily.
Closed Jan 1, May 1, Dec 25. Chambord Festival (evening concerts over 2 weeks in July). **chambord.org**

Transport
Blois, then taxi, bus (2, 4) or shuttle to Chambord (Apr–early Sep only). 02 54 90 41 41.

The Salamander
François I chose the salamander as his enigmatic emblem. It appears over 800 times throughout the château.

Cabinet de François I
The king's barrel-vaulted study *(cabinet)* in the outer north tower was turned into an oratory in the 18th century by Queen Catherine Opalinska, wife of Stanislas Leczinski (Louis XV's father-in-law).

4

Grand Staircase
nis innovative double-helix staircase was upposedly designed by Leonardo da Vinci. ensures that the person going up and the erson going down cannot meet.

Louis XIV's Bedchamber
Louis XIV's bedchamber lies within the Sun King's state apartments, the grandest quarters in the château.

Blois's Cathédrale St-Louis and Hôtel de Ville seen from across the Loire

⑳ Blois

Loir-et-Cher. 60,000.
23 pl du château (02 54 90 41 41).
Wed, Sat. **bloischambord.com**

Once a fief of the counts of Blois, the town rose to prominence as a royal domain in the 15th century, retaining its historic facades and refined atmosphere to this day. Architectural interest abounds in Vieux Blois, the hilly, partially pedestrianized quarter enclosed by the château, cathedral, and river. Four well-signposted walking tours act as a gentle introduction to the noble mansions and romantic courtyards that grace the Loire's most beguiling town.

Set back from the north bank of the river, the **Château Royal de Blois** was the principal royal residence until Henri IV moved the court to Paris in 1598 – Louis XIV's creation of Versailles *(see pp178–81)* was to mark the final eclipse of Blois. The château's four contrasting wings make a harmonious whole. The Salle des Etats Généraux, the only part of the building surviving from the 13th century, housed the council and court, and is the largest and best-preserved Gothic hall in France. The adjoining late 15th-century Louis XII wing, which houses the **Musée des Beaux Arts**, infuses Gothic design with Renaissance spirit, sealed with the king's porcupine symbol.

The 16th-century François I wing is a masterpiece of the French Renaissance containing a monumental spiral staircase in an octagonal tower. By contrast, the 17th-century Gaston d'Orléans wing is a model of Classical sobriety.

Blois is authentically furnished and hung with paintings interpreting its troubled past. These include a portrayal of the murder of the Duc de Guise in 1588. Suspected of heading a Catholic plot against Henri III, he was stabbed to death by guards in the king's chamber.

King Louis XII's porcupine symbol

The most intriguing room is Catherine de' Medici's study where, of the 237 carved woode wall panels, four are secret cabinets said to have stored her poisons. Dominating the easter

François I Staircase

Built between 1515 and 1524, this octagonal staircase is a masterpiece of the early French Renaissance.

The gallery provided an ideal setting for viewing jousts and receptions held in the inner courtyard.
François I's salamander motif adorns the openwor balustrades.
The staircase within the tower slopes appreciably more steeply than the balustrades.

Louis XII wing of the Château Royal de Blois

ctor of the city, the **Cathédrale -Louis** is a 17th-century reconruction of a Gothic church that as almost completely destroyed a hurricane in 1678. Behind e cathedral the former bishop's alace, built in 1700, is the **Hôtel e Ville** (town hall). The surunding terraced gardens have vely views over the city and ver. Opposite the cathedral is e **Maison des Acrobates**, rved with characters from edieval farces including robats and jugglers.

Place Louis-XII, the marketace, is overlooked by splendid 'th-century facades. Rue Pierre e Blois, a quaint alley straddled a Gothic passageway, winds ownhill to the medieval Jewish etto. The rue des Juifs boasts veral distinguished *hôtels articuliers* (mansions), including e galleried **Hôtel de Condé**, th its Renaissance archway d courtyard, and the **Hôtel ssaud**, with magnificent th-century bas-reliefs above e main doorway. On the rue Puits-Châtel, also rich in enaissance mansions, is the lleried **Hôtel Sardini**.

Place Vauvert is the most harming square in Vieux Blois, th a fine example of a halfmbered house.

Château Royal de Blois
l 02 54 90 33 33. **Open** Jan–Mar & v–Dec: 9am–12:30pm, 1:30–5:30pm ily; Apr–Jun & Sep: 9am– 6:30pm ily; Jul–Aug: 9am–7pm daily; Oct: m–6pm daily. **Closed** Jan 1, Dec 25. *Son y lumière* show: Apr–Sep ghtly (in English on Wednesdays).

vered Gothic passageway in rue Pierre Blois

The nave of the abbey church of Notre-Dame in Beaugency

21 Beaugency

Loiret. 7,500. 3 pl de Docteur-Hyvernaud (02 38 44 54 42). Sat. **tourismebeaugency.fr**

Beaugency has long been the eastern gateway to the Loire. This compact medieval town makes a peaceful base for exploring the Orléanais region. Exceptionally for the Loire, it is possible to walk along the river banks and stone *levées*. At quai de l'Abbaye there is a good view of the 11th-century bridge which, until modern times, was the only crossing point between Blois and Orléans. An obvious target for enemy attack, it was captured four times by the English during the Hundred Years' War before being retaken by Joan of Arc in 1429.

The town center is dominated by a ruined 11th-century watchtower. It stands on **place St-Firmin**, along with a 16th-century bell tower (the church was destroyed in the Revolution) and a statue of Joan of Arc. Period houses line the square. Further down is the **Château Dunois**, built on the site of the feudal castle by one of Joan of Arc's *compagnon d'armes*. Its regional museum features an array of costumes, furniture, and antique toys. Facing the Château Dunois is **Notre-Dame**, a Romanesque abbey church that witnessed the annulment of the marriage between Eleanor of Aquitaine and Louis VII in 1152, leaving Eleanor free to marry the future Henry II of England.

Nearby is the medieval clocktower in rue du Change and the Renaissance **Hôtel de Ville**, with its facade adorned with the town's arms. Equally charming is the nearby ancient mill district, around the rue du Pont and the rue du Rü, with its streams and riot of flowers.

Château Dunois (Musée Daniel Vannier)
3 pl Dunois. **Tel** 02 38 44 54 42. **Closed** until 2014; phone for details.

Château Tour of the Sologne

The mysterious Sologne is a secretive landscape of woods and marshes edged by vineyards. Wine-lovers can indulge in tastings of Loire Valley wines accompanied, in season, by a dinner of succulent wild game from the region's forests, popular hunting grounds for centuries. The Sologne is a hunter's paradise and devotees of the sport can see today's hounds, as well as hunting trophies of the past.

This ambling rural route takes in some of the Loire's most varied châteaus. The five on this tour – for which a couple of days is required – represent a delightful encapsulation of regional architecture. All styles are here, from feudal might to Renaissance grace and Classical elegance. Several are inhabited but can still be visited.

② Château de Beauregard
Beauregard was built around 15 as a hunting lodge for François It contains a gallery with 327 portraits of royalty.

① Château de Chaumont
Chaumont is a feudal castle with Renaissance embellishments and lofty views over the river Loire *(see p246)*.

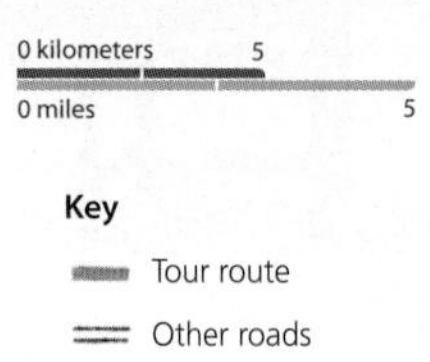

0 kilometers 5
0 miles 5

Key

Tour route

Other roads

㉒ Vendôme

Loir-et-Cher. 18,500. 47 rue Poterie (02 54 77 05 07). Fri & Sun. **vendome-tourisme.fr**

Once an important stop for pilgrims en route to Compostela in Spain, Vendôme is still popular with modern pilgrims, thanks to the TGV rail service. Though a desirable address with Parisian commuters, the town still manages to retain its provincial charm. Vendôme's old stone buildings are encircled by the river Loir, its lush gardens and chic restaurants reflected in the water.

The town's greatest monument is the abbey church of **La Trinité**, founded in 1034. Its Romanesque bell tower (all that remains of the original structure) is overshadowed by the church portal, a masterpiece of Flamboyant Gothic tracery. The interior is embellished with Romanesque capitals and 15th-century choir stalls.

Commanding a rocky spur high above the Loir is the ruined **château**, built by the counts of Vendôme in the 13th–14th centuries. Down below, rowing boats may be rented for gently exploring the meandering backwaters of the Loir, past a medieval *lavoir*, elegant buildings, and a plane tree planted in 1759.

Vendôme's native son Rochambeau, hero of the American Revolution

㉓ The Loir

Loir-et-Cher. Tours. Vendôm Montoire-sur-le-Loir. 16 pl Clémenceau, Montoire-sur-le-Loir (02 54 85 23 30).

Compared with the royal river Loire, the tranquil Loir to the north has a more rural charm. The stretch between Vendôm and Trôo is the most rewardin offering troglodyte caves *(see p296)*, walking trails, wine tasting, fishing, and boat trips.

Les Roches-l'Evêque is a fortified village with cave dwellings visible in the cliff fa Just downstream is **Lavardin**, with its Romanesque church, half-timbered houses, Gothic bridge, and ruined château ringed by ramparts. In **Montoire-sur-le-Loir**, the Chapelle St-Gilles, a former leper colony, has Romanesqu frescoes. **Trôo**, the next major village, is known for its Romar esque Eglise de St-Martin and

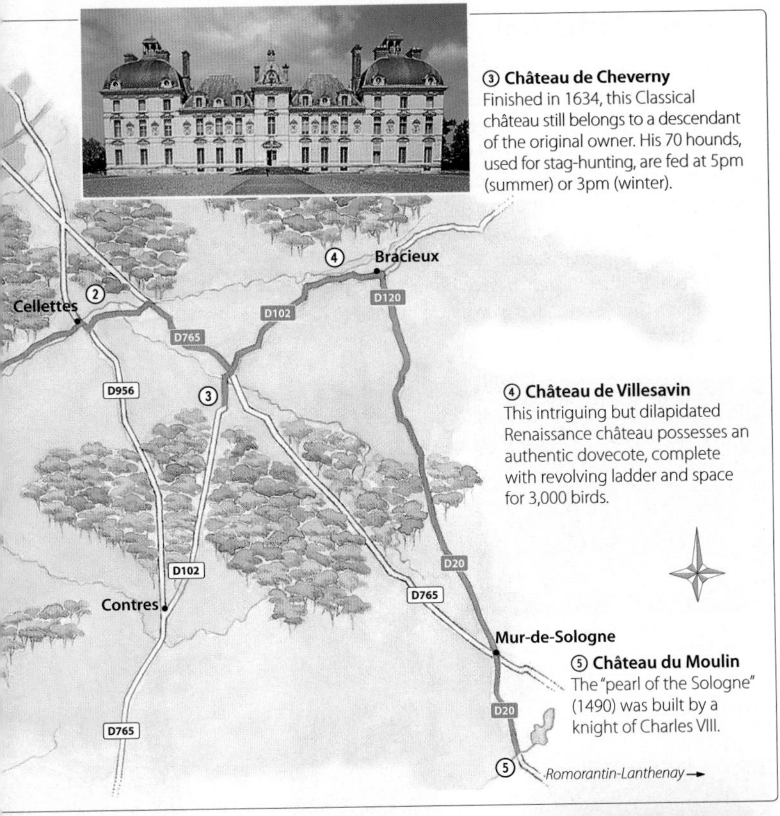

③ **Château de Cheverny**
Finished in 1634, this Classical château still belongs to a descendant of the original owner. His 70 hounds, used for stag-hunting, are fed at 5pm (summer) or 3pm (winter).

④ **Château de Villesavin**
This intriguing but dilapidated Renaissance château possesses an authentic dovecote, complete with revolving ladder and space for 3,000 birds.

⑤ **Château du Moulin**
The "pearl of the Sologne" (1490) was built by a knight of Charles VIII.

Bracieux · Cellettes · Contres · Mur-de-Sologne · Romorantin-Lanthenay → · D102 · D120 · D765 · D956 · D20

abyrinth of troglodyte dwellings. **St-Jacques-des-Guérets**, facing the village of Trôo, has a frescoed Romanesque chapel, as does **Poncé-sur-le-Loir**, farther downstream. On the slopes are vineyards producing Jasnières and Côteaux du Vendômois. Wine tastings enliven sleepy **Poncé** and **La Chartre-sur-le-Loir**. The cliffs on the opposite bank are studded with caves, commonly used as wine cellars.

Northward, the **Forêt de Bercé** abounds with paths and streams, while to the west the small town of **Le Lude** sits on the south bank of the Loir, dominated by its romantic 15th-century château.

Some 12 miles (20 km) west of Le Lude lies the town of **La Flèche**, whose main attraction is the Prytanée Nationale Militaire, originally a Jesuit college founded by Henri IV in 1603. Philosopher René Descartes was one of the college's earliest and most illustrious pupils.

㉔ Chartres

Eure-et-Loir. 42,400.
8–10 rue de la Poissonnerie (02 37 18 26 26). Tue, Thu, Sat.
chartres-tourisme.com

Chartres has the greatest Gothic cathedral in Europe *(see pp312–15)*, and its churches should not be ignored. The Benedictine abbey church of **St-Pierre** has lovely medieval stained-glass windows, while **St-Aignan** abuts 9th-century ramparts. By the river is the Romanesque **Eglise de St-André**, a deconsecrated church used for art exhibitions and concerts. The **Musée des Beaux Arts**, in the former episcopal palace, offers a fine collection of 17th- and 18th-century furniture, Renaissance enamels, and paintings by Vlaminck.

As one of the first urban conservation sites in France, Chartres is a success story. Quirky half-timbered houses abound along such cobbled streets as the rue des Ecuyers. Steep staircases known as *tertres* lead down to the river Eure providing views of mills, humpback stone bridges, washhouses, and the cathedral.

One of the many washhouses along the Eure river

In the Grenier de Loens, next to the cathedral, is the Centre International du Vitrail. The building's 13th-century vaulted storerooms are also used for temporary exhibitions.

Musée des Beaux Arts
29 cloître Notre-Dame.
Tel 02 37 90 45 80. **Open** Wed–Mon. **Closed** Sun am, Jan 1, May 1 & 8, Nov 1 & 11, Dec 25.

Chartres Cathedral

According to art historian Emile Male, "Chartres is the mind of the Middle Ages manifest." Begun in 1020, the Romanesque cathedral was destroyed by fire in 1194. Only the north and south towers, south steeple, west portal, and crypt remained; the sacred *Veil of the Virgin* relic was the sole treasure to survive. Peasant and lord alike helped to rebuild the church in just 25 years. Few alterations were made after 1250 and, fortunately, Chartres was unscathed by the Wars of Religion and the French Revolution. The result is a Gothic cathedral with a true "Bible in stone" reputation.

Elongated Statues
These statues on the Royal Portal represent Old Testament figures.

Gothic Nave
As wide as the Romanesque crypt below it, the nave reaches a lofty height of 121 ft (37 m).

★ Royal Portal
The central tympanum of the Royal Portal (1145–55) shows *Christ in Majesty.*

KEY

① **The lower half** of the west front is a survivor of the original Romanesque church, the portal and the three windows dating from the mid-12th century.

② **The taller** of the two spires dates from the start of the 16th century. Flamboyant Gothic in style, it contrasts sharply with the solemnity of its Romanesque counterpart.

③ **The vaulted ceiling** is supported by a network of ribs.

④ **Labyrinth**

The Labyrinth

The 13th-century labyrinth, inlaid in the nave floor, was a feature of most medieval cathedrals. Pilgrims followed the tortuous route on their knees, echoing the way to Jerusalem and the complexity of life, in order to reach Christ. The journey – 851 ft (262 m) of broken concentric circles – took at least an hour.

VISITORS' CHECKLIST

Practical Information
Pl de la Cathédrale. **Tel** 02 37 21 59 08. **Open** 8:30am–6:45pm daily. 9am Tue & Fri; 11:45am & 6:15pm Mon–Sat (6pm Sat); 9:15am (in Latin) & 11am Sun. for crypt and tower.
cathedrale-chartres.org

Our Lady of the Pillar
Carved from dark pear wood, this 16th-century replica of a 13th-century statue is a striking shrine which is often surrounded by candles.

★ Stained-Glass Windows
The windows cover a surface area of over 28,000 sq ft (2,600 sq m).

★ South Porch
Sculpture on the South Porch (1197–1209) reflects New Testament teaching.

The Crypt
This is the largest crypt in France, most of it dating from the early 11th century. It houses the Veil of the Virgin relic and comprises two galleries, a series of chapels, and the 9th-century St Lubin's vault.

The Stained Glass of Chartres

Donated by royalty, aristocracy, priests, and the merchant brotherhoods between 1210 and 1240, this glorious collection of stained glass is world-renowned. Around 176 windows illustrate biblical stories and daily life in the 13th century. During both World Wars the windows were dismantled piece by piece and removed for safety. There is an on-going program, begun in the 1970s, to restore the windows in the cathedral.

Stained glass above the apse

Redemption Window
Six scenes illustrate *Christ's Passion* and death on the Cross (c.1210).

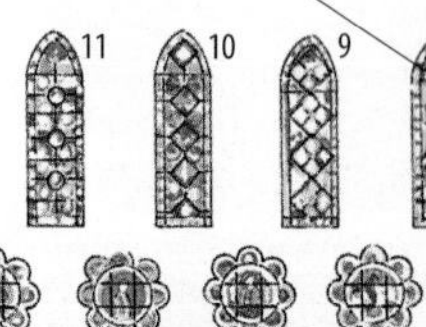

★ Tree of Jesse
This 12th-century stained glass shows Christ's genealogy. The tree rises up from Jesse, father of David, at the bottom, to Christ enthroned at the top.

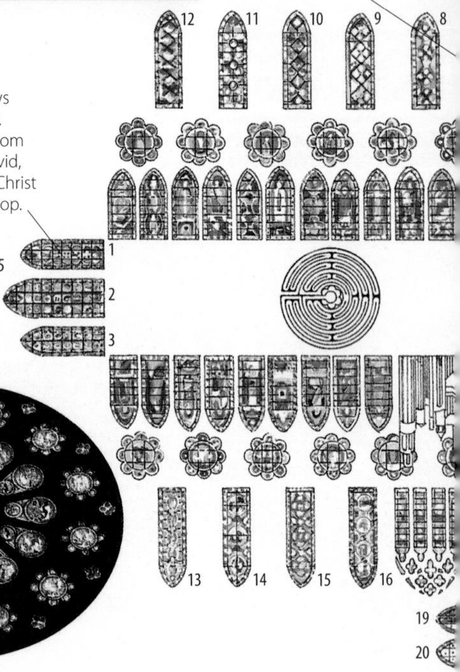

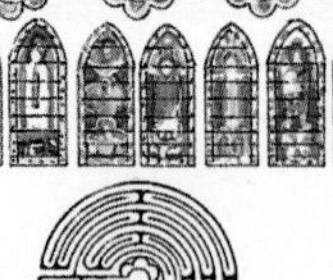

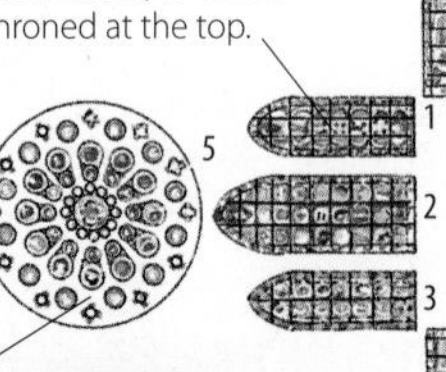

★ West Rose Window
This window (1215), with Christ seated in the center shows the *Last Judgment.*

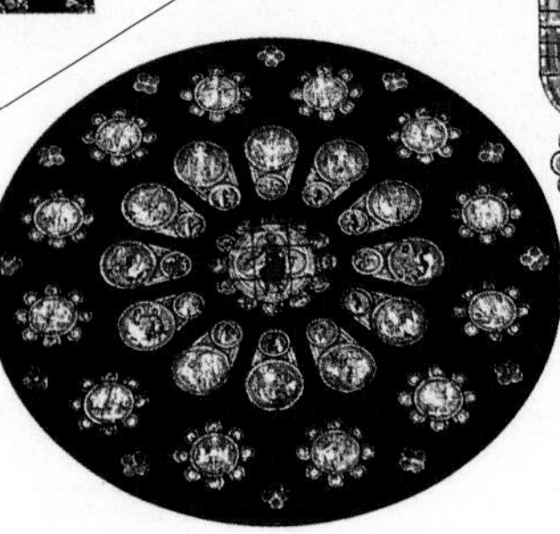

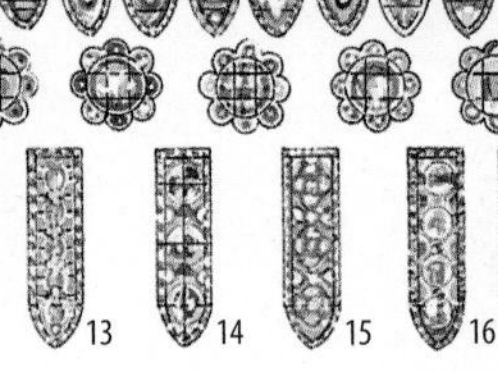

Key

1 Tree of Jesse
2 Incarnation
3 Passion and Resurrection
4 North Rose Window
5 West Rose Window
6 South Rose Window
7 Redemption Window
8 St. Nicholas
9 Joseph
10 St. Eustache
11 St. Lubin
12 Noah
13 St. John the Evangelist
14 Mary Magdalene
15 Good Samaritan and Adam and Eve
16 Assumption
17 Vendôme Chapel Windows
18 Miracles of Mary
19 St. Apollinaris
20 Modern Window
21 St. Fulbert
22 St. Anthony and St. Paul
23 Blue Virgin
24 Life of the Virgin
25 Zodiac Window
26 St. Martin
27 St. Thomas Becket
28 St. Margaret and St. Catherine
29 St. Nicholas
30 St. Remy
31 St. James the Greater
32 Charlemagne
33 St. Theodore and St. Vincent
34 St. Stephen
35 St. Cheron
36 St. Thomas
37 Peace Window
38 Modern Window
39 Prodigal Son
40 Ezekiel and David
41 Aaron
42 Annunciation-Visitatic
43 Isaiah and Moses
44 Daniel and Jeremia

North Rose Window
This depicts the *Glorification of the Virgin*, surrounded by the kings of Judah and the prophets (c.1230).

Guide to Reading the Windows

Each window is divided into panels, usually read from left to right, bottom to top (earth to heaven). The number of figures or abstract shapes used is thought to be symbolic: three stands for divinity, while the number four symbolizes the material world or the four elements.

Mary and Child in the sacred mandorla (c.1150)

Two angels doing homage before the celestial throne

Christ's triumphal entry into Jerusalem on Palm Sunday

Upper panels of the Incarnation Window

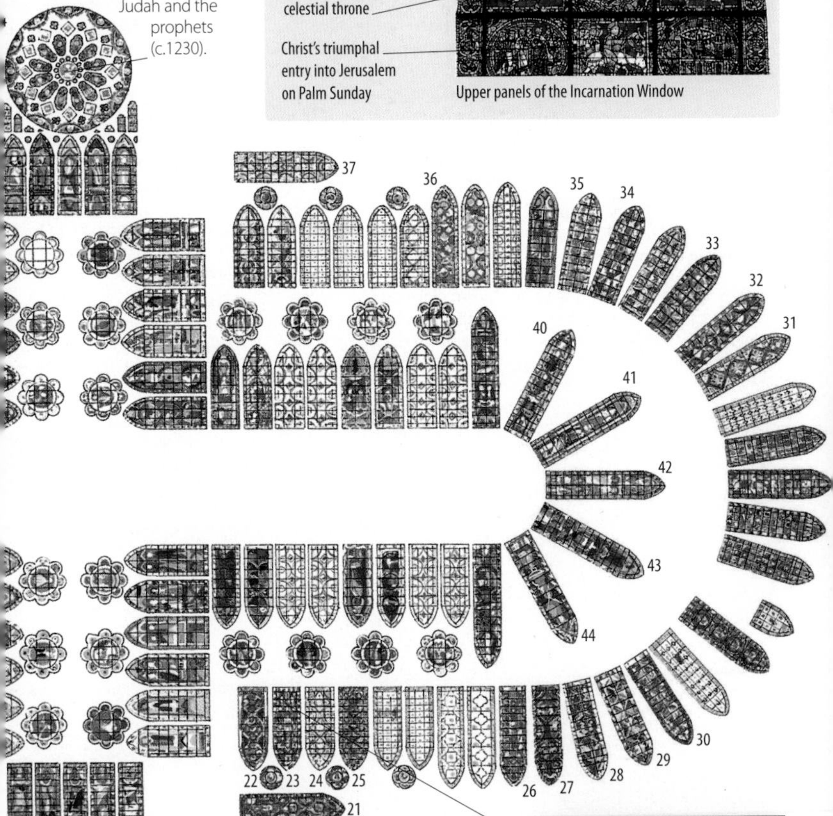

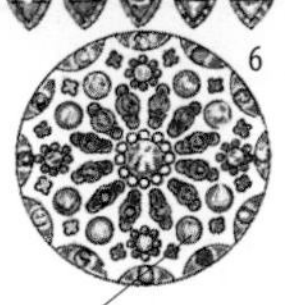

37 36 35 34 33 32 31 40 41 42 43 44 30 29 28 27 26 22 23 24 25 21 6

South Rose Window
This illustrates the *Apocalypse*, with *Christ in Majesty* (c.1225).

★ Blue Virgin Window
The window's bottom panel depicts the conversion of water into wine by Christ at *The Marriage at Cana*.

Orléans' Cathédrale Sainte-Croix

㉕ Orléans

Loiret. 112,500. 2 pl Etape (02 38 24 05 05). Tue–Sun.
tourisme-orleans.com

Orléans' dazzling contemporary bridge symbolizes the city's increasing importance at the geographic heart of both France and Europe. As a tourist, however, one is struck by the city's continued attachment to its past, most particularly to Joan of Arc. It was from here that the Maid of Orléans saved France from the English in 1429 *(see p304)*. Since her martyrdom at Rouen in 1431, Joan remains a presence in Orléans. Every April 29 and May 1, 7, and 8, her liberation of the city is re-enacted in a pageant and a blessing in the cathedral.

Orléans' historic center was badly damaged in World War II, but much has been reconstructed, and a faded grandeur lingers in Vieil Orléans, the quarter bounded by the cathedral, the river Loire, and the **place du Martroi**. The latter, a Classical but rather windswept square, has an equestrian statue of the city's heroine. Nearby the half-timbered **Maison de Jeanne d'Arc,** rebuilt from period dwellings in 1961 on the site where Joan had lodgings in 1429, has multimedia displays telling her story.

From place du Martroi, the rue d'Escures leads past Renaissance mansions to the cathedral. **Hôtel Groslot** is the grandest, a 16th-century red-brick mansion where kings Charles IX, Henri III and Henri IV all stayed. The 17-year-old François II died here in 1560 after attending a meeting of the Etats Généraux with his child-bride, Mary, later Queen of Scots. The building served as Orléans' town hall fro 1790 to 1982, and the sumptuously decorated interior, with i Joan memorabilia, is still used f marriages and official ceremonie

Virtually opposite the Hôtel Groslot and alongside the new town hall is the **Musée des Beaux Arts**, displaying European works of art from the 16th to the 20th centuries.

The **Cathédrale Sainte-Croix** nearby is an imposing edifice begun in the late 13th century, destroyed by the Huguenots (Protestants) in 1568, and then rebuilt in supposedly Gothic style between the 17th and 19th centuries.

Hôtel Groslot
Pl de l'Etape. **Tel** 02 38 79 22 30.
Open daily. **Closed** sporadically.

Musée des Beaux Arts
Pl Ste-Croix. **Tel** 02 38 79 21 55.
Open Tue–Sun. **Closed** Jan 1, May 1 8, Jul 14, Nov 1 & 11, Dec 25. free 1st Sun of month.

Maison de Jeanne d'Arc
3 pl du Général de Gaulle. **Tel** 02 38 5 99 89. **Open** Tue–Sun (Oct–Mar: pms only).

Orléans City Center

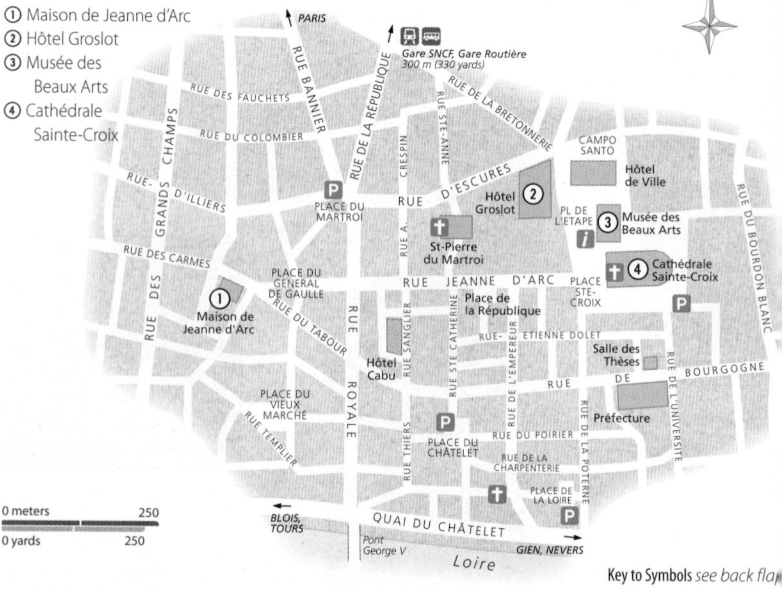

① Maison de Jeanne d'Arc
② Hôtel Groslot
③ Musée des Beaux Arts
④ Cathédrale Sainte-Croix

PARIS
Gare SNCF, Gare Routière 300 m (330 yards)
RUE BANNIER
RUE DE LA RÉPUBLIQUE
RUE DES FAUCHETS
RUE DU COLOMBIER
RUE STE-ANNE
RUE DE LA BRETONNERIE
CAMPO SANTO
Hôtel de Ville
RUE DES GRANDS CHAMPS
RUE D'ILLIERS
PLACE DU MARTROI
RUE CRESPIN
RUE D'ESCURES
Hôtel Groslot
PL DE L'ETAPE
Musée des Beaux Arts
RUE DU BOURDON BLANC
RUE DES CARMES
RUE A. ...
St-Pierre du Martroi
Cathédrale Sainte-Croix
PLACE DU GENERAL DE GAULLE
RUE JEANNE D'ARC
PLACE STE-CROIX
Maison de Jeanne d'Arc
RUE DU TABOUR
RUE ROYALE
Place de la République
RUE SANGLIER
RUE STE CATHERINE
RUE ETIENNE DOLET
Salle des Thèses
Hôtel Cabu
RUE DE L'EMPEREUR
RUE DE BOURGOGNE
RUE DE L'UNIVERSITÉ
PLACE DU VIEUX MARCHÉ
Préfecture
RUE TEMPLIER
RUE DU POIRIER
RUE DE LA POTERNE
PLACE DU CHÂTELET
RUE THIERS
RUE DE LA CHARPENTERIE
PLACE DE LA LOIRE
BLOIS, TOURS
QUAI DU CHÂTELET
Pont George V
GIEN, NEVERS
Loire

0 meters 250
0 yards 250

Key to Symbols *see back fla*

ɜn of Arc stained-glass window in Orléans' :hédrale Sainte-Croix

) St-Benoît-sur-oire

ɔiret. 2,000. 44 rue ·léanaise (02 38 35 79 00). **tourisme-loire-foret.com**

tuated along the river ɔire between Orléans and ien, St-Benoît-sur-Loire boasts ne of the finest Romanesque ɔbey churches in France 067–1108). It is all that ırvives of an important onastery founded in AD 650 ıd named after St. Benedict, ɜtron saint of Europe. His relics ere brought from Italy at ɪe end of the 7th century.

The church's belfry porch graced with carved capitals ɜpicting biblical scenes. ıe nave is tall and light, and ɪe choir floor is an amazing ɜtchwork of Italian marble. aily services with Gregorian ıant are open to the public.

㉗ Bourges

Cher. 80,000. 21 rue Victor Hugo (02 48 23 02 60). Tue–Sun. **bourges-tourisme.com**

This Gallo-Roman city retains its original walls but is best known as the city of Jacques Coeur, financier and foreign minister to Charles VII. The greatest merchant of the Middle Ages and a self-made man *par excellence*, it was in his capacity as an arms dealer that he established a tradition maintained for four centuries, as Napoléon III had cannons manufactured here in 1862.

Built over part of the walls, the **Palais Jacques Coeur** is a Gothic gem and a lasting memorial to its first master. It was finished in 1453, and incorporates Coeur's two emblems, scallop shells and hearts, as well as his motto: *"A vaillan coeur, rien impossible"* – to the valiant heart, nothing is impossible. The guided tour reveals a barrel-vaulted gallery, a painted chapel, and a chamber that had Turkish baths.

Bourges also flourishes as a university town and cultural mecca, renowned for its spring festival of music.

Rue Bourbonnoux leads to **St-Etienne**, the widest Gothic cathedral in France and the one most similar to Paris's Notre-Dame. The west facade has five sculpted portals, the central one depicting an enthralling *Last Judgment*. In the choir are vivid 13th-century stained-glass windows presented by the guilds. The crypt holds the marble tomb of the 14th-century Duc de Berry, best known for commissioning the illuminated manuscript the *Très Riches Heures* (*see pp208–9*). From the top of the north tower stretch views of the beautifully restored medieval quarter and the marshes beyond. Beside the cathedral is a tithe barn and the remains of the Gallo-Roman ramparts. The **Jardin des Prés Fichaux**, set along the river Yèvre, contains pools and an open-air theater. To the north lie the **Marais de Bourges**, where gardeners transport their produce by boat.

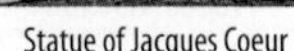

Statue of Jacques Coeur

Palais Jacques Coeur

Rue Jacques Coeur. **Tel** 02 48 24 79 42. **Open** daily. **Closed** Jan 1, May 1, Nov 1 & 11, Dec 25.

Environs

About 22 miles (35 km) south of Bourges in the Berry region is the **Abbaye de Noirlac**. Founded in 1136, it is one of the best-preserved Cistercian abbeys in France.

Statue in the Jardin des Prés Fichaux

CENTRAL FRANCE AND THE ALPS

Introducing Central France and the Alps

The geological contrasts of this region reflect its enormous variety, from the industrial and gastronomic metropolis of Lyon to the largely agricultural landscape of Burgundy. The mountains of the Massif Central and the Alps attract visitors for winter sports, superb walking, and other outdoor activities. The major sights of this richly rewarding area, both natural and architectural, are shown here.

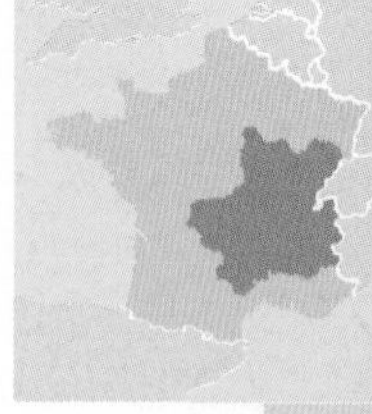

Basilique Ste-Madeleine, the famous pilgrimage church crowning the hill-top village of Vézelay, is a masterpiece of Burgundian Romanesque. It is renowned for its vividly decorated tympanum and capitals *(see pp340–41)*.

The Abbaye de Ste-Foy in the village of Conques *(see pp372–3)* is one of the great pilgrimage churches of France, with a fabulous treasury of medieval and Renaissance gold reliquaries.

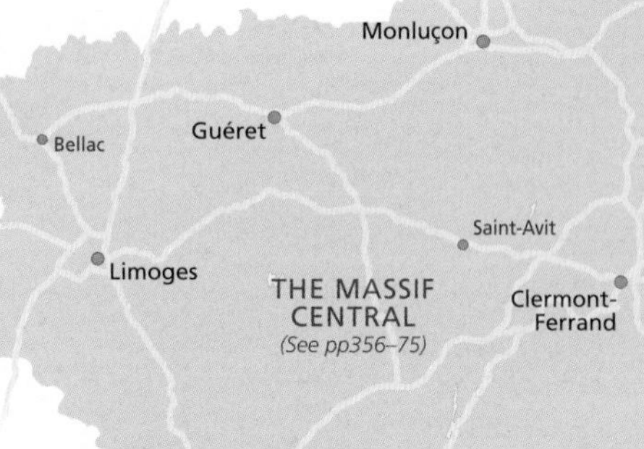

The Gorges du Tarn have some of France's most spectacular natural scenery. The road which follows the plunging course of the river Tarn gives dramatic viewpoints along the canyon and across the limestone Causses *(see pp374–5)*.

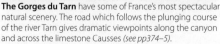

◀ The magnificent peak of Puy de Dôme, the tallest extinct volcano in the Monts Dôme range

The Abbaye de Fontenay, founded by Saint Bernard in the early 12th century, is the oldest Cistercian monastery in France *(see pp336–7)*. This well-preserved Romanesque abbey is a perfect testimony to the severe ideal of the Cistercian life.

Dijon *(see pp344–6)*

Théâtre Romain, Autun *(see p343)*

Brou Abbey Church, Bourg-en-Bresse *(see p380)*

Mont Blanc *(see pp326–7)*

Palais Idéal du Facteur Cheval, Hauterives *(see p387)*

Le Puy *(see pp368–9)*

Temple d'Auguste et Livie, Vienna *(see p386)*

The Flavors of Central France

The renowned gastronomic tradition of Lyon and the rich wine and food of Burgundy combine to make central France a gourmet paradise. The great chefs of the region have a wide choice of excellent local produce: fine Bresse chicken, Charolais beef, and Morvan ham; wildfowl and frogs from the marshes of the Dombe; fish from the Saône and the Rhône; and fat snails called "oysters of Burgundy." Franche-Comté and the Jura contribute smoked sausages, farmhouse cheeses, walnut oil, and fish from glacier-fed lakes. In the Massif Central, sturdy regional fare features salted hams, pork, Cantal cheese, the celebrated green lentils of Le Puy, and wild mushrooms.

Chanterelle mushroom

A mountain farmer shows off his fine salt-cured ham

Burgundy and Franche-Comté

Burgundy is one of France's top wine regions so, not surprisingly, wine plays a major role in the cuisine, such as in the signature dish, *boeuf bourguignon*, made from Charolais beef marinated and then stewed in good red wine, with baby onions, bacon, and mushrooms added. Other specialities include *coq au vin* and *oeufs en meurette*. Dijon's famous mustard appears most classically with steak and in *moutarde au lapin*, rabbit in a creamy mustard sauce. Burgundy and Franche-Comté produce some of the most celebrated French cheeses: Epoisses, a cow's milk cheese washed with *marc de Bourgogne*; Cîteaux, made by monks; and the magnificent Vacherin-Mont d'Or, a winter treat to be scooped straight from its wooden box. Black currants are widely grown and contribute to many desserts as well as the famous Kir: white wine with cassis (black currant liqueur).

The Massif Central

The peasant cuisine of the Auvergne is well known in France due to the many cafés run by

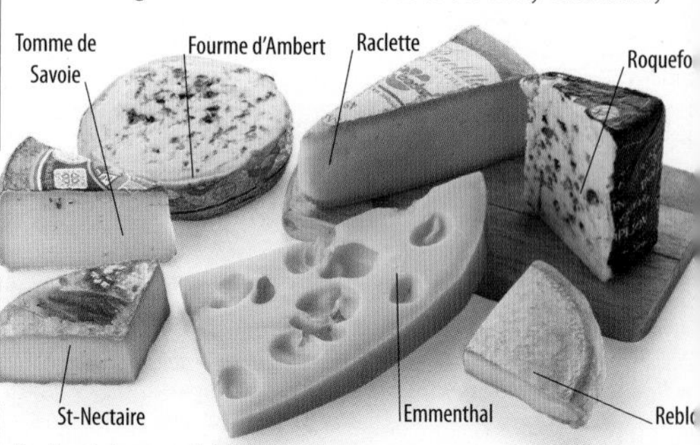

Mouthwatering array of classic French cheeses

Regional Dishes and Specialties

The cuisine of central France is rich with sauces using wine, butter, and cream, which enhance almost every dish: snails in butter and garlic; potatoes cooked with cheese and cream; and beef, lamb, and chicken stewed slowly in reduced wine sauces, often with cream or butter added at the end of cooking. Mushrooms are cooked in cream sauces, and fish is often baked in a creamy gratin. Most indulgent of all is the Alpine fondue, where cheeses are melted, together with Kirsch and wine, in a special earthenware fondue pot. This is placed on a burner on the table, and cubes of bread are speared onto special long forks and dipped into the cheese. Traditionally, anyone who loses their bread in the pot must kiss everyone else at the table.

String of onions

Oeufs en meurette This Burgundian dish is eggs poached in red wine with onions, mushrooms, and bacon.

ditional *charcuterie* on sale in a Lyon market

uvergnats in Paris, where they rve local dishes like pork uffed with cabbage, or *aligot*. Puy lentils, grown in the fertile lcanic soils of the Puy-en-Velay asin, combine well with sausages *petit salé*, or are served cold a salad. Good beef comes om the Salers cattle of the uvergne or from the Limousin, here there is also plentiful game. ild mushrooms are eagerly ought in season. Cheeses include antal, one of the country's dest, and similar in flavor to heddar, and the famous blue oquefort, ripened in the nestone caves of the Lozère.

he Rhône Valley and he French Alps

yon is famous for its aditional bistros, *bouchons*, here the cooks are often omen, known as *mères*, who dish up substantial fare like onion soup, *lyonnais* sausages, and *charcuterie*. The markets of Lyon are equally famous, stocked with the region's wide range of fruit, particularly apricots, peaches, and juicy berries. Vegetables include onions, chard, and cardoons, and the most northerly outpost of the olive is at Nyons. The Bresse region is famous for its high-quality chickens.

The Dombes lakes and the Alps are good sources of fish, such as perch, trout, and lake salmon. Bony perch is most delicious eaten as *quenelles de brochet*, filleted fish blended, made into dumplings, and baked in a creamy sauce. From the Alps comes a wide range of cheeses. As well as being delicious to eat fresh, they will often be found melted in *raclettes* or fondues, or layered with sliced potato to make an unctuous *gratin dauphinois*.

Red currants and blackberries for sale by the punnet

ON THE MENU

Chou farci Cabbage stuffed with pork and herbs.

Gigot Brayaude Leg of lamb baked over sliced potatoes and *lardons* of bacon.

Gougère Cheesy *choux* pastry baked in a ring-shape.

Jambon persillé Ham and parsley in aspic jelly.

Pochouse Freshwater fish (carp, pike, eel, and trout) stewed in white wine.

Potée savoyarde Hotpot made with vegetables, chicken, ham, and sausage.

Salade auvergnate Cubes of Auvergne ham, Cantal cheese, and walnuts.

etit salé A speciality of the uvergne region, salt pork is ooked in wine with tiny green uy lentils.

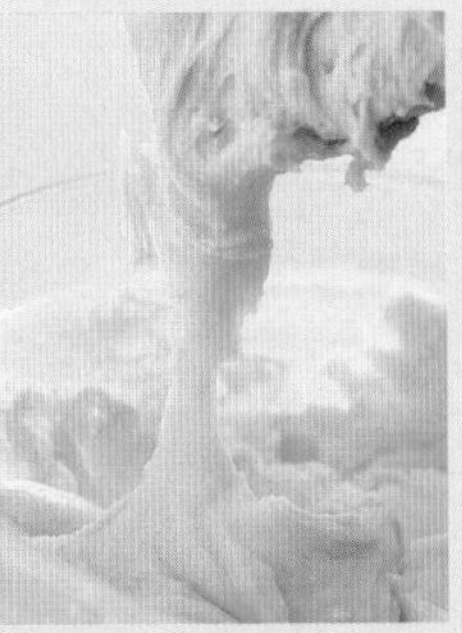
Aligot Slivers of Cantal cheese are beaten into buttery, garlicky mashed potato until the mixture forms long strands.

Clafoutis This is usually made with black cherries, baked in batter, and laced with Kirsch, a cherry liqueur.

France's Wine Regions: Burgundy

Burgundy and its fine wines have inspired awe for centuries. The fame of the region's wines spread throughout Europe in the 14th century, under the Valois Dukes of Burgundy. The system of dividing wine areas into designated *appellations*, of which there are a bewildering number, came into effect in 1935. Even today, the classification system remains dauntingly complex. But despite its impenetrable image, this is unmissable territory for the "serious" wine lover, with its rich vinous history and tradition, and dazzling *grands crus*.

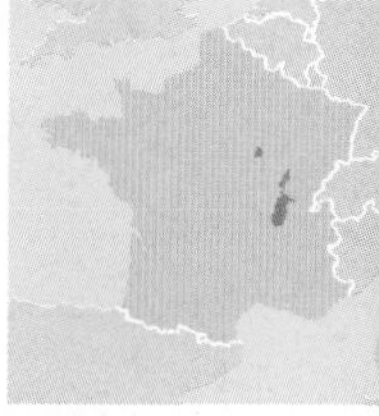

Locator Map

Burgundy wine region

Clos de Vougeot on the Côte de Nuits

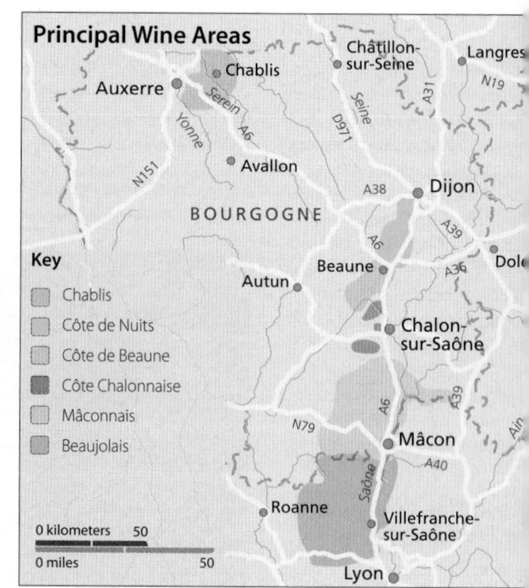

Wine Regions

Between Chablis in the north and the Côte Chalonnaise and Mâconnais in the south is the Côte d'Or, incorporating Côte de Nuits and Côte de Beaune. The Beaujolais region (see p381) *lies below Mâcon.*

Key Facts About Burgundy

Location and Climate

The continental climate (bleak winters and hot summers) can be very variable, making vintages a crucial quality factor. The best vineyards have chalky soil and face south or east.

Grape Varieties

Burgundy is at least relatively simple in its grape varieties. Red Burgundy is made from ***Pinot Noir***, with its sweet flavors of raspberries, cherries, and strawberries, while the ***Gamay*** makes red Mâcon and Beaujolais. ***Chardonnay*** is the principal white variety for Chablis and white Burgundy, though small amounts of ***Aligoté*** and ***Pinot Blanc*** are grown, and the ***Sauvignon*** is a specialty of St-Bris.

Good Producers

White Burgundy: Jean-Marie Raveneau, René Dauvissat, La Chablisienne, Comtes Lafon, Guy Roulot, Etienne Sauzet, Pierre Morey, Louis Carillon, Jean-Marc Boillot, André Ramonet, Hubert Lamy, Jean-Marie Guffens-Heynen, Olivier Merlin, Louis Latour, Louis Jadot, Olivier Leflaive.
Red Burgundy: Denis Bachelet, Daniel Rion, Domaine Dujac, Armand Rousseau, Joseph Roty, De Montille, Domaine de la Pousse d'Or, Domaine de l'Arlot, Jean-Jacques Confuron, Robert Chevillon, Georges Roumier, Leroy, Drouhin.

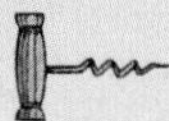

Good Vintages

(Reds) 2009, 2005, 2002, 1999.
(Whites) 2008, 2005, 2001, 1996.

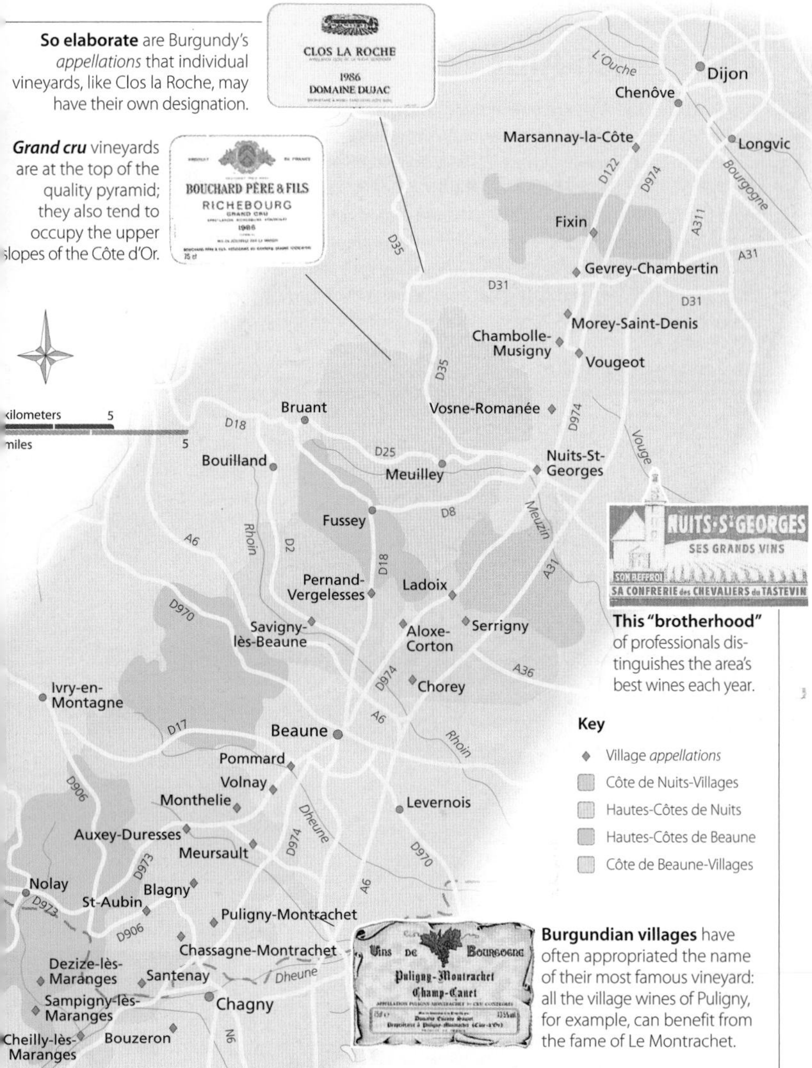

So elaborate are Burgundy's *appellations* that individual vineyards, like Clos la Roche, may have their own designation.

CLOS LA ROCHE
1986
DOMAINE DUJAC

Grand cru vineyards are at the top of the quality pyramid; they also tend to occupy the upper ;lopes of the Côte d'Or.

BOUCHARD PÈRE & FILS
RICHEBOURG
GRAND CRU
1986
75 cl

Dijon
Chenôve
Longvic
L'Ouche
Bourgogne
Marsannay-la-Côte
D122
D974
Fixin
A311
A31
D35
Gevrey-Chambertin
D31
Morey-Saint-Denis
Chambolle-Musigny
Vougeot
Vosne-Romanée
Vouge
Nuits-St-Georges
Bruant
D18
Bouilland
D25
Meuilley
D8
Meuzin
Fussey
A6
Rhoin
D2
Pernand-Vergelesses
Ladoix
Savigny-lès-Beaune
Aloxe-Corton
Serrigny
A36
D970
Chorey
Ivry-en-Montagne
D17
Beaune
Pommard
Volnay
Monthelie
Levernois
D906
Dheune
Auxey-Duresses
Meursault
D973
Nolay
Blagny
St-Aubin
Puligny-Montrachet
Chassagne-Montrachet
Dezize-lès-Maranges
Santenay
Chagny
Sampigny-lès-Maranges
Cheilly-lès-Maranges
Bouzeron
N6

:ilometers 5
niles 5

NUITS-SGEORGES
SES GRANDS VINS
SON BEFFROI
SA CONFRERIE des CHEVALIERS du TASTEVIN

This "brotherhood" of professionals distinguishes the area's best wines each year.

Key

- ◆ Village *appellations*
- Côte de Nuits-Villages
- Hautes-Côtes de Nuits
- Hautes-Côtes de Beaune
- Côte de Beaune-Villages

Vins de Bourgogne
Puligny-Montrachet
Champ-Canet

Burgundian villages have often appropriated the name of their most famous vineyard: all the village wines of Puligny, for example, can benefit from the fame of Le Montrachet.

he Côte d'Or

he Côte de Nuits and Côte e Beaune, together forming he "golden" Côte d'Or (see 348), *meet at the historic own of Beaune, which hosts he most famous annual wine uction in the world* (see p350). Hautes-Côtes" *and* "Villages" *ines, from a different* terroir, *re less sought after than wines om the starry individual* ppellations.

Teams of grape-pickers at the vineyards of Nuits-St-Georges

The French Alps

In any season, the Alps are one of the most spectacular regions of France – a majestic mountain range stretching south from Lake Geneva almost to the Mediterranean, and climaxing in Europe's loftiest peak, the 15,770-ft (4,800-m) Mont Blanc. The area encompasses the old regions of Dauphiné and Savoie, once remote and independent (Savoie only became part of France in 1860). They have prospered since alpine holidays and skiing became popular over the last century, but are still very conscious of their distinct identity.

Children in traditional Savoie costumes

The Alpine landscape in winter: chalets and skiers on the slopes at Courchevel

Winter

The ski season usually starts just before Christmas, and finishes at the end of April. Most resorts offer both cross-country and downhill skiing, with many runs linking two or more ski stations. The less energetic can still enjoy the landscape from some of the highest cable cars *(téléphériques)* in the world.

A cable car at Courchevel, part of Les Trois Vallées complex

Of the 100 or more French Alpine resorts, the most popular include **Chamonix-Mont Blanc**, the historic capital of Alpine skiing and site of the first Winter Olympics in 1924; **Megève**, which boasts one of the best ski schools in Europe; **Morzine**, a year-round resort on the Swiss border, overlooked by the modern, car-free resort of **Avoriaz**; modern **Albertville**, site of the 1992 Winter Olympics; **Les Trois Vallées**, which include glamorous **Courchevel** and **Méribel**, and the lesser-known **Val Thorens/Les Ménuires**; **Tignes**, a year-round resort; **Les Arcs** and **La Plagne**, both purpose-built; and **Val d'Isère**, a favorite among the rich and famous.

A downhill skier at Val d'Isère

Alpine Flowers

In spring and early summer the pastures of the French Alps are ablaze with flowers. These include blue and yellow gentians, bellflowers, lilies, saxifrages, and a variety of orchids. Steep mountain meadows cannot be farmed intensively, and the absence of fertilizers and weed killers enables wild flowers to flourish.

Spring gentian *(Gentiana verna)*

Martagon lily *(Lilium martagon)*

The French Alps in spring: flower-filled meadows overlooked by brilliant white peaks

Spring and Summer

The Alpine summer season starts in late June, extending to early September – most resorts close in October and November between the hiking and skiing seasons. After the spring thaw, flower-filled pastures, snow-fed mountain lakes and a huge number of marked trails make this area a hiker's paradise. In the Chamonix area alone there are over 195 miles (310 km) of hiking trails. The best known long-distance route is the **Tour du Mont Blanc**, a 10-day hike via France, Italy and Switzerland. The **GR5** traverses the entire Alps, passing through the **Parc National de la Vanoise** and **Parc Régional du Queyras** *(see p391)* to the south. *Téléphériques* give access to the higher trails, where the views are even more awesome. Be sure to bring plenty of warm, waterproof clothing: the weather can change very quickly.

Many resorts are now concentrating on broadening their summer appeal – golf, tennis, mountain biking, horseback-riding, paragliding, canoeing, white water rafting, glacier skiing, and mountain climbing are all widely available.

Bell-ringing dairy cows in an Alpine pasture

Mountain climbers scaling the heights around Mont Blanc

Geology of the Massif Central

The Massif Central covers almost one-fifth of France and is over 250 million years old. Most of its peaks have been eroded to form a vast plateau split into deep valleys. The heart of the Massif consists of hard, igneous rocks like granite, with softer rocks such as limestone at its margins. Different rock types are reflected in the landscape and buildings; in the eroded Gorges du Tarn, the houses are built of russet-colored limestone. Massive granite farmhouses are a feature of Limousin, and Le Puy-en-Velay is distinguished by its giant basalt pillars.

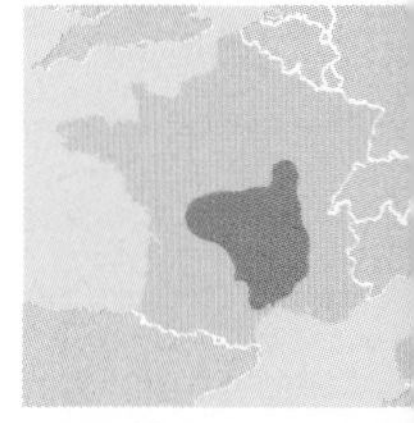

Locator Map

Extent of the Massif Central

This granite portal is found in the Romanesque church at Moutier d'Ahun *(see pp360–1)*. Granite underlies much of the Massif Central.

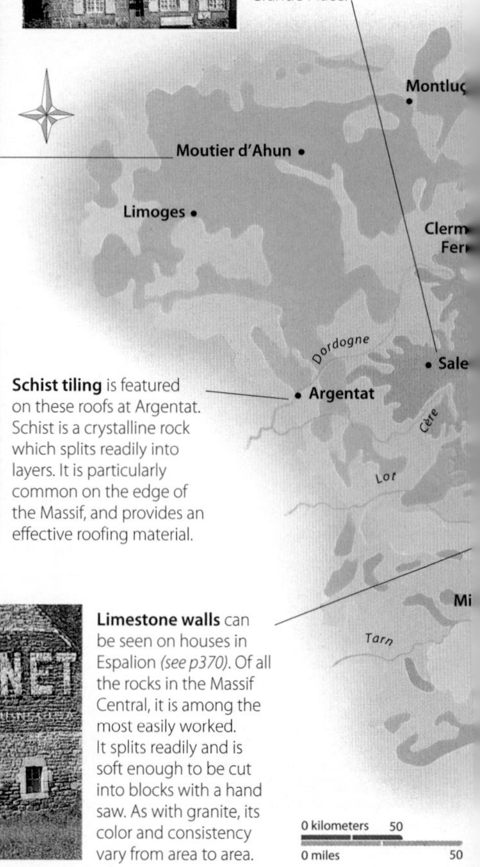

Basalt is a dark, fine-grained rock formed by volcanic lava. A common building stone in the Auvergne, it is often cut into blocks and bonded with lighter-colored mortar. In the medieval town of Salers *(see p367)*, basalt was used for most of the buildings, including this one in the Grande Place.

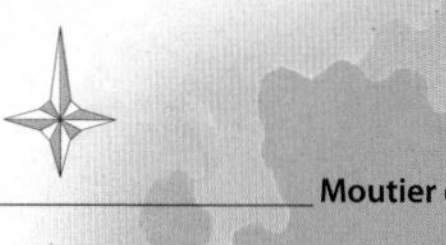

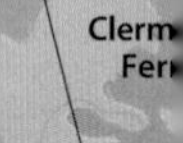

Schist tiling is featured on these roofs at Argentat. Schist is a crystalline rock which splits readily into layers. It is particularly common on the edge of the Massif, and provides an effective roofing material.

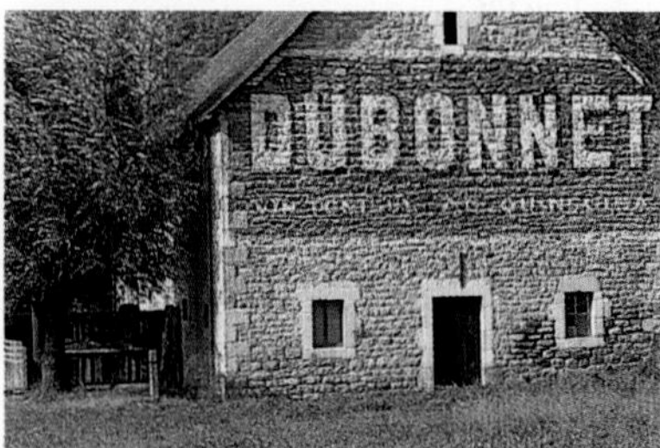

Limestone walls can be seen on houses in Espalion *(see p370)*. Of all the rocks in the Massif Central, it is among the most easily worked. It splits readily and is soft enough to be cut into blocks with a hand saw. As with granite, its color and consistency vary from area to area.

0 kilometers 50

0 miles 50

Crystallized lava, like this dramatic curtain of columns at Prades, formed when liquid basalt seeped through the surrounding rock and solidified to form giant crystals.

Key

- Sedimentary rock
- Surface volcanic rock
- Granite
- Metamorphic rock

ers

Loire

Saône

Lyon

St-Etienne

Le-Puy-en-Velay

Rhône

Limestone plateaus *(causses)* are typical of this region. Gorges, where rivers have cut through layers of this slightly soluble rock, run deep into the Massif Central.

This mature landscape at Mont Aigoual is the highest point in the Cévennes *(see p371)*, dividing rivers flowing into the Atlantic and the Mediterranean. Its granite and schist rocks show erosion.

Recognizing Rocks

Geologists divide rocks into three groups. Igneous rocks, like granite, are formed by volcanic activity and either extruded on to the surface or intrude into other rocks below ground. Sedimentary rocks are produced by sediment build-up. Metamorphic rocks have been transformed by heat or pressure.

Sedimentary Rock

Oolitic limestone often contains fossils and small amounts of quartz.

Surface Volcanic Rock

Basalt, which can form very thick sheets, is the most common lava rock.

Granite

Pink granite, a coarse-grained rock, is formed deep in the earth's crust.

Metamorphic Rock

Muscovite schist is a medium-grained mud or clay-based rock.

BURGUNDY AND FRANCHE-COMTE

onne · Niévre · Côte d'Or
aône-et-Loire · Haute-Saône · Doubs · Jura

urgundy considers itself the heart of France, a prosperous egion with world-renowned wine, earthy but excellent cuisine, nd magnificent architecture. Franche-Comté to the east ombines gentle farmland with lofty Alpine forests.

nder the dukes of Valois, Burgundy was rance's most powerful rival, with territory xtending well beyond its present oundaries. By the 16th century, however, ne duchy was ruled by governors that ere appointed by the French king, but it till retained its privileges and traditions. Once a part of Burgundy, Franche-Comté – ne Free County – struggled to remain ndependent of the French crown, and was a rovince of the Holy Roman Empire until nnexed by Louis XIV in 1674.

Burgundy, now as in the past, is a rich egion, a center of medieval religious faith vhich produced renowned Romanesque nasterpieces at Vézelay, Fontenay, and Cluny. Dijon is a splendid city, filled with the reat palaces of the old Burgundian nobility nd a collection of great paintings and sculptures in the Musée des Beaux Arts. The vineyards of the Côte d'Or, the Côte de Beaune, and Chablis yield some of the world's most venerated wines. Other varied landscapes – from the wild forests of the Morvan to the lush farmland of the Brionnais – produce snails, Bresse chickens, and Charolais beef.

Franche-Comté has none of this opulence, though its capital, Besançon, is a fine 17th-century city with a tradition of clockmaking. Topographically the Franche-Comté is divided into two, with gently-rolling farmland in the Saône valley and high Alpine scenery to the east. This forest country of Alpine torrents filled with trout is also the home of great cheeses, notably Vacherin and Comté, and of the characteristic yellow wine of Arbois.

he prehistoric site of the Roche de Solutré near Mâcon

◀ A view of Semur-en-Auxois, Burgundy, from the banks of the river Armançon

Exploring Burgundy and Franche-Comté

Burgundy is arguably France's richest province – historically, culturally, gastronomically, and economically. This lush kernel of a once great power possesses a concentration of unique Romanesque architecture in Fontenay and Vézelay, along with some of the world's most venerated wines. Dijon is a must for lovers of art, architecture, and food. Franche-Comté is better suited for outdoor holidays, such as trekking and canoeing in wild scenery and crystal-clear rivers.

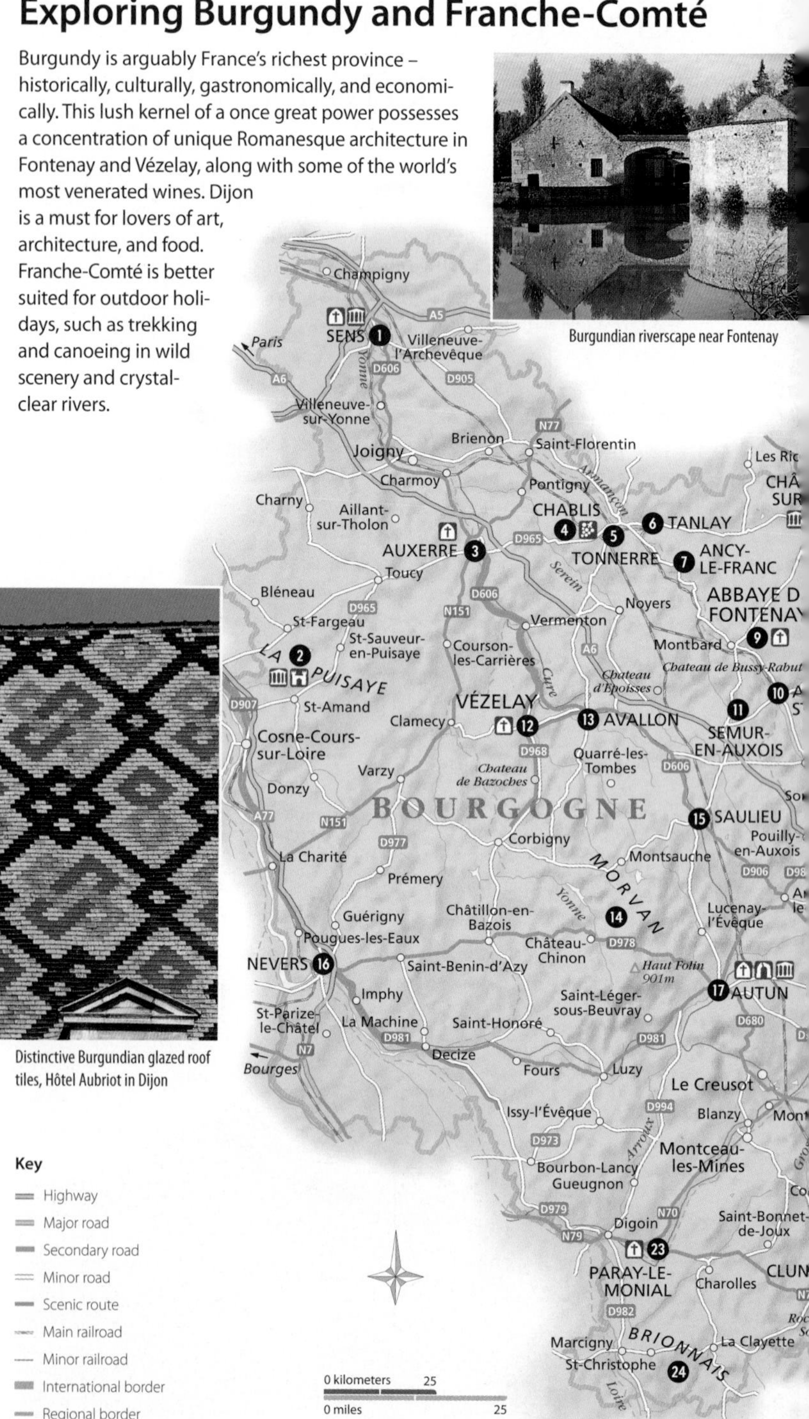

Burgundian riverscape near Fontenay

Distinctive Burgundian glazed roof tiles, Hôtel Aubriot in Dijon

Key

- Highway
- Major road
- Secondary road
- Minor road
- Scenic route
- Main railroad
- Minor railroad
- International border
- Regional border
- Summit

For additional map symbols *see back flap*

ights at a Glance

- Sens
- La Puisaye-Forterre
- Auxerre
- Chablis
- Tonnerre
- Château de Tanlay
- Château d'Ancy-le-Franc
- Châtillon-sur-Seine
- Abbaye de Fontenay
- Alise-Ste-Reine
- Semur-en-Auxois
- Vézelay
- Avallon
- Morvan
- Nevers
- Saulieu
- Autun
- Dijon
- 19 Côte d'Or
- 20 Beaune
- 21 Tournus
- 22 Cluny
- 23 Paray-le-Monial
- 24 Brionnais
- 25 Mâcon
- 26 Cascades du Hérisson
- 27 Arbois
- 28 Dole
- 29 Arc-et-Senans
- 30 Champlitte
- 31 Besançon
- 32 Ornans
- 33 Belfort
- 34 Ronchamp

Wine harvest in Nuits-St-Georges, Côte d'Or

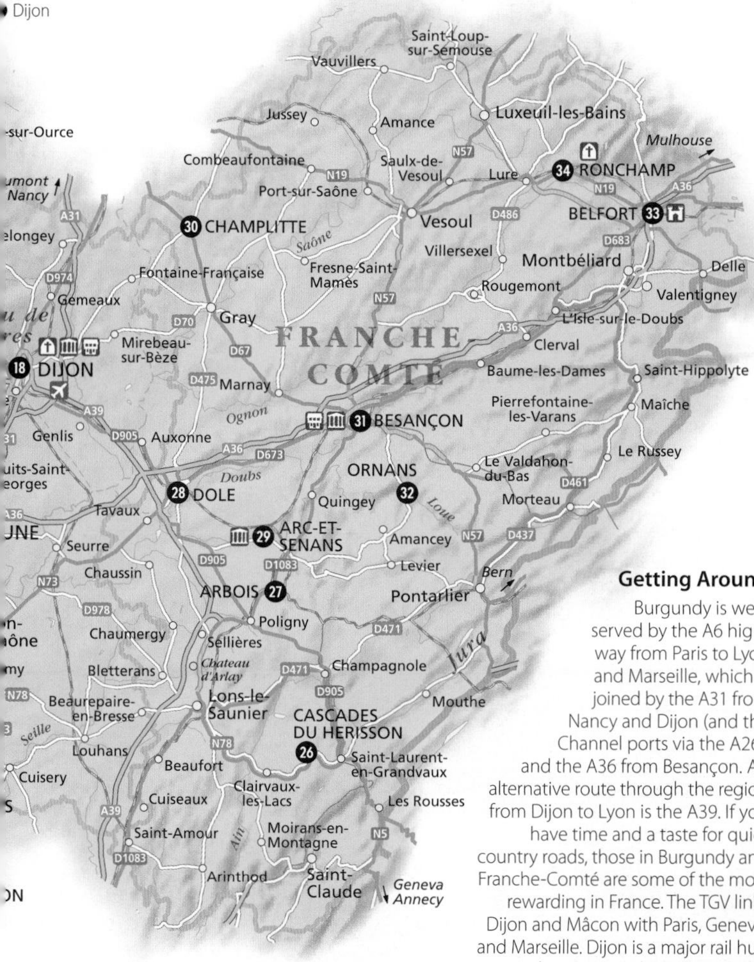

Getting Around

Burgundy is well-served by the A6 highway from Paris to Lyon and Marseille, which is joined by the A31 from Nancy and Dijon (and the Channel ports via the A26), and the A36 from Besançon. An alternative route through the region from Dijon to Lyon is the A39. If you have time and a taste for quiet country roads, those in Burgundy and Franche-Comté are some of the most rewarding in France. The TGV links Dijon and Mâcon with Paris, Geneva, and Marseille. Dijon is a major rail hub and connects other towns in the region; its domestic airport has regular flights to Toulouse and Bordeaux.

La Sainte Châsse, 11th-century reliquary in the Treasury in Sens

❶ Sens

Yonne. 30,000. pl Jean-Jaurès (03 86 65 19 49). Mon, Wed, Fri, Sat & Sun. **office-de-tourisme-sens.com**

The little town of Sens, at the confluence of the rivers Yonne and Vanne, was important before Caesar came to Gaul. It was the Senones whose attempt to sack the Roman Capitol in 390 BC was thwarted by a flock of geese.

The **Cathédrale St-Etienne** is Sens' outstanding glory. Begun before 1140 it is the oldest of the great Gothic cathedrals and its noble simplicity influenced many other churches. Louis IX *(see p55)* did the town the honor of getting married here in 1234.

The exquisite stained-glass windows from the 12th–16th centuries show biblical scenes, including the Tree of Jesse, and a tribute to Thomas Becket who was exiled here. His liturgical robes are in the Treasury (part of the **Musées de Sens**), which has one of the finest collections in France, including a beautiful Byzantine reliquary.

Les Musées de Sens
Pl de la Cathédrale. **Tel** 03 86 64 46 22. **Open** Jun–Sep: Wed–Mon; Oct–May: Wed, Sat, Sun (Mon, Thu, Fri pm only).

❷ La Puisaye-Forterre

Yonne, Nièvre. Auxerre, Clamecy, Bonny-sur-Loire, Cosne-Cours-sur-Loire. St-Fargeau, St-Sauveur-en-Puisaye. Charny (03 86 63 65 51).

The secret forest country of La Puisaye-Forterre was immortalized by Colette (1873–1954), who was born at **St-Sauveur** in "a house that smiled only on its garden side…." This 17th-century château now houses the **Musée Colette**.

The best way to explore the region is on foot or by bike around its watery woodlands, orchards, and meadows. Alternatively, take a ride on the *Transpoyaudin*, a 17 mile (27 km) train ride from St-Sauveur to Villiers St-Benoît.

A hands-on visit can be made to **Château de Guédelon**, a 25-year project begun in 1997 to recreate a medieval castle, using only original building methods and materials found locally. Nearby is the genuine 13th-century **Château de Ratilly**, with pottery, art exhibitions, concerts, and music workshops. More of this can be seen in **St-Amand**, the center of Puisaye stoneware production, much of which was traditionally fired in the 18th-century horizontal kiln at Moutiers. Both the pottery and local frescoes (see the churches at **Moutiers** and **La Ferté-Loupière**) made use of locally mined ocher, a major export in the 19th century. The pink brick **Château de St-Fargeau** housed the exiled Grande Mademoiselle *(p61)*.

Château de St-Fargeau in the Puisaye-Forterre region

Colette in the 1880s at St-Sauveur

Musée Colette
Château St-Sauveur-en-Puisaye. **Tel** 03 86 45 61 95. **Open** Apr–Oct: Wed–Mon.

❸ Auxerre

Yonne. 40,000. 1–2 quai la République (03 86 52 06 19). & Wed. **ot-auxerre.fr**

Beautifully sited overlooking the Yonne river, Auxerre justly prides itself on a fine collectio of churches along with a char ing pedestrianized main squa the place Charles-Surugue.

The Gothic **Cathédrale St-Etienne** took over three centuries to build and was completed in about 1560. It is famous for its intricate 13th-century stained glass. The choir with its slender columns and colonettes is the epitome of Gothic elegance, while the western portals are decorated with beautiful flamboyant sculpture which has been sadly mutilated by w and weather. The Romanesque crypt is adorned by unique 11th–13th-century frescoes, including one depicting Christ a white horse. The badly pillage treasury is less impressive, but still has an interesting collectio of illuminated manuscripts. St. Germanus, mentor of St. Patr nd bishop of Auxerre in the th century, was buried at the ›rmer abbey church of **t-Germain**. The abbey was ›unded by Queen Clothilde, ife of Clovis *(see pp52–3)*, the rst Christian king of France, nd is an important shrine. The rypt is partly Carolingian, with ombs and 11th–13th century escoes. The former abbey ouses the **Musée St-Germain** vith local Gallo-Roman finds.

Musée St-Germain
pl St-Germain. **Tel** 03 86 18 05 50. **pen** Wed–Sun. **Closed** May 1 & 8, ov 1 & 11, last week Dec.

ledieval fresco in Cathédrale St-Etienne t Auxerre

4 Chablis

'onne. 2,700. 1 rue du Maréchal de Lattre de Tassigny (03 86 2 80 80). Sun. **chablis.net**

'here can be no question that Chablis tastes best in Chablis. Although this is one of the most amous wine villages on earth, its narrow stone streets still have an air of sleepy prosperity. February processions in nearby Fyé, attended by the wine brotherhood of Piliers Chablisiens, honor St. Vincent, patron saint of winegrowers.

The intriguing spring of Fosse Dionne in Tonnerre

5 Tonnerre

Yonne. 6,200. pl Marguerite de Bourgogne (03 86 55 14 48). Sat & Wed. **tourisme-tonnerre.fr**

The mystical cloudy-green spring of **Fosse Dionne** is a good reason to visit the small town of Tonnerre. An astonishing volume of water bursts up from the ground into an 18th-century washing-place. Due to its depth and strong currents it has never been thoroughly explored and local legend has it that a serpent lives on undisturbed.

The **Hôtel-Dieu** is 150 years older than the Hôtel-Dieu in Beaune *(see pp350–51)*. It was founded by Margaret of Burgundy in 1293 to care for the poor. In the Revolution it lost its tiling but the barrel-vaulted oak ceiling survived.

Hôtel-Dieu & Musée
Rue du Prieuré. **Tel** 03 86 55 14 48. **Open** daily (Oct–Mar: closed Wed, Sun). **Closed** some public hols.

6 Château de Tanlay

Tanlay. **Tel** 03 86 75 70 61. **Open** Apr–early-Nov: Wed–Mon. oblig.

The moated Château de Tanlay is a beautiful example of French Renaissance, built in the mid-16th century. There is a *trompe l'oeil* in the Grande Galerie and, in the corner tower, an intriguing School of Fontainebleau painted ceiling. Its antique divinities represent famous Protestants and Catholics in the 16th century, such as Diane de Poitiers as Venus.

The Renaissance facade and *cour d'honneur* of Château de Tanlay

❾ Abbaye de Fontenay

The tranquil Abbey of Fontenay is the oldest surviving Cistercian foundation in France and offers a rare insight into the Cistercian way of life. It represents the spirit of the order in the sublime gravity of its Romanesque church and its plain but elegant chapterhouse, in early Gothic style. The abbey was founded in 1118 by St. Bernard. Situated deep in the forest, it offered the peace and seclusion the Cistercians sought. Supported by the local aristocracy, the abbey began to thrive and remained in use until the Revolution when it was sold and converted into a paper mill. In 1906 the abbey came under new ownership and was restored to its original appearance.

Dovecote
A magnificent circular dovecote, built in the 13th century, is situate next to the kennel where the precious hunting dogs of the dukes of Burgundy were guarded by servants.

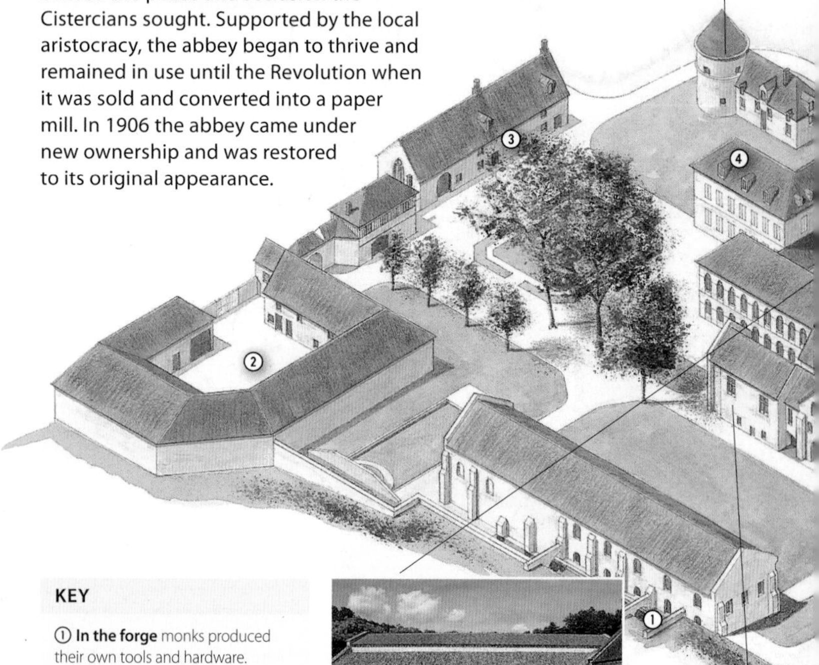

★ Cloisters
For a 12th-century monk a walk through the cloisters was an opportunity for meditation and provided shelter from the weather.

Fontenay "Prison"
It may be that this 15th-century building was actually used to lock up not local miscreants but important abbey archives, in order to protect them against damage by rats.

KEY

① **In the forge** monks produced their own tools and hardware.

② **The visitors' hostel** is where weary wanderers and pilgrims were offered board and lodging by the monks.

③ **The bakehouse** is no longer intact but the 13th-century oven and chimney have survived.

④ **The 17th-century** abbot's lodgings were built when the abbots were appointed by royal favor.

⑤ **Warming Room**

⑥ **The scriptorium** is where manuscripts were copied. The adjacent Warming Room was used to warm chilled hands.

⑦ **The herb garden** was skilfully cultivated by the monks in order to grow healing herbs for medicines and potions.

⑧ **Infirmary**

For hotels and restaurants in this region see pp554–71 and pp576–603

★ Abbey Church
Rich decoration has no place in this church from the 1140s. But the severe architectural forms, the warm color of the stone, and the diffused light convey a grandeur of their own.

VISITORS' CHECKLIST

Practical Information
Marmagne. **Tel** 03 80 92 15 00.
Open 10am–6pm daily (mid-Nov–mid-Apr: 10am–noon, 2–5pm).
abbayedefontenay.com

Transport
Montbard.

Dormitory
Monks slept in long rows on straw mattresses in this large, unheated room. The timberwork roof is from the late 15th century.

Chapterhouse
Once a day, monks and abbot assembled in this room to discuss matters concerning the community. It derives much of its charm from the elegant 12th-century piers and the rib-vaults.

St. Bernard and the Cistercians

In 1112 Bernard, a young Burgundian nobleman, joined the Cistercians. At the time the order was still obscure, founded 14 years earlier by a group of monks who wanted to turn their back on the elaborate lifestyle of Cluny *(see pp52–3)*, renounce the world, and espouse poverty and simplicity of life. During Bernard's lifetime the Cistercians became one of the largest and most famous orders of its time. Part of this success was clearly due to Bernard's powerful personality and his skills as a writer, theologian, and statesman. He reinforced the poverty rule, rejecting all forms of embellishment. In 1174, only 21 years after his death, he was canonized.

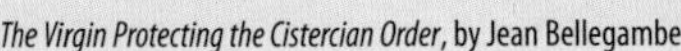

The Virgin Protecting the Cistercian Order, by Jean Bellegambe

❼ Château d'Ancy-le-Franc

Ancy-le-Franc. **Tel** 03 86 75 14 63. **Open** Apr–mid-Nov: Tue–Sun. oblig. **chateau-ancy.com**

The Renaissance facade of Château d'Ancy-le-Franc gives an austere impression. Its inner courtyard, however, has rich ornamentation. The château was built in the 1540s by the Italian Sebastiano Serlio, for the Duke of Clermont-Tonnerre. Most of the interior decorations were carried out by Primaticcio and other members of the Fontainebleau School *(see pp184–5)*. Diane de Poitiers, the duke's sister-in-law and mistress of Henry II, is portrayed in the *Chambre de Judith et Holophernes*.

The château holds monthly classical music concerts and cookery workshops.

The staid facade of Château d'Ancy-le-Franc

The vase of Vix in the Musée du Châtillonnais, Châtillon-sur-Seine

❽ Châtillon-sur-Seine

Côte d'Or. 5,837. rue du Bourg (03 80 91 13 19). Sat. **tourisme-chatillonnais.fr**

World War II left Châtillon a ruin, hence the town's largely modern aspect. But the past is still present in the **Musée du Pays du Châtillonnais**, where the Vix treasure is displayed. In 1953, the tomb of a Gaulish princess, from the 6th century BC, was discovered near Vix at Mont Lassois. The trove of jewelry and artifacts of Greek origin includes a stunning bronze vase, 66 in (164 cm) high and weighing 459 lb (208 kg). Also of interest is the Romanesque **Eglise St-Vorles** containing an *Entombment* with Christ and mourners splendidly sculpted (1527).

At the nearby source of the river Douix, which runs into the Seine, is a beautiful grotto.

Musée du Pays du Châtillonnais
Rue de la Libération. **Tel** 03 80 91 24 67. **Open** Jul–Aug: daily; Sep–Jun: Wed–Mon. **Closed** Jan 1, May 1, Dec 25. **musee-vix.fr**

❾ Abbaye de Fontenay

See pp336–7.

❿ Alise-Ste-Reine

Côte d'Or. 3,275. pl Bingerbrück, Venarey-Les Laumes 21150 (03 80 96 89 13). **alesia-tourisme.net**

Mont Auxois, above the village of Alise-Ste-Reine, was the site of Caesar's final victory over the heroic Gaulish chieftain Vercingétorix in 52 BC after a six-week siege *(see p50)*. The fi[rst] excavations here were undertaken in the mid-19th century, and they uncovered the vestig[es] of a thriving Gallo-Roman tow[n] with theater, forum, and well-laid-out street plan. The **Alésia MuséoParc** includes a historic discovery center with interacti[ve] media displays and lifesize reconstructions of siege engin[es].

Alise is dominated by Aimé Millet's gigantic moustachioe[d] statue of Vercingétorix, which was placed here in 1865 to commemorate the first excavations. Cynics feel that it bears a more than passing resemblance to Napoleon III, who sponsored the dig.

Alésia MuséoParc
Rue de l'Hôpital. **Tel** 03 80 96 96 23 **Open** Feb–Dec: daily. **alesia.com**

Environs

In the vicinity lies **Château de Bussy-Rabutin**. The spiteful 17th-century soldier and wit

Excavations at the Roman site near Alise-Ste-Reine

Roger de Bussy-Rabutin created its highly individualistic decor, while exiled from Louis XIV's court. One room is dedicated to portraits of his many mistresses, as well as a couple of imaginary ones.

Château de Bussy-Rabutin
Bussy-le-Grand. **Tel** 03 80 96 00 03. **Open** daily. **Closed** Jan 1, Nov 1 & 11, Dec 25.

11 Semur-en-Auxois

Côte d'Or. 5,000. 2 pl Gaveau (03 80 97 05 96). Sun.
tourisme-semur.fr

Approached from the west, Semur-en-Auxois comes as a surprise on an otherwise uneventful road. Its massive round bastions built in the 14th century (one of them with an unnerving gash in it) suddenly appear, towering over the Pont Joly and the peaceful river Armançon.

The **Eglise Notre-Dame** dates from the 13th and 14th centuries, and was modeled on the cathedral of Auxerre. The fragile high walls had to be restored in the 15th and 19th centuries. The church houses significant artworks, from the tympanum showing the legend of Doubting Thomas on the north doorway, to the 15th-century *Entombment* by Antoine le Moiturier. The stained glass presents the legend of Saint Barbara, and the work of different guilds such as butchers and drapers.

Environs

The village of Epoisses is the site of the moated **Château d'Epoisses**, its 11th–18th-century construction blending medieval towers with fine Renaissance details, and a huge 15th-century dovecote. Epoisses is also the home of one of Burgundy's most revered cheeses, to be sampled at the local café or *fromagerie*.

Stained-glass window in Eglise Notre-Dame at Semur-en-Auxois

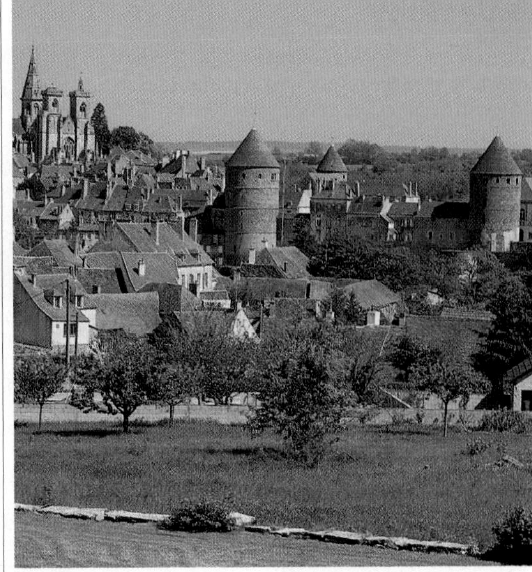

Semur-en-Auxois by the river Armançon

Château d'Epoisses
Epoisses. **Tel** 03 80 96 40 56. **Open** Jul–Aug: Wed–Mon (grounds: all year). ground floor only.

12 Vézelay

See pp340–41.

13 Avallon

Yonne. 9,000. 6 rue Bocquillot (03 86 34 14 19). Sat & Thu. **avallon-morvan.com**

A fine old fortified town, Avallon is situated on a granite spur between two ravines by the river Cousin.

Avallon suffered in the wars of Saracens, Normans, English, and French, which accounts for its defensive aspect. The town is quiet and rather beautiful, full of charming details. The main monument is the 12th-century Romanesque **Eglise St-Lazare**, with two carved doorways. The larger illustrates the signs of the zodiac, the labors of the month, and the horsemen of the Apocalypse. The nave is decorated with sophisticated acanthus capitals and polychrome statuary.

The **Musée de l'Avallonnais** features an intricate Venus mosaic from the 2nd century AD, and Georges Rouault's (1871–1958) series of Expressionist etchings, the *Miserere*.

Musée de l'Avallonnais
5 rue du College. **Tel** 03 86 34 03 19. **Open** Apr–Sep: Wed–Mon pms; Oct–Mar: Sat–Sun pms. **Closed** Dec.

Environs

To the southwest of Avallon is the 12th-century Château de Bazoches, given to Maréchal de Vauban by Louis XIV in 1675, and transformed by him into a military garrison.

Miserere by Georges Rouault in the Musée d'Avallonnais, Avallon

⓬ Vézelay

The golden glow of the Basilique Ste-Madeleine crowning Vézelay's hill is visible from afar. Tourists follow in the footsteps of medieval pilgrims, ascending the narrow street up to the former abbey church. In the 12th century, at the height of its glory, the abbey claimed to house relics of Mary Magdalene and was also an important meeting point for pilgrims en route to Santiago de Compostela in Spain *(see pp404–5)*. Today its attraction lies in the Romanesque church with its magnificent sculpture and Gothic choir.

View of Vézelay
The abbey dominates Vézelay's surroundings as it once dominated the religious and worldly affairs of the area.

Nave of Ste-Madeleine
The nave was rebuilt between 1120–35, using alternate dark and light stone in the transverse arches.

KEY

① **The narthex** used to be a gathering point for medieval processions

② **The facade** dates from 1150 and has a large 13th-century window. It was about to collapse when Viollet-le-Duc was commissioned to restore it according to old plans in 1840.

③ **Tour St-Michel** was built in 1150–1250. It derives its name from the statue of the archangel in the tower's southwest corner.

④ **Nave of Ste-Madeleine**

⑤ **Tour St-Antoine** was built at the same time as the choir, in the late 12th century. Its counterpart on the north side was never finished.

⑥ **The chapterhouse** and cloister are the only parts remaining from the 12th-century monastic buildings. Viollet-le-Duc rebuilt part of the cloister and restored the rib-vaulted chapterhouse, once a graceful background for the monks' daily assemblies.

★ Tympanum
This masterpiece of sculpture (1120–35) shows Christ on His throne, stretching out His hands from which rays of light descend on to the apostles.

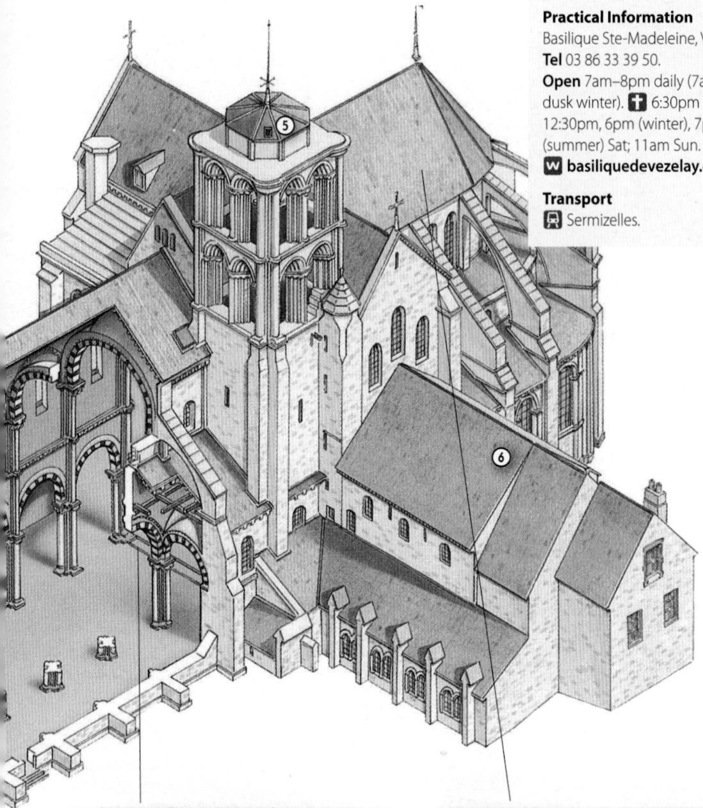

VISITORS' CHECKLIST

Practical Information
Basilique Ste-Madeleine, Vézelay.
Tel 03 86 33 39 50.
Open 7am–8pm daily (7am–dusk winter). 6:30pm Mon–Fri; 12:30pm, 6pm (winter), 7pm (summer) Sat; 11am Sun.
basiliquedevezelay.cef.fr

Transport
Sermizelles.

Crypt of Ste-Madeleine
The Romanesque crypt houses relics once thought to be Mary Magdalene's. The vault was rebuilt in 1165.

★ Capitals
The capitals in the nave and narthex are exquisitely carved, and give a vivid rendering of the stories of Classical antiquity and the Bible. The master who created them remains unknown.

Choir of Ste-Madeleine
The choir was rebuilt in the last quarter of the 12th century in the then modern Gothic style of the Ile de France.

Morvan, a region of rivers and forests, well-suited to fishing and other outdoor pursuits

⓮ Morvan

Yonne, Côte d'Or, Nièvre, Saône et Loire. Dijon. Autun, Mombard. Château-Chinon, Saulieu, Avallon. 6 bd République, Château-Chinon (03 86 85 06 58); Maison du Parc, St-Brisson (03 86 78 79 57). **tourisme.parcdumorvan.org**

Morvan is a Celtic word meaning Black Mountain, which is a good description of this area seen from afar. The immense, sparsely inhabited plateau of granite and woodland appears suddenly in the center of the rich Burgundy hills and farmland. Stretching roughly north to south, it gains altitude as it proceeds southwards, reaching a culminating point of 2,928 ft (901 m) at **Haut-Folin**.

The Morvan's two sources of natural wealth are abundant water and dense forests of oak, beech, and conifer. In the old days lumber used to be floated out of the area to Paris via a network of lakes and rivers. Today it travels by truck, and the Yonne, Cousin, and Cure rivers are instead used for recreation and the production of electricity.

The Morvan has always been a poor, remote area. Each of its largest towns, Château-Chinon in the center and Saulieu on the outskirts, has barely 3,000 inhabitants.

During World War II, the Morvan was a bastion of the French Resistance. Today a Regional Nature Park, its attraction is its wildness. Information on a wide variety of outdoor activities, including cycling, canoeing, skiing, and horse trekking, is available at the **Maison du Parc** at St-Brisson where there is also the very moving **Musée de la Resistance**. There are plenty of short walking trails, and two well-signed long-distance paths: the GR13 (Vézelay to Autun) and the Tour du Morvan par les Grands Lacs.

Musée de la Résistance
Maison du Parc, St-Brisson. **Tel** 03 86 78 72 99. **Open** Easter–mid-Nov: Wed–Mon (Jul & Aug: daily). **Closed** Sat am.

⓯ Saulieu

Côte d'Or. 3,000. 24 rue d'Argentine (03 80 64 00 21). Sat. **saulieu.fr**

On the edge of the Morvan, Saulieu has been a shrine of Burgundian cooking since the 17th century. The town was then a staging post on the Paris to Lyon coach road. Today the tradition is maintained by the **Côte d'Or** restaurant, established by the famous chef Bernard Loiseau. Yet there is more to Saulieu than *ris de veau de lait braisé* or *poularde truffée à la vapeur*. The Romanesque **Basilique St-Andoche**, built in the early 12th century, has decorated capitals with representations of the Flight into Egypt and a comical version of the story of Balaam and his donkey waylaid by the Angel.

⓰ Nevers

Nièvre. 41,000. Palais Ducal, rue Sabatier (03 86 68 46 00). Sat. **nevers-tourisme.com**

Like all Burgundian towns fronting the Loire, Nevers should be approached from the west side of the river for a full appreciation of its noble site. Though lacking historical importance, the town has much to show. Considered to be the earliest of the Loire châteaux, the **Palais Ducal** has a long Renaissance facade framed by polygonal towers and a broad esplanade. The Romanesque 11th-century **Eglise St-Etienne** has graceful monolithic columns and a wreath of radiating chapels.

In the crypt of the Gothic **Cathédrale St-Cyr** is a 16th-century sculpted *Entombment*, and the foundations of a 6th-century baptistry, discovered in 1944, after heavy bombing.

The contemporary stained-glass windows are also noteworthy. The overlordship of Nevers passed to the Gonzaga family in the 16th century. They brought with them an Italian school of artists skilled in faïence making and glassblowing.

Nevers faïence vase

For hotels and restaurants in this region see pp554–71 and pp576–603

'he industry has remained and ne modern pottery is still 'aditionally decorated in blue, vhite, yellow, and green, with its urious trademark, the little green rabesque knot, or *noeud vert*. 'he best place to view it is at the **Ausée Municipal** and the best lace to buy it is the 17th-century **aïencerie Montagnon**.

Musée Municipal 'rédéric Blandin
6 rue Saint-Geneste. **Tel** 03 86 68 44 0. **Open** Tue–Sun (Oct–Apr: Tue–Fri ms only; Sat–Sun all day).

nvirons
ust south of Nevers, the majes- c 19th-century **Pont du Guetin** arries the Loire Canal across ne Allier river. The church at **t-Parize-le-Châtel** has a jolly urgundian menagerie sculpted n the capitals of the crypt.

'he *Temptation of Eve* in Autun

7 Autun

aône-et-Loire. 18,000.
13 rue Général Demetz (03 85 86 0 38). Wed & Fri.
autun-tourisme.com

ugustodunum, the town of ugustus, was founded in the ate 1st century BC. It was a great center of learning, with a population four times what it is today. Its theater, built in the 1st century AD, could seat 20,000 people.

Today Autun is still a delight, deserving gastronomic as well as cultural investigation.

The magical **Cathédrale St-Lazare** was built in the 12th century. It is special because of its sculptures, most of them by the mysterious 12th-century artist Gislebertus. He sculpted both the capitals inside and the glorious Last Judgment tympanum over the main portal. This masterpiece, called a "Romanesque Cézanne" by André Malraux, escaped notice and was saved from destruction during the Revolution because it had been plastered over in the 18th century. Inside, some of the capitals can be seen close-up in a room in the tower. Look also for the sculpture of Pierre Jeannin and his wife. Jeannin was the president of the Dijon parliament who prevented the Massacre of St. Bartholomew *(see pp58–9)* spreading with the perceptive remark, "the commands of very angry monarchs should be obeyed very slowly."

The imposing Porte St-André in Autun, once part of the Roman wall

The brilliant collection of medieval art at the **Musée Rolin** includes the bas-relief *Temptation of Eve,* by Gislebertus. There is also the 15th-century painted stone Virgin of Autun, and the *Nativity of Cardinal Rolin* by the Master of Moulins, from about 1480.

The monumental **Porte St-André** and **Porte d'Arroux**, and the ruins of the **Théâtre Romain** and the **Temple de Janus**, are reminders of Autun's glorious Roman past.

Musée Rolin
3 rue des Bancs. **Tel** 03 85 52 09 76. **Open** Apr–Sep: Wed–Mon; Mar & Oct–mid-Dec: Wed–Sat, Sun am. **Closed** mid-Dec–Feb, public hols.

emains of the Roman theater at Autun, dating from the 1st century AD

⓲ Street by Street: Dijon

The center of Dijon is noted for its architectural splendor – a legacy from the dukes of Burgundy *(see p347)*. Wealthy parliament members also had elegant *hôtels particuliers* built in the 17th–18th centuries. The capital of Burgundy, Dijon today has a rich cultural life and a renowned university. The city's great art treasures are housed in the Palais des Ducs. Dijon is also famous for its mustard *(see p322)* and *pain d'épices* (gingerbread), a reminder of the town's position on the spice route. It became a major rail hub during the 19th century and now has a TGV link to Paris.

Hôtel de Vogüé
This elegant 17th-century mansion is decorated with Burgundian cabbages and fruit garlands by Hugues Sambin.

★ Notre-Dame
This magnificent 13th-century Gothic church has a facade with gargoyles, columns and the popular Jacquemart clock. The *chouette* (owl) is reputed to bring good luck when touched.

Musée des Beaux Arts
The collection of Flemish masters here includes this 14th-century triptych by Jacques de Baerze and Melchior Broederlam.

Place de la Libération was created by Mansart in the 17th century.

★ Palais des Ducs
The dukes of Burgundy held court here, but the building seen today was mainly built in the 17th century for the parliament. It now houses the Musée des Beaux Arts.

Rue Verrerie
This cobbled street in the old merchants' quarter is lined with medieval half-timbered houses. Some have fine wood-carvings, such as Nos. 8, 10 and 12.

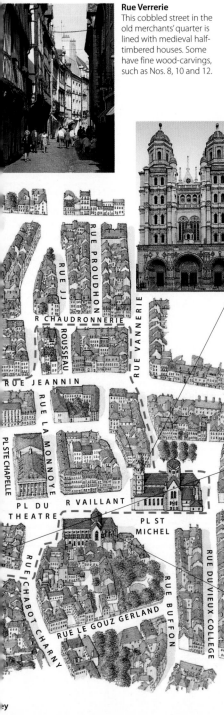

VISITORS' CHECKLIST

Practical Information
Côte d'Or. 155,000. 15 cour de la Gare & 11 rue des Forges (08 92 70 05 58). Tue, Fri, Sat. Florissimo (2014); Fêtes de la Vigne (2014); Festival International de Musique Mécanique (2015). Hôtel de Vogüé: inner courtyard open. Musée Magnin: (03 80 67 11 10). **Open** Tue–Sun. **Closed** Jan 1, Dec 25. **visitdijon.com**

Transport
3 miles (5 km) SSE Dijon. cour de la Gare.

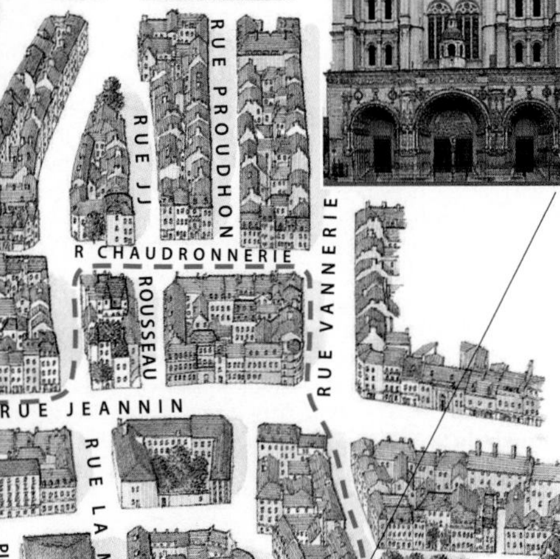

★ St-Michel
Begun in the 15th century and completed in the 17th century, St-Michel's facade combines Flamboyant Gothic with Renaissance details. On the richly carved porch, angels and biblical motifs mingle with mythological themes.

Musée Magnin
A collection of French and foreign 16th–19th-century paintings are displayed among period furniture in this 17th-century mansion.

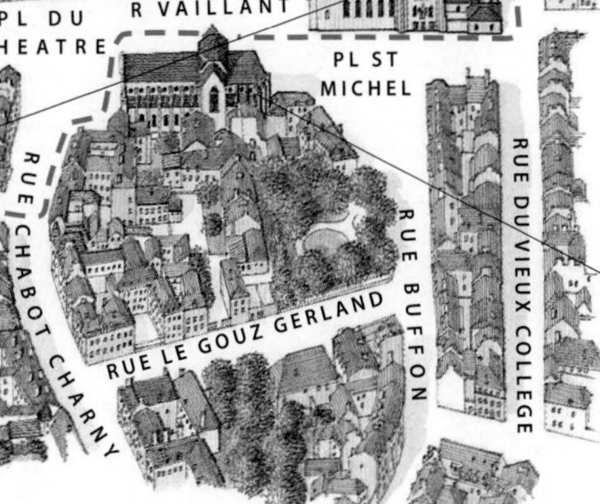

Eglise St-Etienne dates back to the 11th century but has been rebuilt many times. Its characteristic lantern was added in 1686.

0 meters 100
0 yards 100

Key

Suggested route

Well of Moses by Claus Sluter, in the Chartreuse de Champmol

Exploring Dijon

The center of Dijon is a warren of little streets that reward exploration. The rue des Forges, behind the Palais de Ducs, was the main street until the 18th century and is named after the jewelers and goldsmiths who had workshops there. Hôtel Chambellan at No. 34, is Flamboyant Gothic with a stone spiral staircase and wooden galleries. At No. 38 the Maison Maillard, built in 1560, has a stone facade decorated by Hugues Sambin.

Rue Chaudronnerie has a number of houses of note, especially the Maison des Cariatides at No. 28, with ten fine stone carved caryatids framing the windows. Place Darcy is lined with hotels and restaurants; the Jardin Darcy is delightful.

Musée des Beaux Arts

Palais des Etats de Bourgogne, Cour de Bar. **Tel** 03 80 74 52 70. **Open** Wed–Mon. **Closed** Jan 1, May 1 & 8, Jul 14, Nov 1 & 11, Dec 25. limited.

Dijon's prestigious art collection is housed in the former Palais des Ducs *(see p344)*. The Salle des Gardes on the first floor is dominated by the giant mausoleums of the dukes, with tombs sculpted by Claus Sluter (c.1345–1405). Other exhibits include two gilded Flemish retables and a portrait of Philip the Good by Rogier van der Weyden.

The art collection has Dutch and Flemish masters and sculpture by Sluter and Rude as well as Swiss and German primitives 16–18th-century French paintings and the Donation Granville of 19th- and 20th-century French art. Note the ducal kitchens with six fireplaces, and the Tour Philippe le Bon, 150 ft (46 m) tall with a fine view of Burgundian tiled roof tops. The museum is open during renovation, which is due to finish in 2015.

Cathédrale St-Bénigne

Pl Ste-Bénigne. **Tel** 03 80 30 39 33. **Open** daily. for crypt.

Little remains of the 11th-century Benedictine abbey first founded in honor of St. Bénigne. Beneath the church is a Romanesque crypt with a fine rotunda ringed by three circles of columns.

Musée Archéologique

5 rue du Docteur Maret. **Tel** 03 80 · 83 70. **Open** Wed–Sun (Oct–mid-M Wed–Mon). **Closed** most public h

The museum is housed in the c dormitory of the Benedictine abbey of St-Bénigne. The 11th-century chapterhouse, its stock columns supporting a barrel-vaulted roof, houses a fine colle tion of Gallo-Roman sculpture. The ground floor, with its lovely fan vaulting, houses the famou head of Christ by Claus Sluter, originally from the *Well of Mose*

Chartreuse de Champm

1 bd Chanoine Kir. **Open** daily by a (08 92 70 05 58).

This was originally the site of family necropolis built by Phi the Bold, destroyed during th Revolution. All that remains is chapel doorway and the famous *Well of Moses* by Clau Sluter. It is now in the ground of a psychiatric hospital east Dijon train station, not very e to find but definitely worth th effort. Despite its name, it is n a well, but a monument, its lower part probably originally surrounded by water. Sluter is renowned for his deeply cut carving and here his work, depicting six prophets, is exquisitely lifelike.

The tomb of Philip the Bold by Claus Sluter, now in the Salle des Gardes of the Musée des Beaux Arts

The Golden Age of Burgundy

While the French Capetian dynasty fought in the Hundred Years' War *(see pp56–7)*, the dukes of Burgundy built up one of the most powerful states in Europe, which included Flanders and parts of Holland. From the time of Philip the Bold (1342–1404), the ducal court became a cultural force, supporting many of Europe's finest artists, such as painters Rogier van der Weyden and the Van Eyck brothers, and sculptor Claus Sluter. The duchy's dominions were, however, broken up after the death of Duke Charles the Bold in 1477.

The tomb of Philip the Bold in Dijon was made by the Flemish sculptor Claus Sluter, who was among the most brilliant artists of the Burgundian golden age. The dramatic realism of the mourners is one of the most striking features of this spectacular tomb, begun while the duke was still alive.

Burgundy In 1477

Extent of the duchy at its peak

The Marriage of Philip the Good

Philip the Good, duke from 1419–67, married Isabella of Portugal in 1430. This 17th-century copy of a painting by Van Eyck shows the sumptuous wedding feast, when Philip also inaugurated the chivalric Order of the Golden Fleece.

The dukes surrounded themselves with luxury, including fine gold and silverware.

Isabella of Portugal

The Duchess of Bedford, Philip's sister

Greyhounds were popular hunting animals at the Burgundian court.

Philip the Good is dressed in white ceremonial finery.

Burgundian art, such as this Franco-Flemish Book of Hours, reflected the Flemish origins of many of the dukes' favorite artists.

Dijon's Palais des Ducs was rebuilt in 1450 by Philip the Good to reflect the glory of the Burgundian court, a center of art, chivalry, and glorious feasts. Empty after Charles the Bold's death, it was reconstructed in the 17th century.

Wine harvest in the vineyards of Nuits-St-Georges, part of the Côte d'Or district

⓳ Côte d'Or

Côte d'Or. ✈ Dijon. 🚆 🚌 Dijon, Nuits-St-Georges, Beaune, Santenay. ℹ Dijon (08 92 70 05 58). **w cotedor-tourisme.com**

In winemaking terms, the Côte d'Or includes the Côte de Beaune and the Côte de Nuits in a nearly unbroken line of vines from Dijon to Santenay. Squeezed in between the flat plain of the Saône to the southeast and a plateau of woodland to the northwest, this narrow escarpment is about 30 miles (50 km) long. The grapes of the great Burgundy vineyards grow in the golden reddish soil of the slope (hence the area's name).

The classification of the characteristics of the land is fabulously technical and elaborate, but for the layman a rough rule of thumb might be that 95 percent of the best vines are on the uphill side of the D974 thoroughfare *(see pp324–5)*. The names on the signposts haunt the dreams of wine lovers the world over: Gevrey-Chambertin, Vougeot, Chambolle-Musigny, Vosne-Romanée, Nuits-St-Georges, Aloxe-Corton, Meursault, and Chassagne Montrachet.

Narrow street in Beaune's historic centre

Typical grape basket in the Musée du Vin de Bourgogne at Beaune

⓴ Beaune

Côte d'Or. 👥 23,000. 🚆 🚌 ℹ 6 bd Perpeuil (03 80 26 21 30). 🛒 Sat, Wed. 🎭 Baroque Music (Jul). **w ot-beaune.fr**

The old center of Beaune, snug within its ramparts and encircling boulevards, is easy to explore on foot. Its indisputable treasure is the **Hôtel-Dieu** *(see pp350–51)*. The Hôtel des Ducs de Bourgogne, built in the 14th–16th centuries, houses the **Musée du Vin de Bourgogne**. The building, with its flamboyant facade, is as interesting as its display of traditional winemaking equipment.

Farther to the north lies the **Collégiale Notre-Dame**, begun in the early 12th century. Inside this mainly Romanesque church hang five very fine 15th-century woollen and silk tapestries. With hints of early Renaissance style, they delicately illustrate the life of the Virgin Mary in 19 scenes.

Musée du Vin de Bourgogne
Rue d'Enfer. **Tel** 03 80 22 08 19.
Open May–Sep: daily; Oct–Apr: Wed–Mon. **Closed** Jan 1, Dec 25.

㉑ Tournus

Saône-et-Loire. 👥 6,500. 🚆 🚌 ℹ pl de l'Abbaye (03 85 27 00 20). 🛒 Sat. **w tournugeois.fr**

The Abbaye de St-Philibert is one of Burgundy's oldest and greatest Romanesque buildinc It was founded by a group of monks from Noirmoutier who had been driven from their island by invading Normans in the 9th century, who brought with them relics of their patror saint, Philibert (still in the choi Rebuilt in the 10th–12th centu ries, the well-fortified abbey church is made from lovely pa

Dovecote in Cormatin château gardens, Mâconnais

Nave of St-Philibert in Tournus

pink stone, with black and white vaulting inside.

The 17th-century Hôtel-Dieu has its original rooms intact with the furniture, equipment, and pharmacy on display. It also houses the **Musée Greuze** dedicated to Tournus' most famous son, the artist Jean-Baptiste Greuze (1725–1805).

Environs
Southwest of Tournus lies the Mâconnais landscape of hills, vineyards, orchards, red-tiled farmhouses, and Romanesque churches. **Brancion** is a pretty hill village, **Chapaize** has an 11th-century church and there is a sumptuous Renaissance château at **Cormatin**. The village of **Taizé** is the center of a world-famous ecumenical community. To the north, **Chalon-sur-Saône** features the Musée Niepce, dedicated to the inventor of photography.

㉒ Cluny

Saône-et-Loire. 4,800. 6 rue Mercière (03 85 59 05 34). Sat. **cluny-tourisme.com**

The little town of Cluny is overshadowed by the ruins of its great abbey. The **Ancienne Abbaye de Cluny** was once the most powerful monastic foundation in Europe *(see pp48–9)*. The abbey was founded by William the Pious, Duke of Aquitaine in 910. Within 200 years, Cluny had become the head of a major reforming order with monasteries all over Europe. Its abbots were considered as powerful as monarchs or popes, and four of them are venerated as saints. By the 14th century, however, the system was in decline. The abbey was closed in 1790 and the church was later dismantled.

The guided tour presents the abbey remains, notably the Clocher de l'Eau Bénite (Holy Water Belltower); the remains of figured capitals, displayed in the 13th-century flour store; and the **Musée d'Art**, housed in the former abbot's palace. In the town, don't miss the 12th-century **Eglise St-Marcel**.

Southwest of the town, the chapel in **Berzé-la-Ville** is decorated with superb 12th-century frescoes, similar to those once seen at Cluny.

Ancienne Abbaye de Cluny
Tel 03 85 59 15 93. **Open** daily. **Closed** Jan 1, Dec 25.

Musée d'Art
Palais Jean de Bourbon. **Tel** 03 85 59 15 93. **Open** daily. **Closed** Jan 1, May 1, Nov 1 & 11, Dec 25.

㉓ Paray-le-Monial

Saône-et-Loire. 10,000. 25 av Jean-Paul II (03 85 81 10 92). Fri. **paraylemonial.fr**

Dedicated to the cult of the Sacred Heart of Jesus, the **Basilique du Sacré-Coeur** has made Paray-le-Monial one of the most important sites of pilgrimage in modern France. Marguerite-Marie Alacoque, who was born here in 1647, had rather gory visions from which the cult later developed, sweeping across France in the 19th century. The church is a small version of the now lost abbey church of Cluny, with particularly harmonious and pure Romanesque architecture.

A visit to the **Musée de Paul Charnoz** provides an insight into industrial artistic tile production in the 19th and 20th centuries.

Situated on place Guignaud is the ornate **Maison Jayet**, dating from the 16th century, which houses the town hall.

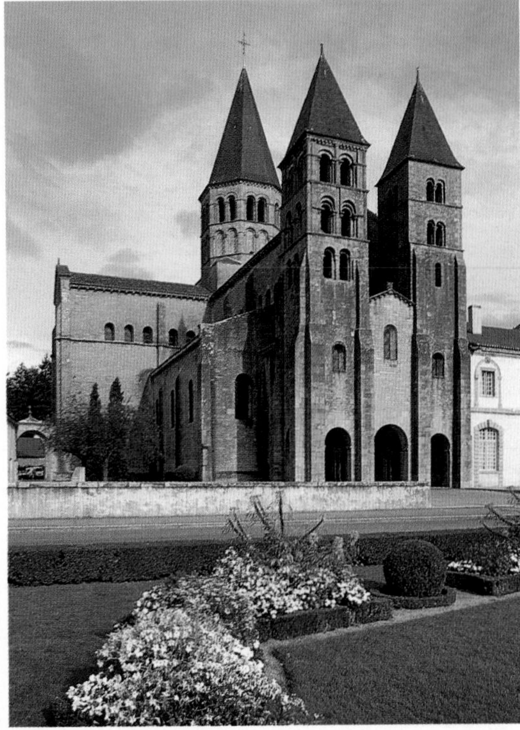
Basilique du Sacré-Coeur at Paray-le-Monial

Hôtel-Dieu

After the Hundred Years' War, many of Beaune's inhabitants suffered the effects of poverty and famine. To remedy this, the chancellor, Nicolas Rolin, and his wife founded a hospice here in 1443, which was inspired by the architecture of Northern French hospitals. The Rolins provided an annual grant and salt-works for income. Today the hospice is considered a medieval jewel, with its superb geometric, multicolored Burgundian roof tiles. It houses two religious masterpieces: the *Christ-de-Pitié* statue, carved from oak, and Rogier van der Weyden's *Last Judgment* polyptych.

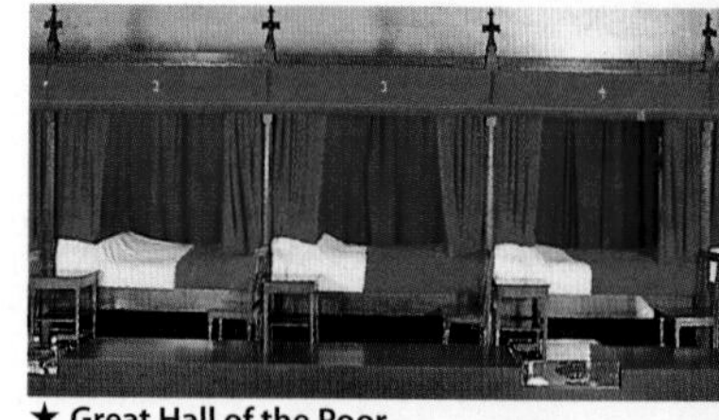

★ Great Hall of the Poor
The hall, with its carved, painted roof, has 28 four-poster beds, each often used by two patients at a time. Meals were served at central tables.

Tribute to Rolin's Wife
A recurring motif features the entwined letters N and G, birds and stars, and the word *"Seulle"* referring to Rolin's wife Guigone, his "one and only."

KEY

① **Saint Anne's Room** has a tableau of nuns working in what was once the linen room, and a colorful feast-day tapestry.

② **Saint Hugues' Room** contains a painting of the saint curing two children. Frescoes by Isaac Moillon show the miracles of Christ.

③ **Glazed roof tiles**, in a colorful geometric pattern, are the most dramatic feature of the Hôtel-Dieu.

④ **St Louis' Room**

Annual Charity Wine Auction

On the third Sunday in November, an annual charity auction in Beaune is the centerpiece of three days of festivities known as *Les Trois Glorieuses*. Saturday sees the banquet of the Confrérie des Chevaliers du Tastevin at the Château Clos de Vougeot. On Sunday the auction of wine from the 151 acres (61 ha) of vineyards, owned by nearby hospitals, takes place. Its prices are the benchmark for the entire vintage. On Monday at La Paulée de Meursault there is a party where growers bring along bottles of their best vintages to enjoy.

Wine sold at the famous auction

Kitchen
The centerpiece of the kitchen is a Gothic fireplace with a dual hearth and a mechanical spit, made in 1698, which is turned by a wooden "robot."

VISITORS' CHECKLIST

Practical Information
Rue de L'Hôtel-Dieu, Beaune.
Tel 03 80 24 45 00. **Open** Apr–mid Nov: 9–6:30pm daily; mid-Nov– Mar: 9–11:30am, 2–5:30pm daily. Wine Auction: 3rd Sun Nov: Les Halles de Beaune (03 80 24 45 00).
hospices-de-beaune.com

Cour d'Honneur
The buildings of Hôtel-Dieu are arranged around a splendid central courtyard. This is flanked by a wooden gallery, above which rise high dormer windows topped by weather vanes. The courtyard well is a fine example of Gothic wrought-iron work.

3

4

Pharmacy
Such unusual potions as woodlouse powder, shrimps' eyes, and vomit nut powder are stored in these earthenware pots. Nearby is a bronze mortar used to prepare the remedies.

★ Last Judgment Polyptych
The naked figures shown in Rogier van der Weyden's 15th-century polyptych were briefly given clothing in the 19th century. At the same time, the altarpiece was cut in half so that the outer and inner panels could be seen together.

Château de Pierreclos in the Mâconnais region

㉔ Brionnais

Saône-et-Loire. Mâcon. Paray-le-Monial, Roanne. Paray-le-Monial. Marcigny (03 85 25 39 06).

The Brionnais is a small and peaceful rural district, squeezed between the river Loire and the Beaujolais foot-hills in the far south of Burgundy.

Its agricultural staple is the white Charolais cow, which can be seen grazing everywhere. For a closer look at this regional symbol, visit the lively cattle-market in **St-Christophe** on Wednesdays.

The area has an abundance of Romanesque churches, most of which are built of the local ocher-colored stone. The 11th-century church of **Anzy-le-Duc** has a majestic three-tiered polygonal tower and exquisitely carved capitals. **Semur-en-Brionnais** was the birthplace of Cluny's famous abbot St. Hugues. Its church is inspired by his great monastery. The church at **St-Julien-de-Jonzy** has a very finely carved tympanum.

Capital in St- Julien-de-Jonzy

A small town by the river Genette, **La Clayette** is graced by a château set in a lake. It is not open to the public, but the gardens can be visited every Tuesday in July and August via the local tourist office.

Southeast of La Clayette the lonely **Montagne de Dun** rises just over 2,300 ft (700 m) and offers a panorama over the gentle, green Brionnais hills. This is some of the best picnic country in Burgundy, full of sleepy corners and quiet byways.

㉕ Mâcon

Saône-et-Loire. 36,000. 1 pl Saint Pierre (03 85 21 07 07). Sat. **macon-tourism.com**

At the frontier between Burgundy and the south, Mâcon is an industrial town and wine center on the Saône.

The lack of churches is due to fervent anticlericalism during the Revolution, when 14 were destroyed. A 17th-century convent has been turned into the **Musée des Ursulines**. Its collections include French and Flemish painting and an exhibition on the prehistoric site of Solutré. On the charming place aux Herbes, where the market is held, the **Maison de Bois** is a 15th-century wooden house covered with bizarre carvings.

Musée des Ursulines
Allée de Matisco. **Tel** 03 85 39 90 38. **Open** Tue–Sat & Sun pm. **Closed** Jan 1, May 1, Jul 14, Nov 1, Dec 25.

Environs

The great **Roche de Solutré** rises dramatically above the Pouilly-Fuissé vineyards in the Mâconnais district *(see p349)*. Below the rock, finds from the Stone Ages have established it as a major archeological site.

Mâconnais is also the land of the Romantic poet Lamartine (1790–1869). Born in Mâcon, he spent his childhood at Milly Lamartine and later lived at Château de St-Point. **Château de Pierreclos** is associated with his epic poem *Jocelyn*.

Charolais cattle grazing on the gentle hills of the Brionnais

ranche-Comté

region of woods and water, e Franche-Comté offers ceptional natural beauty mbined with opportunities canoeing, trekking, and iing. Apart from towns well orth visiting, this is a region explore in the wild. Glorious enery with grottoes and scading waterfalls can be und all along the Vallée du oubs. Farther south are e spectacular sources of e rivers Lison and Loue. The culées is an area of extraor-nary formations of ridges d waterfalls such as Baume-s-Messieurs. In Région des cs, the silent, peaceful lakes e surrounded by mountain aks and virgin forests.

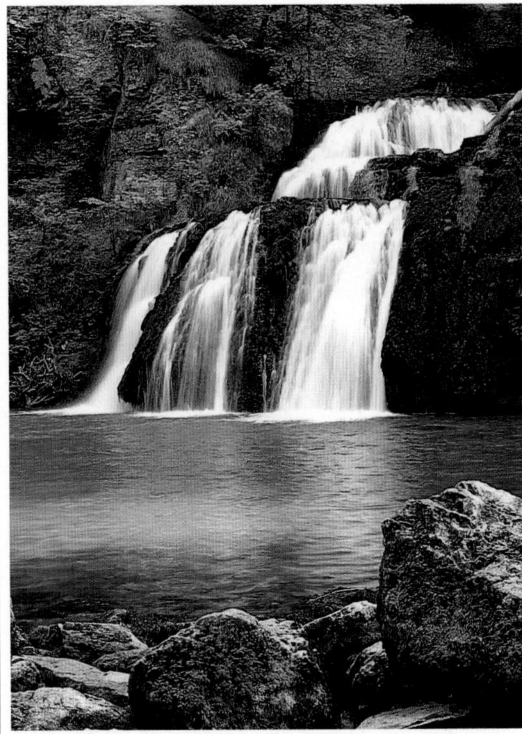

Nature at its purest at Source du Lison in the Franche-Comté

Cascades du érisson

ys-des-Lacs. Clairvaux-les-Lacs 3 84 25 27 47). Wed.

ne village of Doucier, at the ot of the Pic de l'Aigle, is the arting point for the valley of e river Hérisson, one of the nest natural settings in the Jura. ave the car at the park by the oulin Jacquand and walk up e trail through the woods to a ectacular waterfall, the 213-ft 5-m) Cascade de L'Eventail, and eyond to the equally impressive ascade du Grand Saut. The walk, hich takes about two hours ere and back, is steep at times d can be slippery, so proper oes are essential.

Arbois

ra. 3,600. 17 rue de ôtel de Ville (03 84 66 55 50). Fri.
arbois.com

ne jolly wine town of Arbois es on the vine-covered banks the river Cuisance. It is mous for the sherrylike *vin une* (yellow wine) of the strict. On the north side of the wn is **Maison de Pasteur**, the preserved house and laboratory of the great scientist Louis Pasteur (1822–95), the first to test vaccines on humans.

Environs
Southeast of Dole is the 18th-century **Château d'Arlay**, with immaculately kept gardens.

28 Dole

Jura. 28,000. 6 pl Grévy (03 84 72 11 22). Tue & Fri.
tourisme-paysdedole.fr

The busy town of Dole lies where the Doubs meets the Rhine-Rhône canal. The former capital of the Comté was always a symbol of the region's resistance to the French. The region had become used to relative independence, first under the Counts of Burgundy and then as part of the Holy Roman Empire. Though always French-speaking, its people did not appreciate the idea of the French absolute monarchy and in 1636 endured a very long siege. The town finally submitted to Louis XIV, first in 1668, and again in 1674.

There is a charming historic quarter in the center of town, full of winding alleys, houses dating back to the 15th century, and quiet inner courtyards. Place aux Fleurs offers an excellent view of this part of town and the mossy-roofed, 16th-century **Eglise Notre-Dame**.

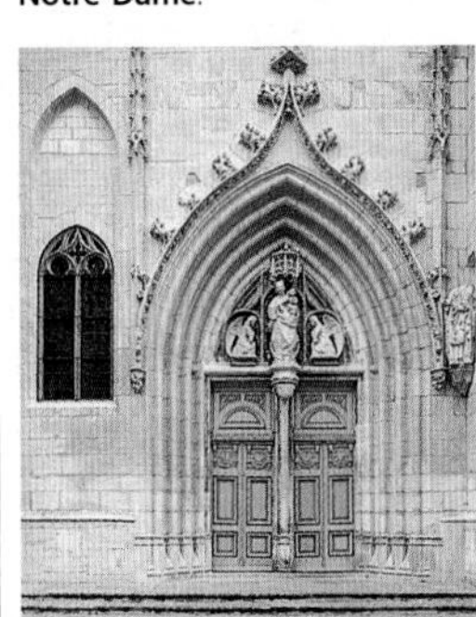

Virgin and Child on the north portal of Eglise Notre-Dame, Dole

The Saline Royale at Arc-et-Senans

29 Arc-et-Senans

Doubs. 1,400. Ancienne Saline Royale (03 81 57 43 21). **ot-arcetsenans.fr**

Designated a World Heritage Site since 1982, the Saline Royale (royal salt works) at Arc-et-Senans were designed by the great French architect Claude-Nicolas Ledoux (1736–1806). He envisaged a development built in concentric circles around the main buildings. However, the only ones to be completed (in 1775) were the buildings used for salt production. Nevertheless, these show the staggering scale of Ledoux's idea: salt water was to be piped from Salins-les-Bains nearby, and fuel to reduce it was to come from the Chaux forest. The enterprise, which was never a success, was closed down in 1895, but the buildings remain.

The **Musée Ledoux Lieu du Sel** displays intriguing models of the grand projects imagined by the visionary architect.

Musée Ledoux Lieu du Sel
Saline Royale. **Tel** 03 81 54 45 45. **Open** daily. **Closed** Jan 1, Dec 25. gr. floor.

30 Champlitte

Haute Saône. 1,900. 2 allée du Sainfoin (03 84 67 67 19).

In the small town of Champlitte, the **Musée des Arts et Traditions Populaires** was created by a local shepherd who collected artifacts connected with disappearing local customs. One of the poignant displays housed in this Renaissance château recalls the emigration of 400 citizens to Mexico in the mid-19th century.

Musée des Arts et Traditions Populaires
Pl de l'Eglise. **Tel** 03 84 67 82 00. **Open** Apr–Jun & Sep: Wed–Fri (Sat–Sun pms only); Jul–Aug: Mon–Fri (Sat–Sun pms only); Oct–Mar: Wed–Mon pm. **Closed** Jan 1, Nov 1, Dec 25.

31 Besançon

Doubs. 120,000. 2 pl de la Première Armée Française (03 81 80 92 55). Tue–Sat & Sun am. **besancon-tourisme.com**

Besançon supplanted Dole as the capital of the Franche-Comté in the 17th century. It began as an ecclesiastical center and is now an industrial one, specializing in precision engineering. The stately architecture of the old town, with its elegant wrought-iron work, is a 17th-century legacy.

Behind the fine Renaissance facade of the Palais Granvelle, in the grande rue, is the **Musée du Temps**, a fine collection of "time-pieces" of all ages – a timely tribute to Besançon's renown as a clock and watch-making center. An interactive exhibition on the third floor invites reflection on the relativity of the notion of time.

Further along the same street are the birthplaces of novelist Victor Hugo (1802–85) at No. 140 and the Lumière brothers *(see p63)* at place Victor Hugo. Behind **Porte Noire**, a Roman arch, is the 12th-century Cathédrale St-Jean. In its bell tower is the **Horloge Astronomique** with its automatons that pop out on the hour.

The stunning **Musée des Beaux Arts et d'Archéologie** occupies the old corn market. Its collection includes works by Bellini, Cranach, Rubens, Fragonard, Boucher, Ingres, Goya, Matisse, and Picasso.

Vauban's citadel overlooking the river Doubs has magnificent views, and the **Musée Comtois** with a collection of local artifacts, an insectarium, and an aquarium.

Musée du Temps
Palais Granvelle, 96 grande rue. **Tel** 03 81 87 81 50. **Open** Tue–Sun. **Closed** Jan 1, May 1, Nov 1, Dec 25.

Horloge Astronomique
Rue de la Convention. **Tel** 03 81 81 12 76. **Open** Apr–Sep: Wed–Mon; (Thu–Mon winter). **Closed** Jan, May 1, Nov 1 & 11, Dec 25.

Musée des Beaux Arts et d'Archéologie
1 pl de la Révolution. **Tel** 03 81 87 80 67. **Closed** for renovation until 201 free Sunday

Musée Comtois
La Citadelle, rue des Fusillés de la Résistance. **Tel** 03 81 87 83 33. **Open** Apr–Oct: daily; Nov–Mar: Wed–Mon. **Closed** Jan 1, Dec 25.

The fantastic astronomical clock in Besançon, made in 1857–60

32 Ornans

Doubs. 4,300. 7 rue Pierre Vernier (03 81 62 21 50). 3rd Tue month. **valleedelaloue.com**

The great Realist painter Gustave Courbet was born at Ornans in 1819. He painted the town in every possible light. His *Enterrement à Ornans* proved to be one of the most influential

striking Chapelle Notre-Dame-du-Haut by Le Corbusier at Ronchamp

intings of the 19th century. urbet's work is displayed in ree historic buildings, including s childhood home, which ake up the **Musée Courbet.**

Musée Courbet

Robert Fernier. **Tel** 03 81 86 22 88. **en** Wed–Mon. **Closed** Jan 1, May 1, v 1, Dec 25.
musee-courbet.fr

virons

canoeist's paradise, the **Vallée la Loue** is the loveliest in the ra. The D67 follows the river om Ornans eastwards to uhans, from where it is only a -minute walk to its magnificent urce. Various belvederes offer lendid views over the area.

Southwest of Ornans, the ectacular **Source du Lison** *ee p353)* is a 20-minute walk om Nans-sous-Ste-Anne.

Belfort

rritoire de Belfort. 52,000. 2 bis rue Clemenceau (03 84 55 90). Wed–Sun. **belfort-urisme.com**

ne symbol of Belfort is an normous pink sandstone lion. It as built (rather than carved) by édéric Bartholdi (1834–1904), whose other major undertaking was the Statue of Liberty.

Belfort's immensely strong **citadel**, designed by Vauban under Louis XIV, withstood three sieges, in 1814, 1815 and 1870. Today this remarkable array of fortifications provides an interesting walk and extensive views of the surroundings. The **Musée d'Histoire** is housed in the citadel and displays models of the original fortifications as well as regional art and artifacts (closed Tue Sep–Jun; open daily Jul–Aug).

34 Ronchamp

Haute Saône. 3,000. 25 rue Le Corbusier (03 84 63 50 82). Sat.
ot-ronchamp.fr

Le Corbusier's **Chapelle Notre-Dame-du-Haut** dominates this former miners' town. A sculpture rather than a building, its swelling concrete form was finalized in 1955. Inside, light, shape, and space form a unity.

There is also a **Musée de la Mine** evoking the industry and the life of local miners.

Le Miroir d'Ornans in the Musée Courbet, Ornans

THE MASSIF CENTRAL

lier · Aveyron · Cantal · Corrèze · Creuse · Haute-Loire
iute-Vienne · Lozère · Puy de Dôme

e Massif Central is a region of strange, wild beauty – one France's best-kept secrets. It is surprisingly little known yond its sprinkling of spas and the major cities of ermont-Ferrand, Vichy, and Limoges. However, the new ghways through the heart of its uplands have started to open this previously remote region.

e huge central plateau of ancient anite and crystalline rock that makes the Massif Central embraces the amatic landscapes of the Auvergne, nousin, Aveyron, and Lozère. Once a sting crossroads for pilgrims, and strung th giant volcanos, it is a region of unsuscted richness, from the ectacular town of Le Puy-en-Velay, the unique treasures at Conques.

With its crater lakes and hot springs, e Auvergne is the Massif Central's lush lcanic core, an outdoor paradise fering activities from hiking in summer to iing in winter. It also has some of France's ost beautiful Romanesque churches, edieval castles, and Renaissance palaces. the east are the mountain ranges of Forez, Livardois, and Velay; to the west are the giant chains of extinct volcanos, the Monts Dômes, Monts Dore and the Monts du Cantal. The Limousin, on the northwestern edge of the Massif Central, is gentler country with green pastures and blissfully empty roads.

The Aveyron spreads into the southwest from the Aubrac mountains, carrying with it the rivers Lot, Aveyron, and Tarn through gorges and valleys with their cliff-hanging villages. To the east in the Lozère are the Grands Causses, the vast, isolated uplands of the Cévennes. These barren plateaus give farmers a poor living, but have been a favorite route with adventurous travelers across the centuries.

ourboule, a spa town in the Monts Dore

A bend in the river in the spectacular Gorges du Tarn

Exploring the Massif Central

Nature is at its most magnificent in the volcanic mountain ranges and wild river gorges of the Massif Central. This is a vast and unspoiled territory which offers spectacular sightseeing and every imaginable outdoor activity, with rafting, paragliding, canoeing, and hiking among the many choices. There are hundreds of churches, châteaux, and museums to nourish lovers of history, architecture, and art; and good, hearty regional cooking and interesting local wines for lovers of good living.

0 kilometers 25

0 miles 25

Key

- Highway
- Major road
- Secondary road
- Minor road
- Scenic route
- Main railroad
- Minor railroad
- Regional border
- △ Summit

Limestone cliffs of the Gorges du Tarn

Getting Around

There are good air and rail services connecting Paris with the major towns of Limoges, Clermont-Ferrand, and Vichy. Many of the most interesting towns and sights are easily accessible only by car, and AutoTrain from Paris to Brive is an effortless way of getting to the region with a car. Most minor roads are well kept, but slow going in the mountains. A few roads are vertiginous, especially the road to the summit of Puy Mary, which is utterly breathtaking. The A71/A75 (toll-free) through the Auvergne is a magnificent road.

For additional map symbols *see back flap*

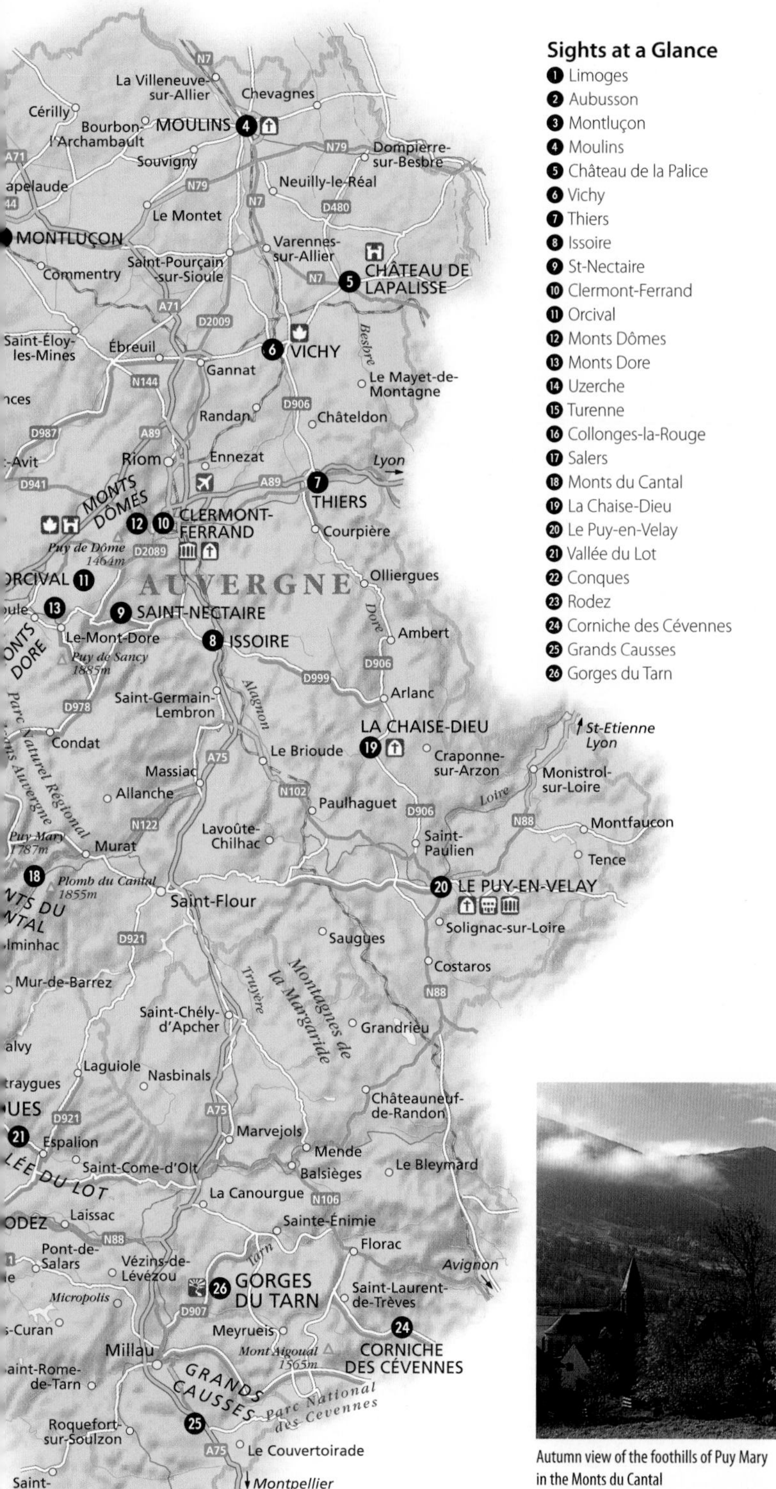

Sights at a Glance

1. Limoges
2. Aubusson
3. Montluçon
4. Moulins
5. Château de la Palice
6. Vichy
7. Thiers
8. Issoire
9. St-Nectaire
10. Clermont-Ferrand
11. Orcival
12. Monts Dômes
13. Monts Dore
14. Uzerche
15. Turenne
16. Collonges-la-Rouge
17. Salers
18. Monts du Cantal
19. La Chaise-Dieu
20. Le Puy-en-Velay
21. Vallée du Lot
22. Conques
23. Rodez
24. Corniche des Cévennes
25. Grands Causses
26. Gorges du Tarn

Autumn view of the foothills of Puy Mary in the Monts du Cantal

IE NY SCAY GVEL REMEDDE METT
RE AVX OVELLES PVSSAYGE
COVRIR TOVES NE LES PVIS SE
COVRIS MIEVX MEVLT VALVT
DEVX ME DEMETRE

A Limoges enamel plaque, *The Bad Shepherd*

❶ Limoges

Haute-Vienne. 200,000. 12 bd de Fleurus (05 55 34 46 87). daily. **limoges-tourisme.com**

The capital of the Limousin has two hearts: the old Cité and the rival château, now the commercial center of the modern city. The Cité was ravaged by the Black Prince during the Hundred Years'War and today it is a quiet place of half-timbered houses and narrow streets.

It was not until the 1770s that Limoges became synonymous with porcelain. The legendary local ware is on display at the superb **Musée National Adrien-Dubouché**. More than 10,000 exhibits trace the history of ceramics. The **Musée des Beaux Arts de Limoges** houses an Egyptian collection, archeological artifacts tracing the history of Limoges, over 600 Limousin enamels, and Impressionist paintings. This area was a center of Resistance operations in World War II; the **Musée de la Résistance et de la Déportation** has a collection of exhibits relating to Resistance acitivities.

Musée National Adrien-Dubouché
Pl Winston Churchill. **Tel** 05 55 33 08 50. **Open** Wed–Mon. **Closed** Jan 1, May 1, Dec 25. **musee-adriendebouche.fr**

Musée des Beaux Arts de Limoges
1 pl de l'Evêché. **Tel** 05 55 45 98 10. **Open** Wed–Mon (Oct–Mar: closed Tue & Sun am). **Closed** Jan 1, May 1, Nov 1 & 11, Dec 25. **museebal.fr**

Musée de la Résistance et de la Déportation
Rue Neuve Saint-Etienne. **Tel** 05 55 45 84 44. **Open** Wed–Mon.

Environs
Resistance activity in the Limousin led to severe reprisals. On June 10, 1944, at the village of **Oradour-sur-Glane**, 16 miles (25 km) north-west of Limoges, SS troops burned alive the entire population. The ruins of the village have been kept as a shrine, and a new village built nearby.

St-Junien close by has been a glove-making town since the Middle Ages, and it still supplies today's designers with luxury leather items.

❷ Aubusson

Creuse. 5,000. rue Vieille (05 55 66 32 12). Sat. **tourisme-aubusson.com**

Aubusson owes its renown to the exceptionally pure waters of the Creuse, perfect for making the delicately colored dyes used for tapestries and rugs. Tapestry production was at its zenith in the 16th and 17th centuries, but by the end of the 18th century the Revolution and patterned wallpaper had swept away the clientele.

In the 1940s, Aubusson was revived, largely due to the artist Jean Lurçat, who persuaded other modern artists to design for tapestry. The **Musée Départemental de la Tapisserie** displays a permanent collection of these modern works. All 30 workshops welcome visitors – at the **Manufacture St-Jean** you can watch tapestries and custom-made carpets being made by hand and restored.

Musée Départemental de la Tapisserie
Av des Lissiers. **Tel** 05 55 83 08 30. **Open** Wed–Mon (Jul–Aug: Tue pm). **Closed** 1 week Apr, 1 week Nov.

Manufacture St-Jean
3 rue St Jean. **Tel** 05 55 66 10 08. **Open** Mon–Fri.

Environs
A single street of 15th-century houses and a Roman bridge comprise **Moûtier-d'Ahun,** tucked into the lush Creuse

Tapestry restoration at the Manufacture St-Jean in Aubusson

For hotels and restaurants in this region see pp554–71 and pp576–603

manesque church at Moûtier-d'Ahun near Aubusson

ılley. Vestiges of a Benedictine ɔbey can still be detected the half-Romanesque, alf-Gothic church with s elaborate stone portal. ɪe choir has wooden stalls, for hich it is worth paying a visit) the church. They are master- ieces of late 17th-century arving with fantastical and ıtricately worked motifs of ɔra and fauna representing ɪe many different facets of ood and Evil in figurative ɔrm. Today there is a garden here the nave once was.

Montluçon

llier. 45,000. 67 ter bd e Courtais (04 70 05 11 44). Tue, Thu–Sun. **montlucontourisme.com**

ıontluçon is the economic enter of the region, a small ɔwn with a medieval core. t its heart there is a Bourbon hâteau, which now houses emporary exhibitions. **ardin Wilson**, a pleasant *ırdin à la française* in the ıedieval quarter, sits on the riginal ramparts of the town. ıostly destroyed in the 8th century, little remains of he ramparts now. The restored ɔse garden and spectacular ower beds are worth a visit. he 12th-century **Eglise de t-Pierre** is a surprise, with ıiant stone columns and a uge barrel-vaulted ceiling.

❹ Moulins

Allier. 23,000. rue François Péron (04 70 44 14 14). Fri, Sun. **moulins-tourisme.com**

Capital of the Bourbonnais and seat of the Bourbon Dukes since the 10th century, Moulins flourished during the early Renaissance. Moulins' most celebrated sight is the Flamboyant Gothic **Cathédrale Notre-Dame**, where members of the Bourbon court appear amid the saints in the 15th- and 16th-century stained-glass windows. The treasury contains a luminous 15th-century Virgin and Child triptych by the "Master of Moulins." Benefactors Pierre II, Duke of Bourbon, and his wife Anne de Beaujeu, bedecked in embroidery and jewels, are shown being introduced to a less richly dressed Madonna.

The tower keep and the single remaining wing of the Bourbon **Vieux Château** house a superb collection of sculpture, painting, and decorative art from the 12th to the 16th centuries. Housed in the former cavalry barracks is a magnificent collection of 10,000 theatrical costumes.

Cathédrale Notre-Dame
Pl des Vosges. **Tel** 04 70 20 89 65.
Treasury: **Open** Tue–Sat & Sun pm.
Closed Dec 25.

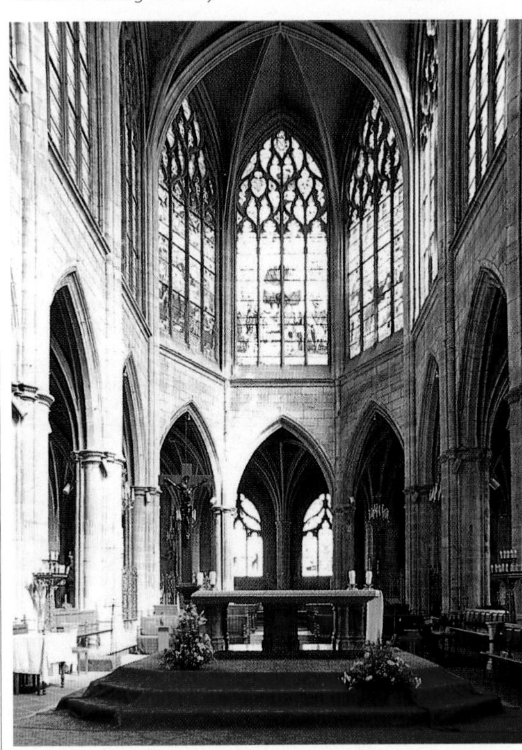
Stained-glass windows at the Cathédrale Notre-Dame in Moulins

❺ Château de la Palice

Allier. **Tel** 04 70 99 37 58. **Open** Easter–Oct: daily.

In the early 16th century, the Marshal of France, Jacques II de Chabannes, hired Florentine architects to reconstruct the feudal château-fort at Lapalisse, creating a refined Renaissance castle, which has been inhabited ever since by his descendants. The *salon doré* (gilded room) has a beamed ceiling paneled in gold, and two huge 15th-century Flemish tapestries showing the Crusader Knight Godefroy de Bouillon and Greek hero Hector, two of the nine classic braves of chivalric legend.

Environs
From Lapalisse, the D480 leads up through the beautiful Besbre valley past a handful of other small, well-preserved châteaus, including **Château de Thoury**.

Château de Thoury
Dompierre. **Tel** 04 70 42 00 41. Courtyard and exterior: **Open** Apr–Nov: daily.

Gilded ceiling, Château de la Palice

❻ Vichy

Allier. 27,000. 19 rue du Parc (04 70 98 71 94). Wed.
vichy-tourisme.com

This small city on the river Allier has long been known for its hot and cold springs, and reputed cures for rheumatism, arthritis, and digestive complaints. The letter-writer Madame de Sévigné and the daughters of Louis XV visited in the late 17th and 18th centuries – the former compared the showers to "a rehearsal for Purgatory." The visits of Napoleon III in the

Interior of the original Thermal Establishment building in Vichy

1860s put Vichy on the map and made taking the waters fashionable. The small town was spruced up and became a favorite among the French nobility and the world's wealthy middle classes. These days, the grand old Thermal Establishment, built in 1900, has been turned into shopping galleries. The modern baths are state-of-the-art and

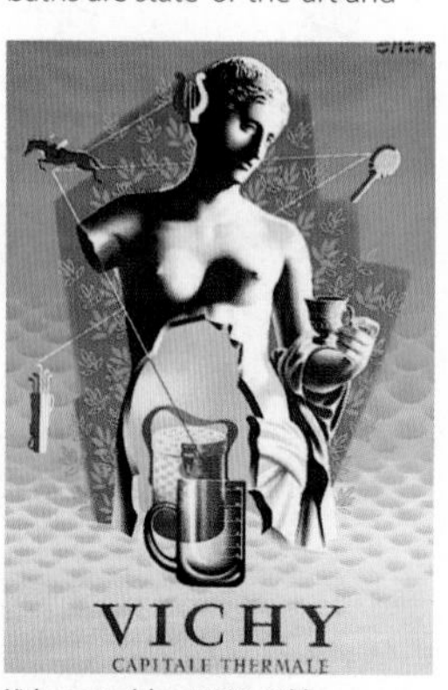

Vichy poster (about 1930–50) by Badia-Vilato

strictly for medical purposes. A doctor's prescription and a reservation 30 days in advance are required for all treatments.

Vichy's fortunes changed for the better once again in the 1960s with the damming of the Allier, creating a huge lake in the middle of town, which rapidly became a thriving centre for watersports and international events. For a small fee, you can have a taste of sports from aikido to waterskiing or learn canoeing on the 2-mile (3-km) long artificial river.

The focal point of life in Vichy is the **Parc des Sources** in the center of town, with its turn-of-the-century bandstand (afternoon concerts in season), Belle Epoque glass-roofed shopping galleries, and the Grand Casino and Opera House. Here there is gambling every afternoon and musical performances in the evenings, and an atmosphere of gaiety pervades. Also open to the public are the beautiful bronze taps of the **Source Célestin**, in verside park containing estiges of a convent bearing ne same name. Only by naking an effort to imagine ne city in grainy black-and-hite newsreel style is there ne slightest reminder of the artime Vichy government hich was based in the town om 1940–44 *(see p69)*.

Source Célestin
d du Président Kennedy. **Open** daily. **losed** Dec–Jan.

Thiers

uy de Dôme. 13,500.
pl de Pirou (04 73 80 65 65).
Thu & Sat. **thiers-tourisme.fr**

According to the writer La ruyère, Thiers "seems painted on the slope of the hill," nanging dramatically as it does n a ravine over a sharp bend n the river Durolle. The city has been renowned for cutlery ince the Middle Ages, when egend has it that Crusaders rought back techniques of netalwork from the Middle ast. With grindstones powered y dozens of waterfalls on the pposite bank of the river, hiers produced everything rom table knives to guillotine lades, and cutlery remains ts major industry today, nuch of it on display in the Cutlery Museum, the **Musée de la Coutellerie**.

The Old Town is filled with nysterious quarters like "the Corner of Chance" and "Hell's Hollow," honeycombed with ortuous streets and well-restored 14th–17th-century nouses. Many have elaborately carved wooden facades, like the Maison du Pirou in place Pirou. The view to the west from the rampart terrace, towards Monts Dômes and Monts Dore, is particularly splendid at sunset.

Musée de la Coutellerie
58 rue de la Coutellerie. **Tel** 04 73 80 58 86. **Open** Jun–Sep: daily; Oct–May: Tue–Sun. **Closed** Jan 1, May 1, Dec 25.

Pilgrimages and Ostensions

Parishes in the Auvergne and the Limousin are renowned for honoring their saints in outdoor processions. Ascension Day sees the Virgin of Orcival carried above the village by night, accompanied by gypsies and their children for baptism. Every seven years a score of villages in the Limousin hold *Ostensions*, when the saints' relics are paraded through the streets into the surrounding woods. The *Ostension* season begins the Sunday after Easter and runs until June. The next event in the seven-year cycle will be held in 2016.

The Virgin of Orcival, carried in procession above the village (1903)

8 Issoire

Puy de Dôme. 15,000.
9 pl St-Paul (04 73 89 15 90).
Sat. **sejours-issoire.com**

Most of old Issoire was destroyed in the 16th-century Wars of Religion. The present-day town has been an important industrial center since the end of World War II. Not only does Issoire have a thriving aeronautical tradition, it is also a mecca for glider pilots who come from miles around to take advantage of the strong local air currents.

Issoire's colorful 12th-century abbey church of **St-Austremoine** is one of the great Romanesque churches of the region. The capitals depict scenes from the *Life of Christ* (one of the Apostles at the Last Supper has fallen asleep at table), and imaginary demons and beasts. The 15th-century fresco of the *Last Judgment* shows Bosch-like figures of sinners being cast into the mouth of a dragon or carted off to hell. The nearby Tour de l'Horloge has scenes of Renaissance history.

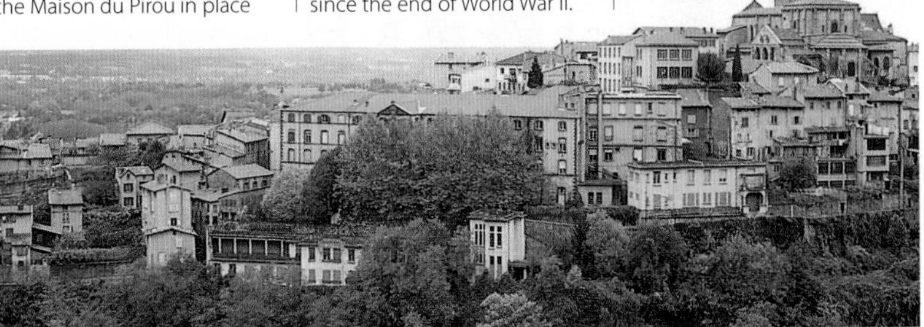

Thiers from the south, spreading over the slopes above the river Durolle

9 St-Nectaire

Puy de Dôme. 750. Les Grands Thermes (04 73 88 50 86). Jul–Aug: Sun am. **sancy.com**

The Auvergne is noted for Romanesque churches. The **Eglise St-Nectaire** in the upper village of St-Nectaire-le Haut, with its soaring, elegant proportions, is one of the most beautiful. The 103 stone capitals, 22 of them polychrome, are vividly carved, and the treasury includes a gold bust of St Baudime and a wooden Notre-Dame-du-Mont-Cornadore, both marvels of 12th-century workmanship. The lower village, St-Nectaire-le-Bas, has more than 40 hot and cold springs.

Environs

The 12th-century citadel of **Château de Murol**, partially in ruins, offers costumed guides demonstrating medieval life and knightly pursuits. It is wonderful for children.

Château de Murol

Murol. **Tel** 04 73 26 02 00. **Open** Apr–Sep: daily; Oct–Mar: Sat & Sun. **chateaudemurol.fr**

Fontaine d'Amboise (1515) in Clermont-Ferrand

10 Clermont-Ferrand

Puy de Dôme. 141,000. pl de la Victoire (04 73 98 65 00). Mon–Sat. **clermont-fd.com**

Clermont-Ferrand began as two distinct cities, united only in 1630. Clermont is a lively commercial centre and student town, with thriving cafés and restaurants. It was a Celtic settlement before the Roman era, had a cathedral as early as the 5th century, and by 1095 was significant enough for the pope to announce the First Crusade there. The Counts of Auvergne, challenging the episcopal power of Clermont, made their base in what is now old Montferrand, a short drive from Clermont city center. Built on a bastide pattern, it is a time warp of quiet streets and Renaissance houses.

Clermont's more ancient origins are well illustrated at the **Musée Bargoin** with its remarkable collections of locally found Roman domestic artifacts (closed Mondays and Sunday mornings).

Place St-Pierre is Clermont's principal marketplace, with a daily food market – especially good on Saturdays. Nearby, the pedestrianized rue du Port leads steeply downhill from the **Fontaine d'Amboise** (1515) to the **Basilique Notre-Dame-du-Port**. This is one of the most important Romanesque churches in the region and has benefited from extensive renovations. The stone interior is beautifully proportioned, with a magnificent raised choir and vivid carved capitals – Charity battles Avarice, in the form of two knights.

The contrast with the black lava **Cathédrale Notre-Dame-de-l'Assomption** is startling, from austere 12th-century

Raised choir in the Basilique Notre-Dame-du-Port

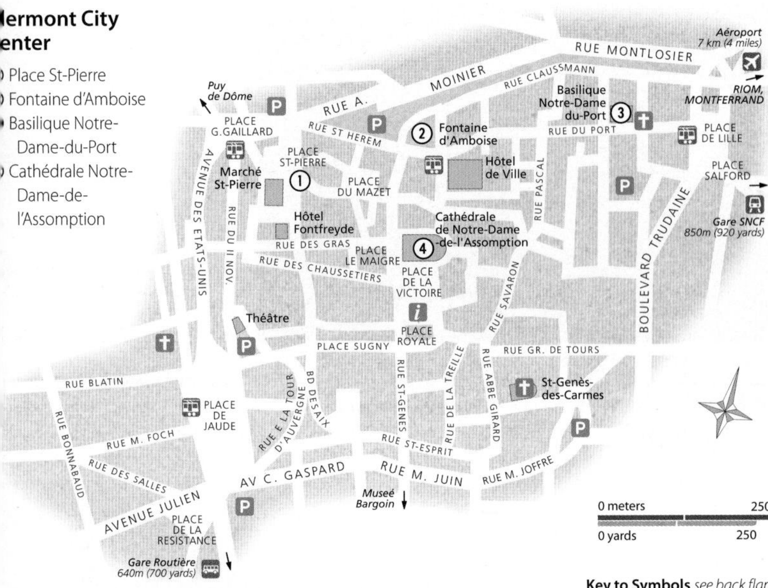

Key to Symbols *see back flap*

omanesque to high-ving 13th-century othic. The graceful nes of the interior e due to the strong cal stone used for onstruction, allow-g pillars to be inner and the hole structure ghter. The dark olcanic rock provides foil for the jewel-like 2th–15th-century ained-glass windows, hich are believed to e from the same workshop as ainte-Chapelle's in Paris *(see p88)*.

The old section of Montferrand rived from the 13th to the 17th enturies, and many fine houses – nown as *hôtels particuliers* – built y prosperous merchants have urvived. Some of the best of

Michelin man, c.1910

these, with Italianate loggias, mullioned windows, and intriguing courtyards, line ancient **rue Kléber**. Between Clermont and old Montferrand lies a third mini-city, the headquarters and factories of the Michelin rubber-and-tire company, founded here in 1830, which dominates the town.

oir inside the Cathédrale Notre-Dame--l'Assomption

Environs

Once the rival of Clermont-Ferrand for supremacy in Auvergne, **Riom** is a somber provincial town of black stone houses and lava fountains. The 14th-century château of Duke Jean de Berry was razed in the 19th century to build the Palais de Justice; all that remains is the delicate Sainte-Chapelle with its lovely 15th-century stained-glass windows.

Riom's greatest treasure is a graceful Madonna holding an infant with a small bird in his hand. The statue is housed in the Eglise de Notre-Dame-du-Marthuret, originally built in the 14th century, but much rearranged since then.

⓫ Orcival

Puy de Dôme. 300. Le Bourg (04 73 65 89 77).
terresdomes-sancy.com

Crowded in summer, Orcival is nevertheless well worth visiting for its Romanesque church, the **Basilique d'Orcival**, which many would say is the best in the region. Completed at the beginning of the 12th century, and typically Auvergne Romanesque in style, the apse is multi-tiered, and the side walls are supported by powerful buttresses and strong arches. Inside, the ornate silver and vermilion *Virgin and Child* (in the forward-facing position known as "in majesty") is enigmatic in its rigid, square chair.

With an interior lit by 14 windows and a spacious crypt, the proportions of the building itself are the most graceful aspect.

Virgin and Child in the Basilique d'Orcival

Aerial view of Puy de Dôme in the Monts Dômes range

⓬ Monts Dômes

Puy de Dôme. Clermont-Ferrand. Montlosier (04 73 65 64 00). parcdesvolcans.fr

The youngest range of the Auvergne volcanos at 4,000 years old, the Monts Dômes, or Chaîne des Puys, encompasses 112 extinct volcanos aligned over a 19-mile (30-km) stretch just west of Clermont-Ferrand. At the center, the **Puy de Dôme** towers above a high plateau. A mountain railroad spirals up the peak at a steady 12 percent gradient, taking 15 minutes to reach the top, while the steeper Roman path is still used by hikers. (No cars or buses ascend the Puy de Dôme; phone 08 26 39 96 15 for train information).

At the summit are the vestiges of the Roman temple of Mercury and a meteorological/telecommunications tower. On a rare clear day, the view across the volcano will take away whatever breath you have left.

The volcanic Roche Tuilière below Col de Guéry in the Monts Dore

The controversial **Parc Européen du Volcanisme, Vulcania**, uses the latest technology to simulate volcanic activity in its 5 acre (2 ha) underground circuit.

In the southwest corner of the Monts Dômes region is the **Château de Cordès**, a small, privately owned 15th-century manor house with formal gardens designed by Le Nôtre *(see p183)*.

Vulcania
D941B, Saint-Ours-les-Roches. **Tel** 04 73 19 70 00. **Open** mid-Mar–Aug: daily; Sep–mid-Nov: Wed–Sun. Documentation center. **vulcania.com**

Château de Cordès
Orcival. **Tel** 04 73 65 81 34. **Open** gardens only (phone 04 73 21 15 89 for times).

⓭ Monts Dore

Puy de Dôme. Clermont-Ferrand. Le Mont-Dore. Montlosier, Aydat (04 73 65 64 00).

Three giant volcanos – the Puy de Sancy, the Banne d'Ordanche, and the Puy de l'Aiguiller – and their secondary cones make up the Monts Dore: dark green, heavily wooded mountains laced with rivers and lakes, and dotted with summer and winter resorts for skiing, hiking, paragliding, canoeing, and sailing.

The 6,185-ft (1,886-m) **Puy de Sancy** is the highest point in Central France. It can be reached by taking a shuttle from the town of Le Mont-Dore to the cable car which goes up to the peak, followed by a long hike across open terrain. From Le Mont-Dore, there is a scenic drive on the D36 which leads to the **Couze-Chambon valley**, a beautiful stretch of high moorland threaded with waterfalls.

The area has two popular spa towns, **La Bourboule**, for children's ailments, with its casino, and Le Mont-Dore, with its grandiose turn-of-the-century **Etablissement Thermal**.

Below the Col de Guéry on the D983, the eroded volcanic **Roche Sanadoire** and **Roche Tuilière** stand up like two gigantic gateposts. From their peaks are far-reaching views over the wooded Cirque de Chausse and beyond.

Church at La Bourboule in the Monts Dore

⓮ Uzerche

Corrèze. 3,000. pl de la Libération (05 55 73 15 71). Sat. **pays-uzerche.fr**

Uzerche is an impressive sight: gray slate roofs, turrets, and belltowers rising from a hill above the Vézère river. This prosperous town never capitulated during the conflicts of the Middle Ages, and earlier withstood a seven-year siege by Moorish forces in 732: the townspeople sent a feast out to their enemy – in fact, the last of their supplies. The Moors, thinking such lavish offerings meant the city had stores to spare, gave up.

The Romanesque **Église St-Pierre** crests the hill above the town. Beyond Uzerche, the Vézère cuts through the green gorges of the Saillant.

Cantal Cheese

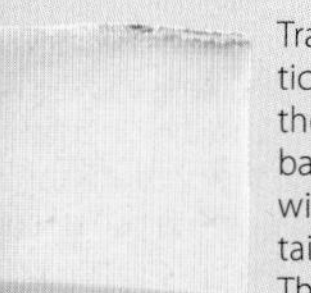

Transhumance is still practiced in the Auvergne, with the local Salers cattle kept in barns in the valleys during winter and led up to mountain pastures for the summer. The robust grasses and flowers – gentian, myrtle, anemone – on which the cows graze produce a flavorsome milk that is the basis for the region's great cheese, Cantal. Curds were once turned and pressed through cheesecloth by hand, but now modern methods prevail. Cantal is the key ingredient in *aligot* – the potato-and-cheese purée flavored with garlic that is one of the region's most famous dishes.

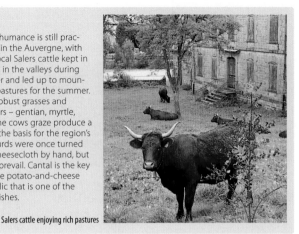

Salers cattle enjoying rich pastures

⓯ Turenne

orrèze. 750. Brive la aillarde (05 55 21 08 80).

urenne is one of the most opealing medieval towns in ne Corrèze. Crescent-shaped nd clustered on the cliffside, ne town was the last indepen-ent feudal fiefdom in France, nder the absolute rule of ne La Tour d'Auvergne family ntil 1738. Henri de la Tour 'Auvergne, their most ustrious member, was a narshal of France under Louis IV, and one of the greatest oldiers of modern times.

Now the sole remains of the **hâteau de Turenne** are the 3th-century Clock Tower and 1th-century Tower of Caesar, om which there is a quite tunning 360-degree view of ne Cantal mountains across to ne Dordogne valley. Not far away is the 16th-century collegiate church and the **Chapelle des Capucins** dating from the 18th century.

Château de Turenne
Tel 05 55 85 90 66. **Open** Apr–Oct: daily; Nov–Mar: Sun pm.
chateau-turenne.com

⓰ Collonges-la-Rouge

Corrèze. 400. Brive, then bus to Collonges. av de l'Auvitrie (05 55 25 47 57). **ot-collonges.fr**

There's something a little unsettling about Collonges' unique carmine sandstone architecture, quite beautiful in individual houses, though the overall effect is both austere and fairytale-like.

Founded in the 8th century, Collonges came under the rule of Turenne, whose burghers built the sturdy turreted houses in the surrounding vineyards. Look out for the communal bread oven in the marketplace, and the 11th-century church, later fortified with a tower keep. The church's unusual carved white limestone tympanum shows a man driving a bear, and other lively figures.

⓱ Salers

Cantal. 400. summer only. pl Tyssandier d'Escous (04 71 40 58 08). Wed. **salers-tourisme.fr**

A handsome town of gray lava houses and 15th-century ramparts, Salers sits atop a steep escarpment at the edge of the Cantal mountains. It is one of few virtually intact Renaissance villages in the region. The church has an admirable polychrome *mise au tombeau* (entombment), dated 1495, and five 17th-century Aubusson tapestries.

From the fountain, streets lead up to the cliff edge, and allow views of the surrounding valleys, with the ever-present sound of cowbells in the distance. The town is very crowded in summer, but it makes a good starting point for excursions to the Puy Mary *(see p368)*, the huge barrage at Bort-les-Orgues, the nearby Château de Val, and the Cère valley to the south.

edieval Château de Val at Bort-les-Orgues near Salers

Puy Mary peak in the volcanic Monts du Cantal

⓲ Monts du Cantal

Cantal. Aurillac. Lioran. Aurillac (04 71 48 46 58). **iaurillac.com**

The Cantal mountains were originally one enormous volcano – the oldest and the largest in Europe, dating from the Tertiary period. The highest peaks, the **Plomb du Cantal** at 6,086 ft (1,855 m) and the **Puy Mary** at 5,863 ft (1,787 m), are surrounded by crests and deep river valleys. Driving the narrow roads is a thrill, compounded by the views at every hairpin turn. Between peaks and gorges, rich mountain pastures provide summer grazing for red-gold Salers cows *(see p367)*. From the **Pas de Peyrol**, the highest road pass in the country at 5,191 ft (1,589 m), it's about a 25-minute journey on foot to the summit of the Puy Mary.

Environs
One of the finest of the Auvergne châteaus, Château d'Anjony was built by Louis II d'Anjony, a supporter of Joan of Arc *(see pp304–5)*. Highlights are the 16th-century frescoes: in the chapel, scenes from the Life and Passion of Christ, and upstairs in the *Salle des Preux* (Knights' Room), a dazzling series of the nine heroes of chivalry. To the south lies the small town of **Aurillac**, a good base for exploring the Cantal region.

Château d'Anjony
Tournemire. **Tel** 04 71 47 61 67.
Open mid-Feb–mid-Nov: daily pms.
obligatory.

⓳ La Chaise-Dieu

Haute-Loire. 700. pl de la Mairie (04 71 00 01 16). Thu.
la-chaise-dieu.info

Somber and massive, midway between Romanesque and Gothic, the 14th-century abbey church of St-Robert is the prime reason to visit the small village of La Chaise-Dieu. The building is an amalgam of styles; the choir, however, is sensational: 144 oak stalls carved with figures of Vice and Virtue. Above them, entirely covering the walls, are some of the loveliest tapestries in France. Made in Brussels and Arras in the early 16th century and depicting scenes from the Old and New Testaments, they are rich in color and detail.

Statue of Notre-Dame-de-France at Le Puy

On the outer walls of the choir the 15th-century wall painting of the *Danse Macabre* shows Death in the form of skeletons leading rich and poor alike to their inevitable end. Beyond the cloister is the Echo room, in which two people whispering in opposite corners can hear one another perfectly. A Baroque Music Festival from mid-August to September makes the abbey crowded.

⓴ Le Puy-en-Velay

Haute-Loire. 20,500. 2 pl de Clauzel (04 71 09 38 41). Sat. Sep.
ot-lepuyenvelay.fr

Located in the bowl of a volcanic cone, the town of Le Puy teeters on a series of rock outcrops and giant basalt pillars. The town has three peaks, each topped with a landmark church or statue. Seen from afar, this is one of the most impressive sights in France.

Now a commercial and tourist-oriented town, Le Puy's star attraction is its medieval **Holy City**. This became a pilgrimage center after the Bishop of Le Puy, Gotescalk, made one of the first pilgrimages to Santiago de Compostela in 962 and built the **Chapelle St-Michel d'Aiguilhe** on his return. Pilgrims from eastern

Detail of *Danse Macabre* at St-Robert, in La Chaise-Dieu

The Auvergne's Black Madonnas

The cult of the Virgin Mary has always been strong in the Auvergne and this is reflected in the concentration of her statues in the region. Carved in dark walnut or cedar, now blackened with age, the Madonnas are believed to originate from the Byzantine influence of the Crusaders. Perhaps the most famous Madonna is the one in Le-Puy-en-Velay, a 17th-century copy of one which belonged to Louis IX in the Middle Ages.

Louis IX's Black Virgin

nce and Germany assembled the **Cathédrale de Notre-me** with its famous Black adonna and "fever stone" – a uid ceremonial stone with aling powers embedded in e of its walls – before setting for Compostela.

Built on an early pagan site, e Cathédrale de Notre-Dame a huge Romanesque struc-re. Multiform arches, carved lm and leaf designs, and a eckerboard facade show the luences of Moorish Spain, d indicate the considerable ltural exchange that took ace with southern France the 11th and 12th centuries. the transept are Romanesque scoes, notably an 11th–th-century St. Michael; in e sacristy, the treasury cludes the Bible of Theo-lphus, a handwritten cument from the era of arlemagne. The cathedral the center of the Holy City mplex that dominates the per town, encompassing a ptistry, cloister, Prior's house, d Penitents' chapel.

The colossal red statue of **tre-Dame-de-France**, on e pinnacle of the Rocher rneille, was erected in 1860, st from 213 cannons captured Sebastopol during the imean War. The statue is ached by a steep pathway, d can be climbed by an iron dder on the inside.

The Chapelle St-Michel, like the cathedral, shows Moorish influences in the trefoil decoration and colored mosaics on the rounded arch over the main entrance. It seems to grow out of a giant finger of lava rock and is reached by a steep climb. The church is thought to be located on the site of a Roman temple to Mercury, and its center dates from the 10th century, although most of the building was constructed a century later. The floor has been constructed to follow the contours of the rock in places, and the interior is ornamented with faded 10th-century murals and 20th-century stained-glass.

In the lower city, narrow streets of 15th- and 16th-century houses lead to the Vinay Garden and the **Musée Crozatier**, which has a collection of handmade lace from the 16th century to the present. The museum also has a good collection of medieval *objets d'art* and 15th-century paintings. The museum will be closed for restoration until 2015.

In mid-September, Le Puy transforms itself entirely for a masked and costumed Renaissance carnival, les Fêtes du Roi de l'Oiseau (the Bird King Festival), an ancient tradition celebrating the skill of the city's best archers *(see p42)*.

Chapelle St-Michel d'Aiguilhe
Aiguilhe. **Tel** 04 71 09 50 03. **Open** mid-Feb–mid-Dec: daily.

Notre-Dame-de-France
Rocher Corneille. **Tel** 04 71 05 45 52. **Open** daily. **Closed** mid-Nov–Jan (except Christmas hols).

Musée Crozatier
Jardin Henri Vinay. **Tel** 04 71 06 62 40. **Closed** for renovations until 2015.

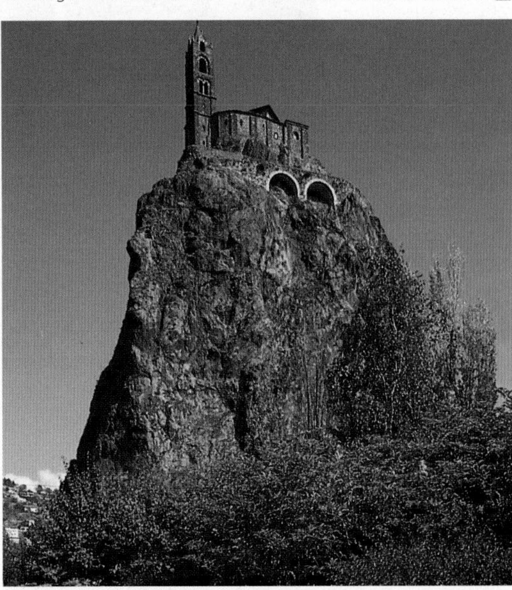

Chapelle St-Michel d'Aiguilhe, standing on a finger of lava rock

Ruins of the Castle of Calmont d… at Espalion in the Lot Va…

㉑ Vallée du Lot

Aveyron. ✈ Aurillac, Rodez. 🚉 Rodez, Séverac-le-Château. 🚌 Espalion, Rodez. ℹ Espalion (05 65 44 10 63). **valleedulot.com**

From Mende and the old river port of La Canourgue all the way to Conques, the river Lot (or Olt in old usage) courses through its fertile valley past orchards, vineyards, and pine forests. **Saint Côme d'Olt**, near the Aubrac mountains, is an unspoiled, fortified village whose 15th-century church is surrounded by Medieval and Renaissance houses. At **Espalion**, the pastel stone houses and a turreted 16th-century castle are reflected in the river, which runs beneath a 13th-century arched stone bridge. The town has one of the best markets in the region on Friday mornings. Just outside town is the 11th-century Perse Church, whose carved capitals portray battling knights and imaginary birds sipping from a chalice.

Estaing was once the fiefdom of one of the greatest families of the Rouergue, dating back to the 13th-century. The village nestles beneath its massive château (open May–Sep) on the river bank. The road passes through the Lot Gorge on the way to **Entraygues** ("between waters") where the old quarter and 13th-century Gothic bridge are worth a visit. Beyond Entraygues the river widens to join the Garonne.

㉒ Conques

See pp368–9.

㉓ Rodez

Aveyron. 26,000. ✈ 🚉 🚌 ℹ place de la Cité (05 65 75 76 77). Wed, Sat. **tourisme.grand-rodez.com**

Like many medieval French cities, Rodez was politically divided: the shop-lined **place du Bourg** on one side of town and **place de la Cité**, near the cathedral, on the other, reflect conflicting secula… and ecclesiastical interests. Rodez's commercial center, th… region's largest, is probably the main attraction now, though t… 13th-century huge pink stone **Cathédrale Notre-Dame** is worth a look, with its fortress-li… west facade, and its magnifice… bell tower. The 15th-century choir stalls show a superb panoply of creatures, including… winged lion and one naughty fellow exposing his derrière.

Entombment in Rodez Cathedral

Environs

Southeast (28 miles/ 45kms) lies Saint Léons, birthplace of Jean-Henr… Fabre, the famous entymologist. Here is **Micropolis**, part interactive museum, part theme park, dedicated to the glory of insects (closed Nov–mi… Feb). Watch the breathtaking film of the same name, if nothing else.

Robert Louis Stevenson

Robert Louis Stevenson (1850–94), best known for his novels *Treasure Island, Kidnapped*, and *Dr Jekyll and Mr Hyde,* was also an accomplished travel writer. In 1878, he set off across the remote Cévennes mountain range with only a small donkey, Modestine, for company. His classic account of this eventful journey, *Travels with a Donkey in the Cévennes*, was published in the following year.

Robert Louis Stevenson

Corniche des Cévennes

ère, Gard. Nîmes. Alès. St-Jean-du-Gard. Parc National Cevennes, 6 bis pl du Palais, Florac 400 (04 66 49 53 00). **cevennes-parcnational.fr**

e dramatic Corniche road m Florac on the Tarn to Jean-du-Gard was cut in the rly 18th century by the army Louis XIV in pursuit of the misards, Protestant rebels no had no uniforms but ught in their ordinary shirts *amiso* in the *langue d'oc*). e route of the D983 makes spectacular drive. Fascination th the history of the misards was one of the asons that Robert Louis evenson undertook his bled trek in the Cévennes th Modestine, recounted his *Travels with a Donkey the Cévennes*.

At St-Laurent-de-Trèves, here fossil remains suggest nosaurs once roamed, there is view of the Grands Causses, d the peaks of Lozère and goual. The Corniche ends in Jean-du-Gard, where the **usée des Vallées Cévenoles**, picting peasant life, is located. is closed for renovation and pected to re-open in 2015.)

Musée des Vallées Cévenoles
grand' rue, St-Jean-du-Gard. 04 66 85 10 48. **Closed** for novation until 2015. **museedescevennes.com**

Dramatic scenery in Corniche des Cévennes national park

㉕ Grands Causses

Aveyron. Rodez-Marcillac. Millau. Millau (05 65 60 02 42). Wed & Fri. **millau-viaduc-tourisme.fr**

The Causses are vast, arid limestone plateaus, alternating with green, fertile canyon valleys. The only sign of life at times is a bird of prey wheeling in the sky, or an isolated stone farm or shepherd's hut. The whole area makes for some desolate hiking for those who like solitude.

The four Grands Causses – Sauveterre, Méjean, Noir, and Larzac – stretch out east of the city of Millau, which boasts the tallest vehicular bridge in the world. They extend from Mende in the north to the valley of the Vis river in the south.

Among the sights in the Causses are the *chaos* – bizarre rock formations reputed to resemble ruined cities, and named accordingly: there's the *chaos* of **Montpellier-le-Vieux**, **Nîmes-le-Vieux**, and **Roquesaltes**. **Aven Armand** and the **Dargilan Grotto** are vast and deep natural underground grottoes.

A good place to head for in the Larzac Causse is the strange, rough-hewn stone village of **La Couvertoirade**, a fully enclosed citadel of the Knights Templar in the 12th century. The unpaved streets and medieval houses are an austere reminder of the dark side of the Middle Ages. Entry to the village is free, with a fee for the tour of the ramparts.

The Causse du Larzac's best-known village is probably **Roquefort-sur-Soulzon**, a small gray town terraced on the side of a crumbled limestone outcrop. It has one main street and one major product, Roquefort cheese. This is made from unpasteurized sheep's milk, seeded with a distinctive blue mould grown on loaves of bread, and aged in the warren of damp caves above the town.

w over Méjean, one of the four plateaus of the Grands Causses

㉒ Conques

The village of Conques clusters around the splendid Abbaye de Ste-Foy, hemmed into a rugged site against the hillside. Saint Foy was a young girl who became an early Christian martyr; her relics were first kept at a rival monastery in Agen. In the 9th century a monk from Conques stole the relics, thereby attracting pilgrims to this remote spot and firmly establishing Conques as a halt on the route to Santiago de Compostela *(see pp404–5)*. The treasury holds the most important collection of medieval and Renaissance gold work in western Europe. Some of it was made in the abbey's own workshops as early as the 9th century. The Romanesque abbey church has beautiful stained-glass windows by Pierre Soulages (1994), and its tympanum is a triumph of medieval sculpture.

View of the church from the village

Nave Interior
Pure and elegantly austere, the Romanesque interior dates from 1050–1135. The short nave soars to a height of 72 ft (22 m), with three tiers of arches topped by 250 decorative carved capitals.

KEY

① **The broad transepts** were able to accommodate crowds of pilgrims.

② **The Cloister** consists of a reconstructed square: only two sections of the original early 12th-century arcades remain. However, 30 of the original carved capitals are displayed in the refectory and in the Musée Fau.

Tympanum
This sculpture from the early 12th century depicts the *Last Judgment*, with the Devil in Hell (shown) in the lower part of the sculpture and Christ in Heaven in the tympanum's central position.

Conques' Treasures

The treasures date from the 9th to the 19th century, and are prized for both their beauty and their rarity. The gold-plated wood and silver reliquary of Ste-Foy is studded with gems, rock crystal, and even an *intaglio* of Roman Emperor Caracalla. The body is 9th century, but the face may be older, possibly 5th century. Other magnificent pieces include an "A"-shaped reliquary said to be a gift from Charlemagne; the small but exquisite Pépin's shrine from AD 1000; and a late 16th-century processional cross.

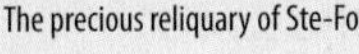

The precious reliquary of Ste-Foy

VISITORS' CHECKLIST

Practical Information
Aveyron. 1,600. Pl de l'Eglise (05 65 72 85 00). Treasury/museum: **Open** daily: Apr–Sep: 9:30am–12:30pm, 2–6:30pm; Oct–Mar: 10am–noon, 2–6pm. 8am Mon–Sat; 11am Sun. restr. **tourisme-conques.fr**

Transport
to St-Christophe, then a bus. from Rodez.

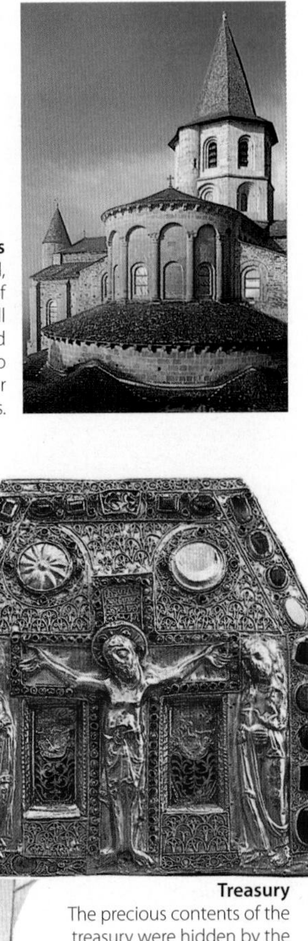

Romanesque Chapels
The east end is three-tiered, topped by the blind arcades of the choir and a central bell tower. Three chapels surround the eastern apse, built to accommodate extra altars for the celebration of mass.

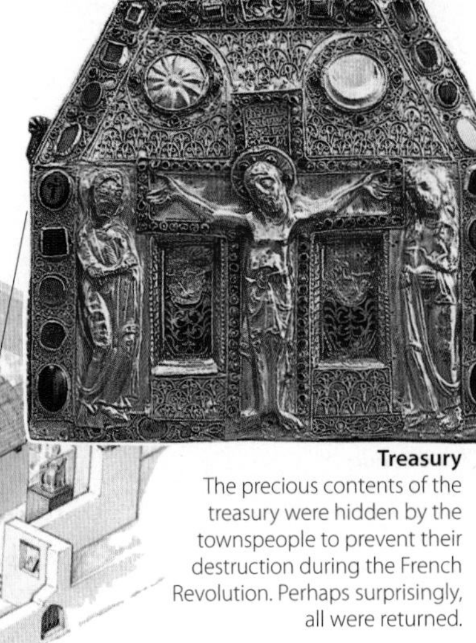

Treasury
The precious contents of the treasury were hidden by the townspeople to prevent their destruction during the French Revolution. Perhaps surprisingly, all were returned.

2

Entrance to Treasury

㉖ Gorges du Tarn

Near the beginning of its journey to meet the river Garonne, the Tarn flows through some of Europe's most spectacular gorges. For millions of years, the Tarn and its tributary the Jonte have eaten their way down through the limestone plateaus of the Cévennes, creating a sinuous forked canyon some 15 miles (25 km) long and nearly 1,300 ft (400 m) deep. The gorges are flanked by rocky bluffs and scaled by roads with dizzying bends and panoramic views, which are incredibly popular in the high season. The surrounding plateaus, or *causses*, are eerily different, forming an open, austere landscape, dry in summer and snow-clad in winter, where wandering sheep and isolated farms are sometimes the only signs of life.

Point Sublime
From 2,600 ft (800 m) up, there are stunning views of a major bend in the Tarn gorge, with the Causse Méjean visible in the distance.

Outdoor Activities
The Tarn and Jonte gorges are popular for canoeing and river rafting. Although relatively placid in summer, melting snow can make the rivers hazardous in spring.

Pas de Souci
Just upriver from Les Vignes, Pas de Souci flanks a narrow point in the gorge as the Tarn makes its way northwards.

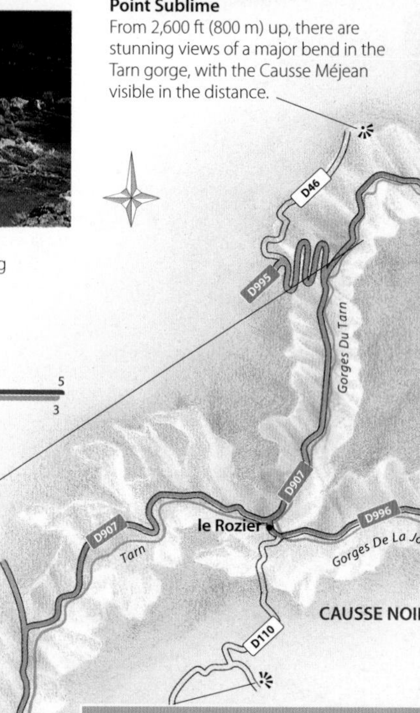

Chaos de Montpellier-le-Vieux
Situated on the flank of the Causse Noir off the D110 is a remarkable geological site – bizarre rock formations created by limestone erosion.

For hotels and restaurants in this region see pp554–71 and pp576–603

La Malène
An old crossing-point between the Causse de Sauveterre and the Causse Méjean, this village, with its 16th-century fortified manor, is a good starting point for boat trips.

VISITORS' CHECKLIST

Practical Information
Lozère. Le Rozier (05 65 62 60 89). St-Enimie (04 66 48 53 44).
gorgesdutarn.net

Transport
Rodez-Marcillac. Mende, Banassac, Séverac-le-Château. Milau.

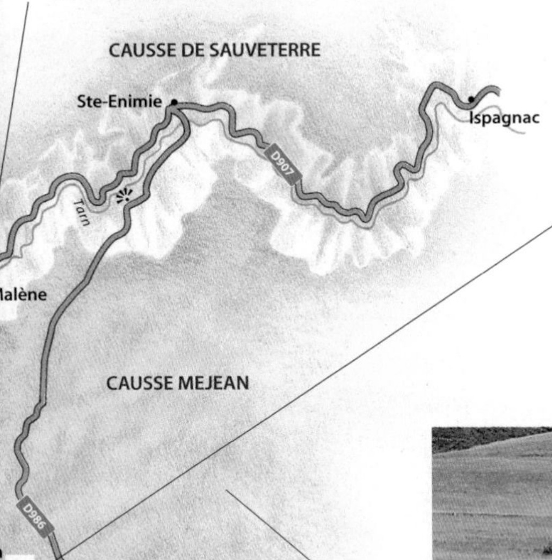

Aven Armand Caves
On the Causse Méjean, many stalactites in the caves are tinted by minerals that are deposited by the slowly trickling water.

Causse Méjean
The high plateaus or *causses* are a botanist's paradise in spring and summer, with over 900 species of wild flowers, including orchids.

The Wild Cevennes

One of the least populated parts of France, this area is well known for its wild flowers and birds of prey, and griffon vultures were once common here. These giant but harmless scavengers nearly died out in the 20th century through being hunted, but now a reintroduction program has led to growing numbers breeding in the Gorges de la Jonte.

Wild flowers found in this thinly populated area include unusual alpine plants.

The griffon vulture, which now breeds in the region, has a wingspan of over 8 ft (2.5 m).

THE RHONE VALLEY AND FRENCH ALPS

Loire · Rhône · Ain · Isèzère · Drôme · Ardèche
Haute-Savoie · Savoie · Hautes-Alpes

Its two most important geographical features, the Alps and the river Rhône, give this region both its name and its dramatic character. The east is dominated by majestic snowcapped peaks, while the Rhône provides a vital conduit between north and south.

The Romans recognized this strategic route when they founded Lyon over 2,000 years ago. Today Lyon, with its great museums and fine Renaissance buildings, is the second city of France. It is one of the country's most vital commercial and cultural centers as well as the undisputed capital of French gastronomy. To the north are the flat marshlands of the Dombes and the rich agricultural Bresse plain. Here, too, are the famous Beaujolais vineyards which, along with the Rhône vineyards, make the region such an important wine producer.

The French Alps are among the most popular year-round resort areas in the world, with internationally renowned ski stations such as Chamonix, Mégève, and Courchevel, and historic cities like Chambéry, capital of Savoy before it joined France. Elegant spa towns line the shores of Lac Léman (Lake Geneva). Grenoble, a bustling university city and high-tech center, is flanked by two of the most spectacular nature reserves in France, the Chartreuse and the Vercors.

To the south, orchards and fields of sunflowers give way to brilliant rows of lavender interspersed with vineyards and olive groves. Châteaus and ancient towns dot the landscape. Mountains and pretty, old-fashioned spa towns characterize the rugged Ardèche, and the deeply scoured gorges along the river Ardèche offer some of the wildest scenery in France.

The restored Ferme de la Forêt at St-Trivier-de-Courtes, north of Bourg-en-Bresse

◀ Chapelle Saint-Marie set against the dramatic scenery of the Vallée de la Clarée, close to Briançon

Exploring the Rhône Valley and French Alps

Lyon is the region's largest city, famed for its historic buildings and gastronomic tradition. Wine lovers can choose between the vineyards of the Beaujolais, Rhône Valley, and Drôme region to the south. To the west, the Ardèche offers rugged wilderness, canoeing, and climbing. Spa devotees from around the world flock to Evian-les-Bains and Aix-les-Bains, while the Alps are a favorite destination for sports enthusiasts *(see pp326–7)*.

Sights at a Glance

1. Bourg-en-Bresse
2. The Dombes
3. Pérouges
4. Lyon
5. Vienne
6. St-Romain-en-Gal
7. St-Étienne
8. Palais Idéal du Facteur Cheval
9. Tournon-sur-Rhône
10. Valence
11. The Ardèche
12. Vals-les-Bains
13. Montélimar
14. Grignan
15. Nyons
16. Briançon
17. Le Bourg d'Oisans
18. Grenoble
19. The Vercors
20. The Chartreuse
21. Chambéry
22. Aix-les-Bains
23. Annecy
24. Lac Léman

The Pont des Amours in Annecy

Key

- Highway
- Major road
- Secondary road
- Minor road
- Scenic route
- Main railroad
- Minor railroad
- International border
- Regional border
- Summit

For additional map symbols *see back flap*

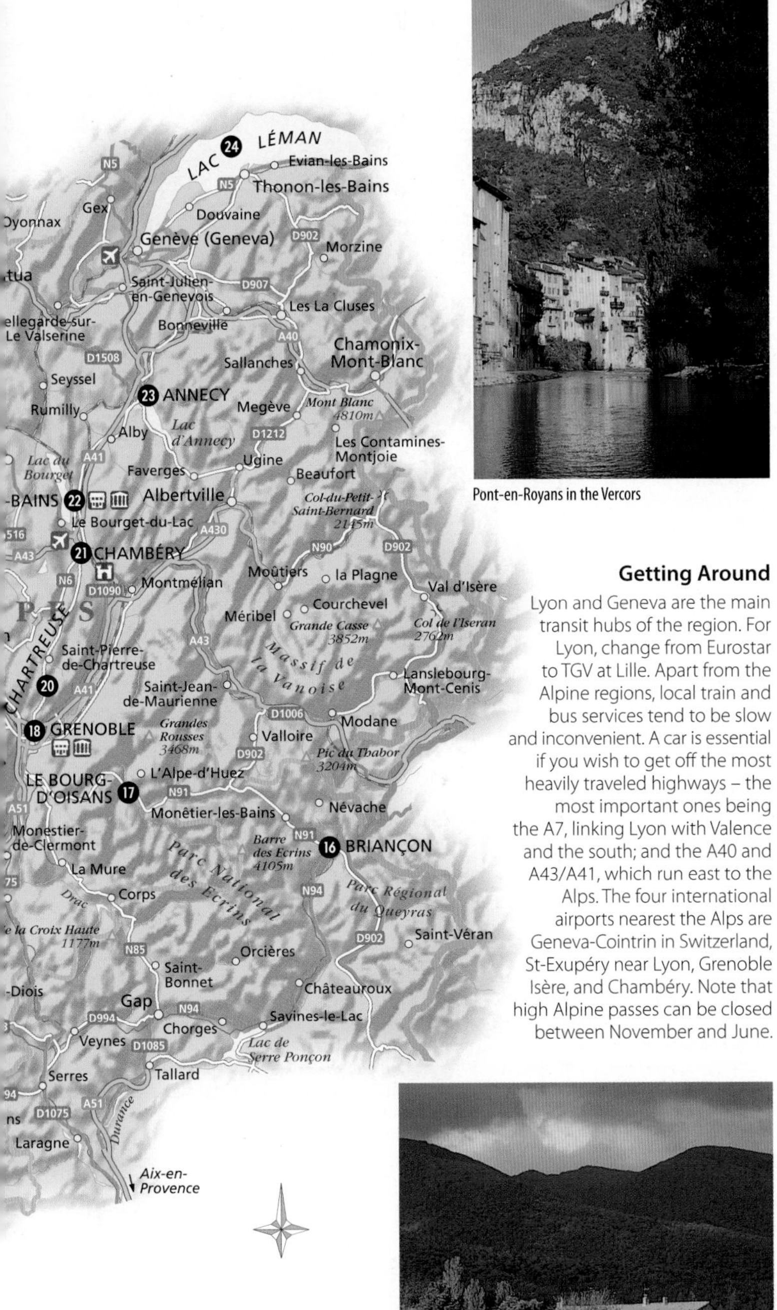

Pont-en-Royans in the Vercors

Getting Around

Lyon and Geneva are the main transit hubs of the region. For Lyon, change from Eurostar to TGV at Lille. Apart from the Alpine regions, local train and bus services tend to be slow and inconvenient. A car is essential if you wish to get off the most heavily traveled highways – the most important ones being the A7, linking Lyon with Valence and the south; and the A40 and A43/A41, which run east to the Alps. The four international airports nearest the Alps are Geneva-Cointrin in Switzerland, St-Exupéry near Lyon, Grenoble Isère, and Chambéry. Note that high Alpine passes can be closed between November and June.

Farms around Le Poët Laval, near Montélimar

❶ Bourg-en-Bresse

Ain. 43,000. Centre Culturel Albert Camus, 6 av Alsace-Lorraine (04 74 22 49 40). Wed & Sat. **bourgenbressetourisme.fr**

Bourg-en-Bresse is a busy market town, with some beautifully restored half-timbered buildings. It is best known for its tasty *poulet de Bresse* (chickens raised in the flat agricultural region of Bresse and designated *appellation contrôlée, see p323*); and its abbey church of **Brou** on the southeast edge of town.

The latter, no longer a place of worship, has become one of the most visited sites in France. Flamboyant Gothic in style, it was built between 1505 and 1536 by Margaret of Austria after the death of her husband Philibert, Duke of Savoy, in 1504.

The couple's finely sculpted Carrara marble tombs can be seen in the choir, along with the tomb of Margaret of Bourbon, Philibert's mother, who died in 1483. Notice also the beautifully carved choir stalls, stained-glass windows, and rood screen with its elegant basket-handle arching.

The adjacent cloisters house a small museum with a good collection of 16th- and 17th-century Dutch and Flemish masters, as well as contemporary works by local artists.

Environs

About 15 miles (24 km) north of Bourg-en-Bresse at St-Trivier-de-Courtes, the restored **Ferme-Musée de la Forêt** offers a look at farm life in the region during the 17th century. The ancient house has what is known locally as a Saracen chimney, with a brick hood in the center of the room, similar to constructions in Sicily and Portugal, and a collection of antique farm implements.

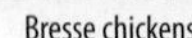

Bresse chickens

Ferme-Musée de la Forêt
Tel 04 74 30 71 89. **Open** call 04 74 30 77 41 for opening hours.

Tomb of Margaret of Austria in the abbey church of Brou at Bourg-en-Bresse

❷ The Dombes

Ain. Lyon. Lyon, Villars les Dombes, Bourg-en-Bresse. Villars-les-Dombes (from Bourg-en-Bresse). 3 pl de Hôtel de Ville, Villars-les-Dombes (04 74 98 06 29).

This flat, glacier-gouged plateau south of Bourg-en-Bresse is dotted with small hills, ponds, and marshes, making it popular with anglers and bird-watchers. In the middle of the area at **Villars-les-Dombes** is an ornithological park, the **Parc des Oiseaux**. Over 400 species of native and exotic birds live here, including tufted herons, vultures, pink flamingos, emus, and ostriches.

Parc des Oiseaux
Route Nationale 83, Villars-les-Dombes.
Tel 04 74 98 05 54. **Open** daily. **Closed** mid-Nov–Feb.

❸ Pérouges

Ain. 900. Meximieux-Pérouges. 04 74 46 70 84. **perouges.org**

Originally the home of immigrants from Perugia, Pérouges is a fortified hilltop village of medieval houses and cobblestone streets. In the 13th century it was a center of linen-weaving, but with the mechanization of the industry in the 19th century, the local population fell from 1,500 to 90.

Restoration of its historic buildings and a new influx of craftsmen have breathed new life into Pérouges. Not surprisingly, the village has often been used as the setting for historical dramas such as *The Three Musketeers* and *Monsieur Vincent*. The village's main square, place de la Halle, is shaded by a huge lime tree planted in 1792 to honor the Revolution.

A Tour of Beaujolais

Beaujolais is an ideal area for wine tasting, offering delicious, affordable wine, and glorious countryside. The south of the region produces most of the Beaujolais Nouveau, released fresh from the cellars on the third Thursday of November each year. In the north are the ten superior quality *cru* wines – St-Amour, Juliénas, Moulin-à-Vent, Chénas, Fleurie, Chiroubles, Morgon, Brouilly, Côte de Brouilly, and Regnié – most of which can be visited in a day's drive. The distinctive *maisons du pays* have living quarters built over the wine cellar. Almost every village has its *cave* (wine cellar), offering tastings and a glimpse of the wine culture that dominates local life.

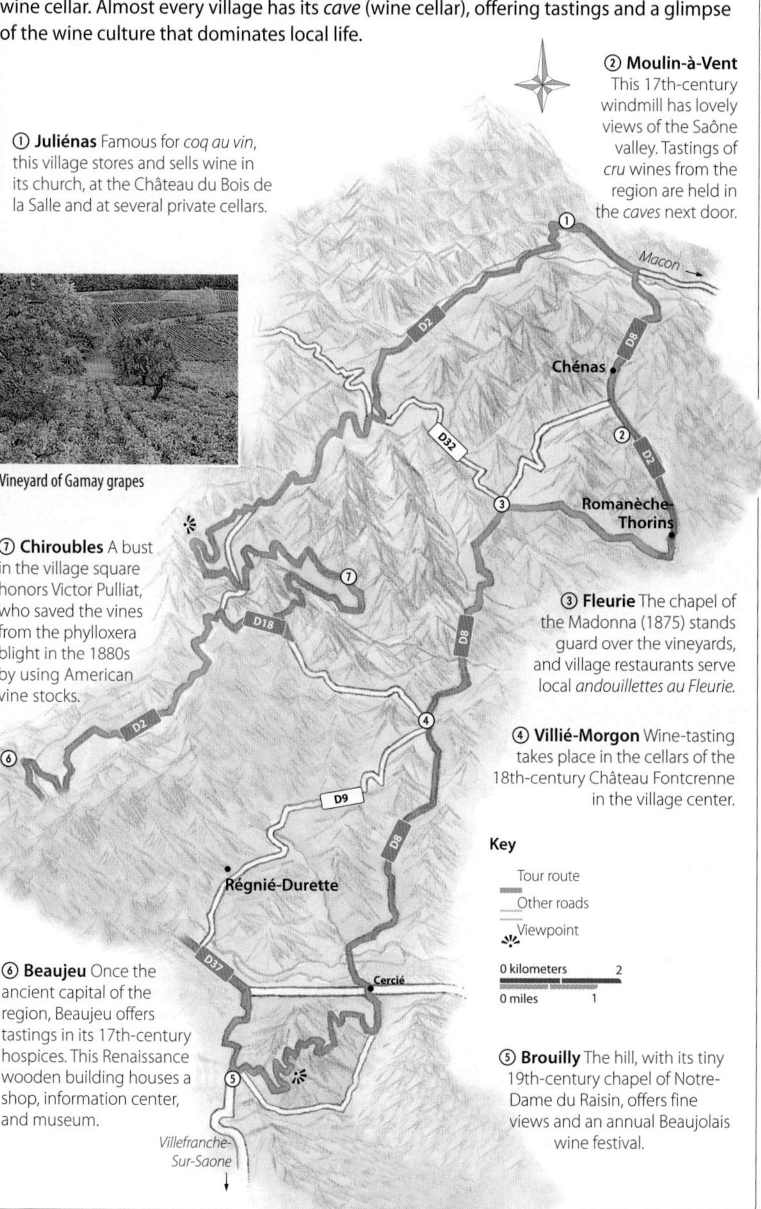

Vineyard of Gamay grapes

① **Juliénas** Famous for *coq au vin*, this village stores and sells wine in its church, at the Château du Bois de la Salle and at several private cellars.

② **Moulin-à-Vent** This 17th-century windmill has lovely views of the Saône valley. Tastings of *cru* wines from the region are held in the *caves* next door.

③ **Fleurie** The chapel of the Madonna (1875) stands guard over the vineyards, and village restaurants serve local *andouillettes au Fleurie*.

④ **Villié-Morgon** Wine-tasting takes place in the cellars of the 18th-century Château Fontcrenne in the village center.

⑤ **Brouilly** The hill, with its tiny 19th-century chapel of Notre-Dame du Raisin, offers fine views and an annual Beaujolais wine festival.

⑥ **Beaujeu** Once the ancient capital of the region, Beaujeu offers tastings in its 17th-century hospices. This Renaissance wooden building houses a shop, information center, and museum.

⑦ **Chiroubles** A bust in the village square honors Victor Pulliat, who saved the vines from the phylloxera blight in the 1880s by using American vine stocks.

❹ Street by Street: Lyon

On the west bank of the river Saône, the restored old quarter of Vieux Lyon is an atmospheric warren of cobbled streets, *traboules* (covered passageways), Renaissance palaces, first-class restaurants, lively *bouchons* (bistros), and bohemian shops. It is also the site of the Roman city of Lugdunum, the commercial and military capital of Gaul founded by Julius Caesar in 44 BC. Vestiges of this prosperous city can be seen in the superb Gallo-Roman museum at the top of Fourvière hill. Two excavated Roman theaters still stage performances from opera to rock concerts. At the foot of the hill is the finest collection of Renaissance mansions in France. The spectacular Musée des Confluences opens in 2014.

★ Théâtres Romains
There are two Roman amphitheaters here: the Grand Théâtre, the oldest theater in France, built in 15 BC to seat 30,000 spectators and still used for modern performances; and the smaller Odéon, with its geometric tiled flooring.

★ Musée de la Civilisation Gallo-Romaine
This underground museum contains a rich collection of statues, mosaics, coins, and inscriptions evoking Lyon's Roman past.

Entrance to funicular

Cathédrale St-Jean
Begun in the late 12th century, the cathedral has a 14th-century astronomical clock that shows religious feast days till the year 2019.

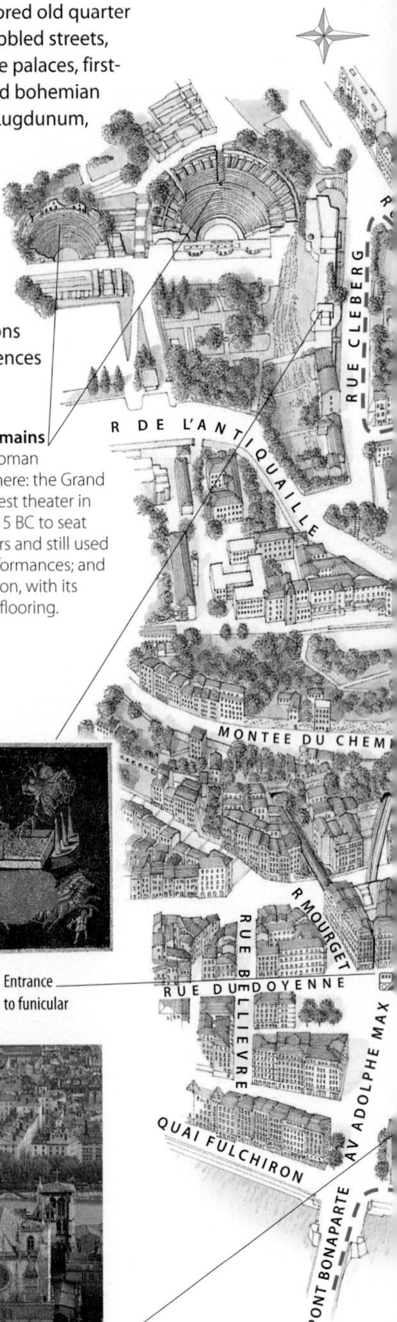

RUE CLEBERG
R DE L'ANTIQUAILLE
MONTEE DU CHEMI
R MOURGET
RUE BELLIEVRE
RUE DU DOYENNE
AV ADOLPHE MAX
QUAI FULCHIRON
PONT BONAPARTE

0 meters 100
0 yards 100

For hotels and restaurants in this region see pp554–71 and pp576–603

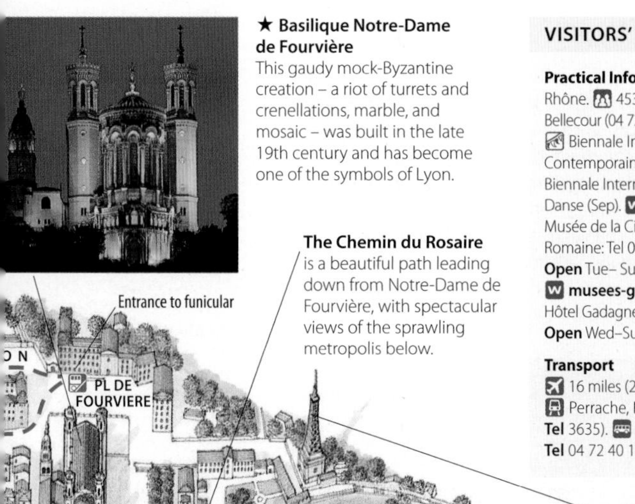

★ Basilique Notre-Dame de Fourvière
This gaudy mock-Byzantine creation – a riot of turrets and crenellations, marble, and mosaic – was built in the late 19th century and has become one of the symbols of Lyon.

The Chemin du Rosaire is a beautiful path leading down from Notre-Dame de Fourvière, with spectacular views of the sprawling metropolis below.

VISITORS' CHECKLIST

Practical Information
Rhône. 453,000. pl Bellecour (04 72 77 69 69). daily. Biennale Internationale d'Art Contemporain (Sep–Jan), Biennale Internationale de la Danse (Sep). **lyon-france.com**
Musée de la Civilisation Gallo-Romaine: Tel 04 72 38 49 30. **Open** Tue–Sun.
musees-gallo-romains.com
Hôtel Gadagne: Tel 04 78 42 03 61. **Open** Wed–Sun.

Transport
16 miles (25 km) E Lyon. Perrache, Part-Dieu (SNCF **Tel** 3635). Perrache (SNCF **Tel** 04 72 40 15 63).

The Tour Métallique was erected in 1893 and is now used as a television transmitter.

Rue Juiverie boasts a number of splendid Renaissance mansions – look out for the Hôtel Paterin at No. 4 and the Hôtel Bullioud at No. 8.

Rue St-Jean and rue du Boeuf are lined with Renaissance mansions, the former homes of bankers and silk merchants.

The 15th-century Hôtel Gadagne houses two museums: the **Musée Historique de Lyon** and the **Musée des Marionnettes du Monde**, which exhibits the famous Lyonnais puppets.

Suggested route

Exploring Lyon

France's second city, dramatically sited on the banks of the Rhône and Saône rivers, has been a vital gateway between the north and south since ancient times. On arriving you immediately feel a *brin du sud*, or touch of the south. The crowds are not as quick-stepping as they are in Paris, and the sun is often shining here when it's rainy and cold in the north. Despite its importance as a banking, textile, and pharmaceutical center, most of the French immediately associate Lyon with their palates. The city is packed with restaurants, ranging from simple *bouchons* (bistros) to some of the most opulent tables in France.

The rue St-Jean in Vieux Lyon

The Presqu'île

The heart of Lyon is the Presqu'île, the narrow peninsula of land between the Saône and Rhône rivers, just north of their confluence. A pedestrianized shopping street, the rue de la République, links the twin poles of civic life: the vast place Bellecour, with its equestrian statue of Louis XIV in the middle, and the **place des Terreaux**. The latter is overlooked by Lyon's ornate 17th-century Hôtel de Ville (town hall) and the Palais St-Pierre, a former Benedictine convent and now the home of the **Musée des Beaux Arts**. In the middle of the square is a monumental 19th-century fountain by Bartholdi, sculptor of the Statue of Liberty.

Behind the town hall, architec Jean Nouvel's futuristic **Opéra d Lyon** – a black barrel vault of steel and glass encased in a Ne Classical shell – was remodeled to a controversial design in 199

A few blocks to the south, the **Musée de l'Imprimerie** illustrates Lyon's contribution to the early days of printing in the late 15th century.

Two other museums worth visiting in the Presqu'île are the **Musée des Tissus**, which house an extraordinary collection of silks and tapestries dating from early Christian times to the present day, and the **Musée de Arts Décoratifs**, which displays a range of tapestries, furniture, porcelain, and *objets d'art*.

Nearby, the **Abbaye St-Mar d'Ainay** is an impressively restored Carolingian church dating from 1107.

Lyon City Center

1. Amphithéâtre des Trois Gaules
2. Eglise St-Polycarpe
3. Opéra de Lyon
4. Hôtel de Ville
5. Musée des Beaux Arts
6. Musée de l'Imprimerie
7. Hôtel Gadagne
8. Tour Métallique
9. Basilique Notre-Dame de Fourvière
10. Musée de la Civilisation Gallo-Romaine
11. Théâtres Romains
12. Cathédrale St-Jean
13. Abbaye St-Martin d'Ainay
14. Musée des Arts Décoratifs
15. Musée Historique des Tissus

0 meters 250
0 yards 250

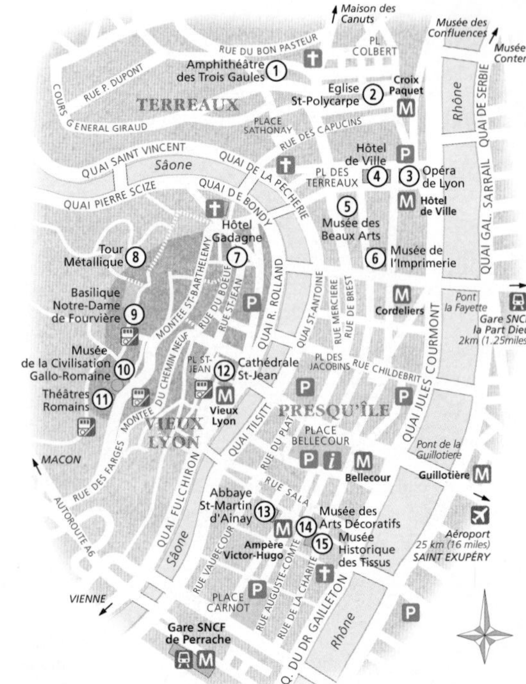

Key to Symbols *see back flap*

ɔod market on quai St-Antoine

a Croix-Rousse

his area north of Presqu'île ecame the center of the city's 'lk-weaving industry in the 15th entury. It is traced with covered assages known as *traboules*, sed by weavers to transport their nished fabrics. To get a sense of nem, enter at No. 6 place des erreaux and continue along until ou reach the **Eglise St-Polycarpe**. rom here, it is a short walk to the uins of the **Amphithéâtre des rois Gaules**, built in AD 19, and ne **Maison des Canuts**, with its 'aditional silk loom.

a Part-Dieu

his modern business area n the east bank of the hône has a TGV station, huge shopping omplex, and the **uditorium Maurice-avel** for important ultural events.

Musée de l'Imprimerie
3 rue de la Poulaillerie. **Tel** 04 3 37 65 98. **Open** Wed–Sun. **losed** public hols.

Musée des Tissus
4 rue de la Charité. **Tel** 04 78 38 42 00. **pen** Tue–Sun. **Closed** public hols.

Musée Arts Décoratifs
) rue de la Charité. **Tel** 04 78 38 42). **Open** Tue–Sun. **Closed** public ols.

Maison des Canuts
)–12 rue d'Ivry. **Tel** 04 78 28 62 04. **pen** Mon–Sat. **Closed** public hols.

nvirons

ourgoin-Jallieu, southeast of yon, still prints silk for fashion ouses, and has a fine textile ollection in its museum.

Musée des Beaux Arts

Lyon's Musée des Beaux Arts showcases the country's largest and probably most important collection of art after the Louvre. The museum is housed in the 17th-century Palais St-Pierre, a former Benedictine convent for the daughters of the nobility. The Musée d'Art Contemporain, formerly located in the Palais St-Pierre, is now at 81 quai Charles de Gaulle, north of the Parc Tête d'Or. Housed in a building designed by Renzo Piano, it specializes in works dating from after the mid-20th century.

Antiquities

Included in this wide-ranging collection on the first floor are Egyptian archeological finds, Etruscan statuettes, and 4,000-year-old Cypriot ceramics. Temporary exhibits, with a separate entrance on 16 rue Edouard Herriott, are also on the ground and first floors.

Sculpture and Objets d'Art

Occupying the old chapel on the ground floor, the sculpture department includes works from the French Romanesque period and Italian Renaissance, as well as late 19th- and early 20th-century pieces. Represented are Rodin and Bourdelle (whose statues also appear in the courtyard), Maillol, Despiau, and Pompon among others. The huge *objets d'art* collection, on the first floor, comprises medieval ivories, bronzes and ceramics, coins, medals, weapons, jewelry, furniture, and tapestries.

Odalisque (1841) by James Pradier

Paintings and Drawings

The museum's superb collection of paintings occupies the first and second floors. It covers all periods and includes works by Spanish and Dutch masters, the French schools of the 17th, 18th, and 19th centuries, Impressionist and modern paintings, as well as works by the Lyon School, whose exquisite flower paintings were used as sources of inspiration by the designers of silk fabrics through the ages. On the first floor, the Cabinet d'Arts Graphiques has over 4,000 drawings and etchings by such artists as Delacroix, Poussin, Géricault, Degas, and Rodin (by appointment only).

Fleurs des Champs (1845) by Louis Janmot of the Lyon School

Musée des Beaux Arts
Palais St-Pierre, 20 pl des Terreaux. **Tel** 04 72 10 17 40. **Open** Wed–Mon. **Closed** public hols.

La Méduse (1923) by Alexeï von Jawlensky

Châtiment de Lycurgue in the Musée Archéologique, St-Romain-en-Gal

❺ Vienne

Isère. 30,000. cours Brillier (04 74 53 80 30). Tue–Sat. International Jazz Festival (end Jun–mid-Jul). **vienne-tourisme.com**

No other city in the Rhône Valley offers such a concentration of architectural history as Vienne. Located in a natural basin of land between the river and the hills, this site was recognized for both its strategic and aesthetic advantages by the Romans, who vastly expanded an existing village when they invaded the area in the 1st century BC.

The center of the Roman town was the **Temple d'Auguste et Livie** (10 BC) on place du Palais, a handsome structure supported by Corinthian columns. Not far away off place de Miremont are the remains of the **Jardin Archéologique de Cybèle**, a temple dedicated to the goddess Cybèle.

Vienne's Temple d'Auguste et Livie (1st century BC)

The **Théâtre Romain**, at the foot of Mont Pipet off rue du Cirque, was one of the largest amphitheaters in Roman France, capable of seating over 13,000 spectators. It was restored in 1938, and is now used for a variety of events, including an international jazz festival. From the very top seats the view of the town and river is spectacular.

Other interesting Roman vestiges include a fragment of Roman road in the public gardens and, on the southern edge of town, the **Pyramide du Cirque**, a curious structure about 65 ft (20 m) high that was once the centerpiece of the chariot racetrack. The **Musée des Beaux Arts et d'Archéologie** also has a good collection of Gallo-Roman artifacts, as well as 18th-century French faïence. This museum may close when the city's museums are regrouped so check before visiting.

The **Cathédrale de St-Maurice** is the city's most important medieval monument. It was built between the 12th and 16th century and represents an unusual hybrid of Romanesque and Gothic styles. Two of Vienne's earliest Christian churches are the 12th-century **Eglise St-André-le-Bas**, with richly carved capitals in its nave and cloister, and the **Eglise St-Pierre** parts of which date from the 5th and 6th centuries. The latter houses the **Musée Lapidaire**, a museum of stone-carving, with bas-reliefs and statues from Gallo-Roman buildings.

Musée des Beaux Arts et d'Archéologie
Pl de Miremont. **Tel** 04 74 85 50 42. **Open** Apr–Oct: Tue–Sun; Nov–Mar: Tue–Fri & Sat–Sun pm. **Closed** Jan 1, May 1, Nov 1 & 11, Dec 25.

Musée Lapidaire
Pl St-Pierre. **Tel** 04 74 85 20 35. **Open** Apr–Oct: Tue–Sun; Nov–Mar: Tue–Fri & Sat–Sun pm. **Closed** Jan 1, May 1, Nov 1 & 11, Dec 25.

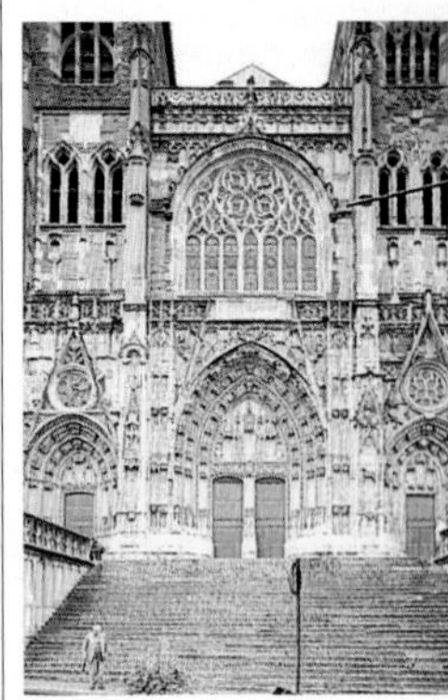

Vienne's Cathédrale de St-Maurice

❻ St-Romain-en-Gal

Rhône. 1,300. Vienne. Vienne (04 74 53 80 30).

In 1967, building work in this commercial town directly across the Rhône from Vienne revealed extensive remains of a significant Roman community dating from 100 BC to AD 300. It comprises the remnants of villas, public baths, shops, and warehouses. Of particular interest is the House of the Ocean Gods, with a magnificent mosaic floor depicting the bearded Neptune and other ocean images.

Much of what has been unearthed during the ongoing excavations is housed in the **Musée Archéologique** adjoining the ıins. The impressive collection ıcludes household objects, ıurals, and mosaics. The star exibit is the *Châtiment de Lycurgue*, mosaic discovered in 1907.

Musée Archéologique
el 04 74 53 74 01. **Open** Tue–Sun. **losed** some publ hols. estr. **musees-gallo-omains.com**

St-Étienne

oire. 180,000. 16 v de la Libération (04 77 49 39 00). daily. **saint-etienne ourisme.com**

he dour industrial renown rought to this city by coalnining and armaments is slowly eing shaken off, with urban edevelopment well underway nd an efficient tramway network. he downtown area around place es Peuple is lively. Nearby, Jean-Aichel Wilmotte has overhauled he **Musée d'Art et d'Industrie**, vhich covers St-Étienne's ndustrial history, including the levelopment of the revolutionary acquard loom, and world-class ollections of cycles and ribbonnaking machines.

To the north of the city, the **Ausée d'Art Moderne** has a collection of 20th-century art, ncluding works by Andy Warhol ınd Frank Stella.

Detail of the bizarre Palais Idéal du Facteur Cheval at Hauterives

Musée d'Art et d'Industrie
2 pl Louis Comte. **Tel** 04 77 49 73 00. **Open** Wed–Mon. **Closed** some public hols.

Musée d'Art Moderne
La Terrasse. **Tel** 04 77 79 52 52. **Open** Wed–Mon. **Closed** some public hols & when exhibitions change. **mam-st-etienne.fr**

The Rhône's Bridges

The Rhône has played a crucial role in French history, transporting armies and commercial traffic between the north and south. It has always been dangerous, a challenge to boatmen and builders for centuries. In 1825 the brilliant engineer, Marc Seguin, built the first suspension bridge using steel wire cables. This was followed by another 20 along the length of the Rhône, forever transforming communications between east and west.

Suspension bridge over the Rhône at Tournon-sur-Rhône

8 Palais Idéal du Facteur Cheval

Hauterives, Drôme. Romans-sur-Isère. **Tel** 04 75 68 81 19. **Open** daily. **Closed** Jan 1, 15–31, Dec 25. restricted. **facteurcheval.com**

At Hauterives, 15 miles (25 km) north of Roman-sur-Isère on the D538, is one of the greatest follies of France, an eccentric "palace" made of stones and evoking Egyptian, Roman, Aztec, and Siamese styles of architecture. It was built by a local postman, Ferdinand Cheval, who collected the stones during his daily rounds. His neighbors thought him mad, but the project attracted the admiring attention of Picasso, the surrealist André Breton, and others.

The interior of the palace is inscribed with numerous mottos and exhortations by Cheval, the most poignant of which refers to his assiduous efforts to realize his lifelong fantasy: "1879–1912: 10,000 days, 93,000 hours, 33 years of toil."

Parc Jouvet in Valence

❾ Tournon-sur-Rhône

Ardèche. 10,000. Hôtel de la Tourette (04 75 08 10 23). Wed & Sat. **ville-tournon.com**

Situated at the foot of impressive granite hills, Tournon is a lovely town with gracious tree-lined promenades and an imposing 11th–16th-century **château**. The latter houses a museum of local history, and has fine views of the town and river from its terraces.

The adjacent **Collégiale St-Julien**, with its square bell tower and elaborate facade, is an interesting example of the Italian influence on architecture in the region during the 14th century. Inside is a powerful *Résurrection*, painted in 1576 by Capassin, a pupil of Raphael.

On quai Charles de Gaulle, the **Lycée Gabriel-Fauré** is the oldest secondary school in France, dating from 1536. Directly across the Rhône from Tournon, the village of **Tain l'Hermitage** is famous for its steep-climbing vineyards which produce both red and white Hermitage, the finest of all Rhône wines.

Environs

From Tournon's main square, the place Jean Jaurès, a narrow, twisting road signposted the **Route Panoramique** leads via the villages of Plats and St-Romain-de-Lerps to St-Péray. This route offers breathtaking views at every turn, and, at St-Romain, you are rewarded with a superb panorama extending over 13 *départements*.

❿ Valence

Drôme. 67,000. 11 bd Bancel (04 75 44 90 40). Thu & Sat. Summer Music (Jul). **valencetourisme.com**

Valence is a large, thriving market town set on the east bank of the Rhône and looking across to the cliffs of the Ardèche. Its principal sight is the Romanesque **Cathédrale St-Apollinaire** on place des Clercs, founded in 1095 and rebuilt in the 17th century.

Alongside the cathedral in the former bishop's palace, the small **Musée des Beaux Arts** contains a collection of late 18th-century chalk drawings of Rome by Hubert Robert.

A short walk from here are two Renaissance mansions. The **Maison des Têtes** at No. 57 Grande Rue was built in 1532 and is embellished with the sculpted heads of ancient Greeks including Aristotle, Homer, and Hippocrates. On ru Pérollerie, the **Maison Dupré-Latour** has a finely sculptured porch and staircase.

The **Parc Jouvet**, south of avenue Gambetta, offers 14 acres (6 ha) of lovely pools and gardens, with fine views across the river to the ruined **Châtea de Crussol**.

Musée des Beaux Arts
4 pl des Ormeaux. **Tel** 04 75 79 20 80. **Open** Tue–Sun.

The limestone Pont d'Arc

⓫ The Ardèche

Ardèche. Avignon. Montélima Montélimar, Vallon Pont d'Arc. Vallon Pont d'Arc (04 75 88 04 01). **vallon-pont-darc.com**

Over the course of thousands of years, wind and water have endowed this south-central region of France with such a

Côtes Du Rhône

Rising in the Swiss Alps and traveling south to the Mediterranean, the mighty Rhône is the common thread that links the many vineyards of the Rhône Valley. A hierarchy of *appellations* divides into three levels of quality: at the base, the regional Côtes du Rhône provides the bulk of the Rhône's wines; next, Côtes du Rhône-Villages comprises a plethora of picturesque villages; and, at the top, there are 13 individual *appellations*. The most famous are the steep slopes of Hermitage and Côte Rôtie in the northern Rhône, and historic Châteauneuf-du-Pape *(see p507)* in the south. The lion's share of production is of red wine, which, based on the syrah grape, is often spicy, full-bodied, and robust.

Harvest in a Côtes du Rhône vineyard

gged landscape that it is more miniscent of the American uthwest than the verdure mmonly associated with the ench countryside. This visible ama is repeated underground well, since the Ardèche is oneycombed with enormous alagmite- and stalactite-namented caves. The most pressive are the **Grotte de la adeleine**, reached via a sign-osted path from the D290, and e cave and museum **La Cité de Préhistoire**, opening in 2014 the south of Vallon-Pont-d'Arc.

For those who prefer to stay ove ground, the most arresting tural scenery in the region is e **Gorges de l'Ardèche**, best en from the D290, a two-lane ad that parallels the recessed ver for 20 miles (32 km). Close the head of the gorge, head-g west, is the **Pont d'Arc**, a tural limestone "bridge" anning the river, created by osion and the elements. earby is **Grotte Chauvet**, a plica of the oldest known ecorated cave in the world, ow closed to the public. inted up to 36,000 years ago, e cave contains hundreds of imal paintings demonstrating tonishing technical ability.

Canoeing and white-water fting are the two most popular orts here. All the equipment ecessary can be rented locally; perators at Vallon-Pont-d'Arc mong many other places) rent ut two-person canoes and ganize return transport from -Martin d'Ardèche, 20 miles 2 km) downstream.

e Gorges de l'Ardèche, between llon-Pont-d'Arc and Pont St-Esprit

The village of Vogüé on the banks of the river Ardèche

The softer side of the region is found in its ancient and picturesque villages, gracious spa towns, vineyards, and plantations of Spanish chestnuts (from which the delectable *marron glacé* is produced).

Some 8 miles (13 km) south of Aubenas, the 12th-century village of **Balazuc** is typical of the region, its stone houses built on a clifftop overlooking a secluded gorge of the river Ardèche. There are fine views as you approach on the D294.

Neighboring **Vogüé** is nestled between the river Ardèche and a limestone cliff. A tiny but atmospheric village, its most commanding sight is the 12th-century **Château de Vogüé**, once the seat of the barons of Languedoc. Rebuilt in the 17th century, the building houses a museum featuring exhibitions about the region.

Château de Vogüé
Tel 04 75 37 01 95. **Open** Easter–Jun: Wed–Sun; Jul–Sep: daily; Oct–mid-Nov: Wed–Sun.
chateaudevogue.net

⓬ Vals-les-Bains

Ardèche. 3,700. Montélimar. rue Jean Jaurès (04 75 89 14 97). Thu & Sun (& Tue in summer).
aubenas-vals.com

This small spa town retains a hint of its past elegance. It is situated in the valley of the Volane, where there are at least 150 springs, of which all but two are cold. The water, which contains bicarbonate of soda and other minerals, is said to help with digestive problems, rheumatism, and diabetes.

Discovered around 1600, Vals-les-Bains is one of the few spas in southern France to have been overlooked by the Romans. The town reached the height of its popularity in the late 19th century, and most of its parks and architecture retain something of the Belle Epoque. Vals is a convenient first stop for an exploration of the Ardèche, with plenty of hotels and restaurants.

Environs

About 5 miles (8 km) east of Vals is the superb Romanesque church of **St-Julien du Serre**.

A farm near Le Poët Laval, east of Montélimar

⓭ Montélimar

Drôme. 33,000.
allées Provençales (04 75 01 00 20).
Wed–Sat.
montelimar-tourisme.com

Whether you choose to make a detour to Montélimar will largely depend on how sweet a tooth you might have. The main curiosity of this market town is its medieval center, chock-full of shops selling almond-studded nougat. This splendid confection has been made here since the start of the 17th century, when the almond tree was first introduced into France from Asia.

The **Château des Adhémar**, a mélange of 12th-, 14th-, and 16th-century architecture, surveys the town from a tall hill to the east.

Château des Adhémar
Tel 04 75 00 62 30. **Open** Apr–Oct: daily; Nov–Mar: Wed–Mon pms (for exhibitions only). **Closed** Jan 1, Dec 25.

Environs

The countryside east of Montélimar is full of picturesque medieval villages and scenic routes. **La Bégude-de-Mazenc** is a thriving little holiday center, with its fortified Old Town perched on a hilltop. Farther east is **Le Poët Laval**, a tiny medieval village set in the Alpine foothills. **Dieulefit**, the capital of this beautiful region, has several small hotels and restaurants, as well as facilities for tennis, swimming, and fishing. To the south, the fortified village of **Taulignan** is known for its truffles.

⓮ Grignan

Drôme. 1,360. pl du Jeu de Ballon (04 75 46 56 75). Tue.
tourisme-paysdegrignan.com

Attractively situated on a rocky hill surrounded by fields of lavender, this charming little village owes its fame to Madame de Sévigné *(see p95)*, who wrote many of her celebrated letters while staying at the **Château de Grignan**.

Built during the 15th and 16th centuries, the château is one of the finest Renaissance structures in this part of France. Its interior contains a good collection of Louis XII furniture and Aubusson tapestries.

From the château's terrace, a panoramic view extends as far as the Vivarais mountains in the Ardèche. Directly below the terrace, the **Eglise de St-Saveur** was built in the 1530s, and contains the tomb of Madame de Sévigné, who died here in 1696 at the age of 69.

Château de Grignan
Tel 04 75 91 83 55. **Open** Apr–Oct: daily; Nov–Mar: Wed–Mon. **Closed** Jan 1, Dec 25.

⓯ Nyons

Drôme. 7,000. pl de la Libération (04 75 26 10 35). Thu.
paysdenyons.com

As a major center of olive production, Nyons is synonymous with olives in France. All manner of olive products are on sale at the Thursday mornin market, from soap to *tapenade*, the olive paste so popular in the south.

The **Quartier des Forts** is Nyons' oldest quarter, a warren of narrow streets and stepped alleyways, the most rewarding of which is the covered rue des Grands Forts. Spanning the rive Aygues is a graceful 13th-centur bridge; on its town side are several old mills turned into shops, where you can see the enormous presses once used t extract olive oil. The **Musée de l'Olivier** further explains the cultivation of the olive tree and the myriad local uses found for its fruit.

There is a fine view of the are from the belvedere overlookin the town. Sheltered by mountains, Nyons enjoys an almost exotic climate, with all the trees and plants of the Riviera to be found here.

Musée de l'Olivier
Pl Olivier de Serres. **Tel** 04 75 26 95 00 **Open** daily. for guide.

Environs

From Nyons, the D94 leads wes to **Suze-la-Rousse**, a pleasant wine-producing village which, during the Middle Ages, was th most important town in the area. Today, it is best known for its "university of wine," one of th most respected centers of enology in the world. It is

The hilltop town of Grignan and its Renaissance château

‹ve groves just outside Nyons

›used in the 14th-century **›âteau de Suze-la-Rousse**, ›e hunting lodge of the ›inces of Orange. The interior ›urtyard is a masterpiece of ›naissance architecture and ›me rooms preserve original ›int and stuccowork.

Château de Suze-la-Rousse
04 75 04 81 44. **Open** Apr–Oct: ›ily; Nov–Mar: Wed–Mon. **›osed** Jan 1, Dec 25.

›ying *boules* in Nyons

Briançon

›autes Alpes. 12,000. 1 pl du Temple (04 92 21 08 50). Wed. Altitude Jazz Festival ›arly Feb). **ot-briancon.fr**

›iançon – the highest town in ›urope at 4,330 ft (1,320 m) – ›as been an important ›ronghold since pre-Roman ›mes, guarding as it does the ›oad to the Col de Montgenèvre, one of the oldest and most important passes into Italy. At the beginning of the 18th century, the town was fortified with ramparts and gates – still splendidly intact – by Louis XIV's military architect, Vauban. If driving, park at the Champs de Mars, and enter the pedestrianized Old Town via the **Porte de Pignerol**.

This leads to the **grande rue**, a steep, narrow street with a stream running down the middle, bordered by lovely period houses. The nearby **Eglise de Notre-Dame** dates from 1718, and was also built by Vauban with an eye to defense. To visit Vauban's **citadel**, stop by the tourist office, which organizes guided tours.

Briançon is a major sports center, with skiing in winter; rafting, cycling, and paragliding in summer *(see pp664–5)*.

Environs
Just west of Briançon, the **Parc National des Ecrins** is the largest of the French national parks, offering lofty peaks and glaciers, and a magnificent variety of Alpine flowers.

The **Parc Régional du Queyras** is reached from Briançon over the rugged Col de l'Izoard. A wall of 9,850-ft (3,000-m) peaks separates this wild and beautiful national park from neighboring Italy.

⓱ Le Bourg d'Oisans

Isère. 3,000. to Grenoble. to Le Bourg d'Oisans. quai Girard (04 76 80 03 25). Sat. **bourgdoisans.com**

Le Bourg d'Oisans is an ideal base from which to explore the Romanche valley, providing numerous opportunities for sports such as cycling, rock-climbing, and skiing, in the nearby resort of **L'Alpe d'Huez**.

Silver and other minerals have been mined here since the Middle Ages, and today the town has a scientific reputation as a center for geology and mineralogy. Its **Musée des Minéraux et de la Faune des Alpes** is renowned for its collection of crystals and precious stones.

Musée des Minéraux et de la Faune des Alpes
Pl de l'Eglise. **Tel** 04 76 80 27 54. **Open** 2–6pm Sat–Sun (school hols: 2–6pm Wed–Mon). **Closed** Jan 1, mid-Nov–mid-Dec, Dec 25.

Life on High

The Alpine ibex is one of the rarest inhabitants of the French Alps, living high above the tree line for all but the coldest part of the year. Until the creation of the Parc National de la Vanoise *(see p323)*, this sure-footed climber had become almost extinct in France, but after rigorous conservation there are now over 500. Both males and females have horns; in the oldest males they can be almost 3 ft (1 m) long.

An ibex in the Parc National de la Vanoise

Grenoble Town Center

① Fort de la Bastille
② Musée Dauphinois
③ Ancien Palais du Parlement du Dauphiné
④ Collégiale St-André
⑤ Musée de Grenoble
⑥ Musée Archéologique Grenoble Saint-Laurent

0 meters 250
0 yards 250

Fort de la Bastille
Jardin Leon Moret
CHAMBERY
Église Saint-Laurent et Musée Archéologique
Parc Guy Pape
Jardins des Dauphins
Musée Dauphinois
Musée de Grenoble
Ancien Palais du Parlement du Dauphiné
Collégiale St-André
Musée de l'Ancien Évêché
Jardin de Ville
Musée de la Résistance et de Deportatio
LYON
QUAI DE FRANCE
Isère
PLACE HUBERT DUBEDOUT
Gare Routiere & Gare SNCF 500 m (550 yards)
PL VICTOR HUGO
COURS LAFONTAINE
Centre National d'Art Contemporain (Le Magasin)
PLACE DE VERDUN
MC2 (Maison de la Culture)
PLACE GRENETTE
PL STE-CLARE
PLACE AUX-HERBES
PLACE NOTRE-DAME
PL ST-ANDRÉ
Pont St-Laurent
Pont de la Citadelle
Pont Gontard

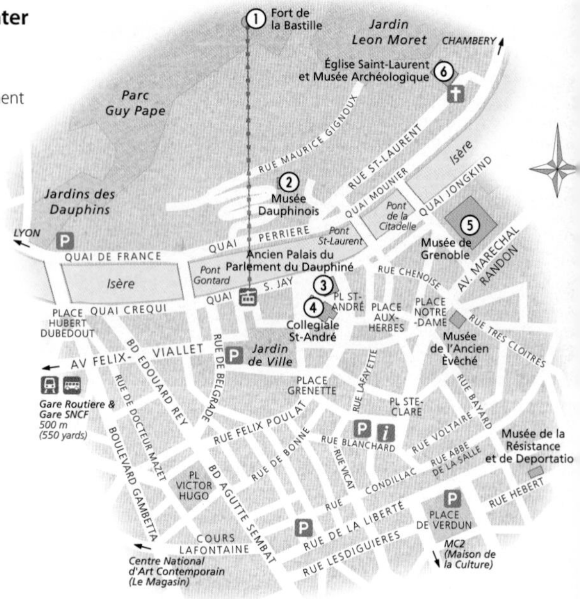

Key to Symbols *see back flap*

Fort de la Bastille on the Chartreuse mountain range, with views of Grenoble

⓲ Grenoble

Isère. 165,000.
14 rue de la République (04 76 42 41 41). Tue–Sun.
grenoble-tourisme.com

Ancient capital of the Dauphiné region and site of the 1968 Winter Olympics, Grenoble is a thriving city at the confluence of the Drac and Isère rivers, with the Vercors and Chartreuse massifs rising to the west and north. It is home to the science-oriented University of Grenoble, and is a center of chemical and electronics industries and nuclear research.

A cable car starting at quai Stéphane-Jay whisks you up to the 19th-century **Fort de la Bastille**, which has superb views of the city and surrounding mountains. Paths lead down through Parc Guy Pape and Jardin des Dauphins to the **Musée Dauphinois**, a regional museum in a 17th-century convent devoted to local history, arts, and crafts. Nearby, **Musée Archéologique Grenoble Saint-Laurent**, located in a former church with a 6th-century crypt, exhibits medieval artifacts and decorative and religious art.

On the left bank of the Isère, the focus of life is the pedestrian area around the place Grenette. Nearby, place St-André is the heart of the medieval city, overlooked by Grenoble's oldest buildings, including the 13th-century **Collégiale St-André** and the 16th-century **Ancien Palais du Parlement du Dauphiné**.

The **Musée de Grenoble** exhibits works by Chagall, Picasso, and Matisse. The **Musée de l'Ancien Evêché** recounts the history of Isère, and includes the 4th-century baptistry. On rue Hébert, the **Musée de la Résistance et de la Déportation** has documents relating to the French Resistance. Displays of contemporary art can be seen at **Le Magasin** (Centre National d'Art Contemporain) a renovated warehouse. In the Quartier Malherbe, **MC2** (Mais de la Culture) hosts concerts, dance, and theater.

Musée Dauphinois
30 rue Maurice Gignoux. **Tel** 04 57 5 89 01. **Open** Wed–Mon. **Closed** Jan May 1, Dec 25.

Musée Archéologique Grenoble Saint-Laurent
Pl St-Laurent. **Tel** 04 76 44 78 68. **Open** Wed–Mon. **musee-archeologique-grenoble.fr**

Musée de Grenoble
5 pl de Lavalette. **Tel** 04 76 63 44 44. **Open** Wed–Mon. **Closed** Jan 1, May Dec 25.

Grenoble's gondola cable car

For hotels and restaurants in this region see pp554–71 and pp576–603

Musée de l'Ancien Evêché
2 rue Très Cloîtres. **Tel** 04 76 03 15 25. **Open** daily. **Closed** Wed am.

Musée de la Résistance et de la Déportation
14 rue Hébert. **Tel** 04 76 42 38 53. **open** daily. **Closed** Tue am, Jan 1, May 1, Dec 25.

Le Magasin (CNAC)
155 cours Berriat. **Tel** 04 76 21 95 84. **Open** Tue–Sun pm only (during exhibs). **magasin-cnac.org**

MC2
4 rue Paul Claudel. **Tel** 04 76 00 79 79. **Open** varies – phone to check. **mc2grenoble.fr**

19 The Vercors

Isère & Drôme. Grenoble. Romans-sur-Isère, St-Marcellin, Grenoble. Pont-en-Royans, Romans-sur-Isère. Pont-en-Royans (04 76 36 09 10). Maison du Parc: 255 chemin des Fusillés, Lans-en-Vercors 38250 (04 76 94 38 26) **parc-du-vercors.fr**

To the south and west of Grenoble, the Vercors is one of France's most magnificent regional parks – a wilderness of pine forests, mountains, waterfalls, caves, and deep, narrow gorges.

The D531 out of Grenoble passes through **Villard-de-Lans** – a good base for excursions – and continues west to the dark **Gorges de la Bournes**. About 5 miles (8 km) further west, the hamlet of **Pont-en-Royans** is sited on a limestone gorge, its stone houses built into the rocks overlooking the river Bourne.

South of Pont-en-Royans along the D76, the **Route de Combe-Laval** snakes along a sheer cliff above the roaring river. The **Grands Goulets**, 4 miles (6.5 km) to the east, is a spectacularly deep, narrow gorge overlooked by sheer cliffs that virtually shut out the sky above. The best-known mountain in the park is the **Mont Aiguille**, a soaring outcrop of 6,844 ft (2,086 m).

The Vercors was a key base for the French Resistance during World War II. In July 1944 the Germans launched an aerial attack on the region, flattening several of its villages. There are Resistance museums at Vassieux and Grenoble.

Cows grazing in the Chartreuse

20 The Chartreuse

Isère & Savoie. Grenoble, Chambéry. Grenoble, Voiron. St-Pierre-de-Chartreuse. St-Pierre-de-Chartreuse (04 76 88 62 08).

From Grenoble, the D512 leads north towards Chambéry into the Chartreuse, a majestic region of mountains and forests where hydroelectricity was invented in the late 19th century. The **Monastère de la Grande Chartreuse** is the main local landmark, situated just west of St-Pierre-de-Chartreuse off the D520-B.

Founded by St Bruno in 1084, the monastery owes its fame to the sticky green and yellow Chartreuse liqueurs first produced by the monks in 1605. The recipe, based on a secret herbal elixir of 130 ingredients, is now produced in the nearby town of Voiron.

The monastery itself is inhabited by about 40 monks who live in silence and seclusion. It is not open to visitors, but there is a museum at the entrance, the **Musée de la Correrie**, which faithfully depicts the daily routine of the Carthusian monks.

Musée de la Correrie
St-Pierre-de-Chartreuse. **Tel** 04 76 88 60 45. **Open** May–Sep: daily; Mar–Apr & Oct–Nov: Mon-Fri pm only, Sat & Sun.

A farm in the pine-clad mountains of the Chartreuse

㉑ Chambéry

Savoie. 61,000.
5 bis pl Palais de Justice (04 79 33 42 47). Tue, Sat.
chambery-tourisme.com

Once the capital of Savoy, this dignified city has aristocratic airs and a distinctly Italianate feel. Its best-loved monument is the extravagant **Fontaine des Eléphants** on rue de Boigne, erected in 1838 to honor the Comte de Boigne, who left to his home town some of the fortune he amassed in India.

The 14th-century **Château des Ducs de Savoie**, at the opposite end of rue de Boigne, is now occupied by the Préfecture. Only parts of the building, such as the late-Gothic Ste-Chapelle, can be visited, via guided tours arranged with the tourist office.

On the southeast edge of town is the 17th-century country house, **Les Charmettes**, where the philosopher Rousseau lived with his mistress Madame de Warens. It is worth a visit for its gardens and museum of memorabilia.

Les Charmettes
892 chemin des Charmettes. **Tel** 04 79 33 39 44. **Open** Wed–Mon. **Closed** public hols. with fee.

Roman statue in the Temple of Diana

The Lac du Bourget at Aix-les-Bains

㉒ Aix-les-Bains

Savoie. 26,000. pl Maurice Mollard (04 79 88 68 00). Wed & Sat am. Festival Musilac (Jul). **aixlesbains.com**

The great Romantic poet Lamartine rhapsodized over the beauty of Lac du Bourget, site of the gracious spa town of Aix-les-Bains. The heart of the town is the 19th-century **Thermes Nationaux**, thermal baths which were first enjoyed by the Romans over 2,000 years ago – in the basement are the remains of the original Roman baths. The ruins are closed to visitors due to safety reasons, but the Thermes Nationaux spa is open all year. Opposite the baths, the 2nd-century AD. **Temple of Diana** contains a collection of Gallo-Roman artifacts. The nearby **Musée Faure** has some stunning Impressionist paintings by Degas and Sisley, Rodin sculptures, and Lamartine memorabilia.

Thermes Nationaux
Pl Maurice Mollard. **Tel** 04 79 35 38 50. **Open** Mon–Sat. for treatment.
valvital.fr

Musée Faure
Villa des Chimères, 10 bd des Côtes. **Tel** 04 79 61 06 57. **Open** Wed–Mon. **Closed** Dec 20–Jan 5, public hols.

Environs

Boats leave from Aix's Grand Port and sail across Lac du Bourget to the **Abbaye d'Hautecombe**, a Benedictine abbey containing the mausoleum of the Savoyard dynasty.

The small town of **Le Revard**, just east of Aix on the D913, has spectacular views of the lake and Mont Blanc.

㉓ Annecy

Haute Savoie. 51,000.
1 rue Jean Jaurès (04 50 45 00 33). Tue, Fri–Sun. Fête du Lac (firework display; 1st Sat Aug).
lac-annecy.com

Annecy is one of the most charming towns in the Alps, set at the northern tip of Lac

Annecy's 12th-century Palais de l'Isle, with the Thiou canal in the foreground

For hotels and restaurants in this region see pp554–71 and pp576–603

Cycling along the shores of Lac Léman (Lake Geneva)

d'Annecy and surrounded by snow-capped mountains. Its small medieval quarter is laced with canals, flower-covered bridges, and arcaded streets. Strolling around is the main attraction here, though there are a couple of specific sights worth having a look at more closely: the formidable **Palais de l'Isle**, a 12th-century prison in the middle of the Thiou canal; and the turreted **Château d'Annecy**, set high on a hill above the town with impressive views of Vieil Annecy and the crystal-clear lake beyond.

The best spot for swimming and watersports is at the eastern end of the avenue d'Albigny near the Imperial Palace hotel, while boat trips leave from quai Napoléon III.

Environs

One of the best ways to enjoy the area's spectacular scenery is to take a boat from Annecy to **Talloires**, a tiny lakeside village celebrated for its hotels and restaurants. Facing Talloires across the lake is the 15th-century **Château de Duingt** (not open to visitors).

On the west bank of the lake, the Semnoz mountain and its summit, the **Crêt de Châtillon**, offer superb views of Mont Blanc and the Alps *(see pp326–7)*.

24 Lac Léman

Haute Savoie & Switzerland. Geneva. Geneva, Thonon-les-Bains, Évian-les-Bains. Thonon-les-Bains (04 50 71 55 55).
thononlesbains.com

The stirring scenery and gentle climate of the French shore of Lake Geneva (Lac Léman to the French) has made it a popular and fashionable resort area since the first spa buildings were erected at Évian-les-Bains in 1839.

Yvoire is a fine place to begin a visit to the area. This medieval port is guarded by a 14th- century castle, and its houses are bedecked with colorful flower boxes.

Further east along Lac Léman is **Thonon-les-Bains**, a prosperous, well-manicured little spa town perched on a cliff overlooking the lake. A funicular takes you down to Rives, the small harbor at the foot of the cliffs, where sailboats can be rented and cruise boats to the Swiss cities of Geneva and Lausanne call in. Just outside the town is the 15th-century **Château de Ripaille**, made famous by its one-time resident, Duke Amadeus VIII, who later became antipope (Felix V).

Though it has been modernized and acquired an international reputation for its eponymous spring water, **Évian-les-Bains** still exudes a polite *vie en rose* charm. The tree-lined lakefront promenade teems with leisurely strollers, while more energetic types can avail themselves of all kinds of sporting facilities including tennis, golf, riding, sailing, and skiing in the winter. State-of-the-art spa treatments are available, and the exotic domed casino is busy at night, offering blackjack, roulette, and baccarat among other games.

From Évian there are daily ferries across Lake Geneva to Lausanne in Switzerland, as well as coach excursions into the surrounding mountains.

The 14th-century castle at Yvoire, overlooking Lac Léman (Lake Geneva)

SOUTHWEST FRANCE

Introducing Southwest France

The southwest is farming France, a green and peaceful land nurturing crops from sunflowers to *foie gras*. Other key country products include Landes forest timber, Bordeaux wines, and Cognac. Major modern industries, including aerospace, are focused on the two chief cities, Bordeaux and Toulouse. Visitors are mainly drawn to the wide Atlantic beaches, the ski slopes of the Pyrenees, and the rural calm of the Dordogne. The major sights of this favored region are shown here and include some of France's most celebrated Romanesque buildings.

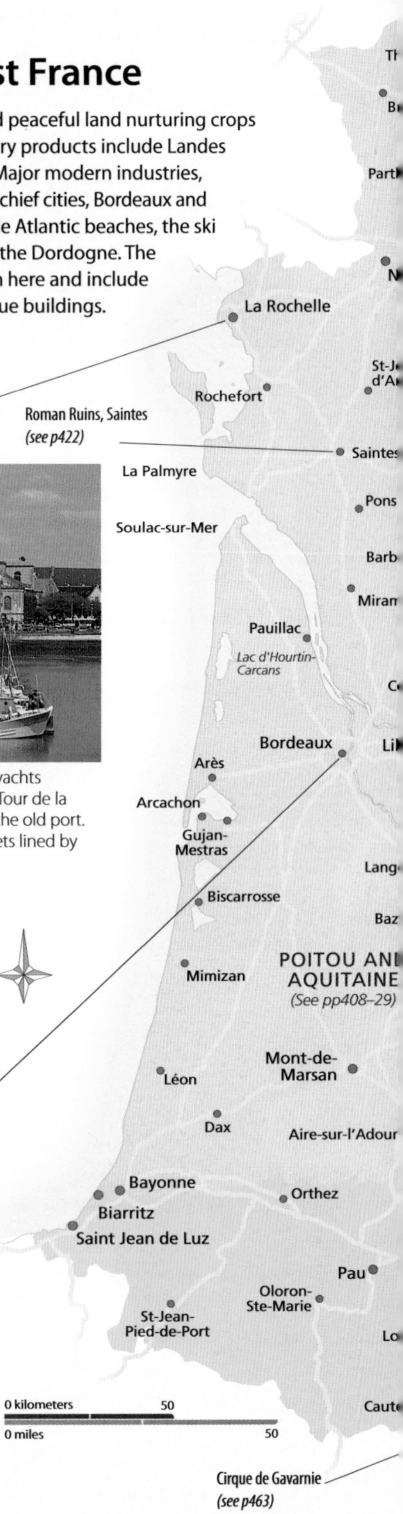

Roman Ruins, Saintes
(see p422)

La Rochelle's harbor is today a haven for pleasure yachts as well as an important commercial port *(see p420)*. Tour de la Chaîne and Tour St-Nicolas protect the entrance of the old port. The town's historic center is filled with cobbled streets lined by merchants' houses.

Bordeaux is a town of grand buildings and monuments, including its theater. The Monument aux Girondins, with its magnificent bronze statues and fountains, stands at the 18th-century Esplanade des Quinconces *(see pp424–5)*.

La Rochelle
Rochefort
Saintes
Pons
La Palmyre
Soulac-sur-Mer
Pauillac
Lac d'Hourtin-Carcans
Bordeaux
Arès
Arcachon
Gujan-Mestras
Biscarrosse
Mimizan
POITOU AND AQUITAINE
(See pp408–29)
Mont-de-Marsan
Léon
Dax
Aire-sur-l'Adour
Bayonne
Biarritz
Saint Jean de Luz
Orthez
Pau
Oloron-Ste-Marie
St-Jean-Pied-de-Port
0 kilometers 50
0 miles 50

Cirque de Gavarnie
(see p463)

◀ Château de Castelnaud, overlooking the river Dordogne

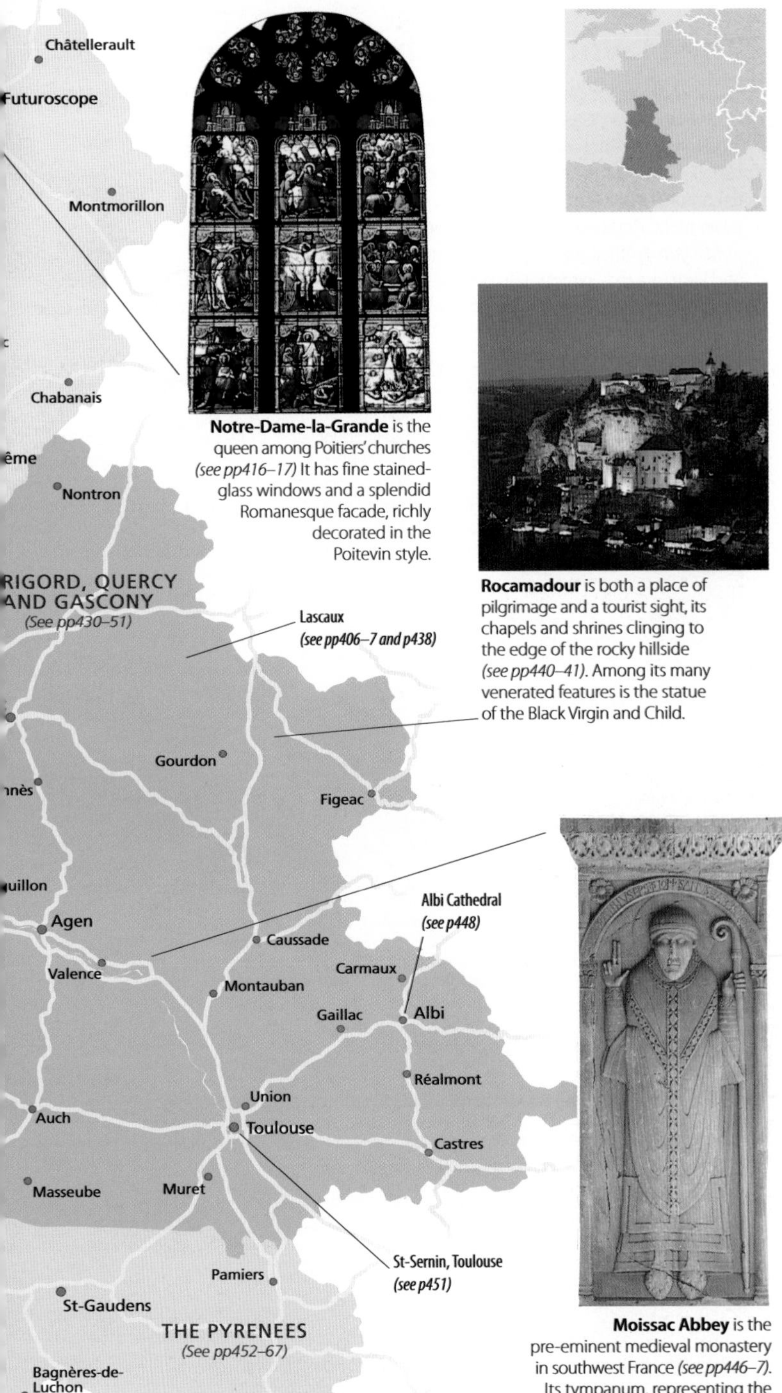

Notre-Dame-la-Grande is the queen among Poitiers' churches *(see pp416–17)* It has fine stained-glass windows and a splendid Romanesque facade, richly decorated in the Poitevin style.

Rocamadour is both a place of pilgrimage and a tourist sight, its chapels and shrines clinging to the edge of the rocky hillside *(see pp440–41)*. Among its many venerated features is the statue of the Black Virgin and Child.

Moissac Abbey is the pre-eminent medieval monastery in southwest France *(see pp446–7)*. Its tympanum, representing the Apocalypse, and the cloister capitals are outstanding examples of Romanesque sculpture.

The Flavors of Southwest France

"Great cooking and great wines make a paradise on earth," said Henri IV of his own region, Gascony. The southwest does indeed fulfill the requirements of the most demanding gourmet. The Atlantic coast supplies fine seafood; Bordeaux produces some of France's best wines to complement its rich cooking; geese and ducks provide the fat that is key to local cuisine; and regional produce includes delicacies such as *foie gras*, truffles, and wild mushrooms. The Pyrenees offer beef and lamb grazed on mountain pastures, cheese, and *charcuterie*, and the Basque country adds the spicy notes of red peppers and fine chocolate.

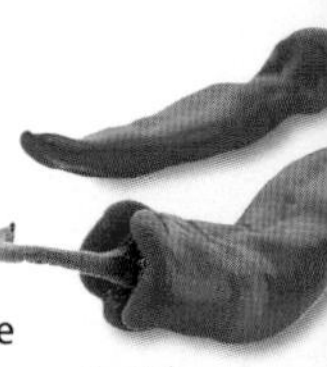

Espelette peppers

Walnuts, one of the southwest's most famous products

Poitou and Aquitaine

The coast is famous for its seafood, and is the most important oyster-producing region of France – the oysters of Marennes-Oleron are of especially high quality. The species of blue algae on which they feed give them a distinctive green coloring. Oysters are usually served simply with lemon or shallot vinegar, but in Bordeaux they like to eat them with little sausages. Mussels are also raised here, and the sea yields a variety of fish. Eels, lamprey, and sturgeon are caught in the Gironde estuary.

Poitou-Charentes is one of France's main goat-rearing areas, producing cheeses such as *chabichou de Poitou*, a small, soft, cylindrical cheese of distinct flavor.

Périgord, Quercy, and Gascony

High-quality ducks, geese, ar poultry form the basis of the cuisine of this region, and th fat is a key ingredient of mar dishes from simple *pommes sarladaises* (potatoes cooked goose fat) to *confit*, where entire duck legs are preserve in their own fat. The ultimate

Selection of traditional southwestern *charcuterie*

Regional Dishes and Specialties

Pink garlic

Duck is one of the essential ingredients of southwestern cooking, and is served in a variety of ways. The *magret* is the breast – the best of all coming from a duck that has been bred for *foie gras*. Usually served pink *(rose)*, it may be served with a variety of sauces but is most perfectly complemented by the smoky flavor of local cèpe mushrooms in season. Duck *confit* is usually made with the legs, but gizzards are also preserved in this way. *Foie gras* is the most expensive (and controversial) product, resulting from the process of *gavage*, when the duck or goose is force-fed maize to enlarge and enrich its liver. *Foie gras* can be eaten freshly cooked, served with sauce or fruit, or preserved and served with toast or brioche, ideally accompanied by a sweet white wine such as Sauternes.

Omelette aux truffes For this luxurious omelette the filling is local black truffles, with more sliced over the top.

attened Toulouse geese, the source of *foie gras*

outhwestern dish has to be *assoulet*, a stew of duck or oose, sausages, pork, and vhite beans topped with a rust of breadcrumbs; it rouses fierce competition mong the dedicated chefs f the region.

Luxury ingredients enhance hese basics: walnut oil is dded to salads, and slivers of xpensive truffles perfume auces or omelettes. Wild nushrooms are eagerly ought in season, and are nost delicious cooked simply vith garlic, shallots, and arsley. The region is one of he main producers of garlic, vhich appears studded into neat or served as whole aked heads. The finest fruits nclude *reines-claudes* (greenages) and the celebrated lums of Agen, which are ried as prunes or added to ishes of rabbit or hare.

The Pyrenees

From the mountain pastures come beef and lamb of high quality, including Barèges mutton, as well as river trout and an array of excellent *charcuterie*. Strong cheeses of goat's or ewe's milk are sometimes served with jam made from the black cherries of Itxassou. One of the most popular dishes is *garbure*, a hearty stew of cabbage, bacon, and confit of duck or goose.

Fishermen opening oysters at a local maritime festival

Basque cuisine has its own distinct identity, with the red Espelette pepper adding a touch of spice to chorizo, *piperade*, or *chipirones* (baby squid cooked in their own ink). Succulent Bayonne ham is made from pigs that forage for acorns and chestnuts. Bayonne was also home to the first chocolatiers in France – 17th-century Jewish refugees from the Inquisition – and the town still makes top-quality dark, bitter chocolate.

On the Menu

Cagouilles à la charentaise Snails with sausage meat, herbs, and wine.

Entrecôte à la bordelaise Steak in sauce of red wine, shallots, and bone marrow.

Farçi poitevin Cabbage stuffed with bacon, pork, and sorrel.

Gasconnade Leg of lamb with garlic and anchovy.

Mouclade Mussels in curry sauce, from the spice port of La Rochelle.

Salade landaise Salad of *foie gras*, gizzards and *confit*.

Ttoro Basque mixed fish and shellfish stew with potatoes, tomatoes, and onions.

Cassoulet This is a stew of vhite beans cooked with a ariety of sausages and cuts of neat, such as pork or duck.

Piperade Eggs are added to a stew of peppers, onions, tomatoes, and garlic, with Bayonne ham laid on top.

Croustade Thin pastry is layered with melted butter and apples, perfumed with Armagnac and vanilla.

France's Wine Regions: Bordeaux

Bordeaux is the world's largest fine wine region, and, for red wines, certainly the most familiar outside France. Following Henry II's marriage to Eleanor of Aquitaine, three centuries of courtly commerce with England ensured that claret was served at the finest foreign tables. In the 19th century, canny merchants capitalized on this fame and brought fantastic financial prosperity to the region, and with it, the famous 1855 Classification of the Médoc, a league table of châteaus that is still very much in force today.

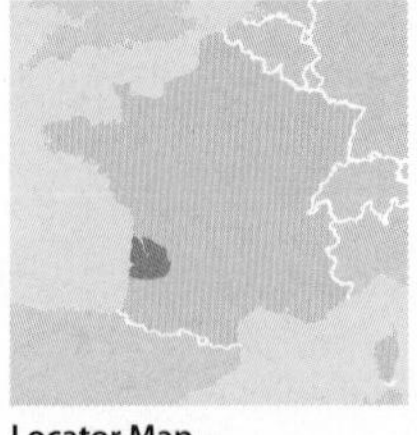

Locator Map

Bordeaux wine region

Picking red Merlot grapes at Château Palmer

Wine Regions

The great wine-producing areas of Bordeaux straddle two great rivers; the land between the rivers ("Entre-Deux-Mers") produces lesser, mainly white wines. The rivers, and the river port of Bordeaux itself, have been crucial to the trade in Bordeaux wines; some of the prettiest châteaus line the river banks, enabling easy transportation.

0 kilometers 15

0 miles 15

Key Facts About Bordeaux Wines

Location and Climate
Climatic conditions may vary not only from one year to another, but also within the region itself. The soils tend to be gravelly in the Médoc and Graves, and clayey on the right bank.

Grape Varieties

The five main red grape varieties are ***Cabernet Franc***, ***Cabernet Sauvignon***, ***Merlot***, ***Petit Verdot***, and ***Malbec***. Cabernet Sauvignon is the dominant grape on the west side of the Gironde, Merlot to the east. Most Bordeaux reds are, however, a blend of grapes. ***Sauvignon Blanc*** and ***Sémillon*** are grown and often blended for both dry and sweet whites.

Good Producers
(reds) Latour, Margaux, Haut-Brion, Cos d'Estournel, Léoville Las Cases, Léoville Barton, Lascombes, Pichon Longueville, Pichon Lalande, Lynch-Bages, Palmer, Rausan-Ségla, Duhart Milon, d'Angludet, Léoville Poyferré, Branaire Ducru, Ducru Beaucaillou, Malescot St-Exupéry, Cantemerle, Phélan-Ségur, Chasse-Spleen, Poujeaux, Domaine de Chevalier, Pape Clément, Cheval Blanc, Canon, Pavie, l'Angelus, Troplong Mondot, La Conseillante, Lafleur, Trotanoy.

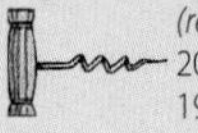

Good Vintages
(reds) 2009, 2006, 2005, 2003, 2000, 1998, 1996.

Key

- Médoc
- Blaye
- Bourg
- Entre-Deux-Mers
- Graves
- Pessac-Léognan
- Cérons
- Barsac
- Sauternes
- Libournais District
- Pomerol
- St-Émilion

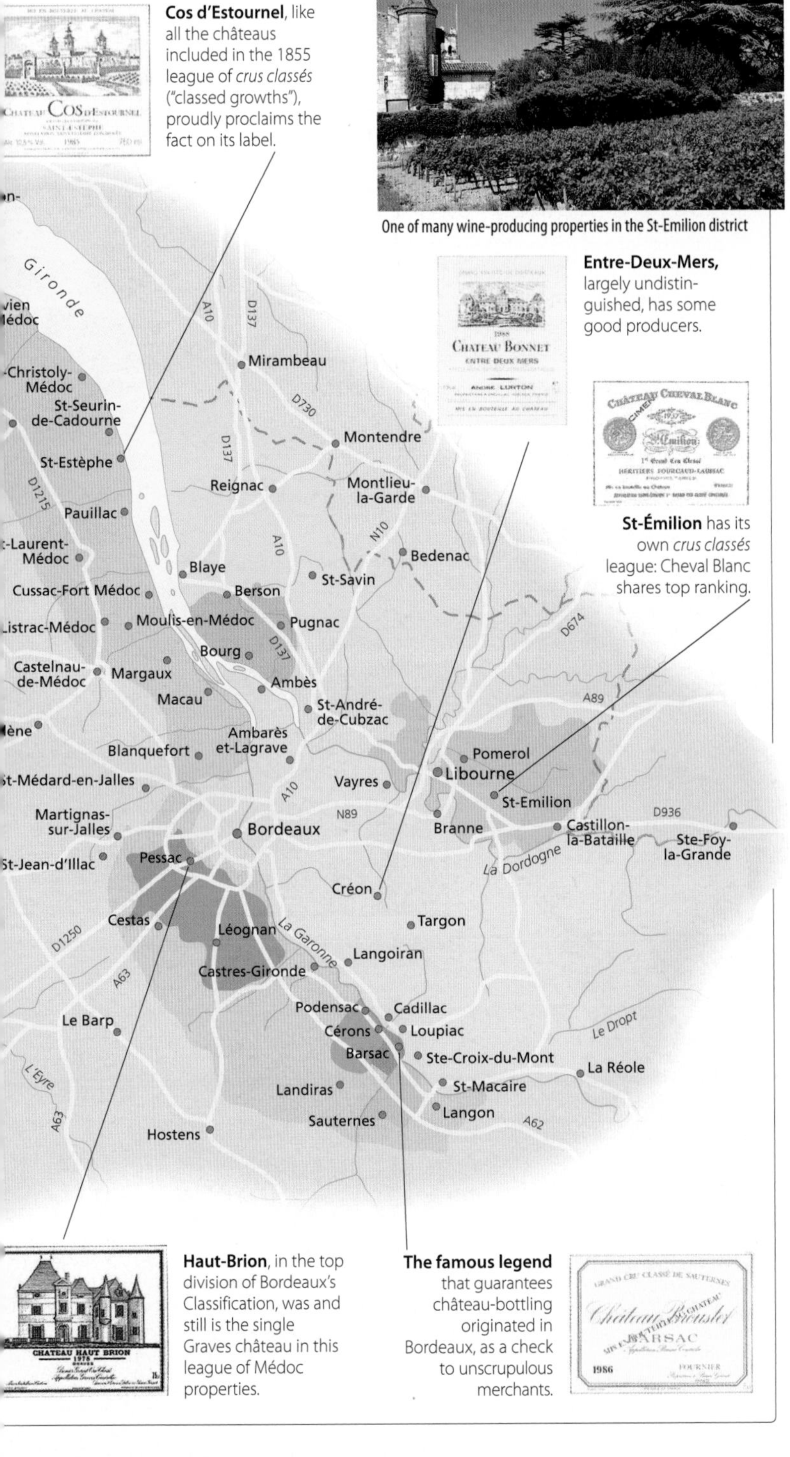

Cos d'Estournel, like all the châteaus included in the 1855 league of *crus classés* ("classed growths"), proudly proclaims the fact on its label.

One of many wine-producing properties in the St-Emilion district

Entre-Deux-Mers, largely undistinguished, has some good producers.

St-Émilion has its own *crus classés* league: Cheval Blanc shares top ranking.

Haut-Brion, in the top division of Bordeaux's Classification, was and still is the single Graves château in this league of Médoc properties.

The famous legend that guarantees château-bottling originated in Bordeaux, as a check to unscrupulous merchants.

The Road to Compostela

Throughout the Middle Ages millions of Christians visited Santiago de Compostela in Spain to pay homage at the shrine of St. James (Santiago). They traveled across France staying in monasteries or simple shelters and would return with a scallop shell, the symbol of St. James, as a souvenir. Most pilgrims went in hope of redemption and were often on the road for years. In 1140, a monk called Picaud wrote one of the world's first travel guides about the pilgrimage. Today, travelers can follow the same routes, passing through ancient towns and villages with their magnificent shrines and churches.

Foreign pilgrims joined at ports such as St-Malo.

The original cathedral of Santiago de Compostela was built in 813 by Alfonso II over the tomb of St. James. In 1075 construction started on the grandiose Romanesque church seen today which has, among other later additions, a resplendent 17th–18th-century Baroque facade.

The routes converged on Santiago de Compostela.

Most pilgrims crossed the Pyrenees at Roncesvalles.

James the Greater, an apostle, came to Spain to spread the Gospel, according to legend. On his return to Judaea, he was martyred by Herod. His remains were taken to Spain by boat and lay hidden for 800 years.

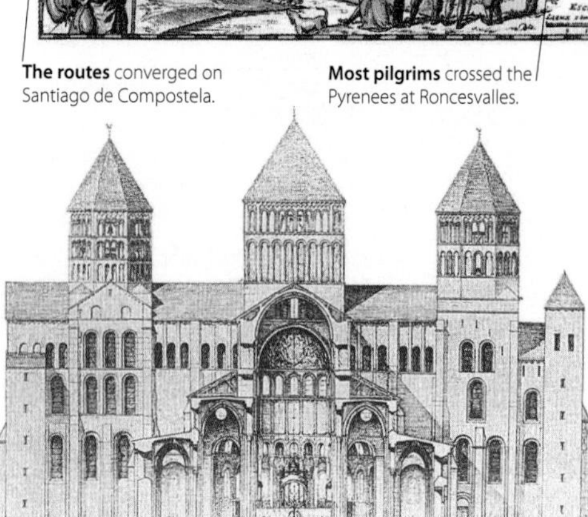

The powerful Cluny monastery in Burgundy *(see pp52–3)*, and its affiliated monasteries, played an important role in promoting the pilgrimage. They built shelters and set up churches and shrines housing precious relics, to encourage the pilgrims on their way.

he Pilgrims' Way

aris, Vézelay (see pp340–41), *Le Puy* (see p368) *and Arles re the rallying points for the four "official" routes across rance. They cross the Pyrenees at Roncesvalles and Somport, nd merge at Puente la Reina to form one route, culminating t the shrine on the Galician coast.*

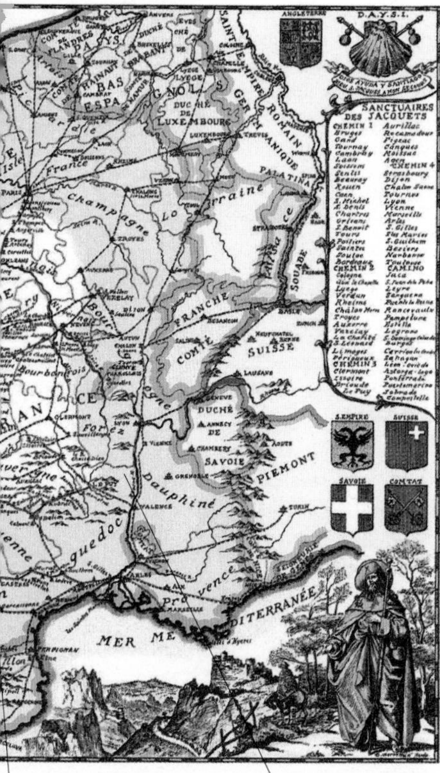

Conques purloined relics to boost its prestige.

Le Puy was a main rallying point for pilgrims.

The reliquary of Ste-Foy, at Conques, is in one of many elaborate shrines on the way which drew crowds of pilgrims. A saint's relics were thought to have miraculous powers.

The name Santiago de Compostela is believed to originate from the Latin *Campus stellae* (field of stars). Legend has it that strange stars were seen hovering over a field in 814 and on July 25, now the feast of Santiago, the saint's remains were found. Subsequent evidence showed that St. James's remains were never in Compostela after all.

What to see Today

Huge Romanesque churches, including Ste-Madeleine at Vézelay *(see p340)*, Ste-Foy at Conques *(pp372–3)*, and St-Sernin at Toulouse *(p451)*, along with many small chapels, were built to accommodate large numbers of pilgrims.

Basilique Ste-Madeleine, Vézelay

The first recorded pilgrim was the bishop of Le Puy in 951. But pilgrims have probably been coming to Santiago since 814, soon after the saint's tomb was found.

Caves of the Southwest

Southwest France is well-known for its spectacular rock formations, created by the slow accumulation of dissolved mineral deposits. Caves and rock shelters exist throughout limestone country in France. But in the foothills of the Pyrenees and the Dordogne they also have something else to offer the visitor: a collection of extraordinary rock paintings, some dating back to the last Ice Age. These art forms were created when prehistoric peoples evolved and began engraving, painting, and carving. This unique artistic tradition lasted for more than 25,000 years, reaching its zenith around 17,000 years ago. Some very fine examples of cave painting are still visible today.

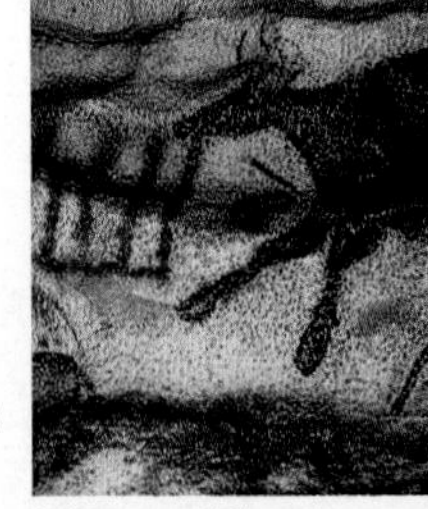

Ancient cave paintings at Lascaux

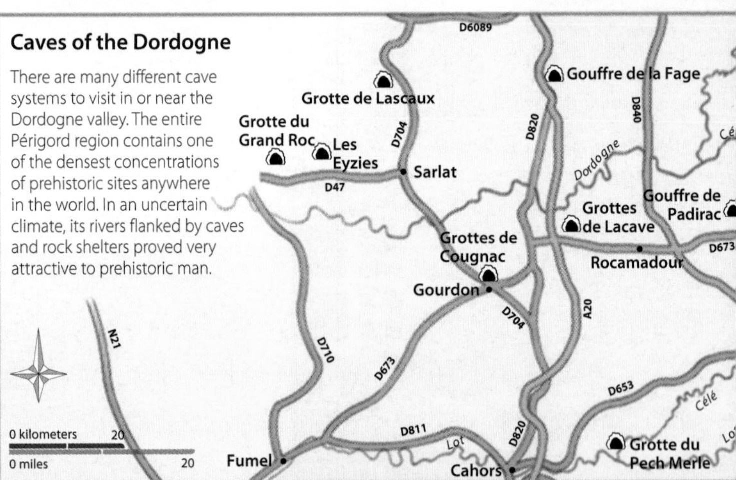

Caves of the Dordogne

There are many different cave systems to visit in or near the Dordogne valley. The entire Périgord region contains one of the densest concentrations of prehistoric sites anywhere in the world. In an uncertain climate, its rivers flanked by caves and rock shelters proved very attractive to prehistoric man.

Cave Formation

Limestone is laid down in layers containing fissures that allow water to penetrate beneath the surface. Over thousands of years, the water slowly dissolves the rock, first forming potholes and then larger caverns. Stalactites develop where water drips from the cave roof; stalagmites grow upwards from the floor.

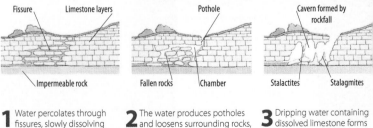

Grotte du Grand Roc in the Vézère valley, Périgord

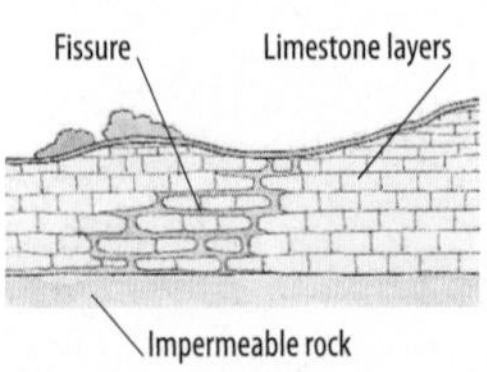

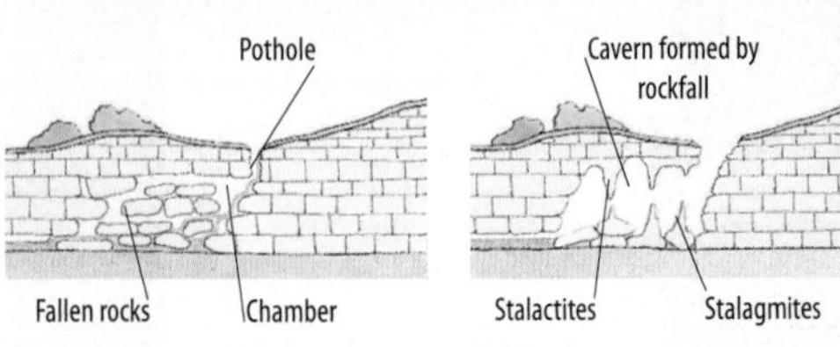

1 Water percolates through fissures, slowly dissolving the surrounding rock.

2 The water produces potholes and loosens surrounding rocks, which gradually fall away.

3 Dripping water containing dissolved limestone forms stalactites and stalagmites.

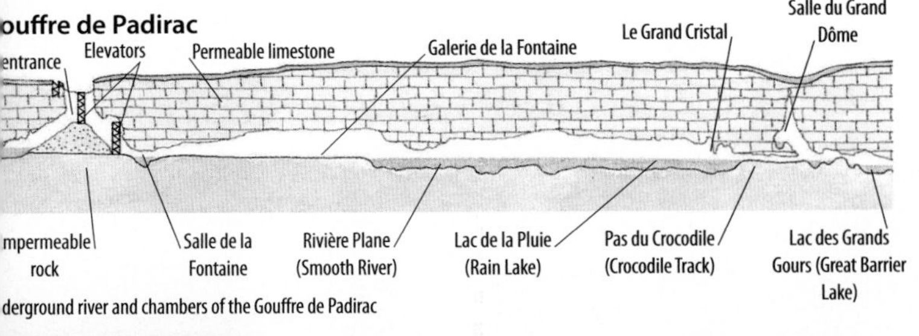

derground river and chambers of the Gouffre de Padirac

ehistoric caves at Les Eyzies

isiting the Caves

ougnac contains chasms gouffres") and galleries and its ehistoric paintings include uman figures. Around **Les yzies** *(see pp438–9)* are the ves of **Les Combarelles**, and **ont de Gaume**, which have eautiful prehistoric paintings, rawings, and engravings, as oes **Rouffignac** in its network f caves. **Grand Roc** has cham- ers containing a profusion of alactites and stalagmites. ortheast of Les Eyzies is the ock shelter of **L'Abri du Cap lanc**, with its rare frieze of orses and bison dating from round 14,000 years ago.

On the south bank of the ordogne, an underground ver and lake with extraordinary ock formations can be seen at **acave**. The gigantic chasm and averns at **Gouffre de Padirac** *442)* are even more spectacular. ne caves at **Lascaux** with the nest prehistoric paintings have een closed but the exceptional eplica at **Lascaux II** *(p438)* is ell worth seeing. Farther outh, **Pech-Merle's** caverns *p442–3)* have impressive ock formations. **Niaux**, in the othills of the Pyrenees, can lso be visited.

The Story of Cave Art

The first prehistoric cave paintings in Europe were discovered in northwest Spain in 1879. Since then, over 200 decorated caves and rock shelters have been found in Spain and France, mainly in the Dordogne region. A wide range of clues, from stone lamps to miraculously preserved footprints, has helped pre-historians to work out the techniques the cave artists used. But their motives are still not clear. Nearly all the paintings are of animals, with few humans, and many of them are in inaccessible underground chambers. The paintings undoubtedly had a symbolic or magical significance; a new theory suggests they were the work of shamans.

The techniques used by Ice Age artists, who worked by lamplight, included cutting outlines into soft rock, using natural contours as part of the design. Black lines and shading were produced by charcoal, while color washes were applied with mineral pigments such as kaolin and haematite. Hand silhouettes were made by sucking up diluted pigment and blowing it through a plant stem to form a fine spray. When the hand was removed from the rock, its eerie shape was left behind.

Decorated stone lamp discovered in Lascaux cave

Kaolin

Charcoal

Haematite

The Great Bull from the Hall of Bulls frieze at Lascaux

POITOU AND AQUITAINE

eux-Sèvres · Vienne · Charente-Maritime · Charente · Gironde · Landes

his vast area of southwest France spans a quarter of the ountry's windswept Atlantic coastline, a great expanse f fine sandy beaches. The region stretches from the arshes of the Marais Poitevin to the great pine forests of the andes. Central to it is the celebrated wine region of Bordeaux nd its great châteaus.

he turbulent history of Poitou and quitaine, fought over for centuries, has ft a rich architectural and cultural eritage. The great arch and mphitheater at Saintes bear witness Roman influence in the area. In the iddle Ages, the pilgrimage route to antiago de Compostela *(see pp404–5)* eated an impressive legacy of omanesque churches, such as those at oitiers and Parthenay, as well as tiny apels and glowing frescoes. The undred Years' War *(see pp56–7)* caused reat upheaval but also resulted in the onstruction of mighty defense keeps by e English Plantagenet kings. As a result f the Wars of Religion *(see pp58–9)*, many towns, churches, and châteaus were destroyed and had to be rebuilt.

Present-day Poitiers is a big, thriving commercial center. To the west are the historic ports of La Rochelle and Rochefort. Farther south, the wine-producing district of Bordeaux combines with Cognac, famous for its brandy, to supply an important part of the region's income. The city of Bordeaux is as prosperous today as in Roman times, combining a lively cultural scene with elegant 18th-century architecture. Its wines complement the region's cuisine: lampreys, mussels, and oysters from the coast; and salty lamb and goat's cheeses from the inland pastures.

uttered houses in St-Martin-de-Ré, on Ile de Ré, off the coast of La Rochelle

Aerial view of Pointe de la Fumée, famous for its seafood restaurants, near Fouras, south of La Rochelle

Exploring Poitou and Aquitaine

Blessed with a seemingly endless Atlantic coastline, abundant navigable waterways, excellent ports, and the finest wine and brandy in the world, the region is ideal for a relaxing holiday. Today most summer visitors head straight for the beaches with their thundering waves, but there is also a lush countryside inland with a lot to offer. Fine medieval architecture can be seen along the pilgrim's route to Santiago de Compostela *(see pp404–5)*, and châteaus of all shapes and sizes characterize the wine districts around Bordeaux. The only modern city of major importance in the region, Bordeaux is worth a visit for its elegant 18th-century architecture as well as for its rich cultural life. The vast man-made forest of Les Landes also adds to this greatly undervalued corner of France.

Beachlife in Bassin d'Arcachon on the Côte d'Argent

Getting Around

The region's main highway is the A10 connecting Paris and Poitiers with Bordeaux and points east, such as Toulouse, west to Rochefort and south to Bayonne and Spain. This road carries most of the area's heavy traffic, relieving the excellent smaller roads. Bordeaux can be reached by TGV direct from Lille (Eurostar interchange), and the Paris–Poitiers–Angoulême–Bordeaux TGV line has halved rail travel times (Paris–Bordeaux 3¼ hrs). Bordeaux, Poitiers, and La Rochelle have international airports (direct flights to UK), and Bordeaux also has bus services to most European capitals. Poitiers has buses to nearby towns.

For additional map symbols *see back flap*

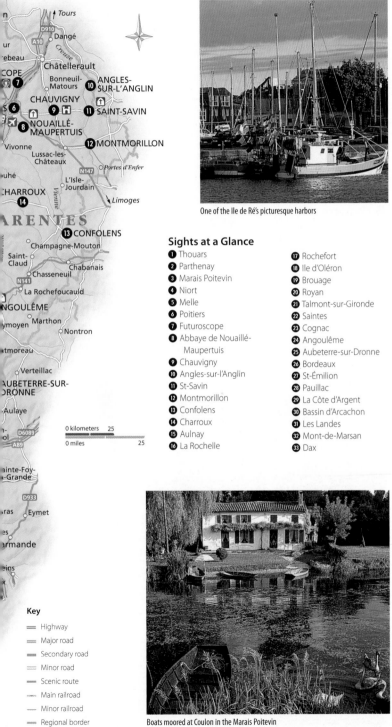

One of the Ile de Ré's picturesque harbors

Sights at a Glance

1. Thouars
2. Parthenay
3. Marais Poitevin
4. Niort
5. Melle
6. Poitiers
7. Futuroscope
8. Abbaye de Nouaillé-Maupertuis
9. Chauvigny
10. Angles-sur-l'Anglin
11. St-Savin
12. Montmorillon
13. Confolens
14. Charroux
15. Aulnay
16. La Rochelle
17. Rochefort
18. Ile d'Oléron
19. Brouage
20. Royan
21. Talmont-sur-Gironde
22. Saintes
23. Cognac
24. Angoulême
25. Aubeterre-sur-Dronne
26. Bordeaux
27. St-Émilion
28. Pauillac
29. La Côte d'Argent
30. Bassin d'Arcachon
31. Les Landes
32. Mont-de-Marsan
33. Dax

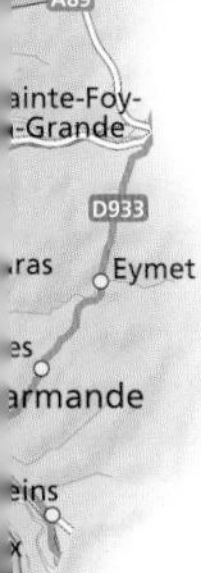

Key

- Highway
- Major road
- Secondary road
- Minor road
- Scenic route
- Main railroad
- Minor railroad
- Regional border

Boats moored at Coulon in the Marais Poitevin

Rose window of St-Médard, Thouars

❶ Thouars

Deux-Sèvres. 10,500. 3 bis bd Pierre Curie (05 49 66 17 65). Tue & Fri. **tourisme-pays-thouarsais.fr**

Thouars, on a rocky outcrop surrounded by the river Thouet, is on the border between Anjou and Poitou. There are as many roofs of northern slate as of southern red tiles.

In the center stands **Eglise St-Médard**. Its Romanesque facade is a perfect example of the Poitevin style that is typical of the region *(see p416)*, although a splendid Gothic rose window has been added. Lined with half-timbered medieval houses, the rue du Château leads up to the 17th-century château which dominates the town. It now houses a school and is open to the public during the summer.

East of Thouars lies the moated **Château d'Oiron**, which now hosts contemporary art exhibitions. A masterpiece of Renaissance architecture, it was largely built from 1518–49.

Château d'Oiron
79100 Oiron. **Tel** 05 49 96 51 25. **Open** daily. **Closed** some public hols.

❷ Parthenay

Deux-Sèvres. 11,000. 8 rue de la Vau-St-Jacques (05 49 94 90 05). Wed. **cc-parthenay.fr**

Parthenay is a classic, sleepy provincial town, except on Wednesday mornings, when France's second biggest livestock market is held here. In the Middle Ages, the town was an important halt on the route to Santiago de Compostela *(see pp404–5)* and it is easy to imagine the processions of pilgrims in the medieval quart Steep and cobbled, rue de la Vau-St-Jacques winds up to th 13th-century ramparts, leading on from the fortified Porte St-Jacques which guards a 13th-century bridge over the river Thouet.

West of Parthenay, the 12th-century church of **St-Pierr de Parthenay-le-Vieux** has a splendid Poitevin façade, featuring Samson and the Lion and a cavalier with a falcon.

Medieval houses lining the cobbled rue de la Vau-St-Jacques in Parthenay

❸ Marais Poitevin

Charente-Maritime, Deux-Sèvres, Vendée. La Rochelle. Niort, La Rochelle. Coulon, Arçais, Marans. pl de la Coutume, Coulo (05 49 35 81 04). **parc-marais-poitevin.fr**

The Poitevin marshes, which have been slowly drained with canals, dikes, and sluices for a thousand years, cover about 309 sq miles (800 sq km) between Niort and the sea. The area is now a regional park, divided into two parts. To the north and south of the Sèvre estuary is the Marais Désséché (dry marsh), where cereal and other crops are grown. The huge swathe of the Marais Mouillé (wet marsh) is upstrear towards Niort.

The wet marshes, known as the Venise Verte (Green Venice) are the most interesting. They are crisscrossed by a labyrinth c weed-choked canals, adorned by waterlilies and irises, shaded by poplars and beeches, and support a rich variety of birds and other wildlife. The *maraîchir* who live here stoutly maintain that much of the huge, waterlogged forest is unexplored. Th picturesque whitewashed villages hereabouts are all built on higher ground, and the customary means of transport a flat-bottomed boat, known as a *platte*.

Coulon, St-Hilaire-la-Palud, La Garette, and Arçais, as well a Damvix and Maillezais in the Vendée, are all convenient

-bottomed boats moored at Coulon in the Marais Poitevin

rting points for boat trips
und the marshes. Boats can
rented with or without a
ide. Make sure you bring
enty of insect repellent.
Coulon is the largest and
st-equipped village, and a
pular base for visiting the
ea. **La Maison du Marais
itevin** presents an account of
in the marshes in times gone
along with details of the
tlands' flora and fauna.

Plantagenet donjon in Niort, now
sing a local museum

❹ Niort

Deux-Sèvres. 60,000. pl de la Brèche (05 49 24 18 79). Thu & Sat. **niortmaraispoitevin.com**

Once a medieval port by the green waters of the Sèvre, Niort is now a prosperous industrial town specializing in machine tools, electronics, chemicals, and insurance.

Its closeness to the marshes is evident in local specialities – eels, snails, and angelica. This herb has been cultivated in the wetlands for centuries and is used for anything from liqueur to ice cream.

The town's immediate attraction is the huge 12th-century donjon overlooking the Vieux Pont. Built by Henry II and Richard the Lion-Heart, it played an important role during the Hundred Years' War and was later used as a prison. One prisoner was the father of Madame de Maintenon *(see p60)*, who spent her childhood in Niort. The donjon is now a museum of local arts and crafts, and archeology. The **Musée d'Agesci** in avenue de Limoges exhibits ceramics, sculpture, and paintings from the 16th to 20th centuries.

Environs

Halfway to Poitiers is the small town of **St-Maixent-L'Ecole**. A marvel of light and space, its abbey church is a Flamboyant Gothic reconstruction by François Le Duc (1670) of a building destroyed during the Wars of Religion. Farther west, the **Tumulus de Bougon** consists of five tumuli (burial mounds), the oldest dating from 4500 BC.

❺ Melle

Deux-Sèvres. 4,000. rue E Traver (05 49 29 15 10). Fri. **ville-melle.fr**

A Roman silver mine was the origin of Melle, which in the 9th century had the only mint in Aquitaine. Later its fame derived from the *baudet du Poitou*, an especially sturdy mule bred in the area. Now Melle is better known for its churches, of which the finest is **St-Hilaire**. It has a 12th-century Poitevin facade with an equestrian statue of the Emperor Constantine above the north door.

Environs

To the northwest, the abbey in **Celles-sur-Belle** has a great Moorish doorway which contrasts strongly with the rest of the church, a 17th-century restoration in Gothic style.

Equestrian statue of Constantine on the facade of St-Hilaire, Melle

Aerial view of a canal in the Marais Poitevin ▶

❻ Poitiers

Three of the greatest battles in French history were fought around Poitiers, the most famous in 732 when Charles Martel halted the Arab invasion. After two periods of English rule *(see p55)* the town thrived during the reign of Jean de Berry (1369–1416), the great sponsor of the arts. Its university, founded in 1431, made Poitiers a major intellectual center and saw Rabelais among its students. The Wars of Religion left Poitiers in chaos and not until the late 19th century did any major development take place. Today, however, the town is a modern and dynamic regional capital with a rich architectural heritage in its historic center.

Fresco in Eglise St-Hilaire-le-Grand

Notre-Dame-la-Grande

Despite its name, Notre-Dame-la-Grande is not a large church. One of Poitiers' great pilgrim churches, it is most celebrated as a masterpiece of lively 12th-century Poitevin sculpture, notably its richly detailed facade. In the choir is a Romanesque fresco of Christ and the Virgin. Most of the chapels were added in the Renaissance.

Palais de Justice

Pl Alphonse Lepetit. **Tel** 05 49 50 22 00. **Open** Mon–Fri.

Behind the bland Renaissance facade is the 12th-century great hall of the palace of the Angevin kings, Henry II and Richard the Lion-Heart. This is thought to be the scene of Joan of Arc's examination by a council of theologians in 1429.

Cathédrale St-Pierre

The 13th-century carved choir stalls in St-Pierre are by far the oldest in France. Note the huge 12th-century east window

Pillars with colorful geometrical patterns in Notre-Dame-la-Grande

Notre-Dame-la-Grande

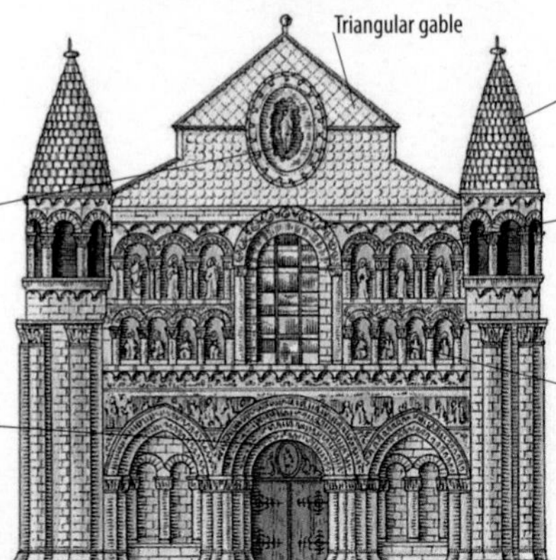

Triangular gable

Cone-shaped pinnacles

Christ in Majesty is shown in the center of the gable, surrounded by symbols of the evangelists.

Blind arcading is a distinctive feature of the Poitevin facade.

The portals on the Poitevin facade are deep and richly sculpted, often showing a pronounced Moorish influence.

The 12 apostles are represented by statues in the arcatures, together with the first bishop St. Hilaire and his disciple St. Martin.

ɿowing the Crucifixion. The tiny gures of the cathedral's patrons Ɨenry II and Eleanor of Aquitaine) ɾe crouched at the foot of the ʋindow. Its organ (1787–91), ɿade by François-Henri Cliquot, is ne of the most prestigious and eautiful in Europe.

Espace Mendès France
pl de la Cathédrale. **Tel** 05 49 50 33 3. **Open** daily. **Closed** Sun in Jun–ug; some public hols.

his museum contains a state-f-the-art planetarium, with ıser shows to help explain the ɿysteries of the universe, plus vents and exhibitions.

Eglise St-Hilaire-le-Grand
ıres and reconstructions have ɿade St-Hilaire a mosaic of ifferent styles. With its origins in ɿe 6th century, the church still isplays an 11th-century bell ɔwer and a 12th-century nave.

Baptistère St-Jean
ue Jean Jaurès. **Open** Wed–Mon.

he polygonal 4th-century aptistère St-Jean is one of the ldest Christian buildings in rance. Many of the earliest onverts were baptized here. ɭow a museum, it contains omanesque frescoes of Christ and Emperor Constantine, and some Merovingian sarcophagi.

VISITORS' CHECKLIST

Practical Information
Vienne. 92,000. 45 pl Charles de Gaulle (05 49 41 21 24). Sat, Tue & Thu. Les Expressifs (Oct). **ot-poitiers.fr**

Transport
3 miles (5 km) W Poitiers.

Musée Sainte-Croix
3 bis rue Jean Jaurès. **Tel** 05 49 41 07 53. **Open** Tue–Sun pms. **Closed** some public hols.

Musée Sainte-Croix exhibits prehistoric, Gallo-Roman and medieval archeology, and a wide range of paintings and 19th-century sculpture. Five bronzes by Camille Claudel are on show, including *La Valse*. There is also a large collection of contemporary art.

Médiathèque François Mitterrand
4 rue de l'Université. **Tel** 05 49 52 31 51. **Open** Tue–Sat. **Closed** public hols.

This modern building, in the historic quarter, is home to the **Maison du Moyen Age**, which displays a collection of medieval manuscripts, maps, and engravings.

One of Futuroscope's most popular attractions: the large-screen cinema

❼ Futuroscope

Jaunay-Clan. **Tel** 05 49 49 30 80. **Open** daily. **Closed** Jan–early Feb. **futuroscope.com**

Futuroscope is a fantastic theme park 4.5 miles (7 km) north of Poitiers, exploring visual technology in a futuristic environment. Attractions evolve yearly and include simulators, 3D and 360° screens, and the "magic carpet" cinema, with one of its screens on the floor, creating the sensation of "flying." The cinema has the biggest screen in Europe.

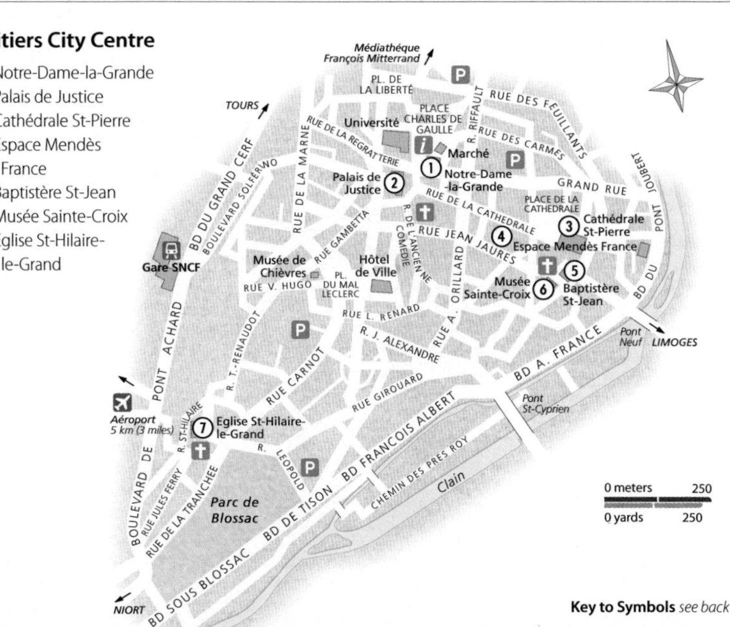

Key to Symbols *see back flap*

The castle ruins of Angles-sur-l'Anglin with the old watermill in the foreground

8 Abbaye de Nouaillé-Maupertuis

Nouaillé-Maupertuis. **Tel** 05 49 55 35 69. Church: **Open** 9am–6pm (7pm in summer). limited. summer only.

On the banks of the river Miosson lies the Abbaye de Nouaillé-Maupertuis. First mentioned in 780, the abbey became independent in 808 and followed the Benedictine rule. Apart from the beauty of the site, it is also worth visiting the church, built in the 11th–12th centuries and reconstructed several times. Behind the altar is the 10th-century sarcophagus of St-Junien, with three great heraldic eagles carved on the front.

More interesting is the nearby battlefield, scene of the great English victory at Poitiers by the Black Prince in 1356. The view has altered little since the 14th century. Drive down the small road to La Cardinerie (to the right off the D142), which leads to the river crossing at Gué de l'Omme, the epicenter of the battle. There is a monument halfway up the hill where the heaviest fighting took place and where the French king Jean le Bon was captured. He had put up a heroic resistance with nothing but his battle-axe, and his small son Philippe to tell him where the next English knight was coming from.

9 Chauvigny

Vienne. 7,000.
5 rue St-Pierre (05 49 46 39 01).
Tue, Thu, Sat. **chauvigny.fr**

Chauvigny, on its steep promontory overlooking the broad river Vienne, displays the ruins of no fewer than four fortified medieval castles. Stone from the local quarry was so plentiful that nobody ever bothered to demolish earlier castles for building material.

Nevertheless, the best thing in this town is the 11th–12th-century **Eglise St-Pierre**, whose decorated capitals are a real treasure – particularly those in the choir stalls. The carvings represent biblical scenes along with monsters, sphinxes, and sirens. Look for the one which says *Gofridus me fecit* (Gofridus made me), with wonderfully natural scenes of the Epiphany.

Monster capitals in Eglise St-Pierre in Chauvigny

Environs

Nearby is the lovely **Château de Touffou**, a Renaissance dream on the banks of the Vienne, with terraces and hanging gardens. Just north of it is the sleepy village of **Bonneuil-Matours**, with fine choir stalls in its Romanesque church.

Château de Touffou

Bonnes. **Tel** 05 49 56 08 48. **Open** May–mid-Jun: Sat, Sun & public hols; mid-Jun–mid-Sep: Wed–Mon.

10 Angles-sur-l'Anglin

Vienne. 400. 2 rue du Four Banal (05 49 48 86 87).
anglessuranglin.com

The village of Angles lies in an extremely beautiful riverside setting, dominated by its castle ruins. Adding to the charm is an old watermill by the slow-running river Anglin, graced by waterlilies and swaying reeds. Try to avoid visiting in summer, as the narrow streets become too crowded for comfort.

Angles is also famous for its tradition of fine needlework, the *jours d'Angles*, which is determinedly maintained by the local women today (their workshops can be visited).

St-Savin

enne. 1,000. 20 pl de la
bération (05 49 84 30 00). Fri.
abbaye-saint-savin.fr

he glory of St-Savin is its 1th-century abbey church with s slender Gothic spire and uge nave.

The abbey had enormous fluence until the Hundred Years' 'ar, when it was burned down. was later pillaged several times uring the Wars of Religion. espite restoration work by ionks in the 17th century and gain in the 19th century, the hurch appears quite untouched.

Its interior contains the most iagnificent series of 2th-century Romanesque escoes in Europe. These wall-aintings were among the very rst in France to be classified as *Monument Historique* in 1836. ome of the frescoes were estored in 1967–74 and have een protected by UNESCO nce 1983. A full-scale replica of ie St-Savin murals can be seen t the Palais de Chaillot in Paris *see pp114–15*). The abbey-iuseum explains the historical ontext and techniques of iese murals.

Bell tower of St-Savin

⓬ Montmorillon

Vienne. 7,000. 2 pl du Maréchal Leclerc (05 49 91 11 96). Wed; la Foire des Hérolles: 29th of each month (28th in Feb).
tourisme-montmorillon.fr

Montmorillon, built on the river Gartempe, has its origins in the 11th century. Like most towns in the region, it had a difficult time during the Hundred Years' War and the Wars of Religion. Some buildings survived, such as **Eglise Notre-Dame**, which has beautiful frescoes in its 12th-century crypt (contact the tourist office for key). They include scenes from the life of St. Catherine of Alexandria.

Environs

A short walk from the Pont de Chez Ragon, south of Montmorillon, is the **Portes d'Enfer**, a dramatically shaped rock above the rapids of the Gartempe.

In nearby Coulonges, the animal market **la Foire des Hérolles** draws people from across France.

St-Savin Wall Paintings

The frescoes of St-Savin represent Old Testament history from the Creation to the Ten Commandments. The sequence starts to the left of the entrance with the Creation of the stars and of Eve.

It continues with scenes from Noah's Ark to the Tower of Babel, the story of Joseph and the parting of the Red Sea. It is believed that all the frescoes were created by the same group of artists, due to the similarity in style. Their harmonious colors – red and yellow ocher, green, black and white – have been softened by time.

Noah's Ark, from a 12th-century wall painting in St-Savin

⓭ Confolens

Charente. 3,000. rue Fontaine des Jardins (05 45 84 14 08. Wed & Sat. **mairie-confolens.fr**

On the border with Limousin, Confolens was once an important frontier town but now suffers from rural exodus. Efforts to prevent the town's isolation include the annual international folklore festival. Every August the town is transformed by a mix of music, costumes, and crafts from all over the world.

Of historical interest is the medieval bridge across the Vienne, heavily restored in the early 18th century.

⓮ Charroux

Vienne. 1,200. 2 route de Chatain (05 49 87 60 12). Thu.
charroux-en-poitou.com

The 8th-century **Abbaye St-Sauveur** in Charroux was once one of the richest abbeys in the region. Today it is a ruin open to the sky (phone the tourist office to arrange a visit).

Its chief contribution to history was made in the 10th century, when the Council of Charroux declared the "Truce of God," the earliest-known attempt to regulate war in the manner of the Geneva convention. Rules included: "Christian soldiers may not plunder churches, strike priests, or steal peasants' livestock while campaigning."

A huge tower marks what was the center of the church, and some superb sculpture from the original abbey portal can be seen in the small museum.

⓯ Aulnay

Charente-Maritime. 1,500. 290 av de l'Eglise (05 46 33 14 44). Thu & Sun. **aulnaytourisme.com**

Perhaps the most unusual fact about the lovely 12th-century **Eglise St-Pierre** at Aulnay is that it was all built at once; there is no ill-fitting apse or transept added to an original nave. Surrounded by nothing but cypresses, it has remained the same since the time of the great pilgrimages.

The church is covered in glorious sculpture, particularly the outside of the south transept. It is a rare example of a complete Romanesque facade, with rank on rank of raucous monsters and graceful human figures. Look for the donkey with a harp. Inside the church there is a pillar decorated with elephants, inscribed "Here be Elephants."

Façade of Eglise St-Pierre at Aulnay

⓰ La Rochelle

Charente-Maritime. 80,000. 2 quai Georges Simenon, Le Gabut (05 46 41 14 68). daily. **larochelle-tourisme.com**

La Rochelle, a commercial center and busy port since the 11th century, has suffered much from a distressing tendency to back the wrong side – the English and the Calvinists, for example. This led to the ruthless siege of the city by Cardinal Richelieu in 1628, during which 23,000 people starved to death. The walls were destroyed and the city's privileges withdrawn.

Tour St-Nicolas in La Rochelle

The glory of La Rochelle is the old harbor surrounded by stately buildings. The harbor is now the biggest yachting center on France's Atlantic coast. On either side of its entrance are **Tour de la Chaîne** and **Tour St-Nicolas**. A huge chain used to be strung between them to ward off attack from the sea.

La Rochelle is easy to explore on foot, though its cobbled streets and arcades can be congested in high summer. To get an overview, climb the 15th-century **Tour de la Lanterne**. Its inner walls were covered in graffiti by prisoners, mostly mariners, in the 17th–19th centuries. Ships are the most common motif.

The study of the 18th-century scientist Clément Lafaille is preserved in the renovated **Muséum d'Histoire Naturelle**, complete with shell collection and display cabinets. There are also stuffed animals and African masks. The town's relation to the New World is treated in the **Musée du Nouveau Monde**. Emigration, commerce, and the slave trade are explained through old maps, paintings, and artifacts.

The richly decorated 16th-century courtyard facade of the **Hôtel de Ville** is worth a visit, as is the delightful collection of perfume bottles in the **Musée du Flacon à Parfum** in the perfumery at No. 33 rue du Temple.

Next to the Vieux Port is the huge **Aquarium**. Transparent tunnels lead through tanks with different marine biotopes, including sharks and turtles.

Tour de la Lanterne
Rue des Murs, Le Port. **Tel** 05 46 41 56 04. **Open** daily. **Closed** Jan 1, May 1, Nov 1 & 11, Dec 25.

Muséum d'Histoire Naturelle
28 rue Albert Premier. **Tel** 05 46 41 18 25. **Open** Tue–Sun. **Closed** Jan 1, May 1, Jul 14, Nov 1 & 11, Dec 25.

Musée du Nouveau Monde
10 rue Fleuriau. **Tel** 05 46 41 46 50. **Open** Wed–Mon. **Closed** Sat am (Oct–Mar), Sun am, Jan 1, May 1, Jul 14, Nov 1 & 11, Dec 25.

Aquarium
Bassin des Grands Yachts, quai Louis Prunier. **Tel** 05 46 34 00 00. **Open** daily. **aquarium-larochelle.com**

Environs
Ile de Ré, known as the white island, is a long stretch of chalky cliffs and dunes, with a rich birdlife. Since 1988 it has been connected to the mainland by a 2-mile (3-km) long bridge. Head for **Ars-en-Ré** or the island's main town, **St-Martin-de-Ré** for seafood restaurants serving locally grown oysters.

Arcade in rue du Palais, La Rochelle

⓱ Rochefort

Charente-Maritime. 27,000. av Sadi-Carnot (05 46 99 08 60). Tue, Thu & Sat; flea market: 2nd Thu at Cour Roy Bry. **rochefort-ocean.com**

The historic rival of La Rochelle, Rochefort was purpose-built by Colbert *(see pp60–61)* in the

are des Baleines on the eastern point of the Ile de Ré, opposite La Rochelle

ʼth century to be the greatest ipyard in France, producing ver 300 sailing vessels per year. This maritime heritage can be aced in the beautifully restored **orderie Royale** from 1670. The uilding houses an exhibition on pemaking. The **Musée de la arine** displays models of the ips built in the arsenal.

Rochefort is also famous as the rthplace of the writer Pierre oti (1850– 1923). The author's xtravagant **Maison de Pierre oti** is filled with lush souvenirs in n oriental decor.

Outside the town is **Pont ansbordeur**, France's last ansporter bridge, built in 1897 o connect Rochefort with outhern points.

La Corderie Royale
entre International de la Mer, rue udebert. **Tel** 05 46 87 01 90. **pen** daily. **Closed** Jan 1, 7–25, Dec 25. **corderie-royale.com**

Musée de la Marine
de la Galissonnière. **Tel** 05 46 99 86 7. **Open** daily. **Closed** Jan, May 1, ec 25. **musee-marine.fr**

Maison de Pierre Loti
41 rue Pierre Loti. **Tel** 05 46 82 91 90. **losed** for renovation; call for formation. only.

Pont Transbordeur
av Maurice Chupin, Parc des ourriers. **Tel** 05 46 83 30 86. **Open** pr–mid-Nov: daily; call for opening mes. **pont-transbordeur.fr**

nvirons

e d'Aix is served by a ferry om Fouras on the mainland. apoleon was briefly kept ere before being exiled to St. Helena. There are Napoleonic mementos in the **Musée Napoléonien**. The camel he rode in the Egyptian campaign is in the **Musée Africain**.

Musée Napoléonien
30 rue Napoléon. **Tel** 05 46 84 66 40. **Open** Wed–Mon. **Closed** May 1.

Musée Africain
Rue Napoléon. **Tel** 05 46 84 66 40. **Open** Wed–Mon. **Closed** May 1.

Napoleon, who was detained at Ile d'Aix in 1814

⑱ Ile d'Oléron

Charente-Maritime. 22,000. La Rochelle. Rochefort, La Rochelle, Saintes then bus. from La Rochelle (in summer). 22 rue Dubois Meynardie (05 46 85 65 23). **ile-oleron-marennes.com**

Accessible from the mainland by bridge, Oleron is the second largest French island after Corsica, and a very popular holiday resort. Its south coast, the **Côte Sauvage**, is all dunes and pine forest, with excellent beaches at Vert Bois and Grande Plage, near the fishing port of La Cotinière. The north is used for farming and fishing.

The train from **St-Trojan** makes an interesting excursion through dunes and woodlands to the Pointe de Maumusson (Easter–October).

⑲ Brouage

Charente-Maritime. 580. 2 rue de Québec (05 46 85 19 16).

Cardinal Richelieu's fortress at Brouage, his base during the Siege of La Rochelle (1627–8), once overlooked a thriving harbor, but its wealth and population declined in the 18th century as the ocean receded. In 1659, Marie Mancini was sent into exile here by her uncle, Cardinal Mazarin, who did not approve of her liaison with Louis XIV. The king never forgot the beautiful Marie. Even on his way back from his wedding, he stayed alone at Brouage in the room once occupied by his first great love. Today the **ramparts** make a peaceful place to stroll and admire the view.

Environs

There are two reasons to go to Marennes, southwest of Brouage: the famous green-tinged oysters and the view from the steeple of Eglise St-Pierre-de-Sales. Nearby is the 18th-century **Château de la Gataudière** with an exhibition of horsedrawn vehicles.

One of Royan's five popular beaches

20 Royan

Charente-Maritime. 20,000. to Verdon only. 1 bd de la Grandière (05 46 23 00 00). Tue–Sun; daily in summer. **royan-tourisme.com**

Badly damaged by Allied bombing in World War II, Royan is now thoroughly modern and different in tone from the rest of the towns on this weather-beaten coast. With five beaches of fine sand, here called *conches*, it becomes a heavily populated resort in the summer months.

Built between 1955 and 1958, **Eglise Notre-Dame** is a remarkable early example of reinforced concrete architecture. Its interior is flooded with color and light by the stained-glass windows.

The outstanding Renaissance **Phare de Cordouan**, visible in the distance from the coast, offers a change from all the modern architecture. Various lighthouses have been erected on the site since the 11th century. The present one was finished in 1611, with a chapel inside. The construction was later reinforced and heightened. Since 1789, nothing has changed but the lighting method. Boat trips in summer ferry visitors to Phare de Cordouan from Royan harbor.

21 Talmont-sur-Gironde

Charente-Maritime. 79. rue de l'Église (05 46 90 16 25).

The tiny Romanesque **Eglise Ste-Radegonde** is perched on a spit of land overlooking the Gironde. Built in 1094, the church's apse was designed to resemble the prow of a ship – which is apt, since the nave has already fallen into the estuary. A 15th-century facade closes off what's left. Inside are richly decorated capitals, including a tableau of St. George and the Dragon.

Talmont is a jewel of a village, packed full of little white houses and colorful hollyhocks in summer.

22 Saintes

Charente-Maritime. 28,000. Place Bassompierre (05 46 74 23 82 Tue–Sun. **saintes-tourisme.fr**

Capital of the Saintonge region, Saintes has an extraordinarily rich architectural heritage. For centuries it boasted the only bridge over the lower Charente, well used by pilgrims on their way to Santiago de Compostela The Roman bridge no longer exists but you can still admire the magnificent **Arch of Germanicus** (AD 19) which used to mark its entrance.

On the same side of the river is the beautiful **Abbaye aux Dames**. Consecrated in 1047, it was modernized in the 12th century. During the 17th–18th centuries noble ladies were educated here. Look for the decorated portal and the vigorous 12th-century head of Christ in the apse.

On the left bank is the 1st-century Roman **amphitheater**. Farther away lies the rather unknown gem, **Eglise St-Eutrope**. In the 15th century, this church had the misfortune to effect a miraculous cure of the dropsy on Louis XI. In a paroxysm of gratitude, he did his best to wreck it with ill-considered Gothic additions. Luckily, its rare Romanesque capitals have survived.

Arch of Germanicus in Saintes

23 Cognac

Charente. 20,000. 16 rue du 14 Juillet (05 45 82 10 71). Tue–Sun. **tourism-cognac.com**

Wherever you spot the black lichen stains from alcohol evaporation on the exterior of the buildings in this river port,

ecropolis in the monolithic Eglise St-Jean in Aubeterre-sur-Dronne

ou may be sure that you re looking at a storehouse f cognac.

All the great cognac houses do ours – a good one is chez **ognac Otard**, situated in he 15th–16th-century hâteau where François was born. The distillery vas established in 1795 y a Scot named Otard, vho demolished an old hapel in the process. uckily much of the enaissance architecture vas saved and can be een during the tour, which ncludes a cognac tasting.

The basic material for cognac s local white wine low in lcohol, which is then distilled. he resultant pale spirit is aged n oak barrels for 4–40 years efore being bottled. The skill es in the blending – therefore he only guide to quality is he name and the duration f aging.

Cognac Otard
hâteau de Cognac, 127 bd Denfert-ochereau. **Tel** 05 45 36 88 86. **Open** pr–Oct: daily; Nov–Mar: by appt. **losed** May 1 & public hols in winter. obligatory. otard.com

24 Angoulême

harente. 46,000. 7 bis ue du Chat (05 45 95 16 84). daily. angouleme-tourisme.com

The celebrated 12th-century **Cathédrale St-Pierre**, which dominates this industrial center, is the fourth to be built on the site. One of its most interesting features is the Romanesque frieze on the facade. Some restoration work was carried out by the 19th-century architect Abadie. In his eagerness to wipe out all details added after the 12th century, he destroyed a 6th-century crypt.

Cognac in traditional snifter

Unforturnately, he was also let loose on the old château, transforming it into a Neo-Gothic **Hôtel de Ville** (town hall). However, the 15th-century tower where Marguerite d'Angoulême was born in 1492 still stands. A statue of her can be seen in the garden. Sister of François I, she spoke six languages, had a major role in foreign policy, and wrote a popular work, *Heptaméron*. The ramparts offer a bracing walk with views over the Charente Valley. A vintage car race takes place there in mid-September. Angoulême has become the capital of comic book art *(band dessinée)*, hosting the prestigious Festival de la Bande Dessinée (Jan/Feb). The **Cité Internationale de la Bande-Dessinée et de l'Image** has a reference collection of French print and film cartoons dating back to 1946. From here, a footbridge leads to the Musée de la Bande Dessinée, where the history, techniques, and aesthetics of the art form are explained.

Cité Internationale de la Bande-Dessinée et de l'Image
121 rue de Bordeaux. **Tel** 05 45 38 65 65. **Open** Tue–Sun (w/e pms only). **Closed** public hols. Cinema: **citebd.org**

25 Aubeterre-sur-Dronne

Charente. 430. 8 pl du Champ de Foine (05 45 98 57 18). Sun. **aubeterresurdronne.com**

The chief ornament of this pretty white village is the staggering monolithic **Eglise St-Jean**. Dug out of the white chalky cliff that gave the village its name (Alba Terra – White Earth), some parts of it date back to the 6th century. Between the Revolution and 1860, it served as the village's cemetery. It contains an early Christian baptismal font and an octagonal reliquary.

The Romanesque Eglise St-Jacques is also of note for its fine sculpted facade.

Detail from the Romanesque façade of Cathédrale St-Pierre in Angoulême

26 Street by Street: Bordeaux

Built on a curve of the river Garonne, Bordeaux has been a major port since pre-Roman times and for centuries a crossroads of European trade. Today Bordeaux shows little visible evidence of the Romans, Franks, English, or the Wars of Religion that have marked its past. This forward-looking town, the seventh largest in France, is an industrial and maritime sprawl surrounding a noble 18th-century center.

Along the waterfront of this wealthy wine metropolis is a long sweep of elegant Classical facades, first built to mask the medieval slums behind. Adding to the magnificence are the Esplanade des Quinconces, the Grand Théâtre, and the place de la Bourse.

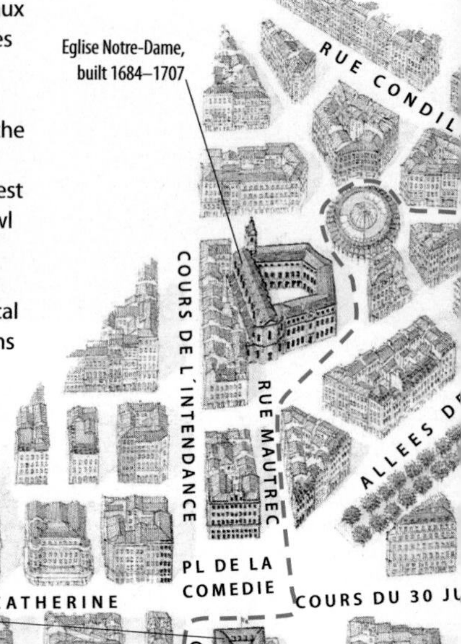

★ Grand Théâtre
Built in 1773–80, the theater is a masterpiece of the Classical style, crowned by nine statues of the muses.

Key

— Suggested route

The *quais*, lined with graceful facades, make a beautiful walk along the Garonne.

★ Place de la Bourse
This elegant and harmonious square is flanked by two majestic 18th-century buildings, Palais de la Bourse and Hôtel des Douanes.

For hotels and restaurants in this region see pp554–71 and pp576–603

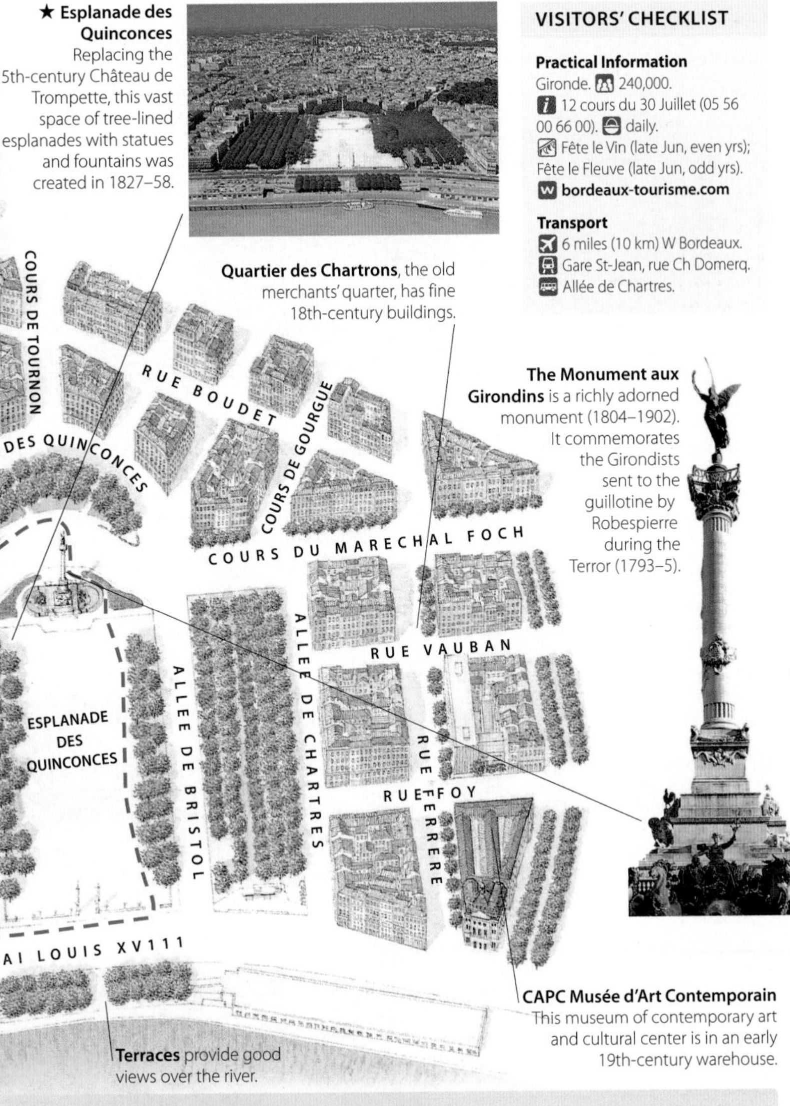

★ Esplanade des Quinconces
Replacing the 15th-century Château de Trompette, this vast space of tree-lined esplanades with statues and fountains was created in 1827–58.

Quartier des Chartrons, the old merchants' quarter, has fine 18th-century buildings.

The Monument aux Girondins is a richly adorned monument (1804–1902). It commemorates the Girondists sent to the guillotine by Robespierre during the Terror (1793–5).

Terraces provide good views over the river.

CAPC Musée d'Art Contemporain
This museum of contemporary art and cultural center is in an early 19th-century warehouse.

VISITORS' CHECKLIST

Practical Information
Gironde. 240,000.
12 cours du 30 Juillet (05 56 00 66 00). daily.
Fête le Vin (late Jun, even yrs); Fête le Fleuve (late Jun, odd yrs).
bordeaux-tourisme.com

Transport
6 miles (10 km) W Bordeaux.
Gare St-Jean, rue Ch Domerq.
Allée de Chartres.

Loading wine barrels in 19th-century Bordeaux

The Bordeaux Wine Trade

After Marseille, Bordeaux is the oldest trading port in France. From Roman times the export of wine was the basis for a modest prosperity, but under English rule (1154–1453, *see pp54–7*), the merchants began making immense fortunes from their monopoly of wine sales to England. After the discovery of the New World, Bordeaux took advantage of its Atlantic position to diversify and extend its wine market. Today the Bordeaux region produces over 60 million cases of wine per year.

Grand Theâtre de Bordeaux

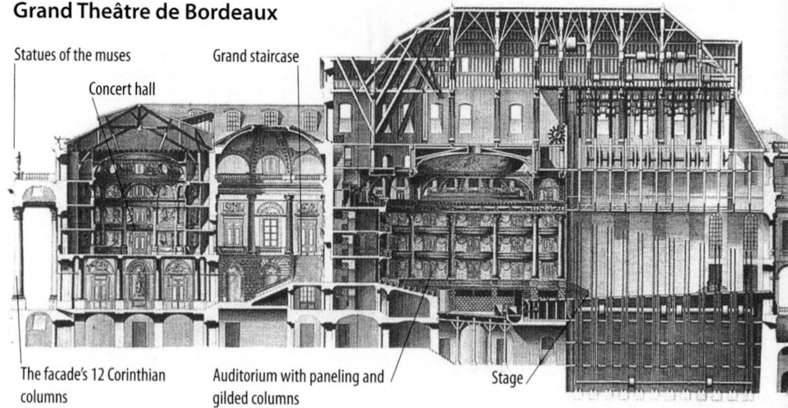

Exploring Bordeaux

Much of central Bordeaux is grand streets and 18th-century mansions. A triangle made by cours Clemenceau, cours de l'Intendance, and allées de Tourny has chic boutiques and cafés. Cathédrale St-André is another focal point, with good museums nearby. Both the *quais* and the Chartrons district around the Jardin Public are worth exploring.

Grand Théâtre

Place de la Comédie. **Tel** 05 56 00 85 95. **Open** by appointment only.

Built by the architect Victor Louis, the 18th-century Grand Théâtre is one of the finest Classical constructions of its type in France. The auditorium is renowned for its extraordinary acoustics. The spectacular main staircase was later imitated by Garnier for the Paris Opéra *(see p101)*.

Eglise St-Seurin

This church is somewhat chaotic with a patchwork of styles ranging from the 11th to the 18th century. Most interesting are the 6th-century Gallo-Roman sarcophagi in the crypt, and a fine 14th-century bishop's throne.

Basilique St-Michel

It took 200 years to build the massive Basilique St-Michel, begun in 1350. This triple-naved edifice has a remarkable statue of St. Ursula with her flock of penitents. Its freestanding belfry, built in 1472–92, is the tallest in southern France (374 ft).

Musée des Beaux-Arts

20 cours d'Albret. **Tel** 05 56 10 20 56. **Open** Wed–Mon. **Closed** public hols.

Housed in two wings of the Hôtel de Ville, the excellent collection of paintings here ranges from the Renaissance to our time. Masterpieces include works by Titian, Veronese, Rubens, Delacroix, Corot, Renoir, Matisse, and Boudin.

Musée des Arts Décoratifs

39 rue Bouffard. **Tel** 05 56 10 14 00. **Open** Wed–Mon. **Closed** public hols.

If you're interested in elegant furnishings and fine porcelain, stop off at this exceptional collection, housed in the suitably refined 18th-century Hôtel de Lalande.

Musée d'Aquitaine

20 cours Pasteur. **Tel** 05 56 01 51 00. **Open** Tue–Sun. **Closed** public hols.

This important museum traces life in the region from prehistoric times to the present, through artifacts, furniture, and viticulture tools. Among its more spectacular exhibits are the Tayac treasure from the 2nd century BC and the Garonne treasure, a hoard of over 4,000 Roman coins.

Calm street in Bordeaux by the Porte de la Grosse Cloche

Cathédrale St-André

The nave of this gigantic church was begun in the 11th century and modified 200 years later. The Gothic choir and transepts were added in the 14th and 15th centuries. The excellent medieval sculptures on the Porte Royale include scenes from the Last Judgement.

CAPC Musée d'Art Contemporain

Entrepôt Lainé, 7 rue Ferrère. **Tel** 05 56 00 81 50. **Open** Tue–Sun. **Closed** public hols.

This superbly converted 19th-century warehouse merits a visit, whatever you make of its high-profile temporary exhibitions and permanent collection of contemporary art.

27 St-Émilion

Gironde. 2,100. pl des Créneaux (05 57 55 28 28). Sun.
saint-emilion-tourisme.com

This charming village in the middle of the red wine district to which it gives its name, dates back to an 8th-century hermit, Émilion, who dug out a cave for himself in the rock. A monastery followed, and by the Middle Ages St-Émilion had become a small town. Today medieval houses still line the narrow streets, and parts of the

:th-century ramparts remain. ıe interior of the church dug ıt of the chalky cliff by llowers of Saint Émilion after s death is somewhat ruined ⁄ concrete columns put up to ·event its collapse.

Famous châteaus in the strict include the elegant **geac**, **Cheval Blanc**, and **ısone**, all of them St-Émilion ·emiers Grands Crus Classés.

Pauillac

ronde. 5,400.
La Verrerie (05 56 59 03 08).
Sat. **pauillac-medoc.com**

ne of the most famous areas the Médoc wine region *ee pp402–3)* is the commune f Pauillac. Three of its châteaus re Médoc Premiers Grands Crus

Vineyard close to Margaux in the Médoc region west of Bordeaux

Classés. The **Château Mouton-Rothschild** uses leading artists to create its wine labels and has a small museum of paintings on wine themes from all over the world. The **Château Lafite-Rothschild** is of medieval origin and the **Château Latour** is recognizable by its distinctive stone turret. They can be visited by appointment (contact the tourist office). The town of Pauillac is situated on the west bank of the Gironde. In the 19th century it was the bustling arrival point for transatlantic steamships, but now the sleepy port is mostly used by pleasure boats. There are picturesque river views from the *quais* and plenty of cafés serving the local wine.

Bordeaux Wine Châteaus

The château is at the heart of the quality system in Bordeaux, the world's largest fine wine region. A château includes a vineyard and a building which can range from the most basic to the grandest, historic as well as modern. But the château is also the symbol of a tradition and the philosophy that a wine's quality and character spring from the soil. Some châteaus welcome visitors for wine tasting as well as buying. Every major wine town has a Maison du Vin, which can provide information on visits to a château.

Latour in Pauillac is famous for its powerful wines and the medieval stone turret that appears on its label.

Cheval Blanc, a great château in the St-Émilion area, boasts a rich, spicy Premier Grand Cru.

Margaux, built in 1802, produces a classic Margaux Premier Cru of the same elegant proportions as its Palladian facade.

Palmer, dating from 1856, is Neo-Renaissance in style and produces a very fine Margaux Troisième Cru.

Gruaud-Larose is a cream-colored château with a Classical facade, distinguished by its full-bodied St-Julien Deuxième Cru Classé.

Vieux Château Certan is Belgian-owned and one of the great historic properties of Pomerol. Its wines are consistently in the first rank in the district, challenged only by Pétrus.

The immense Dune du Pilat, stretching almost 2 miles (3 km) south of the inlet to Bassin d'Arcachon

29 La Côte d'Argent

Gironde, Landes. ✈ Bordeaux, Biarritz. 🚉 Soulac-sur-Mer, Arcachon, Labenne, Dax. 🚌 Lacanau, Arcachon, Mimizan. ℹ Lacanau (05 56 03 21 01), Mimizan-Plage (05 58 09 11 20), Capbreton (05 58 72 12 11).

The long stretch of coast between Pointe de Grave on the Gironde estuary and Bayonne *(see p456)* is called La Côte d'Argent – the Silver Coast. It is virtually one vast beach of shifting sand dunes. Treeplanting has now slowed down their progress.

The coast is dotted with seaside resorts like **Soulac-sur-Mer** in the north, followed by the big **Lacanau-Océan**, and **Mimizan-Plage**. Down in the south is **Hossegor** with its salty lake, and **Capbreton**. Modern holiday resorts have been integrated with the old.

Inland are lakes popular for fishing and boating. They are connected to each other and the ocean by lively water currents, such as the **Courant d'Huchet** from Etang de Léon. Boat trips are available.

30 Bassin d'Arcachon

Gironde. 👥 12,000. ⛴ to Cap Ferret. 🚉 🚌 ℹ espl Georges Pompidou (05 57 52 97 97). 🛒 daily. **W arcachon.com**

In the middle of the Côte d'Argent the straight coastline suddenly forms a lagoon. Famous for its natural beauty, fine beaches, and oysters, the Bassin d'Arcachon is a protected area, perfect for holidaymakers, sailing enthusiasts, and oyster-eaters.

The basin is dotted with smaller amorphous resorts, beaches and fishing/oyster villages, all worth exploring.

Cap Ferret, the northern headland that protects the basin from stiff Atlantic winds, is a preserve of the wealthy, whose luxurious villas stand among the pines. Look for the small road under the trees from Lège, which leads to the wild, magnificent beach of Grand-Crohot.

Between Cap Ferret and Arcachon, near Gujan-Mestras, the **Parc Ornitho-logique du Teich** provides care and shelter for damaged birds and endangered species. For the bird watcher, there are two fascinating walks, each carefully marked: an introductory one, and another of greater length. Both provide concealed observation points from which people can watch the wild fowl without disturbing them.

Arcachon was created as a seaside resort in 1845. Its popularity grew and in the late 19th and early 20th centuries the elegant villas in Ville d'Hiver were built. The livelier Ville d'Eté, facing the lagoon, has a casino and sports facilities.

The immense **Dune du Pilat** is the largest sand dune in Europe. It is nearly 2 miles (3 km) long, 340 ft (104 m) high, and 1,625 ft (500 m) wide. Aside from the view, the dune is a great vantage point in the fall for viewing flocks of migratory birds as they pass overhead on their way to the sanctuary at Le Teich.

Parc Ornithologique du Teich
Le Teich. **Tel** 05 56 22 80 93.
Open daily. **W parc-ornithologique-du-teich.com**

Parc Ornithologique du Teich, a bird sanctuary in Bassin d'Arcachon

For hotels and restaurants in this region see pp554–71 and pp576–603

Landes Forest

The vast, totally artificial 19th-century forest of Les Landes was an ambitious project to make use of an area of sand and marshes. Pines and grasses were planted to anchor the coastal dunes, and inland dunes were stabilized with a mixture of pines, reeds, and broom. In 1855 the land was drained, and is now covered with pine groves and undergrowth, preserving a delicate ecological balance.

Pine trees in the Landes forest

❶ Les Landes

ronde, Landes. ✈ Bordeaux, arritz. 🚉 Morcenx, Dax, Mont-de-arsan. 🚌 Mont-de-Marsan. ℹ Mont-de-Marsan (05 58 05 87 37).

'most entirely covered by an nmense pine forest, the Landes ea extends over the two *épartements* of Gironde and andes. The soil here is uniformly andy. Until a century ago the hole region became a swamp in inter, because of a layer of tufa orous rock) just under the urface which retained water from ne brackish lakes. Any settlement agriculture close to the sea was npossible due to the constantly ifting dunes. Furthermore, the outh of the Adour river kept noving from Capbreton to Vieux-oucau and back, a distance of) miles (32 km).

The Adour was fixed near ayonne by a canal in the 16th entury. This was the start of the ow conquest of the Landes. ne planting of pine trees ltimately wiped out the nigrant shepherds and neir flocks. Today the nner Landes is still very nder-populated, ut wealthy from s pinewood nd pine derivatives. The coastal strip has a large influx of holidaymakers.

In 1970, part of the forest was made into a nature park. At **Marqueze**, in the **Écomusée de la Grande Lande**, a typical 19th-century *airial* (clearing) has been restored. It commemorates the vanished world of Les Landes before the draining of the marshes, when shepherds still used stilts to get about. There are traditional *auberges landaises*, wooden houses with sloping roofs, as well as henhouses built on stilts because of the foxes. In **Luxey** a museum recalls old techniques of tapping and distillation of resin.

Levignacq, near the coast, is a perfect Landais village with a remarkable 14th-century fortified church full of charming native frescoes.

㉜ Mont-de-Marsan

Landes. 👥 32,000. 🚉 🚌 ℹ 1 pl Charles de Gaulle (05 58 05 87 37). 🛒 Tue & Sat. **W tourisme-montdemarsan.fr**

A bullfighting mecca, Mont-de-Marsan attracts all the great bullfighters of France and Spain in summer. A less bloodthirsty local variant of the sport is the *course landaise*, in which the object is to vault over the horns and back of a charging cow.

The administrative capital of the Landes is also known for its hippodrome and the production of poultry and *foie gras*.

Sculpture from the first half of the 20th century can be seen at **Musée Despiau-Wlérick**.

㉝ Dax

Landes. 👥 21,500. 🚉 🚌 ℹ 11 cours Foch (05 58 56 86 86). 🛒 Tue– Sun am. **W dax-tourisme.com**

The thermal spa of Dax is second only to Aix-les-Bains *(see p394)* in importance. Its hot springs, with a constant temperature of 147° F (64° C) and tonic mud from the Adour, have been soothing aches and pains since the time of Emperor Augustus.

Apart from the 13th-century doorway of the otherwise 17th-century **Cathédrale Notre-Dame**, there isn't much of architectural interest in this warm, peaceful town. But the promenade along the river Adour is charming and the bullring is world-renowned.

Force (1937) by Raoul Lamourdieu, in the bullfighting capital of Mont-de-Marsan

?ERIGORD, QUERCY, AND GASCONY

ordogne · Lot · Tarn · Haute-Garonne · Lot-et-Garonne
ırn-et-Garonne · Gers

outhwest France is an archeologist's heaven, for the region as been continuously inhabited by mankind for tens of ıousands of years, longer than any other area in Europe. he landscape of these historic regions seems to have an ncient familiarity, derived from centuries of people living in armony with the land.

he great cave sites around Les Eyzies and ascaux harbor the earliest evidence we ossess of primitive art. The castles, bastides *(see p449)*, and churches that grace the ountryside from Périgueux to the Pyrenees, om the Bay of Biscay to Toulouse, and eyond to the Mediterranean, belong ɔ a far more recent past. From the coming f Christianity until the late 18th century, his lovely region was the battlefield for a tring of conflicts. The English fought and ɔst the Hundred Years' War for Aquitaine 1345–1453); this was followed by ntermittent Wars of Religion, in which Catholics fought Huguenots (French Protestants) in a series of massacres and juerilla wars *(see pp56–7)*.

Today nothing is left of these old struggles ut crumbling ramparts, keeps, and bastides, which are part of the region's cultural and artistic heritage, attracting thousands of visitors every year. Yet it is as well to remember that all the great sights here, from the abbey church at Moissac, whose 12th-century portal is a masterpiece of Romanesque art, to the awesome clifftop site of Rocamadour, have suffered at one time or another from the attacks of marauding soldiers.

Over the last fifty years, the rural southwest has gone through a radical demographic shift. There has been a continual decline in the old peasant way of life with fewer and fewer people cultivating the land. A steady migration by the young to the cities has been matched by an influx of downsizers and commuters looking for a more relaxed way of life.

érigord geese, reared for the area's celebrated *foie gras*

◀ Limestone cliffs tower over the beautiful countryside of the Gorges de l'Aveyron

Exploring Périgord, Quercy, and Gascony

The market towns of Périgueux, Cahors, and Albi make good bases for exploring the region, and are quieter alternatives to Toulouse – the only major urban center. Elsewhere, the green hills and sleepy villages of Gascony and Périgord (also known as the Dordogne) are mainly for those who appreciate the slow pace of life in the countryside. But if you want more than peace and good food, this region offers some of France's finest medieval architecture, and Europe's most important prehistoric caves, notably Lascaux.

The medieval hilltop town of Cordes

Key

- Highway
- Major road
- Secondary road
- Minor road
- Scenic route
- Main railroad
- Minor railroad
- Regional border

D675
Nontron
Mareuil-sur-Belle
Château de Puyguilhem
3 BRANTÔME
BOURDEILLES 4
Dronne
D939
Ribérac
D710
D709
PÉRIGUEUX 5
D6089
Saint-Astier
D708
A89
Montpon-Ménestérol
Mussidan
N21
Verg
Bordeaux
AQUITAINE
Campsegret
LES
BERGERAC 8
Dordogne
D933
N21
Eymet
Castillonnès
Miramont-de-Guyenne
Cancon
Marmande
Tombeboeuf
Bordeaux
D813
Tonneins
Le Temple-sur-Lot
Damazan
L'Aiguillon
N21
A62
Garonne
Lavardac
17 AGEN
Moraix
Laplume
Nérac
D931
Gers
AUVILLAR
LARRESSINGLE 18
19 CONDOM
N21
Cazaubon
Lectoure
D930
Fleurance
Eauze
Manciet
Montestruc-sur-Gers
Vic-Fezensac
N124
Nogaro
MIDI
Mauvez
Baïse
Riscle
Adour
AUCH 20
Aubiet
Castelnau-Rivière-Basse
Gers
D349
Mirande
D935
Maubourguet
N21
Miélan
Masseube
Tarbes
Trie-sur-Baïse
Castelnau-Magnoac

Getting Around

The west–east Autoroute des Deux (A62-A61) is the main road through the region, linking Bordeaux, the Atlantic coast, and the Mediterranean. The A20 from Montauban to Limoges provides access to the Dordogne and Quercy. Buses and mainline railroads, including a Bordeaux–Marseille TGV, pass along the same two axes. They meet at Toulouse, where an international airport has daily flights to and from most European destinations.

For additional map symbols *see back flap*

Sights at a Glance

1. St-Jean-de-Côle
2. Hautefort
3. Brantôme
4. Bourdeilles
5. Périgueux
6. St-Amand-de-Coly
7. Lascaux II
8. Bergerac
9. Les Eyzies
10. Dordogne Valley
11. Sarlat
12. Domme
13. Rocamadour
14. Gouffre de Padirac
15. Autoire
16. Cahors
17. Agen
18. Larressingle
19. Condom
20. Auch
21. Auvillar
22. Moissac
23. Montauban
24. Gorges de l'Aveyron
25. Cordes
26. Albi
27. Castres
28. Toulouse

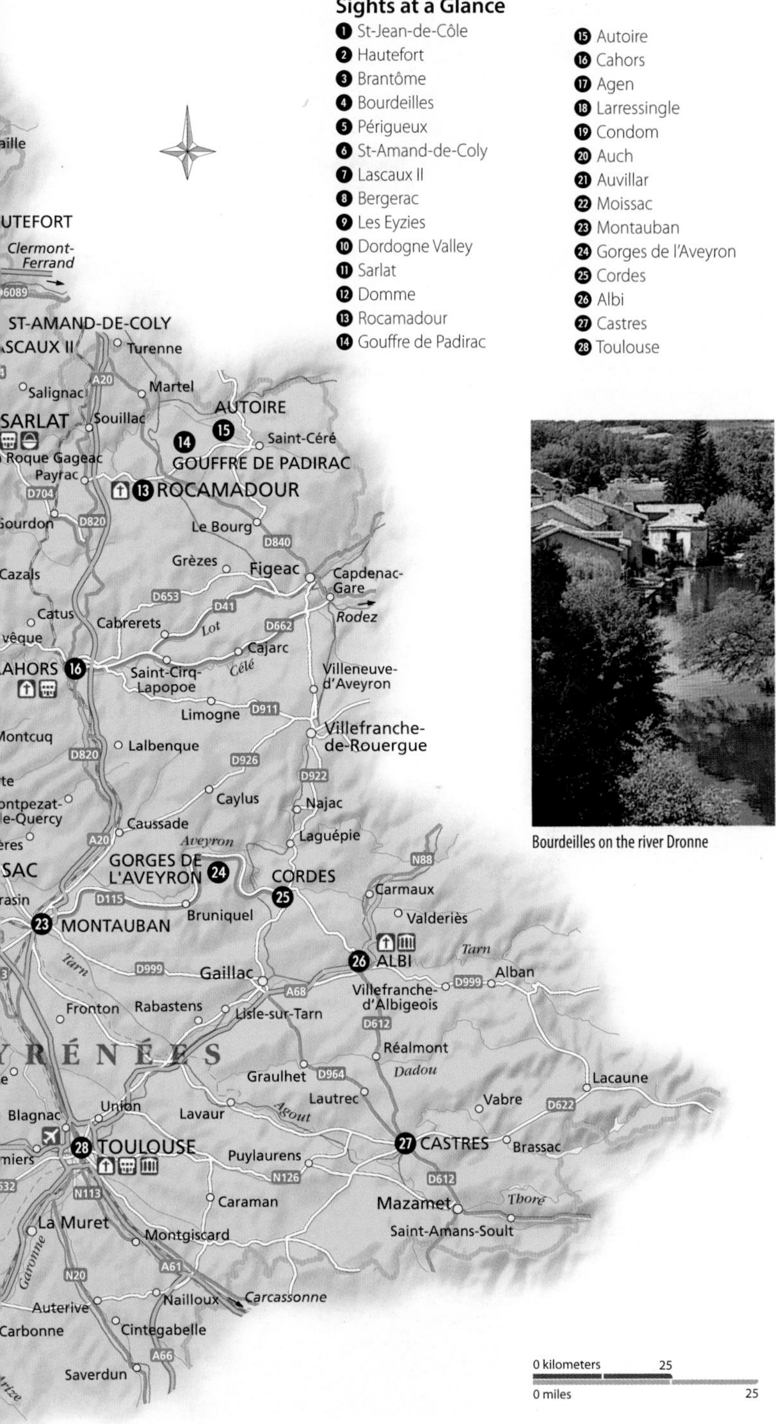

Bourdeilles on the river Dronne

❶ St-Jean-de-Côle

Dordogne. 350. pl du Château (05 53 62 14 15). Floralies (Apr–May). **ville-saint-jean-de-cole.fr**

St-Jean-de-Côle's medieval, humpbacked bridge gives the best view of this lovely Dordogne village set in hilly countryside. Stone and half-timbered houses, roofed with the distinctive red-brown tiles of the region, cram the narrow streets around the main square. Here stand a covered market place, château, and 12th-century church.

The cupola of the church used to be the largest in the region – too large, it seems, for it fell down twice in the 18th and 19th centuries. The second time it happened the builders gave up, and there has been a plank ceiling ever since.

Main square in the lovely village of St-Jean-de-Côle

❷ Hautefort

Tel 05 53 50 40 27. Château: **Open** Apr– Sep: daily (Mar & early Nov: Sat, Sun & hols, pm only; Oct: daily, pm only). **Closed** mid-Nov–Feb. oblig. limited. **chateau-hautefort.com**

Hautefort clings to the sides of a steep hill topped by a massive 17th-century château, one of the finest in southwest France. Partially fortified and built as a pleasure palace in honor of King Louis XIII's secret love, the Marquis de Hautefort's sister Marie, the castle sits among French gardens on terraces with superb views of the rolling countryside of northeast Périgord. In the village, the hospice, of a similar date, has a museum of early medical implements.

Brantôme Abbey, with belfry

❸ Brantôme

Dordogne. 2,200. inside the abbey (05 53 05 80 63). Fri. **ville-brantome.fr**

Surrounded by the river Dronne, Brantôme is often called the Venice of the Périgord Vert. Its medieval abbey and 11th-century belfry (reputedly the oldest in France), together with the verdant rockface behind, provide a dramatic backdrop for this picturesque town.

Pierre de Bourdeille, the poet (1540–1614), was appointed abbot here in his youth. His lovers allegedly included Mary, Queen of Scots. After a crippling fall, Bourdeille retired here in 1569 to write his racy memoirs. It is possible to wander the stone staircases and cloisters, and through the main courtyard to the intriguing troglodyte dwellings in the cliff behind. In one is a huge crucifixion scene cut into the stone during the 16th century. Just 7 miles (12 km) northeast lies the Renaissance **Château de Puyguilhem** and **Grotte de Villars**. Discovered in 1953, these caves lead to several different levels. Apart from spectacular rock formations, there are some marvelous 1,700-year-old cave paintings.

Château de Puyguilhem: Villars. **Tel** 05 53 54 82 18. **Open** Apr–Sep: daily; Oct–Mar: Wed–Sun. **Closed** Jan 1, May 1, Nov 1 &11, Dec 25. **puyguilhem. monuments-nationaux.fr**

Grotte de Villars Villars. **Tel** 05 53 54 82 36. **Open** Apr–mid-Nov: daily. oblig. **grotte-villars.com**

❹ Bourdeilles

Dordogne. 800. 63 place Tilleuls (05 53 03 42 96).

This small town has everything a Gothic bridge with cutwater piers spanning the Dronne, a mill, and a medieval **château**. The 16th-century additions to the castle were designed in a hurry by the châtelaine Jacquette de Montbron, when expecting Queen Catherine de' Medici to visit. When the royal visit was called off, so were the building works. The highlight is the gilded salon, decorated in the 1560s by Ambroise le Noble of the Fontainebleau School.

Château de Bourdeilles **Tel** 05 53 03 73 36. **Open** Feb–Mar & Nov–mid-Dec: Mon, Wed, Thu & Sun; Jul–Aug: daily; Sep–Oct & late Dec: Wed–Mon. **Closed** Jan. **bourdeilles.com**

The impressive Château de Bourdeilles towering above the town

For hotels and restaurants in this region see pp554–71 and pp576–603

Cathédrale St-Front in Périgueux, restored in the 19th century

❺ Périgueux

Dordogne. 31,000.
26 pl Francheville (05 53 53 10 63).
daily. **tourisme-perigueux.fr**

The ancient and truly gastronomic city of Périgueux, like its neighbors Bergerac and Riberac, should be visited on market day, when stalls in the lively squares in the medieval part of town offer the pick of local specialities, including truffles (Nov–Mar), *charcuterie*, and the succulent pies called *pâtés de Périgueux*.

Périgueux, now the busy regional capital, has long been the crossroads of Périgord. The earliest part remaining today is the quarter known as **La Cité**, once the important Gallo-Roman settlement of Vesunna. From Roman times to the Middle Ages, this was the focus of Périgueux. Most of the fabric of Vesunna was pulled down in the 3rd century, but some vestiges of a temple, a huge arena, and a sumptuous villa remain. The **Eglise St-Etienne** nearby dates back to the 12th century. La Domus de Vesonne, a Gallo-Roman museum, is also in La Cité.

Walking up the hill to the city's dazzling white cathedral you pass through bustling streets and squares, each with its market activity. This is the medieval quarter of **Le Puy St-Front**, which began to flourish as pilgrims on their way to Santiago de Compostela *(see p404)* visited the cathedral. As they brought prestige and wealth to the quarter, it gradually eclipsed La Cité.

At the top stands the imposing **Cathédrale St-Front**, the largest in southwestern France. The Romanesque construction was heavily restored in the 19th century, when architect Paul Abadie added the fancy domes and cones. He later used St-Front as inspiration for the Sacré-Coeur in Paris *(see p138)*.

19th-century stained glass in Cathédrale St-Front

Other gems of medieval and Renaissance architecture include **Maison Estignard**, at No. 3 rue Limogeanne, with its unusual corkscrew staircase, and houses along rue Aubergerie and rue de la Constitution.

Also in the cathedral quarter is the **Musée d'Art et d'Archéologie du Périgord**, one of the most comprehensive prehistory museums in France, with remnants of burials dating back 70,000 years. Beautiful Roman glass, mosaics, earthenware, and other artifacts from Vesunna are in the Gallo-Roman museum.

Musée d'Art et d'Archéologie du Périgord
22 cours Tourny. **Tel** 05 53 06 40 70.
Open Wed–Mon. **Closed** public hols.
perigueux-maap.fr

❻ St-Amand-de-Coly

Dordogne. **Tel** Maison du Patrimoine (05 53 51 04 56, summer only); La Mairie (05 53 51 47 85). **Open** daily.
saint-amand-de-coly.org

This abbey church is an outstanding example of fortress architecture, built in the 12th–13th centuries by Augustinian monks to protect their monastery. There are two lines of defence: a high stone rampart and, behind it, the arched tower of the church itself. The tower looks more like a castle keep, and was once pierced by arrow slits.

Inside, the church is beautifully simple, with pure lines, a flat ribbed vault, 12th-century cupola, a soaring nave, and a stone floor sloping up to the altar. Yet even this interior was arranged for defense, with a gallery from which enemies within the building could be attacked.

St-Amand was damaged during the Hundred Years' War. In 1575, it survived a siege by Huguenot cavalry and a 6-day bombardment by cannons. Religious life here ended after the Revolution.

⓫ Sarlat

Sarlat-la-Canéda possesses the highest concentration of medieval, Renaissance, and 17th-century facades of any town in France. Its prosperity was a reflection of the privileged status it was granted in return for loyalty to the French crown during the Hundred Years' War. Behind the nondescript rue de la République are narrow lanes and archways, and ancient, ocher-colored stone town houses rich in ornamental detail. Protected by law since 1962, Sarlat's buildings now form an open-air museum. The town is also famous for one of the best markets in France.

Place de la Liberté
The Renaissance heart of Sarlat is now lined with luxury boutiques and cafés.

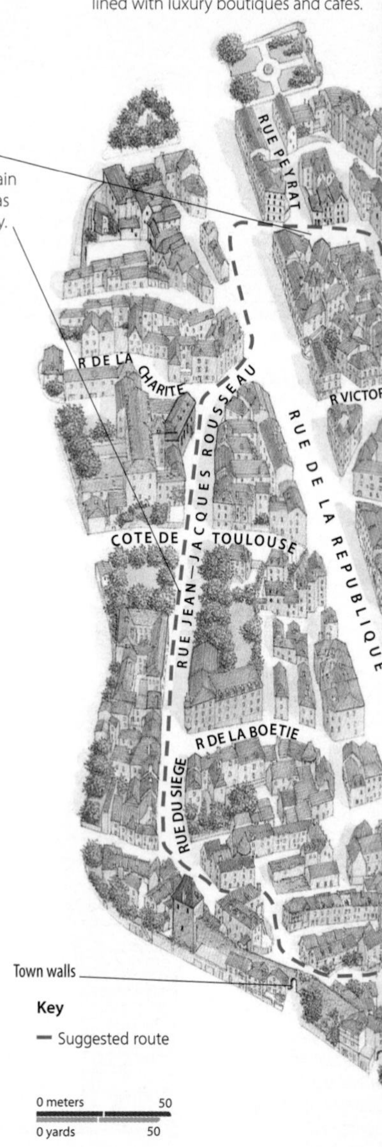

Rue des Consuls contains 15th-, 16th- and 17th-century mansions, built for the town's middle-class merchants, magistrates, and church officials.

Rue Jean-Jacques Rousseau was the main street until rue de la République (known as "La Traverse") was built in the 19th century.

Town walls

Key

— Suggested route

0 meters 50
0 yards 50

Walnuts, a key Périgord crop

Sarlat Market

Every Wednesday, the great Sarlat food market is held in place de la Liberté, every Thursday organic markets meet at 5pm, and every Saturday there is a full-scale fair which attracts locals from all around. There is a daily indoor market at Église Sainte-Marie. Sarlat lies at the heart of the nation's *foie gras* and walnut trades. These typical Périgord products absorb much of the town's attention and supply a good proportion of its revenue, as they did during Sarlat's heyday in the 14th and 15th centuries. Other local specialities are black truffles dug up in the woods in January, and wild mushrooms. Seek out the cheeses of every shape, age, and hue, and the huge range of pork delicacies, potted, fresh, smoked, dried, salted, fried, baked, or boiled.

Bulbs of pink garlic

For hotels and restaurants in this region see pp554–71 and pp576–603

Rue de la Salamandre
This lane was named after the salamander emblem of King François I, seen on many of the town's 16th-century houses.

VISITORS' CHECKLIST

Practical Information
Dordogne. 10,500. 3 rue Tourny (05 53 31 45 45). Wed & Sat. Theater (Jul–Aug); Film (Nov). **sarlat-tourisme.com**

Transport
av de la Gare.

Église Sainte-Marie, built in1365, now houses an indoor market offering local products. A panoramic lift has been built up to the top of the church's steeple, providing a great view of Sarlat from above.

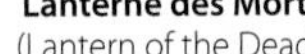

Lanterne des Morts
(Lantern of the Dead) The conical tower in the cemetery was built to commemorate the sermons of St-Bernard in Sarlat in August 1147.

Cathédrale St-Sacerdos
Built largely in the 16th and 17th centuries, the cathedral is remarkable for its magnificent 18th-century organ.

The Chapelle des Pénitents Bleus, built in pure Romanesque style, is the last vestige of the 12th-century abbey.

The former Bishop's Palace, with remains of a 16th-century loggia and a Renaissance interior, is now a tourist office, which puts on excellent summer exhibitions.

Cour des Fontaines
A pure spring here attracted the monks who founded Sarlat's first abbey in the 9th century.

Painting of a bull from the original cave at Lascaux

❼ Lascaux II

Montignac. **Tel** 05 53 05 65 65. **Open** Feb–mid-Nov: daily; mid-Nov–Feb: Tue–Sun; times vary – phone to check. **Closed** Jan, Dec 25. **lascaux.culture.fr**

Lascaux is the most famous of the prehistoric sites clustered around the junction of the rivers Vézère and Beune *(see pp406–7)*. Four boys came across the caves and their astonishing paleolithic paintings in 1940, and the importance of their discovery was swiftly recognized.

Lascaux has been closed to the public since 1963 because of deterioration, but an exact copy has been created a few minutes' walk down the hillside, using the same materials. The replica is beautiful and should not be spurned: high-antlered elk, bison, bulls, and plump horses cover the walls, surrounded by arrows and geometric symbols thought to have had ritual significance.

❽ Bergerac

Dordogne. 26,000. 97 rue Neuve d'Argenson (05 53 57 03 11). Wed & Sat; organic market: Tue. **bergerac-tourisme.com**

This small port, a tobacco farming and commercial center, spreads itself over both sides of the Dordogne. Chief attractions are its extraordinary **Musée du Tabac** (tobacco museum), and its food and wine which are invariably excellent. Bergerac's most celebrated wine is Monbazillac, a sweet white wine, often drunk on ceremonial occasions. On show in the small, lively museum are some Native American pipes.

Musée du Tabac

Maison Peyrarède, pl du Feu. **Tel** 05 53 63 04 13. **Open** Tue–Sun. **Closed** Sun ams (Oct–Mar: Sun all day), public hols.

❾ Les Eyzies

Dordogne. 900. 19 av de la Préhistoire (05 53 06 97 05). Mon (Apr–Oct). **tourisme-vezere.com**

Four major prehistoric sites and a group of smaller caves cluster around the unassuming village of Les Eyzies. Head first for the **Musée National de Préhistoire**, in a new building at the foot of a 16th-century castle overlooking the village. The timelines and other exhibits are useful for putting the vast warren of prehistoric painting and sculpture into context.

The **Grotte de Font de Gaume** is the logical first stop after the museum. This cave, discovered in 1901, contains probably the finest prehistoric paintings still on public view in France.

Close by is the **Grotte des Combarelles**, with engravings of bison, reindeer, magic symbols, and human figures. Farther on, you reach the rock shelter of **Abri du Cap Blanc**, discovered in 1909,

Les Eyzies, a center for the area's concentration of prehistoric caves

vith a rare, lifesize frieze of horses nd bison sculpted in the rock.

On the other side of Les Eyzies s the cave system at **Rouffignac**, favorite place for excursions ince the 15th century. There re 5 miles (8 km) of caves ere, 1.5 miles (2.5 km) of which re served by electric train. he paintings include drawings of mammoths, and a frieze of wo bison challenging each other to combat.

Tickets for the caves sell out ast, especially in summer, so rrive early or book ahead. Tickets for Combarelles and Rouffignac must be purchased at the Grotte de Font de Gaume.

Musée National de Préhistoire

Musée National de Préhistoire
Tel 05 53 06 45 45. **Open** Jul & Aug: daily; Sep–Jun: Wed–Mon. **Closed** Jan 1, Dec 25.

Grotte de Font de Gaume
Tel 05 53 06 86 00. **Open** Sun–Fri by appt; book ahead. **Closed** some public hols.

Grotte des Combarelles
Tel 05 53 06 86 00. **Open** Sun–Fri (book ahead). **Closed** some public hols.

Abri du Cap Blanc
Marquay, Les Eyzies. **Tel** 05 53 06 86 00. **Open** Apr–Oct: daily. **Closed** some public hols.

Grotte de Rouffignac
Tel 05 53 05 41 71. **Open** Apr–Oct: daily (tickets at 9am and 2:30pm).

⑩ Dordogne Valley

Dordogne. Bergerac. Bergerac, Le Buisson de Cadouin. Beynac. Le Buisson de Cadouin (05 53 22 06 09).

Probably no river in France crosses so varied a landscape and such different geological formations as the Dordogne. Starting in deep granite gorges in the Massif Central, it continues through fertile lowlands, then enters the limestone Causse country around Souillac. By the time the Dordogne has wound down to the Garonne, it is almost 2 miles (3 km) wide.

Don't be put off by the valley's touristy image. It is a beautiful area for wandering. Several villages make good stopping-off points, such as Limeuil, Beynac, and La Roque-Gageac from where *gabarres* (river boats) ferry visitors (Easter–Oct).

Perched high above the river, southwest of Sarlat, is the 17th-century **Château de Marqueyssac**. Its topiary park offers panoramic views from Domme to Beynac, and of the Château de Castelnaud on the opposite river bank.

⑪ Sarlat

See pp436–7.

View of Domme from the medieval gateway of Porte de la Combe

⑫ Domme

Dordogne. 1,030. pl de la Halle (05 53 31 71 00). Thu.
ot-domme.com

Henry Miller wrote: "Just to glimpse the black, mysterious river at Domme from the beautiful bluff…is something to be grateful for all one's life." Domme itself is a neat bastide *(see p449)* of golden stone, with medieval gateways still standing. People come here to admire the view, which takes in the Dordogne valley from Beynac in the west to Montfort in the east, and wander the maze of old streets inside the walls. There is also a large cavern under the 17th-century covered market where the inhabitants hid at perilous moments during the Hundred Years' War and the 16th-century Wars of Religion. Despite a seemingly impregnable position, 30 intrepid Huguenots managed to capture Domme by scaling the cliffs under cover of night and opening the gates.

A *cingle* (loop) of the river Dordogne, seen from the town of Domme

⑬ Rocamadour

Rocamadour became one of the most famous centers of pilgrimage following a spate of miracles heralded, it is claimed, by the bell above the Black Virgin and Child in the Chapel of Notre-Dame. This was followed by the discovery in 1166 of an ancient grave and sepulcher containing an undecayed body, said to be that of the early Christian hermit St. Amadour. Although the town suffered with the decline of pilgrimages in the 17th and 18th centuries, it was heavily restored in the 19th century. Still a holy shrine, as well as a popular tourist destination, Rocamadour's site on a rocky plateau above the Alzou valley is phenomenal. The best views are to be had from the ramparts of the château, reached from the hamlet of L'Hospitalet.

General View
Rocamadour is at its most breathtaking in the sunlight of early morning: the cluster of medieval houses, towers, and battlements seems to sprout from the base of the cliff.

KEY

① **The Tomb of St. Amadour** once held the body of the hermit called *roc amator* (lover of rock), from whom the town took its name.

② **St. Michael's Chapel** contains well-preserved 12th-century frescoes.

③ **The château** stands on the site of a fort which protected the sanctuary from the west.

④ **Ramparts**

⑤ **Cross of Jerusalem**

⑥ **The Basilica of St-Sauveur**, a late 12th-century sanctuary, backs on to the bare rock face.

⑦ **The Chapel of St. John the Baptist** faces the fine Gothic portal of the Basilica of St-Sauveur.

⑧ **St. Anne's Chapel** dates from the 13th century, and contains a 17th-century gilded altar screen.

⑨ **Chapel of St. Blaise** (13th century)

Grand Stairway
Pilgrims would climb this broad flight of steps on their knees as they said their rosaries. The stairway leads to a square on the next level, around which the main pilgrim chapels are grouped.

For hotels and restaurants in this region see pp554–71 and pp576–603

VISITORS' CHECKLIST

Practical Information
Lot. 670. L'Hospitalet (05 65 33 22 00). Chapel of Notre-Dame: **Open** 9am–6:30pm daily (to 9pm Jun–Sep). **vallee-dordogne-rocamadour.com**

Transport
3 miles (5 km) SW Rocamadour.

Stations of the Cross
Pilgrims encounter the Cross of Jerusalem and 14 stations marking Jesus's journey to the Cross on their way up the hillside to the château.

Rocamadour Town
Now a pedestrian precinct, its main street is lined with souvenir shops to tempt the throngs of pilgrims.

Chapel of Notre-Dame (Miracles)
St. Amadour's body was found in the cliff, near the Black Virgin Chapel. A statue of the Black Virgin, the supreme object of veneration, stands on the altar.

⓮ Gouffre de Padirac

Lot. **Tel** 05 65 33 64 56. **Open** Apr–Oct: daily. **gouffre-de-padirac.com**

Formed by the collapse of a cave, this huge crater measures 115 ft (35 m) wide and 337 ft (103 m) deep. The underground river and stunning succession of galleries *(see pp406–7)* were discovered in 1889. The immense Salle du Grand Dôme chamber dwarfs the tallest of cathedrals. Take a jacket; the cave is 55° F (13° C).

⓯ Autoire

Lot. 370. Saint Céré (05 65 38 11 85). **saint-cere.fr**

This is one of the loveliest places in Quercy, the fertile area east of Périgord. There are no grand monuments or dramatic history, just an unspoiled site at the mouth of the Autoire gorge. The **Château de Limarque** on the main square, and the **Château de Busqueille** overlooking it, are both built in characteristic Quercy style, with turrets and towers. Elsewhere, elaborate dovecotes stand in fields or are attached to houses.

Outside Autoire, past a 100-ft (30-m) waterfall, a path climbs to a rock amphitheater giving panoramic views of the region.

The picturesque village of Autoire, seen from across the gorge

⓰ Cahors

Lot. 21,200. pl François Mitterrand (05 65 53 20 65). Wed & Sat am. **tourisme-cahors.com**

The capital of the Lot *département*, Cahors is renowned for its dark, heady wine, which was produced as far back as Roman times. It is also famous for being the birthplace of the statesman Léon Gambetta (1838–82), who led France to recovery after the war with Prussia in 1870. The main street of Cahors – like many towns in France – is named after him.

Cathédrale de St-Etienne, entrenched behind the narrow streets of Cahors' Old Town, dates back to 1119. It has some fine medieval details: don't miss the lively figures of the Romanesque north door and tympanum, which depict the Ascension, or the huge cupola above the nave (said to be the

A Tour of Two Rivers

Flanked by spectacular limestone cliffs, the beautiful Lot and Célé valleys feature ancient medieval villages and castles, narrow gorges and rushing waterfalls along lazy stretches of river. An unhurried tour of both valleys, around 100 miles (160 km), is best spread over 2 days, to savor the gastronomic delights as well as the superb views.

From Cahors, the route follows the Lot, then meanders slowly up the peaceful and picturesque Célé valley to reach Figeac, a handsome town full of charming shops, cafés, and restaurants. The return route is via the busier Lot Valley, which has more sights including the spectacular village of St-Cirq-Lapopie (allow time to park above or below the village and enter on foot).

① **Grotte de Pech-Merle**
This 25,000-year-old prehistoric site outside Cabrerets has huge chambers painted with mammoths, horses, bison and human figures.

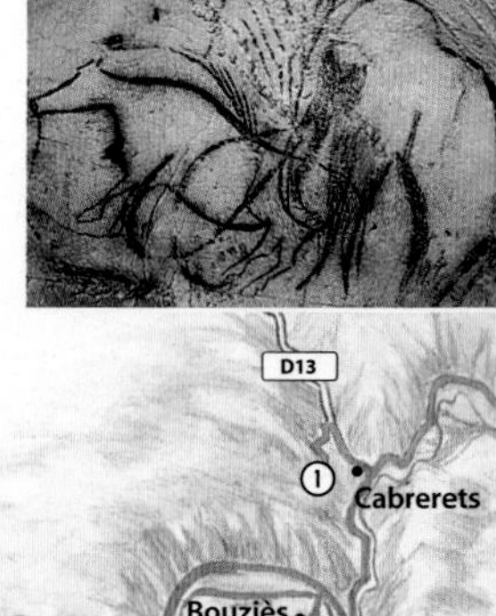

⑥ **St-Cirq-Lapopie**
Perched high above the Lot, one of France's prettiest villages has a 15th-century church and timber-framed houses built into the cliffs.

ırgest in France). They are ɔvered in 14th-century escoes depicting the stoning f St. Stephen (St-Étienne). he Renaissance cloisters are ecorated with some intricate, ɿough damaged, carvings.

Also worth seeking out in the athedral quarter is the ornate 6th-century **Maison de :oaldès**, its north facade ecorated with tree, sun, and ɔse of Quercy motifs. It was here ɿat Henri of Navarre (who later ecame King Henri IV) stayed for ne night in 1580 after besieging nd capturing Cahors.

The town's landmark monu-nent is the **Pont Valentré**, a ɔrtified bridge with seven ointed arches and three ɔwers that spans the river. : was built between 1308 nd 1360, and has withstood nany attacks since then. It is laimed that the bridge is one f the most photographed nonuments in the whole of France. An alternative way to enjoy the scenery is to take a leisurely 90-minute boat trip through the lock from a wharf near the bridge (Apr–Oct).

The fortified Pont Valentré spanning the river Lot at Cahors

Environs

Cahors makes a good base from which to explore the sights of the Lot. Visit the historic towns of Figeac, birthplace of Jean-François Champollion who first deciphered Egyptian hieroglyphics, and the Grotte de Pech-Merle with its extra-ordinary painted walls.

Grotte de Pech-Merle
Cabrerets. **Tel** 05 65 31 27 05. **Open** Apr–Oct daily. **pechmerle.com**

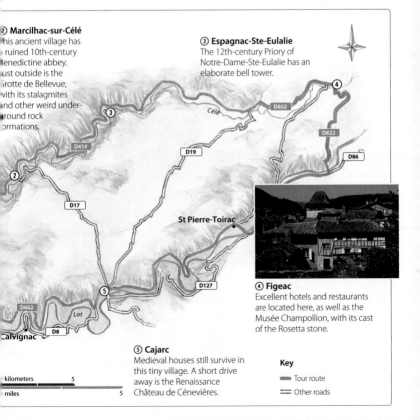

② Marcilhac-sur-Célé
his ancient village has ruined 10th-century Benedictine abbey. ust outside is the Grotte de Bellevue, vith its stalagmites nd other weird under-round rock ɔrmations.

③ Espagnac-Ste-Eulalie
The 12th-century Priory of Notre-Dame-Ste-Eulalie has an elaborate bell tower.

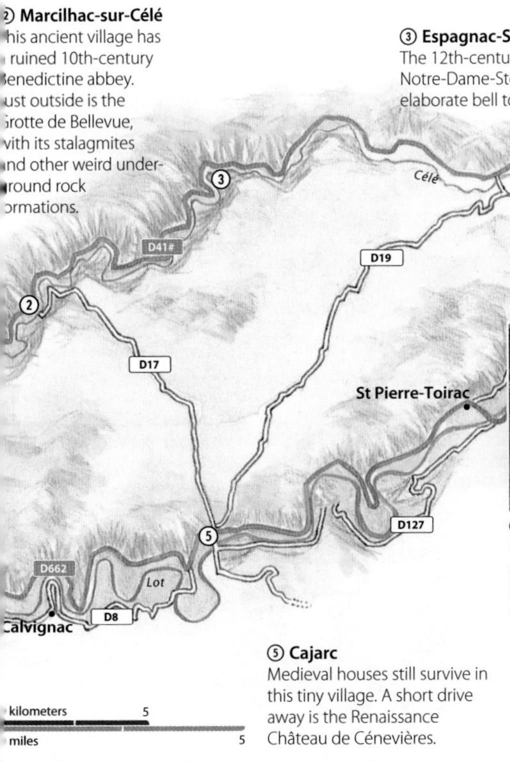

④ Figeac
Excellent hotels and restaurants are located here, as well as the Musée Champollion, with its cast of the Rosetta stone.

⑤ Cajarc
Medieval houses still survive in this tiny village. A short drive away is the Renaissance Château de Cénevières.

Key
Tour route
Other roads

kilometers 5
miles 5

Orchards and vineyards outside Agen

⓱ Agen

Lot-et-Garonne. 35,000. 38 rue Garonne (05 53 47 36 09. Tue–Sun. **ot-agen.org**

Vast orchards of regimented plum trees – producing the celebrated *pruneaux d'Agen* – characterize the landscape around this small provincial city. Crusaders returning from the Middle East brought the fruit to France in the 11th century, and monks in the Lot valley nearby were the first to dry plums for prunes in commercial quantities.

Agen's **Musée Municipal des Beaux-Arts** contains paintings by Goya, including his *Ascent in a Hot-Air Balloon,* Sisley's *September Morning*, Corot's landscape *L'étang de Ville d'Avray*, and works by Picabia. Undisputed jewel of the collection is the *Vénus du Mas*, a beautifully proportioned marble statue dating from the 1st century BC, discovered nearby in 1876.

Musée Municipal des Beaux-Arts
Pl du Docteur Esquirol. **Tel** 05 53 69 47 23. **Open** Wed–Mon. **Closed** Jan 1, May 1, Nov 1, Dec 25.

Environs
The fortified village of Moirax, 5 miles (8 km) south of Agen, has a 12th-century Romanesque church of great beauty and symmetry. Two of the appealing sculpted capitals depict biblical accounts of Daniel in the lions' den, and Original Sin.

The bastide town *(see p449)* of Villeneuve-sur-Lot, 21 miles (34 km) south of Agen stands astride the River Lot. It has a tall 14th-century tower that once formed a defensive gateway. The red-brick Romano-Byzantine church of Ste-Catherine was built in 1909 but contains restored 15th-century stained-glass windows. Just to the east of Villeneuve is the pretty medieval hilltop village of Penne D'Agenais.

⓲ Larressingle

Gers. 200. to Condom. Condom (05 62 28 00 80).

With its ramparts, ruined donjon (defence tower), and fortress gate, Larressingle is a tiny fortified village in the middle of the Gascon countryside. It dates from the 13th century, and is one of the last remaining Gascon villages with its walls still intact. The state of preservation is unique, and gives an idea of what life must have been like for the small, embattled local communities who had to live for decades under conditions of perpetual warfare.

⓳ Condom

Gers. 7,500. 5 pl St-Pierre (05 62 28 00 80). Wed, Sat am & Sun am. **tourisme-tenareze.com**

Long a center for the Armagnac trade, Condom is a market town built around the late-Gothic **Cathédrale St-Pierre**. In 1569 during the Wars of Religion, the Huguenot (French Protestant) army threatened to demolish the cathedral, but Condom's citizens averted this by paying a huge ransom.

The river Baïse skirts the town center. Notable among Condom's fine 17th–18th-century mansions is the **Hôtel de Cugnac** on rue Jean-Jaurès, with its ancient *chai* (wine and spirit storehouse) and distillery. On the other side of the town center, the **Musée de l'Armagnac** is the place to find out, finally, what the difference between the brandy of Armagnac and Cognac really is.

Musée de l'Armagnac
2 rue Jules Ferry. **Tel** 05 62 28 47 17. **Open** Apr–Oct: Wed–Mon; Nov–Mar: Wed–Sun pms. **Closed** Jan, public hols.

Armagnac

Armagnac is one of the world's most expensive brandies. It is also one of the leading products of southwest France: approximately 6 million bottles are produced annually, 45 percent of which are exported to 132 countries. The vineyards of Armagnac roughly straddle the border between the Gers and the Lot-et-Garonne regions, and the Landes. Similar in style to Cognac, its more famous neighbor, Armagnac's single distillation leaves more individual flavors in the spirit. The majority of small, independent producers offer direct sale to the public: look out for the battered, often half-hidden farm signs advertising *Vente Directe*.

A Tenarèze Armagnac

For hotels and restaurants in this region see pp554–71 and pp576–603

D'Artagnan

Gascons call their domain the "Pays d'Artagnan" after Alexandre Dumas' rollicking hero from *The Three Musketeers* (1844). The character of d'Artagnan was based on Charles de Batz, a typical Gascon whose chivalry, passion, and impetuousness made him ideal as a musketeer, or royal bodyguard. De Batz's life was as fast and furious as that of the fictional hero, and he performed a feat of courtliness by arresting Louis XIV's most formidable minister without causing the slightest offence. The French have other opinions on the Gascon nature too: a *promesse de Gascon*, for example, means an empty promise.

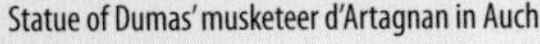
Statue of Dumas' musketeer d'Artagnan in Auch

prophets, patriarchs, and apostles, with 360 individually characterized figures and exceptional colors. Three depict the key biblical events of Creation, the Crucifixion, and the Resurrection.

Auch went through an urbanization program in the 18th century, when the allées d'Etigny, flanked by the grand Hôtel de Ville and Palais de Justice, were built. Some fine houses from this period line the pedestrianized rue Dessoles. Auch's restaurants are known for their hearty dishes, including *foie gras de canard* (fattened duck liver).

) Auch

ers. 23,500. 1 rue essoles (05 62 05 22 89). Tue am, ıu & Sat. **auch-tourisme.com**

ne ancient capital of the ers department, Auch ›ronounced "Ohsh") as long been a sleepy lace which comes alive n market days. The new own by the ation is not a lace which ncourages you › linger. Head ıstead for the Old own on the outcrop verlooking the river Gers. If you climb the 234 stone steps from the river, you arrive directly in front of the restored late-Gothic **Cathédrale Ste-Marie**, begun in 1489. The furnishings of the cathedral are remarkable: highlights are the carved wooden choir stalls depicting more than 1,500 biblical, historical, and mythological characters, and the equally magnificent 15th-century stained glass, attributed to Arnaud de Moles. The windows show a mix of

Medallion from Cathédrale Ste-Marie

㉑ Auvillar

Tarn-et-Garonne. 1,000. pl de la Halle (05 63 39 89 82).

A perfect complement to the high emotion of Moissac *(see pp446–7)*, Auvillar is one of the loveliest hilltop villages in France. It has a triangular marketplace lined with half-timbered arcades at its center, and extensive views from the promenade overlooking the river Garonne. There are picnic spots along this panoramic path plus an orientation map. This includes all but the chimneys visible in the distance, belonging to the nuclear plant at Golfech.

ıunflowers, a popular crop in southwest France grown for their seeds and oil

㉒ Moissac

At the core of this otherwise unremarkable riverside town is the abbey of St-Pierre, one of the undisputed masterpieces of French Romanesque art. Founded in the 7th century by a Benedictine monk, the abbey was subsequently ransacked by Arabs, Normans, and Hungarians. In 1047, Moissac abbey was united with the rich foundation at Cluny and prospered under the direction of Abbot Durand de Bredon. By the 12th century it had become the pre-eminent monastery in southwest France. The superb south portal was created during this period.

Abbey of St-Pierre
The church's exterior belongs to two periods: one part, in stone, is Romanesque; the other, in brick, is Gothic.

Christ in Majesty
The figure of Christ sits in judgment at the center of the scene. He holds the Book of Life in His left hand and raises His right in benediction.

Tympanum
The lower register of the balanced, compact tympanum shows the expressive "24 Elders with crowns of gold" from St. John's vision.

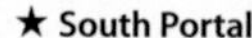

★ South Portal
The carved south portal (1100–1130) is a masterful translation into stone of St. John's dramatic vision of the Apocalypse (Book of Revelation, Chapters 4 and 5). The Evangelists Matthew, Mark, Luke, and John appear as "four beasts full of eyes." Moorish details on the door jambs reflect the contemporary cultural exchange between France and Spain.

VISITORS' CHECKLIST

Practical Information
Tarn-et-Garonne. 13,000. 6 pl Durand de Bredon (05 63 04 01 85). Sat, Sun ams. Abbey: **Open** daily. Cloisters: **Open** daily *(phone for details)*. 6:30pm Mon–Fri, 7:30pm Sat, 10.30am Sun. **tourisme.moissac.fr**

Transport

★ Cloister
The late 11th-century cloister is lined with alternate double and single columns in white, pink, green, and gray marble. In all, there are 76 richly decorated arches.

loorplan: Church and Cloister

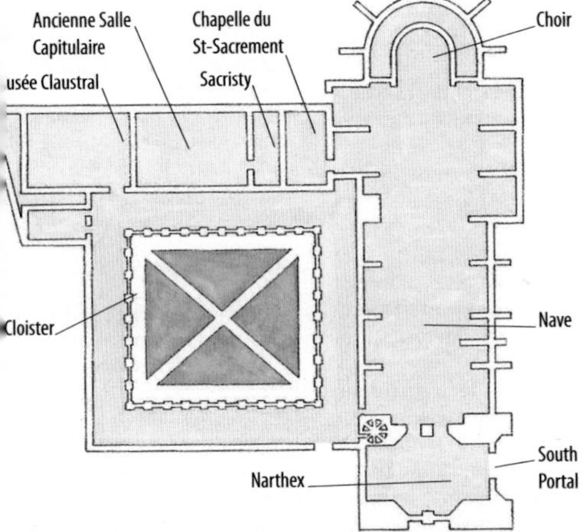

loister Capitals
lowers, beasts, and scenes from both the Old and New Testaments re featured in these superbly sculptured 11th-century omanesque capitals.

㉓ Montauban

Tarn-et-Garonne. 58,000. 4 rue du Collège (05 63 63 60 60). Wed & Sat; organic market: Thu pm. **montauban-tourisme.com**

Montauban deserves more attention than it usually gets, as Toulouse's little pink-brick sister and the capital of the 17th-century "Protestant Republic" of southern France. The painter Ingres was born here in 1780, and the town's great treasure is the **Musée Ingres**, a 17th-century palace with an exceptional bequest of paintings and 4,000 drawings, plus works by Van Dyck, Tintoretto, Courbet, and sculptor Emile Bourdelle, an associate of Rodin, also from here.

Above all, Montauban is a civilized shopping center, with a double-arcaded main square (place Nationale) built in the 17th and 18th centuries. A few streets away lies the stark white **Cathédrale Notre-Dame**, built on the orders of Louis XIV in 1692, in the backlash against Protestant heresy.

Musée Ingres
Palais Episcopal, 19 rue de l'Hôtel de Ville. **Tel** 05 63 22 12 91. **Open** Tue–Sun (Jul–Aug: daily). **Closed** Jan 1, Jul 14, Nov 1, Nov 11, Dec 25.

㉔ Gorges de l'Aveyron

Tarn-et-Garonne. Toulouse. Montauban, Lexos. Montauban. Mairie, St-Antonin-Noble-Val (05 63 30 63 47). **tourisme-saint-antonin-noble-val.com**

At the Gorges de l'Aveyron, the sweltering plains of Montauban change abruptly to cool, chestnut-wooded hills. Here the villages are of a different stamp from those of Périgord and Quercy, displaying an obsession with defense.

The château at Bruniquel, founded in the 6th century, is built over the lip of a precipice. Further along the D115, the village of Penne's position on the tip of a giant rock fang is even more extreme. The gorge narrows and darkens; from St-Antonin-Noble-Val, beside the river, the valley turns towards Cordes.

25 Cordes

Tarn. 1,050. 40 Grand Rue Raimond VII (05 63 56 00 52). Sat. **cordessurciel.fr**

Sometimes known as Cordes-sur-Ciel, this is a fitting description as the town seems suspended against the skyline. During the 13th-century Cathar wars the entire town was excommunicated. Devastating epidemics of plague later sent it into decline, and the town was in an advanced state of decay at the beginning of the 20th century.

Restoration work began in the 1940s and the ramparts and many of the gates built in 1222 have been well preserved. Also intact are Gothic houses like the 14th-century **Maison du Grand Fauconnier**.

Today, Cordes still exudes a sense of loss. The town of which Albert Camus wrote "Everything is beautiful there, even regret," is now dependent on tourism. "Medieval" crafts aimed at visitors abound and a collection at the **Musée d'Art Moderne et Contemporain** evokes Cordes' former embroidery industry. The museum also houses works of modern art by such artists as Picasso and Miro. The **Jardin des Paradis** offers a corner of beauty and hope to reflect in.

Musée d'Art Moderne et Contemporain
Maison du Grand Fauconnier. **Tel** 05 63 56 14 79. **Open** mid-Mar–mid-Nov: daily.

Cathédrale Ste-Cécile perched above the town of Albi

26 Albi

Tarn. 51,275. pl Ste-Cécile (05 63 36 36 00). Tue–Sun. **albi-tourisme.fr**

Like many another large town in this region, Albi is not only red, but also red hot, and not ideal for afternoon visits in summer. You need to get up in the cool early morning to walk the streets around the market and the cathedral.

Then make for the **Musée Henri de Toulouse-Lautrec** in the Palais de la Berbie ahead of the crowds. The museum contains the most complete permanent collection of the artist's work in existence, including paintings, drawings, and his famous posters for the Moulin-Rouge. There are also canvases by Matisse, Dufy, and Yves Brayer. After a stroll around the beautiful terraced gardens, step next door to the vast red-brick **Cathédrale Ste-Cécile**, built in the aftermath of the Albigensian crusade in 1265. It was intended as a reminder to potential heretics that the Church meant business. From a distance, its semi-circular towers and narrow windows give it the appearance more of a fortress than a place of worship. Every feature, from the huge bell tower to the apocalyptic fresco of the *Last Judgement*, is on a giant scale, built deliberately to dwarf the average person. The effect is breathtaking.

Musée Toulouse-Lautrec
Palais de la Berbie. **Tel** 05 63 49 58 97. **Open** Apr–Sep: daily; Oct–Mar: Wed–Mon. **Closed** Jan 1, May 1, Nov 1, Dec 25.
musee-toulouse-lautrec.com

Toulouse-Lautrec

Comte Henri de Toulouse-Lautrec was born in Albi in 1864. Crippled at 15 as a result of two falls, he moved to Paris in 1882, recording the life of the city's cabarets, brothels, racecourses, and circuses. A dedicated craftsman, his bold, vivid posters did much to establish lithography as a major art form. Alcoholism and syphilis led to his early death at the age of 36.

Lautrec's *La Modiste* (1900)

27 Castres

Tarn. 45,000. 2 pl de la République (05 63 62 63 62). Tue–Sun. **tourisme-castres.fr**

Castres has been a center for the cloth industry since the 14th century. Today it is also the headquarters of one of France's biggest pharmaceutical companies. In the large collection of Spanish art in the **Musée Goya** the artist himself is well represented by a large, misty council scene and by a series of powerful prints, *Los Caprichos*. Outside, the formal gardens between the town hall and the river Agout were designed in the 17th century by Le Nôtre *(see p183)*, the landscape architect of Vaux-le-Vicomte and Versailles.

Musée Goya
Hôtel de Ville. **Tel** 05 63 71 59 30 or 05 63 71 59 27. **Open** Jul–Aug: daily; Sep–Jun: Tue–Sun. **Closed** Jan 1, May 1, Nov 1, Dec 25.

Bastide Towns

Bastide towns were hurriedly built in the 13th century by both the English and the French, to encourage settlement of empty areas before the Hundred Years' War. They are the medieval equivalent of "new towns," with their planned grid of streets and fortified perimeters. Over 300 bastide towns and villages still survive between Périgord and the Pyrenees.

A broad arcaded marketplace is the central feature of most bastides. Montauban's arcades still shelter a variety of shops.

Lauzerte, founded in 1241 by the Count of Toulouse, is a typical bastide town of gray stone houses. The town, long an English outpost, is perched for security on the brow of a hill.

The church could be used as a keep when the bastide's outer fortifications had been breached.

The central square is surrounded by a grid of interconnecting streets and alleys. This differs markedly from the usual jumble of medieval houses and lanes.

Stone houses protected the perimeter.

Monflanquin

This military bastide town was built by the French in 1256 on a strategic north–south route. It changed hands several times during the Hundred Years' War.

Today, the bastides form a convenient network of market towns, known as the *route des bastides*. The best time to visit them is on market day, when the central squares are crammed with stalls.

Porte de la Jane in Cordes is a typical bastide feature. These narrow gateways were easily barred by portcullises.

㉘ Toulouse

Toulouse, the most important town in southwest France, is the country's fourth largest metropolis, and a major industrial and university city. The area is also famous for its aerospace industry (Concorde, Airbus, the Ariane space rocket all originated here), as shown by the Cité de l'Espace just outside the city.

Best seen on foot, Toulouse has fine cuisine, one of France's most striking churches, lively street life, and a rose-brick Old Town, which is described as "pink at dawn, red at noon and mauve at dusk."

The river Garonne, crossed by the Pont Neuf

Houseboats at their moorings on the Canal du Midi

Exploring Toulouse

This warm southern city has steadily expanded, crescent-like, from its original Roman site on the Garonne. First it was a flourishing Visigoth city, then a Renaissance town of towered brick palaces built with the wealth generated by the *pastel* (blue pigment) and grain trades. The grandest of these palaces still survive in the Old Town, centered around Place du Capitole and the huge 18th-century **Hôtel de Ville**. Here, and in place St-Georges and rue Alsace-Lorraine, is the main concentration of shops, bars, and cafés. The city's large student population keeps prices down in the numerous cafés, oyster bars, and bookstores, and in the fleamarket, held on Sundays in place St-Sernin.

A ring of 18th- and 19th-century boulevards encircles the city, surrounded in turn by a tangle of autoroutes. The left bank of the Garonne is under development (St-Cyprien) and is linked by Toulouse's driverless metro. The former abattoir has been superbly converted into a center for modern and contemporary art, **Les Abattoirs** (Wed–Sun), the highlight of which is Picasso's theater backdrop *Minotaur disguised as Harlequin*.

Les Jacobins

This church was begun in 1229 and completed over the next two centuries. It was the first Dominican convent, founded to combat dissent. The Jacobins' convent became the founding institution of Toulouse University. Its church, a Gothic masterpiece, features a soaring, 22-branched palm tree vault in the apse. The delicate Gothic Chapelle St-Antonin (1337) contains frescoes of the Apocalypse dating from 1341.

Musée des Augustins

21 rue de Metz. **Tel** 05 61 22 21 82.
Open daily. **Closed** Jan 1, May 1, Dec 25. **augustins.org**

Palm vaulting in the apse of Les Jacobins

MONTAUBAN
BOULEVARD LASCROSSES
RUE LASCROSSES
RUE DE LA CITE
BOULVARD ARMAND DUPORTAL
RUE DES SALE
Université des Sciences Sociales
Aéroport 6 km (3.5 miles)
PLACE A-FRANCE
ALLÉ DE BARCELONE
RUE VALADE
RUE PARGAMIN
QUAI ST PIERRE
PLACE ST-PIERRE
Pont St-Pierre
RUE DES BLANCHERS
QUAI LUCIEN LOMBARD
Les Abattoirs (Espace d'Art Contemporain)
River Garo

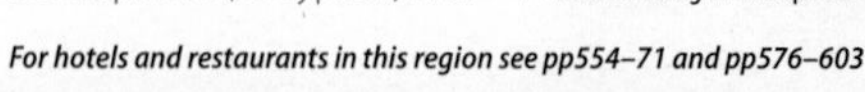

For hotels and restaurants in this region see pp554–71 and pp576–603

›louse became a center of
nanesque art owing to its
sition on the route to Santiago
Compostela *(see pp404–5)*.
› museum has sculpture from
period and 12th-century
nanesque capitals, as well as
isters from a 14th-century
gustinian priory. There are also
h–19th-century French, Italian
d Flemish paintings here,
luding work by Ingres,
acroix, Constant, and Laurens.

Facade of Musée des Augustins

Fondation Bemberg

Hôtel d'Assézat, 7 pl d'Assézat.
Tel 05 61 12 06 89. **Open** Tue–Sun.
Closed 1 Jan, 25 Dec.

This 16th-century palace houses the collection of local art lover Georges Bemberg, and covers Renaissance paintings, 19th–20th-century French paintings, *objets d'art* and bronzes.

VISITORS' CHECKLIST

Practical Information
Haute-Garonne. 446,500.
Donjon du Capitole (08 92 180 180). daily. Piano aux Jacobins (Sep). **toulouse-tourisme.com**

Transport
3.5 miles (6 km) NW Toulouse. bd Pierre Semard (trains: Gare Matabiau). Guided minibus tours: **citytour-toulouse.**

Basilique St-Sernin

Pl St-Sernin. **Tel** 05 61 21 80 45.
Open daily.

This is the largest Romanesque basilica in Europe, built in the 11th–12th centuries to accommodate pilgrims. Highlights are the octagonal brick belfry, with rows of decorative brick arches topped by an enormously tall spire. Beautiful 11th-century marble bas-reliefs of Christ and the symbols of the Evangelists by Bernard Gilduin are in the ambulatory.

Cité de l'Espace

Av Jean Gonord. **Tel** 05 67 22 23 24.
Open daily in summer. **Closed** Jan. **cite-espace.com**

Southeast of the city center, this vast "space park" includes two planetariums, interactive exhibits related to space exploration, the Terradome "film-experience" on the history of the earth, an IMAX cinema, and a lifesize replica of the Ariane 5 rocket, where visitors can learn how, in theory at least, to launch rockets and satellites.

The tiered, 12th-century tower of Basilique St-Sernin

Sights at a Glance

① Basilique St-Sernin
② Le Capitole
③ Les Jacobins
④ Fondation Bemberg
⑤ Musée des Augustins

eters 250
rds 250

r map symbols *see back flap*

THE PYRENEES

rénées-Atlantiques · Hautes-Pyrénées · Ariège · Haute-Garonne

e mountains of the Pyrenees form a conspicuous ontier across southwestern France. Over centuries this mote terrain has fostered tenacious people, many descended om Spanish emigrants and refugees. Today it is the last remaining lderness in southern Europe and a habitat for re animal species.

eading east from the Atlantic coast, the lls are wonderfully lush after the plains of quitaine. The deeper the Pyrenees are enetrated, the steeper the valley sides d the more gigantic the snow-clad eaks become. This is magnificent, empty, ngerous country, to be approached th caution and respect. In summer the gion offers over 1,000 miles (1,600 km) of alking trails, as well as camping, fishing, d climbing. In winter there is both cross-untry and downhill skiing at the busy sorts along the border, much livelier an their Spanish counterparts.

Historically, the Pyrenees are known as the rthplace of Henri IV, who put an end to the Wars of Religion in 1593 and united France, though the region has been characterized more often by independent fiefdoms. The region's oldest inhabitants, the Basque people *(see p459)* have maintained their own language and culture, and their resorts of Bayonne, Biarritz, and St-Jean-de-Luz reflect this, looking to the sea and to summer visitors for their livelihood.

Inland, Pau, Tarbes, and Foix rely on tourism and medium-scale industry, while Lourdes receives four million pilgrims every year. For the rest, life has been regulated by agriculture, though economic constraints today are causing an exodus from the land.

untryside around St-Lizier, in the heart of the Pyrenean countryside

View of the Ariège river in Foix

Exploring the Pyrenees

The towering Pyrenees cut across southwest France from the Mediterranean to the Atlantic coast, encompassing the craggy citadel of Montségur, the pilgrimage center of Lourdes, Pau, capital of the hilly Béarn country, and the Basque port of Bayonne. This formidable range, an unspoiled paradise for walkers, fishermen, and skiers, is as lush on its French side as it is arid in Spain, and contains the wild and beautiful Parc National des Pyrénées. Throughout the region, visitors can expect cool temperatures and grandiose scenery. Lovers of history and architecture will be richly rewarded by St-Bertrand-de-Comminges and St-Jean-de-Luz, among the region's important sights.

Marzipan candies, a specialty of southwest France

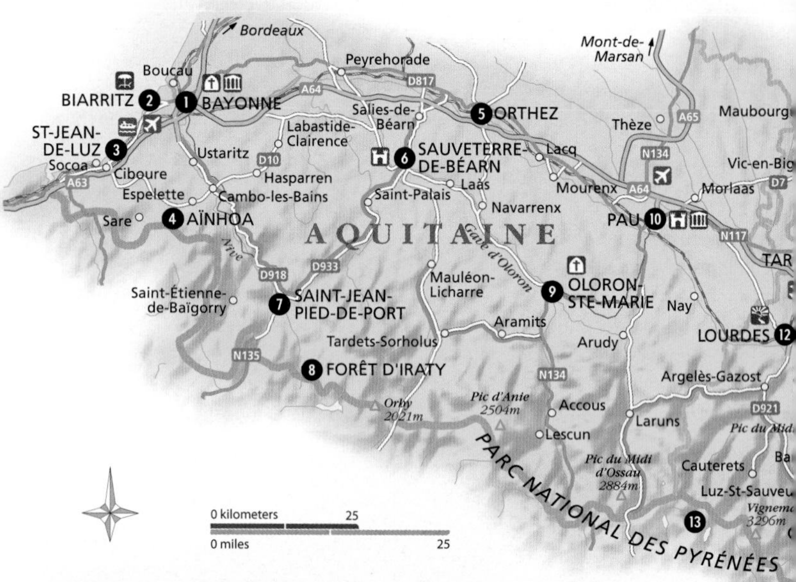

The galleried church in the Basque village of Espelette

Getting Around

Access to the Basque coast in the western Pyrenees is via the A63/N10 from Bordeaux. The length of the Pyrenees, including the mountain valleys, is served by the A64, which runs from Bayonne to Toulouse, via Orthez, Pau, Tarbes, and St-Gaudens. Once you are high up, expect narrow, twisting roads and slow driving. The scenic but demanding D918/D618 road crosses 18 high passes between the Atlantic and the Mediterranean.

There are airports at Biarritz, Pau, and Lourdes. Both Pau and Lourdes, together with Orthez and Tarbes, are on the rail route which loops south between Bordeaux and Toulouse.

For additional map symbols see back flap

ights at a Glance

- Bayonne
- Biarritz
- St-Jean-de-Luz
- Aïnhoa
- Orthez
- Sauveterre-de-Béarn
- St-Jean-Pied-de-Port
- Forêt d'Iraty
- Oloron-Ste-Marie
- Pau
- Tarbes
- Lourdes
- Parc National des Pyrénées
- Luz-St-Sauveur
- Arreau
- St-Bertrand-de-Comminges
- St-Lizier
- Foix
- Montségur
- Mirepoix

Wild *pottock* ponies on moorland in the Forêt d'Iraty

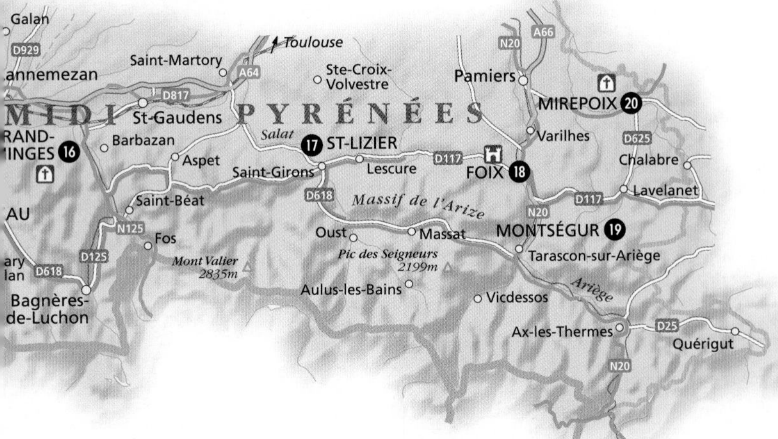

:-Jean-de-Luz seen from Ciboure, across the Nivelle estuary

Key

- Highway
- Major road
- Secondary road
- Minor road
- Scenic route
- Main railroad
- Minor railroad
- International border
- Regional border
- △ Summit

❶ Bayonne

Pyrénées-Atlantiques. 46,000. pl des Basques (08 20 42 64 64). daily. **bayonne-tourisme.com**

Bayonne, capital of the French Basque country, lies between two rivers – the turbulent Nive which arrives straight from the mountains, and the wide, languid Adour. An important town since Roman times because of its command of one of the few easily passable roads to Spain, Bayonne prospered as a free port under English rule from 1154 to 1451. Since then it has successfully withstood 14 sieges, including a particularly bloody one directed by Wellington in 1813.

Grand Bayonne, the district around the cathedral, can be easily explored on foot. The 13th-century **Cathédrale Ste-Marie** was begun under English rule and is northern Gothic in style. Look for the handsome cloister and the 15th-century knocker on the north door – if a fugitive could put a hand to this, he was entitled to sanctuary. The pedestrianized streets around form a lively shopping area, especially the arcaded rue du Port Neuf, with cafés serving hot chocolate, a Bayonne speciality. (Fine-quality chocolate-making was introduced by the Jews who fled Spain at the end of the 15th century, and it has remained a speciality

Grand Bayonne, clustered around the twin-spired cathedral

Lighthouse at Biarritz

of the town.) Bayonne is also famous for its ham.

Petit Bayonne lies on the opposite side of the quay-lined river Nive. The **Musée Basque** gives an excellent introduction to the customs and traditions of the Basque nation, with reconstructed house interiors and exhibits on seafaring. Nearby, the **Musée Bonnat** has a superb art gallery. The first floor here is a must for art lovers, with sketches by Leonardo, Van Dyck, Rubens, and Rembrandt and paintings by Goya, Corot, Ingres, and Constable.

Musée Basque
37 quai des Corsaires. **Tel** 05 59 59 08 98. **Open** Tue–Sun (Jul–Aug: daily). **Closed** public hols.
musee-basque.com

Musée Bonnat
5 rue Jacques Lafitte. **Tel** 05 59 59 08 52. **Closed** for renovation.
musee-bonnat.com

❷ Biarritz

Pyrénées-Atlantiques. 27,000. Javalquinto, square d'Ixelles (05 59 22 37 00). daily.
biarritz.fr

Biarritz, west of Bayonne, has a grandiose center, but has been developed along the coast by residential suburbs. The resort began as a whaling port but was transformed into a playground for the European rich in the 19th century. Its popularity was assured when Empress Eugénie discovered its mild winter climate during the reign of her husband, Napoleon III. The town has three good beaches, with the best surfing in Europe, two casinos, a one of the last great luxury hote in Europe, the Palais, formerly th residence of Eugénie.

In the port des Pêcheurs, th **Musée de la Mer** aquarium is home to specimens of some the marine life found in the B of Biscay. Below it, a narrow causeway leads across to the Rocher de la Vierge, offering far-reaching views along the whole of the Basque coast. The Musée du Chocolat is fine compensation for a rainy day.

Musée de la Mer
Esplanade du Rocher-de-la-Vierge, 14 plateau de l'Atalaye. **Tel** 05 59 22 75 40. **Open** Apr–Oct: daily; Nov–M Tue–Sun. **Closed** Jan 1, 2nd–3rd wk Jan, Dec 25.
museedelamer.com

Altar in Eglise St-Jean-Baptiste

❸ St-Jean-de-Luz

Pyrénées-Atlantiques. 14,500. Biarritz. 20 bd Victor Hugo (05 59 26 03 16). daily.
saint-jean-de-luz.com

St-Jean is a quiet fishing town out of season and a scorching tourist resort in August, with shops to rival the chic rue du Faubourg St-Honoré in Paris. In the 11th century whale carcasses were towed here to feed the whole village. The natural harbor protects th shoreline, making it one of the few beaches safe for swimmin along this stretch of coast.

An important historical ever took place in St-Jean: the wedding of Louis XIV and the Infanta Maria Teresa of Spain ir 1660, a union that had the

t-Jean-de-Luz, a fishing village that explodes into life in summer

ffect of sealing the long-waited alliance between rance and Spain, only to mbroil the two countries ltimately in the War of the panish Succession. This vedding took place at the **glise St-Jean-Baptiste**, still ne biggest and best of the reat Basque churches, a riple-galleried marvel with a littering 17th-century altar-iece and an atmosphere of aiety and fervor. The gate nrough which the Sun King ed his bride was immediately valled up by masons: a laque now marks the place. he **Maison Louis XIV**, with its ontemporary furnishings, is vhere the king stayed in 1660, nd is worth a look.

The port is busy in summer, vhile the restaurants behind ne covered markets serve izzling bowls full of *chipirons* – quid cooked in their own ink – local specialty. Place Louis XIV a lovely place to sit and watch ne world go by.

Maison Louis XIV
lace Louis XIV. **Tel** 05 59 26 27 58.
pen Apr–Oct: daily.
maison-louis-xiv.fr

nvirons

n the other side of the river ivelle, Ciboure was the birth-lace of composer Maurice Ravel. is characterized by 18th-century merchants' houses, steep narrow streets, and seafood restaurants. A 2-hour coastal walk leads to the neighboring village of **Socoa**, where the lighthouse on the clifftop offers a fine view of the coast all the way to Biarritz.

Basque men in traditional berets

4 Aïnhoa

Pyrénées-Atlantiques. 680.
La Mairie (05 59 29 92 60).
ainhoa.fr

A tiny township on the road to the Spanish border, Aïnhoa was founded in the 12th century as a waystation on the road to Santiago de Compostela *(see pp404–5)*. The main street of 17th-century whitewashed Basque houses and a galleried church from the same period survive.

Environs

There is a similar church in the village of Espelette nearby. Typically Basque in style, the galleries boosted the seating capacity and separated the men from the women and children. Espelette is the trading center for *pottocks*, an ancient local breed of pony, auctioned here at the end of January. It is also the shrine of the local crop, the red pimento pepper, especially in October when a pepper festival is held here.

At the foot of the St-Ignace pass lies the mountain village of **Sare**. From the pass you can reach the summit of la Rhune by cog railroad. This provides the best vantage point in the entire Pays Basque. The descent on foot is worthwhile.

11th-century château, Espelette

Sauveterre-de-Béarn and the remains of the fortified bridge over the Gave d'Oloron, the Pont de la Légende

5 Orthez

Pyrénées-Atlantiques. 11,000. Maison Jeanne d'Albret, rue Bourg Vieux (05 59 38 32 84). Tue; Nov–Mar: *foie gras* market Sat. **tourisme-bearn-gaves.com**

Orthez is an important Béarn market town, its 13th–14th-century fortified bridge a vital river-crossing point over the Gave de Pau in the Middle Ages. It has a spectacular Saturday morning market held from November to February, selling *foie gras*, smoked and air-cured Bayonne hams, and all kinds of fresh produce. Fine buildings line the rue Bourg Vieux, especially the house of Jeanne d'Albret, mother of Henry IV, on the corner of rue Roarie. Jeanne's enthusiasm for the Protestant faith alienated both her own subjects and Charles X, and ultimately caused the Béarn region to be drawn into the Wars of Religion (1562–93).

6 Sauveterre-de-Béarn

Pyrénées-Atlantiques. 1,400. pl Royale (05 59 38 32 86). Sat. **tourisme-bearn-gaves.com**

An attractive market town, Sauveterre is well worth a night's stay. It has stunning views southward over the Gave d'Oloron, the graceful single arch of the river's fortified bridge, and the 16th-century **Château de Nays**. Fishermen gather here for the annual world salmon-fishing championships, in the fast-flowing Oloron (April to July).

Be sure to visit the **Château de Laàs**, 5.5 miles (9 km) along the D27 from Sauveterre, which has an excellent collection of 18th-century decorative art and furniture – notably the bed Napoleon slept in on the night after his defeat at Waterloo. There is also a pretty park with a maze.

Château de Laàs
Tel 05 59 38 91 53. **Open** Apr–Oct: Wed– Mon (Apr: pm only; Jul–Aug: daily).

The Château de Nays at Sauveterre in the Béarn region

7 St-Jean-Pied-de-Port

Pyrénées-Atlantiques. 1,700. 14 pl du Général de Gaulle (05 59 37 03 57). Mon. **pyrenees-basques.com**

The old capital of Basse-Navarre lies at the foot of the Roncesvalles Pass. Here the Basques crushed the rear-guard of Charlemagne's army in 778 and killed its commander, Roland, later glorified in the *Chanson de Roland*.

Throughout the Middle Ages this red sandstone fortress-town was famous as the last rallying point before entering Spain on the pilgrim road to Santiago de Compostela *(see pp404–5)*. As soon as a group of pilgrims was spotted, the townsfolk would ring the church bells to show them the way, and the pilgrims would sing in response.

Visitors and pilgrims in all seasons still provide St-Jean with its income. They enter the narrow streets of the upper town on foot from the Porte d'Espagne, and pass cafés, hotels, and restaurants on the way up. The ramparts are worth the steep climb, as is the citadel with panoramic views.

On Mondays the town hosts a craft market, Basque *pelote* matches, and, in summer, shows with bulls.

Forêt d'Iraty

rénées-Aquitaine. St-Jean-Pied-
-Port. St-Jean-Pied-de-Port
5 59 37 03 57), Larrau (05 59 28 62 80).

plateau of beech woods and oorland, the Forêt d'Iraty is mous for its cross-country kiing and walking. Here the ncient breed of Basque ponies, ne *pottocks*, run half-wild. nese creatures have not nanged since the prehistoric habitants of the region traced neir silhouettes on the walls f local caves.

The tourist office at St-Jean-ed-de-Port publishes maps of ocal walks. The best begins at ne Chalet Pedro car park, south f the lake on the Iraty plateau, nd takes you along the GR10 o 3,000-year-old standing tones on the western side of ne Sommet d'Occabé.

Oloron-Ste-Marie

yrénées-Atlantiques. 12,000.
allées du Compte de Tréville
5 59 39 98 00). Fri.
tourisme-oloron.com

)loron, a small town at the unction of the Aspe and the)ssau valleys, has grown from a eltiberian settlement. There are uge agricultural fairs here in May and September, and the own is famed for producing the amous classic French berets.

Basque Culture

Most of Basque country is in Spain, but around 10 percent lies within France. The Basque people have their own complex language, isolated from other European tongues, and their music, games, and folklore are equally distinct. French Basques are less fiercely separatist than their Spanish counterparts, but both are still deeply attached to their unique way of life.

Pelote, the traditional Basque game

Cathédrale Ste-Marie

The town's great glory is the doorway of the Romanesque **Cathédrale Ste-Marie**, with its biblical and Pyrenean scenes. Spain lies just on the other side of the Somport pass at the head of the mountainous Aspe valley, and the influence of Spanish stonemasons is evident in Oloron's **Eglise Sainte-Croix** with its Moorish-style vaulting.

Environs

Head up the Aspe valley to try one of the area's famous ewe's cheeses, or mixed cow and goat's cheeses. A side road leads to Lescun, huddled around its church, beyond which is a spectacular range of saw-toothed peaks topped by the **Pic d'Anie** at 8,215 ft (2,504 m), one of the most beautiful sights in the Pyrenees. This is also one of the last refuges of the Pyrenean brown bear, whose numbers have been drastically diminished by human activity, particularly hunting and the building of roads and houses.

igh moorland above the Forêt d'Iraty, long denuded of timber for use by the French and Spanish navies

Gobelin tapestry in the Château de Pau

⑩ Pau

Pyrénées-Atlantiques. 86,000. pl Royale (05 59 27 27 08). Mon–Sat. **pau-pyrenees.com**

A lively university town, with elegant Belle Epoque architecture and shady parks, Pau is the capital of the Béarn region, and the most interesting big town in the central Pyrenees. The weather in autumn and winter is mild, so this has been a favorite resort of affluent foreigners, especially the English, since the early 19th century.

Pau is chiefly famous as the birthplace of King Henry IV. His mother, Jeanne d'Albret, traveled for 19 days from Picardy, in the eighth month of her pregnancy, just to have her baby here. She sang during her labor, convinced that if she did so, Henry would grow up as tough as she was. As soon as the infant was born, his lips were smeared with garlic and local Jurançon wine, in keeping with the traditional custom.

The town's principal sight is the **Château de Pau**, first remodeled in the 14th century for the ruler of Béarn, Gaston Phoebus *(see p467)*. It was heavily restored 400 years later. Marguerite d'Angoulême, sister of the King of France, resided here in the late 16th century, and transformed the town into a center for the arts and free thinking. The château's 16th-century Gobelin tapestries, made by Flemish weavers working in Paris, are fabulous. (The Maison Carrée in Nay – 11 miles (18 km) towards Lourdes – exhibits the former Musée Béarnais' collection of artifacts retracing the history, traditions, and culture of the Béarn.)

Outside, the boulevard des Pyrénées affords glorious views of some of the highest Pyrenean peaks, often snow-capped year round. Continue from here to the eclectic **Musée des Beaux-Arts**, where there is a splendid Degas, the *Cotton Exchange, New Orleans*; Rubens' *Last Judgment*, and a work by El Greco.

Château de Pau
Rue du Château. **Tel** 05 59 82 38 02. **Open** daily. **Closed** Jan 1, May 1, Dec 25.
musee-chateau-pau.fr

Château de Pau, birthplace of Henry IV in 1553

Musée des Beaux-Arts
Rue Mathieu Lalanne. **Tel** 05 59 27 33 02. **Open** Wed–Mon. **Closed** some public hols. restricted.

⑪ Tarbes

Hautes-Pyrénées. 46,500. 3 cours Gambetta (05 62 51 30 31). Thu. **tarbes.com**

Tarbes is the capital of the Bigorre region and hosts a major agricultural fair. The **Jardin Massey** in the middle of town was designed at the turn of the 19th century and is one of the loveliest parks in the southwest, with many rare plants, including the North American sassafras, and a 14th-century cloister with finely carved capitals.

The **Maison du Cheval** and the Haras National (National Stud), with its thoroughbred stallions, should not be missed.

La Maison du Cheval
Chemin du Mauhourat.
Tel 05 62 56 30 80. **Open** dailys pms. **Closed** public hols. Jul–Aug & school hols.

⑫ Lourdes

Hautes-Pyrénées. 16,000. pl Peyramale (05 62 42 77 40). daily. **lourdes-infotourisme.com**

Lourdes, one of the great shrines of Europe, owes its celebrity to visions of the Virgin experienced by 14-year-old Bernadette Soubirous in 1858. Five million people annually

◀ The lush Forêt d'Iraty and surrounding moorland

it **Grotte Massabielle**, ıere the visions occurred, d rue des Petits-Fossés ıere Bernadette lived, in arch of a miracle cure. e **Musée de Lourdes** gives formation about Bernadette d the shrine.

Visit the **Grottes de Bétharm** for underground rides by oat and train, or the **Musée 'rénéen**, about the pioneers ho opened up these ranges.

Musée de Lourdes
rking de l'Egalité. **Tel** 05 62 94 28 00.
pen Apr–Oct: daily; Nov–Mar: on–Sat.

Grottes de Bétharram
Pé-de-Bigorre. **Tel** 05 62 41 80 04.
pen Feb–late Mar: Mon–Fri pms; e Mar–Oct: daily.
betharram.com

ectacular limestone formations at the ottes de Bétharram

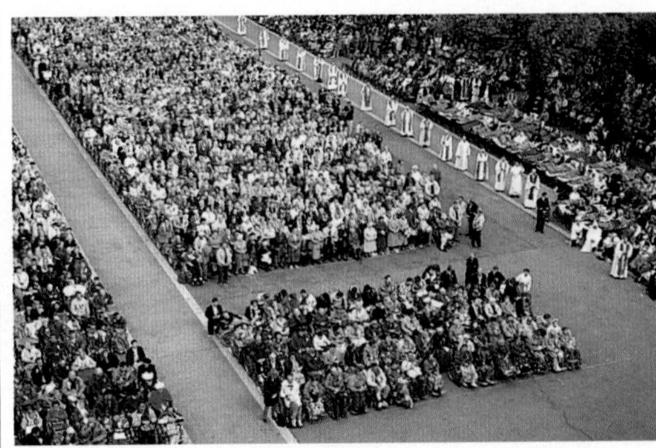

Pilgrims participating in open-air mass at Lourdes

Musée Pyrénéen
Château Fort, rue du Fort.
Tel 05 62 42 37 37. **Open** daily.
Closed Jan 1, Nov 1 & 11, Dec 25.

⓭ Parc National des Pyrénées

See pp464–5.

⓮ Luz-St-Sauveur

Hautes-Pyrénées. 1,200. to Lourdes. pl du 8 mai (05 62 92 30 30). Mon am. **luz.org**

Luz-St-Sauveur is an attractive spa town, with an unusual church built in the 14th century by the Hospitaliers de Saint Jean de Jérusalem (later the Knights of Malta), an order established to protect pilgrims. The church is fortified with gun slits that provided protection for pilgrims on the way to Santiago de Compostela.

Environs

The elegant spa town of **Cauterets** makes a good base for climbing, skiing, and walking in the rugged mountains of the Bigorre region.

Gavarnie is a former way-station on the Santiago de Compostela pilgrim route. A good track, accessible on foot or by donkey, leads from the village to the spectacular natural rock amphitheatre known as the **Cirque de Gavarnie**. Here the longest waterfall in Europe, at 787 ft (240 m), cascades off the mountain into space, encircled by eleven 9,800-ft (3,000-m) peaks.

Tourists can now share much of the **Observatoire Pic du Midi de Bigorre** with scientists. Access is by cable car from La Mongie to Le Taoulet and then up to the summit. Alternatively there are a number of walks up to the Pic (4 hours minimum).

The French are justly proud of the Observatory, which has supplied some of the clearest images of Venus and other planets so far obtained from Earth. The 3.2-ft (1-m) telescope mapped out the moon for NASA's Apollo missions.

Observatoire Pic du Midi de Bigorre
Tel 08 25 00 28 77. **Open** May 6–Nov 4: daily. **Closed** Oct 1.
picdumidi.com

The Miracle of Lourdes

In 1858 a young girl named Bernadette Soubirous experienced 18 visions of the Virgin at the Grotte Massabielle near the town. Despite being told to keep away from the cave by her mother – and the local magistrate – she was guided to a spring with miraculous healing powers. The church endorsed the miracles in the 1860s, and since then, many people claim to have been cured by the holy water. A religious city of shrines, churches and hospices has since grown up around the spring, with a dynamic tourist industry to match.

Bernadette's vision

⓭ Parc National des Pyrénées

The Pyrenees National Park, designated in 1967, extends 62 miles (100 km) along the French and Spanish frontier. It boasts some of the most spectacular scenery in Europe, ranging from meadows glimmering with butterflies to high peaks, snow-capped even in summer. Variations in altitude and climate make the park rich in flora and fauna. One of the most enjoyable ways to see it is on foot: within the park are 217 miles (350 km) of well-marked footpaths.

Vallée d'Aspe
Jagged peaks tower above the Vallée d'Aspe and the Cirque de Lescun. An access road to Somport Tunnel has been built here *(see p459)*.

Pic d'Anie
The limestone-flanked 8,215-ft (2,504-m) Pic d'Anie overlooks rich upland pastures watered by melting snow. In spring, the ground is ablaze with Pyrenean varieties of gentian and columbine, found nowhere else.

OLoron-Ste-Marie
Pic d'Anie 8,215 ft (2,504 m)
VALLEE D'ASPE
N134
VALLEE D'OSSAU
D934
La
Pic du Midi d'Oss
9,462 ft (2,884 m

KEY

① **Col du Somport**, the Somport pass (5,354 ft/1,632 m), is a rugged route into Spain that is now by-passed by a tunnel.

② **The GR10 long-distance trail** is one of the great walks of France, linking the Atlantic with the Mediterranean.

③ **Brèche de Roland**

Pic du Midi d'Ossau
A tough trail leads from the Bious-Artigues lake at the base of the Pic d Midi d'Ossau and encircles the formidabl tooth-shaped summit (9,462 ft/2,884 m).

Pyrenean Wildlife

The Pyrenees are home to a rich variety of wild creatures, many of them unique to the range. The ibex, a member of the antelope family, is still numerous in the valleys of Ossau and Cauterets. Birds of prey include the Egyptian, griffon, and bearded vultures. Ground predators range from the rare Pyrenean lynx, to civet, pine marten, and stoat. The desman, a tiny aquatic mammal related to the mole, is found in many of the mountain streams.

Pyrenean fritillary flowers through late spring and early summer in mountain pastures.

The Turk's Cap Lily flowers J August on rocky slopes at up 7,218 ft (2,200 m).

e de Roland
mous breach in the sheer crest of rque de Gavarnie forms a ay for climbers between France pain.

Tips for Walkers

The park is crossed by a network of numbered trails. Each is well signposted and shows the length of time needed. Mountain huts offer a meal and a bed for the night. For maps and information, visit the Park Office at Cauterets (05 62 92 50 50) or at Luz-St-Sauveur (05 62 92 30 30), both open year round or visit www.parc-pyrenees.com.

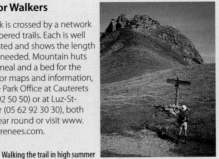

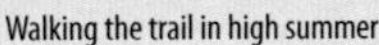

Walking the trail in high summer

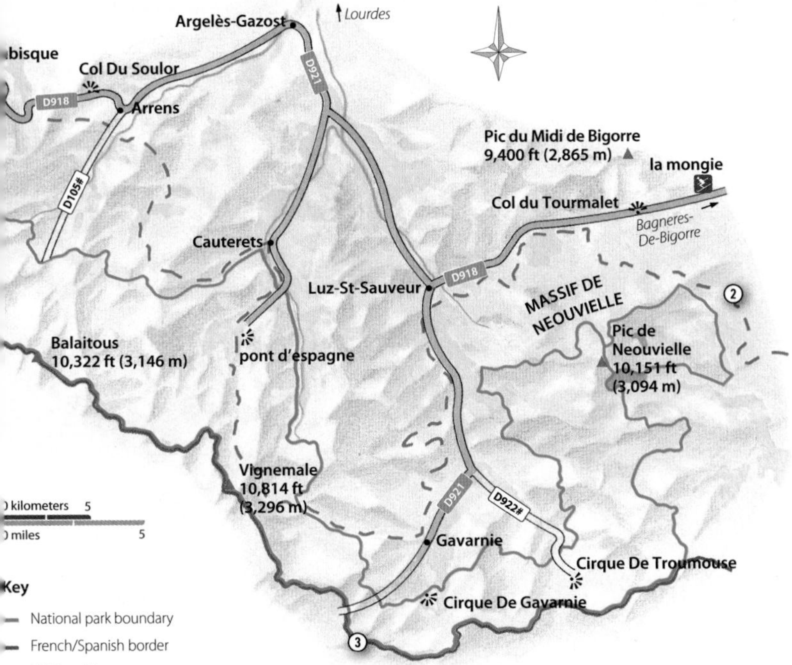

Argelès-Gazost
Lourdes
bisque
Col Du Soulor
D918
Arrens
D921
D105#
Pic du Midi de Bigorre
9,400 ft (2,865 m)
la mongie
Col du Tourmalet
Bagneres-De-Bigorre
Cauterets
Luz-St-Sauveur
D918
MASSIF DE NEOUVIELLE
2
Pic de Neouvielle
10,151 ft
(3,094 m)
Balaitous
10,322 ft (3,146 m)
pont d'espagne
Vignemale
10,814 ft
(3,296 m)
D921
D922#
Gavarnie
Cirque De Troumouse
Cirque De Gavarnie
3

) kilometers 5
) miles 5

Key
National park boundary
French/Spanish border
GR10 walking route

gyptian vulture is seen all the Pyrenees, especially on cliff faces.

Pyrenean bears are close to extinction but a few still live in the Ossau and Aspe valleys.

Cleopatra

Scarce Swallowtail

These butterflies are among several colorful species found at high altitudes.

⓯ Arreau

Hautes-Pyrénées. 865. Château des Nestes (05 62 98 63 15). Thu. **vallee-aure.com**

Arreau stands at the junction of the rivers Aure and Louron. A small, bustling half-timbered town with good shops and restaurants, this is the place to buy the basics for hiking or fishing in the mountains. The town surrounds a handsome town hall with a covered market place beneath it. Next door is a 16th-century house, the Maison de Lys, which has a facade ornamented with the fleur-de-lis motifs.

Environs

St-Lary Soulan is a nearby ski resort and a good base for exploring the entire Massif du Néouvielle. Head for the village of Fabian and the smattering of lakes above it, where the GR10 *(see pp464–5)* and other well-marked trails crisscross the peaks. Here you may see golden eagles or an enormous lammergeier.

⓰ St-Bertrand-de-Comminges

Haute-Garonne. 260. Montrejeau, then taxi. Les Olivetains, parvis de la Cathédrale (05 61 95 44 44). music festival (mid-Jul–end Aug).

The pretty hilltop town of St-Bertrand is the most remarkable artistic and historic site in the Central Pyrenees and the venue for an acclaimed music festival in summer *(see p41)*.

Cloisters in the Cathédrale Ste-Marie, St-Bertrand-de-Comminges

Some of the best sculpture in the region adorns the portal of the **Cathédrale Ste-Marie**. The adjoining Romanesque and Gothic cloisters contain sarcophagi, carved capitals, and statues of the four Evangelists.

St-Bertrand's origins lie on the plain below, in the city founded by the great Roman statesman Pompey in 72 BC. At that time it consisted of two thermal baths, a theater, a temple, a market, and a Christian basilica. All were destroyed by Gontran, the grandson of Clovis *(see p216)* in 585, and six centuries were to pass before the Bishop of Comminges, Bertrand de l'Isle, saw the site as a potential location for a new cathedral and monastery. The town, which was relatively unimportant in political terms, became a major religious centre.

Inside the cathedral, look out for the 66 magnificent carved choirstalls and the 16th-century organ case. The tomb of Bertrand de l'Isle is situated at the far end of the choir, with an altar beside it; the beautiful marble tomb in the Virgin's chapel just off the nave is that of Hugues de Châtillon, a bishop who provided funds for the completion of the cathedral in the 14th century.

Cathédrale Ste-Marie
Tel 05 61 89 04 91. **Open** daily. **Closed** Sun am. cloisters.

Fresco in the Cathédrale St-Lizier

The imposing 12th-century Cathédrale Ste-Marie in St-Bertrand

⓱ St-Lizier

Ariège. 1,500. pl de l'Eglise (05 61 96 77 77). **ariege.com/st-lizier**

St-Lizier is located in the Ariège, a region famous for its steep-sided valleys and wild mountain scenery. The village dates back to Roman times, and by the Middle Ages was an important religious center. St-Lizier has two cathedrals; the finer is the 12th–14th-century **Cathédrale St-Lizier** in the lower town. It boasts Romanesque frescoes and a cloister with carved columns. The **Cathédrale de la Sède** in the upper town has the best view.

For hotels and restaurants in this region see pp554–71 and pp576–603

St-Lizier, with snow-capped mountains in the distance

⑱ Foix

Ariège. 10,000. 29 rue Delcassé (05 61 65 12 12). Fri & 1st, 3rd & 5th Mon of each month, also Tue, Wed all day in Jul–Aug.
tourisme-foix-varilhes.fr

With its battlements and towers, Foix stands foursquare at the junction of the rivers Arget and Ariège. In the Middle Ages, Foix's dynasty of counts ruled the whole of the Béarn area. Count Gaston Phoebus (1331–91) was the most flamboyant, a poet who wrote a famous treatise on hunting. He was a ruthless politician, who had his brother and his son put to death.

Some of the pleasures of the medieval court are recreated in the local summer fair, the largest in the southwest. At any time, the 15th-century keep of the **Château de Foix** is worth climbing just for the view. The restored 14th-century **Eglise de St-Volusien** is delightful in its simplicity and grace.

Château de Foix
Tel 05 34 09 83 83. **Open** Wed–Mon & daily in sch hols. **Closed** Jan 1, Dec 25.

Environs
The **Grotte de Niaux**, 9 miles (15 km) south of Foix, has prehistoric cave paintings.

Grotte de Niaux
Tel 05 61 05 10 10. **Open** by appt only. oblig.

⑲ Montségur

Ariège. 100. 05 61 03 03 03. for the château (summer only).
montsegur.fr

Montségur is famous as the last stronghold of the Cathars *(see p495)*. From the car park at the foot of the mount, a path leads up to the small castle above, occupied in the 13th century by *faidits* (dispossessed aristocrats) and a Cathar community. The Cathars themselves lived outside the fortress, in houses clinging to the rock. Opposed to Catholic authority, Cathar troops marched on Avignonnet in 1243 and massacred members of the Inquisitional tribunal. In retaliation, an army of 10,000 laid siege to Montségur for 10 months. When captured, 205 Cathars refused to convert and were burnt alive.

⑳ Mirepoix

Ariège. 3,300. pl du Maréchal Leclerc (05 61 68 83 76). Mon & Thu.
tourisme-mirepoix.com

Mirepoix is a solid country bastide town *(see p449)* with a huge main square – one of the loveliest in the southwest – surrounded by beamed 13th–15th-century arcades and half-timbered houses.

The **cathedral**, begun in 1317 with the last additions made in 1867, boasts the widest Gothic nave (72 ft/22 m) in France.

The best times to visit the town are on market days, when stalls in the square sell a mass of local produce.

The arcaded main square at Mirepoix

THE SOUTH OF FRANCE

Introducing the South of France

The South is France's most popular holiday region, drawing millions of visitors each year to the Riviera resorts, and modern beach cities to the west. Agriculture is a mainstay of the economy, producing early fruits and an abundance of affordable wine. The new high-tech industries of Nice and Montpellier reflect the region's key role in the developing south coast sunbelt, while Corsica still preserves much of its natural beauty. The map shows the major sights of this sun-blessed region.

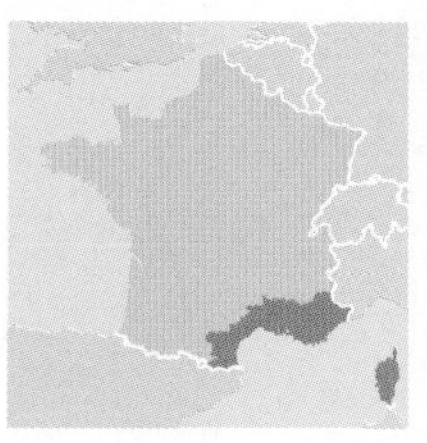

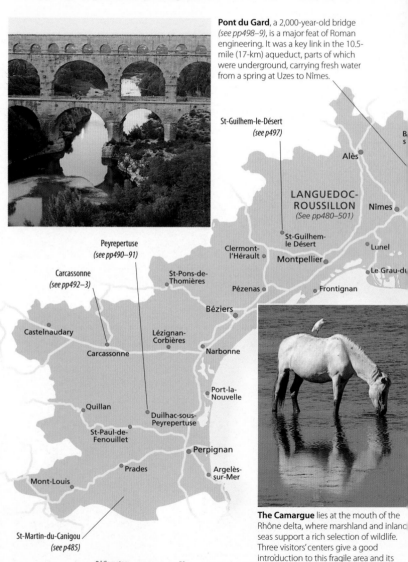

Pont du Gard, a 2,000-year-old bridge *(see pp498–9)*, is a major feat of Roman engineering. It was a key link in the 10.5-mile (17-km) aqueduct, parts of which were underground, carrying fresh water from a spring at Uzes to Nîmes.

St-Guilhem-le-Désert *(see p497)*

Peyrepertuse *(see pp490–91)*

Carcassonne *(see pp492–3)*

LANGUEDOC-ROUSSILLON *(See pp480–501)*

Alès

Nîmes

St-Guilhem-le Désert

Clermont-l'Hérault

Montpellier

Lunel

Le Grau-du

St-Pons-de-Thomières

Pézenas

Frontignan

Béziers

Castelnaudary

Lézignan-Corbières

Carcassonne

Narbonne

Port-la-Nouvelle

Quillan

Duilhac-sous-Peyrepertuse

St-Paul-de-Fenouillet

Perpignan

Prades

Argelès-sur-Mer

Mont-Louis

St-Martin-du-Canigou *(see p485)*

0 kilometers 50

0 miles 50

The Camargue lies at the mouth of the Rhône delta, where marshland and inlanc seas support a rich selection of wildlife. Three visitors' centers give a good introduction to this fragile area and its population of pink flamingos and white horses *(see pp514–15)*.

◀ A field of sunflowers in Languedoc-Roussillon

vignon, enclosed by massive ramparts, became ıpal territory when popes decamped from Rome *ee p507)* in the 14th century, taking up residence the Palais des Papes which towers over the town. the summer the town is the scene of the ɔpular Avignon Festival.

Giacometti Statue, St-Paul-de-Vence *(see pp528–9)*

Musée Matisse, Nice *(see pp530–31)*

Barcelonnette
Seyne
Sisteron
Colmars
Volonne
Digne-les-Bains
Carpentras
Saorge
on
Castellane
Manosque
Cavaillon
Monaco
Vence
Nice
PROVENCE AND THE COTE D'AZUR
(See pp502–35)
Grasse
Salon-de-Provence
Antibes
Aix-en-Provence
Draguignan
Cannes
St-Raphaël
St-Maximin-la Ste-Baume
Brignoles
ʌarignane
Port Grimaud
St-Tropez
Marseille
Cassis
Toulon
Hyères

Statue of Napoleon, Ajaccio *(see p546)*

Bastia
Calvi
CORSICA
(See pp536–47)
Ajaccio
Bonifacio

0 kilometers 50
0 miles 50

he Côte d'Azur has attracted sunworshippers and ɛlebrities since the 1920s *(see pp478–9)*. The coast also ffers some prize collections of 20th-century art *(pp476–7)* nd yearly events such as the Cannes Film Festival and ntibes Jazz Festival.

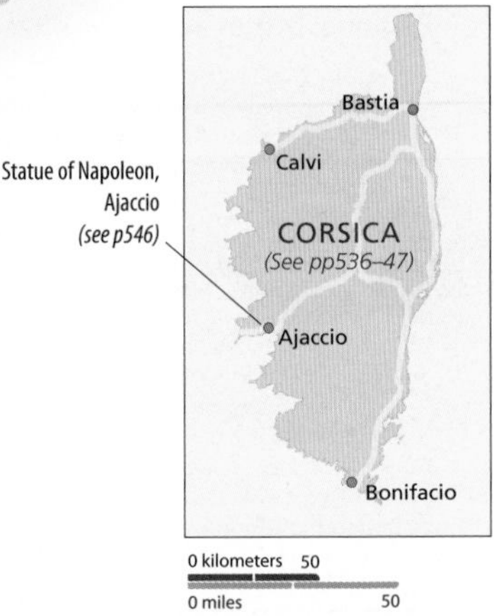

For additional map symbols *see back flap*

The Flavors of the South of France

Mediterranean France has a fresh, sunny cuisine, with ripe and flavorful fruit and vegetables, fresh fish and seafood, and lean meat from mountain pastures. Good dishes are enhanced by key ingredients: olive oil, garlic, and aromatic herbs. Markets are a colorful feast of seasonal produce all year round. Whether you opt for a picnic choice of local hams, sausage, bread, and cheese to eat on the beach, share a simple lunch of tomato salad and grilled fish or lamb in a village bistro, or indulge in the sophisticated cuisine of one of France's top chefs, you can be sure of food that is not only authentic and delicious, but healthy too.

Local olives and olive o

Preserving anchovies in seasoned olive oil in Languedoc-Roussillon

Languedoc-Roussillon

There is a robust Catalan flavor to the food of this region bordering Spain. Spices and almonds add an exotic touch to the fruit and vegetables produced in abundance on the Roussillon plain, and the grass-fed beef and lamb of the Mediterranean Pyrenees. Fish is plentiful: Sète is the largest fishing port on the French Mediterranean, huge oyster and mussel beds thrive in the salt-water lagoons of the coast, and the little fishing port of Collioure is famous for its anchovies. Local dishes include *brandade de morue*, a specialty of Nîmes, as well as squid stuffed with anchovies, and snails with garlic and ham. Roussillon is famous for its peaches and apricots, and the cherries of Ceret are always the first to be harvested in France. Goat's milk is the main source of cheese, with round, orange-rinded Pélardon the most common.

Provence

This is the land of the olive and of rich green olive oil. These are evident in a wide range of dishes, such as *aioli*,

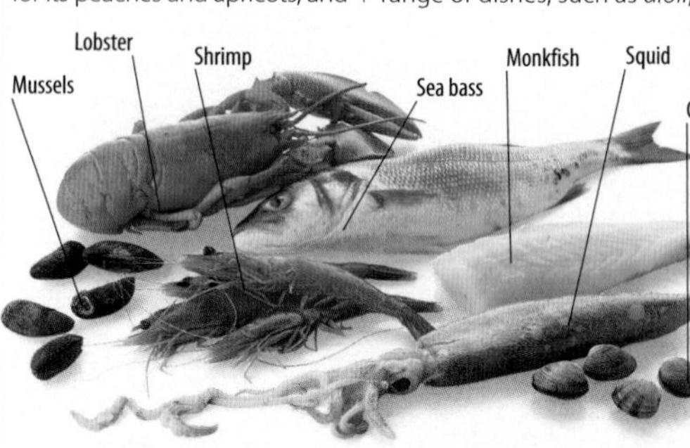

Selection of Mediterranean seafood available in the south of France

Regional Dishes and Specialties

The *cuisine du soleil*, "cuisine of the sun," has produced several classic dishes. *Bouillabaisse* is the most famous. The ingredients of this fish stew vary from place to place, though Marseille claims the original recipe. A variety of local seafood (always including *rascasse*, or scorpion fish) is cooked in stock with tomatoes and saffron. The fish stock is traditionally served first, with croûtons spread with *rouille*, a spicy mayonnaise, and the fish served afterwards. Once a fisherman's supper, it is now a luxury item you may need to order 24 hours in advance. A simpler version is *bourride*, a garlicky fish soup. Rich red wine stews, known as *daubes*, are another specialty, usually made with beef, but sometimes with tuna or calamari. Other classics include *ratatouille* and *salade niçoise*.

Fresh figs

Artichauts à la barigoule Sma violet artichokes are stuffed with bacon and vegetables, cooked in wine.

ried spices and herbs on sale at the market in Nice

rich mayonnaise of olive ›il and garlic, served with 'egetables or fish; *tapenade*, purée of olives, anchovies, nd capers; and *pissaladière*, type of pizza made with ›nions, olives, and anchovies, vith a distinct Italian accent. 'egetables play a leading role: ucchini or tomatoes stuffed 1 the Niçois style with meat, ice, and herbs; baby arti-:hokes sautéed with bacon; ›r aromatic *pistou*, a bean nd vegetable soup laced vith a sauce of basil and jarlic. Mediterranean fish is ıighly prized, and is often ›est appreciated simply jrilled. Meat includes game nd rabbit; Sisteron lamb, jrazed on high mountain ›astures; and the bull's meat tew of the Camargue, served vith nutty local red rice. There s also ripe fruit aplenty, from juicy figs to fragrant Cavaillon melons to the vivid lemons of Menton.

Corsica

The cuisine of Corsica is a robust version of the Mediterranean diet. Chestnuts were once the staple food of the island, and the flour is still widely used. There is a huge variety of *charcuterie*, including flavorsome hams and sausages, smoked, cured or air-dried in the traditional way. Wild boar is a delicacy, stewed with chestnuts in red wine. Roast goat *(cabri roti)* is served as a festive meal, spiked with garlic and rosemary. Game, from rabbit to pigeon and partridge, is also very popular. On the coast there is locally caught fish and seafood, including monkfish, squid, sea urchins, and sardines, the latter most delicious stuffed with herbs and Brocciu, a ricotta-style soft cheese. Local honey is redolent of mountain herbs, and jams are made from a huge variety of ingredients.

Ripe chestnuts on the tree in a Corsican forest

On the Menu

Beignets des fleurs de courgette Zucchini flower fritters.

Estoficada Salt cod stewed with tomatoes, potatoes, garlic, and olives.

Fougasse Flat olive oil bread often studded with olives.

Ratatouille Stew of garlic, onions, eggplant, tomatoes, zucchini, and peppers.

Salade Niçoise Lettuce with hard-boiled egg, olives, green beans, tomatoes, and anchovies.

Socca Garbanzo bean pancakes, a speciality of Nice.

Tourte des blettes Pie of chard, raisins, and pine nuts.

randade de morue Dried alted cod is cooked in water, 'hen beaten with olive oil and nilk to make a purée.

Bœuf en daube Beef is marinated in red wine, onions, and garlic, then stewed with orange peel and tomato.

Crème catalane Originating in Spain, this dessert is an eggy custard topped with a flambéed sugar crust.

France's Wine Regions: the South

A massive arc stretching from Banyuls, in the extreme southern corner of France, to Nice, close to the Italian border, encompasses the Mediterranean vineyards of Languedoc-Roussillon and Provence. This was for a century an area of mass-produced wine, and much is still of *vin de France* quality. Today, however, the more dynamic producers are applying new technology to traditional and classic grape varieties to revive southern France's nobler heritage of generous, warm, aromatic wines, redolent of sun-baked stone, the scent of wild herbs, and the shimmering waters of the Mediterranean.

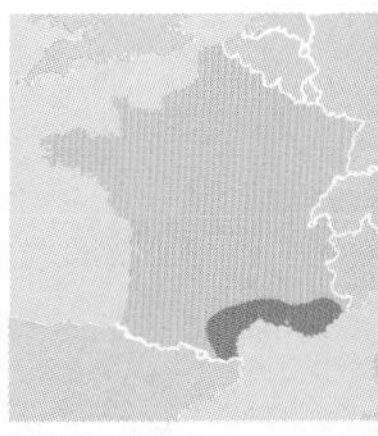

Locator Map

Languedoc-Roussillon & Provence

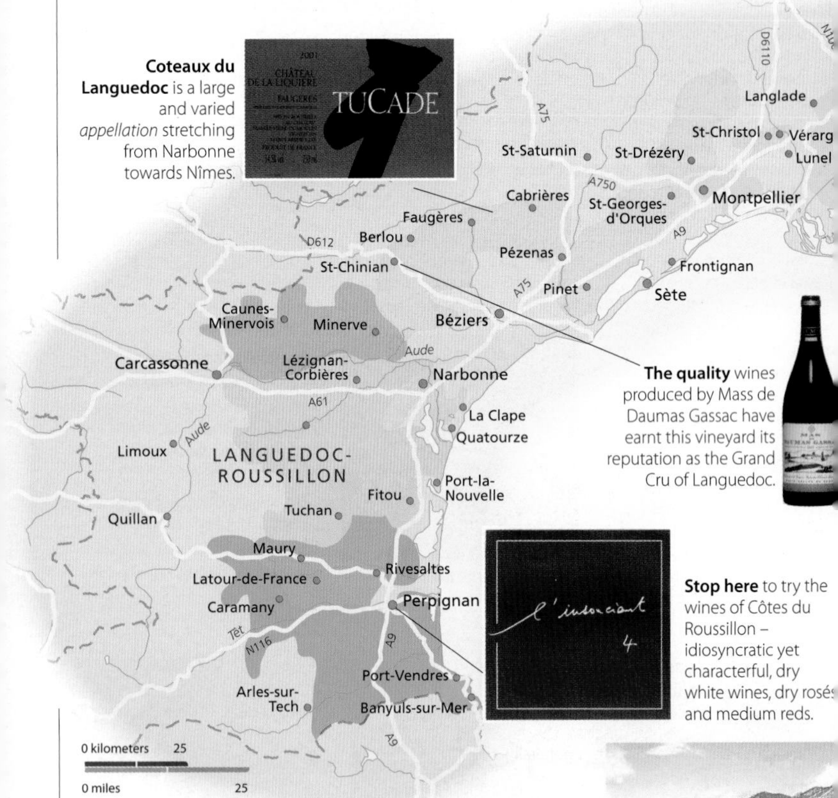

Coteaux du Languedoc is a large and varied *appellation* stretching from Narbonne towards Nîmes.

The quality wines produced by Mass de Daumas Gassac have earnt this vineyard its reputation as the Grand Cru of Languedoc.

Stop here to try the wines of Côtes du Roussillon – idiosyncratic yet characterful, dry white wines, dry rosés and medium reds.

Rugged valley slopes in Corbières

0 kilometers 25

0 miles 25

Key

- Collioure & Banyuls
- Côtes de Roussillon
- Côtes de Roussillon Villages
- Fitou
- Corbières
- Minervois
- Coteaux du Languedoc
- Costières du Gard
- Coteaux d'Aix en Provence
- Côtes de Provence
- Cassis
- Bandol & Côtes de Provence
- Coteaux Varois
- Bellet

ndpicking grapes for Côtes de Provence red wine

Wine Regions

Both in the Provence wine region, east of Aix and Marseille, and in the larger Languedoc-Roussillon area to the west, new quality wine *appellations* such as Cabardès (north of Carcassonne), are joining the more familiar names.

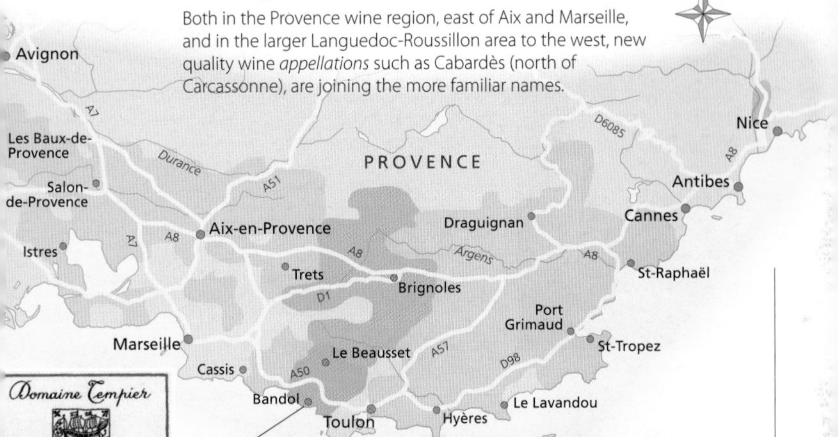

Domaine Tempier
BANDOL
2005

andol is a small *appellation* that ses a traditional southern ench red grape, the *Mourvèdre,* produce its quality reds.

La Courtade reds, whites, and rosés are produced by the Domaine de la Courtade, one of three vineyards located on the Ile de Porquerolles off the coast of Provence.

Key Facts About Wines of The South

Location and Climate

A warm and sunny climate helps to create generously alcoholic wines. The flat coastal plains support acres of vines, but generally the best sites are on the schist and limestone hillsides.

Grape Varieties

Mass-production grapes such as **Aramon** are giving way to quality varieties such as **Syrah**, **Mourvèdre**, and **Grenache**. **Cabernet Sauvignon, Merlot**, and **Syrah**, and the whites **Chardonnay, Sauvignon Blanc**, and **Viognier**, are increasingly used for *IGPs*. Rich, sweet whites are made from the aromatic, honeyed **Muscat** grape.

Good Producers

Corbières & Minervois: La Voulte Gasparets, Saint Auriol, Lastours, Villerambert-Julien. *Faugères*: Château des Estanilles, Châeau de la Liquiere. *St-Chinian*: Château Cazal-Viel, Domaine Navarre, Cave de Roquebrun. *Coteaux du Languedoc and IGPs*: Mas Jullien, Château de Capitoul, Domaine de la Garance, Mas de Daumas Gassac, Pech-Celeyran. *Roussillon*: Domaine Gauby, Domaine Sarda Malet. *Provence:* Domaine Tempier, Château Pibarnon, Domaine de Trévallon, Mas de la Dame, Domaine Richeaume, La Courtade, Château Simone, Château Pradeaux, Château de Bellet.

Artists and Writers in the South of France

Artists and writers have helped create our image of the South of France – the poet Stephen Liégeard even gave the Côte d'Azur its name in 1887. Many writers, French and foreign, found a haven in the warmth of the south. From Cézanne to Van Gogh, Monet to Picasso, artists have been inspired by the special light and brilliant colors of this seductive region. Today it is rich in art museums, some devoted to single artists like Matisse, Picasso, and Chagall, others with varied collections such as those in Céret, Nîmes, Montpellier, St-Tropez, St-Paul-de-Vence, and Nice *(see pp486–531)*.

Picasso and Françoise Gilot on the Golfe Juan, 1948

Paul Cézanne's studio in Aix-en-Provence *(see p511)*

Festive Light

The Impressionists were fascinated by the effects of light, and Monet was entranced by "the glaring festive light" of the south which made colors so intense he said no one would believe they were real if painted accurately. In 1883 Renoir came with him to the south, returning often to paint his voluptuous nudes in the filtered golden light. Bonnard too settled here, painting endless views of the red tiled roofs and palm trees.

Post-Impressionists Van Gogh and Gauguin arrived in 1888, attracted by the region's rich colors. Cézanne, who was born in Aix in 1839, analyzed and painted the structure of nature, above all the landscape of Provence and his beloved Mont-Ste-Victoire. Pointillist Paul Signac came to St-Tropez to paint sea and sky in a rainbow palette of dots.

The Wild Beasts

The Fauves, dubbed "Wild Beasts" for their unnaturally bright and wild colors, led one of the first 20th-century avant-garde movements, founded by Matisse in Collioure in 1905 *(see p33)*. Other Fauves included Derain, Vlaminck, Marquet, Van Dongen, and Dufy. Matisse visited Corsica in 1898, and then St-Tropez, and was inspired by the sensuality of Provence to paint the celebrated *Luxe, Calme, et Volupté*. Eventually he settled in Nice, where he painted his great series of Odalisques. He wrote, "What made me stay are the great colored reflections of January, the luminosity of daylight." The exquisite blue-and-white chapel he designed in Vence is one of the most moving of his later works *(see p527)*.

Vincent Van Gogh's *Sunflowers* (1888)

icasso Country

he South of France is, without uestion, Picasso country. His ymphs and sea urchins, his onumental women running n the beach, his shapes and olors, ceramics and sculpture re all derived from the hard hadows and bright colors of he south.

Pablo Picasso was born Malaga in Spain in 1881, ut he spent much of his life n the French Mediterranean, eveloping Cubism with raque in Céret in 1911, nd arriving in Juan-les-Pins 1920. He was in Antibes hen war broke out in 1939, here he painted *Night ishing at Antibes*, a luminous octurnal eascape. He eturned in 1946 nd was given he Grimaldi alace to use as studio. It is ow a Picasso luseum *(see 525)*. He also vorked in allauris, roducing eramics and culptures *see p526)*.

Deux Femmes Courant sur la Plage (1933) by Pablo Picasso

Lost Caviar Days

Just as F. Scott Fitzgerald wrote the Jazz Age into existence, he created the glittering image of life on the Riviera with *Tender is the Night*. He and Zelda arrived in 1924 attracted, like many expatriate writers, by the warm climate and the cheap, easy living. "One could get away with more on the summer Riviera, and whatever happened seemed to have something to do with art," he wrote. They passed their villa on to another American, Ernest Hemingway. Many other writers flocked there including Katherine Mansfield, D. H. Lawrence, Aldous Huxley, Friedrich Nietzsche, Lawrence Durrell, and Graham Greene. Some, like Somerset Maugham, led a glamorous lifestyle surrounded by exotic guests. Colette was an early visitor to St-Tropez, and in 1954, Françoise Sagan captured the youthful hedonism of the time in her novel, *Bonjour Tristesse*.

Scott and Zelda Fitzgerald with daughter Scottie

lew Realism

n the 1950s Nice produced its wn school of artists, the *louveaux Réalistes*, including 'ves Klein, Arman, Martial Raysse, 'inguely, César, Niki de Saint 'halle, and Daniel Spoerri *see p530)*. They explored the ossibilities of everyday objects - Arman sliced violins, packaged nd displayed trash; Tinguely xploded TV sets and cars. They ad a light-hearted approach, We live in a land of vacations, vhich gives us the spirit of onsense," said Klein. He painted olid blue canvases of his ersonal color, International klein Blue, taking the inspiration f the Mediterranean to its limit.

Provençal Writers

The regions of Provence and Languedoc have always had a distinct literary identity, ever since the troubadours in the 12th–13th centuries composed their love poetry in the *langue d'oc* Provençal, a Latin-based language. In the last century, many regional writers have been inspired by the landscape and local traditions. They were influenced by the 19th-century Felibrige movement to revive the language, led by Nobel prize-winning poet Frédéric Mistral. Some, like Daudet and film-maker turned writer Marcel Pagnol, celebrate the Provençal character; others, such as Jean Giono, explore the connection between nature and humanity.

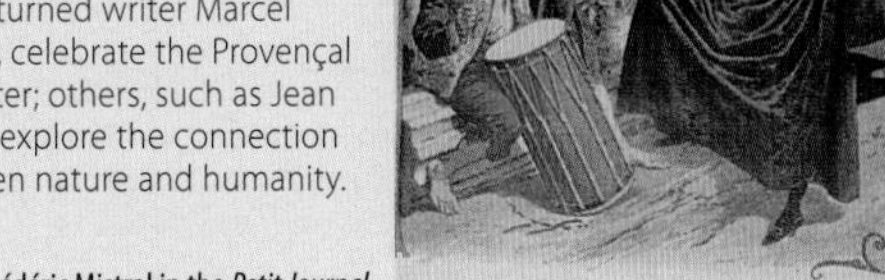

Frédéric Mistral in the *Petit Journal*

Beaches in the South of France

The glamorous Mediterranean coast is France's foremost holiday playground. To the east lie the Riviera's big, traditional resorts such as Menton, Nice, Cannes, and Monte-Carlo. To the west are smaller resorts in coves and bays like St-Tropez and Cassis. Farther on is the Camargue reserve at the mouth of the Rhône. West of the Rhône, making a majestic curve reaching almost to the Spanish border, is the long, sandy shore of Languedoc-Roussillon, where a string of purpose-built resorts range from modernistic beach cities to replicas of fishing villages.

The beaches are sandy west of Antibes; eastwards, they are naturally shingly, so any sand is imported. Antipollution drives mean that most beaches are now clean, except in a few spots west of Marseille and around Nice. Beaches around towns often charge fees but are usually well equipped.

A rail poster by Domergue advertising th Côte d'Azur

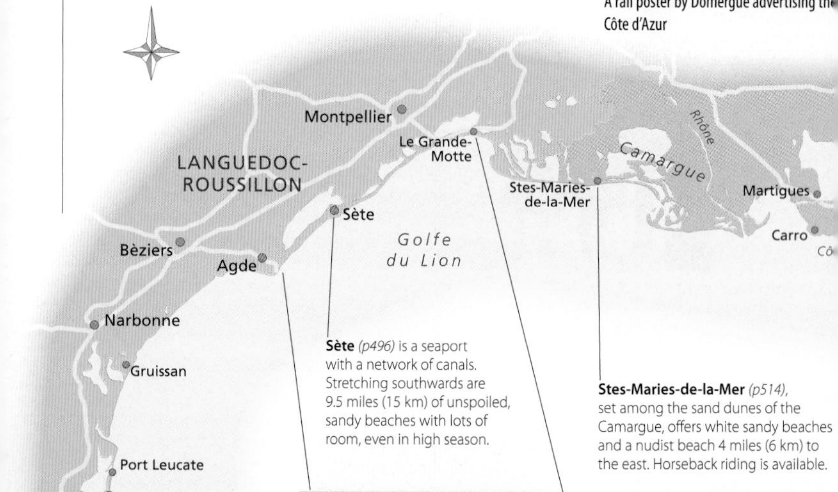

Sète *(p496)* is a seaport with a network of canals. Stretching southwards are 9.5 miles (15 km) of unspoiled, sandy beaches with lots of room, even in high season.

Stes-Maries-de-la-Mer *(p514)*, set among the sand dunes of the Camargue, offers white sandy beaches and a nudist beach 4 miles (6 km) to the east. Horseback riding is available.

Cap d'Agde *(p491)* is a vast modern resort with long, golden sandy beaches and sports facilities of all kinds. It has Europe's largest nudist resort, accommodating 20,000 visitors.

La Grande-Motte *(p499)* is a huge purpose-built beach resort with excellent sports facilities, famous for its bizarre ziggurat architecture.

Victorian times the Côte d'Azur, or Riviera, as the fashionable holiday venue of Europe's yalty and rich. They came to gamble and escape orthern winters. Summer bathing did not come to vogue until the 1920s. Today the Riviera is usy all year round with the glamorous beaches nd nightlife still a major attraction.

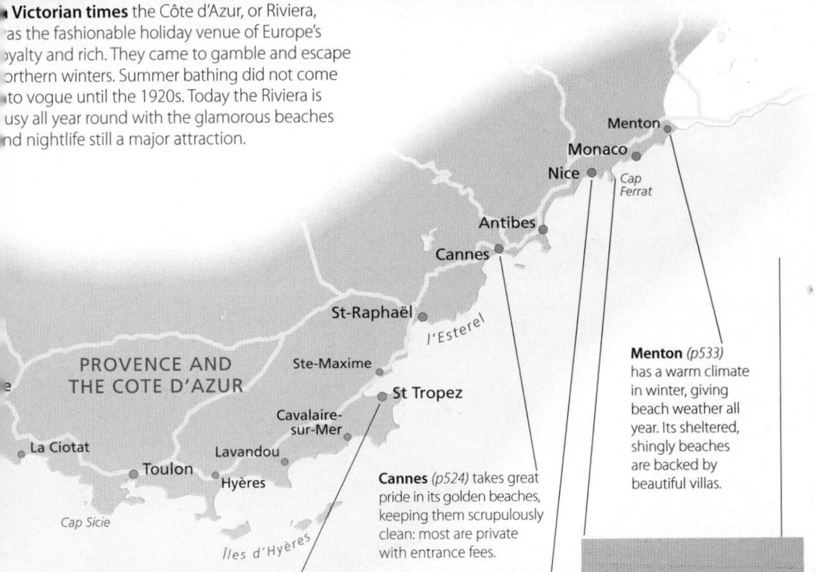

Menton
Monaco
Nice
Cap Ferrat
Antibes
Cannes
St-Raphaël
l'Esterel
PROVENCE AND THE COTE D'AZUR
Ste-Maxime
St Tropez
Cavalaire-sur-Mer
La Ciotat
Toulon
Lavandou
Hyères
Cap Sicie
Îles d'Hyères

Menton *(p533)* has a warm climate in winter, giving beach weather all year. Its sheltered, shingly beaches are backed by beautiful villas.

Cannes *(p524)* takes great pride in its golden beaches, keeping them scrupulously clean: most are private with entrance fees.

assis *(p517)* is a charming fishing village with a popular casino, white cliffs, and some lovely idden creeks nearby.

t-Tropez *(p520)* is flanked by golden beaches mostly occupied by stylish clubs" offering amenities at a price.

Nice *(pp530–31)* has a visually dramatic waterfront with a wide, handsome promenade, but the beach itself is stony and has a busy highway alongside.

Cap Ferrat *(p532)* is a wooded peninsula which has a 6-mile (10-km) craggy cliff walk offering glimpses of grand villas and private beaches.

.ANGUEDOC-ROUSSILLON

ıde · Gard · Hérault · Pyrénées-Orientales

ıe two distinct provinces of Languedoc and Roussillon retch from the foothills of the Pyrenees on the Spanish order to the mouth of the Rhône. The flat beaches and goons of the coast form a purpose-built sunbelt commodating millions of holidaymakers every year. between is a dry, scorched land producing half of France's ble wine and the season's first peaches and cherries.

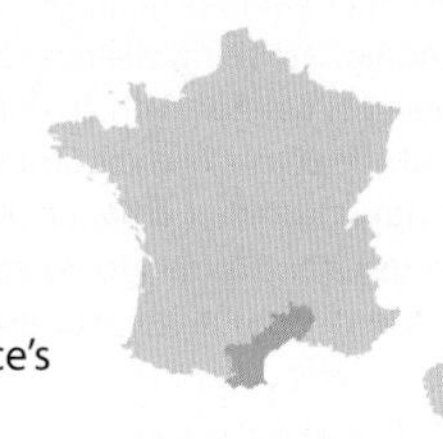

eyond such sensuous pleasures are many yers of history, not least the unification of e two provinces. The formerly dependent Languedoc once spoke ccitan, the tongue of the troubadours, ıd still cherishes its separate identity. oussillon was a Spanish possession ıtil the treaty of the Pyrenees in 1659. s Catalan heritage is displayed everywhere om the road signs to the Sardana dance, ıd the flavor of Spain is evident in the opularity of bullfights, paella, and gaudily ainted facades.

This stretch of coastline was the first place Gaul to be settled by the Romans, their nduring legacy evident in the great mphitheater at Nîmes and the magni-cent engineering of the Pont du Gard. The bbeys of St-Martin-du-Canigou, St-Michel-e-Cuixà, and St-Guilhem-le-Désert are superb examples of early Romanesque architecture, unaffected by Northern Gothic. The great craggy Cathar castles and the perfectly restored medieval Cité of Carcassonne bear witness to the bloody battles of the Middle Ages.

In parts, the region remains wild and untamed: from the high plateaus of the Cerdagne, to the wild hills of the Corbières or the remote uplands of Haut Languedoc. But it also has the most youthful and progressive cities in France: Montpellier, the ancient university city and capital of the region, and Nîmes with its exuberant *feria* and bullfights. The whole area is typified by an insouciant mixture of ancient and modern, from Roman temples and postmodern architecture in its cities to solar power and ancient abbeys in the mountains.

sunny stretch of coastline at Cap d'Agde

◀ The citadel of Carcassonne

Exploring Languedoc-Roussillon

Languedoc-Roussillon combines miles of gentle coastline with a rugged hinterland. Its clean, sandy beaches are perfect for family holidays, with resorts ranging from traditional fishing villages to new purpose-built resorts. Inland is quieter, with acres of vineyards in the Corbières and Minervois, and mountain walks in the Haut Languedoc and Cerdagne. A rich architectural heritage ranges from Roman to Romanesque, contrasting with the modern, vibrant atmosphere of the main cities.

Jousting on the canal, a regular summer event in Sète

Sights at a Glance

1. Cerdagne
2. Villefranche-de-Conflent
3. St-Michel-de-Cuixà
4. St-Martin-du-Canigou
5. Prieuré de Serrabone
6. Céret
7. Côte Vermeille
8. Collioure
9. Elne
10. Perpignan
11. Salses
12. Corbières
13. Narbonne
14. Golfe du Lion
15. Carcassonne
16. Minerve
17. Béziers
18. Sète
19. Pézenas
20. Parc Régional du Haut Languedoc
21. St-Guilhem-le-Désert
22. Montpellier
23. La Grande-Motte
24. Aigues-Mortes
25. Nîmes
26. Pont du Gard

For additional map symbols *see back flap*

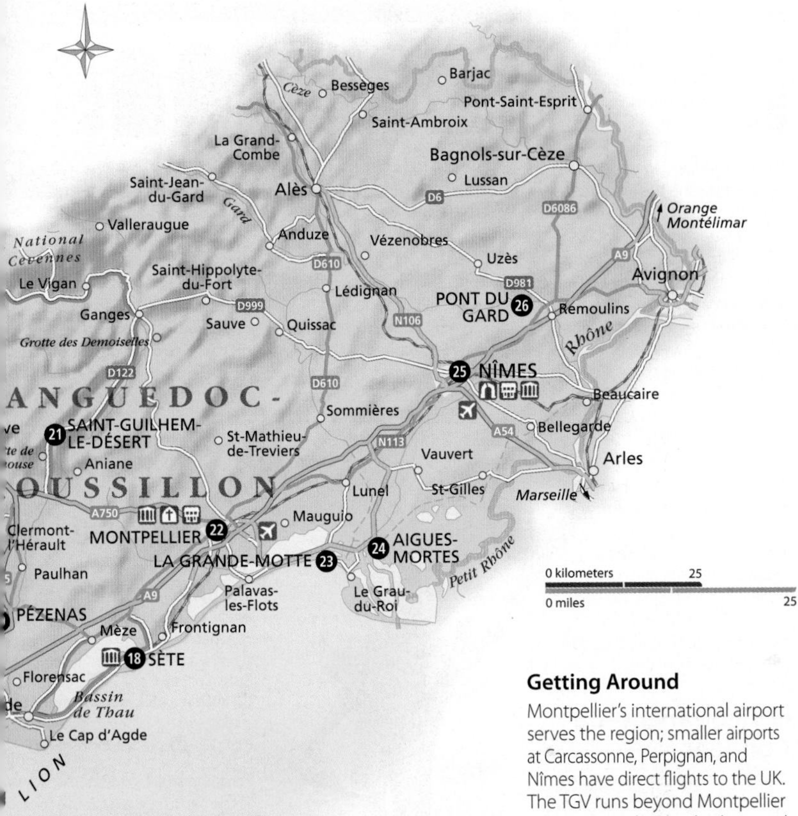

Getting Around

Montpellier's international airport serves the region; smaller airports at Carcassonne, Perpignan, and Nîmes have direct flights to the UK. The TGV runs beyond Montpellier to Béziers, and a good rail network connects the region's main towns. The A61 highway provides access from the west and the A9 follows the coast. The A75 now enters from the north. Smaller roads, even in the mountains, are well maintained. Barges along the Canal du Midi are a leisurely alternative.

The ruined Barbarossa tower at Gruissan on the Golfe du Lion

Key

- Highway
- Major road
- Secondary road
- Minor road
- Scenic route
- Main railroad
- Minor railroad
- International border
- Regional border
- Summit

❶ Cerdagne

Pyrénées-Orientales. ✈ Perpignan. 🚉 🚌 Mont Louis, Bourg Madame, Latour de Carol Enveitg. ℹ 1 pl de Roser, Saillagouse (04 68 04 15 47); Mont Louis (04 68 04 21 97).
pyrenees-cerdagne.com
mont-louis.net

The remote Cerdagne, an independent state in the Middle Ages, is today divided between Spain and France. Its high plateaus offer skiing and walking among clear mountain lakes and pine and chestnut forests. The Little Yellow Train (08 00 88 60 91, www.ter-sncf.com) is an excellent way to sample it in a day. Stops include **Mont Louis**, a town fortified by Vauban, Louis XIV's military architect, which still accommodates French troops; the huge ski resort of **Font-Romeu**; **Latour-de-Carol** and the tiny village of **Yravals** below it. Nearby **Odeillo** is the site of a solar furnace, 150 ft (45 m) tall and 165 ft (50 m) wide; its giant curved mirrors create a remarkable sight in the valley.

❷ Villefranche-de-Conflent

Pyrénées-Orientales. 240. 🚉 🚌 ℹ 2 rue St-Jean, pl de l'Eglise (04 68 96 22 96).

In medieval times Villefranche's position at the narrowest point of the Têt valley made it an eminently defensible fortress against Moorish invasion. Fragments of 11th-century walls remain, along

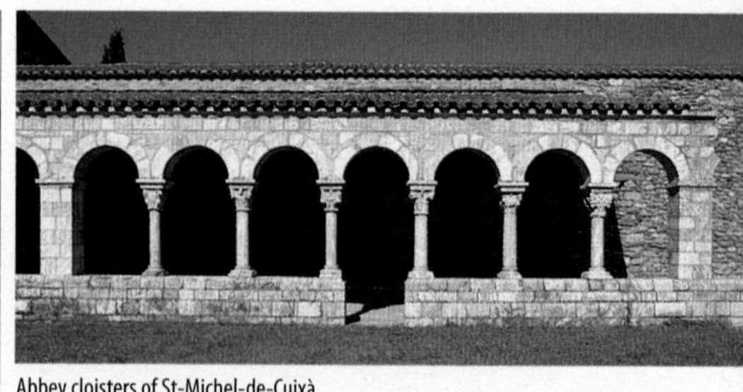

Abbey cloisters of St-Michel-de-Cuixà

with massive ramparts, gates, and Fort Liberia high above the gorge, all built by Vauban in the 17th century. The 12th-century **Eglise de St-Jacques** has fine carved capitals from the workshops of St-Michel-de-Cuixà and Catalan painted wooden statues, including a 14th-century *Virgin and Child*. The 13th-century oak door is embellished with intricate local wrought ironwork, a craft which still features on many of the store signs in town. From the streets of locally quarried pink marble you can make the climb up to the **Grottes des Canalettes**, a superb underground setting for concerts. The Little Yellow Train will take you to the magnificent mountain plain of the Cerdagne (phone 08 06 88 60 91 to book).

Statue in St-Jacques, Villefranche

❸ St-Michel-de-Cuixà

Route de Tourinya Codalet, Prades, Pyrénées-Orientales. **Tel** 04 68 96 15 35. **Open** May–Sep: 9:30–11:50am & 2–6pm; Oct–Apr: 2–5pm. **Closed** Jan 1, Easter Sunday, Dec 25.
abbaye.cuixa.monsite-orange.fr
Prades: 10 pl de la République (04 68 05 41 02). **prades-tourisme.fr**

Prades, a small, pink marble town in the Têt valley, is typical of the local style. The **Eglise St-Pierre** has a southern Gothic wrought-iron belfry and a Baroque Catalan interior. But the town is distinguished by the pre-Romanesque abbey of St-Michel-de-Cuixà which lies 2 miles (3 km) farther up the valley, and by the legacy of the Spanish cellist Pablo Casals. Casals spent many years here in exile from Franco's Spain; every August the abbey provides the setting for the Prades music festival held in his memory.

St-Michel-de-Cuixà abbey was founded by Benedictine monks in 878 and rapidly became renowned throughout France and Spain. Distinctive, Moorish-influenced keyhole arches pierce the massive walls of the abbey church, which was consecrated in 974. The mottled pink marble cloisters, with their superbly carved capitals, were added in the 12th century.

The Little Yellow Train

Arrive early for the best seats in the carriages of *Le Petit Train Jaune*, which winds its way on narrow-gauge tracks through gorges and across towering viaducts up into the Cerdagne, stopping at small mountain stations along the way. Built in 1910 to improve access to the mountains, it now operates mainly for tourists, beginning at Villefranche-de-Conflent and terminating at Latour-de-Carol.

The Little Yellow Train, with open carriages for summer visitors

For hotels and restaurants in this region see pp554–71 and pp576–603

After the Revolution the building was abandoned, and its famous carvings looted. From 1913, George Grey Bernard, a visiting American artist, began to discover some of the capitals incorporated in local buildings. He sold the carvings to the Metropolitan Museum of Art in New York in 1925, where they formed the basis of the Cloisters Museum – a faithful re-creation of a Romanesque abbey in the unlikely setting of Manhattan.

❹ St-Martin-du-Canigou

Casteil. **Tel** 04 68 05 50 03. **Open** (guided tours only: tours last an hour; times vary with seasons) Jun–Sep: daily; Oct–May: Tue–Sun. **Closed** Jan, Good Friday. **W** **stmartinducanigou.org**

Saint-Martin-du-Canigou is situated in a spectacularly remote site a third of the way up Pic du Canigou, on a jagged spur of rock approached only by a 40-minute climb on foot from Casteil, a special shuttle (Jul–Aug: daily) or hired transport. Built at the beginning of the 11th century, the abbey was financed by Guifred, Count of Cerdagne, who entered the monastery in 1035. He was buried there 14 years later in a tomb he carved from the rock himself, which can still be seen. The early-Romanesque church is based on a simple basilican plan. Two churches built quite literally one on top of the other make the lower church the crypt for the upper building.

The abbey complex is best viewed from above, by continuing up the path. From there, its irregular design clinging to the rock is framed by the dramatic mountain setting – the ensemble a tribute to the ingenuity and vitality of its early builders.

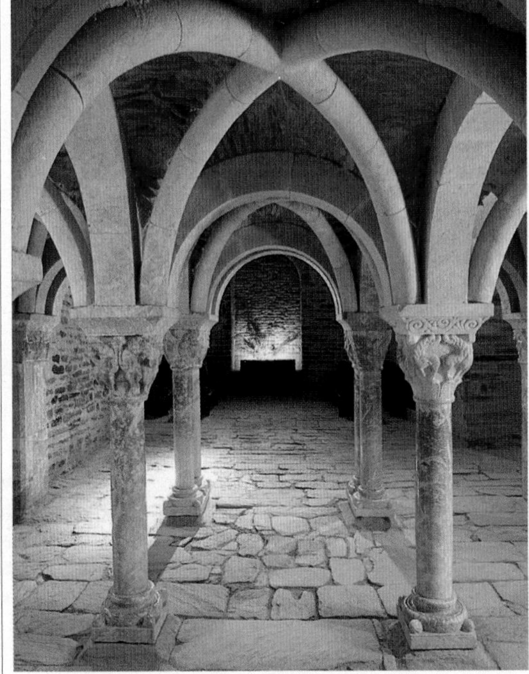

Serrabone priory's chapel tribune, with columns of local marble

The 11th-century cloister of St-Martin-du-Canigou

❺ Prieuré de Serrabone

Boule d'Amont. **Tel** 04 68 84 09 30 (tourist office). **Open** 10am–6pm daily. **Closed** Jan 1, May 1, Nov 1, Dec 25.

Perched high up on the northern flanks of Pic du Canigou, the sacred mountain of the Catalans, is the priory of Serrabone. A final lap of hairpin bends on the approach road (the D618) reveals the simple square tower and round apse of this remote Romanesque abbey, surrounded by a botanical garden of local herbs and woodland plants clinging to the mountain side.

Inside the cool, austere 12th-century building is a surprisingly elaborate chapel tribune, its columns and arches glowing from the local red-veined marble, carved by the anonymous Master of Cuixà, whose work appears throughout the region. Note the strange beasts and verdant flora featured in the capital carvings, especially the rose of Roussillon.

6 Céret

Pyrénées-Orientales. 8,000. av Clémenceau (04 68 87 00 53). Sat, Tue eve Jul–Aug. Fête des Cerises (May/Jun). **ot-ceret.fr**

Céret is a cherry town, surrounded by a cloud of pink blossom in the early spring, and producing the very first fruits of the year. The annual cherry festival is held in early June. The tiled and painted facades and loggias of the buildings have a Spanish feel and the town was popular with Picasso, Braque, and Matisse. Today Céret is distinguished by the **Musée d'Art Moderne**, its sophisticated modern architecture housing a remarkable collection which includes Catalan artists Tapiès and Capdeville; 50 works donated by Picasso, including a series of bowls painted with bullfighting scenes; and works by Matisse, Chagall, Juan Gris, and Salvador Dalí.

The town's Catalan heritage is evident in regular bullfights held in the arena, and in its Sardana dance festivals in July.

Musée d'Art Moderne
8 bd Maréchal Joffre. **Tel** 04 68 87 27 76. **Open** 10am–6pm daily (to 7pm Jul–mid-Sep) . **Closed** Jan 1, May 1, Nov 1 & Dec 25. **musee-ceret.com**

Environs
From Céret the D115 follows the Tech valley to the spa town of

Statue by Aristide Maillol, Banyuls

Amélie-les-Bains, where fragments of Roman baths have been discovered. Beyond, in **Arles-sur-Tech**, the Eglise de Ste-Marie contains 12th-century frescoes, and a sarcophagus beside the church door which, according to local legend, produces drops of unaccountably pure water every year.

Catalan flag

7 Côte Vermeille

Pyrénées-Orientales. Perpignan. Collioure, Cerbère. Collioure, Banyuls-sur-Mer. Collioure (04 68 82 15 47), Cerbère (04 68 88 42 36). **collioure.com**

Here the Pyrenees meet the Mediterranean, the coast road twisting and turning around secluded pebbly coves and rocky outcrops. The *vermeille* (vermilion-tinted) rock of the headlands gives this stretch of coast, the loveliest in the region, its name.

The Côte Vermeille extends all the way to the Costa Brava in northern Spain. With its Catalan character, it is as redolent of Spain as of France. **Argelès-Plage** has three sandy beaches and a palm-fringed promenade, and is the largest camping center in Europe. The small resort of **Cerbère** is the last French town before the border, flying the red and gold Catalan flag to signal its true allegiance. All along the coast, terraced vineyards cling to the rocky hillsides, producing strong, sweet wines like Banyuls and Muscat. The difficult terrain makes harvesting a laborious process. Vines were first cultivated here by Greek settlers in the 7th century BC, and Banyuls itself has wine cellars dating back to the Middle Ages.

Banyuls is also famous as the birthplace of Aristide Maillol, the 19th-century sculptor, whose work can be seen all over the region. **Port Vendres**, with fortifications built by the indefatigable Vauban (architect to Louis XIV) is a fishing port, renowned for its anchovies and sardines.

The spectacular Côte Vermeille, seen from the coast road south of Banyuls

For hotels and restaurants in this region see pp554–71 and pp576–603

Collioure harbor, with one of its beaches and the Eglise Notre-Dame-des-Anges

❽ Collioure

Pyrénées-Orientales. 3,000. pl du 18 juin (04 68 82 15 47). Wed & Sun. **collioure.com**

The colors of Collioure first attracted Matisse here in 1905: brightly stuccoed houses sheltered by cypresses and gaily painted fishing boats, all bathed in the famous luminous light, and washed by a gentle sea. Other artists including André Derain worked here under Matisse's influence and were dubbed *fauves* (wild beasts) for their wild experiments with color. Art galleries and souvenir shops now fill the cobbled streets, but this small fishing port has changed little since then, with anchovies still its main business. Two salting houses, which can be visited, are evidence of this tradition.

Three sheltered beaches, both pebble and sand, nestle round the harbor, dominated by the bulk of the **Château Royal**, which forms part of the harbor wall. It was first built by the Knights Templar in the 13th century, and Collioure became the main port of entry for Perpignan, remaining under the rule of Spanish Aragon until France took over in 1659. The outer fortifications were reinforced ten years later by Vauban, who demolished much of the original town in the process. Today the château can be toured, or visited for its exhibitions of modern art.

The **Eglise Notre-Dame-des-Anges** on Collioure's quayside was rebuilt in the 17th century to replace the church which was destroyed by Vauban. A former lighthouse was incorporated as a bell tower. Inside the church are no fewer than five Baroque altarpieces by Joseph Sunyer and other Catalan masters of the genre.

Be warned that Collioure is extremely popular in July and August, with visitors cramming the tiny streets. Long queues of traffic are possible, too, though the building of another route, the D86, has helped to ease congestion.

Château Royal
Tel 04 68 82 06 43. **Open** daily. **Closed** Jan 1, May 1 & Dec 25.

❾ Elne

Pyrénées-Orientales. 8,000. pl Sant-Jordi (04 68 22 05 07). Mon, Wed, Fri. **ot-elne.fr**

This ancient town accommodated Hannibal and his elephants in 218 BC on his epic journey to Rome, and was one of the most important towns in Roussillon until the 16th century. Today it is famed for the 11th-century **Cathédrale de Ste-Eulalie et Ste-Julie**, with its superb cloister. Milky blue-veined marble has been carved into exquisite capitals, embellished with flowers, figures, and arabesques. The side nearest the cathedral dates from the 1100s; the remaining three are 13th–14th-century.

Cathédrale de Ste-Eulalie et Ste-Julie
Tel 04 68 37 83 71. **Open** daily. **Closed** Jan 1, May 1 & Dec 25.

Carved capital at Elne, showing "The Dream of the Magi"

Entrance to the Palais des Rois de Majorque, Perpignan

⑩ Perpignan

Pyrénées-Orientales. 120,000. Palais des Congrès, place Armand Lanaux (04 68 66 30 30). daily. **perpignantourisme.com**

Catalan Perpignan has a distinctly southern feel, with palm trees lining the place Arago, house and shop facades painted vibrant turquoise and pink, and the streets of the Arab quarter selling aromatic spices, cous-cous, and paella.

Today Perpignan is the vibrant capital of Roussillon, and has an important position on the developing Mediter-ranean sunbelt. But it reached its zenith in the 13th and 14th centuries under the kings of Majorca and the kings of Aragón, who controlled great swathes of northern Spain and southern France. Their vast **Palais des Rois de Majorque** still straddles a substantial area in the southern part of the city. Perpignan's strong Catalan identity is evident during the weekly summer celebrations when the Sardana is danced. It is a key Catalan symbol. Arms raised, concentric circles of dancers keep step to the accompaniment of a Catalan woodwind band.

One of Perpignan's finest buildings, the **Loge de Mer**, lies at the head of the square. Built in 1397 to house the Maritime Exchange, only the eastern section retains the original Gothic design. The rest of the building was rebuilt in Renaissance style in 1540 with sumptuous carved wooden ceilings and sculpted window frames. The Loge de Mer has avoided becoming a hushed museum piece. Instead, it remains the center of Perpignan life – elegant cafés cluster round it, producing a constant buzz of activity.

Next door is the **Hôtel de Ville** with its pebble stone facade and wrought iron gates. Inside, parts of the arcaded courtyard date back to 1315; at the center is Aristide Maillol's allegorical sculpture, *The Mediterranean* (1950). To the east is the laby-rinthine cathedral quarter of St-Jean, made up of small streets and squares containing some fine 14th- and 15th-century buildings.

Devout Christ in St-Jean

Cathédrale St-Jean

Pl de Gambetta. **Tel** 04 68 51 33 72. **Open** 8am–6pm Mon–Sat (to 7pm summer months); 2–6pm Sun.

Topped by a wrought iron belfry, this cathedral was begun in 1324 and was finally ready for use in 1509. It is constructed almost entirely from river pebbles layered with red brick, a style common throughout the region due to the scarcity of other building materials.

Inside the gloomy interior the nave is flanked by gilded altarpieces and painted wood-en statues, with a massive pre-Romanesque marble font. A cloistered cemetery adjoins the church and the Chapel of the Devout Christ with its precious, poignantly realistic medieval wooden Crucifixion. The cathedral replaced the

The Annual Procession de la Sanch

There is a very Catalan atmosphere in Perpignan during the annual Good Friday procession of the Confraternity of La Sanch (Brotherhood of the Holy Blood). Originally dedicated to the comfort of con-demned prisoners in the 15th century, members of the brotherhood still wear macabre red or black robes as they carry sacred relics and the crucifix from the Chapel of the Devout Christ to the cathedral.

th-century church of St-Jean-Vieux, whose superb manesque doorway can be mpsed to the left of the main trance. Some areas may be stricted due to ongoing storation work.

Palais des Rois de ajorque

ue des Archers. **Tel** 04 68 34 48 29. **en** 9am–5pm daily. **Closed** Jan 1, y 1, Nov 1 & Dec 25.

cess to the vast 13th-century tified palace of the Kings of ajorca is as circuitous today as was intended to be for vading soldiers. Flights of eps zigzag within the sheer d-brick ramparts, begun in the th century and added to ccessively over the next two nturies. Eventually, the egant gardens and substantial stle within are revealed, tered by way of the Tour de ommage, from the top of hich is a panoramic view of y, mountains, and sea.

The palace itself is built around central arcaded courtyard, nked on one side by the Salle Majorque, a great hall with a ple fireplace and giant Gothic ched windows. Adjacent, two yal chapels built one above the her show southern Gothic style its best: pointed arches, tterned frescoes, and elabo-te tilework demonstrating a stinct Moorish influence. The ie rose marble doorway of the per King's Chapel is typical of e Roussillon Romanesque style, though the sculpted capitals are othic. Today the great courtyard sometimes used for concerts.

Courtyard in the Hôtel de Ville

Musée de l'Histoire de la Catalogue Nord

pl de Verdun, Le Castillet. **Tel** 04 68 35 42 05. **Open** Tue–Sun. **Closed** public hols.

The red-brick tower and pink belfry of the Castillet, built as the town gate in 1368, was at one time a prison and is all that remains of the town walls. It now houses a collection of Catalan craft objects, agricultural implements, kitchen furniture, looms, and terracotta pots for storing water and oil. It also holds art exhibitions.

Musée des Beaux-Arts Hyacinthe Rigaud

16 rue de l'Ange. **Tel** 04 68 35 43 40. **Open** 10:30am–6pm Tue–Sun. **Closed** public hols.

This magnificent 18th-century mansion has an eclectic art collection dominated by the work of Hyacinthe Rigaud (1659–1743), who was born in Perpignan and was court painter to Louis XIV and Louis XV. The first floor has a room of portraits, including works by David, Greuze, and Ingres; the Dufy, Picasso, and Maillol room; and the Primitifs Catalan, 14th–16th-century Catalan and Spanish paintings, among them the *Retable de la Trinité* (1489) by the Master of Canapost.

The museum also represents the 20th century: Alechinsky, Appel, and others from the late 1940s European Cobra movement; the Catalan artist Pierre Daura; and modern Roussillon painters like Brune, Terrus, and Violet.

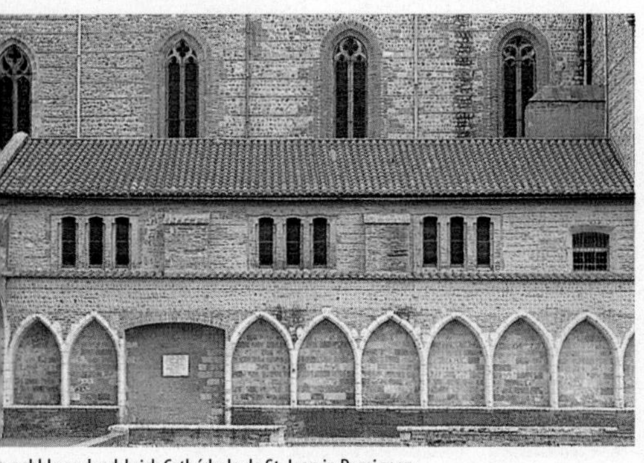

e pebble and red-brick Cathédrale de St-Jean in Perpignan

Fortress tower and ramparts, Salses

⓫ Forteresse de Salses

Pyrénées-Orientales. 3,000. Salses-le-Château 66600 (04 68 38 60 13). Wed. **salses.monuments-nationaux.fr**

Looking like a giant sand-castle against the ocher earth of the Corbières vineyards, the **Forteresse de Salses** stands at the old frontier of Spain and France. It guards the narrow defile between the Mediterranean lagoons and the mountains, and was built by King Ferdinand of Aragon between 1497 and 1506 to defend Spain's possession of Roussillon. Its massive walls and rounded towers are typical of Spanish military architecture, designed to deflect the new threat posed by gunpowder.

Inside were underground stables for 300 horses and a subterranean passageway.

There is a wonderful view from the keep over the lagoons and surrounding coastline.

Vineyards covering the hilly terrain of the Corbières

⓬ Corbières

Aude. ✈ Perpignan. 🚉 Narbonne, Carcassonne, Lézignan-Corbières. 🚌 Narbonne, Carcassonne, Lézignan-Corbières. ℹ 9 cours de la République, Lézignan-Corbières (04 68 27 05 42). **W lezignan-corbieres.fr/tourisme**

Still one of the wildest parts of France with few roads, let alone villages, the Corbières is best known for its wine and the great craggy hulks of the Cathar castles *(see p495)*. Much of the land is untamed *garrigue* (scrubland) fragrant with honeysuckle and broom; south-facing slopes have been cleared and planted with vines.

To the south are the spectacular medieval castles of **Peyrepertuse** and **Quéribus**, the latter one of the last Cathar strongholds. The guided visits around the remarkable Cathar château at **Villerouge-Termenes** reveal some of its turbulent past. To the west is the barren, uninhabited Razès area in the upper Aude valley. Its best-kept secret is the village of **Alet-les-Bains**, with beautifully preserved half-timbered houses and the remains of a Benedictine abbey, battle-scarred from the Wars of Religion.

⓭ Narbonne

Aude. 👥 52,000. 🚉 🚌 ℹ 31 rue Jean Jaurès (04 68 65 15 60). Thu & Sun. **W narbonne-tourisme.com**

Narbonne is a medium-sized, cheerful town profiting from the booming wine region that surrounds it. The town is bisected by the tree-shaded Canal de la Robine; to the north is the restored medieval quarter with many good shops and restaurants. Located here is one of Narbonne's most intriguing tourist attractions, the Roman **Horreum**. This underground warehouse dates from the 1st century BC, when Narbonne was a major port and capital of the largest Roman province in Gaul.

The town prospered through the Middle Ages until the 15th century when the harbor silted up and the course of the river Aude altered, taking Narbonne's fortunes with it. By then, an important bishopric had been established and an ambitious cathedral project, modeled on the great Gothic cathedrals of the North, was underway. However, the full grandiose design was abandoned and just the chancel, begun in 1272, became the **Cathédrale St-Just et St-Pasteur** we see today.

It is still enormous, enhanced by 14th-century sculptures, fine stained-glass windows, and an 18th-century carved organ. Aubusson and Gobelin tapestries adorn the walls, and the Chapel of the Anonciade houses a treasury of manuscripts, jeweled reliquaries, and tapestries.

The unfinished transept now forms a courtyard, and between the cathedral and the **Palais des Archevêques** (Archbishops' Palace), lie cloisters with four galleries of 14th-century vaulting.

This huge palace and cathedral complex dominates the center of Narbonne. Between the Palais des Archevêques' massive 14th-century towers is the town hall, with a 19th-century Neo-Gothic facade by Viollet-le-Duc *(see p200)*, the architect who so determinedly restored medieval France. The palace itself is divided into the Palais Vieux

The vaulted chancel of Cathédrale St-Just St-Pasteur in Narbonne

Tranquil waterway of the Canal du Midi

Canal du Midi

From Sète to Toulouse the 149-mile (240-km) Canal du Midi flows between plane trees, vineyards, and villages. The complex system of locks, aqueducts, and bridges is a remarkable feat of engineering, built by the Béziers salt-tax baron Paul Riquet. Completed in 1681, it encouraged Languedoc trade and created a vital link, via the Garonne river, between the Atlantic and the Mediterranean. Today it is plied by holiday barges (www.canal-du-midi.org).

Cistercian Abbaye de Fontfroide (1093), southwest of Narbonne

ld Palace) and the Palais Neuf ew Palace). Narbonne's most portant museums are in the lais Neuf, on the left as you ter through the low medieval ches of the passage de l'Ancre. e **Musée d'Archéologie et de éhistoire** collection includes gments of Narbonne's Roman ritage, from remarkable Roman scoes, milestones, and parts the original walls to an assem- age of domestic objects, coins, ols, and glassware. The **Chapelle la Madeleine** is decorated th a 14th-century wall painting d houses a collection of Greek ses, sarcophagi, and mosaics. In the archbishops' former artments is the **Musée d'Art et Histoire**, which is as interesting r its luxurious furnishings and hly decorated ceilings as for art collection. This includes me fine paintings by Canaletto, ueghel, Boucher, and Veronese well as a large selection of cal earthenware. In addition, e museum houses an tstanding collection of ddle Eastern paintings.

South of the Canal de la Robine e a number of fine mansions, cluding the Renaissance **aison des Trois Nourrices** on e corner of rue des Trois- urrices and rue Edgard- uinet. Nearby is the **Musée Lapidaire**, with architectural fragments from Gallo-Roman Narbonne, and the 13th-century Gothic **Basilique St-Paul-Serge**. The present building retains the crypt and some sarcophagi of an earlier church on this site.

Horreum
Rue Rouget-de-l'Isle. **Tel** 04 68 32 45 30. **Open** Jun–Sep: daily; Oct–May: Wed–Mon. **Closed** Jan 1, May 1, Nov 1 & 11, Dec 25.

Musée d'Archéologie et de Préhistoire/Musée d'Art et d'Histoire
Palais des Archevêques. **Tel** 04 68 65 15 60. **Open** Jun–Sep: daily; Oct–May: Wed–Mon. **Closed** Jan 1, May 1, Nov 1 & 11, Dec 25.

Musee Lapidaire
Eglise Notre-Dame de Lamourguié. **Tel** 04 68 65 15 60. **Open** Jun–Sep: daily; Oct–May: Wed–Mon. **Closed** Jan 1, May 1, Nov 1, Nov 11, Dec 25.

Environs
Southwest (8 miles /13 km), the Cistercian **Abbaye de Fontfroide** has an elegant cloister. The abbey is tucked away in a quiet valley, surrounded by cypress trees.

⓮ Golfe du Lion

Aude, Hérault. Montpellier. Sète. 35 rue du Port, La Grande Motte (04 67 56 42 00).
ot-lagrandemotte.fr

Languedoc-Roussillon's shore- line (65 miles/100 km) forms an almost unbroken sweep of sandy beach. Only at its southern limits does it break into the rocky inlets of the Côte Vermeille. Purpose- built resorts created since the 1960s emphasize eco-friendly, low-rise family accommodation, some in local styles, others with imaginative architecture.

La Grande Motte marina has distinctive ziggurat-style build- ings *(see p499)*. **Cap d'Agde** has Europe's largest nudist quarter. Inland **Agde**, founded by ancient Greek traders, is built of black basalt and has a fortified cathe- dral. **Port Leucate** and **Port Bacarès** are ideal for watersports. An older town is **Sète** *(see p496)*. A feature of the flat Languedoc coast is its *étangs* – large shallow lagoons. Those nearest the Camargue are the haunt of thousands of wading birds.

A wide, sandy beach on the Cap d'Agde

⓯ Carcassonne

The citadel of Carcassonne is a perfectly restored medieval town, and protected by UNESCO. It crowns a steep bank above the river Aude, a fairy-tale sight of turrets and ramparts overlooking the Basse Ville below. The strategic position of the citadel between the Atlantic and the Mediterranean and on the corridor between the Iberian peninsula and the rest of Europe led to its original settlement, consolidated by the Romans in the 2nd century BC. It became a key element in medieval military conflicts. At its zenith in the 12th century, it was ruled by the Trencavels who built the château and cathedral. Military advances and the Treaty of the Pyrenees in 1659, which relocated the French–Spanish border, hastened its decline. The attentions of architectural historian Viollet-le-Duc *(see p204)* led to its restoration in the 19th century.

The Restored Citadel
Restoration of La Cité has always been controversial. Critics complain it looks too new, favoring a more romantic ruin.

★ Basilique St-Nazaire
Within the Romanesque and Gothic cathedral is the famous Siege Stone, said to depict the 1209 Siege of Carcassonne by crusaders.

②
③
R POR
RUE ST LOUIS
R DAME CARCAS
①
RUE TRENCAV
RUE D
LICES HAUTES

0 meters 50
0 yards 50

KEY

① **The ramparts** were built by Kings Louis VIII, Louis IX, and Philip the Bold, in the 13th century.

② **Bishop's Tower**

③ **Porte d'Aude**

④ **Gallo-Roman walls**

⑤ **The Great Well**

⑥ **The *lices*,** the easily defended spaces between the inner and outer ramparts, were also used for jousting, for crossbow practice, and for storage of timber and other materials.

★ Le Château
A fortress within a fortress, the château has a moat, five towers, and defensive wooden galleries on the walls.

Religious Persecution

Carcassonne's strategic position meant it was often at the center of religious conflict. The Cathars *(see p495)* were given sanctuary here in 1209 by Raymond-Roger Trencavel when besieged by Simon de Montfort in his crusade against heresy. In the 14th century the Inquisition continued to root out the Cathars. This painting depicts intended victims in the Inquisition Tower.

Les Emmurés de Carcassonne, JP Laurens

VISITORS' CHECKLIST

Practical Information
Aude. 49,000. 28 rue Verdun (04 68 10 24 30). Tue, Thu & Sat. Festival de Carcassonne (Jul–Aug); l'Embrasement de la Cité (Jul 14). Le Château: **Open** 9:30am–5pm daily (Apr–Sep: to 6.30pm). **Closed** Jan 1, May 1, July 14, Nov 1 & 11, Dec 25.
carcassonne-tourisme.com

Transport
2 miles (4 km) W Carcassonne.
Port du Canal du Midi.
bd de Varsovie.

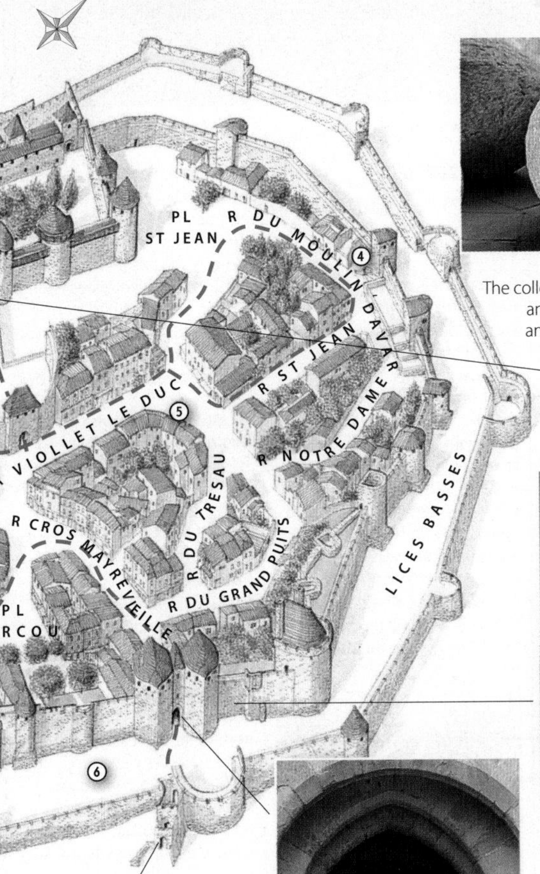

Main entrance to La Cité

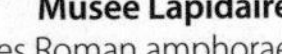

Musée Lapidaire
The collection includes Roman amphorae and terracotta, Romanesque murals and fragments from the cathedral, a set of Gothic windows, and these medieval stone missiles.

Porte Narbonnaise
Flanked by two sandstone towers, built in 1280, the defences included two portcullises, two iron doors, a moat, and a drawbridge.

Old City Entrance
Entering La Cité is still a step back in time, although it is one of France's top tourist destinations, filled with souvenir shops.

Key
— Suggested route

Béziers with its medieval cathedral, seen from Pont Vieux in the southwest

⑯ Minerve

Hérault. 120. rue des Martyrs (04 68 91 81 43). **minerve-tourisme.fr**

In the parched, arid hills of the Minervois, surrounded by vines and not much else, Minerve appears defiant on its rocky outcrop at the confluence of the rivers Cesse and Briant. It is defended by what the Minervois call the "Candela" (Candle), an octagonal tower which is all that remains of the medieval château. In 1210, the small town resisted the vengeful Simon de Montfort, scourge of the Cathars, in a siege lasting seven weeks. This culminated in the execution of 140 Cathars, who were burned at the stake.

Today visitors enter Minerve by a high bridge spanning the gorge. Turn right and follow the route of the Cathars past the Romanesque arch of the Porte des Templiers to the 12th-century **Eglise St-Etienne**. Outside the church is a crudely carved dove, symbol of the Cathars, and within is a 5th-century white marble altar table, one of the oldest artifacts in the region.

A rocky path follows the riverbed below the town, where the water has cut out caves and two bridges – the Grand Pont and the Petit Pont – from the soft limestone.

⑰ Béziers

Hérault. 73,000. 1 av du Président Wilson (04 67 76 20 20). Fri. **beziers-mediteranee.com**

Famous for its bullfights and rugby, and the wine of the surrounding region, Béziers has several other points of interest. The town seems turned in on itself, its roads leading up to the massive 14th-century **Cathédrale St-Nazaire**, with its fine sculpture, stained glass, and frescoes. In 1209, several thousand citizens were massacred in the crusade against the Cathars. The papal legate's troops were ordered not to discriminate between Catholics and Cathars, but to "Kill them all. God will recognize his own!" The **Musée du Biterrois** holds exhibitions on local history, wine, and the Canal du Midi, engineered in the late 17th century by Paul Riquet, Béziers' most famous son *(see p490)*. His statue presides over the Allées Paul Riquet, which is lined by rows of plane trees and large canopied restaurants, a civilized focus to this otherwise businesslike town.

Statue of the engineer Paul Riquet in the allées Paul Riquet, Béziers

Musée du Biterrois
Ramp du 96ème, Caserne St-Jacques. **Tel** 04 67 36 81 60. **Open** 10am–6pm Tue–Sun (Oct–May: to 5pm Tue–Fri). **Closed** Jan 1, Easter, May 1, Dec 25.

Environs

Overlooking the Béziers plain and the mountains to the north is Oppidum d'Ensérune, a superb Roman site. The **Musée de l'Oppidum d'Ensérune** has a good archeological collection, from Celtic, Greek, and Roman vases to jewelry and weapons.

The **Château de Raissac** (between Béziers and Lignan) houses an unusual 19th-century faïence museum in its stables.

Musée de l'Oppidum d'Ensérune
Nissan-lez-Ensérune. **Tel** 04 67 37 01 23. **Open** daily (Sep–Apr: Tue–Sun). **Closed** public hols. limited. **enserune.monuments-nationaux.fr**

Château de Raissac
Rte de Lignan sur Orr. **Tel** 04 67 49 17 60. **Open** by appt. **raissac.com**

The Cathars

The Cathars (from Greek *katharos*, meaning pure) were a 12th–14th-century Christian sect critical of corruption in the established Catholic church. Cathar dissent flourished in independent Languedoc as an expression of separatism, but the rebellion was rapidly exploited for political purposes. Peter II of Aragon was keen to annex Languedoc, and Philippe II of France joined forces with the pope to crush the Cathar heretics in a crusade led by Simon de Montfort in 1209. This heralded the start of over two centuries of ruthless killing and torture.

Cathar Castles

The Cathars took refuge in the defensive castles of the Corbières and Ariège. Peyrepertuse is one of the most remote, difficult to get to even today: a long, narrow stone citadel hacked from a high, craggy peak over 2,000 ft (609 m) high.

Cathars (also known as Albigensians) believed in the duality of good and evil. They considered the material world entirely evil. To be truly pure they had to renounce the world, and be nonviolent, vegetarian, and sexually abstinent.

The crusade against the Cathars was vicious. Heretics' land was promised to the crusaders by the pope, who assured forgiveness in advance of their crimes. In 1209, 20,000 citizens were massacred in Béziers and, the following year, 140 were burned to death in Minerve. In 1244, 225 Cathars died defending one of their last fortresses at Montségur.

Cathar Country

Castles and towns with a Cathar association, some of them spectacular sites, are concentrated in Languedoc-Roussillon, the center of Catharism in the Middle Ages.

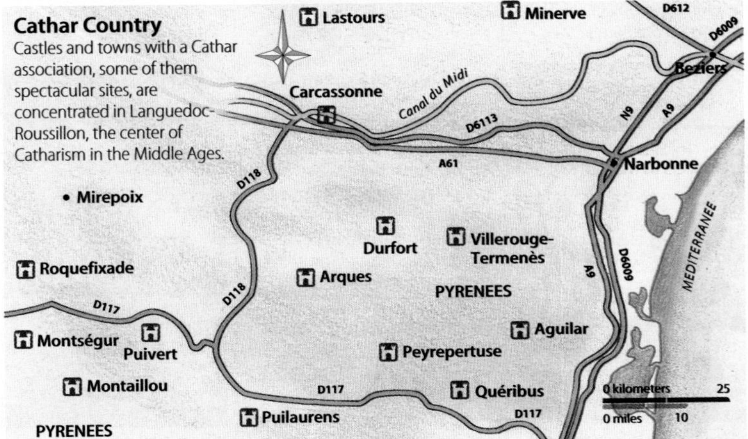

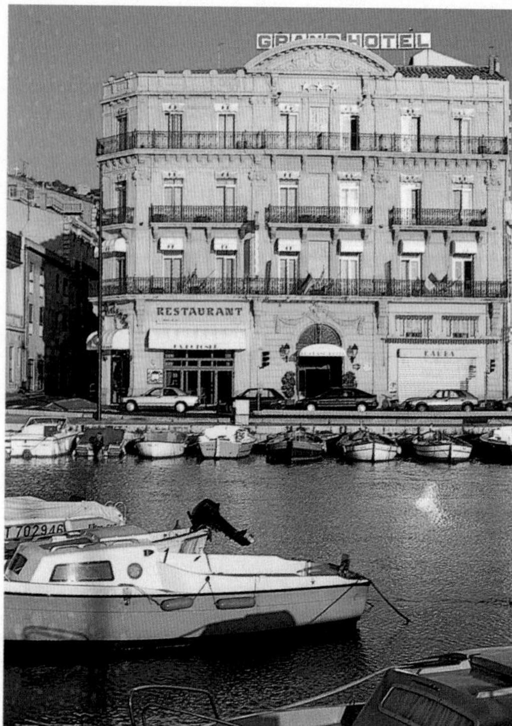

The impressive Grand Hôtel *(see p569)* on quai de la Résistance, Sète

⓲ Sète

Hérault. 43,500. 60 grand' rue Mario Roustan (04 99 04 71 71). Wed–Fri. **tourisme-sete.fr**

Sète is a major fishing and industrial port. It has a gutsier, more raffish air than much of the leisure-oriented Mediterranean, with its shops selling ships' lamps and propellers, and its quayside restaurants full of hungry sailors demolishing vast platters of mussels, oysters, and sea snails straight off the boat. Most of Sète's restaurants can be found in a stroll along the Grand Canal, with its Italianate houses painted in pastel colors and with wrought iron balconies overlooking Sète's network of canals and bridges. Boisterous water jousting tournaments, dating back to 1666, form part of the patron saint's festival in August *(see p42)*.

Cimetière Marin in Sète, burial place of the poet Paul Valéry

The **Musée International des Arts Modestes** displays everyday objects (including some by well-known contemporary designers) in amusing new contexts, within a renovated canalside warehouse.

Above the town is the **Cimetière Marin**, where Sète's most famous son, poet Paul Valéry (1871–1945), is buried. There is a small museum and breathtaking views of the coast and the mountains from the lookout on Mont St-Clair.

Musée International des Arts Modestes
23 quai du Maréchal de Lattre de Tassigny. **Tel** 04 99 04 76 44.
Open Apr–Sep: daily; Oct–Mar: Tue–Sun. **Closed** public hols.
miam.org

⓳ Pézenas

Hérault. 9,000. Pl des Etats de Languedoc (04 67 98 36 40). Sat. **pezenas-tourisme.fr**

Pezenas is a charming little town, easily appreciated in a gentle stroll of its main sights, and abounding in revealing details, fragmentary evidence of its past brilliance as the seat of local government in the 16th–17th centuries. Then the town also played host to many troupes of musicians and actors, including Molière.

Best of all are the glimpses of fine houses through courtyard doorways, such as the **Hôtel des Barons de Lacoste**, at 8 rue François-Oustrin, with its beautiful stone staircase, and the **Maison des Pauvres** at 12 rue Alfred Sabatier, with its three galleries and staircase.

Look out for the medieval shop window on rue Triperie-Vieille, and just within the 14th-century **Porte Faugères**, the narrow streets of the Jewish ghetto, with its chilling feeling of enclosure. Shops selling antiques, secondhand goods, and books abound. All around the town, vines stretch as far as the eye can see.

The stone foyer of the Hôtel des Barons de Lacoste in Pézenas

Parc Naturel égional du Haut anguedoc

rault, Tarn. Béziers. Béziers, darieux. St-Pons-de-Thomières, zamet, Mazamet-Ausillon, Lamalou-Bains St-Pons-de-Thomières 67 97 38 22).
parc-haut-languedoc.fr

e high limestone plateaus d wooded slopes of upper nguedoc are a world away from e coast. From the Montagne ire, a mountainous region tween Béziers and Castres, up to the Cévennes is a landscape remote sheep farms, eroded ck formations, and deep river rges. Much of this area has en designated the Parc Naturel gional du Haut Languedoc, e of the largest of the French tional parks.

You can enter the park at **-Pons-de-Thomières**, with cess to forest and mountain ils for walking and riding, plus wildlife research center, where e can glimpse the mouflons ild mountain sheep), eagles, d wild boar which were once a common sight in the region. You can also enter the park at Revel, Castres, St-Chinian, and Lodéve.

If you take the D908 from St-Pons through the park you pass the village of **Olargues** with its 12th-century bridge over the river Jaur. **Lamalou-les-Bains**, on the park's eastern edge, is a small spa town with a restored Belle Epoque spa building and theater, and a soporifically slow pace.

Outside the park boundaries to the northeast there are spectacular natural phenomena. At the **Cirque de Navacelles**, the river Vis has joined up with itself cutting out an entire island. On it sits the peaceful village of Navacelles, visible from the road higher up. The **Grotte des Demoiselles** is one of the most magnificent in an area full of caves, where you walk through a calcified world. A funicular train takes visitors from the foot of the mountain to the top.

The **Grotte de Clamouse** is also an extraordinary experience, the reflections from underground rivers and pools flickering on the cavern roofs, with stalagmites resembling dripping candles.

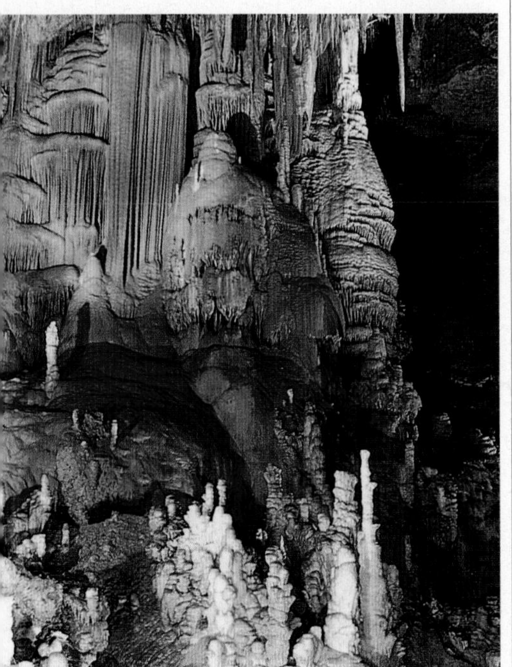

traordinary limestone formations at the Grotte de Clamouse

Grotte des Demoiselles
St-Bauzille-de-Putois. **Tel** 04 67 73 70 02. **Open** daily. **Closed** Jan, Dec 25.
demoiselles.com

Grotte de Clamouse:
Rte de St-Guilhem-le-Désert, St-Jean-de-Fos. **Tel** 04 67 57 71 05. **Open** Feb–mid-Nov: daily. **clamouse.com**

Apse of St-Guilhem-le-Désert

21 St-Guilhem-le-Désert

Hérault. 250.
2 rue Fond de Portal, Maison Communale (04 67 56 41 97).
saintguilhem-valleeherault.fr

Tucked away in the Celette mountains, St-Guilhem-le-Désert is no longer as remote as when Guillaume of Aquitaine retired here as a hermit in the 9th century. After a lifetime as a soldier, Guillaume received a fragment of the True Cross from Emperor Charlemagne and established a monastery in this ravine above the river Hérault.

Vestiges of the first 10th-century church have been discovered but most of the building is a superb example of 11th–12th-century Romanesque architecture. Its lovely apsidal chapels dominate the heights of the village, behind which the carved doorway opens on to a central square.

Within the church is a somber barrel-vaulted central aisle leading to the sunlit central apse. Only two galleries of the cloisters remain: the rest are in New York, along with carvings from St-Michel-de-Cuixà *(see p484–5)*.

Montpellier City Center

1. Château d'Eau
2. Promenade de Peyrou
3. Jardin des Plantes
4. Tours des Pins
5. Cathédrale de St-Pierre
6. Hôtel des Trésoriers de la Bourse
7. Musée Languedocien
8. Hôtel de Manse
9. Hôtel de Mirman
10. Musée Fabre
11. Notre-Dame des Tables
12. CORUM
13. Place de la Comédie
14. Tour de la Babote

0 meters 250
0 yards 100

Key to Symbols *see back flap*

Open-air café in the place de la Comédie, Montpellier

㉒ Montpellier

Hérault. 256,000. 30 allée Jean de Lattré de Tassigny (04 67 60 60 60). daily. Festival International Montpellier Danse (Jun–Jul). **ot-montpellier.fr**

Montpellier is one of the liveliest and most forward-looking cities in the south, with a quarter of its population under 25. Sometimes on a summer evening in university term time it resembles more a rock festival than the capital of Languedoc-Roussillon. Center of the action is the egg-shaped **place de la Comédie**, known as "l'Oeuf" ("the egg"), with its 19th-century opera house fronted by the Fontaine des Trois Graces and surrounded by buzzing cafés. An esplanade of plane trees and fountains leads to the **CORUM**, an opera and conference center typical of the city's brave new architectural projects. The best of these is Ricardo Bofill's Postmodern housing complex known as Antigone, which is modeled on St. Peter's in Rome.

Montpellier was founded relatively late for this region of ancient Roman towns, developing in the 10th century as a result of the spice trade with the Middle East. The city's medical school was founded in 1220, partly as a result of this cross-fertilization of knowledge between the two cultures, and remains one of the most respected in France.

Most of Montpellier was ravaged by the Wars of Religion in the 16th century. Only the **Tour de la Babote** and the **Tours des Pins** remain of the 12th-century fortifications. There are few fine churches, the exceptions being the **Cathédra de St-Pierre** and the 18th-centu **Notre-Dame des Tables**.

Reconstruction in the 17th century saw the building of mansions with elegant courtyards, stone staircases, and balconies. Examples open to th public include **Hôtel de Manse** on rue Embouque-d'Or, **Hôtel Mirman** near place des Martyrs de la Resistance, and **Hôtel des Trésoriers de la Bourse**. The Hôtel des Lunaret houses the **Musée Languedocien** which exhibits Romanesque and prehistoric artifacts.

Another 17th-century buildir houses the renovated **Musée Fabre** with a collection of main French paintings. Highlights

Pont du Gard

← To U

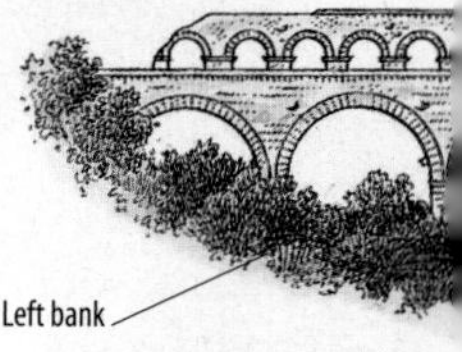

Left bank

The bridge compri three tiers of continuc arch

ude Courbet's famous *Bonjour Courbet*, Berthe Morisot's *L'Eté*, d some evocative paintings of region by Raoul Dufy.

o view the city's position tween mountains and sea go the **Promenade de Peyrou**, a nd 18th-century square minated by the **Château au** and the aqueduct which ed to serve the city. North of re is the **Jardin des Plantes**, nce's oldest botanical gardens 93). Not to be missed is **Mare strum**, the new aquarium in Odysseum leisure zone, which s over 300 marine species.

Musée Languedocien
e Jacques Coeur. **Tel** 04 67 52 93
Open Mon–Sat: pm only.
sed public hols.
musee-languedocien.com

Musée Fabre
bd Bonne Nouvelle. **Tel** 04 67 14 83
Open Tue–Sun.
seefabre.montpellier-agglo.com

teau d'Eau, Montpellier

La Grande-Motte

rault. 8,500. pl du 1er tobre 1974 (04 67 56 42 00). Sun (& Thu: mid-Jun–mid-Sep). **ot-lagrandemotte.fr**

e bizarre white ziggurats of this odern marina exemplify the velopment of the Languedoc-

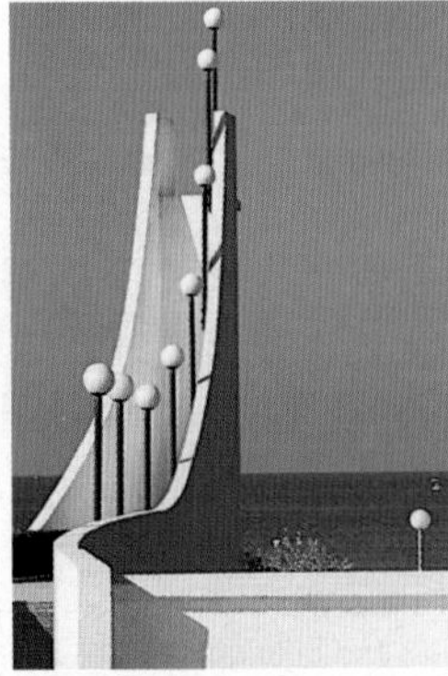

La Grande-Motte

Roussillon coast. One of several on the lagoons south of Montpellier, there are marinas and facilities for every kind of sport from tennis and golf to watersports, all flanked by golden beaches and pine forests. To the east are Le Grau-du-Roi, once a tiny fishing village, and Port-Camargue, with its big marina.

㉔ Aigues-Mortes

Gard. 8,000. pl St Louis (04 66 53 73 00). Wed & Sun.
ot-aiguesmortes.fr

The best approach to this perfectly preserved walled town is across the salt marshes of the Petite Camargue. Now marooned 3 miles (5 km) from the sea, the imposing defenses of this once important port have become a tourist experience, worth visiting more for the effect of the ensemble than the tacky shops within. Aigues-Mortes ("Place of Dead Waters") was established by Louis XI in the 13th century to consolidate his power on the Mediterranean, and built according to a strict grid pattern. By climbing up the **Tour de Constance** you can walk out onto the rectangular walls, which afford a superb view over the Camargue.

Environs

To the northeast is **St-Gilles-du-Gard**, also once an important medieval port. Today it is worth a detour to see the superbly sculpted 12th-century facade of its abbey church. This was originally established by the monks of Cluny abbey as a shrine to St. Gilles, and a resting place on the famous pilgrimage route to Santiago de Compostela *(see pp404–5)*.

㉕ Nîmes

See pp500–1.

㉖ Pont du Gard

400 route du Pont du Gard-La Bégud, Gard. 08 20 90 33 30. from Nîmes. **pontdugard.fr**

No amount of fame can diminish the first sight of the 2,000-year-old Pont du Gard, a UNESCO World Heritage site. The Romans considered it the best testimony to the greatness of their Empire, and at 160 ft (49 m) it was the highest bridge they ever built.

It is made from blocks of stone, hauled into place by slaves using an ingenious system of pulleys. The huge build-up of calcium in the water channels suggests the aqueduct was in continuous use for 400–500 years, carrying water to Nîmes along a 31-mile (50-km) route from the springs at **Uzès**. This charming town has an arcaded marketplace and several fine medieval towers.

Water channel
To Nîmes →
Right bank
Roman inscriptions include a damaged phallus carving as a good luck symbol.
Some stones weighed up to six tons.

㉕ Nîmes

Listed number one on the tourist map of Nîmes is the bus stop designed by Philippe Starck, who is also credited with reworking the city's pedestrian zone. Such innovations are part of the city's design renaissance. Architectural projects range from imaginative housing to a glittering arts complex, under the guidance of a dynamic mayor. An important crossroads in the ancient world, Nîmes is equally well known for its Roman antiquities such as the amphitheater, the best preserved of its kind. The city is also famous for its festivals and bullfights (*feria*). These are good times to see the rest of Nîmes with its museums, archeological collections, and Old Town of narrow streets and intimate squares.

Arches of the Roman amphitheater

Historic Nîmes

Nîmes has had a turbulent history, suffering particularly during the 16th-century Wars of Religion when the Romanesque **Cathédrale Notre-Dame et St-Castor** was badly damaged. During the 17th and 18th centuries the town prospered from textile manufacturing, one of the most enduring products being denim or "de Nîmes." Many of the fine houses of this period have been restored – elegant examples can be seen on rue de l'Aspic, rue des Marchands and rue du Chapitre in the Old Town. Just outside the town center is the futuristic apartment building, **Nemausus I**.

The Roman gate, the **Porte Auguste**, built 20 years before the temple of **Maison Carrée**, was once part of one of the longest city walls in Gaul. Of the original arches still standing, two (large) were for carts and chariots and two (smaller) for pedestrians. The other major Roman remnant is the **Castellum**, where water used to arrive from the Pont du Gard (*see pp498–9*) to be distributed around the city through thick pipes.

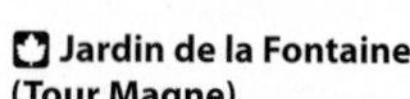

Jug from Musée Archéologique

Jardin de la Fontaine (Tour Magne)

Quai de la Fontaine. **Tel** 04 66 21 82 56. **Open** 7:30am–6:30pm daily (to 10pm summer). reserve at tourist office.

When the Romans arrived in Nîmes, they found a town

Sights at a Glance

① Tour Magne
② Mont Cavalier
③ Jardin de la Fontaine
④ Castellum
⑤ Maison Carrée
⑥ Carré d'Art/Musée d'Art Contemporain
⑦ Porte Auguste
⑧ Cathédrale Notre-Dame et St-Castor
⑨ Musée Archéologique/Musée d'Histoire Naturelle
⑩ Les Arènes
⑪ Musée des Beaux Arts

Jardin de la Fontaine, with a view over the city

ablished by the Gauls, ntered on the source of a ring. They named the town mausus, after their river god. the 18th century, mal gardens were nstructed, and a twork of limpid pools and ol stone terraces remains. gh above the garden on **nt Cavalier** is the octagonal **ur Magne**, once a key part of Roman walls, offering a eat view of the city.

Les Arènes mphithéâtre)
des Arènes. **Tel** 04 66 21 82 56. **en** daily. **Closed** Feria des ndanges performance days. **arenes.nimes.fr**

roads lead to the amphitheater, Arènes. Built at the end of the century AD, the design of the l arena and tiers of stone seats commodated huge crowds of up to 20,000 spectators. Today it is a perfect venue for concerts, sporting events and bullfights.

Arms of the city in a sculpture by Martial Raysse

Maison Carrée
Pl de la Maison Carrée. **Tel** 04 66 21 82 56. **Open** daily. **Closed** Jan 1, May 1, Dec 25.

Square House is a prosaic name for this elegant Roman temple, Built around AD 2, it is one of the best preserved in the world.

Musée des Beaux Arts
Rue Cité Foulc. **Tel** 04 66 28 18 32. **Open** 10am–6pm Tue–Sun. **Closed** Jan 1, May 1, Nov 1, Dec 25.

This fine arts museum houses an eclectic collection of Dutch, French, Italian, and Flemish works, notably Jacopo Bassano's *Susanna and the Elders*, and the *Mystic Marriage of St Catherine* by Michele Giambono. The Gallo-Roman mosaic of *The Marriage of Admetus* is on the main floor.

Musée Archéologique
Musée d'Histoire Naturelle, 13 bis bd Amiral Courbet. **Tel** 04 66 76 74 80. **Open** Tue–Sun. **Closed** Jan 1, May 1, Nov 1, Dec 25.

The museum's collection of Roman statues, ceramics, glass, coins, and mosaics is housed in Nîmes' natural history museum. The exhibits include important Iron Age menhir statues. Nîmes' planetarium is also located here.

VISITORS' CHECKLIST

Practical Information
Gard. 143,000. 6 rue Auguste (04 66 58 38 00). daily. Ferias: de Pentecôte (Pentecost), des Vendanges (Sep). **ot-nimes.fr**.

Transport
7.5 miles (12 km) SSE Nîmes-Arles-Camargues. bd Talabot (SNCF: 36 35). Rue St Félicité (0820 223 030).

The Maison Carrée

Carré d'Art/ Musée d'Art Contemporain
Pl de la Maison Carrée. **Tel** 04 66 76 35 70 (Mon–Fri), 04 66 76 35 35 (Sat–Sun). **Open** 10am–6pm Tue–Sun. **Closed** Jan 1, May 1, Nov 1, Dec 25.

Nîmes' arts complex, by the British architect Sir Norman Foster, opened in 1993. Five floors of this glass and steel temple, which was built in tribute to the Maison Carrée opposite, lie underground. The complex has a library, a roof-terrace restaurant around a huge glass atrium, and the Musée d'Art Contemporain. Works cover the main European art movements from the 1960s on, and include works by French artists Raysse, Boltanski, and Lavier.

Bullfight at Les Arènes in Nîmes

For map symbols *see back flap*

NICE

PROVENCE AND THE COTE D'AZUR

Bouches-du-Rhône · Vaucluse · Var
Alpes-de-Haute-Provence · Alpes-Maritimes

From its herb-scented hills to its yacht-filled harbors, no other region of France fires the imagination as strongly as Provence. The vivid landscape and luminous light have inspired artists and writers from Van Gogh to Picasso, F. Scott Fitzgerald to Pagnol.

The borders of Provence are defined by nature: to the west, the Rhône; south, the Mediterranean; and north, where the olive trees end. To the east are the Alps and a border which has shifted over the centuries between France and Italy. Within is a contrasting terrain of plummeting gorges, Camargue salt flats, lavender fields, and sun-drenched beaches.

Past visitors have left their mark. In Orange and Arles, the buildings of Roman *Provincia* are still in use. Fortified villages like Èze were built to withstand the Saracen pirates who plagued the coast in the 6th century.

In the 19th century, rich Europeans sought winter warmth on the Riviera; by the 1920s, high society was in residence all year, and their elegant villas remain. The warm sunlight nurtures intense flavors and colors. Peppers, garlic, and olives transform a netful of Mediterranean fish into that vibrant epitome of Provençal cuisine, *bouillabaisse*.

The image of Provence bathed in sunshine is marred only when the bitter Mistral wind scours the land. It has shaped a people as hardy as the olive tree, yet quick to embrace life to the full the moment the sun returns.

Cap Martin, seen from the village of Roquebrune

◀ Boats moored in the harbour at Nice

Exploring Provence

This sun-drenched southeastern region is France's most popular holiday destination. Sunworshippers cram the beaches in the summer months, and entertainment includes opera, dance and jazz festivals, bullfights, casinos, and *boules* games. Inland is a paradise for walkers and nature lovers, with remote mountain plateaus, perched villages, and dramatic river gorges.

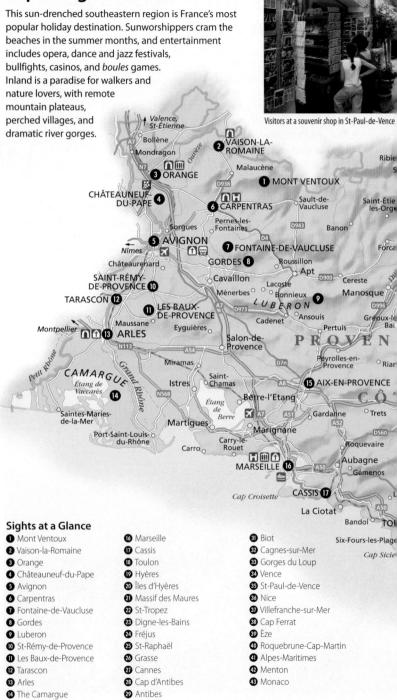

Visitors at a souvenir shop in St-Paul-de-Vence

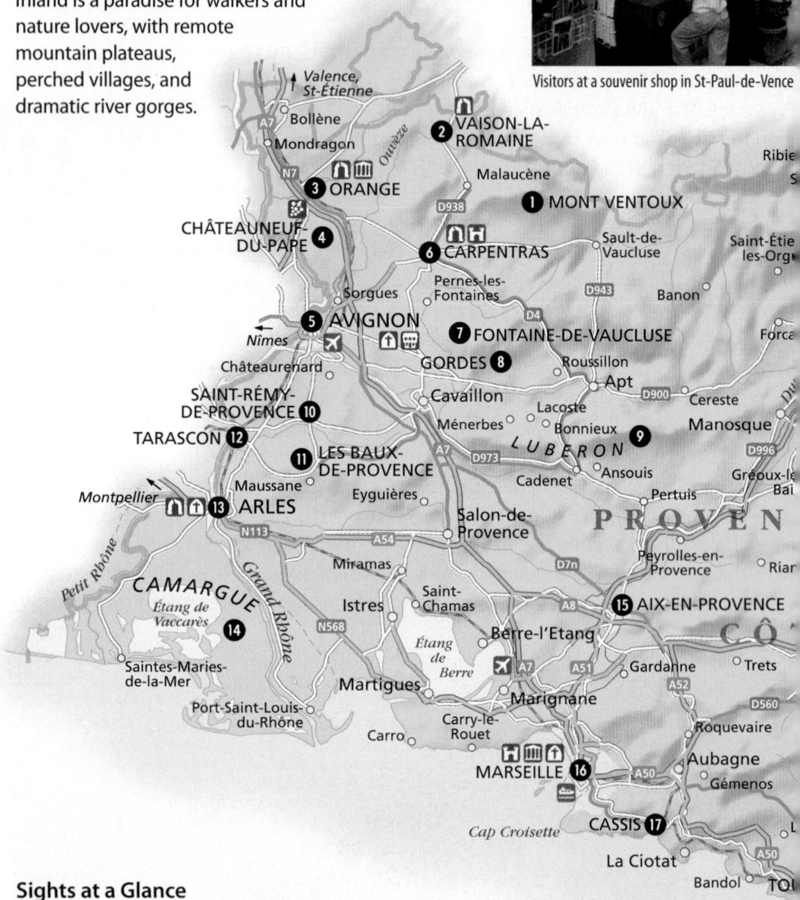

Sights at a Glance

1. Mont Ventoux
2. Vaison-la-Romaine
3. Orange
4. Châteauneuf-du-Pape
5. Avignon
6. Carpentras
7. Fontaine-de-Vaucluse
8. Gordes
9. Luberon
10. St-Rémy-de-Provence
11. Les Baux-de-Provence
12. Tarascon
13. Arles
14. The Camargue
15. Aix-en-Provence
16. Marseille
17. Cassis
18. Toulon
19. Hyères
20. Îles d'Hyères
21. Massif des Maures
22. St-Tropez
23. Digne-les-Bains
24. Fréjus
25. St-Raphaël
26. Grasse
27. Cannes
28. Cap d'Antibes
29. Antibes
30. Vallauris
31. Biot
32. Cagnes-sur-Mer
33. Gorges du Loup
34. Vence
35. St-Paul-de-Vence
36. Nice
37. Villefranche-sur-Mer
38. Cap Ferrat
39. Èze
40. Roquebrune-Cap-Martin
41. Alpes-Maritimes
42. Menton
43. Monaco

For additional map symbols *see back flap*

Getting Around

The largest airport in the region, and second busiest in France, is Nice. Fly-drive packages are popular, although mainly recommended for touring inland. Traffic jams on coastal roads in high season can usually be avoided by using the autoroutes. Main coastal towns have good bus and rail links, and bikes can be rented at most train stations. The Chemin de Fer de Provence railroad runs from Nice to Digne-les-Bains through spectacular mountain scenery. Mountain roads, though tortuous, are good.

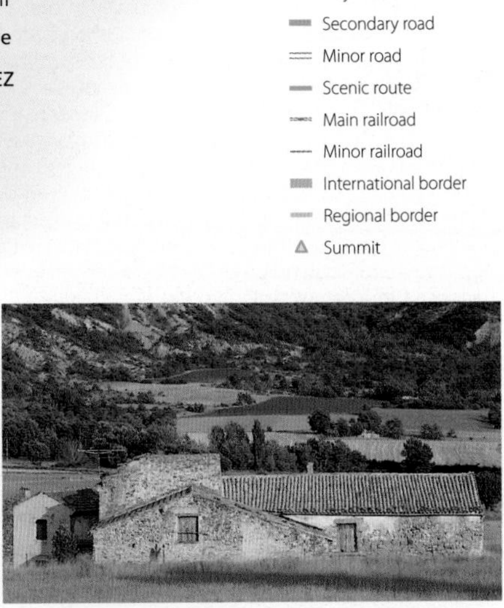

Saint-Paul
D900
Le Lauzet-Ubaye
Colle della Maddalena
Barcelonnette
-du-Caire
Seyne
Pra-Loup
Mont Pelat 3051m
Parc National du Mercantour
Saint-Étienne-de-Tinée
D900
Allos
La Javie
Colmars
Isola 2000
23 DIGNE-LES-BAINS
Valberg
Saint-Sauveur-sur-Tinée
Saint-Martin-Vésubie
Vallée des Merveilles
Tende
Guillaumes
ALPES-MARITIMES
41
Roquebillière
D6204
N85
Saint-André-les-Alpes
Var
Annot
Puget-Théniers
Lantosque
Saorge
Barrême
Entrevaux
Breil-sur-Roya
Sénez
N202
D6202
Sospel
Moustiers-Sainte-Marie
Castellane
Saint-Auban
Plan-du-Var
Escarène
Peille
D952
Mont Cheiron 1777m
Le Logis-du-Pin
D2
ROQUEBRUNE-CAP-MARTIN 40
42 MENTON
Gorges du Verdon
Trigance
GORGES DU LOUP 33
VENCE 34
ÈZE 39
43 MONACO
Lac du Ste-Croix
D6085
NICE 36
37 VILLEFRANCHE-S.-MER
ALPES-
Comps-sur-Artuby
ST-PAUL-DE-VENCE 35
38 CAP FERRAT
GRASSE 26
32
Aups
D955
Fayence
BIOT 31
CAGNES-SUR-MER
VALLAURIS 30
29 ANTIBES
Draguignan
D562
CANNES 27
28 CAP D'ANTIBES
AZUR
La Napoule
Carcès
Lorgues
N7
A8
N98
FRÉJUS 24
Vidauban
25 SAINT-RAPHAËL
Cannet-des-Maures
D25
Saint-Aygulf
MASSIF DES MAURES
Sainte-Maxime
D97
Le Garde-Freinet
21
22 SAINT-TROPEZ
Cogolin
Môle
Ramatuelle
D98
Cavalaire-sur-Mer
HYÈRES
Lavandou
Île du Levant
Porquerolles
Île de Port Cros
20
ÎLES D'HYÈRES

kilometers 25
miles 25

Key

- Highway
- Major road
- Secondary road
- Minor road
- Scenic route
- Main railroad
- Minor railroad
- International border
- Regional border
- △ Summit

Spectacular scenery near the quiet market town of Forcalquier

❶ Mont Ventoux

Vaucluse. Avignon. Avignon. Carpentras. av de la Promenade, Sault-en-Provence (04 90 64 01 21).

The name means "Windy Mountain" in Provençal. A variety of flora and fauna may be found on the lower slopes but only moss survives at the peak, where the temperature can drop to –17° F (–27°C). The bare white scree at the summit makes it look snow-capped even during summer.

Ventoux is the mountain on which the legendary British cyclist Tommy Simpson died during 1967's Tour de France. Today, a road leads to the radio beacon pinnacle, but the trip should not be attempted in bad weather. At other times, spectacular views from the top make the effort worthwhile.

Roman mosaic from the Villa du Paon in Vaison-la-Romaine

❷ Vaison-la-Romaine

Vaucluse. 6,100. pl du Chanoine Sautel (04 90 36 02 11). Tue. **raison-vendoux-tourisme.com**

This site has been settled since the Bronze Age, but its name stems from five centuries as a Roman town. Although the upper town, dominated by the ruins of a 12th-century castle, has some charming narrow streets, stone houses, and fountains, Vaison's main attractions lie on the opposite side of the river.

The **Roman City** is split into two districts: Puymin and La Villasse. At Puymin, an opulent mansion, the Villa du Paon, and a Roman theater have been uncovered.

In 1992, the river Ouvèze burst its banks, taking many lives in Vaison and the nearby area. Damage to some ruins, such as the Roman bridge, has since been repaired. Also at Vaison is the fine Romanesque **Cathédrale Notre-Dame-de-Nazareth**, with medieval cloisters.

Roman City

Fouilles de Puymin & Musée Théo Desplans, pl du Chanoine Sautel. **Tel** 04 90 36 0211. **Open** daily. **Closed** Jan–mid-Feb, Dec 25. restr.

❸ Orange

Vaucluse. 30,000. 5 cours Aristide Briand (04 90 34 70 88). Thu. **otorange.fr**

Orange is a thriving regional center in the Rhône Valley, an important marketplace for produce such as grapes, olives, honey, and truffles. Visitors should explore the area around the 17th-century Hôtel de Ville, where attractive streets open on to quiet, shady squares. Orange also has two of the greatest Roman monuments in Europe: the **Théâtre Antique** and the **Arc de Triomphe**.

Roman Theater (Théâtre Antique)

Rue Madeleine-Roch. **Tel** 04 90 51 17 60. **Open** daily. also valid for Musée d'Orange. restr. **theatreantique.com**

Dating from the 1st-century AD reign of Augustus, the well-preserved theater, a UNESCO World Heritage Site, has perfect acoustics. It is still used for theater performances and concerts. The back wall rises to a height of 120 ft (36 m) and is 338 ft (103 m) wide. In 2006 an immense glass roof, built high above the theater so as not to affect the acoustics, replaced the original roof, which was destroyed in a fire.

Statue of Augustus Caesar in the Roman Theater at Orange

Arc de Triomphe

Av de l'Arc de Triomphe.

The triple-arched monument, built about AD 20, is decorate[d] with battle scenes, trophies, a[nd] inscriptions to the honor of Tiberius and the conquest of Rome after the Battle of Actiu[m].

Musée d'Art et d'Histoire d'Orange

Rue Madeleine-Roch. **Tel** 04 90 51 1[7] 60. **Open** daily.

Relics here reflect the Roman presence in Orange, including 400 marble fragments, some of which date to Emperor Vespasia[n's] reign in the 1st century BC.

❹ Châteauneuf-du-Pape

Vaucluse. 2,100. Sorgues, the taxi. pl du Portail (04 90 83 71 08). Fri. **pays-provence.fr**

Here, in the 14th century, the popes of Avignon chose to buil[d] a new castle *(château neuf)* and plant the vineyards from which one of the finest wines of the

View across the vineyards of Châteauneuf-du-Pape

Côtes du Rhône is produced. Now almost every doorway in this attractive little town seems to open into a *vigneron*'s cellar.

After the Wars of Religion *(see pp58–9)*, all that remained of the papal fortress were a few fragments of walls and tower, but the ruins look spectacular and offer magnificent views across to Avignon and the Vaucluse uplands beyond.

Wine festivals punctuate the year, including the Fête de la Véraison in August *(see p42)*, when the grapes start to ripen, and the Ban des Vendages in September, when the grapes are ready to be harvested.

❺ Avignon

Vaucluse. 90,000. 41 cours Jean Jaurès (04 32 74 32 74). Tue–Sun. Festival d'Avignon (3 wks Jul). May–Sep: Sat.
avignon-tourisme.com

Massive ramparts enclose one of the most fascinating towns in southern France. The **Palais des Papes** *(see pp508–9)* dominates, but there are also other riches. North of the Palais is the 13th-century **Musée du Petit Palais**, once the Archbishop of Avignon's residence. Now a museum, it displays Romanesque and Gothic sculpture and medieval paintings, with works by Botticelli and Carpaccio.

Rue Joseph-Vernet and rue du Roi-René are lined with 17th- and 18th-century houses. There are also fine churches, such as the **Cathédrale de Notre-Dame-des-Doms**, and the 14th-century **Eglise St-Didier**. The **Musée Lapidaire** contains statues, mosaics, and carvings from pre-Roman Provence. The **Musée Calvet** features a superb array of exhibits, such as wrought-iron works and Roman finds. It also gives an overview of French art during the past 500 years, with works by Rodin, Utrillo, and Dufy.

Two major modern and contemporary art collections, the **Musée Angladon** and the **Collection Lambert**, have been added to the city's cultural repertoire. The former has works by Van Gogh, Cézanne, and Modigliani, while the latter features minimalist and conceptual art.

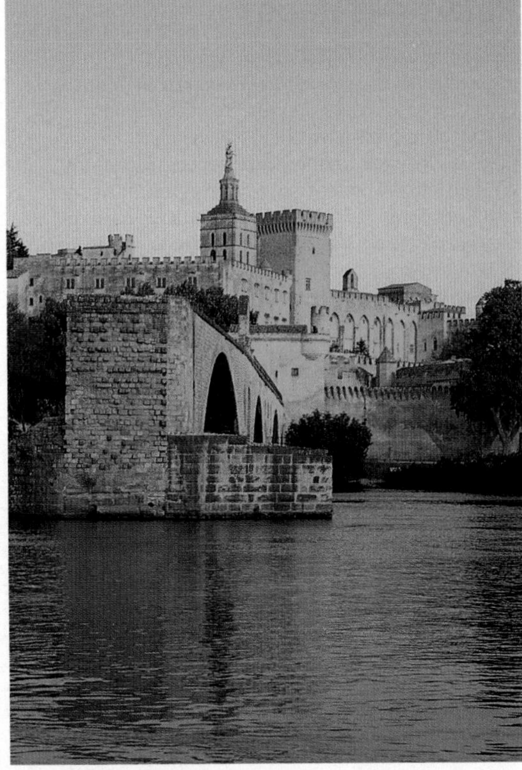

Pont St-Bénézet and the Palais des Papes in Avignon

The place de l'Horloge is the center of Avignon's social life, with sidewalk cafés and a merry-go-round from 1900. One of the prettiest streets is the rue des Teinturiers. Until the 19th century, brightly patterned calico called *indiennes* was printed here – inspiration for today's Provençal patterns. Avignon's renowned 12th-century bridge, the **Pont St-Bénézet**, was largely destroyed by floods in 1668. People danced on an island below the bridge but over the years, as the famous song testifies, *sous* has become *sur*.

Open-air performance at the Avignon Festival

Avignon hosts France's largest festival, which includes ballet, drama, and classical concerts. The "Off" festival features 600 companies from all areas of show business.

Musée du Petit Palais
Pl du Palais. **Tel** 04 90 86 44 58. **Open** Wed–Mon. **Closed** Jan 1, May, Dec 25. **petit-palais.org**

Musée Lapidaire
27 rue de la République. **Tel** 04 90 85 75 38. **Open** Tue–Sun. **Closed** Jan 1, May 1, Dec 25. **musee-lapidaire.org**

Musée Calvet
65 rue Joseph Vernet. **Tel** 04 90 86 33 84. **Open** Wed–Mon. **Closed** Jan 1, May 1, Dec 25. restricted. **musee-calvet-avignon.org**

Palais des Papes

Confronted with factional strife in Rome and encouraged by the scheming of Philippe IV of France, Pope Clement V moved the papal court to Avignon in 1309. Here it remained until 1377, during which time his successors transformed the modest episcopal building into the present magnificent palace. Its heavy fortification was vital to defend against rogue bands of mercenaries. Today it is empty of the luxurious trappings of 14th-century court life, as virtually all the furnishings and works of art were destroyed or looted in the course of the centuries.

★ Consistory Hall
Simone Martini's frescoes (1340) were taken from the cathedral to replace works destroyed by fire in the papal reception hall in 1413.

Military Architecture
The palace and its ten towers were designed as an impregnable fortress. It eventually covered an area of 148,000 sq ft (15,000 sq m).

KEY

① **Champeaux gate**

② **Corner tower**

③ **Belltower**

④ **Trouillas tower**

⑤ **Benedict XII's cloister** incorporates the guest and staff wings, and the Benedictine chapel.

⑥ **La Gache tower**

⑦ **Angels' tower**

⑧ **Pope's chamber**

⑨ **Great courtyard**

⑩ **The Great Chapel** is 66 ft (20 m) high and covers an area of 8,400 sq ft (780 sq m).

⑪ **The Great Audience Hall** is divided into two naves by five columns with bestiary sculpture on their capitals.

The Avignon Popes

Seven "official" popes reigned in Avignon until 1376. They were followed by two "anti-popes," the last of whom, Benedict XIII, fled in 1403. Popes or anti-popes, few were known for their sanctity. Clement V died eating powdered emeralds, prescribed as an indigestion cure; Clement VI (1342–52) thought that the best way to honor God was through luxury. Petrarch was shocked by "the filth of the universe" at court. In 1367, Urban V tried to return the Curia (papal court) to Rome, a move that became permanent in 1377.

Benedict XII (1334–42)

Papal Power
More like a warlord's citadel than a papal palace, the building's heavy fortification reflects the insecure climate of 14th-century religious life.

VISITORS' CHECKLIST

Practical Information
Pl du Palais, Avignon. **Tel** 04 90 27 50 00. **Open** Apr–Aug: 9am–7pm (Jul: to 8pm; Aug: to 8:30pm); Sep–Oct: 9am–7pm; Nov–Mar: 9:30am–6:30pm (Mar: from 9am). Last adm: 1 hr before closing. in 11 languages.
palais-des-papes.com

★ Stag Room
Fourteenth-century hunting frescoes and ceramic tiles adorn Clement VI's study, making it the palace's most lovely room.

Building the Palace

The palace comprises Pope Benedict XII's simple Palais Vieux (1334–42) and Clement VI's flamboyant Palais Neuf (1342–52). Ten towers, some of which are more than 164 ft (50 m) high, are set in the walls to protect its four wings.

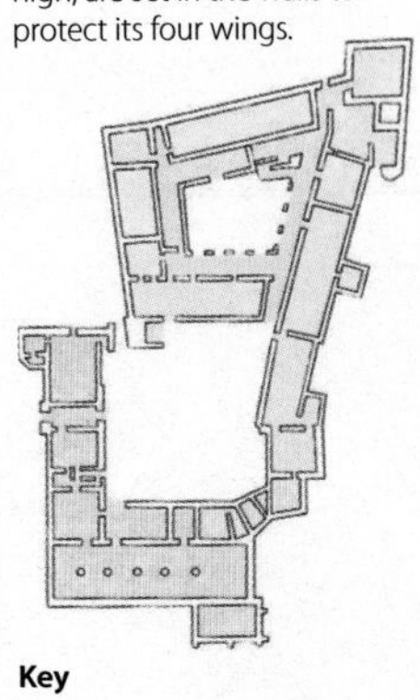

Key

- By Benedict XII (1334–42)
- By Clement VI (1342–52)

❻ Carpentras

Vaucluse. 29,000. Maison de Pays, 97 pl du 25 Août 1944 (04 90 63 00 78). Fri. **carpentras.fr**

In 1320, Carpentras became capital of the papal county of Venaissin, and remained so until 1791. Modern boulevards trace the former ramparts, with only one original gate, the Porte d'Orange, surviving.

In the Middle Ages the town was home to a large Jewish community. The 1367 **Synagogue** is the oldest in France. The Sanctuary has been restored.

While not openly persecuted under papal rule, many Jews changed faith, entering **Cathédrale St-Siffrein** by the Porte Juive (Jews' Door).

The Law Courts were built in 1640 as the episcopal palace. The Criminal Court has 17th-century carved tablets of the local towns. In the pharmacy of the Hôtel-Dieu, the 18th-century cupboards are painted with quaint figures of monkey "doctors." More regional art and history is on show at the **Musée Sobirats**.

Synagogue
Pl de la Mairie. **Tel** 04 90 63 39 97. **Open** Mon–Fri. **Closed** Jewish feast days.

Musée Sobirats
112 rue du Collège. **Tel** 04 90 63 04 92. **Open** Wed–Mon. **Closed** Oct–Mar & public hols.

Riverfront and watermill at Fontaine-de-Vaucluse

❼ Fontaine-de-Vaucluse

Vaucluse. 650. Avignon. chemin du Gouffre, Residence Jean Gardin (04 90 20 32 22). **oti-delasorgue.fr**

The main attraction here is the source of the river Sorgue. It is the most powerful spring in France, gushing at up to 19,800 gallons (90,000 liters) per second from an underground river at the foot of a cliff. It powers the Moulin à Papier Vallis Clausa *(papermill)*, which produces handmade paper using the same methods as in the 15th century, and now sells maps, prints, and lampshades. There are also several museums. One is devoted to the poet Petrarch, who lived and wrote here, and another to the French Resistance of World War II.

Perched village of Gordes

❽ Gordes

Vaucluse. 2,100. pl du Château (04 90 72 02 75). Tue. **gordes-village.com**

Perched villages abound in Provence but Gordes is said to attract the most visitors. Dominated by a 16th-century château, the town forms such a harmonious whole that it might have been designed by an architect. The arcaded medieval lanes add to the attractive hilltop position.

Just south lies the **Village des Bories**, a bizarre, primitive habitat. *Bories* are tiny beehive-shaped huts built of overlapping dry stones. The construction techniques are thought to date back to Neolithic times. This group was inhabited from the 16th to the early 20th century.

The **Abbaye de Sénanque**, to the north, is a fine Romanesque Cistercian monastery.

Château de Gordes
Tel 04 90 72 02 75. **Open** daily in summer. **Closed** Jan 1, Dec 25.

Village des Bories
Rte de Gorde. **Tel** 04 90 72 03 48. **Open** daily. **Closed** Jan 1, Dec 25 & 31.

❾ Luberon

Vaucluse. Avignon. Cavaillon, Avignon. Apt. pl François Tourel, Cavaillon (04 90 71 32 01). **cavaillon-luberon.com**

A huge limestone range, the Montagne du Luberon is one of the most appealing areas of Provence. Rising to 3,690 ft (1,125 m), it combines wild

For hotels and restaurants in this region see pp554–71 and pp576–603

areas with picturesque villages. Almost the entire area is designated a regional nature park. Within it are more than 1,000 plant species and cedar and oak forests. The wildlife is varied, with eagles, vultures, snakes, beavers, wild boar, and the largest European lizards.The park headquarters are in **Apt**, the capital of the Luberon.

Once notorious as the haunt of highwaymen, the Luberon hills now hide sumptuous holiday homes. The major village is **Bonnieux**, with its 12th-century church and 13th-century walls. Also popular are **Roussillon**, with red ocher buildings, **Lacoste**, the site of the ruins of the Marquis de Sade's castle, and **Ansouis**, with its 14th-century Eglise St-Martin and 17th-century castle. **Ménerbes** drew to it the writer Peter Mayle, whose tales of life here brought this quiet region a worldwide audience.

Herb stall at St-Rémy-de-Provence

⑩ St-Rémy-de-Provence

Bouches-du-Rhône. 10,700. Avignon. pl Jean Jaurès (04 90 92 05 22). Wed. **saintremy-de-provence.com**

For centuries St-Rémy, with its boulevards, fountains, and narrow streets, had two claims to fame. One was that Vincent Van Gogh spent a year here, in 1889–90, at the St-Paul-de-Mausole hospital. *Wheat Field with Cypress* and *Ravine* are among the 150 works he produced here. St-Rémy-de-Provence was also, in 1503, the birthplace of Nostradamus, known for his prophecies. But, in 1921, St-Rémy found new fame when archeologists unearthed the Roman ruins at **Glanum**. Little remains of the ancient city, sacked in AD 480 by the Goths, but the site impresses. Around the ruins of a Roman arch is a mausoleum, decorated with scenes such as the death of Adonis.

Glanum
Tel 04 90 92 23 79. **Open** Apr–Aug: daily; Sep–Mar: Tue–Sun. **Closed** Jan 1, May 1, Nov 1 & 11, Dec 25. **glanum.monuments-nationaux.fr**

⑪ Les Baux-de-Provence

Bouches-du-Rhône. 400. Arles. La Maison du Roy (04 90 54 34 39). **lesbauxdeprovence.com**

One of the strangest places in Provence, the deserted citadel of Les Baux stands like a natural extension of a huge rocky plateau. The ruined castle and old houses overlook the Val d'Enfer (Infernal Valley), with its weird rocks.

In the Middle Ages Les Baux was home to powerful feudal lords, who claimed descent from the Magus Balthazar. It was the most famous of the Provençal Cours d'Amour, at which troubadours sang the praises of high-born ladies. The ideal of everlasting but unrequited courtly love contrasts with the warlike nature of the citadel's lords.

The glory of Les Baux ended in 1632. It had become a Protestant stronghold and Louis XIII ordered its destruction. The ruins of **Château de Baux de Provence** are a reminder of a turbulent past and offer spectacular views. The living village below has a pleasant little square, the 12th-century **Eglise St-Vincent** and the **Chapelle des Pénitents Blancs**, decorated by local artist Yves Brayer, whose work can be seen in the **Musée Yves Brayer**.

Deserted medieval citadel of Les Baux-de-Provence

In 1821 bauxite, a deep red mineral, was discovered here and named after the town. Deposits were intensely exploited until they ran out at the end of the 20th century.

To the southwest are the ruins of the **Abbaye de Montmajour** with its 12th-century Romanesque church.

Parading the Tarasque, 1850

⑫ Tarascon

Bouches-du-Rhône. 13,000. Les Panaromiques, av de la République (04 90 91 03 52). Tue & Fri. **tarascon.fr**

According to legend, the town takes its name from the Tarasque, a monster, half-animal and half-fish, which terrorized the countryside. It was tamed by Sainte Marthe, who is buried in the church here. An effigy of the Tarasque is still paraded through the streets each June *(see p41)*.

The striking 15th-century **Château Royal de Provence** on the banks of the Rhône is one of the finest examples of Gothic military architecture in Provence. Its somber exterior gives no hint of the beauties within: the Flemish-Gothic courtyard; the spiral staircase; the painted ceilings of the banqueting hall.

Opposite is Beaucaire, a ruined castle and gardens.

Château Royal de Provence (Tarascon)
Bd du Roi René. **Tel** 04 90 91 01 93. **Open** daily. **Closed** some public hols. **chateau.tarascon.fr**

⓭ Arles

Few other towns in Provence combine all the region's charms so well as Arles. Its position on the Rhône makes it a natural, historic gateway to the Camargue *(see pp514–15)*. Its Roman remains, such as the arena and Constantine's baths, are complemented by the ocher walls and Roman-tiled roofs of later buildings. A bastion of Provençal tradition and culture, its museums are among the best in the region. Van Gogh spent time here in 1888–9, but Arles is no longer the industrial town he painted. Visitors are now its main business, and entertainment ranges from the Arles Festival to bullfights.

Palais Constantine was once a grand imperial palace. Now only its vast Roman baths remain, dating from the 4th century AD. They are remarkably well-preserved and give an idea of the luxury that bathers enjoyed.

Musée Réattu
This museum, in the old Commandery of the Knights of Malta, houses witty Picasso sketches, paintings by the local artist Jacques Réattu (1760–1833), and sculptures by Ossip Zadkine, including *La Grande Odalisque* (1932), above.

Hôtel de ville & entrance to Cryptoportiques

Museon Arlaten
In 1904 the poet Frédéric Mistral used his Nobel Prize money to establish this museum devoted to his beloved native Provence. Parts of the collection are arranged in room settings, and even the museum attendants wear traditional Arles costume.

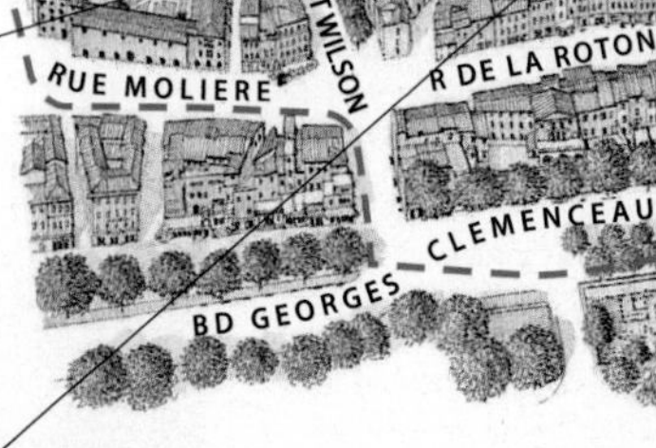

Espace Van Gogh, in a former hospital where the artist was treated in 1889, is a cultural center devoted to his life and work.

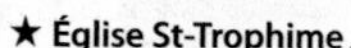

★ Église St-Trophime
This church combines a noble 12th-century Romanesque exterior with superb Romanesque and Gothic cloisters. The ornate main portal is carved with saints and apostles.

Tourist information

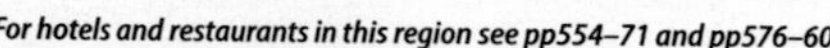

Les Alyscamps by Paul Gauguin

Les Alyscamps

A tree-lined avenue of broken medieval tombs is the focal point of these "Elysian Fields" to the southeast of Arles. It became Christian in the 4th century and was a prestigious burial ground until the 12th century. Some sarcophagi were sold to museums; others have been neglected. Mentioned in Dante's *Inferno*, painted by Van Gogh and Gauguin, it is a place for thought and inspiration.

VISITORS' CHECKLIST

Practical Information
Bouches-du-Rhône. 53,000. **arlestourisme.com** bd des Lices, train station (04 90 18 41 20). Wed, Sat. Arles Festival (Jul); Prémice du Riz (Sep). Musée Réattu: **Open** Tue–Sun. **Closed** Jan 1, May 1, Nov 1, Dec 25. Museon Arlaten: **Closed** for renovation until 2016. **museonarlaten.fr**

Transport
15 miles (25 km) NW Arles. av Paulin Talabot.

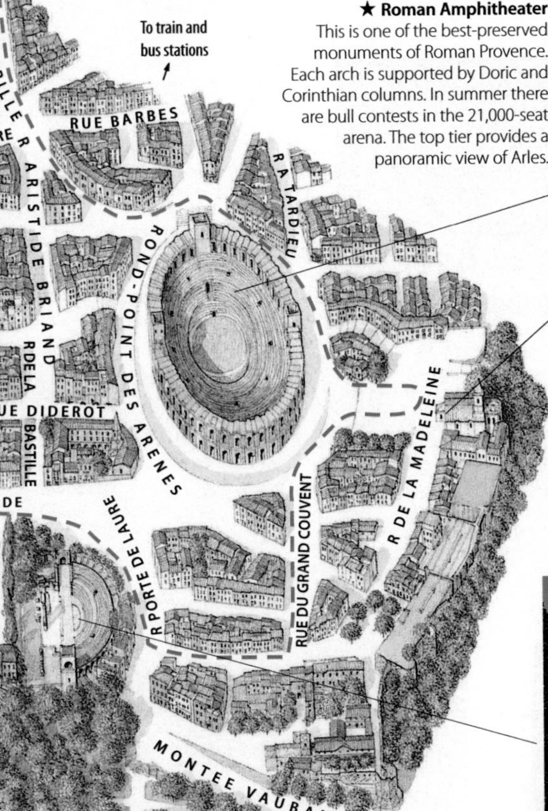

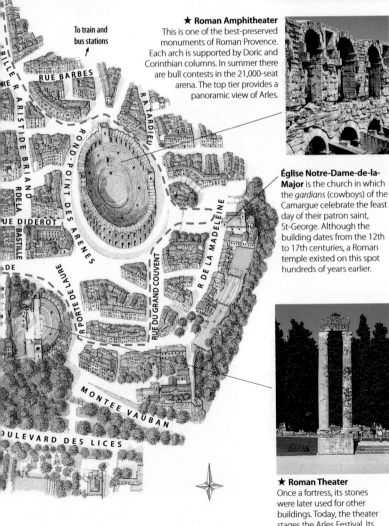

★ Roman Amphitheater
This is one of the best-preserved monuments of Roman Provence. Each arch is supported by Doric and Corinthian columns. In summer there are bull contests in the 21,000-seat arena. The top tier provides a panoramic view of Arles.

Église Notre-Dame-de-la-Major is the church in which the *gardians* (cowboys) of the Camargue celebrate the feast day of their patron saint, St-George. Although the building dates from the 12th to 17th centuries, a Roman temple existed on this spot hundreds of years earlier.

★ Roman Theater
Once a fortress, its stones were later used for other buildings. Today, the theater stages the Arles Festival. Its remaining columns are called the "two widows."

Key

— Suggested route

0 meters 100
0 yards 100

⓮ The Camargue

The Rhône delta was responsible for the formation of more than 424 sq miles (1,120 sq km) of wetlands, pastures, dunes, and salt flats that make up the Camargue, but human efforts are needed to preserve it. The region now maintains a fragile ecological balance, in which a unique collection of flora flourishes, including tamarisk and narcissi, and fauna such as egrets and ibex. The pastures provide grazing for sheep, cattle, and small white Arab-type horses, ridden by the *gardians* or cowboys, a hardy community who traditionally lived in thatched huts *(cabanes)* and still play their part in keeping Camargue traditions alive.

Sunset over the Camargue

Black Bulls
In a Provençal bull contest (known as a *course*), the animals are not killed. Instead, red rosettes are plucked from between their horns with a small hook.

Les Stes-Maries-de-la-Mer
The May gypsy pilgrimage to this fortified church marks the legendary arrival by boat in AD 18 of Mary Magdalene, St. Martha and the sister of the Virgin Mary. Statues in the church depict the event.

Flamingos
These striking birds are always associated with the Camargue, but the region supports many other breeds, including herons, kingfishers, owls, and birds of prey. The area around Ginès is the best place to see them.

For hotels and restaurants in this region see pp554–71 and pp576–603

ey

Nature reserve boundary

Walking routes

Walking and cycling routes

euve

D36

a Capelière

PLAINE DE LA CAMARGUE

Le Grande Rhône

P

D36C

Salin de Giraud

VISITORS' CHECKLIST

Practical Information
Bouches-du-Rhône. Pont de Gau, Saintes-Maries-de-la-Mer. **Tel** 04 90 97 86 32. Les Pèlerinages (end May, end Oct), Festival du Cheval (Jul 14).
Musée Baroncelli: rue Victor Hugo, Saintes-Maries-de-la-Mer. **Tel** 04 90 97 87 60. **Open** phone for information.
saintesmaries.com

Transport
Montpellier-Méditerranée, 56 miles (90 km) east.
av Paulin Talabot, Arles.

White Horses
These small, sturdy horses, which are never stabled, were once used to thresh grain. The foal's dark coat turns white after about 5 years.

Gardians' Cabin
Traditionally, *gardians* lived in thatched cabins. Today, members of the *gardian* brotherhood show off their horsemanship in the Arles arena each April.

Mountains of Salt
Sea salt is by far the largest "harvest" of the Camargue. Throughout the summer, vast brine pans evaporate and the crystals are heaped into shimmering *camelles* up to 26 ft (8 m) high.

⓯ Aix-en-Provence

Bouches du Rhône. 145,000. 2 place du Général-de-Gaulle (04 42 16 11 61). daily.
aixenprovencetourism.com

Founded by the Romans in 103 BC, Aix was frequently attacked, first by the Visigoths in AD 477, later by Lombards, Franks, and Saracens. Despite this, the city prospered. By the end of the 12th century it was capital of Provence. A center of art and learning, it reached its peak in the 15th century during the reign of "Good King" René. He is shown in Nicolas Froment's *Triptych of the Burning Bush* in the 13th-century Gothic **Cathédrale de St-Sauveur**, also noted for its 16th-century walnut doors, Merovingian baptistry, and Romanesque cloisters.

Aix is still a center of art and learning, and its many museums include the **Musée Granet** of fine arts and archeology, and the **Musée des Tapisseries** (tapestries), in the Palais de l'Archevêché.

Aix has been called "the city of a thousand fountains." Three of the best are on cours Mirabeau. On one side are 17th- and 18th-century buildings with wrought-iron balconies; on the other are cafés. The Old Town centers on place de l'Hôtel de Ville, with its colorful flower market. In the northwest of town is the **Pavillon de Vendôme**, housing furniture and works of art by Van Loo.

Aix's most famous son is Paul Cézanne. The **Atelier Cézanne** is kept as it was when he died in 1906. Montagne Ste-Victoire, inspiration for many of his paintings, is 9 miles (15 km) east of Aix.

Musée Granet
pl St-Jean de Malte. **Tel** 04 42 52 88 32. **Open** Tue–Sun (Jun–Oct: daily). **Closed** Jan 1, May 1, Dec 25.
museegranet-aixenprovence.fr

Musée des Tapisseries
28 pl des Martyrs de la Résistance. **Tel** 04 42 23 09 91. **Open** Wed–Mon. **Closed** May 1, Dec 24, 25 & 31, Jan 1.

Atelier Cézanne
9 av Paul Cézanne. **Tel** 04 42 21 06 53. **Open** daily. **Closed** Dec–Feb: Sun; Jan 1–3, May 1.
atelier-cezanne.com

For additional map symbols *see back flap*

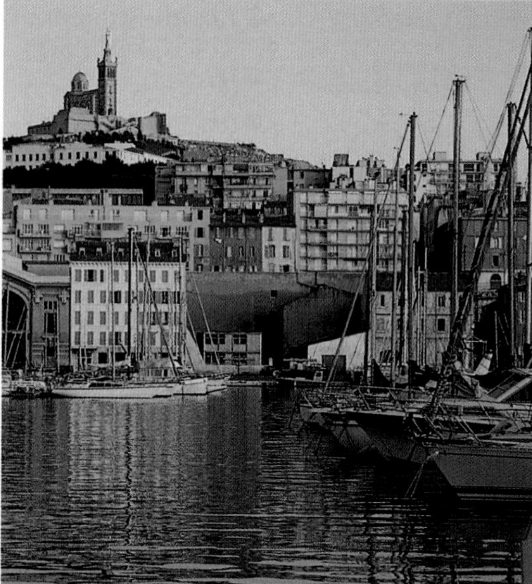

Old harbor of Marseille, looking towards the quai de Rive Neuve

⑯ Marseille

Bouches-du-Rhône. 900,000. 11 La Canebière (0826 500 500). Mon–Sat. **marseille-tourisme.com**

A Greek settlement, founded in the 7th century BC, then called Massilia, Marseille was seized by the Romans in 49 BC. It became the "Gateway to the West" for most Oriental trade. France's largest port and lively second-largest city has close links with the Middle East and North Africa.

Narrow stepped streets, quiet squares, and fine 18th-century facades contrast with the bustle of boulevard Canebière and the Cité Radieuse, Le Corbusier's postwar radical housing complex.

The old harbor now only handles small boats, but its daily fish market is renowned.

Marseille has many excellent museums. Those in the old harbor area include the **Musée des Docks Romains**, the **Musée d'Histoire de Marseille**, and the upbeat **Musée de la Mode**.

The **Musée Cantini**, to the south, houses the 20th-century art collection of sculptor Jules Cantini. It includes Surrealist, Cubist, and Fauve paintings. On the other side of the city is the **Musée Grobet-Labadié**, with its fine furniture, tapestries, and rare musical instruments. Marseille has an extensive streetcar system and has introduced a bike rental scheme that allows people to rent a bike in one part of town and deposit it in another.

Musée des Beaux-Arts

Palais Longchamp, pl Aile Gauche. **Tel** 04 91 14 59 30. **Open** Tue–Sun. **Closed** Jan 1, May 1, Nov 1, Dec 25.

This museum is housed in the handsome 19th-century Palais Longchamp. Works include Michel Serre's graphic views of Marseille's plague of 1721, Pierre Puget's town plans for the city, and murals depicting it in Greek and Roman times.

Château d'If

Tel 04 91 59 02 30. **Open** Apr–Aug: daily; Sep–Mar: Tue–Sun.

The Château d'If (Castle of Yew) stands on a tiny island 1 mile (2 km) southwest of the port. A formidable fortress, it was built in 1529 to house artillery, but never put to military use and later became a prison. Alexandre Dumas' fictional "Count of Monte Cristo" was supposed to have been imprisoned here, and visitors can see a special cell, complete with escape hole. Most real-life inmates were either common criminals or political prisoners.

Basilique de Notre-Dame-de-la-Garde

Built between 1853 and 1864, the Neo-Byzantine basilica dominates the city. Its belfry, 151 ft (46 m) high, is capped by a huge gilded statue of the Virgin. The lavishly decorated interior has colored marble and mosaic facings.

Abbaye de St-Victor

Similar to a fortress in appearance, the abbey was rebuilt in the 11th century after destruction by the Saracens. In the French Revolution, the rebels used it as a barracks and prison.

There is an intriguing crypt in the abbey's church, with an original catacomb chapel and a number of pagan and Christian sarcophagi.

On February 2 each year, St-Victor becomes a place of pilgrimage. Boatshaped cakes are sold to commemorate the legendary arrival of St Mary Magdalene, Lazarus, and St. Martha nearly 2,000 years ago.

Cathédrale de la Major

Built in Neo-Byzantine style, this is the largest 19th-century church in France, 463 ft (141 m) long and 230 ft (70 m) high. In the crypt are the tombs of the

Le Corbusier's innovative Cité Radieuse in Marseille

Fish market at Marseille

bishops of Marseille. By it is the small and beautiful Ancienne Cathédrale de la Major.

La Vieille Charité

2 rue de la Charité. **Tel** 04 91 14 58 11. **Open** Tue–Sun. **Closed** public hols. **vieille-charite-marseille.org**

In 1640, construction of a shelter "for the poor and beggars" of Marseille was begun by royal decree. 100 years later, Pierre Puget's hospital and domed church opened. The restored building houses a fine collection of artifacts in the Musée d'Archéologie Egyptienne; the Musée des Arts Africains is on the second floor.

⑰ Cassis

Bouches-du-Rhône. 8,000. quai des Moulins, Le Port (08 92 25 98 32). Wed & Fri. **ot-cassis.com**

Many villages along this coast have been built up and have all but lost their original charm, but Cassis is still much the same little fishing port that attracted artists such as Dufy, Signac, and Derain. This is a place in which to relax at a waterside café, watching the fishermen or street performers, while enjoying the seafood and a bottle of the local dry white wine for which Cassis is noted.

From Marseille to Cassis the coastline forms narrow inlets, the **Calanques**, their jagged white cliffs (some as much as 1,312 ft/400 m high) reflected in dazzling turquoise water. Wildlife abounds here, with countless seabirds, foxes, stone martens, bats, large snakes, and lizards. The flora is no less impressive, with more than 900 plant species, of which 50 are classified as rare. The En-Vau and Sormiou Calanques are especially lovely.

⑱ Toulon

Var. 170,000. 12 pl Louis-Blanc (04 94 18 53 00). Tue–Sun. **toulontourisme.com**

In 1793 this naval base was captured by an Anglo-Spanish fleet, but was retaken by the young Napoleon Bonaparte. The **Musée National de la Marine** is a focus for history. The **Musée d'Art de Toulon**, housed in an Italian Renaissance building, has a collection representing Fauvism, Minimalism, and Realism. The tower of the former town hall is all that remains of prewar Quai Cronstadt (rebuilt and renamed Quai Stalingrad). The war-damaged Old Town has a few original buildings, and the fish market is worth a visit.

Musée National de la Marine

Pl Monsenergue. **Tel** 04 22 42 02 01. **Open** daily. **Closed** Tue (Sep–Jun), May 1, Dec 25. restr. **musee-marine.fr**

Musée d'Art de Toulon

113 bd Mar Leclerc. **Tel** 04 94 36 81 00. **Open** Tue–Sun pms only. **Closed** public hols.

Paul Signac's *Cap Canaille*, painted at Cassis in 1889

Tour of the Gorges du Verdon

The Verdon Gorges constitute one of the most dramatic natural sights in Europe. The dark green river Verdon flows through a deeply cut valley with twisted rocks and cone-shaped peaks. In places, the Gorges reach depths of 2,300 ft (700 m), passing through largely uninhabited country between the vast natural amphitheater of Moustiers-Ste-Marie and the narrow streets of Castellane. Dramatic viewpoints include the Balcons de la Mescla, beyond the Pont de l'Artuby, and the Point Sublime. A detour southwest of Moutiers to Quinson's Musée de Préhistoire is worthwhile.

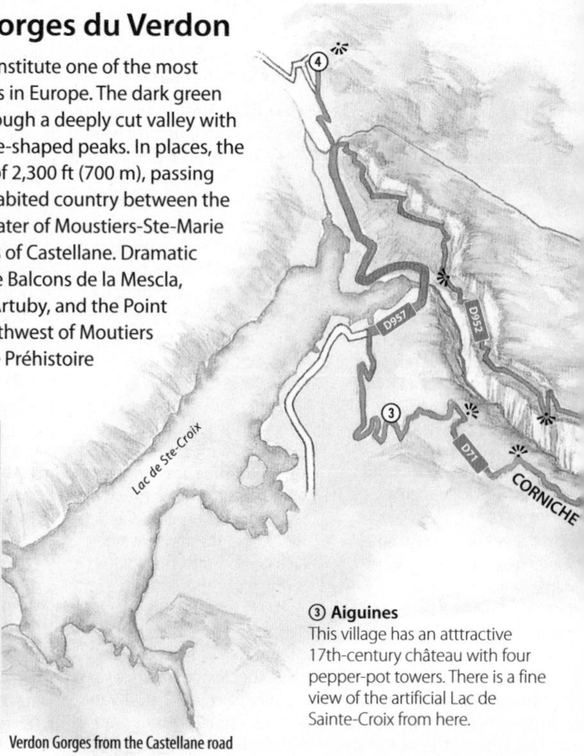

Verdon Gorges from the Castellane road

③ Aiguines
This village has an atttractive 17th-century château with four pepper-pot towers. There is a fine view of the artificial Lac de Sainte-Croix from here.

⓳ Hyères

Var. 50,000.
Rotunda du Park Hotel, av de Belgique (04 94 01 84 50). Tue–Sun. **hyeres-tourisme.com**

Towards the end of the 18th century, Hyères became one of the first health resorts of the Côte d'Azur. Among its subsequent visitors were Queen Victoria and writers Robert Louis Stevenson and Edith Wharton.

The main sights are found in the medieval streets of the Vieille Ville, which lead past the spacious, flagstoned place Massillon to a ruined castle and views over the coast.

Modern Hyères is imbued with a lingering Belle Epoque charm which has become popular with experimental film-makers. It continues to attract a health-conscious crowd and is a major center for aquatic sports.

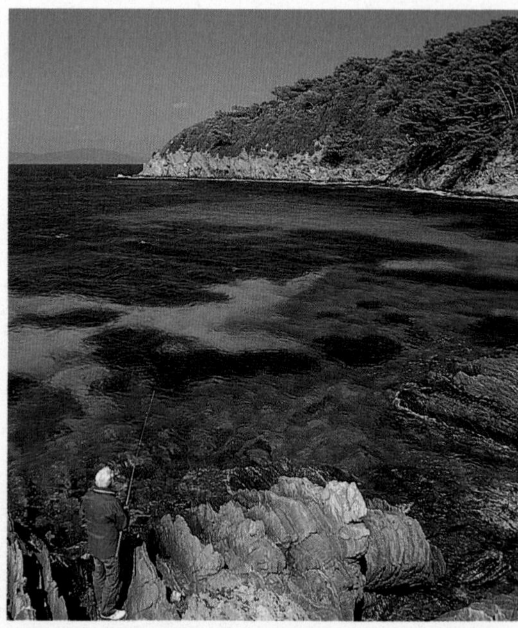

Fishing off Porquerolles, the largest of the Iles d'Hyères

For hotels and restaurants in this region see pp554–71 and pp576–603

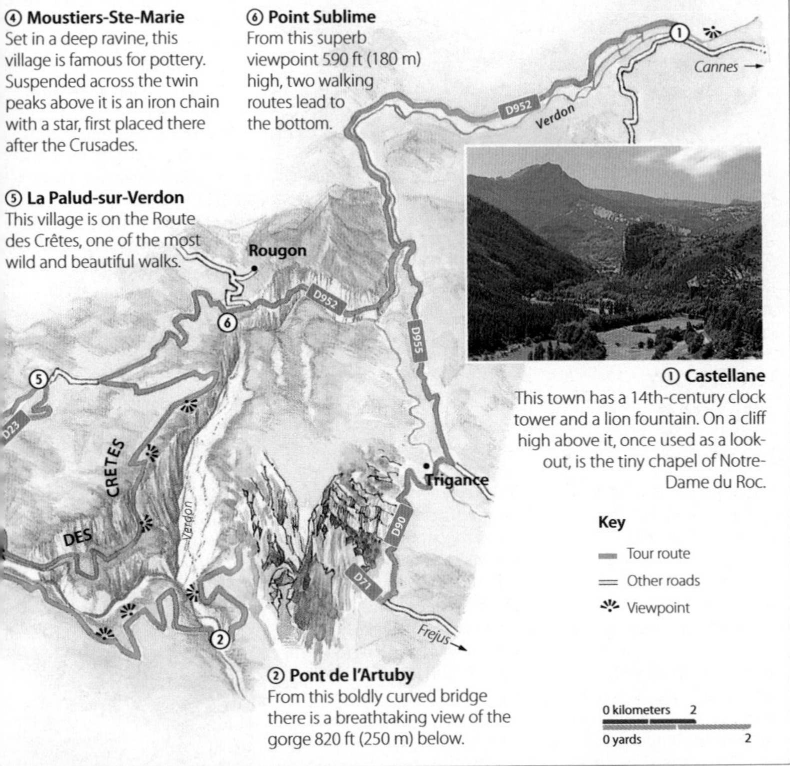

④ Moustiers-Ste-Marie
Set in a deep ravine, this village is famous for pottery. Suspended across the twin peaks above it is an iron chain with a star, first placed there after the Crusades.
⑥ Point Sublime
From this superb viewpoint 590 ft (180 m) high, two walking routes lead to the bottom.
⑤ La Palud-sur-Verdon
This village is on the Route des Crêtes, one of the most wild and beautiful walks.
Cannes
D952
Verdon
Rougon
D952
D955
D23
CRETES
DES
Verdon
Trigance
D90
D71
Frejus
① Castellane
This town has a 14th-century clock tower and a lion fountain. On a cliff high above it, once used as a look-out, is the tiny chapel of Notre-Dame du Roc.
Key
Tour route
Other roads
Viewpoint
② Pont de l'Artuby
From this boldly curved bridge there is a breathtaking view of the gorge 820 ft (250 m) below.
0 kilometers 2
0 yards 2

⑳ Iles d'Hyères

Var. Toulon-Hyères. Hyères. Hyères (Porquerolles office: 04 94 68 33 76). **hyeres-tourisme.com**; **porquerolles.com**

Locally known as the Iles d'Or, after the gold color of their cliffs, this glamorous trio of islands can be reached by boat from Hyères, Le Lavandou, and, in summer, Cavalaire and Port-de-Miramar.

Porquerolles, the largest of the three, measures 4.5 miles (7 km) by 2 miles (3 km). It is covered in rich vegetation, much of which, for instance the Mexican bellombra tree, was introduced from a variety of exotic foreign climes.

The island's main town, also known as Porquerolles, looks more like a north African colonial settlement than a Provençal village. It was established in 1820 as a retirement town for Napoleon's most honored troops. All the island's beaches lie along the northern coastline. The best, the long, sandy Plage Notre-Dame, one of the finest beaches in Provence, sits in a sheltered bay about an hour's walk from Porquerolles.

A stroll around lush, hilly **Port-Cros**, covering just 1 sq mile (2.5 sq km), takes the best part of a day. It rises to 640 ft (195 m), the highest point on any of the islands.

Port-Cros has been a national park since 1963. A unique reserve of flora and fauna, its waters are also protected. There is even a 985-ft (300-m) scenic swimming route. You can buy a waterproof guide to the underwater wildlife.

The wild, virtually treeless **Ile du Levant** is reached by boat from Port-Cros. Its main draw is the oldest nudist resort in France, Héliopolis, founded in 1931. The eastern half of the island, controlled by the French navy, is permanently closed to the public.

㉑ Massif des Maures

Var. Toulon-Hyères. Hyères, Toulon or Fréjus. Bormes-les-Mimosas. Toulon. 1 pl Gambetta, Bormes-les-Mimosas (04 94 01 38 38). **bormeslesmimosas.com**

The dense wilderness of pine, oak, and chestnut, covering the Maures mountains probably gave rise to its name, meaning dark or gloomy. It extends nearly 40 miles (65 km) between Hyères and Fréjus. The D558 north of Cogolin leads to the heart of the Maures. Along the way is La Garde-Freinet, well known for its bottle-cork industry.

Northwest of Cannet-des-Maures lies the Abbaye de Thoronet. With the abbeys at Sénanque, in Vaucluse, and Silvacane, in the Bouches-du-Rhône, it is known as one of the "Three Sisters" of Provence.

Harborside at St-Tropez

22 St-Tropez

Var. 6,000. quai Jean Jaurès (08 92 68 48 28). Tue & Sat.
ot-saint-tropez.com

The geography of St-Tropez kept it untouched by the earliest development of the Côte d'Azur. Tucked away at the tip of a peninsula, it is the only north-facing town on the coast and so did not appeal to those seeking a warm and sheltered winter resort. In 1892 the painter Paul Signac was among the first outsiders to respond to its unspoiled charm, encouraging friends, such as the painters Matisse and Bonnard, to join him. In the 1920s the Parisian writer Colette also made her home here. St-Tropez also began to attract star-spotters, hoping for a glimpse of celebrities such as the Prince of Wales.

During World War II the beaches around St-Tropez were the scene of Allied landings, and part of the town was heavily bombed. Then, in the 1950s, young Parisians began to arrive, and the Bardot-Vadim film helped to create the reputation of modern St-Tropez as a playground for gilded youth. The wild public behavior and turbulent love affairs of Roger Vadim, Brigitte Bardot, Sacha Distel, and others left fiction far behind. Mass tourism followed, with visitors once again more interested in spotting a celebrity than in visiting the **Musée de l'Annonciade** with its outstanding collection of works by Signac, Derain, Rouault, Bonnard, and others. Bardot had a villa at La Madrague, but tourists invaded her privacy, so she left.

Today, there are far more luxury yachts than fishing boats moored in St-Tropez harbor. Its cafés make ideal bases for people- and yacht-watching. Another center of the action is place des Lices, both for the Harley-Davidson set and the morning market. The tiny **Maison des Papillons** (Butterfly House), with its collection of more than 20,000 species, is an increasingly popular attraction.

The best beaches are found outside the town, including the golden curve of Pampelonne, with its beach clubs and restaurants. This is the beach on which to see and be seen. St-Tropez has no train station, so driving and parking can be a nightmare in summer.

It is said that St-Tropez takes its name from a Roman soldier martyred as a Christian by the Emperor Nero. Each year in May a *bravade* in his honor takes place when an effigy of the saint is carried through the town to the accompaniment of musket fire.

Nearby are two small towns of differing character but equal charm. **Port-Grimaud** was only built in 1966 but the sensitive use of traditional architecture makes it seem older. Most of its "streets" are canals. Up in the hills, the winding streets of **Ramatuelle** have been restored to perfection by the largely celebrity population.

Maison des Papillons
9 rue Etienne Berny. **Tel** 04 94 97 63 45. **Open** Apr–Oct, public & school hols: Mon–Sat.

Musée de l'Annonciade
Pl Grammont. **Tel** 04 94 17 84 10. **Open** Wed–Mon. **Closed** Jan 1, Ascension, May 1 & 17, Nov 1, Dec 25.

Stylish solution to the traffic problems in St-Tropez

Brigitte Bardot

Brigitte Bardot in 1956

In 1956, Brigitte Bardot's film, *And God Created Woman*, was shot in St-Tropez by her new husband, Roger Vadim. By settling in St-Tropez, "BB" the sex-goddess changed the fortunes of the sleepy little fishing village and ultimately the Côte d'Azur, making it the center of her hedonistic lifestyle. In 1974, on her 40th birthday, she celebrated her retirement from films at Club 55 on Pampelonne Beach, and now devotes her time to her animal sanctuary.

Digne-les-Bains

ɪpes-de-Haute-Provence. 18,000. pl de Tampinet (04 92 36 2 62). Wed, Sat. ot-dignelesbains.fr

ɦis charming spa town in the ɔothills of the Alps features in ictor Hugo's *Les Misérables*. A ·ip on the *Train des Pignes* from ice offers superb views. Apart om the spa, Digne also offers a ɪvender festival *(see p42)* and e **Jardin des Papillons**, France's nly butterfly garden.

Le Jardin des Papillons
: Benoît. **Tel** 04 92 31 83 34. **Open** ɔr–Sep (appt only). in ɪmmer. **proserpine.org**

Fréjus

ər. 50,000. 249 rue ɛan Jaurès (04 94 51 83 83). Wed, ·i–Sun. **frejus.fr**

he modern town of Fréjus is warfed in importance by wo impressive historic sites. he remains of the Roman port f **Amphithéâtre** (founded by ulius Caesar in 49 BC) may not e as complete as those at)range or Arles but they are f exceptional variety. A great mphitheater, fragments of an queduct, a theater, and part of rampart gateway remain. he sea has receded over the enturies and there are few races of the original harbor.

The cathedral on place Formigé narks the entrance to the **Cité piscopale**. The fortified enclave ncludes the 5th-century baptistry, ne of the oldest in France, and ne cathedral cloister, its coffered nedieval roof decorated with cenes from the Apocalypse.

In 1959 Fréjus was hit by a vall of water as the Malpasset arrage burst. To the north the uined dam can still be seen.

Amphithéâtre
ue Henri Vadon. **Tel** 04 94 51 34 31. **pen** Tue–Sun. **Closed** Jan 1, May 1,)ec 25.

Cité Episcopale
8–58 rue de Fleury. **Tel** 04 94 51 26 0. **Open** Jun–Sep: daily. **Closed** Jan 1, ·lay 1, Nov 1 & 11, Dec 25. cloisters.

The Creation of a Perfume

The best perfumes begin as a formula of essential oils extracted from natural sources. The blend of aromas is created by a perfumer called a "nose" because of his or her exceptional sense of smell. A perfume may use as many as 300 essences, all painstakingly extracted from plants by various methods: steam distillation, extraction by volatile solvents, and *enfluerage a froid* (for costly or potent essences). With this process, pungent blossoms are placed onto layers of fats for several days until the fats are saturated. The oils are then "washed" out with alcohol, and when this evaporates, it leaves the "pure" perfume essence behind.

Lavender water

Grasse flowers

㉕ St-Raphaël

Var. 38,000. 99 quai Albert 1er (04 94 19 52 52). **saint-raphael.com**

Delightfully situated, St-Raphaël is a charming, old-style Côte d'Azur resort with Art Nouveau architecture and a palm-fronded promenade. Aside from its beaches, it offers a marina, a casino, Roman ruins, a 12th-century church, and a museum with treasures from a Roman wreck found by Jacques Cousteau.

It was here that Napoleon Bonaparte landed in 1799 on his return from Egypt.

㉖ Grasse

Alpes-Maritimes. 50,000. pl du Cours Honoré Cresp (04 93 36 66 66) or Grasse Welcome Center, pl de la Foux (04 93 36 21 68). **grasse.fr**

Cradled by hills, with views out to sea, Grasse is surrounded by fields of lavender, mimosa, jasmine, and roses. Grasse has been the center of the world's perfume industry since the 16th century, when Catherine de' Médici set the fashion for scented leather gloves. At that time, Grasse was also known as the center for leather tanning. The tanneries have gone, but the perfume houses founded in the 18th and 19th centuries are still in business, although today Grasse perfumes are made from imported flowers or chemicals. Fragonard and Molinard have museums, but the best place to learn is at the **Musée Internationale de la Parfumerie**, which has a garden of fragrant plants.

Grasse was the birthplace of Jean-Honoré Fragonard, the artist. The **Villa-Musée Fragonard** is decorated with murals by his son. Fragonard's only religious work is in the **Cathédrale de Notre-Dame-du-Puy** in the Old Town, with three paintings by Rubens. The place aux Aires and the place du Cours typify Grasse's charm, surrounded by streets with Renaissance staircases and balconies.

Musée International de la Parfumerie
2 bd de Jeu du Ballon. **Tel** 04 97 05 58 00. **Open** Apr–Sep: daily; Oct–Mar: Wed–Mon. **Closed** Nov; public hols. **musees degrasse.com**

Villa-Musée Fragonard
23 bd Fragonard. **Tel** 04 93 36 80 20. **Open** Wed–Mon. **Closed** 2 wks in Nov; public hols.

Statue honoring Jean-Honoré Fragonard in Grasse

Menton at dusk ▶

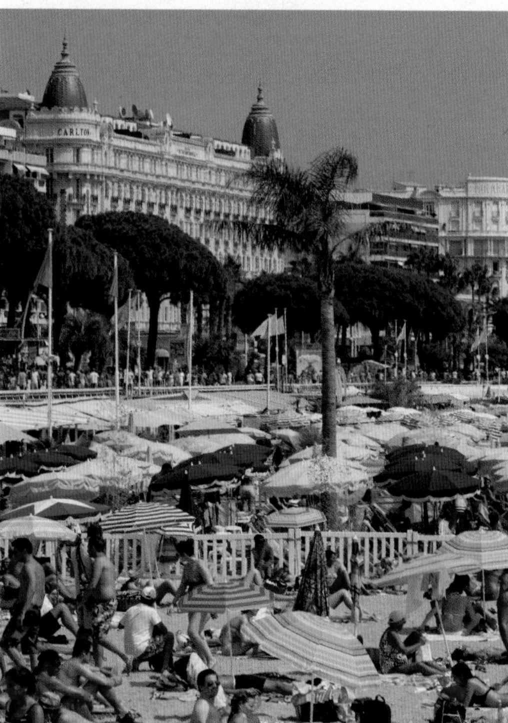

High summer on the beach at Cannes, overlooked by the Carlton Hotel

㉗ Cannes

Alpes-Maritimes. 69,000. Palais des Festivals, 1 La Croisette (04 92 99 84 22). Tue–Sun. **cannes-destination.fr**

Just as Grasse is synonymous with the perfume industry, the first thing that most people associate with Cannes is its many festivals, especially the International Film Festival. There is much more to the city than these glittering events. It was Lord Brougham, the British Lord Chancellor, who put Cannes on the map, although Prosper Mérimée, Inspector of Historic Monuments, allegedly visited Cannes two months before him. Lord Brougham stopped here in 1834, unable to reach Nice due to a cholera outbreak there. Struck by the beauty and mild climate of what was then just a small fishing port, he built a villa here. Other foreigners followe and Cannes became establishe as a top Mediterranean resort.

The Old Town which Lord Brougham knew is centered in the Le Suquet district, on the slopes of Mont Chevalier. Part the old city wall can still be see on place de la Castre, which is dominated by the **Notre-Dam de l'Espérance**, built in the 16 and 17th centuries in the Provençal Gothic style. An 11th century watch tower is anothe attractive feature of the quarte and the castle keep houses the **Musée de la Castre**, the eclect finds of a 19th-century Dutch explorer, Baron Lycklama.

The famed **boulevard de la Croisette** is lined with gardens and palm trees. One side is occupied by luxury boutiques and hotels such as the Carlton, built in Belle Epoque style, whose twin cupolas were modelled on the breasts of La Belle Otero, a famous member of the 19th-century *demi-mond* Opposite are some of the fines sandy beaches on this coast. The glamor of the Croisette, onc one of the world's grandest thoroughfares, seems faded in the noise and fumes of summe

Iles de Lérins

depart from: le Quai des Iles. Horizon (04 92 98 71 36 for Ile Ste Marguerite), Planaria (04 92 98 71 38 for Ile St-Honorat).

Just off the coast from Cannes are the Iles de Lérins. The fort or **Ile Sainte-Marguerite** is where the mysterious Man in the Iron Mask was imprisoned in the late 17th century. A popular theory

Cannes Film Festival

The first Cannes Film Festival took place in 1946 and, for almost 20 years, it remained a small and exclusive affair, attended by the artists and celebrities who lived or were staying on the coast. The arrival of the "starlet," especially Brigitte Bardot, in the mid-1950s marked the change from artistic event to media circus, but Cannes remains the international marketplace for film-makers and distributors, with the *Palme d'Or* award conferring high status on its winner. The annual film festival is held in the huge Palais des Festivals, opened in 1982. It has three auditoriums, two exhibition halls, conference rooms, a casino, night-club, and restaurant.

The Palais at the 2012 Cannes Film Festival

that his face had to be hidden ecause he resembled someone ery important indeed – possibly ven Louis XIV. Visitors can see ie tiny cell that held him for ver ten years.

Ile Saint-Honorat has an th-century tower in which the sident monks took refuge uring raids by the Saracens. here are also five ancient chapels. oth islands offer peaceful wood- nd walks, fine views, and quiet oves for swimming.

side the Boulevard de la Croisette

Cap d'Antibes

pes-Maritimes. Nice. ntibes. Nice. 11 pl du Gén e Gaulle, Antibes (04 97 23 11 11). **antibesjuanlespins.com**

/ith its sumptuous villas in their ish grounds, this rocky, wooded eninsula, known as "the Cap" to s regular visitors, has been a ymbol of luxury life on the iviera since it was frequented by Scott Fitzgerald and the rich merican set in the 1920s. One f the wealthiest of all, magnate rank Jay Gould, invested in the esort of Juan-les-Pins and it ecame the focus of high life on ie Cap. Today, memories of the azz Age live on at the Jazz estival, when international stars erform *(see p41)*.

At the highest point of the eninsula, the sailors' chapel of **a Garoupe** has a collection of otive offerings and a 14th- entury Russian icon. Nearby is ie **Jardin Botanique de la Villa huret**, created in 1856 to cclimatize tropical plants. Much of the exotic flora of the region began its naturalization here.

Jardin Botanique de la Villa Thuret
90 chemin Raymond, Antibes Juan-les-Pins. **Tel** 04 97 21 25 00. **Open** Mon–Fri. **Closed** public hols.

29 Antibes

Alpes-Maritimes. 73,000. 11 pl du Général de Gaulle (04 97 23 11 10). Tue–Sun (Jul–Aug: daily). **antibesjuanlespins.com**

The lively town of Antibes was founded by the Greeks as Antipolis and settled by the Romans. In the 14th century, Savoy's possession of the town was contended by France until it fell to them in 1481, after which **Fort Carré** was built and the port, now a center of Mediterranean yachting, was remodeled by Vauban.

The Château Grimaldi, formerly a residence of Monaco's ruling family, was built in the 12th century. It now houses the **Musée Picasso**. In 1946 the artist used part of the castle as a studio and, in gratitude, donated all 150 works completed during his stay, including *The Goat*. Most are inspired by his love of the sea, including *La Joie de Vivre*.

The Goat (1946) by Pablo Picasso

The pottery in the **Musée d'Histoire et d'Archéologie** includes objects salvaged from shipwrecks from the Middle Ages to the 18th century.

Musée Picasso
Château Grimaldi. **Tel** 04 92 90 54 20. **Open** Tue–Sun. **Closed** Jan 1, May 1, Nov 1, Dec 25.

Musée d'Histoire et d'Archéologie
1 Bastion St-André. **Tel** 04 93 95 85 98. **Open** Tue–Sun. **Closed** public hols.

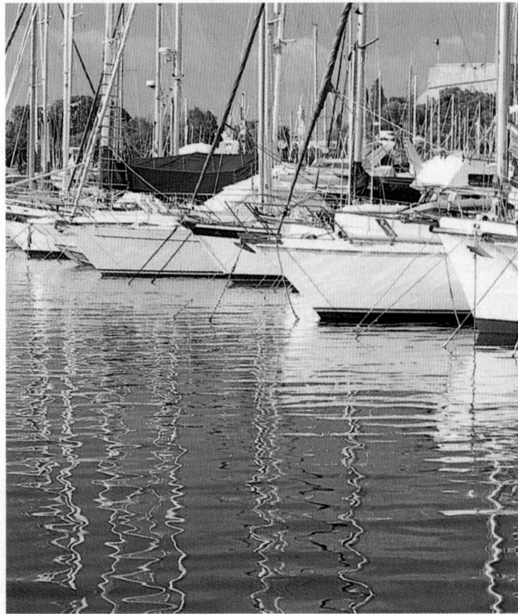

Sailing boats in the harbor at Antibes

⑳ Vallauris

Alpes-Maritimes. 31,000. square 8 mai 1945 (04 93 63 82 58). **vallauris-golfe-juan.fr** Tue–Sun.

Vallauris owes its fame to the influence of Pablo Picasso, who rescued the town's pottery industry. In 1951, the village authorities commissioned Picasso to paint a mural in the deconsecrated chapel next to the castle, and his *War and Peace* (1952) is the chief exhibit of the **Musée National Picasso**. In the main square is a bronze statue, *Man with a Sheep* (1943), donated by Picasso.

Musée National Picasso
Place de la Libération. **Tel** 04 93 64 71 83. **Open** Wed–Mon. **Closed** Jan 1, May 1, Nov 1 & 11, Dec 25. ground floor only.
musee-picasso.vallauris.fr

㉛ Biot

Alpes-Maritimes. 9,000. 46 rue St-Sebastien (04 93 65 78 00). Tue. **biot-tourisme.com**

A typical little hill village, Biot has retained its charm and has always attracted artists and artisans. The best known is Fernand Léger who made his first ceramics here in 1949. Some of these and other work by him are in the **Musée Fernand Léger** outside town.

The town is also famous for its bubble-flecked glassware. The craft of the glassblowers can be seen (and purchased) at the **Verrerie de Biot**.

Musée Fernand Léger
255 chemin du Val-de-Pome. **Tel** 04 92 91 50 30. **Open** Wed–Mon. **Closed** Jan 1, May 1, Dec 25.
musee-fernandleger.fr

La Verrerie de Biot
5 ch des Combes. **Tel** 04 93 65 03 00. **Open** daily. **Closed** public hols.
verreriebiot.com

Exterior of the Musée Fernand Léger in Biot, with a mural by the artist

Renoir's studio at the Musée Renoir, Les Collettes in Cagnes-sur-Mer

㉜ Cagnes-sur-Mer

Alpes-Maritimes. 49,000. 6 bd Maréchal Juin (04 93 20 61 64). Tue–Sun. **cagnes-tourisme.com**

Cagnes-sur-Mer is divided into three districts. The oldest and most interesting is Haut-de-Cagnes, with its steep streets, covered passageways, and ancient buildings, including a number of Renaissance arcaded houses. The other districts are Cagnes-Ville, the modern town where hotels and stores are concentrated, and Cros-de-Cagnes, a seaside fishing resort and yachting harbor.

The **Château Grimaldi** in Haut de-Cagnes was built in the 14t century and reworked in the 17th by Henri Grimaldi. Behinc the fortress walls is a shady courtyard. The surrounding marble columns conceal a museum devoted to the olive tree and a small collection of modern Mediterranean art. There is also a group of paintings bequeathed by *chanteuse* Suzy Solidor. The 40 works, all portraits of her, are b artists such as Marie Laurencin and Cocteau. On the ceiling of the banqueting hall is a vast illusionistic fresco of the *Fall of Phaeton* attributed to Carlone in the 1620s.

The last 12 years of Pierre Auguste Renoir's life were spe in Cagnes, at the **Musée Reno Les Collettes**. The house has been kept almost exactly as it was when he died in 1919 and contains 12 of his paintinc

The artist's great bronze *Venus Victrix* stands amongst olive and citrus trees in the museum's beautiful garden.

Château Grimaldi
pl Grimaldi. **Tel** 04 92 02 47 30.
Open Dec–mid-Nov: Wed–Mon.
Closed Jan 1, Dec 25.

Musée Renoir, Les Collettes
Tel 04 93 20 61 07. **Open** Wed–Mon (call to confirm opening hours).
Closed May 1, Jan 1, Dec 25.

33 Gorges du Loup

Alpes-Maritimes. Nice. Cagnes-sur-Mer. Grasse. Nice. 2 pl de la Libération, Tourrettes-sur-Loup (04 93 24 18 93).
tourrettessurloup.com

The river Loup rises in the Pre-Alps behind Grasse and cuts a deep path down to the Mediterranean. Along its route are dramatic cascades and spectacular views. The superb countryside is crowned by the perched villages for which the region is famous.

Gourdon owes much of its appeal to its ancient houses, grouped around a 12th-century **Château** built on the site of a Saracen stronghold and perched high on the cliffside. Its terraced gardens were laid out by Le Nôtre *(see p183)*.

Tourrettes-sur-Loup is a fortified village in which the ramparts are formed by the outer houses. It is famous for its fields of violets, grown for use in perfume and candied sweets. The **Bastide aux Violettes** museum explores the role of the flower in the village's history and economy.

Bastide aux Violettes
quartier de La Ferrage. **Tel** 04 93 59 06 97. **Open** Tue–Sat.
tourettessurloup.com

34 Vence

Alpes-Maritimes. 20,000. pl du Grand Jardin (04 93 58 06 38). Tue & Fri. **ville-vence.fr**

Vence's gentle climate has always been its main attraction; today it is surrounded by holiday villas. It was an important religious center in the Middle Ages. The **Cathédrale** was restored by Vence's most famous bishop, Antoine Godeau. A 5th-century Roman sarcophagus serves as its altar and there are Carolingian wall carvings. Note, too, the 15th-century carved choir stalls and Godeau's tomb.

Just within the ramparts of the Old Town, which retains its 13th–14th-century town gates, is place du Peyra, once a Roman forum. Its urn-shaped fountain, built in 1822, still provides fresh water. On the edge of town, the **Chapelle du Rosaire** was built from 1947–51 and decorated by Henri Matisse, in gratitude to the nuns who nursed him during an illness. On its white walls, biblical scenes are reduced to simple black lines tinted by splashes of light from the blue and yellow stained-glass windows.

Domed roof in Vence

Chapelle du Rosaire
466 av Henri Matisse. **Tel** 04 93 58 03 26. **Open** Mon–Thu & Sat pm.
Closed mid-Nov–mid-Dec, public hols. Sun 10am.

Market day in the Old Town of Vence

㉟ Street by Street: St-Paul-de-Vence

One of the most famous and visited hill villages of the Nice hinterland, St-Paul-de-Vence was once a French frontier post facing Savoy. Its 16th-century ramparts offer views over a landscape of cypress trees, and red-roofed villas with palm trees and swimming pools. The village has been heavily restored but its winding streets and medieval buildings are authentic. It has proved a magnet for artists, both established and aspiring, throughout the 20th century. Today galleries and studios dominate the village.

View of St-Paul-de-Vence
The local landscape is a favorite subject for artists. Neo-Impressionist Paul Signac (1863–1935) painted this view of St-Paul.

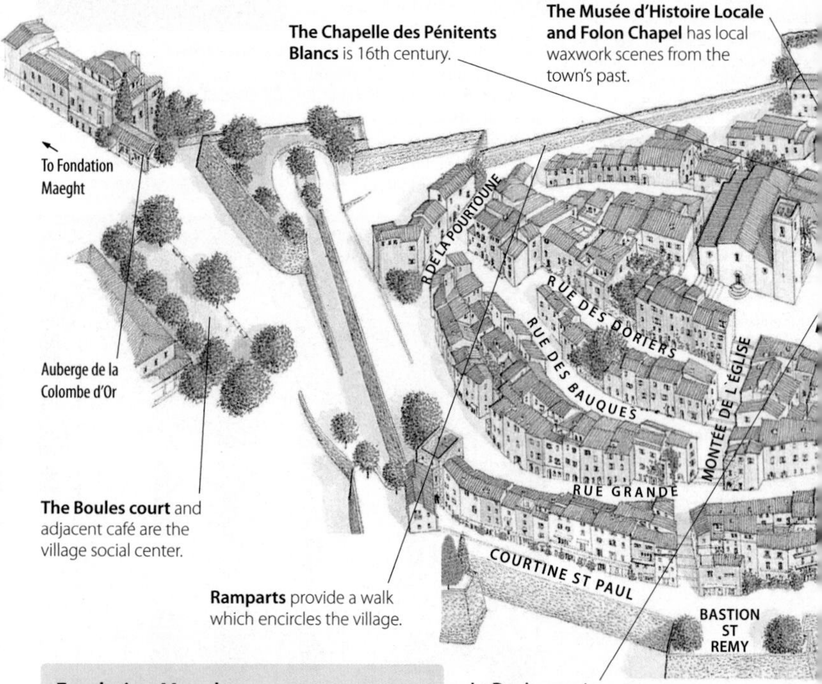

The Chapelle des Pénitents Blancs is 16th century.

The Musée d'Histoire Locale and Folon Chapel has local waxwork scenes from the town's past.

To Fondation Maeght

R DE LA POURTOUNE

RUE DES DORIERS

RUE DES BAUQUES

MONTÉE DE L'ÉGLISE

RUE GRANDE

COURTINE ST PAUL

BASTION ST REMY

Auberge de la Colombe d'Or

The Boules court and adjacent café are the village social center.

Ramparts provide a walk which encircles the village.

Le Donjon, a grim medieval building, was used as a prison until the 19th century.

Fondation Maeght

Built in 1964 by Paris art dealers Aimé and Marguerite Maeght, this is one of Europe's finest museums of modern art. The striking pink and white building, set outside St-Paul, was designed by Catalan architect José-Luis Sert, who worked on it directly with artists such as Miró and Chagall. Inside are paintings by Bonnard, Braque, Kandinsky, Chagall, and others. There are also summer concerts, exhibitions, a library, and lectures. In the terraced gardens, sculptures, mobiles, and mosaics by Arp, Calder, Miró, Giacometti, and Hepworth are set amid the pine trees.

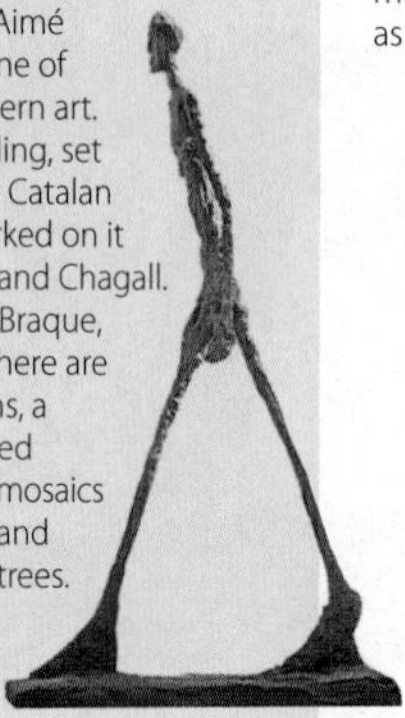

L'Homme qui Marche by Giacometti

The Colombe d'Or
This famous auberge includes a Léger mural (above) on the terrace; a Braque dove by the pool; a Picasso and a Matisse in the dining room.

For hotels and restaurants in this region see pp554–71 and pp576–603

Eglise Collégiale
Begun in the 12th century, the church's treasures include a painting of St Catherine, attributed to Tintoretto.

VISITORS' CHECKLIST

Practical Information
Alpes-Maritimes. 2,900.
2 rue Grande (04 93 32 86 95).
saint-pauldevence.com
Fondation Maeght: 623 Chemin Gardettes (04 93 32 81 63).
Open 10am–6pm daily.

Transport
840 ave Emile Hugues, Vence (04 93 58 37 60).

Grand Fountain
This charming cobble-stoned *place* has a pretty urn-shaped fountain.

Rue Grande
The doors of the 16th- and 17th-century houses bear coats of arms.

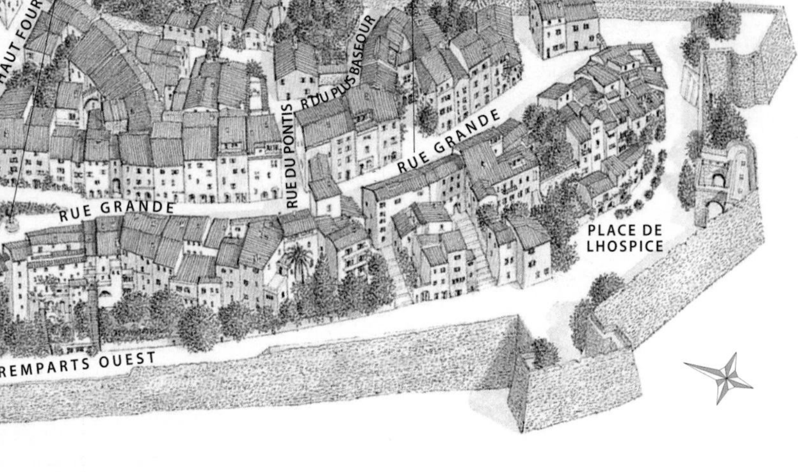

Celebrity Village

The Colombe d'Or (Golden Dove) auberge *(see p603)* was popular with many of the artists and writers who flocked to the Riviera in the 1920s. Early patrons included Picasso, Soutine, Modigliani, Signac, Colette, and Cocteau. Thanks to a friendship with the owners, they often paid for their rooms and meals with paintings, resulting in the priceless collection that can be seen by diners today. The rich and famous have continued to come to St-Paul: Zelda and F. Scott Fitzgerald had a dramatic fight over Isadora Duncan at dinner here one night, and Yves Montand married Simone Signoret on the terrace. Modern-day fans include Elton John, Michael Caine, Roger Moore, and Hugh Grant.

Artist Marc Chagall (1887–1985), who moved to St-Paul-de-Vence in 1950

36 Nice

The largest resort on the Mediterranean coast and the fifth biggest city in France, with its second busiest airport, Nice was founded by the Greeks and colonized by the Romans. Its temperate winter climate and verdant subtropical vegetation have long attracted visitors. Until World War II it was favored by aristocrats, including Tsar Nicholas I's widow who visited in 1856 and Queen Victoria who stayed in 1895. This glittering past has contributed to Nice becoming capital of the Côte d'Azur, and today it is also a center for business conferences and package holidays. Nice has worthy museums, good beaches, and an atmospheric street life. Best of all is Carnival: 18 days of celebrations finishing on Shrove Tuesday in a fireworks display and the Battle of the Flowers *(see p43)*.

Yachts at anchor in Nice harbor

Exploring Nice

The promenade des Anglais, along the seafront, was built in the 1830s with funds raised by the English colony. Today it is an eight-lane, 5-mile (8-km) thoroughfare, with galleries, shops, and grand hotels like the **Negresco**, reflecting Nice's prosperity.

Nice was Italian until 1860, and the pastel facades and balconies of the Old Town have a distinctly Italianate feel. It lies at the foot of a hill still known as the Château for the castle which once stood there. The district's tall, narrow buildings house artists and galleries, boutiques and restaurants. The daily flower market in the cours Saleya should not be missed. The **Cimiez** district, on the hills overlooking the town, is the fashionable quarter of Nice. The old monastery of Notre-Dame-de-Cimiez is well worth a visit. Lower down the hillside are Les Arènes, remains of a Roman settlement with vestiges of the great baths and an amphitheater. Excavated artifacts are on show at the archeological museum, next to the Musée Matisse. At the foot of the Cimiez hill is the **Musée Chagall**. The promenade du Paillon, a strip of park with a central waterway, runs from the Old Town through the center to the promenade des Anglais.

Discover Nice by night on a guided streetcar tour that takes in 14 works of art by celebrated contemporary artists. Book tickets in advance at the tourist office.

Musée Matisse

164 av des Arènes de Cimiez. **Tel** 04 93 81 08 08. **Open** 10am–6pm Wed–Mon. **Closed** some public hols. **W** **musee-matisse-nice.org**

Inspired by the Mediterranean light, Matisse spent many years in Nice. The museum, housed in and below the 17th-century Arena Villa, displays drawings, paintings, bronzes, fabrics, and artifacts. Highlights include *Still Life With Pomegranates* and his last completed work, *Flowers and Fruits*.

Nice's Old Quarter

Palais Lascaris

15 rue Droite. **Tel** 04 93 62 72 40. **Open** Wed–Mon. **Closed** Jan 1, Easte May 1, Dec 25.

This stuccoed 17th-century palace is decorated with ornat woodwork, Flemish tapestries, and illusionistic ceilings thoug to be by Carlone. Its small but delightful collection includes a reconstruction of an 18th-century apothecary's shop.

Musée d'Art Moderne et d'Art Contemporain (MAMAC)

pl Yves Klein. **Tel** 04 97 13 42 01. **Ope** Tue–Sun. **Closed** Jan 1, Easter, May 1 Dec 25. **W** **mamac-nice.or**

The museum occupies a strikingly original complex of four marble-faced towers linke by glass passageways. The collection is particularly strong in Neo-Realism and Pop Art, with works by Andy Warhol, Jean Tinguely, and Niki de Sain Phalle. Also well-represented a such Ecole de Nice artists as César, Arman, and Yves Klein.

Blue Nude IV (1952) by Henri Matisse

\n azure view – relaxing on the promenade des Anglais

VISITORS' CHECKLIST

Practical Information
Alpes-Maritimes. 349,000. 5 prom des Anglais (08 92 70 74 07). Tue–Sun. Carnival. **nicetourism.com**

Transport
4.5 miles (7 km) SW. av Thiers (36 35). 5 bd Jean Jaurès (04 93 85 61 81). quai du Commerce (3260).

Cathédrale Ste-Réparate

ol Rossetti. **Tel** 08 92 70 74 for guided ours. **Open** daily.

A 17th-century Baroque building, with a handsome tiled dome and an interior lavishly decorated with marble and original paneling.

Musée Chagall

36 av du Docteur Ménard. **Tel** 04 93 53 87 20. **Open** Nov–Apr: 10am–5pm Wed–Mon (to 6pm May–Oct). **Closed** Jan 1, May 1, Dec 25. **musee-chagall.fr**

The largest collection of works by Marc Chagall, including paintings, drawings, sculpture, stained glass, mosaics, and the 17 canvases of the artist's *Biblical Message*.

Musée des Beaux-Arts

33 av des Baumettes. **Tel** 04 92 15 28 28. **Open** Tue–Sun. **Closed** Jan 1, Easter, May 1, Dec 25. restr. Thu. **musee-beaux-arts-nice.org**

The 19th-century home of a Ukrainian princess displays works sent to Nice by Napoleon III after Italy ceded the city to France in 1860, as well as paintings by Renoir, Monet, and Dufy.

Villa Masséna

65 rue de France. **Tel** 04 93 91 19 10. **Open** Wed–Mon.

Housed in a 19th-century Italianate mansion, the Villa Masséna exhibits trace the history of Nice from 1800 to the 1930s.

Cathédrale Orthodoxe Russe St-Nicolas

ave Nicolas II and Blvd Tzarevitch. **Open** Tue–Sun 9am–noon & 2pm–6pm. **Closed** during services. **cathedrale-russe-nice.fr**

Built in memory of a young Tsarevitch, with elaborate mosaics outside and dazzling icons inside.

Musée des Arts Asiatiques

405 prom des Anglais. **Tel** 04 92 29 37 00. **Open** May–mid-Oct: 10am–6pm Wed–Mon (to 5pm mid-Oct–Apr). **Closed** Jan 1, May 1, Dec 25. **arts-asiatiques.com**

Ancient and contemporary Asian art in Kenzo Tange's uncluttered white marble and glass setting.

Nice

1. Musée Chagall
2. Hôtel Negresco
3. Palais Masséna
4. Cathédrale Ste-Réparate
5. Palais Lascaris
6. Musée d'Art Moderne et d'Art Contemporain

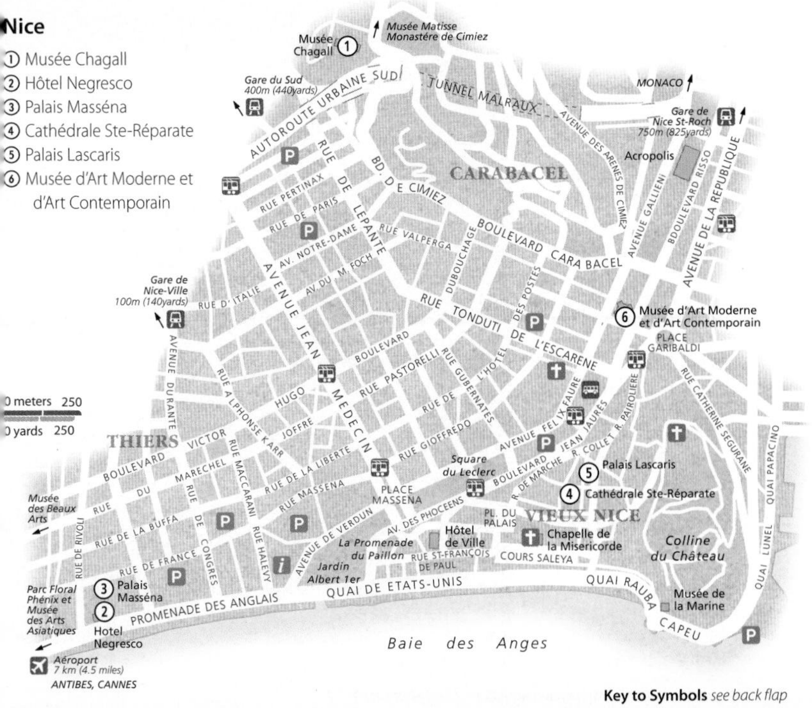

0 meters 250
0 yards 250

Baie des Anges

Key to Symbols *see back flap*

Chapelle de St-Pierre, Villefranche

37 Villefranche-sur-Mer

Alpes-Maritimes. 6,650. Jardin François Binon (04 93 01 73 68). Wed, Sat, Sun. **villefranche-sur-mer.com**

One of the most perfectly situated towns on the coast, Villefranche lies at the foot of hills forming a sheltered amphitheater. The town overlooks a beautiful natural harbor, which is deep enough to be a naval port of call.

The bright and animated waterfront is lined by Italianate facades, with cafés and bars from which to watch the fishermen. Here, too, is the **Chapelle de St-Pierre**, which, after years of service storing fishing nets, was restored in 1957 and decorated by Jean Cocteau. His frescoes depict nonreligious images and the life of St. Peter.

Also worth a visit is the 16th-century **Citadelle St-Elme**, incorporating the town hall and two art galleries.

Behind the harbor, the streets are narrow, winding, and often stepped. Walking through them, you can catch the odd glimpse of the harbor. The vaulted 13th-century rue Obscure has always provided shelter from bombardment, right up to World War II.

Chapelle de St-Pierre
Quai Amiral Courbet. **Tel** 04 93 76 90 70. **Open** Wed–Mon. **Closed** mid-Nov–mid-Dec, Dec 25.

38 Cap Ferrat

Alpes-Maritimes. 2,000. Nice. Nice. Beaulieu-sur-Mer. 5/59 av Denis Femeria (04 93 76 08 90). **saintjeancapferrat.fr**

The peninsula of Cap Ferrat boasts some of the most sumptuous villas found on the Riviera. From 1926 until the author's death, the best-known was Somerset Maugham's Villa Mauresque, where he received celebrities from Noël Coward to Winston Churchill.

High walls shield most of the exclusive villas, but possibly the best one is open to the public. The **Villa Ephrussi de Rothschild** is a terracotta and marble mansion set in themed gardens on the crest of the cape. It belonged to the Baroness Ephrussi de Rothschild, who bequeathed it to the Institut de France in 1934. It is furnished as she left it, with her collections of priceless porcelain, items that belonged to Marie Antoinette, and a unique collection of drawings by Fragonard.

The town of **Beaulieu** lies where the cape joins the mainland. A pleasant marina with an exceptionally mild climate and very fine hotels, it is the site of another unique house, the extraordinary **Villa Kerylos**. Built between 1902 and 1908 for archeologist Theodore Reinach in imitation of an ancient Greek residence, it contains lovingly reproduced mosaics, frescoes, and furniture.

Villa Ephrussi de Rothschild
1 av Ephrussi de Rothschild, Cap Ferrat. **Tel** 04 93 01 45 90. **Open** Mar–Oct: 10am–6pm daily; Nov–Feb: pms daily (10am–6pm w/e & school hols). **villa-ephrussi.com**

Villa Kerylos
Imp Gustave Eiffel, Beaulieu. **Tel** 04 93 01 01 44. **Open** as above. **villa-kerylos.com**

Greek-style Villa Kerylos at Beaulieu on Cap Ferrat

ouis XV salon at the Villa Ephrussi de Rothschild, Cap Ferrat

9 Eze

lpes-Maritimes. 3,100.
pl Général de Gaulle (04 93 41
6 00). **eze-tourisme.com**

or many, Eze is the ultimate erched village, balancing on a ocky pinnacle high above the Aediterranean. Every summer, housands of visitors stream hrough the 14th-century ortified gate. The flower-decked uildings are almost all shops, alleries, and craft workshops. At he top of the village, the château s surrounded by the lush tropical lants of the **Jardin Exotique**. he view from here is superb.

Farther along the Upper Corniche is the Roman Alpine rophy **La Turbie** *(see pp50–51)*. his vast 6 BC structure lominates the surrounding illage, with magnificent views owards Monaco and Italy.

Jardin Exotique
ue du Château. **Tel** 04 93 41 10 30.
Open daily. **Closed** Christmas wk.

Trophée d'Auguste à La Turbie
Open Tue–Sun. **Closed** public hols.
la-turbie.monuments-ationaux.fr

40 Roquebrune-Cap-Martin

lpes-Maritimes. 12,000. Nice.
218 av Aristide Briand
04 93 35 62 87). Wed.
roquebrune-cap-martin.com

The medieval village of Roquebrune overlooks the wooded cape where the villas of he rich and famous still abound. Visitors here have included Coco Chanel and Greta Garbo. The cape has not always been kind – poet W. B. Yeats died here in 1939 and architect Le Corbusier was drowned off the coast in 1965.

In 1467 Roquebrune believed that by performing scenes from the Passion it escaped the plague, and every August it continues this tradition.

View from Roquebrune

41 Alpes-Maritimes

Alpes-Maritimes. Nice. Nice.
Peille. Nice. 15 rue
Centrale, Peille (04 93 82 14 40).
peille.fr

In the hinterland of the Côte d'Azur, it is still possible to find quiet, unspoiled villages off the tourist track. The tiny twin villages of **Peille** and **Peillon** are typical. Both have changed little since the Middle Ages, perched on outcrops over the Paillon river, their streets a mass of steps and arches. Peille, the more remote, even has its own dialect. The Alpes-Maritimes countryside is also unspoiled, its craggy gorges, tumbling rivers, and windswept plateaus just a few hours from the coast. Of note are the ancient rock carvings of the **Vallée des Merveilles** and rare wildlife in the **Parc National du Mercantour**.

42 Menton

Alpes-Maritimes. 30,000.
Palais de l'Europe, 8 av Boyer (04 92 41 76 76). Tue–Sun.
tourisme-menton.fr

Menton's beaches, with the Alps and the golden buildings and Belle Epoque villas of the Old Town as a backdrop, would be enough to lure most visitors. In the 19th century, Queen Victoria and famous writers and poets often holidayed here. Tropical gardens and citrus fruits thrive in the town's perfect climate, mild even in February for the lemon festival *(see p43)*.

The **Basilica St-Michel** is a superb example of Baroque architecture in yellow and pink stone. The square before it is paved with a mosaic of the Grimaldi coat of arms. The **Salle des Mariages** in the Hôtel de Ville was decorated in 1957 by Jean Cocteau. Drawings, paintings, ceramics, and stage designs by the renowned artist are displayed in the **Musée Jean Cocteau**, housed in a 17th-century fort. Inside the Palais Carnolès, the **Musée des Beaux-Arts** features works from the Middle Ages to the 20th century.

Salle des Mariages
Hôtel de Ville. **Tel** 04 92 10 50 00.
Open Mon–Fri. **Closed** public hols.

Musée Jean Cocteau
Bastion du Vieux Port. **Tel** 04 93 57 72 30. **Open** Wed–Mon. **Closed** public hols.

Musée des Beaux-Arts
Palais Carnolès, 3 av de la Madone.
Tel 04 93 35 49 71. **Open** Wed–Mon.
Closed public hols.

Mosaic at the Musée Jean Cocteau in Menton

43 Monaco

Travelers to Monaco by car would do well to take the Moyenne Corniche, one of the most beautiful highways in the world, with incomparable views of the Mediterranean coastline. Arriving among the skyscrapers of Monaco today, it is hard to envisage the turbulence of its history. At first a Greek settlement, later taken by the Romans, it was bought from the Genoese in 1297 by the Grimaldis who, in spite of bitter family feuds and at least one political assassination, still rule as the world's oldest ruling dynasty. Monaco covers 0.74 sq miles (1.9 sq km) and, although its size has increased by one-third in the form of landfills, it still occupies an area smaller than that of New York's Central Park.

Aerial view of Monaco

Grand Casino

Exploring Monaco

Monaco owes its renown principally to its Grand Casino. Source of countless legends, it was instituted in 1878 by Charles III to save himself from bankruptcy. The first casino was opened in 1865 on a barren promontory (later named Monte-Carlo in his honor) across the harbor from ancient Monaco-Ville. So successful was Charles's money-making venture that, by 1870, he was able to abolish taxation for his people. Today, Monaco is a tax haven for thousands, and its residents have the highest per capita income in the world.

Visitors come from all over the world for the Grand Prix de Monaco in May and the Monte-Carlo Rally in January *(see p43)*. Many of the greatest singers perform in the opera season. There is a fireworks festival (July–August), and an international circus festival at the end of January as well as world-class ballet and concerts. Facilities exist for every sort of leisure activity, and there is much else to enjoy without breaking the bank, including **Fort Antoine** and the neo-Romanesque **Cathédrale**.

Grand Casino

Place du Casino. **Tel** 00 377 98 06 21 21. **Open** daily, from noon.
casinomontecarlo.com

Renovated in 1878 by Charles Garnier, architect of the Paris Opéra *(see p101)*, and set in formal gardens, the Casino gives a splendid view over Monaco. The lavish interior is still decorated in Belle Epoque style, recalling an era when this was the rendezvous of Russian Grand Dukes. Anyone can play the odds on the one-armed bandits of the Salon Blanc or the roulette wheels of the Salons Européens. Even the most exclusive of the gaming rooms can be visited at a price, but their tables are for the big spenders only.

Palais Princier

Place du Palais. **Tel** 00 377 93 25 18 31 **Open** Apr–Oct: daily.

Monaco-Ville, the seat of government, is the site of the 13th-century Palais Princier. The interior, with its priceless furniture and carpets and its magnificent frescoes, is only open to the

Skyscrapers and apartment blocks of modern Monte-Carlo

Monaco's Royal Family

Prince Albert II officially assumed the Monaco throne in July 2005, three months after his father died, aged 81, ending a reign of over 55 years. Prince Rainier III was an effective ruler, descended from a Grimaldi who entered the Monaco fortress in 1297. His wife, former film star Grace Kelly, died tragically in 1982. Prince Albert and his sisters, Caroline and Stephanie, remain a focus of media attention.

Prince Rainier III, Princess Grace, and Princess Caroline

VISITORS' CHECKLIST

Practical Information

Monaco. 35,000. 2a bd des Moulins (00 377 92 16 61 16). daily. Festival du Cirque (Jan); International Fireworks Festival (Jul–Aug); Fête Nationale Monégasque (19 Nov). **visitmonaco.com**

Transport

9 miles (15 km) SW Nice. pl Ste-Devoté (08 36 35 35 35).

public in the summer. The changing of the guard is at 11:55am.

Musée des Souvenirs Napoléoniens et Archives Historiques du Palais

Pl du Palais. **Tel** 00 377 93 25 18 31. **Open** daily. **Closed** Jan 1, Dec 25.

A genealogical tree on the wall traces the family links between the Grimaldis and Bonapartes. Also on show are Napoleon's personal effects and numerous portraits.

Guard outside the Palais Princier

Musée Océanographique

Av Saint-Martin. **Tel** 00 377 93 15 36 00. **Open** daily. **Closed** Jan 1, Grand Prix, Dec 25. **oceano.mc**

This museum was founded in 1910 by Prince Albert I. Its aquarium, fed with sea water, holds rare species of marine plants and animals. The museum houses an important scientific collection, diving equipment, and model ships. Marine explorer Jacques Cousteau established his research center here.

Jardin Exotique

62 bd du Jardin Exotique. **Tel** 00 377 93 15 29 80. **Open** daily. **Closed** Nov 19, Dec 25. **jardin-exotique.mc**

These gardens are considered to be the finest in Europe, with a huge range of tropical and subtropical plants. A museum of anthropology offers evidence of mammoths once living on the coast here.

Nouveau Musée National de Monaco

Villa Sauber, 17 av Princesse Grace. **Tel** 00 377 98 98 91 26. **Open** daily. **Closed** Grand Prix, Nov 19, Dec 25.

This museum, housed in two adjoining villas and surrounded by lush gardens, hosts temporary exhibitions. There are usually two a year, on themes of photography and nature.

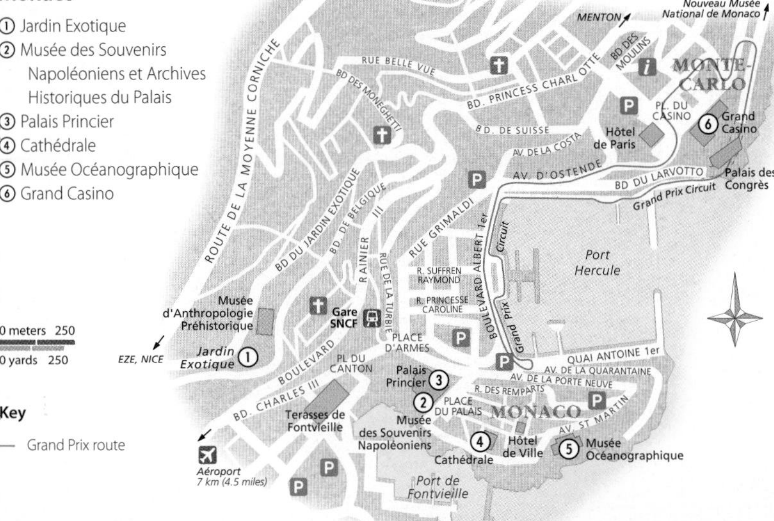

Key to Symbols *see back flap*

CORSICA

Haute-Corse · Corse-du-Sud

Corsica, where the people speak their own language, has all the attributes of a mini-continent. There are tropical palm trees, vineyards, olive and orange groves, forests of chestnut and indigenous pine, alpine lakes and cool mountain torrents filled with trout. Most distinctive of all is the parched maquis (scrub), heavy with the scent of myrtle, which Napoleon swore he could smell from Elba.

The fourth largest island in the Mediterranean after Sicily, Sardinia, and Cyprus, Corsica has been a problem and a bafflement to mainland France ever since 1769, when it was "sold" to Louis XV by the Genoese for 40 million francs. Before that, following years of struggle, the Corsican people had enjoyed 14 years of independence under the revered leadership of Pasquale Paoli. They understandably felt cheated by the deal with the French, and have resented them ever since. To holiday-makers visiting the island – in July and August tourists outnumber the inhabitants six to one – the Corsican–French relationship may be a matter of indifference. However, there is a strong (and sometimes quite violent) separatist movement, which does deter some tourists. As a result, Corsica's wild beauty has been preserved to an extent not seen in the rest of the Mediterranean.

For 200 years, from the 11th to the 13th century, Corsica was a colony of the old Tuscan republic of Pisa, whose builders founded beautifully proportioned Romanesque churches. These buildings are, along with the megalithic stone warriors in Filitosa, the noblest monuments to be seen here. For the rest, the birthplace of Napoleon is a place of wild seacoasts and mountain peaks, one of the last unspoiled corners of the Mediterranean: poor, depopulated, beautiful, old-fashioned, and doggedly aloof.

The village of Oletta in the Nebbio region around St-Florent

◀ Dramatic limestone cliffs at Bonifacio

Exploring Corsica

Corsica's main appeal is its scenery: a wildly beautiful landscape of mountains, forests, myrtle-scented maquis, and countless miles of sandy beaches. Late spring (when the wild flowers are in bloom) and early autumn are the best times to visit – the temperature is moderate and there aren't too many visitors. The island is renowned for its superb hiking trails, some of which become cross-country skiing trails during the winter. Downhill skiing is also possible in February and March.

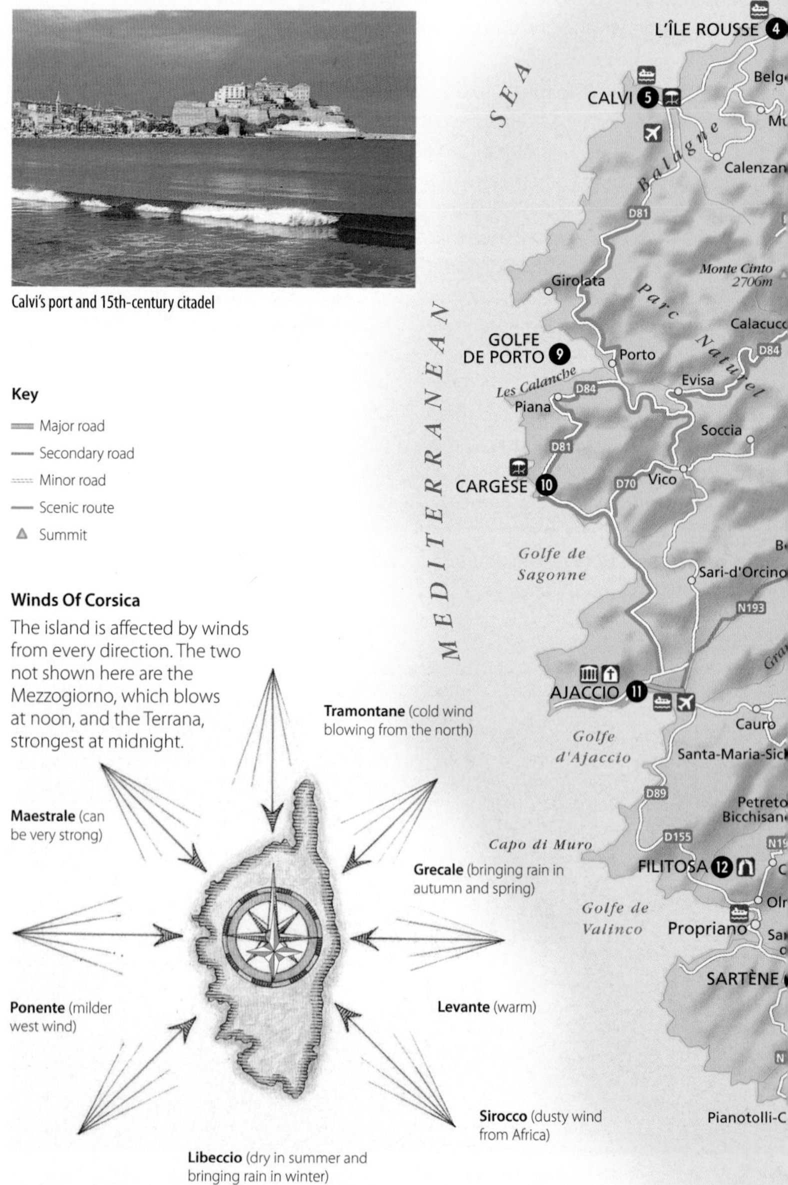

Calvi's port and 15th-century citadel

Key

- Major road
- Secondary road
- Minor road
- Scenic route
- Summit

Winds Of Corsica

The island is affected by winds from every direction. The two not shown here are the Mezzogiorno, which blows at noon, and the Terrana, strongest at midnight.

For additional map symbols *see back flap*

Sights at a Glance

1. Cap Corse
2. Bastia
3. St-Florent
4. L'Ile Rousse
5. Calvi
6. The Niolo
7. Corte
8. The Castagniccia
9. Golfe de Porto
10. Cargèse
11. Ajaccio
12. Filitosa
13. Sartène
14. Bonifacio
15. Côte Orientale

The Calanche cliffs in the Golfe de Porto

Getting Around

Car ferries (which should be booked well in advance) depart from Marseille, Nice, and Toulon, arriving at Bastia, L'Île Rousse, Calvi, Ajaccio, Propriano, and Porto-Vecchio. There are also ferries from Sardinia to Bonifacio, and from Genoa, Livorno, and La Spezia to Bastia. Small airports are at Ajaccio, Bastia, Calvi, and Figari. Corsica's roads are narrow, twisting, and often tortuously slow, though breathtaking views reward the effort. A car is a must for exploring the island, as public transport is limited. Carry extra fuel – gas stations are few and far between.

Corte's Old Town, with its citadel high up on a rocky outcrop

❶ Cap Corse

Haute-Corse. Bastia. Bastia. Bastia. Port de Plaisance, Macinaggio (04 95 35 40 34); Port Toga, Pietrabugna (04 95 31 02 32). **destination-cap-corse.com; macinaggiorogliano-capcorse.fr**

Cap Corse is the northern tip of Corsica, 25 miles (40 km) in length but seldom more than 7.5 miles (12 km) wide, pointing like an accusatory finger towards Genoa.

There are two roads out of Bastia to the cape: the D81 leading west across the mountains and joining up with the D80 after the wine village of Patrimonio; and the D80 traveling north along the eastern shore to **Erbalunga** and **Macinaggio**. The road is narrow and twisting, a taste of what awaits you in Corsica.

From the coastal village of **Lavasina**, the D54 leads left off the D80 to Pozzo; from here it is a 5-hour round trip on foot to the 4,300-ft (1,307-m) summit of **Monte Stello**, the highest peak on the cape. The 360-degree view from the top takes in St-Florent to the west, the massif of central Corsica to the south, and the Italian island of Elba to the east.

Farther up the coast, the restored **Tour de Losse** is one of many 16th-century Genoese towers along the coast – part of an elaborate system which enabled all Corsican towns to be warned within 2 hours of impending barbarian raids.

The charming 18th-century fishing port of **Centuri**, near the tip of the peninsula on the west coast, is an ideal spot for a delicious seafood feast. **Pino**, a pretty little village straggling down the green mountainside farther to the south, has no hotel, only a lovely little church dedicated to the Virgin, full of model ships placed there by mariners grateful for her protection.

On the way south along the vertiginous lower corniche, be sure to turn left up the hill to **Canari**. One of the larger villages in this area, Canari has a jewel of a 12th-century Pisan church, Santa Maria Assunta, a magnificent view across the sea, and a thoroughly convivial hotel-restaurant. All the by-roads in this thickly wooded area seem to lead somewhere interesting. There are dozens of picturesque hamlets in the vicinity, and it should be borne in mind that from this point onward the landscape becomes steadily less attractive as the road winds on past the old asbestos workings and beaches of black sand below the village of **Nonza**.

The village of Erbalunga on the east coast of Cap Corse

Bastia's Vieux Port seen from the Jetée du Dragon

❷ Bastia

Haute-Corse. 39,000. north end of pl St-Nicolas (04 95 54 20 40). Tue–Sun. **bastia-tourisme.com**

A thriving port and the administrative capital of Upper Corsica, Bastia is utterly different in style from its sedate west coast rival, Ajaccio. The Genoese citadel and colorful 19th-century Italianate buildings around the old port are for many people their first taste of the authentic Mediterranean – as it was half a century ago, and as it stubbornly remains in our imagination.

The center of Bastia's life is the **place St-Nicolas**, facing the wharf where ferries from the mainland and Italy arrive. Heading south along the waterfront you come to the **place de l'Hôtel de Ville**, site of a daily food market. Bordering the square are the early 17th-century **Chapelle de l'Immaculée Conception**, with its ornate 18th-century interior, and the mid-17th-century **Eglise de St-Jean-Baptiste**, whose facade dominates the Vieux Port.

From here it is a short walk up to the 16th-century **citadel**, where there are two more churches worth seeing: the Rococo **Chapelle Sainte-Croix**, with its striking *Black Christ*, fished out of the sea by Bastiais fishermen in 1428; and the 15th-century **Sainte-Marie**, which has a *Virgin* made of a ton of solid silver.

❸ St-Florent

Haute-Corse. 1,500.
Bâtiment Administratif (04 95 37 06 04). first Wed of month.
corsica-saintflorent.com

St-Florent is almost a Corsican St-Tropez – chic, affluent, and packed with yachts. Its citadel, which houses photography exhibitions, dates from 1439, and is a fine example of Genoese military architecture. The town itself is pleasant to wander around; its main attraction, the 12th-century Pisan **Cathédrale de Santa Maria Assunta**, lies just inland on the road to Poggio-d'Oletta.

Environs
A leisurely 4-hour circuit by car of the **Nebbio** region, which extends in an amphitheater around St-Florent, might take in the following: **Santo Pietro di Tenda; Murato**, famous for its magnificent **Eglise de San Michele de Murato**, a 12th-century Pisan Romanesque construction built of white and green stone; the **San Stefano** pass, with the sea on either side; **Oletta**, which produces a special blue cheese made from ewes' milk; the **Teghime** pass; and finally the wine village of **Patrimonio**, where there is a strange, big-eared menhir dating from 900–800 BC.

Along the coast to the west of St-Florent lies the barren, uninhabited **Désert des Agriates**. If you can face the 6-mile (10-km) haul to the sea – on foot, by bike, or by motorbike – the Saleccia beach is the most beautiful on the island.

San Michele de Murato

❹ L'Ile Rousse

Haute-Corse. 2,400.
av Calizzi (04 95 60 04 35).
summer: daily; winter: Tue & Fri.
ot-ile-rousse.fr

Founded in 1758 by Pasquale Paoli, leader of independent Corsica, L'Ile Rousse is today a major holiday resort and ferry terminal. The center of town is dominated by a marble statue of Corsica's national hero, Paoli. On the north side of the square is the covered market, with the Old Town just beyond.

In summer, L'Ile Rousse becomes overcrowded, its beaches a mass of bodies. It is worth traveling 6 miles (10 km) up the coast to **Lozari**, which offers a magnificent, virtually unspoiled stretch of sand.

Environs
One very pleasant way to discover the **Balagne** region is to take the tram-train from L'Ile Rousse to Calvi and back. This odd little service runs all year (more frequent in summer), roughly keeping to the coastline and stopping at Algajola, Lumio, and various villages along the way.

❺ Calvi

Haute-Corse. 5,500.
97 Port de Plaisance (04 95 65 16 67).
daily. **balagne-corsica.com**

Calvi, where Nelson lost his eye in an "explosion of stones" in 1794, is today half military town, half cheap holiday resort. Its 15th-century citadel is garrisoned by a crack French regiment of the foreign legion; while beyond the ferry port is a seedy, apparently endless campsite and trailer park.

The town makes a half-hearted case for being the birthplace of Christopher Columbus, but there is no real evidence to support this. A much better claim to fame is the food, which is very good and reasonably priced by Corsican standards. There is also a very respectable jazz festival at Calvi towards the end of June.

Outside town, the 19th-century **Chapelle de Notre-Dame de la Serra** is gloriously sited on a hilltop commanding extensive views in all directions.

French foreign legionnaire

The Chapelle de Notre-Dame de la Serra, 3.5 miles (6 km) southwest of Calvi

Corte's 15th-century citadel seen at dawn

6 The Niolo (Niolu)

Haute-Corse. Corte. route de Cuccia, Calacuccia (04 95 47 12 62). **office-tourisme-niolu.com**

The Niolo, west of Corte, extends westward to the Vergio pass and the upper Golo basin, and to the east as far as the Scala di Santa Regina. It includes Corsica's highest mountain, the 8,860-ft (2,700-m) **Monte Cinto**, and its biggest river, the **Golo**, which meets the sea south of Bastia.

Alone of the various regions of Corsica, the Niolo persists in the cultivation of livestock as its economic mainstay.

The main town, **Calacuccia**, is suitable for excursions to Monte Cinto. The nearby ski resort of **Haut Asco** is best reached by the D147 from **Asco**, but enthusiasts can walk from Calacuccia (8–9 hours). To the south is the huge forest of **Valdu Niello**.

7 Corte

Haute-Corse. 6,700. la Citadelle (04 95 46 26 70). Fri. **corte-tourisme.com**

In the geographical center of Corsica, Corte was the chosen capital of the independence leader Pasqual Paoli from 1755–69, and today is the seat of the island's university. In the Old Town is the 15th-century citadel, housing the **Museu di a Corsica**. Its exhibits relate to traditional Corsican life and anthropology.

Corte is the best base for exploring nearby mountain areas, especially as it stands exactly halfway along the GR20, the legendary 137-mile (220-km) trail from Calenzana to Conca.

Museu di a Corsica
La Citadelle. **Tel** 04 95 45 25 45.
Open Apr–Oct: Tue–Sun (mid-Jun–mid-Sep: daily); Nov–Mar: Tue–Sat.
Closed public hols.
musee-corse.com

Environs
Don't miss the wildly beautiful **Gorges de la Restonica**, about 7.5 miles (12 km) out of town via the D623. Above these gorges adventurous walkers may wish to make the well-marked climb to the snow-fed **Lac de Melo** (allow 60–90 minutes); or the **Lac de Capitello**, 30 minutes farther on, where the snow stays as late as early June. The path – in winter a cross-country ski trail – follows the river.

South of Corte, the **Forêt de Vizzavona** features beech and pine woodland crisscrossed by trout-filled streams and walking trails (notably the GR20). It is a perfect refuge from the summer heat and is also an excuse to take the small-gauge train up from Ajaccio or Bastia, which stops at Vizzavona.

8 The Castagniccia

Haute-Corse. Bastia. Corte, Ponte Leccia. Piedicroce, La Porta, Valle-d'Alesani. Immeuble L'Aiglon, Folelli (04 95 35 82 54). **castagniccia.fr**

East of Corte is the hilly, chestnut-covered region of Castagniccia (literally "small chestnut grove"), which most Corsicans agree is the very heart and kernel of the island. It was here that independence leader Pasquale Paoli was born in 1725, and that the revolts against Genoa and later France began in earnest in 1729. Alas, many of the villages in this beautiful, remote area are nearly empty, their inhabitants having joined the 800,000 or so Corsicans (almost three times the present population) who live and work in mainland France or Italy. It seems hard to believe that in the 17th century, when the great chestnut forests introduced here by the Genoese were at the height of their production, this was the most prosperous and populated region in Corsica.

The D71 from Ponte Leccia (north of Corte) to the east coast winds through the center of the Castagniccia region, and to see it at a leisurely pace will take the best part of a day. Arm yourself with a picnic before you start, as there is little to be had in the way of supplies en route.

◀ View of one of the Genoese towers on the beautiful Iles Sanguinaires

9 Golfe de Porto

Corse-du-Sud. Ajaccio. Porto. Porto marina (04 95 26 10 55). **porto-tourisme.com**

Porto is sited at the head of the Golfe de Porto, one of the most beautiful bays in the Mediterranean, which for the sake of its fauna and flora has been included in UNESCO's list of the world's common cultural heritage sites. The town has a magnificent Genoese watch-tower – the perfect spot for admiring the sunset – and regular boat excursions (Apr–Oct) to the Calanche, Scandola, and Girolata.

The **Calanche** begin 1 mile (2 km) out of Porto, on the road to Piana. These 1,000-ft (300-m) red granite cliffs plunge sheer to the sea, and are quite simply breathtaking. They are accessible only by boat or on foot: well-defined trails start from the Tête du Chien and the Pont de Mezanu, while boat tickets are available at Porto's Hôtel Le Cyrnée.

East of Porto are the Gorges de la Spelunca, accessed by a mule route punctuated by Genoese bridges.

Just south of Porto along a spectacular corniche drive passing under granite arch-ways, lies the pretty village of **Piana**, a good base for visiting this whole area, with infor-mation on recommended walks. One particularly worthwhile destination is the cove at **Ficajola** just below Piana – a truly delightful beach.

Porto's marina and Genoese watchtower

Environs

The road over the mountains from Porto to Calvi offers no more than a taste of this grandiose corner of Corsica – you have to take to the sea to view it properly (ferries from Porto and Galéria). **Girolata**, a tiny hamlet north of Porto, can be reached only by sea or via a mule track (4 hours round trip on foot) from a clearly marked point 14 miles (23 km) north of Porto on the D81.

At the mouth of the Golfe de Girolata, the **Réserve Naturelle de Scandola**, instituted in 1975, is the first land-and-sea reserve in France, covering over 4 sq miles (10 sq km) of sea, and a similar area of cliffs, caves, and maquis. Marine life is abundant in these clear, protected waters; the birds include ospreys, puffins, and falcons.

Corsican Flowers

For lovers of wild flowers, Corsica is a Mediterranean jewel. Much of the island is covered with maquis, a tangle of aromatic shrubs and low trees which flowers from late winter onwards. Among its dense variety are the showy rockroses, which shower the ground with short-lived pink or white petals, and brilliant yellow broom. Grassy and rocky slopes are good places to spot the widespread tassel hyacinth and the Illyrian sea lily which grows only in Corsica and Sardinia.

Rock-rose

The town of Piana with the Calanche in the background

For hotels and restaurants in this region see pp554–71 and pp576–603

Cargèse's Greek rite church

⑩ Cargèse

Corse-du-Sud. 1,000. rue du Docteur Dragacci (04 95 26 41 31). **cargese.net**

Cargèse overlooks the sea from a promontory between the bays of Sagone and Pero. It is a small town with an odd history: many of the people who live here are the descendants of 17th-century Greek refugees from Turkish rule, given asylum in Corsica.

A few Cargèsiens still speak Greek, and their icon-filled Eastern (Greek) rite church faces its Catholic counterpart in an attitude that must once have seemed confrontational. Nowadays the old rivalries have vanished, and the Orthodox priest and Catholic *curé* often stand in for one another.

There are many splendid beaches in the vicinity, notably at **Pero** and **Chiuni** just to the north, and at **Ménasina** and **Stagnoli** to the south.

⑪ Ajaccio

Corse-du-Sud. 60,000. 3 bd du Roi Jérôme (04 95 51 53 03). Tue–Sun. **ajaccio-tourisme.com**

Ajaccio, a noisy, busy town by Corsican standards, was the birthplace of Napoleon Bonaparte in 1769. Napoleon never returned to Corsica after crowning himself emperor of the French in 1804, but the town – modern capital of nationalist Corsica – celebrates his birthday every August 15.

The 16th-century **Cathédrale Notre-Dame de la Miséricorde**, where Napoleon was baptized in 1771, houses Delacroix's painting *Vierge du Sacré-Coeur*.

A few streets away, the **Maison Bonaparte**, where Napoleon was born and spent his childhood, contains family portraits, period furniture, and assorted memorabilia.

Much more interesting is the art collection assembled by Napoleon's unscrupulous uncle, Cardinal Fesch, who merrily looted churches, palaces, and museums during the Italian campaign and brought the swag home to Ajaccio. Housed in the 19th-century Palais Fesch, the **Musée des Beaux Arts** contains the finest collection of Italian primitive art in France after the Louvre. Among its masterpieces are works by Bellini, Botticelli, Titian and Veronese, Bernini, and Poussin. Next to the Palais Fesch stands the **Chapelle Impériale**, built in 1855 by Napoleon III to accommodate the tombs of the Bonapartes. From here, walk back along the quay to the Jetée de la Citadelle, which offers superb views of the town, the marina, and the Golfe d'Ajaccio. The adjacent 16th-century **citadel** is occupied by the army.

Statue of Napoleon by Laboureur in place Maréchal Foch, Ajaccio

Maison Bonaparte
Rue St-Charles. **Tel** 04 95 21 43 89. **Open** Tue–Sun.
musee-maisonbonaparte.fr

Palais Fesch, Musée des Beaux Arts
50–52 rue Cardinal Fesch. **Tel** 04 95 26 26 26. **Open** Wed–Mon.
musee-fesch.com

Environs
From the Quai de la Citadelle there are daily excursions to the **Îles Sanguinaires** at the mouth of the Golfe d'Ajaccio.

At Vero, 13 miles (21 km) northeast on the N193, is an unusual park, **A Cupulatta**, with over 150 species of tortoises and turtles (Apr–Oct).

A statue-menhir at Filitosa

⑫ Filitosa

Centre Préhistorique de Filitosa, Corse-du-Sud. **Tel** 04 95 74 00 91. **Open** Apr–Oct: daily. **filitosa.fr**

The 4,000-year-old, lifesize stone warriors of Filitosa are the most spectacular relics of megalithic man in Corsica. Discovered in 1946, these phallus-like granite menhirs represent an interesting progression from mere silhouettes to more detailed sculpture, etched with human features.

The five most recent and most sophisticated figures (about 1500 BC) stand around

For hotels and restaurants in this region see pp554–71 and pp576–603

The fortified Old Town of Bonifacio, with the harbor in the foreground

a thousand-year-old olive tree, in the field below a tumulus. Other finds, which include a heavily armed warrior with shield, helmet, and sword, can be seen in the site's archeological museum.

⓭ Sartène

Corse-du-Sud. 3,600.
14 cours Soeur Amélie (04 95 77 15 40). summer: daily; winter: Sat.
lacoursedesorigines.com

Sartene is a medieval fortified town of narrow cobbled streets and gray granite houses rising above the Rizzanese valley. Founded by the Genoese in the early 16th century, it has survived attacks by Barbary pirates and centuries of bloody feuding among the town's leading families.

Despite all this, Sartène has a reputation for deep piety, reinforced each year by the oldest and most intense Christian ceremony in Corsica, the Good Friday Catenacciu (literally, the "chained one"). A red-hooded penitent, barefoot and in chains, drags a wooden cross through the Old Town in a reenactment of Christ's ascent to Golgotha.

Environs

In the town center, the **Musée de la Préhistoire Corse** has a collection of Neolithic, Bronze, and Iron Age artifacts.

Musée de la Préhistoire Corse
rue Croce. **Tel** 04 95 77 01 09.
Open Jun–Sep: daily; Oct–May: Mon–Fri. **prehistoire-corse.org**

⓮ Bonifacio

Corse-du-Sud. 2,700.
2 rue Fred Scamaroni (04 95 73 11 88). Wed. **bonifacio.fr**

Bonifacio is the southern-most town in Corsica, dramatically sited on a limestone and granite cliff peninsula with stunning views *(see pp536)*. Its handsome harbor at the foot of the cliffs is the focus of life: cafés, restaurants, and boutiques abound, and boats depart regularly for neighboring Sardinia and the uninhabited island of Lavezzi.

From the harbor, steps lead up to Bonifacio's fortified Old Town. The citadel, which was built by the conquering Genoese at the end of the 12th century, has long been the town's main defensive post, and from 1963–83 was the headquarters of the French foreign legion. From here, wander down to the tip of the promontory to see the three old windmills and the ruins of a Franciscan monastery.

⓯ Côte Orientale

Haute-Corse & Corse-du-Sud.
Bastia. Aléria (04 95 57 01 51); Porto-Vecchio (04 95 70 09 58).
Bastia, Porto-Vecchio.
oriente-corsica.com;
ot-portovecchio.com.

The flat, rather dreary alluvial plain stretching from Bastia to Solenzara has been rich farmland since 1945, the year it was finally drained and rid of malaria. More recently, holiday resorts and even high-rise hotels have mushroomed along the coast, cashing in on its long, sandy beaches.

The best sight in **Mariana**, which is otherwise uncomfortably close to the Bastia-Poretta airport, is the early 12th-century cathedral of Mariana known as **La Canonica**. A short distance away is the slightly older **Eglise de San Perteo**, surrounded by meadows.

About halfway down the coast, the port of **Aléria**, originally a Greek colony and the base for Rome's conquest of Corsica in 259 BC, is interesting for its rich archeological heritage. Just outside town, a museum housed in the 16th-century Fort de Matra chronicles daily life in Roman Aléria.

Towards the southern tip of the island, the fortified town of **Porto-Vecchio**, built by Corsica's Genoese conquerors, is now an extremely popular seaside resort. The setting is perfect for the conventional seaside holiday, with umbrella pines, cork oak forests, and glorious white sandy beaches within easy reach of the town, especially at **Palombaggia** and **Pinarello**.

The Golfe de Porto-Vecchio

TRAVELERS' NEEDS

WHERE TO STAY

France has thousands of registered hotels that range from some of the most glamorous establishments in the world to charming and idiosyncratic little inns buried in the countryside. On these four pages, the types of hotels on offer are summarized with tips on what to expect. The hotel listings pages *(see pp554–71)* describe some of the best hotels around the country in every price category and style. Alternatively choose from the increasingly popular *chambres d'hôtes* (bed and breakfasts), which range from simple farms to grandiose châteaus. As France is one of the most popular countries in the world for holiday-home rental, there is also information on finding a rural home or *gîte*, and how to get the most out of a French camping trip.

Entrance to the Hôtel-Restaurant Euzkadi at Espelette in the Pyrenees *(see p568)*

Gradings

French hotels are graded from one star to five stars, based on the range of facilities they offer. Hotels with two or more stars must have an elevator where appropriate. Eighty percent of the rooms in a three-star hotel must have private bathrooms. Four- and five-star hotels must have room service, air conditioning, and private bathrooms attached to all rooms.

Hotel Chains

France's hotel chains vary from cheap and cheerful pit stops, situated on the outskirts of towns by highways or main roads, to sleek and upmarket four-star business hotels and apartment rentals in city centers. Almost all of them offer the usual conveniences and free Wi-Fi access.

Among the cheapest options are the one-star, no-frills **Formule 1** motels, offering bedrooms with twins, or a double and single bed, and shared bathroom facilities. **Hotels Première Classe** fall under the two-star category – they offer rooms with private bathrooms and charge the same low rates for up to three people sharing. Other options in this category include **Ibis**, which also offers reasonably good deals, and **Campanile**. Three-star chains include **Novotel** and **Mercure** – both offer accommodations with their own bathrooms and usually allow one child with no charge, provided the whole family sleeps in one room. Novotel allows two under-16s. **Adagio** offers apartments in city centers, sleeping up to six for a minimum of four nights. The top spots in the hotel chain accommodations list undoubtedly belong to the boutique-style **MGallery** hotels and the international luxury chain **Sofitel**. Most of these chains are now part of the vast **Accor** hotel empire.

Meals and Facilities

In high season, many resort hotels insist on half board or *demi-pension* (a rate per person for the room, dinner, and breakfast). There is also full board or *pension*, which covers lunch too. While it is cheaper to opt for inclusive rates, set or limited-choice menus often omit the more interesting dishes. And if you do not have *pension* or *demi-pension* accommodations, breakfast is often charged as an extra. Go instead to the local café, as it tends to be cheaper and more filling. Many hotels do not provide meals on Sunday evenings and often stop serving dinner as early as 9pm on other days.

Rooms usually have double beds; twin or single beds must be requested when booking. All midrange hotels, with a few historic exceptions mostly in Paris, have private bathrooms. Elsewhere there are still a handful of budget options with separate bathrooms down the corridor, but the majority now offer attached facilities. A bathroom with a *bain* (bath) is usually more expensive than one with a *douche* (shower).

Imposing white exteriors of Le Negresco in Nice, Côte d'Azur *(see p570)*

◀ Interior of the Galeries Lafayette department store in Paris

Grandiose seating area in the opulent Le Meurice in the Tuileries Quarter, Paris *(see p554)*

Prices

Rates, inclusive of tax and service, are quoted per room (apart from *pension* and *demi-pension* arrangements). There is usually a small surcharge for a third person in a room for two, and little reduction for single travelers.

As a rule, the higher the star rating, the more you pay. Rates for a double room start from about €45 per night for a one-star hotel and upwards of €150 for a four-star hotel. Costs also vary geographically with remote rural areas like Brittany being the cheapest. For equivalent accommodations in fashionable areas such as Dordogne and Provence, expect to pay 20 percent more, plus another 20 percent for Paris and the Côte d'Azur. Prices vary seasonally too, with coastal and alpine areas increasing their tariffs by up to 50 percent during peak periods. The **French Tourist Office** website has an "Affordable France" section dedicated to providing the best deals and offers on vacations in France.

Booking

Advance booking is always wise, especially for Paris and hotels in popular tourist areas over the holiday months of July and August. Places where you think hotels should be easy to find can suddenly fill up, thanks to a sporting event or concert. Even the chain hotels by the highways tend to be full out of season. Choice can also be limited because many hotels are seasonal: at seaside resorts, most shut down from October to March, and ski resort hotels often close in April.

These days most people book their accommodations in France online, either through a hotel booking site or directly on the hotel's home page, paying for at least one night's stay to hold the reservation – although there may be website discounts for paying all in advance. It is advisable to read the small print carefully about cancellations and refunds.

Stone steps leading to the charmingly rustic Hôtel de l'Abbaye in Longpoint *(see p556)*

Those who want to book on arrival can do so from tourist offices in all main cities and towns – they offer reservations up to 8 days in advance.

Holiday Homes

A *gîte* is a rural holiday home, often a converted farmhouse or its outbuildings. *Gîte* vacations are a popular and relatively cheap way to see France, particularly out of season, but you should book many months in advance in order to secure the best properties in summer or for skiing vacations in winter.

Gîtes de France registers some 60,000 *gîtes*, all inspected and graded to indicate the level of facilities. Book directly on their website by region or by theme – country, charm, children, hiking, extreme sports, well-being, and many others. They also list city-break rentals, B&Bs, campgrounds, and cottages.

Clévacances, another reliable national organization, also lists good quality *gîtes* throughout France.

France has numerous other kinds of self-catering options such as stately south-coast villas, stunning ski resort chalets, and modern city and coastal apartments. **Allo Vacances** provides a booking service for vacation rentals throughout the different regions.

Lovely dining area at the Hôtel de la Cité, Carcassonne *(see p569)*

Camping

There are eleven thousand official campgrounds spread around France's diverse countryside. The **Fédération Française de Camping et de Caravaning (FFCC)** publishes a comprehensive list, updated every year. There is a wide range of campgrounds listed on the Gîtes de France website too. **Bienvenue à la Ferme** offers a number of sites, as well as *gîtes* and B&Bs, on farms.

Campgrounds are graded from one to four stars. Three- and four-star sites are usually impressively spacious with plenty of amenities and electricity connections for a percentage of tents and trailers. One- and two-star campgrounds always have toilets, a public phone, and running water, although some one-star sites may have only cold water. However, what they lack in facilities, they often make up for with peaceful surroundings and rural charm.

Camping Card International (CCI), available through various national camping clubs, offers campers, especially in France, numerous discounts and third party liability insurance.

Hostels

Hostels are a money-saving option for single travelers, though cheap hostels don't remain as inexpensive for those traveling with a partner.

The IYHF's hostelling guide details the 220 hostels around France offered by **Fédération Unie des Auberges de Jeunesse (FUAJ)**, open to all ages and providing decent dormitory accommodations. Those who are not members of **Hostelling International** in their home country will have to pay a small surcharge each time they stay in a French youth hostel. **Ethic Etapes** has 50 centers with a cultural bent scattered all over France. All of them have a restaurant and single, shared, and dormitory accommodation for groups, individuals, and families. *Gîtes d'étape* are usually large farmhouses with dormitories close to walking, cycling and horseback riding routes.

Disabled Travelers

A number of associations publish information on accommodations throughout France with wheelchair access, notably the **Association des Paralysés de France (APF)** and the Gîtes de France's guide *Accessibles*. **Les Compagnons du Voyage** can organize escorted door-to-door transport on all public transport networks throughout France.

Guide Accessible (in French) is a useful website which lists, region by region, transport companies and lodgings adapted for wheelchair users.

Further Information

The French National Tourist Office offers a wide range of informative brochures on France and most of them can be downloaded for easy reference. The first port of call for all non-hotel accommodations in the French countryside, however, should be Gîtes de France.

Recommended Hotels

The accommodations options featured in this guide – listed by area and then by price – have been selected across a wide price range for their excellent facilities and unique appeal. They cover categories such as Family, Value for Money, Romantic, Luxury, Boutique, Rooms with Views, and B&Bs.

Family hotels are especially suited for visitors traveling with children, offering either rooms with multiple beds or interconnected rooms. Both independent and chain hotels have rooms and facilities geared to handle guests traveling with their families.

Value for money hotels offer great rates for their facilities, location, or service. Select from a range of independent establishments of character offering excellent deals in cities and the countryside. A large proportion

Vacationers enjoying the pool at a camp site in high season

of these hotels are part of the **Logis de France** organization.

Romantic hotels are aimed at couples, and the hotels that feature in this category may either have a special decor, or four-poster beds, or perhaps a romantic spa.

Hotels labeled as **charming** stand out with their inimitable style and elegant furnishings.

Many of France's châteaus and historic mansions have been converted into **luxury** hotels – from Renaissance piles with sweeping lawns to medieval castles with battlements. Lots of these opulent properties belong to the **Relais et Châteaux** group, which guarantees beautifully designed rooms and top-notch fine dining. From glamorous hotels in Paris to swanky seaside resorts, this category features all the plush places to splurge on.

Chic **boutique** hotels are springing up in many French cities – these are generally small but full of character with smart designs and all the modern conveniences. They

The majestic Carlton InterContinental in Cannes *(see p570)*

tend to be pricey, but the experience is usually worth it.

Rooms with views are hotels set in scenic locations – high in the mountains, on the coast, or in some of France's most beautiful landscapes.

Bed and breakfasts (B&Bs) or *chambres d'hôtes* have increased by a huge margin all over the country in recent years, primarily due to strict EU regulations that have led to the closing of lots of the old family-run hotels, with many B&Bs springing up in their place. Most of these establishments are full of character and range from tiny cottages to elaborate château full of family portraits and antiques, to boutique suites for couples in historic townhouses. B&Bs located on farms are called *fermes-auberges* (farm inns). Besides breakfast, many B&Bs offer dinner on request. Over 10,000 B&Bs are inspected and registered by Gîtes de France. Many others are not registered but information on these is available from local tourist offices or online.

For choosing the very best in hospitality and lodging, look out for hotels marked **DK Choice** – highlighted in recognition of a superlative feature. It may have beautiful surroundings, be a historically important building, have a noteworthy sustainable outlook, or just be incredibly charming. Whatever the reason, it is a guarantee of an especially memorable stay.

DIRECTORY

French Tourist Office

Canada
Tel 1 866 313 7262.
canada@franceguide.com
W ca.franceguide.com

United States
Tel 212 838 7800.
info.us@franceguide.com
W us.franceguide.com

Hotels

Accor (Formule 1, Ibis, MGallery, Mercure, Novotel, Adagio, Sofitel)
Tel 1800 221 4542 (US & Canada); 0805 50 40 30 (France).
W accorhotels.com

Campanile
Tel 0892 230 591 (France).
W campanile.com

Hotel Première Classe
Tel 01 73 21 98 00 (France).
W premiereclasse.com

Logis de France
Tel 01 45 84 83 84 France.
W logishotels.com

Relais et Châteaux
Tel 1800 735 2478 (Canada, US); 0825 82 51 80 (France).
W relaischateaux.com

Holiday Homes & B&Bs

Allo Vacances
W allovacances.com

Clévacances
Tel 05 32 10 82 30.
W clevacances.com

Gîtes de France
W gites-de-france.com

Camping

Bienvenue à la Ferme
Tel 01 53 57 11 50.
W bienvenue-a-la-ferme.com

Camping Card International (CCI)
W campingcard international.com

Fédération Française de Camping et de Caravaning (FFCC)
78 rue de Rivoli, 75004 Paris.
Tel 01 42 72 84 08.
W ffcc.fr

Hostels

Ethic Etapes
27 rue de Turbigo, 75002 Paris.
Tel 01 40 26 57 64.
W ethic-etapes.fr

FUAJ (Fédération Unie des Auberges de Jeunesse)
27 rue Pajol, 75018 Paris.
Tel 01 44 89 87 27.
W fuaj.org

Hostelling International, Canada
205 Catherine St, Suite 400, Ottawa, ON K2P 1C3.
Tel 613 237 7884 or 1800 663 5777.
W hihostels.ca

Hostelling International, USA
8401 Colesville Rd, Suite 600, Silver Spring, MD 20910.
Tel 240 650 2100.
W hiusa.org

Disabled Travelers

Association des Paralysés de France (APF)
17 bd August Blanqui, 75013 Paris.
Tel 08 00 50 0 5 97.
W apf.asso.fr

Guide Accessible
W guide-accessible.com

Les Compagnons du Voyage
34 rue Championnet, LAC CG25, 75018 Paris.
Tel 01 58 76 08 33.
W compagnons.com

Where to Stay

Paris

Ile de la Cité, Marais, & Beaubourg

Hospitel €
B&B **Map** 9 A4
1 pl du Parvis Notre-Dame, 75004
Tel *01 44 32 01 00*
W hotel-hospitel.fr
Bright and comfortable accommodation at this centrally located hotel. Free Wi-Fi.

Britannique €€
Charming **Map** 13 A3
20 av Victoria, 75001
Tel *01 42 33 74 59*
W hotel-britannique.fr
Seascapes and other naval details adorn this hotel with a distinctly British feel.

Caron de Beaumarchais €€
Charming **Map** 9 C3
12 rue Vieille-du-Temple, 75004
Tel *01 42 72 34 12*
W carondebeaumarchais.com
Gracefully decorated hotel with an 18th-century theme in the choice of colors, fabrics, and elegant upholstered furniture.

Hôtel de la Bretonnerie €€
Charming **Map** 9 C3
22 rue Ste-Croix de la Bretonnerie, 75004
Tel *01 48 87 77 63*
W hotelbretonnerie.com
Exposed beams, stone vaulting, and rich fabrics give this hotel a medieval ambience.

DK Choice

Le Petit Moulin €€
Boutique **Map** 10 D2
29–31 rue du Poitou, 75003
Tel *01 42 74 10 10*
W paris-hotel-petitmoulin.com
The oldest *boulangerie* (bakery) in Paris now houses this petite, quirky hotel. All rooms reflect Christian Lacroix's love for color and opulence, and are wildly romantic with audacious murals. There is wheelchair access, free Wi-Fi, and private parking for guests.

St-Louis en l'Isle €€
Romantic **Map** 9 C4
75 rue St-Louis en l'Ile, 75004
Tel *01 46 34 04 80*
W saintlouisenlisle.com
Stylish and intimate hotel with peaceful rooms in neutral shades. Excellent location. Great service.

Jeu du Paume €€€
Luxury **Map** 9 C4
54 rue St-Louis en l'Ile, 75004
Tel *01 43 26 14 18*
W jeudepaumehotel.com
An old-beamed building transformed into a rustic-chic hotel with well-appointed rooms.

DK Choice

Le Pavillon de la Reine €€€
Luxury **Map** 10 D3
28 pl des Vosges, 75003
Tel *01 40 29 19 19*
W pavillon-de-la-reine.com
Overlooking the city's most beautiful square, this hotel has an unrivaled setting. The 17th-century mansion has been refurbished in elegant country-house style with romantic bedrooms and a lovely spa.

Tuileries & Opéra

Chopin €
Charming **Map** 6 F4
46 passage Jouffroy, 75009
Tel *01 47 70 58 10*
W hotelchopin.fr
Simple hotel at the end of a stunning 19th-century glass-roofed arcade. Close to city attractions.

Brighton €€
Charming **Map** 8 D1
218 rue de Rivoli, 75001
Tel *01 47 03 61 61*
W paris-hotel-brighton.com
Enjoy breathtaking views of the Tuileries amid faux marble columns, antique furnishings, and glittering chandeliers.

Entrance to the gorgeous Caron de Beaumarchais hotel

Price Guide
Prices are based on one night's stay in high season for a standard double room, inclusive of service charges and taxes.

€	up to €100
€€	€100 to €250
€€€	over €250

Citadines Prestige Opéra Vendôme €€
Family **Map** 6 D
2 rue Edouard VII, 75009
Tel *01 40 06 56 00*
W citadines.com
Practical rental apartments that are perfect for families.

Le Meurice €€€
Luxury **Map** 8 D
228 rue de Rivoli, 75001
Tel *01 44 58 10 10*
W lemeurice.com
Plush palace with glittering rooms glorious views, and great service

Mandarin Oriental €€
Luxury **Map** 12 D
251 rue St-Honoré, 75001
Tel *01 70 98 78 88*
W mandarinoriental.com
Oriental charm meets Parisian style at this luxurious world-class establishment.

Champs-Elysées & Invalides

Hôtel de la Tour Maubourg €
Romantic **Map** 7 B
150 rue de Grenelle, 75007
Tel *01 47 05 16 16*
W hoteltourmaubourgparis.com
A gracious and welcoming hote with eclectic but charming decc Great location.

Mayet €
Design **Map** 11 B
3 rue Mayet, 75006
Tel *01 47 83 21 35*
W mayet.com
Well-run small boutique hotel with bright, jazzy interiors.

Four Seasons George V €€
Luxury **Map** 2 E
31 av George V, 75008
Tel *01 49 52 70 00*
W fourseasons.com/paris
Modern comforts in an opulent setting at this iconic establishmer

Hôtel Daniel €€
Romantic **Map** 2 F
8 rue Frédéric Bastiat, 75008
Tel *01 42 56 17 00*
W hoteldanielparis.com
Oriental fabrics, wallpaper, and carpets at this flamboyant hote

Le Bristol €€€
Luxury **Map** 3 A4
112 rue de Faubourg St-Honoré, 75008
Tel *01 53 43 43 00*
W lebristolparis.com
Admire the antiques, chandeliers, and tapestries at this elegant hotel. Lovely swimming pool.

Shangri La €€€
Romantic **Map** 6 D1
10 av d'Iéna, 75116
Tel *01 53 67 19 98*
W shangri-la.com/paris/shangrila
A romantic hotel in a Belle Epoque palace with gleaming parquet floor and sparkling chandeliers.

The Left Bank

Degrés de Notre Dame €€
Charming **Map** 9 B4
10 rue des Grands Degrés, 75005
Tel *01 55 42 88 88*
W lesdegreshotel.monsite-orange.fr
Vintage charmer with attractive beamed bedrooms leading off a frescoed stairway.

Hôtel de Buci €€
Romantic **Map** 8 E4
22 rue de Buci, 75006
Tel *01 55 42 74 74*
W buci-hotel.com
Antiques, rich colors and luxurious fabrics lend this hotel a distinctly 18th-century feel.

Hôtel des Grandes Ecoles €€
Charming **Map** 9 B5
75 rue Cardinal Lemoine, 75005
Tel *01 43 26 79 23*
W hotel-grandes-ecoles.com
A family hotel with a leafy garden that is ideal for summer breakfasts.

Hôtel des Grands Hommes €€
Romantic **Map** 13 A1
17 pl du Panthéon, 75005
Tel *01 46 34 19 60*
W hoteldesgrandshommes.com
Enjoy breathtaking views of the panthéon from this glossy Empire-style hotel.

Relais Christine €€€
Luxury **Map** 8 F4
3 rue Christine, 75006
Tel *01 40 51 60 80*
W relais-christine.com
At once luxurious and intimate, with a paneled salon and private garden, Relais Christine never fails to impress.

Relais St-Germain €€€
Romantic **Map** 8 F4
9 carrefour de l'Odéon, 75006
Tel *01 44 27 07 97*
W hotel-paris-relais-saint-germain.com
Irresistibly Parisian, St-Germain has plush, soundproof bedrooms.

Résidence Le Prince Regent €€€
B&B
Map 12 F5
28 rue Monsieur le Prince, 75006
Tel *01 56 24 19 21*
W leprinceregent.com
Gracefully decorated rooms, a top spa, and extremely spacious apartments.

Bright and comfortable seating area, Shangri La hotel

Further Afield

Loft Paris €
B&B
7 cité Véron, 75018
Tel *06 14 48 47 48*
W loft-paris.fr
Quirky decor and lots of character in four neat apartments.

DK Choice

Arvor St-Georges €€
B&B
8 rue Laferrière, 75009
Tel *01 48 78 60 92*
W hotelarvor.com
This family-friendly B&B has been furbished in smart retro-contemporary style. The open-plan reception, which includes a bar and breakfast area, is decorated with conceptual artist Daniel Buren's striped posters.

HotelHome Paris 16 €€
Family
36 rue George Sand, 75016
Tel *01 45 20 61 38*
W hotelhome.fr
Seventeen apartments of various sizes. Great for families.

La Villa Paris €€
Charming
33 rue de la Fontaine à Mulard, 75013
Tel *01 43 47 15 66*
W la-villa-paris.com
All the comforts of home at this lovely B&B, with parquet floors and refined decoration.

Le Relais Montmartre €€
Romantic
6 rue Constance, 75018
Tel *01 70 64 25 25*
W hotel-relais-montmartre.com
Pretty fabric, dainty period furniture, and a lovely courtyard.

L'Ermitage €€
Charming
24 rue Lamarck, 75018
Tel *01 42 64 79 22*
W ermitagesacrecoeur.fr
Light, floral-themed bedrooms with hilltop views over the city and a lovely garden.

Mama Shelter €€
Design
109 rue de Bagnolet, 75020
Tel *01 43 48 48 48*
W mamashelter.com/en/paris
Super-trendy rooms with iMacs, microwaves, and mood lighting.

Manoir de Beauregard €€
Charming
43 rue des Lilas, 75019
Tel *01 42 03 10 20*
W manoir-de-beauregard-paris.com
A B&B in an 18th-century manor with a formal garden. Neat decor and gracious hosts.

DK Choice

Terrass €€
Romantic
12-14 rue Joseph de Maistre, 75018
Tel *01 46 06 72 85*
W terrass-hotel.com
A relaxed four-star hotel with elegant rooms, Terrass is perfect in every season. In winter, guests can enjoy the cozy piano bar, which has an open fire and comfy armchairs to sink into. In summer, sofas dot the roof, allowing visitors to take in the spectacular views.

Ile de France

CERNAY LA VILLE: Abbaye des Vaux de Cernay €€
Rooms with views
Domaine des Vaux de Cernay, 78720
Tel *01 34 85 23 00*
W abbayedecernay.com
A 12th-century ruined abbey restored with breathtaking beauty. Large vaulted rooms and stunning grounds.

LA FERTE SOUS JOUARRE: Château des Bondons €€
Family
47 rue des Bondons, 77260
Tel *01 60 22 00 98*
W chateaudesbondons.com
Attractive 19th-century château with a lovely paneled dining room.

For more information on types of hotels *see pp552–3*

ST-GERMAIN-EN-LAYE: Pavillion Henri IV €€
Rooms with views
19-21 rue Thiers, 78100
Tel *01 39 10 15 15*
W pavillon-henri-4.com
Built by Henri IV, this beautiful château with refurbished rooms has fine views of Paris.

VERSAILLES: Hôtel des Roys €€
Value for money
14, av de Paris, 78000
Tel *01 39 50 56 00*
W hotel-roys-versailles.com
Elegant town house with simple and neat rooms. Great location.

DK Choice

VILLIERS LE MAHIEU: Château de Villiers le Mahieu €€€
Luxury
rue du Centre, 78770
Tel *01 34 87 44 25*
W chateauvilliers.com
Set within a moated, medieval fortress, this 17th-century château has been sensitively modernized to balance conservation and comfort. Superb courtyard and grounds.

Le Nord & Picardy

AMIENS: Victor Hugo €
Value for money
2 rue de l'Oratoire, 80000
Tel *03 22 91 57 91*
W hotel-a-amiens.com
Cheerful family-run hotel with basic rooms next to the cathedral.

Elegant, well-appointed rooms at Hôtel Marrotte in Amiens

AMIENS: Hôtel Marrotte €€€
City centre
3 rue Marotte, 80000
Tel *03 60 12 50 00*
W hotel-marotte.com
Small family-run hotel with gracefully decorated rooms in a beautifully restored building.

DK Choice

BUSNES: Château de Beaulieu €€€
Luxury
1098 rue de Lillers, 62350
Tel *03 21 68 88 88*
W lechateaudebeaulieu.fr
An 18th-century château seamlessly converted into a 21st-century hotel, surrounded by 12 acres (5 ha) of elegant gardens. Herbs from the grounds are used in the luxury Michelin-starred restaurant.

CALAIS: Les Dunes €
Family
48, rte Nationale, Bleriot Plage, 62231
Tel *03 21 34 54 30*
W les-dunes.com
Delightful beach location and vibrant rooms. Pet friendly.

FERE EN TARDENOIS: Château de Fère €€€
Rooms with views
rte de Fismes, 02130
Tel *03 23 82 21 13*
W chateaudefere.com
Stunning 16th-century château hotel just one hour from Paris. Well-stocked wine cellar.

GOSNAY: La Chartreuse du Val St-Esprit €€
Luxury
1 rue de Fouquières, 62199
Tel *03 21 62 80 00*
W lachartreuse.com
An 18th-century château built on medieval ruins with large rooms, a lovely park, and three restaurants.

GOUVIEUX: Château de la Tour €€
Luxury
chemin de la Chaussée, 60270
Tel *03 44 62 38 38*
W lechateaudelatour.fr
Impeccable service, expansive gardens, and a great location.

LAON: La Maison des Trois Rois €
Value for money
17 rue Saint-Martin, 02000
Tel *03 23 20 74 24*
W lamaisondes3rois.com
A friendly and very comfortable B&B set in a beautiful 14th-century mansion with five excellently restored rooms.

LE TOUQUET: Le Castel – Victoria €
Family
11 rue de Paris, 62520
Tel *03 21 90 01 00*
W hotelletouquetparisplage.com
Stylish hotel close to the beach and town center, with a great roof terrace. Decent sized beds.

LILLE: Alliance Couvent des Minimes €€
City centre
17 quai du Wault, 59000
Tel *03 20 30 62 62*
W alliance-lille.com
Converted monastery with lovely cloisters and a spectacular atrium with a trendy bar and restaurant.

LILLE: Hermitage Gantois €€€
Luxury
224 rue de Paris, 59000
Tel *03 20 85 30 30*
W hotelhermitagegantois.com
A 14th-century hospice with large paneled and stylish rooms.

LONGPONT: Hôtel de l'Abbaye €
Value for money
8 rue des Tourelles, 02600
Tel *03 23 96 02 44*
W hotel-abbaye-longpont.fr
Old fashioned and comfortable guest rooms. Located opposite a 12th-century abbey.

LUMBRES: Moulin de Mombreux €€
Family
70 rue Mombreux, 62380
Tel *03 21 39 13 13*
W mombreux.com
Attractive 18th-century mill on the banks of the river Bléquin.

MONTREUIL SUR MER: Le Darnétal €
Value for money
pl Poissonnerie, 62170
Tel *03 21 06 04 87*
W darnetal-montreuil.com
Pub-style hotel in the upper town with an excellent fish restaurant.

MONTREUIL SUR MER: Château de Montreuil €€€
Luxury
4 Chaussée des Capucins, 62170
Tel *03 21 81 53 04*
W chateaudemontreuil.com
Stylish manor house within the ramparts of the town. Lovely gardens and a restaurant.

REUILLY-SAUVIGNY: L'Auberge le Relais €
Value for money
2 rue de Paris, 02850
Tel *03 23 70 35 36*
W relaisreuilly.com
Refined hotel with spacious rooms and a scenic location. Fine service.

Key to Price Guide *see p554*

SAINTE-PREUVE: Château de Barive €€
Rooms with views
Domaine du Château de Barive, 02350
Tel *03 23 22 15 15*
W chateau-de-barive.com
Beautifully converted 18th-century stables. Large rooms, and a gourmet restaurant.

ST-QUENTIN: Hôtel des Cannoniers €
Value for money
15 rue des Cannoniers, 02100
Tel *03 23 62 87 87*
W hotel-cannoniers.com
Period town house with a courtyard for summer breakfasts.

WIMEREUX: Hôtel St-Jean €€
Family
1 rue Georges Romain, 62930
Tel *03 21 83 57 40*
W hotel-saint-jean.fr
Brightly colored, well-decorated rooms. Spa facilities available. Very close to the beach.

Champagne

AUBERIVE: Auberge du Palais Abbatial €
Value for money
pl de l'Abbaye, 52160
Tel *03 25 84 33 66*
W auberge-abbatiale.com
Lovely rooms in a meticulously restored 11th-century building.

AY: Le Castel Jeanson €€
Family
24 rue Jeanson, 51560
Tel *03 26 54 21 75*
W casteljeanson.fr
Neat 18th-century château converted into an excellent hotel. Art Deco veranda by the pool.

CHALONS-EN-CHAMPAGNE: L'Hôtel d'Angleterre €€
City center
19 pl Monseigneur Tissier, 51000
Tel *03 26 68 21 51*
W hotel-dangleterre.fr
Large, beautifully decorated rooms with sleek marble bathrooms. Free Wi-Fi.

DK Choice

CHARLEVILLE MÉZIÈRES: Le Dormeur du Val €€
City center
32 bis rue de la Gravière, 08000
W dormeur.fr
Remarkable hotel with zany modern interiors and vibrant, well-appointed rooms. Rejuvenate with a drink at the lively bar or sit down with a book in the well-stocked hotel library. For the health conscious, there is a gym. The less active can head to the saunas and Turkish baths.

Rustic setting of the grand Château de Barive, Sainte-Preuve

COLOMBEY-LES-DEUX-EGLISES: La Grange du Relais €
Value for money
26 rte Nationale 19, 52330
Tel *03 25 02 03 89*
W lagrangedurelais.fr
A simple, peaceful hotel with an excellent inhouse restaurant.

COURCELLES-SUR-VESLE: Château de Courcelles €€
Luxury
8 rue du Château, 02220
Tel *03 23 74 13 53*
W chateau-de-courcelles.fr
Sumptuous bedrooms and a stately reading room at this magnificent establishment.

EPERNAY: Hôtel de la Cloche €
Value for money
3 pl Mendès-France, 51200
Tel *03 26 55 15 15*
W hotel-la-cloche.com
Cheerful, refurbished hotel with simple rooms. Ideal base to explore neighboring areas.

ETOGES: Château d'Etoges €€
Luxury
4 rue Richebourg, 51270
Tel *03 26 59 30 08*
W etoges.com
Fairytale castle with period rooms, large grounds, a moat, and an excellent restaurant.

GIFFAUMONT CHAMPAUBERT: Le Cheval Blanc €
Family
21 rue du Lac, 51290
Tel *03 26 72 62 65*
W lecheval-blanc.net
Quiet village inn close to Europe's biggest artificial lake.

MESNIL-SAINT-PERE: Auberge du Lac €
Value for money
5-7 rue du 28 Août 1944, 10140
Tel *03 25 41 27 16*
W auberge-du-lac.fr
Family hotel in the Lac et Forêt d'Orient Natural Park, with nicely restored half-timbered buildings.

MOUSSEY: Domaine de la Creuse €€
Value for money
Domaine de la Creuse, 10800
Tel *03 25 41 74 01*
W domainedelacreuse.com
Charming B&B in an old farm with a courtyard. Ideal for sunny evenings.

PEIGNEY: Auberge des Voiliers €
Family
1 chemin du bord de Lac de la Liez, 52200
Tel *03 25 87 05 74*
W hotel-voiliers.com
Good value hotel-restaurant alongside Lac de la Liez.

REIMS: Hôtel de la Paix €€
City center
9 rue de Buirette, 51100
Tel *03 26 40 04 08*
W bestwestern-lapaix-reims.com
Contemporary buildings with medieval ruins and an elegant central courtyard.

REIMS: Château Les Crayères €€€
Luxury
64 bd Henry Vasnier, 51100
Tel *03 26 40 04 08*
W lescrayeres.com
Splendid luxury château in lovely grounds with a wooded park. Excellent on-site restaurant.

ROCROI: Le Saint-Michel €
Value for money
5 pl d'Armes, 08320
W voltolini.fr
Neat, inexpensive rooms in a unique star-shaped fortress rebuilt by Vauban in 1675.

SEDAN: Le Château Fort €€
Value for money
Port des Princes, 08200
Tel *03 24 26 11 00*
W hotelfp-sedan.com
Exceptional hotel in Europe's largest fortress. Some rooms have wheelchair access.

TROYES: Champs des Oiseaux €€
City center
20 rue Linard Gonthier, 10000
Tel *03 25 80 58 50*
W champdesoiseaux.com
Stunningly restored 15th- and 16th-century half-timbered houses. Delightful planted courtyards.

For more information on types of hotels *see pp552–3*

Elegant bedroom at Le Bouclier d'Or in Strasbourg

VIENNE-LE-CHATEAU: Le Tulipier €
Family
rue Saint-Jacques, 51800
Tel *03 26 60 69 90*
W letulipier.com
Modern hotel deep in the forests of the Argonne. Heated indoor pool and a well-stocked bar. Free bicycles.

VILLIERS SUR MARNE: La Source Bleue €
Value for money
La Papeterie, 52320 Gudmont
Tel *03 25 94 70 35*
W hotelsourcebleue.com
Smartly designed rooms and suites, some with balconies, at this old mill in the country.

VINAY: Hostellerie La Briqueterie €€
Luxury
4 rte de Sézanne, 51530
Tel *03 26 59 99 99*
W labriqueterie.fr
Spacious rooms and an excellent gourmet restaurant set in champagne vineyards.

Alsace & Lorraine

AMNEVILLE: Diane €
Family
rue de la source, 57360
Tel *03 87 70 10 40*
W acceuil-amneville.com
Smart and elegant rooms close to the town's famous leisure park.

COLMAR: Hôtel St-Martin €
Value for money
38 grand' rue, 68000
Tel *03 89 24 11 51*
W hotel-saint-martin.com
Gracefully decorated rooms in four 14th–17th-century houses.

COLMAR: Hostellerie Le Marechal €€
City center
4–6 pl des Six Montagnes Noires, Petite Venise, 68000
Tel *03 89 41 60 32*
W le-marechal.com
This museum-like hotel is located right in the heart of Petite Venise.

DIEVE: Hostellerie du Château des Monthairons €€
Family
26 rte de Verdun, Les Monthairons, 55320
Tel *03 29 87 78 55*
W chateaudesmonthairons.com
Palatial château with two chapels, extensive grounds, and a private beach on the Meuse.

DRACHENBRONN: Auberge du Moulin des 7 Fontaines €
Family
1 sept Fontaines, 67160
Tel *03 88 94 50 90*
W auberge7fontaines.com
Set in a working farm, this 18th-century house has simple rooms and great food.

KAYSERSBERG: Hôtel Constantin €
Value for money
10 rue Père Kohlman, 68240
Tel *03 89 47 19 90*
W hotel-constantin.com
This old winemaker's house is now a pleasant, quiet hotel.

LAPOUTROIE: Les Alisiers €€
Rooms with views
5 rue du Faudé, 68650
Tel *03 89 47 52 82*
W alisiers.com
Farmhouse hotel with great rooms, and a terrace with scenic views.

METZ: La Cathédrale €
Value for money
25 pl de Chambre, 57000
Tel *03 87 75 00 02*
W hotelcathedrale-metz.fr
Elegant 400-year-old building in the historic center. Riverside terrace.

MULHOUSE: Hôtel du Parc €€
City center
26 rue de la Sinne, 68100
Tel *03 89 66 12 22*
W hotelduparc-mulhouse.com
Comfortable rooms furnished in an Art Deco style. Piano bar.

NANCY: Grand Hôtel de la Reine €€
Luxury
2 pl Stanislas, 54000
Tel *03 83 35 03 01*
W hoteldelareine.com
Delicately furbished Classical building in one of Europe's finest 18th-century squares.

OBERNAI: Hôtel du Parc €€
Family
169 rte de Otrott, 67210
Tel *03 88 95 50 08*
W hotel-du-parc.com
A historic Alsatian exterior contrasts with modern interiors at this hotel. Excellent facilities.

RIQUEWIHR: L'Oriel €
City center
3 rue Ecuries Seigneuriales, 68340
Tel *03 89 86 03 00*
W hotel-oriel.com
Half-timbered facade and vibrant interiors in a picture-postcard village. Lovely courtyard.

SELESTAT: Hôtel Illwald €
Value for money
Le Schnellenbuhl, 67600
Tel *03 90 56 11 40*
W illwald.fr
Set on the edge of the Illwald forest, this auberge has an attractive mix of traditional and contemporary style.

STRASBOURG: Le Chut €
Value for money
4 rue du Bain aux Plantes, 67000
Tel *03 88 32 05 06*
W hote-strasbourg.fr
Situated in the center of old Strasbourg, this hotel has sleek modern rooms. Great restaurant.

DK Choice

STRASBOURG: Le Bouclier d'Or €€€
Luxury
1 rue du Bouclier, 67000
Tel *03 88 13 73 55*
W hotel-le-bouclier-d-or-strasbourg.fr
Four-star boutique hotel comprising of three elaborately restored Renaissance buildings in the heart of the Petite France district. Le Bouclier d'Or is beautifully furnished with authentic Alsatian antiques. Well-appointed rooms, fully equipped spa with a Turkish bath and sauna, and a wine bar and tea bar.

Normandy

AGNEAUX: Château d'Agneaux €€
Value for money
av Ste-Marie, 50180
Tel *02 33 57 65 88*
W chateau-agneaux.com
A 13th-century hotel with period furniture, parquet floors, and wood paneling.

Key to Price Guide *see p554*

DK Choice

BAGNOLES DE L'ORME: Le Manoir de Lys €€
Family
rte de Juvigny, 61140
Tel *02 33 37 80 69*
manoir-du-lys.fr
A charming family hotel surrounded by a lush deer-filled forest, and offering cozy, up-to-date rooms. Seven family suites, called "The Wood Pavilions," are dotted along the forest's edge – ideal for those seeking solitude. Lots of fun activities on offer for guests.

BAYEAUX: Hôtel Bellefontaine €€
Family
49 rue de Bellefontaine, 14400
Tel *02 31 22 00 10*
hotel-bellefontaine.com
An 18th-century château with huge rooms. Near the city center.

CABOURG: Le Cottage €
Value for money
24 av Général Leclerc, 14390
Tel *02 31 91 65 61*
hotel-cottage-cabourg.com
Smartly decorated rooms in this pretty hotel situated only a few minutes from the beach.

CAEN: Best Western Le Dauphin €€
City center
29 rue Gémare, 14000
Tel *02 31 86 22 26*
le-dauphin-normandie.com
Tastefully renovated 15th-century priory with comfortable rooms.

CAMBREMER: Château les Bruyères €€
Luxury
rte du Cadran, 14340
Tel *02 31 32 22 45*
chateaulesbruyeres.com
Beautiful First Empire château with romantically decorated rooms, some with four-poster beds.

CHERBOURG: Le Louvre €
City center
2 rue Henri Dunant, 50100
Tel *02 33 53 02 28*
hotel-le-louvre-cherbourg.com
No-frills city-center hotel with neat, bright, and modern rooms. Good breakfast buffet.

CREPON: La Ferme de la Rançonnière €
Value for money
rte d'Arromanches, 14480
Tel *02 31 22 21 73*
raconniere.fr
A 13th-century farmhouse with arched gateways and large rooms.

DEAUVILLE: Hôtel Normandy Barrière €€€
Luxury
38 rue J Mermoz, 14800
Tel *02 31 98 66 22*
lucienbarriere.com
This Anglo-Normandy manor house has lavishly decorated rooms with 1920s charm.

DIEPPE: Hôtel La Présidence €€
Rooms with views
1 bvd de Verdun, 76200
Tel *02 35 84 31 31*
hotel-la-presidence.com
Behind the drab exterior, this hotel has smart, modern rooms, some with sea views.

DOUAINS-PACY-SUR-EURE: L'Etape de la Vallée €
Value for money
1 rue Edouard Isambard, 27120
Tel *02 32 36 12 77*
etapedelavallee.com
A lovely villa with cozy rooms, set on the banks of the Eure river, and surrounded by lush greenery.

ETRETAT: Domaine St-Clair €€
Rooms with views
chemin de St-Clair, 76790
Tel *02 35 27 08 23*
hoteletretat.com
A 19th-century Anglo-Norman château with panoramic views of the village and the cliffs of Etretat.

FECAMP: Le Grand Pavois €€
Rooms with views
15 quai Vicomté, 76400
Tel *02 35 10 01 01*
hotel-grand-pavois.com
Quay-side hotel with an attractive marine-themed decor and bright, modern rooms, some with balconies overlooking the port.

Open courtyard leading up to the stately Hôtel Normandy Barrière in Deauville

GRANVILLE: Hôtel Inn Design €
Family
57 av des Matignon, 50400
Tel *02 33 50 05 05*
hotel-inn.fr
Modern chain hotel with rooms for groups of three or four.

HONFLEUR: La Ferme Siméon €€€
Luxury
rue Adolphe Marais, 14600
Tel *02 31 81 78 00*
fermesaintsimeon.fr
Sumptuous rooms at this 19th-century farmhouse mansion, once the haunt of Impressionist artists.

MACE: Hôtel Ile de Sées €
Value for money
Vandel, 61500
Tel *02 33 27 98 65*
ile-sees.fr
An ivy-clad converted dairy with pleasant and comfy rooms. Good restaurant. Fine service.

MESNIL-VAL: Hostellerie de la Vieille Ferme €
Value for money
23 rue de la Mer, 76910
Tel *02 35 86 72 18*
vielle-ferme.net
An 18th-century farmhouse with a lovely garden. Close to the beach.

MONT-ST-MICHEL: Terrasses Poulard €€
Rooms with views
BP 18, 50170
Tel *02 33 89 02 02*
terrasses-poulard.fr
Located in the heart of Mont-St-Michel, with stunning views of the bay and the abbey.

OUISTREHAM: Hôtel de la Plage €
Value for money
39–41 av Pasteur, 14150
Tel *02 31 96 85 16*
hotel-ouistreham.com
A family hotel near the beach, with large and pleasant rooms.

PONT AUDEMER: Belle Ile sur Risle €€
Luxury
112 rte de Rouen, 27500
Tel *02 32 56 96 22*
bellile.com
Elegant hotel on its own island. Superb cuisine served in the 19th-century rotunda.

PONT DE L'ARCHE: Hôtel de la Tour €
Value for money
41 quai Foch, 27340
Tel *02 35 23 00 99*
hoteldelatour.org
Stunning 18th-century Norman architecture and spacious rooms.

For more information on types of hotels *see pp552–3*

ROUEN:
Inter Hôtel Notre Dame €
City center
4 rue de la Savonnerie, 76000
Tel *02 35 71 87 73*
W hotelnotredame.com
Centrally located hotel with guest rooms decorated in a chic contemporary style.

ROUEN:
Hôtel de Bourgtheroulde €€€
Luxury
15 pl de la Pucelle d'Orléans, 76000
Tel *02 35 14 50 50*
W hotelsparouen.com
The ornate Renaissance facade belies all the modern comforts of this boutique hotel. Great spa.

ST-PATERNE:
Château de St-Paterne €€
Luxury
Le Château, 72610
Tel *02 33 27 54 71*
W chateau-saintpaterne.com
Henry IV's 15th-century love nest offers magnificent, stately rooms and dinner by candlelight.

ST-VAAST:
Hôtel de France et Fuchsias €
Value for money
20 rue de Maréchal Foch, 50550
Tel *02 33 54 40 41*
W france-fuchsias.com
A country-house hotel with warm, snug rooms, most overlooking the garden.

Brittany

BENODET:
Domaine de Kereven €
Value for money
Bénodet, 29950
Tel *02 98 57 02 46*
W kereven.fr
Beautifully decorated rooms overlooking the expansive grounds of an 18th-century farm.

BREST: Astoria €
City center
9 rue Traverse, 29200
Tel *02 98 80 19 10*
W astoria-brest-hotel.com
Retro-style hotel very close to the train station. Great buffet breakfast. Free Wi-Fi.

CARNAC: Hôtel Tumulus €€
Rooms with views
rte du Tumulus, 56340
Tel *02 97 52 08 21*
W hotel-tumulus.com
A 1920s villa with elegant, spacious rooms, some with private terraces. Fine views of Quiberon Bay. There is a lovely spa and pool.

DINAN: L'Avaugour €€
Family
1 pl du Champ Clos, 22100
Tel *02 96 39 07 49*
W avaugourhotel.com
Family-run hotel in a traditional granite building near the ramparts.

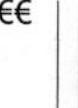

DINARD:
Villa Reine Hortense €€
Rooms with views
19 rue Malouine, 35800
Tel *02 99 46 54 31*
W villa-reine-hortense.com
Relive the splendor of the Belle Epoque at this clifftop hotel.

DOL DE BRETAGNE:
Domaine des Ormes €€
Family
35120
Tel *02 99 73 53 00*
W lesormes.com
Charming guest rooms; part of a holiday resort with a golf course, riding school, and aquapark.

FOUESNANT:
Hôtel l'Orée du Bois €
Value for money
4 rue Kergoadig, 29170
Tel *02 98 56 00 06*
W hotel-oreedubois.com
Simply furnished guest rooms, some with sea views. Lovely outdoor terrace.

ILE DE GROIX:
Hôtel de la Marine €
Value for money
7 rue du Général de Gaulle, 56590
Tel *02 97 86 80 05*
W hoteldelamarine.com
A lovely hotel tucked away on the beautiful island of Groix. Rooms offer sea or garden views.

LANDEDA:
Hôtel La Baie des Anges €€
Family
350 rte des Anges, 29870
Tel *02 98 04 90 04*
W baie-des-anges.com
Seafront mansion with smart rooms and babysitting facilities.

LOCQUIREC:
Le Grand Hôtel des Bains €€€
Luxury
15 rue de l'Eglise, 29241
Tel *02 98 67 41 02*
W grand-hotel-des-bains.com
A Belle Epoque hotel with direct access to the beach. Stylish rooms, most with balconies.

MORLAIX: Hôtel de l'Europe €
City center
1 rue d'Aiguillon, 29600
Tel *02 98 62 11 99*
W hotel-europe-com.fr
Second Empire hotel with pleasant rooms and elegant decor.

Neat, well-kept room at the Manoir du Vaumadeuc, Pleven

PLEVEN:
Manoir du Vaumadeuc €€
Luxury
Le Vaumadeuc, 22130
Tel *02 96 84 46 17*
W vaumadeuc.com
Authentic 15th-cenutry granite manor house with a pretty Renaissance garden and lake.

PLOUBAZLANEC:
Les Agapanthes €€
Rooms with views
1 rue Adrien Rebours, 22620
Tel *02 96 55 89 06*
W hotel-les-agapanthes.com
Beautifully decorated rooms, most with a view of Paimpol Bay.

QUIBERON: Ker Noyal €
Value for money
43 chemin des Dunes, 56170
Tel *02 97 50 33 31*
W ker-noyal.com
Spacious, bright, and modern rooms in a typical seaside hotel on a quiet street near the casino.

QUIMPER: Hôtel Gradlon €€
City center
30 rue de Brest, 29000
Tel *02 98 95 04 39*
W hotel-gradlon.com
Charming, peaceful rooms, some overlooking the hotel's enclosed flower garden and fountain.

RENNES: Coq Gadby €€€
Luxury
156 rue d'Antrain, 35700
Tel *02 99 38 05 55*
W lecoq-gadby.fr
Eco-friendly hotel offering both traditional and contemporary rooms. Great on-site restaurant.

ROSCOFF: La Résidence €
Family
14 rue des Johnnies, 29680
Tel *02 98 69 74 85*
W hotelroscoff-laresidence.fr
Situated close to the port, this hotel is smartly decorated and has a great family room.

Key to Price Guide *see p554*

ST-MALO: La Maison Armateurs €€
City center
6 Grand rue, 35400
Tel *02 99 40 87 70*
W maisondesarmateurs.com
This former shipowners house in the old town is now a chic hotel with bright and modern rooms.

DK Choice

TREBOUL: Ty Mad €€
Rooms with views
Plage St-Jean, 29100
Tel *02 98 74 00 53*
W hoteltymad.com
Frequented in the 1920s by local artists such as Max Jacob, this eco-friendly hotel has 15 individually decorated rooms with sea or garden views. Sauna and spa facilities available.

VANNES: Villa Kerasy €€
City center
20 av Favrel et Lincy, 56000
Tel *02 97 68 36 83*
W villakerasy.com
Charming hotel with decor inspired by the French East India Company and the Spice Route.

The Loire Valley

AMBOISE: Le Choiseul €€
Rooms with views
36 quai Charles-Guinot, 37400
Tel *02 47 30 45 45*
W grandesetapes.fr
18th-century ivy-clad manor house set in flower-filled grounds.

ANGERS: Hôtel Mail €
City center
8 rue des Ursules, 49100
Tel *02 41 25 05 25*
W hotel-du-mail.com
Charming family-run hotel in a 17th-century building that was once part of a convent.

AZAY LE RIDEAU: Manoir de la Rémonière €€
Value for money
La Chapelle Ste-Blaise, 37190
Tel *02 47 45 24 88*
W manoirdelaremoniere.com
Built on the site of a Roman villa, and close to the River Indre. Stately rooms with an old-world feel.

BEAUGENCY: Hôtel de la Sologne €
Value for money
6 pl St-Firmin, 45190
Tel *02 38 44 50 27*
W hoteldelasologne.com
Bright rooms overlooking the ruined castle keep of St-Firmin.

BOURGES: Le Bourbon €€
City center
Bd République, 18000
Tel *02 48 70 70 00*
W hoteldebourbon.fr
Elegant, spacious rooms in this renovated 17th-century abbey. Excellent restaurant.

CHAMPIGNE: Château des Briottières €€
Luxury
rte Marigné, 49330
Tel *02 41 42 00 02*
W briottieres.com
This family-run 18th-century château has stately rooms with luxurious furnishings.

CHARTRES: Le Grand Monarque €€
Family
22 pl des Epars, 28005
Tel *02 37 18 15 15*
W bw-grand-monarque.com
A converted 16th-century staging post with modern rooms. Has a bistro and a fine dining restaurant.

CHENEHUTTE LES TRUFFEAUX: Le Prieuré €€
Rooms with views
Le Prieuré, 49350
Tel *02 41 67 90 14*
W grandesetapes.fr
Former priory with magnificent views over the Loire. Romantic rooms and great service.

CHENONCEAUX: Hôtel du Bon Laboureur €€
Luxury
6 rue de Dr Bretonneau, 37150
Tel *02 47 23 90 02*
W bonlaboureur.com
A picturesque 18th-century inn with lovely gardens. Very close to the Château de Chenonceau.

CHINON: Hôtel Diderot €
Value for money
4 rue Buffon, 37500
Tel *02 47 93 18 87*
W hoteldiderot.com
Elegant hotel on a quiet street near Chinon city center.

CHINON: Château de Marçay €€
Luxury
Le Château, 37500
Tel *02 47 93 03 47*
W chateaudemarcay.com
Sumptuous rooms in a restored 15th-century fortified château.

LA CHARTRE SUR LOIR: Hôtel de France €
Value for money
20 pl de la République, 72340
Tel *02 43 44 40 16*
W hoteldefrance-72.fr
Modestly furnished, comfortable rooms and a pretty garden terrace.

LE CROISIC: Fort de l'Océan €€
Rooms with views
Pointe du Croisic, 44490
Tel *02 40 15 77 77*
W hotelfortocean.com
Stylish and comfortable rooms in a former fortress facing the sea.

LE MANS: Le Charleston €
City center
18 rue Gastelier, 72000
Tel *02 43 24 87 46*
W lecharlestonhotel.com
Attractive rooms at this pleasant and friendly hotel. Small patio for breakfast in good weather.

LOCHES: Hôtel de France €
Value for money
6 rue Picois, 37600
Tel *02 47 59 00 32*
W hoteldefranceloches.com
Modest and comfortable rooms at this former staging post. Good regional food.

LOUE: Hôtel Ricordeau €
Family
13 rue de la Libération, 72540
Tel *02 43 88 40 03*
W hotel-ricordeau.fr
Former coaching inn with individually decorated rooms, some overlooking the garden.

MONTLOUIS SUR LOIRE: Château de la Bourdaisière €€
Luxury
25 rue de la Bourdaisière, 37270
Tel *02 47 45 16 31*
W labourdaisiere.com
A luxury hotel in a magnificent château. Some guest rooms have period furniture.

MUIDES SUR LOIRE: Château de Colliers €€
Rooms with views
rte Départementale 951, 41500
Tel *02 54 87 50 75*
W chateau-colliers.com
Rustic but grand château. Some delightfully romantic rooms.

For more information on types of hotels *see pp552–3*

NANTES: Amiral €
City center
26 bis rue Scribe, 44000
Tel *02 40 69 20 21*
W hotel-nantes.fr
Comfortable and modern rooms with good soundproofing. Excellent location.

NANTES: Hôtel La Pérouse €
Boutique
3 allée Duquesne, 44000
Tel *02 40 89 75 00*
W hotel-laperouse.fr
Chic hotel named after a French navigator. Rooms with designer furniture. Fine service.

NOIRMOITIER EN L'ILE: Hôtel Fleur de Sel €€
Family
rue des Saulniers, 85330
Tel *02 51 39 09 07*
W fleurdesel.fr
Charming hotel with a vast garden and a pool. Some guest rooms have a private terrace.

DK Choice

ONZAIN: Domaine des Hauts de Loire €€€
Luxury
rte d'Herbault, 41150
Tel *02 54 20 72 57*
W domainehautsloire.com
This turreted, ivy-clad hunting lodge with large grounds retains its grandeur with lavishly furnished interiors. Rooms in the old coach-house are the most opulent. The chef prepares cutting-edge food, served with superb local wines.

ORLEANS: Hôtel de l'Abeille €
City center
64 rue Alsace Lorraine, 45000
Tel *02 38 53 54 87*
W hoteldelabeille.com
Grand Neo-Classical building with well-decorated, old-style rooms. Rooftop terrace.

ROMORANTIN-LANTHENAY: Grand Hôtel du Lion d'Or €€
Luxury
69 rue Georges Clémenceau, 41200
Tel *02 54 94 15 15*
W hotel-liondor.fr
Renaissance mansion house with authentic Empire-style decor and well-furnished rooms.

SAUMUR: Hôtel Anne d'Anjou €€
Rooms with views
32–34 quai Mayaud, 49400
Tel *02 41 67 30 30*
W hotel-anneanjou.com
Elegant building on the banks of the Loire river with plush rooms.

SILLE-LE-GUILLAUME: Relais des Etangs de Guibert €
Value for money
Neufchâtel-en-Saosnois, 72600
Tel *02 43 97 15 38*
W lesetangsdeguibert.com
Overlooking a lake, this rustic farmhouse is in a romantic setting deep in the forest.

ST-MARC-SUR-MER: Hôtel de la Plage €€
Rooms with views
Plage de M. Hulot, 44600
Tel *02 40 91 99 01*
W hotel-delaplage.fr
Lovely seaside hotel that featured in the film *Les Vacances de Monsieur Hublot*. Modern rooms.

TOURS: Hôtel l'Adresse €
City center
12 rue de la Rôtisserie, 37000
Tel *02 47 20 85 76*
W hotel-ladresse.com
A modern hotel set within a beautiful 18th-century town house.

Burgundy & Franche-Comté

ARC-ET-SENANS: La Saline Royale €
Family
Arc-et-Senans, 25610
Tel *03 81 54 45 17*
W salineroyale.com
A World Heritage site that combines high-class dormitory accommodations with Louis XVI magnificence. Good service.

AUXERRE: Le Parc des Maréchaux €€
City Center
6 av Foch, 89000
Tel *03 86 51 43 77*
W hotel-parcmarechaux.com
Centrally located Napoleon III building with Empire-style rooms.

Extensive gardens and inviting pool at Hôtel Fleur de Sel, Noirmoitier en L'Ile

BEAUNE: Hôtel Grillon €€
Value for money
21 rte de Seurre, 21200
Tel *03 80 22 44 25*
W hotel-grillon.fr
Charming hotel set in a walled garden. Rooms in the extension are more spacious.

BEAUNE: Hôtel Le Cep €€€
Romantic
27 rue Maufoux, 21200
Tel *03 80 22 35 48*
W hotel-cep-beaune.com
Elegant hotel in the old town. Rooms are named after local wines and furnished with antiques.

BESANCON: Hôtel Charles Quint €€
City center
3 rue du Chapitre, 25000
Tel *03 81 82 05 49*
W hotel-charlesquint.com
Stylish 18th-century hotel in the historic city center. Immaculate service.

CHABLIS: Hostellerie des Clos €€€
Luxury
rue Jules-Rathier, 89800
Tel *03 86 42 10 63*
W hostellerie-des-clos.fr
Delightful rooms and top-notch Michelin dining in this restored medieval convent.

DK Choice

CHAGNY: Lameloise €€€
Luxury
36 pl d'Armes, 71150
Tel *03 85 87 65 65*
W lameloise.fr
Elegant Burgundian house, almost a century old, with classic decor that includes oak-beamed ceilings and period furniture. Large rooms and impeccable bathrooms. Lameloise is also home to one of Burgundy's best restaurants.

DIJON: Le Jacquemart €
Value for money
32 rue Verrerie, 21000
Tel *03 80 60 09 60*
W hotel-lejacquemart.fr
A rambling 17th-century building with rooms in all shapes and sizes.

DIJON: Hostellerie du Chapeau Rouge €€€
Romantic
5 rue Michelet, 21000
Tel *03 80 50 88 88*
W chapeau-rouge.fr
Smart 16th-century hotel offering slick contemporary rooms in the heart of the city. Impressive glass-domed dining room.

Key to Price Guide *see p554*

Beautifully decorated exteriors of Le Relais Bernard Loiseau, Saulieu

DOLE: La Chaumière €€
Family
346 av du Maréchal-Juin, 39100
Tel *03 84 70 72 40*
W lachaumiere-dole.fr
An ancient farmhouse with a chic ambience. Run by one of the region's top chefs.

JOIGNY: La Côte St-Jacques €€€
Luxury
14 faubourg de Paris, 89300
Tel *03 86 62 09 70*
W cotesaintjacques.com
Classy hotel overlooking the Yonne river, with a delightful garden leading to the water's edge.

LEVERNOIS: Hostellerie de Levernois €€€
Romantic
rue du Golf, 21200
Tel *03 80 24 73 58*
W levernois.com
A 17th-century manor-house hotel with a large park and gardens.

MALBUISSON: Le Bon Acceuil €
Value for money
rue de la Source, 25160
Tel *03 81 69 30 58*
W le-bon-accueil.fr
A friendly hotel with rooms done up in simple pine furniture and patterned fabrics. Good restaurant.

MARTAILLY-LES-BRANCION: La Montagne de Brancion €€
Rooms with views
Col de Brancion, 71700
Tel *03 85 51 12 40*
W brancion.fr
Modern hotel on a hillside overlooking vineyards and lush countryside. Impressive cuisine.

NANS-SOUS-STE-ANNE: A l'Ombre du Château €€
Romantic
6 rue du Château, 25330
Tel *03 81 86 54 72*
W frenchcountryretreat.com
Quaint house in vast wooded grounds, with charming rooms.

NEVERS: Clos Ste-Marie €
Value for money
25 rue du Petit-Mouësse, 58000
Tel *03 86 71 94 50*
W clos-sainte-marie.fr
Tranquil hotel with spacious rooms, antique furniture, and quaint decor.

NITRY: Auberge de la Beursaudière €
Value for money
5 & 7 rue Hyacinthe-Gautherin, 89310
Tel *03 86 33 69 70*
W beursaudiere.com
Attractive rooms within a 12th-century former priory. Breakfast is served in a wine cellar.

POLIGNY: Hostellerie des Monts de Vaux €€€
Luxury
Monts Vaux, 39800
Tel *03 84 37 12 50*
W hostellerie.com
Family-run hotel in a former coaching inn with elegant decor.

RULLY: Le Vendangerot €
Value for money
6 pl Sainte-Marie, 71150
Tel *03 85 87 20 09*
W vendangerot.fr
Welcoming hotel with neat and simple rooms, and a popular restaurant serving local delicacies.

SAULIEU: Le Relais Bernard Loiseau €€€
Luxury
2 rue d'Argentine, 21210
Tel *03 80 90 53 53*
W bernard-loiseau.com
Refined rooms and Michelin-starred dining at this upmarket hotel. Impeccable service.

VALLEE DE COUSIN: Hostellerie du Moulin des Ruats €€
Romantic
9 rue des Isles Labaumes, 89200
Tel *03 86 34 97 00*
W moulindesruats.com
Former flour mill transformed into a classic hotel-restaurant. Beautifully furnished rooms.

VONNAS: Georges Blanc €€€
Luxury
pl Marché, 01540
Tel *04 74 50 90 90*
W georgesblanc.com
Plush hotel-restaurant with a glitzy spa and sauna, and one of the region's top restaurants.

YONNE: Hôtel d'Avallon Vauban €
Value for money
53 rue de Paris, 89200
Tel *03 86 34 36 99*
W avallonvaubanhotel.com
Charming ivy-clad hotel. Simple rooms, some with garden views.

The Massif Central

BEAULIEU-SUR-DODOGNE: Manoir de Beaulieu €
Family
4 pl Champ de Mars, 19120
Tel *05 55 91 01 34*
W hotelmanoirdebeaulieu.com
A traditional hotel with nicely renovated rooms – some rustic, some modern.

BELCASTEL: Du Vieux Pont €€
Family
Le Bourg, 12390
Tel *05 65 64 52 29*
W hotelbelcastel.com
Modest hotel by the Aveyron river. The owners run a superb restaurant just across the bridge.

BENEVENT L'ABBAYE: Le Cèdre €
Value for money
rue de l'Oiseau, 23210
Tel *05 55 81 59 99*
W hotelducedre.fr
Contemporary rooms and a terrace shaded by a towering cedar at this classic hotel.

CHAMALIERES: Hôtel Radio €€
Rooms with views
43 av Pierre et Marie Curie, 63400
Tel *04 73 30 87 83*
W hotel-radio.fr
Fans of Art Deco will love the original mosaics, mirrors, and fancy ironwork in this 1930s gem.

CONQUES: Hôtel Ste-Foy €€
Romantic
Le Bourg, 12320
Tel *05 65 69 84 03*
W hotelsaintefoy.fr
A 17th-century Aveyron inn with stone walls, low-beamed ceilings, and modern amenities.

LIMOGES: Hôtel Jeanne d'Arc €€
City center
17 av du Général-de-Gaulle, 87000
Tel *05 55 77 67 77*
W hoteljeannedarc-limoges.fr
Tastefully renovated hotel with stylish, well-equipped rooms.

MENDE: Hôtel de France €€
Family
9 bd Lucien-Arnault, 48000
Tel *04 66 65 00 04*
W hoteldefrance-mende.com
Renovated 1856 staging post with comfortable, chic rooms and a fantastic terrace.

MILLAU: Château de Creissels €€
Romantic
rte de St-Afrique, 12100
Tel *05 65 60 16 59*
W chateau-de-creissels.com
Atmospheric 12th-century château with fine views of the Tarn valley.

For more information on types of hotels *see pp552–3*

Neat, simply furnished room at Château d'Ygrande, Ygrande

MONTSALVY: Auberge Fleurie €
Value for money
pl du Barry, 15120
Tel *04 71 49 20 02*
W auberge-fleurie.com
A village inn full of rustic charm and covered in pretty climbing plants. Beautiful rooms.

MOUDEYRES: Le Pré Bossu €€
Value for money
rd– D361, 43150
Tel *04 71 05 10 70*
W auberge-pre-bossu.com
Thatched Auvergne cottage with bedrooms named after birds. All the modern comforts.

PEYRELEAU: Grand Hôtel de la Muse et du Rozier €€
Rooms with views
rue des Gorges du Tarn, 12720
Tel *05 65 62 60 01*
W hotel-delamuse.fr
Historic country inn in an idyllic wooded setting overlooking the Tarn river.

PONTIGIBAUD: Hôtel Saluces €
Family
rue de la Martille, 15140
Tel *04 71 40 70 82*
W hotel-salers.fr
Spacious, stylish rooms with wooden flooring in a gorgeous family-run 16th-century mansion.

RODEZ: La Ferme de Bourran €€
Rooms with views
Quartier de Bourran, 12000
Tel *05 65 73 62 62*
W fermedebourran.com
Renovated farmhouse on a secluded hillock with airy rooms.

SALERS: Le Bailliage €
Value for money
rue Notre-Dame, 15410
Tel *04 71 40 71 95*
W salers-hotel-bailliage.com
Simple, well-kept rooms in a grand old house with a delightful garden. Some rooms have mountain views.

ST-ALBAN-SUR-LIMAGNOLE: Relais St-Roch €€€
Luxury
Château de la Chastre, chemin du Carreirou, 48120
Tel *04 66 31 55 48*
W relais-saint-roch.fr
An 18th-century mansion with elegant rooms and classy decor. There is a well-stocked lounge bar with over 300 whiskies.

DK Choice

ST-ARCONS-D'ALLIER: Les Deux Abbesses €€€
Romantic
Le Château, 43300
Tel *04 71 74 03 08*
W lesdeuxabbesses.com
A tiny hamlet has been restored to form this outstanding hotel. Four cottages house the rooms, cobbled streets serve as corridors, and the château houses the reception and dining room. All the rooms have an air of romance about them and the bathrooms are simply stunning.

ST-BONNET-LE-FROID: Le Clos des Cimes €€€
Luxury
Le Bourg, 43290
Tel *04 71 59 93 72*
W regismarcon.fr
Luxurious rooms, original works of art, and wonderful valley views at this fabulous country auberge for gourmands.

ST-GERVAIS D'AUVERGNE: Castel-Hôtel 1904 €
Value for money
rue de Castel, 63390
Tel *04 73 85 70 42*
W castel-hotel-1904.com
A turreted château with oak beams, classy wooden floors, and period furniture.

ST-MARTIN-VALMEROUX: Hostellerie de la Maronne €€
Romantic
Le Theil, 15140
Tel *04 71 69 20 33*
W maronne.com
Tastefully renovated 19th-century manor house with well-decorated rooms. Great restaurant.

VICHY: Aletti Palace Hôtel €€
City center
3 pl Joseph-Aletti, 03200
Tel *04 70 30 20 20*
W hotel-aletti.fr
This hotel oozes Belle Epoque grandeur, from its stately reception hall to the crystal chandeliers. Fine restaurant and a terraced pool. Good service.

YGRANDE: Château d'Ygrande €€€
Luxury
Le Mont, 03160
Tel *04 70 66 33 11*
W chateauygrande.fr
Meticulously renovated 19th-century château in vast grounds. Bright and elegant rooms.

The Rhône Valley & French Alps

ANNECY: Hôtel Palais de l'Isle €€
City center
13 rue Perrière, 74000
Tel *04 50 45 86 87*
W hoteldupalaisdelisle.com
Renovated 18th-century house on the Thouin canal. Comfortable rooms and modern decor.

BRIANCON: Hôtel Cristol €
Value for money
6 rte d'Italie, 05100
Tel *04 92 20 20 11*
W hotel-cristol-briancon.fr
Unpretentious hotel with modern, bright, and airy rooms. Family-friendly service.

CHAMBERY: Hôtel des Princes €€
City center
4 rue de Boigne, 73000
Tel *04 79 33 45 36*
W hoteldesprinces.eu
Quiet and comfortable rooms at this lovely hotel near the Fontaine des Eléphants.

CHAMONIX MONT BLANC: Le Hameau Albert 1er €€€
Luxury
119 impasse du Montenvers, 74402
Tel *04 50 53 05 09*
W hameaualbert.fr
Chic hotel complex with various accommodation options. Stunning views of Mont Blanc.

CHANTERMERLE-LES-GRIGNAN: Le Parfum Bleu €€
Value for money
615B rte de Valaurie, 26230
Tel *04 75 98 54 21*
W parfum-bleu.com
Take in the sound of cicadas and the smell of lavender at this stylish, restored farmhouse.

CLIOUSCLAT: La Treille Muscate €
Value for money
Le Village, 26270
Tel *04 75 63 13 10*
W latreillemuscate.com
A pleasant inn with tasteful, individually decorated rooms and a vaulted dining room serving local cuisine.

Key to Price Guide *see p554*

CORDON: Le Cordonant €€
Family
Les Darbaillets, 74700
Tel *04 50 58 34 56*
W lecordonant.fr
Smart chalet with pleasant rooms and pretty, rustic furniture. Alpine fare at the restaurant.

DIVONNE-LES-BAINS: Château de Divonne €€€
Luxury
115 rue des Bains, 01220
Tel *04 50 20 00 32*
W chateau-divonne.com
Charming 19th-century mansion with sumptuous rooms and views of Mont Blanc and Lake Geneva.

GRENOBLE: Splendid Hôtel €
Value for money
22 rue Thiers, 38000
Tel *04 76 46 33 12*
W splendid-hotel.com
Centrally located hotel in a quiet location with a walled garden.

LE POET-LAVAL: Les Hospitaliers €€
Romantic
Vieux Village, 26160
Tel *04 75 46 22 32*
W hotel-les-hospitaliers.com
Classy hotel with spacious rooms in a dreamy hilltop medieval hamlet. Top-notch restaurant.

LYON: Hôtel des Artistes €€
City center
8 rue Gaspard-André, 69002
Tel *04 78 42 04 88*
W hotel-des-artistes.fr
This cozy hotel with bright rooms is a popular haunt of actors from the famous theater opposite.

LYON: Cour des Loges €€€
Luxury
6 rue du Boeuf, 69005
Tel *04 72 77 44 44*
W courdesloges.com
Elegant rooms that blend Renaissance-period features and contemporary decor.

MANIGOD: Hôtel-Chalets de la Croix-Fry €€€
Luxury
rte du Col de la Croix-Fry, 74230
Tel *04 50 44 90 16*
W hotelchaletcroixfry.com
Alpine rustic-chic meets sybaritic comfort at this classy chalet-style hotel. Great log-cabin style rooms.

MEGÈVE: Les Fermes de Marie €€€
Luxury
163 chemin de Riante Colline, 74120
Tel *04 50 93 03 10*
W fermesdemarie.com
Chic Savoyard country-style chalets with an air of relaxed sophistication.

MONTELIMAR: Le Sphinx €
Value for money
19 bd Desmarais, 26200
Tel *04 75 01 86 64*
W sphinx-hotel.fr
Old-school charm greets visitors to this 17th-century townhouse mansion. Delightful terrace.

DK Choice

PEROUGES: Hostellerie du Vieux Pérouges €€
Romantic
pl du Tilleuil, 01800
Tel *04 74 61 00 88*
W hostelleriedeperouges.com
Set in a medieval hilltop village, this historic inn has rooms in four 13th-century timbered houses clustered around the cobbled square – the decor is different in each house. The on-site restaurant serves authentic traditional dishes with flair. A truly unique place.

ROMANS-SUR-ISERE: Hôtel l'Orée du Parc €€
Family
6 av Gambetta, 26100
Tel *04 75 70 26 12*
W hotel-oreeparc.com
An elegant bolthole, perfect for exploring the Drôme region. Impeccably maintained rooms.

SERVAS: Le Nid à Bibi €€
Value for money
Lalleyriat, 01960
Tel *04 74 21 11 47*
W lenidabibi.com
Comfortable and well-equipped rooms at this adorable B&B. Hearty breakfast.

ST-CYR-AU-MONTD'OR: L'Ermitage Hôtel €€
Rooms with views
chemin de l'Ermitage Mont Cindre, 69450
Tel *04 72 19 69 69*
W ermitage-college-hotel.com
Hotel with sleek, luminous, ultra-modern rooms.

Outdoor seating area at the L'Ermitage Hôtel, St-Cyr-au-Montd'Or

TALLOIRES: Hôtel l'Abbaye €€€
Luxury
chemin des Moines, 74290
Tel *04 50 60 77 33*
W abbaye-talloires.com
Wonderful rooms in this 17th-century Benedictine abbey on the shores of Lake Annecy. Cézanne was a fan.

VAL D'ISERE: Christiania €€€
Rooms with views
Chef Lieu, 73152
Tel *04 79 06 08 25*
W hotel-christiania.com
Deluxe Alpine-style rooms with balconies at this modern chalet hotel. Magnificent views.

VALLON PONT D'ARC: Le Clos des Bruyères €€
Family
rte des Gorges, 07150
Tel *04 75 37 18 85*
W closdesbruyeres.net
Modern Provençal-style hotel with rooms that open onto the pool area via a balcony or terrace.

Poitou & Aquitaine

ARCACHON: Hôtel Le Dauphin €€
Family
7 av Gounod, 33120
Tel *05 56 83 02 89*
W dauphin-arcachon.com
Popular hotel a short walk from Arcachon's beaches. Bright rooms and a nice pool.

BORDEAUX: La Maison du Lierre €
Boutique
57 rue Huguerie, 33000
Tel *05 56 51 92 71*
W maisondulierre.com
Charming hotel in central Bordeaux set in a historic house with a pretty garden. Breakfast is served in a lovely inner courtyard.

BORDEAUX: Grand Hôtel de Bordeaux €€€
Luxury
2–5 pl de la Comédie, 33000
Tel *05 57 30 44 44*
W ghbordeaux.com
Magnificent hotel in a great location. Guests can sign up for special wine tours.

CAP-FERRET: La Maison du Bassin €€€
Romantic
5 rue des Pionniers, 33950
Tel *05 56 60 60 63*
W lamaisondubassin.com
Chic, romantic hotel with colonial-style rooms, a bar, a restaurant, and a garden.

For more information on types of hotels *see pp552–3*

COGNAC:
Les Pigeons Blancs €€
Family
110 rue Jules Brisson, 16100
Tel *05 45 82 16 36*
W pigeons-blancs.com
Charming hotel near the Cognac vineyards, with lovely gardens and a renowned restaurant.

COULON: Hôtel Le Central €
Value for money
4 rue d'Autremont, 79510
Tel *05 49 35 90 20*
W hotel-lecentral-coulon.com
Family-run hotel that combines boutique style with comfort. Good location and great food.

EUGENIE-LES-BAINS:
Les Prés d'Eugènie €€€
Luxury
pl de l'Impératrice, 40320
Tel *05 58 05 05 05*
W michelguerard.com
Luxury hotel-restaurant run by chef Michel Guerard. Fabulous spa.

HOSSEGOR:
Les Hortensias du Lac €€
Romantic
1578 av du Tour du Lac, 40150
Tel *05 58 43 42 81*
W hortensias-du-lac.com
Classy rooms in a sprawling villa near France's best surfing beaches.

ILE DE RE: Hôtel Le Sénéchal €€
Value for money
6 rue Gambetta, 17590 Ars-en-Ré
Tel *05 46 29 40 42*
W hotel-le-senechal.com
Laidback village hotel with distinctive rooms and a small pool.

LA ROCHELLE:
Hôtel Les Brises €€
Rooms with views
chemin de la Digue Richelieu, 17000
Tel *05 46 43 89 37*
W hotellesbrises.com
Popular hotel on the seafront, close to several beaches.

MAGESQ:
Relais de la Poste €€€
Luxury
24 av de Maremne, 40140
Tel *05 58 47 70 25*
W relaisposte.com
This peaceful hotel is set in gorgeous gardens with a pool. Spa services available.

MARGAUX:
Le Pavillon de Margaux €€
Romantic
3 rue Georges Mandel, 33460
Tel *05 57 88 77 54*
W pavillonmargaux.fr
Lovely château-style villa with rooms overlooking the famous vineyards. Great wine cellar.

MARTHON:
Château de la Couronne €€€
Luxury
Château de la Couronne, 16380
Tel *05 45 62 29 96*
W chateaudelacouronne.com
Extravagant hotel with five suites set in a 16th-century château. Superb pool and gardens.

PAUILLAC:
Château Cordeillan-Bages €€€
Luxury
rte des Châteaux, 33250
Tel *05 56 59 24 24*
W cordeillanbages.com
Magnificent 17th-century château set in the heart of Médoc vineyards with splendid gardens.

POITIERS: Les Cours du Clain €
Family
117 chemin de la Grotte à Calvin, 86000
Tel *06 10 16 09 55*
W lescoursduclain-poitiers.com
Beautiful, quiet B&B near central Poitiers, set in a historic house with garden and pool.

POITIERS: Château du Clos de la Ribaudière €€
Romantic
10 rue du Champ de Foire, 86360 Chasseneuil du Poitou
Tel *05 49 52 86 66*
W ribaudiere.com
Delightful hotel with elegantly modernized rooms and large gardens. Good service.

ROYAN:
Domaine de Saint-Palais €€
Value for money
50 rue du Logis, 17420 Saint-Palais-sur-Mer
Tel *05 46 39 85 26*
W domainedesaintpalais.eu
Charming former hunting lodge close to both wood and beach. Bright, elegant rooms.

Classy wooden beams and smart decor at the Château de la Couronne, Marthon

SEIGNOSSE:
Villa de l'Etang Blanc €€
Romantic
2265 route de l'Etang Blanc, 40510
Tel *05 58 72 80 15*
W villaetangblanc.fr
Beautifully stylish rooms at this country house by a lake. Excellent restaurant.

ST-EMILION:
Au Logis des Remparts €€
Rooms with views
18 rue Guadet, 33330
Tel *05 57 24 70 43*
W logisdesremparts.com
This pleasant hotel is ideal for wine touring. Some rooms have views of the medieval town.

DK Choice

ST-LOUP-SUR-THOUET:
Château de Saint-Loup €€
Family
79600 St-Loup-sur-Thouet
Tel *05 49 64 81 73*
W chateaudesaint-loup.com
This moated medieval château is tucked away in the atmospheric countryside north of Poitiers. Choose from several exquisite rooms in the 17th-century main house – the most fascinating ones are in a medieval keep and round tower. A magical experience guaranteed.

Périgord, Quercy, & Gascony

AGEN:
Hôtel Château des Jacobins €€
Family
2 rue Jacob, 47000
Tel *05 53 47 03 31*
W chateau-des-jacobins.com
Traditional hotel in a 19th-century mansion near Agen's old town.

ALBI: Hostellerie du Grand-Saint-Antoine €€
Family
17 rue St-Antoine, 81000
Tel *05 63 54 04 04*
W hotel-saint-antoine-albi.com
Historic hotel that has been attractively renovated with all modern comforts.

BERGERAC:
Le Clos d'Argenson €€
Romantic
99 rue Neuve d'Argenson, 24100
Tel *06 12 90 59 58*
W leclosdargenson.com
Located in a delightful Dordogne town, this beautiful B&B offers four ultra-comfortable suites. There is a pool in the garden.

Key to Price Guide *see p554*

BOURDEILLES: Hostellerie Les Griffons €€
Rooms with views
24310 Bourdeilles
Tel *05 53 45 45 35*
W griffons.fr
Lovely 16th-century house in a gorgeous village. Characterful rooms, most with river views.

BRANTOME: Le Chatenet €€
Family
24310 Brantôme
Tel *05 53 05 81 08*
W lechatenet.com
Exceptional B&B housed in a Périgord stone manor house. Huge gardens and a pool.

BRANTOME: Le Moulin de l'Abbaye €€€
Family
1 route de Bourdeilles, 24310
Tel *05 53 05 80 22*
W moulinabbaye.com
Beautiful riverside mill with delightful garden terraces and sumptuous rooms.

CHANCELADE: Château des Reynats €€
Romantic
15 av des Reynats, 24650
Tel *05 53 03 53 59*
W chateau-hotel-perigord.com
Grand Périgord château-hotel with rooms divided between the main house and the orangerie.

CONDOM: Logis des Cordeliers €
Value for money
2bis rue de la Paix, 32100
Tel *05 62 28 03 68*
W logisdescordeliers.com
Convenient modern hotel in the town center with bright and comfortable rooms and a pool.

CORDES-SUR-CIEL: Hostellerie du Vieux Cordes €€
Rooms with views
Haut de la Cité, 81170
Tel *05 63 53 79 20*
W vieuxcordes.fr
Medieval house high up in a superb hill-town, with great views.

DK Choice

CUQ-TOULZA: Hôtel Cuq en Terrasses €€
Rooms with views
Cuq le Château, 81470
Tel *05 63 82 54 00*
W cuqenterrasses.com
Rising up on a hilltop east of Toulouse, this 18th-century manor house feels a part of the Languedoc landscape. The pool is set in lush, picturesque gardens, and the views from the terrace restaurant are glorious.

Bright, well-furnished room at the Le Pont de l'Ouysse

DOMME: L'Esplanade €€
Rooms with views
2 rue Pontcarral, 24250
Tel *05 53 28 31 41*
W esplanade-perigord.com
Clifftop hotel with superb views from most rooms and an excellent restaurant.

GOUDOURVILLE: Château de Goudourville €€
Romantic
Le Bourg, 82400
Tel *05 63 29 09 06*
W chateau-goudourville.fr
Atmospheric B&B with baronial-style rooms, some with four-poster beds, in a medieval castle.

LACAVE: Le Pont de l'Ouysse €€
Luxury
Le Pont de l'Ouysse, 46200
Tel *05 65 37 87 04*
W lepontdelouysse.com
Indulgent retreat with tasteful rooms, a spa, a terrace pool, and an impressive restaurant.

LASCABANES: Le Domaine de Saint-Géry €€
Luxury
Le Bourg, 46800
Tel *05 65 31 82 51*
W saint-gery.com
Palatial B&B set in a historic manor. Magnificent grounds.

LECTOURE: Hôtel de Bastard €€
Value for Money
rue Lagrange, 32700
Tel *05 62 68 82 44*
W hotel-de-bastard.com
Comfortable small-town hotel with a garden pool and restaurant. A beautiful wooden staircase leads to the rooms.

LES EYZIES-DE-TAYAC: Les Glycines €€
Romantic
4 av de Laugerie, 24620
Tel *05 53 06 97 07*
W les-glycines-dordogne.com
Small and mellow hotel that combines country location with boutique style. Especially lovely restaurant, pool, and garden on site.

MAUROUX: Hostellerie Le Vert €€
Family
46700 Mauroux
Tel *05 65 36 51 36*
W hotellevert.com
Rooms with heaps of character in a 17th-century house in the Cahors wine country.

ROCAMADOUR: Domaine de la Rhue €€
Value for money
La Rue, 46500
Tel *05 65 33 71 50*
W domainedelarhue.com
Spacious rooms and pool. Ideal for exploring the countryside.

SARLAT: Le Moulin Pointu €
Value for money
Ste-Nathalène, 24200
Tel *05 53 28 15 54*
W moulinpointu.com
Relaxing B&B with charming rooms surrounded by large gardens and a pool.

SARLAT: La Villa des Consuls €€
Family
3 rue Jean-Jacques Rousseau, 24200
Tel *05 53 31 90 05*
W villaconsuls.fr
No-frills rooms and apartments in old Sarlat, set in different historic buildings.

SEGUENVILLE: Château de Séguenville €€
Romantic
31480 Cabanac-Séguenville
Tel *05 62 13 42 67*
W chateau-de-seguenville.com
Grand B&B with smart rooms and pretty gardens. Meals available on request.

ST-CIRQ-LAPOPIE: Château de Saint-Cirq-Lapopie €€
Rooms with views
Le Bourg, 46330
Tel *05 65 31 27 48*
W chateaudesaintcirqlapopie.com
Imposing stone château with four spacious rooms. Heated indoor swimming pool.

ST-EUTROPE-DE-BORN: Le Moulin de Labique €€
Romantic
47210 St-Eutrope-de-Born
Tel *05 53 01 63 90*
W moulin-de-labique.net
Lovely B&B set in a giant manor house offering rooms decorated with antiques. Fine service.

For more information on types of hotels *see pp552–3*

Elegant, gracefully decorated room at the Hôtel du Palais, Biarritz

TOULOUSE: Les Loges de Saint-Sernin €€
City center
12 rue St-Bernard, 31000
Tel *05 61 24 44 44*
W leslogesdesaintsernin.com
Four spacious B&B rooms in a distinguished Toulouse town-house. Conveniently located.

TOULOUSE: Hôtel des Beaux Arts €€€
City center
1 pl du Pont-Neuf, 31000
Tel *05 34 45 42 42*
W hoteldesbeauxarts.com
Smartly modernized rooms in a Belle Epoque building, some with great river views.

The Pyrenees

AINHOA: Hôtel Ithurria €€
Family
64250 Aïnhoa
Tel *05 59 29 92 11*
W ithurria.com
Charming hotel in a giant Basque-style chalet at the foot of the Pyrenees. Excellent pool.

ANGLET: Château de Brindos €€€
Luxury
1 allée du Château, 64600
Tel *05 59 23 89 80*
W chateaudebrindos.com
Spacious country-house hotel by the lake near Biarritz, with a spa and gourmet lakeside restaurant.

ARGELES-GAZOST: Hôtel Best Western Le Miramont €€
Family
44 av des Pyrénées, 65400
Tel *05 62 97 01 26*
W hotelmiramont.com
Stylishly modernized 1930s spa-town hotel with antique furnishings and smart decor.

ARREAU: Hôtel d'Angleterre €€
Family
rte de Luchon, 65240
Tel *05 62 98 63 30*
W hotel-angleterre-arreau.com
Comfortable hotel in a stunning mountain location. Pretty garden with a lovely pool.

BEAUCENS: Eth Béryè Petit €
Value for money
15 rte de Vielle, 65400
Tel *05 62 97 90 02*
W beryepetit.com
Delightful B&B in the mountains near Lourdes, ideal for walkers. Pretty rooms and friendly owners.

BIARRITZ: Villa le Goëland €€
Rooms with views
12 plateau de l'Atalaye, 64200
Tel *05 59 24 25 76*
W villagoeland-biarritz.com
Grand 19th-century villa set on the cliffs outside Biarritz. Stunning views from the huge B&B rooms.

BIARRITZ: Hôtel du Palais €€€
Luxury
1 av de l'Impératrice, 64200
Tel *05 59 41 64 00*
W hotel-du-palais.com
Palatial hotel in a superb beach location with an opulent spa, pool, and other facilities.

CAMON: L'Abbaye-Château de Camon €€
Luxury
3 Place Philippe de Lévis, 09500
Tel *05 61 60 31 23*
W chateaudecamon.com
Exceptional B&B in a medieval château set in a historic village. Gracefully decorated rooms.

DK Choice

ESPELETTE: Hôtel-Restaurant Euzkadi €
Rooms with views
285 Karrika Nagusia, 64250
Tel *05 59 93 91 88*
W hotel-restaurant-euzkadi.com
A hotel with real warmth and character, the family-run Euzkadi offers well-appointed rooms, lovely terrace views, and a large swimming pool. An ideal place for sampling Basque-influenced dishes. Impeccable service.

FOIX: Hôtel-Restaurant Lons €
Value for money
6 pl Georges Dutilh, 09000
Tel *05 34 09 28 00*
W hotel-lons-foix.com
This traditional hotel has simple but comfortable rooms and a lovely restaurant. Great location. Warm and personable staff.

LASSEUBE: Maison Rancèsamy €
Family
Lieu-dit Rances, 64290
Tel *05 59 04 26 37*
W missbrowne.com
Beautiful rooms and a garden pool in this lovely stone manor.

LOURDES: Grand Hôtel de la Grotte €€
Luxury
66 rue de la Grotte, 65100
Tel *05 62 94 58 87*
W hotel-grotte.com
Large rooms that combine modern features with traditional styling in central Lourdes.

MIREPOIX: Maison des Consuls €€
Rooms with views
6 pl du Maréchal Leclerc, 09500
Tel *05 61 68 81 81*
W maisondesconsuls.com
Imaginatively decorated boutique hotel in a 14th-century house in medieval Mirepoix.

ORTHEZ: Hôtel Reine Jeanne €€
Romantic
44 rue Bourg Vieux, 64300
Tel *05 59 67 00 76*
W hotel-reine-jeanne.fr
Chic modern rooms around a courtyard in an attractive 18th-century building. Fine restaurant.

PAU: Hôtel Bristol €€
Family
3 rue Gambetta, 64000
Tel *05 59 27 72 98*
W hotelbristol-pau.com
Pleasant hotel with good facilities in Pau center. Some rooms have balconies with great views.

SARE: Ttakoinenborda €
Value for money
rte de Lizarrieta, 64310
Tel *05 59 47 51 42*
W chambredhotebasque.fr
Lovely B&B rooms in a Basque farmhouse amid fields. Excellent for exploring the countryside.

ST-ETIENNE-DE-BAIGORRY: Hôtel-Restaurant Arcé €€
Romantic
St-Etienne-de-Baïgorry, 64430
Tel *05 59 37 40 14*
W hotel-arce.com
Striking blend of traditional Basque architecture and boutique style.

ST-JEAN-DE-LUZ: Hôtel La Devinière €€
Romantic
5 rue Louis-Fortuné Loquin, 64500
Tel *05 59 26 05 51*
W hotel-le-deviniere.com
Elegant hotel with antique furnishings and modern comforts.

Key to Price Guide *see p554*

ST-JEAN-PIED-DE-PORT: Hôtel Les Pyrénées €€€
Luxury
19 pl Charles de Gaulle, 64220
Tel *05 59 37 01 01*
W hotel-les-pyrenees.com
Prestigious hotel with elegant rooms and beautiful gardens.

ST-LIZIER: Villa Belisama €
Rooms with views
rue Notre Dame, 09190
Tel *05 61 02 83 24*
W ariege.com/belisama
Charming B&B in a historic hilltop village, with pretty rooms and a pool.

Languedoc-Roussillon

AIGUES-MORTES: Hôtel St-Louis €€
Family
10 rue Amiral Courbet, 30220
Tel *04 66 53 72 68*
W lesaintlouis.fr
Spacious, sunny rooms in an 18th-century building with all modern comforts. Pretty garden patio.

BEZIERS: Hôtel des Poètes €
City center
80 allées Paul Riquet, 34500
Tel *04 67 76 38 66*
W hoteldespoetes.net
Charming budget hotel overlooking the Parc des Poètes. Free bikes for exploring the Canal du Midi. Friendly and helpful owners ensure attentive service.

CARCASSONNE: Hôtel de la Cité €€€
Luxury
pl August-Pierre Pont, 11000
Tel *04 68 71 98 71*
W hoteldelacite.com
Expect immaculate service, opulent period rooms, glorious gardens, and a fine restaurants.

CERET: Le Mas Trilles €€
Family
av du Vallespir, Le Pont de Reynes, 66400
Tel *04 68 87 38 37*
W le-mas-trilles.com
Stone-built 14th-century farmhouse set in beautiful gardens. Charming rooms.

COLLIOURE: Relais des Trois Mas €€
Rooms with views
rte de Port-Vendres, 66190
Tel *04 68 82 05 07*
W relaisdestroismas.com
A calm retreat nestled in pine-shaded gardens. Neat rooms, most with terraces.

DK Choice

MOLITG-LES-BAINS: Château de Riell €€
Rooms with views
66500
Tel *04 68 05 04 40*
W chateauderiell.com
Exuberant Baroque-style château that offers magnificent views over forests and Mount Canigou. The interiors are equally stunning, decorated with antiques and exotic furniture.

MONTPELLIER: Hôtel du Palais €
City center
3 rue Palais des Guilhem, 34000
Tel *04 67 60 47 38*
W hoteldupalais-montpellier.fr
Attractive historic building. Cozy rooms and a relaxed atmosphere.

NARBONNE: Hotel La Résidence €€
City center
6 rue du 1er Mai, 11100
Tel *04 68 32 19 41*
W hotel-laresidence-narbonne.fr
Spacious rooms with high ceilings, and a good wine bar at this hotel.

NIMES: Imperator-Concorde €€
Luxury
Quai de la Fontaine, 30000
Tel *04 66 21 90 30*
W hotel-imperator.com
Favorite of celebrities, with a lovely garden of cedars and palms.

PERPIGNAN: Hôtel de la Loge €
Value for money
1 rue des Fabriques d'en Nabot, 66000
Tel *04 68 34 41 02*
W hoteldelaloge.fr
Unassuming hotel with lots of character set in a 16th-century Catalan mansion.

PERPIGNAN: Villa Duflot €€
Luxury
7 Rond point Albert Donnezan, 66000
Tel *04 68 56 67 67*
W villa-duflot.com
Italian-style villa with stylish decor and striking modern sculptures.

PEZENAS: Aire de Vacances €
Family
1 rue Calquières Basses, 34120
Tel *09 50 58 99 11*
W air-de-vacances.com
Delightful B&B near the town center with welcoming hosts. Delicious breakfasts.

SAILLAGOUSE: L'Atalaya €€
Family
Llo, 66800
Tel *04 68 04 70 04*
W atalaya66.com
Pretty stone auberge and family *gîtes* with a luxury feel, offering spectacular views.

SETE: Grand Hôtel €€
Rooms with views
17 Quai de Tassigny, 34200
Tel *04 67 74 71 77*
W legrandhotelsete.com
Overlooking Sète's grand canal, this 19th-century hotel has an excellent conservatory-restaurant.

UZES: Hostellerie Provençale €€
City center
1–3 rue Grande Bourgade, 30700
Tel *04 66 22 11 06*
W hostellerieprovencale.com
Small, friendly hotel with *tommete* tiled floors, rustic furniture, and up-to-date amenities.

Provence & the Côte d'Azur

AIX-EN-PROVENCE: Hôtel Cézanne €€
Boutique
40 av Victor Hugo, 13100
Tel *04 42 91 11 11*
W cezanne.hotelaix.com
Arty, chic decor at this hotel. Breakfast served until noon.

ANTIBES: Mas Djoliba €€
Family
29 av Provence, 06600
Tel *04 93 34 02 48*
W hotel-djoliba.com
Charming farmhouse with palm trees around its pool and terrace.

Plush room at the Imperator-Concorde, Nîmes

ARLES:
Hôtel de l'Amphithéâtre €
Family
5–7 rue Diderot, 13200
Tel *04 90 96 10 30*
W hoteldelamphitheatrearles.com
Striking Provençal decor and friendly staff. There are several family rooms to choose from.

DK Choice

ARLES:
L'Hôtel Particulier à Arles €€€
Luxury
4 rue de la Monnaie, 13200
Tel *04 90 52 51 40*
W hotel-particulier.com
Step into a world of rich elegance and opulent living at this historic hotel. A walled garden, a swimming pool, and an ultra-sophisticated spa and *hammam* all make for a dreamy stay.

AVIGNON: Hôtel Bristol €€
Family
44 cours Jean Jaurès, 84000
Tel *04 90 16 48 48*
W bristol-avignon.com
Classy hotel with refined rooms, including several for families. Pet friendly. Convenient location.

AVIGNON: La Mirande €€€
Luxury
4 pl de la Mirande, 84000
Tel *04 90 14 20 20*
W la-mirande.fr
Splendid cardinal's mansion by the Palais des Papes. Immaculately renovated in 18th-century style.

BORMES-LES-MIMOSAS:
Domaine du Mirage €€
Family
38 rue de la Vue des Iles, 83230
Tel *04 94 05 32 60*
W domainedumirage.com
Victorian-style hotel with some family rooms, spectacular sea views, and a beautiful pool.

CANNES:
InterContinental Carlton €€€
Luxury
58 la Croisette, 06400
Tel *04 93 06 40 06*
W intercontinental-carlton-cannes.com
Art Deco establishment with breathtaking suites and a private beach. Popular with celebrities.

CAP D'ANTIBES:
La Gardiole et La Garoupe €
Family
60–74 chemin de la Garoupe, 06160
Tel *04 92 93 33 33*
W hotel-lagaroupe-gardiole.com
Quiet, simple rooms at this budget hotel. Friendly service.

Lush trees shade the charming La Bastide de Voulonne in Gordes

CASTELLANE:
Nouvel Hôtel du Commerce €
Family
pl Marcel Sauvaire, 04120
Tel *04 92 83 61 00*
W hotel-du-commerce-verdon.com
Excellent stopover option, with a fine garden restaurant and pool.

DK Choice

CHATEAU-ARNOUX:
La Bonne Etape €€
Classic
chemin du Lac, 04160
Tel *04 92 64 00 09*
W bonneetape.com
An 18th-century post house inherited by current owner and master chef Jany Gleize. Rooms are stunningly done up with antiques. Excellent heated pool amidst the olive groves.

EZE: La Chèvre d'Or €€€
Luxury
rue du Barri, 06360
Tel *04 92 10 66 66*
W chevredor.com
Romantic, individually decorated rooms and suites with Jacuzzis and private gardens.

FAYENCE:
Moulin de la Camandoule €€
Charming
chemin de Notre-Dame des Cyprès, 83440
Tel *04 94 76 00 84*
W camandoule.com
Lovely, well-appointed rooms in a converted 15th-century olive mill.

DK Choice

GORDES:
La Bastide de Voulonne €€
Family
Cabrières d'Avignon, 84220
Tel *04 90 76 77 55*
W bastide-voulonne
This guesthouse is an idyllic spot for a family break – the heated pool and terrace have spectacular views over the Luberon. It has three gracefully decorated family suites.

ILE DE PORT-CROS:
Le Manoir €€€
Romantic
Port-Cros, 83400
Tel *04 94 05 90 52*
W hotel-lemanoirportcros.com
A romantic century-old mansion set on an idyllic island with terraces overlooking the sea.

JUAN-LES-PINS:
Hôtel des Mimosas €
Classic
rue Pauline, 06160
Tel *04 93 61 04 16*
W hotelmimosas.com
Elegant hotel surrounded by a lush park. Comfortable rooms. Free parking.

MARSEILLE: Hotel Résidence du Vieux Port €€
Boutique
18 quai du Port, 13002
Tel *04 91 15 59 00*
W hotel-residence-marseille.com
Colorful 1950s-style decor and spectacular views. Perfect for families.

MONACO: Columbus €€
Boutique
23 av des Papalins, 98000
Tel *00 377 98 06 40 00*
W columbushotels.com
Sleek designer rooms in dark stone and polished metal. Excellent restaurant and cigar bar.

MOUSTIERS-STE-MARIE:
La Bastide de Moustiers €€€
Boutique
chemin de Quinson, 04360
Tel *04 92 70 47 47*
W bastide-moustiers.com
A 17th-century building with gardens, mountain views, and a superb Alain Ducasse restaurant.

NICE: Hôtel Windsor €
Boutique
11 rue Dalpozzo, 06000
Tel *04 93 88 59 35*
W hotelwindsornice.com
Art-filled, individually decorated rooms and a lovely pool inside an exotic garden.

NICE: Le Negresco €€€
Luxury
37 promenade des Anglais, 06000
Tel *04 93 16 64 00*
W hotel-negresco-nice.com
Renowned vintage hotel designed by Henri Négresco. Superb works of art, flawless service, and top-notch facilities.

Key to Price Guide *see p554*

NIMES: Hôtel des Tuileries €
Classic
22 rue Roussy, 30000
Tel *04 66 21 31 15*
W hoteldestuileries.com
Pleasant hotel in the heart of Nîmes. Basic rooms with free Wi-Fi.

SAINTES-MARIES-DE-LA-MER: Mas de la Fouque €€€
Boutique
rte du Petit Rhône, 13460
Tel *04 90 97 81 02*
W masdelafouque.com
Chic hotel and spa overlooking a lagoon, with a fine restaurant, pool, tennis, and riding facilities.

SEILLANS: Hôtel des Deux Rocs €
Charming
pl Font d'Amont, 83440
Tel *04 94 76 87 32*
W hoteldeuxrocs.com
A stately 18th-century mansion with graceful decor and historic charm. Great for families.

ST-PAUL-DE-VENCE: Hostellerie des Remparts €
Historic
72 rue Grande, 06570
Tel *04 93 32 09 88*
W hostellerielesremparts.com
Modern comforts, antique-filled rooms, and marvelous views in a medieval setting.

ST-REMY-DE-PROVENCE: Hôtel Sous Les Figuiers €€
Historic
3 avenue Taillandier, 13210
Tel *04 32 60 15 40*
W hotel-charme-provence.com
Pretty hotel with cozy rooms overlooking centuries-old fig trees and a lovely garden pool.

ST-TROPEZ: Lou Cagnard €€
Charming
av Paul Roussel, 83990
Tel *04 94 97 04 24*
W hotel-lou-cagnard.com
Elegant Provençal town house with airy rooms and a lush garden.

DK Choice

ST-TROPEZ: Pastis Hôtel St-Tropez €€€
Boutique
6 avenue du Général Leclerc, 83990
Tel *04 98 12 56 50*
W pastis-st-tropez.com
An ideal intimate hideaway filled with 20th-century art. The heated garden pool is idyllic, surrounded by centuries-old palm trees – the perfect spot for breakfast or a nightcap.

VAISON LA ROMAINE: Les Tilleuls d'Elisée €
B&B
1 avenue J. Mazen, 84110
Tel *04 90 35 63 04*
W vaisonchambres.info
Charming B&B set in a 19th-century Provençal farmhouse.

VILLEFRANCHE: Hôtel Welcome €€
Boutique
1 quai Amiral Courbet, 06230
Tel *04 93 76 27 62*
W welcomehotel.com
Artist Jean Cocteau's favorite hotel; full of arty, period charm.

Corsica

AJACCIO: Les Mouettes €€
Boutique
9 Cours Lucien Bonaparte, 20000
Tel *04 95 21 71 80*
W hotellesmouettes.fr
Airy Riviera-style rooms in a lovely 19th-century seaside mansion.

BASTIA: Hôtel Pietracap €€
Boutique
rte San Martino, San Martino di Lota, 20200
Tel *04 95 31 64 63*
W pietracap.com
Extremely comfortable hotel swathed in bougainvillea in a beautiful seaside park.

Classy decor in a room at Le Negresco in Nice

BONIFACIO: Hôtel des Etrangers €
Classic
avenue Sylvère Bohn, 20169
Tel *04 95 73 01 09*
W hoteldesetrangers.fr
Bright, beautifully furnished rooms with private bathrooms. Friendly staff.

CALVI: Château Hôtel La Signoria €€€
Luxury
rte de la Forêt de Bonifato, 20260
Tel *04 95 65 93 00*
W hotel-la-signoria.com
An array of chic rooms, suites, and villas, plus a *hammam*, private beach, and gourmet restaurant.

CORTE: Hôtel Dominique Colonna €€
Country
Vallée de la Restonica, BP 83, 20250
Tel *04 95 45 25 65*
W dominique-colonna.com
A beautiful hotel with balconies overhanging the river. Don't miss dinner at the restaurant next door.

DK Choice

ERBALUNGA: Hôtel Demeure Castel Brando €€
Historic
Erbalunga, 20222
Tel *04 95 30 10 30*
W castelbrando.com
Castel Brando is set in a magical park of ancient olive trees and exotic palms. Rooms are spacious and elegant. There are two pools, a breakfast patio, and top-notch staff.

PIANA: Les Roches Rouges €€
Charming
rte de Porto, 20115
Tel *04 95 27 81 81*
W lesrochesrouges.com
Built in 1912, this hotel still exudes genteel charm. Magical views.

PORTO-VECCHIO: Hôtel E Casette €€€
Boutique
rte de Palombaggia, 20137
Tel *04 95 70 13 66*
W ecasette.com
Romantic hotel with a spa and stunning views. All rooms have a private jacuzzi and terrace.

SARTENE: Hôtel San Damianu €€
Classic
Quartier San Damien, 20100
Tel *04 95 70 55 41*
W sandamianu.fr
Airy rooms and terraces with fabulous views. Facilities include a huge pool and garden.

For more information on types of hotels *see pp552–3*

WHERE TO EAT AND DRINK

The French consider eating well an essential part of their national birthright. Restaurant reviews, as well as cooking and food shows on television, are avidly followed, and the general quality of both fresh food and restaurant offerings is excellent. This introduction to the restaurant listings, which are arranged by region and town *(see pp576–603)*, looks at the different types of restaurants in France. Find practical tips on eating out, reading menus, ordering, and service – everything you need to know to enjoy your meal. At the front of the book is a guide to a typical menu and an introduction to French wine *(see pp28–31)*. The main food and wine features are at the beginning of each of the five regional sections.

French Eating Habits

The traditional main meal at midday survives mainly in rural regions. In cities, French families get together for Sunday lunches that can last 3 hours or more. However, a weekday city lunch is increasingly likely to consist of a sandwich, salad, or steak in a café, while dinner is the main meal of the day. Usually, lunch is from noon to 2pm and dinner from 8 to 10pm, with last orders taken 30 minutes before closing time.

Some family-owned places and restaurants in city centers, catering mainly to workers, close on the weekends. A large proportion of French restaurants, even the ones in hotels, close on Sunday night, so be sure to check in advance – though there is likely to be a pizzeria open somewhere. Off the beaten track and in resort towns, restaurants and hotels are often closed out of season or open only on Friday and Saturday nights. It is always advisable to call ahead.

Over the past few decades, French eating habits have changed dramatically, becoming much more international in outlook. The growing popularity of foods from former French colonies and beyond means that North African and Vietnamese establishments are easy to find, as are Chinese and Italian restaurants. Burger and Tex-Mex joints are also popular with young people.

Customers tuck into Lyonnais specialities at the Benoît restaurant, Paris *(see p576)*

Brasseries

The brasserie has its origins in the region of Alsace and were originally attached to breweries; the name brasserie actually means brewery. Usually found in larger cities and towns, they are big, bustling places, many with fresh shellfish stands outside. They serve beer on tap as well as a *vin de la maison* (house wine) and a variety of regional wines. Menus usually include simple fish and grilled meat dishes along with Alsatian specialties such as *choucroute garnie* (sauerkraut with sausage and pork). Prices are very much on par with those charged at bistros. Like cafés, brasseries usually serve food from morning until night.

The *belle époque* interior of La Cigale, a brasserie in Nantes *(see p588)*

Ferme-Auberges

In the country, a simple "farm inn," or *ferme-auberge*, serves good, inexpensive meals prepared with fresh farm produce. *Ferme-auberges* can be dining rooms attached to a working farm, offering in many cases – as in parts of Corsica – an accurate reflection of authentic regional cuisine. Other *ferme-auberges* may be part of a farm's lodgings, where meals are taken with the host's family as part of the room and board.

Cafés

The soul of France, cafés serve drinks, coffee, tea, simple meals, and snacks such as salads, omelettes, and sandwiches throughout the day, and usually provide a cheaper breakfast than most hotels. In addition to serving refreshments, cafés are a good source of information and provide the traveler with endless opportunities to people-watch at leisure.

In villages, almost the entire population may drift in and out of a single café during the course of the day, while large cities have cafés that cater to a specific clientele such as workers or students. Paris's most famous cafés were traditional meeting places for intellectuals and artists to exchange ideas *(see p156)*.

Bistro Annexes, Salons du Thé, and Wine Bars

Over the past few years, bistro annexes have appeared in many cities. They are lower-priced sister eateries of famous – and much more expensive – restaurants run by well-known chefs. Many of them offer *formule* or *prix-fixe* (fixed-price) menus and the chance to sample the cooking of a celebrated chef.

Salons du thé (tea rooms) are also good-value options for light meals, generally offering a choice of salads, savoury tarts, and sandwiches. Wine bars offer light suppers in the evenings, with a choice of Spanish-style tapas, *charcuterie* (cured meats), breads, and cheeses on the menu.

Reservations

In cities, larger towns and major resorts, it is always best to make a reservation, especially from May to September, and for evening meals or a Sunday lunch. But this rarely applies to cafés or in the country, where one can walk into most places. However, when traveling in remote rural and resort areas off season, it is advisable to check whether the restaurant is open all year.

The bar at La Ferme aux Grives in Eugénie-les-Bains ***(see p595)***

If you have a reservation and your plans change, then call and cancel – smaller restaurants, in particular, must fill all their tables to make a profit.

Reading the Menu and Ordering

When the menu is presented, it is common practice for guests to be asked their choice of aperitif, which could be Kir (white wine mixed with a dash of black-currant liqueur), vermouth, light port – drunk in France as a cocktail – or, seeing as many French people do not drink spirits before a meal, a soft drink.

The menu opens with *les entrées* (appetizers) and is followed by *les plats* (main courses); most restaurants will also offer a *plat du jour*, or daily special, for lunch. A selection of dishes from a classic French menu is given on pages 28–9.

Cheese is served as a separate course between the main course and dessert. Coffee is always black, unless one specifies "*crème*," and served after dessert. Alternatively, one can ask for a *tisane* (herbal tea).

Many restaurants offer a choice of fixed-price menus for lunch or dinner. These usually comprise several *entrées*, *plats*, and desserts to choose from in each price category – which generally works out to be cheaper than ordering à la carte. Many chefs in upmarket restaurants also offer a *menu dégustation* (tasting menu) that has numerous courses of small portions, allowing diners to try a variety of the chef's dishes. Because tasting menus are complex for both the chef and wait staff, the whole table is often required to order the same menu.

Wine

As restaurants put a large mark-up on wine, it is more affordable to further your connoisseurship with bottles purchased in stores. Local or house wine, however, is often served in carafes, and is generally quite acceptable. If in doubt, ordering a small carafe is a cheaper way to test it out; ask for a *demi* (50 cl, or 17 fl oz) or *quart* (25 cl, just over 8 fl oz).

French law divides the country's wines into three classes, in ascending order of quality: *Vin de France*, *Indication Géographique Protégée* (IGP), and *Appellation d'Origine Protégée* (AOP). The Vin de France wines are rarely found in restaurants. For help in choosing a regional wine (IGP upwards), refer to the wine features in the regional sections of this book. For an introduction to French wine, see pages 30–31.

Classic wood interiors at Auberge du XIIe Siècle, Saché ***(see p588)***

Tables outside a café in the Old Town of Nice, Côte d'Azur

Water

A carafe of *eau de robinet* (tap water) is supplied on request free of charge and is perfectly safe to drink. The French also pride themselves on their wide range of mineral waters. Favorite mealtime brands include Evian and the slightly fizzy Badoit.

Prices

Prices for restaurants of the same rating are more or less consistent throughout France except in large cities and the more fashionable resort areas, where they can be significantly more expensive. The quality of food and service is the most decisive price factor, and one can easily spend over €150 per head to eat at one of the top establishments – much more if you choose a prestigious wine.

How to Pay

Visa/Carte Bleue (V) is the most widely accepted credit card in France. MasterCard (MC) is also commonly accepted, while American Express (AE) and Diners Club (DC) tend to be accepted only in upmarket establishments. However, it is best to always carry plenty of cash, especially when touring the countryside, as small family-run restaurants and *ferme-auberges* may not take any credit cards. If in doubt, ask when making the reservation.

Service and Tipping

French meals are generally enjoyed at a leisurely pace. People think nothing of spending 4 hours at the table, so if pressed for time, it is better to go to a café, bistro, or brasserie.

A service charge of 12.5 to 15 percent is almost always included in the price of the meal, but most French people leave a few euro cents behind in a café, and an additional 5 percent or so of the total check in other restaurants. In the grander restaurants, which pride themselves on their service, an additional tip of 5 to 10 percent is expected. Around €0.50 to €0.70 is appropriate for coat-check assistants, and €0.30 is sufficient for restroom attendants.

Dress Code

Even when dressed casually, the French are generally well turned out; visitors should aim for the same level of presentable comfort. Running shoes, shorts, beach clothes, or active sportswear are unacceptable everywhere except in cafés or beachside places.

Children

French children are introduced from an early age to restaurants and as a rule are very well behaved. Some restaurants provide equipment such as highchairs or booster seats. There is often not much room for strollers.

Delicious oysters at the popular seafood restaurant A l'Huitrière in Lille *(see p580)*

Pets

Dogs are usually accepted at all but the most elegant restaurants. The French are great dog lovers, so do not be surprised to see your neighbor's lapdog sitting on the next-door *banquette*.

Smoking

The French now adhere to government regulations that prohibit smoking inside restaurants and cafés. However, smoking is generally permitted at outdoor tables.

Wheelchair Access

Though newer restaurants usually provide wheelchair access, it is often restricted elsewhere. A word when booking should ensure that you are given a conveniently located table and assistance, if needed, upon arrival.

Vegetarian Food

France remains difficult for vegetarians, although some progress has been made in recent years. In most restaurants

Bright, spacious sitting area at La Tour d'Argent, Paris *(see p578)*

the main courses are firmly orientated towards meat and fish. However, you can often fare well by ordering from the *entrées* and should not shy away from asking for a dish to be served without its meat content. Provided you make the request in advance, most smart restaurants will prepare a special vegetarian dish.

Only larger cities and university towns are likely to have fully fledged vegetarian restaurants. Otherwise cafés, pizzerias, crêperies, and Oriental restaurants are good places to find vegetarian meals.

Picnics

Picnicking is the best way to enjoy France's wonderful fresh produce while taking in the delights of the French countryside. Select local bread, cheeses, and *charcuterie* from markets and enticing shops.

Picnic areas along major roads are well marked and furnished with tables and chairs, but country lanes are better still.

Recommended Restaurants

The restaurants in this guide have been carefully selected to reflect the wide range that France offers when it comes to eating out – suitable for every budget.

At the top of the list are the country's **fine dining** restaurants, including some of the torch-bearers for the nation's world-renowned culinary art. Some of them, however, still serve classic, sauce-based *haute cuisine*.

Most top chefs take great pride in their individual styles and recipes, adapting *haute cuisine* techniques to modern tastes. Their restaurants are invariably expensive, but often make for an unforgettable dining experience. Many of these establishments are located inside elegant hotels, but are open to nonguests as well.

Traditional French restaurants concentrate on the country's classic dishes such as *escargots* (snails), pâté, *foie gras*, *steak au poivre* (pepper steak), *sole meunière* (sole pan-fried with brown butter sauce and lemon), *crème brûlée* (rich creamy custard topped with hard caramel), and chocolate mousse. Then there are **modern French** restaurants, generally with a casual-chic atmosphere – the heirs of the *nouvelle cuisine* movement that began in the 1960s, emphasizing fresh, top-quality ingredients and inventive food pairings that are beautifully presented and consider modern dietary needs. Contemporary chefs also tend to be more open to inspiration from across a wide spectrum of culinary styles, notably Mediterranean, Asian, North African, and North American.

For a foodie, the best aspect of traveling across France has to be the country's many restaurants that specialize in authentic **regional** cuisine – eateries that lay genuine emphasis on local ingredients and traditional recipes. Many such dishes have now attained popularity around the world, such as the cheese fondues of the Alps, the rich seafood *bouillabaisse* of Marseille in Provence, the *cassoulet* – duck and bean stew – of southwest France, and the crêpes and cider of Brittany.

Although Paris may have the country's most famous restaurants, Lyon as a whole is acknowledged as France's gastronomic capital, known for its fabulous array of hearty meat dishes, such as sausages, duck pâté, and roast pork.

Bistros, varying widely in size and services offered, are often informal and affordable, and stay open later than the average restaurant. Generally they offer a good, moderately priced meal from a traditional menu of an *entrée* or *hors d'oeuvre* (appetizer), *plats mijotés* (simmered dishes) and *grillades* (grilled fish and meats), followed by cheese and dessert. They may also have a reasonably priced three- or four-course meal, usually featuring comfort dishes such as onion soup and *boeuf bourguignon* (beef stewed in red wine).

The establishments labeled **DK Choice** are places that have been highlighted in recognition of a special feature – a celebrity chef, exquisite food, an inviting ambience, or simply great value for money. Most of these eateries are quite popular among locals and visitors, so be sure to inquire regarding reservations well in advance to avoid waiting in a long line. The DK Choice label guarantees not only a delicious meal, but also a superb dining experience.

Lovely wood-finish facade of the Hôtellerie du Bas-Bréau, Barbizon *(see p579)*

Elegant dining room of a hotel in Evian-les-Bains

Where to Eat and Drink

Paris

Ile de la Cite, Marais, & Beaubourg

Chez H'Anna €
Israeli **Map** 9 C3
54 rue des Rosiers, 75004
Tel *01 42 78 23 09* **Closed** *Mon*
Sample creamy homemade hummus and exquisite falafels at this delightful Israeli eatery.

DK Choice

L'As du Fallafel €
Israeli **Map** 9 C3
34 rue des Rosiers, 75004
Tel *01 48 87 63 60* **Closed** *Sat*
The falafels here are arguably the best in town, perhaps even in France – expect to find very long lines for its famous sandwiches snaking down the street at lunchtime. The hummus is a velvety delight.

DK Choice

Les Degrés de Notre Dame €
French/North African **Map** 9 B4
10 rue des Grands Degrés, 75005
Tel *01 55 42 88 88* **Closed** *Sun*
A simple, family-run auberge with beamed interiors and walls crowded with pictures. The food is a mixture of Moroccan and French staples. The couscous and tajines are exceptional.

Frenchie €€
Modern French **Map** 7 A5
5–6 rue du Nil, 75002
Tel *01 40 39 96 19* **Closed** *Sat & Sun*
Book months ahead for a chance to dine at one of Paris's hottest bistros. The exquisite dishes on the fixed-price menus are to die for.

Le Grand Véfour retains much of its original 18th-century decoration

L'Ambassade d'Auvergne €€
Auvergnat **Map** 9 B2
22 rue du Grenier St-Lazare, 75003
Tel *01 42 72 31 22*
Rustic, dark-beamed inn serving Auvergne dishes such as *aligot* (potatoes with cheese and garlic).

Le Garde Robe €€
Tapas **Map** 8 F2
41 rue de Arbre Sec, 75001
Tel *01 49 26 90 60* **Closed** *Sun*
Charcuterie, cheese, and oysters are served as tasty accompaniments to an outstanding wine menu.

Le Hangar €€
Traditional French **Map** 9 B2
12 impasse Berthaud, 75003
Tel *01 42 74 55 44* **Closed** *Sun & Mon*
Delicious food served in a modest setting. Savor pan-fried *foie gras* on pureéd potatoes.

Les Philosophes €€
Traditional French **Map** 9 C3
28 rue Vieille du Temple, 75004
Tel *01 48 87 49 64* **Closed** *Sun*
Visit this all-day café for first-rate onion soup, steak *frites*, and the house speciality, tomato *tarte tatin*.

Benoît €€€
Lyonnais **Map** 9 B3
20 rue St-Martin, 75004
Tel *01 42 72 25 76*
Enjoy hearty food in this quintessential bistro. Don't miss the veal sweetbreads and *cassoulet*.

Spring €€€
Modern French **Map** 8 F2
6 rue Bailleul, 75001
Tel *01 45 96 05 72* **Closed** *Sun & Mon*
Creative versions of French classics paired with outstanding wines. Excellent fixed-price tasting menu.

Yam'Tcha €€€
Asian **Map** 8 F2
4 rue Sauval, 75001
Tel *01 40 26 08 07* **Closed** *Mon & Sun*
The name means "drink tea." Try different brews to complement the mouthwatering Chinese-influenced dishes.

Tuileries & Opéra

Blend €
American **Map** 13 A1
44 rue Argout, 75002
Tel *01 40 26 84 57*
No-frills eatery where the chef prepares high-quality beef in search of the perfect burger.

Price Guide
Price categories are for a three-course meal for one, including tax and all service charges.

€	under €30
€€	€30 to €65
€€€	over €65

Chartier €
Traditional French **Map** 4 F4
7 rue du Faubourg Montmartre, 75009
Tel *01 47 70 86 29*
Great food in glorious Belle Epoque surroundings. Try the house pâté, snails, or meat stew.

Bistrot Victoires €€
Traditional French **Map** 8 F1
6 rue la Vrillière, 75001
Tel *01 42 61 43 78*
Confit, *steak frites*, roast chicken, and other tasty dishes are served in impeccable surroundings.

Chez Georges €€
Traditional French **Map** 8 F1
1 rue du Mail, 75002
Tel *01 42 60 07 11* **Closed** *Sat & Sun*
A vintage treasure, beloved of cookery writer Julia Childs. Try the exceptional *steak au poivre*.

DK Choice

Racines €€
Wine bar **Map** 4 F5
8 passage des Panoramas, 75002
Tel *01 40 13 06 41* **Closed** *Sat & Sun*
A favorite with shoppers and local workers alike, Racines has a short menu that combines French and Italian dishes. Choose from a selection of very good wines, and try the excellent *charcuterie*, ratatouille, lamb, and pork. Make sure you save room for the seriously seductive desserts.

Caviar Kaspia €€€
Russian **Map** 3 C5
17 pl de la Madeleine, 75008
Tel *01 42 65 33 32* **Closed** *Sun*
Sample caviar, smoked salmon, and chilled vodka in the plush surroundings of an early 20th-century Russian aristocrat's salon.

Le Grand Véfour €€€
Fine dining **Map** 8 F1
17 rue de Beaujolais, 75001
Tel *01 42 96 56 27* **Closed** *Sat & Sun*
Savor innovative cuisine in a beautiful 18th-century room. The decor has barely altered since Napoleon brought Josephine here to dine.

Gorgeous dining space with a retractable roof at Lasserre

Champs-Elysées & Invalides

Korean Barbecue Champs-Elysées €
Korean **Map** 3 A5
7 rue de Ponthieu, 75008
Tel *01 42 25 35 41* **Closed** *Sun*
Tuck into unbelievably tender, paper-thin beef teamed with crisp greens. Barbecue heaven.

Bistrot de Paris €€
Traditional French **Map** 8 D3
33 rue de Lille, 75007
Tel *01 42 61 16 83* **Closed** *Mon & Sun*
Delighful Art Nouveau gem that rustles up tasty bistro classics for a busy crowd of loyal customers.

Café Constant €€
Traditional French **Map** 6 E3
139 rue St-Dominique, 75007
Tel *01 47 53 73 34*
Arrive early to get a seat at this popular no-frills café. Comfort food at its best.

La Fontaine de Mars €€
Regional **Map** 6 E3
129 rue St-Dominique, 75007
Tel *01 47 05 46 44*
Duck *cassoulet* is the flagship dish at this archetypal bistro with beautiful interiors and great service.

Le Florimond €€
Traditional French **Map** 6 F3
19 av de la Motte-Picquet, 75007
Tel *01 45 55 40 38* **Closed** *Sun & first Sat of every month*
Hearty food served in a bright interior. Try the tasty lobster ravioli followed by the vanilla *millefeuille*.

Huîtrier €€
Seafood **Map** 2 D2
16 rue Saussier-Leroy, 75017
Tel *01 40 54 83 44*
Oysters steal the show at this modern, minimalist restaurant.

Minipalais €€
Modern French **Map** 7 A1
Grand Palais, 3 av Winston Churchill, 75008
Tel *01 42 56 42 42*
A gastronomic treat in a super-trendy setting, with floor-to-ceiling windows and a fabulous terrace.

DK Choice

Relais de l'Entrecôte €€
Steakhouse **Map** 2 F5
15 rue Marbeuf, 75008
Tel *01 49 52 07 17*
This place is a true carnivore's paradise. The high-quality beef is cut thin, the *frites* are cooked to perfection, and the secret-recipe sauce is really something to write home about.

DK Choice

Antoine €€€
Seafood **Map** 6 E1
10 av de New York, 75116
Tel *01 40 70 19 28*
Sensational seafood and spectacular views across the Seine to the Eiffel Tower. Try the signature sea bass for two, grilled on fennel wood and served with steamed vegetables.

Hiramatsu €€€
Modern French **Map** 5 C1
52 rue de Longchamp, 75116
Tel *01 56 81 08 80* **Closed** *Sat & Sun*
A flawless blend of French and Japanese styles in elegant surroundings. Great service.

L'Arpège €€€
Traditional French **Map** 7 B3
84 rue de Varenne, 75007
Tel *01 47 05 09 06* **Closed** *Sat & Sun*
Homegrown organic vegetables are pride of place in this renowned establishment.

Lasserre €€€
Traditional French **Map** 7 A1
17 av Franklin Delano Roosevelt, 75008
Tel *01 43 59 02 13* **Closed** *Mon & Sun*
Linger over deliciously refined cooking. The retractable roof opens to the stars and the service is impeccable.

L'Astrance €€€
Modern French **Map** 5 C3
4 rue Beethoven, 75016
Tel *01 40 50 84 40* **Closed** *Sat–Mon*
Book months in advance to secure a table at this intimate, globally celebrated restaurant. Sample the inspired tasting menu and excellent wines.

Le Jules Verne €€€
Modern French **Map** 6 D3
5 av Gustave Eiffel, 75007
Tel *01 45 55 61 44*
Alain Ducasse's restaurant on the Eiffel Tower's second platform offers stylish dining to complement the 360-degree views over Paris.

Prunier €€€
Seafood **Map** 2 D4
16 av Victor-Hugo, 75116
Tel *01 44 17 35 85* **Closed** *Sun*
Seasonal menu and an impressive variety of caviars at this beautiful Art Deco gem.

Left Bank

Breakfast in America €
American **Map** 9 A5
17 rue des Ecoles, 75005
Tel *01 43 54 50 28*
All-day breakfast is served at this American diner: bacon, pancakes, burgers, fries, and more.

Café Médicis €
Traditional French **Map** 8 D5
19 rue de Vaugirard, 75006
Tel *01 42 34 37 99*
A varied menu at reasonable prices. The lovely terrace makes this an enticing place for lunch.

El Loubnane €
Lebanese **Map** 13 A4
29 rue Gallande, 75005
Tel *01 43 26 70 60* **Closed** *Mon*
Delicious meze is dished up at this family-run establishment. Don't miss the pistachio-stuffed crêpes.

DK Choice

Brasserie Balzar €€
Traditional French **Map** 9 A5
49 rue des Ecoles, 75005
Tel *01 43 54 13 67*
Skilled waiters in long aprons and waistcoats serve typical brasserie fare at this venerable institution, the former haunt of many great artists and literary figures. There is a separate café and bar section.

Kitchen Galerie Bis €€
Modern French **Map** 8 F4
25 rue des Grands Augustins, 75006
Tel *01 46 33 00 85* **Closed** *Mon & Sun*
Discover contemporary French cuisine with an Asian twist. Fabulous appetizers.

L'Agrume €€
Modern French **Map** 17 C2
15 rue des Fossés St-Marcel, 75005
Tel *01 43 31 86 48* **Closed** *Sun–Tue*
Foodies line up to sample Franck Marchesi-Grandi's delicious five-course tasting menu.

For more information on types of restaurants *see p575*

Le Comptoir du Relais €€
Traditional French **Map** 8 F4
9 carrefour de l'Odéon, 75006
Tel *01 44 27 07 97*
Much celebrated temple to French bistro cuisine. Try the pig's trotters.

Le Procope €€
Traditional French **Map** 8 F4
13 rue de l'Ancienne Comédie, 75006
Tel *01 40 46 79 00*
Opened in 1686, the city's oldest restaurant is delightfully nostalgic. Great selection of desserts.

Le Timbre €€
Traditional French **Map** 12 D1
3 rue Ste-Beuve, 75006
Tel *01 45 49 10 40* **Closed** *Sun & Mon*
All the dishes here are prepared using only the finest, freshest ingredients. Delicious *millefeuille*.

L'Epigramme €€
Traditional French **Map** 8 F4
9 rue de l'Éperon, 75006
Tel *01 44 41 00 09* **Closed** *Sun & Mon*
Serves bistro classics like Basque pork with turnip *choucroute*.

Les Papilles €€
Traditional French **Map** 12 F1
30 rue Gay Lussac, 75005
Tel *01 43 25 20 79* **Closed** *Sun*
A deli, coffee bar, wine shop, and bistro all rolled into one.

Mavrommatis €€
Greek **Map** 17 B2
42 rue Daubenton, 75005
Tel *01 43 31 17 17* **Closed** *Mon*
Superb food and stylish decor teamed with friendly service. Be sure to try the *moussaka*.

Shu €€
Japanese **Map** 8 F4
8 rue Suger, 75006
Tel *01 46 34 25 88* **Closed** *Sun*
There's no menu in this *omakase*-style restaurant. The dishes look and taste stunning.

Terroir Parisien €€
Traditional French **Map** 9 B5
20 rue St-Victor, 75005
Tel *01 44 31 54 54*
Beautifully designed space serving delicious, locally sourced food.

DK Choice

La Tour d'Argent €€€
Traditional French **Map** 9 B5
15 quai de la Tournelle, 75005
Tel *01 43 54 23 31* **Closed** *Sun & Mon*
This Paris institution with its fabulously romantic sixth-floor dining room and panoramic views is world famous. The ground-floor bar doubles as a gastronomic museum.

Vibrant, brightly lit interiors at the popular brasserie Bofinger

Farther Afield

Amici Miei €
Sardinian
44 rue St-Sabin, 75011
Tel *01 42 71 82 62* **Closed** *Sun & Mon*
Unpretentious *trattoria* that rolls out some of the best thin-crust pizzas in Paris.

Arbre de Sel €
Korean
138 rue de Vaugirard, 75015
Tel *01 47 83 29 52* **Closed** *Sun*
Beautifully presented dishes ranging from spicy to very spicy. Vegetarian options available. Friendly and efficient service.

Chez Gladines €
Regional
30 rue des Cinq Diamants, 75013
Tel *01 45 80 70 10*
No-frills eatery where huge salads, smothered with sautéed potatoes, are served in earthenware bowls.

Chez Toinette €
Traditional French
20 rue Germain Pilon, 75018
Tel *01 42 54 44 36* **Closed** *Sun & Mon*
Enjoy delectable duck *foie gras*, snails, lamb shank, and sea bass at this unassuming restaurant.

La Balançoire €
Traditional French
6 rue Aristide Bruant, 75018
Tel *01 42 23 70 83* **Closed** *Sun & Mon*
A child-friendly restaurant filled with jars of sweets. The menu features lots of classics. Try the steak or *foie gras*.

DK Choice

Le Baron Rouge €
Wine bar
1 rue Théophile Roussel, 75012
Tel *01 43 43 14 32*
Fresh, succulent oysters brought directly from the Atlantic coast to be eaten inside the tiny bustling bar or on the sidewalk, standing around large upturned barrels. They also have a great selection of cheese, *charcuterie*, and wine by the glass.

Perraudin €
Traditional French
157 rue St-Jacques, 75005
Tel *01 46 33 15 75*
Hearty fare and a zinc-topped bar that brims with old-world charm. Good selection of desserts.

Rose Bakery €
British vegetarian
46 rue des Martyrs, 75009
Tel *01 42 82 12 80*
Haunt of British expatriates homesick for scones. Fabulous coffee and Neal's Yard cheeses.

Bofinger €€
Regional
5–7 rue de la Bastille, 75004
Tel *01 42 72 87 82*
The city's most beautiful brasserie, with a perfectly preserved Belle Epoque interior.

La Cantine du Troquet €€
Regional
101 rue de l'Ouest, 75014
Tel *01 45 40 04 98* **Closed** *Sat & Sun*
Mouthwatering regional food is served up with a unique touch at this popular restaurant.

La Coupole €€
Traditional French
102 bd du Montparnasse, 75014
Tel *01 43 20 14 20*
Seafood platters draw the crowds at this historic 600-seat brasserie with Art Deco interiors.

La Villa Corse €€
Corsican
164 bd de Grenelle, 75015
Tel *01 53 86 70 81* **Closed** *Sun*
Delicious and varied food in a hospitable setting, with a cozy bar and library.

Le Bistrot Paul Bert €€
Traditional French
18 rue Paul Bert, 75011
Tel *01 43 72 24 01* **Closed** *Sun & Mon*
Top-notch food, a serious wine list, and lovely pre-war decor at this ever-popular bistro.

Key to Price Guide *see p576*

Le Miroir €€
Traditional French
94 rue des Martyrs, 75018
Tel *01 46 06 50 73* **Closed** *Mon*
Bistro-style comfort food from *haute cuisine*–trained chefs.

Marty €€
Traditional French
20 av des Gobelins, 75005
Tel *01 43 31 39 51*
Robust cooking served in original 1913 interiors. Sample the roast duck or the seafood platters.

DK Choice

La Closerie des Lilas €€€
Traditional French
171 bd du Montparnasse, 75006
Tel *01 40 51 34 50*
Splash out on classic cuisine in the restaurant proper, or head for the brasserie and bar where a pianist plays every evening. Hemingway was a regular at this historic establishment.

Ile de France

BARBIZON: Hôtellerie du Bas-Bréau €€€
Regional
22 Grande Rue, 77630
Tel *01 60 66 40 05*
Nestled in the forests of Fontainbleau, this charming restaurant serves wild duck, partridge, pheasant, and hare.

BRAY SUR SEINE: Au Bon Laboureur €
Seafood
2 rue Grande, 77480
Tel *160671081* **Closed** *Wed & Sun eve*
An unassuming exterior belies the delicious fare on offer at this great-value hotel restaurant.

DAMPIERRE: Auberge Saint-Pierre €
Traditional French
1 rue de Chevreuse, 78720
Tel *01 30 52 53 53* **Closed** *Sun eve, Mon & Tue*
A 17th-century half-timbered house with a welcoming dining room and very good food.

FONTAINBLEAU: L'Axel €€
Modern French
43 rue de France, 77300
Tel *01 64 22 01 57* **Closed** *Mon & Tue midday*
Rising star Kunihisa Goto heads the kitchen at this highly recommended restaurant. Try the chef's tasting menu.

LE PERREUX SUR MARNE: Les Magnolias €€
Experimental
48 av de Bry, 94170
Tel *01 48 72 47 43* **Closed** *Mon & Sun; Sat midday*
An avant-garde take on classic dishes. Be sure to try one of the delicious desserts.

NEUILLY-SUR-SEINE: Le Zinc Zinc €
Traditional Bistro
209 ter av du Général-de-Gaulle, 92200
Tel *01 40 88 36 06* **Closed** *Sun*
Lively bistro with great food and wines from all over France.

PROVINS: Au Vieux Remparts €€
Experimental
3 rue Couverte, 77160
Tel *01 64 08 94 00*
Half-timbered eatery with dishes such as mascarpone, white radish with shiso, and smoked salmon.

RAMBOUILLET: Le Cheval Rouge €€
Traditional French
78 rue du Général de Gaulle, 78120
Tel *01 30 88 80 61* **Closed** *Tue midday & Wed*
Top-notch French cuisine. Try *foie gras* and *morilles* mushrooms, and roast lamb with thyme.

ST-GERMAIN-EN-LAYE: Le Saint Exupéry €€
Traditional French
11 av des Loges, 78100
Tel *01 39 21 50 90* **Closed** *Sat & Sun*
Pleasant restaurant with specialities such as shellfish and grilled meat.

DK Choice

VERSAILLES: Ramsay Trianon Palace €€€
Experimental
1 bd de la Reine, 78000
Tel *01 30 84 55 85* **Closed** *Sun, Mon & Tue–Thu lunch*
Gordon Ramsay is the jewel in the crown of this superb royal château hotel. Expect a culinary extravaganza in majestic surroundings but be prepared to feel considerably lighter in the pockets after the meal.

Laid-back outdoor seating area at Hôtellerie du Bas-Bréau, Barbizon

Le Nord & Picardy

AIRE-SUR-LA-LYS: Hostellerie des Trois Mousquetaires €€
Traditional French
Château de la Redoute, rte de Béthune, 62120
Tel *03 21 39 01 11* **Closed** *Sun eve*
Good old-fashioned cooking. Try pike-perch with garden herbs and guinea fowl with mushrooms.

AMIENS: Le Quai €
International
15 Le Quai Bélu, 80000
Tel *03 22 72 10 80* **Closed** *Sun*
Great range of dishes served in a fantastic quayside location.

AMIENS: L'Aubergade €€
Regional
78 rte Nationale
Tel *03 22 89 51 41* **Closed** *Sun & Mon*
Prestigious restaurant located just outside Amiens, with lovely decor and excellent regional dishes.

ARRAS: La Faisanderie €€
Traditional French
45 grand pl, 62000
Tel *03 21 48 20 76* **Closed** *Mon, Sun eve & Thu midday*
Superb restaurant with a Baroque brick-vaulted dining room and traditional menu.

BEAUVAIS: Les Vents d'Ange €€
Bistro
3 rue de Etamine, 60000
Tel *03 44 15 00 08* **Closed** *Mon*
Enjoy inventive cuisine with a great view of the cathedral. Try roasted scallops with vegetables, potatoes, and licorice juice.

BELLE-EGLISE: La Grange de la Belle Eglise €€€
Traditional French
28 bd René-Aimé-la-Gabrielle, 60540
Tel *03 44 08 49 00* **Closed** *Mon, Sun eve & Tue midday*
Well-known luxury restaurant with specialties such as lobster and scallops with truffles.

BOULOGNE-SUR-MER: La Plage €€
Seafood
124 bd Sainte-Beuve, 62200
Tel *03 21 99 90 90* **Closed** *Sun, Mon eve*
A modern take on classic seafood dishes served on the waterfront.

For more information on types of restaurants *see p575*

Take-out counter at A l'Huitrière, a seafood joint in Lille

CALAIS: Histoire Ancienne €
Traditional French
20 rue Royale, 62100
Tel *03 21 34 11 20* **Closed** *Sun & Mon eve; Jul–Aug: Mon*
Old-world bistro-style cooking: marrow bones, snails in garlic butter, and pepper steak.

CALAIS: La Sole Meunière €€
Seafood
1 bd de la Résistance 62100
Tel *03 21 34 43 01* **Closed** *Sun eve & Mon*
Fish served straight from the harbor. Do not miss the seafood platter.

CAMBRAI: L'Escargot €
Bistro
10 rue du Général de Gaulle, 59400
Tel *03 27 81 24 54* **Closed** *Wed & Fri eve*
Unpretentious eatery offering hearty meals at reasonable prices.

CASSEL: Estaminet T'Kasteel Hof €
Traditional French
rue St-Nicolas, 59670
Tel *03 28 40 59 29* **Closed** *Mon–Wed*
No-frills Flanders café with fantastic views. Also has a boutique for local produce.

COMPIEGNE: Alain Blot €€
Seafood
21 rue Maréchal Foch, Rethondes, 60153
Tel *03 44 85 60 24* **Closed** *Mon & Tue; Sat midday; Sun eve*
Excellent seafood at this Louis XVI–style restaurant with an open veranda.

COMPIEGNE: Bistrot de Flandre €€
Traditional French
2 rue d'Amiens, 60200
Tel *03 44 83 26 35* **Closed** *Sun eve*
Classic bistro with hearty meals and a good wine list. Try the roast fillet steak with peppers.

DOUAI: La Terrasse €
Seafood
36 terrasse St-Pierre, 59500
Tel *03 27 88 70 04*
Hidden in a side street, this restaurant dishes up fantastic fresh fish and delectable *fois gras*.

DUNKERQUE: Estouffade €€
Seafood
2 quai de la Citadelle, 59140
Tel *03 28 63 92 78* **Closed** *Sun eve & Mon*
Popular seafood restaurant with port views and refined dishes. Try the turbot or snails with fennel.

FAVIERES: La Clé des Champs €
Traditional French
13 pl Frères Caudron, 80120
Tel *03 22 27 88 00* **Closed** *Mon & Tue*
Great value eatery, with specialties such as beef with Reblochon and turbot with vegetables.

LAON: Zorn-La Petite Auberge €
International
45 bd Brossolette, 02000
Tel *03 23 23 02 38* **Closed** *Sat midday; Sun; Mon eve*
Creative cooking with an emphasis on fish. Stylish decor and an excellent wine list.

LENS: L'Atelier de Marc Meurin €
Regional
Parc du Musée du Louvre-Lens – Rue Paul Bert, 62300
Tel *03 21 68 88 88*
Steps from the Louvre-Lens museum, Marc Meurin creates great dishes from local produce.

LILLE: Au Vieux de la Vieille €
Regional
2–4 rue des Vieux-Murs, 59800
Tel *03 20 63 90 67*
Café specializing in Flemish fare. Try pancakes in *Maroilles* cheese.

LILLE: Le Compostelle €€
Traditional French
4 rue Saint-Étienne, 59800
Tel *03 28 38 08 30*
Great food and delicious desserts are served in a fine 16th-century Renaissance interior.

DK Choice

LILLE: A l'Huitrière €€€
Seafood
3 rue des Chats Bossus, 59800
Tel *03 20 55 43 41* **Closed** *Sun eve*
More than just a restaurant, A l'Huitrière is also an oyster bar and seafood boutique where you can buy the day's catch. Try the vinaigrette salad of smoked eel with *foie gras*, bar with caviar, lobster, crayfish, or the signature turbot.

MONTREUIL SUR MER: Auberge de la Grenouillère €€€
Traditonal
19 rue de la Grenouillère, La Madelaine sous Montreuil, 62170
Tel *03 21 06 07 22* **Closed** *Mon midday, Tue & Wed*
Riverside farm restaurant with traditional interiors and an 11-course tasting menu.

POIX-DE-PICARDIE: L'Auberge de la Forge €€
Traditional French
14 rue du 49ème Régiment BCA Caulières, 80290
Tel *03 22 38 00 91* **Closed** *Sun eve*
Half-timbered Picardy coaching inn with great-value meals and a brasserie for those who just want to grab a quick bite to eat.

ROYE: La Flamiche €€€
Traditional French
20 pl Hôtel de Ville, 80700
Tel *03 22 87 00 56* **Closed** *Mon, Sun eve & Tue midday*
Try tajine of Somme eels or the pan-fried scallops at this Michelin-starred restaurant.

STEENVOORDE: Auberge du Noord Meulen €
Traditional French
rte du Whormhout, 59112
Tel *03 28 48 11 18*
Delicious food served in wonderfully quaint surroundings. Try the *ficelle picarde* (baked pancake with ham, mushrooms, and cream).

Champagne

BAR-SUR-AUBE: La Toque Baralbine €€
Regional
18 rue Nationale 10200
Tel *03 25 27 20 34* **Closed** *Mon*
A great place to try innovative regional dishes. The scallop risotto is particularly good.

CHALONS-EN-CHAMPAGNE: Le Petit Pasteur €
Bistro
42 rue Pasteur, 51000
Tel *03 26 68 24 78* **Closed** *Sun eve, Mon & Wed eve*
Unpretentious decor and a choice of bistro, regional, and traditional menus.

CHALONS-EN-CHAMPAGNE: Au Carillon Gourmand €€
Traditional French
15 pl Monseigneur Tissier, 51000
Tel *03 26 64 45 07* **Closed** *Sun eve, Mon & Wed eve*
Welcoming restaurant offering dishes such as calf's liver in port, cherries, and polenta chips.

Key to Price Guide *see p576*

CHARLEVILLE-MEZIERES:
Au Cochon Qui Louche €
Traditional French
31 rue Victoire Cousin 08000
Tel *03 24 35 49 05* **Closed** *Mon*
Fun restaurant with a bistro menu and homestyle cooking. Excellent chocolate mousse.

COLOMBEY-LES-DEUX-EGLISES:
Hostellerie La Montagne €€
Traditional French
10 rue Pisseloup, 52330
Tel *03 25 01 53 20* **Closed** *Mon & Tue*
Elegant restaurant with friendly service. Don't miss the lobster with spinach shoots.

CUMIERES: Le Caveau €
Traditional French
44 rue de la Coopérative, 51480
Tel *03 26 54 83 23* **Closed** *Sun eve, Mon & Tue eve*
Dine in museum-like rooms on excellent *foie gras* salad and duck breast in red wine.

EPERNAY:
La Cave à Champagne €€
Wine bar
16 rue Gambetta, 51200
Tel *03 26 55 50 70* **Closed** *Tue & Wed*
The perfect place for champagne lovers, offering a wide choice of bubbly. Great appetizers.

FAGNON:
Abbaye des 7 Fontaines €€
Traditional French
rue de Sept Fontaines, 8090
Tel *03 24 37 38 24*
Stately château with a traditional restaurant inside a splendid Louis XVI room.

FOUCHERES:
L'Auberge de la Seine €€
Seafood
1 Faubourg de Bourgogne 10260
Tel *03 25 40 71 11* **Closed** *Sun eve & Mon*
Fresh fish served in a 1930s setting. There is a covered terrace overlooking the Seine.

GIFFAUMONT-CHAMPAUBERT:
La Grange aux Abeilles €
Crêperie
4 rue du Grand Der 51290
Tel *03 26 72 61 97*
An ancient beekeepers' barn now converted into a restaurant and crêperie. Good service.

L'EPINE:
Aux Armes de Champagne €€
Traditional French
31 av du Luxembourg 51460
Tel *03 26 69 30 30* **Closed** *Sun eve, & Mon*
An attractive restaurant serving a wide variety of delectable French classics. Opt for the tasting menu.

LANGRES: Restaurant Diderot €€
Traditional French
4 rue de l'Estres, 52200
Tel *03 25 87 07 00* **Closed** *Wed midday*
Elegant, beamed restaurant with hearty food. Try the *moules-frites*.

MAISONS LES CHAOURCE:
Aux Maisons €
Regional
11 rue Anciens Combattants d'AFN, 10210
Tel *03 25 70 07 19*
Authentic local fare with variations is served in a converted barn. Sample the lamb pastilla.

NOGENT-SUR-SEINE:
Le Beau Rivage €€
Traditional French
20 rue Villiers-aux-Choux, 10400
Tel *03 25 39 84 22* **Closed** *Sun eve & Mon*
Expect delicious food, old-school service, and fantastic views of the Seine. The desserts are superb.

DK Choice

REIMS: Café du Palais €
Traditional French
14 pl Myron Herrick, 51100
Tel *03 26 47 52 54* **Closed** *Sun & Mon*
Enter an Aladdin's cave of theatrical memorabilia under a heritage-listed stained-glass roof. A much-loved family-run brasserie with excellent main dishes, great desserts, and a fine selection of champagne.

REIMS:
Brasserie du Boulingrin €€
Traditional French
48 rue de Mars, 51100
Tel *03 26 40 96 22* **Closed** *Sun*
A very popular meeting place for locals, this eatery serves excellent oysters and steak tartare.

SAINT-DIZIER:
La Palme Rouge
€€
Traditional French
1 rue du Quai d'Ornel, 52100
Tel *03 25 04 92 78*
Closed *Sat midday; Sun eve; Mon eve*
A wide variety of dishes and Parisian brasserie-style decor.

SERMIERS: Lys du Roy
€
Traditional French
1 rte de Damery, 51500
Tel *03 26 97 66 11*
Closed *Mon & Tue eve*
Quaint old-world exteriors and an imaginative menu.

SEZANNE:
Le Relais Champenois €
Traditional French
157 rue Notre Dame, 51120
Tel *03 26 80 58 03* **Closed** *Sun eve*
Eat among rustic beams and copper saucepans. The guinea fowl or monkfish with chorizo are highly recommended.

TINQUEUX:
Assiette Champenoise €€€
Traditional French
40 av Paul Vaillant-Couturier, 51430
Tel *03 26 84 64 64* **Closed** *Tue midday & Wed midday*
Delightful restaurant with stylish modern interiors and exquisitely prepared dishes of lobster, scallops, turbot, and venison.

TROYES: Aux Crieurs de Vin €
Wine bar bistro
4 pl Jean Jaurès, 10000
Tel *03 25 40 01 01* **Closed** *Sun & Mon*
Lively wine bar and bistro with an informal atmosphere; lots of wooden benches and tables.

TROYES: Le Valentino €€
Regional
35 rue Paillot de Montabert, 10000
Tel *03 25 73 14 14* **Closed** *Sun & Mon*
Picturesque half-timbered house with a courtyard for outdoor dining. The menu features dishes such as turbot béarnaise and raspberry omelette.

VILLEMOYENNE: La Parentele €€
Modern
30–32 rue Marcellin Lévèque, 10260
Tel *03 25 43 68 68* **Closed** *Sun–Tue, Wed eve & Thu eve*
Creative, contemporary menu in a sleek setting. Favorites include crayfish with coconut milk, ravioli with *foie gras*, and scallops with sweet and sour sauce.

Exquisite fare laid out at the brasserie Café du Palais

For more information on types of restaurants *see p575*

Gracefully laid table at the refined L'Arnsbourg in Baerenthal

VILLIERS-SUR-SUIZE: Auberge de la Fontaine €
Traditional French
2 pl de la Fontaine, 52210
Tel *03 25 31 22 22* **Closed** *Sat midday & Sun eve*
The menu offers lots of choice, the food is good and prices are easy on the pocket. Great rustic setting.

WILLIERS: Chez Odette €€
Regional
18 rue de l'Ancien Lavoir, 08110
Tel *03 24 55 49 55* **Closed** *Mon–Thu*
Very sleek decor and smart service at this excellent mid-range restaurant. Ask for the larded roast veal.

Alsace & Lorraine

BAERENTHAL: L'Arnsbourg €€€
Traditional French
18 Untermuhlthal, 57230
Tel *03 87 06 50 85* **Closed** *Tue & Wed*
Outstanding dining experience at one of France's finest restaurants tucked away in the countryside.

BITCHE: Le Strasbourg €€
Traditional French
24 rue Col. Teyssier, 57230
Tel *03 87 96 00 44* **Closed** *Mon, Sun eve & Tue midday*
First-class restaurant with a big dining room and a wide range of fish dishes.

COLMAR: Wistub Brenner €
Regional
1 rue de Turenne, 68000
Tel *03 89 41 42 33* **Closed** *Tue & Wed*
Very popular eatery famous for its Alsatian dishes and cheery, unpretentious atmosphere. The salad with potent Munster cheese is especially popular.

COLMAR: JY's €€
International
17 rue de la Poissonerie 68000
Tel *03 89 21 53 60* **Closed** *Sun & Mon*
Contemporary dining hidden away in a 17th-century building. Great international cuisine at reasonable prices.

ILLHAEUSERN: L'Auberge de l'Ill €€€
Regional
2 rue de Collonges, 68970
Tel *03 89 71 89 00* **Closed** *Mon & Tue*
Michelin-starred establishment offering Alsatian dishes. Try the truffle wrapped in *fois gras.*

KAYSERSBERG: Restaurant Saint Alexis €
Traditonal French
Lieu-dit Saint Alexis, 68240
Tel *03 89 73 90 38* **Closed** *Fri*
This eatery in the mountains offers excellent traditional cooking. Serves delicious soups.

KAYSERSBERG: Au Lion d'Or €€
Regional
66 rue Général de Gaulle, 68240
Tel *03 89 47 11 16* **Closed** *Winter: Tue & Wed; Summer: Tue eve & Wed*
Authentic local flavors in an 18th-century setting. Popular dishes include wild game and sauerkraut.

LEMBACH: Gimbelhof €
Traditional French
rte Forestière, 67510
Tel *03 88 94 43 58* **Closed** *Mon & Tue*
Successful family-run hotel-restaurant surrounded by a forest and ruined medieval castles.

LES THONS: Le Couvent des Cordeliers €
Regional
Les Thons, 88410
Tel *03 29 07 90 84* **Closed** *Mon*
Popular, friendly eatery where the owner roasts slices of ham on an open fire. The steak with fried mushrooms is also recommended.

MARLENHEIM: Le Cerf €€€
Traditional French
30 rue Général de Gaulle, 67520
Tel *03 88 87 73 73* **Closed** *Tue & Wed*
Half-timbered coaching inn with a wonderful cobbled courtyard. Delicious lobster gratin.

METZ: Le Bistro des Sommeliers €
Bistro
10 rue Pasteur, 57000
Tel *03 87 63 40 20* **Closed** *Sun*
Excellent food and a wide range of wines. A fine dining experience in a brasserie setting.

METZ: Le Magasin aux Vivres €€€
Traditional French
5 av Ney, 57000
Tel *03 87 17 17 17* **Closed** *Sat midday, Sun eve & Mon*
Good food in elegant historic surroundings. The dessert menu is outstanding. Cookery lessons are also offered.

MULHOUSE: Garden Ice Café €
Brasserie
6 pl de la République 68100
Tel *03 89 66 00 00*
Bright, vibrant interiors, good food, and live music at this charming budget restaurant.

NANCY: Au Grand Serieux €
Brasserie
27 rue Raugraff, 54000
Tel *03 83 36 68 87* **Closed** *Sun*
A popular institution since 1870, this eatery makes a great beef fillet with truffles. Good local wine list. Friendly service.

NANCY: Chez Tanésy Le Gastrolâtre €€
Bistro
23 Grande Rue, 54000
Tel *03 83 35 51 94* **Closed** *Sun, Mon & Tue midday*
A 16th-century town house, made into a small bistro-style restaurant that serves tasty classics – ask for pig trotters and jugged hare.

NIEDERSTEINBACH: Au Wasigenstein €
Regional
32 rue Principale Wengelsbach, 67510
Tel *03 88 09 50 54* **Closed** *Mon & Tue*
Excellent village auberge in a stunning location. Lovely terrace for outdoor dining. Serves superb wild game.

OBERNAI: La Fourchette des Ducs €€€
Traditional French
6 plc de la Gare, 67210
Tel *03 88 48 33 38* **Closed** *Mon, Sun eve & Tue–Sat midday*
A sophisticated dining experience is guaranteed at this luxury restaurant, founded in the 1920s by local motoring genius Ettore Bugatti.

RIQUEWIHR: Le Sarment d'Or €€
Traditional French
4 rue du Cerf, 68340
Tel *03 89 86 02 86* **Closed** *Mon, Sun eve & Tue midday*
Great attention to detail and fantastic food served in a 17th-century house, hidden away in a quiet corner of this pretty village. The elegantly decorated beamed dining room adds to the charm.

Key to Price Guide *see p576*

SAVERNE: Taverne Katz €€
Regional
30 Grand Rue, 67700
Tel *03 88 71 16 56*
Stunning exterior and beautifully paneled interiors. The braised pork cheeks in beer are excellent.

STRASBOURG: Pâtisserie Winter €
Tearoom
25 rue du 22 Novembre, 67000
Tel *03 88 32 85 40* **Closed** *Sun*
Attractive restaurant serving simple and tasty lunches. Great salads, steaks, patés, and cakes.

STRASBOURG: Winstub Zuem Strissel €€
Regional
5 pl de la Grande Boucherie, 67000
Tel *03 88 32 14 73*
Good value brasserie-style food served in a restaurant established in the 14th-century. Try *bibelekäse* (cream cheese and fried potatoes).

DK Choice

STRASBOURG: Buerehiesel €€€
Traditional French
4 Parc de Orangerie, 67000
Tel *038 84 56 65* **Closed** *Sun & Mon*
This is a unique Michelin-starred restaurant that gave up its 3 Rosettes to give clients a better deal. Now it serves without all the bells and whistles that go with such star-rated establishments.

VERDUN: Hostellerie le Coq Hardi €€
Traditional French
av de la Victoire, 55100
Tel *03 29 86 36 36* **Closed** *Fri, Sat midday & Sun eve*
Simple dishes made from local produce served in an elegant dining area with a summer terrace.

WISSEMBOURG: Daniel Rebert €
Bistro
7 pl du Marché aux Choux, 67100
Tel *03 88 94 01 66* **Closed** *Mon*
Lovely bistro with a discreet tearoom at the back serving light lunches and coffee. Exquisite cakes.

Normandy

ACQUIGNY: Hostellerie d'Acquigny €€
Classic
1 rue Evreux, 27400
Tel *02 32 50 20 05* **Closed** *Sun eve, Mon & Tue*
This former coaching inn houses a charming restaurant with inexpensive set menus. It also offers an eclectic wine list and enthusiastic service.

ALENÇON: Le Bistro €
Bistro
21 rue de Sarthe, 61000
Tel *02 33 26 51 69* **Closed** *Sun & Mon*
Classic French bistro with a distinct green-painted facade, red-checkered tablecloths, and old film posters. Well-stocked wine list.

AUMALE: La Villa des Houx €€
Regional
6 av Général de Gaulle, 76390
Tel *02 35 93 93 30* **Closed** *Sun eve & Mon midday; mid-Sep–mid-Jun*
Housed in a former police station, this place offers a taste of real Normandy cuisine. Try the apricot *foie gras* appetizer.

BARNEVILLE-CARTERET: Marine €€
Classic
11 rue de Paris, 50270
Tel *02 33 53 83 31* **Closed** *Apr–May; Sep–Nov*
Modern, stylish dining room with a panoramic view of the port. Wine list matches the great food.

BAYEUX: Le Lion d'Or €€
Traditional French
71 rue St-Jean, 14400
Tel *02 31 92 06 90* **Closed** *Sun eve & Mon, Tue & Sat middays; mid-Nov–mid-Mar: Mon eve*
Well-prepared, traditional Normandy food served in a converted 18th-century post office.

BEUVRON-EN-AUGE: Le Pavé Auge €€
Regional
Les Halles, 14430
Tel *02 31 79 26 71* **Closed** *Mon*
Once a village market hall, this restaurant only uses locally sourced produce. The menu focuses on fish.

Beautiful glass-covered dining area at Buerehiesel in Strasbourg

BLAINVILLE-SUR-MER: Le Mascaret €€€
Modern French
1 rue de Bas, 50560
Tel *02 33 45 86 09* **Closed** *Mon*
Experience top experimental cuisine at Le Mascaret. There is also a bistro in the lovely conservatory where you can snack on oysters, blinis, and sushi.

BRICQUEVILLE-SUR-MER: Couleurs Saveurs €€
Modern French
2 rte de Bretonnière, 50290
Tel *02 33 61 65 62* **Closed** *Sun, Wed & Mon eve*
The modern dining room of this coastal restaurant sets the stage for a menu where regional produce meets Oriental spices.

CAEN: Le Pressoir – Ivan Vautier €€€
Fine dining
3 av Henry-Chéron, 14000
Tel *02 31 73 32 71* **Closed** *Mon & Sun eve*
Award-winning chef Ivan Vautier creates delectable dishes for discerning guests, with emphasis on using the best local produce.

CHERBOURG: Le Faitout €€
Bistro
25 rue Tour-Carrée, 50100
Tel *02 33 04 25 04* **Closed** *Sun & Mon*
A bastion of culinary tradition, Le Faitout is an animated bistro-style restaurant serving wholesome dishes par excellence.

COSQUEVILLE: Au Bouquet de Cosqueville €
Seafood
Hameau Rémond, 50330
Tel *02 33 54 32 81* **Closed** *Winter: Mon*
Set in an ivy-clad house in the village center, this elegantly rustic restaurant serves generous portions of fresh seafood.

DEAUVILLE: Le Spinnaker €€
Seafood
52 rue Mirabeau, 14800
Tel *02 31 88 24 40* **Closed** *Sep–Jun: Mon & Tue*
One of Normandy's finest fish restaurants, Le Spinnaker has an attractive modern dining room. Also offers grilled meat dishes.

DIEPPE: Bistrot du Pollet €
Bistro
23 rue Tête de Boeuf, 76200
Tel *02 35 84 68 57* **Closed** *Sun & Mon*
Small, friendly eatery with a simple but wholesome menu. Try the haddock salad or grilled sardines. Book ahead.

For more information on types of restaurants *see p575*

FALAISE: L'Attache €€
Traditional French
rte de Caen, 14700
Tel *02 31 90 05 38* **Closed** *Tue & Wed*
Beautifully renovated former staging post. The chef uses unusual plants and aromatic herbs to flavor his cooking.

FECAMP: La Marée €€
Seafood
77 quai Bérigny, 76400
Tel *02 35 29 39 15* **Closed** *Mon, Thu eve & Sun eve*
Very popular and lively restaurant that offers huge seafood platters.

GISORS: Le Cappeville €€
Regional
17 rue Cappeville, 27410
Tel *02 32 55 11 08* **Closed** *Wed & Thu*
An elegantly furbished converted town house. Impressive cheeseboard on offer.

GRANVILLE: La Citadelle €€
Seafood
34 rue du Port, 50406
Tel *02 33 50 34 10* **Closed** *Wed; Oct–Mar: Tue*
Overlooking the bay of St-Michel, this charming eatery serves the biggest portions of sole in town.

HONFLEUR:
La Ferme St-Siméon €€€
Fine dining
rue A Marais, 14600
Tel *02 31 81 78 00*
Luxury spa-hotel restaurant with an excellent wine list to go with the delectable fish on offer.

JUVIGNY-SOUS-ANDAINE:
Au Bon Accueil €€
Traditional French
23 pl St-Michel, 61140
Tel *02 33 38 10 04* **Closed** *Sun eve & Mon*
Stylish restaurant offering creative French cuisine. Good menus prepared from fresh local produce.

LA CROIX ST-LEUFROY:
Le Cheval Blanc €€
Traditional French
27 rue de Louviers, 27490
Tel *02 32 34 82 86* **Closed** *Wed, Sun eve & Tue eve*
Drive out to a quiet village in the Eure valley for a taste of top-notch cuisine. Excellent cheese selection.

LA FERRIERE AUX ETANGS:
Auberge de la Mine €€
Regional
Le Gué-Plat, 61450
Tel *02 33 66 91 10* **Closed** *Sun eve, Mon & Tue*
Authentic Norman dishes made with refreshing originality. The desserts are to die for.

Entrance to the ever-popular brasserie La Mère Poulard, Mont-St-Michel

LE BREUIL-EN-AUGE:
Le Dauphin €€€
Fine dining
2 rue de l'Eglise, 14130
Tel *02 31 65 08 11* **Closed** *Sun eve & Mon*
Half-timbered Normandy house where the chef reinvents classics using the best local produce.

LE HAVRE: Jean-Luc Tartarin €€€
Fine dining
73 av Foch, 76600
Tel *02 35 45 46 20* **Closed** *Sun & Mon*
Imaginative dishes based on produce sourced from local farms and fishing harbors. Fine service.

LES ANDELYS: La Chaine d'Or €€€
Traditional French
27 rue Grande, 27700
Tel *02 32 54 00 31* **Closed** *Sun eve & Tue*
Romantic setting on the banks of the Seine, with exquisite culinary classics perfectly prepared.

LYONS-LA-FORET:
Le Grand Cerf €€
Bistro
20 pl Isaac Benserade, 27480
Tel *02 32 49 50 50*
Hearty homemade fare is complemented by the rustic setting. Oak beams and bare red-brick walls add to the charm.

DK Choice

MEZIERES-EN-VEXIN:
Au Pré du Fourneau €€
Traditional French
11 rue de Huis, 27510
Tel *02 32 69 57 44* **Closed** *Mon, Wed & Thu & Sat middays*
This restaurant is passionate about rare herbs and vegetables. Simplicity is the key to the cuisine at this establishment. The chef conjures sensational dishes that delight the eyes and tingle the taste buds. The pot roast pork with honey and pistachio is exceptional.

MONT-ST-MICHEL:
La Mère Poulard €€€
Brasserie
Grande Rue, 50170
Tel *02 33 89 68 68*
Visitors from across the world stop here for omelettes cooked in a long-handled pan over a fire.

PONT L'EVEQUE:
Auberge des Deux Tonneaux €
Bistro
Pierrefitte en Auge, 14130
Tel *02 31 64 09 31* **Closed** *Mon eve & Tue*
Thatched cottage serving robust dishes and local ciders. The shady outdoor terrace offers valley views.

PONT SAINT-PIERRE:
Auberge de l'Andelle €
Traditional French
27 Grande Rue, 27360
Tel *02 32 49 70 18* **Closed** *Oct–mid- Apr: Tue eve*
Rustic dining room with an open fire. Pick a live lobster from the tank and have it cooked to perfection.

ROUEN: Le 37 €
Bistro
37 rue St-Etienne-des-Tonneliers, 76000
Tel *02 35 70 56 65* **Closed** *Sun & Mon*
Attractive city-center bistro serving modern cuisine. Find the daily specials on the blackboard.

ROUEN: Restaurant Gill €€€
Fine dining
8–9 quai de la Bourse, 76000
Tel *02 35 71 16 14* **Closed** *Sun & Mon*
Highly recommended restaurant on the Seine quay with an elegant dining room. Try the sea bass.

STE-CECILE:
Le Manoir de l'Archerie €€
Traditional French
37 rue Michel de l'Epinay, 50800
Tel *02 33 51 13 87* **Closed** *Oct–Mar: Sun eve & Mon*
Fresh Normandy produce served in a beautiful manor house. Good selection of local cheeses.

TROUVILLE-SUR-MER:
La Régence €€
Seafood
132 bd Fernand Moureaux, 14360
Tel *02 31 88 10 71* **Closed** *Winter: Wed & Thu*
Beautiful interior with mirrors and 19th-century wood paneling. The shellfish is a house speciality.

Key to Price Guide *see p576*

VEULES LES ROSES: Les Galets €€
Seafood
3 rue Victor Hugo, 76980
Tel *02 35 97 61 33* **Closed** *Wed (except Aug) & Tue*
Traditional restaurant situated close to the pebbly beach, with a comfortable dining area.

VILLERS BOCAGE: Les Trois Rois €€
Traditional French
2 pl Jeanne d'Arc, 14310
Tel *02 31 77 00 32* **Closed** *Winter: Sun eve*
Set in a vast square surrounded by gardens, this restaurant serves generous portions of local dishes.

Brittany

ARRADON: Les Logoden €
Crêperie
24 rue Albert-Danet, 56610
Tel *02 97 46 79 03* **Closed** *Thu & Sun eve*
Authentic crêpes with a featured filling each week. The produce is sourced from neighboring farms.

AUDIERNE: Le Goyen €€
Seafood
pl Jean-Simon, 29770
Tel *02 98 70 08 88*
Delicious fresh oysters and excellent seafood platters at this hotel-restaurant by the sea. Try the scrumptious pan-fried scallops.

BELLE ILE EN MER: La Désirade €€
Seafood
Le Petit Cosquet, 56360
Tel *02 97 31 70 70* **Closed** *Mon–Fri midday*
This farmhouse restaurant offers a great breakfast menu in addition to fantastic seafood.

BREST: Le M €€€
Fine dining
22 rue du Commandant Drogou, 29200
Tel *02 98 47 90 00* **Closed** *Sun*
Contemporary dining room serving inventive dishes.

CARANTEC: Restaurant Patrick Jeoffroy €€€
Fine dining
20 rue Kélénn, 29660
Tel *02 98 67 00 47* **Closed** *Sun eve Mon & Tue*
Classic food with a modern twist is served in this sleek restaurant with a magnificent view over Kélénn beach. Try the roast fillet of sole.

CARNAC: Le Calypso €€
Seafood
158 rte du Pô, 56340
Tel *02 97 52 06 14* **Closed** *Sep–Jun: Sun eve*
Popular seafood restaurant overlooking the oyster beds of Anse du Pô. Great service.

CONCARNEAU: Le Petit Chaperon Rouge €
Crêperie
7 pl Duguesclin, 29900
Tel *02 98 60 53 32* **Closed** *Sun eve & Mon*
Lovely crêperie near the harbor with a "Little Red Riding Hood" theme to its decor.

DINAN: Ma Mère Pourcel €
Traditional French
3 pl des Merciers, 22100
Tel *02 96 39 03 80* **Closed** *Sun eve, Tue eve & Wed*
Locally reared lamb and a variety of innovative fish dishes at this restaurant inside a medieval half-timbered building.

DOUARNENEZ: Insolite €€
Modern French
4 rue Jean Jaurès, 29100
Tel *02 98 92 00 02*
Stylish restaurant offering original dishes that blend regional produce and Eastern spices.

FOUESNANT CAP COZ: Restaurant de la Pointe du Cap Coz €€
Traditional French
153 av de la Pointe, 29170
Tel *02 98 56 01 63* **Closed** *Mon & Wed; Sep–Jun: Sun eve & Tue eve*
Top-notch cuisine served in a dining room decorated to complement the coastal setting. Excellent wine list.

Spacious dining area at Restaurant Patrick Jeoffroy, Carantec

FOUGERES: Haute Sève €€
Regional French
37 bd Jean Jaurès, 35300
Tel *02 99 94 23 39* **Closed** *Sun eve & Mon*
The timbered facade hides vibrant modern interiors. Regional classics with a twist.

GUIMILIAU: Ar Chupen €
Crêperie
43 rue de Calvaire, 29400
Tel *02 98 68 73 63* **Closed** *Winter: Fri eve & Sat midday*
Traditional galettes and crêpes made to order make this renovated Breton farmhouse a budget winner.

GUINGAMP: Le Clos de la Fontaine €€
Traditional French
9 rue du Général de Gaulle, 22200
Tel *02 96 21 33 63* **Closed** *Sun eve & Mon; Sep–Jun: Tue eve*
Wonderful fish dishes served with delicate sauces. The chef uses only the best local produce.

HEDE: L'Hostellerie du Vieux Moulin €€
Traditional French
Ancienne rte de St-Malo, 35630
Tel *02 99 45 45 70* **Closed** *Mon, Sun midday & Thu midday*
Good-value lunchtime menus at this restaurant overlooking Hédé Castle.

ILE DE NOIRMOUTIER: Le Grand Four €€€
Seafood
1 rue de la Cure, 85330
Tel *02 51 39 61 97* **Closed** *Winter: Sun eve, Thu midday; Jul–Aug: Mon midday*
A 17th-century house cloaked in green ivy with pink shutters. Decent selection of Loire wines.

LORIENT: Le Neptune €€
Seafood
15 av de la Perrière, 56100
Tel *02 97 37 04 56* **Closed** *Sun*
The haul at the nearby Keroman fishing port determines the dish of the day. Trendy modern decor.

LORIENT: L'Amphitryon €€€
Fine dining
127 rue du Colonel Jean Müller, 56100
Tel *02 97 83 34 04* **Closed** *Sun & Mon*
Inspirational cuisine prepared with simplicity in stylish surroundings. Good choice of wines by the glass.

PAIMPOL: L'Islandais €
Crêperie
19 quai Morand, 22500
Tel *02 96 20 93 80*
A quayside restaurant with an aquatic theme. Serves a wide range of tasty sweet and savory galettes.

For more information on types of restaurants *see p575*

DK Choice

PLOMODIERN:
Auberge des Glazicks €€€
Fine dining
7 rue de la Plage,,29550
Tel *02 98 81 52 32* **Closed** *Mon & Tue*
Headed by Olivier Bellin, the award-winning Auberge des Glazicks has stunning views over the Bay of Douarnenez. The celebrated chef works wonders with Breton produce to create sublime and original cuisine.

PLOUBALAY: La Gare €€
Regional French
4 rue des Ormelet, 22650
Tel *02 96 27 25 16* **Closed** *Mon & Wed; Jul–Aug: Mon & Tue midday; Sep–Jun: Mon & Tue eve*
Regional dishes are given a modern twist in this rustic eatery.

QUIMPER: L'Ambroisie €€€
Modern French
49 rue Elie Fréron, 29000
Tel *02 98 95 00 02* **Closed** *Sun eve & Mon*
Located close to the cathedral, this atmospheric restaurant offers both modern and classical cuisine.

RENNES: Léon Le Cochon €
Bistro
1 rue du Maréchal Joffre, 35000
Tel *02 99 79 37 54* **Closed** *Jul–Aug: Sun*
A quirky pork-centric restaurant. The pig's trotters and sausages from Morteau are recommended, but you can also order excellent beef, duck, or prawns.

RENNES: Autre Sens €€
Modern French
11 rue Armand Rébillon, 35000
Tel *02 99 14 25 14* **Closed** *Sat midday & Sun*
Distinct glass cube-shaped restaurant with contemporary bistro-style cuisine.

RENNES:
La Fontaine aux Perles €€€
Fine dining
96 rue de la Poterie, 35000
Tel *02 99 53 90 90* **Closed** *Sun eve & Mon; Aug: Sun–Tue*
Elegant restaurant with dining rooms decorated in varied themes.

ROSCOFF: L'Ecume des Jours €€
Traditional French
quai d'Auxerre, 29680
Tel *02 98 61 22 83* **Closed** *Sep–Jul: Tue & Wed*
An authentic 16th-century ship-owner's house serving a wide selection of local coastal produce.

ST-BRIEUC: Air du Temps €
Bistro
4 rue du Gouët, 22000
Tel *02 96 68 58 40* **Closed** *Sun & Mon*
Pleasant restaurant with modern decor that offsets the 200-year-old stone walls. Try the pork casserole.

ST-MALO: Le Chalut €€
Seafood
8 rue de la Corne de Cerf, 35400
Tel *02 99 56 71 58* **Closed** *Mon & Tue*
Fishing nets, buoys, and an aquarium provide the perfect ambience to this seafood eatery.

TREGUIER: Aigue Marine €€€
Seafood
5 rue Marcelin Berthelot, 22220
Tel *02 96 92 97 00* **Closed** *Oct–May: Sun eve; Jun–Sep: Thu–Sat midday, Mon–Tue midday*
This fine restaurant in a harbor-front hotel serves sublime fish. Fixed-price menus available.

VANNES: Dan Ewen €
Crêperie
3 pl Général de Gaulle, 56000
Tel *02 97 42 44 34* **Closed** *Sun*
Sample buckwheat pancakes and local cider at this rustic crêperie.

VANNES: L'Eden €€
Modern French
3 rue Pasteur, 56000
Tel *02 97 46 42 42* **Closed** *Sat midday & Sun; Winter: Wed eve*
A local favorite, this restaurant prepares contemporary dishes with originality.

The Loire Valley

AMBOISE: Le 36 €€€
Fine dining
36 quai C. Guinot, 37400
Tel *02 47 30 45 45* **Closed** *Tue & Wed*
Lovely restaurant serving seasonal food with a pretty garden and Loire views from the dining room.

Exquisitely decorated dining space at Le 36, Amboise, Loire

ANCENIS:
Les Terrasses de Bel Air €€
Traditional French
rte d'Angers, 44150
Tel *02 40 83 02 87* **Closed** *Sun eve & Mon*
An 18th-century manor house with an enchanting garden. Classic cuisine creatively prepared.

ANGERS: Ma Campagne €€
Traditional French
14 promenade de la Reculée, 49000
Tel *02 41 48 38 06* **Closed** *Mon, Sun eve & Tue eve*
Country-style auberge very close to the town center. Select the chocolate-coated pear for dessert.

BEAUGENCY: Le Petit Bateau €€
Modern French
54 rue du Pont, 45190
Tel *02 38 44 56 38* **Closed** *Mon & Tue*
Appealing restaurant that reinvents classic dishes. Specialties include fresh fish and wild mushrooms.

BLOIS: Côté Loire €
Traditional French
2 pl de la Grève, 41000
Tel *02 54 78 07 86* **Closed** *Sun & Mon*
Old-fashioned hotel-restaurant overlooking the River Loire. Simple but delicious menu.

BLOIS:
Orangerie du Château €€€
Fine dining
1 av Jean Laigret, 41000
Tel *02 54 78 05 36* **Closed** *Sun & Mon*
Excellent regional food and wine served in the beautiful winter gardens of this château.

BOURGES: Le Louis XI €
Bistro
11 rue Porte Jaune, 11000
Tel *02 48 70 92 14* **Closed** *Sep–Jun: Sun & Mon*
Classic no-frills bistro fare served in generous portions. Convivial ambience and good service.

BOURGES: Le Cercle €€
Modern French
44 bd Lahitolle, 18000
Tel *02 48 70 33 27* **Closed** *Sun & Mon*
Contemporary restaurant in a lovely manor house offering modern, inventive cuisine.

BOURGUEIL: Le Moulin Bleu €
Traditional French
7 rue du Moulin-Bleu, 37140
Tel *02 47 97 73 13* **Closed** *Wed & Sun–Tue eve; off-season: Sun–Thu, Fri midday & Sat midday*
Traditional dishes served in two vaulted dining rooms. Great location and friendly service.

Key to Price Guide *see p576*

BRACIEUX: Le Rendez-vous des Gourmets €
Regional
20 rue Roger Brun, 41250
Tel *02 54 46 03 87* **Closed** *Wed, Sat Midday; mid-Aug & mid-Jul: Sun eve & Mon midday*
Very popular auberge serving traditional regional cuisine. Make sure you book in advance.

CHARTRES: Le Grand Monarque, Le Georges €€€
Fine dining
22 pl des Epars, 28000
Tel *02 37 18 15 15* **Closed** *Sun & Mon*
The very best of classic French cuisine at this gourmet restaurant, accompanied by *grands cru* wines.

CHINON: Les Années 30 €€
Modern French
78 rue Haute St-Maurice, 37500
Tel *02 47 93 37 18* **Closed** *Wed; Sep–Jun: Tue*
Elegant eatery offering interesting dishes, such as pigeon and langoustine served with a truffle-flavored vinaigrette.

CLISSON: La Bonne Auberge €€
Traditional French
1 rue Olivier de Clisson, 44190
Tel *02 40 54 01 90* **Closed** *Sun eve, Mon, Tue midday & Wed eve*
Comfortable auberge with three dining rooms. Specialties include seafood, fish, and game (in season).

CONTRES: La Botte d'Asperges €€
Traditional French
52 rue Pierre-Henri Mauger, 41700
Tel *02 54 79 50 49* **Closed** *Sun eve & Mon*
Locally grown asparagus features prominently on the menu, when in season. Delicious food served in a rustic setting.

DOUE LA FONTAINE: Auberge Bienvenue €
Traditional French
104 rte de Cholet, 49700
Tel *02 41 59 22 44* **Closed** *Sun eve & Mon*
A pretty inn offering hearty meals cooked from local produce, often doused in regional wines. Opt for the roast duck cooked in ginger.

FONTEVRAUD ABBAYE: La Licorne €€
Traditional French
allée Sainte-Catherine, 49590
Tel *02 41 51 72 49* **Closed** *Mon, Sun eve & Wed eve*
Next to the splendid abbey, this popular restaurant has a lovely courtyard terrace and an elegant dining room. Serves delicately flavored dishes. Book ahead.

Entrance to Le Georges restaurant, Le Grande Monarque in Chartres

GENNES: Auberge du Moulin de Sarré €
Traditional French
rte de Louerre, 49350
Tel *02 41 51 81 32*
Robust cuisine served in a 16th-century watermill. Ask for *fouées* (warm bread puffs).

GENNES: L'Aubergade €€€
Fine dining
7 av des Cadets, 49350
Tel *02 41 51 81 07* **Closed** *Tue & Wed*
Two elegantly laid out dining rooms serve up a variety of dishes with exotic flavors.

ILE D'YEU: Les Bafouettes €€
Seafood
8 rue Gabriel-Guist'Hau, 84350
Tel *02 51 59 38 38* **Closed** *Mon; Sep–Mar: Sun*
Traditional fish dishes and *foie gras* feature prominently on the menu of this unpretentious restaurant.

LA FERTE IMBAULT: La Tête de Lard €€
Traditional French
13 pl des Tilleuls, 41300
Tel *02 54 96 22 32* **Closed** *Sun eve, Mon & Tue midday*
Housed in a refurbished country hotel, with a menu that offers seasonal choices.

LAMOTTE BEUVRON: Hôtel Tatin €€
Traditional French
5 av de Vierzon, 41600
Tel *02 54 88 00 03* **Closed** *Sun eve, Mon & Tue midday*
Elegant hotel-restaurant serving fresh local produce, *foie gras*, and homemade pâté.

LANGEAIS: Au Coin des Halles €€
Bistro
9 rue Gambetta, 37120
Tel *02 47 96 37 25* **Closed** *Wed & Thu midday*
Top-notch bistro that combines chic interiors with excellent cuisine.

LE CROISIC: Le Fort Océan €€€
Fine dining
Pointe de Croisic, 44490
Tel *02 40 15 77 77* **Closed** *Mon–Fri midday*
Luxury hotel-restaurant with rose-tinted granite walls and stylish, bold cuisine.

LE MANS: Auberge des 7 Plats €
Traditional French
79 Grand Rue
Tel *02 43 24 57 77*
Select from the seven appetizers, seven mains, and 14 desserts on the menu at this unique eatery.

LE MANS: Le Beaulieu €€€
Fine dining
34 bis place de la République, 72000
Tel *02 43 87 78 37* **Closed** *Sat & Sun*
Sophisticated city-center restaurant with well-priced seasonal menus. Fine service.

LES SABLES D'OLONNE: Affiche €
Seafood
21 quai Giné, 85100
Tel *02 51 95 34 74* **Closed** *Mon*
Intimate little fish restaurant with excellent food and great wine. Booking essential.

MALICORNE-SUR-SARTHE: La Petite Auberge €€
Traditional French
5 pl du Guesclin, 72270
Tel *02 43 94 80 52* **Closed** *Sun eve, Mon & Tue eve; Sep–Apr: Sun–Fri eve*
Gourmet food in a charming setting. In summer, dine on the lovely terrace, and in winter, take refuge around the huge fireplace.

MONTBAZON: La Chancelière €€
Modern French
1 pl des Marronniers, 37250
Tel *02 47 26 00 67* **Closed** *Sun & Mon*
Modern, sophisticated cuisine prepared with precision at this chic and elegant restaurant.

For more information on types of restaurants *see p575*

MONTSOREAU:
Diane de Méridor €€
Fine dining
12 quai Philippe de Commines, 49730
Tel *02 41 51 71 76* **Closed** *Tue & Wed*
Carved out of tuffeau rock, this rustic restaurant has exposed beams and an open fireplace. Specializes in freshwater fish dishes.

NANTES: La Cigale €
Brasserie
4 pl Graslin, 44000
Tel *02 51 84 94 94*
This ornate Belle Epoque brasserie dates from 1895. The quality of food perfectly matches the exceptional interiors.

NANTES: L'Océanide €€
Seafood
2 rue Paul Bellamy, 44000
Tel *02 40 20 32 28* **Closed** *Sun & Mon*
A first-class seafood restaurant, designed during World War II to resemble the interior of an ocean liner.

DK Choice

NANTES: L'U.Ni €€
Modern French
36 rue Fouré
Tel *02 40 75 53 05* **Closed** *Mon & Tue*
Serving creative food in a modern setting, this restaurant has made a name for itself in gourmet circles. Specialties include barely-cooked brill with baby turnips and spinach, and desserts such as avocado and white chocolate *millefeuille*.

ONZAIN:
Domaine des Hauts de Loire €€€
Fine dining
rte de Herbault, 41150
Tel *02 54 20 72 57* **Closed** *Mon & Tue*
Award-winning cuisine served in a former hunting lodge set within its own park.

ORLEANS: La Dariole €
Traditional French
25 rue Etienne Dolet, 45000
Tel *02 38 77 26 67* **Closed** *Sat & Sun; Mon eve, Wed eve & Thu eve*
A 15th-century half-timbered building houses this little restaurant and tearoom. The menu includes meat and seafood.

ORLEANS: Le Lièvre Gourmand €€
Modern French
28 quai de Chatelet, 45000
Tel *02 38 53 66 14*
The all-white decor belies the exciting menu at this restaurant. Original dishes include kangaroo. Great wine selection.

ROCHECORBON: Les Hautes Roches €€€
Fine dining
86 quai Loire, 37210
Tel *02 47 52 88 88* **Closed** *Sun eve & Mon*
A château dining room with an elegant contemporary interior. Serves meticulously prepared classic cuisine.

SACHE:
Auberge du XIIème Siècle €€
Traditional French
1 rue du Château, 37190
Tel *02 47 26 88 77* **Closed** *Sun eve, Mon & Tue midday*
A good choice of fixed-price menus built around classic dishes are served in historic surroundings.

SANCERRE:
Auberge La Pomme d'Or €
Traditional French
pl de la Mairie, 18300
Tel *02 48 54 13 30* **Closed** *Tue & Wed; Oct–Mar: Sun eve*
Flavorsome cooking based on seasonal produce from the region. Enjoy the Chavignol goat's cheese with a glass of Sancerre wine.

SANCERRE: La Tour €€
Modern French
31 Nouvelle Place, 18300
Tel *02 48 54 00 81* **Closed** *Sun eve & Mon*
An elegant restaurant with views over the Sancerre vineyards. Serves good contemporary cuisine using the best local produce.

SAUMUR: Auberge St-Pierre €€
Traditional French
6 pl St-Pierre, 49400
Tel *02 41 51 26 25*
Set in a former 15th-century monastery, this atmospheric restaurant dishes out hearty regional fare.

The exterior of Domaine des Hauts de Loire, a popular restaurant in Onzain

ST-OUEN LES VIGNES:
L'Aubinière €€
Traditional French
29 rue Jules Gautier, 37530
Tel *02 47 30 15 29*
A small but lovely restaurant with a pretty garden leading down to the river. Outstanding dishes.

THOUARCE:
Relais de Bonnezeaux €€
Traditional French
rte Angers, 49380
Tel *02 41 54 08 33* **Closed** *Sun eve, Mon & Tue eve*
A converted train station overlooking the vineyards serves creative food using local produce.

TOURS: L'Atelier Gourmand €
Traditional French
37 rue Etienne Marcel, 37000
Tel *02 47 38 59 87* **Closed** *Sat midday–Mon*
A charming restaurant in the old part of Tours. Interesting menu with competitive prices.

TOURS: Les Saveurs €
Bistro
1 pl Gaston Paillhou, 37000
Tel *02 47 37 03 13* **Closed** *Sun & Mon*
Chic, modern city-center bistro serving tasty dishes based around fresh seasonal produce sourced from the daily market.

TOURS: L'Odéon €€
Brasserie
10 pl de la Gare, 37000
Tel *02 47 20 12 65* **Closed** *Sat midday & Sun*
Quality Art Deco-style restaurant that creatively reinvents French regional dishes.

TOURS: La Roche Le Roy €€€
Fine dining
55 rte de St-Avertin, 37000
Tel *02 47 27 22 00* **Closed** *Sun & Mon*
Michelin-starred restaurant serving classic top-notch French cuisine. Fine Loire and Bordeaux wines.

VALAIRE: L'Herbe Rouge €
Bistro
le Bourg, 41120
Tel *02 54 44 98 14* **Closed** *Mon;* Sep–Jun: Sun
An excellent country bistro nestled in tiny Valaire – with plastic stools and other kitsch touches.

VENDOME: La Vallée €€
Traditional French
34 rue Barré-de-St-Venant, 41100
Tel *02 54 77 29 93* **Closed** *Sun eve, Mon & Tue*
Enjoy well-prepared traditional dishes in the rustic dining room. Good regional wines.

Key to Price Guide *see p576*

VIGNOUX-SUR-BARANGEON: Le Prieuré €€
Traditional French
2 rte de St-Laurent, 18500
Tel *02 48 51 58 80* **Closed** *Tue & Wed*
Meals for the discerning diner are served in the elegant dining room or on the covered terrace.

VOUVRAY: Les Geules Noires €€
Classic French
66 vallée Coquette, 37210
Tel *02 47 52 62 18* **Closed** *Sun eve & Mon; Sep–May: Tue*
Carved into a cave, this place is ideal for wine lovers. Be sure to try sweet Vouvray with your dessert.

Burgundy & Franche-Comté

ARBOIS: Jean-Paul Jeunet €€€
Fine dining
9 rue de l'Hôtel de Ville, 39600
Tel *03 84 66 05 67* **Closed** *Sep–Jun; Jul–Aug: midday*
Lovely location, a pretty terrace, courteous staff, and great food.

ARNAY LE DUC: Chez Camille €€
Traditional French
1 pl Edouard Herriot, 21230
Tel *03 80 90 01 38*
Come here to savor hearty dishes such as rabbit paté and game in the stone-walled dining room.

AUTUN: Les Ursulines €€
Fine dining
14 rue de Rivault, 71400
Tel *03 85 86 58 58* **Closed** *Mon–Fri midday*
Elegant restaurant serving gourmet fare. The turbot and duck fillet are superb.

AUXERRE: Le Jardin Gourmand €€€
Modern French
56 bd Vauban, 89000
Tel *03 86 51 53 52* **Closed** *Mon & Tue: Sep–Jun: Sun eve*
Interesting, inventive dishes served in an attractive dining room. Don't miss the veal.

AVALLON: Relais des Gourmets €
Traditional French
45–47 rue de Paris, 89200
Tel *03 86 34 18 90* **Closed** *Sun eve & Mon*
Traditional auberge with two dining rooms. Choose from unpretentious fixed-priced menus.

BEAUNE: La Ciboulette €€
Bistro
69 rue Lorraine, 21200
Tel *03 80 24 70 72* **Closed** *Mon & Tue*
Simple decor belies high culinary standards at this establishment.

Minimalist decor at Hostellerie du Chapeau Rouge

BEAUNE: Le Bistro de L'Hôtel €€
Bistro
3 rue Samuel Legay, 21200
Tel *03 80 25 94 10* **Closed** *Sun midday*
Chic bistro using high-quality ingredients sourced from local suppliers. Boasts an excellent selection of wines.

BEAUNE: L'Ecusson €€
Modern French
pl Malmedy, 21200
Tel *03 80 24 03 82* **Closed** *Wed & Sun*
Daring, inventive cuisine in a pleasant interior with wooden floors and oak beams.

BELFORT: Le Pot au Feu €€
Traditional French
27 bis Grand' rue, 90000
Tel *03 84 28 57 84* **Closed** *Sun*
A 17th-century vaulted cellar is the setting for homestyle dishes, such as the *pot au feu* (braised beef and vegetable stew).

BONLIEU: La Poutre €€
Regional
25 Grande Rue, 39130
Tel *03 84 25 57 77* **Closed** *Sep–Jun: Tue & Wed*
An 18th-century farmhouse dining room with stone walls and oak beams, and hearty home food.

CHABLIS: La Cuisine au Vin €
Regional
16 rue Auxerroise, 89800
Tel *03 86 18 98 52* **Closed** *Sun eve–Tue*
Set in an old wine cellar. Expect innovative takes on classics such as Burgundy snails and *boeuf bourguignon*. Friendly staff.

CHAGNY: Lameloise €€€
Fine dining
36 pl Armes, 71150
Tel *03 85 87 65 65* **Closed** *Oct–Jun: Tue & Wed; Jul–Sep: Tue–Thu midday*
The place for fine Burgundian cooking prepared with only the best, top-quality ingredients.

CHAINTRE: La Table de Chaintré €€
Regional
Le Bourg, 71570
Tel *03 85 32 90 95*
Closed *Sun eve–Tue*
Well-established restaurant with a menu that changes weekly.

CHALON-SUR-SAONE: Le Bistrot €€
Bistro
31 rue de Strasbourg
Tel *03 85 93 22 01*
Closed *Sat & Sun*
Friendly bistro-style restaurant; try seafood risotto or Bresse chicken.

CHAROLLES: Restaurant Frédéric Doucet €€€
Modern French
2 av de la Libération, 71120
Tel *03 85 24 11 32* **Closed** *Sun eve, Mon & Tue midday*
Chic provincial restaurant serving sizzling Charolais steak. Modern spin on traditional dishes.

CHASSAGNE-MONTRACHET: Le Chassagne €€€
Modern French
4 impasse Chenevottes, 21180
Tel *03 80 21 94 94* **Closed** *Sun, Mon & Wed eve*
Innovative cooking in a legendary wine village. Try turbot with hollandaise sauce and asparagus.

DIJON: Le Chabrot €
Bistro
36 rue Monge, 21000
Tel *03 80 30 69 61* **Closed** *Sun*
Relaxed restaurant offering a wide range of regional specialties.

DIJON: DZ'Envies €€
Modern French
12 rue Odebert, 21000
Tel *03 80 50 09 26* **Closed** *Sun*
A popular, contemporary bistro serving simple gourmet cuisine.

DIJON: Hostellerie du Chapeau Rouge €€€
Modern French
5 rue Michelet, 21000
Tel *03 80 50 88 88* **Closed** *Sun & Mon*
Inventive dishes in a sleek setting. Try Bigorre black pork with truffle vinaigrette and pear confit.

DOLE: La Chaumière €€€
Modern French
346 mal-Juin, 39100
Tel *03 84 70 72 40* **Closed** *Sat midday, Sun & Mon midday*
Delightful restaurant serving unusual dishes such as venison with licorice and lemon purée, swede, carrots, and Granny Smith apples.

For more information on types of restaurants *see p575*

FONTANGY: Ferme-Auberge de la Morvandelle €
Traditional French
Précy-sous-Thil, 21390
Tel *03 80 84 33 32* **Closed** *Mon–Fri, Sat midday & Sun eve*
Working farm with rustic weekend-only dining area in a converted barn. Many of the ingredients are home grown.

GEVREY-CHAMBERTIN: Chez Guy €€
Regional
3 pl de la Mairie, 21220
Tel *03 80 58 51 51* **Closed** *Nov–Mar: Sun*
A chic restaurant with exposed oak beams, and a terrace for fine days. Try simple local cuisine such as *coq au vin* and hearty beef cheek cooked slowly in red wine.

IGUERANDE: La Colline du Colombier €€
Modern French
Colombier, 71340
Tel *03 85 84 07 24* **Closed** *Wed; Oct–May: Thu*
Ancient farmhouse renovated by legendary chefs Michel and Marie-Pierre Troigros. The cuisine focuses on local meat and organic produce.

LONS-LE-SAUNIER: Le Relais des Salines €
Brasserie
26 rue des Salines, 39000
Tel *03 84 43 01 57* **Closed** *Sun, Mon & Tue eve*
Lively brasserie dishing up hearty mountain favorites. Ideal place to sample satisfying Franche-Comté dishes. Good service.

MAGNY-COURS: Absolue Renaissance €€
Modern French
2 rue de Paris, 58470
Tel *03 86 58 10 40* **Closed** *Sun & Mon eve*
Set in a vast garden with its own vegetable patch, this restaurant reworks classic dishes with a contemporary flourish.

MALBUISSON: Le Bon Acceuil €€
Modern French
rue de la Source, 25160
Tel *03 81 69 30 58* **Closed** *Sun eve, Mon & Tue midday*
Creative seasonal menus served in a charming converted farmhouse. Sample the turbot with Pontarlier absinthe.

MONTFAUCON: La Cheminée €€
Regional
3 rue de la Vue des Alpes, 25660
Tel *03 81 81 17 48* **Closed** *Sun eve, Mon & Wed eve*
Spectacular Alpine scenery from a rustic dining room serving tasty dishes based on local produce.

NEVERS: Jean-Michel Couron €€
Modern French
21 rue St-Etienne, 58000
Tel *03 86 61 19 28* **Closed** *Sun eve–Tue*
Intimate restaurant that selects top produce to create perfectly balanced flavors.

NITRY: Auberge de la Beursaudière €€
Traditional French
chemin de Ronde, 89310
Tel *03 86 33 69 69*
Hearty local dishes served up by staff in regional dress. Opt for generous portions of veal hock.

NUITS-ST-GEORGES: L'Alambic €€
Regional
rue de Général de Gaulle, 21700
Tel *03 80 61 35 00* **Closed** *Mon & Tue midday; Nov–Mar: Sun eve*
A list of over 450 different wines to go with the classic dishes on offer in this Cistercian dining room.

PORT LESNEY: Le Bistro Pontarlier €
Bistro
Port Lesney, 39600
Tel *03 84 37 83 27* **Closed** *Mon eve, Tue eve, Wed & Thu*
A much-loved bistro in the old schoolhouse of a pretty wine-producing village near Arbois.

Modern dining space at La Table d'Olivier Leflaive, Puligny-Montrachet

PULIGNY-MONTRACHET: La Table d'Olivier Leflaive €€
Regional
pl du Monument, 21190
Tel *03 80 21 37 65* **Closed** *Sun*
Rustic restaurant with a background in wine production. Try the specialty wine-tasting lunches.

QUARRE LES TOMBES: Auberge de Atre €€
Traditional French
Les Lavaults, 89630
Tel *03 86 32 20 79* **Closed** *Tue & Wed*
Classic dishes such as roast lamb with rosemary are served in a cozy dining room.

SAULIEU: Le Relais Bernard Loiseau €€€
Fine dining
2 rue d'Argentine, 21210
Tel *03 80 90 53 53* **Closed** *Tue & Wed*
Renowned across France, this restaurant creates masterful interpretations of traditional dishes.

SENS: La Madeleine €€€
Fine dining
1 rue Alsace-Lorraine, 89100
Tel *03 86 65 09 31* **Closed** *Sun, Mon & Tue midday*
Seasonal menus at this elegant establishment offer dishes such as langoustine *carpaccio.*

ST-PERE-SOUS-VEZELAY: Espérance €€€
Fine dining
St-Père-sous-Vézelay, 89450
Tel *03 86 33 39 10* **Closed** *Mon, Tue & Wed midday*
Chef Marc Meneau presents modern classics such as roast Bresse pigeon and lobster, and pan-fried langoustines with radish.

DK Choice

ST-AMOUR BELLEVUE: L'Auberge du Paradis €€€
Modern French
Le Plâtre Durand, 71570
Tel *03 85 37 10 26* **Closed** *Mon, Tue & Wed & Sat middays*
Surprise the taste buds with daring combinations of spices at this exciting restaurant. Try the lemon tart flavored with curry and served with beet ice cream. The dining room is modern and quirky with an ecletic choice of chairs.

ST-ROMAIN: Les Roches €€
Regional
pl de la Mairie, 21190
Tel *03 80 21 21 63* **Closed** *Tue & Wed*
Small hotel-restaurant with simple no-frills cooking served in a comfortable dining room. Try the four-course set menu.

Key to Price Guide *see p576*

TOURNUS:
Le Restaurant Greuze €€€
Traditional French
1 rue A Thibaudet, 71700
Tel *03 85 51 13 52* **Closed** *Wed & Thu midday*
Enjoy classic cuisine in simple but charming surroundings. Try the Bresse chicken and pair with good Mâcon or Beaujolais wine.

VENOY:
Le Moulin de la Coudre €€
Traditional French
2 rue des Gravottes, La Coudre, 89290
Tel *03 86 40 23 79* **Closed** *Sun eve*
Creatively prepared classic cuisine. The menu changes weekly according to seasonal produce.

VERDUN-SUR-LE-DOUBS:
L'Hostellerie Bourguignonne – Didier Denis €€
Traditional French
2 av Pdt-Borgeot, 71350
Tel *03 85 91 51 45* **Closed** *Tue & Wed midday; winter: Sun eve*
Rustic venue serving honest, straightforward cooking with local ingredients. Superb Charolais beef fillet and good wines.

VILLENEUVE SUR YONNE:
Auberge La Lucarne aux Chouettes €€
Regional
7 quai Bretoche, 89500
Tel *03 86 87 18 26* **Closed** *Sun eve & Mon*
Pretty 17th-century inn by the river Yonne. Menu features dishes such as eggs poached in red wine, snails, and more.

VILLERS-LE-LAC: Le France €€
Modern French
8 pl Cupillard, 25130
Tel *03 81 68 00 06* **Closed** *Sun eve & Mon*
Delicious cooking at this hotel-restaurant. Dishes are infused with herbs from the hotel garden. Try venison with grilled sesame.

VINCELOTTES:
Auberge des Tilleuils €€
Traditional French
12 quai de l'Yonne, 82290
Tel *03 86 42 22 13* **Closed** *Tue & Wed*
Attractive riverside auberge serving mouthwatering cuisine. Game specialities include venison with Epoisses cheese.

VONNAS: Georges Blanc €€€
Fine dining
pl Marché, 01540
Tel *04 74 50 90 90* **Closed** *Mon–Wed & Thu lunch*
A gourmet shrine offering inventive cuisine that includes wagyu beef with bone marrow and truffles. Excellent wines.

Rustic exteriors of the Georges Blanc restaurant in Vonnas

Massif Central

DK Choice

ALLEYRAS: Le Haut Allier €€
Modern French
Pont d'Alleyras, 43580
Tel *04 71 57 57 63* **Closed** *Mon & Tue*
This hotel-restaurant, nestled in the Allier gorge, believes in local produce. Great for traditional dishes such as saddle of Saugues lamb, or imaginative dishes such as pigeon breast in a cocoa crumble with cornflour gnocchi. The set menus are excellent value, with wines to match.

AUMONT-AUBRAC:
Restaurant Prouhèze €€
Regional
2 rte du Languedoc, 48130
Tel *04 66 42 80 07* **Closed** *Mon, Tue & Wed–Fri midday*
Super-fresh ingredients are used to create a unique take on classic dishes from the region.

BELCASTEL: Vieux Pont €€
Modern French
Le Bourg, 12390
Tel *05 65 64 52 29* **Closed** *Mon & Tue midday*
Straddling a medieval cobbled bridge, this restaurant produces creative dishes with flair, such as Mont Royal pigeon with fennel.

BOUDES: La Vigne €€
Modern French
pl de la Mairie, 63340
Tel *04 73 96 55 66* **Closed** *Sun eve, Mon & Tue*
Creative restaurant on the main square of this wine village. The chef constantly seeks out new ideas for his regularly changing repertoire. The set menus are highly recommended.

BOUSSAC: Le Relais Creusois €€
Modern French
40 Maison Dieu, rte de la Châtre, 23600
Tel *05 55 65 02 20* **Closed** *Tue eve & Wed (except summer)*
Award-winning cuisine from a chef who conjures up original dishes such as haddock and leek salad or guinea fowl confit.

BRIVE-LA-GAILLARDE:
Chez Francis €€
Bistro
61 av de Paris, 19100
Tel *05 55 74 41 72* **Closed** *Sun & Mon*
Paris-style bistro that serves well-prepared reworkings of regional favorites. Good selection of southern French wines.

CLERMONT-FERRAND:
Goûts et Couleurs €€
Modern French
6 pl Champgil, 63000
Tel *04 73 19 37 82* **Closed** *Sat midday, Sun & Mon*
The geometric 1980s decor is softened by an ancient vaulted ceiling in this former mirror workshop. Modern, inventive cuisine.

CLERMONT-FERRAND:
Le Caveau €€
Regional
9 rue Philippe Marcombes, 63000
Tel *04 73 14 07 03* **Closed** *Sun*
Rustic and traditional, Le Caveau is a meat eater's paradise serving huge chunks of Salers or Aubrac beef and *coq au vin*.

CLERMONT-FERRAND:
Amphitryon Capucine €€€
Traditional French
50 rue Fontgiève, 63000
Tel *04 73 31 38 39* **Closed** *Sun & Mon*
Stately dining room complete with a fireplace and oak beams. Try the *foie gras* sandwich with cocoa-balsamic. Good wine list.

For more information on types of restaurants *see p575*

COLLONGES-LA-ROUGE: Auberge Le Prieuré €€
Traditional French
pl de l'Eglise, 19500
Tel *05 55 25 41 00* **Closed** *Wed*
Simple, well-prepared dishes, such as pike-perch with lemon butter sauce, at this 18th-century auberge built in local red stone.

FLORAC: La Source du Pêcher €€
Regional
rue Remuret, 48400
Tel *04 66 45 03 01*
Charming little restaurant where regional produce takes pride of place. Try the local lamb and duck with blueberries or ask for the Lozère trout.

LAGUIOLE: Michel Bras €€€
Fine dining
rte de l'Aubrac, 12210
Tel *05 65 51 18 20* **Closed** *Sun*
A wall of glass overlooks the beautiful Aubrac countryside from this hilltop restaurant. This place is renowned for its cutting-edge cuisine.

LE ROUGET: Hôtel des Voyageurs €
Traditional French
20 av de 15 septembre 1945, 15290
Tel *04 71 46 10 14* **Closed** *Sep–May: Sun midday*
Stone-built Cantal hotel-restaurant serving well-prepared traditional dishes. Go for the *menu du terroir*. The rabbit with tarragon is especially good.

LE-PUY-EN-VELAY: Tournayre €€
Regional
12 rue Chênebouterie, 43000
Tel *04 71 09 58 94* **Closed** *Sun eve, Wed eve & Mon*
Vaulted ceilings and stone walls distinguish this 12th-century town house. Typical Auvergnat dishes. Sample the lentils or Velay veal.

LE-PUY-EN-VELAY: François Gagnaire €€€
Modern French
4 av Clément Charbonnier, 43000
Tel *04 71 02 75 55* **Closed** *Sun eve, Mon & Tue midday*
Sophisticated restaurant housed in a good boutique hotel. The monkfish medallions with Arbois wine are the chef's specialty.

LIMOGES: Chez Alphonse €
Bistro
5 pl de la Motte, 87000
Tel *05 55 34 34 14* **Closed** *Sun*
Lively bistro that serves regional cuisine made with fresh ingredients that the chef himself sources daily from the local market. Good *prix-fixe* menus.

Striking, contemporary interiors of the refined Michel Bras restaurant, Laguiole

LIMOGES: Chez François €
Regional
pl de la Motte, 87000
Tel *05 55 32 32 79* **Closed** *Sun*
Simple, no-frills, tasty food is served inside Limoges' covered market hall. Convivial atmosphere.

LIMOGES: L'Amphitryon €€€
Modern French
26 rue de la Boucherie, 87000
Tel *05 55 33 36 39* **Closed** *Sun & Mon*
Contemporary dining space; the food is sophisticated and the flavors delicate. The Limousin beef is a perennial favorite.

MILLAU: La Braconne €€
Traditional French
7 pl Maréchal Foch, 12100
Tel *05 65 60 30 93* **Closed** *Sun eve & Mon*
Classic cuisine in a 13th-century vaulted dining room on an arcaded square. Specialties include flambéed leg of lamb.

MONTLUCON: Le Grenier à Sel €€
Traditional French
10 rue Ste-Anne, 03100
Tel *04 70 05 53 79* **Closed** *Sun eve & Mon*
Elegant pastel-hued dining room set in an ivy-clad 18th-century mansion with huge fireplaces.

MONTSALVY: L'Auberge Fleurie €
Traditional French
pl du Barry, 15120
Tel *04 71 49 20 02* **Closed** *Sun eve; Sep–Jun: Mon*
Charming auberge with oak beams, an open fireplace, and a rustic feel. The grilled duck with cranberry sauce is a must.

MOUDEYRES: Le Pré Bossu €€
Modern French
Le Bourg, 43150
Tel *04 71 05 10 70* **Closed** *May: Mon; Sep–Oct*
Tranquil establishment serving great French cuisine. Much of the fresh produce served is grown on site. There is a vegetarian menu.

MOULINS: Le Trait d'Union €€
Bistro
16 rue Gambette, 3000
Tel *04 70 34 24 61* **Closed** *Sun & Mon*
Sizzling dishes such as Monts du Forez veal and steak Rossini are served at this upmarket bistro.

MURAT: Le Jarrousset €€
Modern French
rte de Clermont-Ferrand, 15300
Tel *04 71 20 10 69* **Closed** *Sep–Jun: Mon & Tue*
The emphasis here is on using top-quality seasonal ingredients, most of them sourced locally. Unpretentious decor.

RODEZ: Goûts en Couleurs €€
Modern French
38 rue Bonald, 12000
Tel *05 65 42 75 10* **Closed** *Sun & Mon*
Charming eatery in the old town. The chef creates imaginative fare such as *carpaccio* of prawns with elderflower and mango.

ST-BONNET-LE-FROID: Auberge des Cimes €€€
Fine dining
Le Bourg, 43290
Tel *04 71 59 93 72* **Closed** *Tue & Wed*
Delicious, seasonally determined dishes such as roast lamb or suckling pig perfumed with sage.

ST-JULIEN-CHAPTEUIL: Vidal €€
Traditional French
pl du Marché, 43260
Tel *04 71 08 70 50* **Closed** *Sun & Mon*
Family-run restaurant in a quaint village. Opt for the juicy stuffed fillet of beef or the Velay lamb.

UZERCHE: Restaurant Jean Teyssier €€
Mediterranean
rue du Pont-Turgot, 19140
Tel *05 55 73 10 05* **Closed** *Sep–Jun: Tue & Wed*
Serves Mediterranean dishes such as *vol-au-vent* with Roquefort sauce. Great views of the Vezère.

Key to Price Guide *see p576*

VICHY: Brasserie du Casino €€
Brasserie
4 rue du Casino, 03200
Tel *04 70 98 23 06* **Closed** *Tue & Wed*
A veritable institution on the Vichy restaurant scene – stylish Art Deco salon decked out with wood and mirrors. Dishes up classic upmarket brasserie fare. Fine service.

VICHY: Jacques Decoret €€€
Modern French
15 rue du Parc, 3200
Tel *04 70 97 65 06* **Closed** *Tue & Wed*
The finest regional produce is used in highly refined dishes that are prepared with great skill. A lovely setting in a huge conservatory.

The Rhône Valley & French Alps

ANNECY: Le Belvédère €€€
Modern French
7 chemin Belvédère, 74000
Tel *04 50 45 04 90* **Closed** *Sun eve & Wed; Oct–May: Tue midday*
Lovely lake views and appetizing contemporary food – *foie gras* perfumed with vanilla, and desserts like chocolate cigar.

BOURG-EN-BRESSE: Les Quatres Saisons €€
Modern French
6 rue de la République, 1000
Tel *04 74 22 01 86* **Closed** *Sat lunch, Sun & Mon*
Mostly traditional dishes, given a contemporary touch by a chef passionate about both wines and local produce.

CHAMBERY: Château de Candie – Orangerie €€€
Modern French
rue de Bois de Candie, Chambéry le Vieux, 73000
Tel *04 79 96 63 00*
Elegant restaurant with experimental dishes such as *omble chevalier* fish with rosemary and lemon confit emulsion.

DK Choice

CHAMONIX: La Calèche €€
Traditional French
rue Dr Paccard, 74400
Tel *04 50 55 94 68*
This traditional mountain restaurant has been run by the same family since 1946. Enjoy typical Savoyard fare such as *tartiflette* (a gratin made with potatoes, onions, and lardon), fondue, and grilled meat. The dining room is crammed with Swiss clocks, copper pans, and a bobsleigh from the 1924 Winter Olympics.

CHAMONIX: Les Jardins du Mont Blanc €€
Modern French
62 allée du Majestic, 74400
Tel *04 50 55 35 42*
A mountain hotel offering savory modern Alpine cuisine using the best produce the region can offer.

COLLONGES MONT D'OR: Paul Bocuse €€€
Fine dining
40 quai de la Plage, 69660
Tel *04 72 42 90 90*
National treasure Paul Bocuse makes superb dishes such as black truffle soup topped with pastry, or the legendary gratin of crayfish.

COURCHEVEL: Le Chabichou €€
Modern French
Quartier des Chenus, 73120
Tel *04 79 08 00 55* **Closed** *summer: Mon*
Experience creative cuisine while enjoying mountain views. Old-school favorites on offer such as pork from the Cantal region.

COURCHEVEL: Le Genépi €€€
Traditional French
Courchevel 1850, 73120
Tel *04 79 08 08 63* **Closed** *Sep–Nov: Sat & Sun*
Excellent dining establishment within this luxury ski resort. Savor traditional mountain fare.

EVIAN-LES-BAINS: Histoire de Goût €€
Bistro
1 av Général Dupas, 74500
Tel *04 50 70 09 98* **Closed** *Mon*
Sleek eatery with a vaulted dining room and wine bar serving gourmet bistro food.

GRENOBLE: A Ma Table €€
Traditional French
92 cours Jean-Jaurès, 38000
Tel *04 76 96 77 04* **Closed** *Sat midday, Sun & Mon*
Beautiful restaurant serving tasty dishes such as caramelized pear and gorgonzola tart with smoked duck breast.

GRENOBLE: Le Mas Bottero €€
Modern French
168 cours Berriat, 38000
Tel *04 76 21 95 33* **Closed** *Sun & Mon*
The dishes at Le Mas Bottero reflect the Provençal roots of the young chef. In summer, tables are set up outside, under the ancient wisteria.

LAMASTRE: Restaurant Barattéro €€
Traditional French
pl Seignobos, 07270
Tel *04 75 06 41 50* **Closed** *Fri eve, Sun eve & Mon*
Pan-fried *foie gras*, Bresse chicken, crayfish, and other such classics are served in this lovely restaurant.

ARGENTIERE: Le Chêne Vert €€
Regional
Rocher, 7110 Tel
Tel *04 75 88 34 02*
Traditional Ardèchois hotel and restaurant serving regional classics. Try the *foie gras* served with a fig confit.

LE BOURGET-LAC: Beaurivage €€
Regional
bd du Lac, 73370
Tel *04 79 25 00 38* **Closed** *Sun & Thu eve*
Lakeside auberge with a dining room opening out onto a lovely terrace overhung with plantain trees. Classic Savoyard cuisine.

LE CLUSAZ: La Scierie €€
Modern French
321–331 rte du Col des Aravis, 74220
Tel *04 50 63 34 68*
Dishes range from local mountain *charcuterie* to John Dory fillet with Mondeuse wine sauce and creamy risotto.

LYON: La Gargotte €
Modern French
15 rue Royale, 69001
Tel *04 78 28 79 20* **Closed** *Sat, Sun, Mon midday & Tue*
Friendly restaurant with retro decor and mirrored walls. Classic dishes reworked with originality.

Brightly lit, vibrant dining room at Le Chabichou in Courchevel

For more information on types of restaurants *see p575*

Contemporary interior at the Troisgros restaurant in Roanne

LYON: 33 Cité €€
Brasserie
33 quai Charles de Gaulle, 69006
Tel *04 37 45 45 45*
Modern city-center brasserie. The stylish dining room offers carefully prepared classic and contemporary cuisine.

LYON: Brasserie Georges €€
Bistro
30 cours Verdun, 69002
Tel *04 72 56 54 54*
Huge, bustling city-center bistro with Art Deco interiors. The menu covers Lyonnais specialties, seafood dishes, and sauerkraut.

LYON: L'Alexandrin €€€
Regional
83 rue Moncey, 69003
Tel *04 72 61 15 69* **Closed** *Sun & Mon*
Exquisite gourmet reinventions of Lyonnais dishes, including fillet of sea bass in a sesame crust.

MEGEVE: La Petite Ravine €€
Traditional French
743 chemin de la Ravine, Demi Quartier Combloux, 74120
Tel *04 50 21 38 67*
Typical alpine chalet restaurant with a warm ambience. A limited selection of dishes includes cheese-based regional classics.

MEGEVE: La Taverne du Mont d'Arbois €€
Modern French
3001 rte Edmond de Rothschild, 74120
Tel *04 50 21 03 53*
This authentic chalet attracts a chic Megève crowd and presents modern reworkings of traditional recipes. Old favorites such as raclette and fondue also on offer.

MORZINE: La Chamade €€
Traditional French
Morzine, 74110
Tel *04 50 79 13 91*
Choose from a wide-ranging menu that features wood oven pizzas and regional fare such as *charcuterie*. Or try the warm Reblochon salad.

ROANNE: Troisgros €€€
Fine dining
pl Jean Troisgros, 42300
Tel *04 77 71 66 97* **Closed** *Tue & Wed*
One of the country's top restaurants, Troisgros has striking contemporary decor, pure lines, and a zen atmosphere. Exceptional high-quality cooking.

ST-AGREVE: Domaine de Rilhac €€
Modern French
Rilhac, 07320
Tel *04 75 30 20 20* **Closed** *Tue eve, Wed & Thu midday*
Chef Ludovic Sinz reinvents classic fare in this smartly renovated farmhouse. Try the pumpkin soup with snails or the pan-fried endive.

ST-ETIENNE: Le Bistrot de Paris €
Bistro
7 pl Jean Jaurès, 42000
Tel *04 77 32 21 50* **Closed** *Sat midday & Sun*
Jovial bistro with a simple menu that changes in accordance with what is in season and looks most delicious at the local market.

ST-MARTIN-DE-BELLEVILLE: La Bouitte €€€
Modern French
St-Marcel, 73440
Tel *04 79 08 96 77*
Alpine chalet restaurant that serves up inventive dishes. Order the quail with truffles and artichoke.

TAIN L'HERMITAGE: Lycée Hotelier de l'Hermitage €
Traditional French
rue Jean Monnet, 26600
Tel *04 75 07 57 14* **Closed** *Sat, Sun, Mon–Wed eve & Fri eve*
Students of this training college for chefs run two restaurants serving classic gourmet dishes. Only open during the school term.

TALLOIRES: La Villa des Fleurs €€
Regional
rte du Port, 74290
Tel *04 50 60 71 14* **Closed** *Sun eve & Mon*
Fish caught in Lake Annecy features prominently on the menu at this lovely waterside villa.

TOURNON: Le Tournesol €€
Modern French
44 av Maréchal Foch, 07300
Tel *04 75 07 08 26* **Closed** *Sun eve, Tue & Wed*
Smart restaurant with views of the Hermitage vineyards. Sample the *foie gras* with rhubarb compôte.

URIAGE-LES-BAINS: Les Terrasses d'Uriage €€€
Modern French
pl de la Déesse-Hygie, 38410
Tel *04 76 89 10 80* **Closed** *Sun eve, Mon, Tue & Wed & Thu middays*
Upscale restaurant in a Napoleon III building that opens out onto a lovely park. Inventive dishes.

VALENCE: Restaurant Pic €€€
Fine dining
285 av Victor Hugo, 26000
Tel *04 75 44 15 32* **Closed** *Sun & Mon*
Elegant restaurant in a luxury hotel with a constantly evolving menu. Excellent Great Rhône wines.

DK Choice

VIENNE: La Pyramide €€€
Fine dining
14 bd Fernand Point, 38200
Tel *04 74 53 01 96* **Closed** *Tue & Wed*
One of France's classic Michelin-starred establishments where all gastronomic creations are based on regional produce – try the Jerusalem artichoke *velouté* with leek ravioli or the sea bream fillet with mango. Excellent wine list.

Poitou & Aquitaine

ANGOULEME: Le Terminus €
Bistro
3 pl de la Gare, 16000
Tel *05 45 95 27 13* **Closed** *Sun*
Stylish and modern restaurant with a lovely summer terrace. Great selection of seafood.

ARCACHON: Chez Yvette €€
Regional
59 bd du Général Leclerc, 33120
Tel *05 56 83 05 11*
Lively and atmospheric local institution. Set on the waterfront, it has been serving generous plates of fish and oysters for over 50 years.

Key to Price Guide *see p576*

ARCINS: Le Lion d'Or €€
Regional
11 rte de Pauillac, 33460
Tel *05 56 58 96 79* **Closed** *Sun & Mon*
Intimate restaurant in a Médoc wine village. Renowned for great local cuisine and superb wines.

BORDEAUX:
Café Andrée Putman €
Brasserie
Entrepôt Lainé, 7 rue Ferrière, 33000
Tel *05 56 44 71 61* **Closed** *Mon*
Stylish and laid-back modern café at the contemporary art museum. Light lunches and larger brunch menu at weekends.

BORDEAUX:
Le Bistrot d'Edouard €
Bistro
16 pl du Parlement, 33000
Tel *05 56 81 48 87*
Lively modern dishes such as prawns cooked in aniseed. Friendly service, exceptional value.

BORDEAUX:
Le Chapon Fin €€€
Fine dining
5 rue Montesquieu, 33000
Tel *05 56 79 10 10* **Closed** *Sun & Mon*
Exquisite creative cuisine is dished up at this historic restaurant with glorious Belle Epoque decor.

COGNAC:
Les Pigeons Blancs €€
Regional
110 rue Jules Brisson, 16100
Tel *05 45 82 16 36*
Charming traditional restaurant that serves locally based cuisine. Succulent beef and duck dishes.

COULON: Hôtel Le Central €€
Modern French
4 rue d'Autremont, 79510
Tel *05 49 35 90 20* **Closed** *Mon*
Innovative cuisine and an excellent range of fruit desserts. The dining room and terrace overlook the Poitevin marshes.

EUGÈNIE-LES-BAINS:
La Ferme aux Grives €€€
Fine dining
11 rue des Thermes, 40320
Tel *05 58 05 06 07* **Closed** *Tue & Wed*
Chef Michel Guérard's rustic upscale restaurant serves sublime French fare with a modern twist.

ILE DE RE: La Baleine Bleue €€
Brasserie
quai Launay Razilly, 17410 St-Martin-de-Ré
Tel *05 46 09 03 30* **Closed** *Oct–Mar: Tue & Wed; Jun & Sep: Tue*
Stylish bar-brasserie specializing in fish, seafood, and fine wines. Great location by the harborside.

ILE D'OLERON: Ecailler €€
Regional
65 rue du Port, 17310 St-Pierre-d'Oléron
Tel *05 46 47 10 31*
Great local oysters, crab and other seafood specialties are served at this harborside eatery.

JARNAC:
Restaurant du Château €€€
Fine dining
15 pl du Château, 16200
Tel *05 45 81 07 17* **Closed** *Mon*
Elegant restaurant with refined dishes such as roast pheasant in cognac sauce.

LA ROCHELLE:
Le Boute en Train €
Bistro
7 rue des Bonnes Femmes, 17000
Tel *05 46 41 73 74* **Closed** *Sun & Mon*
Enjoy hearty classic fare made with market-fresh ingredients.

LA ROCHELLE:
Le Comptoir des Voyages €
Modern French
22 rue St-Jean-du-Pérot, 17000
Tel *05 46 50 62 60*
This renowned eatery combines local produce with exotic spices in refined surroundings.

LA ROCHELLE: L'Entracte €€
Fine dining
35 rue St-Jean-du-Pérot, 17000
Tel *05 46 52 26 69*
An inventive take on regional cuisine, served in a stylish interior.

LANGON: Restaurant Claude Darroze €€€
Fine dining
95 cours du Général Leclerc, 33210
Tel *05 56 63 00 48*
Intimate restaurant with striking decor. Unique, luxurious cooking.

MARGAUX:
Le Pavillon de Margaux €€
Modern French
3 rue Georges Mandel, 33460
Tel *05 57 88 77 54* **Closed** *Jun–Sep: Tue; Oct–May: Tue & Wed*
Mellow dining room set in a villa hotel. Serves great light lunches.

La Ferme aux Grives in Eugènie-les-Bains

Comfortable seating area at the elegant L'Entracte in La Rochelle

MIMIZAN: Hôtel Atlantique €
Regional
38 av de la Côte d'Argent, 40200
Tel *05 58 09 09 42* **Closed** *Oct–Apr: Sun*
Great-value menus feature local favorites such as *tourtière* and Landaise apple pie. Excellent beach location.

MONT-DE-MARSAN:
Restaurant Didier Garbage €€
Fine dining
40090 Uchacq et Parentis
Tel *05 58 75 33 66* **Closed** *Mon*
A rustic restaurant serving inventively presented traditional Landaise dishes.

MONTMORILLON: Le Lucullus €
Regional
4 bd de Strasbourg, 86500
Tel *05 49 84 09 09* **Closed** *Mon & Tue*
Refined regional cuisine and a bar-bistro for casual dining.

NIORT:
La Table des Saveurs €€
Bistro
9 rue Thiers, 79000
Tel *05 49 77 44 35* **Closed** *Sun*
Chic, airy modern bistro where local fish is the highlight of the varied menus.

PAUILLAC:
Château Cordeillan-Bages €€€
Fine dining
rte des Châteaux, 33250
Tel *05 56 59 24 24*
Closed *mid-Mar–Oct: Mon & Tue; Nov–mid-Mar*
Delicious gourmet cuisine is dished up at this lavish Médoc château-hotel. Excellent selection of Bordeaux wines.

For more information on types of restaurants *see p575*

POITIERS: Le Pince Oreille €
Bistro
11 rue Trois Rois, 86000
Tel *05 49 60 25 99* **Closed** *Sun*
Laid-back bar-restaurant with live music. Good selection of fish and meat dishes – simple, wholesome meals and good range of wines.

POITIERS: Les Bons Enfants €
Regional
11bis rue Cloche Perse, 86000
Tel *05 49 41 49 82* **Closed** *Mon*
Snug, tightly packed local eatery serving generous portions of duck and other specialties.

ROCHEFORT: La Belle Poule €€
Regional
102 av du 11 Novembre, 17300
Tel *05 46 99 71 87* **Closed** *Sep–Jun: Fri*
Lovely restaurant with a terrace by the River Charente. Regionally inspired cooking at its best.

SABRES: Auberge des Pins €€€
Fine dining
rte de la Piscine, 40630
Tel *05 58 08 30 00* **Closed** *Sep–Jun: Mon*
Delicate cuisine and serene environs; the menu features pigeon, langoustines, and ice-cream cannelloni.

SAUTERNES: Le Saprien €€
Regional
14 rue Principale, 33210
Tel *05 56 76 60 87* **Closed** *Mon*
Smart village restaurant in a converted farmhouse. Lampreys are the specialty. Fine service.

ST-EMILION:
L'Envers du Décor €€
Bistro
11 rue du Clocher, 33330
Tel *05 57 74 48 31*
Airy, modern bistro, wine-bar, and shop. Serves healthy salads and tasty snacks as well as intricate dishes. Superlative wines.

Cooking wood pigeon over coals, Auberge des Pins, Sabres

DK Choice

ST-EMILION:
Restaurant Le Tertre €€
Fine dining
5 rue du Tertre de la Tente, 33330
Tel *05 57 74 46 33* **Closed** *Apr–mid-Nov: Wed; Feb–Mar: Wed & Thu; mid-Nov–Jan*
An intimate restaurant that has won many fans with its outstanding food, warm service, and superb wines. Choose from a range of classic local dishes such as duck, *foie gras*, or line-caught *maigre* fish – all of which are prepared with great flair.

TALMONT-SUR-GIRONDE:
Hôtel-Restaurant L'Estuaire €€
Regional
1 av de l'Estuaire, 17120
Tel *05 46 90 43 85* **Closed** *Oct–Mar: Mon & Tue*
Local fish and seafood in a lovely, remote location beside the Gironde estuary.

Périgord, Quercy, & Gascony

AGEN: Mariottat €€€
Fine dining
25 rue Louis Vivent, 47000
Tel *05 53 77 99 77* **Closed** *Mon*
Refined food made with fresh produce is served in a beautiful 19th-century town mansion furnished with antiques.

ALBI: Le Jardin des Quatre Saisons €€
Regional
5 rue de la Pompe, 81000
Tel *05 63 60 77 76* **Closed** *Mon*
Located in the heart of historic Albi, this eatery serves great local favorites. Truffle and mushroom dishes are highly recommended.

ALBI: L'Esprit du Vin €€
Fine dining
11 quai Choiseul, 81000
Tel *05 63 54 60 44* **Closed** *Sun & Mon*
Innovative cuisine is dished up in this chic and comfortable restaurant set in a brick cellar. A separate vegetarian menu is available.

AUCH: Le Papillon €€
Regional
rte d'Agen, 32810 Montaut-les-Créneaux
Tel *05 62 65 51 29* **Closed** *Mon*
Gascon specialties such as *cassoulet* and lamb are served in a tranquil room beside a lovely garden. Perfect for big groups.

BERGERAC: La Flambée €€
Regional
49 av Marceau Feyry, 24100
Tel *05 53 57 52 33*
Great place for local fare such as duck, *foie gras*, and goat's cheese.

BRANTOME: Au Fil du Temps €
Bistro
1 chemin du Vert Galant, 24310
Tel *05 53 05 24 12* **Closed** *Mon & Tue*
Very popular bistro with a lively atmosphere and pleasant, nostalgic decor.

BRANTOME: Les Frères Charbonnel €€€
Regional
rue Gambetta, 24310
Tel *05 53 05 70 15* **Closed** *Mon*
Duck and truffles are specialties at this renowned hotel-restaurant beside the River Dronne.

CAHORS:
Auberge du Vieux Cahors €
Regional
144 rue St-Urcisse, 46000
Tel *05 65 35 06 05* **Closed** *Dec–Mar: Tue & Wed*
Atmospheric 15th-century inn that serves generous portions of hearty local dishes. Friendly service.

CAHORS: Le Balandre €€
Fine dining
Hôtel Terminus, 5 av Charles de Freycinet, 46000
Tel *05 65 53 32 00* **Closed** *Mon & Sun*
Cahors' most elegant restaurant presents an entire truffle-based tasting menu – and more.

CASTRES:
La Lanterne des Salvages €
Bistro
1 av du Sidobre, Les Salvages, 81100 Burlats
Tel *05 63 35 08 21* **Closed** *Wed*
Welcoming eatery with a riverside terrace in a village north of Castres. Fresh, seasonal menus and an inviting bar. Good service.

CHAMPAGNAC-DE-BELAIR:
Le Moulin du Roc €€€
Fine dining
24530 Champagnac-de-Bélair
Tel *05 53 02 86 00* **Closed** *Tue; mid-Nov–mid-Mar*
Beautifully presented Périgord cuisine in the romantic environs of a converted 1670s mill.

CONDOM:
La Table des Cordeliers €€
Fine dining
1 rue des Cordeliers, 32100
Tel *05 62 68 43 82* **Closed** *Oct–May: Mon*
Creative cuisine served in a 13th-century convent.

Key to Price Guide *see p576*

CORDES-SUR-CIEL: Bistrot Tonin'ty €€
Regional
Hostellerie du Vieux Cordes, Haut de la Cité, 81170
Tel *05 63 53 79 20* **Closed** *Sep–Apr: Mon*
Irresistible desserts from Yves Thuries, master chocolatier and owner of this hotel-restaurant.

DOMME: L'Esplanade €€
Regional
2 rue Pontcarral, 24250
Tel *05 53 28 31 41* **Closed** *Mon; mid-Nov–mid-Dec; mid-Jan–mid-Feb*
Popular eatery with duck, *foie gras*, and truffles as menu highlights.

FIGEAC: La Cuisine du Marché €€
Bistro
15 rue Clermont, 46100
Tel *05 65 50 18 55* **Closed** *Sun*
Attractively converted stone wine cellar in medieval Figeac. The seasonal menus mix local favorites with Spanish dishes.

FRANCESCAS: Le Relais de la Hire €€
Regional
11 rue Porte Neuve, 47600
Tel *05 53 65 41 59* **Closed** *Mon*
Fresh herbs from the chef's garden add bold flavors to the cuisine in this charming historic building.

GAILLAC: Les Sarments €€
Regional
27 rue Cabrol, 81600
Tel *05 63 57 62 61* **Closed** *Mon–Wed*
Cozy restaurant in a medieval wine cellar. Gascon dishes are cooked with great flair and accompanied by good local wines.

ISSIGEAC: La Brucelière €
Regional
pl de la Chapelle, 24560
Tel *05 53 73 89 61* **Closed** *Wed*
Rugged inn outside Bergerac with a charming terrace. Serves lighter variations of local cuisine.

LACAVE: Le Pont de l'Ouysse €€€
Fine dining
Le Pont de l'Ouysse, 46200
Tel *05 65 37 87 04* **Closed** *mid-Mar–mid-Jul & Sep–Oct: Mon; Nov–mid-Mar*
Gorgeous restaurant with fabulous terrace views. Truffles are from the hotel's own grounds.

LES EYZIES-DE-TAYAC: Au Vieux Moulin €€
Regional
rue du Moulin Bas, 24620
Tel *05 53 06 94 33* **Closed** *Nov–Mar*
Classic local dishes are served in a very pretty old mill overlooking a stream near Lascaux caves.

Beautifully laid table at the ultra sophisticated Michel Sarran, Toulouse

MANCIET: La Bonne Auberge €€
Regional
pl du Pesquèrot, 32370
Tel *05 62 08 50 04* **Closed** *Mon*
Family-run restaurant serving rich Gascon fare and fine Armagnacs.

MONBAZILLAC: La Tour des Vents €€
Fine dining
Moulin de Malfourat, 24240
Tel *05 53 58 30 10* **Closed** *Mon; Jan*
Stunning views of the Dordogne countryside from this hilltop restaurant. Creative menus.

MONTAUBAN: Au Fil de l'Eau €€
Bistro
14 quai du Dr Lafforgue, 82000
Tel *05 63 66 11 85* **Closed** *Jul–Aug: Sun & Mon; Sep–Jun: Mon*
Smart restaurant in the heart of old Montauban. A sizzling *cassoulet* heads the list of local specialties.

PERIGUEUX: Restaurant L'Essentiel €€
Regional
8 rue de la Clarté, 24000
Tel *05 53 35 15 15* **Closed** *Mon & Sun*
Subtle combinations of classic Périgord food and modern innovation at this local favorite.

PUJAUDRAN: Le Puits Saint-Jacques €€€
Fine dining
av Victor Capoul, 32600
Tel *05 62 07 41 11* **Closed** *Mon & Tue*
Prestigious restaurant showcasing exquisite cuisine in a historic farm-house setting. Excellent wine list.

PUJOLS: La Toque Blanche €€
Fine dining
47300 Pujols
Tel *05 53 49 00 30* **Closed** *Sun & Mon*
Long-established restaurant with lovely views and an inventive chef.

ROCAMADOUR: Le Roc du Berger €
Regional
Bois de Belveyre, rte de Padirac, 46500
Tel *05 65 33 19 99* **Closed** *Oct: Mon–Sat; Nov–mid-Mar*
Rustic eatery with tables inside wood cabins or under trees. Menu features local lamb and trout.

SARLAT: La Couleuvrine €€
Regional
1 pl de la Bouquerie, 24200
Tel *05 53 59 27 80*
Hearty bistro-style food served in a tower in Sarlat's grand ramparts.

DK Choice

SORGES: Auberge de la Truffe €€€
Regional
Le Bourg, 24420
Tel *05 53 05 02 05*
Truffles or "black diamonds" figure prominently in Périgord cuisine, and Sorges proclaims itself the "world truffle capital." This inn is the ideal place to sample truffles in all their variety – *consommé*, omelettes, with scallops, and in desserts.

ST-MEDARD: Le Gindreau €€€
Fine dining
Le Bourg, 46150
Tel *05 65 36 22 27* **Closed** *Mon & Tue*
Gourmet luxury in a converted village school. Delicious truffles.

TOULOUSE: Brasserie Flo – Les Beaux Arts €€
Brasserie
1 quai de la Daurade, 31000
Tel *05 61 21 12 12*
Local institution with grand 1900s decor, a bustling atmosphere, and a huge brasserie menu.

TOULOUSE: La Bohème €€
Bistro
3 rue Lafayette, 31000
Tel *05 61 23 24 18* **Closed** *Sun*
Pleasant bistro set in an arching brick cellar serving regional classics.

TOULOUSE: Michel Sarran €€€
Fine dining
21 bd Armand Duportal, 31000
Tel *05 61 12 32 32* **Closed** *Sat & Sun; Aug*
Chic Michelin-starred restaurant. A real gourmet experience.

TURSAC: La Source €
Regional
Le Bourg, 24620
Tel *05 53 06 98 00* **Closed** *Tue & Wed*
Friendly village restaurant serving local dishes that feature freshly-picked herbs and mushrooms.

For more information on types of restaurants *see p575*

VAREN: Le Moulin de Varen €
Regional
Le Bourg, 82330
Tel *05 63 65 45 10* **Closed** *Sep–Jun: Mon*
Enjoy hearty local food at this old stone mill near the Aveyron gorges.

The Pyrenees

AINHOA: La Maison Oppoca €€
Regional
Le Bourg, 64250
Tel *05 59 29 90 72* **Closed** *Mon; Jan–Feb*
Stylish establishment that serves creative Basque cuisine, and specializes in crab.

ARGELES-GAZOST: Au Fond du Gosier €
Bistro
rue du Capitaine Digoy, 65400
Tel *05 62 90 13 40* **Closed** *Jul–Aug: Sun; Sep–Jun: Sun & Mon*
Local dishes prepared with fresh produce and culinary flair.

ASCAIN: L'Atelier Gourmand Basque €€
Regional
pl du Fronton, 64310
Tel *05 59 54 46 82* **Closed** *Wed*
Lively bar-restaurant serving great local cuisine and tapas dishes.

AUDRESSEIN: L'Auberge d'Audressein €€
Regional
Le Bourg, 09800
Tel *05 61 96 11 80* **Closed** *Mon*
Quaint stone inn with sophisticated cuisine. Local trout is a specialty.

AX-LES-THERMES: Auzeraie €–€€
Regional
1 av Théophile Delcassé, 09110
Tel *05 61 64 20 70* **Closed** *Sep–Jun: Mon & Tue*
Slightly old-fashioned eating spot with good-value weekday menus.

BAGNERES-DE-LUCHON: Les Caprices Etigny €
Regional
30 bis allées d'Etigny, 31110
Tel *05 61 94 31 05* **Closed** *Mon*
Local lamb, trout, or pork grilled over an open fire; mountain views.

DK Choice

BAREGES: Auberge du Lienz-Chez Louisette €
Regional
rte de Lienz, 65120
Tel *05 62 92 67 17* **Closed** *Nov*
Few restaurants boast such a spectacular location in the High Pyrenees. In winter, skiers warm up with *garbure* (thick soup); for summer hikers, there are dishes with wildflowers and fruits – the blueberry tart is especially tasty.

Chic, comfortable dining space at Le Sin restaurant, Biarritz

BAYONNE: Le Bayonnais €€
Bistro
38 quai des Corsaires, 64100
Tel *05 59 25 61 19* **Closed** *Jul–Aug: Mon; Sep–Jun: Sun & Mon*
Pleasant restaurant with terrace on a riverside quay. Basque fare on offer, including great squid.

BAYONNE: Auberge du Cheval Blanc €€€
Fine dining
68 rue Bourgneuf, 64100
Tel *05 59 59 01 33* **Closed** *Mon*
Family-run inn with particularly good ham and Atlantic seafood.

BIARRITZ: Le Sin €€
Fine dining
Cité de Océan, 1 av de la Plage, 64200
Tel *05 59 47 82 89* **Closed** *Sep–Jun: Mon*
Modern restaurant with fantastic views and creative Basque cuisine.

BIARRITZ: Chez Albert €€
Brasserie
51bis allée Port des Pêcheurs, 64200
Tel *05 59 24 43 84* **Closed** *Feb–Jun & Sep–Nov: Wed; Dec–Jan*
Bright, bustling seafood brasserie on Biarritz port with great views.

ESPELETTE: Hôtel-Restaurant Euzkadi €€
Regional
285 Karrika Nagusia, 64250
Tel *05 59 93 91 88* **Closed** *Dec–Jun & Sep–Oct: Mon; Nov–mid-Dec*
Charming eatery serving classic Basque cooking, often featuring the village's famous fiery peppers.

FOIX: Le Phoebus €€
Regional
3 cours Irénée Cros, 09000
Tel *05 61 65 10 42* **Closed** *Mon; late July–mid-Aug*
Delicious country cooking with vegetarian options. Great views.

LARRAU: Etchemaïte €
Regional
Le Bourg, 64560
Tel *05 59 28 61 45* **Closed** *Jan–mid-Feb*
Family-run establishment in a gorgeous location. Sea bass in a fresh herb crust is the star dish.

LOURDES: Le Magret €
Bistro
10 rue des 4 Frères Soulas, 65100
Tel *05 62 94 20 55* **Closed** *Wed*
Small, relaxed bistro with good-value seasonal menus and wines.

MIREPOIX: Les Remparts €€
Modern French
6 cours Louis Pons Tande, 09500
Tel *05 61 68 12 15* **Closed** *Mon*
Global touches are given to local produce and traditions at this historic inn.

MONTSEGUR: Auberge de Montségur €
Regional
52 rue du Village, 09300
Tel *05 61 01 10 24* **Closed** *Mon & Tue; Jan*
Pleasant stone inn with delicious local meats on the menu.

ORTHEZ: Au Temps de la Reine Jeanne €€€
Bistro
44 rue Bourg Vieux, 64300
Tel *05 59 67 00 76*
Attractive restaurant and hotel in an 18th-century courtyard building. Fresh, modern food.

PAU: Chez Pierre €€
Regional
14–16 rue Louis Barthou, 64000
Tel *05 59 27 76 86*
Snug restaurant with old-fashioned comfort and an attached pub.

SARE: Baratxartea €€
Regional
Ihalar, 64310
Tel *05 59 54 20 48* **Closed** *Sep–Jun: Tue*
Massive Basque chalet: the chef plates fine local cooking with vegetables from the hotel's garden.

ST-GAUDENS: La Connivence €€
Fine dining
chemin Ample, Valentine, 31800
Tel *05 61 95 29 31* **Closed** *Mon*
Sophisticated restaurant with an excellent selection of wines.

ST-JEAN-DE-LUZ: Chez Pablo €
Regional
5 rue Mlle Etcheto, 64500
Tel *05 59 26 37 81* **Closed** *Wed*
Friendly eatery with bench seating and Basque seafood classics.

ST-JEAN-DE-LUZ: Le Kaïku €
Fine Dining
17 rue de la République, 64500
Tel *05 59 26 13 20* **Closed** *Sep–Jun: Tue & Wed*
Inventive Basque cuisine and chaming service in a lovely old stone house. Superb fish.

ST-JEAN-PIED-DE-PORT: Relais de la Nive €
Brasserie
4 pl Charles de Gaulle, 64220
Tel *05 59 37 04 22*
Spacious brasserie with fine views over the river Nive. Great salads and light meals.

ST-LARY-SOULAN: Restaurant La Grange €
Regional
13 rte d'Autun, 65170
Tel *05 62 40 07 14* **Closed** *Sep–Jun: Tue & Wed*
Large stone farmhouse in the High Pyrenees. Enjoy local bean stews or meats grilled on an open fire.

ST-SULPICE-SUR-LEZE: La Commanderie €
Fine dining
pl de Hôtel de Ville, 31410
Tel *05 61 97 33 61* **Closed** *Jul–Aug: Wed; Sep–June: Tue & Wed*
Elegant cooking in a relaxed rural setting amid lush gardens.

TARBES: L'Ambroisie €€
Fine dining
48 rue Abbé Torné, 65000
Tel *05 62 93 09 34* **Closed** *Mon*
Tarbes' top restaurant, featuring fresh, fine produce. Excellent wines.

Languedoc-Roussillon

AIGUES-MORTES: Le Café des Bouzigues €€
Regional
7 rue Pasteur, 30220
Tel *04 66 53 93 95* **Closed** *most of Jan, late Nov–early Dec*
Cheerful restaurant with terrace; hearty fixed-price menu.

AIGUES-MORTES: Marie Rosé €€
Regional
13 rue Pasteur, 30220
Tel *04 66 53 79 84* **Closed** *Sep–Jun: Mon–Wed*
In an old rectory with tables in the garden. Popular for its delicate seafood creations.

ANDUZE: Auberge Les Trois Barbus €€
Fine dining
rte de Mialet, Générargues, 30140
Tel *04 66 61 72 12* **Closed** *Mon & Tue; Nov–late Mar*
An elegant restaurant in a rustic setting; plenty of *foie gras*, wild mushrooms, and rich desserts.

ARGELLIERS: Auberge de Saugras €
Traditional French
Domaine de Saugras, 34380
Tel *04 67 55 08 71* **Closed** *Tue & Wed*
Traditional farmhouse serving lots of duck and mountain trout. Impressive cellar.

BEZIERS: Octopus €€€
Fine dining
12 rue Boiledieu, 34500
Tel *04 67 49 90 00* **Closed** *Sun & Mon*
Béziers' best with lots of truffles, a touch of Asia, and great wine.

BIZE MINERVOIS: La Bastide Cabezac €
Traditional French
18–20 Hameau de Cabezac, 11120,
Tel *04 68 46 66 10* **Closed** *Mon; 3 weeks in Nov; 2 weeks in Feb*
Attractive 18th-century staging post with refined creative fare such as Cathar chicken fricassee.

CAP D'AGDE: La Manade €
Regional
15 pl Saint-Clair, 34300
Tel *04 67 21 23 38* **Closed** *Tue & Wed*
Tasty, affordable seafood and succulent steaks sourced from the Camargue. Good for families.

DK Choice

CARCASSONNE: La Marquière €€
Regional
13 rue St-Jean, 11000
Tel *04 68 71 52 00* **Closed** *Wed & Thu; 10 Jan–10 Feb*
Located up in the Cité, La Marquière is a popular family-run local favorite. The food is authentic Southwestern – duck breasts and *confits*, *foie gras* and *cassoulet*. Oysters and other seafood are available as well.

Pretty shaded eating area at the popular La Marquiere, Carcassonne

CARCASSONNE: Les Bergers d'Arcadie €€
Modern French
70 rue Trivalle, 11000
Tel *04 68 72 46 01* **Closed** *Wed; 2 weeks in Nov; 2 weeks in Feb*
Unpretentious place serving refined cooking. Try poached quail's eggs or seafood *cassoulet*.

CARCASSONNE: Le Parc Franck Putelat €€€
Fine dining
80 chemin des Anglais, 11000
Tel *04 68 71 80 80* **Closed** *Sun & Mon; 3 weeks in Jan*
Radically creative cuisine at this two-star restaurant. Expensive, but good-value lunch menu.

CERET: Al Catalá €€
Modern French
15 av Georges Clémenceau, 66400
Tel *04 68 87 07 91* **Closed** *Mon*
Creative cooking, exotic flavors, and a dash of Catalan style on a chic bamboo-shaded terrace.

COLLIOURE: Le 5e Péché €€
Fusion
18 rue Fraternité, 66190
Tel *04 68 98 09 76* **Closed** *Mon*
A Japanese chef creates his own remarkable Languedoc-Asian fusion cuisine from a choice of fresh, local ingredients.

COLLIOURE: La Balette €€€
Fine dining
114 rte de Port-Vendres, 66190
Tel *04 68 82 05 07* **Closed** *late Nov–early Feb*
Elaborate gourmet creations in a beautiful setting with magical views of Collioure over the bay.

CUCUGNAN: Auberge du Vigneron €€
Regional
2 rue Achille Mir, 11350
Tel *04 68 45 03 00* **Closed** *Mon; late Nov–early Mar*
Hearty Languedoc cooking, using produce from the kitchen garden, and Corbières wines.

FONTJONCOUSE: Gilles Goujon €€€
Fine dining
av St-Victor, 11360
Tel *04 68 44 07 37* **Closed** *Mon; Jan–late Mar*
Culinary masterpieces are served at this Michelin-starred restaurant. Try the "truffle eggs."

For more information on types of restaurants *see p575*

LE BOULOU: Hostalet de Vivès €€
Regional
Le Village, Vivès, 66490
Tel *04 68 83 05 52* **Closed** *Wed; mid-Jan–Feb*
Grilled snails, rabbit with aioli, and all things Catalan are on offer at this rustic eatery.

MARAUSSAN: Le Parfum des Garrigues €€
Regional
37 rue de l'Ancienne Poste, 34370
Tel *04 67 90 33 76* **Closed** *Mon & Tue*
Fresh seafood, grilled meat, and game dishes in a pretty courtyard.

MINERVE: Relais Chantovent €€
Modern French
17 Grande Rue, 34210
Tel *04 68 91 14 18* **Closed** *Wed; mid-Dec–mid-Mar*
Terrace views over the Gorges du Brian, with creative cooking and homemade ice cream.

MONTPELLIER: Au Bonheur des Tartes €
Traditional French
4 rue des Tresoriers de la Bourse, 34000
Tel *04 67 02 77 38* **Closed** *Sun & Mon*
Perfect cooking and excellent *plats du jour* in this cozy eatery.

MONTPELLIER: La Diligence €€
Traditional French
2 pl Pétrarque, 34000
Tel *04 67 66 12 21* **Closed** *Sun*
City-center restaurant set in a vaulted medieval hall; grilled dishes, wines, and desserts on the menu.

MONTPELLIER: Le Petit Jardin €€
Fine dining
20 rue Jean-Jacques Rousseau, 34000
Tel *04 67 60 78 78* **Closed** *winter: Mon*
Old-world elegance and refined cuisine in a lovely garden setting.

NARBONNE: Chez Bebelle €
Bistro
Halles de Narbonne, 11100
Tel *06 85 40 09 01* **Closed** *Sun & Mon*
Inexpensive, cheerful eatery where the meat comes fresh from the butcher.

NARBONNE: Le Table de St-Crescent €€€
Fine dining
Domaine St-Crescent, 68 av Général Leclerc, 11100
Tel *04 68 41 37 37*
Closed *Mon*
Superb, seasonal menu of imaginative dishes. Perfect setting for a special evening.

NIMES: Le Cheval Blanc €
Wine bar
1 pl des Arènes, 30000
Tel *04 66 76 19 59* **Closed** *Sun*
Lively, classic brasserie-style restaurant with a fantastic cellar and Pyrenean *charcuterie* cheeses.

NIMES: Aux Plaisirs des Halles €€
Traditional French
4 rue Littré, 30000
Tel *04 66 36 01 02* **Closed** *Sun & Mon*
Sample Nîmes' famous *brandade*, or lobster in pleasant wood-paneled surroundings.

PERPIGNAN: Le Grain de Folie €€
Modern French
71 av Général Leclerc, 66000
Tel *04 68 51 00 50* **Closed** *Mon*
An austere dining room but first-rate cooking. Good-value meals.

PERPIGNAN: La Galinette €€€
Fine dining
23 rue Jean Payra, 66000
Tel *04 68 35 00 90* **Closed** *Sun & Mon*
Creative, critically acclaimed Catalan cuisine; huge wine list.

PEZENAS: L'Entre-Pots €€
Modern French
8 av Louis-Montagne, 34120
Tel *04 67 30 00 00* **Closed** *Sun & Mon*
Trendy restaurant in an old warehouse serving inventive food.

PORT CAMARGUE: Le Spinaker €€
Traditional French
Pointe de la Presqu'ile, 30240
Tel *04 66 53 36 37* **Closed** *Mon–Wed (out of season); Jan*
Seafood, grilled beef, and duck on a terrace overlooking the marina. Decadent desserts also on offer.

PORT-VENDRES: La Cote Vermeille €€
Seafood
quai Fanal, 66660
Tel *04 68 82 05 71* **Closed** *Mon*
Perfect quayside location for this famous seafood restaurant; delicious lobster and oysters.

Lovely interiors of La Taverne restaurant, Uzes

PRADES: Le Jardin d'Aymeric €
Traditional French
7 rue du Canigou, 66500
Tel *04 68 96 08 72* **Closed** *Sep–Jun: Wed*
Classic dishes with a twist, served in a tranquil garden setting.

SAILLAGOUSE: La Vielle Maison Cerdane €€
Traditional French
pl de la Cerdagne, 66800
Tel *04 68 04 72 08* **Closed** *Mon; mid-Nov–mid-Dec*
An old family-run coach inn serving venison and other game dishes.

SETE: Terre et Mer €€
Regional
pl de Souras Bas, 34200
Tel *04 67 74 49 43* **Closed** *Wed*
Come here for fresh seafood, meat, and *charcuterie* from the Aveyron.

SOURNIA: Auberge de Sournia €
Traditional French
4 rte de Prades, 66730
Tel *04 68 97 72 82* **Closed** *2 weeks in Feb & Nov*
Hearty mountain cooking makes this a popular village inn. Try steak, duck, and other game dishes.

UZES: La Taverne €€
Traditional French
4 rue Sigalon, 30700
Tel *04 66 22 13 10* **Closed** *winter: Mon*
Snails, *brandade*, and other popular dishes are served in this modest but elegant eatery.

VILLEFRANCHE-DE-CONFLENT: Auberge St-Paul €€
Modern French
7 pl de Eglise, 66500
Tel *04 68 96 30 95* **Closed** *Mon*
Sample creative dishes with a Spanish touch. An excellent seven-course tapas menu.

Provence & the Côte d'Azur

AIGUES-MORTES: Le Dit-Vin €
Bistro **Map** A4
6 rue du 4 Septembre, 30220
Tel *04 66 53 52 76*
A restaurant and tapas bar with a wine cellar visible through the floor and a pretty garden setting.

AIX-EN-PROVENCE: Le Comté Aix €
Regional **Map** C4
17 rue Couronne, 13010
Tel *04 42 26 79 26* **Closed** *Sun*
A blackboard menu shows the fare on offer; plenty of simple but well-prepared local dishes.

Key to Price Guide *see p576*

Beautifully decorated dining area at Les Terraillers in Biot

AIX-EN-PROVENCE: Le Formal €€
Fine dining **Map** C4
32 rue Espariat, 13100
Tel *04 42 27 08 31* **Closed** *Sun & Mon; late Aug–early Sep*
Plenty of truffles to choose from at Le Formal – served in a vaulted cellar with a contemporary design. Good-value lunch menus.

ANTIBES: Aubergine €
Provençal **Map** E3
7 rue Sade, 06600
Tel *04 93 34 55 93* **Closed** *Wed*
Excellent Provençal dishes and lots of aubergines or eggplants, as the name implies.

ARLES: La Grignotte €
Provençal **Map** B3
6 rue Favorin, 13200
Tel *04 90 93 10 43* **Closed** *Sun*
Cheerful, inexpensive eatery. Try the fish soup and beef stew with Camargue rice. Good house wines.

ARLES: Lou Marques €€€
Fine dining **Map** B3
bd Lices, 13200
Tel *04 90 52 52 52* **Closed** *Nov–Mar: Mon*
Elegant restaurant with a garden terrace and classic Provençal dishes.

AVIGNON: La Fourchette €€
Regional **Map** B3
17 rue Racine, 84000
Tel *04 90 85 20 93* **Closed** *Sat & Sun*
Quirky restaurant offering its own innovative take on Provançal classics, with lots of seafood and delicious cheeses.

AVIGNON: Christian Etienne €€€
Fine dining **Map** B3
10 rue Mons, 84000
Tel *04 90 86 16 50* **Closed** *Sun & Mon*
Superb seasonal menus and an elaborate lobster menu are served in a 14th-century dining room.

BIOT: Les Terraillers €€€
Fine dining **Map** E3
11 rte Chemin Neuf, 06410
Tel *04 93 65 01 59* **Closed** *Wed & Thu*
Lobster, truffles, *foie gras*, and other delights; excellent list of Provençal wines.

BONNIEUX: Edouard Loubet €€€
Fine dining **Map** C3
Les Claparèdes, chemin des Cabanes, 84480
Tel *0 4 90 75 89 78* **Closed** *Wed*
Ravishing dishes from one of France's top chefs. Great location.

CAGNES-SUR-MER: Fleur de Sel €€
Modern French **Map** E3
85 montée de la Bourgade, 06800
Tel *04 93 20 33 33* **Closed** *Wed*
The lofty Haut de Cagnes makes a lovely setting for some refined cooking. Great-value set menus and attentive service.

CANNES: Angolo Italiano €€
Italian **Map** E4
6 rue des Batéguiers, 06400
Tel *04 93 68 42 36* **Closed** *Mon*
Neapolitan-run place serving *charcuterie*, cheeses, grilled meat, and seafood.

CANNES: La Palme d'Or €€€
Fine dining **Map** E4
73 la Croisette, 06400
Tel *04 92 98 74 14* **Closed** *Sun–Tue*
Fashionable Michelin-starred restaurant; part of the famous Hôtel Martinez.

CARPENTRAS: Chez Serge €€
Modern French **Map** B3
90 rue Cottier, 84200
Tel *04 90 63 21 24*
Striking contemporary decor and imaginative food featuring fresh fish and wild mushrooms. Huge wine list.

CASTELLANE: Auberge du Teillon €€
Modern French **Map** D3
rte Napoléon le Garde, 04120
Tel *04 92 83 60 88* **Closed** *Mon; Nov–mid-Mar*
Country inn famed for its hand-smoked salmon, *foie gras millefeuille*, Paimpol bean salad, scallop and morel risotto, and local cheeses.

CHATEAUNEUF-DU-PAPE: La Mère Germaine €€
Provençal **Map** B3
3 rue Commandant Lemaitre, 84230
Tel *04 90 83 54 37* **Closed** *Wed*
Wide range of classic Provençal dishes accompanied by an excellent list of wines. Good-value lunch menus.

EZE: Café La Gascogne €
Bistro **Map** F3
151 av de Verdun, 06360
Tel *04 93 41 18 50*
No-frills wholesome fare – everything from *foie gras* to pizza. Fantastic selection of wines.

EZE: Château Eza €€€
Fine dining **Map** F3
rue de la Pise, 06360
Tel *04 93 41 12 24* **Closed** *Mon & Tue*
Stunning terrace views and high quality Michelin-star cooking at Château Eza.

DK Choice

FAYENCE: L'Escourtin €€
Modern French **Map** E3
chemin de Notre Dame des Cyprès, 83440
Tel *04 94 76 00 84* **Closed** *Wed & Thu*
Filled with antiques and flowers, L'Escourtin enjoys an idyllic location inside an ancient olive mill with a delightful garden courtyard. The cuisine is authentic and satisfying, with an emphasis on game dishes, *foie gras*, and fish in subtle sauces – all flavored with the best garden produce and herbs.

ILE DE PORQUEROLLES: L'Olivier €€€
Fine dining **Map** D5
Ile de Porquerolles Ouest, 83400
Tel *04 94 58 34 83* **Closed** *Oct–Apr*
An isolated, semi-tropical island retreat offering a delightful culinary experience. Mostly seafood.

L'ISLE-SUR-LE SORGUE: Le Vivier €€
Fine dining **Map** B3
800 cours Fernande Peyre, 84800
Tel *04 90 38 52 80* **Closed** *Mon*
Ask for the famous pigeon pie and eat it with relish on the magical riverside terrace.

LA TURBIE: Hostellerie Jérôme €€€
Gastronomic **Map** F3
4 av Géneral de Gaulle, 06320
Tel *04 92 41 51 51* **Closed** *Mon & Tue; Nov–mid-Feb*
Michelin-starred establishment. All dishes are prepared using fresh market produce.

LES-BAUX-DE-PROVENCE: L'Oustau de Baumanière €€€
Gastronomic **Map** B3
rte Départementale 27, Le Val d'Enfer 13520
Tel *04 90 54 33 07* **Closed** *Nov–mid-Dec; Jan–Feb*
Gorgeous setting and outstanding food at this Michelin-starred gem. Great for celebrity spotting.

For more information on types of restaurants *see p575*

LES-SAINTES-MARIES-DE-LA-MER: El Campo €
Spanish **Map** A4
13 rue Victor Hugo, 13460
Tel *04 90 97 84 11* **Closed** *Sep–Jun: Wed*
Enjoy an evening with live Flamenco and Gypsy Kings-style guitar music. Paella is a specialty.

MARSEILLE: Toinou €
Seafood **Map** C4
3 cours Saint-Louis, 13001
Tel *08 11 45 45 45*
Fresh oysters, mussels, and prawns served with crusty bread and white wines. Ideal seafood place.

DK Choice

MARSEILLE: L'Epuisette €€€
Seafood **Map** C4
Vallon des Auffes, 13007
Tel *04 91 52 17 82* **Closed** *Sun & Mon*
A gorgeous setting, with a spectacular glass dining room overlooking the turquoise sea. Heavenly *bouillabaisse*, lobster tajine, and other seafood delicacies are accompanied by fine wines and followed by great desserts. Attentive staff ensure a memorable dining experience.

DK Choice

MENTON: Le Mirazur €€€
Fine dining **Map** F3
30 ave Aristide Briand, 06500
Tel *04 92 41 86 86* **Closed** *Mon & Tue*
A Michelin-starred restaurant, Le Mirazur offers aesthetically pleasing, colorful dishes made with seafood, local lamb, and vegetables from the chef's own garden. The views over Menton and the sea are magnificent.

MONACO: Le Louis XV €€€
Fine dining **Map** F3
pl du Casino, Monte Carlo, 98000
Tel *00 377 98 06 88 64* **Closed** *Tue & Wed; Dec; mid-Feb–mid-Mar*
Capital of Alain Ducasse's culinary empire for 25 years, Louis XV is all about luxury dining.

DK Choice

MOUSTIERS-STE-MARIE: La Treille Muscate €
Provençal **Map** D3
pl de l'Eglise, 04360
Tel *04 92 74 64 31* **Closed** *Wed*
Great location near a waterfall, under the crags. There is a shady terrace to sit out in and savor Provençal cuisine, including dishes such as rabbit confit in rosemary, stuffed baby vegetables, and delicious penne with mushrooms and *foie gras*.

NICE: Les Amoureux €
Italian **Map** F3
46 bd Stalingrad, 06000
Tel *04 93 07 59 73* **Closed** *Sun & Mon*
Visit Les Amoureux for some of the best pizzas on the Riviera with the perfect crust.

NICE: Luc Salsedo €€€
Fine dining **Map** F3
14 rue Maccarani, 06000
Tel *04 93 82 24 12* **Closed** *Wed*
Classics such as lamb and ratatouille reinvented and served in style. Good vegetarian choices.

NIMES: Le Vintage €
Bistro **Map** A3
7 rue de Bernis, 30000
Tel *04 66 21 04 45* **Closed** *Sun*
Friendly eatery with tables indoors and out. The blackboard menu features *foie gras*, steaks, and duck.

NIMES: Au Plaisirs des Halles €€
Modern French **Map** A3
4 rue Littré, 30000
Tel *04 66 36 01 02* **Closed** *Sun & Mon*
The contemporary setting matches the cuisine. Do not miss the prawns and scallop tempura.

NIMES: Vincent Croizard €€€
Fine dining **Map** A3
17 rue des Chassaintes, 30900
Tel *04 66 67 04 99* **Closed** *Mon*
Chic hideaway, where the talented chef prepares an exquisite range of little dishes.

ROQUEBRUNE-CAP-MARTIN: Au Grand Inquisiteur €
Traditional French **Map** F3
15 rue du Château, 06190
Tel *04 93 35 05 37* **Closed** *Mon*
An intimate, family-run place rustling up traditional dishes at unbeatable prices. Great snails.

SAINT-REMY-DE-PROVENCE: Alain Assaud €€
Provençal **Map** B3
13 bd Marceau, 13210
Tel *04 90 92 37 11* **Closed** *Wed; mid-Nov–mid-Mar*
Superbly flavored Provençal dishes and desserts are served in this fine rustic restaurant.

STE-AGNES: Le Righi €
Provençal **Map** F3
1 pl du Fort, 06500
Tel *04 92 10 90 88* **Closed** *Wed*
Satisfying home food such as ravioli, gnocchi, and lamb cooked in hay. Amazing views.

ST-JEAN-CAP-FERRAT: Le Pirate €€
Seafood **Map** F3
Nouveau Port, 06230
Tel *04 93 76 12 97*
A perfect setting on a picturesque port. Be sure to try the grilled fish, *bouillabaisse*, and seafood risottos.

ST-PAUL-DE-VENCE: La Colombe d'Or €€
Regional **Map** E3
pl du Général de Gaulle, 06570
Tel *04 93 32 80 02* **Closed** *Nov–mid-Dec*
Legendary artists' retreat that offers simple but excellent Provençal cooking.

ST-REMY-DE-PROVENCE: La Cantina €
Italian **Map** B3
18 bd St-Hugo, 13210
Tel *04 90 90 90 60* **Closed** *mid-Feb–mid-Mar; mid-Nov–early Dec*
Informal restaurant specializing in thin-crust pizzas and pasta dishes. Excellent selection of Italian wines.

ST-TROPEZ: Le Sporting €
Bistro **Map** E4
42 pl des Lices, 83990
Tel *04 94 97 00 65*
Very popular with locals, Le Sporting offers a good range of main dishes, as well as burgers, salads, and omelettes.

ST-TROPEZ: Vague Or €€€
Fine dining **Map** E4
plage de la Bouillabaisse, 83990
Tel *04 94 55 91 00* **Closed** *early Oct–late Apr*
Sample exotic dishes such as cedar, *salicornes*, and chestnut honey in a romantic setting. Excellent service and fine wines.

Refined and graceful dining room at the renowned Le Louis XV in Monaco

Key to Price Guide *see p576*

Classy, vibrant interiors of the stylish seafood restaurant U Callelu, Calvi

VENCE: La Litote €
Contemporary **Map** E3
5 rue de l'Evêché, 06140
Tel *04 93 24 24 82* **Closed** *Mon & Tue*
Laid-back restaurant located on a little square with tables under the trees. Inventive fare on offer.

VILLEFRANCHE-SUR-MER: La Mère Germaine €€
Seafood **Map** F3
9 Quai Courbet, 06230
Tel *04 93 01 71 39* **Closed** *mid-Nov–25 Dec*
A long-established favorite on the port since 1938, serving particularly good *bouillabaisse*.

VILLENEUVE-LES-AVIGNON: Guinguette de Vieux Moulin €
Seafood **Map** B3
5 rue du Vieux Moulin, 30400
Tel *04 90 94 50 72* **Closed** *Mon*
Lively riverside restaurant specializing in grilled sardines and other fish.

Corsica

AJACCIO: Restaurant des Halles €
Corsican **Map** B4
4 rue des Halles, 20000
Tel *04 95 21 42 68* **Closed** *Sun; Dec*
A firm local favorite, with its white tablecloths, crystal glasses, and snug booths. Set menus available.

DK Choice

AJACCIO: Palm Beach €€€
Gastronomic **Map** B4
rte des Sanguinaires, 20000
Tel *04 95 52 01 03*
Located along the road to the Iles Sanguinaires, Palm Beach is one of Ajaccio's top Michelin-starred restaurants. Serves impeccably prepared dishes such as lobster and fennel lasagna, and sublime desserts.

BASTIA: Chez Huguette €€€
Seafood **Map** D2
Vieux Port, 20200
Tel *04 95 31 37 60* **Closed** *2 weeks at Christmas*
A favorite on the Vieux Port, Chez Huguette is ideal for oysters and grilled fish. Excellent wine cellar.

BONIFACIO: The Kissing Pigs €
Bistro **Map** C6
15 quai Banda del Ferro, 20169
Tel *04 95 73 56 09* **Closed** *Wed & Sun*
Portside eatery serving *charcuterie*, omelettes, grills, and a good range of wines to wash it all down.

BONIFACIO: Le Voilier €€€
Gastronomic **Map** C6
81 quai Jérôme Comparetti, 20169
Tel *04 95 73 07 06* **Closed** *Wed; mid-Jan–mid-Feb*
Chic restaurant offering lovely tapas for starters. In summer there is a mozzarella bar, perfect for a light lunch.

CALVI: U Calellu €€€
Seafood **Map** B2
quai Landry, 20260
Tel *04 95 65 22 18* **Closed** *Mon; Oct–Apr*
Run by the elegant La Villa Hotel, this fashionable restaurant is known for its fish soup, swordfish tartare, and rich desserts.

CARGESE: Bel'Mare €
Mediterranean **Map** B3
rte d'Ajaccio, 20130
Tel *04 95 26 40 13* **Closed** *Nov–Feb*
Enjoy the views from the terrace and choose from a range of pizzas, pasta dishes, steaks, and salads.

CORTE: Osteria di l'Orta €
Ferme-auberge **Map** C3
Villa Guelfucci, Pont de l'Orta, 20250
Tel *04 95 61 06 41* **Closed** *Sat & Sun; mid-Nov–Mar*
A young couple dishes out meals featuring homegrown produce, homemade liqueurs, and meat raised and cured by them.

CORTE: U Museu €
Corsican **Map** C3
Rampa Ribanelle, 20260
Tel *04 95 61 08 36* **Closed** *mid-Oct–Apr*
The menu at this lovely tree-shaded spot ranges from pizzas and salads to beautifully prepared traditional Corsican specialities.

ERBALUNGA: Le Pirate €€€
Gastronomic **Map** D1/D2
Port, 20222
Tel *04 95 33 24 20* **Closed** *Mon & Tue; Jan–Feb*
Romantic setting on the water and refined cooking; organic lamb and veal, and tasty desserts. Exceptional Corsican wines.

LEVIE: A Pignata €€
Ferme-auberge **Map** C5
rte du Pianu, 20170
Tel *04 95 78 41 90*
One of the oldest and most beautiful *ferme-auberges* in Corsica guarantees first-rate cooking. Reservations required.

PORTO-VECCHIO: Casadelmar €€€
Gastronomic **Map** C6
rte de Palombaggia, 20137
Tel *04 95 72 34 34* **Closed** *Nov–mid-Apr*
A striking modern pavilion by the sea makes a perfect setting for the sumptuous, Italian-influenced cuisine served here. Reservations are essential.

SAINT-FLORENT: Le Petit Caporal €€
Brasserie **Map** D2
Port de Plaisance, 20217
Tel *04 95 37 20 26* **Closed** *11 Nov–Dec*
Over a century in business, and still serving excellent pizzas, pasta, mussels, and *frites*. Menu also includes steaks and seafood.

Good views and a refined dining area at the waterside restaurant Le Pirate, Erbalunga

For more information on types of restaurants *see p575*

Shopping in France

Shopping in France is a delight. Whether you go to the hypermarkets and department stores, or seek out the small specialist shops and markets, you will be tempted by stylish French presentation and the quality of goods on offer. Renowned for its food and wine, France also offers world-famous fashion, perfume, pottery, porcelain, and crystal. This section provides guidelines on opening hours, and the range of goods stocked by the different types of stores. There are also details of quintessentially French products which are worth hunting down and a size conversion chart to aid clothes shopping.

Fresh nectarines and melons on sale at a market stall

Opening Hours

Food stores open anywhere between 7–8am and close around noon for lunch. In the north, the lunch break generally lasts for 2 hours; in the south, it is 3–4 hours (except in resorts, where it is shorter). After lunch, most food shops reopen until 7pm or later.

Bakeries open early and close early, although many stay open until 1pm or later, to catch the late baguette buyers and to serve a range of lunchtime snacks.

Supermarkets, department stores, and most hypermarkets remain open all day, with no lunchtime closure.

General opening hours for nonfood shops are 9am–6pm Monday through Saturday, often with a break for lunch. Many of these stores are closed on Monday mornings, and the smaller shops may stay closed all day. In the tourist regions, however, shops usually open every day in high season.

Sunday is by far the quietest shopping day, although most food shops (and corner stores) are open in the morning. Virtually every shop in France is closed on Sunday afternoon.

Hypermarkets and Department Stores

Hypermarkets (*hypermarchés* or *grandes surfaces*) can be found on the outskirts of every sizable town: look for signs indicating *centre commercial*. Much bigger than supermarkets, they sell mainly groceries, but their other lines include clothing, home accessories, and electronic equipment. They also sell discount gasoline. **Carrefour**, **Casino**, **Auchan**, **Leclerc**, and **Intermarché** are the biggest.

Department stores *(grands magasins)*, such as **Monoprix** and **Franprix**, are usually found in town centers. The more upmarket **Printemps** and **Galeries Lafayette** also have out-of-town locations.

A local bakery, which often sells pastries as well as bread

Specialist Shops

One of the pleasures of shopping in France is that specialist food stores continue to flourish, despite the influx of supermarkets and hypermarkets. The *boulangerie* (bakery) is frequently combined with a *pâtisserie* selling cakes and pastries. The *traiteur* sells prepared foods. *Fromagers* (cheese shops) and other shops specializing in dairy products *(produits laitiers)* may be combined, but the *boucherie* (butcher) and *charcuterie* (pork butcher/delicatessen) are often separate shops. For general groceries go to an *épicerie* or *alimentation*, but don't confuse this with an *épicerie fine*– a delicatessen.

Cleaning and household products are available from a *droguerie*, while hardware is bought from a *quincaillerie*. The term *papeterie* (stationer) covers both the expensive, specialist retailers and their hypermarket equivalents.

Markets

This guide lists the market day for every town featured in the Area by Area section. To find out where the market is, ask a passerby for *le marché*. Markets are held in the morning and usually finish promptly at noon.

Look for local producers, including those with only one or two special items to sell, as their goods are often more reasonably priced and of better quality than stalls with multiple items. By law (but not always in practice) price tags include the origin of all produce: *pays* means local. Chickens from Bresse are marketed wearing a red, white, and blue badge with the name of the producer.

If you are visiting markets over several weeks, look for items just coming into season, such as fresh walnuts, the first wild asparagus, early artichokes, or wild strawberries. At the market, you can also buy spices and herbs, some offbeat peculiarities (such as decorative cabbages), shoes, and clothing.

The year is full of seasonal regional markets in France, specializing in such things as truffles, hams, garlic, *foie gras* and livestock. *Foires artisanales* may be held at the same time as the seasonal markets, selling local produce and crafts.

Sausages and cheeses, regional specialties on offer in a Lyon market

Regional Produce

French regional specialties are available outside their area of origin, but it is more interesting to buy them locally as their creation and flavor reflect the traditions, tastes, and climate of the region.

Provence, in the south, prides itself on the quality of its olive oil, the best of which is made from the first cold pressing, lovingly decanted every day for a week. If you cannot get to a niche olive oil producer in Provence, head to **Oliviers et Co.** which has branches throughout the country, and sells an excellent selection of oils. Be sure to indulge in a tasting session to sample the flavors.

In the temperate north, the delicious Camembert cheese is the product of fresh Norman milk that has been cured for at least 3 weeks.

Pastis 51, drunk in the south

Popular drinks are also associated with particular regions. Pastis, made from aniseed, is popular in the south. Calvados, made in Normandy from apples, is popular in the north. Crème de Fruit de Dijon, the secret ingredient to many a good cocktail or dessert, comes in many flavors (from peach to wild strawberry), in addition to the well-known black currant – **Crème de Cassis**. Visit local producers to buy good versions of this thick, alcoholic syrup.

To a large extent, location determines the quality of regional produce. For example, the culinary tradition of Lyon *(see pp384–5)*, France's premier gastronomic city, stems from the proximity of Charolais cattle, Bresse chickens and pork, wild game from La Dombes, and the finest Rhône Valley wines.

Alongside sachets of dried herbs from Provence and braided strings of garlic and onions, be sure to buy the seasoning loved by all self-respecting francophile cooks – salt from the Ile de Ré *(see p420)* or Guerande. If you happen to be visiting the area, check out the salt flats and pick up the crumbly coarse grains at a local market. The Fleur de Sel is a delicate flaky variety and the Sel Marin is a gray, coarser type of salt.

Provençal dried herbs for culinary use and for making teas

Beauty Products

French women are renowned for their beauty, and there is a plethora of good beauty products in France. The major French labels, such as **Chanel** and **Guerlain**, are available overseas, but diehard cosmetics fans should scour the local beauty counters to find special products that are only on sale in France.

While in Paris, beauty junkies must visit the Chanel store on the rue Cambon and the Guerlain store on the Champs Elysées to buy scent that is only available in those particular stores. Throughout the rest of the country, supermarket brands such as Evian, Eau Thermale d'Avene, and Barbara Gould, are huge hits with magazine beauty editors. In particular, the cold cream by Eau Thermale d'Avène, the foaming cleanser by Barbara Gould and Evian's facial toning gel can be found in many a fashionista's makeup bag. Similarly, many a groomed Parisian swears by Nuxe's cult body oil *Huile Prodigeuse*, Caudalie's *Vinotherapary Cabernet* body scrub (with grape extracts), and Elancyl's anticellulite toning cream.

Oenobiol tanning supplement capsules and Phytomer's hair care range are considered absolutely necessary by St-Tropez beach lovers looking to lessen sun damage to hair and skin.

A more traditional approach to French grooming can be found by buying *savon de marseilles* – good-quality traditional soap made with plenty of olive oil.

True scent aficionados should head for Grasse *(see p521)*, the perfume capital of the world. Be sure to visit the three largest scent factories, **Fragonard**, **Molinard**, and **Galimard**, all of which have scent available for purchase.

Accessories

French fashion is rightfully famous, but aside from the main couture labels and stores *(see pp146–8)*, the best way to get the French look is to accessorize *à la Français*. In keeping with the French tradition of specialist local trades, there are certain regions that excel in producing accessories.

For a start, a handmade umbrella from Aurillac *(see p368)* is guaranteed to chase away rainy-day blues in style. The best-known umbrella manufacturers are **L'Ondée au Parapluie d'Aurillac**, **Piganiol**, and **Delos**, who will customize one for you with a photograph of whomever you choose to protect you from the storms.

Beautiful hands are easily available courtesy of the glove trade in Millau. Visit **L'Atelier Gantier** (the Glove Workshop) to pick up a stunning pair of expertly hand-stiched leather gloves in one of a seemingly endless array of colors.

More casual chic can be found with brightly colored wicker baskets from local markets and hardware stores. These quickly turn a casual ensemble into a boho-chic outfit. Beachside boutiques are great places for picking up stylish sarongs, beads, and bracelets for any trip to *la plage* (the beach). **K. Jacques** sandals from St-Tropez have long been must-have items among the fashion set.

When it is time to hit the slopes rather than the beach, French skiwear labels such as Rossignol can be a good buy, but only at the end of the season. At the height of *piste* time, ski resort shops are expensive. Once the snow starts to melt, however, exrental gear including skis and boots can be picked up relatively cheaply, while ski jackets, hats, and *après* skiwear tends to be gloriously cut-price.

Household Goods

If you are in the market for housewares, the best stores are **Ikea**, **Alinea**, and **Habitat**. **Truffaut** sells garden furniture, and **Leroy Merlin** is the hypermarket of the DIY, home improvement world.

It is surprisingly rare to see the whole range of kitchen goods in a specialist shop. Instead, try the kitchen section of department stores. General hardware shops stock cast-iron cooking equipment. White china is sold in specialist shops.

Traveling through Normandy provides the perfect excuse for sampling many wonderful products, not least the *crème de chantilly*, but for tableware fans or lingerie lovers, the lace industry here is also guaranteed to please. While the **Alençon** lace is extremely expensive and mainly finds its way onto couture sold in top Parisian stores, hitting the shops in Argentan, Chantilly *(see pp208–9)*, and Bayeux *(see pp256–7)* is likely to yield exquisite yet affordable pieces. It is worth hunting around for lace pieces which can be used to liven up an outfit: lace has made a fashion comeback in recent times and a customized delicate flower on a bag or blouse is *à la mode*.

Lace curtains are easy to come by, as are lovely table-cloths. The easiest way to be sure not to miss anything, is to take "the lace road" and tour the lace museums and boutiques of Alençon, Argentan, Caen *(see pp257–8)*, Courseulles, Villedieu-les-Poêles, and La Perrière.

With a beautiful tablecloth in place, you can proceed to pick up stunning crystal from which to sniff, swirl, and sip great French wine. The most famous French crystal maker, **Baccarat**, has a museum where you can take in some of their amazing creations and a store where you can buy a little Baccarat bauble to take home with you. A cheaper French crystal maker which is still elegant for every-day wear is **Crystal d'Arques**. You can tour the small museum in the factory and buy stemware at discount prices in the factory store.

Pottery is available at reasonable prices, especially near centers of production, such as Quimper *(see p278)* in Brittany, Aubagne near Marseille, and Vallauris *(see p526)* near Grasse.

Porcelain from Limoges *(see p360)* sets off any meal beautifully: a dinner set from the **Royal Limoges** factory store can be a great investment.

Similarly, stunning **Aubusson** tapestries are seriously expensive and unlikely to be an impulse holiday purchase. However, interior design fanatics could do worse than plan their tapestry

Size Chart

Women's dresses, coats, and skirts								
French	36	38	40	42	44	46	48	
British	8	10	12	14	16	18	20	
American	4	6	8	10	12	14	16	
Women's shoes								
French	36	37	38	39	40	41		
British	3	4	5	6	7	8		
American	5	6	7	8	9	10		
Men's suits								
French	44	46	48	50	52	54	56	58
British	34	36	38	40	42	44	46	48
American	34	36	38	40	42	44	46	48
Men's shirts								
French	36	38	39	41	42	43	44	45
British	14	15	151/2	16	161/2	17	171/2	18
American	14	15	151/2	16	161/2	17	171/2	18
Men's shoes								
French	39	40	41	42	43	44	45	46
British	6	7	71/2	8	9	10	11	12
American	7	71/2	8	81/2	91/2	101/2	11	111/2

or rug purchase around a trip to the home of weaving in Aubusson *(see pp360–1)*.

Finishing touches are fun to shop for and can certainly be more frivolous. Be sure to visit the local markets for gingham cotton napkins, linen cleaning cloths, and seafood accoutrements (such as lobster crackers and oyster forks). In Provence be sure to stock up on cheap, brightly colored cookware – tagines, terracotta bowls, and painted plates are all in abundance.

Wine

To buy wine straight from the vineyards *(domaines)* and wine cooperatives, follow the tasting *(dégustation)* signs. You may be expected to buy at least one bottle, except where a small fee is charged for wine-tasting. Wine cooperatives make and sell the wine of small producers. Here you can buy wine in 5- and 10-liter containers *(en tonneau* – about 1.3 and 2.6 gal respectively), as well as in bottles. Wine sold *en tonneau*, once opened, needs to be consumed fairly quickly, as it will deteriorate within a few days. Wine sold in bottles travels better.

Nicolas is France's main wine store, with many branches.

Factory Outlets

The French sales system is very rigid *(see p144)* but true bargain hunters know that factory shops have some items on sale all year round. The biggest factory outlets in France can be found in and around Troyes in outlet malls called **Marques Avenue** (Brands Avenue), **Marques City** (Brands City), and **McArthur Glen**, a large American outlet. They sell everything from Yves Saint Laurent suits to Black and Decker drills, Cristofle silverware and Bonpoint babygros (Onesies). As different an experience as you can get from browsing around French markets and local specialist stores, what factory outlets lack in charm they make up for in bargains. If a whole new wardrobe is in order, it is definitely worth a trip.

DIRECTORY

Hypermarkets and Department Stores

For details of addresses, visit the following websites:

Auchan
W auchan.fr

Carrefour
W carrefour.fr

Casino
W supercasino.fr

Franprix
W franprix.fr

Galeries Lafayette
W galerieslafayette.com

Intermarché
W intermarche.com

Leclerc
W e-leclerc.com

Monoprix
W monoprix.fr

Printemps
W printemps.com

Regional Produce

Crème de Cassis
Gabriel Boudier 14 rue de Cluj 21007 Dijon.
Tel 03 80 74 33 33.

Oliviers et Co.
For details of addresses, visit **W oliviers-co.com**

Beauty Products

Chanel
31 rue Cambon 75008 Paris.
Tel 01 44 50 66 00.
W chanel.com

Fragonard
20 bd Fragonard 06130 Grasse.
Tel 04 93 36 44 65.
W fragonard.com

Galimard
73 route de Cannes 06130 Grasse.
Tel 04 93 09 20 00.
W galimard.com

Guerlain
68 av des Champs Elysées 75008 Paris.
Tel 01 45 62 52 57.
W guerlain.com

Molinard
60 bd Victor Hugo 06130 Grasse.
Tel 04 92 42 33 28.
W molinard.com

Accessories

L'Atelier Gantier
21 rue Droite 12100 Millau. **Tel** 05 65 60 81 50.

Delos
14 rue Rocher 15000 Aurillac.
Tel 04 71 48 86 85.
W delos-france.com

K. Jacques
32 rte Plages 83990 St Tropez.
Tel 04 94 97 41 50.
W kjacques.com

L'Ondée au Parapluie d'Aurillac
27 rue Victor Hugo 15000 Aurillac.
Tel 04 71 48 29 53.

Piganiol
9 rue Ampère 15000 Aurillac.
Tel 04 71 63 42 60.

Household Goods

Alençon Lace Museum
Cour carrée de la Dentelle 61000 Alençon.
Tel 02 33 32 40 07.

Alinea
W alinea.fr

Aubusson
Manufacture Saint-Jean 3 rue Saint-Jean 23200 Aubusson.
Tel 05 55 66 10 08

Baccarat
20 rue des Cristalleries 54120 Baccarat.
Tel 03 83 76 60 06.
W baccarat.com

Cristal d'Arques
Zone industrielle 62510 Arques. **Tel** 03 21 95 46 96.

Habitat
W habitat.net

Ikea
W ikea.com

Leroy Merlin
W leroymerlin.fr

Royal Limoges
28 rue Donzelot Accès par le quai du Port du Naveix 87000 Limoges.
Tel 05 55 33 27 37.
W royal-limoges.fr

Truffaut
W truffaut.com

Wine

Nicolas
W nicolas.com

Factory Outlets

Marques Avenue
Av de la Maille 10800 Saint Julien les Villas.
Tel 03 25 82 80 80.
W marquesavenue.com

Marques City
35 rue Danton 10150 Pont Sainte Marie.
Tel 09 71 27 02 66.
W marquescity.fr

McArthur Glen
ZI des magasin d'usines du Nord 10150 Pont Sainte Marie.
Tel 03 25 70 47 10.
W mcarthurglen.com

Entertainment in France

Paris is one of the world's great entertainment cities, but France's reputation as a center of excellence in the arts extends well beyond the capital. Whether you prefer to attend theater or catch a film, listen to jazz or techno, or watch modern dance, the country has a wide array of choices. The regional chapters in this guide will give you an insight into local gems, while these pages provide an overview of entertainment trends and events. Major festivals, such as Avignon and Cannes, occupy an important place in French hearts, so book well ahead if you plan to attend. For small festivals and local happenings, tourist office websites have up-to-the-minute listings.

The spectacular setting of Avignon Theater at night

Theater

Going to the theater in France can be as formal or intimate as you choose. A trip to a major theater can involve dressing up, making special *souper* (late dinner) reservations at a nearby restaurant specializing in theater-goers, and quaffing exorbitantly priced champagne during the interval. On the other hand, a trip to a small-scale theater can be about casual dress, cheap tickets, and an intimate experience.

Whatever the genre, the French love an evening *au théâtre,* be it a French farce or a festival of street theater.

France's biggest theater festival is at **Avignon** *(see p507).* It is held during three weeks in July and is mainly open air. It also includes ballets, drama, and classical concerts. Many outdoor theaters operate in summer and are often free – contact the town's tourist office for a program.

Circus is also dear to the French. In small towns, summertime is often heralded by the circus loudspeaker strapped to the top of a car cruising the streets and inviting adults and children alike to flock to the big top. For larger circus events, head to Monaco for the Festival International du Cirque de Monte-Carlo or visit the colorful Festival International du Cirque de Bayeux, or the Cirque d'Hiver Bouglione in Paris.

Large-scale *spectacles* or shows are another popular form of theater, be they massive musicals or *son et lumières* performances. Marionettes are also given due respect in France, where puppet shows go beyond traditional Punch and Judy territory.

Film

La Septième Art, as the French refer to film, reveals the respect with which the genre is held. From the Lumière brothers and their innovative technology to contemporary critical smashes, such as *The Chorus*, *Amélie*, *The Artist*, and *The Intouchables*, France's influence on film is undeniable. The French are supportive of local, independent cinemas, and small towns are often fiercely protective of their screening center. So when visiting the cinema, try to avoid the behemoths of UGC and Gaumont, and instead head to a tiny *salle de cinéma*. If your language skills won't stretch to seeing a French film while in France, be sure to catch the VO *(Version Originale)* of any other language films, which will be screened in the film's original language. VF *(Version Française)* denotes a dubbed screening in French. As any expatriate in France knows, hearing a strange French voice coming out of a Hollywood A-lister's mouth is likely to dull any enjoyment of a major blockbuster movie.

Another thing to bear in mind is the French attitude to snacking. Essentially it is only acceptable for children, and even then only at a designated time after school. While French cinemas do have concession stands selling popcorn and sweets, it is only the foreigners who can be heard munching throughout the tense parts of the movie. On the other hand, some French cinemas have bars and restaurants attached, so that movie-goers can dissect the film over a meal. Many cinemas run mini directors' festivals with several films shown back to back, attracting serious film buffs, and those curious to learn more.

As the fame of **Cannes** *(see p524)* reflects, film festivals are taken seriously by the French. Cannes itself is a maelstrom of media hype, old-school glamor, and shiny new cash. It is an amazing experience if you can get tickets to any of the films or parties, but these are notoriously difficult to get as they are by invitation only. An easier way to experience the fabulous side of film is to attend

Poster promoting La Rochelle international film festival

Red carpet and razzmatazz at the Cannes film festival

the lower-key American and Asian film festivals in **Deauville** *(see p259)*. The former is seen as a major launch pad for US independent films looking for European release, and attracts big stars and cult directors alike. The competition section of the festival has ten films in the running each year. The chic town of Deauville is small and accessible and, while the chance of bumping into a huge star is slim, it feels possible.

The film festival in **La Rochelle** *(see p420)*, the second largest in France, does not attract big actors, but film fans will not be disappointed with the selection of movies.

A truly great way to catch a film in France is at an open-air festival. There are many such events throughout the country; check local listings so as not to miss out. And if you are lucky enough to be in Arles *(see pp512–13)*, an epic experience can be had at their annual showing of historical Roman blockbusters, screened against the backdrop of a magnificent Roman amphitheater. Contact **Théâtre Antique** for details.

Dance

Dancing is a way of life in France. From formal lessons to spontaneous outbreaks of grooving in the village square, moving to music is central to all types of celebration. Most foreigners' first experience with French dancers occurs in a nightclub and is, more often than not, accompanied by an expression of surprise. In even the most upscale nightclub, it is not unusual to see trendy twentysomethings jiving away to *le rock*, a formal form of rock and roll dancing. French teens are taught *le rock* before being unleashed on the party scene, and a basic understanding of its signature twirls and twists is considered vital to being a good dancer.

The love affair with formal dance sessions starts young, but lasts until late in life: tea dances are a major fixture of most older people's social calendars. Community centers, sports halls, restaurants, and chic nightclubs often host *thé dansants* (tea dances), normally in the late afternoon or early evening.

Another way to experience French dance culture is to head to a *guingette*, a moored party boat with a convivial, old-fashioned atmosphere. People here dance the *quadrille* or the *musette* to accordion music, spinning around on the banks of the river. While the *guingettes* were traditionally clustered around the Marne river, they have now spread throughout France and are definitely worth seeking out if your travels take you close to a major tributary.

In general, lots of dancing takes place near to water in France. Those looking to get into the groove in the south should take their dancing shoes to the quays in Bordeaux and Marseille.

Of course, once a year, on July 13 and 14, a most unusual impromptu dancing venue springs up around the country with the *Bals des Pompiers*. The "Firemen's Balls" are a national institution when the French of all ages head down to their local fire station to celebrate Bastille day by dancing to everything from Piaf to hip hop until the early hours of the morning.

If you would prefer to watch rather than participate, there are several major dance festivals that celebrate the dance traditions of different regions. The **Gannat festival** held in the Auvergne *(see p357)* is a fine example of a regional dance extravaganza, as is the **Festival Interceltique de Lorient** *(see p274)* which celebrates Celtic music and dance. The main international dance festivals are held in **Montpellier** *(see pp498–9)* and **Lyon** *(see pp382–5)*. These provide a wonderful opportunity to enjoy major contemporary dance talent from around the world.

Wonderful costumes and choreography at the Montpellier dance festival

Music

The French music scene is about far more than Johnny Hallyday, although it must be said that the aging rocker still manages to sell stacks of records, concert tickets, and gossip magazines. It should also be pointed out that he is actually Belgian, but the French have taken him to their hearts anyway. Neither is the scene just about Bob Sinclar, Daft Punk, David Guetta, and "Le French Touch." However, the fact that both dance music and rock happily coexist in the French charts reflects a truism of the music scene over here, which is that there is space for all kinds of tunes. *Chanson* has made a huge comeback over recent years as the success of the movement's poster boy Benjamin Biolay reveals. The new French *chanson* scene is dominated by Biolay, although other well-known artists in this genre include Vincent Delerm and Benabar.

Female crooners are also all the rage; listen to Lara Fabian or reality TV pop star Chimène Badi for confirmation of this.

Hip hop music is also very popular; France is the world's second biggest market for the genre after the USA. The success of artists such as MC Solaar, IAM, and Assassin have ensured international recognition for the country's thriving urban scene.

The event which best symbolizes this musical cornucopia is the Fête de la Musique. Every year on June 21, France resonates to the sound of this national music festival. Amateur and professional musicians alike set up their stages throughout villages and towns and perform. The best way to enjoy this is to walk around and try and take in as many different "concerts" as possible, but be aware that for some wannabe rock stars this is their only chance to shine, regardless of whether or not they can sing. Musical quality aside, what is most impressive about the *Fête de la Musique* is the sheer number of genres that one can hear in a few streets. Ranging from full orchestras to one-man rap artists, you can expect to hear everything from accordion music to panpipes, *chanson*, hip hop, and electro.

If you prefer your festivals a little more specialized, visit one of the events focusing on the very best of everything from chamber music to jazz. The July **Festival of Francofolies** in La Rochelle *(see p420)* brings together French music enthusiasts from around the world just as **Jazz in Antibes** draws top performers to this chic seaside town *(see p525)*. The **Chorégies d'Orange**, France's oldest opera festival, takes place throughout July and August in the well-preserved Roman amphitheater, which retains perfect acoustics. The organ festival in **Aubusson** *(see pp360–61)* focuses around the amazing organ in the Sainte Croix church and **La Roque d'Anthéron** looks set to continue to pull in piano-loving crowds. The **Colmar international festival** *(see p231)* is a major draw for classical music buffs, and the **Aix festival** *(see p515)* is a must for any serious fan, while the **Montpellier** *(see pp498–9)* and **Radio France** event appeals to music lovers throughout the world.

Clubs

Cool clubs and artful partying most definitely exist outside the capital city, despite what Parisians may believe. There are, of course, bars, clubs and discos throughout the country, and night owls looking to dance are unlikely to be disappointed by the range of options on offer. Small local venues can be great fun, and community events such as open-air parties and festivals are almost always worth a peek.

In general, nightclubs open late and even in small towns, don't really get going until after midnight. The French are more likely to nurse a few drinks rather than dash around buying multiple rounds, and shots are almost unheard of over here. It is considered uncouth to drink wine outside of mealtimes, although champagne is always a good thing! The prevailing custom is to club together with friends and buy a bottle of spirits between you. The nightclub will present you with plenty of mixers and – the big benefit of going for this option – you will usually get a table all to yourselves. Tables are generally reserved for those in possession of a full bottle of spirits; a single gin and tonic does not warrant a seat. As extravagant as this may seem, it is generally cheaper than buying individual drinks for four or more people.

In terms of dress code, running shoes are almost always forbidden, and the smarter the better could be seen as the rule. In house or hip-hop clubs strict dress codes tend to be relaxed. However, in more traditional *boites de nuit* (night clubs) getting glammed-up is the way to go. Clubs with difficult door policies can often be out-foxed by late diners. If you are worried about getting in, call ahead and make a dinner reservation. Alternatively flaunt designer labels at the doormen.

To experience one of France's most glamorous clubs head to **Les Planches** – an uber-chic spot outside Deauville *(see p259)*. Aside from its swimming pool in which starlets frolick at 3am, Les Planches is surprisingly inclusive, offering a friendly and fun vibe along with its hedonistic atmosphere. Vintage cars tear around town rounding up party goers to keep the night going.

Up in the mountains **Le Privilege** in Chamonix *(see p326)* and **Le Loft** in Méribel are jumping Alpine party places.

The Côte d'Azur *(see pp503–535)* is, of course, renowned for its hedonistic nightlife. **Les Caves du Roy** in the Hotel Byblos and **Nikki Beach** in St-Tropez *(see p520)* are perfect for the jet set, while **Jimmy'z** in Monaco *(see pp534–5)* is the place to hang out with highrollers.

Spectator Sports

Sporting enthusiasts are spoiled for choice in France, with opportunities to indulge in spectator sport throughout the country. If you don't want to wait to see the *grande finale* of the **Tour de France** in Paris, why not see it start in Brittany *(see pp272–89)*. Alternatively, taking in the spectacle from a tiny village en route is a great experience (drivers beware: the Tour takes precedence and the traffic will be stopped for a very, very long time).

If soccer is more your thing, then head to the Olympic stadiums to catch huge teams, such as **Lyon** and **Marseille**, in action.

Surfing fans should make for Biarritz *(see p456)*, Lacanau *(see p428)*, and Hossegor *(see p428)* to watch the tournaments there, while ski aficionados might want to watch the European Cup in Les Trois Vallées *(see p326)*.

Golfers flock to the **PGA Open** held outside Paris and to the **LPGA in Evian**, which is the world's second most valuable tournament after the US Open.

Riders will be drawn to one of France's national studs at the **Haras National de Pompadour** for dressage, show jumping and other competitions throughout the year. Similarly, equine enthusiasts should not miss out on exciting horse racing at the renowned **Chantilly Racecourse**.

The **Le Mans** 24-hour car race is an institution, as is the famous **Grand Prix** in Monaco *(see pp534–5)*. The **French Grand Prix** at Magny Cours, south of Nevers *(see pp342–3)*, is also well worth a visit.

No visitor to France in the summer should miss out on one of the greatest spectator sports of them all: head to the village square and take in a game of *pétanque* (also known as *boules*).

DIRECTORY

Theater

Avignon Theater Festival
Tel 04 90 14 14 14.
W festival-avignon.com

Film

Cannes Film Festival
W festival-cannes.fr

Deauville Film Festival
W festival-deauville.com
W deauvilleasia.com

La Rochelle Film Festival
W festival-larochelle.org

Théâtre Antique d'Arles
Association Peplum.
Tel 04 90 49 47 11.
W festival-arelate.com

Dance

Festival Interceltique de Lorient
Tel 02 97 64 03 20.
W festival-interceltique.com

Gannat Festival
Tel 04 70 90 12 67.
W cultures-traditions.org

Lyon Festival
Tel 04 27 46 65 60.
W labiennale delyon.com

Montpellier Festival
W montpellierdanse.fr

Music

Aix Festival
Tel 04 42 17 34 00.
W festival-aix.com

Aubusson Festival
Tel 05 55 66 18 36.
W orgue-aubusson.org

Choregies d'Orange
Tel 04 90 34 24 24.
W choregies.fr

Colmar International Festival
Tel 03 89 20 68 97.
W festival-colmar.com

Festival of Francofolies
Tel 05 46 28 28 28.
W francofolies.fr

Jazz in Antibes
Tel 04 97 23 11 10.
W antibesjuanlespins. com

Radio France and Montpellier Festival
Tel 04 67 02 02 01.
W festivalradiofrance montpellier.com

La Roque d'Antheron
Tel 04 42 50 51 15.
W festival-piano.com

Clubs

Les Caves du Roy
Av Paul Signac 83990 St-Tropez.
Tel 04 94 56 68 00.

Jimmy'z
Le Sporting Club
Av Princesse Grace
Monte Carlo.
Tel 00 377 98 06 70 68.

Le Loft
Parc Olympique
La Chaudanne 73550
Méribel.
Tel 06 77 74 72 31.
W loft-club.fr

Nikki Beach
Route de Epi Ramatuelle
83350 St-Tropez.
Tel 04 94 79 82 04.
W nikkibeach.com

Les Planches
Les Longs Champs 14910
Blonville sur Mer.
Tel 02 31 87 58 09.

Le Privilege
52 rue des Moulins 74400
Chamonix.
Tel 04 50 53 29 10.
W barleprivilege.com

Spectator Sports

Chantilly Racecourse
Rue Plaine des Aigles,
Chantilly, Oise.
Tel 03 44 62 44 00.
W france-galop.com

French Grand Prix
Magny Cours 58170.
Tel 03 86 21 80 00.
W circuit magnycours.com

Grand Prix
Automobile Club de Monaco.
Tel 00 377 93 15 26 00.
W formula1 monaco.com

Haras National de Pompadour
Tel 08 11 90 21 31.
W haras-nationaux.fr

LPGA in Evian
W evian championship.com

Le Mans
Tel 02 43 40 24 00.
W lemans.org

Olympique Lyon
350 av Jean Jaurès
69007 Lyon.
W olweb.fr

Olympique de Marseille
3 bd Michelet 13008
Marseille.
W om.net

PGA Open
W pgafrance.net

Tour de France
W letour.fr

Specialist Holidays and Outdoor Activities

France offers an amazing variety of leisure and sport activities, making it a wonderful choice for a specialist holiday. The French take great pride in the *art de vivre*, which entails not only eating and drinking well, but also pursuing special interests and hobbies. For the best in entertainment and spectator sports, festivals and annual events, see *France through the Year* on pages 40–43. Information on leisure and sporting activities in a particular region is available from the tourist offices listed for each town in this guide. The suggestions below cover the most popular, and also the more unusual, pursuits.

Students honing their culinary skills on a Hostellerie Bérard cookery course

Specialist Holidays

French government tourist offices *(see p620)* have a wide range of information on travel companies that offer special interest holidays and can send you a copy of *The Traveler in France Reference Guide*. Their website, www.rendezvousenfrance.com, offers interactive brochures.

If you want to improve your French, many language courses are available. These are very often combined with other activities, such as cooking or painting. For more information, contact your closest **Alliance Française**. They will have links with branches of the foundation in France, where language courses are offered.

Young people can enjoy a French-speaking holiday by working part time on restoration of historic sites with **Union REMPART** *(Union pour la Réhabilitation et Entretien des Monuments et du Patrimoine Artistique)*.

A tantalizing array of gastronomic courses is on offer, to introduce you to classical French cuisine or the cooking of a particular region. For experienced cooks, advanced and specialist courses are available too. Wine-appreciation courses can also be found and are always very popular.

There are numerous arts and crafts courses throughout the country, catering to everyone from the absolute beginner to the most accomplished artist.

Nature lovers can enjoy the national parks *(parcs nationaux)* and join organized bird-watching and botanical trips in many areas, including the Camargue, the Cévennes, and Corsica.

Le Guide des Jardins en France, published by Actes Sud, is a useful reference guide when visiting France's many beautiful gardens.

Painting the picturesque French landscape

Golf

There are golf courses all over France, especially along the north and south coasts and in Aquitaine. Players have to reach a minimum standard and obtain a licence in order to play, so be sure to take your handicap certificate with you. Top courses offer weekend or longer tutored breaks geared to all levels of experience. The **Fédération Française de Golf** will provide a list of all the courses throughout France.

Specialist golf packages, including deluxe hotel accommodation, can be ideal for serious golfers and their non-golfing partners alike. The spectacular Evian Resort and its renowned **Evian Championship** golf course is a very exclusive, pampering option. The 18-hole course is guaranteed to appeal to fans. There is also a spa and five swimming pools, perfect for lazing. The climbing wall, squash and tennis courts will appeal to more active visitors.

In the south, the **American Golf Academy** offers a team of golf pros who are adept at coaching children, beginners, and also experts through their eight different courses and private lessons. Their summer schools and master classes are highly sought after.

The **Hotel de Mougins**, with a lovely address on the "avenue du Golf," is situated near to ten prestigious golf courses, including the Golf Country Club Cannes, the Royal Mougins Golf Club, and the Golf d'Opio-Valbonne. The hotel can arrange rounds at the different clubs, and offers packages which include extras, such as lunch in the clubhouse.

The **Golf Hotel Grenoble Charmeil** can organize green fees for three courses, including the Grenoble International course. In Brittany, the **St-Malo Golf and Country Club** has a 19th-century manor house interior and an impressive 27-hole golf course, surrounded by the Mesnil forest.

Tennis

Tennis is a very popular sport in France, and courts for hourly hire can be found in almost every town. It is a good idea to bring your own equipment with you, as hire facilities may not be available.

Hiking

In France, more than 38,000 miles (60,000 km) of long-distance tracks, known as *Grandes Randonnées* (GR), are clearly marked. There are also 50,000 miles (80,000 km) of the shorter *Petites Randonnées* (PR).

The routes vary in difficulty and include long pilgrim routes, alpine crossings, and tracks through national parks. Some *Grandes* and *Petites Randonnées* are open for mountain biking as well as horseback riding.

Topo Guides, published by **Féderation Française de la Randonnée Pédestre**, describe the tracks, providing details of transport, places for over-night stops, and food shops. A useful book series geared specifically toward families is *Les 200 Plus Belles Balades en France en Famille*, which can be ordered online.

Cycling

For advice on cycling in France, contact the **Fédération Française de Cyclisme**.

Serious cyclists could live their dreams by joining up for a Tour de France stage vacation with the **Velo Echappe** *Etape du Tour* team. The company organizes two types of adventure – a fully guided program or a self-guided option. They handle all the registration forms and paperwork, and on the guided option they will put you up in a hotel a block away from the end of the stage. Applications to the tour company must be received by the end of March every year to have a chance to ride along with the Tour de France professionals.

Mountain biking – a great way to explore

Escaping into the forest at Fontainebleau *(see pp184–5)*

At the other end of the scale, people who enjoy a gentle bike ride could opt for a wine cycling tour through the vineyards of France. Free-wheeling down the Route des Grands Crus in Burgundy may be more than enough holiday exercise for some.

Duvine Adventures organize tours that take in famed vineyards such as La Tache, Romanée-Conti, and Nuit-St-Georges. The riding includes flat spells and hills, and there are excellent lunches.

Local tourist offices provide details about riding facilities in their areas. **Voies Vertes** offers information on "greenways," easy rides through some of France's loveliest countryside. *Gîtes de France (see p551)* offer dormitory accommodation in the vicinity of well-known tracks.

Horseback Riding

There are many reputable companies that offer riding breaks from one-hour treks to long weekends or holidays of a week or more. The best way to choose is to decide which type of countryside you would prefer to see from the saddle. If the Mont-St-Michel (*see pp260–63*) and the beaches of Brittany appeal, then **A La Carte Sportive** offer stables with horses trained in trekking for beginners and intermediates. For more experienced riders, riding a Camargue mount through the countryside of Provence (*see pp514–15*) is a wonderful treat. **Ride in France** organizes rides through beautiful scenery, vineyards, and picturesque villages, allowing riders to experience the flora and fauna of the area. Horse lovers with a taste for the historical, or those hankering after a little luxury, could do worse than to sign up for a break with the **Cheval et Châteaux** company which organizes horseback-riding tours around chateaus in the Loire. Not only do riders get to take in the majesty of the chateaus of the region, the overnight accommodation also comes courtesy of a castle. It makes an ideal way to play lord or lady of the manor while indulging in a passion for trekking.

Hiking along the Gorges du Verdon in Provence *(see pp518–19)*

Mountain Sports

The French mountains, especially the Alps and the Pyrenees, provide a wide range of sporting opportunities. In addition to winter downhill skiing and *ski de fond* (cross-country), the mountains are enjoyed in the summer by rock-climbers and mountaineers, and by those skiers who can't wait for winter and so indulge in some of Europe's best glacier skiing.

Climbers should contact the **Féderation Française de la Montagne et de l'Escalade** for more information on the best climbing locations and other useful tips.

Winter sports fans should join the serious skiers and snowboarders who head to the French hills in droves every season. The mountains here have terrain to satisfy all levels of expertise from toddlers in the kids' club through to death-defying off-piste athletes, adrenalin junkie snowboarders, kite-surfers, and middle-of-the-road snow fans who are happiest cruising blue runs and eating in slope-side restaurants.

Skiing

Undoubtedly, France has some of the best ski resorts anywhere in the world. The sheer scale of some of the larger areas can be quite daunting if you're on a week-long trip – especially to those who insist on covering all the trails on the map. The Trois Vallées ski area *(see p326)*, for example, is made up of three valleys which include the resorts of Courchevel, Méribel, Val Thorens, and Les Ménuires. Added together, they comprise a staggering 375 miles (600 km) worth of runs.

The Trois Vallées is an excellent example of how French ski resorts differ wildly in style. Super-chic stations such as Courchevel and Méribel draw skiers from around the world, often dressed in cutting-edge ski fashion and using the latest high-tech equipment. In these resorts the hotels – especially those dubbed to be "in" – are expensive, and eating and drinking in the see-and-be-seen spots here puts a significant dent in the most generous of holiday budgets. On the other hand, resorts which are considered less glamorous, such as Vals Thorens and Les Menuires, can be enjoyed without designer labels and huge credit card limits.

The main consideration when choosing a resort should be the percentage of terrain to suit your ability. For example, a beginner might be miserable in a resort aimed at experts and offering only a few green runs. Similarly, a confident intermediate looking to improve will be frustrated by a ski area full of easy cruising slopes overrun with beginners.

It is also important to think about whether or not it matters to you if the village is picturesque. Diehard ski fans can overlook ugly concrete architecture in towns such as Flaine, while those looking for the bigger picture would be best off heading to somewhere pretty, such as La Clusaz or Megève *(see p326)*.

The proximity of accommodation to *piste* is also very important; most people find it is worth paying a premium for accommodation near the slopes and ski lifts, rather than having to stagger back in heavy boots carrying your skis after a long day's schussing.

Aside from obvious concerns such as nightlife, children's programs and child care, and the efficiency of ski-lift networks, it can also be useful to look at historic snow reports for the last few years for the time you are planning your trip. The weather can be unpredictable though so be sure to also check the resorts' snow-making capabilities. Armed with these details you should be in a good position to pick the right resort for you but remember, while the Alps get most of the attention, the Pyrenees can offer some seriously good skiing, too.

Aeronautical Sports

Learning to fly in France can be relatively inexpensive. Information on the different flying schools is available from the **Fédération Nationale Aéronautique**. There are also plenty of opportunities to learn the exhilarating skills of gliding, paragliding, and hang gliding. For more information, contact the **Fédération Française de Vol Libre**.

If piloting a plane is a little too much, you can opt for ballooning instead. France has an illustrious ballooning history, being the birthplace of the Montgolfier brothers who pioneered the art in 1783. **Ballon de Paris** provide a tethered taste of adventure in Paris with a trip into the air in the **Parc André-Citroën**, but floating unfettered over the countryside can be arranged by several companies around the country. **France Balloons** can organize trips over Fontainebleau *(see pp184–5)* outside Paris or over the Burgundian vineyards. Alternatively, they offer the opportunity to appreciate the spectacular chateaus of the Loire from a balloon. In Provence **Hot Air Balloon Provence** can float you over the picturesque villages, cornfields, and vines of the Lubéron *(see pp510–11)*.

Water Sports

Whitewater rafting, kayaking, and canoeing all take place on many French rivers, especially in the Massif Central. More information on these sports and the best places to take part can be obtained from the **Fédération Française de Canoë-Kayak**.

The Atlantic coast around Biarritz *(see p456)* offers some of the best surfing and windsurfing in Europe. Excellent windsurfing can also be found in Brittany, with **Wissant** in particular being a big draw. A charming small fishing village, Wissant is considered a decent stop on any windsurf tour.

Surfers who prefer to do it without the sail head to **Hossegor** outside Biarritz *(see p456)* for fantastic waves. The surfing here is world-class and perhaps not ideal for beginners, but the after-surf scene is great fun for anyone who is more interested in lying on the beach or paddling at the shore than carving up the water.

Similarly the town of **Lacanau** *(see p428)* plays host to international surf competitions, drawing wave fans from all over the world.

Sailing and waterskiing are also very popular in France. Contact the **Fédération Française de Voile** for more details. Training schools and equipment hire are found at places along the coast and on lakes.

If cruising on a boat is your kind of thing, there are many outlets that can help. One of the swankier options is to take a **Sunsail** bareboat tour around the Côte d'Azur, although this option is only available to those who have reached a certain level of boatmanship. The company also offers a range of skippered tours around the beautiful coastline.

Swimming facilities throughout the country are generally good, although beaches in the South of France can become very crowded in high season *(see pp478–9)*.

Hunting & Fishing

Although hunting is a popular sport in France, a *permis de chasse* is required, for which there is a fee. You will need a copy of your own national hunting license and to pass an exam in French, which makes it difficult for visitors. There are regional variations on the season, depending on the type of hunting. Since the hunting ban came into force in England, many French hunts have found English hunters a welcome boost to their numbers.

All kinds of fishing, for both fresh and seawater fish, are available, depending on the individual area. Local fishing shops sell the *carte de pêche*, which gives details of regulations.

Nudism

There are nearly 90 nudist centers in France. These are mostly located in the south and southwest of the country, as well as in Corsica. Information in English can be obtained from French Government Tourist Offices *(see p620)*, or from the **Fédération Française de Naturisme**.

Public Events

To join the French as they enjoy their spare time, look out for local soccer and rugby matches, cycling races, or other sporting events suited to spectators.

Special seasonal markets and local *fêtes* often combine antique fairs and *boules* tournaments with rock and pop concerts, making an enjoyable day out.

Spa Holidays

France is renowned for its seawater-based thalassotherapy spa techniques, with many centers, salons, and hotels offering "thalasso" treatments. The seaside towns and resorts seem to be the most logical place to head for ocean-based treatments, and not surprisingly there are some excellent spots dotted around the coastline.

Chic seaside town Deauville *(see p259)* plays host to upscale spa seekers in the **Algotherm Thalassotherapy Spa**. Similarly the **Hôtel Thalasso Sofitel** in Quiberon *(see p282)* offers top-class water therapy. More water therapy can be found near the springs at Vichy *(see pp362–3)* at the **Les Celestins** spa, and at the **Evian Resort** *(see p395)*.

Wine in France is considered to be almost as important as water, so it is not surprising that a spa specialising in "vinotherapy" or wine therapy has hordes of loyal fans. Head to **Les Sources de Caudalie** spa among the vines near Bordeaux and indulge in a vinosource grape facial and cabernet scrub.

If big name treatments are your thing, you should head to **Le Mas Candille** which hosts the first Shiseido spa in continental Europe. The products used are as exceptional as one would expect from such a swanky brand, and the approach is based on Asian techniques.

Finally, if a thoroughly indulgent approach to a spa session is your idea of holiday heaven, then splurge at the **Terre Blanche Hôtel Spa Golf Resort** in Provence. The half-day retreat of total indulgence involves an aromatherapy massage, a Provençale body wrap, and relaxing in the sauna, spa, hammam, or laconium. If you want to go *à la carte*, you can choose from a wide range of delights, such as an eye-lifting facial, a body-toning massage, or an Oshadi clay wrap.

If you can't escape from the city, the Valmont spa at the **Hotel Meurice** and the **Four Seasons** spa at the George V can provide the ultimate escape and spa break right in the center of Paris.

Yoga

The beautiful countryside in France provides the perfect backdrop for a restorative yoga retreat holiday. The **Manolaya Yoga Center** offers relaxing and fun hatha yoga holidays throughout Provence and at its Avignon-based center. For the more relaxing style of hatha yoga, try **Silvananda Ashram Yoga** retreats held near Orléans in the beautiful Loire.

Another excellent option is a break at the **Domaine de la Grausse** in the foothills of the Pyrenees, where walking and visiting local waterfalls, chateaus, medieval villages, and even taking in some cave paintings are all on the agenda. Those with any energy left over can take advantage of options to go mountain biking, horse-back riding, golfing, and fishing.

Beginners and experienced yoga fans alike are welcome at the **Europe Yoga Center**, which specializes in hatha and also astanga yoga. Both individual retreats and group holidays can be arranged at the center.

Gourmet

For gourmets looking to learn how to re-create some of the stunning meals enjoyed in French restaurants, or wine buffs seeking to increase their knowledge and cellar at the same time, there are many excellent options. The sheer number of cookery classes available throughout the country may seem overwhelming, so the first step in choosing an activity holiday of this kind is to consider your initial skill level and what you wish to achieve from the break. From diehard kitchen disasters to budding restaurateurs, there is a gourmet break in France which will suit.

The **Go Learn To** cookery courses offer short breaks or week-long holidays to suit your taste in Provence, Bordeaux, Lyon, Gascony, La Rochelle, Brittany, and the Loire Valley. They provide cookery courses in stunning château settings as well as more specialized courses in Paris, such as cheese and wine pairing, and wine tasting.

Petra Carter, chef and food writer, shows food lovers how to rustle up a menu based on whatever looks great in the market that day, as well as how to prepare foolproof fish recipes and duck confit. These cookery courses, which take place in lovely Languedoc-Roussillon, combine fun with practical tips, and include waterside picnics and visits to saltpans, olive presses, beekeepers, and local markets. There are also tutored wine tastings.

Budding culinary stars might want to head to Alain Ducasse's **Ecole de Cuisine** in Paris, which organizes both cooking and wine courses. It offers day and evening courses, held in an ultra-modern, professionally equipped kitchen. Also in Paris is the **Ecole Ritz Escoffier** (re-opening in 2014 after renovation), which holds workshops, for both adults and children, at the Ritz Hotel. Lessons last from an hour to half a day and cover themes such as chocolate or making the perfect pastry.

Oenophiles, on the other hand, might like to join with the **French Wine Explorers** who offer tours around vineyards. Alternatively, arranging wine classes via the French tourist office can be an excellent idea. **Wine Travel Guides** has an informative website for independent travelers, listing vineyards that are recommended by regional wine experts.

Arts and Crafts

France is a top choice for creative people looking to get away from it all and to express themselves in beautiful surroundings. Whether your preferred method of expression is scribbling in a notebook by yourself on the banks of a river, or perfecting your pastel technique in an art master class, there is an outlet for you somewhere in France.

Mas Saurine offers residential and nonresidential painting holidays in the Pyrenees, 30 minutes from Perpignan. Small group classes, geared to different levels of ability, are taught in an old stone barn by exhibiting artists.

Martine Vaugel, winner of the International Rodin prize, is the founder of the **Vaugel Sculpture Studio** in the Loire Valley, which offers foundation and advanced portrait, standing, and reclining figure courses ranging from one week to two months.

Those with a passion for seeing life through a lens are well catered for with photography courses by **Graham and Belinda Berry** at their farmhouse in Lot, southwest France. Courses suitable for all ages and abilities are offered here.

DIRECTORY

Specialist Holidays

Alliance Française de Washington
Dupont Circle,
2142 Wyoming Ave,
Washington, DC 20008.
Tel (202) 234 7911.
W francedc.org

Union REMPART
1 rue des Guillemites,
75004 Paris.
Tel 01 42 71 96 55.
W rempart.com

Golf

American Golf Academy
Tel 06 81 54 96 42.
W american-golf-academy.com

Evian Resort
South Shore Lake Geneva,
74500 Evian.
Tel 04 50 26 85 00.
W evianresort.com

Fédération Française de Golf
68 rue Anatole France,
92300 Levallois Perret.
Tel 01 41 49 77 00.
W ffgolf.org

Golf Hotel Grenoble Charmeil
38210 Saint Quentin sur Isère. **Tel** 04 76 93 67 28.
W golfhotel charmeil.com

Hotel de Mougins
205 av du Golf
06250 Mougins.
Tel 04 92 92 17 07.
W hotel-de- mougins. com

St-Malo Golf and Country Club
Domaine de St-Yvieux,
35540 Le Tronchet.
Tel 02 99 58 96 69.
W saintmalogolf.com

Hiking

Fédération Française de Randonnée Pédestre
64 rue du Dessous des Berges, 75013 Paris.
Tel 01 44 89 93 90.
W ffrandonnee.fr

Cycling

Duvine Adventures
667 Somerville Ave
Somerville, MA 02143.
Tel 888 396 5383.
W duvine.com

Fédération Française de Cyclisme
5 rue de Rome, 93561
Rosny-sous-Bois.
W ffc.fr

Velo Echappe
W veloechappe.com

Voies Vertes
W voiesvertes.com

Horseback Riding

A La Carte Sportive
W carte-sportive-com. iowners.net

Cheval et Châteaux
W cheval-et- chateaux. com

Ride in France
W rideinfrance.com

DIRECTORY

Mountain Sports

Féderation Française de la Montagne et de l'Escalade
8–10 quai de la Marne, 75019 Paris.
Tel 01 40 18 75 50.
W ffme.fr

Skiing

For information on the different resorts, visit the following websites:

La Clusaz
W laclusaz.com

Courchevel
W courchevel.com

Flaine
W flaine.com

Megève
W megeve.com

Les Menuires
W lesmenuires.com

Méribel
W meribel.net

Les 3 Vallées
W les3vallees.com

Val Thorens
W valthorens.com

Aeronautical Sports

Ballon de Paris
Parc André-Citroën, 75015 Paris.
Tel 01 44 26 20 00.
W ballondeparis.com

Fédération Française de Vol Libre
4 rue de Suisse, 06000 Nice. **Tel** 04 97 03 82 82.
W federation.ffvl.fr

Fédération Nationale Aéronautique
155 av Wagram, 75017 Paris.
Tel 01 44 29 92 00.
W ff-aero.fr

France Balloons
Tel 03 80 97 38 61.
W franceballoons.com

Water Sports

Fédération Française de Canoë-Kayak
87 quai de la Marne, 94340 Joinville-le-Pont.
Tel 01 45 11 08 50.
W ffck.org

Fédération Française de Voile
17 rue Henri Bocquillon, 75015 Paris.
Tel 01 40 60 37 00.
W ffvoile.fr

Hossegor Tourist Office
Pl des Halles – B.P. 6, 40150 Hossegor.
Tel 05 58 41 79 00.
W hossegor.fr

Lacanau Tourist Office
Pl de l'Europe, 33680 Lacanau.
Tel 05 56 03 21 01.
W medococean.com

Sunsail
W sunsail.com

Wissant Tourist Office
Pl de la Mairie, 62179 Wissant.
Tel 03 21 824 800.
W terredes2caps.fr

Nudism

Fédération Française de Naturisme
W ffn-naturisme.com

Spa Holidays

Algotherm
3 rue Sem
14800 Deauville.
Tel 02 31 87 72 00.
W algotherm.fr

Evian Resort
Rive Sud du Lac de Génève 74501 Evian-les-Bains.
Tel 04 50 26 85 00.
W evianresort.com

Terre Blanche Hôtel Spa Golf Resort
Domaine de Terre Blanche, 83440 Tourrettes, Var.
Tel 04 94 39 90 00.
W terre-blanche.com

Hotel Four Seasons George V
31 av George V, 75008 Paris.
Tel 01 49 52 70 00.
W fourseasons.com

Hotel Meurice
228 rue de Rivoli, 75001 Paris.
Tel 01 44 58 10 10.
W lemeurice.com

Le Mas Candille
Bd Clément Rebuffel, 06250 Mougins.
Tel 04 92 28 43 43.
W lemascandille.com

Les Celestins Vichy
111 bd des Etats-Unis, 03200 Vichy.
Tel 04 70 30 82 82.
W vichy-spa-hotel.fr

Hôtel Thalasso Sofitel (Quiberon)
Pointe de Goulvars, BP 10802 Quiberon Cedex, 56178 Quiberon.
Tel 02 97 50 20 00.
W thalasso.quiberon.thalasso-line.com

Les Sources de Caudalie
Chemin de Smith Haut Lafitte 33650 Bordeaux–Martillac.
Tel 05 57 83 83 83.
W sources-caudalie.com

Yoga

Domaine de la Grausse
09420 Clermont la Grausse, Ariège.
Tel 05 61 66 30 53.
W yogafrance.com

Europe Yoga Center
46800 St Matre, Lot.
Tel 05 65 21 76 20.
W europeyoga.com

Manolaya Yoga Center
FFPY 39 rue de la Bonneterie, 84000 Avignon. **Tel** 04 90 82 10 52. **W manolaya.org**

Sivananda Ashram Yoga Group
Neuville aux Bois, Loiret 45170. **Tel** 02 38 91 88 82.
W sivananda.org

Gourmet

Ecole de Cuisine
64 rue du Ranelagh, 75016 Paris. **Tel** 01 44 90 91 00. **W ecolecuisine-alainducasse.com**

Ecole Ritz Escoffier
Tel 01 44 16 30 50.
W ritzescoffier.com

French Wine Explorers
W wine-tours-france.com

Go Learn To
Tel 0845 625 0445 (UK).
W http://euro.golearnto.com

Petra Carter
La Souqueto, 11120 Mirepeisset.
Tel 04 68 40 77 18.
W petracarter.com

Wine Travel Guides
W winetravelguides.com

Arts and Crafts

Graham and Belinda Berry
46800 Montcuq.
Tel 05 65 31 49 72.
W imagefrance.co.uk

Mas Saurine
Comi de l'Estrada, 66320 Joch.
Tel 04 68 05 85 66.
W mas-saurine.com

Vaugel Sculpture Studio
2 rue Petit Anjou, Les Cerqueux Sous Passavant 49310 Vihiers.
Tel 02 41 59 54 14.
W vaugelsculpture.com

SURVIVAL GUIDE

PRACTICAL INFORMATION

France is justifiably proud of its many attractions, for which it has excellent tourist information facilities. Both in France and abroad, French government tourist offices are an invaluable source of reference for practical aspects of your stay. Most towns and large villages have a tourist information office; the relevant address, telephone number and website (if available) are provided for each town and area listed in this guide. Domestic tourism in France creates peak holiday migration periods, especially between July 14 and August 31. Consequently, the hotel and restaurant trades are seasonal. A little forward planning will allow you to avoid the pitfalls of seasonal closure.

Visas and Passports

When traveling to France, visitors from the US, Canada, UK, Ireland, Australia, and New Zealand need a full passport, but do not require a visa for trips shorter than three months. Citizens of other EU countries can enter France with a national identity card. Entry requirements change, so double check with the consulate early in your planning.

Like most EU countries (but not the UK and Ireland) France is part of the Schengen agreement for shared border controls. If you enter the Schengen area through a member country, you are free to cross into all member countries within your 90-day stay.

Non-EU nationals who wish to work or study in France, or stay longer than three months, should obtain a visa from a French consulate in their home country. For more information, check the website of your French embassy and your own country's foreign office.

Customs Information

Residents of countries outside the EU can import up to €430 worth of goods for personal use in their luggage, including 200 cigarettes and 1 liter (33.8 oz) of alcohol above 44 proof. EU residents are allowed to carry any amount of goods between EU countries, as long as the goods are for personal use.

Visitors from outside the EU can reclaim sales tax *(TVA)* on many French goods if more than €175 is spent in one shop in one day. To claim the tax back you must get a *détaxe* form from the store and take your goods out of the EU within three months. Present the receipt at customs when leaving the country, and mail the stamped receipt as instructed. The refund will then be sent to you or credited to your bank card. There are *détaxe* desks at all main airports and in big stores. Full information is available from **Direction Générale des Douanes**.

Office de Tourisme in the Vence region of France

Tourist Information

All cities, towns and many villages have *offices de tourisme*, which provide invaluable free maps and information on local attractions and accommodation. Tourist offices often produce useful guides covering walking and cycling routes, bike rental, local gastronomy, traditional farm produce, and more. Some regional and *département* offices also offer well-priced hotel and tour packages, and many city offices have organized imaginative guided tours and themed routes.

Before traveling to France, you can get basic orientation information and advice, and order brochures, from France's official tourist websites **France Guide** or **Rendezvous en France**. You can also contact your local France tourist office via email. For in-depth regional planning it is best to use the websites of the relevant Regional Tourist Boards *(Comité Régional du Tourisme)* or those of the many *départements (Comités Départementaux du Tourisme)*. The latter provide a valuable range of detailed information. Nearly all websites are available in English. Links to these sites can be found on the FranceGuide website.

Admission Charges

Most museums and monuments in France charge an entry fee, usually from €2 to €10. There are often discounts for families and for students with an ISIC card *(see p622)*. Those under 26 and possessing an EU passport, may also be eligible for discounts.

Several multientry schemes are available that reduce costs if you plan to visit a number of sights. Foremost, the Paris Museum Pass gives unlimited entry to over 60 museums and monuments in and around Paris for either 2, 4, or 6 days. It can be bought in advance online (www.parismuseumpass.com). Other places have local schemes, which often include unlimited use of local transport. Check local tourism websites to see what is available.

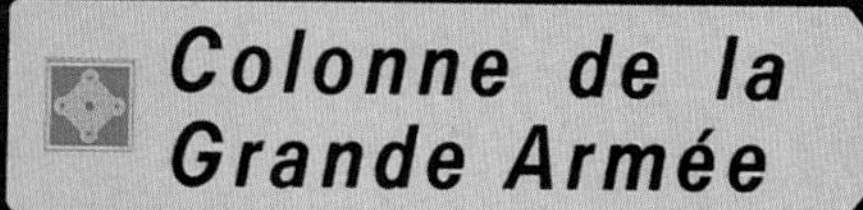

Sign to monument of cultural importance

◀ Evening traffic on the Champs-Elysées, Paris

The Arc de Triomphe du Carrousel and the Musée du Louvre in Paris

Opening Hours

This guide lists which days of the week sights are open. National museums and sights normally close on Tuesdays, with a few exceptions that close on Mondays. Generally, the larger museums and sights are open from 9 or 10am–6pm, sometimes with one late evening a week, often Thursday. Note that smaller museums and churches may close from 12:30–2pm.

Opening times can also vary considerably by season, especially for country châteaux, estates, and gardens. Many are open daily in the peak July to August holiday season and then close completely from November to March, or are only open at weekends. Most sights are closed on Christmas day and New Year's day.

See page 604 for details on opening hours for shops; page 626 for banks; and pages 572–3 for restaurants.

Taxes and Tipping

A service charge of 12.5 to 15 percent is included on all restaurant checks and it is customary to round up the check by a few euros in a restaurant, or a few cents in a café, especially if the service has been good. In grander restaurants, an extra tip of 5–10 percent is the norm.

For taxi drivers, the usual tipping rate is around 10 percent. For hotel porters, it is common to tip around 75 cents to €1.

Travelers with Special Needs

France is working hard to improve access to all its services. There are disabled parking spaces in many streets and all public car parks. However, you need a European Blue Badge to use these. SNCF (French railways) has introduced the *Accès Plus* scheme, through which wheelchair users and others with mobility problems can book ahead to guarantee a space and free assistance. For information go to the "Everyday Life" *(Vie Pratique)* section on the SNCF website and look under *Services + (see p634)*.

In Paris, some buses, some RER lines, and one Métro line (no. 14) are wheelchair accessible *(see pp640–1)*. By law, all taxis must carry wheelchair-users for no extra charge *(see p640)*.

Much has been done to improve access to attractions, but access to smaller historic houses and country châteaus can be difficult at times. The blue *Tourisme & Handicap* label indicates attractions, hotels, restaurants, and other facilities that meet full disabled access criteria. Many hotels and *chambres-d'hôtes* (bed and breakfasts) have adapted rooms, and major booking agencies such as *Logis de France* or *Gîtes de France* indicate this on their websites.

For information on disabled facilities in France, the best resource is the **Association des Paralysés de France** (APF), which produces an annual *Guide Vacances* holiday booklet. The **Infomobi** website also has comprehensive information on transport services for the disabled in and around Paris. Both these resources are in French only. More information in English can be found on the FranceGuide website.

Traveling with Children

Families traveling in France benefit from a range of cost-cutting discounts including reduced or free admission to attractions for children. Children under 4 travel free on most public transport and children aged 4 to 11 (4 to 9, in Paris) travel half price.

Some of the big French hotel chains (notably Novotel) specialize in catering for families, while many small country hotels and *chambres-d'hôtes* have cost-efficient family rooms *(chambres familiales)*. If you base yourself in one area for two days or more, a self-contained *gîte*, with several rooms and a kitchen, can offer exceptional value for money *(see p551)*.

Virtually all French restaurants welcome children *(see p575)*, and many have a children's menu *(menu d'enfants)* for €5–€8.

The FranceGuide website has information on attractions throughout France, while local tourism websites list regional-specific family attractions. The **France for Families** website has plenty of suggestions and loads of useful information.

The Château de Versailles has excellent disabled access

Senior Travelers

Senior visitors to France do not enjoy reduced admission fees at national museums and monuments although some privately owned châteaux and attractions do offer lower prices for older people. Discounted travel on public transport is only available with multijourney passes issued by some cities, and the SNCF *Carte Senior* for the over 60s *(see p634)*. However, these cards are not much use for short visits, as you'll only notice the discount if you make several journeys on each system. Railpasses *(see p634)* bought in advance outside France can be better value.

Student Information

Students aged under 26 with a valid **International Student Identity Card** (ISIC) benefit from many discounts, as well as those available to everyone in France aged 25 or under. The Centre d'Information et de Documentation Jeunesse will provide you with further information (www.cidj.com).

Gay and Lesbian Travelers

France has prominent gay and lesbian communities that are becoming ever more part of the cultural mainstream. The Marais district of Paris is the country's foremost "gay village," but there are gay clubs and services all over the capital. There are gay communities in many other cities, especially in Toulouse, Nantes, Montpellier, and Nice. Tune into Radio FG (98.2 MHz) or consult listings in *Têtu* and *Lesbia* magazines for a wide range of gay-friendly information. For more help, contact **Centre Gai et Lesbien** in Paris.

Traveling on a Budget

How much you spend on a holiday in France will vary enormously depending on what you do. However, in general, two people staying at a basic hotel (an average of €60 for a double room), eating both lunch and dinner in restaurants, visiting a few attractions, and using public transport can roughly expect to spend €160 per day in most parts of France, or €80 each.

Staying in Paris, the Cóte d'Azur, and other fashionable resorts is expensive but less-visited rural regions such as Normandy, inland Brittany, and Lorraine can be more affordable. Traveling in peak season (July–mid-September) will also be costly with high hotel rates, particularly in the most popular regions. December through to March, the winter sports season, can also be

International Student Identity Card

pricey, particularly in the Alps. To keep costs down, it is better to travel during the low season. City hotels, however, can be more reasonable between July and August when most French people head for the country.

Staying in a *chambre-d'hôtes* (bed and breakfast) is a good alternative to costly hotels. Traditionally, these are located in the countryside but they are now popping up in towns and the average price for a comfortable double room is around €40 including breakfast. Another option is a *gîte*, which offers self-catering facilities, though these usually require a minimum stay of a weekend or a week.

When dining, opt for a set menu – ordering from the à la carte menu will be far more expensive. Taking your main meal at midday rather than in the evening will mean you can make the most of the best-value set menus or *formules*. To keep costs down when sightseeing, opt for a City Pass that gives unlimited travel on local transport as well as entry

Waiting to travel at Marseille Gare St-Charles train station

to local monuments *(see p641)*. If you intend to hire a car, book it in advance through an Internet rental agency to get the best rates.

French Time

France is one hour ahead of Greenwich Mean Time (GMT) or British Summer Time (BST).

Electrical Adapters

The voltage in France is 220 volts. Plugs have two small round pins; heavier-duty appliances have two large round pins. Better hotels offer built-in adapters for shavers only or will lend you an adapter. Adapters can also be bought at department stores.

Queueing for the Eiffel Tower

Conversion Chart

Imperial to metric
1 inch = 2.54 centimeters
1 foot = 30 centimeters
1 mile = 1.6 kilometers
1 ounce = 28 grams
1 pound = 454 grams
1 pint = 0.6 liters
1 gallon = 4.6 liters

Metric to imperial
1 millimeter = 0.04 inch
1 centimeter = 0.4 inch
1 meter = 3 feet 3 inches
1 kilometer = 0.6 mile
1 gram = 0.04 ounce
1 kilogram = 2.2 pounds
1 liter = 1.8 pints (33.8 fluid ounces)

Responsible Travel

In France, as in many other countries, there has been a rapid growth in environmental awareness. **Echoway** is one of the leading French ecotourism organizations, encouraging heightened awareness of responsible travel. **Mountain Riders** promotes sustainable winter tourism in the Alps, providing information on how to get to the mountains by public transport and arranging group walks to clean up mountain ski slopes each spring.

France has a long-running rural tourism network, with farmhouse accommodation available through the central Gîtes de France agency *(see p552)*. There are also smaller organizations with a more defined ecological stance such as **Accueil Paysan**, which is a network of small-scale farmers practicing low-impact, sustainable agriculture. Another alternative to staying in a hotel is camping, and there are over 9,000 fully equipped campgrounds across the country to choose from *(see p552)*.

Information on local green tourism (*tourisme vert* or *eco*) initiatives and activities can be found through local tourist offices. Many towns have weekly markets selling only organic and traditional produce (usually called a *marché bio*), which allow visitors to give back to the local community. Market days have been provided throughout the guide.

DIRECTORY

Embassies

Australia
4 Rue Jean Rey, 75015 Paris. **Map** 6 D3. **Tel** 01 40 59 33 00. **W france.embassy.gov.au**

Canada
35 Ave Montaigne, 75008 Paris. **Map** 6 F1. **Tel** 01 44 43 29 00. **W canadainternational.gc.ca**

United Kingdom
35 Rue du Faubourg St-Honoré, 75383 Paris. **Map** 3 C5. **Tel** 01 44 51 31 00. **W gov.uk/government/world/france.fr**

United States
2 Ave Gabriel, 75008 Paris. **Map** 3 A5. **Tel** 01 43 12 22 22. **W france.usembassy.gov**

French Tourist Offices

Official Websites
W franceguide.com
W rendezvousenfrance.com

Australia
Tel (2) 9231 52 44.
W au.franceguide.com

Canada
Tel 1 866 313 7262.
canada@franceguide.com
W franceguide.com

Paris Convention and Visitors Bureau
25 Rue des Pyramides, 75001 Paris.
Tel 01 49 52 42 63.
W parisinfo.com

United Kingdom
Tel 0906 824 4123.
W uk.franceguide.com

United States
Tel (1) 212 838 7800.
info.us@franceguide.com
W us.franceguide.com

Customs Information

Direction Générales des Douanes
Tel 08 11 20 44 44.
W douane.gouv.fr

Gay and Lesbian Travellers

Centre Lesbien, Gai, Bi, et Trans
63 Rue Beaubourg, 75003 Paris. **Tel** 01 43 57 21 47.

Special Needs

APF
W apf.asso.fr

Infomobi
W infomobi.com

Tourisme & Handicaps
W tourisme-handicaps.org

Families and Students

France for Families
W franceforfamilies.com

International Student Identity Card (ISIC)
W isic.org
W isiccard.com

Responsible Travel

Accueil Paysan
Tel 04 76 43 44 83.
W accueil-paysan.com

Echoway
W echoway.org

Mountain Riders
W mountain-riders.org

Personal Security and Health

On the whole France is a safe place for visitors, but it is always a good idea to take the normal precautions of looking after your possessions and avoiding unfamiliar or unfrequented residential urban areas after dark. If you fall ill during your stay, pharmacies generally offer good advice while the emergency services can be contacted for any serious medical problems. Consulates and consular departments *(see p623)* at your embassy can also provide assistance in an emergency.

French pharmacy sign

Gendarmes

Police

Violent crime is not a major problem in France, but as in any country it is advisable to be on your guard against petty theft, especially in cities. If you are robbed, lose any property, or are the victim of any other type of crime, report the incident as soon as possible at the nearest *commissariat de police* (police station). In an emergency, dialing 17 will also connect you to the police department, but you will still have to go to a station to make a statement. In small towns and villages, crime is reported to the *gendarmerie*, the force mainly responsible for rural policing. The *mairie* (town hall) is also a good place to go for help but this will only be open during office hours.

At all police stations you will be required to make a statement, called a *PV* or *procès verbal*, listing any lost or stolen items. You will need your passport, and, if relevant, your vehicle papers. It is important to keep a copy of your police statement for your insurance claim.

Lost and Stolen Property

The likelihood, and impact, of street theft can be considerably reduced by a few simple precautions. In the first instance, ensure that all possessions are covered by a comprehensive travel insurance policy before arrival. Once in France, avoid risky city neighborhoods, and beware of pickpockets, especially on the Paris Métro during rush hour (particularly just as the doors are closing). When you sit at a sidewalk café table, always keep your bag within reach and in sight, preferably on your lap or on the table, and never leave it on the ground or hanging on the back of a chair. Keep bags zipped up and held close to you when walking along, and never leave luggage unattended at train stations or other travel centers. Keep valuables securely concealed and only carry with you as much cash as you think you will need for the day.

For lost or stolen property, it may be worth returning to the station where you reported the incident to check if the police have retrieved some of the items. In addition, all French town halls have a *Bureau d'Objets Trouvés* (lost property office), although they are often inefficient and finding items can take time. Lost property offices can also be found at larger train stations, which will be open during office hours.

If your passport is lost or stolen, notify your consulate immediately *(see p623)*. The loss of credit or debit cards should also be reported as soon as possible to your bank to avoid fraudulent use.

Travel Insurance

All travelers in France should have a comprehensive travel insurance policy providing adequate cover for any eventuality, including potential medical and legal expenses, theft, lost luggage and other personal property, accidents, travel delays, and the option of immediate repatriation by air in the event of a major medical emergency. Winter sports are not covered by standard travel policies so if you are planning to ski or to undertake any other adventure sports in France you will need to pay an additional premium to ensure you are protected. All insurance policies should come with a 24-hour emergency number in case of need.

In an Emergency

The phone number for all emergency services is 112, but in practice it is often quicker to call the relevant authority direct on their traditional two-digit numbers. In a medical emergency call the **Service d'Aide Médicale Urgence** (SAMU), who will send an ambulance. However, it can sometimes be faster to call the **Sapeurs**

DIRECTORY

Emergency Numbers

All Emergency Services
Tel 112.

Ambulance (SAMU)
Tel 15.

Fire (Sapeurs Pompiers)
Tel 18.

Police and Gendarmerie
Tel 17.

Pompiers (fire department) who also offer first aid and can take you to the nearest hospital. This is particularly true in rural areas, where the fire station is likely to be much closer than the ambulance service based in town. The paramedics are called *secouristes*.

Hospitals and Pharmacies

Non-EU nationals must have full private medical insurance while in France and pay for services up front, claiming their costs back in full from their insurance company. Ensure you keep the statement of costs (*feuille de soins*) that is provided by the doctor or hospital. This should include stickers for any prescription drugs, which must be stuck onto the statement by the pharmacist once you have made your purchase.

All European Union nationals holding a European Health Insurance Card (EHIC) are entitled to use the French national health service. However, under the French system patients must pay for all treatments and then reclaim most of the cost from the health authorities. Ensure you keep the *feuille de soins* as described above, as well as any receipts and stickers for prescriptions. Around 80 percent of the cost can be claimed back by following the instructions provided with your EHIC card. This can be a time-consuming process, and it can often be simpler to use private travel insurance.

Well-equipped public hospitals can be found throughout France. In all towns and cities there are hospitals with general emergency departments (called *urgences* or *service des urgences*) that can deal with immediate medical problems. If your hotel cannot direct you to one, call the SAMU or fire department. Should you require an English-speaking doctor, your consulate should be able to recommend one in the area, and in Paris and some other cities in France, there are both American and British private hospitals (these do not have emergency or *urgences* facilities).

Pharmacies, identified by an illuminated green cross sign, are plentiful and easy to find. French pharmacists are highly trained and can diagnose minor health problems and suggest appropriate treatments. When one is closed, a card in the window will give details of the nearest *pharmacie de garde* that is open on Sundays or during the night.

Police car

Fire engine

Ambulance

Natural Hazards

Forest fires are a major risk in many parts of France. High winds can mean fires spread rapidly in winter as well as in summer, so be vigilant about putting out all campfires and cigarette butts. Keep well away from any area where there is a fire, as its direction can change quickly.

Before exploring any of the country's seven national parks or its regional nature parks (*parcs naturels*), visit the relevant park information center to check the regulations and recommendations that apply within the area, and take care to observe them. When walking in mountains or sailing, inform the relevant authority – such as a park information center or a harbormaster – of your intended route and when you expect to return. Never try to walk in remote mountain areas or across tidal marshes without an experienced guide, or against local advice.

Fire hazard poster

During the hunting season (Sep–Feb and especially Sundays) dress in visible colors when out walking and avoid areas where hunters are staked out in hides *(see p615)*.

Safety on Beaches

There are many good family beaches throughout France where bathing is rarely dangerous. Many beaches are guarded in summer by lifeguards *(sauveteurs)* – always heed their instructions and only swim in supervised areas. Also look out for the system of colored flags, indicating whether it is safe to swim. Green flags mean bathing is safe; orange flags warn that bathing may be dangerous and that only the part of the beach marked out by flags is guarded. Swimming outside this area is therefore not recommended. Red flags indicate dangerous conditions (high waves, shifting sands, strong undercurrents), so all bathing is forbidden. Many beaches also display blue flags, which are used throughout the European Union as a sign of cleanliness.

Banking and Local Currency

You may bring any amount of currency into France, but anything over €10,000 (cash and travelers cheques) must be declared on arrival. The same applies when you leave. Travelers cheques are the safest way to carry money abroad, but credit or debit cards, which can be used to withdraw local currency, are by far the most convenient. Bureaux de change are located at airports, large train stations, and in some hotels and shops, although banks usually offer the best rates of exchange.

Using Banks

Most banks will exchange foreign currency and travelers cheques, but the commission rates vary, so it is worth looking around to make sure you get the best deal. Virtually all bank branches have ATMs (automatic teller machines), which accept major credit and debit cards. Most ATMs can give instructions in English.

Travelers cheques can be obtained from **American Express** (AmEx), **Travelex**, or your bank. American Express cheques are widely accepted and no commission is charged if they are exchanged at their offices. In the case of theft, cheques are replaced at once.

Banking Hours

In Paris, and many other cities, banks are generally open from 9 or 10am–5pm Mon–Fri, with some branches open on Saturdays. Elsewhere banks are usually closed on Mondays and generally open from 8 or 9am–12:30pm and 2–5pm Tue–Fri and 8 or 9am–12:30pm on Saturday. There are, however, many variations between banks, and individual branches.

Credit and debit card readers require you to enter your PIN number

All banks close on Sundays and public holidays, and many also close at noon on the working day before the holiday.

Bureaux de Change

Outside Paris, independent bureaux de change are rare except in major train stations and high-density tourist areas. Privately owned bureaux de change can have variable rates: check commission and minimum charges first.

Credit and Debit Cards

Debit and major credit cards, such as **Visa** or **MasterCard**, are essential for most large transactions such as renting a car. Many French businesses do not accept American Express credit cards. French credit and debit cards operate on a chip-and-PIN system so you will need to know your PIN *(code personnel)*. Most American cards do not use chip-and-PIN technology, so must be swiped and you'll need to sign for purchases. Cards without chip-and-PIN cannot be used in train-ticket or autoroute-toll machines.

Given the high commission rates often charged for exchanging travelers cheques, the most economical and convenient way to get local currency is just to withdraw it from an ATM with a debit card. Bear in mind, however, that ATMs may run out of notes during weekends. If an ATM is not working, you can also withdraw up to €300 per day on major credit cards at the foreign counter of a bank. The bank may need to obtain telephone authorization for such withdrawals first.

ATM machine in Paris

DIRECTORY

Bureaux de Change

Travelex

Paris
125 av du Champs-Elysées, 75008.
Tel 01 47 20 25 14.
W travelex.com

Lille
Gare de Lille Flandres, 5980.

Lyon
Gare de Lyon, Part-Dieu Bd Vivier Merle, 69003.

Nice
13 Avenue Thiers, 06000.

Foreign Banks

American Express
11 rue Scribe, 75009 Paris.
Map 4 D5.
Tel 01 47 77 70 00.
W home.americanexpress.com

HSBC
103 av Champs-Elysées, 75008 Paris. **Map** 3 C5.
Tel 08 10 81 58 19.
W hsbc.com

Lost Cards and Travelers Cheques

American Express
Tel 08 00 83 28 20 (cards and cheques).

MasterCard
Tel 08 00 90 13 87.

Visa
Tel 08 00 90 11 79.

The Euro

France was one of the twelve countries taking the euro (€) in 2002, with the original currency, the franc, phased out on February 17, 2002.

EU members using the euro as sole official currency are known as the Eurozone. Several EU members have either opted out or have not met the conditions for adopting the single currency.

Euro banknotes are identical throughout the Eurozone countries, each one including designs of fictional monuments and architectural structures, and the 12 stars of the EU. The coins, however, have one side identical (the value side), and one side with an image unique to each country. Both bills and coins are exchangeable in any of the participating Euro countries.

Banknotes

Euro banknotes have seven denominations. The €5 bill (gray in colour) is the smallest, followed by the €10 bill (pink), €20 bill (blue), €50 bill (orange), €100 bill (green), €200 bill (yellow), and €500 bill (purple). All bills show the stars of the European Union.

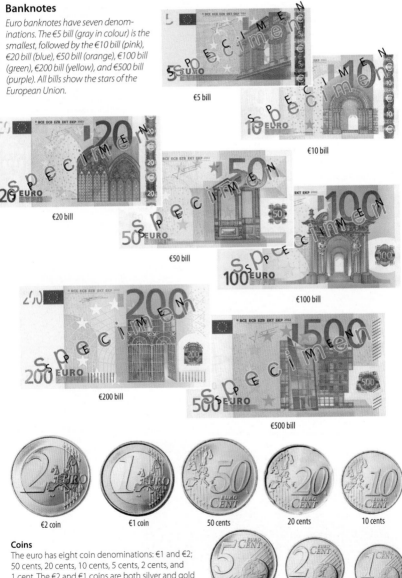

€5 bill

€10 bill

€20 bill

€50 bill

€100 bill

€200 bill

€500 bill

€2 coin

€1 coin

50 cents

20 cents

10 cents

Coins

The euro has eight coin denominations: €1 and €2; 50 cents, 20 cents, 10 cents, 5 cents, 2 cents, and 1 cent. The €2 and €1 coins are both silver and gold in color. The 50-, 20-, and 10-cent coins are gold. The 5-, 2-, and 1-cent coins are bronze.

5 cents

2 cents

1 cent

Communications and Media

French telecommunications are very efficient. Most landline telephones are provided by France Télécom, which also owns Orange, the international mobile phone group. Public telephones can be found in most public places and usually require a phone card *(télécarte)*. Post offices *(bureaux des postes)* are identified by the blue-on-yellow La Poste sign; the postal service was previously known as PTT and this is often still indicated on road signs. Foreign-language newspapers are available in most large towns, and some TV channels and radio stations broadcast foreign-language programs.

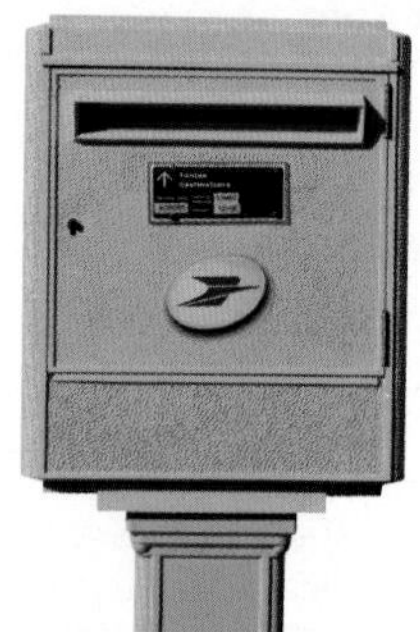

A distinctive yellow French mail box

Local and International Phone Calls

All French telephone numbers have ten digits, and you must key in all the digits even if you are in the same area. In landline numbers the first two digits indicate the region: 01 is for Paris and the Ile de France; 02, the northwest; 03, the northeast; 04, the southeast; and 05, the southwest. French cell phone numbers begin with 06, and 08 indicates a special rate number. All 0800 numbers are free. For landline numbers, cheap rates operate on evenings, weekends and public holidays. It is best to avoid making calls from hotels as most add hefty surcharges.

To call France from abroad, dial 00 33 and omit the initial zero from the 10-digit French number. You cannot call French 08 numbers from outside the country.

To call abroad from France, dial 00 and then the country code (Australia 61, USA and Canada 1, Irish Republic 353, New Zealand 64 and UK 44).

Cell Phones

Mobile phone coverage is generally good throughout France, although signals may be weak in some mountain areas. French cell phones use the European-standard 900 and 1900 MHz frequencies, so UK mobiles work if they have a roaming facility enabled. North American cell phones will only operate in France if they are tri- or quad-band. Always check roaming charges with your service provider before traveling, as making and receiving calls can be very expensive. Some companies offer "packages" for foreign calls which can work out cheaper.

If you expect to use your phone frequently it can be more economical to get a cheap pay-as-you-go French mobile from one of the main local providers such as **Orange France**, **Bouygues Télécom** or **SFR**. All three companies have stores in most towns. You can also insert a local SIM card into your own phone, but this will only work if your phone has not been blocked by your service provider.

People using a French public telephone

Public Telephones

With the rise in the use of cell phones, there are now very few pay phones *(cabine téléphonique)*, and few of these accept coins. Many phones now accept credit cards (with a PIN number), but for some you will need to use a phone card *(télécarte)*. Sold in *tabacs*, post offices, train stations and some convenience stores, cards are available for 50 or 120 telephone units, and are simple to use. For calls abroad, international code cards are available at the Travelex bureaux de change (*see p626*).

There are still a few coin and token-operated pay phones left in some cafés. At some large train stations and post offices there are staffed telephone booths *(cabines)* where you pay after you have made your call. This can be a cheaper option when making long-distance calls.

Internet Access

The Internet is widely used in France, but surprisingly, Internet cafés are a lot less common than you might think. They are plentiful in Paris, and there are usually a few in most cities and resorts, but in small towns and rural areas, they can be hard to find. It is often much easier to get online if you travel with a laptop. In Paris there are free Wi-Fi hotspots in many Métro stations, public libraries and other locations, and similar projects are being introduced in other major cities. Many hotels and even *chambres-d'hôtes* now offer Wi-Fi connections, but check that these are free.

Most hotels use one of several subscription services such as Orange France and **Meteor**, with which you buy a certain amount of time-credit and are then given an access code. Any time-credit remaining can be used anywhere that uses the same service.

French Wi-Fi servers often use different frequencies to those in the UK and North America, so you may need to manually search for the network (for more details, see the Orange Wi-Fi website). If you need to use a cable connection, note that the French modem socket is incompatible with US and UK plugs. Adapters are available, but it is often cheaper and easier to buy a French modem cable.

Postal Services

The postal service in France is fast and usually reliable. There are post offices in most towns, and there are large main offices in all cities. Stamps *(timbres)* can be bought at post offices individually or in a *carnet* of seven or ten, although the most convenient place to buy stamps is often at a *tabac*, where phone cards can also be purchased.

Post offices usually open from 9am–5pm Mon–Fri, often with a break for lunch, and 9am–noon on Saturdays. Post offices in towns and cities are best avoided when they first open as this is when they are at their busiest.

Letters are posted in yellow mail boxes which often have separate slots for post within the town you are in, within the *département*, and for other destinations *(autres destinations)*. There are eight different price zones for international mail. Information on all mail services is provided on the **La Poste** website.

Newspapers and Magazines

Newspapers and magazines can be bought at newsagents *(maisons de la presse)* or newsstands *(kiosques)*. Regional newspapers tend to be more popular than the Paris-based national papers, such as the conservative *Le Figaro*, weighty *Le Monde*, or leftist *Libération*. The daily *International Herald Tribune* can be found in Paris and throughout France. Other foreign newspapers are also often available on the day of publication in resorts and large cities.

The weekly listings magazines *Pariscope* (Thursday) and *L'Officiel des Spectacles* (Wednesday) give the latest on entertainment news in Paris. *Les Inrockuptibles* magazine has information on current music, movies, and the other arts from all over France. Many smaller cities have their own listings magazines, usually in French and often free, which can generally be found at tourist offices.

TV and Radio

All French television networks use Digital Video Broadcasting (DVB). There are 18 free channels, including the major national channels *TF1* and *France 2*. *Canal Plus* (or *Canal +*), a subscription-only channel, offers a broad mix of programs including live sports and movies in English with French subtitles. A film shown in its original language is listed as *VO (Version Originale)*; a film dubbed into French is indicated as *VF (Version Française)*. Most hotels subscribe to *Canal +*, and many also have cable and satellite TV, including English-language stations such as CNN, MTV, Sky, and BBC World.

It is easy to pick up UK radio stations in France, including *Radio 4* (198 long wave). *BBC World Service* broadcasts through the night on the same wavelength. *Voice of America* can be found at 90.5, 98.8 and 102.4 FM. *Radio France International* (738 AM) gives daily news in English from 3–4pm.

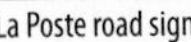

La Poste road sign

Newspapers sold in France

DIRECTORY

Telephone and Internet Service

Bouygues Télécom
Tel 1064 (from a landline).
W **bouyguestelecom.fr**

Meteor
W **meteornetworks.com**

Orange France
Tel 0810 555 421. **W** **orange.fr**
W **orange-wifi.com**

SFR
Tel 1026 (from a landline phone in France). **W** **sfr.fr**

Postal Services

La Poste
W **laposte.fr**

Useful Telephone Numbers and Codes

- **Directory inquiries** 118 712.
- **International directory inquiries** 118 700.
- **France Telecom/Orange** 0800 36 47 75; 0969 363 900 (for English).
- **Free, reduced, and premium numbers** 0800; 0810, 0820, 0825 (free and reduced rate); 0890, 0891, 0892 (premium rate).
- **In case of emergencies** 17.

TRAVEL INFORMATION

France enjoys sophisticated air, road, and rail travel. Direct flights from all over the world serve Paris and some regional airports. Paris is the hub of a vast internal rail network and of Europe's high-speed train network, with the Eurostar to London, Thalys to Brussels and TGVs to Geneva and other destinations. Expressways cross into all surrounding countries including, via the Eurotunnel, the UK. France is also served by frequent Channel and Mediterranean ferries.

Getting to or from France on the national carrier, Air France

Arriving by Air

France is served by nearly all international airlines. Most long-haul flights arrive at Paris Charles de Gaulle airport, but there are flights from Europe and North Africa to many other airports around the country.

From North America there are direct flights to Paris from about 20 cities, mainly on **Air Canada**, **American Airlines**, **Delta**, **United**, and **Air France**. Airlines with regular flights between the UK and France include **British Airways**, **Air France** and low-cost airlines such as **bmibaby**, **Flybe**, **Jet2**, **Ryanair**, and **easyJet**. **Qantas** provides connecting flights from Australia and New Zealand.

Paris Airports

Paris's Charles-de-Gaulle airport (CDG), about 18 miles (30 km) from the city, is the main hub airport in France. Access to central Paris is by RER line B from CDG2, which takes 40 minutes to Gare du Nord and 45 minutes to Châtelet-Les Halles. Regular bus services run from the airport to different parts of Paris, and to Disneyland® Paris theme park. Air France buses run to the Arc de Triomphe and western Paris, and to Montparnasse; each journey takes about 45 minutes. RATP buses (Roissybus) depart every 20 minutes for L'Opéra and take about 50 minutes. Taxis into central Paris cost around €30–€45 and can take up to an hour depending on traffic.

Paris's other main airport, Orly, in the south of the city, serves primarily domestic and short-haul international flights. Shuttle buses link the airport with RER line C at Pont de Rungis and an automatic train, Orlyval, links the airport with RER line B at Antony, from where trains run to Châtelet-Les Halles in 35 minutes. Air France buses for central Paris depart every 30 minutes; RATP Orlybus runs to Denfert- Rochereau Métro; and the Jetbus connects Orly to Châtelet-Les Halles, departing every 15–20 minutes. Taxis take 25–45 minutes to the city center, and cost about €25.

Arriving by Sea

Several regular ferry services operate between the UK and Ireland and France. Dover–Calais is the fastest route: **P&O Ferries** has up to 25 crossings daily, with a journey time of 90 minutes or less. **Seafrance** also offers several crossings a day. **Norfolkline** runs from Dover to Dunkerque in about two hours and has some of the lowest fares. Further west, French operator **Transmanche Ferries/ LD Lines** has crossings between Newhaven and Dieppe (about 4 hrs), and Portsmouth and Le Havre (8 hrs overnight). The biggest operator in the western Channel is **Brittany Ferries**, which sails from Portsmouth to Caen (7 hrs overnight), Poole to Cherbourg (6 hrs overnight), Portsmouth to St Malo (10 hrs overnight), Plymouth to Roscoff (8 hrs overnight), and between Cork and Roscoff (14 hrs). From April/May to September/ October, Brittany Ferries also runs high-speed services on the Poole–Cherbourg and Ports-mouth–Cherbourg routes (4 hrs 30 mins). **Condor Ferries** sails

Plying the Mediterranean with SNCM Ferryterranée

from Portsmouth to Cherbourg in 5 hours (July–September only), and from Poole and Weymouth to St Malo via Jersey or Guernsey (May–September only).

Irish Ferries run between Rosslare and Cherbourg (17 hrs overnight) from January to December, and to Roscoff (15 hrs 30 mins overnight) from mid-May to September. **Southern Ferries (SNCM)** run ferries from a range of European ports *(see p635)*.

EURO TUNNEL

Eurotunnel logo

Arriving by Train

There are at least 20 **Eurostar** trains daily between London St Pancras and the Gare du Nord in Paris. The journey via the Channel Tunnel takes 2 hrs 15 mins. Several trains also stop at Ebbsfleet or Ashford in Kent, Calais–Frethun, Lille (1 hr 30 mins from London) and Disneyland® Paris.

Paris and its six main stations are the great hub of the French rail network. Traveling from Belgium, Holland, and north Germany, you arrive at the Gare du Nord; from other parts of Germany you come into the Gare de l'Est. Trains from Switzerland and Italy arrive at the Gare de Lyons. From Spain you come into the Gare d'Austerlitz. Outside Paris, other major rail hubs include Lille, Tours, Bordeaux, and Lyon. For more information on French rail services and traveling to France by train *(see pp632–4)*.

Arriving by Road

Passengers from the UK can travel to France with their vehicle either by ferry or on the **Eurotunnel** shuttle through the Channel Tunnel. **Eurotunnel** runs at least four trains an hour during the day, and the trip takes about 35 minutes. Fares compete with those of the ferry companies, and similarly vary by season, day, and time of travel. For Eurotunnel crossings, it is possible to turn up and wait for the next available space.

Bus travel is a good-value alternative, and **Eurolines** runs three to five departures daily from Victoria Coach Station in London to Bagnolet in eastern Paris. Buses also run from London and other parts of the UK to Lille, Lyon, Marseille, and several other French towns and cities.

Green Travel

Traveling in France without flying or driving is easier than in many countries thanks to the high quality of public transport, particularly the SNCF rail network. There are daily train services from across Europe, ferries to the UK, Ireland, and Mediterranean destinations, and the Eurostar connection with London.

The French government has introduced an "Ecomobility" program, which aims to make it easier to transfer from trains to local buses, bicycles, or other non-car forms of transport. This includes free cycle schemes like the *Vélib'*, now in use in Paris and other cities *(see p641)*. Many regions have also developed **Voies Vertes**, long-distance paths for cycling or walking, such as the one along the Loire from Orléans to St-Nazaire.

DIRECTORY

Airlines

Air Canada
Tel 01 888 247 2262 (Canada), 0825 880 881 (France).
W **aircanada.com**

Air France
Tel 09 69 39 02 15 (France)
W **airfrance.com**

American Airlines
Tel 01 800 433 7300 (USA), 0826 460 950 (France). **W** **aa.com**

British Airways
Tel 0844 490 0787 (UK), 0825 825 400 (France).
W **britishairways.com**

bmibaby
W **bmibaby.com**

Delta
Tel 01 800 221 1212 (USA), 08 11 64 00 05 (France). **W** **delta.com**

easyJet
Tel 0871 244 2366 (UK), 0826 103 320 (France).
W **easyjet.com**

Flybe
W **flybe.com**

Jet2
Tel 0871 226 1737 (UK), 0821 230 203 (France).
W **jet2.com**

Qantas
Tel 13 13 13 (Australia), 08 11 98 00 02 (France).
W **qantas.com**

Ryanair
Tel 0871 246 000 (UK), 0892 780 270 (France).
W **ryanair.com**

United
Tel 01 800 864 8331 (USA), 0810 72 72 72 (France). **W** **united.com**

Ferry Services

Brittany Ferries
W **brittany-ferries.com**

Condor Ferries
W **condorferries.co.uk**

Irish Ferries
W **irishferries.com**

Norfolkline
W **norfolkline.com**

P&O Ferries
W **poferries.com**

Seafrance
W **seafrance.com**

Southern Ferries (SNCM)
W **sncm.co.uk**

Transmanche Ferries/ LD Lines
W **transmanche ferries. com**

Rail Travel

See also p682

Eurostar
Tel 08705 186 186 (UK), 0892 35 35 39 (France).
W **eurostar.com**

Road Travel

Eurolines
Tel 0871 781 8181 (UK), 0892 899 091 (France).
W **eurolines.com**

Eurotunnel
Tel 08705 35 35 35 (UK), 0810 630 304 (France).
W **eurotunnel.com**

Green Travel

Train+Bicycle Travel
W **velo.sncf.com**

Voies Vertes
W **voiesvertes.com**

Traveling by Train

The French state railway, Société Nationale des Chemins de Fer (**SNCF**), runs Europe's most comprehensive national rail network. Its services include high-speed long-distance TGVs and mainline expresses, overnight sleepers, Motorail and rural branch lines that reach every corner of the country. Lines closed for economic reasons are replaced by SNCF's modern buses, free to railpass holders. Travel off the main lines can be slow, though some cross-country journeys are quicker if you change trains in Paris.

Traveling around France by Train

France has always been known for the punctuality of its trains, and has maintained a high level of investment in the state-owned rail system, SNCF. The pride of the SNCF is its TGV high-speed trains, with journey times such as Lille–Lyon or Paris–Marseille in just 3 hours. In addition, frequent, fast, and comfortable main-line express trains provide a comprehensive city-to-city service, while regional lines provide connections to smaller towns and villages. SNCF is also the largest bus operator in France, filling in the gaps where railway lines have been closed.

Sleeper trains are a convenient way to travel long distances at night, and motorists can travel with their cars on **AutoTrain** trains. Most (but not all) long-distance trains have restaurant cars.

More information on French trains is provided on the main SNCF website *(see p634)* where reservations can also be made. To book a long-distance train from abroad, visit www.voyages-sncf.com. **Rail Europe** also offers a comprehensive information and booking service for travel throughout Europe. For useful links and an invaluable guide to every aspect of using French and other European trains, visit **The Man in Seat 61** website.

RER

Symbol for Paris suburban trains

Local and Scenic Railways

Alongside the national rail network there are several special railways that operate around France. On Corsica, the **Chemins de Fer de la Corse** has narrow-gauge lines between Calvi, Bastia, and Ajaccio. Particularly spectacular is the rail trip along the north-west coast between L'Ile-Rousse and Calvi. In summer, old-style *trains touristiques* run on this and other lines. In Provence, the privately run **Chemins de Fer de Provence** runs the *Train des Pignes* over a magnificent 90-mile (150-km) mountain route from Nice to Digne-les-Bains. SNCF also runs many more *trains touristiques* on particularly scenic sections of its regional network. These are usually in mountainous areas during the winter months and in summer on the coast and in the countryside. *Gentiane Bleu* trains run from Dijon to the winter snows in the Jura, and the *Train des Merveilles* runs from Nice into the Alps at Tende. For a guide to all these routes visit www.trainstouristiques-ter.com.

Several privately or locally owned rail lines around France are kept going by enthusiasts who offer excursions for part of the year, often using steam trains. The *Chemin de Fer de la Baie de la Somme* travels around the Somme Bay in Picardy and the *Chemin de Fer Touristique du Tarn* operates in the Tarn hills near Albi. Nearly all of these companies are members of the **UNECTO** association.

The train to Le Montenvers is a particularly scenic route

Types of Train

SNCF trains are divided into several types. TGV (*Train à Grande Vitesse*) trains are the flagships of the network, traveling on specially built track at around 186 mph (300 kph). There are four main TGV route networks; to the north, west, east, and south-east from Paris, with additional hubs at Lille, Lyon, Bordeaux, and Marseille. In some places, TGVs have separate stations built outside town centers. The trains have first- and second-class coaches, and some of them offer Internet access. Seat reservations are obligatory for all TGV trains: tickets can be bought at stations until shortly before departure time, or booked ahead online.

Within the TGV network there are several international services including Eurostar, linking France with the UK; Thalys, which runs between Paris and Belgium, and Holland and Germany; Lyria, serving Switzerland; and Artesia, which runs a TGV service to Turin and Milan, and a conventional train from Paris to Rome. Non-TGV international trains also operate, notably the nightly Elipsos from Paris to Madrid and Barcelona.

Corail trains are conventional long-distance express trains with modern coaches; Corail Téoz trains run by day; Corail Lunéa trains are overnight with sleepers. Corail Intercités trains are slightly faster with fewer stops. Reservations are obligatory for all Corail trains and can be made through Rail Europe or SNCF.

Motorail trains allow drivers to cut out long distances by traveling overnight with their car on the same train.

The TGV, with its distinctive-looking "nose"

Routes run from Calais to Nice via Avignon, and Calais to Narbonne. AutoTrains run from Paris to Nice, Narbonne, and Bordeaux. Reservations are essential.

TER trains are regional services that usually stop at every station. Reservations are not required and tickets can generally not be bought in advance. Route maps and information (in French only) for each region are available at stations and on the TER website *(see p634)*. Transilien is the TER network for the Ile-de-France around Paris, which is integrated with the RER suburban trains and the Métro.

TGV Rail Service

Trains à Grande Vitesse, or high-speed trains, travel at speeds up to 186 mph (300 kph). There are four routes: TGV Nord from Paris Gare du Nord, TGV Atlantique from Paris Gare Montparnasse, TGV Sud-Est from Paris Gare de Lyon, and TGV Est from Paris Gare de l'Est.

Key

High Speed lines

Other lines

Dunkerque
Tourcoing
Calais
Boulogne
Roubaix
Croix-Wasquehal
St-Omer
Hazebrouck
LILLE
Bethune
Valenciennes
Lens
Yvetot
Rouen
Douai
Charleville Mézières
Cherbourg
Le Havre
Arras
TGV-Haute-Picardie
Sedan
Thionville
Mantes-la-Jolie
Rethel
Metz
Lisieux
Aéroport CDG
Champagne-Ardenne-TGV
Lorraine-TGV
Forbach
Caen
Évreux
Versailles
Reims
Saverne
Lannion
Plouaret-Trégor
Massy-Palaiseau
PARIS
Strasbourg
Morlaix
St-Brieuc
St-Malo
Massy-TGV
Marne La Vallée-Chessy
Châlons-en-Champagne
Sarrebourg
Brest
Dol
Le Mans
Guingamp
Juvisy
Vitry-le-François
Nancy
Luneville
Quimper
Lamballe
Laval
Bar-le-Duc
Colmar
RENNES
Melun
Vendôme-Villiers-TGV
Epinal
St-Dié
Auray
Vannes
Vitré
Sens
Mulhouse
Quimperlé
Redon
Montbard
Remiremont
Lorient
Sablé
Orléans
Laroche-Migennes
Belfort-Montbéliard-TGV
Le Croisic
Savenay
Angers
St-Pierre-des-Corps
Dijon
La Baule
Besançon-Franche-Comte-TGV
Ancenis
Tours
Vierzon
Beaune
Dôle
St-Nazaire
Saumur
Le Creusot-TGV
NANTES
Mouchard
Pontarlier
La Roche-sur-Yon
Châtellerault
Châteauroux
Chalon-sur-Saône
Frasne
Les Sables-d'Olonne
St-Maixent
Futuroscope
GENEVA
Evian-les-Bains
Niort
POITIERS
Mâcon-TGV
La Souterraine
Thonon-les-Bains
Surgères
Bourg-en-Bresse
Bellegarde
Annemasse
La Rochelle
Ruffec
Culoz
St-Gervais
Sallanches
Limoges
LYON
Annecy
Cluses
Angoulême
Bourg-St-Maurice
Lyon St-Expury-TGV
Aix-les-Bains
Brive-la-Gaillarde
Aime-la-Plagne
Libourne
Chambéry
BORDEAUX
St-Étienne
Moutiers-Salins
La Teste
Valence-TGV
Albertville
Arcachon
Facture
Montélimar
GRENOBLE
St-Jean-de-Maurienne
Modane
Agen
Orange
Avignon-TGV
Bayonne
Dax
Nîmes
Menton
Montauban
Aix-en-Provence-TGV
NICE
Monaco
BIARRITZ
MONTPELLIER
Arles
St Jean-de-Luz
Orthez
TOULOUSE
Agde
Cannes
Antibes
Pau
Miramas
Irun
Hendaye
Tarbes
Sète
St-Raphaël
Béziers
MARSEILLE
Les Arcs-Draguignan
Lourdes
Carcassonne
Narbonne
Toulon
Hyères
PERPIGNAN

The automatic ticket machines at the Gare de Lyon in Paris

Fares and Passes

Fare rates vary according to the type of train. For all trains that can be booked online (TGV, Corail, Motorail), there are two or three basic fare rates for each class. The cheapest tickets are called Prem's, which must be booked well in advance and cannot be altered after payment. On most TER and some Corail trains, fares are cheaper at off-peak times *(périodes bleus)*; peak times *(périodes blanches)* are 5–10am Monday and 3–8pm Friday and Sunday.

SNCF sells several travel cards that give fare reductions of around 50 percent. Examples are the *Carte 12–25* for young people, *Carte Senior* for over-60s, *Carte Escapades* for frequent travelers, and *Carte Enfant +* for parents with small children. Details are available on the SNCF website.

For visitors intending to make several train journeys around France it is worth investing in a multijourney rail pass, which can only be bought outside the country. The France Railpass is for visitors from outside Europe and includes 3 to 9 days of unlimited travel within one month. If you're not residing in Europe and traveling beyond France, the **Eurail** Select Pass covers France and neighboring countries. Be aware that some trains, including the TGV, charge additional supplements, which are not included in the price. For more information visit the Rail Europe website.

The **Inter-Rail** pass, for UK and other European residents, is valid for several European countries, giving unlimited travel for 3, 4, 6, or 8 days (not necessarily consecutively) within one month.

Booking Tickets

Train tickets can be bought at any SNCF station and by phone or online. At most stations, there are both staffed counters and automatic ticket machines *(billetterie automatique)*, which accept cash or credit cards and have instructions in English. Tickets for trains that require a reservation (TGV, Corail) can be bought up to 90 days in advance and up until 5 minutes before departure. Tickets bought in advance can be collected from the station, or sent to your address.

From outside France, you can book TGV and Corail tickets through www.voyages-sncf.com, the English arm of the SNCF website, although it can be easier to use Rail Europe. Travelers with mobility problems can arrange assistance through the *Accès Plus* program; more information is available online or from FranceGuide *(see pp620–3)*.

Note that before any train journey in France, you must validate your ticket in a *composteur* machine.

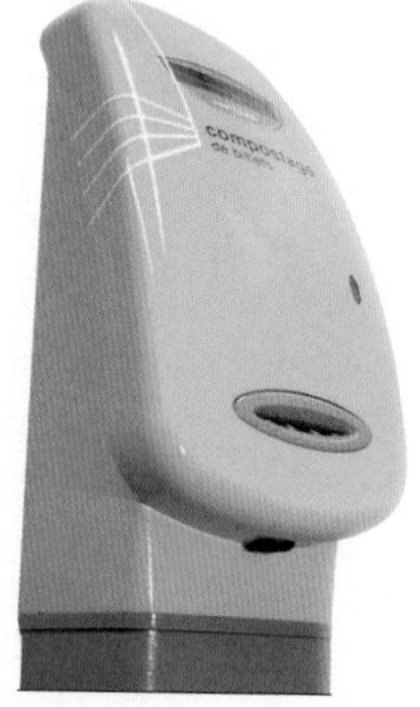

Timetables

French railway timetables change twice a year, in May and September, and all of them can be consulted on the SNCF website. Stations have free regional TER timetables available and information on the TGV network. Other free leaflets provide information on topics such as traveling with children, reduced fares, and travel for the disabled.

DIRECTORY

Rail Information

Autotrain
W **autotrain.voyages-sncf.com**

Corail
W **coraillunea.com**
W **corailteoz.com**

Eurail
W **eurail.com**

Inter-Rail
W **interrail.net**

Rail Europe
W **raileurope.com**

SNCF
W **sncf.com**

TER
W **ter-sncf.com**

The Man in Seat 61
W **seat61.com**

Local Railways

Chemins de Fer de la Corse
W **train-corse.com**

Chemins de Fer de Provence
W **trainprovence.com**

UNECTO
W **trains-fr.org**

Composteur Machine

Yellow *composteur* machines (left) are located in station halls and at the head of each platform. You must validate passes by inserting tickets and reservations separately, printed side up. The *composteur* will punch your ticket and print the time and date on the back. A penalty may be imposed by the train conductor if you fail to validate your ticket.

Traveling by Boat

With both Mediterranean and Atlantic coastlines, France offers excellent opportunities for sailing and has very good facilities. Inland, there is an extensive network of rivers, canals, and other waterways. Cruising through them is an ideal way to discover some of the country's most charming countryside. Frequent scheduled ferries also connect mainland France to Corsica and other parts of the Mediterranean, as well as to the British Channel Islands off Normandy.

Boats moored along the Canal du Midi, Roussillon

Traveling by Ferry

Car ferries sail to Corsica from Marseille, Nice, and Toulon, the main operators being **SNCM** and **Corsica Ferries**. **La Méridionale** sails between Corsica and Sardinia, and **Moby Lines** also connects Corsica with Livorno and Genoa in mainland Italy. **Grimaldi Ferries** sails from France to Morocco, and Italy. Regular ferries also connect France and North Africa; SNCM runs to Algeria and Tunisia, while **Comanav** has a luxury service from Sète to Morocco.

In the Atlantic, **Manche-Iles Express** and **Compagnie Corsaire** sail from St-Malo and the Normandy ports of Granville, Barneville-Carteret, and Diélette to the British Channel Islands. For a guide to all European ferry services visit www.ferrylines.com.

Sailing in France

France has excellent sailing facilities, with marinas all around its coast. On the Atlantic coast, well-equipped ports include Honfleur and St-Vaast-la-Hougue in Normandy, St-Malo and Pleneuf-St-André in Brittany, and La Rochelle and Arcachon on the west coast. Among the best in the Mediterranean are St-Cyprien near the Spanish border, Antibes on the Cote d'Azur, and the small harbors of Corsica. Boats for charter or short-term rental are available at most marinas, and information on rules and permits is available from the **Ministère de l'Ecologie**. The **Fédération Française de Voile** provides updates on sailing conditions.

Canal and River Trips

There are many options for exploring French waterways, from short boat trips to cruises of several days. The official guide to the system is provided by **Voies Navigables de France**. Many companies offer cruises around France, among the best of which are **En Peniche**, which uses traditional barges or *peniches*; **Locaboat**, and **Crown Blue Line**. For canal barges on the Canal du Midi, try **Minervois Cruisers**.

Short excursions are popular around the Marais Poitevin wetlands between La Rochelle and Poitiers, and along the Canal de Bourgogne from Dijon. **Les Caminades** runs trips along the Dordogne in traditional *gabarre* boats. For rides on the River Seine in Paris *see p641*.

DIRECTORY

Ferry Services

Comanav
Tel 04 67 46 68 00. **W aferry.fr**

Compagnie Corsaire
Tel 0825 138 100.
W compagniecorsaire.com

Corsica Ferries
Tel 0825 095 095.
W corsica-ferries.fr

Grimaldi Ferries
Tel 04 94 87 11 45 (in France).
W grimaldi-lines.com

Manche-Iles Express
Tel 0825 133 050 (in France), 01418 7013 (in Jersey).
W manche-iles-express.com

La Méridionale
Tel 0810 201 320.
W lameridionale.fr

Moby Lines
Tel 00 49 (0)611 14020.
W mobylines.com

SNCM
Tel 3260 (24-hrs for all ports), 33 (0) 825 88 80 88 (international).
W sncm.fr

Sailing Information

Fédération Française de Voile
W ffvoile.fr

Ministère de l'Ecologie
W developpement-durable.gouv.fr

Canal and River Trips

Les Caminades
Tel 05 53 29 40 95.
W best-of-perigord.tm.fr

Crown Blue Line
Tel 04 68 94 52 72.
W crownblueline.com

En-Peniche
Tel 04 67 13 19 62.
W en-peniche.com

Locaboat
Tel 03 86 91 72 72.
W locaboat.com

Minervois Cruisers
Tel 01926 811842 (in UK).
W minervoiscruisers.com

Voies Navigables de France
W vnf.fr

On the Road

France's network of modern expressways (autoroutes) allows quick and easy access to all parts of the country. However, you can save money on tolls and explore France in a more leisurely way by using some of the other high-quality roads that dissect the country. This section outlines both alternatives and gives instructions on how to use expressway toll booths *(péage)* and French parking meters (*horodateurs*), as well as some of the rules governing driving in France. There are also tips on how to get weather and traffic forecasts, where to rent a car, and how to get the best road maps.

Highway and main road signs

What to Take

While driving in France you must carry in the car your driving license, passport, the vehicle registration document, and a certificate of insurance. You must also have a set of spare light bulbs, at least one red warning triangle, and a fluorescent reflecting jacket to be worn if you ever have to stop on a highway. You can be fined if you are stopped by the police and do not have this equipment.

European Cars and Insurance

If you're driving into France from another country, it is essential that you have effective car insurance. All car insurance policies in the EU automatically include minimum third-party insurance cover, which is valid in any EU country. However, the extent of cover provided beyond the legal minimum varies between insurance companies, so it is best to check your policy before you travel, and, if necessary, procure additional cover. It is advisable to have breakdown cover with one of the Europe-wide networks with English-speaking call centers.

The car's country of registration should be displayed on a sticker or as part of the license plate. If you're driving from the UK, keep in mind that traffic drives on the right in France, and that British right-hand drive cars need headlamp deflectors – kits are available at most ports.

Buying Gasoline

All gas stations have unleaded and diesel (*gazole* or *gas-oil*, or a high-grade *gas-oil* +). Many stations also have auto propane (*GPL*). The cheapest are attached to big supermarkets, and many major gas stations have 24-hr pumps, with payment by credit card.

Rules of the Road

Wearing seat belts, in the front and back of the car, is compulsory in France, as is the use of booster seats for children under 10. It is illegal to use a mobile phone while driving, even if it's on hands-free mode. Headlights must be on when visibility is bad, and motorcyclists must have their headlights on at all times. Unless road signs indicate otherwise, *Priorité à droite* means that you must give way to any vehicle joining the road from the right except on roundabouts. Flashing headlights mean that the driver is claiming the right of way.

Speed Limits and Fines

Speed limits in France are as follows:

- On autoroutes: 130 kph (80 mph); 110 kph (68 mph) when it rains.
- On major highways: 110 kph (68 mph); 90–100 kph (56–62 mph) when it rains.
- On other roads: 90 kph (56 mph); 80 kph (49 mph) when it rains.
- In towns and villages: 50 kph (31 mph).

There are also lower speed limits on all roads for vehicles towing a trailer.

On-the-spot fines are levied for speeding, not stopping at a Stop sign, for overtaking where forbidden, and exceeding the speed limit by over 40 kph (25 mph). Driving with over 0.05 per cent alcohol in the blood is illegal.

Expressways

Most expressways in France are toll roads (*autoroutes à péage*). The **Societé d'Autoroutes** website *(see p639)* lists the rates charged for each journey. There are also toll-free autoroutes, notably those around big cities like Paris (A3 and A86) and Lille, and some cross-country stretches such as the A84 from Caen to Rennes, and the A75 south of Clermont-Ferrand.

A sign at a gas pump points to *GPL* (auto propane) or *gazole* (gasoline)

The scenic route around Mont Cenis Lake

Much of the autoroute network includes rest areas, petrol stations every 25 miles (40 km) and emergency phones every mile (2 km).

Other Roads

RN (*Route Nationale*) roads are the main alternative to autoroutes for long-distance trips. They are often far more attractive, but can be more congested. To get really off the beaten track, travel by D (*départementale*) roads, which snake around the countryside. Look out for *Bis/Bison Futée* signs, which indicate quieter, alternative routes.

Try to avoid traveling at the French holiday rush periods known as *grands départs*. The worst times are weekends in mid-July, and the beginning and end of August.

Certain signs are particularly useful to know when driving in and out of towns. Follow *Centre Ville* signs for the town center and *Toutes Directions* (all routes) to take you out of the center to where you can find ongoing routes. If your destination is not signposted, follow *Autres Directions*.

Scenic Routes

France's dense web of *Routes Nationales* and D–roads weave through some of the country's most gorgeous scenery. The most celebrated roads are in mountain regions, such as the Col du Galibier road over the Alps east of Grenoble (N91, then D902) but there are many others throughout the country. Some hug the coast, such as the roads along the Côte d'Azur or the rugged coasts of Brittany and Normandy. Information on these *routes touristiques* is available from tourist offices *(see p620)*.

Road Conditions

The French Highway Authorities' **Bison Futé** website *(see p639)* provides essential information for driving in France, with details of weather conditions, winter driving requirements, and road works. Check also www.autoroutes.fr for expressway driving.

The **Michelin** website has maps and an excellent route-finder for France. The websites of the British car clubs **AA** and **RAC** offer similar tools *(see p639)*.

Using the Autoroute Toll

Take a ticket from the toll booth and keep it safe until you reach an exit toll where you will be charged according to the distance traveled and type of vehicle used. To pay at small tolls, just throw your coins into the hopper.

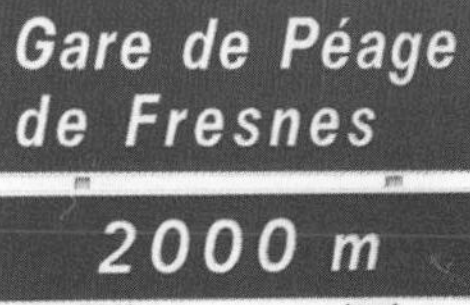

Highway Sign
These signs *(left)* indicate the name and distance to the next toll booth. They are usually blue and white; some show the tariff rates for cars, motorbikes, trucks, trailers, and motor homes.

Toll Booth with Attendant
When you hand in your ticket at a manned toll booth, the attendant will tell you the cost of your journey on the autoroute and the price will be displayed. You can pay with coins, notes, credit cards, or with a check in Euros. A receipt is issued on request.

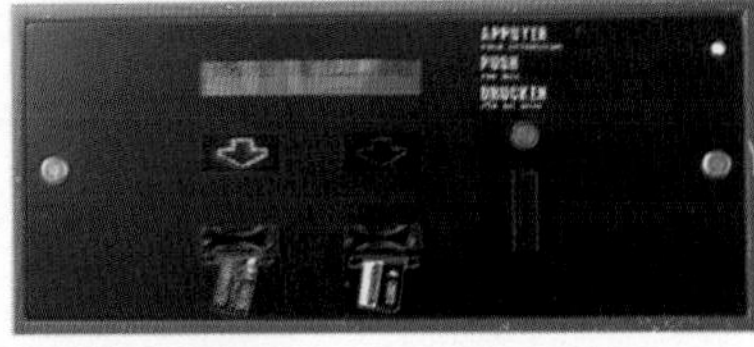

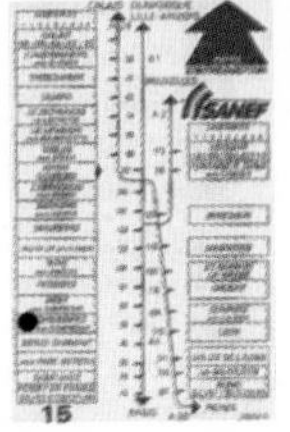

Automatic Machine
On reaching the exit toll, insert your ticket into the machine and the price of your journey is displayed in Euros. You can pay either with coins or by credit card (with chip-and-PIN). The machine will give change and can issue a receipt.

Using an Horodateur Machine

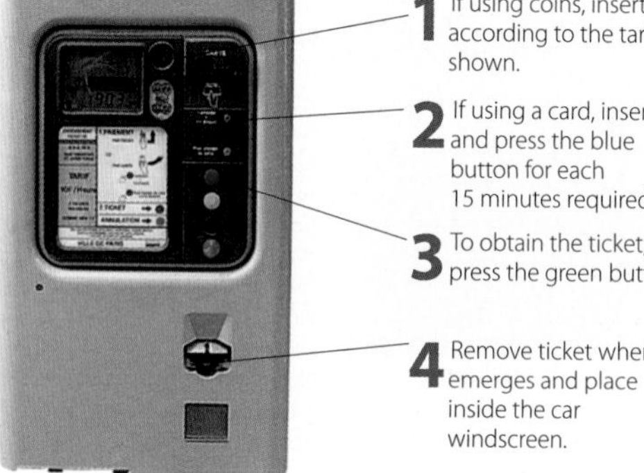

1 If using coins, insert according to the tariff shown.

2 If using a card, insert and press the blue button for each 15 minutes required.

3 To obtain the ticket, press the green button.

4 Remove ticket when it emerges and place inside the car windscreen.

Horodateurs
These parking meters operate from 9am–7pm Mon–Fri. Unless otherwise indicated, parking is free Sat–Sun, public holidays and in August.

Parking

Parking regulations vary from town to town, but most cities have street pay-and-display machines *(horodateurs)*, with spaces marked out in blue. Some machines accept a parking payment card sold at *tabacs*. Parking is normally limited to 2 hours. Charges are relatively low, and in most provincial towns parking is free between noon and 1:30pm. In narrow streets, parking may be confined to one side of the street and this can alternate at different times of the month.

Finding a parking space in larger cities, especially in Paris, can be difficult and it is often easier to use a parking lot. These are well indicated by a large "P" sign accompanied by the word *libre* to indicate that there are spaces available.

Renting a Car

All the main international car-rental companies operate in France, as well as local companies like **ADA** and **Rentacar**, which often have very competitive prices. You will nearly always get the best rates by booking a car in advance through one of the Internet car rental booking services like **Auto Europe** or **Autos Abroad**. Requirements for renting a car vary, but in general you must be over 21 and have held a driving license for at least a year. You will need to present your license, passport, and a credit card against a deposit.

The price quoted should include all taxes and unlimited mileage. All rental contracts include basic third-party insurance, and some companies also include comprehensive insurance. Extras such as car seats or snow chains should be indicated when booking. Note that cars rented in France will have manual transmission. Automatics may be available but will cost extra.

Before you drive away check the general condition of the car and also ensure it has a set of spare bulbs, a warning triangle, and a fluorescent jacket, which are all legal requirements in France *(see p636)*.

Maps

Each chapter in this guide begins with a map of the region showing all the sights and information on getting around. As additional maps, the excellent Michelin Tourist and Motoring Atlas at a scale of 1:200,000 is the most comprehensive driving map available. The red-cover Michelin maps of the whole of France (scale 1:1,000,000) are useful for planning trips, as are the regional maps with orange covers (scale 1:200,000). Larger scale Michelin maps with green covers are only for certain parts of France such as Paris and the French Riviera.

The **Institut Géographique National** (IGN) produces high-quality maps in different scales. Particularly useful are their *Cartes de Randonnée* (scale 1:25,000), an excellent series of walking maps covering every part of the country. Also recommended, are the **Blay Foldex** town maps.

In France, all newsstands and gas stations stock maps and most tourist offices provide good free maps. The online retailers **World of Maps** and **Language Quest** have an impressive selection of maps.

Traveling by Bus

French trains are so fast and reliable that there is not much demand for long-distance buses and they tend to only operate in areas with poor train services.

Eurolines offers a wide range of low-priced international services, many of which make stops within France. These services are centered on the Porte de Bagnolet bus station in Paris (Métro Galliéni).

Veolia Transport runs an extensive network of buses that cover the Ile de France, and **Lignes d'Azur** provides a good service along the Côte d'Azur.

Local buses are definitely an important means of transport, particularly in rural areas. These run in and out of villages from the *gare routière* (bus station), which is often located next to the SNCF train station of the main town of each *département* or area. Buses run mostly at peak times to take people to and from work and school.

Taxis

There are taxi services in every part of France, although in rural areas you will normally have to book a car by phone.

Mountain-biking in the Alps

Hotels, bars, and restaurants will have the numbers of local taxis. Otherwise, in towns look for a taxi stand *(station de taxi)* outside train stations, airports, or in the town center.

All taxis must use meters *(compteurs)*, but prices do vary from one region to another. In general, the pick-up charge should be about €2 plus €0.5 or more per km. It is often possible to agree a fixed price for a long journey. For city taxis, *see pp640–1*.

Cycling

Cycling is extremely popular in France and facilities are steadily improving as part of the government-backed "Eco-mobility" scheme *(see p631)*. Several long-distance **Voies Vertes** hiking trails and cycle tracks have been created, and more are being established. Every local tourist office has a leaflet on nearby *véloroutes*, and many have developed their own schemes, such as the network of cycle routes around the main Loire Valley châteaux *(La Loire à Vélo)*. Details are available from local tourist offices and *département* websites.

Bicycles can be taken on nearly all **SNCF** trains and on some routes you can reserve a rental bike at your destination station when booking a train ticket. There are also cycle rental shops in nearly every town with standard and mountain bikes *(VTT)* for rent at reasonable prices. Tourist offices can advise on local companies.

More information on cycling in France can be found on the Maisons de la France websites and through the **Fédération Française de Cyclisme** (in French only). Most cities offer rental cycling schemes *(see p641)*.

Hitchhiking

It is not easy to get around France by hitchhiking, and it is not advisable to try either. There is, however, a safe car-sharing *(co-voiturage)* scheme called Allostop (www.allostop.net), which has branches in many towns and through which you can set up lifts at reasonable rates.

DIRECTORY

General Driving Information

AA
W **theaa.com**

Bison Futé
W **bison-fute.equipement.gouv.fr**

Michelin
W **viamichelin.com**

RAC
W **rac.co.uk**

Societé d'Autoroutes
W **autoroutes.fr**

Zagaz
W **zagaz.com** (for fuel price guide in French).

Renting a Car

ADA
Tel 0825 169 169.
W **ada.fr**

Auto Europe
Tel 1 888 223 5555 (Canada & US).
W **autoeurope.com**

Avis
Tel 0820 050 505 (France), 1800 331 1084 (Canada & US). W **avis.com**

Budget
Tel 0825 003 564 (France), 800 268 8900 (Canada), 800 218 7992 (US).
W **budget.com**

Europcar
Tel 0825 358 358 (France).
W **europcar.com**

Hertz
Tel 0825 861 861 (France), 1800 654 3001 (Canada & US). W **hertz.com**

National/Citer
Tel 0800 131 211 (France), 1877 222 9058 (Canada & US). W **nationalcar.com**

Rentacar
Tel 0891 700 200.
W **rentacar.fr**

Maps

Blay Foldex
W **blayfoldex.com**

Institut Géographique National
W **ign.fr**

Language Quest
309 N Mt Shasta Blvd, Mt Shasta, CA, US 96067.
Tel (530) 918 9540.
W **languagequest.com**

World of Maps
1235 Wellington St, Ottawa, ON, Canada K1Y 3A3.
Tel 1800 214 8524.
W **worldofmaps.com**

Bus Travel

Eurolines
Tel 0892 899 091.
W **eurolines.fr**

Lignes d'Azur
W **lignesdazur.com**

Veolia Transport
W **veolia- transport.com**

Cycling

Fédération Française de Cyclisme
Tel 01 49 35 69 00.
W **ffc.fr**

SNCF
W **velo.sncf.com** (for train and bicycle travel – in French only).

Voies Vertes
W **voiesvertes.com**

Traveling within Cities

The charming centers of France's cities are best enjoyed on foot. If, however, you need to cover a fair amount of ground in a day, it is best to use the excellent range of public transport available. Paris and many other cities have tram and subway networks, often integrated with local train and bus services, and efforts have been made to create user-friendly ticketing systems. France has led the world in encouraging urban cycle use as an alternative to the car, with easy-access bike-rental schemes. In each city, local tourist offices will provide full information on services, including free maps.

Marseille streetcar traveling along the Boulevard Longchamp

Paris Métro, RER, and Tramway

The **RATP** operates 14 Métro subway lines in Paris. The Métro is the most convenient way to get around the city, and you are never far away from a station in central Paris. Each line can be identified by its color and number. The direction the train is traveling in is indicated by the name of the station on the front of the train – this is always the last station on the route, so it's worth checking the Métro map before boarding. Trains run frequently on each line from 5:20am–1:20am daily (to 2:20am Sat).

The newer RER suburban train lines complement the Métro and run across Paris and the suburbs. There are five lines (A–E), each with branches. The most useful for visitors are B3, from Charles-de-Gaulle airport; A4, to Disneyland Paris Resort; and C5, to Versailles.

Paris also has three streetcar or Tramway lines: from Gare de St-Denis to Noisy-le-Sec; La Défense to Porte de Versailles; and Pont du Garigliano to Porte d'Ivry.

Other Métro and Streetcar Systems

The cities of Lyon, Marseille, Toulouse, Lille, and Rennes all have Métro systems. The Lille Métro serves the whole conurbation known as Lille-Métropole, including towns such as Roubaix and Tourcoing. All Métros connect with SNCF railways at main stations.

Rouen's two-line Métro is actually made up of overground streetcars (light rail lines) that connect the city to the suburbs. Some 22 other cities use streetcars as well as local buses, and Paris too has some suburban streetcar lines that connect with the Métro and RER.

Buses

Every city has local buses. In Paris, RATP buses provide cheap opportunities for sightseeing. Throughout France, most routes operate from around 6am to midnight; routes and times are indicated at bus stops. Most French cities also have several night bus routes, and in Paris and the Ile-de-France, 42 Noctilien bus routes operate throughout the night, passing the main train stations. A fast-growing number of buses in Paris and other cities have wheelchair ramps. On all French city buses, you must board at the front of the bus, and get off through the middle or rear doors. Tickets can be bought from the driver or in advance from a range of outlets, which saves time when boarding.

Local Trains

Regional TER lines *(see p633)* are operated by SNCF and are well integrated with local transport around cities. In some cases, tickets are interchangeable. Around Paris the SNCF Transilien lines form a third level of rail services with the Métro and RER.

Taxis

In Paris and most other cities taxis have a light on top of the car which is white when the taxi is free, and orange, or just switched off, when it is taken. Paris taxi fares are more expensive between 5pm and 10am, Monday–Saturday, and all day Sunday and holidays, and cost more for any journey outside central Paris (limited by but including the Boulevard Périphérique). Many taxis take credit cards, but often only for fares over €15. At busy times the best places to find taxis in Paris are taxi stands *(station de taxis)* marked with a blue T sign. Taxi stands are found at major road junctions and train stations. Though operated by several companies, there is now a single number to phone for taxis in Paris. All taxis in France are required to carry wheelchair users for no extra charge, but in the Paris region **Taxis G7** provide a specialized service for passengers with mobility problems.

In other cities taxis are similarly operated by several companies. Taxi stands are found at airports, most train stations, and around city centers. Otherwise tourist offices and hotels can provide you with local firm numbers.

Taking a bicycle from one of the Vélib' stands in Paris

Cycling

Great efforts are underway in French cities to encourage town cycling. On Sundays, some major streets are closed to traffic to make way for cyclists and roller-bladers. Paris city council has a world-leading procycling program, and expects to have 430 miles of cycle routes by 2014. The centrerpiece of the program is the **Vélib'** scheme, where you can pick up a basic bike at any one of hundreds of Vélib' stations around Paris and leave it at another. To do this you must purchase a Vélib' card, which are available for a day (€1) or a week and can be bought from machines at the bike racks, or by annual subscription. Other cities run similar bike-sharing schemes under different names (**Vélo'V** in Lyon, **Le Vélo** in Marseille, **Vélobleu** in Nice, and **Vélopop** in Avignon). Tourist offices will have full information on them.

Tickets

In Paris, RATP T-tickets are valid for city buses, the Métro, the Tramway, and the RER. Tickets are available singly or for lower prices in carnets of 10 and can be bought at Métro and RER stations, the airports, tourist offices, and *tabacs*. Single tickets can also be bought on board buses but are not valid for other forms of transport. Don't forget to validate your ticket.

An alternative aimed at tourists is the ParisVisite card, which gives unlimited travel on all systems for 1, 2, 3, or 5 days, as well as discounted admission fees to sights. The card is sold at Métro, RER, and train stations, as well as at tourist offices or online.

Nearly all larger cities offer some kind of city pass for visitors, giving unlimited travel and other advantages for one or more days. Inquire at tourist offices for local schemes.

Cruise boats plying the river Seine

Seine Cruises

A boat trip on the Seine is one of the classic ways to see Paris. The long-running **Bateaux-Mouches**, **Bateaux Parisiens**, and **Vedettes du Pont-Neuf** offer traditional cruises along the river with multilingual commentary. The **Batobus** is a more flexible alternative, allowing you to hop on and off as many times as you want during the day. Another option is to see a more intimate side of Paris with a cruise along the St-Martin canal. Full information is available from tourist offices.

DIRECTORY

Transport Authorities

Lille – Transpole
W transpole.fr

Lyon – TCL
Tel 04 26 10 12 12.
W tcl.fr

Marseille – Le Pilote /RTM
Tel 04 91 91 92 10.
W lepilote.com

Paris – RATP
Tel 3246. **W** ratp.fr

Rennes – STAR
Tel 0811 555 535. **W** star.fr

Rouen – TCAR
Tel 02 35 52 52 52. **W** tcar.fr

Toulouse – Tisséo
Tel 05 61 41 70 70. **W** tisseo.fr

Taxis

Paris Taxis
W taxis-paris.fr

Taxis G7
Tel 01 47 39 47 39; specially adapted taxis: 01 47 39 00 91 or 3607. **W** taxisg7.fr

Cycling Schemes

Vélib' (Paris)
Tel 01 30 79 79 30.
W velib.paris.fr

Le Vélo (Marseille)
Tel 0800 801 225.
W levelo-mpm.fr

Vélobleu (Nice)
W velobleu.org

Vélopop (Avignon)
W velopop.fr

Velo'V (Lyon)
Tel 0800 083 568.
W velov.grandlyon.com

Seine Cruises

Bateaux-Mouches
Tel 01 42 25 96 10.
W bateaux-mouches.fr

Bateaux Parisiens
Tel 0825 010 101.
W bateauxparisiens.com

Batobus
Tel 0825 050 101.
W batobus.com

Vedettes du Pont-Neuf
Tel 01 46 33 98 38.
W vedettesdupontneuf.com

General Index

Page numbers in **bold** refer to main entries

A

B

D

E

H

I

J

N

S

Y

Z

Acknowledgments

Dorling Kindersley would like to thank the following people whose contributions and assistance have made the preparation of this book possible.

Main Contributors
John Ardagh, Rosemary Bailey, Judith Fayard, Lisa Gerard-Sharp, Robert Harneis, Alister Kershaw, Alec Lobrano, Anthony Roberts, Alan Tillier, Nigel Tisdall.

Contributors and Consultants
John Ardagh is a writer and broadcaster, and author of many books on France, among them *France Today* and *Writers' France*.

Rosemary Bailey has written and edited several guides to regional France, including *Burgundy*, the *Loire Valley*, and the *Côte d'Azur*.

Alexandra Boyle is a writer and editor who has worked in publishing in England and France for 20 years.

Elsie Burch Donald, editor and writer, is the author of *The French Farmhouse*.

David Burnie B.Sc. has written over 30 books on natural sciences, including *How Nature Works*.

Judith Fayard, an American based in Paris, was Paris bureau chief for *Life* magazine for 10 years, and is now European editor of *Town & Country*. She contributes to various publications, including the *Wall Street Journal*.

Lisa Gerard-Sharp is a broadcaster and author of several regional guides to France and Italy.

Robert Harneis is editorial correspondent for the English language newspaper *French News*.

Colin Jones is Professor of History at Exeter University. His books include *The Longman Companion to the French Revolution* and *The Cambridge Illustrated History of France*.

Alister Kershaw is an Australian writer and broadcaster who has lived in the Loire Valley for 30 years.

Alec Lobrano is an American writer, based in Paris. He is the European editor of *Departures* magazine and contributes to *International Herald Tribune*, *Los Angeles Times*, and *The Independent*.

Anthony Roberts is a writer and translator who has lived in Gascony for 15 years, contributing to various publications including *The Times*, *World of Interiors*, and *Architectural Digest*.

Anthony Rose is the wine correspondent of *The Independent* and co-author of *The Grapevine*.

Jane Sigal is the author of two books on French food, *Normandy Gastronomique* and *Backroom Bistros, Farmhouse Fare*.

Alan Tillier is the main contributor to the *Eyewitness Guide to Paris*. He has lived in Paris for more than 20 years as correspondent for various journals, including the *International Herald Tribune*, *Newsweek*, and *The Times*.

Nigel Tisdall is a travel writer and author of guides to Brittany and Normandy.

Patricia Wells is food critic of the *International Herald Tribune* and author of the *Food Lovers' Guide to Paris* and the *Food Lovers' Guide to France*.

Additional Contributors
Nathalie Boyer, Caroline Bugler, Ann Cremin, Jan Dodd, Bill Echikson, Robin Gauldie, Adrian Gilbert, Peter Graham, Marion Kaplan, Jim Keeble, Alexandra Kennedy, Rolli Lucarotti, Fred Mawer, Lyn Parry, Andrew Sanger, Katherine Spenley, Clive Unger-Hamilton, Roger Williams.

Additional Photography
Jo Craig, Andy Crawford, Michael Crockett, Mike Dunning, Philip Enticknap, Philippe Giraud, Steve Gorton, Alison Harris, John Heseltine, Roger Hilton, Andrew Holligan, Paul Kenwood, Oliver Knight, Eric Meacher, Neil Mersh, Roger Moss, Robert O'Dea, Ian O'Leary, Tony Souter, Alan Williams, Peter Wilson.

Additional Illustrations
Dinwiddie Maclaren, John Fox, Nick Gibbard, Paul Guest, Stephen Gyapay, Kevin Jones Associates, Chris Orr, Robbie Polley, Sue Sharples.

Additional Cartography
Colourmap Scanning Limited; Contour Publishing; Cosmographics; European Map Graphics; Meteo-France. Street Finder maps: ERAMaptec Ltd (Dublin), adapted with permission from original survey and mapping by Shobunsha (Japan).

Cartographic Research
Jennifer Skelley, Rachel Hawtin (Lovell Johns); James Mills-Hicks, Peter Winfield, Claudine Zarte (Dorling Kindersley Cartography).

Design and Editorial Assistance
Peter Adams, Azeem Alam, Michelle Arness Frederic, Elizabeth Ayre, Laetitia Benloulou, Steve Bere, Kate Berens, Sonal Bhatt, Uma Bhattacharya, Hilary Bird, Anna Brooke, Arwen Burnett, Cate Craker, Maggie Crowley, Alison Culliford, Lisa Davidson, Simon Davis, Emer FitzGerald, Helen Foulkes, Fay Franklin, Tom Fraser, Kyra Freestar, Anna Freiberger, Rhiannon Furbear, Catherine Gauthier, Camilla Gersh, Eric Gibory, Emily Green, Vinod Harish, Robert Harneis, Elaine Harries, Victoria Heyworth-Dunne, Paul Hines, Nicholas Inman, Rosa Jackson, Sarah Jackson-Lambert, Stuart James, Laura Jones, Nancy Jones, Kim Laidlaw Adrey, Cécile Landau, Kathryn Lane, Maite Lantaron, Delphine Lawrance, Jude Ledger, Jason Little, Siri Lowe, Francesca Machiavelli, Carly Madden, Hayley Maher, Nicola Malone, Lesley McCave, Ella Milroy, Jason Mitchell, Casper Morris, Claire Naylor, George Nimmo, Malcolm Parchment, Lyn Parry, Helen Partington, Shirin Patel, Susie Peachey, Alice Peebles, Alice Pennington-Mellor, Marianne Petrou, Pollyanna Poulter, Pete Quinlan, Salim Qurashi, Marisa Renzullo, Philippa Richmond, Nick Rider, Ellen Root, Baishakhee Sengupta, Shailesh Sharma, Kunal Singh, Shruti Singhi, Cathy Skipper, Jaynan Spengler, Niamh Smith, Andrew Szudek, Helen Townsend, Conrad van Dyck, Vinita Venugopal, Dora Whitaker, Fiona Wild, Nicholas Wood, Sophie Wright, Irina Zarb.

Special Assistance
Mme Jassinger, French Embassy Press Department; Peter Mills, Christine Lagardère, French Railways Ltd.

Photographic Reference
Altitude, Paris; Sea and See, Paris; Editions Combier, Maçon; Thomas d'Hoste, Paris.

Photography Permissions
Dorling Kindersley would like to thank the following for their assistance and kind permission to photograph at their establishments: The Caisse Nationale des Monuments Historiques et des Sites; M. A. Leonetti, the Abbey of Mont

St-Michel; Chartres Cathedral; M. Voisin, Château de Chenonceau; M. P Mistral, Cité de Carcassonne, M. D. Vingtain, Palais des Papes, Avignon; Château de Fontainebleau; Amiens Cathedral; Conques Abbey; Fontenay Abbey; Moissac Abbey; Vézelay Abbey, Reims Cathedral, and all the other churches, museums, hotels, restaurants, shops, galleries, and sights too numerous to thank individually.

Picture Credits
a = above; b = below/bottom; c = centre; f = far; l = left; r = right; t = top.

Works of art have been reproduced with the permission of the following copyright holders; ©ADAGP, Paris and DACS, London 2011: 33ca, 33crb, 67tl, 68–9, 69tl (d), 94tc, 97cra, 97cb, 97bl, 97br, 103tr, 217bc, 355t, 339br, 486tc, 512ca, 526b, 528bc, 528br, 533br; ©ARS, NY and DACS, London 2011: 96c; ©DACS, London 2011: 97tc, 385br, 426t; © Succession H. Matisse/DACS, London 2011: 33bl, 96bl, 530br; © Succession Picasso/DACS, London 2011: 92cl, 94br, 477t, 525tr.

Photos achieved with the assistance of the EPPV and the CSI: 140–1; Photo of Euro Disneyland ® Park and the Euro Disneyland Paris ® 182crb; The characters, architectural works and trademarks are the property of The Walt Disney Company. All rights reserved; Courtesy of the Maison Victor Hugo, Ville de Paris: 95cra; Musée National des Châteaux de Malmaison et Bois-Preau: 177br; Musée de Montmartre, Paris: 136cb.

The publisher would like to thank the following individuals, companies and picture libraries for permission to reproduce their photographs:
Le 36, Amboise: 586bc.
Alamy Images: amana images inc. 468-9; Jon Arnold Images Ltd 272; Andy Arthur 424bc, Martin Bache 98; Sébastien Baussais 626tr, Tibor Bognar 213tr; Directphoto.org 621br, David R. Frazier Photolibrary, Inc 624cla, FORGET Patrick/SAGAPHOTO.COM 587tr, 597tc; Philippe Hays 627cb, Hemis 53tl, 196, 273bc, 408; Iconotec 285tc; Images & Stories 22; incamerastock 250; Brian Jannsen 222; Joy 174; Neil Juggins 634tl, Michael Juno 243c, Justin Kase Zfivez 625tr, Valerijs Kostreckis 120; LOOK Die Bildagentur der Fotografen GmbH 536; London Entertainment 524br; mcx images 376; nagelstock.com 502; noblelMAGES 460-1; James Osmond Photography 452; a la poste 628tr, 622b, Prisma Bildagentur AG 133; SFL Choice 430; Jack Sullivan 625cra; **Alpine Garden Society/Christopher Grey-Wilson**: 464bc, 464br; **Agence Photo Aquitaine**: D. Lelann 425tc; **Ancient Art and Architecture Collection**: 51crb, 54ca, 54cb, 56br, 61clb, 256–7b, 339bl, 386tl, 438tl, 442crb; **Photo AKG, Berlin**: 49cra, 50bl, 59crb, 406tr, 407br; **Archives Photographiques, Paris/DACS**: 426t; by kind permission of **www.artinswfrance.com**: 612bc; **L'Arnsbourg:** 582tl; **Atelier Brancusi/Centre Georges Pompidou, Paris**: Bernard Prerost 97br; **Atelier du Regard/A Allemand**: 446cl, 446cr, 446br.
Hotellerie de Bas Breau: 575tr, 579bc; **La Bastide de Voulonne:** 570tc; **Hostellerie Berard**: 612cla; **Bibliothèque Nationale, Dijon**: 53cb; **F. Blackburn**: 465bl; **Le Bouclier d'Or:** 558tl; **Gerard Boullay/Photola**: 91bl, 91cra; **Brasserie Bofinger:** 578tc; **Bridgeman Art Library**: Albright Knox Art Gallery, Buffalo, New York 279br; Anthony Crane Collection 215br; Bibliothèque Nationale, Paris 54cr–5cl, 57crb, 73bl; British Library, London 56bl, 72br, 296c, 297br, 297tl; Bonhams, London 63tc; Château de Versailles, France 73tr; Christies, London 33ca, 517b; Giraudon 33tl, 32cla, 60cr–1cl, 61tl, 63tl, 73bc, 185br, 338cl, 347c, 369tl; Guildhall Library, Corporation of London 421c; Hermitage, St Petersburg 33bl; Index 476br; Kress Collection, Washington DC 297bl; Lauros-Giraudon 73br; Musée des Beaux Arts, Quimper 247cr; Musée Condé, Chantilly 61tr, 72bl, 73tc, 73tl, 73cb, 208tr, 297c; Musée d'Orsay, Paris 32bl; Musée du Quai Branly, Paris 116cb; Paul Bremen Collection 259tc; Sotheby's New York 59tl; V&A Museum, London 342crb; Walters Art Gallery, Baltimore, Maryland 360tl; John Brunton 518br; **Buerehiesel:** 583bc.
Cafe du Palais: 581br; **Campagne, Campagne**: 354tl; C. Guy 329t; Lara 195cr; B. Lichtstein 221br, 328clb; Pyszel 194bl; **CNMHS, Paris/DACS**: Longchamps Delehaye 217cla; **Hotel Caron De Beaumarchais:** 554bc; **Castelet/Grotte de Clamouse**: 497bl; **Cephas**: 42crb; Stuart Boreham 264–5; Hervé Champollion 326tr, 338tr, 354crb; Mick Rock 402cla, 475t, 5122–3; **Le Chabichou:** 593br; **Hostellerie du Chapeau Rouge:** 589tc; **Jean Loup Charmet**: 51cb, 54br, 56clb, 66cl, 66clb, 67tl, 67ca, 68bl, 68br, 69crb, 218br, 247b, 269crb, 278tr, 285bc, 304br, 347br, 362bc, 363cra, 365c, 405cr, 405br, 425bl, 479t, 511cr, **Chateau de Barive:** 557tc; **Chateau des Brottieres:** 561br; **Chateau de la Couronne:** Mark Selwood 566bc; **Chateau de La Liquiere:** 474ca; **Chateau d'Ygrande:** 564tl; **Chateau Margaux:** 30crb, 30br; **Cité Des Sciences et L'industrie**: Michel Lamoureux 140ca; NASA/ESA 140tr, 141br; Sylvain Sonnet 140clb; **Bruce Coleman**: Udo Hirsch 375br; Flip de Nooyer 391br; Hans Reinhard 327tc, 327tr; **Collection CDT Gard**: 329bl; **CDT Lot**: 443br; **Photos Editions Combier, Mâcon**: 207tc; **Corbis**: Stuart Black/Robert Harding World Imagery 13bl; Guillaume Bonn 26tl; Gary Braasch 473c; Joel Damase/Photononstop 318-9; Leroy Francis/Hemis 414-5; Owen Franken 16bc; Frumm John/Hemis 238-9; Ray Juno 12cla, Patrice Latron 636br, Douglas Pearson 396-7; Reuters 609tl, Robert Harding World Imagery/Charles Bowman 637tl; Charles E. Rotkin 8-9; Jim Zuckerman 186-7; **Joe Cornish**: 374br.
Dansmuseet, Stockholm/Peter Stenwall: 68cr–69cl; **E. Donard:** 39c, 39clb, 39bc; **Editions D'art Daniel Derveaux**: 404cr–405cl; **Photo Daspet, Avignon**: 508bl; **Doherty**: 249tc; **Domaine De La Courtade**: 475cr; **Domaine des Hauts de Loire:** 588bc; **Domaine Sarda Malet:** 474cb; **Domaine Tempier:** 475cl; **Dreamstime.com:** Adeliepenguin 15bc; Sibel Aisha 179bl; Ihar Balaikin 78; Lesley De Boelpaep 388tl; Flaviu Boerescu 330; Claudio Giovanni Colombo 13tr; Dennis Dolkens 11tc; Radu Razvan Gheorghe 15tc; Gynane 290; Sergey Kelin 84; Mihai-bogdan Lazar 10bc; Martin Molcan 16tl, 522-3; Luciano Mortula 108; Frank Lukasseck 542-3; Oleg Mitiukhin 392cl; Roland Nagy 12bc; Fabio Nodari 2-3; Palaine 17cl; Patrickwang 1c; Beatrice Preve 480; Richair 630cla; Bruce Robbins 618-9; Joern Rynio 356; Richard Semik 210; Jose I. Soto 264-5; Timothy Stirling 548-9; Tehnik83 524tl; Tupungato 74-5; **Alain Ducasse Entreprise:** 572cra.
L'Entracte: Christian Larrit/Gregory Coutanceau 595tr; **L'Ermitage Hotel:** 565bc; **ET Archive**: 304bl; Cathedral Treasury, Aachen 4tr; 52cla; Musée Carnavalet, Paris 65tl; Museum of Fine Arts, Lausanne 59br; Musée d'Orsay, Paris 65cra; Musée de Versailles 60bl; 303bl; National Gallery, Scotland 62br; Victoria and Albert Museum, London 57tl; 347bl; **European Commission**: 679; **Mary Evans Picture Library**: 50br, 54bl, 55c, 57br, 60cla, 62c, 66bc, 67cr, 67br, 69br, 117clb, 181cb, 187c, 195tc, 201bc, 295br, 297tr, 305bl, 370b, 459tr, 477br; Explorer 35br, 58clb.
La Ferme aux Grives: 595bc; Xavier Boymond 573tr; **Festival d'Avignon**: Marc Chaumeil 608cl; **Festival International du Film de la Rochelle**: 608br; **Fleur de Sel:** 562bc; **Fotolia:** Paula Kirsch 14bl.
Georges Blanc: 591tr; **Getty Images:** Axiom Photographic Agency/Ian Cumming 287tl, AFP/Jean Ayissi 641tl, De Agostini Picture Library 488t, Manfred Mehlig 632bl,

National Geographic/Ed George 635cla, Panoramic Images 155br, Sergio Pitamitz 641bl, Peter Scholey 621tl, WireImage/Tony Barson 71bc; **Giraudon, Paris**: 32cla, 21cb, 33cra, 33crb, 50cla, 52clb, 53tl, 54cl, 56cr–57cl, 60clb, 62cl, 64cl, 64cr–65cl, 337br, 351br, 373br, 495cb MS Nero Ell pt.2 fol. 20V0; Lauros-Giraudon 48bc, 49tc, 49crb, 49cb, 49br, 51ca, 53tr, 55crb, 59cr, 64clb, 64br-65bl, 495cl; Musée d'Art Moderne, Paris 32cb; Musée de Beaux Arts, Quimper 32cl; **Le Grand Vefour**: 576bl; **Ronald Grant Archive**: 70clb.
La Halle Saint Pierre: *Untitled* Stavroula Feleggakis 137br; **Sonia Halliday Photographs**: Laura Lushington 313cla; **Robert Harding Picture Library**: 34bl, 41tr, 43tr, 43clb, 47cb, 116br, 247tr, 326bl, 326br, 327br, 353tr, 404cla, 441cr, 465tr, 493bc, C. Bowman 456tc; Explorer, Paris 43cr, 71br, 105bl, 183b, 366tl, 375cra, 464cb, 465tl, 488bl 501br, 613bl, 639tl; D.Hughes 396–7; W.Rawlings 53br, 71tl, 241tl, 260bc; A.Wolfitt 30tr; **Hemispheres Images:** Hervé Hughes 263br; **John Heseltine**: 143c; Honfleur, **Musée Boudin**: 266bl; **David Hughes**: 371t, 371b; **L'Huitriere:** 574tr, 580tl; **The Hulton Deutsch Collection**: 195br, 305br, 477c, 520bc.
Images: 327c, 464cla, 464tr; **Hotel Imperator:** 569br. **Jacana**: JM Labat 465bc; **Restaurant Patrick Jeffroy:** 585bl; **Trevor Jones**: 208bl.
Louis XV Monaco: Bernard Touillon 602br.
Magnum Photos ltd: 25c; Bruno Barbey 24br, 35tr, 40bl; R Capa 476tr; P Halsman 529bl; **La Maison d'Olivier Leflaive:** 590bl; **Manoir du Vaumadeuc:** 560tr; **The Mansell Collection**: 35tl, 286t, 299br, 463bc; **Hotel Marotte:** 556bl; **Le Marquiere:** 599bx; **Mas Daumas Gassac:** 474cr; **Michel Bras:** Aragorn agence de communication 592tr; **John Miller**: 228bl, 340tr, 411br; **Montpellier Danse Festival**: 609br; **Musée de l'Annonciade, St-Tropez**: 528tr; **Musée D'art Moderne et Contemporain de Strasbourg**: Edith Rodeghiero 235tl; **Musée des Beaux Arts, Carcassonne**: 493tl; **Musée des Beaux Arts, Dijon**: 347tl; **Musée des Beaux Arts de Lyon**: 385cra, 385c, 385br; **Musée de la Civilisation Gallo-Romaine, Lyon**: 51cr, 382clb; **Musée Courbet:** Pierre Guénat 355br; **Musée Departmental Breton, Quimper**: 278clb; **Musée Flaubert, Rouen**: 269bl; **Museum National d'Histoire Naturelle, Paris**: 142c; **Courtesy of the Musée Matisse, Nice**: 530br; **Musée National d'Art Moderne, Paris**: 96clb, 97tc, 97cra, 97cb, 339br; Succession Henri Matisse 96bl; **Musée Réattu, Arles**: M Lacanaud 512ca; **Cliché Musée de Sens/ J.P. Elie**: 334tl; **Musée Toulouse-Lautrec, Albi**: 448bc. **Negresco Hotel, Nice:** 571bl; **Network Photographers**: Barry Lewis 342t; Rapho/Mark Buscail 613tc; Rapho/De Sazo 613br; **Hotel Normandy Barriere:** 559bc.
Office de Tourisme de Dijon: Musée Magnin 345fcr; **Office de Tourisme de Vence:** 620c; **Orient-Express Hotels Trains & Cruises**: 552tl; Hotel du Palais 568tl; **OTC Marseille:** 638tl, 640cla.
Paris Tourist Office: Jacques Lebar 26bc; **Photolibrary**: Jean-Marc Romain 625cr, Widmann Widmann/F1 Online 626bl; **Pictures Colour Library**: 406crb, 430, 670–1; **Le Pirate:** 603br; **Michel le Poer Trench**: 34br; **Centre Georges Pompidou**: Bernard Prerost 97b; **Le Pont de l'Ouysse:** 567tc; **Popperfoto**: 255cr; **La Poste:** 629bl; **Pyrenees Magazine/DR**: 404bl.
Redferns: William Gottlieb: 68clb; **Reims Tourisme:** Carmen Moya 214tl, 214cr; **Rennes Tourisme:** Jose Mouret 288bl; **Restaurant de La Tour d'Argent:** 574br; **Retrograph Archive**: M. Breese 478tr; **Réunion des Musées Nationaux**: Musée des Antiquités Nationales 407cr; Musée Guimet 115tl; Musée du Louvre 61ca, 105bl, 106cla, 106bl, 106br, 107tl, 107c, 107bc; Musée Picasso 92cl, 94br, 477tr; Musée de Versailles 183tl; **RF Reynolds**: 249bc. **M Reynard:** 674b; **Rocamadour**: 441tr; **Roger-Viollet**: 117cla; **Foundation Royaumont**: J Johnson 176tl; **Réunion des Musées Nationaux**: *Le Duo* (1937) by Georges Braque, Collections du Centre Pompidou, Musée Nationaux d'Art Moderne, 97cra.
Shangri-La Hotel, Paris: 555tr; **Le Sin:** 598tc; **Sipa Press**: 136bl; **Photo SNCM/Southern Ferries**: 630br; **SNCF – Societe National des Chemins de Fer:** 634bc, Fabro & Leveque 633tr; **Spectrum Colour Library**: P Thompson 253br; **Frank Spooner Pictures**: Bolcina 41bl; Uzan 70bc; Simon 71ca; Gamma Press 43bl, 71crb; **STA Travel Group:** 674tr; **Tony Stone Images**: 326c; **Superstock:** Hemis.fr 596bl; **Sygma**: 535t; C de Bare 40cr; Frederic de la Fosse 524br; L'Illustration 112tl; T Prat 440cl; L de Raemy 70br. **Editions Tallandier**: 46, 48cb, 51tl, 52br, 52br–3bl, 55tl, 55cb, 56cl, 57tr, 58br, 62clb, 62bl, 62cr–63cl, 63crb, 63bc, 65tr, 65crb, 65br, 67bl, 67bc, 68cla, 68crb, 69tc, 69cra; **La Taverne:** 600bc; **Telarci:** 53cr; **Les Terraillers:** 601tl; **TiDenis:** 628bl; **Tourist Office Semur-en-Auxois**: 339tr; **Collection L. Treillard:** © Man Ray Trust/ADAGP, Paris and DACS, London 2011 69tl(d); **Troisgros:** 594tl.
Jean Vertut: 48br–49bl; **La Villa:** U Callelu 603tl; **Visual Arts Library**: 33cr; **View Pictures**: Paul Rafferty 139br.
World Pictures: 327bl. **ZEFA**: 182c, 355t;
O. Zimmerman/Musée d'Unterlinden 6800 Colmar: 231tl.

Front Endpaper
Alamy Images: Jon Arnold Images Ltd Ltl; Hemis Rtl, Lcl; incamerastock Ltc; Brian Jannsen Rtr; LOOK Die Bildagentur der Fotografen GmbH Rbr; mcx images Rcrb; nagelstock.com Rcb; James Osmond Photography Lbl; SFL Choice Lbc; **Dreamstime.com:** Flaviu Boerescu Rca; Gynane Lc; Beatrice Preve Rbl; Joern Rynio Rcra; Richard Semik Rtc.

Back Endpaper
Alamy Images: Martin Bache Rtc; Valerijis Kostreckis Lbc; **Dreamstimecom:** Sergey Kelin Rtr; Luciano Mortula Lclb.

Jacket
Front and spine - **Getty Images:** Guy Edwardes.

Phrase Book

In Emergency

Help!	**Au secours!**	oh se**koor**
Stop!	**Arrêtez!**	aret-**ay**
Call a doctor!	**Appelez un médecin!**	apuh-**lay** uñ med**sañ**
Call an ambulance!	**Appelez une ambulance!**	apuh-**lay** oon oñboo-**loñs**
Call the police!	**Appelez la police!**	apuh-**lay** lah poh-**lees**
Call the fire department!	**Appelez les pompiers!**	apuh-lay leh poñ-**peeyay**
Where is the nearest telephone?	**Où est le téléphone le plus proche?**	oo ay luh tehleh**fon** luh ploo **prosh**
Where is the nearest hospital?	**Où est l'hôpital le plus proche?**	oo ay l'**opee**tal luh ploo **prosh**

Communication Essentials

Yes	**Oui**	wee
No	**Non**	noñ
Please	**S'il vous plaît**	seel voo **play**
Thank you	**Merci**	mer-**see**
Excuse me	**Excusez-moi**	exkoo-**zay** mwah
Hello	**Bonjour**	boñ**zhoor**
Goodbye	**Au revoir**	oh ruh-**vwar**
Good night	**Bonsoir**	boñ-**swar**
Morning	**Le matin**	ma**tañ**
Afternoon	**L'après-midi**	l'apreh-**meedee**
Evening	**Le soir**	swar
Yesterday	**Hier**	ee**yehr**
Today	**Aujourd'hui**	oh-zhoor-**dwee**
Tomorrow	**Demain**	duh**mañ**
Here	**Ici**	ee-**see**
There	**Là**	lah
What?	**Quel, quelle?**	kel, kel
When?	**Quand?**	koñ
Why?	**Pourquoi?**	poor-**kwah**
Where?	**Où?**	oo

Useful Phrases

How are you?	**Comment allez-vous?**	kom-moñ tal**ay voo**
Very well, thank you.	**Très bien, merci.**	treh byañ, mer-**see**
Pleased to meet you.	**Enchanté de faire votre connaissance.**	oñshoñ-**tay** duh fehr votr kon-ay-**sans**
See you soon.	**A bientôt.**	byañ-**toh**
That's fine	**Voilà qui est parfait**	vwalah kee ay par**fay**
Where is/are...?	**Où est/sont...?**	oo ay/soñ
How far is it to...?	**Combien de kilomètres d'ici à...?**	kom-**byañ** duh keelo-**metr** d'ee-**see** ah
Which way to...?	**Quelle est la direction pour...?**	kel ay lah **de**er-ek-**syoñ** poor
Do you speak English?	**Parlez-vous anglais?**	par-**lay** voo oñg-**lay**
I don't understand.	**Je ne comprends pas.**	zhuh nuh kom-**proñ** pah
Could you speak slowly please?	**Pouvez-vous parler moins vite s'il vous plaît?**	poo-**vay** voo par-**lay** mwa**ñ** veet seel voo play
I'm sorry.	**Excusez-moi.**	exkoo-**zay** mwah

Useful Words

big	**grand**	groñ
small	**petit**	puh-**tee**
hot	**chaud**	show
cold	**froid**	frwah
good	**bon**	boñ
bad	**mauvais**	moh-**veh**
enough	**assez**	as**say**
well	**bien**	byañ
open	**ouvert**	oo-**ver**
closed	**fermé**	fer-**meh**
left	**gauche**	gohsh
right	**droit**	drwah
straight ahead	**tout droit**	too drwah
near	**près**	preh
far	**loin**	lwañ
up	**en haut**	oñ **oh**
down	**en bas**	oñ **bah**
early	**de bonne heure**	duh bon **urr**
late	**en retard**	oñ ruh-**tar**
entrance	**l'entrée**	l'on-**tray**
exit	**la sortie**	sor-**tee**
restroom	**les toilettes, les WC**	**twah**-let, vay-**see**
free, unoccupied	**libre**	leebr
free, no charge	**gratuit**	grah-**twee**

Making a Telephone Call

I'd like to make a long-distance call.	**Je voudrais faire un interurbain.**	zhuh voo-dreh fehr uñ añter-oorbañ
I'd like to make a collect call.	**Je voudrais faire une communication PCV.**	zhuh voo**dreh** fehr oon komoonikah-**syoñ** peh-seh-veh
I'll try again later.	**Je rappelerai plus tard.**	zhuh rapel-**eray**ploo tar
Can I leave a message?	**Est-ce que je peux laisser un message?**	es-**keh** zhuh puh leh-**say** uñ meh**sazh**
Hold on.	**Ne quittez pas, s'il vous plaît.**	nuh kee-**tay** pah seel voo play
Could you speak up a little please?	**Pouvez-vous parler un peu plus fort?**	poo-**vay** voo par-**lay** uñ puh ploo for
local call	**la communication locale**	komoonikah-**syoñ** low-**kal**

Shopping

How much does this cost?	**C'est combien s'il vous plaît?**	say kom-**byañ** seel voo play
I would like ...	**je voudrais...**	zhuh voo-**dray**
Do you have?	**Est-ce que vous avez?**	es-**kuh** voo zav**ay**
I'm just looking.	**Je regarde seulement.**	zhuh ruh**gar** suhl**moñ**
Do you take credit cards?	**Est-ce que vous acceptez les cartes de crédit?**	es-**kuh** voo zaksept-**ay** leh kart duh kreh-**dee**
Do you take traveler's cheques?	**Est-ce que vous acceptez les chèques de voyage?**	es-**kuh** voo zaksept-**ay** leh shek duh vwa**yazh**
What time do you open?	**A quelle heure vous êtes ouvert?**	ah kel urr voo zet oo-**ver**
What time do you close?	**A quelle heure vous êtes fermé?**	ah kel urr voo zet fer-**may**
This one.	**Celui-ci.**	suhl-wee-**see**
That one.	**Celui-là.**	suhl-wee-**lah**
expensive	**cher**	shehr
cheap	**pas cher, bon marché**	pah shehr, boñ mar-**shay**
size, clothes	**la taille**	tye
size, shoes	**la pointure**	pwañ-**tur**
white	**blanc**	bloñ
black	**noir**	nwahr
red	**rouge**	roozh
yellow	**jaune**	zhohwn
green	**vert**	vehr
blue	**bleu**	bluh

Types of Shops

antiques shop	**le magasin d'antiquités**	maga-**zañ** d'oñteekee-**tay**
bakery	**la boulangerie**	booloñ-**zhuree**
bank	**la banque**	boñk
bookstore	**la librairie**	lee-**brehree**
butcher	**la boucherie**	boo-**shehree**
cake shop	**la pâtisserie**	patee-**sree**
cheese shop	**la fromagerie**	fromazh-**ree**
dairy	**la crémerie**	krem-**ree**
department store	**le grand magasin**	groñ maga-**zañ**
delicatessen	**la charcuterie**	sharkoot-**ree**
fish seller	**la poissonnerie**	pwasson-**ree**
gift shop	**le magasin de cadeaux**	maga-**zañ** duh ka**doh**
greengrocer	**le marchand de légumes**	mar-**shoñ** duh lay-**goom**
grocery store	**l'alimentation**	alee-moñta-**syoñ**
hairdresser	**le coiffeur**	kwa**fuhr**
market	**le marché**	marsh-**ay**
news stand	**le magasin de journaux**	maga-**zañ** duh zhoor-**no**
pharmacy	**la pharmacie**	farmah-**see**
post office	**la poste, le bureau de poste, le PTT**	pohst, boo**roh** duh pohst, peh-teh-teh
shoe shop	**le magasin de chaussures**	maga-**zañ** duh show-**soor**
supermarket	**le supermarché**	soo pehr-**marshay**
tobacconist	**le tabac**	tabah
travel agent	**l'agence de voyages**	l'azhoñs duh vwayazh

Sightseeing

abbey	**l'abbaye**	l'abay-**ee**
art gallery	**la galerie d'art**	galer-**ree** dart
bus station	**la gare routière**	gahr roo-tee-**yehr**

cathedral	**la cathédrale**	katay-**dral**
church	**l'église**	l'ay**gleez**
garden	**le jardin**	zhar-**dañ**
library	**la bibliothèque**	beeb**leeo**-tek
museum	**le musée**	moo-**zay**
tourist information office	**les renseignements touristiques, le syndicat d'initiative**	roñsayn-**moñ** too-rees-**teek**, sandee-ka d'eenee-sya**teev**
town hall	**l'hôtel de ville**	l'oh**tel** duh veel
train station	**la gare (SNCF)**	gahr (es-en-say-ef)
private mansion	**l'hôtel particulier**	l'oh**tel** partikoo-**lyay**
closed for public holiday	**fermeture jour férié**	fehrmeh-**tur** zhoor fehree-**ay**

Staying in a Hotel

Do you have a vacant room?	**Est-ce que vous avez une chambre?**	es-kuh voo-**zavay** oon shambr
double room, with double bed	**la chambre à deux personnes, avec un grand lit**	shambr ah duh pehr-**son** avek un gronñ lee
twin room	**la chambre à deux lits**	shambr ah duh lee
single room	**la chambre à une personne**	shambr ah oon pehr-**son**
room with a bath, shower	**la chambre avec salle de bains, une douche**	shambr avek sal duh bañ, oon doosh
porter	**le garçon**	gar-**soñ**
key	**la clef**	klay
I have a reservation.	**J'ai fait une réservation.**	zhay fay oon rayzehrva-**syoñ**

Eating Out

Have you got a table?	**Avez-vous une table libre?**	avay-**voo** oon tahbl leebr
I want to reserve a table.	**Je voudrais réserver une table.**	zhuh voo-**dray** rayzehr-**vay** oon tahbl
The check please.	**L'addition s'il vous plaît.**	l'adee-**syoñ** seel voo **play**
I am a vegetarian.	**Je suis végétarien.**	zhuh swee vezhay-**tehryañ**
Waitress/ waiter	**Madame, Mademoiselle/ Monsieur**	mah-**dam**, mah-demwah**zel**/ muh-**syuh**
menu	**le menu, la carte**	men-**oo**, kart
fixed-price menu	**le menu à prix fixe**	men-**oo** ah pree feeks
cover charge	**le couvert**	koo-**vehr**
wine list	**la carte des vins**	**kart**-deh vañ
glass	**le verre**	vehr
bottle	**la bouteille**	boo-**tay**
knife	**le couteau**	koo-**toh**
fork	**la fourchette**	for-**shet**
spoon	**la cuillère**	kwee-**yehr**
breakfast	**le petit déjeuner**	puh-**tee** deh-**zhuh-nay**
lunch	**le déjeuner**	deh-**zhuh-nay**
dinner	**le dîner**	dee-**nay**
main course	**le plat principal**	plah prañsee-**pal**
appetizer, first course	**l'entrée, le hors d'oeuvre**	l'oñ-**tray**, or-duhvr
dish of the day	**le plat du jour**	plah doo zhoor
wine bar	**le bar à vin**	bar ah vañ
café	**le café**	ka-**fay**
rare	**saignant**	**say**-noñ
medium	**à point**	ah **pwañ**
well-done	**bien cuit**	byañ **kwee**

Menu Decoder

l'agneau	l'an**yoh**	lamb
l'ail	l'eye	garlic
la banane	ba**nan**	banana
le beurre	burr	butter
la bière, bière à la pression	bee-**yehr**, bee-**yehr** ah lah pres-**syoñ**	beer, draught beer
le bifteck, le steack	beef-**tek**, stek	steak
le boeuf	buhf	beef
bouilli	boo-**yee**	boiled
le café	kah-**fay**	coffee
le canard	kan**ar**	duck
le chocolat	**shoko**-lah	chocolate
le citron	see-**troñ**	lemon
le citron pressé	see-**troñ** press-**eh**	fresh lemon juice
les crevettes	kruh-**vet**	shrimp
les crustacés	**kroos**-ta-**say**	shellfish
cuit au four	kweet oh foor	baked
le dessert	deh-**ser**	dessert
l'eau minérale	l'oh **meeney**-ral	mineral water
les escargots	leh zes-kar-**goh**	snails
les frites	freet	fries
le fromage	from-**azh**	cheese
le fruit frais	frwee freh	fresh fruit
les fruits de mer	frwee duh mer	seafood
le gâteau	gah-**toh**	cake
la glace	glas	ice, ice cream
grillé	gree-**yay**	grilled
le homard	om**ahr**	lobster
l'huile	l'weel	oil
le jambon	zhoñ-**boñ**	ham
le lait	leh	milk
les légumes	lay-**goom**	vegetables
la moutarde	moo-**tard**	mustard
l'oeuf	l'uf	egg
les oignons	leh zon**yoñ**	onions
les olives	leh zo**leev**	olives
l'orange	l'oroñzh	orange
l'orange pressée	l'oroñzh press-**eh**	fresh orange juice
le pain	pan	bread
le petit pain	puh-**tee** pañ	roll
poché	posh-**ay**	poached
le poisson	pwah-**ssoñ**	fish
le poivre	pwavr	pepper
la pomme	pom	apple
les pommes de terre	pom-duh **tehr**	potatoes
le porc	por	pork
le potage	poh-**tazh**	soup
le poulet	poo-**lay**	chicken
le riz	ree	rice
rôti	row-**tee**	roast
la sauce	sohs	sauce
la saucisse	soh**sees**	sausage, fresh
sec	sek	dry
le sel	sel	salt
la soupe	soop	soup
le sucre	sookr	sugar
le thé	tay	tea
le toast	toast	toast
la viande	vee-**yand**	meat
le vin blanc	vañ **bloñ**	white wine
le vin rouge	vañ **roozh**	red wine
le vinaigre	vee**naygr**	vinegar

Numbers

0	**zéro**	zeh-**roh**
1	**un, une**	uñ, oon
2	**deux**	duh
3	**trois**	trwah
4	**quatre**	katr
5	**cinq**	sañk
6	**six**	sees
7	**sept**	set
8	**huit**	weet
9	**neuf**	nerf
10	**dix**	dees
11	**onze**	oñz
12	**douze**	dooz
13	**treize**	trehz
14	**quatorze**	ka**torz**
15	**quinze**	kañz
16	**seize**	sehz
17	**dix-sept**	dees-**set**
18	**dix-huit**	dees-**weet**
19	**dix-neuf**	dees-**nerf**
20	**vingt**	vañ
30	**trente**	tront
40	**quarante**	kar**oñt**
50	**cinquante**	sañk**oñt**
60	**soixante**	swas**oñt**
70	**soixante-dix**	swasoñt-**dees**
80	**quatre-vingts**	katr-**vañ**
90	**quatre-vingt-dix**	katr-vañ-**dees**
100	**cent**	soñ
1,000	**mille**	meel

Time

one minute	**une minute**	oon mee-**noot**
one hour	**une heure**	oon urr
half an hour	**une demi-heure**	oon **duh-mee** urr
Monday	**lundi**	luñ-**dee**
Tuesday	**mardi**	mar-**dee**
Wednesday	**mercredi**	mehrkruh-**dee**
Thursday	**jeudi**	zhuh-**dee**
Friday	**vendredi**	voñdruh-**dee**
Saturday	**samedi**	sam-**dee**
Sunday	**dimanche**	dee-**moñsh**

Central Paris

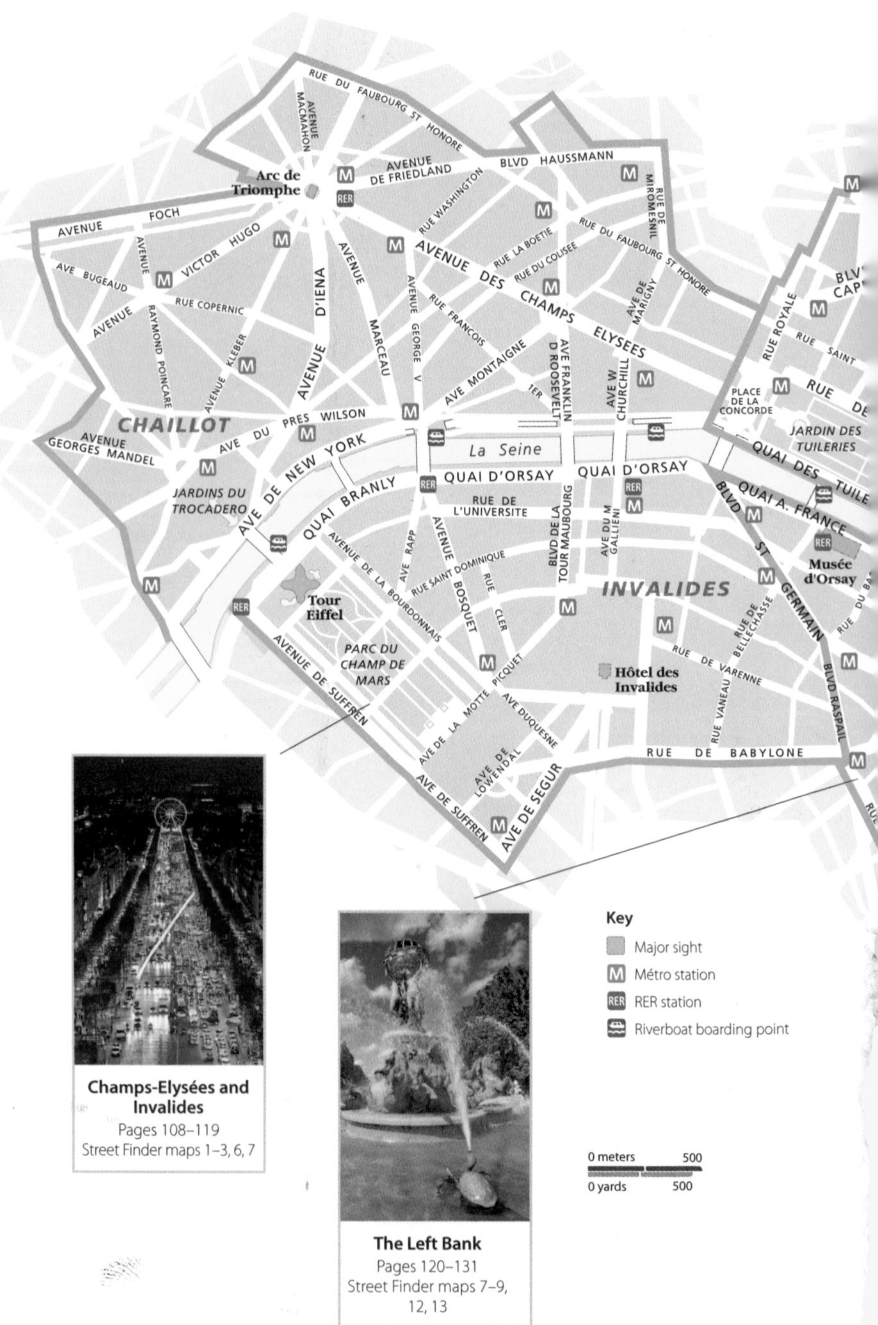

Champs-Elysées and Invalides
Pages 108–119
Street Finder maps 1–3, 6, 7

The Left Bank
Pages 120–131
Street Finder maps 7–9, 12, 13